LW
14.2.06

Blackstone's Statutes
EC Legislation

Blackstone's Statutes
EC Legislation

....

2005/2006

Sixteenth Edition

Edited by

Nigel G. Foster

BA, LLM, Dip German

Jean Monnet Professor of European Law,
Director, LLM in European Legal Studies & Law and German Degree,
Cardiff Law School

OXFORD
UNIVERSITY PRESS

OXFORD
UNIVERSITY PRESS

Great Clarendon Street, Oxford OX2 6DP

Oxford University Press is a department of the University of Oxford.
It furthers the University's objective of excellence in research, scholarship,
and education by publishing worldwide in

Oxford New York

Auckland Cape Town Dar es Salaam Hong Kong Karachi
Kuala Lumpur Madrid Melbourne Mexico City Nairobi
New Delhi Shanghai Taipei Toronto

With offices in

Argentina Austria Brazil Chile Czech Republic France Greece
Guatemala Hungary Italy Japan Poland Portugal Singapore
South Korea Switzerland Thailand Turkey Ukraine Vietnam

Oxford is a registered trade mark of Oxford University Press
in the UK and in certain other countries

Published in the United States
by Oxford University Press Inc., New York

This selection © Nigel G. Foster 2005

First published by Blackstone Press

First edition 1990	Seventh edition 1996	Thirteenth edition 2002
Second edition 1991	reprinted 1997	reprinted 2002
Third edition 1992	Eighth edition 1997	Fourteenth edition 2003
reprinted 1992	Ninth edition 1998	Fifteenth edition 2004
Fourth edition 1993	reprinted 1998	Sixteenth edition 2005
Fifth edition 1994	Tenth edition 1999	
Sixth edition 1995	Eleventh edition 2000	
reprinted 1996	Twelfth edition 2001	

British Library Cataloguing in Publication Data
Data available

Library of Congress Cataloging in Publication Data
Data applied for

Typeset by RefineCatch Limited, Bungay, Suffolk
Printed in Great Britain
on acid-free paper by
Ashford Colour Press Limited, Gosport, Hampshire

ISBN 0–19–928310–9 978–0–19–928310–1
1 3 5 7 9 10 8 6 4 2

CONTENTS

EDITOR'S PREFACE TO THE SIXTEENTH EDITION

It's that time of the year again, when another edition of EC Legislation is prepared. This time, acutely conscious of the unwieldy size of the volume but largely powerless to do anything about it, I have tried to keep changes to the absolutely minimum. It is thankfully appreciated that much of this is to do with the Constitutional Treaty (hereinafter 'CT", to use what appears to be emerging as the most popular term and abbreviation for the 'Treaty Establishing a Constitution for Europe'). Of course, given the present circumstances following the 'No' votes in both the French and Dutch referenda and the consequent postponement of the referenda or the approval process in most other countries not yet having ratified, I could have decision to remove the CT and save all that space (c. 150 pages). However, for reasons outlined in the following introduction to the CT itself, it has been retained.

As for the rest of the content of the 16th edition: a bit of housekeeping has been undertaken on the EC Treaty to remove some of the now superfluous transitional items and I have removed the vestigial Article 3 of Decision 88/591 as its retention was faintly silly. The jurisdiction of the CFI is adequately set out now and governed by Art 225 EC. I have consolidated the changes made to Directive 76/207 by Directive 2002/73 and removed the previous versions of both, and done the same to Directive 80/987 in the Worker Protection section, although the changes to these directives do not officially come into force until the 5 and 8 October 2005 respectively, however, clearing out the dead wood now does have the benefit of cumulatively saving a few pages.

The old competition law hearings' Regulation (2842/98) has been repealed and replaced with Regulation 773/2004 and the technology transfer agreement Regulation (240/96) likewise replaced with its successor, Regulation 772/2004. As usual, I have also made a few amendments to the existing stock as necessitated by various updates and corrections, where noteworthy, duly mentioned.

I acknowledge with thanks the permission of the European Communities to reproduce material taken historically from the OJ printed volumes. More recent provisions and additions have been taken from the online EUR-Lex website and, likewise, permission to reproduce these is gratefully acknowledged but with the clear proviso that 'Only European Union legislation printed in the paper edition of the *Official Journal of the European Union* is deemed authentic'. UK Legislation is reproduced with the permission of HMSO.

I am most thankful for the extensive support work and close attention to detail undertaken by the staff of OUP, in particular I should like to thank Sarah Hyland with whom I continue to work most closely (on four publications now!). Thank you, Sarah. Also in line for thanks are: Kate Whetter, Lucy Graham, Sarah Silvester, Wendy Lynch and, more recently, Gabriella La Cava for all their behind-the-editor work and their enthusiastic support. Thanks also to my wife, Dawn, for her assistance and to my daughter, Lynsey, who helped edit the material added, especially the new table of equivalences – brilliant job!

As ever, I would be most grateful to receive any comments, suggestions, hints, criticisms or advice on the content, style or indeed any other aspect of this publication or to point out errors where they are noticed. Suggestions for additional material are also most welcome. Whilst for each edition I am able to spot a few errors in the OJ and eradicate them, it is possible that I introduce, inadvertently some my own. Thanks to those of you who have made such comments or provided much appreciated advice. I do reflect on each piece of advice provided.

In view ever-changing state of EU law, I thought it useful to provide the main website addresses to the EU and institutions where the latest developments can be viewed.

Entry Portal to the EU	http://europa.eu.int/
EC Commission	http://europa.eu.int/comm/index_en.htm
EC Commission in the UK	http://www.cec.org.uk/
Council of the EU	http://ue.eu.int/en/summ.htm
EP	http://www.europarl.eu.int/home/default_en.htm
ECJ	http://europa.eu.int/cj/en/index.htm
Directory of EC law in force	http://europa.eu.int/eur-lex/en/lif/index.html
The Constitution	http://europa.eu.int/constitution/index_en.htm

Nigel Foster
Cardiff
June 2005

EXTRACTS FROM THE EDITOR'S PREFACE TO THE FIRST EDITION

This collection of European Community legislation has been compiled with two main considerations in mind.

First, to compile an up-to-date selection of the Community primary and secondary legislation which is the subject of frequent reference and is therefore appropriate to include in an accessible reference work which will be useful to both students of Community law and the many others who now come into contact with it.

Secondly, to furnish a basic set of unannotated legislative provisions for those students of Community law who are permitted to take materials into examinations.

In attempting to fulfil these twin tasks, I have been acutely aware of the growing mass of Community law and the danger of trying to incorporate everything which may be considered relevant. Therefore, as demanded by a compilation attempting to achieve specific aims, I have been very selective in the material chosen, particularly with regard to the primary source material of the European Communities.

The first part of the compilation contains Community Treaty and other primary materials.

The second part of the book includes secondary Community legislation taken from a number of areas of substantive law. Once again I have been necessarily selective and confined the scope to areas most commonly covered in Community law courses, although I am certain that I shall be unable to entirely satisfy all courses or perhaps even any course.

Finally I have included as a matter of necessity extracts from the European Communities Act 1972. For the latter item, I gratefully acknowledge HMSO.

The Community source material was taken predominantly from the *Official Journal of the European Communities* unless where otherwise stated and likewise I gratefully acknowledge the permission of the European Commission to reproduce those materials. Wherever they were noticed, errors in this material have been corrected, all other errors and omissions are my responsibility.

Nigel Foster
Cardiff
February 1990

TABLES OF EQUIVALENCES

Tables of equivalences referred to in Article 12 of the Treaty of Amsterdam.

A. Treaty on European Union

Previous numbering	New numbering
Title I	Title I
Article A	Article 1
Article B	Article 2
Article C	Article 3
Article D	Article 4
Article E	Article 5
Article F	Article 6
Article F.1(*)	Article 7
Title II	Title II
Article G	Article 8
Title III	Title III
Article H	Article 9
Title IV	Title IV
Article I	Article 10
Title V(***)	Title V
Article J.1	Article 11
Article J.2	Article 12
Article J.3	Article 13
Article J.4	Article 14
Article J.5	Article 15
Article J.6	Article 16
Article J.7	Article 17
Article J.8	Article 18
Article J.9	Article 19
Article J.10	Article 20
Article J.11	Article 21
Article J.12	Article 22
Article J.13	Article 23
Article J.14	Article 24
Article J.15	Article 25
Article J.16	Article 26
Article J.17	Article 27
Article J.18	Article 28

(*) New Article introduced by the Treaty of Amsterdam.
(***) Title restructured by the Treaty of Amsterdam.

Previous numbering	New numbering
Title VI(***)	Title VI
Article K.1	Article 29
Article K.2	Article 30
Article K.3	Article 31
Article K.4	Article 32
Article K.5	Article 33
Article K.6	Article 34
Article K.7	Article 35
Article K.8	Article 36
Article K.9	Article 37
Article K.10	Article 38
Article K.11	Article 39
Article K.12	Article 40
Article K.13	Article 41
Article K.14	Article 42
Title VIa(**)	Title VII
Article K.15(*)	Article 43
Article K.16(*)	Article 44
Article K.17(*)	Article 45
Title VII	Title VIII
Article L	Article 46
Article M	Article 47
Article N	Article 48
Article O	Article 49
Article P	Article 50
Article Q	Article 51
Article R	Article 52
Article S	Article 53

(*) New Article introduced by the Treaty of Amsterdam.
(**) New Title introduced by the Treaty of Amsterdam.
(***) Title restructured by the Treaty of Amsterdam.

B. Treaty establishing the European Community

Previous numbering	New numbering
Part One	Part One
Article 1	Article 1
Article 2	Article 2
Article 3	Article 3
Article 3a	Article 4
Article 3b	Article 5
Article 3c(*)	Article 6
Article 4	Article 7
Article 4a	Article 8
Article 4b	Article 9
Article 5	Article 10
Article 5a(*)	Article 11

(*) New Article introduced by the Treaty of Amsterdam.

Previous numbering	New numbering
Article 6	Article 12
Article 6a(*)	Article 13
Article 7 (repealed)	–
Article 7a	Article 14
Article 7b (repealed)	–
Article 7c	Article 15
Article 7d(*)	Article 16

Part Two	Part Two
Article 8	Article 17
Article 8a	Article 18
Article 8b	Article 19
Article 8c	Article 20
Article 8d	Article 21
Article 8e	Article 22

Part Three	Part Three
Title I	Title I
Article 9	Article 23
Article 10	Article 24
Article 11 (repealed)	–

Chapter 1	Chapter 1
Section 1 (deleted)	–
Article 12	Article 25
Article 13 (repealed)	–
Article 14 (repealed)	–
Article 15 (repealed)	–
Article 16 (repealed)	–
Article 17 (repealed)	–
Section 2 (deleted)	–
Article 18 (repealed)	–
Article 19 (repealed)	–
Article 20 (repealed)	–
Article 21 (repealed)	–
Article 22 (repealed)	–
Article 23 (repealed)	–
Article 24 (repealed)	–
Article 25 (repealed)	–
Article 26 (repealed)	–
Article 27 (repealed)	Article 26
Article 28	Article 27
Article 29	

Chapter 2	Chapter 2
Article 30	Article 28
Article 31 (repealed)	–
Article 32 (repealed)	–
Article 33 (repealed)	–
Article 34	Article 29
Article 35 (repealed)	–
Article 36	Article 30
Article 37	Article 31

(*) New Article introduced by the Treaty of Amsterdam.

Previous numbering	New numbering
Title II	Title II
Article 38	Article 32
Article 39	Article 33
Article 40	Article 34
Article 41	Article 35
Article 42	Article 36
Article 43	Article 37
Article 44 (repealed)	–
Article 45 (repealed)	–
Article 46	Article 38
Article 47 (repealed)	–
Title III	Title III
Chapter 1	Chapter 1
Article 48	Article 39
Article 49	Article 40
Article 50	Article 41
Article 51	Article 42
Chapter 2	Chapter 2
Article 52	Article 43
Article 53 (repealed)	–
Article 54	Article 44
Article 55	Article 45
Article 56	Article 46
Article 57	Article 47
Article 58	Article 48
Chapter 3	Chapter 3
Article 59	Article 49
Article 60	Article 50
Article 61	Article 51
Article 62 (repealed)	–
Article 63	Article 52
Article 64	Article 53
Article 65	Article 54
Article 66	Article 55
Chapter 4	Chapter 4
Article 67 (repealed)	–
Article 68 (repealed)	–
Article 69 (repealed)	–
Article 70 (repealed)	–
Article 71 (repealed)	–
Article 72 (repealed)	–
Article 73 (repealed)	–
Article 73a (repealed)	–
Article 73b	Article 56
Article 73c	Article 57
Article 73d	Article 58
Article 73e (repealed)	–
Article 73f	Article 59
Article 73g	Article 60
Article 73h (repealed)	–

Previous numbering	New numbering
Title IIIa(**)	Title IV
Article 73i(*)	Article 61
Article 73j(*)	Article 62
Article 73k(*)	Article 63
Article 73l(*)	Article 64
Article 73m(*)	Article 65
Article 73n(*)	Article 66
Article 73o(*)	Article 67
Article 73p(*)	Article 68
Article 73q(*)	Article 69
Title IV	Title V
Article 74	Article 70
Article 75	Article 71
Article 76	Article 72
Article 77	Article 73
Article 78	Article 74
Article 79	Article 75
Article 80	Article 76
Article 81	Article 77
Article 82	Article 78
Article 83	Article 79
Article 84	Article 80
Title V	Title VI
Chapter 1	Chapter 1
Section 1	Section 1
Article 85	Article 81
Article 86	Article 82
Article 87	Article 83
Article 88	Article 84
Article 89	Article 85
Article 90	Article 86
Section 2 (deleted)	–
Article 91 (repealed)	–
Section 3	Section 2
Article 92	Article 87
Article 93	Article 88
Article 94	Article 89
Article 95	Article 90
Article 96	Article 91
Article 97 (repealed)	–
Article 98	Article 92
Article 99	Article 93
Article 100	Article 94
Article 100a	Article 95
Article 100b (repealed)	–
Article 100c (repealed)	–
Article 100d (repealed)	–

(*) New Article introduced by the Treaty of Amsterdam.
(**) New Title introduced by the Treaty of Amsterdam.

Previous numbering	New numbering
Article 101	Article 96
Article 102	Article 97

Title VI	Title VII
Chapter 1	Chapter 1
Article 102a	Article 98
Article 103	Article 99
Article 103a	Article 100
Article 104	Article 101
Article 104a	Article 102
Article 104b	Article 103
Article 104c	Article 104

Chapter 2	Chapter 2
Article 105	Article 105
Article 105a	Article 106
Article 106	Article 107
Article 107	Article 108
Article 108	Article 109
Article 108a	Article 110
Article 109	Article 111

Chapter 3	Chapter 3
Article 109a	Article 112
Article 109b	Article 113
Article 109c	Article 114
Article 109d	Article 115

Chapter 4	Chapter 4
Article 109e	Article 116
Article 109f	Article 117
Article 109g	Article 118
Article 109h	Article 119
Article 109i	Article 120
Article 109j	Article 121
Article 109k	Article 122
Article 109l	Article 123
Article 109m	Article 124

Title VIa(**)	Title VIII
Article 109n(*)	Article 125
Article 109o(*)	Article 126
Article 109p(*)	Article 127
Article 109q(*)	Article 128
Article 109r(*)	Article 129
Article 109s(*)	Article 130

Title VII	Title IX
Article 110	Article 131
Article 111 (repealed)	–
Article 112	Article 132

(*) New Article introduced by the Treaty of Amsterdam.
(**) New Title introduced by the Treaty of Amsterdam.

Previous numbering	New numbering
Title VIIa(**)	Title X
Article 113	Article 133
Article 114 (repealed)	–
Article 115	Article 134
Article 116(*)	Article 135
Title VIII	Title XI
Chapter 1(***)	Chapter 1
Article 117	Article 136
Article 118	Article 137
Article 118a	Article 138
Article 118b	Article 139
Article 118c	Article 140
Article 119	Article 141
Article 119a	Article 142
Article 120	Article 143
Article 121	Article 144
Article 122	Article 145
Chapter 2	Chapter 2
Article 123	Article 146
Article 124	Article 147
Article 125	Article 148
Chapter 3	Chapter 3
Article 126	Article 149
Article 127	Article 150
Title IX	Title XII
Article 128	Article 151
Title X	Title XIII
Article 129	Article 152
Title XI	Title XIV
Article 129a	Article 153
Title XII	Title XV
Article 129b	Article 154
Article 129c	Article 155
Article 129d	Article 156
Title XIII	Title XVI
Article 130	Article 157
Title XIV	Title XVII
Article 130a	Article 158
Article 130b	Article 159
Article 130c	Article 160
Article 130d	Article 161
Article 130e	Article 162

(*) New Article introduced by the Treaty of Amsterdam.
(**) New Title introduced by the Treaty of Amsterdam.
(***) Chapter 1 restructured by the Treaty of Amsterdam.

Previous numbering	New numbering
Title XV	Title XVIII
Article 130f	Article 163
Article 130g	Article 164
Article 130h	Article 165
Article 130i	Article 166
Article 130j	Article 167
Article 130k	Article 168
Article 130l	Article 169
Article 130m	Article 170
Article 130n	Article 171
Article 130o	Article 172
Article 130p	Article 173
Article 130q (repealed)	–
Title XVI	Title XIX
Article 130r	Article 174
Article 130s	Article 175
Article 130t	Article 176
Title XVII	Title XX
Article 130u	Article 177
Article 130v	Article 178
Article 130w	Article 179
Article 130x	Article 180
Article 130y	Article 181
Part Four	Part Four
Article 131	Article 182
Article 132	Article 183
Article 133	Article 184
Article 134	Article 185
Article 135	Article 186
Article 136	Article 187
Article 136a	Article 188
Part Five Title I Chapter 1 Section 1	Part Five Title I Chapter 1 Section 1
Article 137	Article 189
Article 138	Article 190
Article 138a	Article 191
Article 138b	Article 192
Article 138c	Article 193
Article 138d	Article 194
Article 138e	Article 195
Article 139	Article 196
Article 140	Article 197
Article 141	Article 198
Article 142	Article 199
Article 143	Article 200
Article 144	Article 201
Section 2	Section 2
Article 145	Article 202
Article 146	Article 203

Previous numbering	New numbering
Article 189b	Article 251
Article 189c	Article 252
Article 190	Article 253
Article 191	Article 254
Article 191a(*)	Article 255
Article 192	Article 256

Chapter 3	Chapter 3
Article 193	Article 257
Article 194	Article 258
Article 195	Article 259

Article 196	Article 260
Article 197	Article 261
Article 198	Article 262

Chapter 4	Chapter 4
Article 198a	Article 263
Article 198b	Article 264
Article 198c	Article 265

Chapter 5	Chapter 5
Article 198d	Article 266
Article 198e	Article 267

Title II	Title II
Article 199	Article 268
Article 200 (repealed)	–
Article 201	Article 269
Article 201a	Article 270
Article 202	Article 271
Article 203	Article 272
Article 204	Article 273
Article 205	Article 274
Article 205a	Article 275
Article 206	Article 276
Article 206a (repealed)	–
Article 207	Article 277
Article 208	Article 278
Article 209	Article 279
Article 209a	Article 280

Part Six	Part Six
Article 210	Article 281
Article 211	Article 282
Article 212(*)	Article 283
Article 213	Article 284
Article 213a(*)	Article 285
Article 213b(*)	Article 286
Article 214	Article 293
Article 215	Article 288
Article 216	Article 289
Article 217	Article 290

(*) New Article introduced by the Treaty of Amsterdam.

Previous numbering	New numbering
Article 218(*)	Article 291
Article 219	Article 292
Article 220	Article 293
Article 221	Article 294
Article 222	Article 295
Article 223	Article 296
Article 224	Article 297
Article 225	Article 298
Article 226 (repealed)	–
Article 227	Article 299
Article 228	Article 300
Article 228a	Article 301
Article 229	Article 302
Article 230	Article 303
Article 231	Article 304
Article 232	Article 305
Article 233	Article 306
Article 234	Article 307
Article 235	Article 308
Article 236(*)	Article 309
Article 237 (repealed)	–
Article 238	Article 310

Previous numbering	New numbering
Article 239	Article 311
Article 240	Article 312
Article 241 (repealed)	–
Article 242 (repealed)	–
Article 243 (repealed)	–
Article 244 (repealed)	–
Article 245 (repealed)	–
Article 246 (repealed)	–

Final Provisions	Final Provisions
Article 247	Article 313
Article 248	Article 314

(*) New Article introduced by the Treaty of Amsterdam.

EDITOR'S INTRODUCTION TO THE TREATY
ESTABLISHING A CONSTITUTION FOR EUROPE

This version of the Constitutional Treaty ('CT') is the one signed in Rome on 29 October 2004 and subsequently published in the *Official Journal of the European Union* on 16 December 2004 (C series, No. 310). It has been taken from the EC Commission Constitution for Europe website http://europa.eu.int/constitution/index_en.htm and is as published by the Office for Official Publications of the European Communities, Luxembourg 2005,[1] whose permission to reproduce it is gratefully acknowledged.

As was noted in the 15th edition of EC Legislation, the CT is now numbered continuously throughout the four parts which, if it comes into force, will make life even more difficult for those having to concern themselves with EU law in some way (are there any lawyers who do not?). Unfortunately, the helpful cross references provided by the original consolidators in Part III of the CT, which provided the equivalent articles numbers of the EU and EU Treaties from which most of the provisions were drawn, have been omitted in the OJ version of the 16 December. Therefore, as well as re-introducing them into the CT published in this collection, I have provided an additional table of equivalences for Parts III and IV of the CT showing the Constitutional Treaty numbering and the equivalents in either the EC or EU Treaty, unless the provision is a new one, in which case this is simply indicated as 'new'. Please note, this is not an official table of equivalences, as with the Treaty of Amsterdam, but one that I have put together, so whilst every care has been taken in assembling it, it may inadvertently be inaccurate. Thus, if relying on a particular conversion back to the EC or EU Treaties for important reasons, please double check yourself.

As you are no doubt aware, the CT will only enter into force after ratification by all 25 Member States as provided in Article IV-447 (2) CT, however, following its rejection by both the French and Dutch electorates, the ratification process has now been postponed in a number of countries with only 10 so far having ratified the Treaty, see http://europa.eu.int/constitution/referendum_en.htm. There was a plan 'B' drawn up and contained in declaration 30 attached to the Constitutional Treaty which provides:

30. Declaration on the ratification of the Treaty establishing a Constitution for Europe

The Conference notes that if, two years after the signature of the Treaty establishing a Constitution for Europe, four fifths of the Member States have ratified it and one or more Member States have encountered difficulties in proceeding with ratification, the matter will be referred to the European Council.

It seems unlikely though that this can be brought into play under the present circumstances. It is not even clear at this stage whether the CT will survive. In view of this, it crossed my mind to remove the CT from the present collection as this situation will not be completely resolved for two or three years and maybe longer! However, things have a habit of being turned around in the EU, although this is clearly a very serious setback. So much political capital has been invested in agreeing the CT after much effort and horsetrading, that even if the CT does not survive in its present form, the vast majority of the provisions within it are almost certain to find expression in the same or similar form in some future constitutional settlement. The present situation also has perhaps more serious consequences for the condi-

---

[1] http://europa.eu.int/constitution/en/lstoc1_en.htm. See also the legal notice. http://europa.eu.int/geninfo/legal_notices_en.htm

date and applicant countries as there is likely to be severe pressure for a settlement amongst the existing 25 Member States before new members are admitted, despite the agreed timetable already in existence. So, until the fate of the CT is decided, it stays in this collection.

There are a large number of protocols and declarations appended to the Constitutional Treaty but with two exceptions they have not been reproduced at this stage because they largely reproduce those appended to the existing treaties and also run to hundreds of pages! The exceptions are: the Protocol on the transitional provisions relating to the Institutions and bodies of the Union, which will supersede the previously agreed transitional measures when the CT comes into force; and Declaration 40, which provides for further transitional rules in the event that Bulgaria and Romania join the EU after the CT comes into force but before 2009, thus temporarily exceeding the upper limit of 750 of the EP agreed under Art I-20 (2) CT.

However, if the CT does not come into force, then the transitional rules agreed at Nice will continue to apply, although in view of the expansion of the EU in 2004, the Protocol on the Enlargement of the European Union attached to the Nice Treaty would seem to be largely redundant, however it is retained for this present edition. The annexes to the helpful Commission memo reproduced in the 15th edition is retained and can be found in full at: http:// europa.eu.int/rapid/pressReleasesAction.do?reference=MEMO/04/61&format= HTML&aged= 0&language=EN&guiLanguage=en. I am grateful for the permission to re-produce these document annexes from that source in accordance with the legal notice attached to the document.

I sincerely hope the political situation this time next year allows me to start tidying up some of these alternative endings.

Nigel Foster
Editor, Blackstone's EC Legislation

Treaty Establishing a Constitution for Europe[1]

CONTENTS

PREAMBLE

PART I

PART II—THE CHARTER OF FUNDAMENTAL RIGHTS OF THE UNION PREAMBLE

PART III   THE POLICIES AND FUNCTIONING OF THE UNION

[1] **Editor's Note**: This version of the Constitutional Treaty is the one signed in Rome on 29 October 2004, 'Official Journal of the European Union, "Information and Notices" series, C 310 of 16 December 2004. 'The text of the Treaty establishing a Constitution for Europe was signed on 29 October 2004 by the Heads of State or Government of the 25 Member States and the 3 candidate countries. It is subject to ratification by the national authorities of these States, according to their own ratification procedures.' Please note that 'Only European Community official documents printed in the Official Journal of the European Union are deemed authentic.' It has been taken from the EC Commission Constitution for Europe website and as published by the Office for Official Publications of the European Communities, Luxembourg 2005, (http://europa.eu.int/constitution/en/lstoc1_en.htm) whose permission to reproduce it is gratefully acknowledged.

PART IV   GENERAL AND FINAL PROVISIONS

(**Editor's Note**: the list of Protocols and annexes has been omitted.)

FINAL ACT

PREAMBLE

HIS MAJESTY THE KING OF THE BELGIANS, THE PRESIDENT OF THE CZECH REPUBLIC, HER MAJESTY THE QUEEN OF DENMARK, THE PRESIDENT OF THE FEDERAL REPUBLIC OF GERMANY, THE PRESIDENT OF THE REPUBLIC OF ESTONIA, THE PRESIDENT OF THE HELLENIC REPUBLIC, HIS MAJESTY THE KING OF SPAIN, THE PRESIDENT OF THE FRENCH REPUBLIC, THE PRESIDENT OF

IRELAND, THE PRESIDENT OF THE ITALIAN REPUBLIC, THE PRESIDENT OF THE REPUBLIC OF CYPRUS, THE PRESIDENT OF THE REPUBLIC OF LATVIA, THE PRESIDENT OF THE REPUBLIC OF LITHUANIA, HIS ROYAL HIGHNESS THE GRAND DUKE OF LUXEMBOURG, THE PRESIDENT OF THE REPUBLIC OF HUNGARY, THE PRESIDENT OF MALTA, HER MAJESTY THE QUEEN OF THE NETHERLANDS, THE FEDERAL PRESIDENT OF THE REPUBLIC OF AUSTRIA, THE PRESIDENT OF THE REPUBLIC OF POLAND, THE PRESIDENT OF THE PORTUGUESE REPUBLIC, THE PRESIDENT OF THE REPUBLIC OF SLOVENIA, THE PRESIDENT OF THE SLOVAK REPUBLIC, THE PRESIDENT OF THE REPUBLIC OF FINLAND, THE GOVERNMENT OF THE KINGDOM OF SWEDEN, HER MAJESTY THE QUEEN OF THE UNITED KINGDOM OF GREAT BRITAIN AND NORTHERN IRELAND,

DRAWING INSPIRATION from the cultural, religious and humanist inheritance of Europe, from which have developed the universal values of the inviolable and inalienable rights of the human person, freedom, democracy, equality and the rule of law,

BELIEVING that Europe, reunited after bitter experiences, intends to continue along the path of civilisation, progress and prosperity, for the good of all its inhabitants, including the weakest and most deprived; that it wishes to remain a continent open to culture, learning and social progress; and that it wishes to deepen the democratic and transparent nature of its public life, and to strive for peace, justice and solidarity throughout the world,

CONVINCED that, while remaining proud of their own national identities and history, the peoples of Europe are determined to transcend their former divisions and, united ever more closely, to forge a common destiny,

CONVINCED that, thus 'United in diversity', Europe offers them the best chance of pursuing, with due regard for the rights of each individual and in awareness of their responsibilities towards future generations and the Earth, the great venture which makes of it a special area of human hope,

DETERMINED to continue the work accomplished within the framework of the Treaties establishing the European Communities and the Treaty on European Union, by ensuring the continuity of the Community acquis,

GRATEFUL to the members of the European Convention for having prepared the draft of this Constitution on behalf of the citizens and States of Europe,

HAVE DESIGNATED AS THEIR PLENIPOTENTIARIES: (list omitted)

WHO, having exchanged their full powers, found in good and due form, have agreed as follows:

PART I

TITLE I   DEFINITION AND OBJECTIVES OF THE UNION

Article I-1   Establishment of the Union

1.   Reflecting the will of the citizens and States of Europe to build a common future, this Constitution establishes the European Union, on which the Member States confer competences to attain objectives they have in common. The Union shall coordinate the policies by which the Member States aim to achieve these objectives, and shall exercise on a Community basis the competences they confer on it.

2.   The Union shall be open to all European States which respect its values and are committed to promoting them together.

Article I-2   The Union's values

The Union is founded on the values of respect for human dignity, freedom, democracy, equality, the rule of law and respect for human rights, including the rights of persons belonging to minorities. These values are common to the Member States in a society in which pluralism, non-discrimination, tolerance, justice, solidarity and equality between women and men prevail.

Article I-3   The Union's objectives

1.   The Union's aim is to promote peace, its values and the well-being of its peoples.

2.   The Union shall offer its citizens an area of freedom, security and justice without internal frontiers, and an internal market where competition is free and undistorted.

3.   The Union shall work for the sustainable development of Europe based on balanced economic growth and price stability, a highly competitive social market economy, aiming at full employment and social progress, and a high level of protection and improvement of the quality of the environment. It shall promote scientific and technological advance. It shall combat social exclusion and discrimination, and shall promote social justice and protection, equality between women and men, solidarity between generations and protection of the rights of the child. It shall promote economic, social and territorial cohesion, and solidarity among Member States. It shall respect its rich cultural and linguistic diversity, and shall ensure that Europe's cultural heritage is safeguarded and enhanced.

4.   In its relations with the wider world, the Union shall uphold and promote its values and interests. It shall contribute to peace, security, the sustainable development of the Earth, solidarity and mutual respect among peoples, free and fair trade, eradication of poverty and the protection of human rights, in particular the rights of the child, as well as to the strict observance and the development of international law, including respect for the principles of the United Nations Charter.

5.   The Union shall pursue its objectives by appropriate means commensurate with the competences which are conferred upon it in the Constitution.

Article I-4   Fundamental freedoms and non-discrimination

1.   The free movement of persons, services, goods and capital, and freedom of establishment shall be guaranteed within and by the Union, in accordance with the Constitution.

2.   Within the scope of the Constitution, and without prejudice to any of its specific provisions, any discrimination on grounds of nationality shall be prohibited.

Article I-5   Relations between the Union and the Member States

1.   The union shall respect the equality of Member States before the constitution as well as their national identities, inherent in their fundamental structures, political and constitutional, inclusive of regional and local self-government. it shall respect their essential State functions, including ensuring the territorial integrity of the State, maintaining law and order and safeguarding national security.

2.   Pursuant to the principle of sincere cooperation, the Union and the Member States shall, in full mutual respect, assist each other in carrying out tasks which flow from the Constitution.

The Member States shall take any appropriate measure, general or particular, to ensure fulfilment of the obligations arising out of the Constitution or resulting from the acts of the institutions of the Union. The Member States shall facilitate the achievement of the Union's tasks and refrain from any measure which could jeopardise the attainment of the Union's objectives.

Article I-6   Union law

The Constitution and law adopted by the institutions of the Union in exercising competences conferred on it shall have primacy over the law of the Member States.

Article I-7   Legal personality

The Union shall have legal personality.

Article I-8   The symbols of the Union

The flag of the Union shall be a circle of twelve golden stars on a blue background. The anthem of the Union shall be based on the 'Ode to Joy' from the Ninth Symphony by Ludwig van Beethoven.

The motto of the Union shall be: 'United in diversity'.

The currency of the Union shall be the euro.

Europe day shall be celebrated on 9 May throughout the Union.

TITLE II   FUNDAMENTAL RIGHTS AND CITIZENSHIP OF THE UNION

Article I-9   Fundamental rights

1.   The Union shall recognise the rights, freedoms and principles set out in the Charter of Fundamental Rights which constitutes Part II.

2.   The Union shall accede to the European Convention for the Protection of Human Rights and Fundamental Freedoms. Such accession shall not affect the Union's competences as defined in the Constitution.

3.   Fundamental rights, as guaranteed by the European Convention for the Protection of Human Rights and Fundamental Freedoms and as they result from the constitutional traditions common to the Member States, shall constitute general principles of the Union's law.

Article I-10   Citizenship of the Union

1.   Every national of a Member State shall be a citizen of the Union. Citizenship of the Union shall be additional to national citizenship and shall not replace it.

2.   Citizens of the Union shall enjoy the rights and be subject to the duties provided for in the Constitution. They shall have:

(a)   the right to move and reside freely within the territory of the Member States;

(b)   the right to vote and to stand as candidates in elections to the European Parliament and in municipal elections in their Member State of residence, under the same conditions as nationals of that State;

(c)   the right to enjoy, in the territory of a third country in which the Member State of which they are nationals is not represented, the protection of the diplomatic and consular authorities of any Member State on the same conditions as the nationals of that State;

(d)   the right to petition the European Parliament, to apply to the European Ombudsman, and to address the institutions and advisory bodies of the Union in any of the Constitution's languages and to obtain a reply in the same language. These rights shall be exercised in accordance with the conditions and limits defined by the Constitution and by the measures adopted thereunder.

TITLE III   UNION COMPETENCES

Article I-11   Fundamental principles

1.   The limits of Union competences are governed by the principle of conferral. The use of Union competences is governed by the principles of subsidiarity and proportionality.

2.   Under the principle of conferral, the Union shall act within the limits of the competences conferred upon it by the Member States in the Constitution to attain the objectives set out in the Constitution. Competences not conferred upon the Union in the Constitution remain with the Member States.

3.   Under the principle of subsidiarity, in areas which do not fall within its exclusive competence, the Union shall act only if and insofar as the objectives of the proposed action cannot be sufficiently achieved by the Member States, either at central level or at regional and local level, but can rather, by reason of the scale or effects of the proposed action, be better achieved at Union level.

The institutions of the Union shall apply the principle of subsidiarity as laid down in the Protocol on the application of the principles of subsidiarity and proportionality. National Parliaments shall ensure compliance with that principle in accordance with the procedure set out in that Protocol.

4.   Under the principle of proportionality, the content and form of Union action shall not exceed what is necessary to achieve the objectives of the Constitution.

The institutions of the Union shall apply the principle of proportionality as laid down in the Protocol on the application of the principles of subsidiarity and proportionality.

Article I-12   Categories of competence

1.   When the Constitution confers on the Union exclusive competence in a specific area, only the Union may legislate and adopt legally binding acts, the Member States being able to do so themselves only if so empowered by the Union or for the implementation of Union acts.

2.   When the Constitution confers on the Union a competence shared with the Member States in a specific area, the Union and the Member States may legislate and adopt legally binding acts in that area. The Member States shall exercise their competence to the extent that the Union has not exercised, or has decided to cease exercising, its competence.

3.   The Member States shall coordinate their economic and employment policies within arrangements as determined by Part III, which the Union shall have competence to provide.

4.   The Union shall have competence to define and implement a common foreign and security policy, including the progressive framing of a common defence policy.

5.   In certain areas and under the conditions laid down in the Constitution, the Union shall have competence to carry out actions to support, coordinate or supplement the actions of the Member States, without thereby superseding their competence in these areas.

Legally binding acts of the Union adopted on the basis of the provisions in Part III relating to these areas shall not entail harmonisation of Member States' laws or regulations.

6.   The scope of and arrangements for exercising the Union's competences shall be determined by the provisions relating to each area in Part III.

Article I-13   Areas of exclusive competence

1.   The Union shall have exclusive competence in the following areas:
   (a) customs union;
   (b) the establishing of the competition rules necessary for the functioning of the internal market;
   (c) monetary policy for the Member States whose currency is the euro;
   (d) the conservation of marine biological resources under the common fisheries policy;
   (e) common commercial policy.

2.   The Union shall also have exclusive competence for the conclusion of an international agreement when its conclusion is provided for in a legislative act of the Union or is necessary to enable the Union to exercise its internal competence, or insofar as its conclusion may affect common rules or alter their scope.

Article I-14   Areas of shared competence

1.   The Union shall share competence with the Member States where the Constitution confers on it a competence which does not relate to the areas referred to in Articles I-13 and I-17.

2.   Shared competence between the Union and the Member States applies in the following principal areas:
   (a) internal market;
   (b) social policy, for the aspects defined in Part III;
   (c) economic, social and territorial cohesion;
   (d) agriculture and fisheries, excluding the conservation of marine biological resources;
   (e) environment;
   (f) consumer protection;
   (g) transport;
   (h) trans-European networks;

    (i)   energy;
    (j)   area of freedom, security and justice;
    (k) common safety concerns in public health matters, for the aspects defined in Part III.
    3.   In the areas of research, technological development and space, the Union shall have competence to carry out activities, in particular to define and implement programmes; however, the exercise of that competence shall not result in Member States being prevented from exercising theirs.

    4.   In the areas of development cooperation and humanitarian aid, the Union shall have competence to carry out activities and conduct a common policy; however, the exercise of that competence shall not result in Member States being prevented from exercising theirs.

Article I-15   The coordination of economic and employment policies

    1.   The Member States shall coordinate their economic policies within the Union. To this end, the Council of Ministers shall adopt measures, in particular broad guidelines for these policies. Specific provisions shall apply to those Member States whose currency is the euro.

    2.   The Union shall take measures to ensure coordination of the employment policies of the Member States, in particular by defining guidelines for these policies.

    3.   The Union may take initiatives to ensure coordination of Member States' social policies.

Article I-16   The common foreign and security policy

    1.   The Union's competence in matters of common foreign and security policy shall cover all areas of foreign policy and all questions relating to the Union's security, including the progressive framing of a common defence policy that might lead to a common defence.

    2.   Member States shall actively and unreservedly support the Union's common foreign and security policy in a spirit of loyalty and mutual solidarity and shall comply with the Union's action in this area. They shall refrain from action contrary to the Union's interests or likely to impair its effectiveness.

Article I-17   Areas of supporting, coordinating or complementary action

The Union shall have competence to carry out supporting, coordinating or complementary action. The areas of such action shall, at European level, be:
    (a) protection and improvement of human health;
    (b) industry;
    (c) culture;
    (d) tourism;
    (e) education, youth, sport and vocational training;
    (f) civil protection;
    (g) administrative cooperation.

Article I-18   Flexibility clause

    1.   If action by the Union should prove necessary, within the framework of the policies defined in Part III, to attain one of the objectives set out in the Constitution, and the Constitution has not provided the necessary powers, the Council of Ministers, acting unanimously on a proposal from the European Commission and after obtaining the consent of the European Parliament, shall adopt the appropriate measures.

    2.   Using the procedure for monitoring the subsidiarity principle referred to in Article I-11(3), the European Commission shall draw national Parliaments' attention to proposals based on this Article.

    3.   Measures based on this Article shall not entail harmonisation of Member States' laws or regulations in cases where the Constitution excludes such harmonisation.

TITLE IV   THE UNION'S INSTITUTIONS AND BODIES
CHAPTER I   THE INSTITUTIONAL FRAMEWORK

Article I-19   The Union's institutions

1.   The Union shall have an institutional framework which shall aim to:
— promote its values,
— advance its objectives,
— serve its interests, those of its citizens and those of the Member States,
— ensure the consistency, effectiveness and continuity of its policies and actions.
This institutional framework comprises:
— The European Parliament,
— The European Council,
— The Council of Ministers (hereinafter referred to as the 'Council'),
— The European Commission (hereinafter referred to as the 'Commission'),
— The Court of Justice of the European Union.

2.   Each institution shall act within the limits of the powers conferred on it in the Constitution, and in conformity with the procedures and conditions set out in it. The institutions shall practise mutual sincere cooperation.

Article I-20   The European Parliament

1.   The European Parliament shall, jointly with the Council, exercise legislative and budgetary functions. It shall exercise functions of political control and consultation as laid down in the Constitution. It shall elect the President of the Commission.

2.   The European Parliament shall be composed of representatives of the Union's citizens. They shall not exceed seven hundred and fifty in number. Representation of citizens shall be degressively proportional, with a minimum threshold of six members per Member State. No Member State shall be allocated more than ninety-six seats. The European Council shall adopt by unanimity, on the initiative of the European Parliament and with its consent, a European decision establishing the composition of the European Parliament, respecting the principles referred to in the first subparagraph.

3.   The members of the European Parliament shall be elected for a term of five years by direct universal suffrage in a free and secret ballot.

4.   The European Parliament shall elect its President and its officers from among its members.

Article I-21   The European Council

1.   The European Council shall provide the Union with the necessary impetus for its development and shall define the general political directions and priorities thereof. It shall not exercise legislative functions.

2.   The European Council shall consist of the Heads of State or Government of the Member States, together with its President and the President of the Commission. The Union Minister for Foreign Affairs shall take part in its work.

3.   The European Council shall meet quarterly, convened by its President. When the agenda so requires, the members of the European Council may decide each to be assisted by a minister and, in the case of the President of the Commission, by a member of the Commission. When the situation so requires, the President shall convene a special meeting of the European Council.

4.   Except where the Constitution provides otherwise, decisions of the European Council shall be taken by consensus.

Article I-22   The European Council President

1.   The European Council shall elect its President, by a qualified majority, for a term of two and a half years, renewable once. In the event of an impediment or serious misconduct, the European Council can end his or her term of office in accordance with the same procedure.

xxxviii   Treaty Establishing a Constitution for Europe

2.   The President of the European Council:
   (a)   shall chair it and drive forward its work;
   (b)   shall ensure the preparation and continuity of the work of the European Council in cooperation with the President of the Commission, and on the basis of the work of the General Affairs Council;
   (c)   shall endeavour to facilitate cohesion and consensus within the European Council;
   (d)   shall present a report to the European Parliament after each of the meetings of the European Council.

The President of the European Council shall, at his or her level and in that capacity, ensure the external representation of the Union on issues concerning its common foreign and security policy, without prejudice to the powers of the Union Minister for Foreign Affairs.

3.   The President of the European Council shall not hold a national office.

Article I-23   The Council of Ministers

1.   The Council shall, jointly with the European Parliament, exercise legislative and budgetary functions. It shall carry out policy-making and coordinating functions as laid down in the Constitution.

2.   The Council shall consist of a representative of each Member State at ministerial level, who may commit the government of the Member State in question and cast its vote.

3.   The Council shall act by a qualified majority except where the Constitution provides otherwise.

Article I-24   Configurations of the Council of Ministers

1.   The Council shall meet in different configurations.

2.   The General Affairs Council shall ensure consistency in the work of the different Council configurations.

It shall prepare and ensure the follow-up to meetings of the European Council, in liaison with the President of the European Council and the Commission.

3.   The Foreign Affairs Council shall elaborate the Union's external action on the basis of strategic guidelines laid down by the European Council and ensure that the Union's action is consistent.

4.   The European Council shall adopt by a qualified majority a European decision establishing the list of other Council configurations.

5.   A Committee of Permanent Representatives of the Governments of the Member States shall be responsible for preparing the work of the Council.

6.   The Council shall meet in public when it deliberates and votes on a draft legislative act. To this end, each Council meeting shall be divided into two parts, dealing respectively with deliberations on Union legislative acts and non-legislative activities.

7.   The Presidency of Council configurations, other than that of Foreign Affairs, shall be held by Member State representatives in the Council on the basis of equal rotation, in accordance with the conditions established by a European decision of the European Council. The European Council shall act by a qualified majority.

Article I-25   Definition of qualified majority within the European Council and the Council

1.   A qualified majority shall be defined as at least 55% of the members of the Council, comprising at least fifteen of them and representing Member States comprising at least 65% of the population of the Union. A blocking minority must include at least four Council members, failing which the qualified majority shall be deemed attained.

2.   By way of derogation from paragraph 1, when the Council does not act on a proposal from the Commission or from the Union Minister for Foreign Affairs, the qualified majority shall be defined as at least 72% of the members of the Council, representing Member States comprising at least 65% of the population of the Union.

3. Paragraphs 1 and 2 shall apply to the European Council when it is acting by a qualified majority.

4. Within the European Council, its President and the President of the Commission shall not take part in the vote.

Article I-26   The European Commission

1. The Commission shall promote the general interest of the Union and take appropriate initiatives to that end. It shall ensure the application of the Constitution, and measures adopted by the institutions pursuant to the Constitution. It shall oversee the application of Union law under the control of the Court of Justice of the European Union. It shall execute the budget and manage programmes. It shall exercise coordinating, executive and management functions, as laid down in the Constitution. With the exception of the common foreign and security policy, and other cases provided for in the Constitution, it shall ensure the Union's external representation. It shall initiate the Union's annual and multiannual programming with a view to achieving interinstitutional agreements.

2. Union legislative acts may be adopted only on the basis of a Commission proposal, except where the Constitution provides otherwise. Other acts shall be adopted on the basis of a Commission proposal where the Constitution so provides.

3. The Commission's term of office shall be five years.

4. The members of the Commission shall be chosen on the ground of their general competence and European commitment from persons whose independence is beyond doubt.

5. The first Commission appointed under the provisions of the Constitution shall consist of one national of each Member State, including its President and the Union Minister for Foreign Affairs who shall be one of its Vice-Presidents.

6. As from the end of the term of office of the Commission referred to in paragraph 5, the Commission shall consist of a number of members, including its President and the Union Minister for Foreign Affairs, corresponding to two thirds of the number of Member States, unless the European Council, acting unanimously, decides to alter this number. The members of the Commission shall be selected from among the nationals of the Member States on the basis of a system of equal rotation between the Member States. This system shall be established by a European decision adopted unanimously by the European Council and on the basis of the following principles:

(a) Member states shall be treated on a strictly equal footing as regards determination of the sequence of, and the time spent by, their nationals as members of the commission; consequently, the difference between the total number of terms of office held by nationals of any given pair of Member States may never be more than one;

(b) subject to point (a), each successive Commission shall be so composed as to reflect satisfactorily the demographic and geographical range of all the Member States.

7. In carrying out its responsibilities, the Commission shall be completely independent. Without prejudice to Article I-28(2), the members of the Commission shall neither seek nor take instructions from any government or other institution, body, office or entity. They shall refrain from any action incompatible with their duties or the performance of their tasks.

8. The Commission, as a body, shall be responsible to the European Parliament. In accordance with Article III-340, the European Parliament may vote on a censure motion on the Commission. If such a motion is carried, the members of the Commission shall resign as a body and the Union Minister for Foreign Affairs shall resign from the duties that he or she carries out in the Commission.

Article I-27   The President of the European Commission

1. Taking into account the elections to the European Parliament and after having held the appropriate consultations, the European Council, acting by a qualified majority, shall propose to the European Parliament a candidate for President of the Commission. This

candidate shall be elected by the European Parliament by a majority of its component members. If he or she does not obtain the required majority, the European Council, acting by a qualified majority, shall within one month propose a new candidate who shall be elected by the European Parliament following the same procedure.

2.   The Council, by common accord with the President-elect, shall adopt the list of the other persons whom it proposes for appointment as members of the Commission. They shall be selected, on the basis of the suggestions made by Member States, in accordance with the criteria set out in Article I-26 (4) and (6), second subparagraph. The President, the Union Minister for Foreign Affairs and the other members of the Commission shall be subject as a body to a vote of consent by the European Parliament. On the basis of this consent the Commission shall be appointed by the European Council, acting by a qualified majority.

3.   The President of the Commission shall:
   (a)   lay down guidelines within which the Commission is to work;
   (b)   decide on the internal organisation of the Commission, ensuring that it acts consistently, efficiently and as a collegiate body;
   (c)   appoint Vice-Presidents, other than the Union Minister for Foreign Affairs, from among the members of the Commission. A member of the Commission shall resign if the President so requests. The Union Minister for Foreign Affairs shall resign, in accordance with the procedure set out in article I-28(1), if the President so requests.

Article I-28   The Union Minister for Foreign Affairs

1.   The European Council, acting by a qualified majority, with the agreement of the President of the Commission, shall appoint the Union Minister for Foreign Affairs. The European Council may end his or her term of office by the same procedure.

2.   The Union Minister for Foreign Affairs shall conduct the Union's common foreign and security policy. He or she shall contribute by his or her proposals to the development of that policy, which he or she shall carry out as mandated by the Council. The same shall apply to the common security and defence policy.

3.   The Union Minister for Foreign Affairs shall preside over the Foreign Affairs Council.

4.   The Union Minister for Foreign Affairs shall be one of the Vice-Presidents of the Commission. He or she shall ensure the consistency of the Union's external action. He or she shall be responsible within the Commission for responsibilities incumbent on it in external relations and for coordinating other aspects of the Union's external action. In exercising these responsibilities within the Commission, and only for these responsibilities, the Union Minister for Foreign Affairs shall be bound by Commission procedures to the extent that this is consistent with paragraphs 2 and 3.

Article I-29   The Court of Justice of the European Union

1.   The Court of Justice of the European Union shall include the Court of Justice, the General Court and specialised courts. It shall ensure that in the interpretation and application of the Constitution the law is observed.

Member States shall provide remedies sufficient to ensure effective legal protection in the fields covered by Union law.

2.   The Court of Justice shall consist of one judge from each Member State. It shall be assisted by Advocates-General. The General Court shall include at least one judge per Member State.

The Judges and the Advocates-General of the Court of Justice and the Judges of the General Court shall be chosen from persons whose independence is beyond doubt and who satisfy the conditions set out in Articles III-355 and III-356. They shall be appointed by common accord of the governments of the Member States for six years. Retiring Judges and Advocates-General may be reappointed.

3.   The Court of Justice of the European Union shall in accordance with Part III:
   (a)   rule on actions brought by a Member State, an institution or a natural or legal person;
   (b)   give preliminary rulings, at the request of courts or tribunals of the Member States, on the interpretation of Union law or the validity of acts adopted by the institutions;
   (c)   rule in other cases provided for in the Constitution.

CHAPTER II   THE OTHER UNION INSTITUTIONS AND ADVISORY BODIES

Article I-30   The European Central Bank

1.   The European Central Bank, together with the national central banks, shall constitute the European System of Central Banks. The European Central Bank, together with the national central banks of the Member States whose currency is the euro, which constitute the Eurosystem, shall conduct the monetary policy of the Union.

2.   The European System of Central Banks shall be governed by the decision-making bodies of the European Central Bank. The primary objective of the European System of Central Banks shall be to maintain price stability. Without prejudice to that objective, it shall support the general economic policies in the Union in order to contribute to the achievement of the latter's objectives. It shall conduct other Central Bank tasks in accordance with Part III and the Statute of the European System of Central Banks and of the European Central Bank.

3.   The European Central Bank is an institution. It shall have legal personality. It alone may authorise the issue of the euro. It shall be independent in the exercise of its powers and in the management of its finances. Union institutions, bodies, offices and agencies and the governments of the Member States shall respect that independence.

4.   The European Central Bank shall adopt such measures as are necessary to carry out its tasks in accordance with Articles III-185 to III-191 and Article III-196, and with the conditions laid down in the Statute of the European System of Central Banks and of the European Central Bank. In accordance with these same Articles, those Member States whose currency is not the euro, and their central banks, shall retain their powers in monetary matters.

5.   Within the areas falling within its responsibilities, the European Central Bank shall be consulted on all proposed Union acts, and all proposals for regulation at national level, and may give an opinion.

6.   The decision-making organs of the European Central Bank, their composition and operating methods are set out in Articles III-382 and III-383, as well as in the Statute of the European System of Central Banks and of the European Central Bank.

Article I-31   The Court of Auditors

1.   The Court of Auditors is an institution. It shall carry out the Union's audit.

2.   It shall examine the accounts of all Union revenue and expenditure, and shall ensure good financial management.

3.   It shall consist of one national of each Member State. Its members shall be completely independent in the performance of their duties, in the Union's general interest.

Article I-32   The Union's advisory bodies

1.   The European Parliament, the Council and the Commission shall be assisted by a Committee of the Regions and an Economic and Social Committee, exercising advisory functions.

2.   The Committee of the Regions shall consist of representatives of regional and local bodies who either hold a regional or local authority electoral mandate or are politically accountable to an elected assembly.

3.   The Economic and Social Committee shall consist of representatives of organisations

of employers, of the employed, and of other parties representative of civil society, notably in socio- economic, civic, professional and cultural areas.

4.   The members of the Committee of the Regions and the Economic and Social Committee shall not be bound by any mandatory instructions. They shall be completely independent in the performance of their duties, in the Union's general interest.

5.   Rules governing the composition of these Committees, the designation of their members, their powers and their operations are set out in Articles III-386 to III-392. The rules referred to in paragraphs 2 and 3 governing the nature of their composition shall be reviewed at regular intervals by the Council to take account of economic, social and demographic developments within the Union. The Council, on a proposal from the Commission, shall adopt European decisions to that end.

TITLE V   EXERCISE OF UNION COMPETENCE
CHAPTER I   COMMON PROVISIONS

Article I-33   The legal acts of the Union

1.   To exercise the Union's competences the institutions shall use as legal instruments, in accordance with Part III, European laws, European framework laws, European regulations, European decisions, recommendations and opinions. A European law shall be a legislative act of general application. It shall be binding in its entirety and directly applicable in all Member States.

A European framework law shall be a legislative act binding, as to the result to be achieved, upon each Member State to which it is addressed, but shall leave to the national authorities the choice of form and methods. A European regulation shall be a non-legislative act of general application for the implementation of legislative acts and of certain provisions of the Constitution. It may either be binding in its entirety and directly applicable in all Member States, or be binding, as to the result to be achieved, upon each Member State to which it is addressed, but shall leave to the national authorities the choice of form and methods. A European decision shall be a non-legislative act, binding in its entirety. A decision which specifies those to whom it is addressed shall be binding only on them. Recommendations and opinions shall have no binding force.

2.   When considering draft legislative acts, the European Parliament and the Council shall refrain from adopting acts not provided for by the relevant legislative procedure in the area in question.

Article I-34   Legislative acts

1.   European laws and framework laws shall be adopted, on the basis of proposals from the Commission, jointly by the European Parliament and the Council under the ordinary legislative procedure as set out in Article III-396. If the two institutions cannot reach agreement on an act, it shall not be adopted.

2.   In the specific cases provided for in the Constitution, European laws and framework laws shall be adopted by the European Parliament with the participation of the Council, or by the latter with the participation of the European Parliament, in accordance with special legislative procedures.

3.   In the specific cases provided for in the Constitution, European laws and framework laws may be adopted at the initiative of a group of Member States or of the European Parliament, on a recommendation from the European Central Bank or at the request of the Court of Justice or the European Investment Bank.

Article I-35   Non-legislative acts

1.   The European Council shall adopt European decisions in the cases provided for in the Constitution.

2. The Council and the Commission, in particular in the cases referred to in articles I-36 and I-37, and the European Central Bank in the specific cases provided for in the constitution, shall adopt European regulations and decisions.

3. The Council shall adopt recommendations. It shall act on a proposal from the Commission in all cases where the Constitution provides that it shall adopt acts on a proposal from the Commission. It shall act unanimously in those areas in which unanimity is required for the adoption of a Union act. The Commission, and the European Central Bank in the specific cases provided for in the Constitution, shall adopt recommendations.

Article I-36   Delegated European regulations

1. European laws and framework laws may delegate to the Commission the power to adopt delegated European regulations to supplement or amend certain non-essential elements of the law or framework law. The objectives, content, scope and duration of the delegation of power shall be explicitly defined in the European laws and framework laws. The essential elements of an area shall be reserved for the European law or framework law and accordingly shall not be the subject of a delegation of power.

2. European laws and framework laws shall explicitly lay down the conditions to which the delegation is subject; these conditions may be as follows:

    (a) the European Parliament or the Council may decide to revoke the delegation;

    (b) the delegated European regulation may enter into force only if no objection has been expressed by the European Parliament or the Council within a period set by the European law or framework law.

For the purposes of (a) and (b), the European Parliament shall act by a majority of its component members, and the Council by a qualified majority.

Article I-37   Implementing acts

1. Member States shall adopt all measures of national law necessary to implement legally binding Union acts.

2. Where uniform conditions for implementing legally binding Union acts are needed, those acts shall confer implementing powers on the Commission, or, in duly justified specific cases and in the cases provided for in Article I-40, on the Council.

3. For the purposes of paragraph 2, European laws shall lay down in advance the rules and general principles concerning mechanisms for control by Member States of the Commission's exercise of implementing powers.

4. Union implementing acts shall take the form of European implementing regulations or European implementing decisions.

Article I-38   Principles common to the Union's legal acts

1. Where the Constitution does not specify the type of act to be adopted, the institutions shall select it on a case-by-case basis, in compliance with the applicable procedures and with the principle of proportionality referred to in Article I-11.

2. Legal acts shall state the reasons on which they are based and shall refer to any proposals, initiatives, recommendations, requests or opinions required by the Constitution.

Article I-39   Publication and entry into force

1. European laws and framework laws adopted under the ordinary legislative procedure shall be signed by the President of the European Parliament and by the President of the Council.

In other cases they shall be signed by the President of the institution which adopted them. European laws and framework laws shall be published in the Official Journal of the European Union and shall enter into force on the date specified in them or, in the absence thereof, on the twentieth day following their publication.

2. European regulations, and European decisions which do not specify to whom they are addressed, shall be signed by the President of the institution which adopted them. European

regulations, and European decisions when the latter do not specify to whom they are addressed, shall be published in the Official Journal of the European Union and shall enter into force on the date specified in them or, in the absence thereof, on the twentieth day following that of their publication.

3.   European decisions other than those referred to in paragraph 2 shall be notified to those to whom they are addressed and shall take effect upon such notification.

CHAPTER II   SPECIFIC PROVISIONS

Article I-40   Specific provisions relating to the common foreign and security policy

1.   The European Union shall conduct a common foreign and security policy, based on the development of mutual political solidarity among Member States, the identification of questions of general interest and the achievement of an ever increasing degree of convergence of Member States' actions.

2.   The European Council shall identify the Union's strategic interests and determine the objectives of its common foreign and security policy. The Council shall frame this policy within the framework of the strategic guidelines established by the European Council and in accordance with Part III.

3.   The European Council and the Council shall adopt the necessary European decisions.

4.   The common foreign and security policy shall be put into effect by the Union Minister for Foreign Affairs and by the Member States, using national and Union resources.

5.   Member States shall consult one another within the European Council and the Council on any foreign and security policy issue which is of general interest in order to determine a common approach. Before undertaking any action on the international scene or any commitment which could affect the Union's interests, each Member State shall consult the others within the European Council or the Council. Member States shall ensure, through the convergence of their actions, that the Union is able to assert its interests and values on the international scene. Member States shall show mutual solidarity.

6.   European decisions relating to the common foreign and security policy shall be adopted by the European Council and the Council unanimously, except in the cases referred to in Part III. The European Council and the Council shall act on an initiative from a Member State, on a proposal from the Union Minister for Foreign Affairs or on a proposal from that Minister with the Commission's support. European laws and framework laws shall be excluded.

7.   The European Council may, unanimously, adopt a European decision authorising the Council to act by a qualified majority in cases other than those referred to in Part III.

8.   The European Parliament shall be regularly consulted on the main aspects and basic choices of the common foreign and security policy. It shall be kept informed of how it evolves.

Article I-41   Specific provisions relating to the common security and defence policy

1.   The common security and defence policy shall be an integral part of the common foreign and security policy. It shall provide the Union with an operational capacity drawing on civil and military assets. The Union may use them on missions outside the Union for peace-keeping, conflict prevention and strengthening international security in accordance with the principles of the United Nations Charter. The performance of these tasks shall be undertaken using capabilities provided by the Member States.

2.   The common security and defence policy shall include the progressive framing of a common Union defence policy. This will lead to a common defence, when the European Council, acting unanimously, so decides. It shall in that case recommend to the Member States the adoption of such a decision in accordance with their respective constitutional requirements.

The policy of the Union in accordance with this Article shall not prejudice the specific character of the security and defence policy of certain Member States, it shall respect the obligations of certain Member States, which see their common defence realised in the North Atlantic Treaty Organisation, under the North Atlantic Treaty, and be compatible with the common security and defence policy established within that framework.

3.   Member States shall make civilian and military capabilities available to the Union for the implementation of the common security and defence policy, to contribute to the objectives defined by the Council. Those Member States which together establish multinational forces may also make them available to the common security and defence policy. Member States shall undertake progressively to improve their military capabilities. An Agency in the field of defence capabilities development, research, acquisition and armaments (European Defence Agency) shall be established to identify operational requirements, to promote measures to satisfy those requirements, to contribute to identifying and, where appropriate, implementing any measure needed to strengthen the industrial and technological base of the defence sector, to participate in defining a European capabilities and armaments policy, and to assist the Council in evaluating the improvement of military capabilities.

4.   European decisions relating to the common security and defence policy, including those initiating a mission as referred to in this Article, shall be adopted by the Council acting unanimously on a proposal from the Union Minister for Foreign Affairs or an initiative from a Member State. The Union Minister for Foreign Affairs may propose the use of both national resources and Union instruments, together with the Commission where appropriate.

5.   The Council may entrust the execution of a task, within the Union framework, to a group of Member States in order to protect the Union's values and serve its interests. The execution of such a task shall be governed by Article III-310.

6.   Those Member States whose military capabilities fulfil higher criteria and which have made more binding commitments to one another in this area with a view to the most demanding missions shall establish permanent structured cooperation within the Union framework. Such cooperation shall be governed by Article III-312. It shall not affect the provisions of Article III-309.

7.   If a Member State is the victim of armed aggression on its territory, the other Member States shall have towards it an obligation of aid and assistance by all the means in their power, in accordance with Article 51 of the United Nations Charter. This shall not prejudice the specific character of the security and defence policy of certain Member States. Commitments and cooperation in this area shall be consistent with commitments under the North Atlantic Treaty Organisation, which, for those States which are members of it, remains the foundation of their collective defence and the forum for its implementation.

8.   The European Parliament shall be regularly consulted on the main aspects and basic choices of the common security and defence policy. It shall be kept informed of how it evolves.

Article I-42   Specific provisions relating to the area of freedom, security and justice

1.   The Union shall constitute an area of freedom, security and justice:
- (a) by adopting European laws and framework laws intended, where necessary, to approximate laws and regulations of the Member States in the areas referred to in Part III;
- (b) by promoting mutual confidence between the competent authorities of the Member States, in particular on the basis of mutual recognition of judicial and extrajudicial decisions;
- (c) by operational cooperation between the competent authorities of the Member States, including the police, customs and other services specialising in the prevention and detection of criminal offences.

2.   National Parliaments may, within the framework of the area of freedom, security and justice, participate in the evaluation mechanisms provided for in Article III-260. They shall be involved in the political monitoring of Europol and the evaluation of Eurojust's activities in accordance with Articles III-276 and III-273.

3.   Member States shall have a right of initiative in the field of police and judicial cooperation in criminal matters, in accordance with Article III-264.

Article I-43   Solidarity clause

1.   The Union and its Member States shall act jointly in a spirit of solidarity if a Member State is the object of a terrorist attack or the victim of a natural or man-made disaster. The Union shall mobilise all the instruments at its disposal, including the military resources made available by the Member States, to:

(a) —prevent the terrorist threat in the territory of the Member States;
— protect democratic institutions and the civilian population from any terrorist attack;
— assist a Member State in its territory, at the request of its political authorities, in the event of a terrorist attack;

(b) assist a Member State in its territory, at the request of its political authorities, in the event of a natural or man-made disaster.

2.   The detailed arrangements for implementing this Article are set out in Article III-329.

CHAPTER III   ENHANCED COOPERATION

Article I-44   Enhanced cooperation

1.   Member States which wish to establish enhanced cooperation between themselves within the framework of the Union's non-exclusive competences may make use of its institutions and exercise those competences by applying the relevant provisions of the Constitution, subject to the limits and in accordance with the procedures laid down in this Article and in Articles III-416 to III-423. Enhanced cooperation shall aim to further the objectives of the Union, protect its interests and reinforce its integration process. Such cooperation shall be open at any time to all Member States, in accordance with Article III-418.

2.   The European decision authorising enhanced cooperation shall be adopted by the Council as a last resort, when it has established that the objectives of such cooperation cannot be attained within a reasonable period by the Union as a whole, and provided that at least one third of the Member States participate in it. The Council shall act in accordance with the procedure laid down in Article III-419.

3.   All members of the Council may participate in its deliberations, but only members of the Council representing the Member States participating in enhanced cooperation shall take part in the vote. Unanimity shall be constituted by the votes of the representatives of the participating Member States only. A qualified majority shall be defined as at least 55% of the members of the Council representing the participating Member States, comprising at least 65% of the population of these States. A blocking minority must include at least the minimum number of Council members representing more than 35% of the population of the participating Member States, plus one member, failing which the qualified majority shall be deemed attained. By way of derogation from the third and fourth subparagraphs, where the Council does not act on a proposal from the Commission or from the Union Minister for Foreign Affairs, the required qualified majority shall be defined as at least 72% of the members of the Council representing the participating Member States, comprising at least 65% of the population of these States.

4.   Acts adopted in the framework of enhanced cooperation shall bind only participating Member States. They shall not be regarded as part of the acquis which has to be accepted by candidate States for accession to the Union.

TITLE VI   THE DEMOCRATIC LIFE OF THE UNION

Article I-45   The principle of democratic equality

In all its activities, the Union shall observe the principle of the equality of its citizens, who shall receive equal attention from its institutions, bodies, offices and agencies.

Article I-46   The principle of representative democracy

1. The functioning of the Union shall be founded on representative democracy.
2. Citizens are directly represented at Union level in the European Parliament.

Member States are represented in the European Council by their Heads of State or Government and in the Council by their governments, themselves democratically accountable either to their national Parliaments, or to their citizens.

3. Every citizen shall have the right to participate in the democratic life of the Union. Decisions shall be taken as openly and as closely as possible to the citizen.

4. Political parties at European level contribute to forming European political awareness and to expressing the will of citizens of the Union.

Article I-47   The principle of participatory democracy

1. The institutions shall, by appropriate means, give citizens and representative associations the opportunity to make known and publicly exchange their views in all areas of Union action.

2. The institutions shall maintain an open, transparent and regular dialogue with representative associations and civil society.

3. The Commission shall carry out broad consultations with parties concerned in order to ensure that the Union's actions are coherent and transparent.

4. Not less than one million citizens who are nationals of a significant number of Member States may take the initiative of inviting the Commission, within the framework of its powers, to submit any appropriate proposal on matters where citizens consider that a legal act of the Union is required for the purpose of implementing the Constitution. European laws shall determine the provisions for the procedures and conditions required for such a citizens' initiative, including the minimum number of Member States from which such citizens must come.

Article I-48   The social partners and autonomous social dialogue

The Union recognises and promotes the role of the social partners at its level, taking into account the diversity of national systems. It shall facilitate dialogue between the social partners, respecting their autonomy.

The Tripartite Social Summit for Growth and Employment shall contribute to social dialogue.

Article I-49   The European Ombudsman

A European Ombudsman elected by the European Parliament shall receive, examine and report on complaints about maladministration in the activities of the Union institutions, bodies, offices or agencies, under the conditions laid down in the Constitution. The European Ombudsman shall be completely independent in the performance of his or her duties.

Article I-50   Transparency of the proceedings of Union institutions, bodies, offices and agencies

1. In order to promote good governance and ensure the participation of civil society, the Union institutions, bodies, offices and agencies shall conduct their work as openly as possible.

2. The European Parliament shall meet in public, as shall the Council when considering and voting on a draft legislative act.

3. Any citizen of the Union, and any natural or legal person residing or having its registered office in a Member State shall have, under the conditions laid down in Part III, a right of

access to documents of the Union institutions, bodies, offices and agencies, whatever their medium.

European laws shall lay down the general principles and limits which, on grounds of public or private interest, govern the right of access to such documents.

4.   Each institution, body, office or agency shall determine in its own rules of procedure specific provisions regarding access to its documents, in accordance with the European laws referred to in paragraph 3.

Article I-51   Protection of personal data

1.   Everyone has the right to the protection of personal data concerning him or her.

2.   European laws or framework laws shall lay down the rules relating to the protection of individuals with regard to the processing of personal data by Union institutions, bodies, offices and agencies, and by the Member States when carrying out activities which fall within the scope of Union law, and the rules relating to the free movement of such data. Compliance with these rules shall be subject to the control of independent authorities.

Article I-52   Status of churches and non-confessional organisations

1.   The Union respects and does not prejudice the status under national law of churches and religious associations or communities in the Member States.

2.   The Union equally respects the status under national law of philosophical and non-confessional organisations.

3.   Recognising their identity and their specific contribution, the Union shall maintain an open, transparent and regular dialogue with these churches and organisations.

TITLE VII   THE UNION'S FINANCES

Article I-53   Budgetary and financial principles

1.   All items of Union revenue and expenditure shall be included in estimates drawn up for each financial year and shall be shown in the Union's budget, in accordance with Part III.

2.   The revenue and expenditure shown in the budget shall be in balance.

3.   The expenditure shown in the budget shall be authorised for the annual budgetary period in accordance with the European law referred to in Article III-412.

4.   The implementation of expenditure shown in the budget shall require the prior adoption of a legally binding Union act providing a legal basis for its action and for the implementation of the corresponding expenditure in accordance with the European law referred to in Article III-412, except in cases for which that law provides.

5.   With a view to maintaining budgetary discipline, the Union shall not adopt any act which is likely to have appreciable implications for the budget without providing an assurance that the expenditure arising from such an act is capable of being financed within the limit of the Union's own resources and in compliance with the multiannual financial framework referred to in Article I-55.

6.   The budget shall be implemented in accordance with the principle of sound financial management. Member States shall cooperate with the Union to ensure that the appropriations entered in the budget are used in accordance with this principle.

7.   The Union and the Member States, in accordance with Article III-415, shall counter fraud and any other illegal activities affecting the financial interests of the Union.

Article I-54   The Union's own resources

1.   The Union shall provide itself with the means necessary to attain its objectives and carry through its policies.

2.   Without prejudice to other revenue, the Union's budget shall be financed wholly from its own resources.

3.   A European law of the Council shall lay down the provisions relating to the system of

own resources of the Union. In this context it may establish new categories of own resources or abolish an existing category. The Council shall act unanimously after consulting the European Parliament. That law shall not enter into force until it is approved by the Member States in accordance with their respective constitutional requirements.

4.   A European law of the Council shall lay down implementing measures of the Union's own resources system insofar as this is provided for in the European law adopted on the basis of paragraph 3. The Council shall act after obtaining the consent of the European Parliament.

Article I-55   The multiannual financial framework

1.   The multiannual financial framework shall ensure that Union expenditure develops in an orderly manner and within the limits of its own resources. It shall determine the amounts of the annual ceilings of appropriations for commitments by category of expenditure in accordance with Article III-402.

2.   A European law of the Council shall lay down the multiannual financial framework. The Council shall act unanimously after obtaining the consent of the European Parliament, which shall be given by a majority of its component members.

3.   The annual budget of the Union shall comply with the multiannual financial framework.

4.   The European Council may, unanimously, adopt a European decision authorising the Council to act by a qualified majority when adopting the European law of the Council referred to in paragraph 2.

Article I-56   The Union's budget

A European law shall establish the Union's annual budget in accordance with Article III-404.

TITLE VIII   THE UNION AND ITS NEIGHBOURS

Article I-57   The Union and its neighbours

1.   The Union shall develop a special relationship with neighbouring countries, aiming to establish an area of prosperity and good neighbourliness, founded on the values of the Union and characterised by close and peaceful relations based on cooperation.

2.   For the purposes of paragraph 1, the Union may conclude specific agreements with the countries concerned. These agreements may contain reciprocal rights and obligations as well as the possibility of undertaking activities jointly. Their implementation shall be the subject of periodic consultation.

TITLE IX   UNION MEMBERSHIP

Article I-58   Conditions of eligibility and procedure for accession to the Union

1.   The Union shall be open to all European States which respect the values referred to in Article I-2, and are committed to promoting them together.

2.   Any European State which wishes to become a member of the Union shall address its application to the Council. The European Parliament and national Parliaments shall be notified of this application. The Council shall act unanimously after consulting the Commission and after obtaining the consent of the European Parliament, which shall act by a majority of its component members. The conditions and arrangements for admission shall be the subject of an agreement between the Member States and the candidate State. That agreement shall be subject to ratification by each contracting State, in accordance with its respective constitutional requirements.

Article I-59   Suspension of certain rights resulting from Union membership

1.   On the reasoned initiative of one third of the Member States or the reasoned initiative of the European Parliament or on a proposal from the Commission, the Council may

adopt a European decision determining that there is a clear risk of a serious breach by a Member State of the values referred to in Article I-2. The Council shall act by a majority of four fifths of its members after obtaining the consent of the European Parliament. Before making such a determination, the Council shall hear the Member State in question and, acting in accordance with the same procedure, may address recommendations to that State. The Council shall regularly verify that the grounds on which such a determination was made continue to apply.

2.   The European Council, on the initiative of one third of the Member States or on a proposal from the Commission, may adopt a European decision determining the existence of a serious and persistent breach by a Member State of the values mentioned in Article I-2, after inviting the Member State in question to submit its observations. The European Council shall act unanimously after obtaining the consent of the European Parliament.

3.   Where a determination under paragraph 2 has been made, the Council, acting by a qualified majority, may adopt a European decision suspending certain of the rights deriving from the application of the Constitution to the Member State in question, including the voting rights of the member of the Council representing that State. The Council shall take into account the possible consequences of such a suspension for the rights and obligations of natural and legal persons. In any case, that State shall continue to be bound by its obligations under the Constitution.

4.   The Council, acting by a qualified majority, may adopt a European decision varying or revoking measures adopted under paragraph 3 in response to changes in the situation which led to their being imposed.

5.   For the purposes of this Article, the member of the European Council or of the Council representing the Member State in question shall not take part in the vote and the Member State in question shall not be counted in the calculation of the one third or four fifths of Member States referred to in paragraphs 1 and 2. Abstentions by members present in person or represented shall not prevent the adoption of European decisions referred to in paragraph 2.

For the adoption of the European decisions referred to in paragraphs 3 and 4, a qualified majority shall be defined as at least 72% of the members of the Council, representing the participating Member States, comprising at least 65% of the population of these States.

Where, following a decision to suspend voting rights adopted pursuant to paragraph 3, the Council acts by a qualified majority on the basis of a provision of the Constitution, that qualified majority shall be defined as in the second subparagraph, or, where the Council acts on a proposal from the Commission or from the Union Minister for Foreign Affairs, as at least 55% of the members of the Council representing the participating Member States, comprising at least 65% of the population of these States. In the latter case, a blocking minority must include at least the minimum number of Council members representing more than 35% of the population of the participating Member States, plus one member, failing which the qualified majority shall be deemed attained.

6.   For the purposes of this Article, the European Parliament shall act by a two-thirds majority of the votes cast, representing the majority of its component members.

Article I-60   Voluntary withdrawal from the Union

1.   Any Member State may decide to withdraw from the Union in accordance with its own constitutional requirements.

2.   A Member State which decides to withdraw shall notify the European Council of its intention. In the light of the guidelines provided by the European Council, the Union shall negotiate and conclude an agreement with that State, setting out the arrangements for its withdrawal, taking account of the framework for its future relationship with the Union. That agreement shall be negotiated in accordance with Article III-325(3). It shall be concluded by the Council, acting by a qualified majority, after obtaining the consent of the European Parliament.

3.   The Constitution shall cease to apply to the State in question from the date of entry into force of the withdrawal agreement or, failing that, two years after the notification referred to in paragraph 2, unless the European Council, in agreement with the Member State concerned, unanimously decides to extend this period.

4.   For the purposes of paragraphs 2 and 3, the member of the European Council or of the Council representing the withdrawing Member State shall not participate in the discussions of the European Council or Council or in European decisions concerning it.

A qualified majority shall be defined as at least 72% of the members of the Council, representing the participating Member States, comprising at least 65% of the population of these States.

5.   If a State which has withdrawn from the Union asks to rejoin, its request shall be subject to the procedure referred to in Article I-58.

PART II   THE CHARTER OF FUNDAMENTAL RIGHTS OF THE UNION

PREAMBLE

The peoples of Europe, in creating an ever closer union among them, are resolved to share a peaceful future based on common values.

Conscious of its spiritual and moral heritage, the Union is founded on the indivisible, universal values of human dignity, freedom, equality and solidarity; it is based on the principles of democracy and the rule of law. It places the individual at the heart of its activities, by establishing the citizenship of the Union and by creating an area of freedom, security and justice.

The Union contributes to the preservation and to the development of these common values while respecting the diversity of the cultures and traditions of the peoples of Europe as well as the national identities of the Member States and the organisation of their public authorities at national, regional and local levels; it seeks to promote balanced and sustainable development and ensures free movement of persons, services, goods and capital, and the freedom of establishment.

To this end, it is necessary to strengthen the protection of fundamental rights in the light of changes in society, social progress and scientific and technological developments by making those rights more visible in a Charter.

This Charter reaffirms, with due regard for the powers and tasks of the Union and the principle of subsidiarity, the rights as they result, in particular, from the constitutional traditions and international obligations common to the Member States, the European Convention for the Protection of Human Rights and Fundamental Freedoms, the Social Charters adopted by the Union and by the Council of Europe and the case-law of the Court of Justice of the European Union and of the European Court of Human Rights. In this context the Charter will be interpreted by the courts of the Union and the Member States with due regard to the explanations prepared under the authority of the Praesidium of the Convention which drafted the Charter and updated under the responsibility of the Praesidium of the European Convention.

Enjoyment of these rights entails responsibilities and duties with regard to other persons, to the human community and to future generations.

The Union therefore recognises the rights, freedoms and principles set out hereafter.

TITLE I   DIGNITY

Article II-61   Human dignity
Human dignity is inviolable. It must be respected and protected.

Article II-62   Right to life
1. Everyone has the right to life.
2. No one shall be condemned to the death penalty, or executed.

Article II-63   Right to the integrity of the person
1. Everyone has the right to respect for his or her physical and mental integrity.
2. In the fields of medicine and biology, the following must be respected in particular:
    (a) the free and informed consent of the person concerned, according to the procedures laid down by law;
    (b) the prohibition of eugenic practices, in particular those aiming at the selection of persons;
    (c) the prohibition on making the human body and its parts as such a source of financial gain;
    (d) the prohibition of the reproductive cloning of human beings.

Article II-64   Prohibition of torture and inhuman or degrading treatment or punishment
No one shall be subjected to torture or to inhuman or degrading treatment or punishment.

Article II-65   Prohibition of slavery and forced labour
1. No one shall be held in slavery or servitude.
2. No one shall be required to perform forced or compulsory labour.
3. Trafficking in human beings is prohibited.

TITLE II   FREEDOMS

Article II-66   Right to liberty and security
Everyone has the right to liberty and security of person.

Article II-67   Respect for private and family life
Everyone has the right to respect for his or her private and family life, home and communications.

Article II-68   Protection of personal data
1. Everyone has the right to the protection of personal data concerning him or her.
2. Such data must be processed fairly for specified purposes and on the basis of the consent of the person concerned or some other legitimate basis laid down by law. Everyone has the right of access to data which has been collected concerning him or her, and the right to have it rectified.
3. Compliance with these rules shall be subject to control by an independent authority.

Article II-69   Right to marry and right to found a family
The right to marry and the right to found a family shall be guaranteed in accordance with the national laws governing the exercise of these rights.

Article II-70   Freedom of thought, conscience and religion
1. Everyone has the right to freedom of thought, conscience and religion. This right includes freedom to change religion or belief and freedom, either alone or in community with others and in public or in private, to manifest religion or belief, in worship, teaching, practice and observance.
2. The right to conscientious objection is recognised, in accordance with the national laws governing the exercise of this right.

Article II-71   Freedom of expression and information
1. Everyone has the right to freedom of expression. This right shall include freedom to

hold opinions and to receive and impart information and ideas without interference by public authority and regardless of frontiers.

2.   The freedom and pluralism of the media shall be respected.

Article II-72   Freedom of assembly and of association

1.   Everyone has the right to freedom of peaceful assembly and to freedom of association at all levels, in particular in political, trade union and civic matters, which implies the right of everyone to form and to join trade unions for the protection of his or her interests.

2.   Political parties at Union level contribute to expressing the political will of the citizens of the Union.

Article II-73   Freedom of the arts and sciences

The arts and scientific research shall be free of constraint. Academic freedom shall be respected.

Article II-74   Right to education

1.   Everyone has the right to education and to have access to vocational and continuing training.

2.   This right includes the possibility to receive free compulsory education.

3.   The freedom to found educational establishments with due respect for democratic principles and the right of parents to ensure the education and teaching of their children in conformity with their religious, philosophical and pedagogical convictions shall be respected, in accordance with the national laws governing the exercise of such freedom and right.

Article II-75   Freedom to choose an occupation and right to engage in work

1.   Everyone has the right to engage in work and to pursue a freely chosen or accepted occupation.

2.   Every citizen of the Union has the freedom to seek employment, to work, to exercise the right of establishment and to provide services in any Member State.

3.   Nationals of third countries who are authorised to work in the territories of the Member States are entitled to working conditions equivalent to those of citizens of the Union.

Article II-76   Freedom to conduct a business

The freedom to conduct a business in accordance with Union law and national laws and practices is recognised.

Article II-77   Right to property

1.   Everyone has the right to own, use, dispose of and bequeath his or her lawfully acquired possessions. No one may be deprived of his or her possessions, except in the public interest and in the cases and under the conditions provided for by law, subject to fair compensation being paid in good time for their loss. The use of property may be regulated by law insofar as is necessary for the general interest.

2.   Intellectual property shall be protected.

Article II-78   Right to asylum

The right to asylum shall be guaranteed with due respect for the rules of the Geneva Convention of 28 July 1951 and the Protocol of 31 January 1967 relating to the status of refugees and in accordance with the Constitution.

Article II-79   Protection in the event of removal, expulsion or extradition

1.   Collective expulsions are prohibited.

2.   No one may be removed, expelled or extradited to a State where there is a serious risk that he or she would be subjected to the death penalty, torture or other inhuman or degrading treatment or punishment.

TITLE III   EQUALITY

Article II-80   Equality before the law
Everyone is equal before the law.

Article II-81   Non-discrimination
1.   Any discrimination based on any ground such as sex, race, colour, ethnic or social origin, genetic features, language, religion or belief, political or any other opinion, membership of a national minority, property, birth, disability, age or sexual orientation shall be prohibited.

2.   Within the scope of application of the Constitution and without prejudice to any of its specific provisions, any discrimination on grounds of nationality shall be prohibited.

Article II-82   Cultural, religious and linguistic diversity
The Union shall respect cultural, religious and linguistic diversity.

Article II-83   Equality between women and men
Equality between women and men must be ensured in all areas, including employment, work and pay.

The principle of equality shall not prevent the maintenance or adoption of measures providing for specific advantages in favour of the under-represented sex.

Article II-84   The rights of the child
1.   Children shall have the right to such protection and care as is necessary for their well-being. They may express their views freely. Such views shall be taken into consideration on matters which concern them in accordance with their age and maturity.

2.   In all actions relating to children, whether taken by public authorities or private institutions, the child's best interests must be a primary consideration.

3.   Every child shall have the right to maintain on a regular basis a personal relationship and direct contact with both his or her parents, unless that is contrary to his or her interests.

Article II-85   The rights of the elderly
The Union recognises and respects the rights of the elderly to lead a life of dignity and independence and to participate in social and cultural life.

Article II-86   Integration of persons with disabilities
The Union recognises and respects the right of persons with disabilities to benefit from measures designed to ensure their independence, social and occupational integration and participation in the life of the community.

TITLE IV   SOLIDARITY

Article II-87   Workers' right to information and consultation within the undertaking
Workers or their representatives must, at the appropriate levels, be guaranteed information and consultation in good time in the cases and under the conditions provided for by Union law and national laws and practices.

Article II-88   Right of collective bargaining and action
Workers and employers, or their respective organisations, have, in accordance with Union law and national laws and practices, the right to negotiate and conclude collective agreements at the appropriate levels and, in cases of conflicts of interest, to take collective action to defend their interests, including strike action.

Article II-89   Right of access to placement services
Everyone has the right of access to a free placement service.

Article II-90   Protection in the event of unjustified dismissal
Every worker has the right to protection against unjustified dismissal, in accordance with Union law and national laws and practices.

Article II-91   Fair and just working conditions
1.   Every worker has the right to working conditions which respect his or her health, safety and dignity.
2.   Every worker has the right to limitation of maximum working hours, to daily and weekly rest periods and to an annual period of paid leave.

Article II-92   Prohibition of child labour and protection of young people at work
The employment of children is prohibited. The minimum age of admission to employment may not be lower than the minimum school-leaving age, without prejudice to such rules as may be more favourable to young people and except for limited derogations.

Young people admitted to work must have working conditions appropriate to their age and be protected against economic exploitation and any work likely to harm their safety, health or physical, mental, moral or social development or to interfere with their education.

Article II-93   Family and professional life
1.   The family shall enjoy legal, economic and social protection.
2.   To reconcile family and professional life, everyone shall have the right to protection from dismissal for a reason connected with maternity and the right to paid maternity leave and to parental leave following the birth or adoption of a child.

Article II-94   Social security and social assistance
1.   The Union recognises and respects the entitlement to social security benefits and social services providing protection in cases such as maternity, illness, industrial accidents, dependency or old age, and in the case of loss of employment, in accordance with the rules laid down by Union law and national laws and practices.
2.   Everyone residing and moving legally within the European Union is entitled to social security benefits and social advantages in accordance with Union law and national laws and practices.
3.   In order to combat social exclusion and poverty, the Union recognises and respects the right to social and housing assistance so as to ensure a decent existence for all those who lack sufficient resources, in accordance with the rules laid down by Union law and national laws and practices.

Article II-95   Health care
Everyone has the right of access to preventive health care and the right to benefit from medical treatment under the conditions established by national laws and practices. A high level of human health protection shall be ensured in the definition and implementation of all Union policies and activities.

Article II-96   Access to services of general economic interest
The Union recognises and respects access to services of general economic interest as provided for in national laws and practices, in accordance with the Constitution, in order to promote the social and territorial cohesion of the Union.

Article II-97   Environmental protection
A high level of environmental protection and the improvement of the quality of the environment must be integrated into the policies of the Union and ensured in accordance with the principle of sustainable development.

Article II-98   Consumer protection
Union policies shall ensure a high level of consumer protection.

TITLE V   CITIZENS' RIGHTS

Article II-99   Right to vote and to stand as a candidate at elections to the European Parliament

1.   Every citizen of the Union has the right to vote and to stand as a candidate at elections to the European Parliament in the Member State in which he or she resides, under the same conditions as nationals of that State.

2.   Members of the European Parliament shall be elected by direct universal suffrage in a free and secret ballot.

Article II-100   Right to vote and to stand as a candidate at municipal elections

Every citizen of the Union has the right to vote and to stand as a candidate at municipal elections in the Member State in which he or she resides under the same conditions as nationals of that State.

Article II-101   Right to good administration

1.   Every person has the right to have his or her affairs handled impartially, fairly and within a reasonable time by the institutions, bodies, offices and agencies of the Union.

2.   This right includes:
   (a) the right of every person to be heard, before any individual measure which would affect him or her adversely is taken;
   (b) the right of every person to have access to his or her file, while respecting the legitimate interests of confidentiality and of professional and business secrecy;
   (c) the obligation of the administration to give reasons for its decisions.

3.   Every person has the right to have the Union make good any damage caused by its institutions or by its servants in the performance of their duties, in accordance with the general principles common to the laws of the Member States.

4.   Every person may write to the institutions of the Union in one of the languages of the Constitution and must have an answer in the same language.

Article II-102   Right of access to documents

Any citizen of the Union, and any natural or legal person residing or having its registered office in a Member State, has a right of access to documents of the institutions, bodies, offices and agencies of the Union, whatever their medium.

Article II-103   European Ombudsman

Any citizen of the Union and any natural or legal person residing or having its registered office in a Member State has the right to refer to the European Ombudsman cases of maladministration in the activities of the institutions, bodies, offices or agencies of the Union, with the exception of the Court of Justice of the European Union acting in its judicial role.

Article II-104   Right to petition

Any citizen of the Union and any natural or legal person residing or having its registered office in a Member State has the right to petition the European Parliament.

Article II-105   Freedom of movement and of residence

1.   Every citizen of the Union has the right to move and reside freely within the territory of the Member States.

2.   Freedom of movement and residence may be granted, in accordance with the Constitution, to nationals of third countries legally resident in the territory of a Member State.

Article II-106   Diplomatic and consular protection

Every citizen of the Union shall, in the territory of a third country in which the Member State of which he or she is a national is not represented, be entitled to protection by the diplomatic or consular authorities of any Member State, on the same conditions as the nationals of that Member State.

TITLE VI JUSTICE

Article II-107 Right to an effective remedy and to a fair trial

Everyone whose rights and freedoms guaranteed by the law of the Union are violated has the right to an effective remedy before a tribunal in compliance with the conditions laid down in this Article.

Everyone is entitled to a fair and public hearing within a reasonable time by an independent and impartial tribunal previously established by law. Everyone shall have the possibility of being advised, defended and represented.

Legal aid shall be made available to those who lack sufficient resources insofar as such aid is necessary to ensure effective access to justice.

Article II-108 Presumption of innocence and right of defence

1.   Everyone who has been charged shall be presumed innocent until proved guilty according to law.

2.   Respect for the rights of the defence of anyone who has been charged shall be guaranteed.

Article II-109 Principles of legality and proportionality of criminal offences and penalties

1.   No one shall be held guilty of any criminal offence on account of any act or omission which did not constitute a criminal offence under national law or international law at the time when it was committed. Nor shall a heavier penalty be imposed than that which was applicable at the time the criminal offence was committed. If, subsequent to the commission of a criminal offence, the law provides for a lighter penalty, that penalty shall be applicable.

2.   This Article shall not prejudice the trial and punishment of any person for any act or omission which, at the time when it was committed, was criminal according to the general principles recognised by the community of nations.

3.   The severity of penalties must not be disproportionate to the criminal offence.

Article II-110 Right not to be tried or punished twice in criminal proceedings for the same criminal offence

No one shall be liable to be tried or punished again in criminal proceedings for an offence for which he or she has already been finally acquitted or convicted within the Union in accordance with the law.

TITLE VII   GENERAL PROVISIONS GOVERNING THE INTERPRETATION AND APPLICATION OF THE CHARTER

Article II-111 Field of application

1.   The provisions of this Charter are addressed to the institutions, bodies, offices and agencies of the Union with due regard for the principle of subsidiarity and to the Member States only when they are implementing Union law. They shall therefore respect the rights, observe the principles and promote the application thereof in accordance with their respective powers and respecting the limits of the powers of the Union as conferred on it in the other Parts of the Constitution.

2.   This Charter does not extend the field of application of Union law beyond the powers of the Union or establish any new power or task for the Union, or modify powers and tasks defined in the other Parts of the Constitution.

Article II-112 Scope and interpretation of rights and principles

1.   Any limitation on the exercise of the rights and freedoms recognised by this Charter must be provided for by law and respect the essence of those rights and freedoms. Subject to the principle of proportionality, limitations may be made only if they are necessary and

genuinely meet objectives of general interest recognised by the Union or the need to protect the rights and freedoms of others.

2.   Rights recognised by this Charter for which provision is made in other Parts of the Constitution shall be exercised under the conditions and within the limits defined by these relevant Parts.

3.   Insofar as this Charter contains rights which correspond to rights guaranteed by the Convention for the Protection of Human Rights and Fundamental Freedoms, the meaning and scope of those rights shall be the same as those laid down by the said Convention. This provision shall not prevent Union law providing more extensive protection.

4.   Insofar as this Charter recognises fundamental rights as they result from the constitutional traditions common to the Member States, those rights shall be interpreted in harmony with those traditions.

5.   The provisions of this Charter which contain principles may be implemented by legislative and executive acts taken by institutions, bodies, offices and agencies of the Union, and by acts of Member States when they are implementing Union law, in the exercise of their respective powers. They shall be judicially cognisable only in the interpretation of such acts and in the ruling on their legality.

6.   Full account shall be taken of national laws and practices as specified in this Charter.

7.   The explanations drawn up as a way of providing guidance in the interpretation of the Charter of Fundamental Rights shall be given due regard by the courts of the Union and of the Member States.

Article II-113   Level of protection
Nothing in this Charter shall be interpreted as restricting or adversely affecting human rights and fundamental freedoms as recognised, in their respective fields of application, by Union law and international law and by international agreements to which the Union or all the Member States are party, including the European Convention for the Protection of Human Rights and Fundamental Freedoms, and by the Member States' constitutions.

Article II-114   Prohibition of abuse of rights
Nothing in this Charter shall be interpreted as implying any right to engage in any activity or to perform any act aimed at the destruction of any of the rights and freedoms recognised in this Charter or at their limitation to a greater extent than is provided for herein.

PART III[2]   THE POLICIES AND FUNCTIONING OF THE UNION
TITLE I   PROVISIONS OF GENERAL APPLICATION

Article III-115   (new)
The Union shall ensure consistency between the policies and activities referred to in this Part, taking all of its objectives into account and in accordance with the principle of conferral of powers.

Article III-116   (ex Article 3(2) EC)
In all the activities referred to in this Part, the Union shall aim to eliminate inequalities, and to promote equality, between women and men.

---

[2]   **Editor's Note**: The helpful cross references to the corresponding Articles of the EC and TEU Treaties (where they previously existed), which were provided in the provisional consolidated version of this Treaty, have not been included in the Official Treaty version of the Constitutional Treaty. Therefore I have re-introduced these cross references for both Parts III and IV of the Constitutional Treaty. 'EC' refers to the European Community Treaty and 'TEU' refers to the Treaty on European Union.

Article III-117   (new)
In defining and implementing the policies and actions referred to in this Part, the Union shall take into account requirements linked to the promotion of a high level of employment, the guarantee of adequate social protection, the fight against social exclusion, and a high level of education, training and protection of human health.

Article III-118   (new)
In defining and implementing the policies and activities referred to in this Part, the Union shall aim to combat discrimination based on sex, racial or ethnic origin, religion or belief, disability, age or sexual orientation.

Article III-119   (ex Article 6 EC)
Environmental protection requirements must be integrated into the definition and implementation of the policies and activities referred to in this Part, in particular with a view to promoting sustainable development.

Article III-120   (ex Article 153(2) EC)
Consumer protection requirements shall be taken into account in defining and implementing other Union policies and activities.

Article III-121   (new)
In formulating and implementing the Union's agriculture, fisheries, transport, internal market, research and technological development and space policies, the Union and the Member States shall, since animals are sentient beings, pay full regard to the requirements of animal welfare, while respecting the legislative or administrative provisions and customs of Member States relating in particular to religious rites, cultural traditions and regional heritage.

Article III-122   (ex Article 16 EC)
Without prejudice to Articles I-5, III-166, III-167 and III-238, and given the place occupied by services of general economic interest as services to which all in the Union attribute value as well as their role in promoting its social and territorial cohesion, the Union and the Member States, each within their respective competences and within the scope of application of the Constitution, shall take care that such services operate on the basis of principles and conditions, in particular economic and financial conditions, which enable them to fulfil their missions. European laws shall establish these principles and set these conditions without prejudice to the competence of Member States, in compliance with the Constitution, to provide, to commission and to fund such services.

TITLE II   NON-DISCRIMINATION AND CITIZENSHIP

Article III-123   (ex Article 12 EC)
European laws or framework laws may lay down rules to prohibit discrimination on grounds of nationality as referred to in Article I-4(2).

Article III-124   (ex Article 13 EC)
1.   Without prejudice to the other provisions of the Constitution and within the limits of the powers assigned by it to the Union, a European law or framework law of the Council may establish the measures needed to combat discrimination based on sex, racial or ethnic origin, religion or belief, disability, age or sexual orientation. The Council shall act unanimously after obtaining the consent of the European Parliament.

2.   By way of derogation from paragraph 1, European laws or framework laws may establish basic principles for Union incentive measures and define such measures, to support action taken by Member States in order to contribute to the achievement of the objectives referred to in paragraph 1, excluding any harmonisation of their laws and regulations.

Article III-125   (ex Article 18 EC)

1.   If action by the Union should prove necessary to facilitate the exercise of the right, referred to in Article I-10(2)(a), of every citizen of the Union to move and reside freely and the Constitution has not provided the necessary powers, European laws or framework laws may establish measures for that purpose.

2.   For the same purposes as those referred to in paragraph 1 and if the Constitution has not provided the necessary powers, a European law or framework law of the Council may establish measures concerning passports, identity cards, residence permits or any other such document and measures concerning social security or social protection. The Council shall act unanimously after consulting the European Parliament.

Article III-126   (ex Article 19 EC)

A European law or framework law of the Council shall determine the detailed arrangements for exercising the right, referred to in Article I-10(2)(b), for every citizen of the Union to vote and to stand as a candidate in municipal elections and elections to the European Parliament in his or her Member State of residence without being a national of that State. The Council shall act unanimously after consulting the European Parliament. These arrangements may provide for derogations where warranted by problems specific to a Member State. The right to vote and to stand as a candidate in elections to the European Parliament shall be exercised without prejudice to Article III-330(1) and the measures adopted for its implementation.

Article III-127   (ex Article 20 EC)

Member States shall adopt the necessary provisions to secure diplomatic and consular protection of citizens of the Union in third countries, as referred to in Article I-10(2)(c). Member States shall commence the international negotiations required to secure this protection. A European law of the Council may establish the measures necessary to facilitate such protection. The Council shall act after consulting the European Parliament.

Article III-128   (ex Article 21 EC)

The languages in which every citizen of the Union has the right to address the institutions or bodies under Article I-10(2)(d), and to have an answer, are those listed in Article IV-448(1). The institutions and bodies referred to in Article I-10(2)(d) are those listed in Articles I-19(1), second subparagraph, I-30, I-31 and I-32 and also the European Ombudsman.

Article III-129   (ex Article 22 EC)

The Commission shall report to the European Parliament, to the Council and to the Economic and Social Committee every three years on the application of Article I-10 and of this Title. This report shall take account of the development of the Union. On the basis of this report, and without prejudice to the other provisions of the Constitution, a European law or framework law of the Council may add to the rights laid down in Article I-10. The Council shall act unanimously after obtaining the consent of the European Parliament. The law or framework law concerned shall not enter into force until it is approved by the Member States in accordance with their respective constitutional requirements.

TITLE III   INTERNAL POLICIES AND ACTION
CHAPTER I   INTERNAL MARKET

SECTION 1   ESTABLISHMENT AND FUNCTIONING OF THE INTERNAL MARKET

Article III-130   (ex Articles 14 and 15 EC)

1.   The Union shall adopt measures with the aim of establishing or ensuring the functioning of the internal market, in accordance with the relevant provisions of the Constitution.

2.   The internal market shall comprise an area without internal frontiers in which the free movement of persons, services, goods and capital is ensured in accordance with the Constitution.

3.   The Council, on a proposal from the Commission, shall adopt European regulations and decisions determining the guidelines and conditions necessary to ensure balanced progress in all the sectors concerned.

4.   When drawing up its proposals for achieving the objectives set out in paragraphs 1 and 2, the Commission shall take into account the extent of the effort that certain economies showing differences in development will have to sustain for the establishment of the internal market and it may propose appropriate measures. If these measures take the form of derogations, they must be of a temporary nature and must cause the least possible disturbance to the functioning of the internal market.

Article III-131   (ex Article 297 EC)
Member States shall consult each other with a view to taking together the steps needed to prevent the functioning of the Internal market being affected by measures which a Member State may be called upon to take in the event of serious internal disturbances affecting the maintenance of law and order, in the event of war, serious international tension constituting a threat of war, or in order to carry out obligations it has accepted for the purpose of maintaining peace and international security.

Article III-132   (ex Article 298 EC)
If measures taken in the circumstances referred to in Articles III-131 and III-436 have the effect of distorting the conditions of competition in the internal market, the Commission shall, together with the Member State concerned, examine how these measures can be adjusted to the rules laid down in the Constitution. By way of derogation from the procedure laid down in Articles III-360 and III-361, the Commission or any Member State may bring the matter directly before the Court of Justice if the Commission or Member State considers that another Member State is making improper use of the powers provided for in Articles III-131 and III-436. The Court of Justice shall give its ruling in camera.

SECTION 2   FREE MOVEMENT OF PERSONS AND SERVICES

Subsection 1   Workers

Article III-133   (ex Article 39 EC)
1.   Workers shall have the right to move freely within the Union.

2.   Any discrimination based on nationality between workers of the Member States as regards employment, remuneration and other conditions of work and employment shall be prohibited.

3.   Workers shall have the right, subject to limitations justified on grounds of public policy, public security or public health:
   (a)   to accept offers of employment actually made;
   (b)   to move freely within the territory of Member States for this purpose;
   (c)   to stay in a Member State for the purpose of employment in accordance with the provisions governing the employment of nationals of that State laid down by law, regulation or administrative action;
   (d)   to remain in the territory of a Member State after having been employed in that State, subject to conditions which shall be embodied in European regulations adopted by the Commission.

4.   This Article shall not apply to employment in the public service.

Article III-134   (ex Article 40 EC)
European laws or framework laws shall establish the measures needed to bring about freedom

of movement for workers, as defined in Article III-133. They shall be adopted after consultation of the Economic and Social Committee.

Such European laws or framework laws shall aim, in particular, to:

(a) ensure close cooperation between national employment services;

(b) abolish those administrative procedures and practices and those qualifying periods in respect of eligibility for available employment, whether resulting from national legislation or from agreements previously concluded between Member States, the maintenance of which would form an obstacle to liberalisation of the movement of workers;

(c) abolish all such qualifying periods and other restrictions provided for either under national legislation or under agreements previously concluded between Member States as impose on workers of other Member States conditions regarding the free choice of employment other than those imposed on workers of the State concerned;

(d) set up appropriate machinery to bring offers of employment into touch with applications for employment and to facilitate the achievement of a balance between supply and demand in the employment market in such a way as to avoid serious threats to the standard of living and level of employment in the various regions and industries.

Article III-135   (ex Article 41 EC)

Member States shall, within the framework of a joint programme, encourage the exchange of young workers.

Article III-136   (ex Article 42 EC)

1.   In the field of social security, European laws or framework laws shall establish such measures as are necessary to bring about freedom of movement for workers by making arrangements to secure for employed and self-employed migrant workers and their dependants:

(a) aggregation, for the purpose of acquiring and retaining the right to benefit and of calculating the amount of benefit, of all periods taken into account under the laws of the different countries;

(b) payment of benefits to persons resident in the territories of Member States.

2.   Where a member of the Council considers that a draft European law or framework law referred to in paragraph 1 would affect fundamental aspects of its social security system, including its scope, cost or financial structure, or would affect the financial balance of that system, it may request that the matter be referred to the European Council. In that case, the procedure referred to in Article III-396 shall be suspended. After discussion, the European Council shall, within four months of this suspension, either:

(a) refer the draft back to the Council, which shall terminate the suspension of the procedure referred to in Article III-396, or

(b) request the Commission to submit a new proposal; in that case, the act originally proposed shall be deemed not to have been adopted.

Subsection 2   Freedom of establishment

Article III-137   (ex Article 43 EC)

Within the framework of this Subsection, restrictions on the freedom of establishment of nationals of a Member State in the territory of another Member State shall be prohibited. Such prohibition shall also apply to restrictions on the setting-up of agencies, branches or subsidiaries by nationals of any Member State established in the territory of any Member State. Nationals of a Member State shall have the right, in the territory of another Member State, to take up and pursue activities as self-employed persons and to set up and manage undertakings, in particular companies or firms within the meaning of the second paragraph of Article III-142, under the conditions laid down for its own nationals by the law of the Member State where such establishment is effected, subject to Section 4 relating to capital and payments.

Article III-138   (ex Article 44 EC)

1.   European framework laws shall establish measures to attain freedom of establishment as regards a particular activity. They shall be adopted after consultation of the Economic and Social Committee.

2.   The European Parliament, the Council and the Commission shall carry out the duties devolving upon them under paragraph 1, in particular:

(a)   by according, as a general rule, priority treatment to activities where freedom of establishment makes a particularly valuable contribution to the development of production and trade;

(b)   by ensuring close cooperation between the competent authorities in the Member States in order to ascertain the particular situation within the Union of the various activities concerned;

(c)   by abolishing those administrative procedures and practices, whether resulting from national legislation or from agreements previously concluded between Member States, the maintenance of which would form an obstacle to freedom of establishment;

(d)   by ensuring that workers from one Member State employed in the territory of another Member State may remain in that territory for the purpose of taking up activities therein as self-employed persons, where they satisfy the conditions which they would be required to satisfy if they were entering that State at the time when they intended to take up such activities;

(e)   by enabling a national of one Member State to acquire and use land and buildings situated in the territory of another Member State, insofar as this does not conflict with the principles laid down in Article III-227(2);

(f)   by effecting the progressive abolition of restrictions on freedom of establishment in every branch of activity under consideration, both as regards the conditions for setting up agencies, branches or subsidiaries in the territory of a Member State and as regards the conditions governing the entry of personnel belonging to the main establishment into managerial or supervisory posts in such agencies, branches or subsidiaries;

(g)   by coordinating to the necessary extent the safeguards which, for the protection of the interests of members and others, are required by Member States of companies or firms within the meaning of the second paragraph of Article III-142 with a view to making such safeguards equivalent throughout the Union;

(h)   by satisfying themselves that the conditions of establishment are not distorted by aids granted by Member States.

Article III-139   (ex Article 45 EC)

This Subsection shall not apply, so far as any given Member State is concerned, to activities which in that State are connected, even occasionally, with the exercise of official authority.

European laws or framework laws may exclude certain activities from application of this Subsection.

Article III-140   (ex Article 46 EC)

1.   This Subsection and measures adopted in pursuance thereof shall not prejudice the applicability of provisions laid down by law, regulation or administrative action in Member States providing for special treatment for foreign nationals on grounds of public policy, public security or public health.

2.   European framework laws shall coordinate the national provisions referred to in paragraph 1.

Article III-141   (ex Article 47 EC)

1.   European framework laws shall make it easier for persons to take up and pursue activities as self- employed persons. They shall cover:

(a) the mutual recognition of diplomas, certificates and other evidence of formal qualifications;

(b) the coordination of the provisions laid down by law, regulation or administrative action in Member States concerning the taking-up and pursuit of activities as self-employed persons.

2.   In the case of the medical and allied and pharmaceutical professions, the progressive abolition of restrictions shall be dependent upon coordination of the conditions for the exercise of such professions in the various Member States.

Article III-142   (ex Article 48 EC)

Companies or firms formed in accordance with the law of a Member State and having their registered office, central administration or principal place of business within the Union shall, for the purposes of this Subsection, be treated in the same way as natural persons who are nationals of Member States.

'Companies or firms' means companies or firms constituted under civil or commercial law, including cooperative societies, and other legal persons governed by public or private law, save for those which are non-profit-making.

Article III-143   (ex Article 294 EC)

Member States shall accord nationals of the other Member States the same treatment as their own nationals as regards participation in the capital of companies or firms within the meaning of the second paragraph of Article III-142, without prejudice to the application of the other provisions of the Constitution.

Subsection 3   Freedom to provide services

Article III-144   (ex Article 49 EC)

Within the framework of this Subsection, restrictions on freedom to provide services within the Union shall be prohibited in respect of nationals of Member States who are established in a Member State other than that of the person for whom the services are intended.

European laws or framework laws may extend this Subsection to service providers who are nationals of a third State and who are established within the Union.

Article III-145   (ex Article 50 EC)

Services shall be considered to be 'services' for the purposes of the Constitution where they are normally provided for remuneration, insofar as they are not governed by the provisions relating to freedom of movement for persons, goods and capital.

'Services' shall in particular include:

(a) activities of an industrial character;

(b) activities of a commercial character;

(c) activities of craftsmen;

(d) activities of the professions.

Without prejudice to Subsection 2 relating to freedom of establishment, the person providing a service may, in order to do so, temporarily pursue his or her activity in the Member State where the service is provided, under the same conditions as are imposed by that State on its own nationals.

Article III-146   (ex Article 51 EC)

1. Freedom to provide services in the field of transport shall be governed by Section 7 of Chapter III relating to transport.

2. The liberalisation of banking and insurance services connected with movements of capital shall be effected in step with the liberalisation of movement of capital.

Article III-147   (ex Article 52 EC)

1. European framework laws shall establish measures to achieve the liberalisation of a specific service. They shall be adopted after consultation of the Economic and Social Committee.

2. European framework laws referred to in paragraph 1 shall as a general rule give priority to those services which directly affect production costs or the liberalisation of which helps to promote trade in goods.

Article III-148   (ex Article 53 EC)

The Member States shall endeavour to undertake liberalisation of services beyond the extent required by the European framework laws adopted pursuant to Article III-147(1), if their general economic situation and the situation of the economic sector concerned so permit.

To this end, the Commission shall make recommendations to the Member States concerned.

Article III-149   (ex Article 54 EC)

As long as restrictions on freedom to provide services have not been abolished, the Member States shall apply such restrictions without distinction on grounds of nationality or of residence to all persons providing services within the meaning of the first paragraph of Article III-144.

Article III-150   (ex Article 55 EC)

Articles III-139 to III-142 shall apply to the matters covered by this Subsection.

SECTION 3   FREE MOVEMENT OF GOODS

Subsection 1   Customs union

Article III-151   (ex Articles 23 to 27 EC)

1. The Union shall comprise a customs union which shall cover all trade in goods and which shall involve the prohibition between Member States of customs duties on imports and exports and of all charges having equivalent effect, and the adoption of a common customs tariff in their relations with third countries.

2. Paragraph 4 and Subsection 3 on the prohibition of quantitative restrictions shall apply to products originating in Member States and to products coming from third countries which are in free circulation in Member States.

3. Products coming from a third country shall be considered to be in free circulation in a Member State if the import formalities have been complied with and any customs duties or charges having equivalent effect which are payable have been levied in that Member State, and if they have not benefited from a total or partial drawback of such duties or charges.

4. Customs duties on imports and exports and charges having equivalent effect shall be prohibited between Member States. This prohibition shall also apply to customs duties of a fiscal nature.

5. The Council, on a proposal from the Commission, shall adopt the European regulations and decisions fixing Common Customs Tariff duties.

6. In carrying out the tasks entrusted to it under this Article the Commission shall be guided by:

    (a) the need to promote trade between Member States and third countries;

(b) developments in conditions of competition within the Union insofar as they lead to an improvement in the competitive capacity of undertakings;

(c) the requirements of the Union as regards the supply of raw materials and semi-finished goods; in this connection the Commission shall take care to avoid distorting conditions of competition between Member States in respect of finished goods;

(d) the need to avoid serious disturbances in the economies of Member States and to ensure rational development of production and an expansion of consumption within the Union.

Subsection 2   Customs cooperation

Article III-152   (ex Article 135 EC)

Within the scope of application of the Constitution, European laws or framework laws shall establish measures in order to strengthen customs cooperation between Member States and between them and the Commission.

Subsection 3   Prohibition of quantitative restrictions

Article III-153   (ex Articles 28 and 29 EC)

Quantitative restrictions on imports and exports and all measures having equivalent effect shall be prohibited between Member States.

Article III-154   (ex Article 30 EC)

Article III-153 shall not preclude prohibitions or restrictions on imports, exports or goods in transit justified on grounds of public morality, public policy or public security; the protection of health and life of humans, animals or plants; the protection of national treasures possessing artistic, historic or archaeological value; or the protection of industrial and commercial property. Such prohibitions or restrictions shall not, however, constitute a means of arbitrary discrimination or a disguised restriction on trade between Member States.

Article III-155   (ex Article 31 EC)

1. Member States shall adjust any State monopolies of a commercial character so as to ensure that no discrimination regarding the conditions under which goods are procured and marketed exists between nationals of Member States. This Article shall apply to any body through which a Member State, in law or in fact, either directly or indirectly supervises, determines or appreciably influences imports or exports between Member States. It shall likewise apply to monopolies delegated by the State to others.

2. Member States shall refrain from introducing any new measure which is contrary to the principles laid down in paragraph 1 or which restricts the scope of the Articles dealing with the prohibition of customs duties and quantitative restrictions between Member States.

3. If a State monopoly of a commercial character has rules which are designed to make it easier to dispose of agricultural products or obtain for them the best return, steps should be taken in applying this Article to ensure equivalent safeguards for the employment and standard of living of the producers concerned.

SECTION 4   CAPITAL AND PAYMENTS

Article III-156   (ex Article 56 EC)

Within the framework of this Section, restrictions both on the movement of capital and on payments between Member States and between Member States and third countries shall be prohibited.

Article III-157   (ex Article 57 EC)

1.   Article III-156 shall be without prejudice to the application to third countries of any restrictions which existed on 31 December 1993 under national or Union law adopted in respect of the movement of capital to or from third countries involving direct investment—including investment in real estate, establishment, the provision of financial services or the admission of securities to capital markets. With regard to restrictions which exist under national law in Estonia and Hungary, the date in question shall be 31 December 1999.

2.   European laws or framework laws shall enact measures on the movement of capital to or from third countries involving direct investment—including investment in real estate, establishment, the provision of financial services or the admission of securities to capital markets.

The European Parliament and the Council shall endeavour to achieve the objective of free movement of capital between Member States and third countries to the greatest extent possible and without prejudice to other provisions of the Constitution.

3.   Notwithstanding paragraph 2, only a European law or framework law of the Council may enact measures which constitute a step backwards in Union law as regards the liberalisation of the movement of capital to or from third countries. The Council shall act unanimously after consulting the European Parliament.

Article III-158   (ex Article 58 EC)

1.   Article III-156 shall be without prejudice to the right of Member States:
  (a) to apply the relevant provisions of their tax law which distinguish between taxpayers who are not in the same situation with regard to their place of residence or with regard to the place where their capital is invested;
  (b) to take all requisite measures to prevent infringements of national provisions laid down by law or regulation, in particular in the field of taxation and the prudential supervision of financial institutions, or to lay down procedures for the declaration of capital movements for purposes of administrative or statistical information, or to take measures which are justified on grounds of public policy or public security.

2.   This Section shall be without prejudice to the applicability of restrictions on the right of establishment which are compatible with the Constitution.

3.   The measures and procedures referred to in paragraphs 1 and 2 shall not constitute a means of arbitrary discrimination or a disguised restriction on the free movement of capital and payments as defined in Article III-156.

4.   In the absence of a European law or framework law provided for in Article III-157(3), the Commission or, in the absence of a European decision of the Commission within three months from the request of the Member State concerned, the Council, may adopt a European decision stating that restrictive tax measures adopted by a Member State concerning one or more third countries are to be considered compatible with the Constitution insofar as they are justified by one of the objectives of the Union and compatible with the proper functioning of the internal market. The Council shall act unanimously on application by a Member State.

Article III-159   (ex Article 59 EC)

Where, in exceptional circumstances, movements of capital to or from third countries cause, or threaten to cause, serious difficulties for the functioning of economic and monetary union, the Council, on a proposal from the Commission, may adopt European regulations or decisions introducing safeguard measures with regard to third countries for a period not exceeding six months if such measures are strictly necessary. It shall act after consulting the European Central Bank.

Article III-160   (ex Article 60 EC)

Where necessary to achieve the objectives set out in Article III-257, as regards preventing and combating terrorism and related activities, European laws shall define a framework for administrative measures with regard to capital movements and payments, such as the freezing of funds, financial assets or economic gains belonging to, or owned or held by, natural or legal persons, groups or non- State entities.

The Council, on a proposal from the Commission, shall adopt European regulations or European decisions in order to implement the European laws referred to in the first paragraph.

The acts referred to in this Article shall include necessary provisions on legal safeguards.

SECTION 5   RULES ON COMPETITION

Subsection 1   Rules applying to undertakings

Article III-161   (ex Article 81 EC)

1.   The following shall be prohibited as incompatible with the internal market: all agreements between undertakings, decisions by associations of undertakings and concerted practices which may affect trade between Member States and which have as their object or effect the prevention, restriction or distortion of competition within the internal market, and in particular those which:

(a)   directly or indirectly fix purchase or selling prices or any other trading conditions;

(b)   limit or control production, markets, technical development, or investment;

(c)   share markets or sources of supply;

(d)   apply dissimilar conditions to equivalent transactions with other trading parties, thereby placing them at a competitive disadvantage;

(e)   make the conclusion of contracts subject to acceptance by the other parties of supplementary obligations which, by their nature or according to commercial usage, have no connection with the subject of such contracts.

2.   Any agreements or decisions prohibited pursuant to this Article shall be automatically void.

3.   Paragraph 1 may, however, be declared inapplicable in the case of:

— any agreement or category of agreements between undertakings,

— any decision or category of decisions by associations of undertakings,

— any concerted practice or category of concerted practices, which contributes to improving the production or distribution of goods or to promoting technical or economic progress, while allowing consumers a fair share of the resulting benefit, and which does not:

(a)   impose on the undertakings concerned restrictions which are not indispensable to the attainment of these objectives;

(b)   afford such undertakings the possibility of eliminating competition in respect of a substantial part of the products in question.

Article III-162   (ex Article 82 EC)

Any abuse by one or more undertakings of a dominant position within the internal market or in a substantial part of it shall be prohibited as incompatible with the internal market insofar as it may affect trade between Member States.

Such abuse may, in particular, consist in:

(a)   directly or indirectly imposing unfair purchase or selling prices or other unfair trading conditions;

(b)   limiting production, markets or technical development to the prejudice of consumers;

(c)   applying dissimilar conditions to equivalent transactions with other trading parties, thereby placing them at a competitive disadvantage;

(d)   making the conclusion of contracts subject to acceptance by the other parties of supplementary obligations which, by their nature or according to commercial usage, have no connection with the subject of such contracts.

Article III-163   (ex Article 83 EC)

The Council, on a proposal from the Commission, shall adopt the European regulations to give effect to the principles set out in Articles III-161 and III-162. It shall act after consulting the European Parliament.

Such regulations shall be designed in particular:

(a) to ensure compliance with the prohibitions laid down in Article III-161(1) and in Article III-162 by making provision for fines and periodic penalty payments;

(b) to lay down detailed rules for the application of Article III-161(3), taking into account the need to ensure effective supervision on the one hand, and to simplify administration to the greatest possible extent on the other;

(c) to define, if need be, in the various branches of the economy, the scope of Articles III-161 and III-162;

(d) to define the respective functions of the Commission and of the Court of Justice of the European Union in applying the provisions laid down in this paragraph;

(e) to determine the relationship between Member States' laws and this Subsection as well as the European regulations adopted pursuant to this Article.

Article III-164   (ex Article 84 EC)

Until the entry into force of the European regulations adopted pursuant to Article III-163, the authorities in Member States shall rule on the admissibility of agreements, decisions and concerted practices and on abuse of a dominant position in the internal market in accordance with their national law and Article III-161, in particular paragraph 3, and Article III-162.

Article III-165   (ex Article 85 EC)

1.   Without prejudice to Article III-164, the Commission shall ensure the application of the principles set out in Articles III-161 and III-162. On application by a Member State or on its own initiative, and in cooperation with the competent authorities in the Member States, which shall give it their assistance, the Commission shall investigate cases of suspected infringement of these principles. If it finds that there has been an infringement, it shall propose appropriate measures to bring it to an end.

2.   If the infringement referred to in paragraph 1 is not brought to an end, the Commission shall adopt a reasoned European decision recording the infringement of the principles. The Commission may publish its decision and authorise Member States to take the measures, the conditions and details of which it shall determine, needed to remedy the situation.

3.   The Commission may adopt European regulations relating to the categories of agreement in respect of which the Council has adopted a European regulation pursuant to Article III-163, second paragraph, (b).

Article III-166   (ex Article 86 EC)

1.   In the case of public undertakings and undertakings to which Member States grant special or exclusive rights, Member States shall neither enact nor maintain in force any measure contrary to the Constitution, in particular Article I-4(2) and Articles III-161 to III-169.

2.   Undertakings entrusted with the operation of services of general economic interest or having the character of an income-producing monopoly shall be subject to the provisions of the Constitution, in particular to the rules on competition, insofar as the application of such provisions does not obstruct the performance, in law or in fact, of the particular tasks assigned to them. The development of trade must not be affected to such an extent as would be contrary to the Union's interests.

3.   The Commission shall ensure the application of this Article and shall, where necessary, adopt appropriate European regulations or decisions.

Subsection 2   Aid granted by Member States

Article III-167   (ex Article 87 EC)

1.   Save as otherwise provided in the Constitution, any aid granted by a Member State or through State resources in any form whatsoever which distorts or threatens to distort competition by favouring certain undertakings or the production of certain goods shall, insofar as it affects trade between Member States, be incompatible with the internal market.

2.   The following shall be compatible with the internal market:

   (a)   aid having a social character, granted to individual consumers, provided that such aid is granted without discrimination related to the origin of the products concerned;

   (b)   aid to make good the damage caused by natural disasters or exceptional occurrences;

   (c)   aid granted to the economy of certain areas of the Federal Republic of Germany affected by the division of Germany, insofar as such aid is required in order to compensate for the economic disadvantages caused by that division. Five years after the entry into force of the Treaty establishing a Constitution for Europe, the Council, acting on a proposal from the Commission, may adopt a European decision repealing this point.

3.   The following may be considered to be compatible with the internal market:

   (a)   aid to promote the economic development of areas where the standard of living is abnormally low or where there is serious underemployment, and of the regions referred to in Article III-424, in view of their structural, economic and social situation;

   (b)   aid to promote the execution of an important project of common European interest or to remedy a serious disturbance in the economy of a Member State;

   (c)   aid to facilitate the development of certain economic activities or of certain economic areas, where such aid does not adversely affect trading conditions to an extent contrary to the common interest;

   (d)   aid to promote culture and heritage conservation where such aid does not affect trading conditions and competition in the Union to an extent that is contrary to the common interest;

   (e)   such other categories of aid as may be specified by European regulations or decisions adopted by the Council on a proposal from the Commission.

Article III-168   (ex Article 88 EC)

1.   The Commission, in cooperation with Member States, shall keep under constant review all systems of aid existing in those States. It shall propose to the latter any appropriate measures required by the progressive development or by the functioning of the internal market.

2.   If, after giving notice to the parties concerned to submit their comments, the Commission finds that aid granted by a Member State or through State resources is not compatible with the internal market having regard to Article III-167, or that such aid is being misused, it shall adopt a European decision requiring the Member State concerned to abolish or alter such aid within a period of time to be determined by the Commission. If the Member State concerned does not comply with this European decision within the prescribed time, the Commission or any other interested Member State may, in derogation from Articles III-360 and III-361, refer the matter to the Court of Justice of the European Union directly. On application by a Member State, the Council may adopt unanimously a European decision that aid which that State is granting or intends to grant shall be considered to be compatible with the internal market, in derogation from Article III-167 or from European regulations provided for in Article III-169, if such a decision is justified by exceptional circumstances. If, as regards the aid in question, the Commission has already initiated the procedure provided for in the first

subparagraph of this paragraph, the fact that the Member State concerned has made its application to the Council shall have the effect of suspending that procedure until the Council has made its attitude known. If, however, the Council has not made its attitude known within three months of the said application being made, the Commission shall act.

3.   The Commission shall be informed by the Member States, in sufficient time to enable it to submit its comments, of any plans to grant or alter aid. If it considers that any such plan is not compatible with the internal market having regard to Article III-167, it shall without delay initiate the procedure provided for in paragraph 2 of this Article. The Member State concerned shall not put its proposed measures into effect until this procedure has resulted in a final decision.

4.   The Commission may adopt European regulations relating to the categories of State aid that the Council has, pursuant to Article III-169, determined may be exempted from the procedure provided for by paragraph 3 of this Article.

Article III-169   (ex Article 89 EC)
The Council, on a proposal from the Commission, may adopt European regulations for the application of Articles III-167 and III-168 and for determining in particular the conditions in which Article III-168(3) shall apply and the categories of aid exempted from the procedure provided for in Article 168(3). It shall act after consulting the European Parliament.

SECTION 6   FISCAL PROVISIONS

Article III-170   (ex Articles 90 to 92 EC)
1.   No Member State shall impose, directly or indirectly, on the products of other Member States any internal taxation of any kind in excess of that imposed directly or indirectly on similar domestic products. Furthermore, no Member State shall impose on the products of other Member States any internal taxation of such a nature as to afford indirect protection to other products.

2.   Where products are exported by a Member State to the territory of another Member State, any repayment of internal taxation shall not exceed the internal taxation imposed on them whether directly or indirectly.

3.   In the case of charges other than turnover taxes, excise duties and other forms of indirect taxation, remissions and repayments in respect of exports to other Member States may not be granted and countervailing charges in respect of imports from Member States may not be imposed unless the provisions contemplated have been previously approved for a limited period by a European decision adopted by the Council on a proposal from the Commission.

Article III-171   (ex Article 93 EC)
A European law or framework law of the Council shall establish measures for the harmonisation of legislation concerning turnover taxes, excise duties and other forms of indirect taxation provided that such harmonisation is necessary to ensure the establishment and the functioning of the internal market and to avoid distortion of competition. The Council shall act unanimously after consulting the European Parliament and the Economic and Social Committee.

SECTION 7   COMMON PROVISIONS

Article III-172   (ex Article 95 EC)
1.   Save where otherwise provided in the Constitution, this Article shall apply for the achievement of the objectives set out in Article III-130. European laws or framework laws shall establish measures for the approximation of the provisions laid down by law, regulation or administrative action in Member States which have as their object the establishment and functioning of the internal market.

Such laws shall be adopted after consultation of the Economic and Social Committee.

2.   Paragraph 1 shall not apply to fiscal provisions, to those relating to the free movement of persons or to those relating to the rights and interests of employed persons.

3.   The Commission, in its proposals submitted under paragraph 1 concerning health, safety, environmental protection and consumer protection, shall take as a base a high level of protection, taking account in particular of any new development based on scientific facts. Within their respective powers, the European Parliament and the Council shall also seek to achieve this objective.

4.   If, after the adoption of a harmonisation measure by means of a European law or framework law or by means of a European regulation of the Commission, a Member State deems it necessary to maintain national provisions on grounds of major needs referred to in Article III-154, or relating to the protection of the environment or the working environment, it shall notify the Commission of these provisions as well as the grounds for maintaining them.

5.   Moreover, without prejudice to paragraph 4, if, after the adoption of a harmonisation measure by means of a European law or framework law or by means of a European regulation of the Commission, a Member State deems it necessary to introduce national provisions based on new scientific evidence relating to the protection of the environment or the working environment on grounds of a problem specific to that Member State arising after the adoption of the harmonisation measure, it shall notify the Commission of the envisaged provisions and the reasons for them.

6.   The Commission shall, within six months of the notifications referred to in paragraphs 4 and 5, adopt a European decision approving or rejecting the national provisions involved after having verified whether or not they are a means of arbitrary discrimination or a disguised restriction on trade between Member States and whether or not they constitute an obstacle to the functioning of the internal market.

In the absence of a decision by the Commission within this period the national provisions referred to in paragraphs 4 and 5 shall be deemed to have been approved.

When justified by the complexity of the matter and in the absence of danger to human health, the Commission may notify the Member State concerned that the period referred to in this paragraph will be extended for a further period of up to six months.

7.   When, pursuant to paragraph 6, a Member State is authorised to maintain or introduce national provisions derogating from a harmonisation measure, the Commission shall immediately examine whether to propose an adaptation to that measure.

8.   When a Member State raises a specific problem on public health in a field which has been the subject of prior harmonisation measures, it shall bring it to the attention of the Commission which shall immediately examine whether to propose appropriate measures.

9.   By way of derogation from the procedure laid down in Articles III-360 and III-361, the Commission and any Member State may bring the matter directly before the Court of Justice of the European Union if it considers that another Member State is making improper use of the powers provided for in this Article.

10.   The harmonisation measures referred to in this Article shall, in appropriate cases, include a safeguard clause authorising the Member States to take, for one or more of the non-economic reasons referred to in Article III-154, provisional measures subject to a Union control procedure.

Article III-173   (ex Article 94 EC)
Without prejudice to Article III-172, a European framework law of the Council shall establish measures for the approximation of such laws, regulations or administrative provisions of the Member States as directly affect the establishment or functioning of the internal market. The Council shall act unanimously after consulting the European Parliament and the Economic and Social Committee.

Article III-174   (ex Article 96 EC)

Where the Commission finds that a difference between the provisions laid down by law, regulation or administrative action in Member States is distorting the conditions of competition in the internal market and that the resultant distortion needs to be eliminated, it shall consult the Member States concerned. If such consultation does not result in agreement, European framework laws shall establish the measures necessary to eliminate the distortion in question. Any other appropriate measures provided for in the Constitution may be adopted.

Article III-175   (ex Article 97 EC)

1.   Where there is reason to fear that the adoption or amendment of a provision laid down by law, regulation or administrative action of a Member State may cause distortion within the meaning of Article III-174, a Member State desiring to proceed therewith shall consult the Commission. After consulting the Member States, the Commission shall address to the Member States concerned a recommendation on such measures as may be appropriate to avoid the distortion in question.

2.   If a Member State desiring to introduce or amend its own provisions does not comply with the recommendation addressed to it by the Commission, other Member States shall not be required, pursuant to Article III-174, to amend their own provisions in order to eliminate such distortion. If the Member State which has ignored the recommendation of the Commission causes distortion detrimental only to itself, Article III-174 shall not apply.

Article III-176   (new)

In the context of the establishment and functioning of the internal market, European laws or framework laws shall establish measures for the creation of European intellectual property rights to provide uniform intellectual property rights protection throughout the Union and for the setting up of centralised Union-wide authorisation, coordination and supervision arrangements.

A European law of the Council shall establish language arrangements for the European intellectual property rights. The Council shall act unanimously after consulting the European Parliament.

CHAPTER II   ECONOMIC AND MONETARY POLICY

Article III-177   (ex Article 4 EC)

For the purposes set out in Article I-3, the activities of the Member States and the Union shall include, as provided in the Constitution, the adoption of an economic policy which is based on the close coordination of Member States' economic policies, on the internal market and on the definition of common objectives, and conducted in accordance with the principle of an open market economy with free competition. Concurrently with the foregoing, and as provided in the Constitution and in accordance with the procedures set out therein, these activities shall include a single currency, the euro, and the definition and conduct of a single monetary policy and exchange-rate policy, the primary objective of both of which shall be to maintain price stability and, without prejudice to this objective, to support general economic policies in the Union, in accordance with the principle of an open market economy with free competition. These activities of the Member States and the Union shall entail compliance with the following guiding principles: stable prices, sound public finances and monetary conditions and a stable balance of payments.

SECTION 1   ECONOMIC POLICY

Article III-178   (ex Article 98 EC)

Member States shall conduct their economic policies in order to contribute to the achievement of the Union's objectives, as defined in Article I-3, and in the context of the broad guidelines referred to in Article III-179(2). The Member States and the Union shall act in accordance with the principle of an open market economy with free competition, favouring an efficient allocation of resources, and in compliance with the principles set out in Article III-177.

Article III-179   (ex Article 99 EC)

1.   Member States shall regard their economic policies as a matter of common concern and shall coordinate them within the Council, in accordance with Article III-178.

2.   The Council, on a recommendation from the Commission, shall formulate a draft for the broad guidelines of the economic policies of the Member States and of the Union, and shall report its findings to the European Council. The European Council, on the basis of the report from the Council, shall discuss a conclusion on the broad guidelines of the economic policies of the Member States and of the Union. On the basis of this conclusion, the Council shall adopt a recommendation setting out these broad guidelines. It shall inform the European Parliament of its recommendation.

3.   In order to ensure closer coordination of economic policies and sustained convergence of the economic performances of the Member States, the Council, on the basis of reports submitted by the Commission, shall monitor economic developments in each of the Member States and in the Union, as well as the consistency of economic policies with the broad guidelines referred to in paragraph 2, and shall regularly carry out an overall assessment.

For the purpose of this multilateral surveillance, Member States shall forward information to the Commission on important measures taken by them in the field of their economic policy and such other information as they deem necessary.

4.   Where it is established, under the procedure referred to in paragraph 3, that the economic policies of a Member State are not consistent with the broad guidelines referred to in paragraph 2 or that they risk jeopardising the proper functioning of economic and monetary union, the Commission may address a warning to the Member State concerned. The Council, on a recommendation from the Commission, may address the necessary recommendations to the Member State concerned. The Council, on a proposal from the Commission, may decide to make its recommendations public. Within the scope of this paragraph, the Council shall act without taking into account the vote of the member of the Council representing the Member State concerned. A qualified majority shall be defined as at least 55% of the other members of the Council, representing Member States comprising at least 65% of the population of the participating Member States. A blocking minority must include at least the minimum number of these other Council members representing more than 35% of the population of the participating Member States, plus one member, failing which the qualified majority shall be deemed attained.

5.   The President of the Council and the Commission shall report to the European Parliament on the results of multilateral surveillance. The President of the Council may be invited to appear before the competent committee of the European Parliament if the Council has made its recommendations public.

6.   European laws may lay down detailed rules for the multilateral surveillance procedure referred to in paragraphs 3 and 4.

Article III-180   (ex Article 100 EC)

1.   Without prejudice to any other procedures provided for in the Constitution, the Council, on a proposal from the Commission, may adopt a European decision laying down measures appropriate to the economic situation, in particular if severe difficulties arise in the supply of certain products.

2.   Where a Member State is in difficulties or is seriously threatened with severe difficulties caused by natural disasters or exceptional occurrences beyond its control, the Council, on a proposal from the Commission, may adopt a European decision granting, under certain

conditions, Union financial assistance to the Member State concerned. The President of the Council shall inform the European Parliament of the decision adopted.

Article III-181   (ex Article 101 EC)

1.   Overdraft facilities or any other type of credit facility with the European Central Bank or with the central banks of the Member States (hereinafter referred to as 'national central banks') in favour of Union institutions, bodies, offices or agencies, central governments, regional, local or other public authorities, other bodies governed by public law, or public undertakings of Member States shall be prohibited, as shall the purchase directly from them by the European Central Bank or national central banks of debt instruments.

2.   Paragraph 1 shall not apply to publicly owned credit institutions which, in the context of the supply of reserves by central banks, shall be given the same treatment by national central banks and the European Central Bank as private credit institutions.

Article III-182   (ex Article 102 EC)

Any measure or provision, not based on prudential considerations, establishing privileged access by Union institutions, bodies, offices or agencies, central governments, regional, local or other public authorities, other bodies governed by public law, or public undertakings of Member States to financial institutions shall be prohibited.

Article III-183   (ex Article 103 EC)

1.   The Union shall not be liable for or assume the commitments of central governments, regional, local or other public authorities, other bodies governed by public law, or public undertakings of any Member State, without prejudice to mutual financial guarantees for the joint execution of a specific project. A Member State shall not be liable for or assume the commitments of central governments, regional, local or other public authorities, other bodies governed by public law, or public undertakings of another Member State, without prejudice to mutual financial guarantees for the joint execution of a specific project.

2.   The Council, on a proposal from the Commission, may adopt European regulations or decisions specifying definitions for the application of the prohibitions laid down in Articles III-181 and III-182 and in this Article. It shall act after consulting the European Parliament.

Article III-184   (ex Article 104 EC)

1.   Member States shall avoid excessive government deficits.

2.   The Commission shall monitor the development of the budgetary situation and of the stock of government debt in the Member States in order to identify gross errors. In particular it shall examine compliance with budgetary discipline on the basis of the following two criteria:

    (a) whether the ratio of the planned or actual government deficit to gross domestic product exceeds a reference value, unless:

        (i)   either the ratio has declined substantially and continuously and reached a level that comes close to the reference value, or

        (ii) alternatively, the excess over the reference value is only exceptional and temporary and the ratio remains close to the reference value;

    (b) whether the ratio of government debt to gross domestic product exceeds a reference value, unless the ratio is diminishing sufficiently and approaching the reference value at a satisfactory pace.

The reference values are specified in the Protocol on the excessive deficit procedure.

3.   If a Member State does not fulfil the requirements under one or both of these criteria, the Commission shall prepare a report. The Commission's report shall also take into account whether the government deficit exceeds government investment expenditure and take into account all other relevant factors, including the medium-term economic and budgetary position of the Member State.

The Commission may also prepare a report if, notwithstanding the fulfilment of the requirements under the criteria, it is of the opinion that there is a risk of an excessive deficit in a Member State.

4.   The Economic and Financial Committee set up under Article III-192 shall formulate an opinion on the Commission's report.

5.   If the Commission considers that an excessive deficit in a Member State exists or may occur, it shall address an opinion to the Member State concerned and shall inform the Council accordingly.

6.   The Council shall, on a proposal from the Commission, having considered any observations which the Member State concerned may wish to make and after an overall assessment, decide whether an excessive deficit exists. In that case it shall adopt, without undue delay, on a recommendation from the Commission, recommendations addressed to the Member State concerned with a view to bringing that situation to an end within a given period. Subject to paragraph 8, those recommendations shall not be made public. Within the scope of this paragraph, the Council shall act without taking into account the vote of the member of the Council representing the Member State concerned. A qualified majority shall be defined as at least 55% of the other members of the Council, representing Member States comprising at least 65% of the population of the participating Member States. A blocking minority must include at least the minimum number of these other Council members representing more than 35% of the population of the participating Member States, plus one member, failing which the qualified majority shall be deemed attained.

7.   The Council, on a recommendation from the Commission, shall adopt the European decisions and recommendations referred to in paragraphs 8 to 11. It shall act without taking into account the vote of the member of the Council representing the Member State concerned.

A qualified majority shall be defined as at least 55% of the other members of the Council, representing Member States comprising at least 65% of the population of the participating Member States. A blocking minority must include at least the minimum number of these other Council members representing more than 35% of the population of the participating Member States, plus one member, failing which the qualified majority shall be deemed attained.

8.   Where it adopts a European decision establishing that there has been no effective action in response to its recommendations within the period laid down, the Council may make its recommendations public.

9.   If a Member State persists in failing to put the Council's recommendations into practice, the Council may adopt a European decision giving notice to the Member State to take, within a specified time-limit, measures for the deficit reduction which the Council judges necessary to remedy the situation. In such a case, the Council may request the Member State concerned to submit reports in accordance with a specific timetable in order to examine the adjustment efforts of that Member State.

10.   As long as a Member State fails to comply with a European decision adopted in accordance with paragraph 9, the Council may decide to apply or, as the case may be, intensify one or more of the following measures:

(a)   require the Member State concerned to publish additional information, to be specified by the Council, before issuing bonds and securities;

(b)   invite the European Investment Bank to reconsider its lending policy towards the Member State concerned;

(c)   require the Member State concerned to make a non-interest-bearing deposit of an appropriate size with the Union until the Council considers that the excessive deficit has been corrected;

(d)   impose fines of an appropriate size.

The President of the Council shall inform the European Parliament of the measures adopted.

11.   The Council shall repeal some or all of the measures referred to in paragraph 6 and

paragraphs 8, 9 and 10 if it considers the excessive deficit in the Member State concerned to have been corrected. If the Council has previously made public recommendations, it shall state publicly, as soon as the European decision referred to in paragraph 8 has been repealed, that there is no longer an excessive deficit in the Member State concerned.

12.   The rights to bring actions provided for in Articles III-360 and III-361 shall not be exercised within the framework of paragraphs 1 to 6 or paragraphs 8 and 9.

13.   Further provisions relating to the implementation of the procedure laid down in this Article are set out in the Protocol on the excessive deficit procedure.

A European law of the Council shall lay down the appropriate measures to replace the said Protocol. The Council shall act unanimously after consulting the European Parliament and the European Central Bank. Subject to the other provisions of this paragraph, the Council, on a proposal from the Commission, shall adopt European regulations or decisions laying down detailed rules and definitions for the application of the said Protocol. It shall act after consulting the European Parliament.

SECTION 2   MONETARY POLICY

Article III-185   (ex Article 105 EC)

1.   The primary objective of the European System of Central Banks shall be to maintain price stability. Without prejudice to this objective, the European System of Central Banks shall support the general economic policies in the Union in order to contribute to the achievement of its objectives as laid down in Article I-3. The European System of Central Banks shall act in accordance with the principle of an open market economy with free competition, favouring an efficient allocation of resources, and in compliance with the principles set out in Article III-177.

2.   The basic tasks to be carried out through the European System of Central Banks shall be:
   (a)   to define and implement the Union's monetary policy;
   (b)   to conduct foreign-exchange operations consistent with Article III-326;
   (c)   to hold and manage the official foreign reserves of the Member States;
   (d)   to promote the smooth operation of payment systems.

3.   Paragraph 2(c) shall be without prejudice to the holding and management by the governments of Member States of foreign-exchange working balances.

4.   The European Central Bank shall be consulted:
   (a)   on any proposed Union act in areas within its powers;
   (b)   by national authorities regarding any draft legislative provision in areas within its powers, but within the limits and under the conditions set out by the Council in accordance with the procedure laid down in Article III-187(4).

The European Central Bank may submit opinions to the Union institutions, bodies, offices or agencies or to national authorities on matters within its powers.

5.   The European System of Central Banks shall contribute to the smooth conduct of policies pursued by the competent authorities relating to the prudential supervision of credit institutions and the stability of the financial system.

6.   A European law of the Council may confer specific tasks upon the European Central Bank concerning policies relating to the prudential supervision of credit institutions and other financial institutions with the exception of insurance undertakings. The Council shall act unanimously after consulting the European Parliament and the European Central Bank.

Article III-186   (ex Article 106 EC)

1.   The European Central Bank shall have the exclusive right to authorise the issue of euro bank notes in the Union. The European Central Bank and the national central banks may issue such notes. Only the bank notes issued by the European Central Bank and the national central banks shall have the status of legal tender within the Union.

2.   Member States may issue euro coins subject to approval by the European Central Bank of the volume of the issue. The Council, on a proposal from the Commission, may adopt European regulations laying down measures to harmonise the denominations and technical specifications of coins intended for circulation to the extent necessary to permit their smooth circulation within the Union. The Council shall act after consulting the European Parliament and the European Central Bank.

Article III-187   (ex Article 107 EC)

1.   The European System of Central Banks shall be governed by the decision-making bodies of the European Central Bank, which shall be the Governing Council and the Executive Board.

2.   The Statute of the European System of Central Banks is laid down in the Protocol on the Statute of the European System of Central Banks and of the European Central Bank.

3.   Article 5(1), (2) and (3), Articles 17 and 18, Article 19(1), Articles 22, 23, 24 and 26, Article 32(2), (3), (4) and (6), Article 33(1)(a) and Article 36 of the Statute of the European System of Central Banks and of the European Central Bank may be amended by European laws:

(a) either on a proposal from the Commission and after consultation of the European Central Bank;

(b) or on a recommendation from the European Central Bank and after consultation of the Commission.

4.   The Council shall adopt the European regulations and decisions laying down the measures referred to in Article 4, Article 5(4), Article 19(2), Article 20, Article 28(1), Article 29(2), Article 30(4) and Article 34(3) of the Statute of the European System of Central Banks and of the European Central Bank. It shall act after consulting the European Parliament:

(a) either on a proposal from the Commission and after consulting the European Central Bank;

(b) or on a recommendation from the European Central Bank and after consulting the Commission.

Article III-188   (ex Article 108 EC)

When exercising the powers and carrying out the tasks and duties conferred upon them by the Constitution and the Statute of the European System of Central Banks and of the European Central Bank, neither the European Central Bank, nor a national central bank, nor any member of their decision-making bodies shall seek or take instructions from Union institutions, bodies, offices or agencies, from any government of a Member State or from any other body. The Union institutions, bodies, offices or agencies and the governments of the Member States undertake to respect this principle and not to seek to influence the members of the decision-making bodies of the European Central Bank or of the national central banks in the performance of their tasks.

Article III-189   (ex Article 19 EC)

Each Member State shall ensure that its national legislation, including the statutes of its national central bank, is compatible with the Constitution and the Statute of the European System of Central Banks and of the European Central Bank.

Article III-190   (ex Article 110 EC)

1.   In order to carry out the tasks entrusted to the European System of Central Banks, the European Central Bank shall, in accordance with the Constitution and under the conditions laid down in the Statute of the European System of Central Banks and of the European Central Bank, adopt:

(a) European regulations to the extent necessary to implement the tasks defined in Article 3(1)(a), Article 19(1), Article 22 and Article 25(2) of the Statute of the European System of Central Banks and of the European Central Bank and in cases

which shall be laid down in European regulations and decisions as referred to in Article III-187(4);
(b) European decisions necessary for carrying out the tasks entrusted to the European System of Central Banks under the Constitution and the Statute of the European System of Central Banks and of the European Central Bank;
(c) recommendations and opinions.

2.   The European Central Bank may decide to publish its European decisions, recommendations and opinions.

3.   The Council shall, under the procedure laid down in Article III-187(4), adopt the European regulations establishing the limits and conditions under which the European Central Bank shall be entitled to impose fines or periodic penalty payments on undertakings for failure to comply with obligations under its European regulations and decisions.

Article III-191   (ex Article 123 (4) EC)

Without prejudice to the powers of the European Central Bank, European laws or framework laws shall lay down the measures necessary for use of the euro as the single currency. Such laws or framework laws shall be adopted after consultation of the European Central Bank.

SECTION 3   INSTITUTIONAL PROVISIONS

Article III-192   (ex Article 114(2) to (4) EC)

1.   In order to promote coordination of the policies of Member States to the full extent needed for the functioning of the internal market, an Economic and Financial Committee is hereby set up.

2.   The Committee shall have the following tasks:
(a) to deliver opinions at the request of the Council or of the Commission, or on its own initiative, for submission to those institutions;
(b) to keep under review the economic and financial situation of the Member States and of the Union and to report on it regularly to the Council and to the Commission, in particular with regard to financial relations with third countries and international institutions;
(c) without prejudice to Article III-344, to contribute to the preparation of the work of the Council referred to in Article III-159, Article III-179(2), (3), (4) and (6), Articles III-180, III-183 and III-184, Article III-185(6), Article III-186(2), Article III-187(3) and (4), Articles III-191 and III-196, Article III-198(2) and (3), Article III-201, Article III-202(2) and (3) and Articles III-322 and III-326, and to carry out other advisory and preparatory tasks assigned to it by the Council;
(d) to examine, at least once a year, the situation regarding the movement of capital and the freedom of payments, as they result from the application of the Constitution and of Union acts; the examination shall cover all measures relating to capital movements and payments; the Committee shall report to the Commission and to the Council on the outcome of this examination.

The Member States, the Commission and the European Central Bank shall each appoint no more than two members of the Committee.

3.   The Council, on a proposal from the Commission, shall adopt a European decision laying down detailed provisions concerning the composition of the Economic and Financial Committee. It shall act after consulting the European Central Bank and the Committee. The President of the Council shall inform the European Parliament of that decision.

4.   In addition to the tasks referred to in paragraph 2, if and as long as there are Member States with a derogation as referred to in Article III-197, the Committee shall keep under review the monetary and financial situation and the general payments system of those Member States and report regularly to the Council and to the Commission on the matter.

Article III-193   (ex Article 115 EC)

For matters within the scope of Article III-179(4), Article III-184 with the exception of paragraph 13, Articles III-191, III-196, Article III-198(3) and Article III-326, the Council or a Member State may request the Commission to make a recommendation or a proposal, as appropriate. The Commission shall examine this request and submit its conclusions to the Council without delay.

SECTION 4   PROVISIONS SPECIFIC TO MEMBER STATES WHOSE CURRENCY
IS THE EURO

Article III-194   (new)

1.   In order to ensure the proper functioning of economic and monetary union, and in accordance with the relevant provisions of the Constitution, the Council shall, in accordance with the relevant procedure from among those referred to in Articles III-179 and III-184, with the exception of the procedure set out in Article III-184(13), adopt measures specific to those Member States whose currency is the euro:

    (a) to strengthen the coordination and surveillance of their budgetary discipline;
    (b) to set out economic policy guidelines for them, while ensuring that they are compatible with those adopted for the whole of the Union and are kept under surveillance.

2.   For those measures set out in paragraph 1, only members of the Council representing Member States whose currency is the euro shall take part in the vote.

A qualified majority shall be defined as at least 55% of these members of the Council, representing Member States comprising at least 65% of the population of the participating Member States.

A blocking minority must include at least the minimum number of these Council members representing more than 35% of the population of the participating Member States, plus one member, failing which the qualified majority shall be deemed attained.

Article III-195   (new)

Arrangements for meetings between ministers of those Member States whose currency is the euro are laid down by the Protocol on the Euro Group.

Article III-196   (new)

1.   In order to secure the euro's place in the international monetary system, the Council, on a proposal from the Commission, shall adopt a European decision establishing common positions on matters of particular interest for economic and monetary union within the competent international financial institutions and conferences. The Council shall act after consulting the European Central Bank.

2.   The Council, on a proposal from the Commission, may adopt appropriate measures to ensure unified representation within the international financial institutions and conferences. The Council shall act after consulting the European Central Bank.

3.   For the measures referred to in paragraphs 1 and 2, only members of the Council representing Member States whose currency is the euro shall take part in the vote.

A qualified majority shall be defined as at least 55% of these members of the Council, representing Member States comprising at least 65% of the population of the participating Member States.

A blocking minority must include at least the minimum number of these Council members representing more than 35% of the population of the participating Member States, plus one member, failing which the qualified majority shall be deemed attained.

SECTION 5   TRANSITIONAL PROVISIONS

Article III-197   (ex Article 122(1) and (3) to (5) EC)

1.   Member States in respect of which the Council has not decided that they fulfil the necessary conditions for the adoption of the euro shall hereinafter be referred to as 'Member States with a derogation'.

2.   The following provisions of the Constitution shall not apply to Member States with a derogation:

(a) adoption of the parts of the broad economic policy guidelines which concern the euro area generally (Article III-179(2));

(b) coercive means of remedying excessive deficits (Article III-184(9) and (10));

(c) the objectives and tasks of the European System of Central Banks (Article III-185(1), (2), (3) and (5));

(d) issue of the euro (Article III-186);

(e) acts of the European Central Bank (Article III-190);

(f) measures governing the use of the euro (Article III-191);

(g) monetary agreements and other measures relating to exchange-rate policy (Article III-326);

(h) appointment of members of the Executive Board of the European Central Bank (Article III-382(2));

(i) European decisions establishing common positions on issues of particular relevance for economic and monetary union within the competent international financial institutions and conferences (Article III-196(1));

(j) measures to ensure unified representation within the international financial institutions and conferences (Article III-196(2)).

In the Articles referred to in points (a) to (j), 'Member States' shall therefore mean Member States whose currency is the euro.

3.   Under Chapter IX of the Statute of the European System of Central Banks and of the European Central Bank, Member States with a derogation and their national central banks are excluded from rights and obligations within the European System of Central Banks.

4.   The voting rights of members of the Council representing Member States with a derogation shall be suspended for the adoption by the Council of the measures referred to in the Articles listed in paragraph 2, and in the following instances:

(a) recommendations made to those Member States whose currency is the euro in the framework of multilateral surveillance, including on stability programmes and warnings (Article III-179(4));

(b) measures relating to excessive deficits concerning those Member States whose currency is the euro (Article III-184(6), (7), (8) and (11)).

A qualified majority shall be defined as at least 55% of the other members of the Council, representing Member States comprising at least 65% of the population of the participating Member States.

A blocking minority must include at least the minimum number of these other Council members representing more than 35% of the population of the participating Member States, plus one member, failing which the qualified majority shall be deemed attained.

Article III-198   (ex Articles 121, 122(2) and 123(5) EC)

1.   At least once every two years, or at the request of a Member State with a derogation, the Commission and the European Central Bank shall report to the Council on the progress made by the Member States with a derogation in fulfilling their obligations regarding the achievement of economic and monetary union. These reports shall include an examination of the compatibility between the national legislation of each of these Member States, including the statutes of its national central bank, and Articles III-188 and III-189 and the Statute of the European System of Central Banks and of the European Central Bank. The reports shall also

examine whether a high degree of sustainable convergence has been achieved, by analysing how far each of these Member States has fulfilled the following criteria:

(a) the achievement of a high degree of price stability; this is apparent from a rate of inflation which is close to that of, at most, the three best performing Member States in terms of price stability;

(b) the sustainability of the government financial position; this is apparent from having achieved a government budgetary position without a deficit that is excessive as determined in accordance with Article III-184(6);

(c) the observance of the normal fluctuation margins provided for by the exchange-rate mechanism of the European monetary system, for at least two years, without devaluing against the euro;

(d) the durability of convergence achieved by the Member State with a derogation and of its participation in the exchange-rate mechanism, being reflected in the long-term interest-rate levels.

The four criteria laid down in this paragraph and the relevant periods over which they are to be respected are developed further in the protocol on the convergence criteria. the reports from the commission and the european central bank shall also take account of the results of the integration of markets, the situation and development of the balances of payments on current account and an examination of the development of unit labour costs and other price indices.

2.   After consulting the European Parliament and after discussion in the European Council, the Council, on a proposal from the Commission, shall adopt a European decision establishing which Member States with a derogation fulfil the necessary conditions on the basis of the criteria laid down in paragraph 1, and shall abrogate the derogations of the Member States concerned.

The Council shall act having received a recommendation of a qualified majority of those among its members representing Member States whose currency is the euro. These members shall act within six months of the Council receiving the Commission's proposal. The qualified majority referred to in the second subparagraph shall be defined as at least 55% of these members of the Council, representing Member States comprising at least 65% of the population of the participating Member States. A blocking minority must include at least the minimum number of these Council members representing more than 35% of the population of the participating Member States, plus one member, failing which the qualified majority shall be deemed attained.

3.   If it is decided, in accordance with the procedure set out in paragraph 2, to abrogate a derogation, the Council shall, on a proposal from the Commission, adopt the European regulations or decisions irrevocably fixing the rate at which the euro is to be substituted for the currency of the Member State concerned, and laying down the other measures necessary for the introduction of the euro as the single currency in that Member State. The Council shall act with the unanimous agreement of the members representing Member States whose currency is the euro and the Member State concerned, after consulting the European Central Bank.

Article III-199   (ex Articles 123(3) and 117(2) EC)

1.   If and as long as there are Member States with a derogation, and without prejudice to Article III-187(1), the General Council of the European Central Bank referred to in Article 45 of the Statute of the European System of Central Banks and of the European Central Bank shall be constituted as a third decision-making body of the European Central Bank.

2.   If and as long as there are Member States with a derogation, the European Central Bank shall, as regards those Member States:

(a) strengthen cooperation between the national central banks;

(b) strengthen the coordination of the monetary policies of the Member States, with the aim of ensuring price stability;

(c) monitor the functioning of the exchange-rate mechanism;

(d) hold consultations concerning issues falling within the competence of the national central banks and affecting the stability of financial institutions and markets;

(e) carry out the former tasks of the European Monetary Cooperation Fund which had subsequently been taken over by the European Monetary Institute.

Article III-200   (ex Article 124(1) EC)

Each Member State with a derogation shall treat its exchange-rate policy as a matter of common interest. In so doing, it shall take account of the experience acquired in cooperation within the framework of the exchange-rate mechanism.

Article III-201   (ex Article 119 EC)

1.   Where a Member State with a derogation is in difficulties or is seriously threatened with difficulties as regards its balance of payments either as a result of an overall disequilibrium in its balance of payments, or as a result of the type of currency at its disposal, and where such difficulties are liable in particular to jeopardise the functioning of the internal market or the implementation of the common commercial policy, the Commission shall immediately investigate the position of the State in question and the action which, making use of all the means at its disposal, that State has taken or may take in accordance with the Constitution. The Commission shall state what measures it recommends the Member State concerned to adopt.

If the action taken by a Member State with a derogation and the measures suggested by the Commission do not prove sufficient to overcome the difficulties which have arisen or which threaten, the Commission shall, after consulting the Economic and Financial Committee, recommend to the Council the granting of mutual assistance and appropriate methods.

The Commission shall keep the Council regularly informed of the situation and of how it evolves.

2.   The Council shall adopt European regulations or decisions granting such mutual assistance and laying down the conditions and details of such assistance, which may take such forms as:

(a) a concerted approach to or within any other international organisations to which Member States with a derogation may have recourse;

(b) measures needed to avoid deflection of trade where the Member State with a derogation, which is in difficulties, maintains or reintroduces quantitative restrictions against third countries;

(c) the granting of limited credits by other Member States, subject to their agreement.

3.   If the mutual assistance recommended by the Commission is not granted by the Council or if the mutual assistance granted and the measures taken are insufficient, the Commission shall authorise the Member State with a derogation, which is in difficulties, to take protective measures, the conditions and details of which the Commission shall determine.

Such authorisation may be revoked and such conditions and details may be changed by the Council.

Article III-202   (ex Article 120 EC)

1.   Where a sudden crisis in the balance of payments occurs and a European decision as referred to in Article III-201(2) is not immediately adopted, a Member State with a derogation may, as a precaution, take the necessary protective measures. Such measures must cause the least possible disturbance in the functioning of the internal market and must not be wider in scope than is strictly necessary to remedy the sudden difficulties which have arisen.

2.   The Commission and the other Member States shall be informed of the protective measures referred to in paragraph 1 not later than when they enter into force. The Commission may recommend to the Council the granting of mutual assistance under Article III-201.

3.   The Council, acting on a recommendation from the Commission and after consulting the Economic and Financial Committee may adopt a European decision stipulating that the Member State concerned shall amend, suspend or abolish the protective measures referred to in paragraph 1.

CHAPTER III   POLICIES IN OTHER AREAS

SECTION 1   EMPLOYMENT

Article III-203   (ex Article 125 EC)

The Union and the Member States shall, in accordance with this Section, work towards developing a coordinated strategy for employment and particularly for promoting a skilled, trained and adaptable workforce and labour markets responsive to economic change with a view to achieving the objectives referred to in Article I-3.

Article III-204   (ex Article 126 EC)

1.   Member States, through their employment policies, shall contribute to the achievement of the objectives referred to in Article III-203 in a way consistent with the broad guidelines of the economic policies of the Member States and of the Union adopted pursuant to Article III-179(2).

2.   Member States, having regard to national practices related to the responsibilities of management and labour, shall regard promoting employment as a matter of common concern and shall coordinate their action in this respect within the Council, in accordance with article III-206.

Article III-205   (ex Article 127 EC)

1.   The Union shall contribute to a high level of employment by encouraging cooperation between Member States and by supporting and, if necessary, complementing their action. In doing so, the competences of the Member States shall be respected.

2.   The objective of a high level of employment shall be taken into consideration in the formulation and implementation of Union policies and activities.

Article III-206   (ex Article 128 EC)

1.   The European Council shall each year consider the employment situation in the Union and adopt conclusions thereon, on the basis of a joint annual report by the Council and the Commission.

2.   On the basis of the conclusions of the European Council, the Council, on a proposal from the Commission, shall each year adopt guidelines which the Member States shall take into account in their employment policies. It shall act after consulting the European Parliament, the Committee of the Regions, the Economic and Social Committee and the Employment Committee.

These guidelines shall be consistent with the broad guidelines adopted pursuant to Article III-179(2).

3.   Each Member State shall provide the Council and the Commission with an annual report on the principal measures taken to implement its employment policy in the light of the guidelines for employment as referred to in paragraph 2.

4.   The Council, on the basis of the reports referred to in paragraph 3 and having received the views of the Employment Committee, shall each year carry out an examination of the implementation of the employment policies of the Member States in the light of the guidelines for employment. The Council, on a recommendation from the Commission, may adopt recommendations which it shall address to Member States.

5.   On the basis of the results of that examination, the Council and the Commission shall make a joint annual report to the European Council on the employment situation in the Union and on the implementation of the guidelines for employment.

Article III-207   (ex Article 129 EC)

European laws or framework laws may establish incentive measures designed to encourage cooperation between Member States and to support their action in the field of employment through initiatives aimed at developing exchanges of information and best practices, providing comparative analysis and advice as well as promoting innovative approaches and evaluating experiences, in particular by recourse to pilot projects. They shall be adopted after consultation of the Committee of the Regions and the Economic and Social Committee.

Such European laws or framework laws shall not include harmonisation of the laws and regulations of the Member States.

Article III-208   (ex Article 130 EC)

The Council shall, by a simple majority, adopt a European decision establishing an Employment Committee with advisory status to promote coordination between Member States on employment and labour market policies. It shall act after consulting the European Parliament.

The tasks of the Committee shall be:

(a) to monitor the employment situation and employment policies in the Union and the Member States;

(b) without prejudice to Article III-344, to formulate opinions at the request of either the Council or the Commission or on its own initiative, and to contribute to the preparation of the Council proceedings referred to in Article III-206.

In fulfilling its mandate, the Committee shall consult management and labour.

Each Member State and the Commission shall appoint two members of the Committee.

SECTION 2   SOCIAL POLICY

Article III-209   (ex Article 136 EC)

The Union and the Member States, having in mind fundamental social rights such as those set out in the European Social Charter signed at Turin on 18 October 1961 and in the 1989 Community Charter of the Fundamental Social Rights of Workers, shall have as their objectives the promotion of employment, improved living and working conditions, so as to make possible their harmonisation while the improvement is being maintained, proper social protection, dialogue between management and labour, the development of human resources with a view to lasting high employment and the combating of exclusion. To this end the Union and the Member States shall act taking account of the diverse forms of national practices, in particular in the field of contractual relations, and the need to maintain the competitiveness of the Union economy.

They believe that such a development will ensue not only from the functioning of the internal market, which will favour the harmonisation of social systems, but also from the procedures provided for in the Constitution and from the approximation of provisions laid down by law, regulation or administrative action of the Member States.

Article III-210   (ex Article 137 EC)

1.   With a view to achieving the objectives of Article III-209, the Union shall support and complement the activities of the Member States in the following fields:

(a) improvement in particular of the working environment to protect workers' health and safety;

(b) working conditions;

(c) social security and social protection of workers;

(d) protection of workers where their employment contract is terminated;

(e) the information and consultation of workers;

(f) representation and collective defence of the interests of workers and employers, including co- determination, subject to paragraph 6;

    (g) conditions of employment for third-country nationals legally residing in Union territory;

    (h) the integration of persons excluded from the labour market, without prejudice to Article III-283;

    (i) equality between women and men with regard to labour market opportunities and treatment at work;

    (j) the combating of social exclusion;

    (k) the modernisation of social protection systems without prejudice to point (c).

2.   For the purposes of paragraph 1:

    (a) European laws or framework laws may establish measures designed to encourage cooperation between Member States through initiatives aimed at improving knowledge, developing exchanges of information and best practices, promoting innovative approaches and evaluating experiences, excluding any harmonisation of the laws and regulations of the Member States;

    (b) in the fields referred to in paragraph 1(a) to (i), European framework laws may establish minimum requirements for gradual implementation, having regard to the conditions and technical rules obtaining in each of the Member States. Such European framework laws shall avoid imposing administrative, financial and legal constraints in a way which would hold back the creation and development of small and medium-sized undertakings.

In all cases, such European laws or framework laws shall be adopted after consultation of the Committee of the Regions and the Economic and Social Committee.

3.   By way of derogation from paragraph 2, in the fields referred to in paragraph 1(c), (d), (f) and (g), European laws or framework laws shall be adopted by the Council acting unanimously after consulting the European Parliament, the Committee of the Regions and the Economic and Social Committee. The Council may, on a proposal from the Commission, adopt a European decision making the ordinary legislative procedure applicable to paragraph 1(d), (f) and (g). It shall act unanimously after consulting the European Parliament.

4.   A Member State may entrust management and labour, at their joint request, with the implementation of European framework laws adopted pursuant to paragraphs 2 and 3 or, where appropriate, with the implementation of European regulations or decisions adopted in accordance with Article III-212. In this case, it shall ensure that, no later than the date on which a European framework law must be transposed, or a European regulation or decision implemented, management and labour have introduced the necessary measures by agreement, the Member State concerned being required to take any necessary measure enabling it at any time to be in a position to guarantee the results imposed by that framework law, regulation or decision.

5.   The European laws and framework laws adopted pursuant to this Article:

    (a) shall not affect the right of Member States to define the fundamental principles of their social security systems and must not significantly affect the financial equilibrium of such systems;

    (b) shall not prevent any Member State from maintaining or introducing more stringent protective measures compatible with the Constitution.

6.   This Article shall not apply to pay, the right of association, the right to strike or the right to impose lockouts.

Article III-211   (ex Article 138 EC)

1.   The Commission shall promote the consultation of management and labour at Union level and shall adopt any relevant measure to facilitate their dialogue by ensuring balanced support for the parties.

2.   For the purposes of paragraph 1, before submitting proposals in the social policy field,

the Commission shall consult management and labour on the possible direction of Union action.

3. If, after the consultation referred to in paragraph 2, the Commission considers Union action desirable, it shall consult management and labour on the content of the envisaged proposal. Management and labour shall forward to the Commission an opinion or, where appropriate, a recommendation.

4. On the occasion of the consultation referred to in paragraphs 2 and 3, management and labour may inform the Commission of their wish to initiate the process provided for in Article III-212(1). The duration of this process shall not exceed nine months, unless the management and labour concerned and the Commission decide jointly to extend it.

Article III-212   (ex Article 139 EC)

1. Should management and labour so desire, the dialogue between them at Union level may lead to contractual relations, including agreements.

2. Agreements concluded at Union level shall be implemented either in accordance with the procedures and practices specific to management and labour and the Member States or, in matters covered by Article III-210, at the joint request of the signatory parties, by European regulations or decisions adopted by the Council on a proposal from the Commission. The European Parliament shall be informed. Where the agreement in question contains one or more provisions relating to one of the areas for which unanimity is required pursuant to Article III-210(3), the Council shall act unanimously.

Article III-213   (ex Article 140 EC)

With a view to achieving the objectives of Article III-209 and without prejudice to the other provisions of the Constitution, the Commission shall encourage cooperation between the Member States and facilitate the coordination of their action in all social policy fields under this Section, particularly in matters relating to:

(a) employment;

(b) labour law and working conditions;

(c) basic and advanced vocational training;

(d) social security;

(e) prevention of occupational accidents and diseases;

(f) occupational hygiene;

(g) the right of association and collective bargaining between employers and workers.

To this end, the Commission shall act in close contact with Member States by making studies, delivering opinions and arranging consultations both on problems arising at national level and on those of concern to international organisations, in particular initiatives aiming at the establishment of guidelines and indicators, the organisation of exchange of best practice, and the preparation of the necessary elements for periodic monitoring and evaluation. The European Parliament shall be kept fully informed. Before delivering the opinions provided for in this Article, the Commission shall consult the Economic and Social Committee.

Article III-214   (ex Article 141 EC)

1. Each Member State shall ensure that the principle of equal pay for female and male workers for equal work or work of equal value is applied.

2. For the purpose of this Article, 'pay' means the ordinary basic or minimum wage or salary and any other consideration, whether in cash or in kind, which the worker receives directly or indirectly, in respect of his employment, from his employer.

Equal pay without discrimination based on sex means:

(a) that pay for the same work at piece rates shall be calculated on the basis of the same unit of measurement;

(b) that pay for work at time rates shall be the same for the same job.

3. European laws or framework laws shall establish measures to ensure the application

of the principle of equal opportunities and equal treatment of women and men in matters of employment and occupation, including the principle of equal pay for equal work or work of equal value. They shall be adopted after consultation of the Economic and Social Committee.

4.   With a view to ensuring full equality in practice between women and men in working life, the principle of equal treatment shall not prevent any Member State from maintaining or adopting measures providing for specific advantages in order to make it easier for the under-represented sex to pursue a vocational activity, or to prevent or compensate for disadvantages in professional careers.

Article III-215   (ex Article 142 EC)
Member States shall endeavour to maintain the existing equivalence between paid holiday schemes.

Article III-216   (ex Article 143 EC)
The Commission shall draw up a report each year on progress in achieving the objectives of Article III-209, including the demographic situation within the Union. It shall forward the report to the European Parliament, the Council and the Economic and Social Committee.

Article III-217   (ex Article 144 EC)
The Council shall, by a simple majority, adopt a European decision establishing a Social Protection Committee with advisory status to promote cooperation on social protection policies between Member States and with the Commission. The Council shall act after consulting the European Parliament.

The tasks of the Committee shall be:
- (a)   to monitor the social situation and the development of social protection policies in the Member States and within the Union;
- (b)   to promote exchanges of information, experience and good practice between Member States and with the Commission;
- (c)   without prejudice to Article III-344, to prepare reports, formulate opinions or undertake other work within the scope of its powers, at the request of either the Council or the Commission or on its own initiative. In fulfilling its mandate, the Committee shall establish appropriate contacts with management and labour. Each Member State and the Commission shall appoint two members of the Committee.

Article III-218   (ex Article 145 EC)
The Commission shall include a separate chapter on social developments within the Union in its annual report to the European Parliament. The European Parliament may invite the Commission to draw up reports on any particular problems concerning social conditions.

Article III-219   (ex Articles 146-148 EC)
1.   In order to improve employment opportunities for workers in the internal market and to contribute thereby to raising the standard of living, a European Social Fund is hereby established; it shall aim to render the employment of workers easier and to increase their geographical and occupational mobility within the Union, and to facilitate their adaptation to industrial changes and to changes in production systems, in particular through vocational training and retraining.

2.   The Commission shall administer the Fund. It shall be assisted in this task by a Committee presided over by a member of the Commission and composed of representatives of Member States, trade unions and employers' organisations.

3.   European laws shall establish implementing measures relating to the Fund. Such laws shall be adopted after consultation of the Committee of the Regions and the Economic and Social Committee.

SECTION 3   ECONOMIC, SOCIAL AND TERRITORIAL COHESION

Article III-220   (ex Article 158 EC)

In order to promote its overall harmonious development, the Union shall develop and pursue its action leading to the strengthening of its economic, social and territorial cohesion.

In particular, the Union shall aim at reducing disparities between the levels of development of the various regions and the backwardness of the least favoured regions.

Among the regions concerned, particular attention shall be paid to rural areas, areas affected by industrial transition, and regions which suffer from severe and permanent natural or demographic handicaps such as the northernmost regions with very low population density and island, cross-border and mountain regions.

Article III-221   (ex Article 159 EC)

Member States shall conduct their economic policies and shall coordinate them in such a way as, in addition, to attain the objectives set out in Article III-220. The formulation and implementation of the Union's policies and action and the implementation of the internal market shall take into account those objectives and shall contribute to their achievement. The Union shall also support the achievement of these objectives by the action it takes through the Structural Funds (European Agricultural Guidance and Guarantee Fund, Guidance Section; European Social Fund; European Regional Development Fund), the European Investment Bank and the other existing financial instruments.

The Commission shall submit a report to the European Parliament, the Council, the Committee of the Regions and the Economic and Social Committee every three years on the progress made towards achieving economic, social and territorial cohesion and on the manner in which the various means provided for in this Article have contributed to it. This report shall, if necessary, be accompanied by appropriate proposals.

European laws or framework laws may establish any specific measure outside the Funds, without prejudice to measures adopted within the framework of the Union's other policies. They shall be adopted after consultation of the Committee of the Regions and the Economic and Social Committee.

Article III-222   (ex Article 160 EC)

The European Regional Development Fund is intended to help to redress the main regional imbalances in the Union through participation in the development and structural adjustment of regions whose development is lagging behind and in the conversion of declining industrial regions.

Article III-223   (ex Article 161 EC)

1.   Without prejudice to article III-224, European laws shall define the tasks, the priority objectives and the organisation of the structural funds, which may involve grouping the Funds, the general rules applicable to them and the provisions necessary to ensure their effectiveness and the coordination of the Funds with one another and with the other existing Financial Instruments.

A Cohesion Fund set up by a European law shall provide a financial contribution to projects in the fields of environment and trans-European networks in the area of transport infrastructure.

In all cases, such European laws shall be adopted after consultation of the Committee of the Regions and the Economic and Social Committee.

2.   The first provisions on the Structural Funds and the Cohesion Fund to be adopted following those in force on the date on which the Treaty establishing a Constitution for Europe is signed shall be established by a European law of the Council. The Council shall act unanimously after obtaining the consent of the European Parliament.

Article III-224   (ex Article 162 EC)

European laws shall establish implementing measures relating to the European Regional Development Fund. Such laws shall be adopted after consultation of the Committee of the Regions and the Economic and Social Committee.

With regard to the European Agricultural Guidance and Guarantee Fund, Guidance Section, and the European Social Fund, Articles III-231 and III-219(3) respectively shall apply.

SECTION 4   AGRICULTURE AND FISHERIES

Article III-225   (ex Article 32(1), second sentence, EC)

The Union shall define and implement a common agriculture and fisheries policy.

'Agricultural products' means the products of the soil, of stockfarming and of fisheries and products of first-stage processing directly related to these products. References to the common agricultural policy or to agriculture, and the use of the term 'agricultural', shall be understood as also referring to fisheries, having regard to the specific characteristics of this sector.

Article III-226   (ex Article 32(1), first sentence, and (2) to (4) EC)

1.   The internal market shall extend to agriculture and trade in agricultural products.

2.   Save as otherwise provided in articles III-227 to III-232, the rules laid down for the establishment and functioning of the internal market shall apply to agricultural products.

3.   The products listed in Annex I shall be subject to Articles III-227 to III-232.

4.   The operation and development of the internal market for agricultural products must be accompanied by a common agricultural policy.

Article III-227   (ex Article 33 EC)

1.   The objectives of the common agricultural policy shall be:
   (a)   to increase agricultural productivity by promoting technical progress and by ensuring the rational development of agricultural production and the optimum utilisation of the factors of production, in particular labour;
   (b)   thus to ensure a fair standard of living for the agricultural community, in particular by increasing the individual earnings of persons engaged in agriculture;
   (c)   to stabilise markets;
   (d)   to assure the availability of supplies;
   (e)   to ensure that supplies reach consumers at reasonable prices.

2.   In working out the common agricultural policy and the special methods for its application, account shall be taken of:
   (a)   the particular nature of agricultural activity, which results from the social structure of agriculture and from structural and natural disparities between the various agricultural regions;
   (b)   the need to effect the appropriate adjustments by degrees;
   (c)   the fact that in the Member States agriculture constitutes a sector closely linked with the economy as a whole.

Article III-228   (ex Article 34 EC)

1.   In order to attain the objectives set out in Article III-227, a common organisation of agricultural markets shall be established.

This organisation shall take one of the following forms, depending on the product concerned:
   (a)   common rules on competition;
   (b)   compulsory coordination of the various national market organisations;
   (c)   a European market organisation.

2.   The common organisation established in accordance with paragraph 1 may include all measures required to attain the objectives set out in Article III-227, in particular regulation

of prices, aids for the production and marketing of the various products, storage and carryover arrangements and common machinery for stabilising imports or exports.

The common organisation shall be limited to pursuit of the objectives set out in Article III-227 and shall exclude any discrimination between producers or consumers within the Union.

Any common price policy shall be based on common criteria and uniform methods of calculation.

3. In order to enable the common organisation referred to in paragraph 1 to attain its objectives, one or more agricultural guidance and guarantee funds may be set up.

Article III-229   (ex Article 35 EC)

To enable the objectives set out in Article III-227 to be attained, provision may be made within the framework of the common agricultural policy for measures such as:

> (a) an effective coordination of efforts in the spheres of vocational training, of research and of the dissemination of agricultural knowledge; this may include joint financing of projects or institutions;
>
> (b) joint measures to promote consumption of certain products.

Article III-230   (ex Article 36 EC)

1. The Section relating to rules on competition shall apply to production of and trade in agricultural products only to the extent determined by European laws or framework laws in accordance with Article III-231(2), having regard to the objectives set out in Article III-227.

2. The Council, on a proposal from the Commission, may adopt a European regulation or decision authorising the granting of aid:

> (a) for the protection of enterprises handicapped by structural or natural conditions;
>
> (b) within the framework of economic development programmes.

Article III-231   (ex Article 37 EC)

1. The Commission shall submit proposals for working out and implementing the common agricultural policy, including the replacement of the national organisations by one of the forms of common organisation provided for in Article III-228(1), and for implementing the measures referred to in this Section. These proposals shall take account of the inter-dependence of the agricultural matters referred to in this Section.

2. European laws or framework laws shall establish the common organisation of the market provided for in Article III-228(1) and the other provisions necessary for the pursuit of the objectives of the common agricultural policy and the common fisheries policy. They shall be adopted after consultation of the Economic and Social Committee.

3. The Council, on a proposal from the Commission, shall adopt the European regulations or decisions on fixing prices, levies, aid and quantitative limitations and on the fixing and allocation of fishing opportunities.

4. In accordance with paragraph 2, the national market organisations may be replaced by the common organisation provided for in Article III-228(1) if:

> (a) the common organisation offers Member States which are opposed to this measure and which have an organisation of their own for the production in question equivalent safeguards for the employment and standard of living of the producers concerned, account being taken of the adjustments that will be possible and the specialisation that will be needed with the passage of time, and
>
> (b) such an organisation ensures conditions for trade within the Union similar to those existing in a national market.

5. If a common organisation for certain raw materials is established before a common organisation exists for the corresponding processed products, such raw materials as are used for processed products intended for export to third countries may be imported from outside the Union.

Article III-232   (ex Article 38 EC)

Where in a Member State a product is subject to a national market organisation or to internal rules having equivalent effect which affect the competitive position of similar production in another Member State, a countervailing charge shall be applied by Member States to imports of this product coming from the Member State where such organisation or rules exist, unless that State applies a countervailing charge on export.

The Commission shall adopt European regulations or decisions fixing the amount of these charges at the level required to redress the balance. It may also authorise other measures, the conditions and details of which it shall determine.

SECTION 5   ENVIRONMENT

Article III-233   (ex Article 174 EC)

1.   Union policy on the environment shall contribute to the pursuit of the following objectives:
   (a) preserving, protecting and improving the quality of the environment;
   (b) protecting human health;
   (c) prudent and rational utilisation of natural resources;
   (d) promoting measures at international level to deal with regional or worldwide environmental problems.

2.   Union policy on the environment shall aim at a high level of protection taking into account the diversity of situations in the various regions of the Union. It shall be based on the precautionary principle and on the principles that preventive action should be taken, that environmental damage should as a priority be rectified at source and that the polluter should pay.

In this context, harmonisation measures answering environmental protection requirements shall include, where appropriate, a safeguard clause allowing Member States to take provisional steps, for non-economic environmental reasons, subject to a procedure of inspection by the Union.

3.   In preparing its policy on the environment, the Union shall take account of:
   (a) available scientific and technical data;
   (b) environmental conditions in the various regions of the Union;
   (c) the potential benefits and costs of action or lack of action;
   (d) the economic and social development of the Union as a whole and the balanced development of its regions.

4.   Within their respective spheres of competence, the Union and the Member States shall cooperate with third countries and with the competent international organisations. The arrangements for the Union's cooperation may be the subject of agreements between the Union and the third parties concerned.

The first subparagraph shall be without prejudice to Member States' competence to negotiate in international bodies and to conclude international agreements.

Article III-234   (ex Articles 175 and 176 EC)

1.   European laws or framework laws shall establish what action is to be taken in order to achieve the objectives referred to in Article III-233. They shall be adopted after consultation of the Committee of the Regions and the Economic and Social Committee.

2.   By way of derogation from paragraph 1 and without prejudice to Article III-172, the Council shall unanimously adopt European laws or framework laws establishing:
   (a) provisions primarily of a fiscal nature;
   (b) measures affecting:
      (i) town and country planning;
      (ii) quantitative management of water resources or affecting, directly or indirectly, the availability of those resources;

(iii) land use, with the exception of waste management;

(c) measures significantly affecting a Member State's choice between different energy sources and the general structure of its energy supply.

The Council, on a proposal from the Commission, may unanimously adopt a European decision making the ordinary legislative procedure applicable to the matters referred to in the first subparagraph.

In all cases, the Council shall act after consulting the European Parliament, the Committee of the Regions and the Economic and Social Committee.

3.   European laws shall establish general action programmes which set out priority objectives to be attained. Such laws shall be adopted after consultation of the Committee of the Regions and the Economic and Social Committee.

The measures necessary for the implementation of these programmes shall be adopted under the terms of paragraph 1 or 2, as the case may be.

4.   Without prejudice to certain measures adopted by the Union, the Member States shall finance and implement the environment policy.

5.   Without prejudice to the principle that the polluter should pay, if a measure based on paragraph 1 involves costs deemed disproportionate for the public authorities of a Member State, such measure shall provide in appropriate form for:

(a) temporary derogations, and/or

(b) financial support from the Cohesion Fund.

6.   The protective measures adopted pursuant to this Article shall not prevent any Member State from maintaining or introducing more stringent protective measures. Such measures must be compatible with the Constitution. They shall be notified to the Commission.

SECTION 6   CONSUMER PROTECTION

Article III-235   (ex Article 153 EC)

1.   In order to promote the interests of consumers and to ensure a high level of consumer protection, the Union shall contribute to protecting the health, safety and economic interests of consumers, as well as to promoting their right to information, education and to organise themselves in order to safeguard their interests.

2.   The Union shall contribute to the attainment of the objectives referred to in paragraph 1 through:

(a) measures adopted pursuant to Article III-172 in the context of the establishment and functioning of the internal market;

(b) measures which support, supplement and monitor the policy pursued by the Member States.

3.   European laws or framework laws shall establish the measures referred to in paragraph 2(b). Such laws shall be adopted after consultation of the Economic and Social Committee.

4.   Acts adopted pursuant to paragraph 3 shall not prevent any Member State from maintaining or introducing more stringent protective provisions. Such provisions must be compatible with the Constitution. They shall be notified to the Commission.

SECTION 7   TRANSPORT

Article III-236   (ex Articles 133 and 134 EC)

1.   The objectives of the Constitution shall, in matters governed by this Section, be pursued within the framework of a common transport policy.

2.   European laws or framework laws shall implement paragraph 1, taking into account the distinctive features of transport. They shall be adopted after consultation of the Committee of the Regions and the Economic and Social Committee.

Such European laws or framework laws shall establish:

(a) common rules applicable to international transport to or from the territory of a Member State or passing across the territory of one or more Member States;

(b) the conditions under which non-resident carriers may operate transport services within a Member State;

(c) measures to improve transport safety;

(d) any other appropriate measure.

3.   When the European laws or framework laws referred to in paragraph 2 are adopted, account shall be taken of cases where their application might seriously affect the standard of living and level of employment in certain regions, and the operation of transport facilities.

Article III-237   (ex Article 72 EC)

Until the European laws or framework laws referred to in Article III-236(2) have been adopted, no Member State may, unless the Council has unanimously adopted a European decision granting a derogation, make the various provisions governing the subject on 1 January 1958 or, for acceding States, the date of their accession less favourable in their direct or indirect effect on carriers of other Member States as compared with carriers who are nationals of that State.

Article III-238   (ex Article 73 EC)

Aids shall be compatible with the Constitution if they meet the needs of coordination of transport or if they represent reimbursement for the discharge of certain obligations inherent in the concept of a public service.

Article III-239   (ex Article 74 EC)

Any measures adopted within the framework of the Constitution in respect of transport rates and conditions shall take account of the economic circumstances of carriers.

Article III-240   (ex Article 75 EC)

1.   In the case of transport within the Union, discrimination which takes the form of carriers charging different rates and imposing different conditions for the carriage of the same goods over the same transport links on grounds of the Member State of origin or of destination of the goods in question shall be prohibited.

2.   Paragraph 1 shall not prevent the adoption of other European laws or framework laws pursuant to Article III-236(2).

3.   The Council, on a proposal from the Commission, shall adopt European regulations or decisions for implementing paragraph 1. It shall act after consulting the European Parliament and the Economic and Social Committee. The Council may in particular adopt the European regulations and decisions needed to enable the institutions to secure compliance with the rule laid down in paragraph 1 and to ensure that users benefit from it to the full.

4.   The Commission, acting on its own initiative or on application by a Member State, shall investigate any cases of discrimination falling within paragraph 1 and, after consulting any Member State concerned, adopt the necessary European decisions within the framework of the European regulations and decisions referred to in paragraph 3.

Article III-241   (ex Article 76 EC)

1.   The imposition by a Member State, in respect of transport operations carried out within the Union, of rates and conditions involving any element of support or protection in the interest of one or more particular undertakings or industries shall be prohibited, unless authorised by a European decision of the Commission.

2.   The Commission, acting on its own initiative or on application by a Member State, shall examine the rates and conditions referred to in paragraph 1, taking account in particular of the requirements of an appropriate regional economic policy, the needs of underdeveloped areas and the problems of areas seriously affected by political circumstances on the one hand,

and of the effects of such rates and conditions on competition between the different modes of transport on the other.

After consulting each Member State concerned, the Commission shall adopt the necessary European decisions.

3.   The prohibition provided for in paragraph 1 shall not apply to tariffs fixed to meet competition.

Article III-242   (ex Article 77 EC)

Charges or dues in respect of the crossing of frontiers which are charged by a carrier in addition to the transport rates shall not exceed a reasonable level after taking the costs actually incurred thereby into account.

Member States shall endeavour to reduce these costs.

The Commission may make recommendations to Member States for the application of this Article.

Article III-243   (ex Article 78 EC)

The provisions of this Section shall not form an obstacle to the application of measures taken in the Federal Republic of Germany to the extent that such measures are required in order to compensate for the economic disadvantages caused by the division of Germany to the economy of certain areas of the Federal Republic affected by that division. Five years after the entry into force of the Treaty establishing a Constitution for Europe, the Council, acting on a proposal from the Commission, may adopt a European decision repealing this Article.

Article III-244   (ex Article 79 EC)

An Advisory Committee consisting of experts designated by the governments of the Member States shall be attached to the Commission. The Commission, whenever it considers it desirable, shall consult the Committee on transport matters.

Article III-245   (ex Article 80 EC)

1.   This Section shall apply to transport by rail, road and inland waterway.

2.   European laws or framework laws may lay down appropriate measures for sea and air transport. They shall be adopted after consultation of the Committee of the Regions and the Economic and Social Committee.

SECTION 8   TRANS-EUROPEAN NETWORKS

Article III-246   (ex Article 154 EC)

1.   To help achieve the objectives referred to in Articles III-130 and III-220 and to enable citizens of the Union, economic operators and regional and local communities to derive full benefit from the setting-up of an area without internal frontiers, the Union shall contribute to the establishment and development of trans-European networks in the areas of transport, telecommunications and energy infrastructures.

2.   Within the framework of a system of open and competitive markets, action by the Union shall aim at promoting the interconnection and interoperability of national networks as well as access to such networks. It shall take account in particular of the need to link island, landlocked and peripheral regions with the central regions of the Union.

Article III-247   (ex Article 155 EC)

1.   In order to achieve the objectives referred to in Article III-246, the Union:
   (a)   shall establish a series of guidelines covering the objectives, priorities and broad lines of measures envisaged in the sphere of trans-European networks; these guidelines shall identify projects of common interest;
   (b)   shall implement any measures that may prove necessary to ensure the interoperability of the networks, in particular in the field of technical standardisation;

(c) may support projects of common interest supported by Member States, which are identified in the framework of the guidelines referred to in point (a), particularly through feasibility studies, loan guarantees or interest-rate subsidies; the Union may also contribute, through the Cohesion Fund, to the financing of specific projects in Member States in the area of transport infrastructure. The Union's activities shall take into account the potential economic viability of the projects.

2.   European laws or framework laws shall establish the guidelines and other measures referred to in paragraph 1. Such laws shall be adopted after consultation of the Committee of the Regions and the Economic and Social Committee. Guidelines and projects of common interest which relate to the territory of a Member State shall require the agreement of that Member State.

3.   Member States shall, in liaison with the Commission, coordinate among themselves the policies pursued at national level which may have a significant impact on the achievement of the objectives referred to in Article III-246. The Commission may, in close cooperation with the Member States, take any useful initiative to promote such coordination.

4.   The Union may cooperate with third countries to promote projects of mutual interest and to ensure the interoperability of networks.

SECTION 9   RESEARCH AND TECHNOLOGICAL DEVELOPMENT AND SPACE

Article III-248   (ex Article 163 EC)

1.   The Union shall aim to strengthen its scientific and technological bases by achieving a European research area in which researchers, scientific knowledge and technology circulate freely, and encourage it to become more competitive, including in its industry, while promoting all the research activities deemed necessary by virtue of other Chapters of the Constitution.

2.   For the purposes referred to in paragraph 1 the Union shall, throughout the Union, encourage undertakings, including small and medium-sized undertakings, research centres and universities in their research and technological development activities of high quality. It shall support their efforts to cooperate with one another, aiming, notably, at permitting researchers to cooperate freely across borders and at enabling undertakings to exploit the internal market potential, in particular through the opening-up of national public contracts, the definition of common standards and the removal of legal and fiscal obstacles to that cooperation.

3.   All the Union's activities in the area of research and technological development, including demonstration projects, shall be decided on and implemented in accordance with this Section.

Article III-249   (ex Article 164 EC)

In pursuing the objectives referred to in Article III-248, the Union shall carry out the following activities, complementing the activities carried out in the Member States:

(a) implementation of research, technological development and demonstration programmes, by promoting cooperation with and between undertakings, research centres and universities;

(b) promotion of cooperation in the field of the Union's research, technological development and demonstration with third countries and international organisations;

(c) dissemination and optimisation of the results of activities in the Union's research, technological development and demonstration;

(d) stimulation of the training and mobility of researchers in the Union.

Article III-250   (ex Article 165 EC)

1.   The Union and the Member States shall coordinate their research and technological

development activities so as to ensure that national policies and the Union's policy are mutually consistent.

2.   In close cooperation with the Member States, the Commission may take any useful initiative to promote the coordination referred to in paragraph 1, in particular initiatives aiming at the establishment of guidelines and indicators, the organisation of exchange of best practice, and the preparation of the necessary elements for periodic monitoring and evaluation. The European Parliament shall be kept fully informed.

Article III-251   (ex Article 166 EC)

1.   European laws shall establish a multiannual framework programme, setting out all the activities financed by the Union. Such laws shall be adopted after consultation of the Economic and Social Committee.

The framework programme shall:

(a) establish the scientific and technological objectives to be achieved by the activities provided for in Article III-249 and lay down the relevant priorities;

(b) indicate the broad lines of such activities;

(c) lay down the maximum overall amount and the detailed rules for the Union's financial participation in the framework programme and the respective shares in each of the activities provided for.

2.   The multiannual framework programme shall be adapted or supplemented as the situation changes.

3.   A European law of the Council shall establish specific programmes to implement the multiannual framework programme within each activity. Each specific programme shall define the detailed rules for implementing it, fix its duration and provide for the means deemed necessary. The sum of the amounts deemed necessary, fixed in the specific programmes, shall not exceed the overall maximum amount fixed for the framework programme and each activity. Such a law shall be adopted after consulting the European Parliament and the Economic and Social Committee.

4.   As a complement to the activities planned in the multiannual framework programme, European laws shall establish the measures necessary for the implementation of the European research area. Such laws shall be adopted after consulting the Economic and Social Committee.

Article III-252   (ex Articles 167 to 170 and second paragraph of ex Article 172 EC)

1.   For the implementation of the multiannual framework programme, European laws or framework laws shall establish:

(a) the rules for the participation of undertakings, research centres and universities;

(b) the rules governing the dissemination of research results.

Such European laws or framework laws shall be adopted after consultation of the Economic and Social Committee.

2.   In implementing the multiannual framework programme, European laws may establish supplementary programmes involving the participation of certain Member States only, which shall finance them subject to possible participation by the Union.

Such European laws shall determine the rules applicable to supplementary programmes, particularly as regards the dissemination of knowledge as well as access by other Member States. They shall be adopted after consultation of the Economic and Social Committee and with the agreement of the Member States concerned.

3.   In implementing the multiannual framework programme, European laws may make provision, in agreement with the Member States concerned, for participation in research and development programmes undertaken by several Member States, including participation in the structures created for the execution of those programmes. Such European laws shall be adopted after consultation of the Economic and Social Committee.

4.   In implementing the multiannual framework programme the Union may make provision for cooperation in the Union's research, technological development and demonstration with third countries or international organisations. The detailed arrangements for such cooperation may be the subject of agreements between the Union and the third parties concerned.

Article III-253   (ex Article 171 and first paragraph of ex Article 172 EC)

The Council, on a proposal from the Commission, may adopt European regulations or decisions to set up joint undertakings or any other structure necessary for the efficient execution of the Union's research, technological development and demonstration programmes. It shall act after consulting the European Parliament and the Economic and Social Committee.

Article III-254   (new)

1.   To promote scientific and technical progress, industrial competitiveness and the implementation of its policies, the Union shall draw up a European space policy. To this end, it may promote joint initiatives, support research and technological development and coordinate the efforts needed for the exploration and exploitation of space.

2.   To contribute to attaining the objectives referred to in paragraph 1, European laws or framework laws shall establish the necessary measures, which may take the form of a European space programme.

3.   The Union shall establish any appropriate relations with the European Space Agency.

Article III-255   (ex Article 173 EC)

At the beginning of each year the Commission shall send a report to the European Parliament and the Council. The report shall include information on activities relating to research, technological development and the dissemination of results during the previous year, and the work programme for the current year.

SECTION 10   ENERGY

Article III-256   (new)

1.   In the context of the establishment and functioning of the internal market and with regard for the need to preserve and improve the environment, Union policy on energy shall aim to:
- (a) ensure the functioning of the energy market;
- (b) ensure security of energy supply in the Union, and
- (c) promote energy efficiency and energy saving and the development of new and renewable forms of energy.

2.   Without prejudice to the application of other provisions of the Constitution, the objectives in paragraph 1 shall be achieved by measures enacted in European laws or framework laws. Such laws or framework laws shall be adopted after consultation of the Committee of the Regions and the Economic and Social Committee. Such European laws or framework laws shall not affect a Member State's right to determine the conditions for exploiting its energy resources, its choice between different energy sources and the general structure of its energy supply, without prejudice to Article III-234(2)(c).

3.   By way of derogation from paragraph 2, a European law or framework law of the Council shall establish the measures referred to therein when they are primarily of a fiscal nature. The Council shall act unanimously after consulting the European Parliament.

CHAPTER IV   AREA OF FREEDOM, SECURITY AND JUSTICE

SECTION 1   GENERAL PROVISIONS

Article III-257   (ex Articles 29 TEU and 61 EC)

1.   The Union shall constitute an area of freedom, security and justice with respect for fundamental rights and the different legal systems and traditions of the Member States.

2.   It shall ensure the absence of internal border controls for persons and shall frame a common policy on asylum, immigration and external border control, based on solidarity between Member States, which is fair towards third-country nationals. For the purpose of this Chapter, stateless persons shall be treated as third-country nationals.

3.   The Union shall endeavour to ensure a high level of security through measures to prevent and combat crime, racism and xenophobia, and through measures for coordination and cooperation between police and judicial authorities and other competent authorities, as well as through the mutual recognition of judgments in criminal matters and, if necessary, through the approximation of criminal laws.

4.   The Union shall facilitate access to justice, in particular through the principle of mutual recognition of judicial and extrajudicial decisions in civil matters.

Article III-258   (new)

The European Council shall define the strategic guidelines for legislative and operational planning within the area of freedom, security and justice.

Article III-259   (new)

National Parliaments shall ensure that the proposals and legislative initiatives submitted under Sections 4 and 5 of this Chapter comply with the principle of subsidiarity, in accordance with the arrangements laid down by the Protocol on the application of the principles of subsidiarity and proportionality.

Article III-260   (new)

Without prejudice to Articles III-360 to III-362, the Council may, on a proposal from the Commission, adopt European regulations or decisions laying down the arrangements whereby Member States, in collaboration with the Commission, conduct objective and impartial evaluation of the implementation of the Union policies referred to in this Chapter by Member States' authorities, in particular in order to facilitate full application of the principle of mutual recognition. The European Parliament and national Parliaments shall be informed of the content and results of the evaluation.

Article III-261   (ex Article 36 TEU)

A standing committee shall be set up within the Council in order to ensure that operational cooperation on internal security is promoted and strengthened within the Union. Without prejudice to Article III-344, it shall facilitate coordination of the action of Member States' competent authorities. Representatives of the Union bodies, offices and agencies concerned may be involved in the proceedings of this committee. The European Parliament and national Parliaments shall be kept informed of the proceedings.

Article III-262   (ex Articles 33 TEU and 64 EC)

This Chapter shall not affect the exercise of the responsibilities incumbent upon Member States with regard to the maintenance of law and order and the safeguarding of internal security.

Article III-263   (ex Article 66 EC)

The Council shall adopt European regulations to ensure administrative cooperation between the relevant departments of the Member States in the areas covered by this Chapter, as well as between those departments and the Commission. It shall act on a Commission proposal, subject to Article III-264, and after consulting the European Parliament.

Article III-264 (new)

The acts referred to in Sections 4 and 5, together with the European regulations referred to in Article III-263 which ensure administrative cooperation in the areas covered by these Sections, shall be adopted:

    (a) on a proposal from the Commission, or

    (b) on the initiative of a quarter of the Member States.

SECTION 2   POLICIES ON BORDER CHECKS, ASYLUM AND IMMIGRATION

Article III-265 (ex Article 62 EC)

1. The Union shall develop a policy with a view to:

    (a) ensuring the absence of any controls on persons, whatever their nationality, when crossing internal borders;

    (b) carrying out checks on persons and efficient monitoring of the crossing of external borders;

    (c) the gradual introduction of an integrated management system for external borders.

2. For the purposes of paragraph 1, European laws or framework laws shall establish measures concerning:

    (a) the common policy on visas and other short-stay residence permits;

    (b) the checks to which persons crossing external borders are subject;

    (c) the conditions under which nationals of third countries shall have the freedom to travel within the Union for a short period;

    (d) any measure necessary for the gradual establishment of an integrated management system for external borders;

    (e) the absence of any controls on persons, whatever their nationality, when crossing internal borders.

3. This Article shall not affect the competence of the Member States concerning the geographical demarcation of their borders, in accordance with international law.

Article III-266 (ex Article 63, points 1 and 2, and ex Article 64(2) EC)

1. The Union shall develop a common policy on asylum, subsidiary protection and temporary protection with a view to offering appropriate status to any third-country national requiring international protection and ensuring compliance with the principle of non-defilement. This policy must be in accordance with the Geneva Convention of 28 July 1951 and the Protocol of 31 January 1967 relating to the status of refugees, and other relevant treaties.

2. For the purposes of paragraph 1, European laws or framework laws shall lay down measures for a common European asylum system comprising:

    (a) a uniform status of asylum for nationals of third countries, valid throughout the Union;

    (b) a uniform status of subsidiary protection for nationals of third countries who, without obtaining European asylum, are in need of international protection;

    (c) a common system of temporary protection for displaced persons in the event of a massive inflow;

    (d) common procedures for the granting and withdrawing of uniform asylum or subsidiary protection status;

    (e) criteria and mechanisms for determining which Member State is responsible for considering an application for asylum or subsidiary protection;

    (f) standards concerning the conditions for the reception of applicants for asylum or subsidiary protection;

    (g) partnership and cooperation with third countries for the purpose of managing inflows of people applying for asylum or subsidiary or temporary protection.

3.   In the event of one or more Member States being confronted by an emergency situation characterised by a sudden inflow of nationals of third countries, the Council, on a proposal from the Commission, may adopt European regulations or decisions comprising provisional measures for the benefit of the Member State(s) concerned. It shall act after consulting the European Parliament.

Article III-267   (ex Article 63, points 3 and 4, EC)

1.   The Union shall develop a common immigration policy aimed at ensuring, at all stages, the efficient management of migration flows, fair treatment of third-country nationals residing legally in Member States, and the prevention of, and enhanced measures to combat, illegal immigration and trafficking in human beings.

2.   For the purposes of paragraph 1, European laws or framework laws shall establish measures in the following areas:

(a)   the conditions of entry and residence, and standards on the issue by Member States of long-term visas and residence permits, including those for the purpose of family reunion;

(b)   the definition of the rights of third-country nationals residing legally in a Member State, including the conditions governing freedom of movement and of residence in other Member States;

(c)   illegal immigration and unauthorised residence, including removal and repatriation of persons residing without authorisation;

(d)   combating trafficking in persons, in particular women and children.

3.   The Union may conclude agreements with third countries for the readmission to their countries of origin or provenance of third-country nationals who do not or who no longer fulfil the conditions for entry, presence or residence in the territory of one of the Member States.

4.   European laws or framework laws may establish measures to provide incentives and support for the action of Member States with a view to promoting the integration of third-country nationals residing legally in their territories, excluding any harmonisation of the laws and regulations of the Member States.

5.   This Article shall not affect the right of Member States to determine volumes of admission of third-country nationals coming from third countries to their territory in order to seek work, whether employed or self-employed.

Article III-268   (new)

The policies of the Union set out in this Section and their implementation shall be governed by the principle of solidarity and fair sharing of responsibility, including its financial implications, between the Member States. Whenever necessary, the Union acts adopted pursuant to this Section shall contain appropriate measures to give effect to this principle.

SECTION 3   JUDICIAL COOPERATION IN CIVIL MATTERS

Article III-269   (ex Article 65 EC)

1.   The Union shall develop judicial cooperation in civil matters having cross-border implications, based on the principle of mutual recognition of judgments and decisions in extrajudicial cases. Such cooperation may include the adoption of measures for the approximation of the laws and regulations of the Member States.

2.   For the purposes of paragraph 1, European laws or framework laws shall establish measures, particularly when necessary for the proper functioning of the internal market, aimed at ensuring:

(a)   the mutual recognition and enforcement between Member States of judgments and decisions in extrajudicial cases;

(b)   the cross-border service of judicial and extrajudicial documents;

(c) the compatibility of the rules applicable in the Member States concerning conflict of laws and of jurisdiction;

(d) cooperation in the taking of evidence;

(e) effective access to justice;

(f) the elimination of obstacles to the proper functioning of civil proceedings, if necessary by promoting the compatibility of the rules on civil procedure applicable in the Member States;

(g) the development of alternative methods of dispute settlement;

(h) support for the training of the judiciary and judicial staff.

3.   Notwithstanding paragraph 2, a European law or framework law of the Council shall establish measures concerning family law with cross-border implications. The Council shall act unanimously after consulting the European Parliament. The Council, on a proposal from the Commission, may adopt a European decision determining those aspects of family law with cross-border implications which may be the subject of acts adopted by the ordinary legislative procedure. The Council shall act unanimously after consulting the European Parliament.

SECTION 4   JUDICIAL COOPERATION IN CRIMINAL MATTERS

Article III-270   **(ex Article 31(1) TEU)**

1.   Judicial cooperation in criminal matters in the Union shall be based on the principle of mutual recognition of judgments and judicial decisions and shall include the approximation of the laws and regulations of the Member States in the areas referred to in paragraph 2 and in Article III-271.

European laws or framework laws shall establish measures to:

(a) lay down rules and procedures for ensuring recognition throughout the Union of all forms of judgments and judicial decisions;

(b) prevent and settle conflicts of jurisdiction between Member States;

(c) support the training of the judiciary and judicial staff;

(d) facilitate cooperation between judicial or equivalent authorities of the Member States in relation to proceedings in criminal matters and the enforcement of decisions.

2.   To the extent necessary to facilitate mutual recognition of judgments and judicial decisions and police and judicial cooperation in criminal matters having a cross-border dimension, European framework laws may establish minimum rules. Such rules shall take into account the differences between the legal traditions and systems of the Member States.

They shall concern:

(a) mutual admissibility of evidence between Member States;

(b) the rights of individuals in criminal procedure;

(c) the rights of victims of crime;

(d) any other specific aspects of criminal procedure which the Council has identified in advance by a European decision; for the adoption of such a decision, the Council shall act unanimously after obtaining the consent of the European Parliament.

Adoption of the minimum rules referred to in this paragraph shall not prevent Member States from maintaining or introducing a higher level of protection for individuals.

3.   Where a member of the Council considers that a draft European framework law as referred to in paragraph 2 would affect fundamental aspects of its criminal justice system, it may request that the draft framework law be referred to the European Council. In that case, the procedure referred to in Article III-396 shall be suspended. After discussion, the European Council shall, within four months of this suspension, either:

(a) refer the draft back to the Council, which shall terminate the suspension of the procedure referred to in Article III-396, or

(b) request the Commission or the group of Member States from which the draft originates to submit a new draft; in that case, the act originally proposed shall be deemed not to have been adopted.

4.   If, by the end of the period referred to in paragraph 3, either no action has been taken by the European Council or if, within 12 months from the submission of a new draft under paragraph 3(b), the European framework law has not been adopted, and at least one third of the Member States wish to establish enhanced cooperation on the basis of the draft framework law concerned, they shall notify the European Parliament, the Council and the Commission accordingly.

In such a case, the authorisation to proceed with enhanced cooperation referred to in Articles I-44(2) and III-419(1) shall be deemed to be granted and the provisions on enhanced cooperation shall apply.

Article III-271   (new)

1.   European framework laws may establish minimum rules concerning the definition of criminal offences and sanctions in the areas of particularly serious crime with a cross-border dimension resulting from the nature or impact of such offences or from a special need to combat them on a common basis.

These areas of crime are the following: terrorism, trafficking in human beings and sexual exploitation of women and children, illicit drug trafficking, illicit arms trafficking, money laundering, corruption, counterfeiting of means of payment, computer crime and organised crime.

On the basis of developments in crime, the Council may adopt a European decision identifying other areas of crime that meet the criteria specified in this paragraph. It shall act unanimously after obtaining the consent of the European Parliament.

2.   If the approximation of criminal laws and regulations of the Member States proves essential to ensure the effective implementation of a Union policy in an area which has been subject to harmonisation measures, European framework laws may establish minimum rules with regard to the definition of criminal offences and sanctions in the area concerned. Such framework laws shall be adopted by the same procedure as was followed for the adoption of the harmonisation measures in question, without prejudice to Article III-264.

3.   Where a member of the Council considers that a draft European framework law as referred to in paragraph 1 or 2 would affect fundamental aspects of its criminal justice system, it may request that the draft framework law be referred to the European Council. In that case, where the procedure referred to in Article III-396 is applicable, it shall be suspended. After discussion, the European Council shall, within four months of this suspension, either:

(a) refer the draft back to the Council, which shall terminate the suspension of the procedure referred to in Article III-396 where it is applicable, or

(b) request the Commission or the group of Member States from which the draft originates to submit a new draft; in that case, the act originally proposed shall be deemed not to have been adopted.

4.   If, by the end of the period referred to in paragraph 3, either no action has been taken by the European Council or if, within 12 months from the submission of a new draft under paragraph 3(b), the European framework law has not been adopted, and at least one third of the Member States wish to establish enhanced cooperation on the basis of the draft framework law concerned, they shall notify the European Parliament, the Council and the Commission accordingly. In such a case, the authorisation to proceed with enhanced cooperation referred to in Articles I-44(2) and III-419(1) shall be deemed to be granted and the provisions on enhanced cooperation shall apply.

Article III-272   (new)

European laws or framework laws may establish measures to promote and support the action of Member States in the field of crime prevention, excluding any harmonisation of the laws and regulations of the Member States.

Article III-273   (ex Article 31(2) TEU)

1.   Eurojust's mission shall be to support and strengthen coordination and cooperation between national investigating and prosecuting authorities in relation to serious crime affecting two or more Member States or requiring a prosecution on common bases, on the basis of operations conducted and information supplied by the Member States' authorities and by Europol.

In this context, European laws shall determine Eurojust's structure, operation, field of action and tasks. Those tasks may include:

(a)   the initiation of criminal investigations, as well as proposing the initiation of prosecutions, conducted by competent national authorities, particularly those relating to offences against the financial interests of the Union;

(b)   the coordination of investigations and prosecutions referred to in point (a);

(c)   the strengthening of judicial cooperation, including by resolution of conflicts of jurisdiction and by close cooperation with the European Judicial Network.

European laws shall also determine arrangements for involving the European Parliament and national Parliaments in the evaluation of Eurojust's activities.

2.   In the prosecutions referred to in paragraph 1, and without prejudice to Article III-274, formal acts of judicial procedure shall be carried out by the competent national officials.

Article III-274   (new)

1.   In order to combat crimes affecting the financial interests of the Union, a European law of the Council may establish a European Public Prosecutor's Office from Eurojust. The Council shall act unanimously after obtaining the consent of the European Parliament.

2.   The European Public Prosecutor's Office shall be responsible for investigating, prosecuting and bringing to judgment, where appropriate in liaison with Europol, the perpetrators of, and accomplices in, offences against the Union's financial interests, as determined by the European law provided for in paragraph 1. It shall exercise the functions of prosecutor in the competent courts of the Member States in relation to such offences.

3.   The European law referred to in paragraph 1 shall determine the general rules applicable to the European Public Prosecutor's Office, the conditions governing the performance of its functions, the rules of procedure applicable to its activities, as well as those governing the admissibility of evidence, and the rules applicable to the judicial review of procedural measures taken by it in the performance of its functions.

4.   The European Council may, at the same time or subsequently, adopt a European decision amending paragraph 1 in order to extend the powers of the European Public Prosecutor's Office to include serious crime having a cross-border dimension and amending accordingly paragraph 2 as regards the perpetrators of, and accomplices in, serious crimes affecting more than one Member State. The European Council shall act unanimously after obtaining the consent of the European Parliament and after consulting the Commission.

SECTION 5   POLICE COOPERATION

Article III-275   (ex Article 30(1) TEU)

1.   The Union shall establish police cooperation involving all the Member States' competent authorities, including police, customs and other specialised law enforcement services in relation to the prevention, detection and investigation of criminal offences.

2.   For the purposes of paragraph 1, European laws or framework laws may establish measures concerning:

(a)   the collection, storage, processing, analysis and exchange of relevant information;

(b) support for the training of staff, and cooperation on the exchange of staff, on equipment and on research into crime-detection;

(c) common investigative techniques in relation to the detection of serious forms of organised crime.

3. A European law or framework law of the Council may establish measures concerning operational cooperation between the authorities referred to in this Article. The Council shall act unanimously after consulting the European Parliament.

Article III-276   (ex Article 30(2) TEU)

1. Europol's mission shall be to support and strengthen action by the Member States' police authorities and other law enforcement services and their mutual cooperation in preventing and combating serious crime affecting two or more Member States, terrorism and forms of crime which affect a common interest covered by a Union policy.

2. European laws shall determine Europol's structure, operation, field of action and tasks. These tasks may include:

(a) the collection, storage, processing, analysis and exchange of information forwarded particularly by the authorities of the Member States or third countries or bodies;

(b) the coordination, organisation and implementation of investigative and operational action carried out jointly with the Member States' competent authorities or in the context of joint investigative teams, where appropriate in liaison with Eurojust.

European laws shall also lay down the procedures for scrutiny of Europol's activities by the European Parliament, together with national Parliaments.

3. Any operational action by Europol must be carried out in liaison and in agreement with the authorities of the Member State or States whose territory is concerned. The application of coercive measures shall be the exclusive responsibility of the competent national authorities.

Article III-277   (ex Article 32 TEU)

A European law or framework law of the Council shall lay down the conditions and limitations under which the competent authorities of the Member States referred to in Articles III-270 and III-275 may operate in the territory of another Member State in liaison and in agreement with the authorities of that State. The Council shall act unanimously after consulting the European Parliament.

CHAPTER V   AREAS WHERE THE UNION MAY TAKE COORDINATING, COMPLEMENTARY OR SUPPORTING ACTION

SECTION 1   PUBLIC HEALTH

Article III-278   (ex Article 152 EC)

1. A high level of human health protection shall be ensured in the definition and implementation of all the Union's policies and activities.

Action by the Union, which shall complement national policies, shall be directed towards improving public health, preventing human illness and diseases, and obviating sources of danger to physical and mental health. Such action shall cover:

(a) the fight against the major health scourges, by promoting research into their causes, their transmission and their prevention, as well as health information and education;

(b) monitoring, early warning of and combating serious cross-border threats to health.

The Union shall complement the Member States' action in reducing drug-related health damage, including information and prevention.

2.   The Union shall encourage cooperation between the Member States in the areas referred to in this Article and, if necessary, lend support to their action. It shall in particular encourage cooperation between the Member States to improve the complementarity of their health services in cross-border areas.

Member States shall, in liaison with the Commission, coordinate among themselves their policies and programmes in the areas referred to in paragraph 1. The Commission may, in close contact with the Member States, take any useful initiative to promote such coordination, in particular initiatives aiming at the establishment of guidelines and indicators, the organisation of exchange of best practice, and the preparation of the necessary elements for periodic monitoring and evaluation. The European Parliament shall be kept fully informed.

3.   The Union and the Member States shall foster cooperation with third countries and the competent international organisations in the sphere of public health.

4.   By way of derogation from Article I-12(5) and Article I-17(a) and in accordance with Article I-14 (2)(k), European laws or framework laws shall contribute to the achievement of the objectives referred to in this Article by establishing the following measures in order to meet common safety concerns:

(a)   measures setting high standards of quality and safety of organs and substances of human origin, blood and blood derivatives; these measures shall not prevent any Member State from maintaining or introducing more stringent protective measures;

(b)   measures in the veterinary and phytosanitary fields which have as their direct objective the protection of public health;

(c)   measures setting high standards of quality and safety for medicinal products and devices for medical use;

(d)   measures concerning monitoring, early warning of and combating serious cross-border threats to health.

Such European laws or framework laws shall be adopted after consultation of the Committee of the Regions and the Economic and Social Committee.

5.   European laws or framework laws may also establish incentive measures designed to protect and improve human health and in particular to combat the major cross-border health scourges, as well as measures which have as their direct objective the protection of public health regarding tobacco and the abuse of alcohol, excluding any harmonisation of the laws and regulations of the Member States. They shall be adopted after consultation of the Committee of the Regions and the Economic and Social Committee.

6.   For the purposes of this Article, the Council, on a proposal from the Commission, may also adopt recommendations.

7.   Union action shall respect the responsibilities of the Member States for the definition of their health policy and for the organisation and delivery of health services and medical care. The responsibilities of the Member States shall include the management of health services and medical care and the allocation of the resources assigned to them. The measures referred to in paragraph 4(a) shall not affect national provisions on the donation or medical use of organs and blood.

SECTION 2   INDUSTRY

Article III-279   (ex Article 157 EC)

1.   The Union and the Member States shall ensure that the conditions necessary for the competitiveness of the Union's industry exist.

For that purpose, in accordance with a system of open and competitive markets, their action shall be aimed at:

(a)   speeding up the adjustment of industry to structural changes;

(b)   encouraging an environment favourable to initiative and to the development of undertakings throughout the Union, particularly small and medium-sized undertakings;

(c) encouraging an environment favourable to cooperation between undertakings;

(d) fostering better exploitation of the industrial potential of policies of innovation, research and technological development.

2.   The Member States shall consult each other in liaison with the Commission and, where necessary, shall coordinate their action. The Commission may take any useful initiative to promote such coordination, in particular initiatives aiming at the establishment of guidelines and indicators, the organisation of exchange of best practice, and the preparation of the necessary elements for periodic monitoring and evaluation. The European Parliament shall be kept fully informed.

3.   The Union shall contribute to the achievement of the objectives set out in paragraph 1 through the policies and activities it pursues under other provisions of the Constitution. European laws or framework laws may establish specific measures in support of action taken in the Member States to achieve the objectives set out in paragraph 1, excluding any harmonisation of the laws and regulations of the Member States. They shall be adopted after consultation of the Economic and Social Committee.

This Section shall not provide a basis for the introduction by the Union of any measure which could lead to distortion of competition or contains tax provisions or provisions relating to the rights and interests of employed persons.

SECTION 3   CULTURE

Article III-280   (ex Article 151 EC)

1.   The Union shall contribute to the flowering of the cultures of the Member States, while respecting their national and regional diversity and at the same time bringing the common cultural heritage to the fore.

2.   Action by the Union shall be aimed at encouraging cooperation between Member States and, if necessary, supporting and complementing their action in the following areas:

(a) improvement of the knowledge and dissemination of the culture and history of the European peoples;

(b) conservation and safeguarding of cultural heritage of European significance;

(c) non-commercial cultural exchanges;

(d) artistic and literary creation, including in the audiovisual sector.

3.   The Union and the Member States shall foster cooperation with third countries and the competent international organisations in the sphere of culture, in particular the Council of Europe.

4.   The Union shall take cultural aspects into account in its action under other provisions of the Constitution, in particular in order to respect and to promote the diversity of its cultures.

5.   In order to contribute to the achievement of the objectives referred to in this Article:

(a) European laws or framework laws shall establish incentive measures, excluding any harmonisation of the laws and regulations of the Member States. They shall be adopted after consultation of the Committee of the Regions;

(b) the Council, on a proposal from the Commission, shall adopt recommendations.

SECTION 4   (NEW) TOURISM

Article III-281   (new)

1.   The Union shall complement the action of the Member States in the tourism sector, in particular by promoting the competitiveness of Union undertakings in that sector.

To that end, Union action shall be aimed at:

(a) encouraging the creation of a favourable environment for the development of undertakings in this sector;
(b) promoting cooperation between the Member States, particularly by the exchange of good practice;

2. European laws or framework laws shall establish specific measures to complement actions within the Member States to achieve the objectives referred to in this Article, excluding any harmonisation of the laws and regulations of the Member States.

SECTION 5   EDUCATION, YOUTH, SPORT AND VOCATIONAL TRAINING

Article III-282   (ex Article 149 EC)

1. The Union shall contribute to the development of quality education by encouraging cooperation between Member States and, if necessary, by supporting and complementing their action. It shall fully respect the responsibility of the Member States for the content of teaching and the organisation of education systems and their cultural and linguistic diversity. The Union shall contribute to the promotion of European sporting issues, while taking account of the specific nature of sport, its structures based on voluntary activity and its social and educational function.

Union action shall be aimed at:
(a) developing the European dimension in education, particularly through the teaching and dissemination of the languages of the Member States;
(b) encouraging mobility of students and teachers, inter alia by encouraging the academic recognition of diplomas and periods of study;
(c) promoting cooperation between educational establishments;
(d) developing exchanges of information and experience on issues common to the education systems of the Member States;
(e) encouraging the development of youth exchanges and of exchanges of socio-educational instructors and encouraging the participation of young people in democratic life in Europe;
(f) encouraging the development of distance education;
(g) developing the European dimension in sport, by promoting fairness and openness in sporting competitions and cooperation between bodies responsible for sports, and by protecting the physical and moral integrity of sportsmen and sportswomen, especially young sportsmen and sportswomen.

2. The Union and the Member States shall foster cooperation with third countries and the competent international organisations in the field of education and sport, in particular the Council of Europe.

3. In order to contribute to the achievement of the objectives referred to in this Article:
(a) European laws or framework laws shall establish incentive measures, excluding any harmonisation of the laws and regulations of the Member States. They shall be adopted after consultation of the Committee of the Regions and the Economic and Social Committee;
(b) the Council, on a proposal from the Commission, shall adopt recommendations.

Article III-283   (ex Article 150 EC)

1. The Union shall implement a vocational training policy which shall support and complement the action of the Member States, while fully respecting the responsibility of the Member States for the content and organisation of vocational training.

Union action shall aim to:
(a) facilitate adaptation to industrial change, in particular through vocational training and retraining;
(b) improve initial and continuing vocational training in order to facilitate vocational integration and reintegration into the labour market;

(c) facilitate access to vocational training and encourage mobility of instructors and trainees and particularly young people;

(d) stimulate cooperation on training between educational or training establishments and firms;

(e) develop exchanges of information and experience on issues common to the training systems of the Member States.

2. The Union and the Member States shall foster cooperation with third countries and the competent international organisations in the sphere of vocational training.

3. In order to contribute to the achievement of the objectives referred to in this Article:

(a) European laws or framework laws shall establish the necessary measures, excluding any harmonisation of the laws and regulations of the Member States. They shall be adopted after consultation of the Committee of the Regions and the Economic and Social Committee;

(b) the Council, on a proposal from the Commission, shall adopt recommendations.

SECTION 6   CIVIL PROTECTION

Article III-284   (new)

1. The Union shall encourage cooperation between Member States in order to improve the effectiveness of systems for preventing and protecting against natural or man-made disasters.

Union action shall aim to:

(a) support and complement Member States' action at national, regional and local level in risk prevention, in preparing their civil-protection personnel and in responding to natural or Man-made disasters within the Union;

(b) promote swift, effective operational cooperation within the Union between national civil-protection services;

(c) promote consistency in international civil-protection work.

2. European laws or framework laws shall establish the measures necessary to help achieve the objectives referred to in paragraph 1, excluding any harmonisation of the laws and regulations of the Member States.

SECTION 7   ADMINISTRATIVE COOPERATION

Article III-285   (new)

1. Effective implementation of Union law by the Member States, which is essential for the proper functioning of the Union, shall be regarded as a matter of common interest.

2. The Union may support the efforts of Member States to improve their administrative capacity to implement Union law. Such action may include facilitating the exchange of information and of civil servants as well as supporting training schemes. No Member State shall be obliged to avail itself of such support. European laws shall establish the necessary measures to this end, excluding any harmonisation of the laws and regulations of the Member States.

3. This Article shall be without prejudice to the obligations of the Member States to implement Union law or to the prerogatives and duties of the Commission. It shall also be without prejudice to other provisions of the Constitution providing for administrative cooperation among the Member States and between them and the Union.

TITLE IV   ASSOCIATION OF THE OVERSEAS COUNTRIES AND TERRITORIES

Article III-286   (ex Article 182 EC)

1.   The non-European countries and territories which have special relations with Denmark, France, the Netherlands and the United Kingdom shall be associated with the Union. These countries and territories, hereinafter called the 'countries and territories', are listed in Annex II.

This title shall apply to Greenland, subject to the specific provisions of the Protocol on special arrangements for Greenland.

2.   The purpose of association shall be to promote the economic and social development of the countries and territories and to establish close economic relations between them and the Union. Association shall serve primarily to further the interests and prosperity of the inhabitants of these countries and territories in order to lead them to the economic, social and cultural development to which they aspire.

Article III-287   (ex Article 183 EC)

Association shall have the following objectives:

   (a)   Member States shall apply to their trade with the countries and territories the same treatment as they accord each other pursuant to the Constitution;
   (b)   each country or territory shall apply to its trade with Member States and with the other countries and territories the same treatment as that which it applies to the European State with which it has special relations;
   (c)   Member States shall contribute to the investments required for the progressive development of these countries and territories;
   (d)   for investments financed by the Union, participation in tenders and supplies shall be open on equal terms to all natural and legal persons who are nationals of a Member State or of one of the countries and territories;
   (e)   in relations between Member States and the countries and territories, the right of establishment of nationals and companies or firms shall be regulated in accordance with the provisions of Subsection 2 of Section 2 of Chapter I of Title III relating to the freedom of establishment and under the procedures laid down in that Subsection, and on a non-discriminatory basis, subject to any acts adopted pursuant to Article III-291.

Article III-288   (ex Article 184 EC)

1.   Customs duties on imports into the Member States of goods originating in the countries and territories shall be prohibited in conformity with the prohibition of customs duties between Member States provided for in the Constitution.

2.   Customs duties on imports into each country or territory from Member States or from the other countries or territories shall be prohibited in accordance with Article III-151(4).

3.   The countries and territories may, however, levy customs duties which meet the needs of their development and industrialisation or produce revenue for their budgets. The duties referred to in the first subparagraph shall not exceed the level of those imposed on imports of products from the Member State with which each country or territory has special relations.

4.   Paragraph 2 shall not apply to countries and territories which, by reason of the particular international obligations by which they are bound, already apply a non-discriminatory customs tariff.

5.   The introduction of or any change in customs duties imposed on goods imported into the countries and territories shall not, either in law or in fact, give rise to any direct or indirect discrimination between imports from the various Member States.

Article III-289   (ex Article 185 EC)

If the level of the duties applicable to goods from a third country on entry into a country or territory is liable, when Article III-288(1) has been applied, to cause deflections of trade to the detriment of any Member State, the latter may request the Commission to propose to the other Member States that they take the necessary measures to remedy the situation.

Article III-290 (ex Article 186 EC)
Subject to the provisions relating to public health, public security or public policy, freedom of movement within Member States for workers from the countries and territories, and within the countries and territories for workers from Member States, shall be regulated by acts adopted in accordance with Article III-291.

Article III-291 (ex Article 187 EC)
The Council, on a proposal from the Commission, shall adopt unanimously, on the basis of the experience acquired under the association of the countries and territories with the Union, European laws, framework laws, regulations and decisions as regards the detailed rules and the procedure for the association of the countries and territories with the Union. These laws and framework laws shall be adopted after consultation of the European Parliament.

TITLE V   THE UNION'S EXTERNAL ACTION
CHAPTER I   PROVISIONS HAVING GENERAL APPLICATION

Article III-292 (ex Article 3, second paragraph and ex Article 11 TEU)
1.   The Union's action on the international scene shall be guided by the principles which have inspired its own creation, development and enlargement, and which it seeks to advance in the wider world: democracy, the rule of law, the universality and indivisibility of human rights and fundamental freedoms, respect for human dignity, the principles of equality and solidarity, and respect for the principles of the United Nations Charter and international law. The Union shall seek to develop relations and build partnerships with third countries, and international, regional or global organisations which share the principles referred to in the first subparagraph. It shall promote multilateral solutions to common problems, in particular in the framework of the United Nations.

2.   The Union shall define and pursue common policies and actions, and shall work for a high degree of cooperation in all fields of international relations, in order to:
  (a) safeguard its values, fundamental interests, security, independence and integrity;
  (b) consolidate and support democracy, the rule of law, human rights and the principles of international law;
  (c) preserve peace, prevent conflicts and strengthen international security, in accordance with the purposes and principles of the United Nations Charter, with the principles of the Helsinki Final Act and with the aims of the Charter of Paris, including those relating to external borders;
  (d) foster the sustainable economic, social and environmental development of developing countries, with the primary aim of eradicating poverty;
  (e) encourage the integration of all countries into the world economy, including through the progressive abolition of restrictions on international trade;
  (f) help develop international measures to preserve and improve the quality of the environment and the sustainable management of global natural resources, in order to ensure sustainable development;
  (g) assist populations, countries and regions confronting natural or man-made disasters;
  (h) promote an international system based on stronger multilateral cooperation and good global governance.

3.   The Union shall respect the principles and pursue the objectives set out in paragraphs 1 and 2 in the development and implementation of the different areas of the Union's external action covered by this Title and the external aspects of its other policies.

The Union shall ensure consistency between the different areas of its external action and between these and its other policies. The Council and the Commission, assisted by the Union Minister for Foreign Affairs, shall ensure that consistency and shall cooperate to that effect.

Article III-293   (new)

1.   On the basis of the principles and objectives set out in Article III-292, the European Council shall identify the strategic interests and objectives of the Union. European decisions of the European Council on the strategic interests and objectives of the Union shall relate to the common foreign and security policy and to other areas of the external action of the Union. Such decisions may concern the relations of the Union with a specific country or region or may be thematic in approach. They shall define their duration, and the means to be made available by the Union and the Member States. The European Council shall act unanimously on a recommendation from the Council, adopted by the latter under the arrangements laid down for each area. European decisions of the European Council shall be implemented in accordance with the procedures provided for in the Constitution.

2.   The Union Minister for Foreign Affairs, for the area of common foreign and security policy, and the Commission, for other areas of external action, may submit joint proposals to the Council.

CHAPTER II   COMMON FOREIGN AND SECURITY POLICY

SECTION 1   COMMON PROVISIONS

Article III-294   (ex Articles 11 and 12 TEU)

1.   In the context of the principles and objectives of its external action, the Union shall define and implement a common foreign and security policy covering all areas of foreign and security policy.

2.   The Member States shall support the common foreign and security policy actively and unreservedly in a spirit of loyalty and mutual solidarity.

The Member States shall work together to enhance and develop their mutual political solidarity. They shall refrain from any action which is contrary to the interests of the Union or likely to impair its effectiveness as a cohesive force in international relations.

The Council and the Union Minister for Foreign Affairs shall ensure that these principles are complied with.

3.   The Union shall conduct the common foreign and security policy by:
  (a) defining the general guidelines;
  (b) adopting European decisions defining:
      (i)   actions to be undertaken by the Union;
      (ii) positions to be taken by the Union;
      (iii) arrangements for the implementation of the European decisions referred to in points (i) and (ii);
  (c) strengthening systematic cooperation between Member States in the conduct of policy.

Article III-295   (ex Article 13 TEU)

1.   The European Council shall define the general guidelines for the common foreign and security policy, including for matters with defence implications.

If international developments so require, the President of the European Council shall convene an extraordinary meeting of the European Council in order to define the strategic lines of the Union's policy in the face of such developments.

2.   The Council shall adopt the European decisions necessary for defining and implementing the common foreign and security policy on the basis of the general guidelines and strategic lines defined by the European Council.

Article III-296   (ex Articles 18 and 26 TEU)

1.   The Union Minister for Foreign Affairs, who shall chair the Foreign Affairs Council, shall contribute through his or her proposals towards the preparation of the common foreign and security policy and shall ensure implementation of the European decisions adopted by the European Council and the Council.

2.   The Minister for Foreign Affairs shall represent the Union for matters relating to the common foreign and security policy. He or she shall conduct political dialogue with third parties on the Union's behalf and shall express the Union's position in international organisations and at international conferences.

3.   In fulfilling his or her mandate, the Union Minister for Foreign Affairs shall be assisted by a European External Action Service. This service shall work in cooperation with the diplomatic services of the Member States and shall comprise officials from relevant departments of the General Secretariat of the Council and of the Commission as well as staff seconded from national diplomatic services of the Member States. The organisation and functioning of the European External Action Service shall be established by a European decision of the Council. The Council shall act on a proposal from the Union Minister for Foreign Affairs after consulting the European Parliament and after obtaining the consent of the Commission.

Article III-297   (ex Article 14 TEU)

1.   Where the international situation requires operational action by the Union, the Council shall adopt the necessary European decisions. Such decisions shall lay down the objectives, the scope, the means to be made available to the Union, if necessary the duration, and the conditions for implementation of the action. If there is a change in circumstances having a substantial effect on a question subject to such a European decision, the Council shall review the principles and objectives of that decision and adopt the necessary European decisions.

2.   The European decisions referred to in paragraph 1 shall commit the Member States in the positions they adopt and in the conduct of their activity.

3.   Whenever there is any plan to adopt a national position or take national action pursuant to a European decision as referred to in paragraph 1, information shall be provided by the Member State concerned in time to allow, if necessary, for prior consultations within the Council. The obligation to provide prior information shall not apply to measures which are merely a national transposition of such a decision.

4.   In cases of imperative need arising from changes in the situation and failing a review of the European decision pursuant to the second subparagraph of paragraph 1, Member States may take the necessary measures as a matter of urgency, having regard to the general objectives of that decision. The Member State concerned shall inform the Council immediately of any such measures.

5.   Should there be any major difficulties in implementing a European decision as referred to in this Article, a Member State shall refer them to the Council which shall discuss them and seek appropriate solutions. Such solutions shall not run counter to the objectives of the action or impair its effectiveness.

Article III-298   (ex Article 15 TEU)

The Council shall adopt European decisions which shall define the approach of the Union to a particular matter of a geographical or thematic nature. Member States shall ensure that their national policies conform to the positions of the Union.

Article III-299   (ex Article 22 TEU)

1.   Any Member State, the Union Minister for Foreign Affairs, or that Minister with the Commission's support, may refer any question relating to the common foreign and security policy to the Council and may submit to it initiatives or proposals as appropriate.

2.   In cases requiring a rapid decision, the Union Minister for Foreign Affairs, of the Minister's own motion or at the request of a Member State, shall convene an extraordinary meeting of the Council within forty-eight hours or, in an emergency, within a shorter period.

Article III-300   (ex Article 23 TEU)

1.   The European decisions referred to in this Chapter shall be adopted by the Council acting unanimously. When abstaining in a vote, any member of the Council may qualify its abstention by making a formal declaration. In that case, it shall not be obliged to apply the European decision, but shall accept that the latter commits the Union. In a spirit of mutual solidarity, the Member State concerned shall refrain from any action likely to conflict with or impede Union action based on that decision and the other Member States shall respect its position. If the members of the Council qualifying their abstention in this way represent at least one third of the Member States comprising at least one third of the population of the Union, the decision shall not be adopted.

2.   By way of derogation from paragraph 1, the Council shall act by a qualified majority:
   (a) when adopting European decisions defining a Union action or position on the basis of a European decision of the European Council relating to the Union's strategic interests and objectives, as referred to in Article III-293(1);
   (b) when adopting a European decision defining a Union action or position, on a proposal which the Union Minister for Foreign Affairs has presented following a specific request to him or her from the European Council, made on its own initiative or that of the Minister;
   (c) when adopting a European decision implementing a European decision defining a Union action or position;
   (d) when adopting a European decision concerning the appointment of a special representative in accordance with Article III-302.

If a member of the Council declares that, for vital and stated reasons of national policy, it intends to oppose the adoption of a European decision to be adopted by a qualified majority, a vote shall not be taken. The Union Minister for Foreign Affairs will, in close consultation with the Member State involved, search for a solution acceptable to it. If he or she does not succeed, the Council may, acting by a qualified majority, request that the matter be referred to the European Council for a European decision by unanimity.

3.   In accordance with Article I-40(7) the European Council may unanimously adopt a European decision stipulating that the Council shall act by a qualified majority in cases other than those referred to in paragraph 2 of this Article.

4.   Paragraphs 2 and 3 shall not apply to decisions having military or defence implications.

Article III-301   (new)

1.   When the European Council or the Council has defined a common approach of the Union within the meaning of Article I-40(5), the Union Minister for Foreign Affairs and the Ministers for Foreign Affairs of the Member States shall coordinate their activities within the Council.

2.   The diplomatic missions of the Member States and the Union delegations in third countries and at international organisations shall cooperate and shall contribute to formulating and implementing the common approach referred to in paragraph 1.

Article III-302   (ex Article 18(5) TEU)

The Council may appoint, on a proposal from the Union Minister for Foreign Affairs, a special representative with a mandate in relation to particular policy issues. The special representative shall carry out his or her mandate under the Minister's authority.

Article III-303   (ex Article 24 TEU)
The Union may conclude agreements with one or more States or international organisations in areas covered by this Chapter.

Article III-304   (ex Article 21 TEU)
1.   The Union Minister for Foreign Affairs shall consult and inform the European Parliament in accordance with Article I-40(8) and Article I-41(8). He or she shall ensure that the views of the European Parliament are duly taken into consideration. Special representatives may be involved in briefing the European Parliament.

2.   The European Parliament may ask questions of the Council and of the Union Minister for Foreign Affairs or make recommendations to them. Twice a year it shall hold a debate on progress in implementing the common foreign and security policy, including the common security and defence policy.

Article III-305   (ex Article 19 TEU)
1.   Member States shall coordinate their action in international organisations and at international conferences. They shall uphold the Union's positions in such fora. The Union Minister for Foreign Affairs shall organise this coordination.

In international organisations and at international conferences where not all the Member States participate, those which do take part shall uphold the Union's positions.

2.   In accordance with Article I-16(2), Member States represented in international organisations or international conferences where not all the Member States participate shall keep the latter, as well as the Union Minister for Foreign Affairs, informed of any matter of common interest.

Member States which are also members of the United Nations Security Council shall concert and keep the other Member States and the Union Minister for Foreign Affairs fully informed. Member States which are members of the Security Council will, in the execution of their functions, defend the positions and the interests of the Union, without prejudice to their responsibilities under the United Nations Charter.

When the Union has defined a position on a subject which is on the United Nations Security Council agenda, those Member States which sit on the Security Council shall request that the Union Minister for Foreign Affairs be asked to present the Union's position.

Article III-306   (ex Article 20 TEU)
The diplomatic and consular missions of the Member States and the Union delegations in third countries and international conferences, and their representations to international organisations, shall cooperate in ensuring that the European decisions defining Union positions and actions adopted pursuant to this Chapter are complied with and implemented. They shall step up cooperation by exchanging information and carrying out joint assessments.

They shall contribute to the implementation of the right of European citizens to protection in the territory of third countries as referred to in Article I-10(2)(c) and the measures adopted pursuant to Article III-127.

Article III-307   (ex Article 25 EC)
1.   Without prejudice to Article III-344, a Political and Security Committee shall monitor the international situation in the areas covered by the common foreign and security policy and contribute to the definition of policies by delivering opinions to the Council at the request of the latter, or of the Union Minister for Foreign Affairs, or on its own initiative. It shall also monitor the implementation of agreed policies, without prejudice to the powers of the Union Minister for Foreign Affairs.

2.   Within the scope of this Chapter, the Political and Security Committee shall exercise, under the responsibility of the Council and of the Union Minister for Foreign Affairs, the political control and strategic direction of the crisis management operations referred to in Article III-309.

The Council may authorise the Committee, for the purpose and for the duration of a crisis management operation, as determined by the Council, to take the relevant measures concerning the political control and strategic direction of the operation.

Article III-308   (ex Articles 46(f) and 47 TEU)

The implementation of the common foreign and security policy shall not affect the application of the procedures and the extent of the powers of the institutions laid down by the Constitution for the exercise of the Union competences referred to in Articles I-13 to I-15 and I-17.

Similarly, the implementation of the policies listed in those Articles shall not affect the application of the procedures and the extent of the powers of the institutions laid down by the Constitution for the exercise of the Union competences under this Chapter.

SECTION 2   THE COMMON SECURITY AND DEFENCE POLICY

Article III-309   (ex Article 17 TEU)

1.   The tasks referred to in Article I-41(1), in the course of which the Union may use civilian and military means, shall include joint disarmament operations, humanitarian and rescue tasks, military advice and assistance tasks, conflict prevention and peace-keeping tasks, tasks of combat forces in crisis management, including peace-making and post-conflict stabilisation. All these tasks may contribute to the fight against terrorism, including by supporting third countries in combating terrorism in their territories.

2.   The Council shall adopt European decisions relating to the tasks referred to in paragraph 1, defining their objectives and scope and the general conditions for their implementation. The Union Minister for Foreign Affairs, acting under the authority of the Council and in close and constant contact with the Political and Security Committee, shall ensure coordination of the civilian and military aspects of such tasks.

Article III-310   (new)

1.   Within the framework of the European decisions adopted in accordance with Article III-309, the Council may entrust the implementation of a task to a group of Member States which are willing and have the necessary capability for such a task. Those Member States, in association with the Union Minister for Foreign Affairs, shall agree among themselves on the management of the task.

2.   Member States participating in the task shall keep the Council regularly informed of its progress on their own initiative or at the request of another Member State. Those States shall inform the Council immediately should the completion of the task entail major consequences or require amendment of the objective, scope and conditions determined for the task in the European decisions referred to in paragraph 1. In such cases, the Council shall adopt the necessary European decisions.

Article III-311   (new)

1.   The Agency in the field of defence capabilities development, research, acquisition and armaments (European Defence Agency), established by Article I-41(3) and subject to the authority of the Council, shall have as its task to:

(a) contribute to identifying the Member States' military capability objectives and evaluating observance of the capability commitments given by the Member States;

(b) promote harmonisation of operational needs and adoption of effective, compatible procurement methods;

(c) propose multilateral projects to fulfil the objectives in terms of military capabilities, ensure coordination of the programmes implemented by the Member States and management of specific cooperation programmes;

(d) support defence technology research, and coordinate and plan joint research activities and the study of technical solutions meeting future operational needs;

(e) contribute to identifying and, if necessary, implementing any useful measure for strengthening the industrial and technological base of the defence sector and for improving the effectiveness of military expenditure.

2.   The European Defence Agency shall be open to all Member States wishing to be part of it. The Council, acting by a qualified majority, shall adopt a European decision defining the Agency's statute, seat and operational rules. That decision should take account of the level of effective participation in the Agency's activities. Specific groups shall be set up within the Agency bringing together Member States engaged in joint projects. The Agency shall carry out its tasks in liaison with the Commission where necessary.

Article III-312   (new)

1.   Those Member States which wish to participate in the permanent structured cooperation referred to in Article I-41(6), which fulfil the criteria and have made the commitments on military capabilities set out in the Protocol on permanent structured cooperation shall notify their intention to the Council and to the Union Minister for Foreign Affairs.

2.   Within three months following the notification referred to in paragraph 1 the Council shall adopt a European decision establishing permanent structured cooperation and determining the list of participating Member States. The Council shall act by a qualified majority after consulting the Union Minister for Foreign Affairs.

3.   Any Member State which, at a later stage, wishes to participate in the permanent structured cooperation shall notify its intention to the Council and to the Union Minister for Foreign Affairs. The Council shall adopt a European decision confirming the participation of the Member State concerned which fulfils the criteria and makes the commitments referred to in Articles 1 and 2 of the Protocol on permanent structured cooperation. The Council shall act by a qualified majority after consulting the Union Minister for Foreign Affairs. Only members of the Council representing the participating Member States shall take part in the vote.

A qualified majority shall be defined as at least 55% of the members of the Council representing the participating Member States, comprising at least 65% of the population of these States.

A blocking minority must include at least the minimum number of Council members representing more than 35% of the population of the participating Member States, plus one member, failing which the qualified majority shall be deemed attained.

4.   If a participating Member State no longer fulfils the criteria or is no longer able to meet the commitments referred to in Articles 1 and 2 of the Protocol on permanent structured cooperation, the Council may adopt a European decision suspending the participation of the Member State concerned. The Council shall act by a qualified majority. Only members of the Council representing the participating Member States, with the exception of the Member State in question, shall take part in the vote. A qualified majority shall be defined as at least 55% of the members of the Council representing the participating Member States, comprising at least 65% of the population of these States. A blocking minority must include at least the minimum number of Council members representing more than 35% of the population of the participating Member States, plus one member, failing which the qualified majority shall be deemed attained.

5.   Any participating Member State which wishes to withdraw from permanent structured cooperation shall notify its intention to the Council, which shall take note that the Member State in question has ceased to participate.

6.   The European decisions and recommendations of the Council within the framework of permanent structured cooperation, other than those provided for in paragraphs 2 to 5, shall be adopted by unanimity. For the purposes of this paragraph, unanimity shall be constituted by the votes of the representatives of the participating Member States only.

SECTION 3   FINANCIAL PROVISIONS

Article III-313   (ex Article 28 TEU)

1.   Administrative expenditure which the implementation of this Chapter entails for the institutions shall be charged to the Union budget.

2.   Operating expenditure to which the implementation of this Chapter gives rise shall also be charged to the Union budget, except for such expenditure arising from operations having military or defence implications and cases where the Council decides otherwise.

In cases where expenditure is not charged to the Union budget it shall be charged to the Member States in accordance with the gross national product scale, unless the Council decides otherwise. As for expenditure arising from operations having military or defence implications, Member States whose representatives in the Council have made a formal declaration under Article III-300(1), second subparagraph, shall not be obliged to contribute to the financing thereof.

3.   The Council shall adopt a European decision establishing the specific procedures for guaranteeing rapid access to appropriations in the Union budget for urgent financing of initiatives in the framework of the common foreign and security policy, and in particular for preparatory activities for the tasks referred to in Article I-41(1) and Article III-309. It shall act after consulting the European Parliament.

Preparatory activities for the tasks referred to in Article I-41(1) and Article III-309 which are not charged to the Union budget shall be financed by a start-up fund made up of Member States' contributions.

The Council shall adopt by a qualified majority, on a proposal from the Union Minister for Foreign Affairs, European decisions establishing:

(a)   the procedures for setting up and financing the start-up fund, in particular the amounts allocated to the fund;

(b)   the procedures for administering the start-up fund;

(c)   the financial control procedures.

When the task planned in accordance with Article I-41(1) and Article III-309 cannot be charged to the Union budget, the Council shall authorise the Union Minister for Foreign Affairs to use the fund. The Union Minister for Foreign Affairs shall report to the Council on the implementation of this remit.

CHAPTER III   COMMON COMMERCIAL POLICY

Article III-314   (ex Article 131 EC)

By establishing a customs union in accordance with Article III-151, the Union shall contribute, in the common interest, to the harmonious development of world trade, the progressive abolition of restrictions on international trade and on foreign direct investment, and the lowering of customs and other barriers.

Article III-315   (ex Article 133 EC)

1.   The common commercial policy shall be based on uniform principles, particularly with regard to changes in tariff rates, the conclusion of tariff and trade agreements relating to trade in goods and services, and the commercial aspects of intellectual property, foreign direct investment, the achievement of uniformity in measures of liberalisation, export policy and measures to protect trade such as those to be taken in the event of dumping or subsidies. The common commercial policy shall be conducted in the context of the principles and objectives of the Union's external action.

2.   European laws shall establish the measures defining the framework for implementing the common commercial policy.

3.   Where agreements with one or more third countries or international organisations need to be negotiated and concluded, Article III-325 shall apply, subject to the special

provisions of this Article. The Commission shall make recommendations to the Council, which shall authorise it to open the necessary negotiations. The Council and the Commission shall be responsible for ensuring that the agreements negotiated are compatible with internal Union policies and rules. The Commission shall conduct these negotiations in consultation with a special committee appointed by the Council to assist the Commission in this task and within the framework of such directives as the Council may issue to it. The Commission shall report regularly to the special committee and to the European Parliament on the progress of negotiations.

4.   For the negotiation and conclusion of the agreements referred to in paragraph 3, the Council shall act by a qualified majority. For the negotiation and conclusion of agreements in the fields of trade in services and the commercial aspects of intellectual property, as well as foreign direct investment, the Council shall act unanimously where such agreements include provisions for which unanimity is required for the adoption of internal rules. The Council shall also act unanimously for the negotiation and conclusion of agreements:

(a) in the field of trade in cultural and audiovisual services, where these agreements risk prejudicing the Union's cultural and linguistic diversity;

(b) in the field of trade in social, education and health services, where these agreements risk seriously disturbing the national organisation of such services and prejudicing the responsibility of Member States to deliver them.

5.   The negotiation and conclusion of international agreements in the field of transport shall be subject to Section 7 of Chapter III of Title III and to Article III-325.

6.   The exercise of the competences conferred by this Article in the field of the common commercial policy shall not affect the delimitation of competences between the Union and the Member States, and shall not lead to harmonisation of legislative or regulatory provisions of the Member States insofar as the Constitution excludes such harmonisation.

CHAPTER IV   COOPERATION WITH THIRD COUNTRIES AND HUMANITARIAN AID

SECTION 1   DEVELOPMENT COOPERATION

Article III-316   (ex Article 177 EC)

1.   Union policy in the field of development cooperation shall be conducted within the framework of the principles and objectives of the Union's external action. The Union's development cooperation policy and that of the Member States shall complement and reinforce each other.

Union development cooperation policy shall have as its primary objective the reduction and, in the long term, the eradication of poverty. The Union shall take account of the objectives of development cooperation in the policies that it implements which are likely to affect developing countries.

2.   The Union and the Member States shall comply with the commitments and take account of the objectives they have approved in the context of the United Nations and other competent international organisations.

Article III-317   (ex Articles 179 and 181 EC)

1.   European laws or framework laws shall establish the measures necessary for the implementation of development cooperation policy, which may relate to multiannual cooperation programmes with developing countries or programmes with a thematic approach.

2.   The Union may conclude with third countries and competent international organisations any agreement helping to achieve the objectives referred to in Articles III-292 and III-316.

The first subparagraph shall be without prejudice to Member States' competence to negotiate in international bodies and to conclude agreements.

3.   The European Investment Bank shall contribute, under the terms laid down in its Statute, to the implementation of the measures referred to in paragraph 1.

Article III-318   (ex Articles 180 and 181 EC)

1.   In order to promote the complementarity and efficiency of their action, the Union and the Member States shall coordinate their policies on development cooperation and shall consult each other on their aid programmes, including in international organisations and during international conferences. They may undertake joint action. Member States shall contribute if necessary to the implementation of Union aid programmes.

2.   The Commission may take any useful initiative to promote the coordination referred to in paragraph 1.

3.   Within their respective spheres of competence, the Union and the Member States shall cooperate with third countries and the competent international organisations.

SECTION 2   ECONOMIC, FINANCIAL AND TECHNICAL COOPERATION WITH
THIRD COUNTRIES

Article III-319   (ex Article 181a EC)

1.   Without prejudice to the other provisions of the Constitution, and in particular Articles III-316 to III-318, the Union shall carry out economic, financial and technical cooperation measures, including assistance, in particular financial assistance, with third countries other than developing countries. Such measures shall be consistent with the development policy of the Union and shall be carried out within the framework of the principles and objectives of its external action. The Union's measures and those of the Member States shall complement and reinforce each other.

2.   European laws or framework laws shall establish the measures necessary for the implementation of paragraph 1.

3.   Within their respective spheres of competence, the Union and the Member States shall cooperate with third countries and the competent international organisations. The arrangements for Union cooperation may be the subject of agreements between the Union and the third parties concerned. The first subparagraph shall be without prejudice to Member States' competence to negotiate in international bodies and to conclude agreements.

Article III-320   (new)

When the situation in a third country requires urgent financial assistance from the Union, the Council shall adopt the necessary European decisions on a proposal from the Commission.

SECTION 3   HUMANITARIAN AID

Article III-321   (new)

1.   The Union's operations in the field of humanitarian aid shall be conducted within the framework of the principles and objectives of the external action of the Union. Such operations shall be intended to provide ad hoc assistance and relief and protection for people in third countries who are victims of natural or man-made disasters, in order to meet the humanitarian needs resulting from these different situations. The Union's operations and those of the Member States shall complement and reinforce each other.

2.   Humanitarian aid operations shall be conducted in compliance with the principles of international law and with the principles of impartiality, neutrality and non-discrimination.

3.   European laws or framework laws shall establish the measures defining the framework within which the Union's humanitarian aid operations shall be implemented.

4.   The Union may conclude with third countries and competent international organisations any agreement helping to achieve the objectives referred to in paragraph 1 and in Article III-292.

The first subparagraph shall be without prejudice to Member States' competence to negotiate in international bodies and to conclude agreements.

　　5.　In order to establish a framework for joint contributions from young Europeans to the humanitarian aid operations of the Union, a European Voluntary Humanitarian Aid Corps shall be set up. European laws shall determine the rules and procedures for the operation of the Corps.

　　6.　The Commission may take any useful initiative to promote coordination between actions of the Union and those of the Member States, in order to enhance the efficiency and complementarity of Union and national humanitarian aid measures.

　　7.　The Union shall ensure that its humanitarian aid operations are coordinated and consistent with those of international organisations and bodies, in particular those forming part of the United Nations system.

CHAPTER V　RESTRICTIVE MEASURES

Article III-322　(ex Article 301 EC)

　　1.　Where a European decision, adopted in accordance with Chapter II, provides for the interruption or reduction, in part or completely, of economic and financial relations with one or more third countries, the Council, acting by a qualified majority on a joint proposal from the Union Minister for Foreign Affairs and the Commission, shall adopt the necessary European regulations or decisions. It shall inform the European Parliament thereof.

　　2.　Where a European decision adopted in accordance with Chapter II so provides, the Council may adopt restrictive measures under the procedure referred to in paragraph 1 against natural or legal persons and groups or non-State entities.

　　3.　The acts referred to in this Article shall include necessary provisions on legal safeguards.

CHAPTER VI　INTERNATIONAL AGREEMENTS

Article III-323　(ex Article 300(7) EC)

　　1.　The Union may conclude an agreement with one or more third countries or international organisations where the Constitution so provides or where the conclusion of an agreement is necessary in order to achieve, within the framework of the Union's policies, one of the objectives referred to in the Constitution, or is provided for in a legally binding Union act or is likely to affect common rules or alter their scope.

　　2.　Agreements concluded by the Union are binding on the institutions of the Union and on its Member States.

Article III-324　(ex Article 310 EC)

The Union may conclude an association agreement with one or more third countries or international organisations in order to establish an association involving reciprocal rights and obligations, common actions and special procedures.

Article III-325　(ex Article 300 EC)

　　1.　Without prejudice to the specific provisions laid down in Article III-315, agreements between the Union and third countries or international organisations shall be negotiated and concluded in accordance with the following procedure.

　　2.　The Council shall authorise the opening of negotiations, adopt negotiating directives, authorise the signing of agreements and conclude them.

　　3.　The Commission, or the Union Minister for Foreign Affairs where the agreement envisaged relates exclusively or principally to the common foreign and security policy, shall submit recommendations to the Council, which shall adopt a European decision authorising the opening of negotiations and, depending on the subject of the agreement envisaged, nominating the Union negotiator or head of the Union's negotiating team.

4.   The Council may address directives to the negotiator and designate a special committee in consultation with which the negotiations must be conducted.

5.   The Council, on a proposal by the negotiator, shall adopt a European decision authorising the signing of the agreement and, if necessary, its provisional application before entry into force.

6.   The Council, on a proposal by the negotiator, shall adopt a European decision concluding the agreement. Except where agreements relate exclusively to the common foreign and security policy, the Council shall adopt the European decision concluding the agreement:

(a)   after obtaining the consent of the European Parliament in the following cases:
  (i)   association agreements;
  (ii) Union accession to the European Convention for the Protection of Human Rights and Fundamental Freedoms;
  (iii) agreements establishing a specific institutional framework by organising cooperation procedures;
  (iv) agreements with important budgetary implications for the Union;
  (v)   agreements covering fields to which either the ordinary legislative procedure applies, or the special legislative procedure where consent by the European Parliament is required.
The European Parliament and the Council may, in an urgent situation, agree upon a time-limit for consent.

(b)   after consulting the European Parliament in other cases. The European Parliament shall deliver its opinion within a time-limit which the Council may set depending on the urgency of the matter. In the absence of an opinion within that time-limit, the Council may act.

7.   When concluding an agreement, the Council may, by way of derogation from paragraphs 5, 6 and 9, authorise the negotiator to approve on the Union's behalf modifications to the agreement where it provides for them to be adopted by a simplified procedure or by a body set up by the agreement. The Council may attach specific conditions to such authorisation.

8.   The Council shall act by a qualified majority throughout the procedure.

However, it shall act unanimously when the agreement covers a field for which unanimity is required for the adoption of a Union act as well as for association agreements and the agreements referred to in Article III-319 with the States which are candidates for accession.

9.   The Council, on a proposal from the Commission or the Union Minister for Foreign Affairs, shall adopt a European decision suspending application of an agreement and establishing the positions to be adopted on the Union's behalf in a body set up by an agreement, when that body is called upon to adopt acts having legal effects, with the exception of acts supplementing or amending the institutional framework of the agreement.

10.   The European Parliament shall be immediately and fully informed at all stages of the procedure.

11.   A Member State, the European Parliament, the Council or the Commission may obtain the opinion of the Court of Justice as to whether an agreement envisaged is compatible with the Constitution. Where the opinion of the Court of Justice is adverse, the agreement envisaged may not enter into force unless it is amended or the Constitution is revised.

Article III-326   (ex Article 111 EC)

1.   By way of derogation from Article III-325, the Council, either on a recommendation from the European Central Bank or on a recommendation from the Commission and after consulting the European Central Bank, in an endeavour to reach a consensus consistent with the objective of price stability, may conclude formal agreements on an exchange-rate system

for the euro in relation to the currencies of third States. The Council shall act unanimously after consulting the European Parliament and in accordance with the procedure provided for in paragraph 3. The Council, either on a recommendation from the European Central Bank or on a recommendation from the Commission and after consulting the European Central Bank, in an endeavour to reach a consensus consistent with the objective of price stability, may adopt, adjust or abandon the central rates of the euro within the exchange-rate system. The President of the Council shall inform the European Parliament of the adoption, adjustment or abandonment of the central rates of the euro.

2.   In the absence of an exchange-rate system in relation to one or more currencies of third States as referred to in paragraph 1, the Council, acting either on a recommendation from the European Central Bank or on a recommendation from the Commission and after consulting the European Central Bank, may formulate general orientations for exchange-rate policy in relation to these currencies. These general orientations shall be without prejudice to the primary objective of the European System of Central Banks, to maintain price stability.

3.   By way of derogation from Article III-325, where agreements on matters relating to the monetary or exchange-rate system are to be the subject of negotiations between the Union and one or more third States or international organisations, the Council, acting on a recommendation from the Commission and after consulting the European Central Bank, shall decide the arrangements for the negotiation and for the conclusion of such agreements. These arrangements shall ensure that the Union expresses a single position. The Commission shall be fully associated with the negotiations.

4.   Without prejudice to Union competence and Union agreements as regards economic and monetary union, Member States may negotiate in international bodies and conclude agreements.

CHAPTER VII   THE UNION'S RELATIONS WITH INTERNATIONAL ORGANISATIONS
                       AND THIRD COUNTRIES AND UNION DELEGATIONS

Article III-327   (ex Articles 302 and 303 EC)

1.   The Union shall establish all appropriate forms of cooperation with the organs of the United Nations and its specialised agencies, the Council of Europe, the Organisation for Security and Cooperation in Europe and the Organisation for Economic Cooperation and Development.

The Union shall also maintain such relations as are appropriate with other international organisations.

2.   The Union Minister for Foreign Affairs and the Commission shall be instructed to implement this Article.

Article III-328   (new)

1.   Union delegations in third countries and at international organisations shall represent the Union.

2.   Union delegations shall be placed under the authority of the Union Minister for Foreign Affairs. They shall act in close cooperation with Member States' diplomatic and consular missions.

CHAPTER VIII   IMPLEMENTATION OF THE SOLIDARITY CLAUSE

Article III-329   (new)

1.   Should a Member State be the object of a terrorist attack or the victim of a natural or man-made disaster, the other Member States shall assist it at the request of its political authorities. To that end, the Member States shall coordinate between themselves in the Council.

2.   The arrangements for the implementation by the Union of the solidarity clause

referred to in Article I-43 shall be defined by a European decision adopted by the Council acting on a joint proposal by the Commission and the Union Minister for Foreign Affairs. The Council shall act in accordance with Article III-300(1) where this decision has defence implications. The European Parliament shall be informed.

For the purposes of this paragraph and without prejudice to Article III-344, the Council shall be assisted by the Political and Security Committee with the support of the structures developed in the context of the common security and defence policy and by the Committee referred to in Article III-261; the two committees shall, if necessary, submit joint opinions.

3.   The European Council shall regularly assess the threats facing the Union in order to enable the Union and its Member States to take effective action.

TITLE VI   THE FUNCTIONING OF THE UNION
CHAPTER I   PROVISIONS GOVERNING THE INSTITUTIONS

SECTION 1   THE INSTITUTIONS

Subsection 1   The European Parliament

Article III-330   (ex Article 190 EC)
1.   A European law or framework law of the Council shall establish the necessary measures for the election of the Members of the European Parliament by direct universal suffrage in accordance with a uniform procedure in all Member States or in accordance with principles common to all Member States. The Council shall act unanimously on initiative from, and after obtaining the consent of, the European Parliament, which shall act by a majority of its component members. This law or framework law shall enter into force after it has been approved by the Member States in accordance with their respective constitutional requirements.

2.   A European law of the European Parliament shall lay down the regulations and general conditions governing the performance of the duties of its Members. The European Parliament shall act on its own initiative after seeking an opinion from the Commission and after obtaining the consent of the Council. The Council shall act unanimously on all rules or conditions relating to the taxation of Members or former Members.

Article III-331   (ex Article 191 EC)
European laws shall lay down the regulations governing the political parties at European level referred to in Article I-46(4), and in particular the rules regarding their funding.

Article III-332   (ex Article 192 EC)
The European Parliament may, by a majority of its component Members, request the Commission to submit any appropriate proposal on matters on which it considers that a Union act is required for the purpose of implementing the Constitution. If the Commission does not submit a proposal, it shall inform the European Parliament of the reasons.

Article III-333   (ex Article 193 EC)
In the course of its duties, the European Parliament may, at the request of a quarter of its component Members, set up a temporary Committee of Inquiry to investigate, without prejudice to the powers conferred by the Constitution on other institutions or bodies, alleged contraventions or maladministration in the implementation of Union law, except where the alleged facts are being examined before a court and while the case is still subject to legal proceedings.

The temporary Committee of Inquiry shall cease to exist on submission of its report.

A European law of the European Parliament shall lay down the detailed provisions governing the exercise of the right of inquiry. The European Parliament shall act on its own initiative after obtaining the consent of the Council and of the Commission.

Article III-334   (ex Article 194 EC)
In accordance with Article I-10(2)(d), any citizen of the Union, and any natural or legal person residing or having its registered office in a Member State, shall have the right to address, individually or in association with other persons, a petition to the European Parliament on a matter which comes within the Union's fields of activity and which affects him, her or it directly.

Article III-335   (ex Article 195 EC)
   1.   The European Parliament shall elect a European Ombudsman. In accordance with Articles I-10 (2)(d) and I-49, he or she shall be empowered to receive complaints from any citizen of the Union or any natural or legal person residing or having its registered office in a Member State concerning instances of maladministration in the activities of the Union's institutions, bodies, offices or agencies, with the exception of the Court of Justice of the European Union acting in its judicial role. In accordance with his or her duties, the Ombuds-man shall conduct inquiries for which he or she finds grounds, either on his or her own initiative or on the basis of complaints submitted to him or her direct or through a member of the European Parliament, except where the alleged facts are or have been the subject of legal proceedings. Where the Ombudsman establishes an instance of maladministration, he or she shall refer the matter to the institution, body, office or agency concerned, which shall have a period of three months in which to inform him or her of its views. The European Ombudsman shall then forward a report to the European Parliament and the institution, body, office or agency concerned. The person lodging the complaint shall be informed of the outcome of such inquiries. The Ombudsman shall submit an annual report to the European Parliament on the outcome of his or her inquiries.
   2.   The Ombudsman shall be elected after each election of the European Parliament for the duration of its term of office. The Ombudsman shall be eligible for reappointment.
   The Ombudsman may be dismissed by the Court of Justice at the request of the European Parliament if he or she no longer fulfils the conditions required for the performance of his or her duties or if he or she is guilty of serious misconduct.
   3.   The Ombudsman shall be completely independent in the performance of his or her duties. In the performance of those duties he or she shall neither seek nor take instructions from any institution, body, office or agency. The Ombudsman shall not, during his or her term of office, engage in any other occupation, whether gainful or not.
   4.   A European law of the European Parliament shall lay down the regulations and gen-eral conditions governing the performance of the Ombudsman's duties. The European Parliament shall act on its own initiative after seeking an opinion from the Commission and after obtaining the consent of the Council.

Article III-336   (ex Article 196 EC)
The European Parliament shall hold an annual session. It shall meet, without requiring to be convened, on the second Tuesday in March.
   The European Parliament may meet in extraordinary part-session at the request of a majority of its component members or at the request of the Council or of the Commission.

Article III-337   (ex Articles 197 and 200 EC)
   1.   The European Council and the Council shall be heard by the European Parliament in accordance with the conditions laid down in the Rules of Procedure of the European Council and those of the Council.
   2.   The Commission may attend all the meetings of the European Parliament and shall, at its request, be heard. It shall reply orally or in writing to questions put to it by the European Parliament or by its members.
   3.   The European Parliament shall discuss in open session the annual general report submitted to it by the Commission.

Article III-338   (ex Article 198 EC)

Save as otherwise provided in the Constitution, the European Parliament shall act by a majority of the votes cast. Its Rules of Procedure shall determine the quorum.

Article III-339   (ex Article 199 EC)

The European Parliament shall adopt its Rules of Procedure, by a majority of its component members.

The proceedings of the European Parliament shall be published in the manner laid down in the Constitution and the Rules of Procedure of the European Parliament.

Article III-340   (ex Article 201 EC)

If a motion of censure on the activities of the Commission is tabled before it, the European Parliament shall not vote thereon until at least three days after the motion has been tabled and shall do so only by open vote. If the motion of censure is carried by a two-thirds majority of the votes cast, representing a majority of the component members of the European Parliament, the members of the Commission shall resign as a body and the Union Minister for Foreign Affairs shall resign from duties that he or she carries out in the Commission. They shall remain in office and continue to deal with current business until they are replaced in accordance with Articles I-26 and I-27. In this case, the term of office of the members of the Commission appointed to replace them shall expire on the date on which the term of office of the members of the Commission obliged to resign as a body would have expired.

Subsection 2   *The European Council*

Article III-341   (new)

1.   Where a vote is taken, any member of the European Council may also act on behalf of not more than one other member.

Abstentions by members present in person or represented shall not prevent the adoption by the European Council of acts which require unanimity.

2.   The President of the European Parliament may be invited to be heard by the European Council.

3.   The European Council shall act by a simple majority for procedural questions and for the adoption of its Rules of Procedure.

4.   The European Council shall be assisted by the General Secretariat of the Council.

Subsection 3   *The Council of Ministers*

Article III-342   (ex Articles 203 and 204 EC)

The Council shall meet when convened by its President on his or her own initiative, or at the request of one of its members or of the Commission.

Article III-343   (ex Articles 205 and 206 EC)

1.   Where a vote is taken, any member of the Council may act on behalf of not more than one other member.

2.   Where it is required to act by a simple majority, the Council shall act by a majority of its component members.

3.   Abstentions by members present in person or represented shall not prevent the adoption by the Council of acts which require unanimity.

Article III-344   (ex Article 207 EC)

1.   A committee consisting of the Permanent Representatives of the Governments of the Member States shall be responsible for preparing the work of the Council and for carrying out the tasks assigned to it by the latter. The Committee may adopt procedural decisions in cases provided for in the Council's Rules of Procedure.

2.   The Council shall be assisted by a General Secretariat, under the responsibility of a Secretary-General appointed by the Council.

The Council shall decide on the organisation of the General Secretariat by a simple majority.

3.   The Council shall act by a simple majority regarding procedural matters and for the adoption of its Rules of Procedure.

Article III-345   (ex Article 208 EC)

The Council, by a simple majority, may request the Commission to undertake any studies the Council considers desirable for the attainment of the common objectives, and to submit any appropriate proposals to it. If the Commission does not submit a proposal, it shall inform the Council of the reasons.

Article III-346   (ex Article 209 EC)

The Council shall adopt European decisions laying down the rules governing the committees provided for in the Constitution. It shall act by a simple majority after consulting the Commission.

Subsection 4   The European Commission

Article III-347   (ex Article 214(2) EC)

The members of the Commission shall refrain from any action incompatible with their duties. Member States shall respect their independence and shall not seek to influence them in the performance of their tasks. The members of the Commission shall not, during their term of office, engage in any other occupation, whether gainful or not. When entering upon their duties they shall give a solemn undertaking that, both during and after their term of office, they will respect the obligations arising therefrom and in particular their duty to behave with integrity and discretion as regards the acceptance, after they have ceased to hold office, of certain appointments or benefits. In the event of any breach of these obligations, the Court of Justice may, on application by the Council, acting by a simple majority, or the Commission, rule that the person concerned be, according to the circumstances, either compulsorily retired in accordance with Article III-349 or deprived of his or her right to a pension or other benefits in its stead.

Article III-348   (ex Article 215 EC)

1.   Apart from normal replacement, or death, the duties of a member of the Commission shall end when he or she resigns or is compulsorily retired.

2.   A vacancy caused by resignation, compulsory retirement or death shall be filled for the remainder of the member's term of office by a new member of the same nationality appointed by the Council, by common accord with the President of the Commission, after consulting the European Parliament and in accordance with the criteria set out in Article I-26(4). The Council may, acting unanimously on a proposal from the President of the Commission, decide that such a vacancy need not be filled, in particular when the remainder of the member's term of office is short.

3.   In the event of resignation, compulsory retirement or death, the President shall be replaced for the remainder of his or her term of office in accordance with Article I-27(1).

4.   In the event of resignation, compulsory retirement or death, the Union Minister for Foreign Affairs shall be replaced, for the remainder of his or her term of office, in accordance with Article I-28(1).

5.   In the case of the resignation of all the members of the Commission, they shall remain in office and continue to deal with current business until they have been replaced, for the remainder of their term of office, in accordance with Articles I-26 and I-27.

Article III-349   (ex Article 216 EC)

If any member of the Commission no longer fulfils the conditions required for the performance of his or her duties or if he or she has been guilty of serious misconduct, the Court of Justice may, on application by the Council, acting by a simple majority, or by the Commission, compulsorily retire him or her.

Article III-350   (ex Article 217 EC)

Without prejudice to Article I-28(4), the responsibilities incumbent upon the Commission shall be structured and allocated among its members by its President, in accordance with Article I-27(3). The President may reshuffle the allocation of those responsibilities during the Commission's term of office. The members of the Commission shall carry out the duties devolved upon them by the President under his or her authority.

Article III-351   (ex Article 219 EC)

The Commission shall act by a majority of its members. Its Rules of Procedure shall determine the quorum.

Article III-352   (ex Articles 212 and 218 EC)

1.   The Commission shall adopt its Rules of Procedure so as to ensure both its own operation and that of its departments. It shall ensure that these rules are published.

2.   The Commission shall publish annually, not later than one month before the opening of the session of the European Parliament, a general report on the activities of the Union.

Subsection 5   The Court of Justice of the European Union

Article III-353   (ex Article 221 EC)

The Court of Justice shall sit in chambers, as a Grand Chamber or as a full Court, in accordance with the Statute of the Court of Justice of the European Union.

Article III-354   (ex Article 222 EC)

The Court of Justice shall be assisted by eight Advocates-General. Should the Court of Justice so request, the Council may, acting unanimously, adopt a European decision to increase the number of Advocates-General. It shall be the duty of the Advocate-General, acting with complete impartiality and independence, to make, in open court, reasoned submissions on cases which, in accordance with the Statute of the Court of Justice of the European Union, require his or her involvement.

Article III-355   (ex Article 223 EC)

The Judges and Advocates-General of the Court of Justice shall be chosen from persons whose independence is beyond doubt and who possess the qualifications required for appointment to the highest judicial offices in their respective countries or who are jurisconsults of recognised competence; they shall be appointed by common accord of the governments of the Member States after consultation of the panel provided for in Article III-357. Every three years there shall be a partial replacement of the Judges and Advocates-General, in accordance with the conditions laid down in the Statute of the Court of Justice of the European Union.

The Judges shall elect the President of the Court of Justice from among their number for a term of three years. He or she may be re-elected. The Court of Justice shall adopt its Rules of Procedure. Those Rules shall require the consent of the Council.

Article III-356   (ex Article 224 EC)

The number of Judges of the General Court shall be determined by the Statute of the Court of Justice of the European Union. The Statute may provide for the General Court to be assisted by Advocates- General. The members of the General Court shall be chosen from persons whose independence is beyond doubt and who possess the ability required for appointment to high judicial office. They shall be appointed by common accord of the governments of the

Member States after consultation of the panel provided for in Article III-357. The membership of the General Court shall be partially renewed every three years. The Judges shall elect the President of the General Court from among their number for a term of three years. He or she may be re-elected. The General Court shall establish its Rules of Procedure in agreement with the Court of Justice. The Rules shall be subject to the consent of the Council. Unless the Statute provides otherwise, the provisions of the Constitution relating to the Court of Justice shall apply to the General Court.

Article III-357   (new)

A panel shall be set up in order to give an opinion on candidates' suitability to perform the duties of Judge and Advocate-General of the Court of Justice and the General Court before the governments of the Member States make the appointments referred to in Articles III-355 and III-356.

The panel shall comprise seven persons chosen from among former members of the Court of Justice and the General Court, members of national supreme courts and lawyers of recognised competence, one of whom shall be proposed by the European Parliament. The Council shall adopt a European decision establishing the panel's operating rules and a European decision appointing its members. It shall act on the initiative of the President of the Court of Justice.

Article III-358   (ex Article 225 EC)

1.   The General Court shall have jurisdiction to hear and determine at first instance actions or proceedings referred to in Articles III-365, III-367, III-370, III-372 and III-374, with the exception of those assigned to a specialised court set up under Article III-359 and those reserved in the Statute of the Court of Justice of the European Union for the Court of Justice. The Statute may provide for the General Court to have jurisdiction for other classes of action or proceeding.

Decisions given by the General Court under this paragraph may be subject to a right of appeal to the Court of Justice on points of law only, under the conditions and within the limits laid down by the Statute.

2.   The General Court shall have jurisdiction to hear and determine actions or proceedings brought against decisions of the specialised courts.

Decisions given by the General Court under this paragraph may exceptionally be subject to review by the Court of Justice, under the conditions and within the limits laid down by the Statute of the Court of Justice of the European Union, where there is a serious risk of the unity or consistency of Union law being affected.

3.   The General Court shall have jurisdiction to hear and determine questions referred for a preliminary ruling under Article III-369, in specific areas laid down by the Statute of the Court of Justice of the European Union.

Where the General Court considers that the case requires a decision of principle likely to affect the unity or consistency of Union law, it may refer the case to the Court of Justice for a ruling.

Decisions given by the General Court on questions referred for a preliminary ruling may exceptionally be subject to review by the Court of Justice, under the conditions and within the limits laid down by the Statute, where there is a serious risk of the unity or consistency of Union law being affected.

Article III-359   (ex Article 225a EC)

1.   European laws may establish specialised courts attached to the General Court to hear and determine at first instance certain classes of action or proceeding brought in specific areas. They shall be adopted either on a proposal from the Commission after consultation of the Court of Justice or at the request of the Court of Justice after consultation of the Commission.

2.   The European law establishing a specialised court shall lay down the rules on the organisation of the court and the extent of the jurisdiction conferred upon it.

3.   Decisions given by specialised courts may be subject to a right of appeal on points of law only or, when provided for in the European law establishing the specialised court, a right of appeal also on matters of fact, before the General Court.

4.   The members of the specialised courts shall be chosen from persons whose independence is beyond doubt and who possess the ability required for appointment to judicial office. They shall be appointed by the Council, acting unanimously.

5.   The specialised courts shall establish their Rules of Procedure in agreement with the Court of Justice. Those Rules shall require the consent of the Council.

6.   Unless the European law establishing the specialised court provides otherwise, the provisions of the Constitution relating to the Court of Justice of the European Union and the provisions of the Statute of the Court of Justice of the European Union shall apply to the specialised courts. Title I of the Statute and Article 64 thereof shall in any case apply to the specialised courts.

Article III-360   (ex Article 226 EC)

If the Commission considers that a Member State has failed to fulfil an obligation under the Constitution, it shall deliver a reasoned opinion on the matter after giving the State concerned the opportunity to submit its observations. If the State concerned does not comply with the opinion within the period laid down by the Commission, the latter may bring the matter before the Court of Justice of the European Union.

Article III-361   (ex Article 227 EC)

A Member State which considers that another Member State has failed to fulfil an obligation under the Constitution may bring the matter before the Court of Justice of the European Union. Before a Member State brings an action against another Member State for an alleged infringement of an obligation under the Constitution, it shall bring the matter before the Commission. The Commission shall deliver a reasoned opinion after each of the States concerned has been given the opportunity to submit its own case and its observations on the other party's case both orally and in writing. If the Commission has not delivered an opinion within three months of the date on which the matter was brought before it, the absence of such opinion shall not prevent the matter from being brought before the Court.

Article III-362   (ex Article 228 EC)

1.   If the Court of Justice of the European Union finds that a Member State has failed to fulfil an obligation under the Constitution, that State shall be required to take the necessary measures to comply with the judgment of the Court.

2.   If the Commission considers that the Member State concerned has not taken the necessary measures to comply with the judgment referred to in paragraph 1, it may bring the case before the Court of Justice of the European Union after giving that State the opportunity to submit its observations. It shall specify the amount of the lump sum or penalty payment to be paid by the Member State concerned which it considers appropriate in the circumstances.

If the Court finds that the Member State concerned has not complied with its judgment it may impose a lump sum or penalty payment on it.

This procedure shall be without prejudice to Article III-361.

3.   When the Commission brings a case before the Court of Justice of the European Union pursuant to Article III-360 on the grounds that the Member State concerned has failed to fulfil its obligation to notify measures transposing a European framework law, it may, when it deems appropriate, specify the amount of the lump sum or penalty payment to be paid by the Member State concerned which it considers appropriate in the circumstances. If the Court finds that there is an infringement it may impose a lump sum or penalty payment on the Member State concerned not exceeding the amount specified by the Commission. The payment obligation shall take effect on the date set by the Court in its judgment.

Article III-363   (ex Article 229 EC)

European laws and regulations of the Council may give the Court of Justice of the European Union unlimited jurisdiction with regard to the penalties provided for in them.

Article III-364   (ex Article 229a EC)

Without prejudice to the other provisions of the Constitution, a European law may confer on the Court of Justice of the European Union, to the extent that it shall determine, jurisdiction in disputes relating to the application of acts adopted on the basis of the Constitution which create European intellectual property rights.

Article III-365   (ex Article 270 EC)

1.   The Court of Justice of the European Union shall review the legality of European laws and framework laws, of acts of the Council, of the Commission and of the European Central Bank, other than recommendations and opinions, and of acts of the European Parliament and of the European Council intended to produce legal effects vis-à-vis third parties. It shall also review the legality of acts of bodies, offices or agencies of the Union intended to produce legal effects vis-à-vis third parties.

2.   For the purposes of paragraph 1, the Court of Justice of the European Union shall have jurisdiction in actions brought by a Member State, the European Parliament, the Council or the Commission on grounds of lack of competence, infringement of an essential procedural requirement, infringement of the Constitution or of any rule of law relating to its application, or misuse of powers.

3.   The Court of Justice of the European Union shall have jurisdiction under the conditions laid down in paragraphs 1 and 2 in actions brought by the Court of Auditors, by the European Central Bank and by the Committee of the Regions for the purpose of protecting their prerogatives.

4.   Any natural or legal person may, under the conditions laid down in paragraphs 1 and 2, institute proceedings against an act addressed to that person or which is of direct and individual concern to him or her, and against a regulatory act which is of direct concern to him or her and does not entail implementing measures.

5.   Acts setting up bodies, offices and agencies of the Union may lay down specific conditions and arrangements concerning actions brought by natural or legal persons against acts of these bodies, offices or agencies intended to produce legal effects in relation to them.

6.   The proceedings provided for in this Article shall be instituted within two months of the publication of the act, or of its notification to the plaintiff, or, in the absence thereof, of the day on which it came to the plaintiff's knowledge, as the case may be.

Article III-366   (ex Article 231 EC)

If the action is well founded, the Court of Justice of the European Union shall declare the act concerned to be void. However, the Court shall, if it considers this necessary, state which of the effects of the act which it has declared void shall be considered as definitive.

Article III-367   (ex Article 232 EC)

Should the European Parliament, the European Council, the Council, the Commission or the European Central Bank, in infringement of the Constitution, fail to act, the Member States and the other institutions of the Union may bring an action before the Court of Justice of the European Union to have the infringement established. This Article shall apply, under the same conditions, to bodies, offices and agencies of the Union which fail to act. The action shall be admissible only if the institution, body, office or agency concerned has first been called upon to act. If, within two months of being so called upon, the institution, body, office or agency concerned has not defined its position, the action may be brought within a further period of two months. Any natural or legal person may, under the conditions laid down in the first and second paragraphs, complain to the Court that an institution, body, office or agency of the Union has failed to address to that person any act other than a recommendation or an opinion.

Article III-368   (ex Article 233 EC)

The institution, body, office or agency whose act has been declared void, or whose failure to act has been declared contrary to the Constitution, shall be required to take the necessary measures to comply with the judgment of the Court of Justice of the European Union. This obligation shall not affect any obligation which may result from the application of the second paragraph of Article III-431.

Article III-369   (ex Article 234 EC)

The Court of Justice of the European Union shall have jurisdiction to give preliminary rulings concerning:

- a)   the interpretation of the Constitution;
- b)   the validity and interpretation of acts of the institutions, bodies, offices and agencies of the Union.

Where such a question is raised before any court or tribunal of a Member State, that court or tribunal may, if it considers that a decision on the question is necessary to enable it to give judgment, request the Court to give a ruling thereon.

Where any such question is raised in a case pending before a court or tribunal of a Member State against whose decisions there is no judicial remedy under national law, that court or tribunal shall bring the matter before the Court.

If such a question is raised in a case pending before a court or tribunal of a Member State with regard to a person in custody, the Court shall act with the minimum of delay.

Article III-370   (ex Article 235 EC)

The Court of Justice of the European Union shall have jurisdiction in disputes relating to compensation for damage provided for in the second and third paragraphs of Article III-431.

Article III-371   (ex Article 46(e) TEU)

The Court of Justice shall have jurisdiction to decide on the legality of an act adopted by the European Council or by the Council pursuant to Article I-59 solely at the request of the Member State concerned by a determination of the European Council or of the Council and in respect solely of the procedural stipulations contained in that Article. Such a request must be made within one month from the date of such determination. The Court shall rule within one month from the date of the request.

Article III-372   (ex Article 236 EC)

The Court of Justice of the European Union shall have jurisdiction in any dispute between the Union and its servants within the limits and under the conditions laid down in the Staff Regulations of Officials and the Conditions of Employment of other servants of the Union.

Article III-373   (ex Article 237 EC)

The Court of Justice of the European Union shall, within the limits hereinafter laid down, have jurisdiction in disputes concerning:

- (a)   the fulfilment by Member States of obligations under the Statute of the European Investment Bank. In this connection, the Board of Directors of the Bank shall enjoy the powers conferred upon the Commission by Article III-360;
- (b)   measures adopted by the Board of Governors of the European Investment Bank. In this connection, any Member State, the Commission or the Board of Directors of the Bank may institute proceedings under the conditions laid down in Article III-365;
- (c)   measures adopted by the Board of Directors of the European Investment Bank. Proceedings against such measures may be instituted only by Member States or by the Commission, under the conditions laid down in Article III-365, and solely on

the grounds of non-compliance with the procedure provided for in Article 19(2), (5), (6) and (7) of the Statute of the Bank;

(d) the fulfilment by national central banks of obligations under the Constitution and the Statute of the European System of Central Banks and of the European Central Bank. In this connection, the powers of the Governing Council of the European Central Bank in respect of national central banks shall be the same as those conferred upon the Commission in respect of Member States by Article III-360. If the Court of Justice of the European Union finds that a national central bank has failed to fulfil an obligation under the Constitution, that bank shall be required to take the necessary measures to comply with the judgment of the Court.

Article III-374   (ex Article 238 EC)

The Court of Justice of the European Union shall have jurisdiction to give judgment pursuant to any arbitration clause contained in a contract concluded by or on behalf of the Union, whether that contract be governed by public or private law.

Article III-375   (ex Articles 239, 240 and 292 EC)

1.   Save where jurisdiction is conferred on the Court of Justice of the European Union by the Constitution, disputes to which the Union is a party shall not on that ground be excluded from the jurisdiction of the courts or tribunals of the Member States.

2.   Member States undertake not to submit a dispute concerning the interpretation or application of the Constitution to any method of settlement other than those provided for therein.

3.   The Court of Justice shall have jurisdiction in any dispute between Member States which relates to the subject-matter of the Constitution if the dispute is submitted to it under a special agreement between the parties.

Article III-376   (new)

The Court of Justice of the European Union shall not have jurisdiction with respect to Articles I-40 and I-41 and the provisions of Chapter II of Title V concerning the common foreign and security policy and Article III-293 insofar as it concerns the common foreign and security policy.

However, the Court shall have jurisdiction to monitor compliance with Article III-308 and to rule on proceedings, brought in accordance with the conditions laid down in Article III-365(4), reviewing the legality of European decisions providing for restrictive measures against natural or legal persons adopted by the Council on the basis of Chapter II of Title V.

Article III-377   (new)

In exercising its powers regarding the provisions of Sections 4 and 5 of Chapter IV of Title III relating to the area of freedom, security and justice, the Court of Justice of the European Union shall have no jurisdiction to review the validity or proportionality of operations carried out by the police or other law-enforcement services of a Member State or the exercise of the responsibilities incumbent upon Member States with regard to the maintenance of law and order and the safeguarding of internal security.

Article III-378   (ex Article 241 EC)

Notwithstanding the expiry of the period laid down in Article III-365(6), any party may, in proceedings in which an act of general application adopted by an institution, body, office or agency of the Union is at issue, plead the grounds specified in Article III-365(2) in order to invoke before the Court of Justice of the European Union the inapplicability of that act.

Article III-379   (ex Articles 242 and 243 EC)

1.   Actions brought before the Court of Justice of the European Union shall not have suspensory effect. The Court may, however, if it considers that circumstances so require, order that application of the contested act be suspended.

2.   The Court of Justice of the European Union may in any cases before it prescribe any necessary interim measures.

Article III-380   (ex Article 244 EC)

The judgments of the Court of Justice of the European Union shall be enforceable under the conditions laid down in Article III-401.

Article III-381   (ex Article 245 EC)

The Statute of the Court of Justice of the European Union shall be laid down in a Protocol. A European law may amend the provisions of the Statute, with the exception of Title I and Article 64. It shall be adopted either at the request of the Court of Justice and after consultation of the Commission, or on a proposal from the Commission and after consultation of the Court of Justice.

Subsection 6 The European Central Bank

Article III-382   (ex Article 112 EC)

1.   The Governing Council of the European Central Bank shall comprise the members of the Executive Board of the European Central Bank and the Governors of the national central banks of the Member States without a derogation as referred to in Article III-197.

2.   The Executive Board shall comprise the President, the Vice-President and four other members. The President, the Vice-President and the other members of the Executive Board shall be appointed by the European Council, acting by a qualified majority, from among persons of recognised standing and professional experience in monetary or banking matters, on a recommendation from the Council and after consulting the European Parliament and the Governing Council of the European Central Bank. Their term of office shall be eight years and shall not be renewable.

Only nationals of Member States may be members of the Executive Board.

Article III-383   (ex Article 113 EC)

1.   The President of the Council and a member of the Commission may participate, without having the right to vote, in meetings of the Governing Council of the European Central Bank.

The President of the Council may submit a motion for deliberation to the Governing Council of the European Central Bank.

2.   The President of the European Central Bank shall be invited to participate in meetings of the Council when it is discussing matters relating to the objectives and tasks of the European System of Central Banks.

3.   The European Central Bank shall address an annual report on the activities of the European System of Central Banks and on the monetary policy of both the previous and the current year to the European Parliament, the European Council, the Council and the Commission. The President of the European Central Bank shall present this report to the European Parliament, which may hold a general debate on that basis, and to the Council.

The President of the European Central Bank and the other members of the Executive Board may, at the request of the European Parliament or on their own initiative, be heard by the competent bodies of the European Parliament.

Subsection 7   The Court of Auditors

Article III-384   (ex Article 248 EC)

1.   The Court of Auditors shall examine the accounts of all revenue and expenditure of the Union. It shall also examine the accounts of all revenue and expenditure of any body, office or agency set up by the Union insofar as the instrument establishing that body, office or agency does not preclude such examination. The Court of Auditors shall provide the Euro-

pean Parliament and the Council with a statement of assurance as to the reliability of the accounts and the legality and regularity of the underlying transactions which shall be published in the Official Journal of the European Union. This statement may be supplemented by specific assessments for each major area of Union activity.

2. The Court of Auditors shall examine whether all revenue has been received and all expenditure incurred in a lawful and regular manner and whether the financial management has been sound. In doing so, it shall report in particular on any cases of irregularity. The audit of revenue shall be carried out on the basis of the amounts established as due and the amounts actually paid to the Union. The audit of expenditure shall be carried out on the basis both of commitments undertaken and payments made. These audits may be carried out before the closure of accounts for the financial year in question.

3. The audit shall be based on records and, if necessary, performed on the spot in the other institutions, or on the premises of any body, office or agency which manages revenue or expenditure on behalf of the Union and in the Member States, including on the premises of any natural or legal person in receipt of payments from the budget. In the Member States the audit shall be carried out in liaison with national audit bodies or, if these do not have the necessary powers, with the competent national departments. The Court of Auditors and the national audit bodies of the Member States shall cooperate in a spirit of trust while maintaining their independence. These bodies or departments shall inform the Court of Auditors whether they intend to take part in the audit. The other institutions, any bodies, offices or agencies managing revenue or expenditure on behalf of the Union, any natural or legal person in receipt of payments from the budget, and the national audit bodies or, if these do not have the necessary powers, the competent national departments, shall forward to the Court of Auditors, at its request, any document or information necessary to carry out its task. In respect of the European Investment Bank's activity in managing Union revenue and expenditure, rights of access by the Court of Auditors to information held by the Bank shall be governed by an agreement between the Court of Auditors, the Bank and the Commission. In the absence of an agreement, the Court of Auditors shall nevertheless have access to information necessary for the audit of Union expenditure and revenue managed by the Bank.

4. The Court of Auditors shall draw up an annual report after the close of each financial year. It shall be forwarded to the other institutions and shall be published, together with the replies of these institutions to the observations of the Court of Auditors, in the Official Journal of the European Union. The Court of Auditors may also, at any time, submit observations, particularly in the form of special reports, on specific questions and deliver opinions at the request of one of the other institutions. It shall adopt its annual reports, special reports or opinions by a majority of its component members. However, it may establish internal chambers in order to adopt certain categories of reports or opinions under the conditions laid down by its Rules of Procedure.

It shall assist the European Parliament and the Council in exercising their powers of control over the implementation of the budget. It shall adopt its Rules of Procedure. Those rules shall require the consent of the Council.

Article III-385   (ex Article 247 EC)

1. The members of the Court of Auditors shall be chosen from among persons who belong or have belonged in their respective States to external audit bodies or who are especially qualified for this office. Their independence must be beyond doubt.

2. The members of the Court of Auditors shall be appointed for a term of six years. Their term of office shall be renewable. The Council shall adopt a European decision establishing the list of members drawn up in accordance with the proposals made by each Member State. It shall act after consulting the European Parliament. The members of the Court of Auditors shall elect their President from among their number for a term of three years. He or she may be re-elected.

3.   In the performance of their duties, members of the Court of Auditors shall neither seek nor take instructions from any government or from any other body. They shall refrain from any action incompatible with their duties.

4.   Members of the Court of Auditors shall not, during their term of office, engage in any other occupation, whether gainful or not. When entering upon their duties they shall give a solemn undertaking that, both during and after their term of office, they will respect the obligations arising therefrom and in particular their duty to behave with integrity and discretion as regards the acceptance, after they have ceased to hold office, of certain appointments or benefits.

5.   Apart from normal replacement, or death, the duties of a member of the Court of Auditors shall end when he or she resigns, or is compulsorily retired by a ruling of the Court of Justice pursuant to paragraph 6. The vacancy thus caused shall be filled for the remainder of the member's term of office. Save in the case of compulsory retirement, members of the Court of Auditors shall remain in office until they have been replaced.

6.   A member of the Court of Auditors may be deprived of his or her office or of his or her right to a pension or other benefits in its stead only if the Court of Justice, at the request of the Court of Auditors, finds that he or she no longer fulfils the requisite conditions or meets the obligations arising from his or her office.

SECTION 2   THE UNION'S ADVISORY BODIES

Subsection 1   The Committee of the Regions

Article III-386   (ex Article 263 EC)
The number of members of the Committee of the Regions shall not exceed 350. The Council, acting unanimously on a proposal from the Commission, shall adopt a European decision determining the Committee's composition. The members of the Committee and an equal number of alternate members shall be appointed for five years. Their term of office shall be renewable. No member of the Committee shall at the same time be a member of the European Parliament. The Council shall adopt the European decision establishing the list of members and alternate members drawn up in accordance with the proposals made by each Member State. When the mandate referred to in Article I-32(2) on the basis of which they were proposed comes to an end, the term of office of members of the Committee shall terminate automatically and they shall then be replaced for the remainder of the said term of office in accordance with the same procedure.

Article III-387   (ex Article 264 EC)
The Committee of the Regions shall elect its chairman and officers from among its members for a term of two and a half years. It shall be convened by its chairman at the request of the European Parliament, of the Council or of the Commission. It may also meet on its own initiative.

It shall adopt its Rules of Procedure.

Article III-388   (ex Article 265 EC)
The Committee of the Regions shall be consulted by the European Parliament, by the Council or by the Commission where the Constitution so provides and in all other cases in which one of these institutions considers it appropriate, in particular those which concern cross-border cooperation. The European Parliament, the Council or the Commission shall, if it considers it necessary, set the Committee, for the submission of its opinion, a time-limit which shall not be less than one month from the date on which the chairman receives notification to this effect. Upon expiry of the time- limit, the absence of an opinion shall not prevent further action.

Where the Economic and Social Committee is consulted, the Committee of the Regions shall be informed by the European Parliament, the Council or the Commission of the request for an opinion. Where it considers that specific regional interests are involved, the Committee of the Regions may issue an opinion on the matter. It may also issue an opinion on its own initiative.

The opinion of the Committee, together with a record of its proceedings, shall be forwarded to the European Parliament, to the Council and to the Commission.

Subsection 2   The Economic and Social Committee

Article III-389   (ex Article 258 EC)
The number of members of the Economic and Social Committee shall not exceed 350. The Council, acting unanimously on a proposal from the Commission, shall adopt a European decision determining the Committee's composition.

Article III-390   (ex Article 259 EC)
The members of the Economic and Social Committee shall be appointed for five years. Their term of office shall be renewable. The Council shall adopt the European decision establishing the list of members drawn up in accordance with the proposals made by each Member State.

The Council shall act after consulting the Commission. It may obtain the opinion of European bodies which are representative of the various economic and social sectors and of civil society to which the Union's activities are of concern.

Article III-391   (ex Article 260 EC)
The Economic and Social Committee shall elect its chairman and officers from among its members for a term of two and a half years. It shall be convened by its chairman at the request of the European Parliament, of the Council or of the Commission. It may also meet on its own initiative.

It shall adopt its Rules of Procedure.

Article III-392   (ex Article 262 EC)
The Economic and Social Committee shall be consulted by the European Parliament, by the Council or by the Commission where the Constitution so provides. It may be consulted by these institutions in all cases in which they consider it appropriate. It may also issue an opinion on its own initiative. The European Parliament, the Council or the Commission shall, if it considers it necessary, set the Committee, for the submission of its opinion, a time-limit which shall not be less than one month from the date on which the chairman receives notification to this effect. Upon expiry of the time-limit, the absence of an opinion shall not prevent further action.

The opinion of the Committee, together with a record of its proceedings, shall be forwarded to the European Parliament, to the Council and to the Commission.

SECTION 3   THE EUROPEAN INVESTMENT BANK

Article III-393   (ex Article 266 EC)
The European Investment Bank shall have legal personality. Its members shall be the Member States. The Statute of the European Investment Bank is laid down in a Protocol. A European law of the Council may amend the Statute of the European Investment Bank. The Council shall act unanimously, either at the request of the European Investment Bank and after consulting the European Parliament and the Commission, or on a proposal from the Commission and after consulting the European Parliament and the European Investment Bank.

Article III-394   (ex Article 267 EC)
The task of the European Investment Bank shall be to contribute, by having recourse to the capital markets and utilising its own resources, to the balanced and steady development of the internal market in the Union's interest. For this purpose the European Investment Bank

shall, operating on a non-profit-making basis, in particular grant loans and give guarantees which facilitate the financing of the following projects in all sectors of the economy:

(a) projects for developing less-developed regions

(b) projects for modernising or converting undertakings or for developing fresh activities called for by the establishment or functioning of the internal market, where these projects are of such a size or nature that they cannot be entirely financed by the various means available in the individual Member States;

(c) projects of common interest to several Member States which are of such a size or nature that they cannot be entirely financed by the various means available in the individual Member States.

In carrying out its task, the European Investment Bank shall facilitate the financing of investment programmes in conjunction with assistance from the Structural Funds and other Union financial instruments.

SECTION 4   PROVISIONS COMMON TO UNION INSTITUTIONS, BODIES, OFFICES AND AGENCIES

Article III-395   (ex Article 250 EC)

1.   Where, pursuant to the Constitution, the Council acts on a proposal from the Commission, it may amend that proposal only by acting unanimously, except in the cases referred to in Articles I-55, I-56, III-396(10) and (13), III-404 and III-405(2).

2.   As long as the Council has not acted, the Commission may alter its proposal at any time during the procedures leading to the adoption of a Union act.

Article III-396   (ex Article 251 EC)

1.   Where, pursuant to the Constitution, European laws or framework laws are adopted under the ordinary legislative procedure, the following provisions shall apply.

2.   The Commission shall submit a proposal to the European Parliament and the Council.

First reading

3.   The European Parliament shall adopt its position at first reading and communicate it to the Council.

4.   If the Council approves the European Parliament's position, the act concerned shall be adopted in the wording which corresponds to the position of the European Parliament.

5.   If the Council does not approve the European Parliament's position, it shall adopt its position at first reading and communicate it to the European Parliament.

6.   The Council shall inform the European Parliament fully of the reasons which led it to adopt its position at first reading. The Commission shall inform the European Parliament fully of its position.

Second reading

7.   If, within three months of such communication, the European Parliament:

(a) approves the Council's position at first reading or has not taken a decision, the act concerned shall be deemed to have been adopted in the wording which corresponds to the position of the Council;

(b) rejects, by a majority of its component members, the Council's position at first reading, the proposed act shall be deemed not to have been adopted;

(c) proposes, by a majority of its component members, amendments to the Council's position at first reading, the text thus amended shall be forwarded to the Council and to the Commission, which shall deliver an opinion on those amendments.

8.   If, within three months of receiving the European Parliament's amendments, the Council, acting by a qualified majority:

(a) approves all those amendments, the act in question shall be deemed to have been adopted;

(b) does not approve all the amendments, the President of the Council, in agreement with the President of the European Parliament, shall within six weeks convene a meeting of the Conciliation Committee.

9.   The Council shall act unanimously on the amendments on which the Commission has delivered a negative opinion.

Conciliation

10.   The Conciliation Committee, which shall be composed of the members of the Council or their representatives and an equal number of members representing the European Parliament, shall have the task of reaching agreement on a joint text, by a qualified majority of the members of the Council or their representatives and by a majority of the members representing the European Parliament within six weeks of its being convened, on the basis of the positions of the European Parliament and the Council at second reading.

11.   The Commission shall take part in the Conciliation Committee's proceedings and shall take all necessary initiatives with a view to reconciling the positions of the European Parliament and the Council.

12.   If, within six weeks of its being convened, the Conciliation Committee does not approve the joint text, the proposed act shall be deemed not to have been adopted.

Third reading

13.   If, within that period, the Conciliation Committee approves a joint text, the European Parliament, acting by a majority of the votes cast, and the Council, acting by a qualified majority, shall each have a period of six weeks from that approval in which to adopt the act in question in accordance with the joint text. If they fail to do so, the proposed act shall be deemed not to have been adopted.

14.   The periods of three months and six weeks referred to in this Article shall be extended by a maximum of one month and two weeks respectively at the initiative of the European Parliament or the Council.

Special provisions

15.   Where, in the cases provided for in the Constitution, a law or framework law is submitted to the ordinary legislative procedure on the initiative of a group of Member States, on a recommendation by the European Central Bank, or at the request of the Court of Justice, paragraph 2, the second sentence of paragraph 6, and paragraph 9 shall not apply.

In such cases, the European Parliament and the Council shall communicate the proposed act to the Commission with their positions at first and second readings. The European Parliament or the Council may request the opinion of the Commission throughout the procedure, which the Commission may also deliver on its own initiative. It may also, if it deems it necessary, take part in the Conciliation Committee in accordance with paragraph 11.

Article III-397   (ex Article 218 EC and new provision)

The European Parliament, the Council and the Commission shall consult each other and by common agreement make arrangements for their cooperation. To that end, they may, in compliance with the Constitution, conclude interinstitutional agreements which may be of a binding nature.

Article III-398   (new)

1.   In carrying out their missions, the institutions, bodies, offices and agencies of the Union shall have the support of an open, efficient and independent European administration.

2.   In compliance with the Staff Regulations and the Conditions of employment adopted on the basis of Article III-427, European laws shall establish provisions to that end.

Article III-399   (ex Article 255 EC)

1.   The institutions, bodies, offices and agencies of the Union shall ensure transparency in their work and shall, pursuant to Article I-50, determine in their rules of procedure specific

provisions for public access to their documents. The Court of Justice of the European Union, the European Central Bank and the European Investment Bank shall be subject to the provisions of Article I-50(3) and to this Article only when exercising their administrative tasks.

2.   The European Parliament and the Council shall ensure publication of the documents relating to the legislative procedures under the terms laid down by the European law referred to in Article I-50(3).

Article III-400   (ex Articles 210 and 247(8) EC)

1.   The Council shall adopt European regulations and decisions determining:
    (a)   the salaries, allowances and pensions of the President of the European Council, the President of the Commission, the Union Minister for Foreign Affairs, the members of the Commission, the Presidents, members and Registrars of the Court of Justice of the European Union, and the Secretary-General of the Council;
    (b)   the conditions of employment, in particular the salaries, allowances and pensions, of the President and members of the Court of Auditors;
    (c)   any payment to be made instead of remuneration to the persons referred to in points (a) and (b).

2.   The Council shall adopt European regulations and decisions determining the allowances of the members of the Economic and Social Committee.

Article III-401   (ex Article 256 EC)

Acts of the Council, of the Commission or of the European Central Bank which impose a pecuniary obligation on persons other than Member States shall be enforceable.

Enforcement shall be governed by the rules of civil procedure in force in the Member State in the territory of which it is carried out. The order for its enforcement shall be appended to the decision, without other formality than verification of the authenticity of the decision, by the national authority which the government of each Member State shall designate for this purpose and shall make known to the Commission and the Court of Justice of the European Union. When these formalities have been completed on application by the party concerned, the latter may proceed to enforcement by bringing the matter directly before the competent authority, in accordance with the national law. Enforcement may be suspended only by a decision of the Court of Justice of the European Union. However, the courts of the country concerned shall have jurisdiction over complaints that enforcement is being carried out in an irregular manner.

CHAPTER II   FINANCIAL PROVISIONS

SECTION 1   THE MULTIANNUAL FINANCIAL FRAMEWORK

Article III-402   (new)

1.   The multiannual financial framework shall be established for a period of at least five years in accordance with Article I-55.

2.   The financial framework shall determine the amounts of the annual ceilings on commitment appropriations by category of expenditure and of the annual ceiling on payment appropriations. The categories of expenditure, limited in number, shall correspond to the Union's major sectors of activity.

3.   The financial framework shall lay down any other provisions required for the annual budgetary procedure to run smoothly.

4.   Where no European law of the Council determining a new financial framework has been adopted by the end of the previous financial framework, the ceilings and other provisions corresponding to the last year of that framework shall be extended until such time as that law is adopted.

5.   Throughout the procedure leading to the adoption of the financial framework, the

European Parliament, the Council and the Commission shall take any measure necessary to facilitate the successful completion of the procedure.

SECTION 2   THE UNION'S ANNUAL BUDGET

Article III-403   (ex Article 272 EC)
The financial year shall run from 1 January to 31 December.

Article III-404   (ex Article 272 EC)
European laws shall establish the Union's annual budget in accordance with the following provisions:

1. Each institution shall, before 1 July, draw up estimates of its expenditure for the following financial year. The Commission shall consolidate these estimates in a draft budget which may contain different estimates. The draft budget shall contain an estimate of revenue and an estimate of expenditure.

2. The Commission shall submit a proposal containing the draft budget to the European Parliament and to the Council not later than 1 September of the year preceding that in which the budget is to be implemented. The Commission may amend the draft budget during the procedure until such time as the Conciliation Committee, referred to in paragraph 5, is convened.

3. The Council shall adopt its position on the draft budget and forward it to the European Parliament not later than 1 October of the year preceding that in which the budget is to be implemented. The Council shall inform the European Parliament in full of the reasons which led it to adopt its position.

4. If, within forty-two days of such communication, the European Parliament:
    (a) approves the position of the Council, the European law establishing the budget shall be adopted;
    (b) has not taken a decision, the European law establishing the budget shall be deemed to have been adopted
    (c) adopts amendments by a majority of its component members, the amended draft shall be forwarded to the Council and to the Commission. The President of the European Parliament, in agreement with the President of the Council, shall immediately convene a meeting of the Conciliation Committee. However, if within ten days of the draft being forwarded the Council informs the European Parliament that it has approved all its amendments, the Conciliation Committee shall not meet.

5. The Conciliation Committee, which shall be composed of the members of the Council or their representatives and an equal number of members representing the European Parliament, shall have the task of reaching agreement on a joint text, by a qualified majority of the members of the Council or their representatives and by a majority of the representatives of the European Parliament within twenty-one days of its being convened, on the basis of the positions of the European Parliament and the Council. The Commission shall take part in the Conciliation Committee's proceedings and shall take all the necessary initiatives with a view to reconciling the positions of the European Parliament and the Council.

6. If, within the twenty-one days referred to in paragraph 5, the Conciliation Committee agrees on a joint text, the European Parliament and the Council shall each have a period of fourteen days from the date of that agreement in which to approve the joint text.

7. If, within the period of fourteen days referred to in paragraph 6:
    (a) the European Parliament and the Council both approve the joint text or fail to take a decision, or if one of these institutions approves the joint text while the other one fails to take a decision, the European law establishing the budget shall be deemed to be definitively adopted in accordance with the joint text, or

    (b) the European Parliament, acting by a majority of its component members, and the Council both reject the joint text, or if one of these institutions rejects the joint text while the other one fails to take a decision, a new draft budget shall be submitted by the Commission, or

    (c) the European Parliament, acting by a majority of its component members, rejects the joint text while the Council approves it, a new draft budget shall be submitted by the Commission, or

    (d) the European Parliament approves the joint text whilst the Council rejects it, the European Parliament may, within fourteen days from the date of the rejection by the Council and acting by a majority of its component members and three-fifths of the votes cast, decide to confirm all or some of the amendments referred to in paragraph 4(c). Where a European Parliament amendment is not confirmed, the position agreed in the Conciliation committee on the budget heading which is the subject of the amendment shall be retained. The European law establishing the budget shall be deemed to be definitively adopted on this basis.

8.   If, within the twenty-one days referred to in paragraph 5, the Conciliation Committee does not agree on a joint text, a new draft budget shall be submitted by the Commission.

9.   When the procedure provided for in this Article has been completed, the President of the European Parliament shall declare that the European law establishing the budget has been definitively adopted.

10.   Each institution shall exercise the powers conferred upon it under this Article in compliance with the Constitution and the acts adopted thereunder, with particular regard to the Union's own resources and the balance between revenue and expenditure.

Article III-405   (ex Article 273 EC)

1.   If at the beginning of a financial year no European law establishing the budget has been definitively adopted, a sum equivalent to not more than one twelfth of the budget appropriations entered in the chapter in question of the budget for the preceding financial year may be spent each month in respect of any chapter in accordance with the European law referred to in Article III-412; that sum shall not, however, exceed one twelfth of the appropriations provided for in the same chapter of the draft budget.

2.   The Council, on a proposal by the Commission and in compliance with the other conditions laid down in paragraph 1, may adopt a European decision authorising expenditure in excess of one twelfth, in accordance with the European law referred to in Article III-412. The Council shall forward the decision immediately to the European Parliament.

The European decision shall lay down the necessary measures relating to resources to ensure application of this Article, in accordance with the European laws referred to in Article I-54(3) and (4).

It shall enter into force thirty days following its adoption if the European Parliament, acting by a majority of its component members, has not decided to reduce this expenditure within that time-limit.

Article III-406   (ex Article 271 EC)

In accordance with the conditions laid down by the European law referred to in Article III-412, any appropriations, other than those relating to staff expenditure, that are unexpended at the end of the financial year may be carried forward to the next financial year only.

Appropriations shall be classified under different chapters grouping items of expenditure according to their nature or purpose and subdivided in accordance with the European law referred to in Article III-412.

The expenditure of:

    — the European Parliament,

    — the European Council and the Council,

— the Commission, and
— the Court of Justice of the European Union

shall be set out in separate sections of the budget, without prejudice to special arrangements for certain common items of expenditure.

SECTION 3   IMPLEMENTATION OF THE BUDGET AND DISCHARGE

Article III-407   (ex Article 274 EC)

The Commission shall implement the budget in cooperation with the Member States, in accordance with the European law referred to in Article III-412, on its own responsibility and within the limits of the appropriations allocated, having regard to the principles of sound financial management. Member States shall cooperate with the Commission to ensure that the appropriations are used in accordance with those principles. The European law referred to in Article III-412 shall establish the control and audit obligations of the Member States in the implementation of the budget and the resulting responsibilities. It shall establish the responsibilities and detailed rules for each institution concerning its part in effecting its own expenditure. Within the budget the Commission may, subject to the limits and conditions laid down by the European law referred to in Article III-412, transfer appropriations from one chapter to another or from one subdivision to another.

Article III-408   (ex Article 275 EC)

The Commission shall submit annually to the European Parliament and to the Council the accounts of the preceding financial year relating to the implementation of the budget. The Commission shall also forward to them a financial statement of the Union's assets and liabilities.

The Commission shall also submit to the European Parliament and to the Council an evaluation report on the Union's finances based on the results achieved, in particular in relation to the indications given by the European Parliament and the Council pursuant to Article III-409.

Article III-409   (ex Article 276 EC)

1.   The European Parliament, on a recommendation from the Council, shall give a discharge to the Commission in respect of the implementation of the budget. To this end, the Council and the European Parliament in turn shall examine the accounts, the financial statement and the evaluation report referred to in Article III-408, the annual report by the Court of Auditors together with the replies of the institutions under audit to the observations of the Court of Auditors, the statement of assurance referred to in the second subparagraph of Article III-384(1) and any relevant special reports by the Court of Auditors.

2.   Before giving a discharge to the Commission, or for any other purpose in connection with the exercise of its powers over the implementation of the budget, the European Parliament may ask to hear the Commission give evidence with regard to the execution of expenditure or the operation of financial control systems. The Commission shall submit any necessary information to the European Parliament at the latter's request.

3.   The Commission shall take all appropriate steps to act on the observations in the decisions giving discharge and on other observations by the European Parliament relating to the execution of expenditure, as well as on comments accompanying the recommendations on discharge adopted by the Council.

4.   At the request of the European Parliament or the Council, the Commission shall report on the measures taken in the light of these observations and comments and in particular on the instructions given to the departments which are responsible for the implementation of the budget. These reports shall also be forwarded to the Court of Auditors.

SECTION 4   COMMON PROVISIONS

Article III-410   (ex Article 277 EC)

The multiannual financial framework and the annual budget shall be drawn up in euro.

Article III-411   (ex Article 278 EC)

The Commission may, provided it notifies the competent authorities of the Member States concerned, transfer into the currency of one of the Member States its holdings in the currency of another Member State, to the extent necessary to enable them to be used for purposes which come within the scope of the Constitution. The Commission shall as far as possible avoid making such transfers if it possesses cash or liquid assets in the currencies which it needs.

The Commission shall deal with each Member State concerned through the authority designated by that State. In carrying out financial operations the Commission shall employ the services of the bank of issue of the Member State concerned or of any other financial institution approved by that State.

Article III-412   (ex Article 279 EC)

1.   European laws shall establish:
   (a) the financial rules which determine in particular the procedure to be adopted for establishing and implementing the budget and for presenting and auditing accounts;
   (b) rules providing for checks on the responsibility of financial actors, in particular authorising officers and accounting officers.

Such European laws shall be adopted after consultation of the Court of Auditors.

2.   The Council shall, on a proposal from the Commission, adopt a European regulation laying down the methods and procedure whereby the budget revenue provided under the arrangements relating to the Union's own resources shall be made available to the Commission, and the measures to be applied, if need be, to meet cash requirements. The Council shall act after consulting the European Parliament and the Court of Auditors.

3.   The Council shall act unanimously until 31 December 2006 in all the cases referred to by this Article.

Article III-413   (new)

The European Parliament, the Council and the Commission shall ensure that the financial means are made available to allow the Union to fulfil its legal obligations in respect of third parties.

Article III-414   (new)

Regular meetings between the Presidents of the European Parliament, the Council and the Commission shall be convened, on the initiative of the Commission, under the budgetary procedures referred to in this Chapter. The Presidents shall take all the necessary steps to promote consultation and the reconciliation of the positions of the institutions over which they preside in order to facilitate the implementation of this Chapter.

SECTION 5   COMBATING FRAUD

Article III-415   (ex Article 280 EC)

1.   The Union and the Member States shall counter fraud and any other illegal activities affecting the Union's financial interests through measures taken in accordance with this Article. These measures shall act as a deterrent and be such as to afford effective protection in the Member States and in all the Union's institutions, bodies, offices and agencies.

2.   Member States shall take the same measures to counter fraud affecting the Union's financial interests as they take to counter fraud affecting their own financial interests.

3.   Without prejudice to other provisions of the Constitution, the Member States shall coordinate their action aimed at protecting the Union's financial interests against fraud. To

this end they shall organise, together with the Commission, close and regular cooperation between the competent authorities.

4. European laws or framework laws shall lay down the necessary measures in the fields of the prevention of and fight against fraud affecting the Union's financial interests with a view to affording effective and equivalent protection in the Member States and in all the Union's institutions, bodies, offices and agencies. They shall be adopted after consultation of the Court of Auditors.

5. The Commission, in cooperation with Member States, shall each year submit to the European Parliament and to the Council a report on the measures taken for the implementation of this Article.

CHAPTER III   ENHANCED COOPERATION

Article III-416   (ex Article 43 TEU)
Any enhanced cooperation shall comply with the Constitution and the law of the Union.

Such cooperation shall not undermine the internal market or economic, social and territorial cohesion. It shall not constitute a barrier to or discrimination in trade between Member States, nor shall it distort competition between them.

Article III-417   (ex Articles 43(h) and 44(2) TEU)
Any enhanced cooperation shall respect the competences, rights and obligations of those Member States which do not participate in it. Those Member States shall not impede its implementation by the participating Member States.

Article III-418   (ex Article 43B TEU and new provisions)
1. When enhanced cooperation is being established, it shall be open to all Member States, subject to compliance with any conditions of participation laid down by the European authorising decision. It shall also be open to them at any other time, subject to compliance with the acts already adopted within that framework, in addition to any such conditions.

The Commission and the Member States participating in enhanced cooperation shall ensure that they promote participation by as many Member States as possible.

2. The Commission and, where appropriate, the Union Minister for Foreign Affairs shall keep the European Parliament and the Council regularly informed regarding developments in enhanced cooperation.

Article III-419   (ex Article 27C TEU)
1. Member States which wish to establish enhanced cooperation between themselves in one of the areas covered by the Constitution, with the exception of fields of exclusive competence and the common foreign and security policy, shall address a request to the Commission, specifying the scope and objectives of the enhanced cooperation proposed. The Commission may submit a proposal to the Council to that effect. In the event of the Commission not submitting a proposal, it shall inform the Member States concerned of the reasons for not doing so. Authorisation to proceed with enhanced cooperation shall be granted by a European decision of the Council, which shall act on a proposal from the Commission and after obtaining the consent of the European Parliament.

2. The request of the Member States which wish to establish enhanced cooperation between themselves within the framework of the common foreign and security policy shall be addressed to the Council. It shall be forwarded to the Union Minister for Foreign Affairs, who shall give an opinion on whether the enhanced cooperation proposed is consistent with the Union's common foreign and security policy, and to the Commission, which shall give its opinion in particular on whether the enhanced cooperation proposed is consistent with other Union policies. It shall also be forwarded to the European Parliament for information.

Authorisation to proceed with enhanced cooperation shall be granted by a European decision of the Council acting unanimously.

Article III-420   (ex Article 27E TEU)

1.   Any Member State which wishes to participate in enhanced cooperation in progress in one of the areas referred to in Article III-419(1) shall notify its intention to the Council and the Commission. The Commission shall, within four months of the date of receipt of the notification, confirm the participation of the Member State concerned. It shall note where necessary that the conditions of participation have been fulfilled and shall adopt any transitional measures necessary with regard to the application of the acts already adopted within the framework of enhanced cooperation. However, if the Commission considers that the conditions of participation have not been fulfilled, it shall indicate the arrangements to be adopted to fulfil those conditions and shall set a deadline for re- examining the request. On the expiry of that deadline, it shall re-examine the request, in accordance with the procedure set out in the second subparagraph. If the Commission considers that the conditions of participation have still not been met, the Member State concerned may refer the matter to the Council, which shall decide on the request. The Council shall act in accordance with Article I-44(3). It may also adopt the transitional measures referred to in the second subparagraph on a proposal from the Commission.

2.   Any Member State which wishes to participate in enhanced cooperation in progress in the framework of the common foreign and security policy shall notify its intention to the Council, the Union Minister for Foreign Affairs and the Commission. The Council shall confirm the participation of the Member State concerned, after consulting the Union Minister for Foreign Affairs and after noting, where necessary, that the conditions of participation have been fulfilled. The Council, on a proposal from the Union Minister for Foreign Affairs, may also adopt any transitional measures necessary with regard to the application of the acts already adopted within the framework of enhanced cooperation. However, if the Council considers that the conditions of participation have not been fulfilled, it shall indicate the arrangements to be adopted to fulfil those conditions and shall set a deadline for re-examining the request for participation. For the purposes of this paragraph, the Council shall act unanimously and in accordance with Article I-44(3).

Article III-421   (ex Article 44A TEU)

Expenditure resulting from implementation of enhanced cooperation, other than administrative costs entailed for the institutions, shall be borne by the participating Member States, unless all members of the Council, acting unanimously after consulting the European Parliament, decide otherwise.

Article III-422   (new)

1.   Where a provision of the Constitution which may be applied in the context of enhanced cooperation stipulates that the Council shall act unanimously, the Council, acting unanimously in accordance with the arrangements laid down in Article I-44(3), may adopt a European decision stipulating that it will act by a qualified majority.

2.   Where a provision of the Constitution which may be applied in the context of enhanced cooperation stipulates that the Council shall adopt European laws or framework laws under a special legislative procedure, the Council, acting unanimously in accordance with the arrangements laid down in Article I-44(3), may adopt a European decision stipulating that it will act under the ordinary legislative procedure. The Council shall act after consulting the European Parliament.

3.   Paragraphs 1 and 2 shall not apply to decisions having military or defence implications.

Article III-423   (ex Article 45 TEU)

The Council and the Commission shall ensure the consistency of activities undertaken in the context of enhanced cooperation and the consistency of such activities with the policies of the Union, and shall cooperate to that end.

TITLE VII COMMON PROVISIONS

Article III-424 (ex Article 299 EC)

Taking account of the structural economic and social situation of Guadeloupe, French Guiana, Martinique, Réunion, the Azores, Madeira and the Canary Islands, which is compounded by their remoteness, insularity, small size, difficult topography and climate, economic dependence on a few products, the permanence and combination of which severely restrain their development, the Council, on a proposal from the Commission, shall adopt European laws, framework laws, regulations and decisions aimed, in particular, at laying down the conditions of application of the Constitution to those regions, including common policies. It shall act after consulting the European Parliament. The acts referred to in the first paragraph concern in particular areas such as customs and trade policies, fiscal policy, free zones, agriculture and fisheries policies, conditions for supply of raw materials and essential consumer goods, State aids and conditions of access to structural funds and to horizontal Union programmes. The Council shall adopt the acts referred to in the first paragraph taking into account the special characteristics and constraints of the outermost regions without undermining the integrity and the coherence of the Union legal order, including the internal market and common policies.

Article III-425 (ex Article 295 EC)

The Constitution shall in no way prejudice the rules in Member States governing the system of property ownership.

Article III-426 (ex Article 282 EC)

In each of the Member States, the Union shall enjoy the most extensive legal capacity accorded to legal persons under their laws; it may, in particular, acquire or dispose of movable and immovable property and may be a party to legal proceedings. To this end, the Union shall be represented by the Commission. However, the Union shall be represented by each of the institutions, by virtue of their administrative autonomy, in matters relating to their respective operation.

Article III-427 (ex Article 282 EC)

The Staff Regulations of officials and the Conditions of employment of other servants of the Union shall be laid down by a European law. It shall be adopted after consultation of the institutions concerned.

Article III-428 (ex Article 284 EC)

The Commission may, within the limits and under conditions laid down by a European regulation or decision adopted by a simple majority by the Council, collect any information and carry out any checks required for the performance of the tasks entrusted to it.

Article III-429 (ex Article 285 EC)

1. Without prejudice to Article 5 of the Protocol on the Statute of the European System of Central Banks and of the European Central Bank, measures for the production of statistics shall be laid down by a European law or framework law where necessary for the performance of the Union's activities.

2. The production of statistics shall conform to impartiality, reliability, objectivity, scientific independence, cost-effectiveness and statistical confidentiality. It shall not entail excessive burdens on economic operators.

Article III-430 (ex Article 287 EC)

The members of the Union's institutions, the members of committees, and the officials and other servants of the Union shall be required, even after their duties have ceased, not to disclose information of the kind covered by the obligation of professional secrecy, in particular information about undertakings, their business relations or their cost components.

Article III-431   (ex Article 288 EC)

The Union's contractual liability shall be governed by the law applicable to the contract in question. In the case of non-contractual liability, the Union shall, in accordance with the general principles common to the laws of the Member States, make good any damage caused by its institutions or by its servants in the performance of their duties. Notwithstanding the second paragraph, the European Central Bank shall, in accordance with the general principles common to the laws of the Member States, make good any damage caused by it or by its servants in the performance of their duties. The personal liability of its servants towards the Union shall be governed by the provisions laid down in their Staff Regulations or in the Conditions of Employment applicable to them.

Article III-432   (ex Article 289 EC)

The seat of the Union's institutions shall be determined by common accord of the governments of the Member States.

Article III-433   (ex Article 290 EC)

The Council shall adopt unanimously a European regulation laying down the rules governing the languages of the Union's institutions, without prejudice to the Statute of the Court of Justice of the European Union.

Article III-434   (ex Article 291 EC)

The Union shall enjoy in the territories of the Member States such privileges and immunities as are necessary for the performance of its tasks, under the conditions laid down in the Protocol on the privileges and immunities of the European Union.

Article III-435   (ex Article 307 EC)

The rights and obligations arising from agreements concluded before 1 January 1958 or, for acceding States, before the date of their accession, between one or more Member States on the one hand, and one or more third countries on the other, shall not be affected by the Constitution.

To the extent that such agreements are not compatible with the Constitution, the Member State or States concerned shall take all appropriate steps to eliminate the incompatibilities established. Member States shall, where necessary, assist each other to this end and shall, where appropriate, adopt a common attitude. In applying the agreements referred to in the first paragraph, Member States shall take into account the fact that the advantages accorded under the Constitution by each Member State form an integral part of the Union and are thereby inseparably linked with the creation of institutions on which powers have been conferred by the Constitution and the granting of identical advantages by all the other Member States.

Article III-436   (ex Article 296 EC)

1.   The Constitution shall not preclude the application of the following rules:
   (a) no Member State shall be obliged to supply information the disclosure of which it considers contrary to the essential interests of its security;
   (b) any Member State may take such measures as it considers necessary for the protection of the essential interests of its security which are connected with the production of or trade in arms, munitions and war material; such measures shall not adversely affect the conditions of competition in the internal market regarding products which are not intended for specifically military purposes.

2.   The Council, on a proposal from the Commission, may unanimously adopt a European decision making changes to the list of 15 April 1958 of the products to which the provisions of paragraph 1(b) apply.

PART IV   GENERAL AND FINAL PROVISIONS

Article IV-437   (new) Repeal of earlier Treaties

1.   This Treaty establishing a Constitution for Europe shall repeal the Treaty establishing the European Community, the Treaty on European Union and, under the conditions laid down in the Protocol on the acts and treaties having supplemented or amended the Treaty establishing the European Community and the Treaty on European Union, the acts and treaties which have supplemented or amended them, subject to paragraph 2 of this Article.

2.   The Treaties on the Accession:
  (a) of the Kingdom of Denmark, Ireland and the United Kingdom of Great Britain and Northern Ireland;
  (b) of the Hellenic Republic;
  (c) of the Kingdom of Spain and the Portuguese Republic;
  (d) of the Republic of Austria, the Republic of Finland and the Kingdom of Sweden, and
  (e) of the Czech Republic, the Republic of Estonia, the Republic of Cyprus, the Republic of Latvia, the Republic of Lithuania, the Republic of Hungary, the Republic of Malta, the Republic of Poland, the Republic of Slovenia and the Slovak Republic, shall be repealed.

Nevertheless:
  — the provisions of the Treaties referred to in points (a) to (d) and set out or referred to in the Protocol on the Treaties and Acts of Accession of the Kingdom of Denmark, Ireland and the United Kingdom of Great Britain and Northern Ireland, of the Hellenic Republic, of the Kingdom of Spain and the Portuguese Republic, and of the Republic of Austria, the Republic of Finland and the Kingdom of Sweden shall remain in force and their legal effects shall be preserved in accordance with that Protocol,
  — the provisions of the Treaty referred to in point (e) and which are set out or referred to in the Protocol on the Treaty and Act of Accession of the Czech Republic, the Republic of Estonia, the Republic of Cyprus, the Republic of Latvia, the Republic of Lithuania, the Republic of Hungary, the Republic of Malta, the Republic of Poland, the Republic of Slovenia and the Slovak Republic shall remain in force and their legal effects shall be preserved in accordance with that Protocol.

Article IV-438   (new) Succession and legal continuity

1.   The European Union established by this Treaty shall be the successor to the European Union established by the Treaty on European Union and to the European Community.

2.   Until new provisions have been adopted in implementation of this Treaty or until the end of their term of office, the institutions, bodies, offices and agencies existing on the date of the entry into force of this Treaty shall, subject to Article IV-439, exercise their powers within the meaning of this Treaty in their composition on that date.

3.   The acts of the institutions, bodies, offices and agencies adopted on the basis of the treaties and acts repealed by Article IV-437 shall remain in force. Their legal effects shall be preserved until those acts are repealed, annulled or amended in implementation of this Treaty. The same shall apply to agreements concluded between Member States on the basis of the treaties and acts repealed by Article IV-437. The other components of the acquis of the Community and of the Union existing at the time of the entry into force of this Treaty, in particular the interinstitutional agreements, decisions and agreements arrived at by the Representatives of the Governments of the Member States, meeting within the Council, the agreements concluded by the Member States on the functioning of the Union or of the Community or linked to action by the Union or by the Community, the declarations, including those made in the context of intergovernmental conferences, as well as the resolutions or other positions adopted by the European Council or the Council and those relating to the Union or

to the Community adopted by common accord by the Member States, shall also be preserved until they have been deleted or amended.

4.   The case-law of the Court of Justice of the European Communities and of the Court of First Instance on the interpretation and application of the treaties and acts repealed by Article IV-437, as well as of the acts and conventions adopted for their application, shall remain, mutatis mutandis, the source of interpretation of Union law and in particular of the comparable provisions of the Constitution.

5.   Continuity in administrative and legal procedures commenced prior to the date of entry into force of this Treaty shall be ensured in compliance with the Constitution. The institutions, bodies, offices and agencies responsible for those procedures shall take all appropriate measures to that effect.

Article IV-439   (new) Transitional provisions relating to certain institutions

The transitional provisions relating to the composition of the European Parliament, to the definition of a qualified majority in the European Council and in the Council, including those cases where not all members of the European Council or Council vote, and to the composition of the Commission, including the Union Minister for Foreign Affairs, shall be laid down in the Protocol on the transitional provisions relating to the institutions and bodies of the Union.

Article IV-440   (ex Article 299 EC) Scope

1.   This Treaty shall apply to the Kingdom of Belgium, the Czech Republic, the Kingdom of Denmark, the Federal Republic of Germany, the Republic of Estonia, the Hellenic Republic, the Kingdom of Spain, the French Republic, Ireland, the Italian Republic, the Republic of Cyprus, the Republic of Latvia, the Republic of Lithuania, the Grand Duchy of Luxembourg, the Republic of Hungary, the Republic of Malta, the Kingdom of the Netherlands, the Republic of Austria, the Republic of Poland, the Portuguese Republic, the Republic of Slovenia, the Slovak Republic, the Republic of Finland, the Kingdom of Sweden and the United Kingdom of Great Britain and Northern Ireland.

2.   This Treaty shall apply to Guadeloupe, French Guiana, Martinique, Réunion, the Azores, Madeira and the Canary Islands in accordance with Article III-424.

3.   The special arrangements for association set out in Title IV of Part III shall apply to the overseas countries and territories listed in Annex II.

This Treaty shall not apply to overseas countries and territories having special relations with the United Kingdom of Great Britain and Northern Ireland which are not included in that list.

4.   This Treaty shall apply to the European territories for whose external relations a Member State is responsible.

5.   This Treaty shall apply to the Åland Islands with the derogations which originally appeared in the Treaty referred to in Article IV-437(2)(d) and which have been incorporated in Section 5 of Title V of the Protocol on the Treaties and Acts of Accession of the Kingdom of Denmark, Ireland and the United Kingdom of Great Britain and Northern Ireland, of the Hellenic Republic, of the Kingdom of Spain and the Portuguese Republic, and of the Republic of Austria, the Republic of Finland and the Kingdom of Sweden.

6.   Notwithstanding paragraphs 1 to 5:

   (a) this Treaty shall not apply to the Faeroe Islands;

   (b) this Treaty shall apply to Akrotiri and Dhekelia, the sovereign base areas of the United Kingdom of Great Britain and Northern Ireland in Cyprus, only to the extent necessary to ensure the implementation of the arrangements originally provided for in the Protocol on the Sovereign Base Areas of the United Kingdom of Great Britain and Northern Ireland in Cyprus, annexed to the Act of Accession which is an integral part of the Treaty referred to in Article IV-437(2)(e), and which have been incorporated in Title III of Part II of the Protocol on the Treaty and Act of Accession of the Czech Republic, the Republic of Estonia, the Republic of Cyprus, the Republic of Latvia, the Republic of Lithuania, the Republic of Hungary, the Republic of Malta, the Republic of Poland, the Republic of Slovenia and the Slovak Republic;

(c) this Treaty shall apply to the Channel Islands and the Isle of Man only to the extent necessary to ensure the implementation of the arrangements for those islands originally set out in the Treaty referred to in Article IV-437(2)(a), and which have been incorporated in Section 3 of Title II of Part IV the Protocol on the Treaties and Acts of Accession of the Kingdom of Denmark, Ireland and the United Kingdom of Great Britain and Northern Ireland, of the Hellenic Republic, of the Kingdom of Spain and the Portuguese Republic, and of the Republic of Austria, the Republic of Finland and the Kingdom of Sweden.

7.　The European Council may, on the initiative of the Member State concerned, adopt a European decision amending the status, with regard to the Union, of a Danish, French or Netherlands country or territory referred to in paragraphs 2 and 3. The European Council shall act unanimously after consulting the Commission.

Article IV-441　(ex Article 306 EC) Regional unions
This Treaty shall not preclude the existence or completion of regional unions between Belgium and Luxembourg, or between Belgium, Luxembourg and the Netherlands, to the extent that the objectives of these regional unions are not attained by application of the said Treaty.

Article IV-442　(ex Article 311 EC) Protocols and Annexes
The Protocols and Annexes to this Treaty shall form an integral part thereof.

Article IV-443　(ex Article 48 TEU) Ordinary revision procedure
1.　The government of any Member State, the European Parliament or the Commission may submit to the Council proposals for the amendment of this Treaty. These proposals shall be submitted to the European Council by the Council and the national Parliaments shall be notified.

2.　If the European Council, after consulting the European Parliament and the Commission, adopts by a simple majority a decision in favour of examining the proposed amendments, the President of the European Council shall convene a Convention composed of representatives of the national Parliaments, of the Heads of State or Government of the Member States, of the European Parliament and of the Commission. The European Central Bank shall also be consulted in the case of institutional changes in the monetary area. The Convention shall examine the proposals for amendments and shall adopt by consensus a recommendation to a conference of representatives of the governments of the Member States as provided for in paragraph 3.

The European Council may decide by a simple majority, after obtaining the consent of the European Parliament, not to convene a Convention should this not be justified by the extent of the proposed amendments. In the latter case, the European Council shall define the terms of reference for a conference of representatives of the governments of the Member States.

3.　A conference of representatives of the governments of the Member States shall be convened by the President of the Council for the purpose of determining by common accord the amendments to be made to this Treaty.

The amendments shall enter into force after being ratified by all the Member States in accordance with their respective constitutional requirements.

4.　If, two years after the signature of the treaty amending this Treaty, four fifths of the Member States have ratified it and one or more Member States have encountered difficulties in proceeding with ratification, the matter shall be referred to the European Council.

Article IV-444   (new) Simplified revision procedure

1.   Where Part III provides for the Council to act by unanimity in a given area or case, the European Council may adopt a European decision authorising the Council to act by a qualified majority in that area or in that case. This paragraph shall not apply to decisions with military implications or those in the area of defence.

2.   Where Part III provides for European laws and framework laws to be adopted by the Council in accordance with a special legislative procedure, the European Council may adopt a European decision allowing for the adoption of such European laws or framework laws in accordance with the ordinary legislative procedure.

3.   Any initiative taken by the European Council on the basis of paragraphs 1 or 2 shall be notified to the national Parliaments. If a national Parliament makes known its opposition within six months of the date of such notification, the European decision referred to in paragraphs 1 or 2 shall not be adopted. In the absence of opposition, the European Council may adopt the decision.

For the adoption of the European decisions referred to in paragraphs 1 and 2, the European Council shall act by unanimity after obtaining the consent of the European Parliament, which shall be given by a majority of its component members.

Article IV-445   (new) Simplified revision procedure concerning internal Union policies and action

1.   The Government of any Member State, the European Parliament or the Commission may submit to the European Council proposals for revising all or part of the provisions of Title III of Part III on the internal policies and action of the Union.

2.   The European Council may adopt a European decision amending all or part of the provisions of Title III of Part III. The European Council shall act by unanimity after consulting the European Parliament and the Commission, and the European Central Bank in the case of institutional changes in the monetary area.

Such a European decision shall not come into force until it has been approved by the Member States in accordance with their respective constitutional requirements.

3.   The European decision referred to in paragraph 2 shall not increase the competences conferred on the Union in this Treaty.

Article IV-446   (ex Articles 51 TEU and 312 EC) Duration

This Treaty is concluded for an unlimited period.

Article IV-447   (ex Articles 52 TEU and 313 EC) Ratification and entry into force

1.   This Treaty shall be ratified by the High Contracting Parties in accordance with their respective constitutional requirements. The instruments of ratification shall be deposited with the Government of the Italian Republic.

2.   This Treaty shall enter into force on 1 November 2006, provided that all the instruments of ratification have been deposited, or, failing that, on the first day of the second month following the deposit of the instrument of ratification by the last signatory State to take this step.

Article IV-448   (ex Articles 53 TEU and 314 EC) Authentic texts and translations

1.   This Treaty, drawn up in a single original in the Czech, Danish, Dutch, English, Estonian, Finnish, French, German, Greek, Hungarian, Irish, Italian, Latvian, Lithuanian, Maltese, Polish, Portuguese, Slovak, Slovenian, Spanish and Swedish languages, the texts in each of these languages being equally authentic, shall be deposited in the archives of the Government of the Italian Republic, which will transmit a certified copy to each of the governments of the other signatory States.

2.   This Treaty may also be translated into any other languages as determined by Member States among those which, in accordance with their constitutional order, enjoy official status

in all or part of their territory. A certified copy of such translations shall be provided by the Member States concerned to be deposited in the archives of the Council.

In witness whereof, the undersigned plenipotentiaries have signed this Treaty.

Done at . . . this . . .

(**Editor's Note:** Final Act list of signatories omitted.)

FINAL ACT[3]

THE CONFERENCE OF THE REPRESENTATIVES OF THE GOVERNMENTS OF THE MEMBER STATES, convened in Brussels on 30 September 2003 to adopt by common accord the Treaty establishing a Constitution for Europe, has adopted the following texts:

I. Treaty establishing a Constitution for Europe

II. Protocols annexed to the Treaty establishing a Constitution for Europe
1. Protocol on the role of national Parliaments in the European Union
2. Protocol on the application of the principles of subsidiarity and proportionality
3. Protocol on the Statute of the Court of Justice of the European Union
4. Protocol on the Statute of the European System of Central Banks and of the European Central Bank
5. Protocol on the Statute of the European Investment Bank
6. Protocol on the location of the seats of the institutions and of certain bodies, offices, agencies and departments of the European Union
7. Protocol on the privileges and immunities of the European Union
8. Protocol on the Treaties and Acts of Accession of the Kingdom of Denmark, Ireland and the United Kingdom of Great Britain and Northern Ireland, of the Hellenic Republic, of the Kingdom of Spain and the Portuguese Republic, and of the Republic of Austria, the Republic of Finland and the Kingdom of Sweden
9. Protocol on the Treaty and the Act of Accession of the Czech Republic, the Republic of Estonia, the Republic of Cyprus, the Republic of Latvia, the Republic of Lithuania, the Republic of Hungary, the Republic of Malta, the Republic of Poland, the Republic of Slovenia and the Slovak Republic
10. Protocol on the excessive deficit procedure
11. Protocol on the convergence criteria
12. Protocol on the Euro Group
13. Protocol on certain provisions relating to the United Kingdom of Great Britain and Northern Ireland as regards economic and monetary union
14. Protocol on certain provisions relating to Denmark as regards economic and monetary union
15. Protocol on certain tasks of the National Bank of Denmark
16. Protocol on the Pacific Financial Community franc system
17. Protocol on the Schengen acquis integrated into the framework of the European Union
18. Protocol on the application of certain aspects of Article III-130 of the Constitution to the United Kingdom and to Ireland

---

[3] Until the Constitutional Treaty comes into force, this collection will carry only the list, and not the text, of Annexes, Protocols and Declarations with the exception of the Protocol on the transitional provisions relating to the institutions and bodies of the Union and Declaration 40 on transitional arrangements for Bulgaria and Romania which are reproduced following.

19. Protocol on the position of the United Kingdom and Ireland on policies in respect of border controls, asylum and immigration, judicial cooperation in civil matters and on police cooperation
20. Protocol on the position of Denmark
21. Protocol on external relations of the Member States with regard to the crossing of external borders
22. Protocol on asylum for nationals of Member States
23. Protocol on permanent structured cooperation established by Article I-41(6) and Article III-312 of the Constitution
24. Protocol on Article I-41(2) of the Constitution
25. Protocol concerning imports into the European Union of petroleum products refined in the Netherlands Antilles
26. Protocol on the acquisition of property in Denmark
27. Protocol on the system of public broadcasting in the Member States
28. Protocol concerning Article III-214 of the Constitution
29. Protocol on economic, social and territorial cohesion
30. Protocol on special arrangements for Greenland
31. Protocol on Article 40.3.3 of the Constitution of Ireland
32. Protocol relating to Article I-9(2) of the Constitution on the accession of the Union to the European Convention on the Protection of Human Rights and Fundamental Freedoms Treaty establishing a Constitution for Europe
33. Protocol on the Acts and Treaties which have supplemented or amended the Treaty establishing the European Community and the Treaty on European Union
34. Protocol on the transitional provisions relating to the institutions and bodies of the Union
35. Protocol on the financial consequences of the expiry of the Treaty establishing the European Coal and Steel Community and on the Research Fund for Coal and Steel
36. Protocol amending the Treaty establishing the European Atomic Energy Community

III. Annexes to the Treaty establishing a Constitution for Europe:
1. Annex I—List referred to in Article III-226 of the Constitution
2. Annex II—Overseas countries and territories to which Title IV of Part III of the Constitution applies

The Conference has adopted the following declarations annexed to this Final Act.

A. Declarations concerning provisions of the Constitution
1. Declaration on Article I-6
2. Declaration on Article I-9(2)
3. Declaration on Articles I-22, 1–27 and 1–28
4. Declaration on Article I-24(7) concerning the European Council decision on the exercise of the Presidency of the Council
5. Declaration on Article I-25
6. Declaration on Article I-26
7. Declaration on Article I-27
8. Declaration on Article I-36
9. Declaration on Articles I-43 and III-329
10. Declaration on Article I-51
11. Declaration on Article I-57
12. Declaration concerning the explanations relating to the Charter of Fundamental Rights
13. Declaration on Article III-116
14. Declaration on Articles III-136 and III-267
15. Declaration on Articles III-160 and III-322
16. Declaration on Article III-167(2)(c)

17. Declaration on Article III-184
18. Declaration on Article III-213
19. Declaration on Article III-220
20. Declaration on Article III-243
21. Declaration on Article III-248
22. Declaration on Article III-256
23. Declaration on Article III-273(1), second subparagraph
24. Declaration on Article III-296
25. Declaration on Article III-325 concerning the negotiation and conclusion of international agreements by Member States relating to the area of freedom, security and justice
26. Declaration on Article III-402(4)
27. Declaration on Article III-419
28. Declaration on Article IV-440(7)
29. Declaration on Article IV-448(2)
30. Declaration on the ratification of the Treaty establishing a Constitution for Europe

B. Declarations concerning Protocols annexed to the Constitution
Declarations concerning the Protocol on the Treaties and Acts of Accession of the Kingdom of Denmark, Ireland and the United Kingdom of Great Britain and Northern Ireland, of the Hellenic Republic, of the Kingdom of Spain and the Portuguese Republic, and of the Republic of Austria, the Republic of Finland and the Kingdom of Sweden

31. Declaration on the Åland islands
32. Declaration on the Sami people

Declarations concerning the Protocol on the Treaty and the Act of Accession of the Czech Republic, the Republic of Estonia, the Republic of Cyprus, the Republic of Latvia, the Republic of Lithuania, the Republic of Hungary, the Republic of Malta, the Republic of Poland, the Republic of Slovenia and the Slovak Republic

33. Declaration on the Sovereign Base Areas of the United Kingdom of Great Britain and Northern Ireland in Cyprus
34. Declaration by the Commission on the Sovereign Base Areas of the United Kingdom of Great Britain and Northern Ireland in Cyprus
35. Declaration on the Ignalina Nuclear Power Plant in Lithuania
36. Declaration on the transit of persons by land between the region of Kaliningrad and other parts of the Russian Federation
37. Declaration on Unit 1 and Unit 2 of the Bohunice V1 nuclear power plant in Slovakia
38. Declaration on Cyprus
39. Declaration concerning the Protocol on the position of Denmark
40. Declaration concerning the Protocol on the transitional provisions relating to the institutions and Bodies of the Union
41. Declaration concerning Italy

Furthermore, the Conference has noted the declarations listed hereafter and annexed to this Final Act:

42. Declaration by the Kingdom of the Netherlands on Article I-55
43. Declaration by the Kingdom of the Netherlands on Article IV-440
44. Declaration by the Federal Republic of Germany, Ireland, the Republic of Hungary, the Republic of Austria and the Kingdom of Sweden
45. Declaration by the Kingdom of Spain and the United Kingdom of Great Britain and Northern Ireland
46. Declaration by the United Kingdom of Great Britain and Northern Ireland on the definition of the term 'nationals'
47. Declaration by the Kingdom of Spain on the definition of the term 'nationals'

48. Declaration by the United Kingdom of Great Britain and Northern Ireland on the franchise for elections to the European Parliament
49. Declaration by the Kingdom of Belgium on national parliaments
50. Declaration by the Republic of Latvia and the Republic of Hungary on the spelling of the name of the single currency in the Treaty establishing a Constitution for Europe.

Table of Equivalences between the Constitutional Treaty and the EC and EU Treaties*

Constitutional Treaty Numbers	EC & TEU Numbers
Article III-115	new
Article III-116	Article 32 EC
Article III-125	Article 18 EC
Article III-126	Article 19 EC
Article III-127	Article 20 EC
Article III-128	Article 21 EC
Article III-129	Article 22 EC
Article III-130	Articles 14 and 15 EC
Article III-131	Article 297 EC
Article III-132	Article 298 EC
Article III-133	Article 39 EC
Article III-134	Article 40 EC
Article III-135	Article 41 EC
Article III-136	Article 42 EC
Article III-137	Article 43 EC
Article III-138	Article 44 EC
Article III-139	Article 45 EC
Article III-140	Article 46 EC
Article III-141	Article 47 EC
Article III-142	Article 48 EC
Article III-143	Article 294 EC
Article III-144	Article 49 EC
Article III-145	Article 50 EC
Article III-146	Article 51 EC
Article III-147	Article 52 EC
Article III-148	Article 53 EC
Article III-149	Article 54 EC
Article III-150	Article 55 EC
Article III-151	Articles 23 to 27 EC
Article III-152	Article 135 EC
Article III-153	Articles 28 and 29 EC
Article III-154	Article 30 EC
Article III-155	Article 31 EC
Article III-156	Article 56 EC
Article III-157	Article 57 EC
Article III-158	Article 58 EC
Article III-159	Article 59 EC
Article III-160	Article 60 EC
Article III-161	Article 81 EC
Article III-162	Article 82 EC
Article III-163	Article 83 EC

* **Editor's Note:** This is not an official table, it is one compiled by the editor.

Constitutional Treaty Numbers	EC & TEU Numbers
Article III-164	Article 84 EC
Article III-165	Article 85 EC
Article III-166	Article 86 EC
Article III-167	Article 87 EC
Article III-168	Article 88 EC
Article III-169	Article 89 EC
Article III-170	Articles 90 to 92 EC
Article III-170	Articles 90 to 92 EC
Article III-171	Article 93 EC
Article III-172	Article 95 EC
Article III-173	Article 94 EC
Article III-174	Article 96 EC
Article III-175	Article 97 EC
Article III-176	new
Article III-177	Article 4 EC
Article III-178	Article 98 EC
Article III-179	Article 99 EC
Article III-180	Article 100 EC
Article III-181	Article 101 EC
Article III-182	Article 102 EC
Article III-183	Article 103 EC
Article III-184	Article 104 EC
Article III-185	Article 105 EC
Article III-186	Article 106 EC
Article III-187	Article 107 EC
Article III-188	Article 108 EC
Article III-189	Article 109 EC
Article III-190	Article 110 EC
Article III-191	Article 123 4 EC
Article III-192	Article 114 2 to 4 EC
Article III-193	Article 115 EC)
Article III-194	new
Article III-195	new
Article III-196	new
Article III-197	Article 1221 and 3 to 5 EC
Article III-198	Articles 121, 122 2 and 123 5 EC
Article III-199	Articles 123 3 and 117 2 EC
Article III-200	Article 124 1 EC
Article III-201	Article 119 EC
Article III-202	Article 120 EC
Article III-203	Article 125 EC
Article III-204	Article 126 EC
Article III-205	Article 127 EC
Article III-206	Article 128 EC
Article III-207	Article 129 EC
Article III-208	Article 130 EC
Article III-209	Article 136 EC
Article III-210	Article 137 EC
Article III-211	Article 138 EC
Article III-212	Article 139 EC
Article III-213	Article 140 EC
Article III-214	Article 141 EC
Article III-215	Article 142 EC
Article III-216	Article 143 EC
Article III-217	Article 144 EC

Constitutional Treaty Numbers	EC & TEU Numbers
Article III-218	Article 145 EC
Article III-219	Articles 146–148 EC
Article III-220	Article 158 EC
Article III-221	Article 159 EC
Article III-222	Article 160 EC
Article III-223	Article 161 EC
Article III-224	Article 162 EC
Article III-225	Article 32 1, second sentence, EC
Article III-226	Article 32 1, first sentence, and 2 to 4 EC
Article III-227	Article 33 EC
Article III-228	Article 34 EC
Article III-229	Article 35 EC
Article III-230	Article 36 EC
Article III-231	Article 37 EC
Article III-232	Article 38 EC
Article III-233	Article 174 EC
Article III-234	Articles 175 and 176 EC
Article III-235	Article 153 EC
Article III-236	Articles 133 and 134 EC
Article III-237	Article 72 EC
Article III-238	Article 73 EC
Article III-239	Article 74 EC
Article III-240	Article 75 EC
Article III-241	Article 76 EC
Article III-242	Article 77 EC
Article III-243	Article 78 EC
Article III-244	Article 79 EC
Article III-245	Article 80 EC
Article III-246	Article 154 EC
Article III-247	Article 155 EC
Article III-248	Article 163 EC
Article III-249	Article 164 EC
Article III-250	Article 165 EC
Article III-251	Article 166 EC
Article III-252	Articles 167 to 170 & 2nd paragraph of ex Article 172 EC
Article III-253	Article 171 & 1st paragraph of Article 172 EC
Article III-254	new
Article III-255	Article 173 EC
Article III-256	new
Article III-257	Articles 29 TEU and 61 EC
Article III-258	new
Article III-259	new
Article III-260	new
Article III-261	Article 36 TEU
Article III-262	Articles 33 TEU and 64 EC
Article III-263	Article 66 EC
Article III-264	new
Article III-265	Article 62 EC
Article III-266	Article 63, points 1 and 2, and Article 64 2 EC
Article III-267	Article 63, points 3 and 4, EC
Article III-268	new

Constitutional Treaty Numbers	EC & TEU Numbers
Article III-269	Article 65 EC
Article III-270	Article 31 1 TEU
Article III-271	new
Article III-272	new
Article III-273	Article 31 2 TEU
Article III-274	new
Article III-275	Article 30 1 TEU
Article III-276	Article 30 2 TEU
Article III-277	Article 32 TEU
Article III-278	Article 152 EC
Article III-279	Article 157 EC
Article III-280	Article 151 EC
Article III-281	new
Article III-282	Article 149 EC
Article III-283	Article 150 EC
Article III-284	new
Article III-285	new
Article III-286	Article 182 EC
Article III-287	Article 183 EC
Article III-288	Article 184 EC
Article III-288	Article 184 EC
Article III-290	Article 186 EC
Article III-291	Article 187 EC
Article III-292	Article 3, second paragraph & Article 11 TEU
Article III-293	new
Article III-294	Articles 11 and 12 TEU
Article III-295	Article 13 TEU
Article III-296	Articles 18 and 26 TEU
Article III-297	Article 14 TEU
Article III-298	Article 15 TEU
Article III-299	Article 22 TEU
Article III-300	Article 23 TEU
Article III-301	new
Article III-302	Article 18 5 TEU
Article III-303	Article 24 TEU
Article III-304	Article 21 TEU
Article III-305	Article 19 TEU
Article III-306	Article 20 TEU
Article III-307	Article 25 EC
Article III-308	Articles 46 f and 47 TEU
Article III-309	Article 17 TEU
Article III-310	new
Article III-311	new
Article III-312	new
Article III-313	Article 28 TEU
Article III-314	Article 131 EC
Article III-315	Article 133 EC
Article III-316	Article 177 EC
Article III-317	Articles 179 and 181 EC
Article III-318	Articles 180 and 181 EC
Article III-319	Article 181a EC
Article III-320	new
Article III-321	new
Article III-322	Article 301 EC

Constitutional Treaty Numbers	EC & TEU Numbers
Article III-323	Article 300 7 EC
Article III-324	Article 310 EC
Article III-325	Article 300 EC
Article III-326	Article 111 EC
Article III-327	Articles 302 and 303 EC
Article III-328	new
Article III-329	new
Article III-330	Article 190 EC
Article III-331	Article 191 EC
Article III-332	Article 192 EC
Article III-333	Article 193 EC
Article III-334	Article 194 EC
Article III-335	Article 195 EC
Article III-336	Article 196 EC
Article III-337	Articles 197 and 200 EC
Article III-338	Article 198 EC
Article III-339	Article 199 EC
Article III-340	Article 201 EC
Article III-341	new
Article III-342	Articles 203 and 204 EC
Article III-343	Articles 205 and 206 EC
Article III-344	Article 207 EC
Article III-345	Article 208 EC
Article III-347	Article 214 2 EC
Article III-348	Article 215 EC
Article III-349	Article 216 EC
Article III-350	Article 217 EC
Article III-351	Article 219 EC
Article III-352	Articles 212 and 218 EC
Article III-353	Article 221 EC
Article III-354	Article 222 EC
Article III-355	Article 223 EC
Article III-356	Article 224 EC
Article III-357	new
Article III-358	Article 225 EC
Article III-359	Article 225a EC
Article III-360	Article 226 EC
Article III-361	Article 227 EC
Article III-362	Article 228 EC
Article III-363	Article 229 EC
Article III-364	Article 229 a EC
Article III-365	Article 270 EC
Article III-366	Article 231 EC
Article III-367	Article 232 EC
Article III-368	Article 233 EC
Article III-369	Article 234 EC
Article III-370	Article 235 EC
Article III-371	Article 46 e TEU
Article III-372	Article 236 EC
Article III-373	Article 237 EC
Article III-374	Article 238 EC
Article III-375	Articles 239, 240 and 292 EC
Article III-376	new
Article III-377	new
Article III-378	Article 241 EC

Constitutional Treaty Numbers	EC & TEU Numbers
Article III-379	Articles 242 and 243 EC
Article III-380	Article 244 EC
Article III-381	Article 245 EC
Article III-382	Article 112 EC
Article III-383	Article 113 EC
Article III-384	Article 248 EC
Article III-385	Article 247 EC
Article III-386	Article 263 EC
Article III-387	Article 264 EC
Article III-388	Article 265 EC
Article III-389	Article 258 EC
Article III-390	Article 259 EC
Article III-391	Article 260 EC
Article III-392	Article 262 EC
Article III-393	Article 266 EC
Article III-394	Article 267 EC
Article III-395	Article 250 EC
Article III 396	Article 251 EC
Article III-397	Article 218 EC and new provision
Article III-398	new
Article III-399	Article 255 EC
Article III-400	Articles 210 and 247 8 EC
Article III-401	Article 256 EC
Article III-402	new
Article III-403	Article 272 EC
Article III-404	Article 272 EC
Article III-405	Article 273 EC
Article III-406	Article 271 EC
Article III-407	Article 274 EC
Article III-408	Article 275 EC
Article III-409	Article 276 EC
Article III-410	Article 277 EC
Article III-411	Article 278 EC
Article III-412	Article 279 EC
Article III-413	new
Article III-414	new
Article III-415	Article 280 EC
Article III-416	Article 43 TEU
Article III-417	Articles 43 h and 44 2 TEU
Article III-418	Article 43B TEU and new provisions
Article III-419	Article 27C TEU
Article III-420	Article 27E TEU
Article III-421	Article 44A TEU
Article III-422	new
Article III-423	Article 45 TEU
Article III-424	Article 299 EC
Article III-425	Article 295 EC
Article III-426	Article 282 EC
Article III-427	Article 282 EC
Article III-428	Article 284 EC
Article III-429	Article 285 EC
Article III-430	Article 287 EC
Article III-431	Article 288 EC
Article III-432	Article 289 EC
Article III-433	Article 290 EC

Constitutional Treaty Numbers	EC & TEU Numbers
Article III-434	Article 291 EC
Article III-435	Article 307 EC
Article III-436	Article 296 EC
PART IV	
Article IV-437	new
Article IV-438	new
Article IV-439	new
Article IV-440	Article 299 EC
Article IV-441	Article 306 EC
Article IV-442	Article 311 EC
Article IV-443	Article 48 TEU
Article IV-444	new
Article IV-445	new
Article IV-446	Articles 51 TEU and 312 EC
Article IV-447	Articles 52 TEU and 313 EC
Article IV-448	Articles 53 TEU and 314 EC

Compiled by Nigel Foster, May 2005

Protocol on the Transitional Provisions relating to the Institutions and Bodies of the Union

THE HIGH CONTRACTING PARTIES,

WHEREAS, in order to organise the transition between the European Union established by the Treaty on European Union and the European Community and the European Union established by the Treaty establishing a Constitution for Europe which is their successor, it is necessary to lay down transitional provisions which will apply before all the provisions of the Constitution and the instruments necessary for their implementation take full effect,

HAVE AGREED UPON the following provisions, which shall be annexed to the Treaty establishing a Constitution for Europe and to the Treaty establishing the European Atomic Energy Community:

TITLE 1   PROVISIONS CONCERNING THE EUROPEAN PARLIAMENT

Article 1

1.   In accordance with Article I-19(2) of the Constitution, the European Council shall adopt a European decision determining the composition of the European Parliament sufficiently in advance of the 2009 parliamentary elections.

2.   During the 2004–2009 parliamentary term, the composition and the number of representatives elected to the European Parliament in each Member State shall remain the same as on the date of the entry into force of the Treaty establishing a Constitution for Europe, the number of representatives being as follows:

Belgium 24
Czech Republic 24
Denmark 14
Germany 99
Estonia 6
Greece 24

Spain 54
France 78
Ireland 13
Italy 78
Cyprus 6
Latvia 9
Lithuania 13
Luxembourg 6
Hungary 24
Malta 5
Netherlands 27
Austria 18
Poland 54
Portugal 24
Slovenia 7
Slovakia 14
Finland 14
Sweden 19
United Kingdom 78

TITLE 2   PROVISIONS CONCERNING THE EUROPEAN COUNCIL AND THE COUNCIL OF MINISTERS

Article 2

1.   The provisions of Article I-24(1) (2) and (2a) of the Constitution on the definition of the qualified majority in the European Council and the Council shall take effect on 1 November 2009, after the 2009 European Parliament elections have taken place in accordance with Article I-19(2).

2.   The following provisions shall remain in force until 31 October 2009, without prejudice to Article I-24 of the Constitution.

For acts of the European Council and of the Council requiring a qualified majority, Members' votes shall be weighted as follows:
Belgium 12
Czech Republic 12
Denmark 7
Germany 29
Estonia 4
Greece 12
Spain 27
France 29
Ireland 7
Italy 29
Cyprus 4
Latvia 4
Lithuania 7
Luxembourg 4
Hungary 12
Malta 3
Netherlands 13
Austria 10
Poland 27
Portugal 12

Slovenia 4
Slovakia 7
Finland 7
Sweden 10
United Kingdom 29

Acts shall be adopted if there are at least 232 votes in favour representing a majority of the members where, under the Constitution, they must be adopted on a proposal from the Commission.

In other cases decisions shall be adopted if there are at least 232 votes in favour representing at least two thirds of the members.

A member of the European Council or the Council may request that, where an act is adopted by the European Council or the Council by a qualified majority, a check is made to ensure that the Member States comprising the qualified majority represent at least 62% of the total population of the Union. If that proves not to be the case, the act shall not be adopted.

    3.   For subsequent accessions, the threshold referred to in paragraph 2 shall be calculated to ensure that the qualified majority threshold expressed in votes does not exceed that resulting from the table in the Declaration on the enlargement of the European Union in the Final Act of the Conference which adopted the Treaty of Nice.

    4.   The provisions of the following Articles shall take effect on 1 November 2009:
— Article I-43(3), third, fourth and fifth subparagraphs, of the Constitution;
— Article I-58(5), second and third subparagraphs, of the Constitution;
— Article I-59(3a), second subparagraph, of the Constitution;
— Article III-71(4), third and fourth subparagraphs, of the Constitution;
— Article III-76(6), third and fourth subparagraphs, of the Constitution;
— Article III-76(7), third and fourth subparagraphs, of the Constitution;
— Article III-88(2), second and third subparagraphs, of the Constitution;
— Article III-90(3), second and third subparagraphs, of the Constitution;
— Article III-91(4), second and third subparagraphs, of the Constitution;
— Article III-92(2), third subparagraph, of the Constitution;
— Article III-213(3), third and fourth subparagraphs, of the Constitution;
— Article III-213(4) third and fourth subparagraphs, of the Constitution;
— Article 1, second, third and fourth subparagraphs, and Article 3(1), second, third and fourth subparagraphs, of the Protocol on the position of the United Kingdom and Ireland on policies in respect of border controls, asylum and immigration, on judicial cooperation in civil matters and on police cooperation;
— Article 1, second, third and fourth subparagraphs, of the Protocol on the position on Denmark and Article 1, second, third and fourth subparagraphs, of the Annex to that Protocol.

Until 31 October 2009, the qualified majority shall, in cases where not all the members of the Council participate in voting, namely in the cases referred to in the articles mentioned in the first subparagraph, be defined as the same proportion of the weighted votes and the same proportion of the number of the Council members and, if appropriate, the same percentage of the population of the Member States concerned as laid down in paragraph 2.

Article 3

Until entry into force of the decision referred to in Article I-23(3) of the Constitution, the Council may meet in the configurations laid down in Article I-23(1) and (2) and in the other configurations on the list established by a decision of the General Affairs Council, acting by a simple majority.

TITLE 3   PROVISIONS CONCERNING THE COMMISSION, INCLUDING THE UNION'S MINISTER OF FOREIGN AFFAIRS

Article 4

The Members of the Commission in office on the date of entry into force of the Treaty establishing a Constitution for Europe shall remain in office until the end of their term of office. However, on the day of the appointment of the Union Minister for Foreign Affairs, the term of office of the Member having the same nationality as the Union Minister for Foreign Affairs shall end.

TITLE 3A   PROVISIONS CONCERNING THE SECRETARY-GENERAL OF THE COUNCIL, HIGH REPRESENTATIVE FOR THE COMMON FOREIGN AND SECURITY POLICY AND THE DEPUTY SECRETARY-GENERAL OF THE COUNCIL

Article 4a

The terms of office of the Secretary-General of the Council, High Representative for the common foreign and security policy and the Deputy Secretary-General of the Council shall end on the date of entry into force of the Treaty establishing a Constitution for Europe. The Council shall appoint a Secretary-General in conformity with Article III-247(2) of the Constitution.

TITLE 4   PROVISIONS CONCERNING ADVISORY BODIES

Article 5

Until entry into force of the decision referred to in Article III-292, the allocation of members of the Committee of the Regions shall be as follows:

Belgium 12
Czech Republic 12
Denmark 9
Germany 24
Estonia 7
Greece 12
Spain 21
France 24
Ireland 9
Italy 24
Cyprus 6
Latvia 7
Lithuania 9
Luxembourg 6
Hungary 12
Malta 5
Netherlands 12
Austria 12
Poland 21
Portugal 12
Slovenia 7
Slovakia 9
Finland 9
Sweden 12
United Kingdom 24

Article 6

Until entry into force of the decision referred to in Article III-295, the allocation of members of the Economic and Social Committee shall be as follows:

Belgium 12
Czech Republic 12
Denmark 9
Germany 24
Estonia 7
Greece 12
Spain 21
France 24
Ireland 9
Italy 24
Cyprus 6
Latvia 7
Lithuania 9
Luxembourg 6
Hungary 12
Malta 5
Netherlands 12
Austria 12
Poland 21
Portugal 12
Slovenia 7
Slovakia 9
Finland 9
Sweden 12
United Kingdom 24

Declaration 40 on Bulgaria and Romania

40.　Declaration concerning the Protocol on the transitional provisions relating to the institutions and bodies of the Union

The common position which will be taken by the Member States at the conferences on the accession to the Union of Romania and/or Bulgaria regarding the allocation of seats in the European Parliament and the weighting of votes in the European Council and the Council will be as follows.

1.　If the accession to the Union of Romania and/or Bulgaria takes place before the entry into force of the European Council Decision referred to in Article I-20(2), the allocation of seats in the European Parliament throughout the 2004–2009 parliamentary term will be in accordance with the following table for a Union of 27 Member States.

Member States	Seats in the EP
Germany	99
United Kingdom	78
France	78
Italy	78
Spain	54
Poland	54
Romania	35
Netherlands	27
Greece	24
Czech Republic	24
Belgium	24
Hungary	24
Portugal	24
Sweden	19
Bulgaria	18
Austria	18
Slovakia	14
Denmark	14
Finland	14
Ireland	13
Lithuania	13
Latvia	9
Slovenia	7
Estonia	6
Cyprus	6
Luxembourg	6
Malta	5
TOTAL	785

The Treaty of Accession to the Union will therefore, by way of derogation from Article I-20(2) of the Constitution, stipulate that the number of members of the European Parliament may temporarily exceed 750 for the remainder of the 2004 to 2009 Parliamentary term.

2. In Article 2(2) of the Protocol on the transitional provisions relating to the institutions and bodies of the Union, the weighting of the votes of Romania and Bulgaria in the European Council and the Council will be set at 14 and 10 respectively.

3. At the time of each accession, the threshold referred to in the Protocol on the transitional provisions relating to the institutions and bodies of the Union will be calculated according to Article 2(3) of that Protocol.

Annexes referred to in Commission Memo/04/61
16th March 2004*

ANNEX I   THE COUNCIL OF THE EUROPEAN UNION

Member States	Current vote weighting EU-15	Vote weighting EU-25 01.05.04 to 31.10.04	Vote weighting EU-25 from 1.11.04	Vote weighting EU-27
Germany	10	10	29	29
United Kingdom	10	10	29	29
France	10	10	29	29
Italy	10	10	29	29
Spain	8	8	27	27
Poland	—	8	27	27
Romania	—	—	—	14
Netherlands	5	5	13	13
Greece	5	5	12	12
Czech Republic	—	5	12	12
Belgium	5	5	12	12
Hungary	—	5	12	12
Portugal	5	5	12	12
Sweden	4	4	10	10
Bulgaria	—	—	—	10
Austria	4	4	10	10
Slovakia	—	3	7	7
Denmark	3	3	7	7
Finland	3	3	7	7
Ireland	3	3	7	7
Lithuania	—	3	7	7
Latvia	—	3	4	4
Slovenia	—	3	4	4
Estonia	—	3	4	4
Cyprus	—	2	4	4
Luxembourg	2	2	4	4
Malta	—	2	3	3
Total	87	124	321	345
Qualified majority	62 (71.26%)	88 (70.97%)	232 (72.27%)	255 (73.91%)
Blocking minority	26	37	90	91

* To be found at and taken from http://europa.eu.int/rapid/pressReleaseAction.do?reference=MEMO/04/61&format=HTML&aged=0&language=EN&guiLanguage=en. I am grateful for the permission to reproduce these document annexes from that source in accordance with the legal notice attached to the document. Please note though that 'Only European Community official documents printed in the Official Journal of the European Union are deemed authentic'.

ANNEX II   THE EUROPEAN PARLIAMENT

Member States	Seats until 01.05.04	Seats EU-25 (2004–2009)	Seats EU-27	EU-25 Seat % under Nice	% of EU-25 Population*
Germany	99	99	99	13.52%	18.17%
United Kingdom	87	78	72	10.66%	13.18%
France	87	78	72	10.66%	13.06%
Italy	87	78	72	10.66%	12.75%
Spain	64	54	50	7.38%	8.89%
Poland	—	54	50	7.38%	8.53%
Romania	—	—	33	—	—
Netherlands	31	27	25	3.69%	3.54%
Greece	25	24	22	3.28%	2.33%
Portugal	25	24	22	3.28%	2.27%
Belgium	25	24	22	3.28%	2.27%
Czech Republic	—	24	20	3.28%	2.27%
Hungary	—	24	20	3.28%	2.25%
Sweden	22	19	18	2.60%	1.96%
Austria	21	18	17	2.46%	1.79%
Bulgaria	—	—	17	—	—
Slovakia	—	14	13	1.91%	1.19%
Denmark	16	14	13	1.91%	1.18%
Finland	16	14	13	1.91%	1.14%
Ireland	15	13	12	1.78%	0.85%
Lithuania	—	13	12	1.78%	0.77%
Latvia	—	9	8	1.23%	0.52%
Slovenia	—	7	7	0.96%	0.44%
Estonia	—	6	6	0.82%	0.30%
Cyprus	—	6	6	0.82%	0.17%
Luxembourg	6	6	6	0.82%	0.10%
Malta	—	5	5	0.68%	0.09%
Total	626	732	732	100%	100%

Note: the draft Constitution as proposed by the Convention foresees a total number of 736 MEPs[1]

* Based on Eurostat 2001 population figures, except for Italy, UK, Cyprus, Estonia and Romania (2000 figures) and Greece (1999 figures).
[1] **Editor's Note:** Agreed under the Constitutional Treaty to be raised to 750 from 2009.

PART I

Primary Legislation

Consolidated Version of the Treaty Establishing the European Community[1]

PREAMBLE

HIS MAJESTY THE KING OF THE BELGIANS, THE PRESIDENT OF THE FEDERAL REPUBLIC OF GERMANY, THE PRESIDENT OF THE FRENCH REPUBLIC, THE PRESIDENT OF THE ITALIAN REPUBLIC, HER ROYAL HIGHNESS THE GRAND DUCHESS OF LUXEMBOURG, HER MAJESTY THE QUEEN OF THE NETHERLANDS,[2]

DETERMINED to lay the foundations of an ever closer union among the peoples of Europe,

RESOLVED to ensure the economic and social progress of their countries by common action to eliminate the barriers which divide Europe,

AFFIRMING as the essential objective of their efforts the constant improvements of the living and working conditions of their peoples,

RECOGNISING that the removal of existing obstacles calls for concerted action in order to guarantee steady expansion, balanced trade and fair competition,

ANXIOUS to strengthen the unity of their economies and to ensure their harmonious development by reducing the differences existing between the various regions and the backwardness of the less-favoured regions,

DESIRING to contribute, by means of a common commercial policy, to the progressive abolition of restrictions on international trade,

INTENDING to confirm the solidarity which binds Europe and the overseas countries and desiring to ensure the development of their prosperity, in accordance with the principles of the Charter of the United Nations,

RESOLVED by thus pooling their resources to preserve and strengthen peace and liberty, and calling upon the other peoples of Europe who share their ideal to join in their efforts,

DETERMINED to promote the development of the highest possible level of knowledge for their peoples through a wide access to education and through its continuous updating,

HAVE DECIDED to create a EUROPEAN COMMUNITY and to this end have designated as their Plenipotentiaries:

HIS MAJESTY THE KING OF THE BELGIANS:
Mr Paul Henri SPAAK, Minister for Foreign Affairs,

---

[1] **Editor's Note:** As amended in accordance with the Treaty of Nice Consolidated Version (OJ 2002 C325/1–184) and the 2003 Accession Treaty (OJ 2003 L236/17).

[2] The Kingdom of Denmark, the Hellenic Republic, the Kingdom of Spain, Ireland, the Republic of Austria, the Portuguese Republic, the Republic of Finland, the Kingdom of Sweden and the United Kingdom of Great Britain and Northern Ireland have since become members of the European Community, as have since 1st May 2004, the Czech Republic, Estonia, Cyprus, Latvia, Lithuania, Hungary, Malta, Poland, Slovenia and Slovakia.

Baron J. Ch. SNOY ET D'OPPUERS, Secretary General of the Ministry of Economic Affairs, Head of the Belgian Delegation to the Intergovernmental Conference;

THE PRESIDENT OF THE FEDERAL REPUBLIC OF GERMANY:
Dr. Konrad ADENAUER, Federal Chancellor,
Professor Dr. Walter HALLSTEIN, State Secretary of the Federal Foreign Office;

THE PRESIDENT OF THE FRENCH REPUBLIC:
Mr Christian PINEAU, Minister for Foreign Affairs,
Mr Maurice FAURE, Under Secretary of State for Foreign Affairs;

THE PRESIDENT OF THE ITALIAN REPUBLIC:
Mr Antonio SEGNI, President of the Council of Ministers,
Professor Gaetano MARTINO, Minister for Foreign Affairs;

HER ROYAL HIGHNESS THE GRAND DUCHESS OF LUXEMBOURG:
Mr Joseph BECH, President of the Government, Minister for Foreign Affairs,
Mr Lambert SCHAUS, Ambassador, Head of the Luxembourg Delegation to the Intergovernmental Conference;

HER MAJESTY THE QUEEN OF THE NETHERLANDS:
Mr Joseph LUNS, Minister for Foreign Affairs,
Mr J. LINTHORST HOMAN, Head of the Netherlands Delegation to the Intergovernmental Conference;

WHO, having exchanged their full powers, found in good and due form, have agreed as follows.

PART ONE   PRINCIPLES

Article 1   (ex Article 1)
By this Treaty, the HIGH CONTRACTING PARTIES establish among themselves a EUROPEAN COMMUNITY.

Article 2   (ex Article 2)
The Community shall have as its task, by establishing a common market and an economic and monetary union and by implementing common policies or activities referred to in Articles 3 and 4, to promote throughout the Community a harmonious, balanced and sustainable development of economic activities, a high level of employment and of social protection, equality between men and women, sustainable and non inflationary growth, a high degree of competitiveness and convergence of economic performance, a high level of protection and improvement of the quality of the environment, the raising of the standard of living and quality of life, and economic and social cohesion and solidarity among Member States.

Article 3   (ex Article 3)
   1.   For the purposes set out in Article 2, the activities of the Community shall include, as provided in this Treaty and in accordance with the timetable set out therein:
   (a) the prohibition, as between Member States, of customs duties and quantitative restrictions on the import and export of goods, and of all other measures having equivalent effect;
   (b) a common commercial policy;
   (c) an internal market characterised by the abolition, as between Member States, of obstacles to the free movement of goods, persons, services and capital;
   (d) measures concerning the entry and movement of persons as provided for in Title IV;

(e) a common policy in the sphere of agriculture and fisheries;

(f) a common policy in the sphere of transport;

(g) a system ensuring that competition in the internal market is not distorted;

(h) the approximation of the laws of Member States to the extent required for the functioning of the common market;

(i) the promotion of coordination between employment policies of the Member States with a view to enhancing their effectiveness by developing a coordinated strategy for employment;

(j) a policy in the social sphere comprising a European Social Fund;

(k) the strengthening of economic and social cohesion;

(l) a policy in the sphere of the environment;

(m) the strengthening of the competitiveness of Community industry;

(n) the promotion of research and technological development;

(o) encouragement for the establishment and development of trans-European networks;

(p) a contribution to the attainment of a high level of health protection;

(q) a contribution to education and training of quality and to the flowering of the cultures of the Member States;

(r) a policy in the sphere of development cooperation;

(s) the association of the overseas countries and territories in order to increase trade and promote jointly economic and social development;

(t) a contribution to the strengthening of consumer protection;

(u) measures in the spheres of energy, civil protection and tourism.

2. In all the activities referred to in this Article, the Community shall aim to eliminate inequalities, and to promote equality, between men and women.

Article 4   (ex Article 3a)

1. For the purposes set out in Article 2, the activities of the Member States and the Community shall include, as provided in this Treaty and in accordance with the timetable set out therein, the adoption of an economic policy which is based on the close coordination of Member States' economic policies, on the internal market and on the definition of common objectives, and conducted in accordance with the principle of an open market economy with free competition.

2. Concurrently with the foregoing, and as provided in this Treaty and in accordance with the timetable and the procedures set out therein, these activities shall include the irrevocable fixing of exchange rates leading to the introduction of a single currency, the ECU, and the definition and conduct of a single monetary policy and exchange rate policy the primary objective of both of which shall be to maintain price stability and, without prejudice to this objective, to support the general economic policies in the Community, in accordance with the principle of an open market economy with free competition.

3. These activities of the Member States and the Community shall entail compliance with the following guiding principles: stable prices, sound public finances and monetary conditions and a sustainable balance of payments.

Article 5   (ex Article 3b)

The Community shall act within the limits of the powers conferred upon it by this Treaty and of the objectives assigned to it therein.

In areas which do not fall within its exclusive competence, the Community shall take action, in accordance with the principle of subsidiarity, only if and insofar as the objectives of the proposed action cannot be sufficiently achieved by the Member States and can therefore, by reason of the scale or effects of the proposed action, be better achieved by the Community.

Any action by the Community shall not go beyond what is necessary to achieve the objectives of this Treaty.

Article 6   (ex Article 3c)

Environmental protection requirements must be integrated into the definition and implementation of the Community policies and activities referred to in Article 3, in particular with a view to promoting sustainable development.

Article 7   (ex Article 4)

1.   The tasks entrusted to the Community shall be carried out by the following institutions:

— a EUROPEAN PARLIAMENT,
— a COUNCIL,
— a COMMISSION,
— a COURT OF JUSTICE,
— a COURT OF AUDITORS.

Each institution shall act within the limits of the powers conferred upon it by this Treaty.

2.   The Council and the Commission shall be assisted by an Economic and Social Committee and a Committee of the Regions acting in an advisory capacity.

Article 8   (ex Article 4a)

A European System of Central Banks (hereinafter referred to as 'ESCB') and a European Central Bank (hereinafter referred to as 'ECB') shall be established in accordance with the procedures laid down in this Treaty; they shall act within the limits of the powers conferred upon them by this Treaty and by the Statute of the ESCB and of the ECB (hereinafter referred to as 'Statute of the ESCB') annexed thereto.

Article 9   (ex Article 4b)

A European Investment Bank is hereby established, which shall act within the limits of the powers conferred upon it by this Treaty and the Statute annexed thereto.

Article 10   (ex Article 5)

Member States shall take all appropriate measures, whether general or particular, to ensure fulfilment of the obligations arising out of this Treaty or resulting from action taken by the institutions of the Community. They shall facilitate the achievement of the Community's tasks.

They shall abstain from any measure which could jeopardise the attainment of the objectives of this Treaty.

Article 11   (ex Article 5a) **(As amended by the Treaty of Nice)**

1.   Member States which intend to establish enhanced cooperation between themselves in one of the areas referred to in this Treaty shall address a request to the Commission, which may submit a proposal to the Council to that effect. In the event of the Commission not submitting a proposal, it shall inform the Member States concerned of the reasons for not doing so.

2.   Authorisation to establish enhanced cooperation as referred to in paragraph 1 shall be granted, in compliance with Articles 43 to 45 of the Treaty on European Union, by the Council, acting by a qualified majority on a proposal from the Commission and after consulting the European Parliament. When enhanced cooperation relates to an area covered by the procedure referred to in Article 251 of this Treaty, the assent of the European Parliament shall be required.

A member of the Council may request that the matter be referred to the European Council. After that matter has been raised before the European Council, the Council may act in accordance with the first subparagraph of this paragraph.

3.   The acts and decisions necessary for the implementation of enhanced cooperation activities shall be subject to all the relevant provisions of this Treaty, save as otherwise provided in this Article and in Articles 43 to 45 of the Treaty on European Union.

Article 11a   (Inserted by the Treaty of Nice (former Article 11(3))

Any Member State which wishes to participate in enhanced cooperation established in accordance with Article 11 shall notify its intention to the Council and to the Commission, which shall give an opinion to the Council within three months of the date of receipt of that notification. Within four months of the date of receipt of that notification, the Commission shall take a decision on it, and on such specific arrangements as it may deem necessary.

Article 12   (ex Article 6)

Within the scope of application of this Treaty, and without prejudice to any special provisions contained therein, any discrimination on grounds of nationality shall be prohibited.

The Council, acting in accordance with the procedure referred to in Article 251, may adopt rules designed to prohibit such discrimination.

Article 13   (ex Article 6a) (As amended by the Treaty of Nice)

1.   Without prejudice to the other provisions of this Treaty and within the limits of the powers conferred by it upon the Community, the Council, acting unanimously on a proposal from the Commission and after consulting the European Parliament, may take appropriate action to combat discrimination based on sex, racial or ethnic origin, religion or belief, disability, age or sexual orientation.

2.   By way of derogation from paragraph 1, when the Council adopts Community incentive measures, excluding any harmonisation of the laws and regulations of the Member States, to support action taken by the Member States in order to contribute to the achievement of the objectives referred to in paragraph 1, it shall act in accordance with the procedure referred to in Article 251.

Article 14   (ex Article 7a)

1.   The Community shall adopt measures with the aim of progressively establishing the internal market over a period expiring on 31 December 1992, in accordance with the provisions of this Article and of Articles 15, 26, 47(2), 49, 80, 93 and 95 and without prejudice to the other provisions of this Treaty.

2.   The internal market shall comprise an area without internal frontiers in which the free movement of goods, persons, services and capital is ensured in accordance with the provisions of this Treaty.

3.   The Council, acting by a qualified majority on a proposal from the Commission, shall determine the guidelines and conditions necessary to ensure balanced progress in all the sectors concerned.

Article 15   (ex Article 7c)

When drawing up its proposals with a view to achieving the objectives set out in Article 14, the Commission shall take into account the extent of the effort that certain economies showing differences in development will have to sustain during the period of establishment of the internal market and it may propose appropriate provisions.

If these provisions take the form of derogations, they must be of a temporary nature and must cause the least possible disturbance to the functioning of the common market.

Article 16   (ex Article 7d)

Without prejudice to Articles 73, 86 and 87, and given the place occupied by services of general economic interest in the shared values of the Union as well as their role in promoting social and territorial cohesion, the Community and the Member States, each within their respective powers and within the scope of application of this Treaty, shall take care that such services operate on the basis of principles and conditions which enable them to fulfil their missions.

PART TWO   CITIZENSHIP OF THE UNION

Article 17   (ex Article 8)

1.   Citizenship of the Union is hereby established. Every person holding the nationality of a Member State shall be a citizen of the Union. Citizenship of the Union shall complement and not replace national citizenship.

2.   Citizens of the Union shall enjoy the rights conferred by this Treaty and shall be subject to the duties imposed thereby.

Article 18   (ex Article 8a) (As amended by the Treaty of Nice)

1.   Every citizen of the Union shall have the right to move and reside freely within the territory of the Member States, subject to the limitations and conditions laid down in this Treaty and by the measures adopted to give it effect.

2.   If action by the Community should prove necessary to attain this objective and this Treaty has not provided the necessary powers, the Council may adopt provisions with a view to facilitating the exercise of the rights referred to in paragraph 1. The Council shall act in accordance with the procedure referred to in Article 251.

3.   Paragraph 2 shall not apply to provisions on passports, identity cards, residence permits or any other such document or to provisions on social security or social protection.

Article 19   (ex Article 8b)

1.   Every citizen of the Union residing in a Member State of which he is not a national shall have the right to vote and to stand as a candidate at municipal elections in the Member State in which he resides, under the same conditions as nationals of that State. This right shall be exercised subject to detailed arrangements adopted by the Council, acting unanimously on a proposal from the Commission and after consulting the European Parliament; these arrangements may provide for derogations where warranted by problems specific to a Member State.

2.   Without prejudice to Article 190(4) and to the provisions adopted for its implementation, every citizen of the Union residing in a Member State of which he is not a national shall have the right to vote and to stand as a candidate in elections to the European Parliament in the Member State in which he resides, under the same conditions as nationals of that State. This right shall be exercised subject to detailed arrangements adopted by the Council, acting unanimously on a proposal from the Commission and after consulting the European Parliament; these arrangements may provide for derogations where warranted by problems specific to a Member State.

Article 20   (ex Article 8c)

Every citizen of the Union shall, in the territory of a third country in which the Member State of which he is a national is not represented, be entitled to protection by the diplomatic or consular authorities of any Member State, on the same conditions as the nationals of that State. Member States shall establish the necessary rules among themselves and start the international negotiations required to secure this protection.

Article 21   (ex Article 8d)

Every citizen of the Union shall have the right to petition the European Parliament in accordance with Article 194.

Every citizen of the Union may apply to the Ombudsman established in accordance with Article 195.

Every citizen of the Union may write to any of the institutions or bodies referred to in this Article or in Article 7 in one of the languages mentioned in Article 314 and have an answer in the same language.

Article 22   (ex Article 8e)

The Commission shall report to the European Parliament, to the Council and to the Economic and Social Committee every three years on the application of the provisions of this Part. This report shall take account of the development of the Union.

On this basis, and without prejudice to the other provisions of this Treaty, the Council, acting unanimously on a proposal from the Commission and after consulting the European Parliament, may adopt provisions to strengthen or to add to the rights laid down in this Part, which it shall recommend to the Member States for adoption in accordance with their respective constitutional requirements.

PART THREE   COMMUNITY POLICIES

TITLE I   FREE MOVEMENT OF GOODS

Article 23   (ex Article 9)

1.   The Community shall be based upon a customs union which shall cover all trade in goods and which shall involve the prohibition between Member States of customs duties on imports and exports and of all charges having equivalent effect, and the adoption of a common customs tariff in their relations with third countries.

2.   The provisions of Article 25 and of Chapter 2 of this Title shall apply to products originating in Member States and to products coming from third countries which are in free circulation in Member States.

Article 24   (ex Article 10)

Products coming from a third country shall be considered to be in free circulation in a Member State if the import formalities have been complied with and any customs duties or charges having equivalent effect which are payable have been levied in that Member State, and if they have not benefited from a total or partial drawback of such duties or charges.

CHAPTER 1   THE CUSTOMS UNION

Article 25   (ex Article 12)

Customs duties on imports and exports and charges having equivalent effect shall be prohibited between Member States. This prohibition shall also apply to customs duties of a fiscal nature.

Article 26   (ex Article 28)

Common Customs Tariff duties shall fixed by the Council acting by a qualified majority on a proposal from the Commission.

Article 27   (ex Article 29)

In carrying out the tasks entrusted to it under this Chapter the Commission shall be guided by:

(a)   the need to promote trade between Member States and third countries;

(b)   developments in conditions of competition within the Community insofar as they lead to an improvement in the competitive capacity of undertakings;

(c)   the requirements of the Community as regards the supply of raw materials and semi-finished goods; in this connection the Commission shall take care to avoid distorting conditions of competition between Member States in respect of finished goods;

(d)   the need to avoid serious disturbances in the economies of Member States and to ensure rational development of production and an expansion of consumption within the Community.

CHAPTER 2   PROHIBITION OF QUANTITATIVE RESTRICTIONS BETWEEN
MEMBER STATES

Article 28   (ex Article 30)

Quantitative restrictions on imports and all measures having equivalent effect shall be prohibited between Member States.

Article 29   (ex Article 34)

Quantitative restrictions on exports, and all measures having equivalent effect, shall be prohibited between Member States.

Article 30   (ex Article 36)

The provisions of Articles 28 and 29 shall not preclude prohibitions or restrictions on imports, exports or goods in transit justified on grounds of public morality, public policy or public security; the protection of health and life of humans, animals or plants; the protection of national treasures possessing artistic, historic or archaeological value; or the protection of industrial and commercial property. Such prohibitions or restrictions shall not, however, constitute a means of arbitrary discrimination or a disguised restriction on trade between Member States.

Article 31   (ex Article 37)

1.   Member States shall adjust any State monopolies of a commercial character so as to ensure that no discrimination regarding the conditions under which goods are procured and marketed exists between nationals of Member States.

The provisions of this Article shall apply to any body through which a Member State, in law or in fact, either directly or indirectly supervises, determines or appreciably influences imports or exports between Member States. These provisions shall likewise apply to monopolies delegated by the State to others.

2.   Member States shall refrain from introducing any new measure which is contrary to the principles laid down in paragraph 1 or which restricts the scope of the Articles dealing with the prohibition of customs duties and quantitative restrictions between Member States.

3.   If a State monopoly of a commercial character has rules which are designed to make it easier to dispose of agricultural products or obtain for them the best return, steps should be taken in applying the rules contained in this Article to ensure equivalent safeguards for the employment and standard of living of the producers concerned.

TITLE II   AGRICULTURE

Article 32   (ex Article 38)

1.   The common market shall extend to agriculture and trade in agricultural products. 'Agricultural products' means the products of the soil, of stockfarming and of fisheries and products of first stage processing directly related to these products.

2.   Save as otherwise provided in Articles 33 to 38, the rules laid down for the establishment of the common market shall apply to agricultural products.

3.   The products subject to the provisions of Articles 33 to 38 are listed in Annex I to this Treaty.

4.   The operation and development of the common market for agricultural products must be accompanied by the establishment of a common agricultural policy.

Article 33   (ex Article 39)

1.   The objectives of the common agricultural policy shall be:
   (a)   to increase agricultural productivity by promoting technical progress and by ensuring the rational development of agricultural production and the optimum utilisation of the factors of production, in particular labour;

(b) thus to ensure a fair standard of living for the agricultural community, in particular by increasing the individual earnings of persons engaged in agriculture;

(c) to stabilise markets;

(d) to assure the availability of supplies;

(e) to ensure that supplies reach consumers at reasonable prices.

2. In working out the common agricultural policy and the special methods for its application, account shall be taken of:

(a) the particular nature of agricultural activity, which results from the social structure of agriculture and from structural and natural disparities between the various agricultural regions;

(b) the need to effect the appropriate adjustments by degrees;

(c) the fact that in the Member States agriculture constitutes a sector closely linked with the economy as a whole.

Article 34   (ex Article 40)

1. In order to attain the objectives set out in Article 33, a common organisation of agricultural markets shall be established. This organisation shall take one of the following forms, depending on the product concerned:

(a) common rules on competition;

(b) compulsory coordination of the various national market organisations;

(c) a European market organisation.

2. The common organisation established in accordance with paragraph 1 may include all measures required to attain the objectives set out in Article 33, in particular regulation of prices, aids for the production and marketing of the various products, storage and carry-over arrangements and common machinery for stabilising imports or exports. The common organisation shall be limited to pursuit of the objectives set out in Article 33 and shall exclude any discrimination between producers or consumers within the Community.

Any common price policy shall be based on common criteria and uniform methods of calculation.

3. In order to enable the common organisation referred to in paragraph 1 to attain its objectives, one or more agricultural guidance and guarantee funds may be set up.

Article 35   (ex Article 41)

To enable the objectives set out in Article 33 to be attained, provision may be made within the framework of the common agricultural policy for measures such as:

(a) an effective coordination of efforts in the spheres of vocational training, of research and of the dissemination of agricultural knowledge; this may include joint financing of projects or institutions;

(b) joint measures to promote consumption of certain products.

Article 36   (ex Article 42)

The provisions of the Chapter relating to rules on competition shall apply to production of and trade in agricultural products only to the extent determined by the Council within the framework of Article 37(2) and (3) and in accordance with the procedure laid down therein, account being taken of the objectives set out in Article 33.

The Council may, in particular, authorise the granting of aid:

(a) for the protection of enterprises handicapped by structural or natural conditions;

(b) within the framework of economic development programmes.

Article 37   (ex Article 43)

1. In order to evolve the broad lines of a common agricultural policy, the Commission shall, immediately this Treaty enters into force, convene a conference of the Member States with a view to making a comparison of their agricultural policies, in particular by producing a statement of their resources and needs.

2.   Having taken into account the work of the Conference provided for in paragraph 1, after consulting the Economic and Social Committee and within two years of the entry into force of this Treaty, the Commission shall submit proposals for working out and implementing the common agricultural policy, including the replacement of the national organisations by one of the forms of common organisation provided for in Article 34(1), and for implementing the measures specified in this Title.

These proposals shall take account of the interdependence of the agricultural matters mentioned in this Title.

The Council shall, on a proposal from the Commission and after consulting the European Parliament, acting by a qualified majority, make regulations, issue directives, or take decisions, without prejudice to any recommendations it may also make.

3.   The Council may, acting by a qualified majority and in accordance with paragraph 2, replace the national market organisations by the common organisation provided for in Article 34(1) if:

(a) the common organisation offers Member States which are opposed to this measure and which have an organisation of their own for the production in question equivalent safeguards for the employment and standard of living of the producers concerned, account being taken of the adjustments that will be possible and the specialisation that will be needed with the passage of time;

(b) such an organisation ensures conditions for trade within the Community similar to those existing in a national market.

4.   If a common organisation for certain raw materials is established before a common organisation exists for the corresponding processed products, such raw materials as are used for processed products intended for export to third countries may be imported from outside the Community.

Article 38   (ex Article 46)

Where in a Member State a product is subject to a national market organisation or to internal rules having equivalent effect which affect the competitive position of similar production in another Member State, a countervailing charge shall be applied by Member States to imports of this product coming from the Member State where such organisation or rules exist, unless that State applies a countervailing charge on export.

The Commission shall fix the amount of these charges at the level required to redress the balance; it may also authorise other measures, the conditions and details of which it shall determine.

TITLE III   FREE MOVEMENT OF PERSONS, SERVICES AND CAPITAL

CHAPTER 1   WORKERS

Article 39   (ex Article 48)

1.   Freedom of movement for workers shall be secured within the Community.

2.   Such freedom of movement shall entail the abolition of any discrimination based on nationality between workers of the Member States as regards employment, remuneration and other conditions of work and employment.

3.   It shall entail the right, subject to limitations justified on grounds of public policy, public security or public health:

(a) to accept offers of employment actually made;

(b) to move freely within the territory of Member States for this purpose;

(c) to stay in a Member State for the purpose of employment in accordance with the provisions governing the employment of nationals of that State laid down by law, regulation or administrative action;

   (d) to remain in the territory of a Member State after having been employed in that State, subject to conditions which shall be embodied in implementing regulations to be drawn up by the Commission.
   4. The provisions of this Article shall not apply to employment in the public service.

Article 40   (ex Article 49)

The Council shall, acting in accordance with the procedure referred to in Article 251 and after consulting the Economic and Social Committee, issue directives or make regulations setting out the measures required to bring about freedom of movement for workers, as defined in Article 39, in particular:

   (a) by ensuring close cooperation between national employment services;
   (b) by abolishing those administrative procedures and practices and those qualifying periods in respect of eligibility for available employment, whether resulting from national legislation or from agreements previously concluded between Member States, the maintenance of which would form an obstacle to liberalisation of the movement of workers;
   (c) by abolishing all such qualifying periods and other restrictions provided for either under national legislation or under agreements previously concluded between Member States as imposed on workers of other Member States conditions regarding the free choice of employment other than those imposed on workers of the State concerned;
   (d) by setting up appropriate machinery to bring offers of employment into touch with applications for employment and to facilitate the achievement of a balance between supply and demand in the employment market in such a way as to avoid serious threats to the standard of living and level of employment in the various regions and industries.

Article 41   (ex Article 50)

Member States shall, within the framework of a joint programme, encourage the exchange of young workers.

Article 42   (ex Article 51)

The Council shall, acting in accordance with the procedure referred to in Article 251, adopt such measures in the field of social security as are necessary to provide freedom of movement for workers; to this end, it shall make arrangements to secure for migrant workers and their dependants:

   (a) aggregation, for the purpose of acquiring and retaining the right to benefit and of calculating the amount of benefit, of all periods taken into account under the laws of the several countries;
   (b) payment of benefits to persons resident in the territories of Member States.
   The Council shall act unanimously throughout the procedure referred to in Article 251.

CHAPTER 2   RIGHT OF ESTABLISHMENT

Article 43   (ex Article 52)

Within the framework of the provisions set out below, restrictions on the freedom of establishment of nationals of a Member State in the territory of another Member State shall be prohibited. Such prohibition shall also apply to restrictions on the setting up of agencies, branches or subsidiaries by nationals of any Member State established in the territory of any Member State.
   Freedom of establishment shall include the right to take up and pursue activities as self employed persons and to set up and manage undertakings, in particular companies or firms within the meaning of the second paragraph of Article 48, under the conditions laid down for

its own nationals by the law of the country where such establishment is effected, subject to the provisions of the Chapter relating to capital.

Article 44   (ex Article 54)

1.   In order to attain freedom of establishment as regards a particular activity, the Council, acting in accordance with the procedure referred to in Article 251 and after consulting the Economic and Social Committee, shall act by means of directives.

2.   The Council and the Commission shall carry out the duties devolving upon them under the preceding provisions, in particular:

    (a) by according, as a general rule, priority treatment to activities where freedom of establishment makes a particularly valuable contribution to the development of production and trade;

    (b) by ensuring close cooperation between the competent authorities in the Member States in order to ascertain the particular situation within the Community of the various activities concerned;

    (c) by abolishing those administrative procedures and practices, whether resulting from national legislation or from agreements previously concluded between Member States, the maintenance of which would form an obstacle to freedom of establishment;

    (d) by ensuring that workers of one Member State employed in the territory of another Member State may remain in that territory for the purpose of taking up activities therein as self-employed persons, where they satisfy the conditions which they would be required to satisfy if they were entering that State at the time when they intended to take up such activities;

    (e) by enabling a national of one Member State to acquire and use land and buildings situated in the territory of another Member State, insofar as this does not conflict with the principles laid down in Article 33(2);

    (f) by effecting the progressive abolition of restrictions on freedom of establishment in every branch of activity under consideration, both as regards the conditions for setting up agencies, branches or subsidiaries in the territory of a Member State and as regards the subsidiaries in the territory of a Member State and as regards the conditions governing the entry of personnel belonging to the main establishment into managerial or supervisory posts in such agencies, branches or subsidiaries;

    (g) by coordinating to the necessary extent the safeguards which, for the protection of the interests of members and other, are required by Member States of companies or firms within the meaning of the second paragraph of Article 48 with a view to making such safeguards equivalent throughout the Community;

    (h) by satisfying themselves that the conditions of establishment are not distorted by aids granted by Member States.

Article 45   (ex Article 55)

The provisions of this Chapter shall not apply, so far as any given Member State is concerned, to activities which in that State are connected, even occasionally, with the exercise of official authority.

The Council may, acting by a qualified majority on a proposal from the Commission, rule that the provisions of this Chapter shall not apply to certain activities.

Article 46   (ex Article 56)

1.   The provisions of this Chapter and measures taken in pursuance thereof shall not prejudice the applicability of provisions laid down by law, regulation or administrative action providing for special treatment for foreign nationals on grounds of public policy, public security or public health.

2.   The Council shall, acting in accordance with the procedure referred to in Article 251, issue directives for the coordination of the abovementioned provisions.

Article 47   (ex Article 57)

1.   In order to make it easier for persons to take up and pursue activities as self-employed persons, the Council shall, acting in accordance with the procedure referred to in Article 251, issue directives for the mutual recognition of diplomas, certificates and other evidence of formal qualifications.

2.   For the same purpose, the Council shall, acting in accordance with the procedure referred to in Article 251, issue directives for the coordination of the provisions laid down by law, regulation or administrative action in Member States concerning the taking up and pursuit of activities as self-employed persons. The Council, acting unanimously throughout the procedure referred to in Article 251, shall decide on directives the implementation of which involves in at least one Member State amendment of the existing principles laid down by law governing the professions with respect to training and conditions of access for natural persons. In other cases the Council shall act by qualified majority.

3.   In the case of the medical and allied and pharmaceutical professions, the progressive abolition of restrictions shall be dependent upon coordination of the conditions for their exercise in the various Member States.

Article 48   (ex Article 58)

Companies or firms formed in accordance with the law of a Member State and having their registered office, central administration or principal place of business within the Community shall, for the purposes of this Chapter, be treated in the same way as natural persons who are nationals of Member States.

'Companies or firms' means companies or firms constituted under civil or commercial law, including cooperative societies, and other legal persons governed by public or private law, save for those which are non-profit-making.

CHAPTER 3   SERVICES

Article 49   (ex Article 59)

Within the framework of the provisions set out below, restrictions on freedom to provide services within the Community shall be prohibited in respect of nationals of Member States who are established in a State of the Community other than that of the person for whom the services are intended.

The Council may, acting by a qualified majority on a proposal from the Commission, extend the provisions of the Chapter to nationals of a third country who provide services and who are established within the Community.

Article 50   (ex Article 60)

Services shall be considered to be 'services' within the meaning of this Treaty where they are normally provided for remuneration, insofar as they are not governed by the provisions relating to freedom of movement for goods, capital and persons. 'Services' shall in particular include:

   (a) activities of an industrial character;
   (b) activities of a commercial character;
   (c) activities of craftsmen;
   (d) activities of the professions.

Without prejudice to the provisions of the Chapter relating to the right of establishment, the person providing a service may, in order to do so, temporarily pursue his activity in the State where the service is provided, under the same conditions as are imposed by that State on its own nationals.

Article 51   (ex Article 61)

1.   Freedom to provide services in the field of transport shall be governed by the provisions of the Title relating to transport.

2.   The liberalisation of banking and insurance services connected with movements of capital shall be effected in step with the liberalisation of movement of capital.

Article 52   (ex Article 63)

1.   In order to achieve the liberalisation of a specific service, the Council shall, on a proposal from the Commission and after consulting the Economic and Social Committee and the European Parliament, issue directives acting by a qualified majority.

2.   As regards the directives referred to in paragraph 1, priority shall as a general rule be given to those services which directly affect production costs or the liberalisation of which helps to promote trade in goods.

Article 53   (ex Article 64)

The Member States declare their readiness to undertake the liberalisation of services beyond the extent required by the directives issued pursuant to Article 52(1), if their general economic situation and the situation of the economic sector concerned so permit.

To this end, the Commission shall make recommendations to the Member States concerned.

Article 54   (ex Article 65)

As long as restrictions on freedom to provide services have not been abolished, each Member State shall apply such restrictions without distinction on grounds of nationality or residence to all persons providing services within the meaning of the first paragraph of Article 49.

Article 55   (ex Article 66)

The provisions of Articles 45 to 48 shall apply to the matters covered by this Chapter.

—   the Council, acting unanimously after consulting the European Parliament, shall take a decision with a view to providing for all or parts of the areas covered by this Title to be governed by the procedure referred to in Article 251 and adapting the provisions relating to the powers of the Court of Justice.

CHAPTER 4   CAPITAL AND PAYMENTS

Article 56   (ex Article 73b)

1.   Within the framework of the provisions set out in this Chapter, all restrictions on the movement of capital between Member States and between Member States and third countries shall be prohibited.

2.   Within the framework of the provisions set out in this Chapter, all restrictions on payments between Member States and between Member States and third countries shall be prohibited.

Article 57   (ex Article 73c)

1.   The provisions of Article 56 shall be without prejudice to the application to third countries of any restrictions which exist on 31 December 1993 under national or Community law adopted in respect of the movement of capital to or from third countries involving direct investment—including in real estate—establishment, the provision of financial services or the admission of securities to capital markets. In respect of restrictions existing under national law in Estonia and Hungary, the relevant date shall be 31 December 1999.

2.   Whilst endeavouring to achieve the objective of free movement of capital between Member States and third countries to the greatest extent possible and without prejudice to the other Chapters of this Treaty, the Council may, acting by a qualified majority on a proposal from the Commission, adopt measures on the movement of capital to or from third countries involving direct investment—including investment in real estate—establishment,

the provision of financial services or the admission of securities to capital markets. Unanimity shall be required for measures under this paragraph which constitute a step back in Community law as regards the liberalisation of the movement of capital to or from third countries.

Article 58   (ex Article 73d)
1. The provisions of Article 56 shall be without prejudice to the right of Member States:
    (a) to apply the relevant provisions of their tax law which distinguish between taxpayers who are not in the same situation with regard to their place of residence or with regard to the place where their capital is invested;
    (b) to take all requisite measures to prevent infringements of national law and regulations, in particular in the field of taxation and the prudential supervision of financial institutions, or to lay down procedures for the declaration of capital movements for purposes of administrative or statistical information, or to take measures which are justified on grounds of public policy or public security.
2. The provisions of this Chapter shall be without prejudice to the applicability of restrictions on the right of establishment which are compatible with this Treaty.
3. The measures and procedures referred to in paragraphs 1 and 2 shall not constitute a means of arbitrary discrimination or a disguised restriction on the free movement of capital and payments as defined in Article 56.

Article 59   (ex Article 73f)
Where, in exceptional circumstances, movements of capital to or from third countries cause, or threaten to cause, serious difficulties for the operation of economic and monetary union, the Council, acting by a qualified majority on a proposal from the Commission and after consulting the ECB, may take safeguard measures with regard to third countries for a period not exceeding six months if such measures are strictly necessary.

Article 60   (ex Article 73g)
1. If, in the cases envisaged in Article 301, action by the Community is deemed necessary, the Council may, in accordance with the procedure provided for in Article 301, take the necessary urgent measures on the movement of capital and on payments as regards the third countries concerned.
2. Without prejudice to Article 297 and as long as the Council has not taken measures pursuant to paragraph 1, a Member State may, for serious political reasons and on grounds of urgency, take unilateral measures against a third country with regard to capital movements and payments. The Commission and the other Member States shall be informed of such measures by the date of their entry into force at the latest.
    The Council may, acting by a qualified majority on a proposal from the Commission, decide that the Member State concerned shall amend or abolish such measures. The President of the Council shall inform the European Parliament of any such decision taken by the Council.

TITLE IV (ex Title IIIa)   VISAS, ASYLUM, IMMIGRATION AND OTHER POLICIES RELATED TO FREE MOVEMENT OF PERSONS

Article 61   (ex Article 73i)
In order to establish progressively an area of freedom, security and justice, the Council shall adopt:
    (a) within a period of five years after the entry into force of the Treaty of Amsterdam, measures aimed at ensuring the free movement of persons in accordance with Article 14, in conjunction with directly related flanking measures with respect to external border controls, asylum and immigration, in accordance with the provisions of Article 62(2) and (3) and Article 63(1)(a) and (2)(a), and measures to

prevent and combat crime in accordance with the provisions of Article 31(e) of the Treaty on European Union;

(b) other measures in the fields of asylum, immigration and safeguarding the rights of nationals of third countries, in accordance with the provisions of Article 63;

(c) measures in the field of judicial cooperation in civil matters as provided for in Article 65;

(d) appropriate measures to encourage and strengthen administrative cooperation, as provided for in Article 66;

(e) measures in the field of police and judicial cooperation in criminal matters aimed at a high level of security by preventing and combating crime within the Union in accordance with the provisions of the Treaty on European Union.

Article 62   (ex Article 73j)

The Council, acting in accordance with the procedure referred to in Article 67, shall, within a period of five years after the entry into force of the Treaty of Amsterdam, adopt:

(1) measures with a view to ensuring, in compliance with Article 14, the absence of any controls on persons, be they citizens of the Union or nationals of third countries, when crossing internal borders;

(2) measures on the crossing of the external borders of the Member States which shall establish:

(a) standards and procedures to be followed by Member States in carrying out checks on persons at such borders;

(b) rules on visas for intended stays of no more than three months, including:

(i) the list of third countries whose nationals must be in position of visas when crossing the external borders and those whose nationals are exempt from that requirement;

(ii) the procedures and conditions for issuing visas by Member States;

(iii) a uniform format for visas;

(iv) rules on a uniform visa;

(3) measures setting out the conditions under which nationals of third countries shall have the freedom to travel within the territory of the Member States during a period of no more than three months.

Article 63   (ex Article 73k)

The Council, acting in accordance with the procedure referred to in Article 67, shall, within a period of five years after the entry into force of the Treaty of Amsterdam, adopt:

(1) measures on asylum, in accordance with the Geneva Convention of 28 July 1951 and the Protocol of 31 January 1967 relating to the status of refugees and other relevant treaties, within the following areas:

(a) criteria and mechanisms for determining which Member State is responsible for considering an application for asylum submitted by a national of a third country in one of the Member States,

(b) minimum standards on the reception of asylum seekers in Member States,

(c) minimum standards with respect to the qualification of nationals of third countries as refugees,

(d) minimum standards on procedures in Member States for granting or withdrawing refugee status;

(2) measures on refugees and displaced persons within the following areas:

(a) minimum standards for giving temporary protection to displaced persons from third countries who cannot return to their country of origin and for persons who otherwise need international protection,

(b) promoting a balance of effort between Member States in receiving and bearing the consequences of receiving refugees and displaced persons;

(3) measures on immigration policy within the following areas:
    (a) conditions of entry and residence, and standards on procedures for the issue by Member States of long term visas and residence permits, including those for the purpose of family reunion,
    (b) illegal immigration and illegal residence, including repatriation of illegal residents;
(4) measures defining the rights and conditions under which nationals of third countries who are legally resident in a Member State may reside in other Member States.

Measures adopted by the Council pursuant to points 3 and 4 shall not prevent any Member State from maintaining or introducing in the areas concerned national provisions which are compatible with this Treaty and with international agreements.

Measures to be adopted pursuant to points 2(b), 3(a) and 4 shall not be subject to the five year period referred to above.

Article 64   (ex Article 73l)

1.   This Title shall not affect the exercise of the responsibilities incumbent upon Member States with regard to the maintenance of law and order and the safeguarding of internal security.

2.   In the event of one or more Member States being confronted with an emergency situation characterised by a sudden inflow of nationals of third countries and without prejudice to paragraph 1, the Council may, acting by qualified majority on a proposal from the Commission, adopt provisional measures of a duration not exceeding six months for the benefit of the Member States concerned.

Article 65   (ex Article 73m)

Measures in the field of judicial cooperation in civil matters having cross border implications, to be taken in accordance with Article 67 and insofar as necessary for the proper functioning of the internal market, shall include:
    (a) improving and simplifying:
        — the system for cross border service of judicial and extrajudicial documents;
        — cooperation in the taking of evidence;
        — the recognition and enforcement of decisions in civil and commercial cases, including decisions in extrajudicial cases;
    (b) promoting the compatibility of the rules applicable in the Member States concerning the conflict of laws and of jurisdiction;
    (c) eliminating obstacles to the good functioning of civil proceedings, if necessary by promoting the compatibility of the rules on civil procedure applicable in the Member States.

Article 66   (ex Article 73n)

The Council, acting in accordance with the procedure referred to in Article 67, shall take measures to ensure cooperation between the relevant departments of the administrations of the Member States in the areas covered by this Title, as well as between those departments and the Commission.

Article 67   (ex Article 73o) (As amended by the Treaty of Nice)

1.   During a transitional period of five years following the entry into force of the Treaty of Amsterdam, the Council shall act unanimously on a proposal from the Commission or on the initiative of a Member State and after consulting the European Parliament.

2.   After this period of five years:
    — the Council shall act on proposals from the Commission; the Commission shall examine any request made by a Member State that it submit a proposal to the Council;
    — the Council, acting unanimously after consulting the European Parliament, shall take a decision with a view to providing for all or parts of the areas covered by this

Title to be governed by the procedure referred to in Article 251 and adapting the provisions relating to the powers of the Court of Justice.

3.   By derogation from paragraphs 1 and 2, measures referred to in Article 62(2)(b) (i) and (iii) shall, from the entry into force of the Treaty of Amsterdam, be adopted by the Council acting by a qualified majority on a proposal from the Commission and after consulting the European Parliament;

4.   By derogation from paragraph 2, measures referred to in Article 62(2)(b) (ii) and (iv) shall, after a period of five years following the entry into force of the Treaty of Amsterdam, be adopted by the Council acting in accordance with the procedure referred to in Article 251.

5.   By derogation from paragraph 1, the Council shall adopt, in accordance with the procedure referred to in Article 251:

— the measures provided for in Article 63(1) and (2)(a) provided that the Council has previously adopted, in accordance with paragraph 1 of this Article, Community legislation defining the common rules and basic principles governing these issues;
— the measures provided for in Article 65 with the exception of aspects relating to family law.

Article 68   (ex Article 73p)

1.   Article 234 shall apply to this Title under the following circumstances and conditions: where a question on the interpretation of this Title or on the validity or interpretation of acts of the institutions of the Community based on this Title is raised in a case pending before a court or a tribunal of a Member State against whose decisions there is no judicial remedy under national law, that court or tribunal shall, if it considers that a decision on the question is necessary to enable it to give judgment, request the Court of Justice to give a ruling thereon.

2.   In any event, the Court of Justice shall not have jurisdiction to rule on any measure or decision taken pursuant to Article 62(1) relating to the maintenance of law and order and the safeguarding of internal security.

3.   The Council, the Commission or a Member State may request the Court of Justice to give a ruling on a question of interpretation of this Title or of acts of the institutions of the Community based on this Title. The ruling given by the Court of Justice in response to such a request shall not apply to judgments of courts or tribunals of the Member States which have become res judicata.

Article 69   (ex Article 73q)

The applicationof this Title shall be subject to the provisions of the Protocol on the position of the United Kingdom and Ireland and to the Protocol on the position of Denmark and without prejudice to the Protocol on the application of certain aspects of Article 14 of the Treaty establishing the European Community to the United Kingdom and to Ireland.

TITLE V (ex Title IV)   TRANSPORT

Article 70   (ex Article 74)

The objectives of this Treaty shall, in matters governed by this Title, be pursued by Member States within the framework of a common transport policy.

Article 71   (ex Article 75)

1.   For the purpose of implementing Article 70, and taking into account the distinctive features of transport, the Council shall, acting in accordance with the procedure referred to in Article 251 and after consulting the Economic and Social Committee and the Committee of the Regions, lay down:

    (a) common rules applicable to international transport to or from the territory of a Member State or passing across the territory of one or more Member States;

    (b) the conditions under which non-resident carriers may operate transport services within a Member State;

    (c) measures to improve transport safety;

    (d) any other appropriate provisions.

2. By way of derogation from the procedure provided for in paragraph 1, where the application of provisions concerning the principles of the regulatory system for transport would be liable to have a serious effect on the standard of living and on employment in certain areas and on the operation of transport facilities, they shall be laid down by the Council acting unanimously on a proposal from the Commission, after consulting the European Parliament and the Economic and Social Committee. In so doing, the Council shall take into account the need for adaptation to the economic development which will result from establishing the common market.

Article 72   (ex Article 76)

Until the provisions referred to in Article 71(1) have been laid down, no Member State may, without the unanimous approval of the Council, make the various provisions governing the subject on 1 January 1958 or, for acceding States, the date of their accession less favourable in their direct or indirect effect on carriers of other Member States as compared with carriers who are nationals of that State.

Article 73   (ex Article 77)

Aids shall be compatible with this Treaty if they meet the needs of coordination of transport or if they represent reimbursement for the discharge of certain obligations inherent in the concept of a public service.

Article 74   (ex Article 78)

Any measures taken within the framework of this Treaty in respect of transport rates and conditions shall take account of the economic circumstances of carriers.

Article 75   (ex Article 79)

1. In the case of transport within the Community, discrimination which takes the form of carriers charging different rates and imposing different conditions for the carriage of the same goods over the same transport links on grounds of the country of origin or of destination of the goods in question shall be abolished.

2. Paragraph 1 shall not prevent the Council from adopting other measures in pursuance of Article 71(1).

3. The Council shall, acting by a qualified majority on a proposal from the Commission and after consulting the Economic and Social Committee, lay down rules for implementing the provisions of paragraph 1. The Council may in particular lay down the provisions needed to enable the institutions of the Community to secure compliance with the rule laid down in paragraph 1 and to ensure that users benefit from it to the full.

4. The Commission shall, acting on its own initiative or on application by a Member State, investigate any cases of discrimination falling within paragraph 1 and, after consulting any Member State concerned, shall take the necessary decisions within the framework of the rules laid down in accordance with the provisions of paragraph 3.

Article 76   (ex Article 80)

1. The imposition by a Member State, in respect of transport operations carried out within the Community, of rates and conditions involving any element of support or protection in the interest of one or more particular undertakings or industries shall be prohibited, unless authorised by the Commission.

2.   The Commission shall, acting on its own initiative or on application by a Member State, examine the rates and conditions referred to in paragraph 1, taking account in particular of the requirements of an appropriate regional economic policy, the needs of underdeveloped areas and the problems of areas seriously affected by political circumstances on the one hand, and of the effects of such rates and conditions on competition between the different modes of transport on the other.

After consulting each Member State concerned, the Commission shall take the necessary decisions.

3.   The prohibition provided for in paragraph 1 shall not apply to tariffs fixed to meet competition.

Article 77   (ex Article 81)

Charges or dues in respect of the crossing of frontiers which are charged by a carrier in addition to the transport rates shall not exceed a reasonable level after taking the costs actually incurred thereby into account.

Member States shall endeavour to reduce these costs progressively.

The Commission may make recommendations to Member States for the application of this Article.

Article 78   (ex Article 82)

The provisions of this Title shall not form an obstacle to the application of measures taken in the Federal Republic of Germany to the extent that such measures are required in order to compensate for the economic disadvantages caused by the division of Germany to the economy of certain areas of the Federal Republic affected by that division.

Article 79   (ex Article 83)

An Advisory Committee consisting of experts designated by the governments of Member States shall be attached to the Commission. The Commission, whenever it considers it desirable, shall consult the Committee on transport matters without prejudice to the powers of the Economic and Social Committee.

Article 80   (ex Article 84)

1.   The provisions of this Title shall apply to transport by rail, road and inland waterway.

2.   The Council may, acting by a qualified majority, decide whether, to what extent and by what procedure appropriate provisions may be laid down for sea and air transport.

The procedural provisions of Article 71 shall apply.

TITLE VI (ex Title V)   COMMON RULES ON COMPETITION, TAXATION AND APPROXIMATION OF LAWS

CHAPTER 1   RULES ON COMPETITION

SECTION 1   RULES APPLYING TO UNDERTAKINGS

Article 81   (ex Article 85)

1.   The following shall be prohibited as incompatible with the common market: all agreements between undertakings, decisions by associations of undertakings and concerted practices which may affect trade between Member States and which have as their object or effect the prevention, restriction or distortion of competition within the common market, and in particular those which:

(a)   directly or indirectly fix purchase or selling prices or any other trading conditions;

(b)   limit or control production, markets, technical development, or investment;

(c)   share markets or sources of supply;

(d)   apply dissimilar conditions to equivalent transactions with other trading parties, thereby placing them at a competitive disadvantage;

(e) make the conclusion of contracts subject to acceptance by the other parties of supplementary obligations which, by their nature or according to commercial usage, have no connection with the subject of such contracts.

2. Any agreements or decisions prohibited pursuant to this Article shall be automatically void.

3. The provisions of paragraph 1 may, however, be declared inapplicable in the case of:
— any agreement or category of agreements between undertakings;
— any decision or category of decisions by associations of undertakings;
— any concerted practice or category of concerted practices,

which contributes to improving the production or distribution of goods or to promoting technical or economic progress, while allowing consumers a fair share of the resulting benefit, and which does not:
(a) impose on the undertakings concerned restrictions which are not indispensable to the attainment of these objectives;
(b) afford such undertakings the possibility of eliminating competition in respect of a substantial part of the products in question.

Article 82   (ex Article 86)

Any abuse by one or more undertakings a dominant position within the common market or in a substantial part of it shall be prohibited as incompatible with the common market insofar as it may affect trade between Member States.

Such abuse may, in particular, consist in:
(a) directly or indirectly imposing unfair purchase or selling prices or other unfair trading conditions;
(b) limiting production, markets or technical development to the prejudice of consumers;
(c) applying dissimilar conditions to equivalent transactions with other trading parties, thereby placing them at a competitive disadvantage;
(d) making the conclusion of contracts subject to acceptance by the other parties of supplementary obligations which, by their nature or according to commercial usage, have no connection with the subject of such contracts.

Article 83   (ex Article 87)

1. The appropriate regulations or directives to give effect to the principles set out in Articles 81 and 82 shall be laid down by the Council, acting by a qualified majority on a proposal from the Commission and after consulting the European Parliament.

2. The regulations or directives referred to in paragraph 1 shall be designed in particular:
(a) to ensure compliance with the prohibitions laid down in Article 81(1) and in Article 82 by making provision for fines and periodic penalty payments;
(b) to lay down detailed rules for the application of Article 81(3), taking into account the need to ensure effective supervision on the one hand, and to simplify administration to the greatest possible extent on the other;
(c) to define, if need be, in the various branches of the economy, the scope of the provisions of Articles 81 and 82;
(d) to define the respective functions of the Commission and of the Court of Justice in applying the provisions laid down in this paragraph;
(e) to determine the relationship between national laws and the provisions contained in this Section or adopted pursuant to this Article.

Article 84   (ex Article 88)

Until the entry into force of the provisions adopted in pursuance of Article 83, the authorities in Member States shall rule on the admissibility of agreements, decisions and concerted practices and on abuse of a dominant position in the common market in accordance with the law of their country and with the provisions of Article 81, in particular paragraph 3, and of Article 82.

Article 85   (ex Article 89)

1.   Without prejudice to Article 84, the Commission shall ensure the application of the principles laid down in Articles 81 and 82. On application by a Member State or on its own initiative, and in cooperation with the competent authorities in the Member States, who shall give it their assistance, the Commission shall investigate cases of suspected infringement of these principles. If it finds that there has been an infringement, it shall propose appropriate measures to bring it to an end.

2.   If the infringement is not brought to an end, the Commission shall record such infringement of the principles in a reasoned decision. The Commission may publish its decision and authorise Member States to take the measures, the conditions and details of which it shall determine, needed to remedy the situation.

Article 86   (ex Article 90)

1.   In the case of public undertakings and undertakings to which Member States grant special or exclusive rights, Member States shall neither enact nor maintain in force any measure contrary to the rules contained in this Treaty, in particular to those rules provided for in Article 12 and Articles 81 to 89.

2.   Undertakings entrusted with the operation of services of general economic interest or having the character of a revenue producing monopoly shall be subject to the rules contained in this Treaty, in particular to the rules on competition, insofar as the application of such rules does not obstruct the performance, in law or in fact, of the particular tasks assigned to them. The development of trade must not be affected to such an extent as would be contrary to the interests of the Community.

3.   The Commission shall ensure the application of the provisions of this Article and shall, where necessary, address appropriate directives or decisions to Member States.

SECTION 2   AIDS GRANTED BY STATES

Article 87   (ex Article 92)

1.   Save as otherwise provided in this Treaty, any aid granted by a Member State or through State resources in any form whatsoever which distorts or threatens to distort competition by favouring certain undertakings or the production of certain goods shall, insofar as it affects trade between Member States, be incompatible with the common market.

2.   The following shall be compatible with the common market:

   (a)   aid having a social character, granted to individual consumers, provided that such aid is granted without discrimination related to the origin of the products concerned;

   (b)   aid to make good the damage caused by natural disasters or exceptional occurrences;

   (c)   aid granted to the economy of certain areas of the Federal Republic of Germany affected by the division of Germany, insofar as such aid is required in order to compensate for the economic disadvantages caused by that division.

3.   The following may be considered to be compatible with the common market:

   (a)   aid to promote the economic development of areas where the standard of living is abnormally low or where there is serious underemployment;

   (b)   aid to promote the execution of an important project of common European interest or to remedy a serious disturbance in the economy of a Member State;

   (c)   aid to facilitate the development of certain economic activities or of certain economic areas, where such aid does not adversely affect trading conditions to an extent contrary to the common interest;

(d) aid to promote culture and heritage conservation where such aid does not affect trading conditions and competition in the Community to an extent that is contrary to the common interest;

(e) such other categories of aid as may be specified by decision of the Council acting by a qualified majority on a proposal from the Commission.

Article 88 (ex Article 93)

1. The Commission shall, in cooperation with Member States, keep under constant review all systems of aid existing in those States. It shall propose to the latter any appropriate measures required by the progressive development or by the functioning of the common market.

2. If, after giving notice to the parties concerned to submit their comments, the Commission finds that aid granted by a State or through State resources is not compatible with the common market having regard to Article 87, or that such aid is being misused, it shall decide that the State concerned shall abolish or alter such aid within a period of time to be determined by the Commission.

If the State concerned does not comply with this decision within the prescribed time, the Commission or any other interested State may, in derogation from the provisions of Articles 226 and 227, refer the matter to the Court of Justice direct.

On application by a Member State, the Council may, acting unanimously, decide that aid which that State is granting or intends to grant shall be considered to be compatible with the common market, in derogation from the provisions of Article 87 or from the regulations provided for in Article 89, if such a decision is justified by exceptional circumstances. If, as regards the aid in question, the Commission has already initiated the procedure provided for in the first sub-paragraph of this paragraph, the fact that the State concerned has made its application to the Council shall have the effect of suspending that procedure until the Council has made its attitude known.

If, however, the Council has not made its attitude known within three months of the said application being made, the Commission shall give its decision on the case.

3. The Commission shall be informed, in sufficient time to enable it to submit its comments, of any plans to grant or alter aid. If it considers that any such plan is not compatible with the common market having regard to Article 87, it shall without delay initiate the procedure provided for in paragraph 2. The Member State concerned shall not put its proposed measures into effect until this procedure has resulted in a final decision.

Article 89 (ex Article 94)

The Council, acting by a qualified majority on a proposal from the Commission and after consulting the European Parliament, may make any appropriate regulations for the application of Articles 87 and 88 and may in particular determine the conditions in which Article 88(3) shall apply and the categories of aid exempted from this procedure.

CHAPTER 2 TAX PROVISIONS

Article 90 (ex Article 95)

No Member State shall impose, directly or indirectly, on the products of other Member States any internal taxation of any kind in excess of that imposed directly or indirectly on similar domestic products.

Furthermore, no Member State shall impose on the products of other Member States any internal taxation of such a nature as to afford indirect protection to other products.

Article 91 (ex Article 96)

Where products are exported to the territory of any Member State, any repayment of internal taxation shall not exceed the internal taxation imposed on them whether directly or indirectly.

Article 92   (ex Article 98)

In the case of charges other than turnover taxes, excise duties and other forms of indirect taxation, remissions and repayments in respect of exports to other Member States may not be granted and countervailing charges in respect of imports from Member States may not be imposed unless the measures contemplated have been previously approved for a limited period by the Council acting by a qualified majority on a proposal from the Commission.

Article 93   (ex Article 99)

The Council shall, acting unanimously on a proposal from the Commission and after consulting the European Parliament and the Economic and Social Committee, adopt provisions for the harmonisation of legislation concerning turnover taxes, excise duties and other forms of indirect taxation to the extent that such harmonisation is necessary to ensure the establishment and the functioning of the internal market within the time limit laid down in Article 14.

CHAPTER 3   APPROXIMATION OF LAWS

Article 94   (ex Article 100)

The Council shall, acting unanimously on a proposal from the Commission and after consulting the European Parliament and the Economic and Social Committee, issue directives for the approximation of such laws, regulations or administrative provisions of the Member States as directly affect the establishment or functioning of the common market.

Article 95   (ex Article 100a)

1.   By way of derogation from Article 94 and save where otherwise provided in this Treaty, the following provisions shall apply for the achievement of the objectives set out in Article 14. The Council shall, acting in accordance with the procedure referred to in Article 251 and after consulting the Economic and Social Committee, adopt the measures for the approximation of the provisions laid down by law, regulation or administrative action in Member States which have as their object the establishment and functioning of the internal market.

2.   Paragraph 1 shall not apply to fiscal provisions, to those relating to the free movement of persons nor to those relating to the rights and interests of employed persons.

3.   The Commission, in its proposals envisaged in paragraph 1 concerning health, safety, environmental protection and consumer protection, will take as a base a high level of protection, taking account in particular of any new development based on scientific facts. Within their respective powers, the European Parliament and the Council will also seek to achieve this objective.

4.   If, after the adoption by the Council or by the Commission of a harmonisation measure, a Member State deems it necessary to maintain national provisions on grounds of major needs referred to in Article 30, or relating to the protection of the environment or the working environment, it shall notify the Commission of these provisions as well as the grounds for maintaining them.

5.   Moreover, without prejudice to paragraph 4, if, after the adoption by the Council or by the Commission of a harmonisation measure, a Member State deems it necessary to introduce national provisions based on new scientific evidence relating to the protection of the environment or the working environment on grounds of a problem specific to that Member State arising after the adoption of the harmonisation measure, it shall notify the Commission of the envisaged provisions as well as the grounds for introducing them.

6.   The Commission shall, within six months of the notifications as referred to in paragraphs 4 and 5, approve or reject the national provisions involved after having verified whether or not they are a means of arbitrary discrimination or a disguised restriction on trade

between Member States and whether or not they shall constitute an obstacle to the functioning of the internal market.

In the absence of a decision by the Commission within this period the national provisions referred to in paragraphs 4 and 5 shall be deemed to have been approved.

When justified by the complexity of the matter and in the absence of danger for human health, the Commission may notify the Member State concerned that the period referred to in this paragraph may be extended for a further period of up to six months.

7.   When, pursuant to paragraph 6, a Member State is authorised to maintain or introduce national provisions derogating from a harmonisation measure, the Commission shall immediately examine whether to propose an adaptation to that measure.

8.   When a Member State raises a specific problem on public health in a field which has been the subject of prior harmonisation measures, it shall bring it to the attention of the Commission which shall immediately examine whether to propose appropriate measures to the Council.

9.   By way of derogation from the procedure laid down in Articles 226 and 227, the Commission and any Member State may bring the matter directly before the Court of Justice if it considers that another Member State is making improper use of the powers provided for in this Article.

10.   The harmonisation measures referred to above shall, in appropriate cases, include a safeguard clause authorising the Member States to take, for one or more of the non-economic reasons referred to in Article 30, provisional measures subject to a Community control procedure.

Article 96   (ex Article 101)

Where the Commission finds that a difference between the provisions laid down by law, regulation or administrative action in Member States is distorting the conditions of competition in the common market and that the resultant distortion needs to be eliminated, it shall consult the Member States concerned.

If such consultation does not result in an agreement eliminating the distortion in question, the Council shall, on a proposal from the Commission, acting by a qualified majority, issue the necessary directives. The Commission and the Council may take any other appropriate measures provided for in this Treaty.

Article 97   (ex Article 102)

1.   Where there is a reason to fear that the adoption or amendment of a provision laid down by law, regulation or administrative action may cause distortion within the meaning of Article 96, a Member State desiring to proceed therewith shall consult the Commission. After consulting the Member States, the Commission shall recommend to the States concerned such measures as may be appropriate to avoid the distortion in question.

2.   If a State desiring to introduce or amend its own provisions does not comply with the recommendation addressed to it by the Commission, other Member States shall not be required, in pursuance of Article 96, to amend their own provisions in order to eliminate such distortion. If the Member State which has ignored the recommendation of the Commission causes distortion detrimental only to itself, the provisions of Article 96 shall not apply.

TITLE VII (ex Title VI)   ECONOMIC AND MONETARY POLICY

CHAPTER 1   ECONOMIC POLICY

Article 98   (ex Article 102a)

Member States shall conduct their economic policies with a view to contributing to the achievement of the objectives of the Community, as defined in Article 2, and in the context of the broad guidelines referred to in Article 99(2). The Member States and the Community shall act in accordance with the principle of an open market economy with free competition, favouring an efficient allocation of resources, and in compliance with the principles set out in Article 4.

Article 99   (ex Article 103)

1.   Member States shall regard their economic policies as a matter of common concern and shall coordinate them within the Council, in accordance with the provisions of Article 98.

2.   The Council shall, acting by a qualified majority on a recommendation from the Commission, formulate a draft for the broad guidelines of the economic policies of the Member States and of the Community, and shall report its findings to the European Council.

The European Council shall, acting on the basis of the report from the Council, discuss a conclusion on the broad guidelines of the economic policies of the Member States and of the Community.

On the basis of this conclusion, the Council shall, acting by a qualified majority, adopt a recommendation setting out these broad guidelines. The Council shall inform the European Parliament of its recommendation.

3.   In order to ensure closer coordination of economic policies and sustained convergence of the economic performances of the Member States, the Council shall, on the basis of reports submitted by the Commission, monitor economic developments in each of the Member States and in the Community as well as the consistency of economic policies with the broad guidelines referred to in paragraph 2, and regularly carry out an overall assessment.

For the purpose of this multilateral surveillance, Member States shall forward information to the Commission about important measures taken by them in the field of their economic policy and such other information as they deem necessary.

4.   Where it is established, under the procedure referred to in paragraph 3, that the economic policies of a Member State are not consistent with the broad guidelines referred to in paragraph 2 or that they risk jeopardising the proper functioning of economic and monetary union, the Council may, acting by a qualified majority on a recommendation from the Commission, make the necessary recommendations to the Member State concerned. The Council may, acting by a qualified majority on a proposal from the Commission, decide to make its recommendations public.

The President of the Council and the Commission shall report to the European Parliament on the results of multilateral surveillance. The President of the Council may be invited to appear before the competent committee of the European Parliament if the Council has made its recommendations public.

5.   The Council, acting in accordance with the procedure referred to in Article 252, may adopt detailed rules for the multilateral surveillance procedure referred to in paragraphs 3 and 4 of this Article.

Article 100   (ex Article 103a) (As amended by the Treaty of Nice)

1.   Without prejudice to any other procedures provided for in this Treaty, the Council, acting by a qualified majority on a proposal from the Commission, may decide upon the measures appropriate to the economic situation, in particular if severe difficulties arise in the supply of certain products.

2.   Where a Member State is in difficulties or is seriously threatened with severe difficulties caused by natural disasters or exceptional occurrences beyond its control, the Council, acting by a qualified majority on a proposal from the Commission, may grant, under certain conditions, Community financial assistance to the Member State concerned. The President of the Council shall inform the European Parliament of the decision taken.

Article 101   (ex Article 104)

1.   Overdraft facilities or any other type of credit facility with the ECB or with the central banks of the Member States (hereinafter referred to as 'national central banks') in favour of

Community institutions or bodies, central governments, regional, local or other public authorities, other bodies governed by public law, or public undertakings of Member States shall be prohibited, as shall the purchase directly from them by the ECB or national central banks of debt instruments.

2.   Paragraph 1 shall not apply to publicly owned credit institutions which, in the context of the supply of reserves by central banks, shall be given the same treatment by national central banks and the ECB as private credit institutions.

Article 102   (ex Article 104a)

1.   Any measure, not based on prudential considerations, establishing privileged access by Community institutions or bodies, central governments, regional, local or other public authorities, other bodies governed by public law, or public undertakings of Member States to financial institutions, shall be prohibited.

2.   The Council, acting in accordance with the procedure referred to in Article 252, shall, before 1 January 1994, specify definitions for the application of the prohibition referred to in paragraph 1.

Article 103   (ex Article 104b)

1.   The Community shall not be liable for or assume the commitments of central governments, regional, local or other public authorities, other bodies governed by public law, or public undertakings of any Member State, without prejudice to mutual financial guarantees for the joint execution of a specific project. A Member State shall not be liable for or assume the commitments of central governments, regional, local or other public authorities, other bodies governed by public law, or public undertakings of another Member State, without prejudice to mutual financial guarantees for the joint execution of a specific project.

2.   If necessary, the Council, acting in accordance with the procedure referred to in Article 252, may specify definitions for the application of the prohibition referred to in Article 101 and in this Article.

Article 104   (ex Article 104c)

1.   Member States shall avoid excessive government deficits.

2.   The Commission shall monitor the development of the budgetary situation and of the stock of government debt in the Member States with a view to identifying gross errors. In particular it shall examine compliance with budgetary discipline on the basis of the following two criteria:

(a) whether the ratio of the planned or actual government deficit to gross domestic product exceeds a reference value, unless:
   — either the ratio has declined substantially and continuously and reached a level that comes close to the reference value;
   — or, alternatively, the excess over the reference value is only exceptional and temporary and the ratio remains close to the reference value;

(b) whether the ratio of government debt to gross domestic product exceeds a reference value, unless the ratio is sufficiently diminishing and approaching the reference value at a satisfactory pace.

The reference values are specified in the Protocol on the excessive deficit procedure annexed to this Treaty.

3.   If a Member State does not fulfil the requirements under one or both of these criteria, the Commission shall prepare a report. The report of the Commission shall also take into account whether the government deficit exceeds government investment expenditure and take into account all other relevant factors, including the medium-term economic and budgetary position of the Member State.

The Commission may also prepare a report if, notwithstanding the fulfilment of the requirements under the criteria, it is of the opinion that there is a risk of an excessive deficit in a Member State.

4. The Committee provided for in Article 114 shall formulate an opinion on the report of the Commission.

5. If the Commission considers that an excessive deficit in a Member State exists or may occur, the Commission shall address an opinion to the Council.

6. The Council shall, acting by a qualified majority on a recommendation from the Commission, and having considered any observations which the Member State concerned may wish to make, decide after an overall assessment whether an excessive deficit exists.

7. Where the existence of an excessive deficit is decided according to paragraph 6, the Council shall make recommendations to the Member State concerned with a view to bringing that situation to an end within a given period. Subject to the provisions of paragraph 8, these recommendations shall not be made public.

8. Where it establishes that there has been no effective action in response to its recommendations within the period laid down, the Council may make its recommendations public.

9. If a Member State persists in failing to put into practice the recommendations of the Council, the Council may decide to give notice to the Member State to take, within a specified time limit, measures for the deficit reduction which is judged necessary by the Council in order to remedy the situation.

In such a case, the Council may request the Member State concerned to submit reports in accordance with a specific timetable in order to examine the adjustment efforts of that Member State.

10. The rights to bring actions provided for in Articles 226 and 227 may not be exercised within the framework of paragraphs 1 to 9 of this Article.

11. As long as a Member State fails to comply with a decision taken in accordance with paragraph 9, the Council may decide to apply or, as the case may be, intensify one or more of the following measures:

— to require the Member State concerned to publish additional information, to be specified by the Council, before issuing bonds and securities;
— to invite the European Investment Bank to reconsider its lending policy towards the Member State concerned;
— to require the Member State concerned to make a non-interest-bearing deposit of an appropriate size with the Community until the excessive deficit has, in the view of the Council, been corrected;
— to impose fines of an appropriate size.

The President of the Council shall inform the European Parliament of the decisions taken.

12. The Council shall abrogate some or all of its decisions referred to in paragraphs 6 to 9 and 11 to the extent that the excessive deficit in the Member State concerned has, in the view of the Council, been corrected. If the Council has previously made public recommendations, it shall, as soon as the decision under paragraph 8 has been abrogated, make a public statement that an excessive deficit in the Member State concerned no longer exists.

13. When taking the decisions referred to in paragraphs 7 to 9, 11 and 12, the Council shall act on a recommendation from the Commission by a majority of two thirds of the votes of its members weighted in accordance with Article 205(2), excluding the votes of the representative of the Member State concerned.

14. Further provisions relating to the implementation of the procedure described in this Articleare set out in the Protocol on the excessive deficit procedure annexed to this Treaty.

The Council shall, acting unanimously on a proposal from the Commission and after consulting the European Parliament and the ECB, adopt the appropriate provisions which shall then replace the said Protocol.

Subject to the other provisions of this paragraph, the Council shall, before 1 January 1994, acting by a qualified majority on a proposal from the Commission and after consulting the European Parliament, lay down detailed rules and definitions for the application of the provisions of the said Protocol.

CHAPTER 2   MONETARY POLICY

Article 105   (ex Article 105)

1.   The primary objective of the ESCB shall be to maintain price stability. Without prejudice to the objective of price stability, the ESCB shall support the general economic policies in the Community with a view to contributing to the achievement of the objectives of the Community as laid down in Article 2. The ESCB shall act in accordance with the principle of an open market economy with free competition, favouring an efficient allocation of resources, and in compliance with the principles set out in Article 4.

2.   The basic tasks to be carried out through the ESCB shall be:
   — to define and implement the monetary policy of the Community;
   — to conduct foreign exchange operations consistent with the provisions of Article111;
   — to hold and manage the official foreign reserves of the Member States;
   — to promote the smooth operation of payment systems.

3.   The third indent of paragraph 2 shall be without prejudice to the holding and management by the governments of Member States of foreign exchange working balances.

4.   The ECB shall be consulted:
   — on any proposed Community act in its fields of competence;
   — by national authorities regarding any draft legislative provision in its fields of competence, but within the limits and under the conditions set out by the Council in accordance with the procedure laid down in Article 107(6).
The ECB may submit opinions to the appropriate Community institutions or bodies or to national authorities on matters in its fields of competence.

5.   The ESCB shall contribute to the smooth conduct of policies pursued by the competent authorities relating to the prudential supervision of credit institutions and the stability of the financial system.

6.   The Council may, acting unanimously on a proposal from the Commission and after consulting the ECB and after receiving the assent of the European Parliament, confer upon the ECB specific tasks concerning policies relating to the prudential supervision of credit institutions and other financial institutions with the exception of insurance undertakings.

Article 106   (ex Article 105a)

1.   The ECB shall have the exclusive right to authorise the issue of banknotes within the Community. The ECB and the national central banks may issue such notes. The banknotes issued by the ECB and the national central banks shall be the only such notes to have the status of legal tender within the Community.

2.   Member States may issue coins subject to approval by the ECB of the volume of the issue. The Council may, acting in accordance with the procedure referred to in Article 252 and after consulting the ECB, adopt measures to harmonise the denominations and technical specifications of all coins intended for circulation to the extent necessary to permit their smooth circulation within the Community.

Article 107   (ex Article 106)

1.   The ESCB shall be composed of the ECB and of the national central banks.

2.   The ECB shall have legal personality.

3.   The ESCB shall be governed by the decision making bodies of the ECB which shall be the Governing Council and the Executive Board.

4.   The Statute of the ESCB is laid down in a Protocol annexed to this Treaty.

5.   Articles 5.1, 5.2, 5.3, 17, 18, 19.1, 22, 23, 24, 26, 32.2, 32.3, 32.4, 32.6, 33.1(a) and 36 of the Statute of the ESCB may be amended by the Council, acting either by a qualified majority on a recommendation from the ECB and after consulting the Commission or unanimously on a proposal from the Commission and after consulting the ECB. In either case, the assent of the European Parliament shall be required.

6.   The Council, acting by a qualified majority either on a proposal from the Commission and after consulting the European Parliament and the ECB or on a recommendation from the ECB and after consulting the European Parliament and the Commission, shall adopt the provisions referred to in Articles 4, 5.4, 19.2, 20, 28.1, 29.2, 30.4 and 34.3 of the Statute of the ESCB.

Article 108   (ex Article 107)

When exercising the powers and carrying out the tasks and duties conferred upon them by this Treaty and the Statute of the ESCB, neither the ECB, nor a national central bank, nor any member of their decision making bodies shall seek or take instructions from Community institutions or bodies, from any government of a Member State or from any other body. The Community institutions and bodies and the governments of the Member States undertake to respect this principle and not to seek to influence the members of the decision making bodies of the ECB or of the national central banks in the performance of their tasks.

Article 109   (ex Article 108)

Each Member State shall ensure, at the latest at the date of the establishment of the ESCB, that its national legislation including the statutes of its national central bank is compatible with this Treaty and the Statute of the ESCB.

Article 110   (ex Article 108a)

1.   In order to carry out the tasks entrusted to the ESCB, the ECB shall, in accordance with the provisions of this Treaty and under the conditions laid down in the Statute of the ESCB:
  — make regulations to the extent necessary to implement the tasks defined in Article 3.1, first indent, Articles 19.1, 22 and 25.2 of the Statute of the ESCB and in cases which shall be laid down in the acts of the Council referred to in Article 107(6);
  — take decisions necessary for carrying out the tasks entrusted to the ESCB under this Treaty and the Statute of the ESCB;
  — make recommendations and deliver opinions.

2.   A regulation shall have general application. It shall be binding in its entirety and directly applicable in all Member States.

Recommendations and opinions shall have no binding force.

A decision shall be binding in its entirety upon those to whom it is addressed.

Articles 253 to 256 shall apply to regulations and decisions adopted by the ECB.

The ECB may decide to publish its decisions, recommendations and opinions.

3.   Within the limits and under the conditions adopted by the Council under the procedure laid down in Article 107(6), the ECB shall be entitled to impose fines or periodic penalty payments on undertakings for failure to comply with obligations under its regulations and decisions.

Article 111   (ex Article 109) (As amended by the Treaty of Nice)

1.   By way of derogation from Article 300, the Council may, acting unanimously on a recommendation from the ECB or from the Commission, and after consulting the ECB in an endeavour to reach a consensus consistent with the objective of price stability, after consulting the European Parliament, in accordance with the procedure in paragraph 3 for determining the arrangements, conclude formal agreements on an exchange-rate system for the ECU in relation to non-Community currencies. The Council may, acting by a qualified

majority on a recommendation from the ECB or from the Commission, and after consulting the ECB in an endeavour to reach a consensus consistent with the objective of price stability, adopt, adjust or abandon the central rates of the ECU within the exchange-rate system. The President of the Council shall inform the European Parliament of the adoption, adjustment or abandonment of the ECU central rates.

2.   In the absence of an exchange-rate system in relation to one or more non-Community currencies as referred to in paragraph 1, the Council, acting by a qualified majority either on a recommendation from the Commission and after consulting the ECB or on a recommendation from the ECB, may formulate general orientations for exchange rate policy in relation to these currencies. These general orientations shall be without prejudice to the primary objective of the ESCB to maintain price stability.

3.   By way of derogation from Article 300, where agreements concerning monetary or foreign exchange regime matters need to be negotiated by the Community with one or more States or international organisations, the Council, acting by a qualified majority on a recommendation from the Commission and after consulting the ECB, shall decide the arrangements for the negotiation and for the conclusion of such agreements. These arrangements shall ensure that the Community expresses a single position. The Commission shall be fully associated with the negotiations.

Agreements concluded in accordance with this paragraph shall be binding on the institutions of the Community, on the ECB and on Member States.

4.   Subject to paragraph 1, the Council, acting by a qualified majority on a proposal from the Commission and after consulting the ECB, shall decide on the position of the Community at international level as regards issues of particular relevance to economic and monetary union and on its representation, in compliance with the allocation of powers laid down in Articles 99 and 105.

5.   Without prejudice to Community competence and Community agreements as regards economic and monetary union, Member States may negotiate in international bodies and conclude international agreements.

CHAPTER 3   INSTITUTIONAL PROVISIONS

Article 112   (ex Article 109a)

1.   The Governing Council of the ECB shall comprise the members of the Executive Board of the ECB and the Governors of the national central banks.

2.   (a) The Executive Board shall comprise the President, the Vice-President and four other members.

(b) The President, the Vice-President and the other members of the Executive Board shall be appointed from among persons of recognised standing and professional experience in monetary or banking matters by common accord of the governments of the Member States at the level of Heads of State or Government, on a recommendation from the Council, after it has consulted the European Parliament and the Governing Council of the ECB.

Their term of office shall be eight years and shall not be renewable.

Only nationals of Member States may be members of the Executive Board.

Article 113   (ex Article 109b)

1.   The President of the Council and a member of the Commission may participate, without having the right to vote, in meetings of the Governing Council of the ECB.

The President of the Council may submit a motion for deliberation to the Governing Council of the ECB.

2.   The President of the ECB shall be invited to participate in Council meetings when the Council is discussing matters relating to the objectives and tasks of the ESCB.

3.   The ECB shall address an annual report on the activities of the ESCB and on the monetary policy of both the previous and current year to the European Parliament, the Council and the Commission, and also to the European Council. The President of the ECB shall present this report to the Council and to the European Parliament, which may hold a general debate on that basis.

The President of the ECB and the other members of the Executive Board may, at the request of the European Parliament or on their own initiative, be heard by the competent committees of the European Parliament.

Article 114   (ex Article 109c)

1.   In order to promote coordination of the policies of Member States to the full extent needed for the functioning of the internal market, a Monetary Committee with advisory status is hereby set up.

It shall have the following tasks:

- to keep under review the monetary and financial situation of the Member States and of the Community and the general payments system of the Member States and to report regularly thereon to the Council and to the Commission;
- to deliver opinions at the request of the Council or of the Commission, or on its own initiative for submission to those institutions;
- without prejudice to Article 207, to contribute to the preparation of the work of the Council referred to in Articles 59, 60, 99(2), (3), (4) and (5), 100, 102, 103, 104, 116(2), 117(6), 119, 120, 121(2) and 122(1);
- to examine, at least once a year, the situation regarding the movement of capital and the freedom of payments, as they result from the application of this Treaty and of measures adopted by the Council; the examination shall cover all measures relating to capital movements and payments; the Committee shall report to the Commission and to the Council on the outcome of this examination.

The Member States and the Commission shall each appoint two members of the Monetary Committee.

2.   At the start of the third stage, an Economic and Financial Committee shall be set up. The Monetary Committee provided for in paragraph 1 shall be dissolved.

The Economic and Financial Committee shall have the following tasks:

- to deliver opinions at the request of the Council or of the Commission, or on its own initiative for submission to those institutions;
- to keep under review the economic and financial situation of the Member States and of the Community and to report regularly thereon to the Council and to the Commission, in particular on financial relations with third countries and international institutions;
- without prejudice to Article 207, to contribute to the preparation of the work of the Council referred to in Articles 59, 60, 99(2), (3), (4) and (5), 100, 102, 103, 104, 105(6), 106(2), 107(5) and (6), 111, 119, 120(2) and (3), 122(2), 123(4) and (5), and to carry out other advisory and preparatory tasks assigned to it by the Council;
- to examine, at least once a year, the situation regarding the movement of capital and the freedom of payments, as they result from the application of this Treaty and of measures adopted by the Council; the examination shall cover all measures relating to capital movements and payments; the Committee shall report to the Commission and to the Council on the outcome of this examination.

The Member States, the Commission and the ECB shall each appoint no more than two members of the Committee.

3.   The Council shall, acting by a qualified majority on a proposal from the Commission and after consulting the ECB and the Committee referred to in this Article, lay down detailed

provisions concerning the composition of the Economic and Financial Committee. The President of the Council shall inform the European Parliament of such a decision.

4.   In addition to the tasks set out in paragraph 2, if and as long as there are Member States with a derogation as referred to in Articles 122 and 123, the Committee shall keep under review the monetary and financial situation and the general payments system of those Member States and report regularly thereon to the Council and to the Commission.

Article 115   (ex Article 109d)

For matters within the scope of Articles 99(4), 104 with the exception of paragraph 14, 111, 121, 122 and 123(4) and (5), the Council or a Member State may request the Commission to make a recommendation or a proposal, as appropriate. The Commission shall examine this request and submit its conclusions to the Council without delay.

CHAPTER 4   TRANSITIONAL PROVISIONS

Article 116   (ex Article 109e)

1.   The second stage for achieving economic and monetary union shall begin on 1 January 1994.

2.   Before that date:
  (a) each Member State shall:
      — adopt, where necessary, appropriate measures to comply with the prohibitions laid down in Article 56 and in Articles 101 and 102(1);
      — adopt, if necessary, with a view to permitting the assessment provided for in sub-paragraph (b), multiannual programmes intended to ensure the lasting convergence necessary for the achievement of economic and monetary union, in particular with regard to price stability and sound public finances;
  (b) the Council shall, on the basis of a report from the Commission, assess the progress made with regard to economic and monetary convergence, in particular with regard to price stability and sound public finances, and the progress made with the implementation of Community law concerning the internal market.

3.   The provisions of Articles 101, 102(1), 103(1) and 104 with the exception of paragraphs 1, 9, 11 and 14 shall apply from the beginning of the second stage.

The provisions of Articles 100(2), 104(1), (9) and (11), 105, 106, 108, 111, 112, 113 and 114(2) and (4) shall apply from the beginning of the third stage.

4.   In the second stage, Member States shall endeavour to avoid excessive government deficits.

5.   During the second stage, each Member State shall, as appropriate, start the process leading to the independence of its central bank, in accordance with Article 109.

Article 117   (ex Article 109f)

1.   At the start of the second stage, a European Monetary Institute (hereinafter referred to as 'EMI') shall be established and take up its duties; it shall have legal personality and be directed and managed by a Council, consisting of a President and the Governors of the national central banks, one of whom shall be Vice-President.

The President shall be appointed by common accord of the governments of the Member States at the level of Heads of State or Government, on a recommendation from the Council of the EMI, and after consulting the European Parliament and the Council. The President shall be selected from among persons of recognised standing and professional experience in monetary or banking matters. Only nationals of Member States may be President of the EMI. The Council of the EMI shall appoint the Vice-President.

The Statute of the EMI is laid down in a Protocol annexed to this Treaty.

2.   The EMI shall:

— strengthen cooperation between the national central banks;
— strengthen the coordination of the monetary policies of the Member States, with the aim of ensuring price stability;
— monitor the functioning of the European Monetary System;
— hold consultations concerning issues falling within the competence of the national central banks and affecting the stability of financial institutions and markets;
— take over the tasks of the European Monetary Cooperation Fund, which shall be dissolved; the modalities of dissolution are laid down in the Statute of the EMI;
— facilitate the use of the ECU and oversee its development, including the smooth functioning of the ECU clearing system.

3. For the preparation of the third stage, the EMI shall:
— prepare the instruments and the procedures necessary for carrying out a single monetary policy in the third stage;
— promote the harmonisation, where necessary, of the rules and practices governing the collection, compilation and distribution of statistics in the areas within its field of competence;
— prepare the rules for operations to be undertaken by the national central banks within the framework of the ESCB;
— promote the efficiency of cross border payments;
— supervise the technical preparation of ECU banknotes.

At the latest by 31 December 1996, the EMI shall specify the regulatory, organisational and logistical framework necessary for the ESCB to perform its tasks in the third stage. This framework shall be submitted for decision to the ECB at the date of its establishment.

4. The EMI, acting by a majority of two thirds of the members of its Council, may:
— formulate opinions or recommendations on the overall orientation of monetary policy and exchange rate policy as well as on related measures introduced in each Member State;
— submit opinions or recommendations to governments and to the Council on policies which might affect the internal or external monetary situation in the Community and, in particular, the functioning of the European Monetary System;
— make recommendations to the monetary authorities of the Member States concerning the conduct of their monetary policy.

5. The EMI, acting unanimously, may decide to publish its opinions and its recommendations.

6. The EMI shall be consulted by the Council regarding any proposed Community act within its field of competence.

Within the limits and under the conditions set out by the Council, acting by a qualified majority on a proposal from the Commission and after consulting the European Parliament and the EMI, the EMI shall be consulted by the authorities of the Member States on any draft legislative provision within its field of competence.

7. The Council may, acting unanimously on a proposal from the Commission and after consulting the European Parliament and the EMI, confer upon the EMI other tasks for the preparation of the third stage.

8. Where this Treaty provides for a consultative role for the ECB, references to the ECB shall be read as referring to the EMI before the establishment of the ECB.

9. During the second stage, the term 'ECB' used in Articles 230, 232, 233, 234, 237 and 288 shall be read as referring to the EMI.

Article 118   (ex Article 109g)

The currency composition of the ECU basket shall not be changed.

From the start of the third stage, the value of the ECU shall be irrevocably fixed in accordance with Article 123(4).

Article 119   (ex Article 109h)

1.   Where a Member State is in difficulties or is seriously threatened with difficulties as regards its balance of payments either as a result of an overall disequilibrium in its balance of payments, or as a result of the type of currency at its disposal, and where such difficulties are liable in particular to jeopardise the functioning of the common market or the progressive implementation of the common commercial policy, the Commission shall immediately investigate the position of the State in question and the action which, making use of all the means at its disposal, that State has taken or may take in accordance with the provisions of this Treaty. The Commission shall state what measures it recommends the State concerned to take.

If the action taken by a Member State and the measures suggested by the Commission do not prove sufficient to overcome the difficulties which have arisen or which threaten, the Commission shall, after consulting the Committee referred to in Article 114, recommend to the Council the granting of mutual assistance and appropriate methods therefor.

The Commission shall keep the Council regularly informed of the situation and of how it is developing.

2.   The Council, acting by a qualified majority, shall grant such mutual assistance; it shall adopt directives or decisions laying down the conditions and details of such assistance, which may take such forms as:

(a)   a concerted approach to or within any other international organisations to which Member States may have recourse;

(b)   measures needed to avoid deflection of trade where the State which is in difficulties maintains or reintroduces quantitative restrictions against third countries;

(c)   the granting of limited credits by other Member States, subject to their agreement.

3.   If the mutual assistance recommended by the Commission is not granted by the Council or if the mutual assistance granted and the measures taken are insufficient, the Commission shall authorise the State which is in difficulties to take protective measures, the conditions and details of which the Commission shall determine. Such authorisation may be revoked and such conditions and details may be changed by the Council acting by a qualified majority.

4.   Subject to Article 122(6), this Article shall cease to apply from the beginning of the third stage.

Article 120   (ex Article 109i)

1.   Where a sudden crisis in the balance of payments occurs and a decision within the meaning of Article 119(2) is not immediately taken, the Member State concerned may, as a precaution, take the necessary protective measures.

Such measures must cause the least possible disturbance in the functioning of the common market and must not be wider in scope than is strictly necessary to remedy the sudden difficulties which have arisen.

2.   The Commission and the other Member States shall be informed of such protective measures not later than when they enter into force. The Commission may recommend to the Council the granting of mutual assistance under Article 119.

3.   After the Commission has delivered an opinion and the Committee referred to in Article 114 has been consulted, the Council may, acting by a qualified majority, decide that the State concerned shall amend, suspend or abolish the protective measures referred to above.

4.   Subject to Article 122(6), this Article shall cease to apply from the beginning of the third stage.

Article 121   (ex Article 109j)

1.   The Commission and the EMI shall report to the Council on the progress made in the fulfilment by the Member States of their obligations regarding the achievement of economic

and monetary union. These reports shall include an examination of the compatibility between each Member State's national legislation, including the statutes of its national central bank, and Articles 108 and 109 of this Treaty and the Statute of the ESCB. The reports shall also examine the achievement of a high degree of sustainable convergence by reference to the fulfilment by each Member State of the following criteria:

— the achievement of a high degree of price stability; this will be apparent from a rate of inflation which is close to that of, at most, the three best performing Member States in terms of price stability;

— the sustainability of the government financial position; this will be apparent from having achieved a government budgetary position without a deficit that is excessive as determined in accordance with Article 104(6);

— the observance of the normal fluctuation margins provided for by the exchange-rate mechanism of the European Monetary System, for at least two years, without devaluing against the currency of any other Member State;

— the durability of convergence achieved by the Member State and of its participation in the exchange rate mechanism of the European Monetary System being reflected in the long-term interest rate levels.

The four criteria mentioned in this paragraph and the relevant periods over which they are to be respected are developed further in a Protocol annexed to this Treaty. The reports of the Commission and the EMI shall also take account of the development of the ECU, the results of the integration of markets, the situation and development of the balances of payments on current account and an examination of the development of unit labour costs and other price indices.

2.   On the basis of these reports, the Council, acting by a qualified majority on a recommendation from the Commission, shall assess:

— for each Member State, whether it fulfils the necessary conditions for the adoption of a single currency;

— whether a majority of the Member States fulfil the necessary conditions for the adoption of a single currency, and recommend its findings to the Council, meeting in the composition of the Heads of State or Government. The European Parliament shall be consulted and forward its opinion to the Council, meeting in the composition of the Heads of State or Government.

3.   Taking due account of the reports referred to in paragraph 1 and the opinion of the European Parliament referred to in paragraph 2, the Council, meeting in the composition of the Heads of State or Government, shall, acting by a qualified majority, not later than 31 December 1996:

— decide, on the basis of the recommendations of the Council referred to in paragraph 2, whether a majority of the Member States fulfil the necessary conditions for the adoption of a single currency;

— decide whether it is appropriate for the Community to enter the third stage, and if so:

— set the date for the beginning of the third stage.

4.   If by the end of 1997 the date for the beginning of the third stage has not been set, the third stage shall start on 1 January 1999. Before 1 July 1998, the Council, meeting in the composition of the Heads of State or Government, after a repetition of the procedure provided for in paragraphs 1 and 2, with the exception of the second indent of paragraph 2, taking into account the reports referred to in paragraph 1 and the opinion of the European Parliament, shall, acting by a qualified majority and on the basis of the recommendations of the Council referred to in paragraph 2, confirm which Member States fulfil the necessary conditions for the adoption of a single currency.

Article 122   (ex Article 109k)

1.   If the decision has been taken to set the date in accordance with Article 121(3), the Council shall, on the basis of its recommendations referred to in Article 121(2), acting by a qualified majority on a recommendation from the Commission, decide whether any, and if so which, Member States shall have a derogation as defined in paragraph 3 of this Article. Such Member States shall in this Treaty be referred to as 'Member States with a derogation'.

If the Council has confirmed which Member States fulfil the necessary conditions for the adoption of a single currency, in accordance with Article 121(4), those Member States which do not fulfil the conditions shall have a derogation as defined in paragraph 3 of this Article. Such Member States shall in this Treaty be referred to as 'Member States with a derogation'.

2.   At least once every two years, or at the request of a Member State with a derogation, the Commission and the ECB shall report to the Council in accordance with the procedure laid down in Article 121(1). After consulting the European Parliament and after discussion in the Council, meeting in the composition of the Heads of State or Government, the Council shall, acting by a qualified majority on a proposal from the Commission, decide which Member States with a derogation fulfil the necessary conditions on the basis of the criteria set out in Article 121(1), and abrogate the derogations of the Member States concerned.

3.   A derogation referred to in paragraph 1 shall entail that the following Articles do not apply to the Member State concerned: Articles 104(9) and (11), 105(1), (2), (3) and (5), 106, 110, 111, and 112(2)(b). The exclusion of such a Member State and its national central bank from rights and obligations within the ESCB is laid down in Chapter IX of the Statute of the ESCB.

4.   In Articles 105(1), (2) and (3), 106, 110, 111 and 112(2)(b), 'Member States' shall be read as 'Member States without a derogation'.

5.   The voting rights of Member States with a derogation shall be suspended for the Council decisions referred to in the Articles of this Treaty mentioned in paragraph 3. In that case, by way of derogation from Articles 205 and 250(1), a qualified majority shall be defined as two thirds of the votes of the representatives of the Member States without a derogation weighted in accordance with Article 205(2), and unanimity of those Member States shall be required for an act requiring unanimity.

6.   Articles 119 and 120 shall continue to apply to a Member State with a derogation.

Article 123   (ex Article 109l) (As amended by the Treaty of Nice)

1.   Immediately after the decision on the date for the beginning of the third stage has been taken in accordance with Article 121(3), or, as the case may be, immediately after 1 July 1998:

— the Council shall adopt the provisions referred to in Article 107(6);

— the governments of the Member States without a derogation shall appoint, in accordance with the procedure set out in Article 50 of the Statute of the ESCB, the President, the Vice-President and the other members of the Executive Board of the ECB. If there are Member States with a derogation, the number of members of the Executive Board may be smaller than provided for in Article 11.1 of the Statute of the ESCB, but in no circumstances shall it be less than four.

As soon as the Executive Board is appointed, the ESCB and the ECB shall be established and shall prepare for their full operation as described in this Treaty and the Statute of the ESCB. The full exercise of their powers shall start from the first day of the third stage.

2.   As soon as the ECBis established, it shall, if necessary, take over tasks of the EMI. The EMI shall go into liquidation upon the establishment of the ECB; the modalities of liquidation are laid down in the Statute of the EMI.

3.   If and as long as there are Member States with a derogation, and without prejudice to Article 107(3) of this Treaty, the General Council of the ECB referred to in Article 45 of the Statute of the ESCB shall be constituted as a third decision-making body of the ECB.

4.   At the starting date of the third stage, the Council shall, acting with the unanimity of the Member States without a derogation, on a proposal from the Commission and after consulting the ECB, adopt the conversion rates at which their currencies shall be irrevocably fixed and at which irrevocably fixed rate the ECU shall be substituted for these currencies, and the ECU will become a currency in its own right. This measure shall by itself not modify the external value of the ECU. The Council, acting by a qualified majority of the said Member States, on a proposal from the Commission and after consulting the ECB, shall take the other measures necessary for the rapid introduction of the ECU as the single currency of those Member States. The second sentence of Article 122(5) shall apply.

5.   If it is decided, according to the procedure set out in Article 122(2), to abrogate a derogation, the Council shall, acting with the unanimity of the Member States without a derogation and the Member State concerned, on a proposal from the Commission and after consulting the ECB, adopt the rate at which the ECU shall be substituted for the currency of the Member State concerned, and take the other measures necessary for the introduction of the ECU as the single currency in the Member State concerned.

Article 124   (ex Article 109m)

1.   Until the beginning of the third stage, each Member State shall treat its exchange rate policy as a matter of common interest. In so doing, Member States shall take account of the experience acquired in cooperation within the framework of the European Monetary System (EMS) and in developing the ECU, and shall respect existing powers in this field.

2.   From the beginning of the third stage and for as long as a Member State has a derogation, paragraph 1 shall apply by analogy to the exchange rate policy of that Member State.

TITLE VIII (ex Title VIa)   EMPLOYMENT

Article 125   (ex Article 109n)

Member States and the Community shall, in accordance with this Title, work towards developing a coordinated strategy for employment and particularly for promoting a skilled, trained and adaptable workforce and labour markets responsive to economic change with a view to achieving the objectives defined in Article 2 of the Treaty on European Union and in Article 2 of this Treaty.

Article 126   (ex Article 109o)

1.   Member States, through their employment policies, shall contribute to the achievement of the objectives referred to in Article 125 in a way consistent with the broad guidelines of the economic policies of the Member States and of the Community adopted pursuant to Article 99(2).

2.   Member States, having regard to national practices related to the responsibilities of management and labour, shall regard promoting employment as a matter of common concern and shall coordinate their action in this respect within the Council, in accordance with the provisions of Article 128.

Article 127   (ex Article 109p)

1.   The Community shall contribute to a high level of employment by encouraging cooperation between Member States and by supporting and, if necessary, complementing their action. In doing so, the competences of the Member States shall be respected.

2.   The objective of a high level of employment shall be taken into consideration in the formulation and implementation of Community policies and activities.

Article 128   (ex Article 109q)

1.   The European Council shall each year consider the employment situation in the

Community and adopt conclusions thereon, on the basis of a joint annual report by the Council and the Commission.

2.   On the basis of the conclusions of the European Council, the Council, acting by a qualified majority on a proposal from the Commission and after consulting the European Parliament, the Economic and Social Committee, the Committee of the Regions and the Employment Committee referred to in Article 130, shall each year draw up guidelines which the Member States shall take into account in their employment policies. These guidelines shall be consistent with the broad guidelines adopted pursuant to Article 99(2).

3.   Each Member State shall provide the Council and the Commission with an annual report on the principal measures taken to implement its employment policy in the light of the guidelines for employment as referred to in paragraph 2.

4.   The Council, on the basis of the reports referred to in paragraph 3 and having received the views of the Employment Committee, shall each year carry out an examination of the implementation of the employment policies of the Member States in the light of the guidelines for employment. The Council, acting by a qualified majority on a recommendation from the Commission, may, if it considers it appropriate in the light of that examination, make recommendations to Member States.

5.   On the basis of the results of that examination, the Council and the Commission shall make a joint annual report to the European Council on the employment situation in the Community and on the implementation of the guidelines for employment.

Article 129   (ex Article 109r)
The Council, acting in accordance with the procedure referred to in Article 251 and after consulting the Economic and Social Committee and the Committee of the Regions, may adopt incentive measures designed to encourage cooperation between Member States and to support their action in the field of employment through initiatives aimed at developing exchanges of information and best practices, providing comparative analysis and advice as well as promoting innovative approaches and evaluating experiences, in particular by recourse to pilot projects. Those measures shall not include harmonisation of the laws and regulations of the Member States.

Article 130   (ex Article 109s)
The Council, after consulting the European Parliament, shall establish an Employment Committee with advisory status to promote coordination between Member States on employment and labour market policies. The tasks of the Committee shall be:
— to monitor the employment situation and employment policies in the Member States and the Community;
— without prejudice to Article 207, to formulate opinions at the request of either the Council or the Commission or on its own initiative, and to contribute to the preparation of the Council proceedings referred to in Article 128. In fulfilling its mandate, the Committee shall consult management and labour. Each Member State and the Commission shall appoint two members of the Committee.

TITLE IX (ex Title VII)   COMMON COMMERCIAL POLICY

Article 131   (ex Article 110)
By establishing a customs union between themselves Member States aim to contribute, in the common interest, to the harmonious development of world trade, the progressive abolition of restrictions on international trade and the lowering of customs barriers.

The common commercial policy shall take into account the favourable effect which the abolition of customs duties between Member States may have on the increase in the competitive strength of undertakings in those States.

Article 132   (ex Article 112)

1.   Without prejudice to obligations undertaken by them within the framework of other international organisations, Member States shall progressively harmonise the systems whereby they grant aid for exports to third countries, to the extent necessary to ensure that competition between undertakings of the Community is not distorted.

On a proposal from the Commission, the Council shall, acting by a qualified majority, issue any directives needed for this purpose.

2.   The preceding provisions shall not apply to such a drawback of customs duties or charges having equivalent effect nor to such a repayment of indirect taxation including turn-over taxes, excise duties and other indirect taxes as is allowed when goods are exported from a Member State to a third country, insofar as such a drawback or repayment does not exceed the amount imposed, directly or indirectly, on the products exported.

Article 133   (ex Article 113) (As amended by the Treaty of Nice)

1.   The common commercial policy shall be based on uniform principles, particularly in regard to changes in tariff rates, the conclusion of tariff and trade agreements, the achievement of uniformity in measures of liberalisation, export policy and measures to protect trade such as those to be taken in the event of dumping or subsidies.

2.   The Commission shall submit proposals to the Council for implementing the common commercial policy.

3.   Where agreements with one or more States or international organisations need to be negotiated, the Commission shall make recommendations to the Council, which shall authorise the Commission to open the necessary negotiations. The Council and the Commission shall be responsible for ensuring that the agreements negotiated are compatible with internal Community policies and rules.

The Commission shall conduct these negotiations in consultation with a special committee appointed by the Council to assist the Commission in this task and within the framework of such directives as the Council may issue to it. The Commission shall report regularly to the special committee on the progress of negotiations.

The relevant provisions of Article 300 shall apply.

4.   In exercising the powers conferred upon it by this Article, the Council shall act by a qualified majority.

5.   Paragraphs 1 to 4 shall also apply to the negotiation and conclusion of agreements in the fields of trade in services and the commercial aspects of intellectual property, in so far as those agreements are not covered by the said paragraphs and without prejudice to paragraph 6.

By way of derogation from paragraph 4, the Council shall act unanimously when negotiating and concluding an agreement in one of the fields referred to in the first sub-paragraph, where that agreement includes provisions for which unanimity is required for the adoption of internal rules or where it relates to a field in which the Community has not yet exercised the powers conferred upon it by this Treaty by adopting internal rules.

The Council shall act unanimously with respect to the negotiation and conclusion of a horizontal agreement insofar as it also concerns the preceding subparagraph or the second subparagraph of paragraph 6.

This paragraph shall not affect the right of the Member States to maintain and conclude agreements with third countries or international organisations in so far as such agreements comply with Community law and other relevant international agreements.

6.   An agreement may not be concluded by the Council if it includes provisions which would go beyond the Community's internal powers, in particular by leading to harmonisation of the laws or regulations of the Member States in an area for which this Treaty rules out such harmonisation.

In this regard, by way of derogation from the first subparagraph of paragraph 5, agreements relating to trade in cultural and audiovisual services, educational services, and social and human health services, shall fall within the shared competence of the Community and its Member States. Consequently, in addition to a Community decision taken in accordance with the relevant provisions of Article 300, the negotiation of such agreements shall require the common accord of the Member States. Agreements thus negotiated shall be concluded jointly by the Community and the Member States.

The negotiation and conclusion of international agreements in the field of transport shall continue to be governed by the provisions of Title V and Article 300.

7.   Without prejudice to the first subparagraph of paragraph 6, the Council, acting unanimously on a proposal from the Commission and after consulting the European Parliament, may extend the application of paragraphs 1 to 4 to international negotiations and agreements on intellectual property in so far as they are not covered by paragraph 5.

Article 134   (ex Article 115)
In order to ensure that the execution of measures of commercial policy taken in accordance with this Treaty by any Member State is not obstructed by deflection of trade, or where differences between such measures lead to economic difficulties in one or more Member States, the Commission shall recommend the methods for the requisite cooperation between Member States. Failing this, the Commission may authorise Member States to take the necessary protective measures, the conditions and details of which it shall determine.

In case of urgency, Member States shall request authorisation to take the necessary measures themselves from the Commission, which shall take a decision as soon as possible; the Member States concerned shall then notify the measures to the other Member States. The Commission may decide at any time that the Member States concerned shall amend or abolish the measures in question.

In the selection of such measures, priority shall be given to those which cause the least disturbance of the functioning of the common market.

TITLE X (ex Title VIIa)   CUSTOMS COOPERATION

Article 135   (ex Article 116)
Within the scope of application of this Treaty, the Council, acting in accordance with the procedure referred to in Article 251, shall take measures in order to strengthen customs co-operation between Member States and between the latter and the Commission. These measures shall not concern the application of national criminal law or the national administration of justice.

TITLE XI (ex Title VIII)   SOCIAL POLICY, EDUCATION, VOCATIONAL TRAINING AND YOUTH

CHAPTER 1   SOCIAL PROVISIONS

Article 136   (ex Article 117)
The Community and the Member States, having in mind fundamental social rights such as those set out in the European Social Charter signed at Turin on 18 October1961 and in the 1989 Community Charter of the Fundamental Social Rights of Workers, shall have as their objectives the promotion of employment, improved living and working conditions, so as to make possible their harmonisation while the improvement is being maintained, proper social protection, dialogue between management and labour, the development of human resources with a view to lasting high employment and the combating of exclusion.

To this end the Community and the Member States shall implement measures which take account of the diverse forms of national practices, in particular in the field of contractual relations, and the need to maintain the competitiveness of the Community economy.

They believe that such a development will ensue not only from the functioning of the common market, which will favour the harmonisation of social systems, but also from the procedures provided for in this Treaty and from the approximation of provisions laid down by law, regulation or administrative action.

Article 137   (ex Article 118) (As amended by the Treaty of Nice)

1.   With a view to achieving the objectives of Article 136, the Community shall support and complement the activities of the Member States in the following fields:

    (a) improvement in particular of the working environment to protect workers' health and safety;

    (b) working conditions;

    (c) social security and social protection of workers;

    (d) protection of workers where their employment contract is terminated;

    (e) the information and consultation of workers;

    (f) representation and collective defence of the interests of workers and employers, including co-determination, subject to paragraph 5;

    (g) conditions of employment for third-country nationals legally residing in Community territory;

    (h) the integration of persons excluded from the labour market, without prejudice to Article 150;

    (i) equality between men and women with regard to labour market opportunities and treatment at work;

    (j) the combating of social exclusion;

    (k) the modernisation of social protection systems without prejudice to point (c).

2.   To this end, the Council:

    (a) may adopt measures designed to encourage cooperation between Member States through initiatives aimed at improving knowledge, developing exchanges of information and best practices, promoting innovative approaches and evaluating experiences, excluding any harmonisation of the laws and regulations of the Member States;

    (b) may adopt, in the fields referred to in paragraph 1(a) to (i), by means of directives, minimum requirements for gradual implementation, having regard to the conditions and technical rules obtaining in each of the Member States. Such directives shall avoid imposing administrative, financial and legal constraints in a way which would hold back the creation and development of small and medium-sized undertakings.

The Council shall act in accordance with the procedure referred to in Article 251 after consulting the Economic and Social Committee and the Committee of the Regions, except in the fields referred to in paragraph 1(c), (d), (f) and (g) of this Article, where the Council shall act unanimously on a proposal from the Commission, after consulting the European Parliament and the said Committees. The Council, acting unanimously on a proposal from the Commission, after consulting the European Parliament, may decide to render the procedure referred to in Article 251 applicable to paragraph 1(d), (f) and (g) of this Article.

3.   A Member State may entrust management and labour, at their joint request, with the implementation of directives adopted pursuant to paragraph 2.

In this case, it shall ensure that, no later than the date on which a directive must be transposed in accordance with Article 249, management and labour have introduced the necessary measures by agreement, the Member State concerned being required to take any necessary measure enabling it at any time to be in a position to guarantee the results imposed by that directive.

4. The provisions adopted pursuant to this Article:
   — shall not affect the right of Member States to define the fundamental principles of their social security systems and must not significantly affect the financial equilibrium thereof;
   — shall not prevent any Member State from maintaining or introducing more stringent protective measures compatible with this Treaty.

5. The provisions of this Article shall not apply to pay, the right of association, the right to strike or the right to impose lock-outs.

Article 138   (ex Article 118a)

1. The Commission shall have the task of promoting the consultation of management and labour at Community level and shall take any relevant measure to facilitate their dialogue by ensuring balanced support for the parties.

2. To this end, before submitting proposals in the social policy field, the Commission shall consult management and labour on the possible direction of Community action.

3. If, after such consultation, the Commission considers Community action advisable, it shall consult management and labour on the content of the envisaged proposal. Management and labour shall forward to the Commission an opinion or, where appropriate, a recommendation.

4. On the occasion of such consultation, management and labour may inform the Commission of their wish to initiate the process provided for in Article 139. The duration of the procedure shall not exceed nine months, unless the management and labour concerned and the Commission decide jointly to extend it.

Article 139   (ex Article 118b)

1. Should management and labour so desire, the dialogue between them at Community level may lead to contractual relations, including agreements.

2. Agreements concluded at Community level shall be implemented either in accordance with the procedures and practices specific to management and labour and the Member States or, in matters covered by Article 137, at the joint request of the signatory parties, by a Council decision on a proposal from the Commission.

The Council shall act by qualified majority, except where the agreement in question contains one or more provisions relating to one of the areas for which unanimity is required pursuant to Article 137(2). In that case, it shall act unanimously.

Article 140   (ex Article 118c)

With a view to achieving the objectives of Article 136 and without prejudice to the other provisions of this Treaty, the Commission shall encourage cooperation between the Member States and facilitate the coordination of their action in all social policy fields under this chapter, particularly in matters relating to:
   — employment;
   — labour law and working conditions;
   — basic and advanced vocational training;
   — social security;
   — prevention of occupational accidents and diseases;
   — occupational hygiene;
   — the right of association and collective bargaining between employers and workers.

To this end, the Commission shall act in close contact with Member States by making studies, delivering opinions and arranging consultations both on problems arising at national level and on those of concern to international organisations.

Before delivering the opinions provided for in this Article, the Commission shall consult the Economic and Social Committee.

Article 141   (ex Article 119)

1.   Each Member State shall ensure that the principle of equal pay for male and female workers for equal work or work of equal value is applied.

2.   For the purpose of this Article, 'pay' means the ordinary basic or minimum wage or salary and any other consideration, whether in cash or in kind, which the worker receives directly or indirectly, in respect of his employment, from his employer.

Equal pay without discrimination based on sex means:

(a) that pay for the same work at piece rates shall be calculated on the basis of the same unit of measurement;

(b) that pay for work at time rates shall be the same for the same job.

3.   The Council, acting in accordance with the procedure referred to in Article 251, and after consulting the Economic and Social Committee, shall adopt measures to ensure the application of the principle of equal opportunities and equal treatment of men and women in matters of employment and occupation, including the principle of equal pay for equal work or work of equal value.

4.   With a view to ensuring full equality in practice between men and women in working life, the principle of equal treatment shall not prevent any Member State from maintaining or adopting measures providing for specific advantages in order to make it easier for the under-represented sex to pursue a vocational activity or to prevent or compensate for disadvantages in professional careers.

Article 142   (ex Article 119a)

Member States shall endeavour to maintain the existing equivalence between paid holiday schemes.

Article 143   (ex Article 120)

The Commission shall draw up a report each year on progress in achieving the objectives of Article 136, including the demographic situation in the Community. It shall forward the report to the European Parliament, the Council and the Economic and Social Committee.

The European Parliament may invite the Commission to draw up reports on particular problems concerning the social situation.

Article 144   (ex Article 121) (As amended by the Treaty of Nice)

The Council, after consulting the European Parliament, shall establish a Social Protection Committee with advisory status to promote cooperation on social protection policies between Member States and with the Commission. The tasks of the Committee shall be:

— to monitor the social situation and the development of social protection policies in the Member States and the Community;

— to promote exchanges of information, experience and good practice between Member States and with the Commission;

— without prejudice to Article 207, to prepare reports, formulate opinions or undertake other work within its fields of competence, at the request of either the Council or the Commission or on its own initiative.

In fulfilling its mandate, the Committee shall establish appropriate contacts with management and labour.

Each Member State and the Commission shall appoint two members of the Committee.

Article 145   (ex Article 122)

The Commission shall include a separate chapter on social developments within the Community in its annual report to the European Parliament.

The European Parliament may invite the Commission to draw up reports on any particular problems concerning social conditions.

CHAPTER 2   THE EUROPEAN SOCIAL FUND

Article 146   (ex Article 123)

In order to improve employment opportunities for workers in the internal market and to contribute thereby to raising the standard of living, a European Social Fund is hereby established in accordance with the provisions set out below; it shall aim to render the employment of workers easier and to increase their geographical and occupational mobility within the Community, and to facilitate their adaptation to industrial changes and to changes in production systems, in particular through vocational training and retraining.

Article 147   (ex Article 124)

The Fund shall be administered by the Commission.

The Commission shall be assisted in this task by a Committee presided over by a Member of the Commission and composed of representatives of governments, trade unions and employers' organisations.

Article 148   (ex Article 125)

The Council, acting in accordance with the procedure referred to in Article 251 and after consulting the Economic and Social Committee and the Committee of the Regions, shall adopt implementing decisions relating to the European Social Fund.

CHAPTER 3   EDUCATION, VOCATIONAL TRAINING AND YOUTH

Article 149   (ex Article 126)

1. The Community shall contribute to the development of quality education by encouraging cooperation between Member States and, if necessary, by supporting and supplementing their action, while fully respecting the responsibility of the Member States for the content of teaching and the organisation of education systems and their cultural and linguistic diversity.

2. Community action shall be aimed at:
   — developing the European dimension in education, particularly through the teaching and dissemination of the languages of the Member States;
   — encouraging mobility of students and teachers, inter alia by encouraging the academic recognition of diplomas and periods of study;
   — promoting cooperation between educational establishments;
   — developing exchanges of information and experience on issues common to the education systems of the Member States;
   — encouraging the development of youth exchanges and of exchanges of socio-educational instructors;
   — encouraging the development of distance education.

3. The Community and the Member States shall foster cooperation with third countries and the competent international organisations in the field of education, in particular the Council of Europe.

4. In order to contribute to the achievement of the objectives referred to in this Article, the Council:
   — acting in accordance with the procedure referred to in Article 251, after consulting the Economic and Social Committee and the Committee of the Regions, shall adopt incentive measures, excluding any harmonisation of the laws and regulations of the Member States;

— acting by a qualified majority on a proposal from the Commission, shall adopt recommendations.

Article 150   (ex Article 127)

1.   The Community shall implement a vocational training policy which shall support and supplement the action of the Member States, while fully respecting the responsibility of the Member States for the content and organisation of vocational training.

2.   Community action shall aim to:
— facilitate adaptation to industrial changes, in particular through vocational training and retraining;
— improve initial and continuing vocational training in order to facilitate vocational integration and reintegration into the labour market;
— facilitate access to vocational training and encourage mobility of instructors and trainees and particularly young people;
— stimulate cooperation on training between educational or training establishments and firms;
— develop exchanges of information and experience on issues common to the training systems of the Member States.

3.   The Community and the Member States shall foster cooperation with third countries and the competent international organisations in the sphere of vocational training.

4.   The Council, acting in accordance with the procedure referred to in Article 251 and after consulting the Economic and Social Committee and the Committee of the Regions, shall adopt measures to contribute to the achievement of the objectives referred to in this Article, excluding any harmonisation of the laws and regulations of the Member States.tes.

TITLE XII (ex Title IX)   CULTURE

Article 151   (ex Article 128)

1.   The Community shall contribute to the flowering of the cultures of the Member States, while respecting their national and regional diversity and at the same time bringing the common cultural heritage to the fore.

2.   Action by the Community shall be aimed at encouraging cooperation between Member States and, if necessary, supporting and supplementing their action in the following areas:
— improvement of the knowledge and dissemination of the culture and history of the European peoples;
— conservation and safeguarding of cultural heritage of European significance;
— non-commercial cultural exchanges;
— artistic and literary creation, including in the audiovisual sector.

3.   The Community and the Member States shall foster cooperation with third countries and the competent international organisations in the sphere of culture, in particular the Council of Europe.

4.   The Community shall take cultural aspects into account in its action under other provisions of this Treaty, in particular in order to respect and to promote the diversity of its cultures.

5.   In order to contribute to the achievement of the objectives referred to in this Article, the Council:
— acting in accordance with the procedure referred to in Article 251 and after consulting the Committee of the Regions, shall adopt incentive measures, excluding any harmonisation of the laws and regulations of the Member States. The Council shall act unanimously throughout the procedure referred to in Article 251;
— acting unanimously on a proposal from the Commission, shall adopt recommendations.

TITLE XIII (ex Title X)   PUBLIC HEALTH

Article 152   **(ex Article 129)**

1.   A high level of human health protection shall be ensured in the definition and implementation of all Community policies and activities.

Community action, which shall complement national policies, shall be directed towards improving public health, preventing human illness and diseases, and obviating sources of danger to human health. Such action shall cover the fight against the major health scourges, by promoting research into their causes, their transmission and their prevention, as well as health information and education.

The Community shall complement the Member States' action in reducing drugs-related health damage, including information and prevention.

2.   The Community shall encourage cooperation between the Member States in the areas referred to in this Article and, if necessary, lend support to their action.

Member States shall, in liaison with the Commission, coordinate among themselves their policies and programmes in the areas referred to in paragraph 1. The Commission may, in close contact with the Member States, take any useful initiative to promote such coordination.

3.   The Community and the Member States shall foster cooperation with third countries and the competent international organisations in the sphere of public health.

4.   The Council, acting in accordance with the procedure referred to in Article 251 and after consulting the Economic and Social Committee and the Committee of the Regions, shall contribute to the achievement of the objectives referred to in this Article through adopting:

   (a) measures setting high standards of quality and safety of organs and substances of human origin, blood and blood derivatives; these measures shall not prevent any Member State from maintaining or introducing more stringent protective measures;

   (b) by way of derogation from Article 37, measures in the veterinary and phyto-sanitary fields which have as their direct objective the protection of public health;

   (c) incentive measures designed to protect and improve human health, excluding any harmonisation of the laws and regulations of the Member States.

The Council, acting by a qualified majority on a proposal from the Commission, may also adopt recommendations for the purposes set out in this Article.

5.   Community action in the field of public health shall fully respect the responsibilities of the Member States for the organisation and delivery of health services and medical care. In particular, measures referred to in paragraph 4(a) shall not affect national provisions on the donation or medical use of organs and blood.

TITLE XIV (ex Title XI)   CONSUMER PROTECTION

Article 153   **(ex Article 129a)**

1.   In order to promote the interests of consumers and to ensure a high level of consumer protection, the Community shall contribute to protecting the health, safety and economic interests of consumers, as well as to promoting their right to information, education and to organise themselves in order to safeguard their interests.

2.   Consumer protection requirements shall be taken into account in defining and implementing other Community policies and activities.

3.   The Community shall contribute to the attainment of the objectives referred to in paragraph 1 through:

   (a) measures adopted pursuant to Article 95 in the context of the completion of the internal market;

   (b) measures which support, supplement and monitor the policy pursued by the Member States.

4.   The Council, acting in accordance with the procedure referred to in Article 251 and after consulting the Economic and Social Committee, shall adopt the measures referred to in paragraph 3(b).

5.   Measures adopted pursuant to paragraph 4 shall not prevent any Member State from maintaining or introducing more stringent protective measures. Such measures must be compatible with this Treaty. The Commission shall be notified of them.

TITLE XV (ex Title XII)   TRANS-EUROPEAN NETWORKS

Article 154   (ex Article 129b)

1.   To help achieve the objectives referred to in Articles 14 and 158 and to enable citizens of the Union, economic operators and regional and local communities to derive full benefit from the setting up of an area without internal frontiers, the Community shall contribute to the establishment and development of trans-European networks in the areas of transport, telecommunications and energy infrastructures.

2.   Within the framework of a system of open and competitive markets, action by the Community shall aim at promoting the interconnection and interoperability of national networks as well as access to such networks. It shall take account in particular of the need to link island, landlocked and peripheral regions with the central regions of the Community.

Article 155   (ex Article 129c)

1.   In order to achieve the objectives referred to in Article 154, the Community:
   — shall establish a series of guidelines covering the objectives, priorities and broad lines of measures envisaged in the sphere of trans-European networks; these guidelines shall identify projects of common interest;
   — shall implement any measures that may prove necessary to ensure the interoperability of the networks, in particular in the field of technical standardisation;
   — may support projects of common interest supported by Member States, which are identified in the framework of the guidelines referred to in the first indent, particularly through feasibility studies, loan guarantees or interest rate subsidies; the Community may also contribute, through the Cohesion Fund set up pursuant to Article 161, to the financing of specific projects in Member States in the area of transport infrastructure.

The Community's activities shall take into account the potential economic viability of the projects.

2.   Member States shall, in liaison with the Commission, coordinate among themselves the policies pursued at national level which may have a significant impact on the achievement of the objectives referred to in Article 154. The Commission may, in close cooperation with the Member State, take any useful initiative to promote such coordination.

3.   The Community may decide to cooperate with third countries to promote projects of mutual interest and to ensure the interoperability of networks.

Article 156   (ex Article 129d)

The guidelines and other measures referred to in Article 155(1) shall be adopted by the Council, acting in accordance with the procedure referred to in Article 251 and after consulting the Economic and Social Committee and the Committee of the Regions.

Guidelines and projects of common interest which relate to the territory of a Member State shall require the approval of the Member State concerned.

TITLE XVI (ex Title XIII)   INDUSTRY

Article 157   (ex Article 130) (As amended by the Treaty of Nice)

1.   The Community and the Member States shall ensure that the conditions necessary for the competitiveness of the Community's industry exist.

For that purpose, in accordance with a system of open and competitive markets, their action shall be aimed at:

— speeding up the adjustment of industry to structural changes;

— encouraging an environment favourable to initiative and to the development of undertakings throughout the Community, particularly small and medium-sized undertakings;

— encouraging an environment favourable to cooperation between undertakings;

— fostering better exploitation of the industrial potential of policies of innovation, research and technological development.

2.   The Member States shall consult each other in liaison with the Commission and, where necessary, shall coordinate their action. The Commission may take any useful initiative to promote such coordination.

3.   The Community shall contribute to the achievement of the objectives set out in paragraph 1 through the policies and activities it pursues under other provisions of this Treaty. The Council, acting in accordance with the procedure referred to in Article 251 and after consulting the Economic and Social Committee, may decide on specific measures in support of action taken in the Member States to achieve the objectives set out in paragraph 1.

This Title shall not provide a basis for the introduction by the Community of any measure which could lead to a distortion of competition or contains tax provisions or provisions relating to the rights and interests of employed persons.

TITLE XVII (ex Title XIV)   ECONOMIC AND SOCIAL COHESION

Article 158   (ex Article 130a)

In order to promote its overall harmonious development, the Community shall develop and pursue its actions leading to the strengthening of its economic and social cohesion.

In particular, the Community shall aim at reducing disparities between the levels of development of the various regions and the backwardness of the least favoured regions or islands, including rural areas.

Article 159   (ex Article 130b) (As amended by the Treaty of Nice)

Member States shall conduct their economic policies and shall coordinate them in such a way as, in addition, to attain the objectives set out in Article 158. The formulation and implementation of the Community's policies and actions and the implementation of the internal market shall take into account the objectives set out in Article 158 and shall contribute to their achievement. The Community shall also support the achievement of these objectives by the action it takes through the Structural Funds (European Agricultural Guidance and Guarantee Fund, Guidance Section; European Social Fund; European Regional Development Fund), the European Investment Bank and the other existing financial instruments.

The Commission shall submit a report to the European Parliament, the Council, the Economic and Social Committee and the Committee of the Regions every three years on the progress made towards achieving economic and social cohesion and on the manner in which the various means provided for in this Article have contributed to it. This report shall, if necessary, be accompanied by appropriate proposals.

If specific actions prove necessary outside the Funds and without prejudice to the measures decided upon within the framework of the other Community policies, such actions may be adopted by the Council acting in accordance with the procedure referred to in Article 251 and after consulting the Economic and Social Committee and the Committee of the Regions.

Article 160   (ex Article 130c)

The European Regional Development Fund is intended to help to redress the main regional imbalances in the Community through participation in the development and structural adjustment of regions whose development is lagging behind and in the conversion of declining industrial regions.

Article 161   (ex Article 130d) (As amended by the Treaty of Nice)

Without prejudice to Article 162, the Council, acting unanimously on a proposal from the Commission and after obtaining the assent of the European Parliament and consulting the Economic and Social Committee and the Committee of the Regions, shall define the tasks, priority objectives and the organisation of the Structural Funds, which may involve grouping the Funds. The Council, acting by the same procedure, shall also define the general rules applicable to them and the provisions necessary to ensure their effectiveness and the coordination of the Funds with one another and with the other existing financial instruments.

A Cohesion Fund set up by the Council in accordance with the same procedure shall provide a financial contribution to projects in the fields of environment and trans-European networks in the area of transport infrastructure.

From 1 January 2007, the Council shall act by a qualified majority on a proposal from the Commission after obtaining the assent of the European Parliament and after consulting the Economic and Social Committee and the Committee of the Regions if, by that date, the multiannual financial perspective applicable from 1 January 2007 and the Interinstitutional Agreement relating thereto have been adopted. If such is not the case, the procedure laid down by this paragraph shall apply from the date of their adoption.

Article 162   (ex Article 130e)

Implementing decisions relating to the European Regional Development Fund shall be taken by the Council, acting in accordance with the procedure referred to in Article 251 and after consulting the Economic and Social Committee and the Committee of the Regions.

With regard to the European Agricultural Guidance and Guarantee Fund, Guidance Section, and the European Social Fund, Articles 37 and 148 respectively shall continue to apply.

TITLE XVIII (ex Title XV)   RESEARCH AND TECHNOLOGICAL DEVELOPMENT

Article 163   (ex Article 130f)

1.   The Community shall have the objective of strengthening the scientific and techno-logical bases of Community industry and encouraging it to become more competitive at international level, while promoting all the research activities deemed necessary by virtue of other Chapters of this Treaty.

2.   For this purpose the Community shall, throughout the Community, encourage undertakings, including small and medium sized undertakings, research centres and uni-versities in their research and technological development activities of high quality; it shall support their efforts to cooperate with one another, aiming, notably, at enabling undertakings to exploit the internal market potential to the full, in particular through the opening up of national public contracts, the definition of common standards and the removal of legal and fiscal obstacles to that cooperation.

3.   All Community activities under this Treaty in the area of research and technological development, including demonstration projects, shall be decided on and implemented in accordance with the provisions of this Title.

Article 164   (ex Article 130g)

In pursuing these objectives, the Community shall carry out the following activities, complementing the activities carried out in the Member States:

(a) implementation of research, technological development and demonstration programmes, by promoting cooperation with and between undertakings, research
centres and universities;

(b) promotion of cooperation in the field of Community research, technological
development and demonstration with third countries and international
organisations;

(c) dissemination and optimisation of the results of activities in Community
research, technological development and demonstration;

(d) stimulation of the training and mobility of researchers in the Community.

Article 165   (ex Article 130h)

1. The Community and the Member States shall coordinate their research and technological development activities so as to ensure that national policies and Community policy
are mutually consistent.

2. In close cooperation with the Member State, the Commission may take any useful
initiative to promote the coordination referred to in paragraph 1.

Article 166   (ex Article 130i)

1. A multi-annual framework programme, setting out all the activities of the Community, shall be adopted by the Council, acting in accordance with the procedure referred to
in Article 251 after consulting the Economic and Social Committee.

The framework programme shall:

— establish the scientific and technological objectives to be achieved by the activities
provided for in Article 164 and fix the relevant priorities;

— indicate the broad lines of such activities;

— fix the maximum overall amount and the detailed rules for Community financial
participation in the framework programme and the respective shares in each of the
activities provided for.

2. The framework programme shall be adapted or supplemented as the situation
changes.

3. The framework programme shall be implemented through specific programmes
developed within each activity. Each specific programme shall define the detailed rules for
implementing it, fix its duration and provide for the means deemed necessary. The sum of the
amounts deemed necessary, fixed in the specific programmes, may not exceed the overall
maximum amount fixed for the framework programme and each activity.

4. The Council, acting by a qualified majority on a proposal from the Commission and
after consulting the European Parliament and the Economic and Social Committee, shall
adopt the specific programmes.

Article 167   (ex Article 130j)

For the implementation of the multiannual framework programme the Council shall:

— determine the rules for the participation of undertakings, research centres and
universities;

— lay down the rules governing the dissemination of research results.

Article 168   (ex Article 130k)

In implementing the multiannual framework programme, supplementary programmes
may be decided on involving the participation of certain Member States only, which shall
finance them subject to possible Community participation. The Council shall adopt the

rules applicable to supplementary programmes, particularly as regards the dissemination of knowledge and access by other Member States.

Article 169   (ex Article 130l)
In implementing the multiannual framework programme the Community may make provision, in agreement with the Member States concerned, for participation in research and development programmes undertaken by several Member States, including participation in the structures created for the execution of those programmes.

Article 170   (ex Article 130m)
In implementing the multiannual framework programme the Community may make provision for cooperation in Community research, technological development and demonstration with third countries or international organisations.

The detailed arrangements for such cooperation may be the subject of agreements between the Community and the third parties concerned, which shall be negotiated and concluded in accordance with Article 300.

Article 171   (ex Article 130n)
The Community may set up joint undertakings or any other structure necessary for the efficient execution of Community research, technological development and demonstration programmes.

Article 172   (ex Article 130o)
The Council, acting by qualified majority on a proposal from the Commission and after consulting the European Parliament and the Economic and Social Committee, shall adopt the provisions referred to in Article 171.

The Council, acting in accordance with the procedure referred to in Article 251 and after consulting the Economic and Social Committee, shall adopt the provisions referred to in Articles 167, 168 and 169. Adoption of the supplementary programmes shall require the agreement of the Member States concerned.

Article 173   (ex Article 130p)
At the beginning of each year the Commission shall send a report to the European Parliament and the Council. The report shall include information on research and technological development activities and the dissemination of results during the previous year, and the work programme for the current year.

TITLE XIX (ex Title XVI)   ENVIRONMENT

Article 174   (ex Article 130r)
   1.   Community policy on the environment shall contribute to pursuit of the following objectives:
> — preserving, protecting and improving the quality of the environment;
> — protecting human health;
> — prudent and rational utilisation of natural resources;
> — promoting measures at international level to deal with regional or worldwide environmental problems.
   2.   Community policy on the environment shall aim at a high level of protection taking into account the diversity of situations in the various regions of the Community. It shall be based on the precautionary principle and on the principles that preventive action should be taken, that environmental damage should as a priority be rectified at source and that the polluter should pay.

In this context, harmonisation measures answering environmental protection requirements shall include, where appropriate, a safeguard clause allowing Member States to take provisional measures, for non-economic environmental reasons, subject to a Community inspection procedure.

3.   In preparing its policy on the environment, the Community shall take account of:
— available scientific and technical data;
— environmental conditions in the various regions of the Community;
— the potential benefits and costs of action or lack of action;
— the economic and social development of the Community as a whole and the balanced development of its regions.

4.   Within their respective spheres of competence, the Community and the Member States shall cooperate with third countries and with the competent international organisations. The arrangements for Community cooperation may be the subject of agreements between the Community and the third parties concerned, which shall be negotiated and concluded in accordance with Article 300.

The previous sub-paragraph shall be without prejudice to Member States' competence to negotiate in international bodies and to conclude international agreements.

Article 175   (ex Article 130s) (As amended by the Treaty of Nice)

1.   The Council, acting in accordance with the procedure referred to in Article 251 and after consulting the Economic and Social Committee and the Committee of the Regions, shall decide what action is to be taken by the Community in order to achieve the objectives referred to in Article 174.

2.   By way of derogation from the decision-making procedure provided for in paragraph 1 and without prejudice to Article 95, the Council, acting unanimously on a proposal from the Commission and after consulting the European Parliament, the Economic and Social Committee and the Committee of the Regions, shall adopt:
(a) provisions primarily of a fiscal nature;
(b) measures affecting:
— town and country planning;
— quantitative management of water resources or affecting, directly or indirectly, the availability of those resources;
— land use, with the exception of waste management;
(c) measures significantly affecting a Member State's choice between different energy sources and the general structure of its energy supply.

The Council may, under the conditions laid down in the first subparagraph, define those matters referred to in this paragraph on which decisions are to be taken by a qualified majority.

3.   In other areas, general action programmes setting out priority objectives to be attained shall be adopted by the Council, acting in accordance with the procedure referred to in Article 251 and after consulting the Economic and Social Committee and the Committee of the Regions.

The Council, acting under the terms of paragraph 1 or paragraph 2 according to the case, shall adopt the measures necessary for the implementation of these programmes.

4.   Without prejudice to certain measures of a Community nature, the Member States shall finance and implement the environment policy.

5.   Without prejudice to the principle that the polluter should pay, if a measure based on the provisions of paragraph 1 involves costs deemed disproportionate for the public authorities of a Member State, the Council shall, in the act adopting that measure, lay down appropriate provisions in the form of:
— temporary derogations, and/or
— financial support from the Cohesion Fund set up pursuant to Article 161.

Article 176   (ex Article 130t)

The protective measures adopted pursuant to Article 175 shall not prevent any Member State from maintaining or introducing more stringent protective measures. Such measures must be compatible with this Treaty. They shall be notified to the Commission.

TITLE XX (ex Title XVII)   DEVELOPMENT COOPERATION

Article 177   (ex Article 130u)

1.   Community policy in the sphere of development cooperation, which shall be complementary to the policies pursued by the Member States, shall foster:
— the sustainable economic and social development of the developing countries, and more particularly the most disadvantaged among them;
— the smooth and gradual integration of the developing countries into the world economy;
— the campaign against poverty in the developing countries.

2.   Community policy in this area shall contribute to the general objective of developing and consolidating democracy and the rule of law, and to that of respecting human rights and fundamental freedoms.

3.   The Community and the Member States shall comply with the commitments and take account of the objectives they have approved in the context of the United Nations and other competent international organisations.

Article 178   (ex Article 130v)

The Community shall take account of the objectives referred to in Article 177 in the policies that it implements which are likely to affect developing countries.

Article 179   (ex Article 130w)

1.   Without prejudice to the other provisions of this Treaty, the Council, acting in accordance with the procedure referred to in Article 251, shall adopt the measures necessary to further the objectives referred to in Article 177. Such measures may take the form of multiannual programmes.

2.   The European Investment Bank shall contribute, under the terms laid down in its Statute, to the implementation of the measures referred to in paragraph 1.

3.   The provisions of this Article shall not affect cooperation with the African, Caribbean and Pacific countries in the framework of the ACP-EC Convention.

Article 180   (ex Article 130x)

1.   The Community and the Member States shall coordinate their policies on development cooperation and shall consult each other on their aid programmes, including in international organisations and during international conferences. They may undertake joint action. Member States shall contribute if necessary to the implementation of Community aid programmes.

2.   The Commission may take any useful initiative to promote the coordination referred to in paragraph 1.

Article 181   (ex Article 130y)

Within their respective spheres of competence, the Community and the Member States shall cooperate with third countries and with the competent international organisations. The arrangements for Community cooperation may be the subject of agreements between the Community and the third parties concerned, which shall be negotiated and concluded in accordance with Article 300.

The previous paragraph shall be without prejudice to Member States' competence to negotiate in international bodies and to conclude international agreements.

TITLE XXI (Title added by the Treaty of Nice)
ECONOMIC, FINANCIAL AND TECHNICAL
COOPERATION WITH THIRD COUNTRIES

Article 181a

1. Without prejudice to the other provisions of this Treaty, and in particular those of Title XX, the Community shall carry out, within its spheres of competence, economic, financial and technical cooperation measures with third countries. Such measures shall be complementary to those carried out by the Member States and consistent with the development policy of the Community.

Community policy in this area shall contribute to the general objective of developing and consolidating democracy and the rule of law, and to the objective of respecting human rights and fundamental freedoms.

2. The Council, acting by a qualified majority on a proposal from the Commission and after consulting the European Parliament, shall adopt the measures necessary for the implementation of paragraph 1. The Council shall act unanimously for the association agreements referred to in Article 310 and for the agreements to be concluded with the States which are candidates for accession to the Union.

3. Within their respective spheres of competence, the Community and the Member States shall cooperate with third countries and the competent international organisations. The arrangements for Community cooperation may be the subject of agreements between the Community and the third parties concerned, which shall be negotiated and concluded in accordance with Article 300.

The first subparagraph shall be without prejudice to the Member States' competence to negotiate in international bodies and to conclude international agreements.

PART FOUR   ASSOCIATION OF THE OVERSEAS COUNTRIES
AND TERRITORIES

Article 182   (ex Article 131)

The Member States agree to associate with the Community the non-European countries and territories which have special relations with Denmark, France, the Netherlands and the United Kingdom. These countries and territories (hereinafter called the 'countries and territories') are listed in Annex II to this Treaty.

The purpose of association shall be to promote the economic and social development of the countries and territories and to establish close economic relations between them and the Community as a whole.

In accordance with the principles set out in the Preamble to this Treaty, association shall serve primarily to further the interests and prosperity of the inhabitants of these countries and territories in order to lead them to the economic, social and cultural development to which they aspire.

Article 183   (ex Article 132)

Association shall have the following objectives.

(1) Member States shall apply to their trade with the countries and territories the same treatment as they accord each other pursuant to this Treaty.

(2) Each country or territory shall apply to its trade with Member States and with the other countries and territories the same treatment as that which it applies to the European State with which it has special relations.

(3) The Member States shall contribute to the investments required for the progressive development of these countries and territories.

(4) For investments financed by the Community, participation in tenders and supplies shall be open on equal terms to all natural and legal persons who are nationals of a Member State or of one of the countries and territories.

(5) In relations between Member States and the countries and territories the right of establishment of nationals and companies or firms shall be regulated in accordance with the provisions and procedures laid down in the Chapter relating to the right of establishment and on a non-discriminatory basis, subject to any special provisions laid down pursuant to Article 187.

Article 184   (ex Article 133)

1.   Customs duties on imports into the Member States of goods originating in the countries and territories shall be prohibited in conformity with the prohibition of customs duties between Member States in accordance with the provisions of this Treaty.

2.   Customs duties on imports into each country or territory from Member States or from the other countries or territories shall be prohibited in accordance with the provisions of Article 25.

3.   The countries and territories may, however, levy customs duties which meet the needs of their development and industrialisation or produce revenue for their budgets.

The duties referred to in the preceding sub-paragraph may not exceed the level of those imposed on imports of products from the Member State with which each country or territory has special relations.

4.   Paragraph 2 shall not apply to countries and territories which, by reason of the particular international obligations by which they are bound, already apply a non-discriminatory customs tariff.

5.   The introduction of or any change in customs duties imposed on goods imported into the countries and territories shall not, either in law or in fact, give rise to any direct or indirect discrimination between imports from the various Member States.

Article 185   (ex Article 134)

If the level of the duties applicable to goods from a third country on entry into a country or territory is liable, when the provisions of Article 184(1) have been applied, to cause deflections of trade to the detriment of any Member State, the latter may request the Commission to propose to the other Member States the measures needed to remedy the situation.

Article 186   (ex Article 135)

Subject to the provisions relating to public health, public security or public policy, freedom of movement within Member States for workers from the countries and territories, and within the countries and territories for workers from Member States, shall be governed by agreements to be concluded subsequently with the unanimous approval of Member States.

Article 187   (ex Article 136)

The Council, acting unanimously, shall, on the basis of the experience acquired under the association of the countries and territories with the Community and of the principles set out in this Treaty, lay down provisions as regards the detailed rules and the procedure for the association of the countries and territories with the Community.

Article 188   (ex Article 136a)

The provisions of Articles 182 to 187 shall apply to Greenland, subject to the specific provisions for Greenland set out in the Protocol on special arrangements for Greenland, annexed to this Treaty.

PART FIVE   INSTITUTIONS OF THE COMMUNITY
TITLE I   PROVISIONS GOVERNING THE INSTITUTIONS
CHAPTER 1   THE INSTITUTIONS
SECTION 1   THE EUROPEAN PARLIAMENT

Article 189   (ex Article 137) (As amended by the Treaty of Nice and the 2003 Accession Treaty)

The European Parliament, which shall consist of representatives of the peoples of the States brought together in the Community, shall exercise the powers conferred upon it by this Treaty.

The number of Members of the European Parliament shall not exceed 732.[1]

Article 190   (ex Article 138) (As amended by the Treaty of Nice and the 2003 Accession Treaty)

1.   The representatives in the European Parliament of the peoples of the States brought together in the Community shall be elected by direct universal suffrage.

2.   The number of representatives elected in each Member State shall be as follows:[2]

Belgium	24
Czech Republic	24
Denmark	14
Germany	99
Estonia	6
Greece	24
Spain	54
France	78
Ireland	13
Italy	78
Cyprus	6
Latvia	9
Lithuania	13
Luxembourg	6
Hungary	24
Malta	5
Netherlands	27
Austria	18
Poland	54
Portugal	24
Slovenia	7
Slovakia	14
Finland	14
Sweden	19
United Kingdom	78

In the event of amendments to this paragraph, the number of representatives elected in each Member State must ensure appropriate representation of the peoples of the States brought together in the Community.

---

[1] **Editor's Note:** Agreed under the Constitutional Treaty to be raised to 750 from 2009 but with contingency plans in the event of Bulgaria and Romania joining, see Declaration 40 at Prelim clxvi.

[2] **Editor's Note:** Transitional until 2009 unless Bulgaria and Romania join and/or the CT comes into force. See the Protocol on the Enlargement of the European Union and the Declaration on the enlargement of the European Union, both attached to the Nice Treaty (p. 119 and p. 133) or the Constitutional Treaty for Europe (see above at Prelim xxix) and the Annexes to a Commission memo on transitional numbers (Prelim clxviii above).

3.   Representatives shall be elected for a term of five years.

4.   The European Parliament shall draw up a proposal for elections by direct universal suffrage in accordance with a uniform procedure in all Member States or in accordance with principles common to all Member States.

The Council shall, acting unanimously after obtaining the assent of the European Parliament, which shall act by a majority of its component members, lay down the appropriate provisions, which it shall recommend to Member States for adoption in accordance with their respective constitutional requirements.

5.   The European Parliament, after seeking an opinion from the Commission and with the approval of the Council acting by a qualified majority, shall lay down the regulations and general conditions governing the performance of the duties of its Members. All rules or conditions relating to the taxation of Members or former Members shall require unanimity within the Council.

Article 191   (ex Article 138a) (As amended by the Treaty of Nice)
Political parties at European level are important as a factor for integration within the Union. They contribute to forming a European awareness and to expressing the political will of the citizens of the Union.

The Council, acting in accordance with the procedure referred to in Article 251, shall lay down the regulations governing political parties at European level and in particular the rules regarding their funding.

Article 192   (ex Article 138b)
Insofar as provided in this Treaty, the European Parliament shall participate in the process leading up to the adoption of Community acts by exercising its powers under the procedures laid down in Articles 251 and 252 and by giving its assent or delivering advisory opinions.

The European Parliament may, acting by a majority of its Members, request the Commission to submit any appropriate proposal on matters on which it considers that a Community act is required for the purpose of implementing this Treaty.

Article 193   (ex Article 138c)
In the course of its duties, the European Parliament may, at the request of a quarter of its Members, set up a temporary Committee of Inquiry to investigate, without prejudice to the powers conferred by this Treaty on other institutions or bodies, alleged contraventions or maladministration in the implementation of Community law, except where the alleged facts are being examined before a court and while the case is still subject to legal proceedings.

The temporary Committee of Inquiry shall cease to exist on the submission of its report.

The detailed provisions governing the exercise of the right of inquiry shall be determined by common accord of the European Parliament, the Council and the Commission.

Article 194   (ex Article 138d)
Any citizen of the Union, and any natural or legal person residing or having its registered office in a Member State, shall have the right to address, individually or in association with other citizens or persons, a petition to the European Parliament on a matter which comes within the Community's fields of activity and which affects him, her or it directly.

Article 195   (ex Article 138e)
1.   The European Parliament shall appoint an Ombudsman empowered to receive complaints from any citizen of the Union or any natural or legal person residing or having its registered office in a Member State concerning instances of maladministration in the activities of the Community institutions or bodies, with the exception of the Court of Justice and the Court of First Instance acting in their judicial role.

In accordance with his duties, the Ombudsman shall conduct inquiries for which he finds grounds, either on his own initiative or on the basis of complaints submitted to him direct or through a Member of the European Parliament, except where the alleged facts are or have been the subject of legal proceedings. Where the Ombudsman establishes an instance of maladministration, he shall refer the matter to the institution concerned, which shall have a period of three months in which to inform him of its views. The Ombudsman shall then forward a report to the European Parliament and the institution concerned. The person lodging the complaint shall be informed of the outcome of such inquiries.

The Ombudsman shall submit an annual report to the European Parliament on the outcome of his inquiries.

2.   The Ombudsman shall be appointed after each election of the European Parliament for the duration of its term of office. The Ombudsman shall be eligible for reappointment.

The Ombudsman may be dismissed by the Court of Justice at the request of the European Parliament if he no longer fulfils the conditions required for the performance of his duties or if he is guilty of serious misconduct.

3.   The Ombudsman shall be completely independent in the performance of his duties. In the performance of those duties he shall neither seek nor take instructions from any body. The Ombudsman may not, during his term of office, engage in any other occupation, whether gainful or not.

4.   The European Parliament shall, after seeking an opinion from the Commission and with the approval of the Council acting by a qualified majority, lay down the regulations and general conditions governing the performance of the Ombudsman's duties.

Article 196   (ex Article 139)

The European Parliament shall hold an annual session. It shall meet, without requiring to be convened, on the second Tuesday in March.

The European Parliament may meet in extraordinary session at the request of a majority of its Members or at the request of the Council or of the Commission.

Article 197   (ex Article 140)

The European Parliament shall elect its President and its officers from among its Members.

Members of the Commission may attend all meetings and shall, at their request, be heard on behalf of the Commission.

The Commission shall reply orally or in writing to questions put to it by the European Parliament or by its Members.

The Council shall be heard by the European Parliament in accordance with the conditions laid down by the Council in its Rules of Procedure.

Article 198   (ex Article 141)

Save as otherwise provided in this Treaty, the European Parliament shall act by an absolute majority of the votes cast. The Rules of Procedure shall determine the quorum.

Article 199   (ex Article 142)

The European Parliament shall adopt its Rules of Procedure, acting by a majority of its Members.

The proceedings of the European Parliament shall be published in the manner laid down in its Rules of Procedure.

Article 200   (ex Article 143)

The European Parliament shall discuss in open session the annual general report submitted to it by the Commission.

Article 201   (ex Article 144)

If a motion of censure on the activities of the Commission is tabled before it, the European Parliament shall not vote thereon until at least three days after the motion has been tabled and only by open vote.

If the motion of censure is carried by a two-thirds majority of the votes cast, representing a majority of the Members of the European Parliament, the Members of the Commission shall resign as a body. They shall continue to deal with current business until they are replaced in accordance with Article 214. In this case, the term of office of the Members of the Commission appointed to replace them shall expire on the date on which the term of office of the Members of the Commission obliged to resign as a body would have expired.

SECTION 2   THE COUNCIL

Article 202   (ex Article 145)
To ensure that the objectives set out in this Treaty are attained the Council shall, in accordance with the provisions of this Treaty:
— ensure coordination of the general economic policies of the Member States;
— have power to take decisions;
— confer on the Commission, in the acts which the Council adopts, powers for the implementation of the rules which the Council lays down. The Council may impose certain requirements in respect of the exercise of these powers. The Council may also reserve the right, in specific cases, to exercise directly implementing powers itself. The procedures referred to above must be consonant with principles and rules to be laid down in advance by the Council, acting unanimously on a proposal from the Commission and after obtaining the Opinion of the European Parliament.

Article 203   (ex Article 146)
The Council shall consist of a representative of each Member State at ministerial level, authorised to commit the government of that Member State.
   The office of President shall be held in turn by each Member State in the Council for a term of six months in the order decided by the Council acting unanimously.

Article 204   (ex Article 147)
The Council shall meet when convened by its President on his own initiative or at the request of one of its members or of the Commission.

Article 205[1]   (ex Article 148)
   1.   Save as otherwise provided in this Treaty, the Council shall act by a majority of its members.
   2.   Where the Council is required to act by a qualified majority, the votes of its members shall be weighted as follows:

Editor's Note: Article 12 Accession Treaty 2003, vote weighting from 01.11.04:

Belgium	12
Czech Republic	12
Denmark	7
Germany	29
Estonia	4
Greece	12
Spain	27
France	29
Ireland	7

[1] **Editor's Note:** The figures show the increased numbers valid from 1 November 2004 in accordance with the Nice Declaration on the enlargement of the European Union (see below at p. 133). See the Commission prepared annex at Prelim. clxviii above. The numbers, according to the Constitutional Treaty for Europe will not then change, but a revised definition of a qualified majority will make them less important than the 2003 Accession Treaty (see above at Prelim xxxviii, Art I–25).

Italy 29
Cyprus 4
Latvia 4
Lithuania 7
Luxembourg 4
Hungary 12
Malta 3
Netherlands 13
Austria 10
Poland 27
Portugal 12
Slovenia 4
Slovakia 7
Finland 7
Sweden 10
United Kingdom 29

Acts of the Council shall require for their adoption at least 232 votes in favour cast by a majority of the members where this Treaty requires them to be adopted on a proposal from the Commission.

In other cases, for their adoption acts of the Council shall require at least 232 votes in favour, cast by at least two-thirds of the members.

3.   Abstentions by members present in person or represented shall not prevent the adoption by the Council of acts which require unanimity.

4.   When a decision is to be adopted by the Council by a qualified majority, a member of the Council may request verification that the Member States constituting the qualified majority represent at least 62% of the total population of the Union. If that condition is shown not to have been met, the decision in question shall not be adopted.

Article 206   (ex Article 150)

Where a vote is taken, any member of the Council may also act on behalf of not more than one other member.

Article 207   (ex Article 151) (As amended by the Treaty of Nice)

1.   A committee consisting of the Permanent Representatives of the Member States shall be responsible for preparing the work of the Council and for carrying out the tasks assigned to it by the Council. The Committee may adopt procedural decisions in cases provided for in the Council's Rules of Procedure.

2.   The Council shall be assisted by a General Secretariat, under the responsibility of a Secretary-General, High Representative for the common foreign and security policy, who shall be assisted by a Deputy Secretary-General responsible for the running of the General Secretariat. The Secretary-General and the Deputy Secretary-General shall be appointed by the Council, acting by a qualified majority.

The Council shall decide on the organisation of the General Secretariat.

3.   The Council shall adopt its Rules of Procedure.

For the purpose of applying Article 255(3), the Council shall elaborate in these Rules the conditions under which the public shall have access to Council documents. For the purpose of this paragraph, the Council shall define the cases in which it is to be regarded as acting in its legislative capacity, with a view to allowing greater access to documents in those cases, while at the same time preserving the effectiveness of its decision making process. In any event, when the Council acts in its legislative capacity, the results of votes and explanations of vote as well as statements in the minutes shall be made public.

Article 208   (ex Article 152)

The Council may request the Commission to undertake any studies the Council considers desirable for the attainment of the common objectives, and to submit to it any appropriate proposals.

Article 209   (ex Article 153)

The Council shall, after receiving an opinion from the Commission, determine the rules governing the committees provided for in this Treaty.

Article 210   (ex Article 154) (As amended by the Treaty of Nice)

The Council shall, acting by a qualified majority, determine the salaries, allowances and pensions of the President and Members of the Commission, and of the President, Judges, Advocates-General and Registrar of the Court of Justice and of the Members and Registrar of the Court of First Instance. It shall also, again by a qualified majority, determine any payment to be made instead of remuneration.

SECTION 3   THE COMMISSION

Article 211   (ex Article 155)

In order to ensure the proper functioning and development of the common market, the Commission shall:

— ensure that the provisions of this Treaty and the measures taken by the institutions pursuant thereto are applied;

— formulate recommendations or deliver opinions on matters dealt with in this Treaty, if it expressly so provides or if the Commission considers it necessary;

— have its own power of decision and participate in the shaping of measures taken by the Council and by the European Parliament in the manner provided for in this Treaty;

— exercise the powers conferred on it by the Council for the implementation of the rules laid down by the latter.

Article 212   (ex Article 156)

The Commission shall publish annually, not later than one month before the opening of the session of the European Parliament, a general report on the activities of the Community.

Article 213[1]   (ex Article 157)

1.   The Commission shall consist of 20 Members, who shall be chosen on the grounds of their general competence and whose independence is beyond doubt.

The number of Members of the Commission may be altered by the Council, acting unanimously.

---

[1] **Editor's Note:** Without formally amending this Article, article 45 of the 2003 Accession Treaty, provides for the following changes which will be altered by the Constitutional Treaty when in force (see at Prelim xxviii, Art I–25).

(a) a national of each new Member State shall be appointed to the Commission as from the date of its accession. The new Members of the Commission shall be appointed by the Council, acting by qualified majority and by common accord with the President of the Commission,

(b) the term of office of the Members of the Commission appointed pursuant to (a) as well as of those who were appointed as from 23 January 2000 shall expire on 31 October 2004,

(c) a new Commission composed of one national of each Member State shall take up its duties on 1 November 2004; the term of office of the Members of this new Commission shall expire on 31 October 2009,

(d) the date of 1 November 2004 is substituted for the date of 1 January 2005 in Article 4(1) of the Protocol on the enlargement of the European Union annexed to the EU Treaty and to the Treaties establishing the European Communities.

Only nationals of Member States may be Members of the Commission.

The Commission must include at least one national of each of the Member States, but may not include more than two Members having the nationality of the same State.

2.   The Members of the Commission shall, in the general interest of the Community, be completely independent in the performance of their duties.

In the performance of these duties, they shall neither seek nor take instructions from any government or from any other body. They shall refrain from any action incompatible with their duties. Each Member State undertakes to respect this principle and not to seek to influence the Members of the Commission in the performance of their tasks.

The Members of the Commission may not, during their term of office, engage in any other occupation, whether gainful or not. When entering upon their duties they shall give a solemn undertaking that, both during and after their term of office, they will respect the obligations arising there from and in particular their duty to behave with integrity and discretion as regards the acceptance, after they have ceased to hold office, of certain appointments or benefits. In the event of any breach of these obligations, the Court of Justice may, on application by the Council or the Commission, rule that the Member concerned be, according to the circumstances, either compulsorily retired in accordance with Article 216 or deprived of his right to a pension or other benefits in its stead.

Article 214   (ex Article 158) (As amended by the Treaty of Nice)

1.   The Members of the Commission shall be appointed, in accordance with the procedure referred to in paragraph 2, for a period of five years, subject, if need be, to Article 201.

Their term of office shall be renewable.

2.   The Council, meeting in the composition of Heads of State or Government and acting by a qualified majority, shall nominate the person it intends to appoint as President of the Commission; the nomination shall be approved by the European Parliament.

The Council, acting by a qualified majority and by common accord with the nominee for President, shall adopt the list of the other persons whom it intends to appoint as Members of the Commission, drawn up in accordance with the proposals made by each Member State.

The President and the other Members of the Commission thus nominated shall be subject as a body to a vote of approval by the European Parliament. After approval by the European Parliament, the President and the other Members of the Commission shall be appointed by the Council, acting by a qualified majority.

Article 215   (ex Article 159) (As amended by the Treaty of Nice)

Apart from normal replacement, or death, the duties of a Member of the Commission shall end when he resigns or is compulsorily retired.

A vacancy caused by resignation, compulsory retirement or death shall be filled for the remainder of the Member's term of office by a new Member appointed by the Council, acting by a qualified majority. The Council may, acting unanimously, decide that such a vacancy need not be filled.

In the event of resignation, compulsory retirement or death, the President shall be replaced for the remainder of his term of office. The procedure laid down in Article 214(2) shall be applicable for the replacement of the President.

Save in the case of compulsory retirement under Article 216, Members of the Commission shall remain in office until they have been replaced or until the Council has decided that the vacancy need not be filled, as provided for in the second paragraph of this Article.

Article 216   (ex Article 160)

If any Member of the Commission no longer fulfils the conditions required for the performance of his duties or if he has been guilty of serious misconduct, the Court of Justice may, on application by the Council or the Commission, compulsorily retire him.

Article 217   (ex Article 161) (As amended by the Treaty of Nice)

1.   The Commission shall work under the political guidance of its President, who shall decide on its internal organisation in order to ensure that it acts consistently, efficiently and on the basis of collegiality.

2.   The responsibilities incumbent upon the Commission shall be structured and allocated among its Members by its President. The President may reshuffle the allocation of those responsibilities during the Commission's term of office. The Members of the Commission shall carry out the duties devolved upon them by the President under his authority.

3.   After obtaining the approval of the College, the President shall appoint Vice-Presidents from among its Members.

4.   A Member of the Commission shall resign if the President so requests, after obtaining the approval of the College.

Article 218   (ex Article 162)

1.   The Council and the Commission shall consult each other and shall settle by common accord their methods of cooperation.

2.   The Commission shall adopt its Rules of Procedure so as to ensure that both it and its departments operate in accordance with the provisions of this Treaty. It shall ensure that these rules are published.

Article 219   (ex Article 163) (As amended by the Treaty of Nice)

The Commission shall act by a majority of the number of Members provided for in Article 213.

A meeting of the Commission shall be valid only if the number of Members laid down in its Rules of Procedure is present.

SECTION 4   THE COURT OF JUSTICE

Article 220   (ex Article 164) (As amended by the Treaty of Nice)

The Court of Justice and the Court of First Instance, each within its jurisdiction, shall ensure that in the interpretation and application of this Treaty the law is observed

In addition, judicial panels may be attached to the Court of First Instance under the conditions laid down in Article 225a in order to exercise, in certain specific areas, the judicial competence laid down in this Treaty.

Article 221   (ex Article 165) (As amended by the Treaty of Nice)

The Court of Justice shall consist of one judge per Member State.

The Court of Justice shall sit in chambers or in a Grand Chamber, in accordance with the rules laid down for that purpose in the Statute of the Court of Justice.

When provided for in the Statute, the Court of Justice may also sit as a full Court.

Article 222   (ex Article 166) (As amended by the Treaty of Nice)

The Court of Justice shall be assisted by eight Advocates-General. Should the Court of Justice so request, the Council, acting unanimously, may increase the number of Advocates-General.

It shall be the duty of the Advocate-General, acting with complete impartiality and independence, to make, in open court, reasoned submissions on cases which, in accordance with the Statute of the Court of Justice, require his involvement.

Article 223   (ex Article 167) (As amended by the Treaty of Nice)

The Judges and Advocates-General of the Court of Justice shall be chosen from persons whose independence is beyond doubt and who possess the qualifications required for appointment to the highest judicial offices in their respective countries or who are jurisconsults of recognised competence; they shall be appointed by common accord of the governments of the Member States for a term of six years.

Every three years there shall be a partial replacement of the Judges and Advocates-General, in accordance with the conditions laid down in the Statute of the Court of Justice.

The Judges shall elect the President of the Court of Justice from among their number for a term of three years. He may be re-elected.

Retiring Judges and Advocates-General may be reappointed.

The Court of Justice shall appoint its Registrar and lay down the rules governing his service.

The Court of Justice shall establish its Rules of Procedure. Those Rules shall require the approval of the Council, acting by a qualified majority.

Article 224   (ex Article 168) (As amended by the Treaty of Nice)

The Court of First Instance shall comprise at least one judge per Member State. The number of Judges shall be determined by the Statute of the Court of Justice. The Statute may provide for the Court of First Instance to be assisted by Advocates-General.

The members of the Court of First Instance shall be chosen from persons whose independence is beyond doubt and who possess the ability required for appointment to high judicial office. They shall be appointed by common accord of the governments of the Member States for a term of six years. The membership shall be partially renewed every three years. Retiring members shall be eligible for reappointment.

The Judges shall elect the President of the Court of First Instance from among their number for a term of three years. He may be re-elected.

The Court of First Instance shall appoint its Registrar and lay down the rules governing his service.

The Court of First Instance shall establish its Rules of Procedure in agreement with the Court of Justice. Those Rules shall require the approval of the Council, acting by a qualified majority.

Unless the Statute of the Court of Justice provides otherwise, the provisions of this Treaty relating to the Court of Justice shall apply to the Court of First Instance.

Article 225   (ex Article 168a) (As amended by the Treaty of Nice)

1. The Court of First Instance shall have jurisdiction to hear and determine at first instance actions or proceedings referred to in Articles 230, 232, 235, 236 and 238, with the exception of those assigned to a judicial panel and those reserved in the Statute for the Court of Justice. The Statute may provide for the Court of First Instance to have jurisdiction for other classes of action or proceeding.

Decisions given by the Court of First Instance under this paragraph may be subject to a right of appeal to the Court of Justice on points of law only, under the conditions and within the limits laid down by the Statute.

2. The Court of First Instance shall have jurisdiction to hear and determine actions or proceedings brought against decisions of the judicial panels set up under Article 225a.

Decisions given by the Court of First Instance under this paragraph may exceptionally be subject to review by the Court of Justice, under the conditions and within the limits laid down by the Statute, where there is a serious risk of the unity or consistency of Community law being affected.

3. The Court of First Instance shall have jurisdiction to hear and determine questions referred for a preliminary ruling under Article 234, in specific areas laid down by the Statute.

Where the Court of First Instance considers that the case requires a decision of principle likely to affect the unity or consistency of Community law, it may refer the case to the Court of Justice for a ruling.

Decisions given by the Court of First Instance on questions referred for a preliminary ruling may exceptionally be subject to review by the Court of Justice, under the conditions and within the limits laid down by the Statute, where there is a serious risk of the unity or consistency of Community law being affected.

Article 225a   (Article inserted by the Treaty of Nice)

The Council, acting unanimously on a proposal from the Commission and after consulting the European Parliament and the Court of Justice or at the request of the Court of Justice and after consulting the European Parliament and the Commission, may create judicial panels to hear and determine at first instance certain classes of action or proceeding brought in specific areas.

The decision establishing a judicial panel shall lay down the rules on the organisation of the panel and the extent of the jurisdiction conferred upon it.

Decisions given by judicial panels may be subject to a right of appeal on points of law only or, when provided for in the decision establishing the panel, a right of appeal also on matters of fact, before the Court of First Instance.

The members of the judicial panels shall be chosen from persons whose independence is beyond doubt and who possess the ability required for appointment to judicial office. They shall be appointed by the Council, acting unanimously.

The judicial panels shall establish their Rules of Procedure in agreement with the Court of Justice. Those Rules shall require the approval of the Council, acting by a qualified majority.

Unless the decision establishing the judicial panel provides otherwise, the provisions of this Treaty relating to the Court of Justice and the provisions of the Statute of the Court of Justice shall apply to the judicial panels.

Article 226   (ex Article 169)

If the Commission considers that a Member State has failed to fulfil an obligation under this Treaty, it shall deliver a reasoned opinion on the matter after giving the State concerned the opportunity to submit its observations.

If the State concerned does not comply with the opinion within the period laid down by the Commission, the latter may bring the matter before the Court of Justice.

Article 227   (ex Article 170)

A Member State which considers that another Member State has failed to fulfil an obligation under this Treaty may bring the matter before the Court of Justice.

Before a Member State brings an action against another Member State for an alleged infringement of an obligation under this Treaty, it shall bring the matter before the Commission.

The Commission shall deliver a reasoned opinion after each of the States concerned has been given the opportunity to submit its own case and its observations on the other party's case both orally and in writing.

If the Commission has not delivered an opinion within three months of the date on which the matter was brought before it, the absence of such opinion shall not prevent the matter from being brought before the Court of Justice.

Article 228   (ex Article 171)

1.   If the Court of Justice finds that a Member State has failed to fulfil an obligation under this Treaty, the State shall be required to take the necessary measures to comply with the judgment of the Court of Justice.

2.   If the Commission considers that the Member State concerned has not taken such measures it shall, after giving that State the opportunity to submit its observations, issue a reasoned opinion specifying the points on which the Member State concerned has not complied with the judgment of the Court of Justice.

If the Member State concerned fails to take the necessary measures to comply with the Court's judgment within the time-limit laid down by the Commission, the latter may bring the case before the Court of Justice. In so doing it shall specify the amount of the lump sum or penalty payment to be paid by the Member State concerned which it considers appropriate in the circumstances.

If the Court of Justice finds that the Member State concerned has not complied with its judgment it may impose a lump sum or penalty payment on it.

This procedure shall be without prejudice to Article 227.

Article 229   (ex Article 172)

Regulations adopted jointly by the European Parliament and the Council, and by the Council, pursuant to the provisions of this Treaty, may give the Court of Justice unlimited jurisdiction with regard to the penalties provided for in such regulations.

Article 229a   (Article inserted by the Treaty of Nice)

Without prejudice to the other provisions of this Treaty, the Council, acting unanimously on a proposal from the Commission and after consulting the European Parliament, may adopt provisions to confer jurisdiction, to the extent that it shall determine, on the Court of Justice in disputes relating to the application of acts adopted on the basis of this Treaty which create Community industrial property rights. The Council shall recommend those provisions to the Member States for adoption in accordance with their respective constitutional requirements.

Article 230   (ex Article 173) (As amended by the Treaty of Nice)

The Court of Justice shall review the legality of acts adopted jointly by the European Parliament and the Council, of acts of the Council, of the Commission and of the ECB, other than recommendations and opinions, and of acts of the European Parliament intended to produce legal effects vis-à-vis third parties.

It shall for this purpose have jurisdiction in actions brought by a Member State, the European Parliament, the Council or the Commission on grounds of lack of competence, infringement of an essential procedural requirement, infringement of this Treaty or of any rule of law relating to its application, or misuse of powers.

The Court of Justice shall have jurisdiction under the same conditions in actions brought by the Court of Auditors and by the ECB for the purpose of protecting their prerogatives.

Any natural or legal person may, under the same conditions, institute proceedings against a decision addressed to that person or against a decision which, although in the form of a regulation or a decision addressed to another person, is of direct and individual concern to the former.

The proceedings provided for in this Article shall be instituted within two months of the publication of the measure, or of its notification to the plaintiff, or, in the absence thereof, of the day on which it came to the knowledge of the latter, as the case may be.

Article 231   (ex Article 174)

If the action is well founded, the Court of Justice shall declare the act concerned to be void.

In the case of a regulation, however, the Court of Justice shall, if it considers this necessary, state which of the effects of the regulation which it has declared void shall be considered as definitive.

Article 232   (ex Article 175)

Should the European Parliament, the Council or the Commission, in infringement of this Treaty, fail to act, the Member States and the other institutions of the Community may bring an action before the Court of Justice to have the infringement established.

The action shall be admissible only if the institution concerned has first been called upon to act. If, within two months of being so called upon, the institution concerned has not defined its position, the action may be brought within a further period of two months.

Any natural or legal person may, under the conditions laid down in the preceding paragraphs, complain to the Court of Justice that an institution of the Community has failed to address to that person any act other than a recommendation or an opinion.

The Court of Justice shall have jurisdiction, under the same conditions, in actions or proceedings brought by the ECB in the areas falling within the latter's field of competence and in actions or proceedings brought against the latter.

Article 233   (ex Article 176)

The institution or institutions whose act has been declared void or whose failure to act has been declared contrary to this Treaty shall be required to take the necessary measures to comply with the judgment of the Court of Justice.

This obligation shall not affect any obligation which may result from the application of the second paragraph of Article 288.

This Article shall also apply to the ECB.

Article 234   (ex Article 177)

The Court of Justice shall have jurisdiction to give preliminary rulings concerning:

    (a) the interpretation of this Treaty;

    (b) the validity and interpretation of acts of the institutions of the Community and of the ECB;

    (c) the interpretation of the statutes of bodies established by an act of the Council, where those statutes so provide.

Where such a question is raised before any court or tribunal of a Member State, that court or tribunal may, if it considers that a decision on the question is necessary to enable it to give judgment, request the Court of Justice to give a ruling thereon.

Where any such question is raised in a case pending before a court or tribunal of a Member State against whose decisions there is no judicial remedy under national law, that court or tribunal shall bring the matter before the Court of Justice.

Article 235   (ex Article 178)

The Court of Justice shall have jurisdiction in disputes relating to compensation for damage provided for in the second paragraph of Article 288.

Article 236   (ex Article 179)

The Court of Justice shall have jurisdiction in any dispute between the Community and its servants within the limits and under the conditions laid down in the Staff Regulations or the Conditions of Employment.

Article 237   (ex Article 180)

The Court of Justice shall, within the limits hereinafter laid down, have jurisdiction in disputes concerning:

    (a) the fulfilment by Member States of obligations under the Statute of the European Investment Bank. In this connection, the Board of Directors of the Bank shall enjoy the powers conferred upon the Commission by Article 226;

    (b) measures adopted by the Board of Governors of the European Investment Bank. In this connection, any Member State, the Commission or the Board of Directors of the Bank may institute proceedings under the conditions laid down in Article 230;

    (c) measures adopted by the Board of Directors of the European Investment Bank. Proceedings against such measures may be instituted only by Member States or by the Commission, under the conditions laid down in Article 230, and solely on the grounds of non-compliance with the procedure provided for in Article 21(2), (5), (6) and (7) of the Statute of the Bank;

    (d) the fulfilment by national central banks of obligations under this Treaty and the Statute of the ESCB. In this connection the powers of the Council of the ECB in respect of national central banks shall be the same as those conferred upon the Commission in respect of Member States by Article 226. If the Court of Justice finds that a national central bank has failed to fulfil an obligation under this

Treaty, that bank shall be required to take the necessary measures to comply with the judgment of the Court of Justice.

Article 238   (ex Article 181)
The Court of Justice shall have jurisdiction to give judgment pursuant to any arbitration clause contained in a contract concluded by or on behalf of the Community, whether that contract be governed by public or private law.

Article 239   (ex Article 182)
The Court of Justice shall have jurisdiction in any dispute between Member States which relates to the subject matter of this Treaty if the dispute is submitted to it under a special agreement between the parties.

Article 240   (ex Article 183)
Save where jurisdiction is conferred on the Court of Justice by this Treaty, disputes to which the Community is a party shall not on that ground be excluded from the jurisdiction of the courts or tribunals of the Member States.

Article 241   (ex Article 184)
Notwithstanding the expiry of the period laid down in the fifth paragraph of Article 230, any party may, in proceedings in which a regulation adopted jointly by the European Parliament and the Council, or a regulation of the Council, of the Commission, or of the ECB is at issue, plead the grounds specified in the second paragraph of Article 230 in order to invoke before the Court of Justice the inapplicability of that regulation.

Article 242   (ex Article 185)
Actions brought before the Court of Justice shall not have suspensory effect. The Court of Justice may, however, if it considers that circumstances so require, order that application of the contested act be suspended.

Article 243   (ex Article 186)
The Court of Justice may in any cases before it prescribe any necessary interim measures.

Article 244   (ex Article 187)
The judgments of the Court of Justice shall be enforceable under the conditions laid down in Article 256.

Article 245   (ex Article 188) (As amended by the Treaty of Nice)
The Statute of the Court of Justice shall be laid down in a separate Protocol.

   The Council, acting unanimously at the request of the Court of Justice and after consulting the European Parliament and the Commission, or at the request of the Commission and after consulting the European Parliament and the Court of Justice, may amend the provisions of the Statute, with the exception of Title I.

SECTION 5   THE COURT OF AUDITORS

Article 246   (ex Article 188a)
The Court of Auditors shall carry out the audit.

Article 247   (ex Article 188b) (As amended by the Treaty of Nice)
   1.   The Court of Auditors shall consist of one national from each Member State.
   2.   The Members of the Court of Auditors shall be chosen from among persons who belong or have belonged in their respective countries to external audit bodies or who are especially qualified for this office. Their independence must be beyond doubt.
   3.   The Members of the Court of Auditors shall be appointed for a term of six years. The Council, acting by a qualified majority after consulting the European Parliament, shall adopt

the list of Members drawn up in accordance with the proposals made by each Member State. The term of office of the Members of the Court of Auditors shall be renewable.

They shall elect the President of the Court of Auditors from among their number for a term of three years. The President may be re-elected.

4.   The Members of the Court of Auditors shall, in the general interest of the Community, be completely independent in the performance of their duties.

In the performance of these duties, they shall neither seek nor take instructions from any government or from any other body. They shall refrain from any action incompatible with their duties.

5.   The Members of the Court of Auditors may not, during their term of office, engage in any other occupation, whether gainful or not. When entering upon their duties they shall give a solemn undertaking that, both during and after their term of office, they will respect the obligations arising therefrom and in particular their duty to behave with integrity and discretion as regards the acceptance, after they have ceased to hold office, of certain appointments or benefits.

6.   Apart from normal replacement, or death, the duties of a Member of the Court of Auditors shall end when he resigns, or is compulsorily retired by a ruling of the Court of Justice pursuant to paragraph 7.

The vacancy thus caused shall be filled for the remainder of the Member's term of office.

Save in the case of compulsory retirement, Members of the Court of Auditors shall remain in office until they have been replaced.

7.   A Member of the Court of Auditors may be deprived of his office or of his right to a pension or other benefits in its stead only if the Court of Justice, at the request of the Court of Auditors, finds that he no longer fulfils the requisite conditions or meets the obligations arising from his office.

8.   The Council, acting by a qualified majority, shall determine the conditions of employment of the President and the Members of the Court of Auditors and in particular their salaries, allowances and pensions. It shall also, by the same majority, determine any payment to be made instead of remuneration.

9.   The provisions of the Protocol on the privileges and immunities of the European Communities applicable to the Judges of the Court of Justice shall also apply to the Members of the Court of Auditors.

Article 248   (ex Article 188c) (As amended by the Treaty of Nice)
1.   The Court of Auditors shall examine the accounts of all revenue and expenditure of the Community. It shall also examine the accounts of all revenue and expenditure of all bodies set up by the Community insofar as the relevant constituent instrument does not preclude such examination.

The Court of Auditors shall provide the European Parliament and the Council with a statement of assurance as to the reliability of the accounts and the legality and regularity of the underlying transactions which shall be published in the Official Journal of the European Union. This statement may be supplemented by specific assessments for each major area of Community activity.

2.   The Court of Auditors shall examine whether all revenue has been received and all expenditure incurred in a lawful and regular manner and whether the financial management has been sound. In doing so, it shall report in particular on any cases of irregularity.

The audit of revenue shall be carried out on the basis both of the amounts established as due and the amounts actually paid to the Community.

The audit of expenditure shall be carried out on the basis both of commitments undertaken and payments made.

These audits may be carried out before the closure of accounts for the financial year in question.

3. The audit shall be based on records and, if necessary, performed on the spot in the other institutions of the Community, on the premises of any body which manages revenue or expenditure on behalf of the Community and in the Member States, including on the premises of any natural or legal person in receipt of payments from the budget. In the Member States the audit shall be carried out in liaison with national audit bodies or, if these do not have the necessary powers, with the competent national departments. The Court of Auditors and the national audit bodies of the Member States shall cooperate in a spirit of trust while maintaining their independence. These bodies or departments shall inform the Court of Auditors whether they intend to take part in the audit.

The other institutions of the Community, any bodies managing revenue or expenditure on behalf of the Community, any natural or legal person in receipt of payments from the budget, and the national audit bodies or, if these do not have the necessary powers, the competent national departments, shall forward to the Court of Auditors, at its request, any document or information necessary to carry out its task.

In respect of the European Investment Bank's activity in managing Community expenditure and revenue, the Court's rights of access to information held by the Bank shall be governed by an agreement between the Court, the Bank and the Commission. In the absence of an agreement, the Court shall nevertheless have access to information necessary for the audit of Community expenditure and revenue managed by the Bank.

4. The Court of Auditors shall draw up an annual report after the close of each financial year. It shall be forwarded to the other institutions of the Community and shall be published, together with the replies of these institutions to the observations of the Court of Auditors, in the Official Journal of the European Union.

The Court of Auditors may also, at any time, submit observations, particularly in the form of special reports, on specific questions and deliver opinions at the request of one of the other institutions of the Community.

It shall adopt its annual reports, special reports or opinions by a majority of its Members. However, it may establish internal chambers in order to adopt certain categories of reports or opinions under the conditions laid down by its Rules of Procedure.

It shall assist the European Parliament and the Council in exercising their powers of control over the implementation of the budget.

The Court of Auditors shall draw up its Rules of Procedure. Those rules shall require the approval of the Council, acting by a qualified majority.

CHAPTER 2   PROVISIONS COMMON TO SEVERAL INSTITUTIONS

Article 249   (ex Article 189)

In order to carry out their task and in accordance with the provisions of this Treaty, the European Parliament acting jointly with the Council, the Council and the Commission shall make regulations and issue directives, take decisions, make recommendations or deliver opinions.

A regulation shall have general application. It shall be binding in its entirety and directly applicable in all Member States.

A directive shall be binding, as to the result to be achieved, upon each Member State to which it is addressed, but shall leave to the national authorities the choice of form and methods.

A decision shall be binding in its entirety upon those to whom it is addressed.

Recommendations and opinions shall have no binding force.

Article 250   (ex Article 189a)

1. Where, in pursuance of this Treaty, the Council acts on a proposal from the Commission, unanimity shall be required for an act constituting an amendment to that proposal, subject to Article 251(4) and (5).

2. As long as the Council has not acted, the Commission may alter its proposal at any time during the procedures leading to the adoption of a Community act.

Article 251 (ex Article 189b)

1. Where reference is made in this Treaty to this Article for the adoption of an act, the following procedure shall apply.

2. The Commission shall submit a proposal to the European Parliament and the Council. The Council, acting by a qualified majority after obtaining the opinion of the European Parliament,

— if it approves all the amendments contained in the European Parliament's opinion, may adopt the proposed act thus amended;

— if the European Parliament does not propose any amendments, may adopt the proposed act;

— shall otherwise adopt a common position and communicate it to the European Parliament. The Council shall inform the European Parliament fully of the reasons which led it to adopt its common position. The Commission shall inform the European Parliament fully of its position.

If, within three months of such communication, the European Parliament:

(a) approves the common position or has not taken a decision, the act in question shall be deemed to have been adopted in accordance with that common position;

(b) rejects, by an absolute majority of its component members, the common position, the proposed act shall be deemed not to have been adopted;

(c) proposes amendments to the common position by an absolute majority of its component members, the amended text shall be forwarded to the Council and to the Commission, which shall deliver an opinion on those amendments.

3. If, within three months of the matter being referred to it, the Council, acting by a qualified majority, approves all the amendments of the European Parliament, the act in question shall be deemed to have been adopted in the form of the common position thus amended; however, the Council shall act unanimously on the amendments on which the Commission has delivered a negative opinion. If the Council does not approve all the amendments, the President of the Council, in agreement with the President of the European Parliament, shall within six weeks convene a meeting of the Conciliation Committee.

4. The Conciliation Committee, which shall be composed of the members of the Council or their representatives and an equal number of representatives of the European Parliament, shall have the task of reaching agreement on a joint text, by a qualified majority of the members of the Council or their representatives and by a majority of the representatives of the European Parliament. The Commission shall take part in the Conciliation Committee's proceedings and shall take all the necessary initiatives with a view to reconciling the positions of the European Parliament and the Council. In fulfilling this task, the Conciliation Committee shall address the common position on the basis of the amendments proposed by the European Parliament.

5. If, within six weeks of its being convened, the Conciliation Committee approves a joint text, the European Parliament, acting by an absolute majority of the votes cast, and the Council, acting by a qualified majority, shall each have a period of six weeks from that approval in which to adopt the act in question in accordance with the joint text. If either of the two institutions fails to approve the proposed act within that period, it shall be deemed not to have been adopted.

6. Where the Conciliation Committee does not approve a joint text, the proposed act shall be deemed not to have been adopted.

7. The periods of three months and six weeks referred to in this Article shall be extended by a maximum of one month and two weeks respectively at the initiative of the European Parliament or the Council.

Article 252   (ex Article 189c)

Where reference is made in this Treaty to this Article for the adoption of an act, the following procedure shall apply:

(a) The Council, acting by a qualified majority on a proposal from the Commission and after obtaining the opinion of the European Parliament, shall adopt a common position.

(b) The Council's common position shall be communicated to the European Parliament. The Council and the Commission shall inform the European Parliament fully of the reasons which led the Council to adopt its common position and also of the Commission's position.

If, within three months of such communication, the European Parliament approves this common position or has not taken a decision within that period, the Council shall definitively adopt the act in question in accordance with the common position.

(c) The European Parliament may, within the period of three months referred to in point (b), by an absolute majority of its component Members, propose amendments to the Council's common position. The European Parliament may also, by the same majority, reject the Council's common position. The result of the proceedings shall be transmitted to the Council and the Commission.

If the European Parliament has rejected the Council's common position, unanimity shall be required for the Council to act on a second reading.

(d) The Commission shall, within a period of one month, re-examine the proposal on the basis of which the Council adopted its common position, by taking into account the amendments proposed by the European Parliament.

The Commission shall forward to the Council, at the same time as its re-examined proposal, the amendments of the European Parliament which it has not accepted, and shall express its opinion on them. The Council may adopt these amendments unanimously.

(e) The Council, acting by a qualified majority, shall adopt the proposal as re-examined by the Commission.

Unanimity shall be required for the Council to amend the proposal as re-examined by the Commission.

(f) In the cases referred to in points (c), (d) and (e), the Council shall be required to act within a period of three months. If no decision is taken within this period, the Commission proposal shall be deemed not to have been adopted.

(g) The periods referred to in points (b) and (f) may be extended by a maximum of one month by common accord between the Council and the European Parliament.

Article 253   (ex Article 190)

Regulations, directives and decisions adopted jointly by the European Parliament and the Council, and such acts adopted by the Council or the Commission, shall state the reasons on which they are based and shall refer to any proposals or opinions which were required to be obtained pursuant to this Treaty.

Article 254   (ex Article 191) (As amended by the Treaty of Nice)

1. Regulations, directives and decisions adopted in accordance with the procedure referred to in Article 251 shall be signed by the President of the European Parliament and by the President of the Council and published in the *Official Journal of the European Union*. They shall enter into force on the date specified in them or, in the absence thereof, on the twentieth day following that of their publication.

2. Regulations of the Council and of the Commission, as well as directives of those institutions which are addressed to all Member States, shall be published in the *Official Journal of the European Union*. They shall enter into force on the date specified in them or, in the absence thereof, on the twentieth day following that of their publication.

3.   Other directives, and decisions, shall be notified to those to whom they are addressed and shall take effect upon such notification.

Article 255   (ex Article 191a)

1.   Any citizen of the Union, and any natural or legal person residing or having its registered office in a Member State, shall have a right of access to European Parliament, Council and Commission documents, subject to the principles and the conditions to be defined in accordance with paragraphs 2 and 3.

2.   General principles and limits on grounds of public or private interest governing this right of access to documents shall be determined by the Council, acting in accordance with the procedure referred to in Article 251 within two years of the entry into force of the Treaty of Amsterdam.

3.   Each institution referred to above shall elaborate in its own Rules of Procedure specific provisions regarding access to its documents.

Article 256   (ex Article 192)

Decisions of the Council or of the Commission which impose a pecuniary obligation on persons other than States, shall be enforceable.

Enforcement shall be governed by the rules of civil procedure in force in the State in the territory of which it is carried out. The order for its enforcement shall be appended to the decision, without other formality than verification of the authenticity of the decision, by the national authority which the government of each Member State shall designate for this purpose and shall make known to the Commission and to the Court of Justice.

When these formalities have been completed on application by the party concerned, the latter may proceed to enforcement in accordance with the national law, by bringing the matter directly before the competent authority.

Enforcement may be suspended only by a decision of the Court of Justice. However, the courts of the country concerned shall have jurisdiction over complaints that enforcement is being carried out in an irregular manner.

CHAPTER 3   THE ECONOMIC AND SOCIAL COMMITTEE

Article 257   (ex Article 193) (As amended by the Treaty of Nice)

An Economic and Social Committee is hereby established. It shall have advisory status.

The Committee shall consist of representatives of the various economic and social components of organised civil society, and in particular representatives of producers, farmers, carriers, workers, dealers, craftsmen, professional occupations, consumers and the general interest.

Article 258   (ex Article 194) (As amended by the Treaty of Nice and the 2003 Accession Treaty)

The number of members of the Economic and Social Committee shall not exceed 350.

The number of members of the Committee shall be as follows:

Belgium	12
Czech Republic	12
Denmark	9
Germany	24
Estonia	7
Greece	12
Spain	21
France	24
Ireland	9
Italy	24

The members of the Committee may not be bound by any mandatory instructions. They shall be completely independent in the performance of their duties, in the general interest of the Community.

The Council, acting by a qualified majority, shall determine the allowances of members of the Committee.

Article 259   (ex Article 195) (As amended by the Treaty of Nice)

1.   The members of the Committee shall be appointed for four years, on proposals from the Member States. The Council, acting by a qualified majority, shall adopt the list of members drawn up in accordance with the proposals made by each Member State. The term of office of the members of the Committee shall be renewable.

The composition of the Committee shall take account of the need to ensure adequate representation of the various categories of economic and social activity.

2.   The Council shall consult the Commission. It may obtain the opinion of European bodies which are representative of the various economic and social sectors to which the activities of the Community are of concern.

Article 260   (ex Article 196)

The Committee shall elect its chairman and officers from among its members for a term of two years.

It shall adopt its Rules of Procedure.

The Committee shall be convened by its chairman at the request of the Council or of the Commission. It may also meet on its own initiative.

Article 261   (ex Article 197)

The Committee shall include specialised sections for the principal fields covered by this Treaty.

These specialised sections shall operate within the general terms of reference of the Committee. They may not be consulted independently of the Committee.

Subcommittees may also be established within the Committee to prepare on specific questions or in specific fields, draft opinions to be submitted to the Committee for its consideration.

The Rules of Procedure shall lay down the methods of composition and the terms of reference of the specialised sections and of the subcommittees.

Article 262   (ex Article 198)

The Committee must be consulted by the Council or by the Commission where this Treaty so provides. The Committee may be consulted by these institutions in all cases in which they consider it appropriate. It may issue an opinion on its own initiative in cases in which it considers such action appropriate.

The Council or the Commission shall, if it considers it necessary, set the Committee, for the submission of its opinion, a time-limit which may not be less than one month from the date on which the chairman receives notification to this effect. Upon expiry of the time limit, the absence of an opinion shall not prevent further action.

The opinion of the Committee and that of the specialised section, together with a record of the proceedings, shall be forwarded to the Council and to the Commission.

The Committee may be consulted by the European Parliament.

CHAPTER 4   THE COMMITTEE OF THE REGIONS

Article 263   (ex Article 198a) (As amended by the Treaty of Nice and the 2003 Accession Treaty)

A Committee, hereinafter referred to as 'the Committee of the Regions', consisting of representatives of regional and local bodies who either hold a regional or local authority electoral mandate or are politically accountable to an elected assembly, is hereby established with advisory status.

The number of members of the Committee of the Regions shall not exceed 350.

The number of members of the Committee shall be as follows:

Belgium	12
Czech Republic	12
Denmark	9
Germany	24
Estonia	7
Greece	12
Spain	21
France	24
Ireland	9
Italy	24
Cyprus	6
Latvia	7
Lithuania	9
Luxembourg	6
Hungary	12
Malta	5
Netherlands	12
Austria	12
Poland	21
Portugal	12
Slovenia	7
Slovakia	9
Finland	9
Sweden	12
United Kingdom	24

The members of the Committee and an equal number of alternate members shall be appointed for four years, on proposals from the respective Member States. Their term of office shall be renewable. The Council, acting by a qualified majority, shall adopt the list of members and alternate members drawn up in accordance with the proposals made by each Member State. When the mandate referred to in the first paragraph on the basis of which they were proposed comes to an end, the term of office of members of the Committee shall terminate automatically and they shall then be replaced for the remainder of the said term of office in accordance with the same procedure. No member of the Committee shall at the same time be a Member of the European Parliament.

The members of the Committee may not be bound by any mandatory instructions. They shall be completely independent in the performance of their duties, in the general interest of the Community.

Article 264   (ex Article 198b)

The Committee of the Regions shall elect its chairman and officers from among its members for a term of two years. It shall adopt its Rules of Procedure.

The Committee shall be convened by its chairman at the request of the Council or of the Commission. It may also meet on its own initiative.

Article 265   (ex Article 198c)

The Committee of the Regions shall be consulted by the Council or by the Commission where this Treaty so provides and in all other cases, in particular those which concern cross border cooperation, in which one of these two institutions considers it appropriate.

The Council or the Commission shall, if it considers it necessary, set the Committee, for the submission of its opinion, a time-limit which may not be less than one month from the date on which the chairman receives notification to this effect. Upon expiry of the time limit, the absence of an opinion shall not prevent further action.

Where the Economic and Social Committee is consulted pursuant to Article 262, the Committee of the Regions shall be informed by the Council or the Commission of the request for an opinion. Where it considers that specific regional interests are involved, the Committee of the Regions may issue an opinion on the matter.

The Committee of the Regions may be consulted by the European Parliament.

It may issue an opinion on its own initiative in cases in which it considers such action appropriate.

The opinion of the Committee, together with a record of the proceedings, shall be forwarded to the Council and to the Commission.

CHAPTER 5   THE EUROPEAN INVESTMENT BANK

Article 266   (ex Article 198d) (As amended by the Treaty of Nice)

The European Investment Bank shall have legal personality.

The members of the European Investment Bank shall be the Member States.

The Statute of the European Investment Bank is laid down in a Protocol annexed to this Treaty. The Council, acting unanimously, at the request of the European Investment Bank and after consulting the European Parliament and the Commission, or at the request of the Commission and after consulting the European Parliament and the European Investment Bank, may amend Articles 4, 11 and 12 and Article 18(5) of the Statute of the Bank.

Article 267   (ex Article 198e)

The task of the European Investment Bank shall be to contribute, by having recourse to the capital market and utilising its own resources, to the balanced and steady development of the common market in the interest of the Community. For this purpose the Bank shall, operating on a non-profit-making basis, grant loans and give guarantees which facilitate the financing of the following projects in all sectors of the economy:

(a) projects for developing less-developed regions;

(b) projects for modernising or converting undertakings or for developing fresh activities called for by the progressive establishment of the common market, where these projects are of such a size or nature that they cannot be entirely financed by the various means available in the individual Member States;

(c) projects of common interest to several Member States which are of such a size or nature that they cannot be entirely financed by the various means available in the individual Member States.

In carrying out its task, the Bank shall facilitate the financing of investment programmes in conjunction with assistance from the Structural Funds and other Community financial instruments.

TITLE II   FINANCIAL PROVISIONS

Article 268   (ex Article 199)

All items of revenue and expenditure of the Community, including those relating to the European Social Fund, shall be included in estimates to be drawn up for each financial year and shall be shown in the budget.

Administrative expenditure occasioned for the institutions by the provisions of the Treaty on European Union relating to common foreign and security policy and to cooperation in the fields of justice and home affairs shall be charged to the budget. The operational expenditure occasioned by the implementation of the said provisions may, under the conditions referred to therein, be charged to the budget.

The revenue and expenditure shown in the budget shall be in balance.

Article 269   (ex Article 201)

Without prejudice to other revenue, the budget shall be financed wholly from own resources.

The Council, acting unanimously on a proposal from the Commission and after consulting the European Parliament, shall lay down provisions relating to the system of own resources of the Community, which it shall recommend to the Member States for adoption in accordance with their respective constitutional requirements.

Article 270   (ex Article 201a)

With a view to maintaining budgetary discipline, the Commission shall not make any proposal for a Community act, or alter its proposals, or adopt any implementing measure which is likely to have appreciable implications for the budget without providing the assurance that that proposal or that measure is capable of being financed within the limit of the Community's own resources arising under provisions laid down by the Council pursuant to Article 269.

Article 271   (ex Article 202)

The expenditure shown in the budget shall be authorised for one financial year, unless the regulations made pursuant to Article 279 provide otherwise.

In accordance with conditions to be laid down pursuant to Article 279, any appropriations, other than those relating to staff expenditure, that are unexpended at the end of the financial year may be carried forward to the next financial year only.

Appropriations shall be classified under different chapters grouping items of expenditure according to their nature or purpose and subdivided, as far as may be necessary, in accordance with the regulations made pursuant to Article 279. The expenditure of the European Parliament, the Council, the Commission and the Court of Justice shall be set out in separate parts of the budget, without prejudice to special arrangements for certain common items of expenditure.

Article 272   (ex Article 203)

1.   The financial year shall run from 1 January to 31 December.

2.   Each institution of the Community shall, before 1 July, draw up estimates of its expenditure. The Commission shall consolidate these estimates in a preliminary draft budget. It shall attach thereto an opinion which may contain different estimates.

The preliminary draft budget shall contain an estimate of revenue and an estimate of expenditure.

3.   The Commission shall place the preliminary draft budget before the Council not later than 1 September of the year preceding that in which the budget is to be implemented.

The Council shall consult the Commission and, where appropriate, the other institutions concerned whenever it intends to depart from the preliminary draft budget.

The Council, acting by a qualified majority, shall establish the draft budget and forward it to the European Parliament.

4. The draft budget shall be placed before the European Parliament not later than 5 October of the year preceding that in which the budget is to be implemented.

The European Parliament shall have the right to amend the draft budget, acting by a majority of its Members, and to propose to the Council, acting by an absolute majority of the votes cast, modifications to the draft budget relating to expenditure necessarily resulting from this Treaty or from acts adopted in accordance therewith.

If, within 45 days of the draft budget being placed before it, the European Parliament has given its approval, the budget shall stand as finally adopted. If within this period the European Parliament has not amended the draft budget nor proposed any modifications thereto, the budget shall be deemed to be finally adopted.

If within this period the European Parliament has adopted amendments or proposed modifications, the draft budget together with the amendments or proposed modifications shall be forwarded to the Council.

5. After discussing the draft budget with the Commission and, where appropriate, with the other institutions concerned, the Council shall act under the following conditions:

(a) the Council may, acting by a qualified majority, modify any of the amendments adopted by the European Parliament;

(b) with regard to the proposed modifications:

— where a modification proposed by the European Parliament does not have the effect of increasing the total amount of the expenditure of an institution, owing in particular to the fact that the increase in expenditure which it would involve would be expressly compensated by one or more proposed modifications correspondingly reducing expenditure, the Council may, acting by a qualified majority, reject the proposed modification. In the absence of a decision to reject it, the proposed modification shall stand as accepted;

— where a modification proposed by the European Parliament has the effect of increasing the total amount of the expenditure of an institution, the Council may, acting by a qualified majority, accept this proposed modification. In the absence of a decision to accept it, the proposed modification shall stand as rejected;

— where, in pursuance of one of the two preceding sub-paragraphs, the Council has rejected a proposed modification, it may, acting by a qualified majority, either retain the amount shown in the draft budget or fix another amount.

The draft budget shall be modified on the basis of the proposed modifications accepted by the Council.

If, within 15 days of the draft being placed before it, the Council has not modified any of the amendments adopted by the European Parliament and if the modifications proposed by the latter have been accepted, the budget shall be deemed to be finally adopted. The Council shall inform the European Parliament that it has not modified any of the amendments and that the proposed modifications have been accepted.

If within this period the Council has modified one or more of the amendments adopted by the European Parliament or if the modifications proposed by the latter have been rejected or modified, the modified draft budget shall again be forwarded to the European Parliament. The Council shall inform the European Parliament of the results of its deliberations.

6. Within 15 days of the draft budget being placed before it, the European Parliament, which shall have been notified of the action taken on its proposed modifications, may, acting by a majority of its Members and three-fifths of the votes cast, amend or reject the modifications to its amendments made by the Council and shall adopt the budget accordingly. If

within this period the European Parliament has not acted, the budget shall be deemed to be finally adopted.

7.   When the procedure provided for in this Article has been completed, the President of the European Parliament shall declare that the budget has been finally adopted.

8.   However, the European Parliament, acting by a majority of its Members and two-thirds of the votes cast, may, if there are important reasons, reject the draft budget and ask for a new draft to be submitted to it.

9.   A maximum rate of increase in relation to the expenditure of the same type to be incurred during the current year shall be fixed annually for the total expenditure other than that necessarily resulting from this Treaty or from acts adopted in accordance therewith.

The Commission shall, after consulting the Economic Policy Committee, declare what this maximum rate is as it results from:

— the trend, in terms of volume, of the gross national product within the Community;
— the average variation in the budgets of the Member States; and
— the trend of the cost of living during the preceding financial year.

The maximum rate shall be communicated, before 1 May, to all the institutions of the Community. The latter shall be required to conform to this during the budgetary procedure, subject to the provisions of the fourth and fifth sub-paragraphs of this paragraph.

If, in respect of expenditure other than that necessarily resulting from this Treaty or from acts adopted in accordance therewith, the actual rate of increase in the draft budget established by the Council is over half the maximum rate, the European Parliament may, exercising its right of amendment, further increase the total amount of that expenditure to a limit not exceeding half the maximum rate.

Where the European Parliament, the Council or the Commission consider that the activities of the Communities require that the rate determined according to the procedure laid down in this paragraph should be exceeded, another rate may be fixed by agreement between the Council, acting by a qualified majority, and the European Parliament, acting by a majority of its Members and three-fifths of the votes cast.

10.   Each institution shall exercise the powers conferred upon it by this Article, with due regard for the provisions of the Treaty and for acts adopted in accordance therewith, in particular those relating to the Communities' own resources and to the balance between revenue and expenditure.

Article 273   (ex Article 204)

If, at the beginning of a financial year, the budget has not yet been voted, a sum equivalent to not more than one-twelfth of the budget appropriations for the preceding financial year may be spent each month in respect of any chapter or other subdivision of the budget in accordance with the provisions of the Regulations made pursuant to Article 279; this arrangement shall not, however, have the effect of placing at the disposal of the Commission appropriations in excess of one twelfth of those provided for in the draft budget in course of preparation.

The Council may, acting by a qualified majority, provided that the other conditions laid down in the first sub-paragraph are observed, authorise expenditure in excess of one twelfth.

If the decision relates to expenditure which does not necessarily result from this Treaty or from acts adopted in accordance therewith, the Council shall forward it immediately to the European Parliament; within 30 days the European Parliament, acting by a majority of its Members and three-fifths of the votes cast, may adopt a different decision on the expenditure in excess of the one-twelfth referred to in the first sub-paragraph. This part of the decision of the Council shall be suspended until the European Parliament has taken its decision. If within the said period the European Parliament has not taken a decision which differs from the decision of the Council, the latter shall be deemed to be finally adopted.

The decisions referred to in the second and third sub-paragraphs shall lay down the necessary measures relating to resources to ensure application of this Article.

Article 274   (ex Article 205)

The Commission shall implement the budget, in accordance with the provisions of the regulations made pursuant to Article 279, on its own responsibility and within the limits of the appropriations, having regard to the principles of sound financial management.

Member States shall cooperate with the Commission to ensure that the appropriations are used in accordance with the principles of sound financial management.

The regulations shall lay down detailed rules for each institution concerning its part in effecting its own expenditure. Within the budget, the Commission may, subject to the limits and conditions laid down in the regulations made pursuant to Article 279, transfer appropriations from one chapter to another or from one subdivision to another.

Article 275   (ex Article 205a)

The Commission shall submit annually to the Council and to the European Parliament the accounts of the preceding financial year relating to the implementation of the budget. The Commission shall also forward to them a financial statement of the assets and liabilities of the Community.

Article 276   (ex Article 206)

1.   The European Parliament, acting on a recommendation from the Council which shall act by a qualified majority, shall give a discharge to the Commission in respect of the implementation of the budget. To this end, the Council and the European Parliament in turn shall examine the accounts and the financial statement referred to in Article 275, the annual report by the Court of Auditors together with the replies of the institutions under audit to the observations of the Court of Auditors, the statement of assurance referred to in Article 248(1), second sub-paragraph and any relevant special reports by the Court of Auditors.

2.   Before giving a discharge to the Commission, or for any other purpose in connection with the exercise of its powers over the implementation of the budget, the European Parliament may ask to hear the Commission give evidence with regard to the execution of expenditure or the operation of financial control systems. The Commission shall submit any necessary information to the European Parliament at the latter's request.

3.   The Commission shall take all appropriate steps to act on the observations in the decisions giving discharge and on other observations by the European Parliament relating to the execution of expenditure, as well as on comments accompanying the recommendations on discharge adopted by the Council.

At the request of the EuropeanParliament or the Council, the Commission shall report on the measures taken in the light of these observations and comments and in particular on the instructions given to the departments which are responsible for the implementation of the budget. These reports shall also be forwarded to the Court of Auditors.

Article 277   (ex Article 207)

The budget shall be drawn up in the unit of account determined in accordance with the provisions of the regulations made pursuant to Article 279.

Article 278   (ex Article 208)

The Commission may, provided it notifies the competent authorities of the Member States concerned, transfer into the currency of one of the Member States its holdings in the currency of another Member State, to the extent necessary to enable them to be used for purposes which come within the scope of this Treaty. The Commission shall as far as possible avoid making such transfers if it possesses cash or liquid assets in the currencies which it needs.

The Commission shall deal with each Member State through the authority designated by the State concerned. In carrying out financial operations the Commission shall employ the services of the bank of issue of the Member State concerned or of any other financial institution approved by that State.

Article 279   (ex Article 209) (As amended by the Treaty of Nice)

1.   The Council, acting unanimously on a proposal from the Commission and after consulting the European Parliament and obtaining the opinion of the Court of Auditors, shall:

(a) make Financial Regulations specifying in particular the procedure to be adopted for establishing and implementing the budget and for presenting and auditing accounts;

(b) lay down rules concerning the responsibility of financial controllers, authorising officers and accounting officers, and concerning appropriate arrangements for inspection.

From 1 January 2007, the Council shall act by a qualified majority on a proposal from the Commission and after consulting the European Parliament and obtaining the opinion of the Court of Auditors.

2.   The Council, acting unanimously on a proposal from the Commission and after consulting the European Parliament and obtaining the opinion of the Court of Auditors, shall determine the methods and procedure whereby the budget revenue provided under the arrangements relating to the Community's own resources shall be made available to the Commission, and determine the measures to be applied, if need be, to meet cash requirements.

Article 280   (ex Article 209a)

1.   The Community and the Member States shall counter fraud and any other illegal activities affecting the financial interests of the Community through measures to be taken in accordance with this Article, which shall act as a deterrent and be such as to afford effective protection in the Member States.

2.   Member States shall take the same measures to counter fraud affecting the financial interests of the Community as they take to counter fraud affecting their own financial interests.

3.   Without prejudice to other provisions of this Treaty, the Member States shall co-ordinate their action aimed at protecting the financial interests of the Community against fraud. To this end they shall organise, together with the Commission, close and regular cooperation between the competent authorities.

4.   The Council, acting in accordance with the procedure referred to in Article 251, after consulting the Court of Auditors, shall adopt the necessary measures in the fields of the prevention of and fight against fraud affecting the financial interests of the Community with a view to affording effective and equivalent protection in the Member States. These measures shall not concern the application of national criminal law or the national administration of justice.

5.   The Commission, in cooperation with Member States, shall each year submit to the European Parliament and to the Council a report on the measures taken for the implementation of this Article.

PART SIX   GENERAL AND FINAL PROVISIONS

Article 281   (ex Article 210)

The Community shall have legal personality.

Article 282   (ex Article 211)

In each of the Member States, the Community shall enjoy the most extensive legal capacity accorded to legal persons under their laws; it may, in particular, acquire or dispose of movable and immovable property and may be a party to legal proceedings. To this end, the Community shall be represented by the Commission.

Article 283　(ex Article 212)

The Council shall, acting by a qualified majority on a proposal from the Commission and after consulting the other institutions concerned, lay down the Staff Regulations of officials of the European Communities and the Conditions of Employment of other servants of those Communities.

Article 284　(ex Article 213)

The Commission may, within the limits and under conditions laid down by the Council in accordance with the provisions of this Treaty, collect any information and carry out any checks required for the performance of the tasks entrusted to it.

Article 285　(ex Article 213a)

1.　Without prejudice to Article 5 of the Protocol on the Statute of the European System of Central Banks and of the European Central Bank, the Council, acting in accordance with the procedure referred to in Article 251, shall adopt measures for the production of statistics where necessary for the performance of the activities of the Community.

2.　The production of Community statistics shall conform to impartiality, reliability, objectivity, scientific independence, cost effectiveness and statistical confidentiality; it shall not entail excessive burdens on economic operators.

Article 286　(ex Article 213b)

1.　From 1 January 1999, Community acts on the protection of individuals with regard to the processing of personal data and the free movement of such data shall apply to the institutions and bodies set up by, or on the basis of, this Treaty.

2.　Before the date referred to in paragraph 1, the Council, acting in accordance with the procedure referred to in Article 251, shall establish an independent supervisory body responsible for monitoring the application of such Community acts to Community institutions and bodies and shall adopt any other relevant provisions as appropriate.

Article 287　(ex Article 214)

The members of the institutions of the Community, the members of committees, and the officials and other servants of the Community shall be required, even after their duties have ceased, not to disclose information of the kind covered by the obligation of professional secrecy, in particular information about undertakings, their business relations or their cost components.

Article 288　(ex Article 215)

The contractual liability of the Community shall be governed by the law applicable to the contract in question.

In the case of non-contractual liability, the Community shall, in accordance with the general principles common to the laws of the Member States, make good any damage caused by its institutions or by its servants in the performance of their duties.

The preceding paragraph shall apply under the same conditions to damage caused by the ECB or by its servants in the performance of their duties.

The personal liability of its servants towards the Community shall be governed by the provisions laid down in their Staff Regulations or in the Conditions of Employment applicable to them.

Article 289　(ex Article 216)

The seat of the institutions of the Community shall be determined by common accord of the Governments of the Member States.

Article 290　(ex Article 217)

The rules governing the languages of the institutions of the Community shall, without prejudice to the provisions contained in the Statute of the Court of Justice, be determined by the Council, acting unanimously.

Article 291   (ex Article 218)

The Community shall enjoy in the territories of the Member States such privileges and immunities as are necessary for the performance of its tasks, under the conditions laid down in the Protocol of 8 April 1965 on the privileges and immunities of the European Communities. The same shall apply to the European Central Bank, the European Monetary Institute, and the European Investment Bank.

Article 292   (ex Article 219)

Member States undertake not to submit a dispute concerning the interpretation or application of this Treaty to any method of settlement other than those provided for therein.

Article 293   (ex Article 220)

Member States shall, so far as is necessary, enter into negotiations with each other with a view to securing for the benefit of their nationals:

— the protection of persons and the enjoyment and protection of rights under the same conditions as those accorded by each State to its own nationals;

— the abolition of double taxation within the Community;

— the mutual recognition of companies or firms within the meaning of the second paragraph of Article 48, the retention of legal personality in the event of transfer of their seat from one country to another, and the possibility of mergers between companies or firms governed by the laws of different countries;

— the simplification of formalities governing the reciprocal recognition and enforcement of judgments of courts or tribunals and of arbitration awards.

Article 294   (ex Article 221)

Member States shall accord nationals of the other Member States the same treatment as their own nationals as regards participation in the capital of companies or firms within the meaning of Article 48, without prejudice to the application of the other provisions of this Treaty.

Article 295   (ex Article 222)

This Treaty shall in no way prejudice the rules in Member States governing the system of property ownership.

Article 296   (ex Article 223)

1.   The provisions of this Treaty shall not preclude the application of the following rules:

(a) no Member State shall be obliged to supply information the disclosure of which it considers contrary to the essential interests of its security;

(b) any Member State may take such measures as it considers necessary for the protection of the essential interests of its security which are connected with the production of or trade in arms, munitions and war material; such measures shall not adversely affect the conditions of competition in the common market regarding products which are not intended for specifically military purposes.

2.   The Council may, acting unanimously on a proposal from the Commission, make changes to the list, which it drew up on 15 April 1958, of the products to which the provisions of paragraph 1(b) apply.

Article 297   (ex Article 224)

Member States shall consult each other with a view to taking together the steps needed to prevent the functioning of the common market being affected by measures which a Member State may be called upon to take in the event of serious internal disturbances affecting the maintenance of law and order, in the event of war, serious international tension constituting a threat of war, or in order to carry out obligations it has accepted for the purpose of maintaining peace and international security.

Article 298   (ex Article 225)

If measures taken in the circumstances referred to in Articles 296 and 297 have the effect of distorting the conditions of competition in the common market, the Commission shall, together with the State concerned, examine how these measures can be adjusted to the rules laid down in the Treaty.

By way of derogation from the procedure laid down in Articles 226 and 227, the Commission or any Member State may bring the matter directly before the Court of Justice if it considers that another Member State is making improper use of the powers provided for in Articles 296 and 297. The Court of Justice shall give its ruling in camera.

Article 299   (ex Article 227) (as amended by the 2003 Accession Treaty)

   1.   This Treaty shall apply to the Kingdom of Belgium, the Czech Republic, the Kingdom of Denmark, the Federal Republic of Germany, the Republic of Estonia, the Hellenic Republic, the Kingdom of Spain, the French Republic, Ireland, the Italian Republic, the Republic of Cyprus, the Republic of Latvia, the Republic of Lithuania, the Grand Duchy of Luxembourg, the Republic of Hungary, the Republic of Malta, the Kingdom of the Netherlands, the Republic of Austria, the Republic of Poland, the Portuguese Republic, the Republic of Slovenia, the Slovak Republic, the Republic of Finland, the Kingdom of Sweden and the United Kingdom of Great Britain and Northern Ireland.

   2.   The provisions of this Treaty shall apply to the French overseas departments, the Azores, Madeira and the Canary Islands.

   However, taking account of the structural social and economic situation of the French overseas departments, the Azores, Madeira and the Canary Islands, which is compounded by their remoteness, insularity, small size, difficult topography and climate, economic dependence on a few products, the permanence and combination of which severely restrain their development, the Council, acting by a qualified majority on a proposal from the Commission and after consulting the European Parliament, shall adopt specific measures aimed, in particular, at laying down the conditions of application of the present Treaty to those regions, including common policies.

   The Council shall, when adopting the relevant measures referred to in the second sub-paragraph, take into account areas such as customs and trade policies, fiscal policy, free zones, agriculture and fisheries policies, conditions for supply of raw materials and essential consumer goods, State aids and conditions of access to structural funds and to horizontal Community programmes.

   The Council shall adopt the measures referred to in the second sub-paragraph taking into account the special characteristics and constraints of the outermost regions without undermining the integrity and the coherence of the Community legal order, including the internal market and common policies.

   3.   The special arrangements for association set out in Part Four of this Treaty shall apply to the overseas countries and territories listed in Annex II to this Treaty.

   This Treaty shall not apply to those overseas countries and territories having special relations with the United Kingdom of Great Britain and Northern Ireland which are not included in the aforementioned list.

   4.   The provisions of this Treaty shall apply to the European territories for whose external relations a Member State is responsible.

   5.   The provisions of this Treaty shall apply to the Åland Islands in accordance with the provisions set out in Protocol No 2 to the Act concerning the conditions of accession of the Republic of Austria, the Republic of Finland and the Kingdom of Sweden.

   6.   Notwithstanding the preceding paragraphs:
      (a) this Treaty shall not apply to the Faeroe Islands;
      (b) this Treaty shall not apply to the Sovereign Base Areas of the United Kingdom of Great Britain and Northern Ireland in Cyprus;

(c) this Treaty shall apply to the Channel Islands and the Isle of Man only to the extent necessary to ensure the implementation of the arrangements for those islands set out in the Treaty concerning the accession of new Member States to the European Economic Community and to the European Atomic Energy Community signed on 22 January 1972.

Article 300   (ex Article 228) (As amended by the Treaty of Nice)

1.   Where this Treaty provides for the conclusion of agreements between the Community and one or more States or international organisations, the Commission shall make recommendations to the Council, which shall authorise the Commission to open the necessary negotiations. The Commission shall conduct these negotiations in consultation with special committees appointed by the Council to assist it in this task and within the framework of such directives as the Council may issue to it.

In exercising the powers conferred upon it by this paragraph, the Council shall act by a qualified majority, except in the cases where the first sub-paragraph of paragraph 2 provides that the Council shall act unanimously.

2.   Subject to the powers vested in the Commission in this field, the signing, which may be accompanied by a decision on provisional application before entry into force, and the conclusion of the agreements shall be decided on by the Council, acting by a qualified majority on a proposal from the Commission. The Council shall act unanimously when the agreement covers a field for which unanimity is required for the adoption of internal rules and for the agreements referred to in Article 310.

By way of derogation from the rules laid down in paragraph 3, the same procedures shall apply for a decision to suspend the application of an agreement, and for the purpose of establishing the positions to be adopted on behalf of the Community in a body set up by an agreement, when that body is called upon to adopt decisions having legal effects, with the exception of decisions supplementing or amending the institutional framework of the agreement.

The European Parliament shall be immediately and fully informed of any decision under this paragraph concerning the provisional application or the suspension of agreements, or the establishment of the Community position in a body set up by an agreement.

3.   The Council shall conclude agreements after consulting the European Parliament, except for the agreements referred to in Article 133(3), including cases where the agreement covers a field for which the procedure referred to in Article 251 or that referred to in Article 252 is required for the adoption of internal rules. The European Parliament shall deliver its opinion within a time-limit which the Council may lay down according to the urgency of the matter. In the absence of an opinion within that time limit, the Council may act.

By way of derogation from the previous sub-paragraph, agreements referred to in Article 310, other agreements establishing a specific institutional framework by organising cooperation procedures, agreements having important budgetary implications for the Community and agreements entailing amendment of an act adopted under the procedure referred to in Article 251 shall be concluded after the assent of the European Parliament has been obtained.

The Council and the European Parliament may, in an urgent situation, agree upon a time-limit for the assent.

4.   When concluding an agreement, the Council may, by way of derogation from paragraph 2, authorise the Commission to approve modifications on behalf of the Community where the agreement provides for them to be adopted by a simplified procedure or by a body set up by the agreement; it may attach specific conditions to such authorisation.

5.   When the Council envisages concluding an agreement which calls for amendments to this Treaty, the amendments must first be adopted in accordance with the procedure laid down in Article 48 of the Treaty on European Union.

6.   The European Parliament, the Council, the Commission or a Member State may obtain the opinion of the Court of Justice as to whether an agreement envisaged is compatible with the provisions of this Treaty. Where the opinion of the Court of Justice is adverse, the agreement may enter into force only in accordance with Article 48 of the Treaty on European Union.

7.   Agreements concluded under the conditions set out in this Article shall be binding on the institutions of the Community and on Member States.

Article 301   (ex Article 228a)

Where it is provided, in a common position or in a joint action adopted according to the provisions of the Treaty on European Union relating to the common foreign and security policy, for an action by the Community to interrupt or to reduce, in part or completely, economic relations with one or more third countries, the Council shall take the necessary urgent measures. The Council shall act by a qualified majority on a proposal from the Commission.

Article 302   (ex Article 229)

It shall be for the Commission to ensure the maintenance of all appropriate relations with the organs of the United Nations and of its specialised agencies.

The Commission shall also maintain such relations as are appropriate with all international organisations.

Article 303   (ex Article 230)

The Community shall establish all appropriate forms of cooperation with the Council of Europe.

Article 304   (ex Article 231)

The Community shall establish close cooperation with the Organisation for Economic Cooperation and Development, the details of which shall be determined by common accord.

Article 305   (ex Article 232)

1.   The provisions of this Treaty shall not affect the provisions of the Treaty establishing the European Coal and Steel Community, in particular as regards the rights and obligations of Member States, the powers of the institutions of that Community and the rules laid down by that Treaty for the functioning of the common market in coal and steel.

2.   The provisions of this Treaty shall not derogate from those of the Treaty establishing the European Atomic Energy Community.

Article 306   (ex Article 233)

The provisions of this Treaty shall not preclude the existence or completion of regional unions between Belgium and Luxembourg, or between Belgium, Luxembourg and the Netherlands, to the extent that the objectives of these regional unions are not attained by application of this Treaty.

Article 307   (ex Article 234)

The rights and obligations arising from agreements concluded before 1 January 1958 or, for acceding States, before the date of their accession, between one or more Member States on the one hand, and one or more third countries on the other, shall not be affected by the provisions of this Treaty.

To the extent that such agreements are not compatible with this Treaty, the Member State or States concerned shall take all appropriate steps to eliminate the incompatibilities established. Member States shall, where necessary, assist each other to this end and shall, where appropriate, adopt a common attitude.

In applying the agreements referred to in the first paragraph, Member States shall take into account the fact that the advantages accorded under this Treaty by each Member State form an integral part of the establishment of the Community and are thereby inseparably linked with the creation of common institutions, the conferring of powers upon them and the granting of the same advantages by all the other Member States.

Article 308   (ex Article 235)

If action by the Community should prove necessary to attain, in the course of the operation of the common market, one of the objectives of the Community and this Treaty has not provided the necessary powers, the Council shall, acting unanimously on a proposal from the Commission and after consulting the European Parliament, take the appropriate measures.

Article 309   (ex Article 236) (As amended by the Treaty of Nice)

1.   Where a decision has been taken to suspend the voting rights of the representative of the government of a Member State in accordance with Article 7(3) of the Treaty on European Union, these voting rights shall also be suspended with regard to this Treaty.

2.   Moreover, where the existence of a serious and persistent breach by a Member State of principles mentioned in Article 6(1) of the Treaty on European Union has been determined in accordance with Article 7(2) of that Treaty, the Council, acting by a qualified majority, may decide to suspend certain of the rights deriving from the application of this Treaty to the Member State in question. In doing so, the Council shall take into account the possible consequences of such a suspension on the rights and obligations of natural and legal persons.

The obligations of the Member State in question under this Treaty shall in any case continue to be binding on that State.

3.   The Council, acting by a qualified majority, may decide subsequently to vary or revoke measures taken in accordance with paragraph 2 in response to changes in the situation which led to their being imposed.

4.   When taking decisions referred to in paragraphs 2 and 3, the Council shall act without taking into account the votes of the representative of the government of the Member State in question. By way of derogation from Article 205(2) a qualified majority shall be defined as the same proportion of the weighted votes of the members of the Council concerned as laid down in Article 205(2).

This paragraph shall also apply in the event of voting rights being suspended in accordance with paragraph 1. In such cases, a decision requiring unanimity shall be taken without the vote of the representative of the government of the Member State in question.

Article 310   (ex Article 238)

The Community may conclude with one or more States or international organisations agreements establishing an association involving reciprocal rights and obligations, common action and special procedure.

Article 311   (ex Article 239)

The protocols annexed to this Treaty by common accord of the Member States shall form an integral part thereof.

Article 312   (ex Article 240)

This Treaty is concluded for an unlimited period.

FINAL PROVISIONS

Article 313   (ex Article 247)

This Treaty shall be ratified by the High Contracting Parties in accordance with their respective constitutional requirements. The instruments of ratification shall be deposited with the Government of the Italian Republic.

This Treaty shall enter into force on the first day of the month following the deposit of the instrument of ratification by the last signatory State to take this step. If, however, such deposit is made less than 15 days before the beginning of the following month, this Treaty shall not enter into force until the first day of the second month after the date of such deposit.

Article 314   (ex Article 248)

This Treaty, drawn up in a single original in the Dutch, French, German, and Italian languages, all four texts being equally authentic, shall be deposited in the archives of the Government of the Italian Republic, which shall transmit a certified copy to each of the Governments of the other signatory States.

Pursuant to the Accession Treaties, the Danish, English, Finnish, Greek, Irish, Portuguese, Spanish and Swedish versions of this Treaty shall also be authentic.

IN WITNESS WHEREOF, the undersigned Plenipotentiaries have signed this Treaty. Done at Rome this twenty fifth day of March in the year one thousand nine hundred and fifty seven.

P. H. SPAAK	J. Ch. SNOY ET D' OPPUERS
ADENAUER	HALLSTEIN
PINEAU	M. FAURE
Antonio SEGNI	Gaetano MARTINO
BECH	Lambert SCHAUS
J. LUNS	J. LINTHORST HOMAN

ANNEX II   OVERSEAS COUNTRIES AND TERRITORIES

to which the provisions of Part Four of the Treaty apply

—Greenland,
—New Caledonia and Dependencies,
—French Polynesia,
—French Southern and Antarctic Territories,
—Wallis and Futuna Islands,
—Mayotte,
—Saint Pierre and Miquelon,
—Aruba,
—Netherlands Antilles:
  —Bonaire,
  —Curaçao,
  —Saba,
  —Sint Eustatius,
  —Sint Maarten.

—Anguilla,
—Cayman Islands,
—Falkland Islands,
—South Georgia and the South Sandwich Islands,
—Montserrat,
—Pitcairn,
—Saint Helena and Dependencies,
—British Antarctic Territory,
—British Indian Ocean Territory,
—Turks and Caicos Islands,
—British Virgin Islands,
—Bermuda.

Consolidated Version of the Treaty on European Union[1]

HIS MAJESTY THE KING OF THE BELGIANS, HER MAJESTY THE QUEEN OF DENMARK, THE PRESIDENT OF THE FEDERAL REPUBLIC OF GERMANY, THE PRESIDENT OF THE HELLENIC REPUBLIC, HIS MAJESTY THE KING OF SPAIN, THE PRESIDENT OF THE

---

[1] **Editor's Note:** As amended in accordance with the Treaty of Nice Consolidated Version (OJ 2002 C325/1–184) and the 2003 Accession Treaty (OJ 2003, L236/17).

FRENCH REPUBLIC, THE PRESIDENT OF IRELAND, THE PRESIDENT OF THE ITALIAN REPUBLIC, HIS ROYAL HIGHNESS THE GRAND DUKE OF LUXEMBOURG, HER MAJESTY THE QUEEN OF THE NETHERLANDS, THE PRESIDENT OF THE PORTUGUESE REPUBLIC, HER MAJESTY THE QUEEN OF THE UNITED KINGDOM OF GREAT BRITAIN AND NORTH-ERN IRELAND,

RESOLVED to mark a new stage in the process of European integration undertaken with the establishment of the European Communities,

RECALLING the historic importance of the ending of the division of the European continent and the need to create firm bases for the construction of the future Europe,

CONFIRMING their attachment to the principles of liberty, democracy and respect for human rights and fundamental freedoms and of the rule of law,

CONFIRMING their attachment to fundamental social rights as defined in the European Social Charter signed at Turin on 18 October 1961 and in the 1989 Community Charter of the Fundamental Social Rights of Workers,

DESIRING to deepen the solidarity between their peoples while respecting their history, their culture and their traditions,

DESIRING to enhance further the democratic and efficient functioning of the institutions so as to enable them better to carry out, within a single institutional framework, the tasks entrusted to them,

RESOLVED to achieve the strengthening and the convergence of their economies and to establish an economic and monetary union including, in accordance with the provisions of this Treaty, a single and stable currency,

DETERMINED to promote economic and social progress for their peoples, taking into account the principle of sustainable development and within the context of the accomplish-ment of the internal market and of reinforced cohesion and environmental protection, and to implement policies ensuring that advances in economic integration are accompanied by parallel progress in other fields,

RESOLVED to establish a citizenship common to nationals of their countries,

RESOLVED to implement a common foreign and security policy including the progressive framing of a common defence policy, which might lead to a common defence in accordance with the provisions of Article 17, thereby reinforcing the European identity and its independ-ence in order to promote peace, security and progress in Europe and in the world,

RESOLVED to facilitate the free movement of persons, while ensuring the safety and security of their peoples, by establishing an area of freedom, security and justice, in accordance with the provisions of this Treaty,

RESOLVED to continue the process of creating an ever closer union among the peoples of Europe, in which decisions are taken as closely as possible to the citizen in accordance with the principle of subsidiarity,

IN VIEW of further steps to be taken in order to advance European integration,

HAVE DECIDED to establish a European Union and to this end have designated as their Plenipotentiaries:

HIS MAJESTY THE KING OF THE BELGIANS:
Mark EYSKENS, Minister for Foreign Affairs,
Philippe MAYSTADT, Minister for Finance;

HER MAJESTY THE QUEEN OF DENMARK:
Uffe ELLEMANN-JENSEN, Minister for Foreign Affairs,
Anders FOGH RASMUSSEN, Minister for Economic Affairs;

THE PRESIDENT OF THE FEDERAL REPUBLIC OF GERMANY:
Hans Dietrich GENSCHER, Federal Minister for Foreign Affairs,
Theodor WAIGEL, Federal Minister for Finance;

THE PRESIDENT OF THE HELLENIC REPUBLIC:
Antonios SAMARAS, Minister for Foreign Affairs,
Efthymios CHRISTODOULOU, Minister for Economic Affairs;

HIS MAJESTY THE KING OF SPAIN:
Francisco FERNÁNDEZ ORDÓÑEZ, Minister for Foreign Affairs,
Carlos SOLCHAGA CATALÁN, Minister for Economic Affairs and Finance;

THE PRESIDENT OF THE FRENCH REPUBLIC:
Roland DUMAS, Minister for Foreign Affairs,
Pierre BÉRÉGOVOY, Minister for Economic and Financial Affairs and the Budget;

THE PRESIDENT OF IRELAND:
Gerard COLLINS, Minister for Foreign Affairs,
Bertie AHERN, Minister for Finance;

THE PRESIDENT OF THE ITALIAN REPUBLIC:
Gianni DE MICHELIS, Minister for Foreign Affairs,
Guido CARLI, Minister for the Treasury;

HIS ROYAL HIGHNESS THE GRAND DUKE OF LUXEMBOURG:
Jacques F. POOS, Deputy Prime Minister, Minister for Foreign Affairs,
Jean-Claude JUNCKER, Minister for Finance;

HER MAJESTY THE QUEEN OF THE NETHERLANDS:
Hans VAN DEN BROEK, Minister for Foreign Affairs,
Willem KOK, Minister for Finance;

THE PRESIDENT OF THE PORTUGUESE REPUBLIC:
João de Deus PINHEIRO, Minister for Foreign Affairs,
Jorge BRAGA DE MACEDO, Minister for Finance;

HER MAJESTY THE QUEEN OF THE UNITED KINGDOM OF GREAT BRITAIN AND NORTHERN IRELAND:
The Rt. Hon. Douglas HURD, Secretary of State for Foreign and Commonwealth Affairs,
The Hon. Francis MAUDE, Financial Secretary to the Treasury;

WHO, having exchanged their full powers, found in good and due form, have agreed as follows.

TITLE I　COMMON PROVISIONS

Article 1　(ex Article A)
By this Treaty, the HIGH CONTRACTING PARTIES establish among themselves a EUROPEAN UNION, hereinafter called 'the Union'.

This Treaty marks a new stage in the process of creating an ever closer union among the peoples of Europe, in which decisions are taken as openly as possible and as closely as possible to the citizen.

The Union shall be founded on the European Communities, supplemented by the policies and forms of cooperation established by this Treaty. Its task shall be to organise, in a manner demonstrating consistency and solidarity, relations between the Member States and between their peoples.

Article 2　(ex Article B)
The Union shall set itself the following objectives:
— to promote economic and social progress and a high level of employment and to achieve balanced and sustainable development, in particular through the creation

of an area without internal frontiers, through the strengthening of economic and social cohesion and through the establishment of economic and monetary union, ultimately including a single currency in accordance with the provisions of this Treaty;

— to assert its identity on the international scene, in particular through the implementation of a common foreign and security policy including the progressive framing of a common defence policy, which might lead to a common defence, in accordance with the provisions of Article 17;

— to strengthen the protection of the rights and interests of the nationals of its Member States through the introduction of a citizenship of the Union;

— to maintain and develop the Union as an area of freedom, security and justice, in which the free movement of persons is assured in conjunction with appropriate measures with respect to external border controls, asylum, immigration and the prevention and combating of crime;

— to maintain in full the acquis communautaire and build on it with a view to considering to what extent the policies and forms of cooperation introduced by this Treaty may need to be revised with the aim of ensuring the effectiveness of the mechanisms and the institutions of the Community.

The objectives of the Union shall be achieved as provided in this Treaty and in accordance with the conditions and the timetable set out therein while respecting the principle of subsidiarity as defined in Article 5 of the Treaty establishing the European Community.

Article 3   (ex Article C)

The Union shall be served by a single institutional framework which shall ensure the consistency and the continuity of the activities carried out in order to attain its objectives while respecting and building upon the acquis communautaire.

The Union shall in particular ensure the consistency of its external activities as a whole in the context of its external relations, security, economic and development policies. The Council and the Commission shall be responsible for ensuring such consistency and shall cooperate to this end. They shall ensure the implementation of these policies, each in accordance with its respective powers.

Article 4   (ex Article D)

The European Council shall provide the Union with the necessary impetus for its development and shall define the general political guidelines thereof.

The European Council shall bring together the Heads of State or Government of the Member States and the President of the Commission. They shall be assisted by the Ministers for Foreign Affairs of the Member States and by a Member of the Commission. The European Council shall meet at least twice a year, under the chairmanship of the Head of State or Government of the Member State which holds the Presidency of the Council. The European Council shall submit to the European Parliament a report after each of its meetings and a yearly written report on the progress achieved by the Union.

Article 5   (ex Article E)

The European Parliament, the Council, the Commission, the Court of Justice and the Court of Auditors shall exercise their powers under the conditions and for the purposes provided for, on the one hand, by the provisions of the Treaties establishing the European Communities and of the subsequent Treaties and Acts modifying and supplementing them and, on the other hand, by the other provisions of this Treaty.

Article 6   (ex Article F)

1.   The Union is founded on the principles of liberty, democracy, respect for human rights and fundamental freedoms, and the rule of law, principles which are common to the Member States.

2.   The Union shall respect fundamental rights, as guaranteed by the European Convention for the Protection of Human Rights and Fundamental Freedoms signed in Rome on 4 November 1950 and as they result from the constitutional traditions common to the Member States, as general principles of Community law.

3.   The Union shall respect the national identities of its Member States.

4.   The Union shall provide itself with the means necessary to attain its objectives and carry through its policies.

Article 7   **(ex Article F.1) (As amended by the Treaty of Nice)**

1.   On a reasoned proposal by one third of the Member States, by the European Parliament or by the Commission, the Council, acting by a majority of four-fifths of its members after obtaining the assent of the European Parliament, may determine that there is a clear risk of a serious breach by a Member State of principles mentioned in Article 6(1), and address appropriate recommendations to that State. Before making such a determination, the Council shall hear the Member State in question and, acting in accordance with the same procedure, may call on independent persons to submit within a reasonable time limit a report on the situation in the Member State in question.

The Council shall regularly verify that the grounds on which such a determination was made continue to apply.

2.   The Council, meeting in the composition of the Heads of State or Government and acting by unanimity on a proposal by one third of the Member States or by the Commission and after obtaining the assent of the European Parliament, may determine the existence of a serious and persistent breach by a Member State of principles mentioned in Article 6(1), after inviting the government of the Member State in question to submit its observations.

3.   Where a determination under paragraph 2 has been made, the Council, acting by a qualified majority, may decide to suspend certain of the rights deriving from the application of this Treaty to the Member State in question, including the voting rights of the representative of the government of that Member State in the Council. In doing so, the Council shall take into account the possible consequences of such a suspension on the rights and obligations of natural and legal persons.

The obligations of the Member State in question under this Treaty shall in any case continue to be binding on that State.

4.   The Council, acting by a qualified majority, may decide subsequently to vary or revoke measures taken under paragraph 3 in response to changes in the situation which led to their being imposed.

5.   For the purposes of this Article, the Council shall act without taking into account the vote of the representative of the government of the Member State in question. Abstentions by members present in person or represented shall not prevent the adoption of decisions referred to in paragraph 2. A qualified majority shall be defined as the same proportion of the weighted votes of the members of the Council concerned as laid down in Article 205(2) of the Treaty establishing the European Community.

This paragraph shall also apply in the event of voting rights being suspended pursuant to paragraph 3.

6.   For the purposes of paragraphs 1 and 2, the European Parliament shall act by a two-thirds majority of the votes cast, representing a majority of its Members.

TITLE II   PROVISIONS AMENDING THE TREATY ESTABLISHING THE EUROPEAN ECONOMIC COMMUNITY WITH A VIEW TO ESTABLISHING THE EUROPEAN COMMUNITY

Article 8   (ex Article G)[2]

TITLE III   PROVISIONS AMENDING THE TREATY ESTABLISHING THE EUROPEAN COAL AND STEEL COMMUNITY

Article 9   (ex Article H)[3]

TITLE IV   PROVISIONS AMENDING THE TREATY ESTABLISHING THE EUROPEAN ATOMIC ENERGY COMMUNITY

Article 10   (ex Article I)[4]

TITLE V   PROVISIONS ON A COMMON FOREIGN AND SECURITY POLICY

Article 11   (ex Article J.1)

1.   The Union shall define and implement a common foreign and security policy covering all areas of foreign and security policy, the objectives of which shall be:
— to safeguard the common values, fundamental interests, independence and integrity of the Union in conformity with the principles of the United Nations Charter;
— to strengthen the security of the Union in all ways;
— to preserve peace and strengthen international security, in accordance with the principles of the United Nations Charter, as well as the principles of the Helsinki Final Act and the objectives of the Paris Charter, including those on external borders;
— to promote international cooperation;
— to develop and consolidate democracy and the rule of law, and respect for human rights and fundamental freedoms.

2.   The Member States shall support the Union's external and security policy actively and unreservedly in a spirit of loyalty and mutual solidarity.

The Member States shall work together to enhance and develop their mutual political solidarity. They shall refrain from any action which is contrary to the interests of the Union or likely to impair its effectiveness as a cohesive force in international relations.

The Council shall ensure that these principles are complied with.

Article 12   (ex Article J.2)

The Union shall pursue the objectives set out in Article 11 by:
— defining the principles of and general guidelines for the common foreign and security policy;

---

[2] **Editor's Note:** This is the article which made the numerous amendments to the EC Treaty and is not reproduced.
[3] **Editor's Note:** This is the article which made the numerous amendments to the ECSC Treaty and is not reproduced.
[4] **Editor's Note:** This is the article which made the numerous amendments to the Euratom Treaty and is not reproduced.

— deciding on common strategies;
— adopting joint actions;
— adopting common positions;
— strengthening systematic cooperation between Member States in the conduct of policy.

Article 13   (ex Article J.3)

1.   The European Council shall define the principles of and general guidelines for the common foreign and security policy, including for matters with defence implications.

2.   The European Council shall decide on common strategies to be implemented by the Union in areas where the Member States have important interests in common.

Common strategies shall set out their objectives, duration and the means to be made available by the Union and the Member States.

3.   The Council shall take the decisions necessary for defining and implementing the common foreign and security policy on the basis of the general guidelines defined by the European Council.

The Council shall recommend common strategies to the European Council and shall implement them, in particular by adopting joint actions and common positions.

The Council shall ensure the unity, consistency and effectiveness of action by the Union.

Article 14   (ex Article J.4)

1.   The Council shall adopt joint actions. Joint actions shall address specific situations where operational action by the Union is deemed to be required. They shall lay down their objectives, scope, the means to be made available to the Union, if necessary their duration, and the conditions for their implementation.

2.   If there is a change in circumstances having a substantial effect on a question subject to joint action, the Council shall review the principles and objectives of that action and take the necessary decisions. As long as the Council has not acted, the joint action shall stand.

3.   Joint actions shall commit the Member States in the positions they adopt and in the conduct of their activity.

4.   The Council may request the Commission to submit to it any appropriate proposals relating to the common foreign and security policy to ensure the implementation of a joint action.

5.   Whenever there is any plan to adopt a national position or take national action pursuant to a joint action, information shall be provided in time to allow, if necessary, for prior consultations within the Council. The obligation to provide prior information shall not apply to measures which are merely a national transposition of Council decisions.

6.   In cases of imperative need arising from changes in the situation and failing a Council decision, Member States may take the necessary measures as a matter of urgency having regard to the general objectives of the joint action. The Member State concerned shall inform the Council immediately of any such measures.

7.   Should there be any major difficulties in implementing a joint action, a Member State shall refer them to the Council which shall discuss them and seek appropriate solutions. Such solutions shall not run counter to the objectives of the joint action or impair its effectiveness.

Article 15   (ex Article J.5)

The Council shall adopt common positions. Common positions shall define the approach of the Union to a particular matter of a geographical or thematic nature. Member States shall ensure that their national policies conform to the common positions.

Article 16   (ex Article J.6)

Member States shall inform and consult one another within the Council on any matter of foreign and security policy of general interest in order to ensure that the Union's influence is exerted as effectively as possible by means of concerted and convergent action.

Article 17   (ex Article J.7) (As amended by the Treaty of Nice)

1.   The common foreign and security policy shall include all questions relating to the security of the Union, including the progressive framing of a common defence policy, which might lead to a common defence, should the European Council so decide. It shall in that case recommend to the Member States the adoption of such a decision in accordance with their respective constitutional requirements.

The policy of the Union in accordance with this Article shall not prejudice the specific character of the security and defence policy of certain Member States and shall respect the obligations of certain Member States, which see their common defence realised in the North Atlantic Treaty Organisation (NATO), under the North Atlantic Treaty and be compatible with the common security and defence policy established within that framework.

The progressive framing of a common defence policy will be supported, as Member States consider appropriate, by cooperation between them in the field of armaments.

2.   Questions referred to in this Article shall include humanitarian and rescue tasks, peacekeeping tasks and tasks of combat forces in crisis management, including peacemaking.

3.   Decisions having defence implications dealt with under this Article shall be taken without prejudice to the policies and obligations referred to in paragraph 1, second subparagraph.

4.   The provisions of this Article shall not prevent the development of closer cooperation between two or more Member States on a bilateral level, in the framework of the Western European Union (WEU) and NATO, provided such cooperation does not run counter to or impede that provided for in this Title.

5.   With a view to furthering the objectives of this Article, the provisions of this Article will be reviewed in accordance with Article 48.

Article 18   (ex Article J.8)

1.   The Presidency shall represent the Union in matters coming within the common foreign and security policy.

2.   The Presidency shall be responsible for the implementation of decisions taken under this Title; in that capacity it shall in principle express the position of the Union in international organisations and international conferences.

3.   The Presidency shall be assisted by the Secretary-General of the Council who shall exercise the function of High Representative for the commonforeign and security policy.

4.   The Commission shall be fully associated in the tasks referred to in paragraphs 1 and 2. The Presidency shall be assisted in those tasks if need be by the next Member State to hold the Presidency.

5.   The Council may, whenever it deems it necessary, appoint a special representative with a mandate in relation to particular policy issues.

Article 19   (ex Article J.9)

1.   Member States shall coordinate their action in international organisations and at international conferences. They shall uphold the common positions in such fora.

In international organisations and at international conferences where not all the Member States participate, those which do take part shall uphold the common positions.

2.   Without prejudice to paragraph 1 and Article 14(3), Member States represented in international organisations or international conferences where not all the Member States participate shall keep the latter informed of any matter of common interest.

Member States which are also members of the United Nations Security Council will concert and keep the other Member States fully informed. Member States which are permanent members of the Security Council will, in the execution of their functions, ensure the defence of the positions and the interests of the Union, without prejudice to their responsibilities under the provisions of the United Nations Charter.

Article 20   (ex Article J.10)

The diplomatic and consular missions of the Member States and the Commission Delegations in third countries and international conferences, and their representations to international organisations, shall cooperate in ensuring that the common positions and joint actions adopted by the Council are complied with and implemented.

They shall step up cooperation by exchanging information, carrying out joint assessments and contributing to the implementation of the provisions referred to in Article 20 of the Treaty establishing the European Community.

Article 21   (ex Article J.11)

The Presidency shall consult the European Parliament on the main aspects and the basic choices of the common foreign and security policy and shall ensure that the views of the European Parliament are duly taken into consideration. The European Parliament shall be kept regularly informed by the Presidency and the Commission of the development of the Union's foreign and security policy.

The European Parliament may ask questions of the Council or make recommendations to it. It shall hold an annual debate on progress in implementing the common foreign and security policy.

Article 22   (ex Article J.12)

   1.   Any Member State or the Commission may refer to the Council any question relating to the common foreign and security policy and may submit proposals to the Council.

   2.   In cases requiring a rapid decision, the Presidency, of its own motion, or at the request of the Commission or a Member State, shall convene an extraordinary Council meeting within forty-eight hours or, in an emergency, within a shorter period.

Article 23   (ex Article J.13) (As amended by the Treaty of Nice)

   1.   Decisions under this Title shall be taken by the Council acting unanimously. Abstentions by members present in person or represented shall not prevent the adoption of such decisions.

   When abstaining in a vote, any member of the Council may qualify its abstention by making a formal declaration under the present sub-paragraph. In that case, it shall not be obliged to apply the decision, but shall accept that the decision commits the Union. In a spirit of mutual solidarity, the Member State concerned shall refrain from any action likely to conflict with or impede Union action based on that decision and the other Member States shall respect its position. If the members of the Council qualifying their abstention in this way represent more than one third of the votes weighted in accordance with Article 205(2) of the Treaty establishing the European Community, the decision shall not be adopted.

   2.   By derogation from the provisions of paragraph 1, the Council shall act by qualified majority:

> — when adopting joint actions, common positions or taking any other decision on the basis of a common strategy;
> — when adopting any decision implementing a joint action or a common position.
> — when appointing a special representative in accordance with Article 18(5)

If a member of the Council declares that, for important and stated reasons of national policy, it intends to oppose the adoption of a decision to be taken by qualified majority, a vote shall not be taken. The Council may, acting by a qualified majority, request that the matter be referred to the European Council for decision by unanimity.

   The votes of the members of the Council shall be weighted in accordance with Article 205(2) of the Treaty establishing the European Community. For their adoption, decisions shall require at least 232 votes in favour cast by at least two-thirds of the members. When a decision is to be adopted by the Council by a qualified majority, a member of the Council may request verification that the Member States constituting the qualified majority represent at least 62% of the total population of the Union. If that condition is shown not to have been met, the decision in question shall not be adopted.*

This paragraph shall not apply to decisions having military or defence implications.

3.   For procedural questions, the Council shall act by a majority of its members.

Article 24   (ex Article J.14) (As amended by the Treaty of Nice)

1.   When it is necessary to conclude an agreement with one or more States or international organisations in implementation of this Title, the Council may authorise the Presidency, assisted by the Commission as appropriate, to open negotiations to that effect. Such agreements shall be concluded by the Council on a recommendation from the Presidency.

2.   The Council shall act unanimously when the agreement covers an issue for which unanimity is required for the adoption of internal decisions.

3.   When the agreement is envisaged in order to implement a joint action or common position, the Council shall act by a qualified majority in accordance with Article 23(2).

4.   The provisions of this Article shall also apply to matters falling under Title VI. When the agreement covers an issue for which a qualified majority is required for the adoption of internal decisions or measures, the Council shall act by a qualified majority in accordance with Article 34(3).

5.   No agreement shall be binding on a Member State whose representative in the Council states that it has to comply with the requirements of its own constitutional procedure; the other members of the Council may agree that the agreement shall nevertheless apply provisionally.

6.   Agreements concluded under the conditions set out by this Article shall be binding on the institutions of the Union.

Article 25   (ex Article J.15) (As amended by the Treaty of Nice)

Without prejudice to Article 207 of the Treaty establishing the European Community, a Political and Security Committee shall monitor the international situation in the areas covered by the common foreign and security policy and contribute to the definition of policies by delivering opinions to the Council at the request of the Council or on its own initiative. It shall also monitor the implementation of agreed policies, without prejudice to the responsibility of the Presidency and the Commission.

Within the scope of this Title, this Committee shall exercise, under the responsibility of the Council, political control and strategic direction of crisis management operations.

The Council may authorise the Committee, for the purpose and for the duration of a crisis management operation, as determined by the Council, to take the relevant decisions concerning the political control and strategic direction of the operation, without prejudice to Article 47.

Article 26   (ex Article J.16)

The Secretary General of the Council, High Representative for the common foreign and security policy, shall assist the Council in matters coming within the scope of the common foreign and security policy, in particular through contributing to the formulation, preparation and implementation of policy decisions, and, when appropriate and acting on behalf of the Council at the request of the Presidency, through conducting political dialogue with third parties.

Article 27   (ex Article J.17)

The Commission shall be fully associated with the work carried out in the common foreign and security policy field.

---

* **Editor's Note**: As amended by Article 12 of the 2003 Accession Treaties. The figures have not been altered by the Constitutional Treaty, but the definition of a qualified majority has changed; refer to Prelim xxxviii.

Article 27a   (Article inserted by the Treaty of Nice)
    1. Enhanced cooperation in any of the areas referred to in this Title shall be aimed at safeguarding the values and serving the interests of the Union as a whole by asserting its identity as a coherent force on the international scene. It shall respect:
       — the principles, objectives, general guidelines and consistency of the common foreign and security policy and the decisions taken within the framework of that policy;
       — the powers of the European Community, and
       — consistency between all the Union's policies and its external activities.
    2. Articles 11 to 27 and Articles 27b to 28 shall apply to the enhanced cooperation provided for in this Article, save as otherwise provided in Article 27c and Articles 43 to 45.

Article 27b   (Article inserted by the Treaty of Nice)
Enhanced cooperation pursuant to this Title shall relate to implementation of a joint action or a common position. It shall not relate to matters having military or defence implications.

Article 27c   (Article inserted by the Treaty of Nice)
Member States which intend to establish enhanced cooperation between themselves under Article 27b shall address a request to the Council to that effect.
    The request shall be forwarded to the Commission and to the European Parliament for information. The Commission shall give its opinion particularly on whether the enhanced cooperation proposed is consistent with Union policies. Authorisation shall be granted by the Council, acting in accordance with the second and third subparagraphs of Article 23(2) and in compliance with Articles 43 to 45.

Article 27d   (Article inserted by the Treaty of Nice)
Without prejudice to the powers of the Presidency or of the Commission, the Secretary-General of the Council, High Representative for the common foreign and security policy, shall in particular ensure that the European Parliament and all members of the Council are kept fully informed of the implementation of enhanced cooperation in the field of the common foreign and security policy.

Article 27e   (Article inserted by the Treaty of Nice)
Any Member State which wishes to participate in enhanced cooperation established in accordance with Article 27c shall notify its intention to the Council and inform the Commission. The Commission shall give an opinion to the Council within three months of the date of receipt of that notification. Within four months of the date of receipt of that notification, the Council shall take a decision on the request and on such specific arrangements as it may deem necessary. The decision shall be deemed to be taken unless the Council, acting by a qualified majority within the same period, decides to hold it in abeyance; in that case, the Council shall state the reasons for its decision and set a deadline for re-examining it.
    For the purposes of this Article, the Council shall act by a qualified majority. The qualified majority shall be defined as the same proportion of the weighted votes and the same proportion of the number of the members of the Council concerned as those laid down in the third subparagraph of Article 23(2).

Article 28   (ex Article J.18)
    1. Articles 189, 190, 196 to 199, 203, 204, 206 to 209, 213 to 219, 255 and 290 of the Treaty establishing the European Community shall apply to the provisions relating to the areas referred to in this Title.
    2. Administrative expenditure which the provisions relating to the areas referred to in this Title entail for the institutions shall be charged to the budget of the European Communities.

3.   Operational expenditure to which the implementation of those provisions gives rise shall also be charged to the budget of the European Communities, except for such expenditure arising from operations having military or defence implications and cases where the Council acting unanimously decides otherwise.

In cases where expenditure is not charged to the budget of the European Communities it shall be charged to the Member States in accordance with the gross national product scale, unless the Council acting unanimously decides otherwise. As for expenditure arising from operations having military or defence implications, Member States whose representatives in the Council have made a formal declaration under Article 23(1), second sub-paragraph, shall not be obliged to contribute to the financing thereof.

4.   The budgetary procedure laid down in the Treaty establishing the European Community shall apply to the expenditure charged to the budget of the European Communities.

TITLE VI   PROVISIONS ON POLICE AND JUDICIAL COOPERATION IN CRIMINAL MATTERS

Article 29   **(ex Article K.1) (As amended by the Treaty of Nice)**
Without prejudice to the powers of the European Community, the Union's objective shall be to provide citizens with a high level of safety within an area of freedom, security and justice by developing common action among the Member States in the fields of police and judicial cooperation in criminal matters and by preventing and combating racism and xenophobia.

That objective shall be achieved by preventing and combating crime, organised or otherwise, in particular terrorism, trafficking in persons and offences against children, illicit drug trafficking and illicit arms trafficking, corruption and fraud, through:
— closer cooperation between police forces, customs authorities and other competent authorities in the Member States, both directly and through the European Police Office (Europol), in accordance with the provisions of Articles 30 and 32;
— closer cooperation between judicial and other competent authorities of the Member States including cooperation through the European Judicial Cooperation Unit ('Eurojust'), in accordance with the provisions of Articles 31 and 32;
— approximation, where necessary, of rules on criminal matters in the Member States, in accordance with the provisions of Article 31(e).

Article 30   **(ex Article K.2)**
1.   Common action in the field of police cooperation shall include:
   (a) operational cooperation between the competent authorities, including the police, customs and other specialised law enforcement services of the Member States in relation to the prevention, detection and investigation of criminal offences;
   (b) the collection, storage, processing, analysis and exchange of relevant information, including information held by law enforcement services on reports on suspicious financial transactions, in particular through Europol, subject to appropriate provisions on the protection of personal data;
   (c) cooperation and joint initiatives in training, the exchange of liaison officers, secondments, the use of equipment, and forensic research;
   (d) the common evaluation of particular investigative techniques in relation to the detection of serious forms of organised crime.
2.   The Council shall promote cooperation through Europol and shall in particular, within a period of five years after the date of entry into force of the Treaty of Amsterdam:
   (a) enable Europol to facilitate and support the preparation, and to encourage the coordination and carrying out, of specific investigative actions by the competent

authorities of the Member States, including operational actions of joint teams comprising representatives of Europol in a support capacity;
(b) adopt measures allowing Europol to ask the competent authorities of the Member States to conduct and coordinate their investigations in specific cases and to develop specific expertise which may be put at the disposal of Member States to assist them in investigating cases of organised crime;
(c) promote liaison arrangements between prosecuting/investigating officials specialising in the fight against organised crime in close cooperation with Europol;
(d) establish a research, documentation and statistical network on cross-border crime.

Article 31 (ex Article K.3) (As amended by the Treaty of Nice)

1. Common action on judicial cooperation in criminal matters shall include:
   (a) facilitating and accelerating cooperation between competent ministries and judicial or equivalent authorities of the Member States, including, where appropriate, cooperation through Eurojust, in relation to proceedings and the enforcement of decisions;
   (b) facilitating extradition between Member States;
   (c) ensuring compatibility in rules applicable in the Member States, as may be necessary to improve such cooperation;
   (d) preventing conflicts of jurisdiction between Member States;
   (e) progressively adopting measures establishing minimum rules relating to the constituent elements of criminal acts and to penalties in the fields of organised crime, terrorism and illicit drug trafficking.
2. The Council shall encourage cooperation through Eurojust by:
   (a) enabling Eurojust to facilitate proper coordination between Member States' national prosecuting authorities;
   (b) promoting support by Eurojust for criminal investigations in cases of serious cross-border crime, particularly in the case of organised crime, taking account, in particular, of analyses carried out by Europol;
   (c) facilitating close cooperation between Eurojust and the European Judicial Network, particularly, in order to facilitate the execution of letters rogatory and the implementation of extradition requests.

Article 32 (ex Article K.4)

The Council shall lay down the conditions and limitations under which the competent authorities referred to in Articles 30 and 31 may operate in the territory of another Member State in liaison and in agreement with the authorities of that State.

Article 33 (ex Article K.5)

This Title shall not affect the exercise of the responsibilities incumbent upon Member States with regard to the maintenance of law and order and the safeguarding of internal security.

Article 34 (ex Article K.6)

1. In the areas referred to in this Title, Member States shall inform and consult one another within the Council with a view to coordinating their action. To that end, they shall establish collaboration between the relevant departments of their administrations.
2. The Council shall take measures and promote cooperation, using the appropriate form and procedures as set out in this Title, contributing to the pursuit of the objectives of the Union. To that end, acting unanimously on the initiative of any Member State or of the Commission, the Council may:
   (a) adopt common positions defining the approach of the Union to a particular matter;
   (b) adopt framework decisions for the purpose of approximation of the laws and regulations of the Member States. Framework decisions shall be binding upon the

Member States as to the result to be achieved but shall leave to the national authorities the choice of form and methods. They shall not entail direct effect;

(c) adopt decisions for any other purpose consistent with the objectives of this Title, excluding any approximation of the laws and regulations of the Member States. These decisions shall be binding and shall not entail direct effect; the Council, acting by a qualified majority, shall adopt measures necessary to implement those decisions at the level of the Union;

(d) establish conventions which it shall recommend to the Member States for adoption in accordance with their respective constitutional requirements. Member States shall begin the procedures applicable within a time limit to be set by the Council.

Unless they provide otherwise, conventions shall, once adopted by at least half of the Member States, enter into force for those Member States. Measures implementing conventions shall be adopted within the Council by a majority of two-thirds of the Contracting Parties.

3.   Where the Council is required to act by a qualified majority, the votes of its members shall be weighted as laid down in Article 205(2) of the Treaty establishing the European Community, and for their adoption acts of the Council shall require at least 232 votes in favour cast by at least two-thirds of the members. When a decision is to be adopted by the Council by a qualified majority, a member of the Council may request verification that the Member States constituting the qualified majority represent at least 62% of the total population of the Union. If that condition is shown not to have been met, the decision in question shall not be adopted.*

4.   For procedural questions, the Council shall act by a majority of its members.

Article 35   (ex Article K.7)

1.   The Court of Justice of the European Communities shall have jurisdiction, subject to the conditions laid down in this Article, to give preliminary rulings on the validity and interpretation of framework decisions and decisions, on the interpretation of conventions established under this Title and on the validity and interpretation of the measures implementing them.

2.   By a declaration made at the time of signature of the Treaty of Amsterdam or at any time thereafter, any Member State shall be able to accept the jurisdiction of the Court of Justice to give preliminary rulings as specified in paragraph 1.

3.   A Member State making a declaration pursuant to paragraph 2 shall specify that either:

(a) any court or tribunal of that State against whose decisions there is no judicial remedy under national law may request the Court of Justice to give a preliminary ruling on a question raised in a case pending before it and concerning the validity or interpretation of an act referred to in paragraph 1 if that court or tribunal considers that a decision on the question is necessary to enable it to give judgment, or

(b) any court or tribunal of that State may request the Court of Justice to give a preliminary ruling on a question raised in a case pending before it and concerning the validity or interpretation of an act referred to in paragraph 1 if that court or tribunal considers that a decision on the question is necessary to enable it to give judgment.

4.   Any Member State, whether or not it has made a declaration pursuant to paragraph 2, shall be entitled to submit statements of case or written observations to the Court in cases which arise under paragraph 1.

---

* **Editor's Note**: As amended by Article 12 of the 2003 Accession Treaties. The figures have not been altered by the Constitutional Treaty, but the definition of qualified majority has; refer to Prelim xxxviii.

5. The Court of Justice shall have no jurisdiction to review the validity or pro-portionality of operations carried out by the police or other law enforcement services of a Member State or the exercise of the responsibilities incumbent upon Member States with regard to the maintenance of law and order and the safeguarding of internal security.

6. The Court of Justice shall have jurisdiction to review the legality of framework decisions and decisions in actions brought by a Member State or the Commission on grounds of lack of competence, infringement of an essential procedural requirement, infringement of this Treaty or of any rule of law relating to its application, or misuse of powers. The proceedings provided for in this paragraph shall be instituted within two months of the publication of the measure.

7. The Court of Justice shall have jurisdiction to rule on any dispute between Member States regarding the interpretation or the application of acts adopted under Article 34(2) whenever such dispute cannot be settled by the Council within six months of its being referred to the Council by one of its members. The Court shall also have jurisdiction to rule on any dispute between Member States and the Commission regarding the interpretation or the application of conventions established under Article 34(2)(d).

Article 36   (ex Article K.8)

1. A Coordinating Committee shall be set up consisting of senior officials. In addition to its coordinating role, it shall be the task of the Committee to:
   — give opinions for the attention of the Council, either at the Council's request or on its own initiative;
   — contribute, without prejudice to Article 207 of the Treaty establishing the European Community, to the preparation of the Council's discussions in the areas referred to in Article 29.

2. The Commission shall be fully associated with the work in the areas referred to in this Title.

Article 37   (ex Article K.9)

Within international organisations and at international conferences in which they take part, Member States shall defend the common positions adopted under the provisions of this Title.

Articles 18 and 19 shall apply as appropriate to matters falling under this Title.

Article 38   (ex Article K.10)

Agreements referred to in Article 24 may cover matters falling under this Title.

Article 39   (ex Article K.11)

1. The Council shall consult the European Parliament before adopting any measure referred to in Article 34(2)(b), (c) and (d). The European Parliament shall deliver its opinion within a time limit which the Council may lay down, which shall not be less than three months. In the absence of an opinion within that time limit, the Council may act.

2. The Presidency and the Commission shall regularly inform the European Parliament of discussions in the areas covered by this Title.

3. The European Parliament may ask questions of the Council or make recommenda-tions to it. Each year, it shall hold a debate on the progress made in the areas referred to in this Title.

Article 40   (ex Article K.12) (As amended by the Treaty of Nice)

1. Enhanced cooperation in any of the areas referred to in this Title shall have the aim of enabling the Union to develop more rapidly into an area of freedom, security and justice, while respecting the powers of the European Community and the objectives laid down in this Title.

2. Articles 29 to 39 and Articles 40a to 41 shall apply to the enhanced cooperation provided for by this Article, save as otherwise provided in Article 40a and in Articles 43 to 45.

3. The provisions of the Treaty establishing the European Community concerning the powers of the Court of Justice and the exercise of those powers shall apply to this Article and to Articles 40a and 40b.

Article 40a   (Article inserted by the Treaty of Nice)

1. Member States which intend to establish enhanced cooperation between themselves under Article 40 shall address a request to the Commission, which may submit a proposal to the Council to that effect. In the event of the Commission not submitting a proposal, it shall inform the Member States concerned of the reasons for not doing so. Those Member States may then submit an initiative to the Council designed to obtain authorisation for the enhanced cooperation concerned.

2. The authorisation referred to in paragraph 1 shall be granted, in compliance with Articles 43 to 45, by the Council, acting by a qualified majority, on a proposal from the Commission or on the initiative of at least eight Member States, and after consulting the European Parliament. The votes of the members of the Council shall be weighted in accordance with Article 205(2) of the Treaty establishing the European Community.

A member of the Council may request that the matter be referred to the European Council. After that matter has been raised before the European Council, the Council may act in accordance with the first subparagraph of this paragraph.

Article 40b   (Article inserted by the Treaty of Nice)

Any Member State which wishes to participate in enhanced cooperation established in accordance with Article 40a shall notify its intention to the Council and to the Commission, which shall give an opinion to the Council within three months of the date of receipt of that notification, possibly accompanied by a recommendation for such specific arrangements as it may deem necessary for that Member State to become a party to the cooperation in question. The Council shall take a decision on the request within four months of the date of receipt of that notification. The decision shall be deemed to be taken unless the Council, acting by a qualified majority within the same period, decides to hold it in abeyance; in that case, the Council shall state the reasons for its decision and set a deadline for re-examining it.

For the purposes of this Article, the Council shall act under the conditions set out in Article 44(1).

Article 41   (ex Article K.13)

1. Articles 189, 190, 195, 196 to 199, 203, 204, 205(3), 206 to 209, 213 to 219, 255 and 290 of the Treaty establishing the European Community shall apply to the provisions relating to the areas referred to in this Title.

2. Administrative expenditure which the provisions relating to the areas referred to in this Title entail for the institutions shall be charged to the budget of the European Communities.

3. Operational expenditure to which the implementation of those provisions gives rise shall also be charged to the budget of the European Communities, except where the Council acting unanimously decides otherwise. In cases where expenditure is not charged to the budget of the European Communities it shall be charged to the Member States in accordance with the gross national product scale, unless the Council acting unanimously decides otherwise.

4. The budgetary procedure laid down in the Treaty establishing the European Community shall apply to the expenditure charged to the budget of the European Communities.

Article 42   (ex Article K.14)

The Council, acting unanimously on the initiative of the Commission or a Member State, and after consulting the European Parliament, may decide that action in areas referred to in Article 29 shall fall under Title IV of the Treaty establishing the European Community, and at the same time determine the relevant voting conditions relating to it. It shall recommend the

Member States to adopt that decision in accordance with their respective constitutional requirements.

TITLE VII (ex Title VIa)   PROVISIONS ON CLOSER COOPERATION

Article 43   (ex Article K.15) (As amended by the Treaty of Nice)
Member States which intend to establish enhanced cooperation between themselves may make use of the institutions, procedures and mechanisms laid down by this Treaty and by the Treaty establishing the European Community provided that the proposed cooperation:

(a) is aimed at furthering the objectives of the Union and of the Community, at protecting and serving their interests and at reinforcing their process of integration;

(b) respects the said Treaties and the single institutional framework of the Union;

(c) respects the acquis communautaire and the measures adopted under the other provisions of the said Treaties;

(d) remains within the limits of the powers of the Union or of the Community and does not concern the areas which fall within the exclusive competence of the Community;

(e) does not undermine the internal market as defined in Article 14(2) of the Treaty establishing the European Community, or the economic and social cohesion established in accordance with Title XVII of that Treaty;

(f) does not constitute a barrier to or discrimination in trade between the Member States and does not distort competition between them;

(g) involves a minimum of eight Member States;

(h) respects the competences, rights and obligations of those Member States which do not participate therein;

(i) does not affect the provisions of the Protocol integrating the Schengen acquis into the framework of the European Union;

(j) is open to all the Member States, in accordance with Article 43b.

Article 43a   (Article inserted by the Treaty of Nice)
Enhanced cooperation may be undertaken only as a last resort, when it has been established within the Council that the objectives of such cooperation cannot be attained within a reasonable period by applying the relevant provisions of the Treaties.

Article 43b   (Article inserted by the Treaty of Nice)
When enhanced cooperation is being established, it shall be open to all Member States. It shall also be open to them at any time, in accordance with Articles 27e and 40b of this Treaty and with Article 11a of the Treaty establishing the European Community, subject to compliance with the basic decision and with the decisions taken within that framework. The Commission and the Member States participating in enhanced cooperation shall ensure that as many Member States as possible are encouraged to take part.

Article 44   (As amended by the Treaty of Nice)
    1.   For the purposes of the adoption of the acts and decisions necessary for the implementation of enhanced cooperation referred to in Article 43, the relevant institutional provisions of this Treaty and of the Treaty establishing the European Community shall apply. However, while all members of the Council shall be able to take part in the deliberations, only those representing Member States participating in enhanced cooperation shall take part in the adoption of decisions. The qualified majority shall be defined as the same proportion of the weighted votes and the same proportion of the number of the Council members concerned as laid down in Article 205(2) of the Treaty establishing the European Community, and in the second and third subparagraphs of Article 23(2) of this Treaty as regards enhanced

cooperation established on the basis of Article 27c. Unanimity shall be constituted by only those Council members concerned.

Such acts and decisions shall not form part of the Union acquis.

2.   Member States shall apply, as far as they are concerned, the acts and decisions adopted for the implementation of the enhanced cooperation in which they participate. Such acts and decisions shall be binding only on those Member States which participate in such cooperation and, as appropriate, shall be directly applicable only in those States. Member States which do not participate in such cooperation shall not impede the implementation thereof by the participating Member States.

Article 44a   **(Article inserted by the Treaty of Nice)**
Expenditure resulting from implementation of enhanced cooperation, other than administrative costs entailed for the institutions, shall be borne by the participating Member States, unless all members of the Council, acting unanimously after consulting the European Parliament, decide otherwise.

Article 45   **(As amended by the Treaty of Nice)**
The Council and the Commission shall ensure the consistency of activities undertaken on the basis of this Title and the consistency of such activities with the policies of the Union and the Community, and shall cooperate to that end.

TITLE VIII (ex Title VII)   FINAL PROVISIONS

Article 46   **(ex Article L) (As amended by the Treaty of Nice)**
The provisions of the Treaty establishing the European Community, the Treaty establishing the European Coal and Steel Community and the Treaty establishing the European Atomic Energy Community concerning the powers of the Court of Justice of the European Communities and the exercise of those powers shall apply only to the following provisions of this Treaty:

(a)   provisions amending the Treaty establishing the European Economic Community with a view to establishing the European Community, the Treaty establishing the European Coal and Steel Community and the Treaty establishing the European Atomic Energy Community;

(b)   provisions of Title VI, under the conditions provided for by Article 35;

(c)   provisions of Title VII, under the conditions provided for by Articles 11 and 11a of the Treaty establishing the European Community and Article 40 of this Treaty;

(d)   Article 6(2) with regard to action of the institutions, insofar as the Court has jurisdiction under the Treaties establishing the European Communities and under this Treaty;

(e)   the purely procedural stipulations in Article 7, with the Court acting at the request of the Member State concerned within one month from the date of the determination by the Council provided for in that Article;

(f)   Articles 46 to 53.

Article 47   **(ex Article M)**
Subject to the provisions amending the Treaty establishing the European Economic Community with a view to establishing the European Community, the Treaty establishing the European Coal and Steel Community and the Treaty establishing the European Atomic Energy Community, and to these final provisions, nothing in this Treaty shall affect the Treaties establishing the European Communities or the subsequent Treaties and Acts modifying or supplementing them.

Article 48   **(ex Article N)**
The government of any Member State or the Commission may submit to the Council proposals for the amendment of the Treaties on which the Union is founded.

If the Council, after consulting the European Parliament and, where appropriate, the Commission, delivers an opinion in favour of calling a conference of representatives of the governments of the Member States, the conference shall be convened by the President of the Council for the purpose of determining by common accord the amendments to be made to those Treaties. The European Central Bank shall also be consulted in the case of institutional changes in the monetary area.

The amendments shall enter into force after being ratified by all the Member States in accordance with their respective constitutional requirements.

Article 49   (ex Article O)

Any European State which respects the principles set out in Article 6(1) may apply to become a member of the Union. It shall address its application to the Council, which shall act unanimously after consulting the Commission and after receiving the assent of the European Parliament, which shall act by an absolute majority of its component members.

The conditions of admission and the adjustments to the Treaties on which the Union is founded which such admission entails shall be the subject of an agreement between the Member States and the applicant State. This agreement shall be submitted for ratification by all the contracting States in accordance with their respective constitutional requirements.

Article 50   (ex Article P)

1.   Articles 2 to 7 and 10 to 19 of the Treaty establishing a Single Council and a Single Commission of the European Communities, signed in Brussels on 8 April 1965, are hereby repealed.

2.   Article 2, Article 3(2) and Title III of the Single European Act signed in Luxembourg on 17 February 1986 and in The Hague on 28 February 1986 are hereby repealed.

Article 51   (ex Article Q)

This Treaty is concluded for an unlimited period.

Article 52   (ex Article R)

1.   This Treaty shall be ratified by the High Contracting Parties in accordance with their respective constitutional requirements. The instruments of ratification shall be deposited with the Government of the Italian Republic.

2.   This Treaty shall enter into force on 1 January 1993, provided that all the instruments of ratification have been deposited, or, failing that, on the first day of the month following the deposit of the instrument of ratification by the last signatory State to take this step.

Article 53   (ex Article S)

This Treaty, drawn up in a single original in the Danish, Dutch, English, French, German, Greek, Irish, Italian, Portuguese and Spanish languages, the texts in each of these languages being equally authentic, shall be deposited in the archives of the government of the Italian Republic, which will transmit a certified copy to each of the governments of the other signatory States.

Pursuant to the Accession Treaty of 1994, the Finnish and Swedish versions of this Treaty shall also be authentic.

IN WITNESS WHEREOF the undersigned Plenipotentiaries have signed this Treaty. Done at Maastricht on the seventh day of February in the year one thousand nine hundred and ninety two.

Mark EYSKENS	Philippe MAYSTADT
Uffe ELLEMANN-JENSEN	Anders FOGH RASMUSSEN
Hans Dietrich GENSCHER	Theodor WAIGEL
Antonios SAMARAS	Efthymios CHRISTODOULOU
Francisco FERNÁNDEZ ORDÓÑEZ	Carlos SOLCHAGA CATALÁN

Roland DUMAS
Gerard COLLINS
Gianni DE MICHELIS
Jacques F. POOS
Hans VAN DEN BROEK
João de Deus PINHEIRO
Douglas HURD

Pierre BÉRÉGOVOY
Bertie AHERN
Guido CARLI
Jean-Claude JUNCKER
Willem KOK
Jorge BRAGA DE MACEDO
Francis MAUDE

TEXTS OF PROTOCOLS ATTACHED TO TREATIES

Protocols added by the Treaty of Maastricht

PROTOCOL CONCERNING ARTICLE 141 OF THE TREATY ESTABLISHING THE EUROPEAN COMMUNITY (NO. 17)

THE HIGH CONTRACTING PARTIES,

HAVE AGREED UPON the following provision, which shall be annexed to the Treaty establishing the European Community:

For the purposes of Article 141 of this Treaty, benefits under occupational social security schemes shall not be considered as remuneration if and in so far as they are attributable to periods of employment prior to 17 May 1990, except in the case of workers or those claiming under them who have before that date initiated legal proceedings or introduced an equivalent claim under the applicable national law.

PROTOCOL ANNEXED TO THE TREATY ON EUROPEAN UNION AND TO THE TREATIES ESTABLISHING THE EUROPEAN COMMUNITIES (Ireland)

THE HIGH CONTRACTING PARTIES,

HAVE AGREED upon the following provision, which shall be annexed to the Treaty on European Union and to the Treaties establishing the European Communities:

Nothing in the Treaty on European Union, or in the Treaties establishing the European Communities, or in the Treaties or Acts modifying or supplementing those Treaties, shall affect the application in Ireland of Article 40.3.3 of the Constitution of Ireland.

DECLARATION ON NATIONALITY OF A MEMBER STATE

The Conference declares that, wherever in the Treaty establishing the European Community reference is made to nationals of the Member States, the question whether an individual possesses the nationality of a Member State shall be settled solely by reference to the national law of the Member State concerned. Member States may declare, for information, who are to be considered their nationals for Community purposes by way of a declaration lodged with the Presidency and may amend any such declaration when necessary.

Protocols added by the Treaty of Amsterdam*

PROTOCOL INTEGRATING THE SCHENGEN ACQUIS INTO THE FRAMEWORK OF THE EUROPEAN UNION

THE HIGH CONTRACTING PARTIES,

NOTING that the Agreements on the gradual abolition of checks at common borders signed by some Member States of the European Union in Schengen on 14 June 1985 and on 19 June 1990, as well as related agreements and the rules adopted on the basis of these agreements, are aimed at enhancing European integration and, in particular, at enabling the European Union to develop more rapidly into an area of freedom, security and justice,

DESIRING to incorporate the abovementioned agreements and rules into the framework of the European Union,

CONFIRMING that the provisions of the Schengen acquis are applicable only if and as far as they are compatible with the European Union and Community law,

TAKING INTO ACCOUNT the special position of Denmark,

TAKING INTO ACCOUNT the fact that Ireland and the United Kingdom of Great Britain and Northern Ireland are not parties to and have not signed the abovementioned agreements; that provision should, however, be made to allow those Member States to accept some or all of the provisions thereof,

RECOGNISING that, as a consequence, it is necessary to make use of the provisions of the Treaty on European Union and of the Treaty establishing the European Community concerning closer cooperation between some Member States and that those provisions should only be used as a last resort,

TAKING INTO ACCOUNT the need to maintain a special relationship with the Republic of Iceland and the Kingdom of Norway, both States having confirmed their intention to become bound by the provisions mentioned above, on the basis of the Agreement signed in Luxembourg on 19 December 1996,

HAVE AGREED UPON the following provisions, which shall be annexed to the Treaty on European Union and to the Treaty establishing the European Community,

Article 1

The Kingdom of Belgium, the Kingdom of Denmark, the Federal Republic of Germany, the Hellenic Republic, the Kingdomof Spain, the French Republic, the Italian Republic, the Grand Duchy of Luxembourg, the Kingdom of the Netherlands, the Republic of Austria, the Portuguese Republic, the Republic of Finland and the Kingdom of Sweden, signatories to the Schengen agreements, are authorised to establish closer cooperation among themselves within the scope of those agreements and related provisions, as they are listed in the Annex to this Protocol, hereinafter referred to as the 'Schengen acquis'. This cooperation shall be conducted within the institutional and legal framework of the European Union and with respect for the relevant provisions of the Treaty on European Union and of the Treaty establishing the European Community.

Article 2

1. From the date of entry into force of the Treaty of Amsterdam, the Schengen acquis, including the decisions of the Executive Committee established by the Schengen agreements which have been adopted before this date, shall immediately apply to the thirteen Member States referred to in Article 1, without prejudice to the provisions of paragraph 2

---

* **Editor's Note:** To be found at OJ 1997 C340/92–114 but note that a different order of presentation of the same protocols can be found at http://europa.eu.int/eur-lex/en/treaties/selected/livre3_c.html.

of this Article. From the same date, the Council will substitute itself for the said Executive Committee.

The Council, acting by the unanimity of its Members referred to in Article 1, shall take any measure necessary for the implementation of this paragraph. The Council, acting unanimously, shall determine, in conformity with the relevant provisions of the Treaties, the legal basis for each of the provisions or decisions which constitute the Schengen acquis.

With regard to such provisions and decisions and in accordance with that determination, the Court of Justice of the European Communities shall exercise the powers conferred upon it by the relevant applicable provisions of the Treaties. In any event, the Court of Justice shall have no jurisdiction on measures or decisions relating to the maintenance of law and order and the safeguarding of internal security.

As long as the measures referred to above have not been taken and without prejudice to Article 5(2), the provisions or decisions which constitute the Schengen acquis shall be regarded as acts based on Title VI of the Treaty on European Union.

2. The provisions of paragraph 1 shall apply to the Member States which have signed accession protocols to the Schengen agreements, from the dates decided by the Council, acting with the unanimity of its Members mentioned in Article 1, unless the conditions for the accession of any of those States to the Schengen acquis are met before the date of the entry into force of the Treaty of Amsterdam.

Article 3

Following the determination referred to in Article 2(1), second sub-paragraph, Denmark shall maintain the same rights and obligations in relation to the other signatories to the Schengen agreements, as before the said determination with regard to those parts of the Schengen acquis that are determined to have a legal basis in Title IIIa of the Treaty establishing the European Community.

With regard to those parts of the Schengen acquis that are determined to have legal base in Title VI of the Treaty on European Union, Denmark shall continue to have the same rights and obligations as the other signatories to the Schengen agreements.

Article 4

Ireland and the United Kingdom of Great Britain and Northern Ireland, which are not bound by the Schengen acquis, may at any time request to take part in some or all of the provisions of this acquis.

The Council shall decide on the request with the unanimity of its members referred to in Article 1 and of the representative of the Government of the State concerned.

Article 5

1. Proposals and initiatives to build upon the Schengen acquis shall be subject to the relevant provisions of the Treaties.

In this context, where either Ireland or the United Kingdom or both have not notified the President of the Council in writing within a reasonable period that they wish to take part, the authorisation referred to in Article 5a of the Treaty establishing the European Community or Article K.12 of the Treaty on European Union shall be deemed to have been granted to the Members States referred to in Article 1 and to Ireland or the United Kingdomwhere either of them wishes to take part in the areas of cooperation in question.

2. The relevant provisions of the Treaties referred to in the first sub-paragraph of paragraph 1 shall apply even if the Council has not adopted the measures referred to in Article 2(1), second sub-paragraph.

Article 6

The Republic of Iceland and the Kingdom of Norway shall be associated with the implementation of the Schengen acquis and its further development on the basis of the Agreement signed in Luxembourg on 19 December 1996. Appropriate procedures shall be agreed to that effect in an Agreement to be concluded with those States by the Council, acting by the unanimity of its Members mentioned in Article 1. Such Agreement shall include provisions on the contribution of Iceland and Norway to any financial consequences resulting from the implementation of this Protocol.

A separate Agreement shall be concluded with Iceland and Norway by the Council, acting unanimously, for the establishment of rights and obligations between Ireland and the United Kingdomof Great Britain and Northern Ireland on the one hand, and Iceland and Norway on the other, in domains of the Schengen acquis which apply to these States.

Article 7
The Council shall, acting by a qualified majority, adopt the detailed arrangements for the integration of the Schengen Secretariat into the General Secretariat of the Council.

Article 8
For the purposes of the negotiations for the admission of new Member States into the European Union, the Schengen acquis and further measures taken by the institutions within its scope shall be regarded as an acquis which must be accepted in full by all State candidates for admission.

ANNEX   SCHENGEN ACQUIS

1. The Agreement, signed in Schengen on 14 June 1985, between the Governments of the States of the Benelux Economic Union, the Federal Republic of Germany and the French Republic on the gradual abolition of checks at their common borders.

2. The Convention, signed in Schengen on 19 June 1990, between the Kingdom of Belgium, the Federal Republic of Germany, the French Republic, the Grand Duchy of Luxembourg and the Kingdom of the Netherlands, implementing the Agreement on the gradual abolition of checks at their common borders, signed in Schengen on 14 June 1985, with related Final Act and common declarations.

3. The Accession Protocols and Agreements to the 1985 Agreement and the 1990 Implementation Convention with Italy (signed in Paris on 27 November 1990), Spain and Portugal (signed in Bonn on 25 June 1991), Greece (signed in Madrid on 6 November 1992), Austria (signed in Brussels on 28 April 1995) and Denmark, Finland and Sweden (signed in Luxembourg on 19 December 1996), with related Final Acts and declarations.

4. Decisions and declarations adopted by the Executive Committee established by the 1990 Implementation Convention, as well as acts adopted for the implementation of the Convention by the organs upon which the Executive Committee has conferred decision making powers.

PROTOCOL ON THE APPLICATION OF CERTAIN ASPECTS OF ARTICLE 14 OF THE TREATY ESTABLISHING THE EUROPEAN COMMUNITY TO THE UNITED KINGDOM AND TO IRELAND*

THE HIGH CONTRACTING PARTIES,

DESIRING to settle certain questions relating to the United Kingdom and Ireland,

HAVING REGARD to the existence for many years of special travel arrangements between the United Kingdom and Ireland,

HAVE AGREED UPON the following provisions, which shall be annexed to the Treaty establishing the European Community and to the Treaty on European Union,

* **Editor's Note:** Although the Article numbers have been changed to the new numbering in the title, the numbering within the text of the protocol remains as it is in the *Official Journal*.

Article 1

The United Kingdom shall be entitled, notwithstanding Article 7a of the Treaty establishing the European Community, any other provision of that Treaty or of the Treaty on European Union, any measure adopted under those Treaties, or any international agreement concluded by the Community or by the Community and its Member States with one or more third States, to exercise at its frontiers with other Member States such controls on persons seeking to enter the United Kingdom as it may consider necessary for the purpose:

    (a) of verifying the right to enter the United Kingdom of citizens of States which are Contracting parties to the Agreement on the European Economic Area and of their dependants exercising rights conferred by Community law, as well as citizens of other States on whom such rights have been conferred by an agreement by which the United Kingdom is bound; and

    (b) of determining whether or not to grant other persons permission to enter the United Kingdom.

Nothing in Article 7a of the Treaty establishing the European Community or in any other provision of that Treaty or of the Treaty on European Union or in any measure adopted under them shall prejudice the right of the United Kingdom to adopt or exercise any such controls. References to the United Kingdom in this Article shall include territories for whose external relations the United Kingdom is responsible.

Article 2

The United Kingdom and Ireland may continue to make arrangements between themselves relating to the movement of persons between their territories ('the Common Travel Area'), while fully respecting the rights of persons referred to in Article 1, first paragraph, point (a) of this Protocol. Accordingly, as long as they maintain such arrangements, the provisions of Article 1 of this Protocol shall apply to Ireland under the same terms and conditions as for the United Kingdom. Nothing in Article 7a of the Treaty establishing the European Community, in any other provision of that Treaty or of the Treaty on European Union or in any measure adopted under them, shall affect any such arrangements.

Article 3

The other Member States shall be entitled to exercise at their frontiers or at any point of entry into their territory such controls on persons seeking to enter their territory from the United Kingdom or any territories whose external relations are under its responsibility for the same purposes stated in Article 1 of this Protocol, or from Ireland as long as the provisions of Article 1 of this Protocol apply to Ireland.

Nothing in Article 7a of the Treaty establishing the European Community or in any other provision of that Treaty or of the Treaty on European Union or in any measure adopted under them shall prejudice the right of the other Member States to adopt or exercise any such controls.

PROTOCOL ON THE POSITION OF THE UNITED KINGDOM AND IRELAND

THE HIGH CONTRACTING PARTIES,

    DESIRING to settle certain questions relating to the United Kingdom and Ireland,

    HAVING REGARD to the Protocol on the application of certain aspects of Article 7a of the Treaty establishing the European Community to the United Kingdom and to Ireland,

    HAVE AGREED UPON the following provisions which shall be annexed to the Treaty establishing the European Community and to the Treaty on European Union,

Article 1

Subject to Article 3, the United Kingdom and Ireland shall not take part in the adoption by the Council of proposed measures pursuant to Title IIIa of the Treaty establishing the

European Community. By way of derogation from Article 148(2) of the Treaty establishing the European Community, a qualified majority shall be defined as the same proportion of the weighted votes of the members of the Council concerned as laid down in the said Article 148(2). The unanimity of the members of the Council, with the exception of the representatives of the governments of the United Kingdom and Ireland, shall be necessary for decisions of the Council which must be adopted unanimously.

Article 2

In consequence of Article 1 and subject to Articles 3, 4 and 6, none of the provisions of Title IIIa of the Treaty establishing the European Community, no measure adopted pursuant to that Title, no provision of any international agreement concluded by the Community pursuant to that Title, and no decision of the Court of Justice interpreting any such provision or measure shall be binding upon or applicable in the United Kingdom or Ireland; and no such provision, measure or decision shall in any way affect the competences, rights and obligations of those States; and no such provision, measure or decision shall in any way affect the acquis communautaire nor form part of Community law as they apply to the United Kingdom or Ireland.

Article 3

1.   The United Kingdom or Ireland may notify the President of the Council in writing, within three months after a proposal or initiative has been presented to the Council pursuant to Title IIIa of the Treaty establishing the European Community, that it wishes to take part in the adoption and application of any such proposed measure, whereupon that State shall be entitled to do so. By way of derogation from Article 148(2) of the Treaty establishing the European Community, a qualified majority shall be defined as the same proportion of the weighted votes of the members of the Council concerned as laid down in the said Article 148(2).

The unanimity of the members of the Council, with the exception of a member which has not made such a notification, shall be necessary for decisions of the Council which must be adopted unanimously. A measure adopted under this paragraph shall be binding upon all Member States which took part in its adoption.

2.   If after a reasonable period of time a measure referred to in paragraph 1 cannot be adopted with the United Kingdom or Ireland taking part, the Council may adopt such measure in accordance with Article 1 without the participation of the United Kingdom or Ireland. In that case Article 2 applies.

Article 4

The United Kingdom or Ireland may at any time after the adoption of a measure by the Council pursuant to Title IIIa of the Treaty establishing the European Community notify its intention to the Council and to the Commission that it wishes to accept that measure. In that case, the procedure provided for in Article 5a(3) of the Treaty establishing the European Community shall apply mutatis mutandis.

Article 5

A Member State which is not bound by a measure adopted pursuant to Title IIIa of the Treaty establishing the European Community shall bear no financial consequences of that measure other than administrative costs entailed for the institutions.

Article 6

Where, in cases referred to in this Protocol, the United Kingdom or Ireland is bound by a measure adopted by the Council pursuant to Title IIIa of the Treaty establishing the European Community, the relevant provisions of that Treaty, including Article 73p, shall apply to that State in relation to that measure.

Article 7

Articles 3 and 4 shall be without prejudice to the Protocol integrating the Schengen acquis into the framework of the European Union.

Article 8

Ireland may notify the President of the Council in writing that it no longer wishes to be covered by the terms of this Protocol. In that case, the normal treaty provisions will apply to Ireland.

PROTOCOL ON THE POSITION OF DENMARK

THE HIGH CONTRACTING PARTIES,

RECALLINGthe Decision of the Heads of State or Government, meeting within the European Council at Edinburgh on 12 December 1992, concerning certain problems raised by Denmark on the Treaty on European Union,

HAVING NOTED the position of Denmark with regard to Citizenship, Economic and Monetary Union, Defence Policy and Justice and Home Affairs as laid down in the Edinburgh Decision,

BEARING IN MIND Article 3 of the Protocol integrating the Schengen acquis into the framework of the European Union,

HAVE AGREED UPON the following provisions, which shall be annexed to the Treaty establishing the European Community and to the Treaty on European Union,

PART I

Article 1

Denmark shall not take part in the adoption by the Council of proposed measures pursuant to Title IIIa of the Treaty establishing the European Community. By way of derogation from Article 148(2) of the Treaty establishing the European Community, a qualified majority shall be defined as the same proportion of the weighted votes of the members of the Council concerned as laid down in the said Article 148(2). The unanimity of the members of the Council, with the exception of the representative of the government of Denmark, shall be necessary for the decisions of the Council which must be adopted unanimously.

Article 2

None of the provisions of Title IIIa of the Treaty establishing the European Community, no measure adopted pursuant to that Title, no provision of any international agreement concluded by the Community pursuant to that Title, and no decision of the Court of Justice interpreting any such provision or measure shall be binding upon or applicable in Denmark; and no such provision, measure or decision shall in any way affect the competences, rights and obligations of Denmark; and no such provision, measure or decision shall in any way affect the acquis communautaire nor form part of Community law as they apply to Denmark.

Article 3

Denmark shall bear no financial consequences of measures referred to in Article 1, other than administrative costs entailed for the institutions.

Article 4

Articles 1, 2 and 3 shall not apply to measures determining the third countries whose nationals must be in possession of a visa when crossing the external borders of the Member States, or measures relating to a uniform format for visas.

Article 5

1. Denmark shall decide within a period of 6 months after the Council has decided on a

proposal or initiative to build upon the Schengen acquis under the provisions of Title IIIa of the Treaty establishing the European Community, whether it will implement this decision in its national law. If it decides to do so, this decision will create an obligation under international law between Denmark and the other Member States referred to in Article 1 of the Protocol integrating the Schengen acquis into the framework of the European Union as well as Ireland or the United Kingdom if those Member States take part in the areas of cooperation in question.

2. If Denmark decides not to implement a decision of the Council as referred to in paragraph 1, the Member States referred to in Article 1 of the Protocol integrating the Schengen acquis into the framework of the European Union will consider appropriate measures to be taken.

PART II

Article 6

With regard to measures adopted by the Council in the field of Articles J.3(1) and J.7 of the Treaty on European Union, Denmark does not participate in the elaboration and the implementation of decisions and actions of the Union which have defence implications, but will not prevent the development of closer cooperation between Member States in this area. Therefore Denmark shall not participate in their adoption. Denmark shall not be obliged to contribute to the financing of operational expenditure arising from such measures.

PART III

Article 7

At any time Denmark may, in accordance with its constitutional requirements, inform the other Member States that it no longer wishes to avail itself of all or part of this Protocol. In that event, Denmark will apply in full all relevant measures then in force taken within the framework of the European Union.

PROTOCOL ON ASYLUM FOR NATIONALS OF MEMBER STATES OF THE EUROPEAN UNION

THE HIGH CONTRACTING PARTIES;

WHEREAS pursuant to the provisions of Article F(2) of the Treaty on European Union the Union shall respect fundamental rights as guaranteed by the European Convention for the Protection of Human Rights and Fundamental Freedoms signed in Rome on 4 November 1950;

WHEREAS the Court of Justice of the European Communities has jurisdiction to ensure that in the interpretation and application of Article F(2) of the Treaty on European Union the law is observed by the European Community;

WHEREAS pursuant to Article O of the Treaty on European Union any European State, when applying to become a Member of the Union, must respect the principles set out in Article F(1) of the Treaty on European Union,

BEARING IN MIND that Article 236 of the Treaty establishing the European Community establishes a mechanism for the suspension of certain rights in the event of a serious and persistent breach by a Member State of those principles;

RECALLING that each national of a Member State, as a citizen of the Union, enjoys a special status and protection which shall be guaranteed by the Member States inaccordance with the provisions of Part Two of the Treaty establishing the European Community;

BEARING IN MIND that the Treaty establishing the European Community establishes an area without internal frontiers and grants every citizen of the Union the right to move and reside freely within the territory of the Member States;

RECALLING that the question of extradition of nationals of Member States of the Union is addressed in the European Convention on Extradition of 13 December 1957 and the Convention of 27 September 1996 drawn up on the basis of Article K.3 of the Treaty on European Union relating to extradition between the Member States of the European Union;

WISHING to prevent the institution of asylum being resorted to for purposes alien to those for which it is intended;

WHEREAS this Protocol respects the finality and the objectives of the Geneva Convention of 28 July 1951 relating to the status of refugees;

HAVE AGREED UPON the following provisions which shall be annexed to the Treaty establishing the European Community,

Sole Article
Given the level of protection of fundamental rights and freedoms by the Member States of the European Union, Member States shall be regarded as constituting safe countries of origin in respect of each other for all legal and practical purposes in relation to asylum matters. Accordingly, any application for asylum made by a national of a Member State may be taken into consideration or declared admissible for processing by another Member State only in the following cases:

(a) if the Member State of which the applicant is a national proceeds after the entry into force of the Treaty of Amsterdam, availing itself of the provisions of Article 15 of the Convention for the Protection of Human Rights and Fundamental Freedoms, to take measures derogating in its territory from its obligations under that Convention;

(b) if the procedure referred to in Article F.1(1) of the Treaty on European Union has been initiated and until the Council takes a decision in respect thereof;

(c) if the Council, acting on the basis of Article F.1(1) of the Treaty on European Union, has determined, in respect of the Member State which the applicant is a national, the existence of a serious and persistent breach by that Member State of principles mentioned in Article F(1);

(d) if a Member State should so decide unilaterally in respect of the application of a national of another Member State; in that case the Council shall be immediately informed; the application shall be dealt with on the basis of the presumption that it is manifestly unfounded without affecting in any way, whatever the cases may be, the decision-making power of the Member State.

PROTOCOL ON THE APPLICATION OF THE PRINCIPLES OF SUBSIDIARITY AND PROPORTIONALITY

THE HIGH CONTRACTING PARTIES,

DETERMINED to establish the conditions for the application of the principles of subsidiarity and proportionality enshrined in Article 3b of the Treaty establishing the European Community with a view to defining more precisely the criteria for applying them and to ensure their strict observance and consistent implementation by all institutions;

WISHING to ensure that decisions are taken as closely as possible to the citizens of the Union;

TAKING ACCOUNT of the Interinstitutional Agreement of 25 October 1993 between the European Parliament, the Council and the Commission on procedures for implementing the principle of subsidiarity;

HAVE CONFIRMED that the conclusions of the Birmingham European Council on 16

October 1992 and the overall approach to the application of the subsidiarity principle agreed by the European Council meeting in Edinburgh on 11–12 December 1992 will continue to guide the action of the Union's institutions as well as the development of the application of the principle of subsidiarity, and, for this purpose,

HAVE AGREED UPON the following provisions which shall be annexed to the Treaty establishing the European Community:

(1) In exercising the powers conferred on it, each institution shall ensure that the principle of subsidiarity is complied with. It shall also ensure compliance with the principle of proportionality, according to which any action by the Community shall not go beyond what is necessary to achieve the objectives of the Treaty.

(2) The application of the principles of subsidiarity and proportionality shall respect the general provisions and the objectives of the Treaty, particularly as regards the maintaining in full of the acquis communautaire and the institutional balance; it shall not affect the principles developed by the Court of Justice regarding the relationship between national and Community law, and it should take into account Article F(4) of the Treaty on European Union, according to which 'the Union shall provide itself with the means necessary to attain its objectives and carry through its policies'.

(3) The principle of subsidiarity does not call into question the powers conferred on the European Community by the Treaty, as interpreted by the Court of Justice. The criteria referred to in the second paragraph of Article 3b of the Treaty shall relate to areas for which the Community does not have exclusive competence. The principle of subsidiarity provides a guide as to how those powers are to be exercised at the Community level. Subsidiarity is a dynamic concept and should be applied in the light of the objectives set out in the Treaty. It allows Community action within the limits of its powers to be expanded where circumstances so require, and conversely, to be restricted or discontinued where it is no longer justified.

(4) For any proposed Community legislation, the reasons on which it is based shall be stated with a view to justifying its compliance with the principles of subsidiarity and proportionality; the reasons for concluding that a Community objective can be better achieved by the Community must be substantiated by qualitative or, wherever possible, quantitative indicators.

(5) For Community action to be justified, both aspects of the subsidiarity principle shall be met: the objectives of the proposed action cannot be sufficiently achieved by Member States' action in the framework of their national constitutional system and can therefore be better achieved by action on the part of the Community.

The following guidelines should be used in examining whether the abovementioned condition is fulfilled:

— the issue under consideration has transnational aspects which cannot be satisfactorily regulated by action by Member States;

— actions by Member States alone or lack of Community action would conflict with the requirements of the Treaty (such as the need to correct distortion of competition or avoid disguised restrictions on trade or strengthen economic and social cohesion) or would otherwise significantly damage Member States' interests;

— action at Community level would produce clear benefits by reason of its scale or effects compared with action at the level of the Member States.

(6) The form of Community action shall be as simple as possible, consistent with satisfactory achievement of the objective of the measure and the need for effective enforcement. The Community shall legislate only to the extent necessary. Other things being equal, directives should be preferred to regulations and framework directives to detailed measures. Directives as provided for in Article 189 of the Treaty, while binding upon each Member State to which they are addressed as to the result to be achieved, shall leave to the national authorities the choice of form and methods.

(7) Regarding the nature and the extent of Community action, Community measures should leave as much scope for national decision as possible, consistent with securing the aim of the measure and observing the requirements of the Treaty. While respecting Community law, care should be taken to respect well established national arrangements and the organisation and working of Member States' legal systems. Where appropriate and subject to the need for proper enforcement, Community measures should provide Member States with alternative ways to achieve the objectives of the measures.

(8) Where the application of the principle of subsidiarity leads to no action being taken by the Community, Member States are required in their action to comply with the general rules laid down in Article 5 of the Treaty, by taking all appropriate measures to ensure fulfilment of their obligations under the Treaty and by abstaining from any measure which could jeopardise the attainment of the objectives of the Treaty.

(9) Without prejudice to its right of initiative, the Commission should:
— except in cases of particular urgency or confidentiality, consult widely before proposing legislation and, wherever appropriate, publish consultation documents;
— justify the relevance of its proposals with regard to the principle of subsidiarity: whenever necessary, the explanatory memorandum accompanying a proposal will give details in this respect. The financing of Community action in whole or in part from the Community budget shall require an explanation;
— take duly into account the need for any burden, whether financial or administrative, falling upon the Community, national governments, local authorities, economic operators and citizens, to be minimised and proportionate to the objective to be achieved;
— submit an annual report to the European Council, the European Parliament and the Council on the application of Article 3b of the Treaty. This annual report shall also be sent to the Committee of the Regions and to the Economic and Social Committee.

(10) The European Council shall take account of the Commission report referred to in the fourth indent of point 9 within the report on the progress achieved by the Union which it is required to submit to the European Parliament in accordance with Article D of the Treaty on European Union.

(11) While fully observing the procedures applicable, the European Parliament and the Council shall, as an integral part of the overall examination of Commission proposals, consider their consistency with Article 3b of the Treaty. This concerns the original Commission proposal as well as amendments which the European Parliament and the Council envisage making to the proposal.

(12) In the course of the procedures referred to in Articles 189b and 189c of the Treaty, the European Parliament shall be informed of the Council's position on the application of Article 3b of the Treaty, by way of a statement of the reasons which led the Council to adopt its common position. The Council shall inform the European Parliament of the reasons on the basis of which all or part of a Commission proposal is deemed to be inconsistent with Article 3b of the Treaty.

(13) Compliance with the principle of subsidiarity shall be reviewed in accordance with the rules laid down by the Treaty.

PROTOCOL ON EXTERNAL RELATIONS OF THE MEMBER STATES WITH REGARD TO THE CROSSING OF EXTERNAL BORDERS

THE HIGH CONTRACTING PARTIES,
TAKING INTO ACCOUNT the need of the Member States to ensure effective controls at

their external borders, in cooperation with third countries where appropriate,

HAVE AGREED UPON the following provision, which shall be annexed to the Treaty establishing the European Community,

The provisions on the measures on the crossing of external borders included in Article 73j(2)(a) of Title IIIa of the Treaty shall be without prejudice to the competence of Member States to negotiate or conclude agreements with third countries as long as they respect Community law and other relevant international agreements.

Protocols added by the Treaty of Nice

PROTOCOL ON THE ENLARGEMENT OF THE EUROPEAN UNION

THE HIGH CONTRACTING PARTIES

HAVE AGREED UPON the following provisions, which shall be annexed to the Treaty on European Union and to the Treaties establishing the European Communities:

Article 1   Repeal of the Protocol on the institutions

The Protocol on the institutions with the prospect of enlargement of the European Union, annexed to the Treaty on European Union and to the Treaties establishing the European Communities, is hereby repealed.

Article 2   Provisions concerning the European Parliament

1.   On 1 January 2004 and with effect from the start of the 2004–2009 term, in Article 190(2) of the Treaty establishing the European Community and in Article 108(2) of the Treaty establishing the European Atomic Energy Community, the first sub-paragraph shall be replaced by the following:

'The number of representatives elected in each Member State shall be as follows:

Belgium	22
Denmark	13
Germany	99
Greece	22
Spain	50
France	72
Ireland	12
Italy	72
Luxembourg	6
Netherlands	25
Austria	17
Portugal	22
Finland	13
Sweden	18
United Kingdom	72'

2.   Subject to paragraph 3, the total number of representatives in the European Parliament for the 2004–2009 term shall be equal to the number of representatives specified in Article 190(2) of the Treaty establishing the European Community and in Article 108(2) of the Treaty establishing the European Atomic Energy Community plus the number of representatives of the new Member States resulting from the accession treaties signed by 1 January 2004 at the latest.

3.   If the total number of members referred to in paragraph 2 is less than 732, a pro rata

correction shall be applied to the number of representatives to be elected in each Member State, so that the total number is as close as possible to 732, without such a correction leading to the number of representatives to be elected in each Member State being higher than that provided for in Article 190(2) of the Treaty establishing the European Community and in Article 108(2) of the Treaty establishing the European Atomic Energy Community for the 1999–2004 term.

The Council shall adopt a decision to that effect.

4.   By way of derogation from the second paragraph of Article 189 of the Treaty establishing the European Community and from the second paragraph of Article 107 of the Treaty establishing the European Atomic Energy Community, in the event of the entry into force of accession treaties after the adoption of the Council decision provided for in the second sub-paragraph of paragraph 3 of this Article, the number of members of the European Parliament may temporarily exceed 732 for the period for which that decision applies. The same correction as that referred to in the first sub-paragraph of paragraph 3 of this Article shall be applied to the number of representatives to be elected in the Member States in question.

Article 3   Provisions concerning the weighting of votes in the Council*

2.   At the time of each accession, the threshold referred to in the second sub-paragraph of Article 205(2) of the Treaty establishing the European Community and in the second sub-paragraph of Article 118(2) of the Treaty establishing the European Atomic Energy Community shall be calculated in such a way that the qualified majority threshold expressed in votes does not exceed the threshold resulting from the table in the Declaration on the enlargement of the European Union, included in the Final Act of the Conference which adopted the Treaty of Nice.

Article 4   Provisions concerning the Commission

1.   On 1 January 2005 and with effect from when the first Commission following that date takes up its duties, Article 213(1) of the Treaty establishing the European Community and Article 126(1) of the Treaty establishing the European Atomic Energy Community shall be replaced by the following:

'1. The Members of the Commission shall be chosen on the grounds of their general competence and their independence shall be beyond doubt.

The Commission shall include one national of each of the Member States.

The number of Members of the Commission may be altered by the Council, acting unanimously.'

2.   When the Union consists of 27 Member States, Article 213(1) of the Treaty establishing the European Community and Article 126(1) of the Treaty establishing the European Atomic Energy Community shall be replaced by the following:

'1. The Members of the Commission shall be chosen on the grounds of their general competence and their independence shall be beyond doubt.

The number of Members of the Commission shall be less than the number of Member States. The Members of the Commission shall be chosen according to a rotation system based on the principle of equality, the implementing arrangements for which shall be adopted by the Council, acting unanimously.

The number of Members of the Commission shall be set by the Council, acting unanimously.'

This amendment shall apply as from the date on which the first Commission following the date of accession of the twenty-seventh Member State of the Union takes up its duties.

3.   The Council, acting unanimously after signing the treaty of accession of the twenty-seventh Member State of the Union, shall adopt:

---

* **Editor's Note**: Repealed by Article 12(2) of the 2003 Accession Treaties.

— the number of Members of the Commission;

— the implementing arrangements for a rotation system based on the principle of equality containing all the criteria and rules necessary for determining the composition of successive colleges automatically on the basis of the following principles:

   (a) Member States shall be treated on a strictly equal footing as regards determination of the sequence of, and the time spent by, their nationals as Members of the Commission; consequently, the difference between the total number of terms of office held by nationals of any given pair of Member States may never be more than one;

   (b) subject to point (a), each successive college shall be so composed as to reflect satisfactorily the demographic and geographical range of all the Member States of the Union.

4.   Any State which accedes to the Union shall be entitled, at the time of its accession, to have one of its nationals as a Member of the Commission until paragraph 2 applies.

PROTOCOL ON THE STATUTE OF THE COURT OF JUSTICE*

THE HIGH CONTRACTING PARTIES

DESIRING to lay down the Statute of the Court of Justice provided for in Article 245 of the Treaty establishing the European Community and in Article 160 of the Treaty establishing the European Atomic Energy Community,

HAVE AGREED upon the following provisions, which shall be annexed to the Treaty on European Union, the Treaty establishing the European Community and the Treaty establishing the European Atomic Energy Community:

Article 1

The Court of Justice shall be constituted and shall function in accordance with the provisions of the Treaty on European Union (EU Treaty), of the Treaty establishing the European Community (EC Treaty), of the Treaty establishing the European Atomic Energy Community (EAEC Treaty) and of this Statute.

TITLE I   JUDGES AND ADVOCATES-GENERAL

Article 2

Before taking up his duties each Judge shall, in open court, take an oath to perform his duties impartially and conscientiously and to preserve the secrecy of the deliberations of the Court.

Article 3

The Judges shall be immune from legal proceedings. After they have ceased to hold office, they shall continue to enjoy immunity in respect of acts performed by them in their official capacity, including words spoken or written.

The Court, sitting as a full Court, may waive the immunity. Where immunity has been waived and criminal proceedings are instituted against a Judge, he shall be tried, in any of the Member States, only by the court competent to judge the members of the highest national judiciary.

Articles 12 to 15 and Article 18 of the Protocol on the privileges and immunities of the European Communities shall apply to the Judges, Advocates-General, Registrar and Assistant Rapporteurs of the Court, without prejudice to the provisions relating to immunity from legal proceedings of Judges which are set out in the preceding paragraphs.

---

* **Editor's Note:** As amended by Article 13 of the 2003 Accession Treaties.

Article 4

The Judges may not hold any political or administrative office.

They may not engage in any occupation, whether gainful or not, unless exemption is exceptionally granted by the Council.

When taking up their duties, they shall give a solemn undertaking that, both during and after their term of office, they will respect the obligations arising therefrom, in particular the duty to behave with integrity and discretion as regards the acceptance, after they have ceased to hold office, of certain appointments or benefits.

Any doubt on this point shall be settled by decision of the Court.

Article 5

Apart from normal replacement, or death, the duties of a Judge shall end when he resigns.

Where a Judge resigns, his letter of resignation shall be addressed to the President of the Court for transmission to the President of the Council. Upon this notification a vacancy shall arise on the bench.

Save where Article 6 applies, a Judge shall continue to hold office until his successor takes up his duties.

Article 6

A Judge may be deprived of his office or of his right to a pension or other benefits in its stead only if, in the unanimous opinion of the Judges and Advocates-General of the Court, he no longer fulfils the requisite conditions or meets the obligations arising from his office. The Judge concerned shall not take part in any such deliberations.

The Registrar of the Court shall communicate the decision of the Court to the President of the European Parliament and to the President of the Commission and shall notify it to the President of the Council.

In the case of a decision depriving a Judge of his office, a vacancy shall arise on the bench upon this latter notification.

Article 7

A Judge who is to replace a member of the Court whose term of office has not expired shall be appointed for the remainder of his predecessor's term.

Article 8

The provisions of Articles 2 to 7 shall apply to the Advocates-General.

TITLE II   ORGANISATION

Article 9

When, every three years, the Judges are partially replaced, thirteen and twelve Judges shall be replaced alternately.

When, every three years, the Advocates-General are partially replaced, four Advocates-General shall be replaced on each occasion.

Article 10

The Registrar shall take an oath before the Court to perform his duties impartially and conscientiously and to preserve the secrecy of the deliberations of the Court.

Article 11

The Court shall arrange for replacement of the Registrar on occasions when he is prevented from attending the Court.

Article 12

Officials and other servants shall be attached to the Court to enable it to function. They shall be responsible to the Registrar under the authority of the President.

Article 13

On a proposal from the Court, the Council may, acting unanimously, provide for the appointment of Assistant Rapporteurs and lay down the rules governing their service. The Assistant Rapporteurs may be required, under conditions laid down in the Rules of Procedure, to participate in preparatory inquiries in cases pending before the Court and to cooperate with the Judge who acts as Rapporteur.

The Assistant Rapporteurs shall be chosen from persons whose independence is beyond doubt and who possess the necessary legal qualifications; they shall be appointed by the Council. They shall take an oath before the Court to perform their duties impartially and conscientiously and to preserve the secrecy of the deliberations of the Court.

Article 14

The Judges, the Advocates-General and the Registrar shall be required to reside at the place where the Court has its seat.

Article 15

The Court shall remain permanently in session. The duration of the judicial vacations shall be determined by the Court with due regard to the needs of its business.

Article 16

The Court shall form chambers consisting of three and five Judges. The Judges shall elect the Presidents of the chambers from among their number. The Presidents of the chambers of five Judges shall be elected for three years. They may be re-elected once.

The Grand Chamber shall consist of eleven Judges. It shall be presided over by the President of the Court. The Presidents of the chambers of five Judges and other Judges appointed in accordance with the conditions laid down in the Rules of Procedure shall also form part of the Grand Chamber.

The Court shall sit in a Grand Chamber when a Member State or an institution of the Communities that is party to the proceedings so requests.

The Court shall sit as a full Court where cases are brought before it pursuant to Article 195(2), Article 213(2), Article 216 or Article 247(7) of the EC Treaty or Article 107d(2), Article 126(2), Article 129 or Article 160b(7) of the EAEC Treaty.

Moreover, where it considers that a case before it is of exceptional importance, the Court may decide, after hearing the Advocate-General, to refer the case to the full Court.

Article 17

Decisions of the Court shall be valid only when an uneven number of its members is sitting in the deliberations.

Decisions of the chambers consisting of either three or five Judges shall be valid only if they are taken by three Judges.

Decisions of the Grand Chamber shall be valid only if nine Judges are sitting. Decisions of the full Court shall be valid only if eleven Judges are sitting.

In the event of one of the Judges of a chamber being prevented from attending, a Judge of another chamber may be called upon to sit in accordance with conditions laid down in the Rules of Procedure.

Article 18

No Judge or Advocate-General may take part in the disposal of any case in which he has previously taken part as agent or adviser or has acted for one of the parties, or in which he has been called upon to pronounce as a member of a court or tribunal, of a commission of inquiry or in any other capacity.

If, for some special reason, any Judge or Advocate-General considers that he should not take part in the judgment or examination of a particular case, he shall so inform the President.

If, for some special reason, the President considers that any Judge or Advocate-General should not sit or make submissions in a particular case, he shall notify him accordingly.

Any difficulty arising as to the application of this Article shall be settled by decision of the Court.

A party may not apply for a change in the composition of the Court or of one of its chambers on the grounds of either the nationality of a Judge or the absence from the Court or from the chamber of a Judge of the nationality of that party.

TITLE III   PROCEDURE

Article 19

The Member States and the institutions of the Communities shall be represented before the Court by an agent appointed for each case; the agent may be assisted by an adviser or by a lawyer.

The States, other than the Member States, which are parties to the Agreement on the European Economic Area and also the EFTA Surveillance Authority referred to in that Agreement shall be represented in same manner.

Other parties must be represented by a lawyer. Only a lawyer authorised to practise before a court of a Member State or of another State which is a party to the Agreement on the European Economic Area may represent or assist a party before the Court.

Such agents, advisers and lawyers shall, when they appear before the Court, enjoy the rights and immunities necessary to the independent exercise of their duties, under conditions laid down in the Rules of Procedure.

As regards such advisers and lawyers who appear before it, the Court shall have the powers normally accorded to courts of law, under conditions laid down in the Rules of Procedure.

University teachers being nationals of a Member State whose law accords them a right of audience shall have the same rights before the Court as are accorded by this Article to lawyers.

Article 20

The procedure before the Court shall consist of two parts: written and oral.

The written procedure shall consist of the communication to the parties and to the institutions of the Communities whose decisions are in dispute, of applications, statements of case, defences and observations, and of replies, if any, as well as of all papers and documents in support or of certified copies of them.

Communications shall be made by the Registrar in the order and within the time laid down in the Rules of Procedure.

The oral procedure shall consist of the reading of the report presented by a Judge acting as Rapporteur, the hearing by the Court of agents, advisers and lawyers and of the submissions of the Advocate-General, as well as the hearing, if any, of witnesses and experts.

Where it considers that the case raises no new point of law, the Court may decide, after hearing the Advocate-General, that the case shall be determined without a submission from the Advocate-General.

Article 21

A case shall be brought before the Court by a written application addressed to the Registrar. The application shall contain the applicant's name and permanent address and the description of the signatory, the name of the party or names of the parties against whom the application is made, the subject-matter of the dispute, the form of order sought and a brief statement of the pleas in law on which the application is based.

The application shall be accompanied, where appropriate, by the measure the annulment of which is sought or, in the circumstances referred to in Article 232 of the EC Treaty and Article 148 of the EAEC Treaty, by documentary evidence of the date on which an institution was, in accordance with those Articles, requested to act. If the documents are not submitted with the application, the Registrar shall ask the party concerned to produce them within a reasonable period, but in that event the rights of the party shall not lapse even if such documents are produced after the time-limit for bringing proceedings.

Article 22

A case governed by Article 18 of the EAEC Treaty shall be brought before the Court by an appeal addressed to the Registrar. The appeal shall contain the name and permanent address of the applicant and the description of the signatory, a reference to the decision against which the appeal is brought, the names of the respondents, the subject-matter of the dispute, the submissions and a brief statement of the grounds on which the appeal is based.

The appeal shall be accompanied by a certified copy of the decision of the Arbitration Committee which is contested.

If the Court rejects the appeal, the decision of the Arbitration Committee shall become final.

If the Court annuls the decision of the Arbitration Committee, the matter may be re-opened, where appropriate, on the initiative of one of the parties in the case, before the Arbitration Committee. The latter shall conform to any decisions on points of law given by the Court.

Article 23

In the cases governed by Article 35(1) of the EU Treaty, by Article 234 of the EC Treaty and by Article 150 of the EAEC Treaty, the decision of the court or tribunal of a Member State which suspends its proceedings and refers a case to the Court shall be notified to the Court by the court or tribunal concerned. The decision shall then be notified by the Registrar of the Court to the parties, to the Member States and to the Commission, and also to the Council or to the European Central Bank if the act the validity or interpretation of which is in dispute originates from one of them, and to the European Parliament and the Council if the act the validity or interpretation of which is in dispute was adopted jointly by those two institutions.

Within two months of this notification, the parties, the Member States, the Commission and, where appropriate, the European Parliament, the Council and the European Central Bank, shall be entitled to submit statements of case or written observations to the Court.

In the cases governed by Article 234 of the EC Treaty, the decision of the national court or tribunal shall, moreover, be notified by the Registrar of the Court to the States, other than the Member States, which are parties to the Agreement on the European Economic Area and also to the EFTA Surveillance Authority referred to in that Agreement which may, within two months of notification, where one of the fields of application of that Agreement is concerned, submit statements of case or written observations to the Court.

Article 24

The Court may require the parties to produce all documents and to supply all information which the Court considers desirable. Formal note shall be taken of any refusal.

The Court may also require the Member States and institutions not being parties to the case to supply all information which the Court considers necessary for the proceedings.

Article 25

The Court may at any time entrust any individual, body, authority, committee or other organisation it chooses with the task of giving an expert opinion.

Article 26

Witnesses may be heard under conditions laid down in the Rules of Procedure.

Article 27

With respect to defaulting witnesses the Court shall have the powers generally granted to courts and tribunals and may impose pecuniary penalties under conditions laid down in the Rules of Procedure.

Article 28

Witnesses and experts may be heard on oath taken in the form laid down in the Rules of Procedure or in the manner laid down by the law of the country of the witness or expert.

Article 29

The Court may order that a witness or expert be heard by the judicial authority of his place of permanent residence.

The order shall be sent for implementation to the competent judicial authority under conditions laid down in the Rules of Procedure. The documents drawn up in compliance with the letters rogatory shall be returned to the Court under the same conditions.

The Court shall defray the expenses, without prejudice to the right to charge them, where appropriate, to the parties.

Article 30

A Member State shall treat any violation of an oath by a witness or expert in the same manner as if the offence had been committed before one of its courts with jurisdiction in civil proceedings. At the instance of the Court, the Member State concerned shall prosecute the offender before its competent court.

Article 31

The hearing in court shall be public, unless the Court, of its own motion or on application by the parties, decides otherwise for serious reasons.

Article 32

During the hearings the Court may examine the experts, the witnesses and the parties themselves. The latter, however, may address the Court only through their representatives.

Article 33

Minutes shall be made of each hearing and signed by the President and the Registrar.

Article 34

The case list shall be established by the President.

Article 35

The deliberations of the Court shall be and shall remain secret.

Article 36

Judgments shall state the reasons on which they are based. They shall contain the names of the Judges who took part in the deliberations.

Article 37

Judgments shall be signed by the President and the Registrar. They shall be read in open court.

Article 38

The Court shall adjudicate upon costs.

Article 39

The President of the Court may, by way of summary procedure, which may, in so far as necessary, differ from some of the rules contained in this Statute and which shall be laid down in the Rules of Procedure, adjudicate upon applications to suspend execution, as provided for in Article 242 of the EC Treaty and Article 157 of the EAEC Treaty, or to prescribe interim measures in pursuance of Article 243 of the EC Treaty or Article 158 of the EAEC Treaty, or to suspend enforcement in accordance with the fourth paragraph of Article 256 of the EC Treaty or the third paragraph of Article 164 of the EAEC Treaty.

Should the President be prevented from attending, his place shall be taken by another Judge under conditions laid down in the Rules of Procedure.

The ruling of the President or of the Judge replacing him shall be provisional and shall in no way prejudice the decision of the Court on the substance of the case.

Article 40
Member States and institutions of the Communities may intervene in cases before the Court.

The same right shall be open to any other person establishing an interest in the result of any case submitted to the Court, save in cases between Member States, between institutions of the Communities or between Member States and institutions of the Communities.

Without prejudice to the second paragraph, the States, other than the Member States, which are parties to the Agreement on the European Economic Area, and also the EFTA Surveillance Authority referred to in that Agreement, may intervene in cases before the Court where one of the fields of application of that Agreement is concerned.

An application to intervene shall be limited to supporting the form of order sought by one of the parties.

Article 41
Where the defending party, after having been duly summoned, fails to file written submissions in defence, judgment shall be given against that party by default. An objection may be lodged against the judgment within one month of it being notified. The objection shall not have the effect of staying enforcement of the judgment by default unless the Court decides otherwise.

Article 42
Member States, institutions of the Communities and any other natural or legal persons may, in cases and under conditions to be determined by the Rules of Procedure, institute third-party proceedings to contest a judgment rendered without their being heard, where the judgment is prejudicial to their rights.

Article 43
If the meaning or scope of a judgment is in doubt, the Court shall construe it on application by any party or any institution of the Communities establishing an interest therein.

Article 44
An application for revision of a judgment may be made to the Court only on discovery of a fact which is of such a nature as to be a decisive factor, and which, when the judgment was given, was unknown to the Court and to the party claiming the revision.

The revision shall be opened by a judgment of the Court expressly recording the existence of a new fact, recognising that it is of such a character as to lay the case open to revision and declaring the application admissible on this ground.

No application for revision may be made after the lapse of 10 years from the date of the judgment.

Article 45
Periods of grace based on considerations of distance shall be determined by the Rules of Procedure.

No right shall be prejudiced in consequence of the expiry of a time-limit if the party concerned proves the existence of unforeseeable circumstances or of force majeure.

Article 46
Proceedings against the Communities in matters arising from non-contractual liability shall be barred after a period of five years from the occurrence of the event giving rise thereto. The period of limitation shall be interrupted if proceedings are instituted before the Court or if prior to such proceedings an application is made by the aggrieved party to the relevant institution of the Communities. In the latter event the proceedings must be instituted within the period of two months provided for in Article 230 of the EC Treaty and Article 146 of the EAEC Treaty; the provisions of the second paragraph of Article 232 of the EC Treaty and the second paragraph of Article 148 of the EAEC Treaty, respectively, shall apply where appropriate.

TITLE IV   THE COURT OF FIRST INSTANCE OF THE EUROPEAN COMMUNITIES

Article 47

Articles 2 to 8, Articles 14 and 15, the first, second, fourth and fifth paragraphs of Article 17 and Article 18 shall apply to the Court of First Instance and its members. The oath referred to in Article 2 shall be taken before the Court of Justice and the decisions referred to in Articles 3, 4 and 6 shall be adopted by that Court after hearing the Court of First Instance.

The fourth paragraph of Article 3 and Articles 10, 11 and 14 shall apply to the Registrar of the Court of First Instance mutatis mutandis.

Article 48

The Court of First Instance shall consist of twenty-five Judges.

Article 49

The members of the Court of First Instance may be called upon to perform the task of an Advocate-General.

It shall be the duty of the Advocate-General, acting with complete impartiality and independence, to make, in open court, reasoned submissions on certain cases brought before the Court of First Instance in order to assist the Court of First Instance in the performance of its task.

The criteria for selecting such cases, as well as the procedures for designating the Advocates-General, shall be laid down in the Rules of Procedure of the Court of First Instance.

A member called upon to perform the task of Advocate-General in a case may not take part in the judgment of the case.

Article 50

The Court of First Instance shall sit in chambers of three or five Judges. The Judges shall elect the Presidents of the chambers from among their number. The Presidents of the chambers of five Judges shall be elected for three years. They may be re-elected once.

The composition of the chambers and the assignment of cases to them shall be governed by the Rules of Procedure. In certain cases governed by the Rules of Procedure, the Court of First Instance may sit as a full court or be constituted by a single Judge.

The Rules of Procedure may also provide that the Court of First Instance may sit in a Grand Chamber in cases and under the conditions specified therein.

Article 51

By way of exception to the rule laid down in Article 225(1) of the EC Treaty and Article 140a(1) of the EAEC Treaty, the Court of Justice shall have jurisdiction in actions brought by the Member States, by the institutions of the Communities and by the European Central Bank.

Article 52

The President of the Court of Justice and the President of the Court of First Instance shall determine, by common accord, the conditions under which officials and other servants attached to the Court of Justice shall render their services to the Court of First Instance to enable it to function. Certain officials or other servants shall be responsible to the Registrar of the Court of First Instance under the authority of the President of the Court of First Instance.

Article 53

The procedure before the Court of First Instance shall be governed by Title III.

Such further and more detailed provisions as may be necessary shall be laid down in its Rules of Procedure. The Rules of Procedure may derogate from the fourth paragraph of Article 40 and from Article 41 in order to take account of the specific features of litigation in the field of intellectual property.

Notwithstanding the fourth paragraph of Article 20, the Advocate-General may make his reasoned submissions in writing.

Article 54

Where an application or other procedural document addressed to the Court of First Instance is lodged by mistake with the Registrar of the Court of Justice, it shall be transmitted immediately by that Registrar to the Registrar of the Court of First Instance; likewise, where an application or other procedural document addressed to the Court of Justice is lodged by mistake with the Registrar of the Court of First Instance, it shall be transmitted immediately by that Registrar to the Registrar of the Court of Justice.

Where the Court of First Instance finds that it does not have jurisdiction to hear and determine an action in respect of which the Court of Justice has jurisdiction, it shall refer that action to the Court of Justice; likewise, where the Court of Justice finds that an action falls within the jurisdiction of the Court of First Instance, it shall refer that action to the Court of First Instance, whereupon that Court may not decline jurisdiction.

Where the Court of Justice and the Court of First Instance are seised of cases in which the same relief is sought, the same issue of interpretation is raised or the validity of the same act is called in question, the Court of First Instance may, after hearing the parties, stay the proceedings before it until such time as the Court of Justice shall have delivered judgment. Where applications are made for the same act to be declared void, the Court of First Instance may also decline jurisdiction in order that the Court of Justice may rule on such applications. In the cases referred to in this paragraph, the Court of Justice may also decide to stay the proceedings before it; in that event, the proceedings before the Court of First Instance shall continue.

Article 55

Final decisions of the Court of First Instance, decisions disposing of the substantive issues in part only or disposing of a procedural issue concerning a plea of lack of competence or inadmissibility, shall be notified by the Registrar of the Court of First Instance to all parties as well as all Member States and the institutions of the Communities even if they did not intervene in the case before the Court of First Instance.

Article 56

An appeal may be brought before the Court of Justice, within two months of the notification of the decision appealed against, against final decisions of the Court of First Instance and decisions of that Court disposing of the substantive issues in part only or disposing of a procedural issue concerning a plea of lack of competence or inadmissibility.

Such an appeal may be brought by any party which has been unsuccessful, in whole or in part, in its submissions. However, interveners other than the Member States and the institutions of the Communities may bring such an appeal only where the decision of the Court of First Instance directly affects them.

With the exception of cases relating to disputes between the Communities and their servants, an appeal may also be brought by Member States and institutions of the Communities which did not intervene in the proceedings before the Court of First Instance. Such Member States and institutions shall be in the same position as Member States or institutions which intervened at first instance.

Article 57

Any person whose application to intervene has been dismissed by the Court of First Instance may appeal to the Court of Justice within two weeks from the notification of the decision dismissing the application.

The parties to the proceedings may appeal to the Court of Justice against any decision of the Court of First Instance made pursuant to Article 242 or Article 243 or the fourth paragraph of Article 256 of the EC Treaty or Article 157 or Article 158 or the third paragraph of Article 164 of the EAEC Treaty within two months from their notification.

The appeal referred to in the first two paragraphs of this Article shall be heard and determined under the procedure referred to in Article 39.

Article 58

An appeal to the Court of Justice shall be limited to points of law. It shall lie on the grounds of lack of competence of the Court of First Instance, a breach of procedure before it which adversely affects the interests of the appellant as well as the infringement of Community law by the Court of First Instance.

No appeal shall lie regarding only the amount of the costs or the party ordered to pay them.

Article 59

Where an appeal is brought against a decision of the Court of First Instance, the procedure before the Court of Justice shall consist of a written part and an oral part. In accordance with conditions laid down in the Rules of Procedure, the Court of Justice, having heard the Advocate-General and the parties, may dispense with the oral procedure.

Article 60

Without prejudice to Articles 242 and 243 of the EC Treaty or Articles 157 and 158 of the EAEC Treaty, an appeal shall not have suspensory effect.

By way of derogation from Article 244 of the EC Treaty and Article 159 of the EAEC Treaty, decisions of the Court of First Instance declaring a regulation to be void shall take effect only as from the date of expiry of the period referred to in the first paragraph of Article 56 of this Statute or, if an appeal shall have been brought within that period, as from the date of dismissal of the appeal, without prejudice, however, to the right of a party to apply to the Court of Justice, pursuant to Articles 242 and 243 of the EC Treaty or Articles 157 and 158 of the EAEC Treaty, for the suspension of the effects of the regulation which has been declared void or for the prescription of any other interim measure.

Article 61

If the appeal is well founded, the Court of Justice shall quash the decision of the Court of First Instance. It may itself give final judgment in the matter, where the state of the proceedings so permits, or refer the case back to the Court of First Instance for judgment.

Where a case is referred back to the Court of First Instance, that Court shall be bound by the decision of the Court of Justice on points of law.

When an appeal brought by a Member State or an institution of the Communities, which did not intervene in the proceedings before the Court of First Instance, is well founded, the Court of Justice may, if it considers this necessary, state which of the effects of the decision of the Court of First Instance which has been quashed shall be considered as definitive in respect of the parties to the litigation.

Article 62

In the cases provided for in Article 225(2) and (3) of the EC Treaty and Article 140a(2) and (3) of the EAEC Treaty, where the First Advocate-General considers that there is a serious risk of the unity or consistency of Community law being affected, he may propose that the Court of Justice review the decision of the Court of First Instance.

The proposal must be made within one month of delivery of the decision by the Court of First Instance. Within one month of receiving the proposal made by the First Advocate-General, the Court of Justice shall decide whether or not the decision should be reviewed.

TITLE V   FINAL PROVISIONS

Article 63

The Rules of Procedure of the Court of Justice and of the Court of First Instance shall contain any provisions necessary for applying and, where required, supplementing this Statute.

Article 64

Until the rules governing the language arrangements applicable at the Court of Justice and the Court of First Instance have been adopted in this Statute, the provisions of the Rules of Procedure of the Court of Justice and of the Rules of Procedure of the Court of First Instance governing language arrangements shall continue to apply. Those provisions may only be amended or repealed in accordance with the procedure laid down for amending this Statute.

Declarations adopted by the Nice Intergovernmental Conference

1. **Declaration on the European security and defence policy**

In accordance with the texts approved by the European Council in Nice concerning the European security and defence policy (Presidency report and Annexes), the objective for the European Union is for that policy to become operational quickly. A decision to that end will be taken by the European Council as soon as possible in 2001 and no later than at its meeting in Laeken/Brussels, on the basis of the existing provisions of the Treaty on European Union. Consequently, the entry into force of the Treaty of Nice does not constitute a precondition.

2. **Declaration on Article 31(2) of the Treaty on European Union**

The Conference recalls that:

- the decision to set up a unit composed of national prosecutors, magistrates or police officers of equivalent competence, detached from each Member State (Eurojust), having the task of facilitating proper coordination between national prosecuting authorities and of supporting criminal investigations in organised crime cases, was provided for in the Presidency conclusions of the European Council at Tampere on 15 and 16 October 1999;
- the European Judicial Network was set up by Joint Action 98/428/JHA adopted by the Council on 29 June 1998 (OJ L 191, 7.7.1998, p. 4).

3. **Declaration on Article 10 of the Treaty establishing the European Community**

The Conference recalls that the duty of sincere cooperation which derives from Article 10 of the Treaty establishing the European Community and governs relations between the Member States and the Community institutions also governs relations between the Community institutions themselves. In relations between those institutions, when it proves necessary, in the context of that duty of sincere cooperation, to facilitate the application of the provisions of the Treaty establishing the European Community, the European Parliament, the Council and the Commission may conclude interinstitutional agreements. Such agreements may not amend or supplement the provisions of the Treaty and may be concluded only with the agreement of these three institutions.

4. **Declaration on the third paragraph of Article 21 of the Treaty establishing the European Community**

The Conference calls upon the institutions and bodies referred to in the third paragraph of Article 21 or in Article 7 to ensure that the reply to any written request by a citizen of the Union is made within a reasonable period.

5. **Declaration on Article 67 of the Treaty establishing the European Community**

The High Contracting Parties agree that the Council, in the decision it is required to take pursuant to the second indent of Article 67(2):

- will decide, from 1 May 2004, to act in accordance with the procedure referred to in Article 251 in order to adopt the measures referred to in Article 62(3) and Article 63(3)(b);
- will decide to act in accordance with the procedure referred to in Article 251 in order to adopt the measures referred to in Article 62(2)(a) from the date on which agreement is reached on the scope of the measures concerning the crossing by persons of the external borders of the Member States.

The Council will, moreover, endeavour to make the procedure referred to in Article 251 applicable from 1 May 2004 or as soon as possible thereafter to the other areas covered by Title IV or to parts of them.

6.   Declaration on Article 100 of the Treaty establishing the European Community

The Conference recalls that decisions regarding financial assistance, such as are provided for in Article 100 and are compatible with the 'no bail-out' rule laid down in Article 103, must comply with the 2000–2006 financial perspective, and in particular paragraph 11 of the Interinstitutional Agreement of 6 May 1999 between the European Parliament, the Council and the Commission on budgetary discipline and improvement of the budgetary procedure, and with the corresponding provisions of future interinstitutional agreements and financial perspectives.

7.   Declaration on Article 111 of the Treaty establishing the European Community

The Conference agrees that procedures shall be such as to enable all the Member States in the Euro area to be fully involved in each stage of preparing the position of the Community at international level as regards issues of particular relevance to economic and monetary union.

8.   Declaration on Article 137 of the Treaty establishing the European Community

The Conference agrees that any expenditure incurred by virtue of Article 137 is to be charged to heading 3 of the financial perspective.

9.   Declaration on Article 175 of the Treaty establishing the European Community

The High Contracting Parties are determined to see the European Union play a leading role in promoting environmental protection in the Union and in international efforts pursuing the same objective at global level. Full use should be made of all possibilities offered by the Treaty with a view to pursuing this objective, including the use of incentives and instruments which are market-oriented and intended to promote sustainable development.

10.   Declaration on Article 181a of the Treaty establishing the European Community

The Conference confirms that, without prejudice to other provisions of the Treaty establishing the European Community, balance-of-payments aid to third countries falls outside the scope of Article 181a.

11.   Declaration on Article 191 of the Treaty establishing the European Community

The Conference recalls that the provisions of Article 191 do not imply any transfer of powers to the European Community and do not affect the application of the relevant national constitutional rules.

The funding for political parties at European level provided out of the budget of the European Communities may not be used to fund, either directly or indirectly, political parties at national level.

The provisions on the funding for political parties shall apply, on the same basis, to all the political forces represented in the European Parliament.

12.   Declaration on Article 225 of the Treaty establishing the European Community

The Conference calls on the Court of Justice and the Commission to give overall consideration as soon as possible to the division of jurisdiction between the Court of Justice and the Court of First Instance, in particular in the area of direct actions, and to submit suitable proposals for examination by the competent bodies as soon as the Treaty of Nice enters into force.

13.   Declaration on Article 225(2) and (3) of the Treaty establishing the European Community

The Conference considers that the essential provisions of the review procedure in Article 225(2) and (3) should be defined in the Statute of the Court of Justice. Those provisions should in particular specify:

— the role of the parties in proceedings before the Court of Justice, in order to safeguard their rights;
— the effect of the review procedure on the enforceability of the decision of the Court of First Instance;
— the effect of the Court of Justice decision on the dispute between the parties.

14. Declaration on Article 225(2) and (3) of the Treaty establishing the European Community

The Conference considers that when the Council adopts the provisions of the Statute which are necessary to implement Article 225(2) and (3), it should put a procedure in place to ensure that the practical operation of those provisions is evaluated no later than three years after the entry into force of the Treaty of Nice.

15. Declaration on Article 225(3) of the Treaty establishing the European Community

The Conference considers that, in exceptional cases in which the Court of Justice decides to review a decision of the Court of First Instance on a question referred for a preliminary ruling, it should act under an emergency procedure.

16. Declaration on Article 225a of the Treaty establishing the European Community

The Conference asks the Court of Justice and the Commission to prepare as swiftly as possible a draft decision establishing a judicial panel which has jurisdiction to deliver judgments at first instance on disputes between the Community and its servants.

17. Declaration on Article 229a of the Treaty establishing the European Community

The Conference considers that Article 229a does not prejudge the choice of the judicial framework which may be set up to deal with disputes relating to the application of acts adopted on the basis of the Treaty establishing the European Community which create Community industrial property rights.

18. Declaration on the Court of Auditors

The Conference invites the Court of Auditors and the national audit institutions to improve the framework and conditions for cooperation between them, while maintaining the autonomy of each. To that end, the President of the Court of Auditors may set up a contact committee with the chairmen of the national audit institutions.

19. Declaration on Article 10.6 of the Statute of the European System of Central Banks and of the European Central Bank

The Conference expects that a recommendation within the meaning of Article 10.6 of the Statute of the European System of Central Banks and of the European Central Bank will be presented as soon as possible.

20. Declaration on the enlargement of the European Union *

The common position to be adopted by the Member States at the accession conferences, as regards the distribution of seats at the European Parliament, the weighting of votes in the Council, the composition of the Economic and Social Committee and the composition of the Committee of the Regions will correspond to the following tables for a Union of 27 Member States.

(1) The tables in this declaration take account only of those candidate countries with which accession negotiations have actually started.

1.   THE EUROPEAN PARLIAMENT

Member States	EP seats
Germany	99
United Kingdom	72
France	72
Italy	72
Spain	50
Poland	50
Romania	33
Netherlands	25
Greece	22
Czech Republic	20
Belgium	22
Hungary	20

---

* **Editor's Note:** This Declaration will be superseded when the Constitutional Treaty enters into force.

Member States	EP seats
Portugal	22
Sweden	18
Bulgaria	17
Austria	17
Slovakia	13
Denmark	13
Finland	13
Ireland	12
Lithuania	12
Latvia	8
Slovenia	7
Estonia	6
Cyprus	6
Luxembourg	6
Malta	5
Total	732

2. THE WEIGHTING OF VOTES IN THE COUNCIL

Members of the Council	Weighted votes
Germany	29
United Kingdom	29
France	29
Italy	29
Spain	27
Poland	27
Romania	14
Netherlands	13
Greece	12
Czech Republic	12
Belgium	12
Hungary	12
Portugal	12
Sweden	10
Bulgaria	10
Austria	10
Slovakia	7
Denmark	7
Finland	7
Ireland	7
Lithuania	4
Latvia	4
Slovenia	4
Estonia	4
Cyprus	4
Luxembourg	4
Malta	3
Total	344

Acts of the Council shall require for their adoption at least 258 votes in favour, cast by a majority of members, where this Treaty requires them to be adopted on a proposal from the Commission.

In other cases, for their adoption acts of the Council shall require at least 258 votes in favour cast by at least two-thirds of the members.

When a decision is to be adopted by the Council by a qualified majority, a member of the Council may request verification that the Member States constituting the qualified majority represent at least 62% of the total population of the Union. If that condition is shown not to have been met, the decision in question shall not be adopted.

3. THE ECONOMIC AND SOCIAL COMMITTEE

Member States	Members
Germany	24
United Kingdom	24
France	24
Italy	24
Spain	21
Poland	21
Romania	15
Netherlands	12
Greece	12
Czech Republic	12
Belgium	12
Hungary	12
Portugal	12
Sweden	12
Bulgaria	12
Austria	12
Slovakia	9
Denmark	9
Finland	9
Ireland	9
Lithuania	9
Latvia	7
Slovenia	7
Estonia	7
Cyprus	6
Luxembourg	6
Malta	5
Total	344

4. THE COMMITTEE OF THE REGIONS

Member States	Members
Germany	24
United Kingdom	24
France	24
Italy	24
Spain	21
Poland	21
Romania	15
Netherlands	12
Greece	12
Czech Republic	12
Belgium	12
Hungary	12
Portugal	12
Sweden	12
Bulgaria	12
Austria	12
Slovakia	9
Denmark	9
Finland	9
Ireland	9
Lithuania	9
Latvia	7
Slovenia	7
Estonia	7

Member States	Members
Cyprus	6
Luxembourg	6
Malta	5
Total	344

21.   **Declaration on the qualified majority threshold and the number of votes for a blocking minority in an enlarged Union.***

Insofar as all the candidate countries listed in the Declaration on the enlargement of the European Union have not yet acceded to the Union when the new vote weightings take effect (1 January 2005), the threshold for a qualified majority will move, according to the pace of accessions, from a percentage below the current one to a maximum of 73,4%. When all the candidate countries mentioned above have acceded, the blocking minority, in a Union of 27, will be raised to 91 votes, and the qualified majority threshold resulting from the table given in the Declaration on enlargement of the European Union will be automatically adjusted accordingly.

22.   **Declaration on the venue for European Councils**

As from 2002, one European Council meeting per Presidency will be held in Brussels. When the Union comprises 18 members, all European Council meetings will be held in Brussels.

23.   **Declaration on the future of the Union**

1.   Important reforms have been decided in Nice. The Conference welcomes the successful conclusion of the Conference of Representatives of the Governments of the Member States and commits the Member States to pursue the early ratification of the Treaty of Nice.

2.   It agrees that the conclusion of the Conference of Representatives of the Governments of the Member States opens the way for enlargement of the European Union and underlines that, with ratification of the Treaty of Nice, the European Union will have completed the institutional changes necessary for the accession of new Member States.

3.   Having thus opened the way to enlargement, the Conference calls for a deeper and wider debate about the future of the European Union. In 2001, the Swedish and Belgian Presidencies, in cooperation with the Commission and involving the European Parliament, will encourage wide-ranging discussions with all interested parties: representatives of national parliaments and all those reflecting public opinion, namely political, economic and university circles, representatives of civil society, etc. The candidate States will be associated with this process in ways to be defined.

4.   Following a report to be drawn up for the European Council in Goteborg in June 2001, the European Council, at its meeting in Laeken/Brussels in December 2001, will agree on a declaration containing appropriate initiatives for the continuation of this process.

5.   The process should address, inter alia, the following questions:
— how to establish and monitor a more precise delimitation of powers between the European Union and the Member States, reflecting the principle of subsidiarity;
— the status of the Charter of Fundamental Rights of the European Union, proclaimed in Nice, in accordance with the conclusions of the European Council in Cologne;
— a simplification of the Treaties with a view to making them clearer and better understood without changing their meaning;
— the role of national parliaments in the European architecture.

6.   Addressing the abovementioned issues, the Conference recognises the need to improve and to monitor the democratic legitimacy and transparency of the Union and its institutions, in order to bring them closer to the citizens of the Member States.

7.   After these preparatory steps, the Conference agrees that a new Conference of the Representatives of the Governments of the Member States will be convened in 2004, to address the abovementioned items with a view to making corresponding changes to the Treaties.

8.   The Conference of Member States shall not constitute any form of obstacle or

* **Editor's Note**: This Declaration will be superseded when the Constitutional Treaty enters into force.

pre-condition to the enlargement process. Moreover, those candidate States which have concluded accession negotiations with the Union will be invited to participate in the Conference. Those candidate States which have not concluded their accession negotiations will be invited as observers.

24.   Declaration on Article 2 of the Protocol on the financial consequences of the expiry of the ECSC Treaty and on the research fund for coal and steel

The Conference invites the Council to ensure, under Article 2 of the Protocol, the prolongation of the ECSC statistics system after the expiry of the ECSC Treaty until 31 December 2002 and to invite the Commission to make the appropriate recommendations.

DECLARATIONS OF WHICH THE CONFERENCE TOOK NOTE

1.   Declaration by Luxembourg

Without prejudice to the Decision of 8 April 1965 and the provisions and possibilities contained therein regarding the seats of institutions, bodies and departments to be set up, the Luxembourg Government undertakes not to claim the seat of the Boards of Appeal of the Office for Harmonisation in the Internal Market (trade marks and designs), which will remain in Alicante, even if those Boards were to become judicial panels within the meaning of Article 220 of the Treaty establishing the European Community.

2.   Declaration by Greece, Spain and Portugal on Article 161 of the Treaty establishing the European Community

Greece, Spain and Portugal have agreed to the move to a qualified majority in Article 161 of the Treaty establishing the European Community on the basis that the word 'multiannual' in the third paragraph means that the financial perspective applicable from 1 January 2007 and the Interinstitutional Agreement relating thereto will have the same duration as the current financial perspective.

3.   Declaration by Denmark, Germany, the Netherlands and Austria on Article 161 of the Treaty establishing the European Community

With regard to the Declaration by Greece, Spain and Portugal on Article 161 of the Treaty establishing the European Community, Denmark, Germany, the Netherlands and Austria declare that that Declaration is without prejudice to actions of the European Commission, in particular with respect to its right of initiative.

ADDITIONAL LEGISLATION AND AGREEMENTS AFFECTING THE INSTITUTIONS

Interinstitutional Agreement of 6 May 1999 between the European Parliament, the Council and the Commission on budgetary discipline and improvement of the budgetary procedure
[OJ 1999, C172/1]

1.   The purpose of this Agreement concluded between the European parliament, the Council and the Commission, hereafter referred to as the 'institutions', is to implement budgetary discipline and to improve the functioning of the annual budgetary procedure and cooperation between the institutions on budgetary matters.

2.   Budgetary discipline under this Agreement covers all expenditure. It is binding on all the institutions involved in its implementation for as long as the Agreement is in force.

3.   This Agreement does not alter the respective budgetary powers of the various institutions, as laid down in the Treaties.

4.   Any amendment of this Agreement requires the consent of all the institutions which are party to it. Changes to the financial perspective must be made in accordance with the procedures laid down for this purpose in this Agreement.

5.   This Agreement is in two parts:
- — Part I contains a definition and implementing provisions for the financial perspective 2000 to 2006 and applies for the duration of that financial perspective,
- — Part II relates to improvement of Interinstitutional collaboration during the budgetary procedure.

6.   Whenever it considers it necessary and at all events at the same time as any proposal for a new financial perspective presented pursuant to paragraph 26, the Commission will present a report on the application of this Agreement, accompanied where necessary by proposed amendments.

7.   This Agreement enters into force on 1 January 2000. It replaces with effect from the same date:
- — the Joint Declaration by the European Parliament, the Council and the Commission of 30 June 1982 on various measures to improve the budgetary procedure,[1]
- — the Interinstitutional Agreement of 29 October 1993 between the European Parliament, the Council and the Commission on budgetary discipline and improvement of the budgetary procedure,[2]
- — the Declaration by the European Parliament, the Council and the Commission of 6 March 1995 on the incorporation of financial provisions into legislative acts,[3]
- — the Joint Declaration of 12 December 1996 concerning the improvement of information to the budgetary authority on fisheries agreements,[4]
- — the Interinstitutional Agreement between the European Parliament, the Council and the European Commission of 16 July 1997 on provisions regarding financing of the common foreign and security policy,[5]
- — the Interinstitutional Agreement of 13 October 1998 between the European Parliament, the Council and the Commission on legal bases and implementation of the budget.[6]

PART I   FINANCIAL PERSPECTIVE 2000 TO 2006: DEFINITION AND IMPLEMENTING PROVISIONS

A   Contents and scope of the financial perspective

8.   The 2000 to 2006 financial perspective, set out in Annex I, forms an integral part of this Agreement. It constitutes the reference framework for Interinstitutional budgetary discipline. Its contents are consistent with the conclusions of the Berlin European Council of 24 and 25 March 1999.

9.   The financial perspective is intended to ensure that, in the medium term, European Union expenditure, broken down by broad category, develops in an orderly manner and within the limits of own resources.

10.   The 2000 to 2006 financial perspective establishes, for each of the years and for each heading or subheading, amounts of expenditure in terms of appropriations for commitments. Overall annual totals of expenditure are also shown in terms of both appropriations for commitments and appropriations for payments. The appropriations for payments left available for the enlargement and to be used in accordance with the second sub-paragraph of paragraph 25 are also identified. All these amounts are expressed in 1999 prices, except for the monetary

---

[1] OJ C 194, 28.7.1982, p. 1.   [2] OJ C 331, 7.12.1993, p. 1.   [3] OJ C 102, 4.4.1996, p. 4.
[4] OJ C 20, 20.1.1997, p. 109.   [5] OJ C 286, 22.9.1997, p. 80.   [6] OJ C 344, 12.11.1998, p. 1.

reserve, where the amounts are expressed in current prices. The financial perspective does not take account of budget items financed by earmarked revenue within the meaning of Article 4 of the Financial Regulation of 21 December 1977 applicable to the general budget of the European Communities,[7] hereafter referred to as the 'Financial Regulation'. Specific items of expenditure may be financed only up to the ceiling fixed for this purpose and without prejudice to the second sub-paragraph of paragraph 11. Information relating to operations not included in the general budget of the European Communities and the foreseeable development of the various categories of Community own resources are set out, by way of indication, in separate tables. This information is updated annually when the technical adjustment is made to the financial perspective. The agricultural guideline remains unchanged. It will be re-examined on the basis of a report which the Commission will present to the Council before the next enlargement of the European Union in order to make any adjustment considered necessary.

11.   The institutions acknowledge that each of the absolute amounts shown in the 2000 to 2006 financial perspective represents an annual ceiling on expenditure under the general budget of the European Communities. Without prejudice to any changes in these ceilings in accordance with the provisions contained in this Agreement, they undertake to use their respective powers in such a way as to comply with the various annual expenditure ceilings during each budgetary procedure and when implementing the budget for the year concerned. However, the ceilings under heading 7 of the financial perspective (pre-accession aid) are indicative by nature and the two arms of the budgetary authority may jointly decide to alter the breakdown in the course of the budgetary procedure.

12.   The two arms of the budgetary authority agree to accept, for the duration of the 2000 to 2006 financial perspective, the maximum rates of increase for non-compulsory expenditure deriving from the budgets established within the ceilings set by the financial perspective. Except in heading 2 of the financial perspective (structural operations), for the purposes of sound financial management, the institutions will ensure as far as possible during the budgetary procedure and at the time of the budget's adoption that sufficient margins are left available beneath the ceilings for the various headings. Within the maximum rates of increase for non-compulsory expenditure specified in the first sub-paragraph, the European Parliament and the Council undertake to respect the allocations of commitment appropriations provided in the financial perspective for structural operations.

13.   No act adopted under the co-decision procedure by the European Parliament and the council nor any act adopted by the Council which involves exceeding the appropriations available in the budget or the allocations available in the financial perspective in accordance with paragraph 11 may be implemented in financial terms until the budget has been amended and, if necessary, the financial perspective has been appropriately revised in accordance with the relevant procedure for each of these cases.

14.   For each of the years covered by the financial perspective, the total appropriations for payments required, after annual adjustment and taking account of any other adjustments or revisions, must not be such as to produce a call-in rate for own resource that exceeds the ceiling in force for these resources. If need be, the two arms of the budgetary authority will decide, acting on a proposal from the Commission and in accordance with the voting rules laid down in the fifth sub-paragraph of Article 272(9) of the Treaty establishing the European Community (hereafter referred to as the 'EC Treaty'), to lower the ceilings set in the financial perspective in order to ensure compliance with the ceiling on own resources.

B   Annual adjustments of the financial perspective

Technical adjustments

15.   Each year the commission, acting ahead of the budgetary procedure for year n + 1,

---

[7] OJ L 356, 31.12.1977, p. 1.

will determine the agricultural guideline and make the following technical adjustments to the financial perspective in line with movements in gross national product (GNP) and prices:

    (a) revaluation, at year n + 1 prices, of the ceilings and of the overall figures for appropriations for commitments and appropriations for payments, with the exception of the monetary reserve;

    (b) calculation of the margin available under the own resources ceiling.

The Commission will make these technical adjustments on the basis of the most recent economic data and forecasts available. However, the technical adjustment of the ceiling for heading 1 of the financial perspective (agriculture) will be based on a deflator of 2% a year. The technical adjustment of the ceiling for the 'Structural Funds' subheading will be based on the overall deflator stipulated in the Structural Funds regulations for determining the programming of the corresponding operations. The index base against which the allocations for 2004 to 2006 are pegged will be reviewed by way of technical adjustment, if necessary, by the Commission before 31 December 2003 on the basis of the most recent information available. There will be no ex-post adjustment of the allocations for earlier years. The results of such adjustments and the underlying economic forecasts will be communicated to the two arms of the budgetary authority. No further technical adjustments will be made in respect of the year concerned, either during the year or as ex-post corrections during subsequent years.

Adjustments connected with implementation

    16.   When notifying the two arms of the budgetary authority of the technical adjustments to the financial perspective, the Commission will present any proposals for adjustments to the total appropriations for payments which it considers necessary, in the light of implementation, to ensure an orderly progression in relation to the appropriations for commitments.

    17.   For the adjustment exercise an 2001 and in the event of delays in the adoption of the programmes for structural operations, the two arms of the budgetary authority undertake to authorise, on a proposal from the Commission, the transfer to subsequent years, in excess of the corresponding ceilings on expenditure, of the allocations not used in 2000.

    18.   The European Parliament and the Council will take decisions on these proposals before 1 May of year n, in accordance with the voting rules laid down in the fifth sub-paragraph of Article 272(9) of the EC Treaty.

C   Revision of the financial perspective

    19.   In addition to the regular technical adjustments and adjustments in line with the conditions of implementation, the financial perspective may be revised in compliance with the own resources ceiling, on a proposal from the Commission, in the event of unforeseen circumstances.

    20.   As a general rule, any such proposal for revision must be presented and adopted before the start of the budgetary procedure for the year or the first of the years concerned. Any decision to revise the financial perspective by up to 0,03% of the Community GNP within the margin for unforeseen expenditure will be taken jointly by the two arms of the budgetary authority acting in accordance with the voting rules laid down in the fifth sub-paragraph of Article 272(9) of the EC Treaty. Any revision of the financial perspective above 0,03% of the Community GNP within the margin for unforeseen expenditure will be taken jointly by the two arms of the budgetary authority, with the Council acting unanimously.

    21.   Except for expenditure under heading 2, the institutions will examine the scope for reallocating expenditure between the programmes covered by the heading concerned by the revision, with particular reference to any expected under-utilisation of appropriations. The objective should be that a significant amount, in absolute terms and as a percentage of the new expenditure planned, should be within the existing ceiling for the heading. The instructions will also examine the scope for offsetting raising the ceiling for one heading by lowering the ceiling for another. Amounts available under headings 1 to 6 of the financial perspective (pre-accession assistance) and, conversely, expenditure reserved for pre-accession assistance

cannot be used for headings 1 to 6. Amounts available for accession can be used only in order to cover expenditure arising as a direct consequence of enlargement, and cannot cover unforeseen expenditure arising as a direct consequence of enlargement, and cannot cover unforeseen expenditure arising under headings 1 to 7 of the financial perspective. Conversely, expenditure earmarked for headings 1 to 7 cannot be used to supplement the cost of new accessions. Any revision of the compulsory expenditure in the financial perspective may not lead to a reduction in the amount available for non-compulsory expenditure. Any revision must maintain an appropriate relationship between commitments and payments.

D Consequences of the absence of a joint decision on the adjustment or revision of the financial perspective

22. In the absence of a joint decision by the European Parliament and the Council on any adjustment or revision of the financial perspective proposed by the Commission, the amounts set previously will, after the annual technical adjustment, continue to apply as the expenditure ceilings for the year in question.

E Reserves

23. The three reserves appearing in heading 6 of the financial perspective are entered in the general budget of the European Communities. The necessary resources will be called in only when these reserves are implemented:

(a) the monetary reserve is intended to cover, during the years 2000 to 2002, the impact on agricultural budget expenditure of significant and unforeseen movements in the Euro/United States dollar parity in relation to the parity used in the budget;

(b) the reserve for guaranteeing loans to non-member countries is intended to endow the budget headings which will be drawn on to constitute the Guarantee Fund[8] and for any additional payments to be made should a debtor default;

(c) the purpose of the emergency aid reserve is to provide a rapid response to the specific aid requirements of non-member countries following events which could not be foreseen when the budget was established, first and foremost for humanitarian operations. When the Commission considers that one of these reserves needs to be called on, it will present a proposal for a corresponding transfer to the two arms of the budgetary authority. Any Commission proposal to draw on the reserve for emergency aid must, however, be preceded by an examination of the scope for reallocating appropriations. At the same time as it presents its proposal for a transfer, the Commission will initiate a trialogue procedure, if necessary in a simplified form, to secure the agreement of the two arms of the budgetary authority on the need to use the reserve and on the amount required. If the Commission's proposal fails to secure the agreement of the two arms of the budgetary authority, and if the European Parliament and the Council are unable to agree on a common position, they will refrain from taking a decision on the Commission's proposal for a transfer.

F Flexibility instrument

24. The flexibility instrument with an annual ceiling of EUR200 million is intended to allow financing, for a given financial year and up to the amount indicated, of clearly identified expenditure which could not be financed within the limits of the ceilings available for one or more other headings. The portion of the annual amount which is not used may be carried over up to year n + 2. If the instrument is mobilised, any carryovers will be drawn on first, in order of age. The portion of the annual amount from year n which is not used in year n + 2 will lapse. The flexibility instrument should not, as a rule, be used to cover the same needs two

---

[8] Set up by Council Regulation (EC, Euratom) No. 2728/94 (OJ L293, 12.11.1994, p. 1).

years running. The Commission will make a proposal for the flexibility instrument to be used after it has examined all possibilities for re-allocating appropriations under the heading requiring additional expenditure. The proposal will concern the principle of making use of the instrument and will identify the needs to be covered and the amount required. It may be presented, for any given financial year, during the budgetary procedure. The Commission proposal will be included in the preliminary draft budget or accompanied, in accordance with the financial Regulation, by the appropriate budgetary instrument. The decision to deploy the flexibility instrument will be taken jointly by the two arms of the budgetary authority in accordance with the voting rules under the fifth sub-paragraph of Article 272(9) of the EC Treaty. Agreement will be reached by means of the conciliation procedure provided for in Part II, Section A and Annex III to this Agreement.

G   Adjustment of the financial perspective to cater for enlargement
25.   Where the Union is enlarged to include new Member States during the period covered by the financial perspective, the European Parliament and the Council, acting on a proposal from the Commission and in accordance with the voting rules under the fifth sub-paragraph of Article 272(9) of the EC Treaty, will jointly adjust the financial perspective to take account of the expenditure requirements resulting from this enlargement. Without prejudice to the outcome of the accession negotiations, the change in the headings concerned should not exceed the amounts shown in the indicative financial framework based on the assumption of an enlarged Union with six new Member States from 2002 and contained in Annex II, which forms an integral part of this Agreement. The additional requirements will be covered by the available amounts set aside for this purpose in the financial perspective and, if necessary, by using the additional own resources resulting from the increased Community GNP after enlargement of the Union.

H   Duration of the financial perspective and consequences of the absence of a financial perspective
26.   Before 1 July 2005, the Commission will present proposals for a new medium-term financial perspective. Should the two arms of the budgetary authority fail to agree on a new financial perspective, and unless the existing financial perspective is expressly denounced by one of the parties to this Agreement, the ceilings for the last year covered by the existing financial perspective will be adjusted in accordance with paragraph 15 by applying to these amounts the average rate of increase observed over the preceding period, excluding any adjustments made to take account of enlargement of the Union. This rate of increase may not, however, exceed the rate of growth of Community GNP for the year concerned.

PART II   IMPROVEMENT OF INTERINSTITUTIONAL COLLABORATION DURING THE BUDGETARY PROCEDURE

A   The Interinstitutional collaboration procedure
27.   The institutions agree to set up a procedure for Interinstitutional collaboration in budgetary matters. The details of this collaboration are set out in Annex III, which forms an integral part of this Agreement.

B   Establishment of the budget
28.   The Commission will present each year a preliminary draft budget showing the Community's actual financing requirements.
   It will take into account:
      — the capacity for utilising appropriations, endeavouring to maintain a strict relationship between appropriations for commitments and appropriations for payments,
      — the possibilities for starting up new policies through pilot projects and/or new

preparatory operations or continuing multiannual operations which are coming to an end, after assessing whether it will be possible to secure a basic act, within the meaning of paragraph 36,

— the need to ensure that any change in expenditure in relation to the previous year is in accordance with the constraints of budgetary discipline.

29.   The institutions will, as far as possible, avoid entering items in the budget carrying insignificant amounts of expenditure on operations. The two arms of the budgetary authority also undertake to bear in mind the assessment of the possibilities for implementing the budget made by the Commission in its preliminary drafts and in connection with implementation of the current budget.

C   Classification of expenditure

30.   the institutions consider compulsory expenditure to be such expenditure as the budgetary authority is obliged to enter in the budget by virtue of a legal undertaking entered into under the treaties or acts adopted by virtue of the said Treaties.

31.   The preliminary draft budget is to contain a proposal for the classification of each new budget item and each item with an amended legal base. If they do not accept the classification proposed in the preliminary draft budget, the European Parliament and the Council will examine classification of the budget item concerned on the basis of Annex IV, which forms an integral part of this Agreement. Agreement will be sought during the conciliation procedure provided for the Annex III.

D   Maximum rate of increase of non-compulsory expenditure in the absence of a financial perspective

32.   Without prejudice to the first sub-paragraph of paragraph 12, the institutions agree on the following provisions:

(a)   the European Parliament's autonomous margin for manoeuvre for the purposes of the fourth sub-paragraph of Article 272(9) of the EC Treaty—which is to be half the maximum rate—applies as from the draft budget established by the council at first reading, including any letters of amendment. The maximum rate is to be observed in respect of the annual budget, including any supplementary and/or amending budgets. Without prejudice to the setting of a new rate, any portion of the maximum rate which has not been utilised will remain available for use and may be used when draft supplementary and/or amending budgets are considered;

(b)   without prejudice to point (a), if it appears in the course of the budgetary procedure that completion of the procedure might require agreement on setting a new rate of increase for non-compulsory expenditure to apply to payment appropriations and/or a new rate to apply to commitment appropriations (the latter rate may be at a different level from the former), the institutions will endeavour to secure an agreement between the two arms of the budgetary authority by the conciliation procedure provided for in Annex III.

E   Incorporation of financial provisions in legislative acts

33.   Legislative acts concerning multiannual programmes adopted under the co-decision procedure contain a provision in which the legislative authority lays down the financial framework for the programme for its entire duration. That amount will constitute the prime reference for the budgetary authority during the annual budgetary procedure. The budgetary authority and the Commission, when drawing up its preliminary draft budget, undertake not to depart from this amount unless new, objective, long-term circumstances arise for which explicit and precise reasons are given, with account being taken of the results obtained from implementing the programme, in particular on the basis of assessments.

34.   Legislative instruments concerning multiannual programmes not subject to the co-decision procedure will not contain an 'amount deemed necessary'. Should the Council wish

to include a financial reference, this will be taken as illustrating the will of the legislative authority and will not affect the powers of the budgetary authority as defined by the Treaty. This provision will be mentioned in all instruments which include such a financial reference. If the amount concerned has been the subject of an agreement pursuant to the conciliation procedure provided for in the Joint Declaration of the European Parliament, Council and the Commission of 4 March 1975,[9] it will be considered a reference amount within the meaning of paragraph 33 of this Agreement.

35.   The financial statement provided for in Article 3 of the Financial Regulation will reflect in financial terms the objectives of the proposed programme and include a schedule covering the duration of the programme. It will be revised, where necessary, when the preliminary draft budget is drawn up, taking account of the extent of implementation of the programme. The revised statement will be forwarded to the budgetary authority when the preliminary draft budget is presented and after the budget is adopted.

F   Legal bases

36.   Under the system of the Treaty, implementation of appropriation entered in the budget for any Community action requires the prior adoption of a basic act. A 'basic act' is an act of secondary legislation which provides a legal basis for the Community action and for the implementation of the corresponding expenditure entered in the budget. Such an act must take the form of a Regulation, a Directive or a Decision (Entscheidung or Beschluß). Recommendations and opinions do not constitute basic acts, nor do resolutions or declarations.

37.   However, the following may be implemented without a basic act as long as the actions which they are intended to finance fall within the competence of the Community:

    (a) (i)   appropriations for pilot schemes of an experimental nature aimed at testing the feasibility of an action and its usefulness. The relevant commitment appropriations may be entered in the Budget for only two financial years. Their total amount may not exceed EUR 32 million;

        (ii)   appropriations relating to preparatory actions intended to prepare proposals with a view to the adoption of future Community actions. The preparatory actions are to follow a coherent approach and may take various forms. The relevant commitment appropriations may be entered in the budget for only three financial years at most. The legislative procedure should be concluded before the end of the third financial year. During the course of the legislative procedure, the commitment of appropriations must correspond to the particular features of the preparatory action as regards the activities envisaged, the aims pursued and the persons benefited. Consequently, the means implemented cannot correspond in volume to those envisaged for financing the definitive action itself. The total amount of the new headings concerned may not exceed EUR 30 million per financial year and the total amount of the appropriations actually committed in respect of the preparatory actions may not exceed EUR 75 million. When the preliminary draft budget is presented, the Commission will submit a report on the actions referred to in points (i) and (ii) which will also cover the objective of the action, an assessment of results and the follow-up envisaged;

    (b) appropriations concerning actions of a specific, or even indefinite, nature carried out by the Commission by virtue of tasks resulting from its prerogatives at institutional level, other than its right of legislative initiative as referred to in point (a), and specific powers directly conferred upon it by the EC Treaty. A list is contained in Annex V, which forms an integral part of this Agreement. The list may be supplemented, in the presentation of the preliminary draft budget, with an indication of the Articles in question and the amounts concerned;

[9] OJ C 89, 22.4.1975, p. 1.

(c) appropriations intended for the operation of each institution under its administrative autonomy.

G   Expenditure relating to fisheries agreements

38.   The institutions agree to finance expenditure on fisheries agreements in accordance with the arrangements set out in Annex VI, which forms an integral part of this Agreement.

H   Financing of the common foreign and security policy (CFSP)

39.   For the CFSP expenditure charged to the general budget of the European Communities in accordance with Article 28 of the Treaty on European Union, the institutions will endeavour, in the conciliation procedure provided for in Annex III and on the basis of the preliminary draft budget established by the Commission, to secure each year agreement on the amount of the operational expenditure to be charged to the Community budget and on the distribution of this amount between the articles of the CFSP budget chapter suggested in the fourth sub-paragraph of this paragraph. In the absence of agreement, it is understood that the European Parliament and the Council will enter in the budget the amount contained in the previous budget or the amount proposed in the preliminary draft budget, whichever is the lower. The total amount of operational CFSP expenditure will be entered entirely in one budget chapter (CFSP) and distributed between the articles of this chapter as suggested in the fourth sub-paragraph of this paragraph. This amount is to cover the real predictable needs and a reasonable margin for unforeseen actions. No funds will be entered in a reserve. Each article covers common strategies or joint actions already adopted, measures which are foreseen but not adopted and all future—i.e. unforeseen—action to be adopted by the Council during the financial year concerned. Since, under the Financial Regulation, the Commission has the authority, within the framework of a CFSP action, to transfer appropriations autonomously between articles within one budget chapter, i.e. the CFSP allocation, the flexibility deemed necessary for speedy implementation of CFSP actions will accordingly be assured. In the event of the amount of the CFSP budget during the financial year being insufficient to cover the necessary expenses, the European Parliament and the Council will seek a solution as a matter of urgency, on a proposal from the Commission. Within the CFSP budget chapter, the articles into which the CFSP actions are to be entered could read along the following lines:

— observation and organisation or elections/participation in democratic transition processes,
— Union envoys,
— prevention of conflicts/ peace and security processes,
— financial assistance to disarmament processes,
— contributions to international conferences,
— urgent actions.

The European Parliament, the Council and the Commission agree that the amount for actions entered under the article mentioned in the sixth indent may not exceed 20% of the overall amount of the CFSP budget chapter.

40.   Once a year, the Council Presidency will consult the European Parliament on a Council document setting out the main aspects and basic choices of the CFSP, including the financial implications for the general budget of the European Communities. Furthermore, the Presidency will regularly inform the European Parliament about the development and implementation of CFSP actions. Whenever it adopts a decision in the field of CFSP entailing expenditure, the Council will immediately and in each case send the European Parliament an estimate of the costs envisaged ('financial statement'), in particular those regarding timeframe, staff employed, use of premises and other infrastructure, transport facilities, training requirements and security arrangements. Once a quarter the Commission will inform the budgetary authority about the implementation of CFSP actions and the financial forecasts for the remaining period of the year.

Commitment appropriations	2000	2001	2002	2003	2004	2005	2006
1. AGRICULTURE	40,920	42,800	43,900	43,770	42,760	41,930	41,660
Common agricultural policy (not including rural development)	36,620	38,480	39,570	39,430	38,410	37,570	37,290
Rural development and accompanying measures	4,300	4,320	4,330	4,340	4,350	4,360	4,370
2. STRUCTURAL OPERATIONS	32,045	31,455	30,865	30,285	29,595	29,595	29,170
Structural funds	29,430	28,840	28,250	27,670	27,080	27,080	26,660
Cohesion Fund	2,615	2,615	2,615	2,615	2,515	2,515	2,510
3. INTERNAL POLICIES[1]	5,930	6,040	6,150	6,260	6,370	6,480	6,600
4. EXTERNAL ACTION	4,500	4,560	4,570	4,580	4,590	4,600	4,610
5. ADMINISTRATION[2]	4,560	4,600	4,700	4,800	4,900	5,000	5,100
6. RESERVES	900	900	650	400	400	400	4,900
Monetary reserve	500	500	250	0	0	0	0
Emergency aid reserve	200	200	200	200	200	200	200
Loan guarantee reserve	200	200	200	200	200	200	200
7. PRE-ACCESSION AID	3,120	3,120	3,120	3,120	3,120	3,120	3,120
Agriculture	520	520	520	520	520	520	520
Pre-accession structural instruments	1,040	1,040	1,040	1,040	1,040	1,040	1,040
PHARE (applicant countries)	1,560	1,560	1,560	1,560	1,560	1,560	1,560
TOTAL COMMITMENT APPROPRIATIONS	92,025	93,475	93,955	93,215	91,735	91,125	90,660

[1] In accordance with Article 2 of Decision No. 182/1999/EC of the European Parliament and of the Council and Council Decision 1999/64/Euratom (OJ L26, 1.2.1999, p. 1 and p. 34), the amount of expenditure available during the period 2000 to 2002 for research amounts to EUR 11,510 million at current prices.

[2] The experience on pensions included under the ceilings for this heading is calculated net of staff contributions to the relevant scheme, within the limity of EUR 1,100 million at 1999 prices for the period 2000 to 2006.

ANNEX I —continued (EUR million—1999 prices)

Commitment appropriations	2000	2001	2002	2003	2004	2005	2006
TOTAL PAYMENT APPROPRIATIONS	89,600	91,110	94,220	94,880	91,910	90,160	89,620
Payment appropriations as % of GNP	1,13%	1,12%	1,13%	1,11%	1,05%	1,00%	0,97%
AVAILABLE FOR ACCESSION (payment appopriations)							
Agriculture			4,140	6,710	8,890	11,440	14,220
Other expenditure			1,600	2,030	2,450	2,930	3,400
			2,540	4,680	6,440	8,510	10,820
CEILING ON PAYMENT APPROPRIATIONS	89,600	91,110	98,360	101,590	100,800	101,600	103,840
Ceiling on payment appropriations as % of GNP	1,13%	1,12%	1,18%	1,19%	1,15%	1,13%	1,13%
Margin for unforeseen expenditure	0,14%	0,15%	0,09%	0,08%	0,12%	0,14%	0,14%
Own resources ceiling	1,27%	1,27%	1,27%	1,27%	1,27%	1,27%	1,27%

ANNEX II FINANCIAL FRAMEWORK (EU-21)
(EUR million—1999 prices)

Commitment appropriations	2000	2001	2002	2003	2004	2005	2006
1. AGRICULTURE	40,920	42,800	43,900	43,770	42,760	41,930	41,660
Common agricultural policy (not including rural development)	36,620	38,480	39,570	39,430	38,410	37,570	37,290
Rural development and accompanying measures	4,300	4,320	4,330	4,340	4,350	4,360	4,370
2. STRUCTURAL OPERATIONS	32,045	31,455	30,865	30,285	29,595	29,595	29,170
Structural funds	29,430	28,840	28,250	27,670	27,080	27,080	26,660
Cohesion Fund	2,615	2,615	2,615	2,615	2,515	2,515	2,510
3. INTERNAL POLICIES[1]	5,930	6,040	6,150	6,260	6,370	6,480	6,600
4. EXTERNAL ACTION	4,500	4,560	4,570	4,580	4,590	4,600	4,610
5. ADMINISTRATION[2]	4,560	4,600	4,700	4,800	4,900	5,000	5,100
6. RESERVES	900	900	650	400	400	400	400
Monetary reserve	500	500	250	0	0	0	0
Emergency aid reserve	200	200	200	200	200	200	200
Loan guarantee reserve	200	200	200	200	200	200	200
7. PRE-ACCESSION AID	3,120	3,120	3,120	3,120	3,120	3,120	3,120
Agriculture	520	520	520	520	520	520	520
Pre-accession structural instruments	1,040	1,040	1,040	1,040	1,040	1,040	1,040
PHARE (applicant countries)	1,560	1,560	1,560	1,560	1,560	1,560	1,560

[1] In accordance with Article 2 of Decision No. 182/1999/EC of the European Parliament and of the Council and Council Decision 1999/64/Euratom (OJ L26, 1.2.1999, p. 1 and p. 34), the amount of expenditure available during the period 2000 to 2002 for research amounts to EUR 11,510 million at current prices.

[2] The expenditure on pensions included under the ceilings for this heading is calculated net of staff contributions to the relevant scheme, within the limity of EUR 1,100 million at 1999 prices for the period 2000 to 2006.

ANNEX II—continued (EUR million—1999 prices)

Commitment appropriations	2000	2001	2002	2003	2004	2005	2006
8. ENLARGEMENT			6,450	9,030	11,610	14,200	16,780
Agriculture			1,600	2,030	2,450	2,930	3,400
Structural operations			3,730	5,830	7,920	10,000	12,080
Internal policies			730	760	790	820	850
Administration			370	410	450	450	450
TOTAL COMMITMENT APPROPRIATIONS	92,025	93,475	100,405	102,245	103,345	105,325	107,440
TOTAL PAYMENT APPROPRIATIONS	89,600	91,110	98,360	101,590	100,800	101,600	103,840
Of which: enlargement			*4,140*	*6,710*	*8,890*	*11,440*	*14,220*
Payment appropriations as % of GNP	1,13%	1,12%	1,14%	1,15%	1,11%	1,09%	0,09%
Margin for unforeseen expenditure	0,14%	0,15%	0,09%	0,08%	0,12%	0,14%	0,14%
Own resources ceiling	1,27%	1,27%	1,27%	1,27%	1,27%	1,27%	1,27%

ANNEX III   INTERINSTITUTIONAL COLLABORATION IN THE BUDGETARY SECTOR

A. After the technical adjustment of the financial perspective for the forthcoming financial year and prior to the Commission's decision on the preliminary draft budget, a meeting of the trialogue will be convened to discuss the possible priorities for the budget of that year, with due account being taken of the institutions' powers.

B. 1. A conciliation procedure is set up for all expenditure.

2. As regards compulsory expenditure, the Commission, in presenting its preliminary draft budget, will identify:

(a) appropriations connected with new or planned legislation;

(b) appropriations arising from the application of legislation existing when the previous budget was adopted. The Commission will make a careful estimate of the financial implications of the Community's obligations based on the rules. If necessary it will update its estimates in the course of the budgetary procedure. It will supply the budgetary authority with all the duly justified reasons it may require. If it considers it necessary, the Commission may present to the budgetary authority an ad hoc letter of amendment to update the figures underlying the estimate of agricultural expenditure in the preliminary draft budget and/or to correct, on the basis of the most recent information available concerning fisheries agreements in force on 1 January of the financial year concerned, the breakdown between the appropriations entered in the operational items for international fisheries agreements and those entered in reserve. This letter of amendment must be sent to the budgetary authority before the end of October. If it is presented to the Council less than a month before the European Parliament's first reading, the Council will as a rule consider the ad hoc letter of amendment when giving the draft budget its second reading. As a consequence, before the Council's second reading of the budget, the two arms of the budgetary authority will try to meet the conditions necessary for the letter of amendment to be adopted on a single reading by each of the institutions concerned.

3. The purpose of the conciliation procedure is to:

(a) continue discussions on the general trend of expenditure and, in this framework, on the broad lines of the budget for the coming year in the light of the Commission's preliminary draft budget;

(b) secure agreement between the two arms of the budgetary authority on:

— the appropriations referred to in point 2(a) and (b), including those proposed in the ad hoc letter of amendment referred to at point 2,

— the amounts to be entered in the budget for non-compulsory expenditure, in accordance with the third sub-paragraph of paragraph 12 of this Agreement,

— and, particularly, matters for which reference to this procedure is made in this Agreement.

4. The procedure will begin with a trialogue meeting convened in time to allow the institutions to seek an agreement by no later than the date set by the Council for establishing its draft budget. There will be conciliation on the results of this trialogue between the Council and a European Parliament delegation, with the Commission also taking part. Unless decided otherwise during the trialogue, the conciliation meeting will be held at the traditional meeting between the same participants on the date set by the Council for establishing the draft budget.

5. A new trialogue meeting will be held before the European Parliament's first reading to enable the institutions to identify the programmes on which the conciliation is to focus so as to reach an agreement on their allocations. At that meeting the institutions will also exchange views on the state of implementation of the current budget with a view to discussing the omnibus transfer or a possible supplementary and amending budget.

6.   The institutions will continue the conciliation after the first reading of the budget by each of the two arms of the budgetary authority in order to secure agreement on compulsory and non-compulsory expenditure and, in particular, to discuss the ad hoc letter of amendment referred to in point 2. A trialogue meeting will be held for this purpose after the European Parliament's first reading. The results of the trialogue will be discussed at a second conciliation meeting to be held the day before the Council's second reading. If necessary, the institutions will continue their discussions on non-compulsory expenditure after the Council's second reading.

7.   At these trialogue meetings, the institutions' delegations will be led by the President of the Council (Budgets), the Chairman of the European Parliament's Committee on Budgets and the Member of the Commission with responsibility for the budget.

8.   Each arm of the budgetary authority will take whatever steps are required to ensure that the results which may be secured in the conciliation process are respected throughout the current budgetary procedure.

ANNEX IV   CLASSIFICATION OF EXPENDITURE[1]

Heading 1 —Expenditure of the common agricultural policy and expenditure on animal and plant health —Rural development and accompanying measures	Compulsory Non-compulsory
Heading 2	Non-compulsory
Heading 3	Non-compulsory
Heading 4 —Expenditure resulting from international agreements which the European Union or Community has concluded with third parties, including fisheries agreements —Contributions to international organisations or institutions —Other items covered by heading 4 of the financial perspective	Compulsory Compulsory Non-compulsory
Heading 5 —Alowances and miscellaneous contributions on termination of service —Pensions and serverance grants —Legal expenses —Damages —Compensation —Other items covered by heading 5 of the financial perspective	Compulsory Compulsory Compulsory Compulsory Compulsory Non-compulsory
Heading 6 —Monetary reserve —Loan guarantee reserve —Emergency aid reserve	Compulsory Compulsory Non-compulsory
Heading 7 —Agriculture (rural development measures and accompanying measures) —Pre-accession structural instrument —PHARE (applicant countries)	Non-compulsory Non-compulsory Non-compulsory

[1] Compulsory expenditure.
  Non-compulsory expenditure.

ANNEX V

List of Articles of the EC and EAEC Treaties which directly confer powers on the Commission which are specific and likely to have financial implications in Part B (operating appropriations) of Section III—Commission—of the budget

I   EC TREATY

Article 138	Social dialogue
Article 140	Studies, opinions, consultations on social matters
Articles 143 and 145	Special reports in the social field
Article 152(2)	Initiatives to promote coordination with regard to health protection
Article 155(2)	Initiative to promote coordination with regard to trans-European networks
Article 157(2)	Initiatives to promote industrial coordination
Article 159, second paragraph	Report on progress made towards achieving economic and social cohesion
Article 165(2)	Initiatives to promote coordination with regard to technological research and development
Article 173	Report on technological research and development
Article 180(2)	Initiatives to promote the coordination of development cooperation policies

II   EURATOM TREATY

Chapter 6, Section 5 Article 70	Supply policy Financial support, within the limits set by the budget, to prospecting programmes in the territories of Member States
Chapter 7, Articles 77 *et seq*	Safeguards

ANNEX VI   FINANCING OF EXPENDITURE DERIVING FROM FISHERIES AGREEMENTS

A.   Expenditure relating to fisheries agreements is financed by two items (by reference to the 1998 budget nomenclature):
   (a) international fisheries agreements (B7–8000);
   (b) contributions to international organisations (B7–8001).
All the amounts relating to agreements and protocols which will be in force on 1 January of the year in question will be entered under heading B7–8000. Amounts relating to all new or renewable agreements which will come into force after 1 January of the year in question will be assigned to heading B7–8000 but entered in the reserve B0–40.

B.   In the conciliation procedure provided for in Annex III, the European Parliament and the Council will seek to agree on the amount to be entered in the budget headings and in the reserve on the basis of the proposal made by the Commission.

C.   The Commission undertakes to keep the European Parliament regularly informed about the preparation and conduct of the negotiations, including the budgetary implications. In the course of the legislative process relating to fisheries agreements, the institutions undertake to make every effort to ensure that all procedures are carried out as quickly as possible. If appropriations relating to fisheries agreements (including the reserve) prove insufficient, the Commission will provide the budgetary authority with the necessary information for an exchange of views in the form of a trialogue, possibly simplified, on the causes of the situation, and on the measures which might be adopted under established procedures. Where necessary, the commission will propose appropriate measures.

Each quarter the commission will present to the budgetary authority detailed information about the implementation of agreements in force and financial forecasts for the remainder of the year.

DECLARATIONS

Declaration on the adjustment of Structural Fund allocations in the light of the circumstances of their implementation
The institutions agree that, in the event of any significant delay in the adoption of the new rules governing the Structural Funds, the possibility of re-entering appropriations in the budget could be extended to those not used in the first two years of the financial perspective.

Declaration on the conciliation procedure applicable to legislative acts with significant financial implications
The institutions confirm that the Joint Declaration of the European Parliament, the Council and the Commission of 4 March 1975 concerning the institution of a conciliation procedure remains fully applicable.

Declaration on the principles and mechanism of the agricultural guideline
In accordance with the decision on budgetary discipline, the institutions confirm the principles and mechanisms of the agricultural guideline.

Declaration on the URBAN initiative
In view of the reduction in the amount provided for innovatory measures, relating to the URBAN initiative, the institutions agree that they will examine the possibility of allocating up to EUR 200 million for this purpose, by mobilising the flexibility instrument during the period 2000 to 2006.

Declaration of the European Parliament and the Council on the Balkan situation
In view of developments in the Balkan situation, particularly in Kosovo, the two arms of the budgetary authority request the Commission, when needs have been ascertained and estimated, to submit the necessary budget proposals, including, if appropriate, a proposal for revision of the financial perspective.

Commission Declaration on paragraph 6 of the Agreement
In the case of paragraph 6 of the Agreement, the Commission states that it will take account of any request by one of the two arms of the budgetary authority when examining the need to present the report referred to in that paragraph.

Commission Declaration on paragraph 37(a)(ii) of the Agreement
The Commission declares that it reserves the right to propose that the ceiling of EUR 30 million be exceeded in the event of exceptional external circumstances.

Declaration by the European Parliament on Annex VI to the Agreement
The European Parliament considers that, as far as possible, fisheries agreements will leave six months between the initialling of the agreement and payment of the first financial compensation so as to allow the European Parliament time to deliver its opinion.

Council Declaration on point 6 of Annex III
The Council states that the conciliation meeting with Parliament need not automatically and in every case be held the day before the Council meeting but that there may be objective grounds for holding the conciliation meeting on the morning of the Council meeting.

Council Decision 2000/597 of 29 September 2000 on the system of the European Communities' own resources
[OJ 2000, L253/42]

THE COUNCIL OF THE EUROPEAN UNION,
    Having regard to the Treaty establishing the European Community, and in particular Article 269 thereof,
    Having regard to the Treaty establishing the European Atomic Energy Community, and in particular Article 173 thereof,
    Having regard to the proposal from the Commission,[1]
    Having regard to the opinion of the European Parliament,[2]
    Having regard to the opinion of the Court of Auditors,[3]
    Having regard to the opinion of the Economic and Social Committee,[4]
    Whereas:
    (1) The European Council meeting in Berlin on 24 and 25 March 1999 concluded, inter alia, that the system of the Communities' own resources should be equitable, transparent, cost-effective, simple and based on criteria which best express each Member State's ability to contribute.
    (2) The Communities' own resources system must ensure adequate resources for the orderly development of the Communities' policies, subject to the need for strict budgetary discipline.
    (3) It is appropriate that the best quality data be used for the purposes of the budget of the European Union and the Communities' own resources. The application of the European system of integrated economic accounts (hereinafter referred to as the 'ESA 95') in accordance with Council Regulation (EC) No 2223/96[5] will improve the quality of measurement of national accounts data.
    (4) It is appropriate to use the most recent statistical concepts for the purposes of own resources and accordingly to define gross national product (GNP) as being equal for these purposes to gross national income (GNI) as provided by the Commission in application of the ESA 95 in accordance with Regulation (EC) No 2223/96.
    (5) It is, moreover, appropriate, should modifications to the ESA 95 result in significant changes in GNI as provided by the Commission in accordance with Regulation (EC) No 2223/96, that the Council decide whether these modifications apply for the purposes of own resources.

[1] OJ C 274 E, 28.9.1999, p. 39.
[2] Opinion delivered on 17 November 1999 (OJ C 189, 7.7.2000, p. 79).
[3] OJ C 310, 28.10.1999, p. 1.
[4] OJ C 368, 20.12.1999, p. 16.
[5] OJ L 310, 30.11.1996, p. 1. Regulation as amended by Regulation (EC) No 448/98 (OJ L 58, 27.2.1998).

(6) According to Council Decision 94/728/EC, Euratom of 31 October 1994 on the system of the European Communities' own resources,[6] the maximum ceiling of own resources for 1999 was set equal to 1,27% of the Communities' GNP at market prices and an overall ceiling of 1,335% of the Communities' GNP was set for appropriations for commitments.

(7) It is appropriate to adapt these ceilings expressed as a percent of GNP in order to maintain unchanged the amount of financial resources put at the disposal of the Communities by establishing a formula for the determination of the new ceilings, in relation to GNP as defined for the present purposes, to be applied after the entry into force of this Decision.

(8) It is appropriate that the same method be used in the future on the occasion of changes in the ESA 95 which may have effects on the level of GNP.

(9) In order further to continue the process of making allowance for each Member State's ability to contribute to the system of own resources and of correcting the regressive aspects of the current system for the least prosperous Member States, the European Council meeting in Berlin of 24 and 25 March 1999 concluded that the Union's financing rules would be amended as follows:

— the maximum rate of call of the VAT resource would be reduced from 1% to 0,75% in 2002 and 2003 and to 0,50% from 2004 onwards,

— the value added tax base of the Member States would continue to be restricted to 50% of their GNP.

(10) The European Council of 24 and 25 March 1999 concluded that it is appropriate to adapt the amount retained by Member States to cover the costs related to collection in connection with the so-called traditional own resources paid to the budget of the European Union.

(11) Budgetary imbalances should be corrected in such a way as not to affect the own resources available for the Communities' policies and be resolved, to the extent possible, by means of expenditure policy.

(12) The European Council of 24 and 25 March 1999 concluded that the manner for calculating the correction of budgetary imbalances in favour of the United Kingdom as defined in Decision 88/376/EEC, Euratom[7] and confirmed by Decision 94/728/EC, Euratom, should not include the windfall gains resulting from changes in the financing systems and from future enlargement. Accordingly, at the time of enlargement, an adjustment will reduce 'total Allocated Expenditure' by an amount equivalent to the annual pre-accession expenditure in the acceding countries, thereby ensuring that expenditure which is unabated remains so.

(13) For reasons of clarity, the description of the calculation of the correction in respect of budgetary imbalances granted to the United Kingdom has been simplified. This simplification has no impact on the determination of the amount of this correction granted to the United Kingdom.

(14) The European Council of 24 and 25 March 1999 concluded that the financing of the correction of budgetary imbalances in favour of the United Kingdom should be modified to allow Austria, Germany, the Netherlands and Sweden to see a reduction in their financing share to 25% of the normal share.

(15) The monetary reserve, hereinafter referred to as 'the EAGGF monetary reserve', the reserve for the financing of the Loan Guarantee Fund and the reserve for emergency aid in non-member countries are covered by specific provisions.

(16) The Commission should undertake, before 1 January 2006, a general review of the operation of the own resources system, accompanied, if necessary, by appropriate proposals, in the light of all relevant factors including the effects of enlargement on the financing of the budget of the European Union, the possibility of modifying the own resources structure by

---

[6] OJ L 293, 12.11.1994, p. 9.
[7] OJ L 185, 15.7.1988, p. 24.

creating new autonomous own resources and the correction of budgetary imbalances granted to the United Kingdom as well as the granting to Austria, Germany, the Netherlands and Sweden of the reduction in the financing of the budgetary imbalances in favour of the United Kingdom.

(17) Provisions must be laid down to cover the changeover from the system introduced by Decision 94/728/EC, Euratom to that arising from this Decision.

(18) The European Council of 24 and 25 March 1999 concluded that this Decision should take effect on 1 January 2002,

HAS LAID DOWN THESE PROVISIONS, WHICH IT RECOMMENDS TO THE MEMBER STATES FOR ADOPTION:

Article 1

The Communities shall be allocated own resources in accordance with the rules laid down in the following Articles in order to ensure, in accordance with Article 269 of the Treaty establishing the European Community (hereinafter referred to as the 'EC Treaty') and Article 173 of the Treaty establishing the European Atomic Energy Community (hereinafter referred to as the 'Euratom Treaty'), the financing of the budget of the European Union.

The budget of the European Union shall, without prejudice to other revenue, be financed wholly from the Communities' own resources.

Article 2

1.   Revenue from the following shall constitute own resources entered in the budget of the European Union:

(a) levies, premiums, additional or compensatory amounts, additional amounts or factors and other duties established or to be established by the institutions of the Communities in respect of trade with non-member countries within the framework of the common agricultural policy, and also contributions and other duties provided for within the framework of the common organisation of the markets in sugar;

(b) Common Customs Tariff duties and other duties established or to be established by the institutions of the Communities in respect of trade with non-member countries and customs duties on products coming under the Treaty establishing the European Coal and Steel Community;

(c) the application of a uniform rate valid for all Member States to the harmonised VAT assessment bases determined according to Community rules. The assessment base to be taken into account for this purpose shall not exceed 50% of GNP for each Member State, as defined in paragraph 7;

(d) the application of a rate—to be determined pursuant to the budgetary procedure in the light of the total of all other revenue—to the sum of all the Member States' GNPs.

2.   Revenue deriving from any new charges introduced within the framework of a common policy, in accordance with the EC Treaty or the Euratom Treaty, provided that the procedure laid down in Article 269 of the EC Treaty or in Article 173 of the Euratom Treaty has been followed, shall also constitute own resources entered in the budget of the European Union.

3.   Member States shall retain, by way of collection costs, 25% of the amounts referred to in paragraph 1(a) and (b), which shall be established after 31 December 2000.

4.   The uniform rate referred to in paragraph 1(c) shall correspond to the rate resulting from the difference between:

(a) the maximum rate of call of the VAT resource, which is fixed at:
0,75% in 2002 and 2003,

0,50% from 2004 onwards,
and
(b) a rate ('frozen rate') equivalent to the ratio between the amount of the compensation referred to in Article 4 and the sum of the VAT assessment bases (established in accordance with paragraph (1)(c)) of all Member States, taking into account the fact that the United Kingdom is excluded from the financing of its correction and that the share of Austria, Germany, the Netherlands and Sweden in the financing of the United Kingdom correction is reduced to one fourth of its normal value.

5. The rate fixed under paragraph 1(d) shall apply to the GNP of each Member State.

6. If, at the beginning of the financial year, the budget has not been adopted, the previous uniform VAT rate and rate applicable to Member States' GNPs, without prejudice to the provisions adopted in accordance with Article 8(2) as regards the EAGGF monetary reserve, the reserve for financing the Loan Guarantee Fund and the reserve for emergency aid in third countries, shall remain applicable until the entry into force of the new rates.

7. For the purposes of applying this Decision, GNP shall mean GNI for the year at market prices as provided by the Commission in application of the ESA 95 in accordance with Regulation (EC) No. 2223/96.

Should modifications to the ESA 95 result in significant changes in the GNI as provided by the Commission, the Council, acting unanimously on a proposal of the Commission and after consulting the European Parliament, shall decide whether these modifications shall apply for the purposes of this Decision.

Article 3

1. The total amount of own resources assigned to the Communities to cover appropriations for payments may not exceed a certain percentage of the total GNPs of the Member States. This percentage, expressed in two decimal places, will be calculated by the Commission in December 2001 on the basis of the following formula:

Maximum own resources = 1,27% × 1998 + 1999 + 2000 GNP ESA second edition/1998 + 1999 + 2000 GNP ESA 95

2. Appropriations for commitments entered in the general budget of the European Union must follow an orderly progression resulting in a total amount, which does not exceed a certain percentage of the total GNPs of the Member States. This percentage, expressed in two decimal places, shall be calculated by the Commission in December 2001 on the basis of the following formula:

Maximum appropriations for commitments = 1,335% × 1998 + 1999 + 2000 GNP ESA second edition/1998 + 1999 + 2000 GNP ESA 95

An orderly ratio between appropriations for commitments and appropriations for payments shall be maintained to guarantee their compatibility and to enable the ceilings pursuant to paragraph 1 to be respected in subsequent years.

3. The Commission shall communicate to the budgetary authority the new ceilings for own resources before 31 December 2001.

4. The method described in paragraphs 1 and 2 will be followed in the case of modifications to the ESA 95 which result in changes in the level of GNP.

Article 4

The United Kingdom shall be granted a correction in respect of budgetary imbalances. This correction shall be established by:
(a) calculating the difference, in the preceding financial year, between:
   — the percentage share of the United Kingdom in the sum of uncapped VAT assessment bases, and
   — the percentage share of the United Kingdom in total allocated expenditure;

(b) multiplying the difference thus obtained by total allocated expenditure;

(c) multiplying the result under (b) by 0,66;

(d) subtracting from the result under (c) the effects arising for the United Kingdom from the changeover to capped VAT and the payments referred to in Article 2(1)(d), namely the difference between:

— what the United Kingdom would have had to pay for the amounts financed by the resources referred to in Article 2(1)(c) and (d), if the uniform rate had been applied to non-capped VAT bases, and

— the payments of the United Kingdom pursuant to Article 2(1)(c) and (d);

(e) from the year 2001 onwards, subtracting from the result under (d) the net gains of the United Kingdom resulting from the increase in the percentage of resources referred to in Article 2(1)(a) and (b) retained by Member States to cover collection and related costs;

(f) calculating, at the time of each enlargement of the European Union, an adjustment to the result under (e) so as to reduce the compensation, thereby ensuring that expenditure which is unabated before enlargement remains so after enlargement. This adjustment shall be made by reducing total allocated expenditure by an amount equivalent to the annual pre-accession expenditure in the acceding countries. All amounts so calculated shall be carried forward to subsequent years and shall be adjusted annually by applying the euro GNP deflator used for the adaptation of the Financial Perspective.

Article 5

1. The cost of the correction shall be borne by the other Member States in accordance with the following arrangements:

The distribution of the cost shall first be calculated by reference to each Member State's share of the payments referred to in Article 2(1)(d), the United Kingdom being excluded; it shall then be adjusted in such a way as to restrict the financing share of Austria, Germany, the Netherlands and Sweden to one fourth of their normal share resulting from this calculation.

2. The correction shall be granted to the United Kingdom by a reduction in its payments resulting from the application of Article 2(1)(c) and (d). The costs borne by the other Member States shall be added to their payments resulting from the application for each Member State of Article 2(1)(c) and (d).

3. The Commission shall perform the calculations required for the application of Article 4 and this Article.

4. If, at the beginning of the financial year, the budget has not been adopted, the correction granted to the United Kingdom and the costs borne by the other Member States as entered in the last budget finally adopted shall remain applicable.

Article 6

The revenue referred to in Article 2 shall be used without distinction to finance, all expenditure entered in the budget. The revenue needed to cover in full or in part the EAGGF monetary reserve, the reserve for the financing of the Loan Guarantee Fund and the reserve for emergency aid in third countries, entered in the budget shall not be called up from the Member States until the reserves are implemented. Provisions for the operation of those reserves shall be adopted as necessary in accordance with Article 8(2).

Article 7

Any surplus of the Communities' revenue over total actual expenditure during a financial year shall be carried over to the following financial year.

Any surpluses generated by a transfer from EAGGF Guarantee Section chapters, or surplus from the Guarantee Fund arising from external measures, transferred to the revenue account in the budget, shall be regarded as constituting own resources.

Article 8

1. The Communities' own resources referred to in Article 2(1)(a) and (b) shall be collected by the Member States in accordance with the national provisions imposed by law, regulation or administrative action, which shall, where appropriate, be adapted to meet the requirements of Community rules.

The Commission shall examine at regular intervals the national provisions communicated to it by the Member States, transmit to the Member States the adjustments it deems necessary in order to ensure that they comply with Community rules and report to the budget authority.

Member States shall make the resources provided for in Article 2(1)(a) to (d) available to the Commission.

2. Without prejudice to the auditing of the accounts and to checks that they are lawful and regular as laid down in Article 248 of the EC Treaty and Article 160C of the Euratom Treaty, such auditing and checks being mainly concerned with the reliability and effectiveness of national systems and procedures for determining the base for own resources accruing from VAT and GNP and without prejudice to the inspection arrangements made pursuant to Article 279(c) of the EC Treaty and Article 183 point (c) of the Euratom Treaty, the Council shall, acting unanimously on a proposal from the Commission and after consulting the European Parliament, adopt the provisions necessary to apply this Decision and to make possible the inspection of the collection, the making available to the Commission and payment of the revenue referred to in Articles 2 and 5.

Article 9

The Commission shall undertake, before 1 January 2006, a general review of the own resources system, accompanied, if necessary, by appropriate proposals, in the light of all relevant factors, including the effects of enlargement on the financing of the budget, the possibility of modifying the structure of the own resources by creating new autonomous own resources and the correction of budgetary imbalances granted to the United Kingdom as well as the granting to Austria, Germany, the Netherlands and Sweden of the reduction pursuant to Article 5(1).

Article 10

1. Member States shall be notified of this Decision by the Secretary-General of the Council and the Decision shall be published in the Official Journal of the European Communities. Member States shall notify the Secretary-General of the Council without delay of the completion of the procedures for the adoption of this Decision in accordance with their respective constitutional requirements.

This Decision shall enter into force on the first day of the month following receipt of the last of the notifications referred to in the second sub-paragraph. It shall take effect on 1 January 2002 except for Article 2(3) and Article 4, which shall take effect on 1 January 2001.

2. (a) Subject to (b), Decision 94/728/EC, Euratom shall be repealed as of 1 January 2002. Any references to the Council Decision of 21 April 1970 on the replacement of financial contributions from Member States by the Communities' own resources,[8] to Council Decision 85/257/EEC, Euratom of 7 May 1985 on the Communities' system of own resources,[9] to Decision 88/376/EEC, Euratom, or to Decision 94/728/EC, Euratom shall be construed as references to this Decision.

(b) Articles 2, 4 and 5 of Decisions 88/376/EEC, Euratom and 94/728/EC, Euratom shall continue to apply to the calculation and adjustment of revenue accruing from the application of a uniform rate valid for all Member States to the VAT base determined in a uniform manner and limited between 50% to 55% of the GNP of

[8] OJ L 94, 28.4.1970, p. 19.
[9] OJ L 128, 14.5.1985, p. 15. Decision repealed by Decision 88/376/EEC, Euratom.

each Member State, depending on the relevant year, and to the calculation of the correction of budgetary imbalances granted to the United Kingdom for the years 1988 to 2000.

(c) For amounts referred to in Article 2(1)(a) and (b) which should have been made available by the Member States before 28 February 2001 in accordance with the applicable Community rules,

Member States shall continue to retain 10% of these amounts by way of collection costs.

Done at Brussels, 29 September 2000.

For the Council
The President
L. FABIUS

Council Decision 1999/468 of 28 June 1999 laying down the procedures for the exercise of implementing powers conferred on the Commission[1]

[OJ 1999, L184/23]

THE COUNCIL OF THE EUROPEAN UNION,

Having regard to the Treaty establishing the European Community, and in particular the third indent of Article 202 thereof,

Having regard to the proposal from the Commission,[2]

Having regard to the opinion of the European Parliament,[3]

Whereas:

(1) in the instruments which it adopts, the Council has to confer on the Commission powers for the implementation of the rules which the Council lays down; the Council may impose certain requirements in respect of the exercise of these powers; it may also reserve to itself the right, in specific and substantiated cases, to exercise directly implementing powers;

(2) the Council adopted Decision 87/373/EEC of 13 July 1987 laying down the procedures for the exercise of implementing powers conferred on the Commission;[4] that Decision has provided for a limited number of procedures for the exercise of such powers;

(3) declaration No 31 annexed to the Final Act of the Intergovernmental Conference which adopted the Amsterdam Treaty calls on the Commission to submit to the Council a proposal amending Decision 87/373/EEC;

(4) for reasons of clarity, rather than amending Decision 87/373/EEC, it has been considered more appropriate to replace that Decision by a new Decision and, therefore, to repeal Decision 87/373/EEC;

(5) the first purpose of this Decision is, with a view to achieving greater consistency and predictability in the choice of type of committee, to provide for criteria relating to the choice of committee procedures, it being understood that such criteria are of a non-binding nature;

---

[1] Three statements in the Council minutes relating to this Decision are set out in OJ C 203 of 17 June, p. 1.

[2] OJ C 279, 8.9.1998, p. 5.

[3] Opinion delivered on 6 May 1999 (not yet published in the Official Journal).

[4] OJ L 197, 18.7.1987, p. 33.

(6) in this regard, the management procedure should be followed as regards management measures such as those relating to the application of the common agricultural and common fisheries policies or to the implementation of programmes with substantial budgetary implications; such management measures should be taken by the Commission by a procedure ensuring decision-making within suitable periods; however, where non-urgent measures are referred to the Council, the Commission should exercise its discretion to defer application of the measures;

(7) the regulatory procedure should be followed as regards measures of general scope designed to apply essential provisions of basic instruments, including measures concerning the protection of the health or safety of humans, animals or plants, as well as measures designed to adapt or update certain non-essential provisions of a basic instrument; such implementing measures should be adopted by an effective procedure which complies in full with the Commission's right of initiative in legislative matters;

(8) the advisory procedure should be followed in any case in which it is considered to be the most appropriate; the advisory procedure will continue to be used in those cases where it currently applies;

(9) the second purpose of this Decision is to simplify the requirements for the exercise of implementing powers conferred on the Commission as well as to improve the involvement of the European Parliament in those cases where the basic instrument conferring implementation powers on the Commission was adopted in accordance with the procedure laid down in Article 251 of the Treaty; it has been accordingly considered appropriate to reduce the number of procedures as well as to adjust them in line with the respective powers of the institutions involved and notably to give the European Parliament an opportunity to have its views taken into consideration by, respectively, the Commission or the Council in cases where it considers that, respectively, a draft measure submitted to a committee or a proposal submitted to the Council under the regulatory procedure exceeds the implementing powers provided for in the basic instrument;

(10) the third purpose of this Decision is to improve information to the European Parliament by providing that the Commission should inform it on a regular basis of committee proceedings, that the Commission should transmit to it documents related to activities of committees and inform it whenever the Commission transmits to the Council measures or proposals for measures to be taken;

(11) the fourth purpose of this Decision is to improve information to the public concerning committee procedures and therefore to make applicable to committees the principles and conditions on public access to documents applicable to the Commission, to provide for a list of all committees which assist the Commission in the exercise of implementing powers and for an annual report on the working of committees to be published as well as to provide for all references to documents related to committees which have been transmitted to the European Parliament to be made public in a register;

(12) the specific committee procedures created for the implementation of the common commercial policy and the competition rules laid down by the Treaties that are not currently based upon Decision 87/373/EEC are not in any way affected by this Decision,
HAS DECIDED AS FOLLOWS:

Article 1
Other than in specific and substantiated cases where the basic instrument reserves to the Council the right to exercise directly certain implementing powers itself, such powers shall be conferred on the Commission in accordance with the relevant provisions in the basic instrument. These provisions shall stipulate the essential elements of the powers thus conferred.

Where the basic instrument imposes specific procedural requirements for the adoption of implementing measures, such requirements shall be in conformity with the procedures provided for by Articles 3, 4, 5 and 6.

Article 2

The choice of procedural methods for the adoption of implementing measures shall be guided by the following criteria:

(a) management measures, such as those relating to the application of the common agricultural and common fisheries policies, or to the implementation of programmes with substantial budgetary implications, should be adopted by use of the management procedure;

(b) measures of general scope designed to apply essential provisions of basic instruments, including measures concerning the protection of the health or safety of humans, animals or plants, should be adopted by use of the regulatory procedure; where a basic instrument stipulates that certain non-essential provisions of the instrument may be adapted or updated by way of implementing procedures, such measures should be adopted by use of the regulatory procedure;

(c) without prejudice to points (a) and (b), the advisory procedure shall be used in any case in which it is considered to be the most appropriate.

Article 3   Advisory procedure

1. The Commission shall be assisted by an advisory committee composed of the representatives of the Member States and chaired by the representative of the Commission.

2. The representative of the Commission shall submit to the Committee a draft of the measures to be taken. The committee shall deliver its opinion on the draft, within a time-limit which the chairman may lay down according to the urgency of the matter, if necessary by taking a vote.

3. The opinion shall be recorded in the minutes; in addition, each Member State shall have the right to ask to have its position recorded in the minutes.

4. The Commission shall take the utmost account of the opinion delivered by the committee. It shall inform the committee of the manner in which the opinion has been taken into account.

Article 4   Management procedure

1. The Commission shall be assisted by a management committee composed of the representatives of the Member States and chaired by the representative of the Commission.

2. The representative of the Commission shall submit to the committee a draft of the measures to be taken. The committee shall deliver its opinion on the draft within a time-limit which the chairman may lay down according to the urgency of the matter. The opinion shall be delivered by the majority laid down in Article 205(2) of the Treaty, in the case of decisions which the Council is required to adopt on a proposal from the Commission. The votes of the representatives of the Member States within the committee shall be weighted in the manner set out in that Article. The chairman shall not vote.

3. The Commission shall, without prejudice to Article 8, adopt measures which shall apply immediately. However, if these measures are not in accordance with the opinion of the committee, they shall be communicated by the Commission to the Council forthwith. In that event, the Commission may defer application of the measures which it has decided on for a period to be laid down in each basic instrument but which shall in no case exceed three months from the date of such communication.

4. The Council, acting by qualified majority, may take a different decision within the period provided for by paragraph 3.

Article 5   Regulatory procedure

1. The Commission shall be assisted by a regulatory committee composed of the representatives of the Member States and chaired by the representative of the Commission.

2. The representative of the Commission shall submit to the committee a draft of the measures to be taken. The committee shall deliver its opinion on the draft within a time-limit

which the chairman may lay down according to the urgency of the matter. The opinion shall be delivered by the majority laid down in Article 205(2) of the Treaty in the case of decisions which the Council is required to adopt on a proposal from the Commission. The votes of the representatives of the Member States within the Committee shall be weighted in the manner set out in that Article. The chairman shall not vote.

3.   The Commission shall, without prejudice to Article 8, adopt the measures envisaged if they are in accordance with the opinion of the committee.

4.   If the measures envisaged are not in accordance with the opinion of the committee, or if no opinion is delivered, the Commission shall, without delay, submit to the Council a proposal relating to the measures to be taken and shall inform the European Parliament.

5.   If the European Parliament considers that a proposal submitted by the Commission pursuant to a basic instrument adopted in accordance with the procedure laid down in Article 251 of the Treaty exceeds the implementing powers provided for in that basic instrument, it shall inform the Council of its position.

6.   The Council may, where appropriate in view of any such position, act by qualified majority on the proposal, within a period to be laid down in each basic instrument but which shall in no case exceed three months from the date of referral to the Council.

If within that period the Council has indicated by qualified majority that it opposes the proposal, the Commission shall re-examine it. It may submit an amended proposal to the Council, re-submit its proposal or present a legislative proposal on the basis of the Treaty.

If on the expiry of that period the Council has neither adopted the proposed implementing act nor indicated its opposition to the proposal for implementing measures, the proposed implementing act shall be adopted by the Commission.

Article 6   Safeguard procedure

The following procedure may be applied where the basic instrument confers on the Commission the power to decide on safeguard measures:

(a) the Commission shall notify the Council and the Member States of any decision regarding safeguard measures. It may be stipulated that before adopting its decision, the Commission shall consult the Member States in accordance with procedures to be determined in each case;

(b) Any Member State may refer the Commission's decision to the Council within a time-limit to be determined within the basic instrument in question;

(c) the Council, acting by a qualified majority, may take a different decision within a time-limit to be determined in the basic instrument in question. Alternatively, it may be stipulated in the basic instrument that the Council, acting by qualified majority, may confirm, amend or revoke the decision adopted by the Commission and that, if the Council has not taken a decision within the above mentioned time-limit, the decision of the Commission is deemed to be revoked.

Article 7

1.   Each committee shall adopt its own rules of procedure on the proposal of its chairman, on the basis of standard rules of procedure which shall be published in the Official Journal of the European Communities. Insofar as necessary existing committees shall adapt their rules of procedure to the standard rules of procedure.

2.   The principles and conditions on public access to documents applicable to the Commission shall apply to the committees.

3.   The European Parliament shall be informed by the Commission of committee proceedings on a regular basis. To that end, it shall receive agendas for committee meetings, draft measures submitted to the committees for the implementation of instruments adopted by the procedure provided for by Article 251 of the Treaty, and the results of voting and summary records of the meetings and lists of the authorities and organisations to which the persons designated by the Member States to represent them belong. The European Parliament

shall also be kept informed whenever the Commission transmits to the Council measures or proposals for measures to be taken.

4. The Commission shall, within six months of the date on which this Decision takes effect, publish in the Official Journal of the European Communities, a list of all committees which assist the Commission in the exercise of implementing powers. This list shall specify, in relation to each committee, the basic instrument(s) under which the committee is established. From 2000 onwards, the Commission shall also publish an annual report on the working of committees.

5. The references of all documents sent to the European Parliament pursuant to paragraph 3 shall be made public in a register to be set up by the Commission in 2001.

Article 8

If the European Parliament indicates, in a Resolution setting out the grounds on which it is based, that draft implementing measures, the adoption of which is contemplated and which have been submitted to a committee pursuant to a basic instrument adopted under Article 251 of the Treaty, would exceed the implementing powers provided for in the basic instrument, the Commission shall re-examine the draft measures. Taking the Resolution into account and within the time-limits of the procedure under way, the Commission may submit new draft measures to the committee, continue with the procedure or submit a proposal to the European Parliament and the Council on the basis of the Treaty. The Commission shall inform the European Parliament and the committee of the action which it intends to take on the Resolution of the European Parliament and of its reasons for doing so.

Article 9

Decision 87/373/EEC shall be repealed.

Article 10

This Decision shall take effect on the day following that of its publication in the Official Journal of the European Communities.

Done at Luxembourg, 28 June 1999.

For the Council
The President
M. NAUMANN

Declarations of 17th July 1999 on Council Decision 1999/468/EC of 28 June 1999 laying down the procedures for the exercise of implementing powers conferred on the Commission

[OJ 1999, C203/1]

1 Commission statement (ad Article 4)

Under the management procedure, the Commission would recall that its constant practice is to try to secure a satisfactory decision which will also muster the widest possible support within the Committee. The commission will take account of the position of the members of the Committee and act in such a way as to avoid going against any predominant position which might emerge against the appropriateness of an implementing measure.

2 Council and commission statement

The Commission and the Council agree that provisions relating to committees assisting the Commission in the exercise of implementing powers provided for in application of Decision

87/373/EEC should be adjusted without delay in order to align them with Articles 3, 4, 5 and 6 of Decision 1999/468/EC in accordance with the appropriate legislative procedures.

Such adjustment should be made as follows:

— current procedure I would be turned into the new advisory procedure;
— current procedures II(a) and II(b) would be turned into the new management procedure;
— current procedures III(a) and III(b) would be turned into the new regulatory procedure.

A modification of the type of committee provided for in a basic instrument should be made, on a case by case basis, in the course of normal revision of legislation, guided inter alia by the criteria provided for in Article 2.

Such adjustment or modification should be made in compliance with the obligations incumbent on the Community institutions. It should not have the effect of jeopardising attainment of the objectives of the basic instrument or the effectiveness of Community action.

3   Commission statement (ad Article 5)

In the review of proposals for implementing measures concerning particularly sensitive sectors, the Commission, in order to find a balanced solution, will act in such a way as to avoid going against any predominant position which might emerge within the Council against the appropriateness of an implementing measure.

Agreement of the 10th October 2000 between the European Parliament and the Commission on Procedures for implementing Council Decision 1999/468/EC of 28 June 1999 laying down the procedures for the exercise of implementing powers conferred on the Commission

[OJ 2000, L256/19]

1.   Pursuant to Article 7(3) of Decision 1999/468/EC,[1] the European Parliament is to be informed by the Commission on a regular basis of the proceedings of the committees involved in committee procedures. To that end, it is to receive, at the same time as the members of the committees and on the same terms, the draft agendas for committee meetings, the draft implementing measures submitted to the committees under basic instruments adopted by the procedure provided for by Article 251 of the EC Treaty, and the results of voting and summary records of the meetings and lists of the authorities to which the persons designated by the Member States to represent them belong.

2.   Furthermore, the Commission agrees to forward to the European Parliament, for information, at the request of the parliamentary committee responsible, specific draft measures for implementing basic instruments which, although not adopted under the codecision procedure, are of particular importance to the European Parliament. Pursuant to the judgment of the Court of First Instance of the European Communities of 19 July 1999 (Case T-188/97, Rothmans v Commission),[2] the European Parliament may request access to minutes of committee meetings.

3.   The European Parliament and the Commission consider the following agreements superseded and thus of no effect in so far as they themselves are concerned: the 1988 Plumb/Delors agreement, the 1996 Samland/Williamson agreement and the 1994 modus vivendi.[3]

[1] OJ L 184, 17.7.1999, p. 23.
[2] (1999) ECR II-2463.
[3] OJ C 102, 4.4.1996, p. 1.

4.   Once the appropriate technical arrangements have been made, the documents referred to in Article 7(3) of Decision 1999/468/EC will be forwarded electronically. Confidential documents will be processed in accordance with internal administrative procedures drawn up by each institution with a view to providing all the requisite guarantees.

5.   Pursuant to Article 8 of Decision 1999/468/EC, the European Parliament may indicate, in a resolution setting out the grounds on which it is based, that draft measures for implementing a basic instrument adopted by the procedure provided for by Article 251 of the Treaty exceed the implementing powers provided for in that basic instrument.

6.   The European Parliament is to adopt such resolutions in plenary; it is to have a period of one month in which to do so, beginning on the date of receipt of the final draft of the implementing measures in the language versions submitted to the Commission.

7.   In urgent cases, and in the case of measures relating to day-to-day administrative matters and/or having a limited period of validity, the time limit will be shorter. That time limit may be very short in extremely urgent cases, and in particular on public health grounds. The Member of the Commission responsible is to set the appropriate time limit and to state the reason for that time limit. The European Parliament may then use a procedure whereby application of Article 8 of Decision 1999/468/EC, within the relevant time limit, may be delegated to the parliamentary committee responsible.

8.   Following adoption by the European Parliament of a resolution setting out the grounds on which it is based, the Member of the Commission responsible is to inform the European Parliament or, where appropriate, the parliamentary committee responsible, of the action the Commission intends to take thereon.

9.   The European Parliament supports the aim and the procedures set out in Declaration No 2 of the Council and the Commission.[4] That Declaration is aimed at simplifying Community implementing arrangements by bringing the committee procedures currently in force into line with those contained in Decision 1999/468/EC.

Majority Voting Procedure Extract from the Luxembourg Accords
[EEC Bulletin 1966 No. 3, p. 9]*

I. Where, in the case of decisions which may be taken by majority vote on a proposal of the Commission, very important interests of one or more partners are at stake, the Members of the Council will endeavour, within a reasonable time, to reach solutions which can be adopted by all the Members of the Council while respecting their mutual interests and those of the Community, in accordance with Article 2 of the Treaty.

II. With regard to the preceding paragraph, the French delegation considers that where very important interests are at stake the discussion must be continued until unanimous agreement is reached.

III. The six delegations note that there is a divergence of views on what should be done in the event of a failure to reach complete agreement.

IV. The six delegations nevertheless consider that this divergence does not prevent the Community's work being resumed in accordance with the normal procedure.

[4] OJ C 203, 17.7.1999, p. 1.

* **Editor's Note:** Permission to reproduce gratefully acknowledged but please note that 'Only European Community legislation printed in the paper edition of the Official Journal of the European Union is deemed authentic'.

Protocol on the Privileges and Immunities of the European Communities

[Annex to the Merger Treaty (OJ 1967, No. 152, 13 July 1967)][1]

The High Contracting Parties,

Considering that, in accordance with Article 28 of the Treaty establishing a Single Council and a Single Commission of the European Communities, these Communities and the European Investment Bank shall enjoy in the territories of the Member States such privileges and immunities as are necessary for the performance of their tasks,

Have agreed upon the following provisions, which shall be annexed to this Treaty:

CHAPTER I   PROPERTY, FUNDS, ASSETS AND OPERATIONS OF THE EUROPEAN COMMUNITIES

Article 1

The premises and buildings of the Communities shall be inviolable. They shall be exempt from search, requisition, confiscation or expropriation. The property and assets of the Communities shall not be the subject of any administrative or legal measure of constraint without the authorisation of the Court of Justice.

Article 2

The archives of the Communities shall be inviolable.

Article 3

The Communities, their assets, revenues and other property shall be exempt from all direct taxes.

The Governments of the Member States shall, wherever possible, take the appropriate measures to remit or refund the amount of indirect taxes or sales taxes included in the price of movable or immovable property, where the Communities make, for their official use, substantial purchases the price of which includes taxes of this kind. These provisions shall not be applied, however, so as to have the effect of distorting competition within the Communities.

No exemption shall be granted in respect of taxes and dues which amount merely to charges for public utility services.

Article 4

The Communities shall be exempt from all customs duties, prohibitions and restrictions on imports and exports in respect of articles intended for their official use: articles so imported shall not be disposed of, whether or not in return for payment, in the territory of the country into which they have been imported, except under conditions approved by the Government of that country.

The Communities shall also be exempt from any customs duties and any prohibitions and restrictions on imports and exports in respect of their publications.

Article 5

The European Coal and Steel Community may hold currency of any kind and operate accounts in any currency.

---

[1] **Editor's Note:** As amended by the Treaty on European Union Protocol and Article 6 of the Treaty of Nice.

CHAPTER II   COMMUNICATIONS AND LAISSEZ-PASSER

Article 6

For their official communications and the transmission of all their documents, the institutions of the Communities shall enjoy in the territory of each Member State the treatment accorded by that State to diplomatic missions.

Official correspondence and other official communications of the institutions of the Communities shall not be subject to censorship.

Article 7

1.   Laissez-passer in a form to be prescribed by the Council, which shall be recognised as valid travel documents by the authorities of the Member States, may be issued to members and servants of the institutions of the Communities by the Presidents of these institutions. The laissez-passer shall be issued to officials and other servants under conditions laid down in the Staff Regulations of officials and the Conditions of Employment of other servants of the Communities.

The Commission may conclude agreements for these laissez-passer to be recognised as valid travel documents within the territory of third countries.

2.   The provisions of Article 6 of the Protocol on the Privileges and Immunities of the European Coal and Steel Community shall, however, remain applicable to members and servants of the institutions who are at the date of entry into force of this Treaty in possession of the laissez-passer provided for in that Article, until the provisions of paragraph 1 of this Article are applied.

CHAPTER III   MEMBERS OF THE EUROPEAN PARLIAMENT

Article 8

No administrative or other restriction shall be imposed on the free movement of members of the European Parliament travelling to or from the place of meeting of the European Parliament.

Members of the European Parliament shall, in respect of customs and exchange control, be accorded:

(a) by their own Government, the same facilities as those accorded to senior officials travelling abroad on temporary official missions;

(b) by the Governments of other Member States, the same facilities as those accorded to representatives of foreign Governments on temporary official missions.

Article 9

Members of the European Parliament shall not be subject to any form of inquiry, detention or legal proceedings in respect of opinions expressed or votes cast by them in the performance of their duties.

Article 10

During the sessions of the European Parliament, its members shall enjoy:

(a) in the territory of their own State, the immunities accorded to members of their parliament;

(b) in the territory of any other Member State, immunity from any measure of detention and from legal proceedings.

Immunity shall likewise apply to members while they are travelling to and from the place of meeting of the European Parliament.

Immunity cannot be claimed when a member is found in the act of committing an offence and shall not prevent the European Parliament from exercising its right to waive the immunity of one of its members.

CHAPTER IV   REPRESENTATIVES OF MEMBER STATES TAKING PART IN THE WORK OF THE INSTITUTIONS OF THE EUROPEAN COMMUNITIES

Article 11

Representatives of Member States taking part in the work of the institutions of the Communities, their advisers and technical experts shall, in the performance of their duties and during their travel to and from the place of meeting, enjoy the customary privileges, immunities and facilities.

This Article shall also apply to members of the advisory bodies of the Communities.

CHAPTER V   OFFICIALS AND OTHER SERVANTS OF THE EUROPEAN COMMUNITIES

Article 12

In the territory of each Member State and whatever their nationality, officials and other servants of the Communities shall:

(a) subject to the provisions of the Treaties relating, on the one hand, to the rules on the liability of officials and other servants towards the Communities and, on the other hand, to the jurisdiction of the Court in disputes between the Communities and their officials and other servants, be immune from legal proceedings in respect of acts performed by them in their official capacity, including their words spoken or written. They shall continue to enjoy this immunity after they have ceased to hold office.

(b) together with their spouses and dependent members of their families, not be subject to immigration restrictions or to formalities for the registration of aliens;

(c) in respect of currency or exchange regulations, be accorded the same facilities as are customarily accorded to officials of international organisations;

(d) enjoy the right to import free of duty their furniture and effects at the time of first taking up their post in the country concerned, and the right to re-export free of duty their furniture and effects, on termination of their duties in that country, subject in either case to the conditions considered to be necessary by the Government of the country in which this right is exercised;

(e) have the right to import free of duty a motor car for their personal use, acquired either in the country of their last residence or in the country of which they are nationals on the terms ruling in the home market in that country, and to re-export it free of duty, subject in either case to the conditions considered to be necessary by the Government of the country concerned.

Article 13

Officials and other servants of the Communities shall be liable to a tax for the benefit of the Communities on salaries, wages and emoluments paid to them by the Communities, in accordance with the conditions and procedure laid down by the Council, acting on a proposal from the Commission.

They shall be exempt from national taxes on salaries, wages and emoluments paid by the Communities.

Article 14

In the application of income tax, wealth tax and death duties and in the application of conventions on the avoidance of double taxation concluded between Member States of the Communities, officials and other servants of the Communities who, solely by reason of the performance of their duties in the service of the Communities, establish their residence in the territory of a Member State other than their country of domicile for tax purposes at the time of entering the service of the Communities, shall be considered, both in the country of their actual residence and in the country of domicile for tax purposes, as having maintained their domicile in the latter country provided that it is a member of the Communities. This provision shall also apply to a spouse, to the extent that the latter is not separately engaged in a gainful occupation, and to children dependent on and in the care of the persons referred to in this Article.

Movable property belonging to persons referred to in the preceding paragraph and situated in the territory of the country where they are staying shall be exempt from death duties in that country; such property shall, for the assessment of such duty, be considered as being in the country of domicile for tax purposes, subject to the rights of third countries and to the possible application of provisions of international conventions on double taxation.

Any domicile acquired solely by reason of the performance of duties in the service of other international organisations shall not be taken into consideration in applying the provisions of this Article.

Article 15
The Council shall, acting unanimously on a proposal from the Commission, lay down the scheme of social security benefits for officials and other servants of the Communities.

Article 16
The Council shall, acting on a proposal from the Commission and after consulting the other institutions concerned, determine the categories of officials and other servants of the Communities to whom the provisions of Article 12, the second paragraph of Article 13, and Article 14 shall apply, in whole or in part.

The names, grades and addresses of officials and other servants included in such categories shall be communicated periodically to the Governments of the Member States.

CHAPTER VI   PRIVILEGES AND IMMUNITIES OF MISSIONS OF THIRD COUNTRIES ACCREDITED TO THE EUROPEAN COMMUNITIES

Article 17
The Member State in whose territory the Communities have their seat shall accord the customary diplomatic immunities and privileges to missions of third countries accredited to the Communities.

CHAPTER VII   GENERAL PROVISIONS

Article 18
Privileges, immunities and facilities shall be accorded to officials and other servants of the Communities solely in the interests of the Communities.

Each institution of the Communities shall be required to waive the immunity accorded to an official or other servant wherever that institution considers that the waiver of such immunity is not contrary to the interests of the Communities.

Article 19
The institutions of the Communities shall, for the purpose of applying this Protocol, cooperate with the responsible authorities of the Member States concerned.

Article 20
Articles 12 to 15 and Article 18 shall apply to members of the Commission.

Article 21*

Articles 12 to 15 and Article 18 shall apply to the Judges, the Advocates-General, the Registrar and the Assistant Rapporteurs of the Court of Justice and to the Members and Registrar of the Court of First Instance, without prejudice to the provisions of Article 3 of the Protocols on the Statute of the Court of Justice concerning immunity from legal proceedings of Judges and Advocates-General.

Article 22

This Protocol shall also apply to the European Investment Bank, to the members of its organs, to its staff and to the representatives of the Member States taking part in its activities, without prejudice to the provisions of the Protocol on the Statute of the Bank.

The European Investment Bank shall in addition be exempt from any form of taxation or imposition of a like nature on the occasion of any increase in its capital and from the various formalities which may be connected therewith in the State where the Bank has its seat. Similarly, its dissolution or liquidation shall not give rise to any imposition. Finally, the activities of the Bank and of its organs carried on in accordance with its Statute shall not be subject to any turnover tax.

Article 23†

The Protocol shall also apply to the European Central Bank, to the members of its organs and to its staff, without prejudice to the provisions of the Protocol on the Statute of the European System of Central Banks and the European Central Bank.

The European Central Bank shall, in addition, be exempt from any form of taxation or imposition of a like nature on the occasion of any increase in its capital and from the various formalities which may be connected therewith in the State where the bank has its seat. The activities of the Bank and of its organs carried on in accordance with the Statute of the European System of Central Banks and of the European Central Bank shall not be subject to any turnover tax.

The above provisions shall also apply to the European Monetary Institute. Its dissolution or liquidation shall not give rise to any imposition.

(Signatures omitted.)

Regulation (EC) No. 1049/2001 of the European Parliament and of the Council of 30 May 2001 regarding public access to European Parliament, Council and Commission documents

[OJ 2001, L145/43]

THE EUROPEAN PARLIAMENT AND THE COUNCIL OF THE EUROPEAN UNION,

Having regard to the Treaty establishing the European Community, and in particular Article 255(2) thereof,

Having regard to the proposal from the Commission([1]),

Acting in accordance with the procedure referred to in Article 251 of the Treaty([2]),

Whereas:

---

* **Editor's Note:** amended by Article 6 Treaty of Nice.
† Article added by Article 9(5) of the Treaty of Amsterdam.
[1] OJ C 177 E, 27.6.2000, p. 70.
[2] Opinion of the European Parliament of 3 May 2001 (not yet published in the Official Journal) and Council Decision of 28 May 2001.

(1) The second sub-paragraph of Article 1 of the Treaty on European Union enshrines the concept of openness, stating that the Treaty marks a new stage in the process of creating an ever closer union among the peoples of Europe, in which decisions are taken as openly as possible and as closely as possible to the citizen.

(2) Openness enables citizens to participate more closely in the decision-making process and guarantees that the administration enjoys greater legitimacy and is more effective and more accountable to the citizen in a democratic system. Openness contributes to strengthening the principles of democracy and respect for fundamental rights as laid down in Article 6 of the EU Treaty and in the Charter of Fundamental Rights of the European Union.

(3) The conclusions of the European Council meetings held at Birmingham, Edinburgh and Copenhagen stressed the need to introduce greater transparency into the work of the Union institutions. This Regulation consolidates the initiatives that the institutions have already taken with a view to improving the transparency of the decision-making process.

(4) The purpose of this Regulation is to give the fullest possible effect to the right of public access to documents and to lay down the general principles and limits on such access in accordance with Article 255 (2) of the EC Treaty.

(5) Since the question of access of documents is not covered by provisions of the Treaty establishing the European Coal and Steel Community and the Treaty establishing the European Atomic Energy Community, the European Parliament, the Council and the Commission should, in accordance with Declaration No 41 attached to the Final Act of the Treaty of Amsterdam, draw guidance from this Regulation as regards documents concerning the activities covered by those two Treaties.

(6) Wider access should be granted to documents in cases where the institutions are acting in their legislative capacity, including under delegated powers, while at the same time preserving the effectiveness of the institutions' decision making process. Such documents should be made directly accessible to the greatest possible extent.

(7) In accordance with Articles 28(1) and 41(1) of the Eu Treaty, the right of access also applies to documents relating to the common foreign and security policy and to police and judicial cooperation in criminal matters. Each institution should respect its security rules.

(8) In order to ensure the full application of this Regulation to all activities of the Union, all agencies established by the institutions should apply the principles laid down in this Regulation.

(9) On account of their highly sensitive content, certain documents should be given special treatment. Arrangements for informing the European Parliament of the content of such documents should be made through interinstitutional agreement.

(10) In order to bring about greater openness in the work of the institutions, access to documents should be granted by the European Parliament, the Council and the Commission not only to documents drawn up by the institutions, but also to documents received by them. In this context, it is recalled that Declaration No 35 attached to the Final Act of the Treaty of Amsterdam provides that a Member State may request the Commission or the Council not to communicate to third parties a document originating from that State without its prior agreement.

(11) In priciple, all documents of the institutions should be accessible to the public. However, certain public and private interests should be protected by way of exceptions. The institutions should be entitled to protect their internal consultations and eeliberations where necessary to safeguard thcir ability to carry out their tasks. In assessing the exceptions, the institutions should take account of the principles in Community legislation concerning the protection of personal data, in all areas of Union activities.

(12) All rules concerning access to documents of the institutions should be in conformity with this Regulation.

(13) In order to ensure that the right of access is fully respected, a two-stage administra-

tive procedure should apply, with the additional possibility of court proceedings or complaints to the Ombudsman.

(14) Each institution should take the measures necessary to inform the public of the new provisions in force and to train its staff to assist citizens exercising their rights under this Regulation. In order to make it easier for citizens to exercise their rights, each institution should provide access to a register of documents.

(15) Even though it is neither the object nor the effect of this Regulation to amend national legislation on access to documents, it is nevertheless clear that, by virtue of the principle of loyal cooperation which governs relations between the institutions and the Member States, Member States should take care not to hamper the proper application of this Regulation and should respect the security rules of the institutions.

(16) This Regulation is without prejudice to existing rights of access to documents for Member States, judicial authorities or investigative bodies.

(17) In accordance with Article 255(3) of the EC Treaty, each institution lays down specific provisions regarding access to its documents in its rules of procedure. Council Decision 93/731/EC of 20 December 1993 on public access to Council documents([3]), Commission Decision 94/90/ECSC, EC, Euratom of 8 February 1994 on public access to Commission documents([4]), European Parliament Decision 97/632/EC, ECSC, Euratom of 10 July 1997 on public access to European Parliament documents([5]), and the rules on confidentiality of Schengen documents should therefore, if necessary, be modified or be repealed,

HAVE ADOPTED THIS REGULATION:

Article 1 Purpose
The purpose of this Regulation is:
- (a) to define the principles, conditions and limits on grounds of public or private interest governing the right of access to European Parliament, Council and Commission (hereinafter referred to as 'the institutions') documents provided for in Article 255 of the EC Treaty in such a way as to ensure the widest possible access to documents,
- (b) to establish rules ensuring the easiest possible exercise of this right, and
- (c) to promote good administrative practice on access to documents.

Article 2 Beneficiaries and scope
1.   Any citizen of the Union, and any natural or legal person residing or having its registered office in a Member State, has a right of access to documents of the institutions, subject to the principles, conditions and limits defined in this Regulation.

2.   The institutions may, subject to the same principles, conditions and limits, grant access to documents to any natural or legal person not residing or not having its registered office in a Member State.

3.   This Regulation shall apply to all documents held by an institution, that is to say, documents drawn up or received by it and in its possession, in all areas of activity of the European Union.

4.   Without prejudice to Articles 4 and 9, documents shall be made accessible to the public either following a written application or directly in electronic form or through a register. In particular, documents drawn up or received in the course of a legislative procedure shall be made directly accessible in accordance with Article 12.

5.   Sensitive documents as defined in Article 9(1) shall be subject to special treatment in accordance with that Article.

---

[3] OJ L 340, 31.12.1993, p. 43. Decision as last amended by Decision 2000/527/EC (OJ L 212, 23.8.2000, p. 9).
[4] OJ L 46, 18.2.1994, p. 58. Decision as amended by Decision 96/567/EC, ECSC, Euratom (OJ L 247, 28.9.1996, p. 45).
[5] OJ L 263, 25.9.1997, p. 27.

6. This Regulation shall be without prejudice to rights of public access to documents held by the institutions which might follow from instruments of international law or acts of the institutions implementing them.

Article 3   Definitions
For the purpose of this Regulation:
- (a) 'document' shall mean any content whatever its medium (written on paper or stored in electronic form or as a sound, visual or audiovisual recording) concerning a matter relating to the policies, activities and decisions falling within the institution's sphere of responsibility;
- (b) 'third party' shall mean any natural or legal person, or any entity outside the institution concerned, including the Member States, other Community or non-Community institutions and bodies and third countries.

Article 4   Exceptions
1. The institutions shall refuse access to a document where disclosure would undermine the protection of:
- (a) the public interest as regards:
  - — public security,
  - — defence and military matters,
  - — international relations,
  - — the financial, monetary or economic policy of the Community or a Member State;
- (b) privacy and the integrity of the individual, in particular in accordance with Community legislation regarding the protection of personal data.

2. The institutions shall refuse access to a document where disclosure would undermine the protection of:
- — commercial interests of a natural or legal person, including intellectual property,
- — court proceedings and legal advice,
- — the purpose of inspections, investigations and audits,

unless there is an overriding public interest in disclosure.

3. Access to a document, drawn up by an institution for internal use or received by an institution, which relates to a matter where the decision has not been taken by the institution, shall be refused if disclosure of the document would seriously undermine the institution's decision-making process, unless there is an overriding public interest in disclosure. Access to a document containing opinions for internal use as part of deliberations and preliminary consultations within the institution concerned shall be refused even after the decision has been taken if disclosure of the document would seriously undermine the institution's decision-making process, unless there is an overriding public interest in disclosure.

4. As regards third-party documents, the institution shall consult the third party with a view to assessing whether an exception in paragraph 1 or 2 is applicable, unless it is clear that the document shall or shall not be disclosed.

5. A Member State may request the institution not to disclose a document originating from that Member State without its prior agreement.

6. If only parts of the requested document are covered by any of the exceptions, the remaining parts of the document shall be released.

7. The exceptions as laid down in paragraphs 1 to 3 shall only apply for the period during which protection is justified on the basis of the content of the document. The exceptions may apply for a maximum period of 30 years. In the case of documents covered by the exceptions relating to privacy or commercial interests and in the case of sensitive documents, the exceptions may, if necessary, continue to apply after this period.

Article 5   Documents in the Member States

Where a Member State receives a request for a document in its possession, originating from an institution, unless it is clear that the document shall or shall not be disclosed, the Member State shall consult with the institution concerned in order to take a decision that does not jeopardise the attainment of the objectives of this Regulation. The Member State may instead refer the request to the institution.

Article 6   Applications

1.   Applications for access to a document shall be made in any written form, including electronic form, in one of the languages referred to in Article 314 of the EC Treaty and in a sufficiently precise manner to enable the institution to identify the document. The applicant is not obliged to state reasons for the application.

2.   If an application is not sufficiently precise, the institution shall ask the applicant to clarify the application and shall assist the applicant in doing so, for example, by providing information on the use of the public registers of documents.

3.   In the event of an application relating to a very long document or to a very large number of documents, the institution concerned may confer with the applicant informally, with a view to finding a fair solution.

4.   The institutions shall provide information and assistance to citizens on how and where applications for access to documents can be made.

Article 7   Processing of initial applications

1.   An application for access to a document shall be handled promptly. An acknowledge-ment of receipt shall be sent to the applicant. Within 15 working days from registration of the application, the institution shall either grant access to the document requested and provide access in accordance with Article 10 within that period or, in a written reply, state the reasons for the total or partial refusal and inform the applicant of his or her right to make a confirmatory application in accordance with paragraph 2 of this Article.

2.   In the event of a total or partial refusal, the applicant may, within 15 working days of receiving the institution's reply, make a confirmatory application asking the institution to reconsider its position.

3.   In exceptional cases, for example, in the event of an application relating to a very long document or to a very large number of documents, the time-limit provided for in paragraph 1 may be extended by 15 working days, provided that the applicant is notified in advance and that detailed reasons are given.

4.   Failure by the institution to reply within the prescribed time-limit shall entitle the applicant to make a confirmatory application.

Article 8   Processing of confirmatory applications

1.   A confirmatory application shall be handled promptly. Within 15 working days from registration of such an application, the institution shall either grant access to the document requested and provide access in accordance with Article 10 within that period or, in a written reply, state the reasons for the total or partial refusal. In the event of a total or partial refusal, the institution shall inform the applicant of the remedies open to him or her, namely instituting court proceedings against the institution and/or making a complaint to the Ombudsman, under the conditions laid down in Articles 230 and 195 of the EC Treaty, respectively.

2.   In exceptional cases, for example, in the event of an application relating to a very long document or to a very large number of documents, the time limit provided for in paragraph 1 may be extended by 15 working days, provided that the applicant is notified in advance and that detailed reasons are given.

3.   Failure by the institution to reply within the prescribed time limit shall be considered as a negative reply and entitle the applicant to institute court proceedings against the institu-

tion and/or make a complaint to the Ombudsman, under the relevant provisions of the EC Treaty.

Article 9   Treatment of sensitive documents

1.   Sensitive documents are documents originating from the institutions or the agencies established by them, from Member States, third countries or International Organisations, classified as 'TRÈS SECRET/TOP SECRET', 'SECRET' or 'CONFIDENTIEL' in accordance with the rules of the institution concerned, which protect essential interests of the European Union or of one or more of its Member States in the areas covered by Article 4(1)(a), notably public security, defence and military matters.

2.   Applications for access to sensitive documents under the procedures laid down in Articles 7 and 8 shall be handled only by those persons who have a right to acquaint themselves with those documents. These persons shall also, without prejudice to Article 11(2), assess which references to sensitive documents could be made in the public register.

3.   Sensitive documents shall be recorded in the register or released only with the consent of the originator.

4.   An institution which decides to refuse access to a sensitive document shall give the reasons for its decision in a manner which does not harm the interests protected in Article 4.

5.   Member States shall take appropriate measures to ensure that when handling applications for sensitive documents the principles in this Article and Article 4 are respected.

6.   The rules of the institutions concerning sensitive documents shall be made public.

7.   The Commission and the Council shall inform the European Parliament regarding sensitive documents in accordance with arrangements agreed between the institutions.

Article 10   Access following an application

1.   The applicant shall have access to documents either by consulting them on the spot or by receiving a copy, including, where available, an electronic copy, according to the applicant's preference. The cost of producing and sending copies may be charged to the applicant. This charge shall not exceed the real cost of producing and sending the copies. Consultation on the spot, copies of less than 20 A4 pages and direct access in electronic form or through the register shall be free of charge.

2.   If a document has already been released by the institution concerned and is easily accessible to the applicant, the institution may fulfil its obligation of granting access to documents by informing the applicant how to obtain the requested document.

3.   Documents shall be supplied in an existing version and format (including electronically or in an alternative format such as Braille, large print or tape) with full regard to the applicant's preference.

Article 11   Registers

1.   To make citizens' rights under this Regulation effective, each institution shall provide public access to a register of documents. Access to the register should be provided in electronic form. References to documents shall be recorded in the register without delay.

2.   For each document the register shall contain a reference number (including, where applicable, the interinstitutional reference), the subject matter and/or a short description of the content of the document and the date on which it was received or drawn up and recorded in the register. References shall be made in a manner which does not undermine protection of the interests in Article 4.

3.   The institutions shall immediately take the measures necessary to establish a register which shall be operational by 3 June 2002.

Article 12   Direct access in electronic form or through a register

1.   The institutions shall as far as possible make documents directly accessible to the public in electronic form or through a register in accordance with the rules of the institution concerned.

2.   In particular, legislative documents, that is to say, documents drawn up or received in the course of procedures for the adoption of acts which are legally binding in or for the Member States, should, subject to Articles 4 and 9, be made directly accessible.

3.   Where possible, other documents, notably documents relating to the development of policy or strategy, should be made directly accessible.

4.   Where direct access is not given through the register, the register shall as far as possible indicate where the document is located.

Article 13   Publication in the Official Journal

1.   In addition to the acts referred to in Article 254(1) and (2) of the EC Treaty and the first paragraph of Article 163 of the Euratom Treaty, the following documents shall, subject to Articles 4 and 9 of this Regulation, be published in the Official Journal:

(a) Commission proposals;

(b) common positions adopted by the Council in accordance with the procedures referred to in Articles 251 and 252 of the EC Treaty and the reasons underlying those common positions, as well as the European Parliament's positions in these procedures;

(c) framework decisions and decisions referred to in Article 34(2) of the EU Treaty;

(d) conventions established by the Council in accordance with Article 34(2) of the EU Treaty;

(e) conventions signed between Member States on the basis of Article 293 of the EC Treaty;

(f) international agreements concluded by the Community or in accordance with Article 24 of the EU Treaty.

2.   As far as possible, the following documents shall be published in the Official Journal:

(a) initiatives presented to the Council by a Member State pursuant to Article 67(1) of the EC Treaty or pursuant to Article 34(2) of the EU Treaty;

(b) common positions referred to in Article 34(2) of the EU Treaty;

(c) directives other than those referred to in Article 254(1) and (2) of the EC Treaty, decisions other than those referred to in Article 254(1) of the EC Treaty, recommendations and opinions.

3.   Each institution may in its rules of procedure establish which further documents shall be published in the Official Journal.

Article 14   Information

1.   Each institution shall take the requisite measures to inform the public of the rights they enjoy under this Regulation.

2.   The Member States shall cooperate with the institutions in providing information to the citizens.

Article 15   Administrative practice in the institutions

1.   The institutions shall develop good administrative practices in order to facilitate the exercise of the right of access guaranteed by this Regulation.

2.   The institutions shall establish an interinstitutional committee to examine best practice, address possible conflicts and discuss future developments on public access to documents.

Article 16   Reproduction of documents

This Regulation shall be without prejudice to any existing rules on copyright which may limit a third party's right to reproduce or exploit released documents.

Article 17   Reports

1.   Each institution shall publish annually a report for the preceding year including the number of cases in which the institution refused to grant access to documents, the reasons for such refusals and the number of sensitive documents not recorded in the register.

2.   At the latest by 31 January 2004, the Commission shall publish a report on the implementation of the principles of this Regulation and shall make recommendations, including, if appropriate, proposals for the revision of this Regulation and an action programme of measures to be taken by the institutions.

Article 18   Application measures

1.   Each institution shall adapt its rules of procedure to the provisions of this Regulation. The adaptations shall take effect from 3 December 2001.

2.   Within six months of the entry into force of this Regulation, the Commission shall examine the conformity of Council Regulation (EEC, Euratom) No 354/83 of 1 February 1983 concerning the opening to the public of the historical archives of the European Economic Community and the European Atomic Energy Community([6]) with this Regulation in order to ensure the preservation and archiving of documents to the fullest extent possible.

3.   Within six months of the entry into force of this Regulation, the Commission shall examine the conformity of the existing rules on access to documents with this Regulation.

Article 19   Entry into force

This Regulation shall enter into force on the third day following that of its publication in the Official Journal of the European Communities. It shall be applicable from 3 December 2001.

This Regulation shall be binding in its entirety and directly applicable in all Member States.
    Done at Brussels, 30 May 2001.

Joint declaration relating to Regulation 1049/2001 of the European Parliament and of the Council regarding public access to European Parliament, Council and Commission documents

[OJ 2001, L173/5]

1.   The European Parliament, the Council and the Commission agree that the agencies and similar bodies created by the legislator should have rules on access to their documents which conform to those of this Regulation. To this effect, the European Parliament and the Council welcome the Commission's intention to propose, as soon as possible, amendments to the acts establishing the existing agencies and bodies and to include provisions in future proposals concerning the establishment of such agencies and bodies. They undertake to adopt the necessary acts rapidly.

2.   The European Parliament, the Council and the Commission call on the institutions and bodies not covered by paragraph 1 to adopt internal rules on public access to documents which take account of the principles and limits in this Regulation.

[6] OJ L 43, 15.2.1983, p. 1.

THE EUROPEAN COURT OF JUSTICE

INFORMATION NOTE ON REFERENCES BY NATIONAL COURTS FOR PRELIMINARY RULINGS*

The development of the Community legal order is largely the result of cooperation established between the Court of Justice of the European Communities and the national courts and tribunals through the preliminary ruling procedure provided for in Article 177 of the EC Treaty and the corresponding provisions of the ECSC and Euratom Treaties.[1]

In order to make this cooperation more effective, and thus to enable the Court of Justice to meet the expectations of national courts more suitably by providing answers to preliminary questions which are of assistance to them, this Note provides information for all interested parties, in particular the national courts.

The Note is for information only and does not have any regulatory or interpretative effect in relation to the provisions which govern the preliminary ruling procedure. It merely contains practical information which, in the light of experience accumulated in the application of the preliminary ruling procedure, may help to prevent the kind of difficulties which the Court has sometimes encountered.

1. Any court or tribunal of a Member State may ask the Court of Justice to interpret a rule of Community law, whether contained in the Treaties or in acts of secondary law, if it considers that that is necessary for it to give judgment in a case pending before it.

Courts against whose decisions there is no judicial remedy under national law must refer questions of interpretation arising before them to the Court of Justice, unless the Court has already ruled on the point or unless the correct application of the rule of Community law is obvious.[2]

2. The Court of Justice has jurisdiction to rule on the validity of acts of the Community institutions. National courts may reject a pleas challenging the validity of an act. All national courts – even those whose decisions are still open to appeal – raising the question of the validity of a Community act must refer that question to the Court of Justice.[3]

However, if a national court has serious doubts about the validity of a Community act on which a national measure is based, it may exceptionally suspend application of that measure temporarily or grant other interim relief with respect to it. It must then refer the question of validity to the Court of Justice, stating the reasons for which it considers that the Community act is not valid.[4]

3. Questions referred for a preliminary ruling must concern the interpretation or validity of a provision of Community law only, since the Court of Justice does not have jurisdiction to interpret national law or assess its validity. It is for the referring court to apply the relevant provision of Community law in the specific case pending before it.

4. The decision by which a national court or tribunal refers a question to the Court of Justice for a preliminary ruling may be in any form allowed by national law as regards pro-

---

* **Editor's Note:** Taken from the ECJ website at http://europa.eu.int/cj/en/instit/txtdocfr/autrestxts/ txt8.pdf. This text may also be found at [1997] 1 CMLR 78 and in the Weekly Proceedings of the Court of Justice 34/96 at p. 1. Reproduction authorised and acknowledged, see http://europa.eu.int/cj/en/ avertissement.htm.

[1] A preliminary ruling procedure is also provided for by the protocols to several conventions concluded by the Member States, in particular the Brussels Convention on Jurisdiction and the Enforcement of Judgments in Civil and Commercial Matters.

[2] Judgment in Case 283/81 *CILFIT* v *Ministry of Health* [1982] ECR 3415.

[3] Judgment in Case 314/85 *Foto-Frost* v *Hauptzollamt Lübeck-Ost* [1987] ECR 4199.

[4] Judgments in Joined Cases C-143/88 and C-92/89 *Zuckerfabrik Süderdithmarschen and Zuckerfabrik Soest* [1991] ECR I-415 and in Case C-465/93 *Atlanta Fruchthandelsgesellschaft* [1995] ECR I-3761.

cedural steps. The reference of a question or questions to the Court of Justice generally causes the national proceedings to be stayed until the Court gives its ruling, but the decision to stay proceedings is one which the national court alone must take in accordance with its own national law.

5.   The decision making the reference and containing the question or questions referred to the Court will have to be translated by the Court's translators into the other official languages of the Community. Questions concerning the interpretation or validity of Community law are frequently of general interest and the Member States and Community institutions are entitled to submit observations. It is therefore desirable that the decision making the reference should be drafted as clearly and precisely as possible.

6.   It must contain a statement of reasons which is succinct but sufficiently complete to give the Court, and those to whom the decision must be notified (the Member States, the Commission, and in certain cases the Council and the European Parliament), a clear understanding of the factual and legal context of the main proceedings.[5]

In particular, it must include an account of the facts which are essential for understanding the full legal significance of the main proceedings, an account of the points of law which may apply, a statement of the reasons which prompted the national court to refer the question or questions to the Court of Justice and, if need be, a summary of the arguments of the parties. The purpose of all this is to put the Court of Justice in a position to give the national court an answer which will be of assistance to it.

The decision making the reference must also be accompanied by copies of the documents needed for a proper understanding of the case, especially the text of the applicable national provisions. However, as the case-file or documents annexed to the decision making the reference are not always translated in full into the other official languages of the Community, the national court must make sure that its decision includes all the relevant information.

7.   A national court or tribunal may refer a question to the Court of Justice for a preliminary ruling as soon as it finds that a ruling on the point or points of interpretation or validity is necessary to enable it to give judgment. It must be stressed, however, that it is not for the Court of Justice to decide issues of fact or differences of opinion as to the interpretation or application of rules of national law. It is therefore desirable that a decision to make a reference should not be taken until the national proceedings have reached a stage where the national court is able to define, if only hypothetically, the factual and legal context of the question. In any event, the administration of justice may well be best served by waiting to refer a question for a preliminary ruling until both sides have been heard.[6]

8.   The decision making the reference and the relevant documents are to be sent by the national court directly to the Court of Justice, by registered post (addressed to the Registry of the Court of Justice of the European Communities, L-2925 Luxembourg, telephone 352–43031). The Court Registry will stay in contact with the national court until judgment is given, and will send it copies of the various documents (written observations, Report for the Hearing, Opinion of the Advocate General). The Court will also send its judgment to the national court. It would be grateful to receive word that its judgment has been applied in the national proceedings and a copy of the national court's final decision.

9.   Proceedings for a preliminary ruling before the Court of Justice are free of charge. The Court does not rule on costs.

---

[5] Judgment in Joined Cases C-320/90, C-321/90 and C-322/90 *Telemarsicabruzzo* [1993] ECR I-393.
[6] Judgment in Case 70/77 *Simmenthal* v *Amministrazione delle Finanze dello Stato* [1978] ECR 1453.

Rules of Procedure of the Court of Justice of the European Communities of 19 June 1991

[OJ 1991, L176/7][1]

THE COURT OF JUSTICE,

Having regard to the powers conferred on the Court of Justice by the Treaty establishing the European Coal and Steel Community, the Treaty establishing the European Economic Community and the Treaty establishing the European Atomic Energy Community (EAEC),

Having regard to Article 55 of the Protocol on the Statute of the Court of Justice of the European Coal and Steel Community,

Having regard to the third paragraph of Article 188 of the Treaty establishing the European Economic Community,

Having regard to the third paragraph of Article 160 of the Treaty establishing the European Atomic Energy Community (EAEC),

Whereas it is necessary to revise the text of its Rules of Procedure in the various languages in order to ensure coherence and uniformity between those language versions;

With the unanimous approval of that revision, given by the Council on 29 April 1991; And whereas, after the numerous amendments to its Rules of Procedure, it is necessary, in the interests of clarity and simplicity to establish a coherent authentic text,

With the unanimous approval of the Council, given on 7 June 1991,

REPLACES ITS RULES OF PROCEDURE BY THE FOLLOWING RULES:

INTERPRETATION

Article 1

In these Rules:
— 'Union Treaty' means the Treaty on European Union,
— 'EC Treaty' means the Treaty establishing the European Community,
— 'EAEC Treaty' means the Treaty establishing the European Atomic Energy Community,
— 'Statute' means the Protocol on the Statute of the Court of Justice,
— 'EEA Agreement' means the Agreement on the European Economic Area.

For the purposes of these Rules:
— 'institutions' means the institutions of the Community and bodies which are established by the Treaties, or by an act adopted in implementation thereof, and which may be parties before the Court,
— 'EFTA Surveillance Authority' means the surveillance authority referred to in the EEA Agreement.

TITLE I   ORGANIZATION OF THE COURT

CHAPTER 1   JUDGES AND ADVOCATES-GENERAL

Article 2

The term of office of a Judge shall begin on the date laid down in his instrument of appointment. In the absence of any provisions regarding the date, the term shall begin on the date of the instrument.

---

[1] As corrected by OJ 1992 L383/117 and amended by OJ 1995 L44/61, OJ 1997 L103/1 and Decision 97/419 OJ 1997 L103/3, OJ 2000 L122/43, OJ 2000 L322/1, OJ 2001 L119/1–2, OJ 2002 L272/24 and OJ 2003 L147/17.

Article 3

1.   Before taking up his duties, a Judge shall at the first public sitting of the Court which he attends after his appointment take the following oath: 'I swear that I will perform my duties impartially and conscientiously; I swear that I will preserve the secrecy of the deliberations of the Court'.

2.   Immediately after taking the oath, a Judge shall sign a declaration by which he solemnly undertakes that, both during and after his term of office, he will respect the obligations arising therefrom, and in particular the duty to behave with integrity and discretion as regards the acceptance, after he has ceased to hold office, of certain appointments and benefits.

Article 4

When the Court is called upon to decide whether a Judge no longer fulfils the requisite conditions or no longer meets the obligations arising from his office, the President shall invite the Judge concerned to make representations to the Court, in closed session and in the absence of the Registrar.

Article 5

Articles 2, 3 and 4 of these Rules shall apply in a corresponding manner to Advocates-General.

Article 6

Judges and Advocates-General shall rank equally in precedence according to their seniority in office. Where there is equal seniority in office, precedence shall be determined by age.

Retiring Judges and Advocates-General who are re-appointed shall retain their former precedence.

CHAPTER 2   PRESIDENCY OF THE COURT AND CONSTITUTION
OF THE CHAMBERS

Article 7

1.   The Judges shall, immediately after the partial replacement provided for in Article 223 of the EC Treaty and Article 139 of the EAEC Treaty, elect one of their number as President of the Court for a term of three years.

2.   If the office of the President of the Court falls vacant before the normal date of expiry thereof, the Court shall elect a successor for the remainder of the term.

3.   The elections provided for in this Article shall be by secret ballot. If a Judge obtains an absolute majority he shall be elected. If no Judge obtains an absolute majority, a second ballot shall be held and the Judge obtaining the most votes shall be elected. Where two or more Judges obtain an equal number of votes the oldest of them shall be deemed elected.

Article 8

The President shall direct the judicial business and the administration of the Court; he shall preside at hearings and deliberations.

Article 9

1.   The Court shall set up Chambers of five and three Judges in accordance with Article 16 of the Statute and shall decide which Judges shall be attached to them. The assignment of Judges to the Judges shall be published in the Official Journal of the European Union.

2.   As soon as an application initiating proceedings has been lodged, the President shall assign the case to one of the Chambers of three Judges for any preparatory inquiries and shall designate a Judge from that Chamber to act as Rapporteur.

3.   For cases assigned to a formation of the Court in accordance with Article 44(3), the word 'Court' in these Rules shall mean that formation.

4.   In cases assigned to a Chamber of five or three Judges the powers of the President of the Court shall be exercised by the President of the Chamber.

Article 10

1.   The Judges shall, immediately after the election of the President of the Court, elect the Presidents of the Chambers of five Judges for a term of three years The Judges shall elect the Presidents of the Chambers of three Judges for a term of one year. The Court shall appoint for a period of one year the First Advocate General. The provisions of Article 7(2) and (3) shall apply. The elections and appointment made in pursuance of this paragraph shall be published in the Official Journal of the European Union.

2.   The First Advocate-General shall assign each case to an Advocate-General as soon as the Judge-Rapporteur has been designated by the President. He shall take the necessary steps if an Advocate-General is absent or prevented from acting.

Article 11

When the President of the Court is absent or prevented from attending or when the office of President is vacant, the functions of President shall be exercised by a President of a Chamber of five Judges according to the order of precedence laid down in Article 6 of these Rules. When the President of the Court and the Presidents of the Chambers of five Judges are all prevented from attending at the same time, or their posts are vacant at the same time, the functions of President shall be exercised by one of the Presidents of the Chambers of three Judges according to the order of precedence laid down in Article 6 of these Rules. If the President of the Court and all the Presidents of Chambers are all prevented from attending at the same time, or their posts are vacant at the same time, the functions of President shall be exercised by one of the other Judges according to the order of precedence laid down in Article 6 of these Rules.

CHAPTER 2(a)   FORMATIONS OF THE COURT

Article 11(a)

The Court shall sit in the following formations:
- the full Court, composed of all the Judges,
- the Grand Chamber, composed of eleven Judges in accordance with Article 11(b),
- Chambers composed of five or three Judges in accordance with Article 11(c).

Article 11(b)

1.   For each case the Grand Chamber shall be composed of the President of the Court, the Presidents of the Chambers of five Judges, the Judge-Rapporteur and the number of Judges necessary to reach eleven. The last-mentioned Judges shall be designated from the list referred to in paragraph (2), following the order laid down therein, the starting-point moving on by one name at each general meeting of the Court.

2.   After the election of the President of the Court and of the Presidents of the Chambers of five Judges, a list of the other Judges shall be drawn up for the purposes of determining the composition of the Grand Chamber. That list shall follow the order laid down in Article 6 of these Rules, alternating with the reverse order: the first Judge on that list shall be the first according to the order laid down in that Article, the second Judge shall be the last according to that order, the third Judge shall be the second according to that order, the fourth Judge the penultimate according to that order, and so on.
The list shall be published in the Official Journal of the European Union.

Article 11(c)

1.   The Chambers of five Judges and three Judges shall, for each case, be composed of the President of the Chamber, the Judge-Rapporteur and the number of Judges required to attain the number of five and three Judges respectively. Those last-mentioned Judges shall be

designated from the lists referred to in paragraph (2) and following the order laid down in them, the starting-point being moved on by one name at each general meeting of the Court.

2.   For the composition of the Chambers of five Judges, after the election of the Presidents of those Chambers lists shall be drawn up including all the Judges attached to the Chamber concerned, with the exception of its President. The lists shall be drawn up in the same way as the list referred to in Article 11(b)(2).

For the composition of the Chambers of three Judges, after the election of the Presidents of those Chambers lists shall be drawn up including all the Judges attached to the Chamber concerned, with the exception of its President. The lists shall be drawn up according to the order laid down in Article 6 of these Rules.

The lists referred to in this paragraph shall be published in the Official Journal of the European Union.

Article 11(d)

Where the Court considers that several cases must be heard and determined together by one and the same formation of the Court, the composition of that formation shall be that fixed for the case in respect of which the preliminary report was first examined.

Article 11(e)

When a member of the formation determining a case is prevented from attending, he shall be replaced by a Judge according to the order of the lists referred to in Article 11(b)(2) or 11(c)(2).

When the President of the Court is prevented from attending, the functions of the President of the Grand Chamber shall be exercised in accordance with the provisions of Article 11.

When the President of a Chamber of five Judges is prevented from attending, the functions of President of the Chamber shall be exercised by a President of a Chamber of three Judges, where necessary according to the order laid down in Article 6 of these Rules or, if that Chamber does not include a President of a Chamber of three Judges, by one of the other Judges according to the order laid down in Article 6.

When the President of a Chamber of three Judges is prevented from attending, the functions of President of the Chamber shall be exercised by a Judge of that Chamber according to the order laid down in Article 6 of these Rules.

CHAPTER 3   REGISTRY

SECTION 1   THE REGISTRAR AND ASSISTANT REGISTRAR

Article 12

1.   The Court shall appoint the Registrar. Two weeks before the date fixed for making the appointment, the President shall inform the Members of the Court of the applications which have been made for the post.

2.   An application shall be accompanied by full details of the candidate's age, nationality, university degrees, knowledge of any languages, present and past occupations and experience, if any, in judicial and international fields.

3.   The appointment shall be made following the procedure laid down in Article 7 (3) of these Rules.

4.   The Registrar shall be appointed for a term of six years. He may be re-appointed.

5.   The Registrar shall take the oath in accordance with Article 3 of these Rules.

6.   The Registrar may be deprived of his office only if he no longer fulfils the requisite conditions or no longer meets the obligations arising from his office; the Court shall take its decision after giving the Registrar an opportunity to make representations.

7.   If the office of Registrar falls vacant before the normal date of expiry of the term thereof, the Court shall appoint a new Registrar for a term of six years.

Article 13

The Court may, following the procedure laid down in respect of the Registrar, appoint one or more Assistant Registrars to assist the Registrar and to take his place in so far as the Instructions to the Registrar referred in Article 15 of these Rules allow.

Article 14

Where the Registrar and the Assistant Registrar are absent or prevented from attending or their posts are vacant, the President shall designate an official to carry out temporarily the duties of Registrar.

Article 15

Instructions to the Registrar shall be adopted by the Court acting on a proposal from the President.

Article 16

1. There shall be kept in the Registry, under the control of the Registrar, a register initialled by the President, in which all pleadings and supporting documents shall be entered in the order in which they are lodged.

2. When a document has been registered, the Registrar shall make a note to that effect on the original and, if a party so requests, on any copy submitted for the purpose.

3. Entries in the register and the notes provided for in the preceding paragraph shall be authentic.

4. Rules for keeping the register shall be prescribed by the Instructions to the Registrar referred to in Article 15 of the Rules.

5. Persons having an interest may consult the register at the Registry and may obtain copies or extracts on payment of a charge on a scale fixed by the Court on a proposal from the Registrar.

The parties to a case may on payment of the appropriate charge also obtain copies of pleadings and authenticated copies of judgments and orders.

6. Notice shall be given in the Official Journal of the European Union of the date of registration of an application initiating proceedings, the names and addresses of the parties, the subject-matter of the proceedings, the form of order sought by the applicant and a summary of the pleas in law and of the main supporting arguments.

7. Where the Council or the Commission is not a party to a case, the Court shall send to it copies of the application and of the defence, without the annexes thereto, to enable it to assess whether the inapplicability of one of its acts is being invoked under the third paragraph of Article 241 of the EC Treaty or Article 156 of the EAEC Treaty. Copies of the application and of the defence shall likewise be sent to the European Parliament, to enable it to assess whether the inapplicability of an act adopted jointly by that institution and by the Council is being invoked under Article 241 of the EC Treaty.

Article 17

1. The Registrar shall be responsible, under the authority of the President, for the acceptance, transmission and custody of documents and for effecting service as provided for by these Rules.

2. The Registrar shall assist the Court, the President and the Presidents of Chambers and the Judges in all their official functions.

Article 18

The Registrar shall have custody of the seals. He shall be responsible for the records and be in charge of the publications of the Court.

Article 19

Subject to Articles 4 and 27 of these Rules, the Registrar shall attend the sittings of the Court and of the Chambers.

SECTION 2   OTHER DEPARTMENTS

Article 20

1.   The officials and other servants of the Court shall be appointed in accordance with the provisions of the Staff Regulations.

2.   Before taking up his duties, an official shall take the following oath before the President, in the presence of the Registrar: 'I swear that I will perform loyally, discreetly and conscientiously the duties assigned to me by the Court of Justice of the European Communities'.

Article 21

The organization of the departments of the Court shall be laid down, and may be modified, by the Court on a proposal from the Registrar.

Article 22

The Court shall set up a translating service staffed by experts with adequate legal training and a thorough knowledge of several official languages of the Court.

Article 23

The Registrar shall be responsible, under the authority of the President, for the administration of the Court, its financial management and its accounts; he shall be assisted in this by an administrator.

CHAPTER 4   ASSISTANT RAPPORTEURS

Article 24

1.   Where the Court is of the opinion that the consideration of and preparatory inquiries in cases before it so require, it shall, pursuant to Article 13 of the Statute, propose the appointment of Assistant Rapporteurs.

2.   Assistant Rapporteurs shall in particular assist the President in connection with applications for the adoption of interim measures and assist the Judge-Rapporteurs in their work.

3.   In the performance of their duties the Assistant Rapporteurs shall be responsible to the President of the Court, the President of a Chamber or a Judge-Rapporteur, as the case may be.

4.   Before taking up his duties, an Assistant Rapporteur shall take before the Court the oath set out in Article 3 of these Rules.

CHAPTER 5   THE WORKING OF THE COURT

Article 25

1.   The dates and times of the sittings of the Grand Chamber and the full of Court shall be fixed by the President.

2.   The dates and times of the sittings of the Chambers of five and three Judges shall be fixed by their respective Presidents.

3.   The Court and the Chambers may choose to hold one or more sittings in a place other than that in which the Court has its seat.

Article 26

1.   Where, by reason of a Judge being absent or prevented from attending, there is an even number of Judges, the most junior Judge within the meaning of Article 6 of these Rules shall abstain from taking part in the deliberations unless he is the Judge-Rapporteur. In that case the Judge immediately senior to him shall abstain from taking part in the deliberations.

2.   If, after the Grand Chamber or full Court has been convened, it is found that the quorum referred to in the third or rourth paragraph of Article 17 of the Statute has not been attained, the President shall adjourn the sitting until there is a quorum.

3.   If, in any Chamber five or three Judges the quorum referred to in the second paragraph of Article 17 and if it is not possible to replace the Judges prevented from attending in accordance with Article 11(e), of the Statute has not been attained the President of that Chamber shall so inform the President of the Court, who shall designate another Judge to complete the Chamber.

Article 27

1.   The Court shall deliberate in closed session.

2.   Only those Judges who were present at the oral proceedings and the Assistant Rapporteur, if any, entrusted with the consideration of the case may take part in the deliberations.

3.   Every Judge taking part in the deliberations shall state his opinion and the reasons for it.

4.   Any Judge may require that any questions be formulated in the language of his choice and communicated in writing to the Court before being put to the vote.

5.   The conclusions reached by the majority of the Judges after final discussion shall determine the decision of the Court. Votes shall be cast in reverse order to the order of precedence laid down in Article 6 of these Rules.

6.   Differences of view on the substance, wording or order of questions, or on the interpretation of the voting shall be settled by decision of the Court.

7.   Where the deliberations of the Court concern questions of its own administration, the Advocates-General shall take part and have a vote. The Registrar shall be present, unless the Court decides to the contrary.

8.   Where the court sits without the Registrar being present it shall, if necessary, instruct the most junior Judge within the meaning of Article 6 of these rules to draw up minutes. The minutes shall be signed by this Judge and by the President.

Article 28

1.   Subject to any special decision of the Court, its vacations shall be as follows:
   — from 18 December to 10 January,
   — from the Sunday before Easter to the second Sunday after Easter,
   — from 15 July to 15 September.
During the vacations, the functions of President shall be exercised at the place where the Court has its seat either by the President himself, keeping in touch with the Registrar, or by a President of Chamber or other Judge invited by the President to take his place.

2.   In a case of urgency, the President may convene the Judges and the Advocates-General during the vacations.

3.   The Court shall observe the official holidays of the place where it has its seat.

4.   The Court may, in proper circumstances, grant leave of absence to any Judge or Advocate-General.

CHAPTER 6   LANGUAGES

Article 29

1.   The language of a case shall be Danish, Dutch, English, French, Finnish, German, Greek, Irish, Italian, Portuguese, Spanish or Swedish.

2.   The language of the case shall be chosen by the applicant, except that:
   (a) where the defendant is a Member State or a natural or legal person having the nationality of a Member State, the language of the case shall be the official language of that State; where that State has more than one official language, the applicant may choose between them;

(b) at the joint request of the parties, the use of another of the languages mentioned in paragraph 1 for all or part of the proceedings may be authorised;

(c) at the request of one of the parties, and after the opposite party and the Advocate-General have been heard, the use of another of the languages mentioned in paragraph 1 as the language of the case for all or part of the proceedings may be authorised by way of derogation from sub-paragraphs (a) and (b). In cases to which Article 103 of these Rules applies, the language of the case shall be the language of the national court or tribunal which refers the matter to the Court. At the duly substantiated request of one of the parties to the main proceedings, and after the opposite party and the Advocate-General have been heard, the use of another of the languages mentioned in paragraph 1 may be authorised for the oral procedure. Requests as above may be decided on by the President; the latter may and, where he wishes to accede to a request without the agreement of all the parties, must refer the request to the Court.

3. The language of the case shall be used in the written and oral pleadings of the parties and in supporting documents, and also in the minutes and decisions of the Court.

Any supporting documents expressed in another language must be accompanied by a translation into the language of the case. In the case of lengthy documents, translations may be confined to extracts. However, the Court may, of its own motion or at the request of a party, at any time call for a complete or fuller translation.

Notwithstanding the foregoing provisions, a Member State shall be entitled to use its official language when intervening in a case before the Court or when taking part in any reference of a kind mentioned in Article 103. This provision shall apply both to written statements and to oral addresses. The Registrar shall cause any such statement or address to be translated into the language of the case.

The States, other than the Member States, which are parties to the EEA Agreement, and also the EFTA Surveillance Authority, may be authorised to use one of the languages mentioned in paragraph 1, other than the language of the case, when they intervene in a case before the Court or participate in preliminary ruling proceedings envisaged by Article 23 of the Statute. This provision shall apply both to written statements and oral addresses. The Registrar shall cause any such statement or address to be translated into the language of the case. Non-member States taking part in proceedings for a preliminary ruling pursuant to the fourth paragraph of Article 23 of the Statute may be authorised to use one of the languages mentioned in paragraph 1 of this Article other than the language of the case. This provision shall apply both to written documents and to oral statements. The Registrar shall in each case arrange for their translation into the language of the case.

4. Where a witness or expert states that he is unable adequately to express himself in one of the languages referred to in paragraph (1) of this Article, the Court may authorise him to give his evidence in another language. The Registrar shall arrange for translation into the language of the case.

5. The President of the Court and the Presidents of Chambers in conducting oral proceedings, the Judge-Rapporteur both in his preliminary report and in his report for the hearing, Judges and Advocates-General in putting questions and AdvocatesGeneral in delivering their opinions may use one of the languages referred to in paragraph (1) of this Article other than the language of the case. The Registrar shall arrange for translation into the language of the case.

Article 30

1. The Registrar shall, at the request of any Judge, of the Advocate-General or of a party, arrange for anything said or written in the course of the proceedings before the Court to be translated into the languages he chooses from those referred to in Article 29(1).

2.   Publications of the Court shall be issued in the languages referred to in Article 1 of Council Regulation No 1.

Article 31
The texts of documents drawn up in the language of the case or in any other language authorised by the Court pursuant to Article 29 of these rules shall be authentic.

CHAPTER 7   RIGHTS AND OBLIGATIONS OF AGENTS, ADVISERS AND LAWYERS

Article 32
1.   Agents, advisers and lawyers appearing before the Court or before any judicial authority to which the Court has addressed letters rogatory, shall enjoy immunity in respect of words spoken or written by them concerning the case or the parties.
2.   Agents, advisers and lawyers shall enjoy the following further privileges and facilities:
   (a) papers and documents relating to the proceedings shall be exempt from both search and seizure; in the event of a dispute the customs officials or police may seal those papers and documents; they shall then be immediately forwarded to the Court for inspection in the presence of the Registrar and of the person concerned;
   (b) agents, advisers and lawyers shall be entitled to such allocation of foreign currency as may be necessary for the performance of their duties;
   (c) agents, advisers and lawyers shall be entitled to travel in the course of duty without hindrance.

Article 33
In order to qualify for the privileges, immunities and facilities specified in Article 32, persons entitled to them shall furnish proof of their status as follows:
   (a) agents shall produce an official document issued by the party for whom they act, and shall forward without delay a copy thereof to the Registrar;
   (b) advisers and lawyers shall produce a certificate signed by the Registrar. The validity of this certificate shall be limited to a specified period, which may be extended or curtailed according to the length of the proceedings.

Article 34
The privileges, immunities and facilities specified in Article 32 of these Rules are granted exclusively in the interests of the proper conduct of proceedings.
   The Court may waive the immunity where it considers that the proper conduct of proceedings will not be hindered thereby.

Article 35
1.   Any adviser or lawyer whose conduct towards the Court, a Judge, an Advocate-General or the Registrar is incompatible with the dignity of the Court, or who uses his rights for purposes other than those for which they were granted, may at any time be excluded from the proceedings by an order of the Court, after the Advocate-General has been heard; the person concerned shall be given an opportunity to defend himself.
   The order shall have immediate effect.
2.   Where an adviser or lawyer is excluded from the proceedings, the proceedings shall be suspended for a period fixed by the President in order to allow the party concerned to appoint another adviser or lawyer.
3.   Decisions taken under this Article may be rescinded.

Article 36
The provisions of this Chapter shall apply to university teachers who have a right of audience before the Court in accordance with Article 19 of the Statute.

TITLE II   PROCEDURE

CHAPTER 1   WRITTEN PROCEDURE

Article 37

1.   The original of every pleading must be signed by the party's agent or lawyer. The original, accompanied by all annexes referred to therein, shall be lodged together with five copies for the Court and a copy for every other party to the proceedings. Copies shall be certified by the party lodging them.

2.   Institutions shall in addition produce, within time-limits laid down by the Court, translations of all pleadings into the other languages provided for by Article 1 of Council Regulation No 1. The second sub-paragraph of paragraph (1) of this Article shall apply.

3.   All pleadings shall bear a date. In the reckoning of time-limits for taking steps in proceedings, only the date of lodgment at the Registry shall be taken into account.

4.   To every pleading there shall be annexed a file containing the documents relied on in support of it, together with a schedule listing them.

5.   Where in view of the length of a document only extracts from it are annexed to the pleading, the whole document or a full copy of it shall be lodged at the Registry.

6.   Without prejudice to the provisions of paragraphs 1 to 5, the date on which a copy of the signed original of a pleading, including the schedule of documents referred to in paragraph 4, is received at the Registry by telefax or other technical means of communication available to the Court shall be deemed to be the date of lodgment for the purposes of compliance with the time-limits for taking steps in proceedings, provided that the signed original of the pleading, accompanied by the annexes and copies referred to in the second sub-paragraph of paragraph 1 above, is lodged at the Registry no later than ten days thereafter.

Article 38

1.   An application of the kind referred to in Article 21 of the Statute shall state:
   (a)   the name and address of the applicant;
   (b)   the designation of the party against whom the application is made;
   (c)   the subject-matter of the proceedings and a summary of the pleas in law on which the application is based;
   (d)   the form of order sought by the applicant;
   (e)   where appropriate, the nature of any evidence offered in support.

2.   For the purpose of the proceedings, the application shall state an address for service in the place where the Court has its seat and the name of the person who is authorised and has expressed willingness to accept service.

In addition to, or instead of, specifying an address for service as referred to in the first sub-paragraph, the application may state that the lawyer or agent agrees that service is to be effected on him by telefax or other technical means of communication.

If the application does not comply with the requirements referred to in the first and second sub-paragraphs, all service on the party concerned for the purpose of the proceedings shall be effected, for so long as the defect has not been cured, by registered letter addressed to the agent or lawyer of that party. By way of derogation from Article 79(1), service shall then be deemed to be duly effected by the lodging of the registered letter at the post office of the place where the Court has its seat.

3.   The lawyer acting for a party must lodge at the Registry a certificate that he is authorised to practise before a court of a Member State or of another State which is a party to the EEA Agreement.

4.   The application shall be accompanied, where appropriate, by the documents specified in the second paragraph of Article 21 of the.

5.   An application made by a legal person governed by private law shall be accompanied by:

(a) the instrument or instruments constituting or regulating that legal person or a recent extract from the register of companies, firms or associations or any other proof of its existence in law;

(b) proof that the authority granted to the applicant's lawyer has been properly conferred on him by someone authorised for the purpose.

6.   An application submitted under Articles 238 and 239 of the EC Treaty, and Articles 153 and 154 of the EAEC Treaty shall be accompanied by a copy of the arbitration clause contained in the contract governed by private or public law entered into by the Communities or on their behalf, or, as the case may be, by a copy of the special agreement concluded between the Member States concerned.

7.   If an application does not comply with the requirements set out in paragraphs (3) to (6) of this Article, the Registrar shall prescribe a reasonable period within which the applicant is to comply with them whether by putting the application itself in order or by producing any of the abovementioned documents. If the applicant fails to put the application in order or to produce the required documents within the time prescribed, the Court shall, after hearing the Advocate-General, decide whether the noncompliance with these conditions renders the application formally inadmissible.

Article 39

The application shall be served on the defendant. In a case where Article 38 (7) applies, service shall be effected as soon as the application has been put in order or the Court has declared it admissible notwithstanding the failure to observe the formal requirements set out in that Article.

Article 40

1.   Within one month after service on him of the application, the defendant shall lodge a defence, stating:

(a) the name and address of the defendant;

(b) the arguments of fact and law relied on;

(c) the form of order sought by the defendant;

(d) the nature of any evidence offered by him.

The provisions of Article 38 (2) to (5) of these Rules shall apply to the defence.

2.   The time-limit laid down in paragraph (1) of this Article may be extended by the President on a reasoned application by the defendant.

Article 41

1.   The application initiating the proceedings and the defence may be supplemented by a reply from the applicant and by a rejoinder from the defendant.

2.   The President shall fix the time-limits within which these pleadings are to be lodged.

Article 42

1.   In reply or rejoinder a party may offer further evidence. The party must however, give reasons for the delay in offering it.

2.   No new plea in law may be introduced in the course of proceedings unless it is based on matters of law or of fact which come to light in the course of the procedure.

If in the course of the procedure one of the parties puts forward a new plea in law which is so based, the President may, even after the expiry of the normal procedural time-limits, acting on a report of the Judge-Rapporteur and after hearing the Advocate-General, allow the other party time to answer on that plea.

The decision on the admissibility of the plea shall be reserved for the final judgment.

Article 43

The Court may, at any time, after hearing the parties and the Advocate-General, if the assignment referred to in Article 10 (2) has taken place, order that two or more cases concerning the same subject-matter shall, on account of the connection between them, be joined for the purposes of the written or oral procedure or of the final judgment. The cases may subsequently be disjoined. The President may refer these matters to the Court.

CHAPTER 1(a)   THE PRELIMINARY REPORT AND ASSIGNMENT OF CASES TO FORMATIONS

Article 44

1.   The President shall fix a date on which the Judge-Rapporteur is to present his preliminary report to the general meeting of the Court, either:
   (a) after the rejoinder has been lodged; or
   (b) where no reply or no rejoinder has been lodged within the time-limit fixed in accordance with Article 41(2); or
   (c) where the party concerned has waived his right to lodge a reply or rejoinder; or
   (d) where the expedited procedure referred to in Article 62(a) is to be applied, when the President fixes a date for the hearing.

2.   The preliminary report shall contain recommendations as to whether a preparatory inquiry or any other preparatory step should be undertaken and as to the formation to which the case should be assigned. It shall also contain the Judge-Rapporteur's recommendation, if any, as to whether to dispense with a hearing as provided for in Article 44(a) and as to whether to dispense with an opinion of the Advocate General pursuant to the fifth subparagraph of Article 20 of the Statute.

The Court shall decide, after hearing the Advocate General, what action to take upon the recommendations of the Judge-Rapporteur.

3.   The Court shall assign to the Chambers of five and three Judges any case brought before it in so far as the difficulty or importance of the case or particular circumstances are not such as to require that it should be assigned to the Grand Chamber.

However, a case may not be assigned to a Chamber of five or three Judges if a Member State or an institution of the Communities, being a party to the proceedings, has requested that the case be decided by the Grand Chamber. For the purposes of this provision, 'party to the proceedings' means any Member State or any institution which is a party to or an intervener in the proceedings or which has submitted written observations in any reference of a kind mentioned in Article 103. A request such as that referred to in this subparagraph may not be made in proceedings between the Communities and their servants.

The Court shall sit as a full Court where cases are brought before it pursuant to the provisions referred to in the fourth paragraph of Article 16 of the Statute. It may assign a case to the full Court where, in accordance with the fifth paragraph of Article 16 of the Statute, it considers that the case is of exceptional importance.

4.   The formation to which a case has been assigned may, at any stage of the proceedings, refer the case back to the Court in order that it may be reassigned to a formation composed of a greater number of Judges.

5.   Where a preparatory inquiry has been opened, the formation determining the case may, if it does not undertake it itself, assign the inquiry to the Chamber referred to in Article 9(2) of these Rules.

Where the oral procedure is opened without an inquiry, the President of the formation determining the case shall fix the opening date.

Article 44a

Without prejudice to any special provisions laid down in these Rules, the procedure before the Court shall also include an oral part. However, after the pleadings referred to in Article 40(1) and, as the case may be, in Article 41(1) have been lodged, the Court, acting on a report from the Judge-Rapporteur and after hearing the Advocate-General, and if none of the parties has submitted an application setting out the reasons for which he wishes to be heard, may decide otherwise. The application shall be submitted within a period of one month from notification to the party of the close of the written procedure. That period may be extended by the President.

CHAPTER 2   PREPARATORY INQUIRIES AND OTHER PREPARATORY MEASURES

SECTION 1   MEASURES OF INQUIRY

Article 45

1.   The Court, after hearing the Advocate-General, shall prescribe the measures of inquiry that it considers appropriate by means of an order setting out the facts to be proved. Before the Court decides on the measures of inquiry referred to in paragraph (2)(c), (d) and (e) the parties shall be heard. The order shall be served on the parties.

2.   Without prejudice to Articles 24 and 25 of the Statute, the following measures of inquiry may be adopted:

    (a) the personal appearance of the parties;

    (b) a request for information and production of documents;

    (c) oral testimony;

    (d) the commissioning of an expert's report;

    (e) an inspection of the place or thing in question.

3.   The measures of inquiry which the Court has ordered may be conducted by the Court itself, or be assigned to the Judge-Rapporteur. The Advocate-General shall take part in the measures of inquiry.

4.   Evidence may be submitted in rebuttal and previous evidence may be amplified.

Article 46

1.   A Chamber to which a preparatory inquiry has been assigned may exercise the powers vested in the Court by Articles 45 and 47 to 53 of these Rules; the powers vested in the President of the Court may be exercised by the President of the Chamber.

2.   Articles 56 and 57 of the Rules shall apply in a corresponding manner to proceedings before the Chamber.

3.   The parties shall be entitled to attend the measures of inquiry.

SECTION 2   THE SUMMONING AND EXAMINATION OF WITNESSES AND EXPERTS

Article 47

1.   The Court may, either of its own motion or an application by a party, and after hearing the Advocate-General, order that certain facts be proved by witnesses. The order of the Court shall set out the facts to be established.

The Court may summon a witness of its own motion or on application by a party or at the instance of the Advocate-General.

An application by a party for the examination of a witness shall state precisely about what facts and for what reasons the witness should be examined.

2.   The witness shall be summoned by an order of the Court containing the following information:

    (a) the surname, forenames, description and address of the witness;

    (b) an indication of the facts about which the witness is to be examined;

    (c) where appropriate, particulars of the arrangements made by the Court for reimbursement of expenses incurred by the witness, and of the penalties which may be imposed on defaulting witnesses. The order shall be served on the parties and the witnesses.

3.   The Court may make the summoning of a witness for whose examination a party has

applied conditional upon the deposit with the cashier of the Court of a sum sufficient to cover the taxed costs thereof; the Court shall fix the amount of the payment. The cashier shall advance the funds necessary in connection with the examination of any witness summoned by the Court of its own motion.

4.   After the identity of the witness has been established, the President shall inform him that he will be required to vouch the truth of his evidence in the manner laid down in these Rules.

The witness shall give his evidence to the Court, the parties having been given notice to attend. After the witness has given his main evidence the President may, at the request of a party or of his own motion, put questions to him. The other Judges and the Advocate-General may do likewise. Subject to the control of the President, questions may be put to witnesses by the representatives of the parties.

5.   After giving his evidence, the witness shall take the following oath: 'I swear that I have spoken the truth, the whole truth and nothing but the truth.'

The Court may, after hearing the parties, exempt a witness from taking the oath.

6.   The Registrar shall draw up minutes in which the evidence of each witness is reproduced.

The minutes shall be signed by the President or by the Judge-Rapporteur responsible for conducting the examination of the witness, and by the Registrar. Before the minutes are thus signed, witnesses must be given an opportunity to check the content of the minutes and to sign them. The minutes shall constitute an official record.

Article 48

1.   Witnesses who have been duly summoned shall obey the summons and attend for examination.

2.   If a witness who has been duly summoned fails to appear before the Court, the Court may impose upon him a pecuniary penalty not exceeding ECU 5000 and may order that a further summons be served on the witness at his own expense. The same penalty may be imposed upon a witness who, without good reason, refuses to give evidence or to take the oath or where appropriate to make a solemn affirmation equivalent thereto.

3.   If the witness proffers a valid excuse to the Court, the pecuniary penalty imposed on him may be cancelled. The pecuniary penalty imposed may be reduced at the request of the witness where he establishes that it is disproportionate to his income.

4.   Penalties imposed and other measures ordered under this Article shall be enforced in accordance with Articles 244 and 256 of the EC Treaty, and Articles 159 and 164 of the EAEC Treaty.

Article 49

1.   The Court may order that an expert's report be obtained. The order appointing the expert shall define his task and set a time-limit within which he is to make his report.

2.   The expert shall receive a copy of the order, together with all the documents necessary for carrying out his task. He shall be under the supervision of the Judge-Rapporteur, who may be present during his investigation and who shall be kept informed of his progress in carrying out his task. The Court may request the parties or one of them to lodge security for the costs of the expert's report.

3.   At the request of the expert, the Court may order the examination of witnesses. Their examination shall be carried out in accordance with Article 47 of these Rules.

4.   The expert may give his opinion only on points which have been expressly referred to him.

5.   After the expert has made his report, the Court may order that he be examined, the parties having been given notice to attend. Subject to the control of the President, questions may be put to the expert by the representatives of the parties.

6.   After making his report, the expert shall take the following oath before the Court: 'I swear that I have conscientiously and impartially carried out my task.'

The Court may, after hearing the parties, exempt the expert from taking the oath.

Article 50

1.   If one of the parties objects to a witness or to an expert on the ground that he is not a competent or proper person to act as witness or expert or for any other reason, or if a witness or expert refuses to give evidence, to take the oath or to make a solemn affirmation equivalent thereto, the matter shall be resolved by the Court.

2.   An objection to a witness or to an expert shall be raised within two weeks after service of the order summoning the witness or appointing the expert; the statement of objection must set out the grounds of objection and indicate the nature of any evidence offered.

Article 51

1.   Witnesses and experts shall be entitled to reimbursement of their travel and subsistence expenses. The cashier of the Court may make a payment to them towards these expenses in advance.

2.   Witnesses shall be entitled to compensation for loss of earnings, and experts to fees for their services. The cashier of the Court shall pay witnesses and experts their compensation or fees after they have carried out their respective duties or tasks.

Article 52

The Court may, on application by a party or of its own motion, issue letters rogatory for the examination of witnesses or experts, as provided for in the supplementary rules mentioned in Article 125 of these Rules.

Article 53

1.   The Registrar shall draw up minutes of every hearing. The minutes shall be signed by the President and by the Registrar and shall constitute an official record.

2.   The parties may inspect the minutes and any expert's report at the Registry and obtain copies at their own expense.

SECTION 4

Article 54a

The Judge-Rapporteur and the Advocate-General may request the parties to submit within a specified period all such information relating to the facts, and all such documents or other particulars, as they may consider relevant. The information and/or documents provided shall be communicated to the other parties.

SECTION 3   CLOSURE OF THE PREPARATORY INQUIRY

Article 54

Unless the Court prescribes a period within which the parties may lodge written observations, the President shall fix the date for the opening of the oral procedure after the preparatory inquiry has been completed. Where a period had been prescribed for the lodging of written observations, the President shall fix the date for the opening of the oral procedure after that period has expired.

CHAPTER 3   ORAL PROCEDURE

Article 55

1.   Subject to the priority of decisions provided for in Article 85 of these Rules, the Court shall deal with the cases before it in the order in which the preparatory inquiries in

them have been completed. Where the preparatory inquiries in several cases are completed simultaneously, the order in which they are to be dealt with shall be determined by the dates of entry in the register of the applications initiating them respectively.

2.   The President may in special circumstances order that a case be given priority over others. The President may in special circumstances, after hearing the parties and the Advocate-General, either on his own initiative or at the request of one of the parties, defer a case to be dealt with at a later date. On a joint application by the parties the President may order that a case be deferred.

Article 56

1.   The proceedings shall be opened and directed by the President, who shall be responsible for the proper conduct of the hearing.

2.   The oral proceedings in cases heard in camera shall not be published.

Article 57

The President may in the course of the hearing put questions to the agents, advisers or lawyers of the parties. The other Judges and the Advocate-General may do likewise.

Article 58

A party may address the Court only through his agent, adviser or lawyer.

Article 59

1.   The Advocate-General shall deliver his opinion orally at the end of the oral procedure.

2.   After the Advocate-General has delivered his opinion, the President shall declare the oral procedure closed.

Article 60

The Court may at any time, in accordance with Article 45 (1), after hearing the Advocate-General, order any measure of inquiry to be taken or that a previous inquiry be repeated or expanded. The Court may direct the Chamber or the Judge-Rapporteur to carry out the measures so ordered.

Article 61

The Court may after hearing the Advocate-General order the reopening of the oral procedure.

Article 62

1.   The Registrar shall draw up minutes of every hearing. The minutes shall be signed by the President and by the Registrar and shall constitute an official record.

2.   The parties may inspect the minutes at the Registry and obtain copies at their own expense.

CHAPTER 3a   EXPEDITED PROCEDURES

Article 62a

1.   On application by the applicant or the defendant, the President may exceptionally decide, on the basis of a recommendation by the Judge-Rapporteur and after hearing the other party and the Advocate-General, that a case is to be determined pursuant to an expedited procedure derogating from the provisions of these Rules, where the particular urgency of the case requires the Court to give its ruling with the minimum of delay. An application for a case to be decided under an expedited procedure shall be made by a separate document lodged at the same time as the application initiating the proceedings or the defence, as the case may be.

2.   Under the expedited procedure, the originating application and the defence may be supplemented by a reply and a rejoinder only if the President considers this to be necessary. An intervener may lodge a statement in intervention only if the President considers this to be necessary.

3.   Once the defence has been lodged or, if the decision to adjudicate under an expedited procedure is not made until after that pleading has been lodged, once that decision has been taken, the President shall fix a date for the hearing, which shall be communicated forthwith to the parties. He may postpone the date of the hearing where the organisation of measures of inquiry or of other preparatory measures so requires. Without prejudice to Article 42, the parties may supplement their arguments and offer further evidence in the course of the oral procedure. They must, however, give reasons for the delay in offering such further evidence.

4.   The Court shall give its ruling after hearing the Advocate-General.

CHAPTER 4   JUDGMENTS

Article 63
The judgment shall contain:
- a statement that it is the judgment of the Court,
- the date of its delivery,
- the names of the President and of the Judges taking part in it,
- the name of the Advocate-General,
- the name of the Registrar,
- the description of the parties,
- the names of the agents, advisers and lawyers of the parties,
- a statement of the forms of order sought by the parties,
- a statement that the Advocate-General has been heard,
- a summary of the facts,
- the grounds for the decision,
- the operative part of the judgment, including the decision as to costs.

Article 64
1.   The judgment shall be delivered in open court; the parties shall be given notice to attend to hear it.

2.   The original of the judgment, signed by the President, by the Judges who took part in the deliberations and by the Registrar, shall be sealed and deposited at the Registry; the parties shall be served with certified copies of the judgment.

3.   The Registrar shall record on the original of the judgment the date on which it was delivered.

Article 65
The judgment shall be binding from the date of its delivery.

Article 66
1.   Without prejudice to the provisions relating to the interpretation of judgments the Court may, of its own motion or on application by a party made within two weeks after the delivery of a judgment, rectify clerical mistakes, errors in calculation and obvious slips in it.

2.   The parties, whom the Registrar shall duly notify, may lodge written observations within a period prescribed by the President.

3.   The Court shall take its decision in closed session after hearing the Advocate-General.

4.   The original of the rectification order shall be annexed to the original of the rectified judgment. A note of this order shall be made in the margin of the original of the rectified judgment.

Article 67
If the Court should omit to give a decision on a specific head of claim or on costs, any party may within a month after service of the judgment apply to the Court to supplement its judgment. The application shall be served on the opposite party and the President shall prescribe a period within which that party may lodge written observations. After these

observations have been lodged, the Court shall, after hearing the Advocate-General, decide both on the admissibility and on the substance of the application.

Article 68
The Registrar shall arrange for the publication of reports of cases before the Court.

CHAPTER 5   COSTS

Article 69
1.   A decision as to costs shall be given in the final judgment or in the order which closes the proceedings.

2.   The unsuccessful party shall be ordered to pay the costs if they have been applied for in the successful party's pleadings. Where there are several unsuccessful parties the Court shall decide how the costs are to be shared.

3.   Where each party succeeds on some and fails on other heads, or where the circumstances are exceptional, the Court may order that the costs be shared or that the parties bear their own costs. The States, other than the Member States, which are parties to the EEA Agreement, and also the EFTA Surveillance Authority, shall bear their own costs if they intervene in the proceedings. The Court may order a party, even if successful, to pay costs which the Court considers that party to have unreasonably or vexatiously caused the opposite party to incur.

4.   The Member States and institutions which intervene in the proceedings shall bear their own costs. The Court may order an intervener other than those mentioned in the preceding sub-paragraph to bear his own costs.

5.   A party who discontinues or withdraws from proceedings shall be ordered to pay the costs if they have been applied for in the other party's observations on the discontinuance pleadings.

However, upon application by the party who discontinues or withdraws from proceedings, the costs shall be borne by the other party if this appears justified by the conduct of that party.

If costs are not applied for, the parties shall bear their own costs.

6.   Where a case does not proceed to judgment the costs shall be in the discretion of the Court.

Article 70
Without prejudice to the second sub-paragraph of Article 69 (3) of these Rules, in proceedings between the Communities and their servants the institutions shall bear their own costs.

Article 71
Costs necessarily incurred by a party in enforcing a judgment or order of the Court shall be refunded by the opposite party on the scale in force in the State where the enforcement takes place.

Article 72
Proceedings before the Court shall be free of charge, except that:
- (a) where a party has caused the Court to incur avoidable costs the Court may, after hearing the Advocate-General, order that party to refund them;
- (b) where copying or translation work is carried out at the request of a party, the cost shall, in so far as the Registrar considers it excessive, be paid for by that party on the scale of charges referred to in Article 16 (5) of these Rules.

Article 73
Without prejudice to the preceding Article, the following shall be regarded as recoverable costs:

(a) sums payable to witnesses and experts under Article 51 of these Rules;

(b) expenses necessarily incurred by the parties for the purpose of the proceedings, in particular the travel and subsistence expenses and the remuneration of agents, advisers or lawyers.

Article 74

1.   If there is a dispute concerning the costs to be recovered, the Chamber referred to in Article 9(2) of these Rules to which the case has been assigned shall, on application by the party concerned and after hearing the opposite party and the Advocate-General, make an order, from which no appeal shall lie.

2.   The parties may, for the purposes of enforcement, apply for an authenticated copy of the order.

Article 75

1.   Sums due from the cashier of the Court shall be paid in the currency of the country where the Court has its seat. At the request of the person entitled to any sum, it shall be paid in the currency of the country where the expenses to be refunded were incurred or where the steps in respect of which payment is due were taken.

2.   Other debtors shall make payment in the currency of their country of origin.

3.   Conversions of currency shall be made at the official rates of exchange ruling on the day of payment in the country where the Court has its seat.

CHAPTER 6   LEGAL AID

Article 76

1.   A party who is wholly or in part unable to meet the costs of the proceedings may at any time apply for legal aid. The application shall be accompanied by evidence of the applicant's need of assistance, and in particular by a document from the competent authority certifying his lack of means.

2.   If the application is made prior to proceedings which the applicant wishes to commence, it shall briefly state the subject of such proceedings. The application need not be made through a lawyer.

3.   The President shall designate a Judge to act as Rapporteur. The Chamber of three Judges to which the latter belongs shall, after considering the written observations of the opposite party and after hearing the Advocate-General, decide whether legal aid should be granted in full or in part, or whether it should be refused. The Chamber shall consider whether there is manifestly no cause of action. The Chamber shall make an order without giving reasons, and no appeal shall lie therefrom.

4.   The Chamber may at any time, either of its own motion or on application, withdraw legal aid if the circumstances which led to its being granted alter during the proceedings.

5.   Where legal aid is granted, the cashier of the Court shall advance the funds necessary to meet the expenses. In its decision as to costs the Court may order the payment to the cashier of the Court of the whole or any part of amounts advanced as legal aid. The Registrar shall take steps to obtain the recovery of these sums from the party ordered to pay them.

CHAPTER 7   DISCONTINUANCE

Article 77

If, before the Court has given its decision, the parties reach a settlement of their dispute and intimate to the Court the abandonment of their claims, the President shall order the case to be removed from the register and shall give a decision as to costs in accordance with Article 69(5), having regard to any proposals made by the parties on the matter.

This provision shall not apply to proceedings under Articles 230 and 232 of the EC Treaty or Articles 146 and 148 of the EC Treaty.

Article 78

If the applicant informs the Court in writing that he wishes to discontinue the proceedings, the President shall order the case to be removed from the register and shall give a decision as to costs in accordance with Article 69(5).

CHAPTER 8   SERVICE

Article 79

1.   Where these Rules require that a document be served on a person, the Registrar shall ensure that service is effected at that person's address for service either by the dispatch of a copy of the document by registered post with a form for acknowledgement of receipt or by personal delivery of the copy against a receipt. The Registrar shall prepare and certify the copies of documents to be served, save where the parties themselves supply the copies in accordance with Article 37(1) of these Rules.

2.   Where, in accordance with the second sub-paragraph of Article 38(2), the addressee has agreed that service is to be effected on him by telefax or other technical means of communication, any procedural document other than a judgment or order of the Court may be served by the transmission of a copy of the document by such means. Where, for technical reasons or on account of the nature or length of the document, such transmission is impossible or impracticable, the document shall be served, if the addressee has failed to state an address for service, at his address in accordance with the procedures laid down in paragraph 1 of this article. The addressee shall be so advised by telefax or other technical means of communication. Service shall then be deemed to have been effected on the addressee by registered post on the tenth day following the lodging of the registered letter at the post office of the place where the Court has its seat, unless it is shown by the acknowledgement of receipt that the letter was received on a different date or the addressee informs the Registrar, within three weeks of being advised by telefax or other technical means of communication, that the document to be served has not reached him.

CHAPTER 9   TIME LIMITS

Article 80

1.   Any period of time prescribed by the Union Treaty, the EC Treaty and the EAEC Treaty, the Statute of the Court or these Rules for the taking of any procedural step shall be reckoned as follows:

    (a)   where a period expressed in days, weeks, months or years is to be calculated from the moment at which an event occurs or an action takes place, the day during which that event occurs or that action takes place shall not be counted as falling within the period in question;

    (b)   a period expressed in weeks, months or in years shall end with the expiry of whichever day in the last week, month or year is the same day of the week, or falls on the same date, as the day during which the event or action from which the period is to be calculated occurred or took place. If, in a period expressed in months or in years, the day on which it should expire does not occur in the last month, the period shall end with the expiry of the last day of that month;

    (c)   where a period is expressed in months and days, it shall first be reckoned in whole months, then in days;

    (d)   periods shall include official holidays, Sundays and Saturdays;

    (e)   periods shall not be suspended during the judicial vacations.

2.   If the period would otherwise end on a Saturday, Sunday or an official holiday, it shall be extended until the end of the first following working day. A list of official holidays drawn up by the Court shall be published in the Official Journal of the European Union.

Article 81

1.   Where the period of time allowed for initiating proceedings against a measure adopted by an institution runs from the publication of that measure, that period shall be calculated, for the purposes of Article 80 (1) (a), from the end of the 14th day after publication thereof in the Official Journal of the European Union.

2.   The prescribed time-limits shall be extended on account of distance by a single period of ten days.

Article 82

Any time limit prescribed pursuant to these Rules may be extended by whoever prescribed it.

The President and the Presidents of Chambers may delegate to the Registrar power of signature for the purpose of fixing time limits which, pursuant to these Rules, it falls to them to prescribe or of extending such time limits.

CHAPTER 10   STAY OF PROCEEDINGS

Article 82a

1.   The proceedings may be stayed:
   (a)   in the circumstances specified in the third paragraph of Article 54 of the Statute, by order of the Court, made after hearing the Advocate-General;
   (b)   in all other cases, by decision of the President adopted after hearing the Advocate-General and, save in the case of references for a preliminary ruling as referred to in Article 103, the parties. The proceedings may be resumed by order or decision, following the same procedure. The orders or decisions referred to in this paragraph shall be served on the parties.

2.   The stay of proceedings shall take effect on the date indicated in the order or decision of stay or, in the absence of such indication, on the date of that order or decision. While proceedings are stayed time shall cease to run for the purposes of prescribed time limits for all parties.

3.   Where the order or decision of stay does not fix the length of stay, it shall end on the date indicated in the order or decision of resumption or, in the absence of such indication, on the date of the order or decision of resumption. From the date of resumption time shall begin to run afresh for the purposes of the time limits.

TITLE III   SPECIAL FORMS OF PROCEDURE

CHAPTER 1   SUSPENSION OF OPERATION OR ENFORCEMENT AND OTHER INTERIM MEASURES

Article 83

1.   An application to suspend the operation of any measure adopted by an institution, made pursuant to Article 242 of the EC Treaty, or Article 157 of the EAEC Treaty shall be admissible only if the applicant is challenging that measure in proceedings before the Court.

An application for the adoption of any other interim measure referred to in Article 243 of the EC Treaty or Article 158 of the EAEC Treaty shall be admissible only if it is made by a party to a case before the Court and relates to that case.

2.   An application of a kind referred to in paragraph (1) of this Article shall state the subject-matter of the proceedings, the circumstances giving rise to urgency and the pleas of fact and law establishing a prima facie case for the interim measures applied for.

3.   The application shall be made by a separate document and in accordance with the provisions of Articles 37 and 38 of these Rules.

Article 84

1.   The application shall be served on the opposite party, and the President shall prescribe a short period within which that party may submit written or oral observations.

2.   The President may order a preparatory inquiry.

The President may grant the application even before the observations of the opposite party have been submitted. This decision may be varied or cancelled even without any application being made by any party.

Article 85

The President shall either decide on the application himself or refer it to the Court.

If the President is absent or prevented from attending, Article 11 of these Rules shall apply.

Where the application is referred to it, the Court shall postpone all other cases, and shall give a decision after hearing the Advocate-General. Article 84 shall apply.

Article 86

1.   The decision on the application shall take the form of a reasoned order, from which no appeal shall lie. The order shall be served on the parties forthwith.

2.   The enforcement of the order may be made conditional on the lodging by the applicant of security, of an amount and nature to be fixed in the light of the circumstances.

3.   Unless the order fixes the date on which the interim measure is to lapse, the measure shall lapse when final judgment is delivered.

4.   The order shall have only an interim effect, and shall be without prejudice to the decision of the Court on the substance of the case.

Article 87

On application by a party, the order may at any time be varied or cancelled on account of a change in circumstances.

Article 88

Rejection of an application for an interim measure shall not bar the party who made it from making a further application on the basis of new facts.

Article 89

The provisions of this Chapter shall apply to applications to suspend the enforcement of a decision of the Court or of any measure adopted by another institution, submitted pursuant to Articles 244 and 256 of the EC Treaty or Articles 159 and 164 of the EAEC Treaty. The order granting the application shall fix, where appropriate, a date on which the interim measure is to lapse.

Article 90

1.   An application of a kind referred to in the third and fourth paragraphs of Article 81 of the EAEC Treaty shall contain:

(a)   the names and addresses of the persons or undertakings to be inspected;

(b)   an indication of what is to be inspected and of the purpose of the inspection.

2.   The President shall give his decision in the form of an order. Article 86 of these Rules shall apply.

If the President is absent or prevented from attending, Article 11 of these Rules shall apply.

CHAPTER 2   PRELIMINARY ISSUES

Article 91

1.   A party applying to the Court for a decision on a preliminary objection or other preliminary plea not going to the substance of the case shall make the application by a

separate document. The application must state the pleas of fact and law relied on and the form of order sought by the applicant; any supporting documents must be annexed to it.

2.   As soon as the application has been lodged, the President shall prescribe a period within which the opposite party may lodge a document containing a statement of the form of order sought by that party and its pleas in law.

3.   Unless the Court decides otherwise, the remainder of the proceedings shall be oral.

4.   The Court shall, after hearing the Advocate-General, decide on the application or reserve its decision for the final judgment. If the Court refuses the application or reserves its decision, the President shall prescribe new time-limits for the further steps in the proceedings.

Article 92

1.   Where it is clear that the Court has no jurisdiction to take cognisance of an action or where the action is manifestly inadmissible, the Court may, by reasoned order, after hearing the Advocate-General and without taking further steps in the proceedings, give a decision on the action.

2.   The Court may at any time of its own motion consider whether there exists any absolute bar to proceeding with a case or declare, after hearing the parties, that the action has become devoid of purpose and that there is no need to adjudicate on it; it shall give its decision in accordance with Article 91 (3) and (4) of these Rules.

CHAPTER 3   INTERVENTION

Article 93

1.   An application to intervene must be made within six weeks of the publication of the notice referred to in Article 16 (6) of these Rules.

The application shall contain:
- (a) the description of the case;
- (b) the description of the parties;
- (c) the name and address of the intervener;
- (d) the intervener's address for service at the place where the Court has its seat;
- (e) the form of order sought, by one or more of the parties, in support of which the intervener is applying for leave to intervene;
- (f) a statement of the circumstances establishing the right to intervene, where the application is submitted pursuant to the second or third paragraph of Article 40 of of the Statute.

The intervener shall be represented in accordance with Article 19 of the Statute. Articles 37 and 38 of these Rules shall apply.

2.   The application shall be served on the parties.

The President shall give the parties an opportunity to submit their written or oral observations before deciding on the application. The President shall decide on the application by order or shall refer the application to the Court.

3.   If the President allows the intervention, the intervener shall receive a copy of every document served on the parties. The President may, however, on application by one of the parties, omit secret or confidential documents.

4.   The intervener must accept the case as he finds it at the time of his intervention.

5.   The President shall prescribe a period within which the intervener may submit a statement in intervention.

The statement in intervention shall contain:
- (a) a statement of the form of order sought by the intervener in support of or opposing, in whole or in part, the form of order sought by one of the parties;
- (b) the pleas in law and arguments relied on by the intervener;
- (c) where appropriate, the nature of any evidence offered.

6.   After the statement in intervention has been lodged, the President shall, where necessary, prescribe a time-limit within which the parties may reply to that statement.

7.   Consideration may be given to an application to intervene which is made after the expiry of the period prescribed in paragraph 1 but before the decision to open the oral procedure provided for in Article 44(3). In that event, if the President allows the intervention, the intervener may, on the basis of the Report for the Hearing communicated to him, submit his observations during the oral procedure, if that procedure takes place.

CHAPTER 4   JUDGMENTS BY DEFAULT AND APPLICATIONS TO SET THEM ASIDE

Article 94

1.   If a defendant on whom an application initiating proceedings has been duly served fails to lodge a defence to the application in the proper form within the time prescribed, the applicant may apply for judgment by default. The application shall be served on the defendant. The President shall fix a date for the opening of the oral procedure.

2.   Before giving judgment by default the Court shall, after hearing the Advocate-General, consider whether the application initiating proceedings is admissible, whether the appropriate formalities have been complied with, and whether the application appears well founded. The Court may decide to open the oral procedure on the application.

3.   A judgment by default shall be enforceable. The Court may, however, grant a stay of execution until the Court has given its decision on any application under paragraph (4) to set aside the judgment, or it may make execution subject to the provision of security of an amount and nature to be fixed in the light of the circumstances; this security shall be released if no such application is made or if the application fails.

4.   Application may be made to set aside a judgment by default. The application to set aside the judgment must be made within one month from the date of service of the judgment and must be lodged in the form prescribed by Articles 37 and 38 of these Rules.

5.   After the application has been served, the President shall prescribe a period within which the other party may submit his written observations. The proceedings shall be conducted in accordance with Articles 44 et seq. of these Rules.

6.   The Court shall decide by way of a judgment which may not be set aside. The original of this judgment shall be annexed to the original of the judgment by default. A note of the judgment on the application to set aside shall be made in the margin of the original of the judgment by default.

Article 95
(repealed)

Article 96
(repealed)

CHAPTER 6   EXCEPTIONAL REVIEW PROCEDURES

SECTION 1   THIRD-PARTY PROCEEDINGS

Article 97

1.   Articles 37 and 38 of these Rules shall apply to an application initiating third-party proceedings. In addition such an application shall:
  (a) specify the judgment contested;
  (b) state how that judgment is prejudicial to the rights of the third party;
  (c) indicate the reasons for which the third party was unable to take part in the original case.

The application must be made against all the parties to the original case. Where the judgment has been published in the Official Journal of the European Union, the application must be lodged within two months of the publication.

2.   The Court may, on application by the third party, order a stay of execution of the judgment. The provisions of Title III, Chapter I, of these Rules shall apply.

3.   The contested judgment shall be varied on the points on which the submissions of the third party are upheld. The original of the judgment in the third-party proceedings shall be annexed to the original of the contested judgment. A note of the judgment in the third-party proceedings shall be made in the margin of the original of the contested judgment.

SECTION 2   REVISION

Article 98
An application for revision of a judgment shall be made within three months of the date on which the facts on which the application is based came to the applicant's knowledge.

Article 99
1.   Articles 37 and 38 of these Rules shall apply to an application for revision. In addition such an application shall:
   (a) specify the judgment contested;
   (b) indicate the points on which the judgment is contested;
   (c) set out the facts on which the application is based;
   (d) indicate the nature of the evidence to show that there are facts justifying revision of the judgment, and that the time-limit laid down in Article 98 has been observed.

2.   The application must be made against all parties to the case in which the contested judgment was given.

Article 100
1.   Without prejudice to its decision on the substance, the Court, in closed session, shall, after hearing the Advocate-General and having regard to the written observations of the parties, give in the form of a judgment its decision on the admissibility of the application.

2.   If the Court finds the application admissible, it shall proceed to consider the substance of the application and shall give its decision in the form of a judgment in accordance with these Rules.

3.   The original of the revising judgment shall be annexed to the original of the judgment revised. A note of the revising judgment shall be made in the margin of the original of the judgment revised.

CHAPTER 7   APPEALS AGAINST DECISIONS OF THE ARBITRATION COMMITTEE

Article 101
1.   An application initiating an appeal under the second paragraph of Article 18 of the EAEC Treaty shall state:
   (a) the name and address of the applicant;
   (b) the description of the signatory;
   (c) a reference to the arbitration committee's decision against which the appeal is made;
   (d) the description of the parties;
   (e) a summary of the facts;
   (f) the pleas in law of and the form of order sought by the applicant.

2.   Articles 37 (3) and (4) and 38 (2), (3) and (5) of these Rules shall apply. A certified copy of the contested decision shall be annexed to the application.

3.   As soon as the application has been lodged, the Registrar of the Court shall request the arbitration committee registry to transmit to the Court the papers in the case.

4.   Articles 39, 40, 55 et seq. of these Rules shall apply to these papers.

5.   The Court shall give its decision in the form of a judgment. Where the Court sets aside the decision of the arbitration committee it may refer the case back to the committee.

CHAPTER 8   INTERPRETATION OF JUDGMENTS

Article 102

1.   An application for interpretation of a judgment shall be made in accordance with Articles 37 and 38 of these Rules. In addition it shall specify:
  (a) the judgment in question;
  (b) the passages of which interpretation is sought.

The application must be made against all the parties to the case in which the judgment was given.

2.   The Court shall give its decision in the form of a judgment after having given the parties an opportunity to submit their observations and after hearing the Advocate-General.

The original of the interpreting judgment shall be annexed to the original of the judgment interpreted. A note of the interpreting judgment shall be made in the margin of the original of the judgment interpreted.

CHAPTER 9   PRELIMINARY RULINGS AND OTHER REFERENCES
FOR INTERPRETATION

Article 103

1.   In cases governed by Article 23 of the Statute the procedure shall be governed by the provisions of these Rules, subject to adaptations necessitated by the nature of the reference for a preliminary ruling.

2.   The provisions of paragraph (1) shall apply to the references for a preliminary ruling provided for in the Protocol concerning the interpretation by the Court of Justice of the Convention of 29 February 1968 on the mutual recognition of companies and legal persons and the Protocol concerning the interpretation by the Court of Justice of the Convention of 27 September 1968 on jurisdiction and the enforcement of judgments in civil and commercial matters, signed at Luxembourg on 3 June 1971, and to the references provided for by Article 4 of the latter Protocol. The provisions of paragraph (1) shall apply also to references for interpretation provided for by other existing or future agreements.

Article 104

1.   The decisions of national courts or tribunals referred to in Article 103 shall be communicated to the Member States in the original version, accompanied by a translation into the official language of the State to which they are addressed.

In the cases governed by the third paragraph of Article 23 of the Statute, the decisions of national courts or tribunals shall be notified to the States, other than the Member States, which are parties to the EEA Agreement, and also to the EFTA Surveillance Authority, in the original version, accompanied by a translation into one of the languages mentioned in Article 29 (1), to be chosen by the addressee of the notification.

Where a non-member State has the right to take part in proceedings for a preliminary ruling pursuant to the fourth paragraph of Article 23 of the Statute, the original version of the decision of the national court or tribunal shall be communicated to it together with a translation into one of the languages mentioned in Article 29(1), to be chosen by the non-member State concerned.

2.   As regards the representation and attendance of the parties to the main proceedings

in the preliminary ruling procedure the Court shall take account of the rules of procedure of the national court or tribunal which made the reference.

3.   Where a question referred to the Court for a preliminary ruling is identical to a question on which the Court has already ruled, where the answer to such a question may be clearly deduced from existing case-law or where the answer to the question admits of no reasonable doubt, the Court may, after informing the court or tribunal which referred the question to it, after hearing any observations submitted by the persons referred to in Article 23 of the Statute, and after hearing the Advocate-General, give its decision by reasoned order in which, if appropriate, reference is made to its previous judgment or to the relevant case-law.

4.   Without prejudice to paragraph 3 of this Article, the procedure before the Court in the case of a reference for a preliminary ruling shall also include an oral part. However, after the statements of case or written observations referred to in Article 23 of the Statute, have been submitted, the Court, acting on a report from the Judge-Rapporteur, after informing the persons who under the aforementioned provisions are entitled to submit such statements or observations, may, after hearing the Advocate-General, decide otherwise, provided that none of those persons has submitted an application setting out the reasons for which he wishes to be heard. The application shall be submitted within a period of one month from service on the party or person of the written statements of case or written observations which have been lodged. That period may be extended by the President.

5.   The Court may, after hearing the Advocate-General, request clarification from the national court.

6.   It shall be for the national court or tribunal to decide as to the costs of the reference.

In special circumstances the Court may grant, by way of legal aid, assistance for the purpose of facilitating the representation or attendance of a party.

Article 104a

At the request of the national court, the President may exceptionally decide, on a proposal from the Judge-Rapporteur and after hearing the Advocate-General, to apply an accelerated procedure derogating from the provisions of these Rules to a reference for a preliminary ruling, where the circumstances referred to establish that a ruling on the question put to the Court is a matter of exceptional urgency. In that event, the President may immediately fix the date for the hearing, which shall be notified to the parties in the main proceedings and to the other persons referred to in Article 23 of the Statute when the decision making the reference is served. The parties and other interested persons referred to in the preceding paragraph may lodge statements of case or written observations within a period prescribed by the President, which shall not be less than 15 days. The President may request the parties and other interested persons to restrict the matters addressed in their statement of case or written observations to the essential points of law raised by the question referred. The statements of case or written observations, if any, shall be notified to the parties and to the other persons referred to above prior to the hearing. The Court shall rule after hearing the Advocate-General.

CHAPTER 10   SPECIAL PROCEDURES UNDER ARTICLES 103 TO 105 OF
THE EAEC TREATY

Article 105

1.   Four certified copies shall be lodged of an application under the third paragraph of Article 103 of the EAEC Treaty. The Commission shall be served with a copy.

2.   The application shall be accompanied by the draft of the agreement or contract in question, by the observations of the Commission addressed to the State concerned and by all other supporting documents. The Commission shall submit its observations to the Court within a period of 10 days, which may be extended by the President after the State concerned has been heard. A certified copy of the observations shall be served on that State.

3.   As soon as the application has been lodged the President shall designate a Judge to act as Rapporteur. The First Advocate-General shall assign the case to an Advocate-General as soon as the Judge-Rapporteur has been designated.

4.   The decision shall be taken in closed session after the Advocate-General has been heard.

The agents and advisers of the State concerned and of the Commission shall be heard if they so request.

Article 106

1.   In cases provided for in the last paragraph of Article 104 and the last paragraph of Article 105 of the EAEC Treaty, the provisions of Articles 37 *et seq.* of these Rules shall apply.

2.   The application shall be served on the State to which the respondent person or undertaking belongs.

CHAPTER 11   OPINIONS

Article 107

1.   A request by the European Parliament for an opinion pursuant to Article 300 of the EC Treaty shall be served on the Council, on the Commission and on the Member States. Such a request by the Council shall be served on the Commission and on the European Parliament. Such a request by the Commission shall be served on the Council, on the European Parliament and on the Member States. Such a request by a Member State shall be served on the Council, on the Commission, on the European Parliament and on the other Member States.

2.   The Opinion may deal not only with the question whether the envisaged agreement is compatible with the provisions of the EC Treaty but also with the question whether the Community or any Community institution has the power to enter into that agreement.

Article 108

1.   As soon as the request for an Opinion has been lodged, the President shall designate a Judge to act as Rapporteur.

2.   The Court sitting in closed session shall, after hearing the Advocates-General, deliver a reasoned Opinion.

3.   The Opinion, signed by the President, by the Judges who took part in the deliberations and by the Registrar, shall be served on the Council, the Commission, the European Parliament and the Member States.

Article 109

(repealed)

CHAPTER 12   REQUESTS FOR INTERPRETATION UNDER ARTICLE 68
OF THE EC TREATY

Article 109a

1.   A request for a ruling on a question of interpretation under Article 68(3) of the EC Treaty shall be served on the Commission and the Member States if the request is submitted by the Council, on the Council and the Member States if the request is submitted by the Commission and on the Council, the Commission and the other Member States if the request is submitted by a Member State. The President shall prescribe a time limit within which the institutions and the Member States on which the request has been served are to submit their written observations.

2.   As soon as the request referred to in paragraph 1 has been submitted, the President shall designate the Judge-Rapporteur. The First Advocate-General shall thereupon assign the request to an Advocate-General.

3.   The Court shall, after the Advocate-General has delivered his opinion, give its decision on the request by way of judgment. The procedure relating to the request shall include an oral part where a Member State or one of the institutions referred to in paragraph 1 so requests.

CHAPTER 13   SETTLEMENT OF THE DISPUTES REFERRED TO IN ARTICLE 35
OF THE UNION TREATY

Article 109b
1.   In the case of disputes between Member States as referred to in Article 35(7) of the Union Treaty, the matter shall be brought before the Court by an application by a party to the dispute. The application shall be served on the other Member States and on the Commission. In the case of disputes between Member States and the Commission as referred to in Article 35(7) of the Union Treaty, the matter shall be brought before the Court by an application by a party to the dispute. The application shall be served on the other Member States, the Council and the Commission if it was made by a Member State. The application shall be served on the Member States and on the Council if it was made by the Commission. The President shall prescribe a time limit within which the institutions and the Member States on which the application has been served are to submit their written observations.

2.   As soon as the application referred to in paragraph 1 has been submitted, the President shall designate the Judge-Rapporteur. The First Advocate-General shall thereupon assign the application to an Advocate-General.

3.   The Court shall, after the Advocate-General has delivered his opinion, give its ruling on the dispute by way of judgment. The procedure relating to the application shall include an oral part where a Member State or one of the institutions referred to in paragraph 1 so requests.

4.   The same procedure shall apply where an agreement concluded between the Member States confers jurisdiction on the Court to rule on a dispute between Member States or between Member States and an institution.

TITLE IV   APPEALS AGAINST DECISIONS OF THE COURT
OF FIRST INSTANCE

Article 110
Without prejudice to the arrangements laid down in Article 29 (2) (b) and (c) and the fourth sub-paragraph of Article 29 (3) of these Rules, in appeals against decisions of the Court of First Instance as referred to in Articles Articles 56 and 57 of the Statute, the language of the case shall be the language of the decision of the Court of First Instance against which the appeal is brought.

Article 111
1.   An appeal shall be brought by lodging an application at the Registry of the Court of Justice or of the Court of First Instance.

2.   The Registry of the Court of First Instance shall immediately transmit to the Registry of the Court of Justice the papers in the case at first instance and, where necessary, the appeal.

Article 112
1.   An appeal shall contain:
   (a) the name and address of the appellant;
   (b) the names of the other parties to the proceedings before the Court of First Instance;
   (c) the pleas in law and legal arguments relied on;
   (d) the form or order sought by the appellant.

Article 37 and Article 38 (2) and (3) of these Rules shall apply to appeals.

2.   The decision of the Court of First Instance appealed against shall be attached to the appeal. The appeal shall state the date on which the decision appealed against was notified to the appellant.

3.   If an appeal does not comply with Article 38 (3) or with paragraph (2) of this Article, Article 38 (7) of these Rules shall apply.

Article 113

1.   An appeal may seek:
— to set aside, in whole or in part, the decision of the Court of First Instance;
— the same form of order, in whole or in part, as that sought at first instance and shall not seek a different form of order.

2.   The subject-matter of the proceedings before the Court of First Instance may not be changed in the appeal.

Article 114

Notice of the appeal shall be served on all the parties to the proceedings before the Court of First Instance. Article 39 of these Rules shall apply.

Article 115

1.   Any party to the proceedings before the Court of First Instance may lodge a response within two months after service on him of notice of the appeal.
    The time-limit for lodging a response shall not be extended.

2.   A response shall contain:
(a) the name and address of the party lodging it;
(b) the date on which notice of the appeal was served on him;
(c) the pleas in law and legal arguments relied on;
(d) the form of order sought by the respondent.
Article 37 and Article 38(2) and (3) of these Rules shall apply.

Article 116

1.   A response may seek:
— to dismiss, in whole or in part, the appeal or to set aside, in whole or in part, the decision of the Court of First Instance;
— the same form of order, in whole or in part, as that sought at first instance and shall not seek a different form of order.

2.   The subject-matter of the proceedings before the Court of First Instance may not be changed in the response.

Article 117

1.   The appeal and the response may be supplemented by a reply and a rejoinder where the President, on application made by the appellant within seven days of service of the response, considers such further pleading necessary and expressly allows the submission of a reply in order to enable the appellant to put forward his point of view or in order to provide a basis for the decision on the appeal. The President shall prescribe the date by which the reply is to be submitted and, upon service of that pleading, the date by which the rejoinder is to be submitted.

2.   Where the response seeks to set aside, in whole or in part, the decision of the Court of First Instance on a plea in law which was not raised in the appeal, the appellant or any other party may submit a reply on that plea alone within two months of the service of the response in question. Paragraph (1) shall apply to any further pleading following such a reply.

Article 118

Subject to the following provisions, Articles 42 (2), 43, 44, 55 to 90, 93, 95 to 100 and 102 of these Rules shall apply to the procedure before the Court of Justice on appeal from a decision of the Court of First Instance.

Article 119
Where the appeal is, in whole or in part, clearly inadmissible or clearly unfounded, the Court may at any time, acting on a report from the Judge-Rapporteur and after hearing the Advocate-General, by reasoned order dismiss the appeal in whole or in part.

Article 120
After the submission of pleadings as provided for in Article 115(1) and, if any, Article 117(1) and (2) of these Rules, the Court, acting on a report from the Judge-Rapporteur and after hearing the Advocate-General and the parties, may decide to dispense with the oral part of the procedure unless one of the parties submits an application setting out the reasons for which he wishes to be heard. The application shall be submitted within a period of one month from notification to the party of the close of the written procedure. That period may be extended by the President.

Article 121
The report referred to in Article 44(2) shall be presented to the Court after the pleadings provided for in Article 115(1) and, where appropriate, Article 117(1) and (2) have been lodged. Where no such pleadings are lodged, the same procedure shall apply after the expiry of the period prescribed for lodging them.

Article 122
Where the appeal is unfounded or where the appeal is well founded and the Court itself gives final judgment in the case, the Court shall make a decision as to costs.
 In proceedings between the Communities and their servants:
   — Article 70 of these Rules shall apply only to appeals brought by institutions.
   — by way of derogation from Article 69 (2) of these Rules, the Court may, in appeals brought by officials or other servants of an institution, order the parties to share the costs where equity so requires. If the appeal is withdrawn Article 69 (5) shall apply.
 When an appeal brought by a Member State or an institution which did not intervene in the proceedings before the Court of First Instance is well founded, the Court of Justice may order that the parties share the costs or that the successful appellant pay the costs which the appeal has caused an unsuccessful party to incur.

Article 123
An application to intervene made to the Court in appeal proceedings shall be lodged before the expiry of a period of one month running from the publication referred to in Article 16 (6).

TITLE V   PROCEDURES PROVIDED FOR BY THE EEA AGREEMENT

Article 123a
 1.   In the case governed by Article 111 (3) of the EEA Agreement (1), the matter shall be brought before the Court by a request submitted by the Contracting Parties to the dispute. The request shall be served on the other Contracting Parties, on the Commission, on the EFTA Surveillance Authority and, where appropriate, on the other persons to whom a reference for a preliminary ruling raising the same question of interpretation of Community legislation would be notified.
 The President shall prescribe a period within which the Contracting Parties and the other persons on whom the request has been served may submit written observations.

The request shall be made in one of the languages mentioned in Article 29 (1). Paragraphs (3) and (5) of that Article shall apply. The provisions of Article 104 (1) shall apply *mutatis mutandis*.

2.   As soon as the request referred to in paragraph 1 of this Article has been submitted, the President shall appoint a Judge-Rapporteur. The First Advocate-General shall, immediately afterwards, assign the request to an Advocate-General.

The Court shall, after hearing the Advocate-General, give a reasoned decision on the request in closed session.

3.   The decision of the Court, signed by the President, by the Judges who took part in the deliberations and by the Registrar, shall be served on the Contracting Parties and on the other persons referred to in paragraph 1.

Article 123b

In the case governed by Article 1 of Protocol 34 to the EEA Agreement, the request of a court or tribunal of an EFTA State shall be served on the parties to the case, on the Contracting Parties, on the Commission, on the EFTA Surveillance Authority and, where appropriate, on the other persons to whom a reference for a preliminary ruling raising the same question of interpretation of Community legislation would be notified.

If the request is not submitted in one of the languages mentioned in Article 29 (1), it shall be accompanied by a translation into one of those languages.

Within two months of this notification, the parties to the case, the Contracting Parties and the other persons referred to in the first paragraph shall be entitled to submit statements of case or written observations.

The procedure shall be governed by the provisions of these Rules, subject to the adaptations called for by the nature of the request.

MISCELLANEOUS PROVISIONS

Article 124

1.   The President shall instruct any person who is required to take an oath before the Court, as witness or expert, to tell the truth or to carry out his task conscientiously and impartially, as the case may be, and shall warn him of the criminal liability provided for in his national law in the event of any breach of this duty.

2.   The witness shall take the oath either in accordance with the first sub-paragraph of Article 47 (5) of these Rules or in the manner laid down by his national law. Where his national law provides the opportunity to make, in judicial proceedings, a solemn affirmation equivalent to an oath as well as or instead of taking an oath, the witness may make such an affirmation under the conditions and in the form prescribed in his national law. Where his national law provides neither for taking an oath nor for making a solemn affirmation, the procedure described in paragraph (1) shall be followed.

3.   Paragraph (2) shall apply mutatis mutandis to experts, a reference to the first sub-paragraph of Article 49 (6) replacing in this case the reference to the first sub-paragraph of Article 47 (5) of these Rules.

Article 125

Subject to the provisions of Article 223 of the EC Treaty and Article 139 of the EAEC Treaty and after consultation with the Governments concerned, the Court shall adopt supplementary rules concerning its practice in relation to:

(a) letters rogatory;
(b) applications for legal aid;
(c) reports of perjury by witnesses or experts, delivered pursuant to Article 30 of the Statute.

Article 125a

The Court may issue practice directions relating in particular to the preparation and conduct of the hearings before it and to the lodging of written statements of case or written observations.

Article 126

These Rules replace the Rules of Procedure of the Court of Justice of the European Communities adopted on 4 December 1974 (Official Journal of the European Communities No L 350 of 28 December 1974, p. 1), as last amended on 15 May 1991.

Article 127

These Rules, which are authentic in the languages mentioned in Article 29 (1) of these Rules, shall be published in the Official Journal of the European Communities and shall enter into force on the first day of the second month following their publication.

Done at Luxembourg, 19 June 1991.

ANNEX I   DECISION ON OFFICIAL HOLIDAYS

THE COURT OF JUSTICE OF THE EUROPEAN COMMUNITIES

Having regard to Article 80 (2) of the Rules of Procedure, which requires the Court to draw up a list of official holidays;

DECIDES:

Article 1

For the purposes of Article 80 (2) of the Rules of Procedure the following shall be official holidays:

New Year's Day;
Easter Monday;
1 May;
Ascension Day;
Whit Monday;
23 June;
24 June, where 23 June is a Sunday;
15 August;
1 November;
25 December;
26 December.

The official holidays referred to in the first paragraph hereof shall be those observed at the place where the Court of Justice has its seat.

Article 2

Article 80 (2) of the Rules of Procedure shall apply only to the official holidays mentioned in Article 1 of this Decision.

Article 3

This Decision, which shall constitute Annex I to the Rules of Procedure, shall enter into force on the same day as those Rules.

It shall be published in the Official Journal of the European Communities.

Done at Luxembourg, 19 June 1991.

ANNEX II   DECISION ON EXTENSION OF TIME LIMITS ON ACCOUNT OF DISTANCE

THE COURT OF JUSTICE OF THE EUROPEAN COMMUNITIES,

Having regard to Article 81 (2) of the Rules of Procedure relating to the extension, on account of distance, of prescribed time limits;

DECIDES:

Article 1

In order to take account of distance, procedural time limits for all parties save those habitually resident in the Grand Duchy of Luxembourg shall be extended as follows:

— for the Kingdom of Belgium: two days,

— for the Federal Republic of Germany, the European territory of the French Republic and the European territory of the Kingdom of the Netherlands: six days,

— for the European territory of the Kingdom of Denmark, for the Kingdom of Spain, for Ireland, for the Hellenic Republic, for the Italian Republic, for the Republic of Austria, for the Portuguese Republic (with the exception of the Azores and Madeira), for the Republic of Finland, for the Kingdom of Sweden and for the United Kingdom: 10 days.

— for other European countries and territories: two weeks,

— for the autonomous regions of the Azores and Madeira of the Portuguese Republic: three weeks,

— for other countries, departments and territories: one month.

Article 2

This Decision, which shall constitute Annex II to the Rules of Procedure, shall enter into force on the same day as those Rules.

It shall be published in the Official Journal of the European Communities.

Secondary Legislation

FREE MOVEMENT OF GOODS

Commission Directive of 22 December 1969 based on the provisions of Article 33(7), on the abolition of measures which have an effect equivalent to quantitative restrictions on imports and are not covered by other provisions adopted in pursuance of the EEC Treaty (70/50/EEC)

[OJ Sp. Ed. 1970, I No. L13/29, p. 17]

(Preamble omitted.)

Article 1
The purpose of this Directive is to abolish the measures referred to in Articles 2 and 3, which were operative at the date of entry into force of the EEC Treaty.

Article 2
1.   This Directive covers measures, other than those applicable equally to domestic or imported products, which hinder imports which could otherwise take place, including measures which make importation more difficult or costly than the disposal of domestic production.

2.   In particular, it covers measures which make imports or the disposal, at any marketing stage, of imported products subject to a condition—other than a formality—which is required in respect of imported products only, or a condition differing from that required for domestic products and more difficult to satisfy. Equally, it covers, in particular, measures which favour domestic products or grant them a preference, other than an aid, to which conditions may or may not be attached.

3.   The measures referred to must be taken to include those measures which:
   (a) lay down, for imported products only, minimum or maximum prices below or above which imports are prohibited, reduced or made subject to conditions liable to hinder importation;
   (b) lay down less favourable prices for imported products than for domestic products;
   (c) fix profit margins or any other price components for imported products only or fix these differently for domestic products and for imported products, to the detriment of the latter;
   (d) preclude any increase in the price of the imported product corresponding to the supplementary costs and charges inherent in importation;
   (e) fix the prices of products solely on the basis of the cost price or the quality of domestic products at such a level as to create a hindrance to importation;

(f) lower the value of an imported product, in particular by causing a reduction in its intrinsic value, or increase its costs;

(g) make access of imported products to the domestic market conditional upon having an agent or representative in the territory of the importing Member State;

(h) lay down conditions of payment in respect of imported products only, or subject imported products to conditions which are different from those laid down for domestic products and more difficult to satisfy;

(i) require, for imports only, the giving of guarantees or making of payments on account;

(j) subject imported products only to conditions, in respect, in particular of shape, size, weight, composition, presentation, identification or putting up, or subject imported products to conditions which are different from those for domestic products and more difficult to satisfy;

(k) hinder the purchase by private individuals of imported products only, or encourage, require or give preference to the purchase of domestic products only;

(l) totally or partially preclude the use of national facilities or equipment in respect of imported products only, or totally or partially confine the use of such facilities or equipment to domestic products only;

(m) prohibit or limit publicity in respect of imported products only, or totally or partially confine publicity to domestic products only;

(n) prohibit, limit or require stocking in respect of imported products only; totally or partially confine the use of stocking facilities to domestic products only, or make the stocking of imported products subject to conditions which are different from those required for domestic products and more difficult to satisfy;

(o) make importation subject to the granting of reciprocity by one or more Member States;

(p) prescribe that imported products are to conform, totally or partially, to rules other than those of the importing country;

(q) specify time limits for imported products which are insufficient or excessive in relation to the normal course of the various transactions to which these time limits apply;

(r) subject imported products to controls or, other than those inherent in the customs clearance procedure, to which domestic products are not subject or which are stricter in respect of imported products than they are in respect of domestic products, without this being necessary in order to ensure equivalent protection;

(s) confine names which are not indicative of origin or source to domestic products only.

Article 3

This Directive also covers measures governing the marketing of products which deal, in particular, with shape, size, weight, composition, presentation, identification or putting up and which are equally applicable to domestic and imported products, where the restrictive effect of such measures on the free movement of goods exceeds the effects intrinsic to trade rules.

This is the case, in particular, where:

— the restrictive effects on the free movement of goods are out of proportion to their purpose;

— the same objective can be attained by other means which are less of a hindrance to trade.

(All remaining provisions omitted.)

Commission Practice Note on Import Prohibitions

Communication from the Commission concerning the consequences of the judgment given by the Court of Justice on 20 February 1979 in Case 120/78 ('Cassis de Dijon')

[OJ 1980, C256/2]

The following is the text of a letter which has been sent to the Member States; the European Parliament and the Council have also been notified of it.

In the Commission's Communication of 6 November 1978 on 'Safeguarding free trade within the Community', it was emphasised that the free movement of goods is being affected by a growing number of restrictive measures.

The judgment delivered by the Court of Justice on 20 February 1979 in Case 120/78 (the 'Cassis de Dijon' case), and recently reaffirmed in the judgment of 26 June 1980 in Case 788/79, has given the Commission some interpretative guidance enabling it to monitor more strictly the application of the Treaty rules on the free movement of goods, particularly Articles 30 to 36 of the EEC Treaty.

The Court gives a very general definition of the barriers to free trade which are prohibited by the provisions of Article 30 *et seq.* of the EEC Treaty. These are taken to include 'any national measure capable of hindering, directly or indirectly, actually or potentially, intra-Community trade'.

In its judgment of 20 February 1979 the Court indicates the scope of this definition as it applies to technical and commercial rules.

Any product lawfully produced and marketed in one Member State must, in principle, be admitted to the market of any other Member State.

Technical and commercial rules, even those equally applicable to national and imported products, may create barriers to trade only where those rules are necessary to satisfy mandatory requirements and to serve a purpose which is in the general interest and for which they are an essential guarantee. This purpose must be such as to take precedence over the requirements of the free movement of goods, which constitutes one of the fundamental rules of the Community.

The conclusions in terms of policy which the Commission draws from this new guidance are set out below.

— Whereas Member States may, with respect to domestic products and in the absence of relevant Community provisions, regulate the terms on which such products are marketed, the case is different for products imported from other Member States.

Any product imported from another Member State must in principle be admitted to the territory of the importing Member State if it has been lawfully produced, that is, conforms to the rules and processes of manufacture that are customarily and traditionally accepted in the exporting country, and is marketed in the territory of the latter.

This principle implies that Member States, when drawing up commercial or technical rules liable to affect the free movement of goods, may not take an exclusively national viewpoint and take account only of requirements confined to domestic products. The proper functioning of the common market demands that each Member State also give consideration to the legitimate requirements of the other Member States.

— Only under very strict conditions does the Court accept exceptions to this principle; barriers to trade resulting from differences between commercial and technical rules are only admissible:

— if the rules are necessary, that is appropriate and not excessive, in order to satisfy mandatory requirements (public health, protection of consumers or the environment, the fairness of commercial transactions, etc.);

— if the rules serve a purpose in the general interest which is compelling enough to justify an exception to a fundamental rule of the Treaty such as the free movement of goods;

— if the rules are essential for such a purpose to be attained, i.e., are the means which are the most appropriate and at the same time least hinder trade.

The Court's interpretation has induced the Commission to set out a number of guidelines.

— The principles deduced by the Court imply that a Member State may not in principle prohibit the sale in its territory of a product lawfully produced and marketed in another Member State even if the product is produced according to technical or quality requirements which differ from those imposed on its domestic products. Where a product 'suitably and satisfactorily' fulfils the legitimate objective of a Member State's own rules (public safety, protection of the consumer or the environment, etc.), the importing country cannot justify prohibiting its sale in its territory by claiming that the way it fulfils the objective is different from that imposed on domestic products.

In such a case, an absolute prohibition of sale could not be considered 'necessary' to satisfy a 'mandatory requirement' because it would not be an 'essential guarantee' in the sense defined in the Court's judgment.

The Commission will therefore have to tackle a whole body of commercial rules which lay down that products manufactured and marketed in one Member State must fulfil technical or qualitative conditions in order to be admitted to the market of another and specifically in all cases where the trade barriers occasioned by such rules are inadmissible according to the very strict criteria set out by the Court.

The Commission is referring in particular to rules covering the composition, designation, presentation and packaging of products as well as rules requiring compliance with certain technical standards.

— The Commission's work of harmonisation will henceforth have to be directed mainly at national laws having an impact on the functioning of the common market where barriers to trade to be removed arise from national provisions which are admissible under the criteria set by the Court.

The Commission will be concentrating on sectors deserving priority because of their economic relevance to the creation of a single internal market.

To forestall later difficulties, the Commission will be informing Member States of potential objections, under the terms of Community law, to provisions they may be considering introducing which come to the attention of the Commission.

It will be producing suggestions soon on the procedures to be followed in such cases.

The Commission is confident that this approach will secure greater freedom of trade for the Community's manufacturers, so strengthening the industrial base of the Community, while meeting the expectations of consumers.

Council Regulation 2679/98 of 7 December 1998 on the functioning of the internal market in relation to the free movement of goods among the Member States
[OJ 1998, L337/8]

The Council of the European Union,

Having regard to the Treaty establishing the European Community, and in particular Article 235 thereof,

Having regard to the proposal from the Commission,[1]
Having regard to the opinion of the European Parliament,[2]
Having regard to the opinion of the Economic and Social Committee,[3]

(1) Whereas, as provided for in Article 7a of the Treaty, the internal market comprises an area without internal frontiers in which, in particular, the free movement of goods is ensured in accordance with Articles 30 to 36 of the Treaty;

(2) Whereas breaches of this principle, such as occur when in a given Member State the free movement of goods is obstructed by actions of private individuals, may cause grave disruption to the proper functioning of the internal market and inflict serious losses on the individuals affected;

(3) Whereas, in order to ensure fulfilment of the obligations arising from the Treaty, and, in particular, to ensure the proper functioning of the internal market, Member States should, on the one hand, abstain from adopting measures or engaging in conduct liable to constitute an obstacle to trade and, on the other hand, take all necessary and proportionate measures with a view to facilitating the free movement of goods in their territory;

(4) Whereas such measures must not affect the exercise of fundamental rights, including the right or freedom to strike;

(5) Whereas this Regulation does not prevent any actions which may be necessary in certain cases at Community level to respond to problems in the functioning of the internal market, taking into account, where appropriate, the application of this Regulation;

(6) Whereas Member States have exclusive competence as regards the maintenance of public order and the safeguarding of internal security as well as in determining whether, when and which measures are necessary and proportionate in order to facilitate the free movement of goods in their territory in a given situation;

(7) Whereas there should be adequate and rapid exchange of information between the Member States and the Commission on obstacles to the free movement of goods;

(8) Whereas a Member State on the territory of which obstacles to the free movement of goods occur should take all necessary and proportionate measures to restore as soon as possible the free movement of goods in their territory in order to avoid the risk that the disruption or loss in question will continue, increase or intensify and that there may be a breakdown in trade and in the contractual relations which underlie it; whereas such Member State should inform the Commission and, if requested, other Member States of the measures it has taken or intends to take in order to fulfil this objective;

(9) Whereas the Commission, in fulfilment of its duty under the Treaty, should notify the Member State concerned of its view that a breach has occurred and the Member State should respond to that notification;

(10) Whereas the Treaty provides for no powers, other than those in Article 235 thereof, for the adoption of this Regulation,

Has adopted this Regulation:

Article 1

For the purpose of this Regulation:

1. the term 'obstacle' shall mean an obstacle to the free movement of goods among Member States which is attributable to a Member State, whether it involves action or inaction on its part, which may constitute a breach of Articles 30 to 36 of the Treaty and which:

    (a) leads to serious disruption of the free movement of goods by physically or other-

[1] OJ C 10, 15.1.1998, p. 14.
[2] OJ C 359, 23.11.1998.
[3] OJ C 214, 10.7.1998, p. 90.

wise preventing, delaying or diverting their import into, export from or transport across a Member State,

(b) causes serious loss to the individuals affected, and

(c) requires immediate action in order to prevent any continuation, increase or intensification of the disruption or loss in question;

2.   the term 'inaction' shall cover the case when the competent authorities of a Member State, in the presence of an obstacle caused by actions taken by private individuals, fail to take all necessary and proportionate measures within their powers with a view to removing the obstacle and ensuring the free movement of goods in their territory.

Article 2

This Regulation may not be interpreted as affecting in any way the exercise of fundamental rights as recognised in Member States, including the right or freedom to strike. These rights may also include the right or freedom to take other actions covered by the specific industrial relations systems in Member States.

Article 3

1.   When an obstacle occurs or when there is a threat thereof

(a) any Member State (whether or not it is the Member State concerned) which has relevant information shall immediately transmit it to the Commission, and

(b) the Commission shall immediately transmit to the Member States that information and any information from any other source which it may consider relevant.

2.   The Member State concerned shall respond as soon as possible to requests for information from the Commission and from other Member States concerning the nature of the obstacle or threat and the action which it has taken or proposes to take. Information exchange between Member States shall also be transmitted to the Commission.

Article 4

1.   When an obstacle occurs, and subject to Article 2, the Member State concerned shall

(a) take all necessary and proportionate measures so that the free movement of goods is assured in the territory of the Member State in accordance with the Treaty, and

(b) inform the Commission of the actions which its authorities have taken or intend to take.

2.   The Commission shall immediately transmit the information received under paragraph 1(b) to the other Member States.

Article 5

1.   Where the Commission considers that an obstacle is occurring in a Member State, it shall notify the Member State concerned of the reasons that have led the Commission to such a conclusion and shall request the Member State to take all necessary and proportionate measures to remove the said obstacle within a period which it shall determine with reference to the urgency of the case.

2.   In reaching its conclusion, the Commission shall have regard to Article 2.

3.   The Commission may publish in the Official Journal of the European Communities the text of the notification which it has sent to the Member State concerned and shall immediately transmit the text to any party which requests it.

4.   The Member State shall, within five working days of receipt of the text, either:

— inform the Commission of the steps which it has taken or intends to take to implement paragraph 1, or

— communicate a reasoned submission as to why there is no obstacle constituting a breach of Articles 30 to 36 of the Treaty.

5.   In exceptional cases, the Commission may allow an extension of the deadline mentioned in paragraph 4 if the Member State submits a duly substantiated request and the grounds cited are deemed acceptable.

This Regulation shall be binding in its entirety and directly applicable in all Member States. Done at Brussels, 7 December 1998.
For the Council
The President
J. FARNLEITNER

FREE MOVEMENT OF PERSONS*

Regulation (EEC) No. 1612/68 of the Council of 15 October 1968 on freedom of movement for workers within the Community**

[OJ Sp. Ed. 1968, No. L257/2, p. 475]

(Preamble omitted.)

PART I   EMPLOYMENT AND WORKERS' FAMILIES

TITLE I   ELIGIBILITY FOR EMPLOYMENT

Article 1

1. Any national of a Member State, shall, irrespective of his place of residence, have the right to take up an activity as an employed person, and to pursue such activity, within the territory of another Member State in accordance with the provisions laid down by law, regulation or administrative action governing the employment of nationals of that State.

2. He shall, in particular, have the right to take up available employment in the territory of another Member State with the same priority as nationals of the State.

Article 2

Any national of a Member State and any employer pursuing an activity in the territory of a Member State may exchange their applications for and offers of employment, and may conclude and perform contracts of employment in accordance with the provisions in force laid down by law, regulation or administrative action, without any discrimination resulting therefrom.

Article 3

1. Under this Regulation, provisions laid down by law, regulation or administrative action or administrative practices of a Member State shall not apply:
   — where they limit application for and offers of employment, or the right of foreign nationals to take up and pursue employment or subject these to conditions not applicable in respect of their own nationals; or
   — where, though applicable irrespective of nationality, their exclusive or principal aim or effect is to keep nationals of other Member States away from the employment offered.

---

* **Editor's Note:** There will be considerable changes to this area of law as a result of the enactment of Directive 2004/38 (Citizens' Free Movement Rights Directive) below, p. 277 and which enters into force on 30 April 2006 repealing many of the following directives at the same time.

** **Editor's Note:** As corrected and amended up to and including Regulation 2434/92, parts of which will be amended and part repealed by Directive 2004/38, see p. 277.

This provision shall not apply to conditions relating to linguistic knowledge required by reason of the nature of the post to be filled.

2.   There shall be included in particular among the provisions or practices of a Member State referred to in the first sub-paragraph of paragraph 1 those which:

(a) prescribe a special recruitment procedure for foreign nationals;

(b) limit or restrict the advertising or vacancies in the press or through any other medium or subject it to conditions other than those applicable in respect of employers pursuing their activities in the territory of that Member State;

(c) subject eligibility for employment to conditions of registration with employment offices or impede recruitment of individual workers, where persons who do not reside in the territory of that State are concerned.

Article 4

1.   Provisions laid down by law, regulation or administrative action of the Member States which restrict by number of percentage the employment of foreign nationals in any undertaking, branch of activity or region, or at a national level, shall not apply to nationals of the other Member States.

2.   When in a Member State the granting of any benefit to undertakings is subject to a minimum percentage of national workers being employed, nationals of the other Member States shall be counted as national workers, subject to the provisions of the Council Directive of 15 October 1963.

Article 5

A national of a Member State who seeks employment in the territory of another Member State shall receive the same assistance there as that afforded by the employment offices in that State to their own nationals seeking employment.

Article 6

1.   The engagement and recruitment of a national of one Member State for a post in another Member State shall not depend on medical, vocational or other criteria which are discriminatory on grounds of nationality by comparison with those applied to nationals of the other Member State who wish to pursue the same activity.

2.   Nevertheless, a national who holds an offer in his name from an employer in a Member State other than that of which he is a national may have to undergo a vocational test, if the employer expressly requests this when making his offer of employment.

TITLE II   EMPLOYMENT AND EQUALITY OF TREATMENT

Article 7

1.   A worker who is a national of a Member State may not, in the territory of another Member State, be treated differently from national workers by reason of his nationality in respect of any conditions of employment and work, in particular as regards remuneration, dismissal, and should he become unemployed, reinstatement or reemployment.

2.   He shall enjoy the same social and tax advantages as national workers.

3.   He shall also, by virtue of the same right and under the same conditions as national workers, have access to training in vocational schools and retraining centres.

4.   Any clause of a collective or individual agreement or of any other collective regulation concerning eligibility for employment, employment, remuneration and other conditions of work or dismissal shall be null and void in so far as it lays down or authorises discriminatory conditions in respect of workers who are nationals of the other Member States.

Article 8

A worker who is a national of a Member State and who is employed in the territory of another Member State shall enjoy equality of treatment as regards membership of trade unions and the exercise of rights attaching thereto, including the right to vote and to be eligible for the administration or management posts of a trade union; he may be excluded from taking part in the management of bodies governed by public law and from holding an office governed by public law. Furthermore, he shall have the right of eligibility for workers' representative bodies in the undertaking. The provisions of this Article shall not affect laws or regulations in certain Member States which grant more extensive rights to workers coming from the other Member States.

Article 9

1.   A worker who is a national of a Member State and who is employed in the territory of another Member State shall enjoy all the rights and benefits accorded to national workers in matters of housing, including ownership of the housing he needs.

2.   Such worker may, with the same right as nationals, put his name down on the housing lists in the region in which he is employed, where such lists exist; he shall enjoy the resultant benefits and priorities.

If his family has remained in the country whence he came, they shall be considered for this purpose as residing in the said region, where national workers benefit from a similar presumption.

TITLE III   WORKERS' FAMILIES

Article 10

1.   The following shall, irrespective of their nationality, have the right to install themselves with a worker who is a national of one Member State and who is employed in the territory of another Member State:
>   (a) his spouse and their descendants who are under the age of 21 years or are dependants;
>   (b) dependent relatives in the ascending line of the worker and his spouse.

2.   Member States shall facilitate the admission of any member of the family not coming within the provisions of paragraph 1 if dependent on the worker referred to above or living under his roof in the country whence he comes.

3.   For the purposes of paragraphs 1 and 2, the worker must have available for his family housing considered as normal for national workers in the region where he is employed; this provision, however must not give rise to discrimination between national workers and workers from the other Member States.

Article 11

Where a national of a Member State is pursuing an activity as an employed or self-employed person in the territory of another Member State, his spouse and those of the children who are under the age of 21 years or dependent on him shall have the right to take up any activity as an employed person throughout the territory of that same State, even if they are not nationals of any Member State.

Article 12

The children of a national of a Member State who is or has been employed in the territory of another Member State shall be admitted to that State's general educational, apprenticeship and vocational training courses under the same conditions as the nationals of that State, if such children are residing in its territory.

Member States shall encourage all efforts to enable such children to attend these courses under the best possible conditions.

(All remaining provisions omitted.)

Council Directive of 25 February 1964 on the co-ordination of special measures concerning the movement and residence of foreign nationals which are justified on grounds of public policy, public security or public health (64/221/EEC)

[OJ Sp. Ed. 1964, No. 850/64, p. 117]

[Note: To be repealed on 30 April 2006 when Directive 2004/38 enters into force.]

(Preamble omitted.)

Article 1

1.   The provisions of this Directive shall apply to any national of a Member State who resides in or travels to another Member State of the Community, either in order to pursue an activity as an employed or self-employed person, or as a recipient of services.

2.   These provisions shall apply also to the spouse and to members of the family who come within the provisions of the regulations and directives adopted in this field in pursuance of the Treaty.

Article 2

1.   This Directive relates to all measures concerning entry into their territory, issue or renewal of residence permits, or expulsion from their territory, taken by Member States on grounds of public policy, public security or public health.

2.   Such grounds shall not be invoked to service economic ends.

Article 3

1.   Measures taken on grounds of public policy or of public security shall be based exclusively on the personal conduct of the individual concerned.

2.   Previous criminal convictions shall not in themselves constitute grounds for the taking of such measures.

3.   Expiry of the identity card or passport used by the person concerned to enter the host country and to obtain a residence permit shall not justify expulsion from the territory.

4.   The State which issued the identity card or passport shall allow the holder of such document to re-enter its territory without any formality even if the document is no longer valid or the nationality of the holder is in dispute.

Article 4

1.   The only diseases or disabilities justifying refusal of entry into a territory or refusal to issue a first residence permit shall be those listed in the Annex to this Directive.

2.   Diseases or disabilities occurring after a first residence permit has been issued shall not justify refusal to renew the residence permit or expulsion from the territory.

3.   Member States shall not introduce new provisions or practices which are more restrictive than those in force at the date of notification of this Directive.

Article 5

1.   A decision to grant or to refuse a first residence permit shall be taken as soon as possible and in any event not later than six months from the date of application for the permit.

The person concerned shall be allowed to remain temporarily in the territory pending a decision either to grant or to refuse a residence permit.

2.   The host country may, in cases where this is considered essential, request the Member State of origin of the applicant, and if need be other Member States, to provide information

concerning any previous police record. Such enquiries shall not be made as a matter of routine. The Member State consulted shall give its reply within two months.

Article 6

The person concerned shall be informed of the grounds of public policy, public security, or public health upon which the decision taken in his case is based, unless this is contrary to the interests of the security of the State involved.

Article 7

The person concerned shall be officially notified of any decision to refuse the issue or renewal of a residence permit or to expel him from the territory. The period allowed for leaving the territory shall be stated in this notification. Save in cases of urgency, this period shall be not less than fifteen days if the person concerned has not yet been granted a residence permit and not less than one month in all other cases.

Article 8

The person concerned shall have the same legal remedies in respect of any decision concerning entry, or refusing the issue or renewal of a residence permit, or ordering expulsion from the territory, as are available to nationals of the State concerned in respect of acts of the administration.

Article 9

1.   Where there is no right of appeal to a court of law, or where such appeal may be only in respect the legal validity of the decision, or where the appeal cannot have suspensory effect, a decision refusing renewal of a residence permit or ordering the expulsion of the holder of a residence permit from the territory shall not be taken by the administrative authority, save in cases of urgency, until an opinion has been obtained from a competent authority of the host country before which the person concerned enjoys such rights of defence and of assistance or representation as the domestic law of that country provides for.

This authority shall not be the same as that empowered to take the decision refusing renewal of the residence permit or ordering expulsion.

2.   Any decision refusing the issue of a first residence permit or ordering expulsion of the person concerned before the issue of the permit shall, where that person so requests, be referred for consideration to the authority whose prior opinion is required under paragraph I. The person concerned shall then be entitled to submit his defence in person, except where this would be contrary to the interests of national security.

Article 10

1.   Member States shall within six months of notification of this Directive put into force the measures necessary to comply with its provisions and shall forthwith inform the Commission thereof.

2.   Member States shall ensure that the texts of the main provisions of national law which they adopt in the field governed by this Directive are communicated to the Commission.

Article 11

This Directive is addressed to the Member States.
Done at Brussels, 25 February 1964.

ANNEX

A.   *Diseases which might endanger public health:*

1.   Diseases subject to quarantine listed in International Health Regulation No. 2 of the World Health Organisation of 25 May 1951;

2.   Tuberculosis of the respiratory system in an active state or showing a tendency to develop;

3.   Syphilis;

4.   Other infectious diseases or contagious parasitic diseases if they are the subject of provisions for the protection of nationals of the host country.

B.   *Diseases and disabilities which might threaten public policy or public security:*
1.   Drug addiction;
2.   Profound mental disturbance; manifest conditions of psychotic disturbance with agitation, delirium, hallucinations or confusion.

Council Directive of 15 October 1968 on the abolition of restrictions on movement and residence within the Community for workers of Member States and their families (68/360/EEC)

[OJ Sp. Ed. 1968, No. L257/13, p. 485]

[Note: To be repealed on 30 April 2006 when Directive 2004/38 enters into force.]

(Preamble omitted.)

Article 1
Member States shall, acting as provided in this Directive, abolish restrictions on the movement and residence of nationals of the said States and of members of their families to whom Regulation (EEC) No 1612/68 applies.

Article 2
1.   Member States shall grant the nationals referred to in Article 1 the right to leave their territory in order to take up activities as employed persons and to pursue such activities in the territory of another Member State. Such right shall be exercised simply on production of a valid identity card or passport. Members of the family shall enjoy the same right as the national on whom they are dependent.

2.   Member States shall, acting in accordance with their laws, issue to such nationals, or renew, an identity card or passport, which shall state in particular the holder's nationality.

3.   The passport must be valid at least for all Member States and for countries through which the holder must pass when travelling between Member States. Where a passport is the only document on which the holder may lawfully leave the country, its period of validity shall be not less than five years.

4.   Member States may not demand from the nationals referred to in Article 1 any exit visa or any equivalent document.

Article 3
1.   Member States shall allow the persons referred to in Article 1 to enter their territory simply on production of a valid identity card or passport.

2.   No entry visa or equivalent document may be demanded save from members of the family who are not nationals of a Member State. Member States shall accord to such persons every facility for obtaining any necessary visas.

Article 4
1.   Member States shall grant the right of residence in their territory to the persons referred to in Article 1 who are able to produce the documents listed in paragraph 3.

2.   As proof of the right of residence, a document entitled 'Residence Permit for a National of a Member State of the EEC' shall be issued. This document must include a statement that it

has been issued pursuant to Regulation (EEC) No 1612/68 and to the measures taken by the Member States for the implementation of the present Directive. The text of such statement is given in the Annex to this Directive.

3. For the issue of a Residence Permit for a National of a Member State of the EEC, Member States may require only the production of the following documents;
— by the worker:
    (a) the document with which he entered their territory;
    (b) a confirmation of engagement from the employer or a certificate of employment;
— by the members of the worker's family:
    (c) the document with which they entered the territory;
    (d) a document issued by the competent authority of the State of origin or the State whence they came, proving their relationship;
    (e) in the cases referred to in Article 10(1) and (2) of Regulation (EEC) No 1612/68, a document issued by the competent authority of the State of origin or the State whence they came, testifying that they are dependent on the worker or that they live under his roof in such country.

4. A member of the family who is not a national of a Member State shall be issued with a residence document which shall have the same validity as that issued to the worker on whom he is dependent.

Article 5
Completion of the formalities for obtaining a residence permit shall not hinder the immediate beginning of employment under a contract concluded by the applicants.

Article 6
1. The residence permit:
    (a) must be valid throughout the territory of the Member State which issued it;
    (b) must be valid for at least five years from the date of issue and be automatically renewable.

2. Breaks in residence not exceeding six consecutive months and absence on military service shall not affect the validity of a residence permit.

3. Where a worker is employed for a period exceeding three months but not exceeding a year in the service of an employer in the host State or in the employ of a person providing services, the host Member State shall issue him a temporary residence permit, the validity of which may be limited to the expected period of the employment. Subject to the provisions of Article 8(1)(c), a temporary residence permit shall be issued also to a seasonal worker employed for a period of more than three months. The period of employment must be shown in the documents referred to in paragraph 4(3)(b).

Article 7
1. A valid residence permit may not be withdrawn from a worker solely on the grounds that he is no longer in employment, either because he is temporarily incapable of work as a result of illness or accident, or because he is involuntarily unemployed, this being duly confirmed by the competent employment office.

2. When the residence permit is renewed for the first time, the period of residence may be restricted, but not to less than twelve months, where the worker has been involuntarily unemployed in the Member State for more than twelve consecutive months.

Article 8
1. Member States shall, without issuing a residence permit, recognise the right of residence in their territory of:
    (a) a worker pursuing an activity as an employed person, where the activity is not expected to last for more than three months. The document with which the

person concerned entered the territory and a statement by the employer on the expected duration of the employment shall be sufficient to cover his stay; a statement by the employer shall not, however, be required in the case of workers coming within the provisions of the Council Directive of 25 February 1964 on the attainment of freedom of establishment and freedom to provide services in respect of the activities of intermediaries in commerce, industry and small craft industries;

(b) a worker who, while having his residence in the territory of a Member State to which he returns as a rule, each day or at least once a week, is employed in the territory of another Member State. The competent authority of the State where he is employed may issue such worker with a special permit valid for five years and automatically renewable;

(c) a seasonal worker who holds a contract of employment stamped by the competent authority of the Member State on whose territory he has come to pursue his activity.

2.   In all cases referred to in paragraph 1, the competent authorities of the host Member State may require the worker to report his presence in the territory.

Article 9

1.   The residence documents granted to nationals of a Member State of the EEC referred to in this Directive shall be issued and renewed free of charge or on payment of an amount not exceeding the dues and taxes charged for the issue of identity cards to nationals.

2.   The visa referred to in Article 3(2) and the stamp referred to in Article 8(1)(c) shall be free of charge.

3.   Member States shall take the necessary steps to simplify as much as possible the formalities and procedure for obtaining the documents mentioned in paragraph 1.

Article 10

Member States shall not derogate from the provisions of this Directive save on grounds of public policy, public security or public health.

(All remaining provisions omitted.)

Regulation (EEC) No. 1251/70 of the Commission of 29 June 1970 on the right of workers to remain in the territory of a Member State after having been employed in that State

[OJ Sp. Ed. 1970, No. L142/24, p. 402]

(Preamble omitted.)

Article 1

The provisions of this Regulation shall apply to nationals of a Member State who have worked as employed persons in the territory of another Member State and to members of their families, as defined in Article 10 of Council Regulation (EEC) No 1612/68 on freedom of movement for workers within the Community.

Article 2

1.   The following shall have the right to remain permanently in the territory of a Member State:

(a) a worker who, at the time of termination of his activity, has reached the age laid down by the law of that Member State for entitlement to an old-age pension and

who has been employed in that State for at least the last twelve months and has resided there continuously for more than three years;
(b) a worker who, having resided continuously in the territory of that State for more than two years, ceases to work there as an employed person as a result of permanent incapacity to work. If such incapacity is the result of an accident at work or an occupational disease entitling him to a pension for which an institution of that State is entirely or partially responsible, no condition shall be imposed as to length of residence;
(c) a worker who, after three years' continuous employment and resident in the territory of that State, works as an employed person in the territory of another Member State, while retaining his residence in the territory of the first State, to which he returns, as a rule, each day or at least once a week.

Periods of employment completed in this way in the territory of the other Member State shall, for the purposes of entitlement to the rights referred to in sub-paragraphs (a) and (b), be considered as having been completed in the territory of the State of residence.

2. The conditions as to length of residence and employment laid down in paragraph 1(a) and the condition as to length of residence laid down in paragraph 1(b) shall not apply if the worker's spouse is a national of the Member State concerned or has lost the nationality of that State by marriage to that worker.

Article 3

1. The members of a worker's family referred to in Article 1 of this Regulation who are residing with him in the territory of a Member State shall be entitled to remain there permanently if the worker has acquired the right to remain in the territory of that State in accordance with Article 2, and to do so even after his death.

2. If, however, the worker dies during his working life and before having acquired the right to remain in the territory of the State concerned, members of his family shall be entitled to remain there permanently on condition that:
— the worker, on the date of his decease, had resided continuously in the territory of that Member State for at least 2 years; or
— his death resulted from an accident at work or an occupational disease; or
— the surviving spouse is a national of the State of residence or lost the nationality of that State by marriage to that worker.

Article 4

1. Continuity of residence as provided for in Articles 2(1) and 3(2) may be attested by any means of proof in use in the country of residence. It shall not be affected by temporary absences not exceeding a total of three months per year, nor by longer absences due to compliance with the obligations of military service.

2. Periods of involuntary unemployment, duly recorded by the competent employment office, and absences due to illness or accident shall be considered as periods of employment within the meaning of Article 2(1).

Article 5

1. The person entitled to the right to remain shall be allowed to exercise it within two years from the time of becoming entitled to such right pursuant to Article 2(1)(a) and (b) and Article 3. During such period he may leave the territory of the Member State without adversely affecting such right.

2. No formality shall be required on the part of the person concerned in respect of the exercise of the right to remain.

Article 6

1. Persons coming under the provisions of this Regulation shall be entitled to a residence permit which:

(a) shall be issued and renewed free of charge or on paymentof a sumnot exceeding the dues and taxes payable by nationals for the issue or renewal identity documents;

(b) must be valid throughout the territory of the Member State issuing it;

(c) must be valid for at least five years and be renewable automatically.

2. Periods of non-residence not exceeding six consecutive months shall not affect the validity of the residence permit.

Article 7

The right to equality of treatment, established by Council Regulation (EEC) No 1612/68, shall apply also to persons coming under the provisions of this Regulation.

Article 8

1. This Regulation shall not affect any provisions laid down by law, regulation or administrative action of one Member State which would be more favourable to nationals of other Member States.

2. Member States shall facilitate re-admission to their territories of workers who have left those territories after having resided there permanently for a long period and having been employed there and who wish to return there when they have reached retirement age or are permanently incapacitated for work.

(All remaining provisions omitted.)

Council Directive of 21 May 1973 on the abolition of restrictions on movement and residence within the Community for nationals of Member States with regard to establishment and the provision of services (73/148/EEC)

[OJ 1973, L172/14]

[Note: To be repealed on 30 April 2006 when Directive 2004/38 enters into force.]

(Preamble omitted.)

Article 1

1. The Member States shall, acting as provided in this Directive, abolish restrictions on the movement and residence of:

(a) nationals of a Member State who are established or who wish to establish themselves in another Member State in order to pursue activities as self-employed persons, or who wish to provide services in that State;

(b) nationals of Member States wishing to go to another Member State as recipients of services;

(c) the spouse and the children under twenty-one years of age of such nationals, irrespective of their nationality;

(d) the relatives in the ascending and descending lines of such nationals and of the spouse of such nationals, which relatives are dependent on them, irrespective of their nationality.

2. Member States shall favour the admission of any other member of the family of a national referred to in paragraph 1(a) and (b) or of the spouse of that national, which member is dependent on that national or spouse of that national or who in the country of origin was living under the same roof.

Article 2

1.   Member States shall grant the persons referred to in Article 1 the right to leave their territory. Such right shall be exercised simply on production of a valid identity card or passport. Members of the family shall enjoy the same right as the national on whom they are dependent.

2.   Member States shall, acting in accordance with their laws, issue to their nationals, or renew, an identity card or passport, which shall state in particular the holder's nationality.

3.   The passport must be valid at least for all Member States and for countries through which the holder must pass when travelling between Member States. Where a passport is the only document on which the holder may lawfully leave the country, its period of validity shall be not less than five years.

4.   Member States may not demand from the persons referred to in Article 1 any exit visa or any equivalent requirement.

Article 3

1.   Member States shall grant to the persons referred to in Article 1 right to enter their territory merely on production of a valid identity card or passport.

2.   No entry visa or equivalent requirement may be demanded save in respect of members of the family who do have the nationality of a Member State. Member States shall afford to such persons every facility for obtaining any necessary visas.

Article 4

1.   Each Member State shall grant the right of permanent residence to nationals of other Member States who establish themselves within its territory in order to pursue activities as self-employed persons, when the restrictions on these activities have been abolished pursuant to the Treaty.

As proof of the right of residence, a document entitled 'Residence Permit for a National of a Member State of the European Communities' shall be issued. This document shall be valid for not less than five years from the date of issue and shall be automatically renewable.

Breaks in residence not exceeding six consecutive months and absence on military service shall not affect the validity of a residence permit.

A valid residence permit may not be withdrawn from a national referred to in Article 1(1)(a) solely on the grounds that he is no longer in employment because he is temporarily incapable of work as a result of illness or accident.

Any national of a Member State who is not specified in the first sub-paragraph but who is authorised under the laws of another Member State to pursue an activity within its territory shall be granted a right of abode for a period not less than that of the authorisation granted for the pursuit of the activity in question.

However, any national referred to in sub-paragraph 1 and to whom the provisions of the preceding sub-paragraph apply as a result of a change of employment shall retain his residence permit until the date on which it expires.

2.   The right of residence for persons providing and receiving services shall be of equal duration with the period during which the services are provided.

Where such period exceeds three months, the Member State in the territory of which the services are performed shall issue a right of abode as proof of the right of residence.

Where the period does not exceed three months, the identity card or passport with which the person concerned entered the territory shall be sufficient to cover his stay. The Member State may, however, require the person concerned to report his presence in the territory.

3.   A member of the family who is not a national of a Member State shall be issued with a residence document which shall have the same validity as that issued to that national on whom he is dependent.

Article 5

The right of residence shall be effective throughout the territory of the Member State concerned.

Article 6

An applicant for a residence permit or right of abode shall not be required by a Member State to produce anything other than the following, namely:

  (a) the identity card or passport with which he or she entered its territory;
  (b) proof that he or she comes within one of the classes of person referred to in Articles 1 and 4.

Article 7

1. The residence documents granted to nationals of a Member State shall be issued and renewed free of charge or on payment of an amount not exceeding the dues and taxes charged for the issue of identity cards to nationals. These provisions shall also apply to documents and certificates required for the issue and renewal of such residence documents.

2. The visas referred to in Article 3(2) shall be free of charge.

3. Member States shall take the necessary steps to simplify as much as possible the formalities and the procedure for obtaining the documents mentioned in paragraph 1.

Article 8

Member States shall not derogate from the provisions of this Directive save on grounds of public policy, public security or public health.

(All remaining provisions omitted.)

Council Directive of 17 December 1974 concerning the right of nationals of a Member State to remain in the territory of another Member State after having pursued therein an activity in a self-employed capacity (75/34/EEC)

[OJ 1975, L14/10]

[Note: To be repealed on 30 April 2006 when Directive 2004/38 enters into force.]

(Preamble omitted.)

Article 1

Member States shall, under the conditions laid down in this Directive, abolish restrictions on the right to remain in their territory in favour of nationals of another Member State who have pursued activities as self-employed persons in their territory, and members of their families, as defined in Article 1 of Directive No 73/148/EEC.

Article 2

1. Each Member State shall recognise the right to remain permanently in its territory of:

  (a) any person who, at the time of termination of his activity, has reached the age laid down by the law of that State for entitlement to an old-age pension and who has pursued his activity in that State for at least the previous twelve months and has resided there continuously for more than three years.

Where the law of that Member State does not grant the right to an old-age pension to certain categories of self-employed workers, the age requirement shall be considered as satisfied when the beneficiary reaches 65 years of age;

  (b) any person who, having resided continuously in the territory of that State for more than two years, ceases to pursue his activity there as a result of permanent incapacity to work.

If such incapacity is the result of an accident at work or an occupational illness entitling him to a pension which is payable in whole or in part by an institution of that State no condition shall be imposed as to length of residence;

      (c) any person who, after three years' continuous activity and residence in the territory of that State, pursues his activity in the territory of another Member State, while retaining his residence in the territory of the first State, to which he returns, as a rule, each day or at least once a week.

Periods of activity so completed in the territory of the other Member State shall, for the purposes of entitlement to the rights referred to in (a) and (b), be considered as having been completed in the territory of the State of residence.

    2. The conditions as to length of residence and activity laid down in paragraph 1(a) and the condition as to length of residence laid down in paragraph 1(b) shall not apply if the spouse of the self-employed person is a national of the Member State concerned or has lost the nationality of that State by marriage to that person.

Article 3

    1. Each Member State shall recognise the right of the members of the self-employed person's family referred to in Article 1 who are residing with him in the territory of that State to remain there permanently, if the person concerned has acquired the right to remain in the territory of that State in accordance with Article 2. This provision shall continue to apply even after the death of the person concerned.

    2. If, however, the self-employed person dies during his working life and before having acquired the right to remain in the territory of the State concerned, that State shall recognise the right of the members of his family to remain there permanently on condition that:

— the person concerned, on the date of his decease, had resided continuously in its territory for at least two years; or

— his death resulted from an accident at work or an occupational illness; or

— the surviving spouse is a national of that State or lost such nationality by marriage to the person concerned.

Article 4

    1. Continuity of residence as provided for in Articles 2(1) and 3(2) may be attested by any means of proof in use in the country of residence. It may not be affected by temporary absences not exceeding a total of three months per year, nor by longer absences due to compliance with the obligations of military service.

    2. Periods of inactivity due to circumstances outside the control of the person concerned or of inactivity owing to illness or accident must be considered as periods of activity within the meaning of Article 2(1).

Article 5

    1. Member States shall allow the person entitled to the right to remain to exercise such right within two years from the time of becoming entitled thereto pursuant to Article 2(1)(a) and (b) and Article 3. During this period the beneficiary must be able to leave the territory of the Member State without adversely affecting such right.

    2. Member States shall not require the person concerned to comply with any particular formality in order to exercise the right to remain.

Article 6

    1. Member States shall recognise the right of persons having the right to remain in their territory to a residence permit, which must:

      (a) be issued and renewed free of charge or on payment of a sum not exceeding the dues and taxes payable by nationals for the issue or renewal of identity cards;

      (b) be valid throughout the territory of the Member State issuing it;

      (c) be valid for five years and renewable automatically.

2.   Periods of non-residence not exceeding six consecutive months and longer absences due to compliance with the obligations of military service may not affect the validity of a residence permit.

Article 7
Member States shall apply to persons having the right to remain in their territory the right of equality of treatment recognised by the Council Directives on the abolition of restrictions on freedom of establishment pursuant to Title III of the General Programme which provides for such abolition.

Article 8
1.   This Directive shall not affect any provisions laid down by law, regulation or administrative action of any Member State which would be more favourable to nationals of other Member States.

2.   Member States shall facilitate re-admission to their territories of self-employed persons who left those territories after having resided there permanently for a long period while pursuing an activity there and who wish to return when they have reached retirement age as defined in Article 2(1)(a) or are permanently incapacitated for work.

Article 9
Member States may not derogate from the provisions of this Directive save on grounds of public policy, public security or public health.

(All remaining provisions omitted.)

Council Directive of 22 March 1977 to facilitate the effective exercise by lawyers of freedom to provide services (77/249/EEC)
[OJ 1977, L78/17]*

THE COUNCIL OF THE EUROPEAN COMMUNITIES,
Having regard to the Treaty establishing the European Economic Community, and in particular Articles 57 and 66 thereof,
Having regard to the proposal from the Commission,
Having regard to the opinion of the European Parliament (1),
Having regard to the opinion of the Economic and Social Committee (2),
(1) OJ No C 103, 5. 10. 1972, p. 19 and OJ No C 53, 8. 3. 1976, p. 33.
(2) OJ No C 36, 28. 3. 1970, p. 37 and OJ No C .SO, 4. 3. 1976, p. 17.

Whereas, pursuant to the Treaty, any restriction on the provision of services which is based on nationality or on conditions of residence has been prohibited since the end of the transitional period;
Whereas this Directive deals only with measures to facilitate the effective pursuit of the activities of lawyers by way of provision of services;
whereas more detailed measures will be necessary to facilitate the effective exercise of the right of establishment;
Whereas if lawyers are to exercise effectively the freedom to provide services host Member States must recognize as lawyers those persons practising the profession in the various Member States;

---

* As amended up to and including OJ 2003 L236/257.

Whereas, since this Directive solely concerns provision of services and does not contain provisions on the mutual recognition of diplomas, a person to whom the Directive applies must adopt the professional title used in the Member State in which he is established, hereinafter referred to as 'the Member State from which he comes', HAS ADOPTED THIS DIRECTIVE:

Article 1

1. This Directive shall apply, within the limits and under the conditions laid down herein, to the activities of lawyers pursued by way of provision of services.

Notwithstanding anything contained in this Directive, Member States may reserve to prescribed categories of lawyers the preparation of formal documents for obtaining title to administer estates of deceased persons, and the drafting of formal documents creating or transferring interests in land.

2. 'Lawyers' means any person entitled to pursue his professional activities under one of the following designations:[1]

Belgium:	Avocat/Advocaat
Czech Republic:	Advokáat
Denmark:	Advokat
Germany:	Rechtsanwalt
Estonia:	Vandeadvokaat
Greece:	Dikigoros
France:	Avocat
Ireland:	Barrister
	Solicitor
Italy:	Avvocato
Cyprus:	Δικηγορός
Latvia:	Zvērināts/Advokats
Lithuania:	Advokāts
Luxembourg:	Avocat-avoue
Hungary:	Ügyvéd
Malta:	Avukat/Prokuratur Legali
Netherlands:	Advocaat
Austria:	Rechtsanwalt
Poland:	Adwokat/Radca prawny
Portugal:	Advogado
Slovenia:	Odvetnik/Odvetnica
Slovakia	Advokát/Komerčný právnik
Finland:	Asianajaja — Advokat
Spain:	Abogado
Sweden:	Advokat
United Kingdom:	Advocate
	Barrister
	Solicitor

Article 2

Each Member State shall recognise as a lawyer for the purpose of pursuing the activities specified in Article 1(1) any person listed in paragraph 2 of that Article.

Article 3

A person referred to in Article 1 shall adopt the professional title used in the Member State from which he comes, expressed in the language or one of the languages, of that State, with an

---

[1] As amended by the Accession Acts.

indication of the professional organisation by which he is authorised to practise or the court of law before which he is entitled to practise pursuant to the laws of that State.

Article 4

1. Activities relating to the representation of a client in legal proceedings or before public authorities shall be pursued in each host Member State under the conditions laid down for lawyers established in that State, with the exception of any conditions requiring residence, or registration with a professional organisation, in that State.

2. A lawyer pursuing these activities shall observe the rules of professional conduct of the host Member State, without prejudice to his obligations in the Member State from which he comes.

3. When these activities are pursued in the United Kingdom, 'rules of professional conduct of the host Member State' means the rules of professional conduct applicable to solicitors, where such activities are not reserved for barristers and advocates. Otherwise the rules of professional conduct applicable to the latter shall apply. However, barristers from Ireland shall always be subject to the rules of professional conduct applicable in the United Kingdom to barristers and advocates.

When these activities are pursued in Ireland 'rules of professional conduct of the host Member State' means, in so far as they govern the oral presentation of a case in court, the rules of professional conduct applicable to barristers. In all other cases the rules of professional conduct applicable to solicitors shall apply. However, barristers and advocates from the United Kingdom shall always be subject to the rules of professional conduct applicable in Ireland to barristers.

4. A lawyer pursuing activities other than those referred to in paragraph 1 shall remain subject to the conditions and rules of professional conduct of the Member State from which he comes without prejudice to respect for the rules, whatever their source, which govern the profession in the host Member State, especially those concerning the incompatibility of the exercise of the activities of a lawyer with the exercise of other activities in that State, professional secrecy, relation with other lawyers, the prohibition on the same lawyer acting for parties with mutually conflicting interests, and publicity. The latter rules are applicable only if they are capable of being observed by a lawyer who is not established in the host Member State and to the extent to which their observance is objectively justified to ensure, in that State, the proper exercise of a lawyer's activities, the standing of the profession and respect for the rules concerning incompatibility.

Article 5

For the pursuit of activities relating to the representation of a client in legal proceedings, a Member State may require lawyers to whom Article 1 applies:

— to be introduced, in accordance with local rules or customs, to the presiding judge and, where appropriate, to the President of the relevant Bar in the host Member State;

— to work in conjunction with a lawyer who practises before the judicial authority in question and who would, where necessary, be answerable to that authority, or with an 'avoué' or 'procuratore' practising before it.

Article 6

Any Member State may exclude lawyers who are in the salaried employment of a public or private undertaking from pursuing activities relating to the representation of that undertaking in legal proceedings in so far as lawyers established in that State are not permitted to pursue those activities.

Article 7

1. The competent authority of the host Member State may request the person providing the services to establish his qualifications as a lawyer.

2.   In the event of non-compliance with the obligations referred to in Article 4 and in force in the host Member State, the competent authority of the latter shall determine in accordance with its own rules and procedures the consequences of such noncompliance, and to this end may obtain an appropriate professional information concerning the person providing services. It shall notify the competent authority of the Member State from which the person comes of any decision taken. Such exchanges shall not affect the confidential nature of the information supplied.

(All remaining provisions omitted.)

Council Directive of 21 December 1988 on a general system for the recognition of higher-education diplomas awarded on completion of professional education and training of at least three years' duration (89/48/EEC)

[OJ 1989, L19/16]*

The Council of the European Communities,

Having regard to the Treaty establishing the European Economic Community, and in particular Articles 49, 57(1) and 66 thereof,

Having regard to the proposal from the Commission,

In cooperation with the European Parliament,

Having regard to the opinion of the Economic and Social Committee,

Whereas, pursuant to Article 3(c) of the Treaty the abolition, as between Member States, of obstacles to freedom of movement for persons and services constitutes one of the objectives of the Community; whereas, for nationals of the Member States, this means in particular the possibility of pursuing a profession, whether in a self-employed or employed capacity, in a Member State other than that in which they acquired their professional qualifications;

Whereas the provisions so far adopted by the Council, and pursuant to which Member States recognise mutually and for professional purposes higher-education diplomas issued within their territory, concern only a few professions; whereas the level and duration of the education and training governing access to those professions have been regulated in a similar fashion in all the Member States or have been the subject of the minimal harmonisation needed to establish sectoral systems for the mutual recognition of diplomas;

Whereas, in order to provide a rapid response to the expectations of nationals of Community countries who hold higher-education diplomas awarded on completion of professional education and training issued in a Member State other than that in which they wish to pursue their profession, another method of recognition of such diplomas should also be put in place such as to enable those concerned to pursue all those professional activities which in a host Member State are dependent on the completion of post-secondary education and training, provided they hold such a diploma preparing them for those activities awarded on completion of a course of studies lasting at least three years and issued in another Member State;

Whereas this objective can be achieved by the introduction of a general system for the recognition of higher-education diplomas awarded on completion of professional education and training of at least three years' duration;

* **Editor's Note**: As corrected and amended up to and including Directive 2001/19 of 14/5/2001 (OJ 2001, L206/1).

Whereas, for those professions for the pursuit of which the Community has not laid down the necessary minimum level of qualification, Member States reserve the option of fixing such a level with a view to guaranteeing the quality of services provided in their territory; whereas, however, they may not, without infringing their obligations laid down in Article 5 of the Treaty, require a national of a Member State to obtain those qualifications which in general they determine only by reference to diplomas issued under their own national education systems, where the person concerned has already acquired all or part of those qualifications in another Member State; whereas, as a result, any host Member State in which a profession is regulated is required to take account of qualifications acquired in another Member State and to determine whether those qualifications correspond to the qualifications which the Member State concerned requires;

Whereas collaboration between the Member States is appropriate in order to facilitate their compliance with those obligations; whereas, therefore, the means of organising such collaboration should be established;

Whereas the term 'regulated professional activity' should be defined so as to take account of differing national sociological situations; whereas the term should cover not only professional activities access to which is subject, in a Member State, to the possession of a diploma, but also professional activities, access to which is unrestricted when they are practised under a professional title reserved for the holders of certain qualifications; whereas the professional associations and organisations which confer such titles on their members and are recognised by the public authorities cannot invoke their private status to avoid application of the system provided for by this Directive;

Whereas it is also necessary to determine the characteristics of the professional experience or adaptation period which the host Member State may require of the person concerned in addition to the higher-education diploma, where the person's qualifications do not correspond to those laid down by national provisions;

Whereas an aptitude test may also be introduced in place of the adaptation period; whereas the effect of both will be to improve the existing situation with regard to the mutual recognition of diplomas between Member States and therefore to facilitate the free movement of persons within the Community; whereas their function is to assess the ability of the migrant, who is a person who has already received his professional training in another Member State, to adapt to this new professional environment; whereas, from the migrant's point of view, an aptitude test will have the advantage of reducing the length of the practice period; whereas, in principle, the choice between the adaptation period and the aptitude test should be made by the migrant; whereas, however, the nature of certain professions is such that Member States must be allowed to prescribe, under certain conditions, either the adaptation period or the test; whereas, in particular, the differences between the legal systems of the Member States, whilst they may vary in extent from one Member State to another, warrant special provisions since, as a rule, the education or training attested by the diploma, certificate or other evidence of formal qualifications in a field of law in the Member State of origin does not cover thelegalknowledgerequired in the host Member State with respect to the corresponding legal field;

Whereas, moreover, the general system for the recognition of higher-education diplomas is intended neither to amend the rules, including those relating to professional ethics, applicable to any person pursuing a profession in the territory of a Member State nor to exclude migrants from the application of those rules; whereas that system is confined to laying down appropriate arrangements to ensure that migrants comply with the professional rules of the host Member State;

Whereas Articles 49, 57(1) and 66 of the Treaty empower the Community to adopt provisions necessary for the introduction and operation of such a system;

Whereas the general system for the recognition of higher-education diplomas is entirely without prejudice to the application of Article 48(4) and Article 55 of the Treaty;

Whereas such a system, by strengthening the right of a Community national to use his professional skills in any Member State, supplements and reinforces his right to acquire such skills wherever he wishes;

Whereas this system should be evaluated, after being in force for a certain time, to determine how efficiently it operates and in particular how it can be improved or its field of application extended,

Has adopted this Directive:

Article 1

For the purposes of this Directive following definitions shall apply:

(a) diploma: any diploma, certificate or other evidence of formal qualifications or any set of such diplomas, certificates or other evidence:

— which has been awarded by a competent authority in a Member State, designated in accordance with its own laws, regulations or administrative provisions;

— which shows that the holder has successfully completed a post-secondary course of at least three years' duration, or of an equivalent duration part-time, at a university or establishment of higher education or another establishment of equivalent level and, where appropriate, that he has successfully completed the professional training required in addition to the post-secondary course, and

— which shows that the holder has the professional qualifications required for the taking up or pursuit of a regulated profession in that Member State,

provided that the education and training attested by the diploma, certificate or other evidence of formal qualifications were received mainly in the Community, or the holder thereof has three years' professional experience certified by the Member State which recognised a third-country diploma, certificate or other evidence of formal qualifications.

The following shall be treated in the same way as a diploma, within the meaning of the first sub-paragraph: any diploma, certificate or other evidence of formal qualifications or any set of such diplomas, certificates or other evidence awarded by a competent authority in a Member State if it is awarded on the successful completion of education and training received in the Community and recognised by a competent authority in that Member State as being of an equivalent level and if it confers the same rights in respect of the taking up and pursuit of a regulated profession in that Member State;

(b) host Member State: any Member State in which a national of a Member State applies to pursue a profession subject to regulation in that Member State, other than the State in which he obtained his diploma or first pursued the profession in question;

(c) a regulated profession: the regulated professional activity or range of activities which constitute this profession in a Member State;

(d) regulated professional activity: a professional activity, in so far as the taking up or pursuit of such activity or one of its modes of pursuit in a Member State is subject, directly or indirectly by virtue of laws, regulations or administrative provisions, to the possession of a diploma. The following in particular shall constitute a mode of pursuit of a regulated professional activity:

— pursuit of an activity under a professional title, in so far as the use of such a title is reserved to the holders of a diploma governed by laws, regulations or administrative provisions,

— pursuit of a professional activity relating to health, in so far as remuneration and/or reimbursement for such an activity is subject by virtue of national social security arrangements to the possession of a diploma.

Where the first sub-paragraph does not apply, a professional activity shall be deemed to be a regulated professional activity if it is pursued by the members of an association or organisation the purpose of which is, in particular, to promote and maintain a high standard in the professional field concerned and which, to achieve that purpose, is recognised in a special form by a Member State and:

— awards a diploma to its members,

— ensures that its members respect the rules of professional conduct which it prescribes, and

— confers on them the right to use a title or designatory letters, or to benefit from a status corresponding to that diploma.

A non-exhaustive list of associations or organisations which, when this Directive is adopted, satisfy the conditions of the second sub-paragraph is contained in the Annex. Whenever a Member State grants the recognition referred to in the second sub-paragraph to an association or organisation, it shall inform the Commission thereof, which shall publish this information in the *Official Journal of the European Communities*;

(d)* a regulated education and training: any education and training which:

— is directly geared to the practice of a defined profession, and

— comprises a post-secondary course of at least three years' duration, or an equivalent duration part-time, at a university or higher education establishment or in another establishment of equivalent level and, where appropriate, the professional training, professional traineeship or professional practice required in addition to the post-secondary course; the structure and level of the professional training, professional traineeship or professional practice shall be determined by the laws, regulations or administrative provisions of the Member State concerned or monitored or approved by the authority designated for that purpose.

(e) professional experience: the actual and lawful pursuit of the profession concerned in a Member State;

(f) adaptation period: the pursuit of a regulated profession in the host Member State under the responsibility of a qualified member of that profession, such period of supervised practice possibly being accompanied by further training. This period of supervised practice shall be the subject of an assessment. The detailed rules governing the adaptation period and its assessment as well as the status of a migrant person under supervision shall be laid down by the competent authority in the host Member States;

(g) aptitude test: a test limited to the professional knowledge of the applicant, made by the competent authorities of the host Member State with the aim of assessing the ability of the applicant to pursue a regulated profession in that Member State.

In order to permit this test to be carried out, the competent authorities shall draw up a list of subjects which, on the basis of a comparison of the education and training required in the Member State and that received by the applicant, are not covered by the diploma or other evidence of formal qualifications possessed by the applicant.

The aptitude test must take account of the fact that the applicant is a qualified professional in the Member State of origin or the Member State from which he comes. It shall cover subjects to be selected from those on the list, knowledge of which is essential in order to be able to exercise the profession in the host Member State. The test may also include knowledge of the professional rules applicable to the activities in question in the host Member State. The detailed application of the aptitude test shall be determined by the competent authorities of that State with due regard to the rules of Community law.

The status, in the host Member State, of the applicant who wishes to prepare himself for the aptitude test in that State shall be determined by the competent authorities in that State.

---

* **Editor's Note**: Second (d) inserted by the amendment! See OJ 2001 L206/3.

Article 2

This Directive shall apply to any national of a Member State wishing to pursue a regulated profession in a host Member State in a self-employed capacity or as an employed person.

This Directive shall not apply to professions which are the subject of a separate Directive establishing arrangements for the mutual recognition of diplomas by Member States.

Article 3

Where, in a host Member State, the taking up or pursuit of a regulated profession is subject to possession of a diploma, the competent authority may not, on the grounds of inadequate qualifications, refuse to authorise a national of a Member State to take up or pursue that profession on the same conditions as apply to its own nationals:

(a) if the applicant holds the diploma required in another Member State for the taking up or pursuit of the profession in question in its territory, such diploma having been awarded in a Member State; or

(b) if the applicant has pursued the profession in question full-time for two years during the previous ten years in another Member State which does not regulate that profession, within the meaning of Article 1(c) and the first sub-paragraph of Article 1(d), and possesses evidence of one or more formal qualifications:

— which have been awarded by a competent authority in a Member State, designated in accordance with the laws, regulations or administrative provisions of such State,

— which show that the holder has successfully completed a post-secondary course of at least three years' duration, or of an equivalent duration part-time, at a university or establishment of higher education or another establishment of similar level of a Member State and, where appropriate, that he has successfully completed the professional training required in addition to the post-secondary course, and

— which have prepared the holder for the pursuit of his profession.

However, the two years' of professional experience referred to in the first sub-paragraph may not be required where the qualification or qualifications held by the applicant and referred to in this point were awarded on completion of regulated education and training.

The following shall be treated in the same way as the evidence of formal qualifications referred to in the first sub-paragraph: any formal qualifications or any set of such formal qualifications awarded by a competent authority in a Member State if it is awarded on the successful completion of training received in the Community and is recognised by that Member State as being of an equivalent level, provided that the other Member States and the Commission have been notified of this recognition.

Article 4

1. Notwithstanding Article 3, the host Member State may also require the applicant:

(a) to provide evidence of professional experience, where the duration of the education and training adduced in support of his application, as laid down in Article 3(a) and (b), is at least one year less than that required in the host Member State. In this event, the period of professional experience required:

— may not exceed twice the shortfall in duration of education and training where the shortfall relates to post-secondary studies and/or to a period of probationary practice carried out under the control of a supervising professional person and ending with an examination,

— may not exceed the shortfall where the shortfall relates to professional practice acquired with the assistance of a qualified member of the profession.

In the case of diplomas within the meaning of the last sub-paragraph of Article 1(a), the duration of education and training recognised as being of an equivalent level shall be determined as for the education and training defined in the first sub-paragraph of Article 1(a).

When applying these provisions, account must be taken of the professional experience referred to in Article 3(b).

At all events, the professional, experience required may not exceed four years;

(b) to complete an adaptation period not exceeding three years or take an aptitude test:

— where the matters covered by the education and training he has received as laid down in Article 3 (a) and (b), differ substantially from those covered by the diploma required in the host Member State, or

— where, in the case referred to in Article 3(a), the profession regulated in the host Member State comprises one or more regulated professional activities which are not in the profession regulated in the Member State from which the applicant originates or comes and that difference corresponds to specific education and training required in the host Member State and covers matters which differ substantially from those covered by the diploma adduced by the applicant, or

— where, in the case referred to in Article 3(b), the profession regulated in the host Member State comprises one or more regulated professional activities which are not in the profession pursued by the applicant in the Member State from which he originates or comes, and that difference corresponds to specific education and training required in the host Member State and covers matters which differ substantially from those covered by the evidence of formal qualifications adduced by the applicant.

If the host Member State intends to require the applicant to complete an adaption period or take an aptitude test, it must first examine whether the knowledge acquired by the applicant in the course of his professional experience is such that it fully or partly covers the substantial difference referred to in the first sub-paragraph.

Should the host Member State make use of this possibility, it must give the applicant the right to choose between an adaptation period and an aptitude test. By way of derogation from this principle, for professions whose practice requires precise knowledge of national law and in respect of which the provision of advice and/or assistance concerning national law is an essential and constant aspect of the professional activity, the host Member State may stipulate either an adaptation period or an aptitude test. Where the host Member State intends to introduce derogations for other professions as regards an applicant's right to choose, the procedure laid down in Article 10 shall apply.

2.   However, the host Member State may not apply the provisions of paragraph 1(a) and (b) cumulatively.

Article 5

Without prejudice to Articles 3 and 4, a host Member State may allow the applicant, with a view to improving his possibilities of adapting to the professional environment in that State, to undergo there, on the basis of equivalence, that part of his professional education and training represented by professional practice, acquired with the assistance of a qualified member of the profession, which he has not undergone in his Member State of origin or the Member State from which he has come.

Article 6

1.   Where the competent authority of a host Member State requires of persons wishing to take up a regulated profession proof that they are of good character or repute or that they have not been declared bankrupt, or suspends or prohibits the pursuit of this profession in the event of serious professional misconduct or a criminal offence, that State shall accept as sufficient evidence, in respect of nationals of Member States wishing to pursue that profession in its territory, the production of documents issued by competent authorities in the Member State of origin or the Member State from which the foreign national comes showing that those requirements are met.

Where the competent authorities of the Member State of origin or of the Member State from which the foreign national comes do not issue the documents referred to in the first sub-paragraph, such documents shall be replaced by a declaration on oath—or, in States where there is no provision for declaration on oath, by a solemn declaration—made by the person concerned before a competent judicial or administrative authority or, where appropriate, a notary or qualified professional body of the Member State of origin or the Member State from which the person comes; such authority or notary shall issue a certificate attesting the authenticity of the declaration on oath or solemn declaration.

2.   Where the competent authority of a host Member State requires of nationals of that Member State wishing to take up or pursue a regulated profession a certificate of physical or mental health, that authority shall accept as sufficient evidence in this respect the production of the document required in the Member State of origin or the Member State from which the foreign national comes.

Where the Member State of origin or the Member State from which the foreign national comes does not impose any requirements of this nature on those wishing to take up or pursue the profession in question, the host Member State shall accept from such nationals a certificate issued by a competent authority in that State corresponding to the certificates issued in the host Member State.

3.   The competent authorities of host Member States may require that the documents and certificates referred to in paragraphs 1 and 2 are presented no more than three months after their date of issue.

4.   Where the competent authority of a host Member State requires nationals of that Member State wishing to take up or pursue a regulated profession to take an oath or make a solemn declaration and where the form of such oath or declaration cannot be used by nationals of other Member States, that authority shall ensure that an appropriate and equivalent form of oath or declaration is offered to the person concerned.

5.   Where proof of financial standing is required in order to take up or pursue a regulated profession in the host Member State, that Member State shall regard certificates issued by banks in the Member State of origin or in the Member State from where the foreign national comes as equivalent to those issued in its own territory.

6.   Where the competent authority of the host Member State requires of its own nationals wishing to take up or pursue a regulated profession proof that they are insured against the financial risks arising from their professional liability, that Member State shall accept certificates issued by insurance undertakings of other Member States as equivalent to those issued in its own territory. Such certificates shall state that the insurer has complied with the laws and regulations in force in the host Member State regarding the terms and extent of cover. They may not be presented more than three months after their date of issue.

Article 7

1.   The competent authorities of host Member States shall recognise the right of nationals of Member States who fulfil the conditions for the taking up and pursuit of a regulated profession in their territory to use the professional title of the host Member State corresponding to that profession.

2.   The competent authorities of host Member States shall recognise the right of nationals of Member States who fulfil the conditions for the taking up and pursuit of a regulated profession in their territory to use their lawful academic title and, where appropriate, the abbreviation thereof deriving from their Member State of origin or the Member State from which they come, in the language of that State. Host Member State may require this title to be followed by the name and location of the establishment or examining board which awarded it.

3.   Where a profession is regulated in the host Member State by an association or organisation referred to in Article 1(d), nationals of Member States shall only be entitled to use

the professional title or designatory letters conferred by that organisation or association on proof of membership.

Where the association or organisation makes membership subject to certain qualification requirements, it may apply these to nationals of other Member States who are in possession of a diploma within the meaning of Article 1(a) or a formal qualification within the meaning of Article 3(b) only in accordance with this Directive, in particular Articles 3 and 4.

Article 8

1.   The host Member State shall accept as proof that the conditions laid down in Articles 3 and 4 are satisfied the certificates and documents issued by the competent authorities in the Member States, which the person concerned shall submit in support of his application to pursue the profession concerned.

2.   The procedure for examining an application to pursue a regulated profession shall be completed as soon as possible and the outcome communicated in a reasoned decision of the competent authority in the host Member State not later than four months after presentation of all the documents relating to the person concerned. A remedy shall be available against this decision, or the absence thereof, before a court or tribunal in accordance with the provisions of national law.

Article 9

1.   Member States shall designate, within the period provided for in Article 12, the competent authorities empowered to receive the applications and take the decisions referred to in this Directive.

They shall communicate this information to the other Member States and to the Commission.

2.   Each Member State shall designate a person responsible for coordinating the activities of the authorities referred to in paragraph 1 and shall inform the other Member States and the Commission to that effect. His role shall be to promote uniform application of this Directive to all the professions concerned. A coordinating group shall be set up under the aegis of the Commission, composed of the coordinators appointed by each Member State or their deputies and chaired by a representative of the Commission.

The task of this group shall be:
— to facilitate the implementation of this Directive, in particular by adopting and publishing opinions on the questions referred to it by the Commission,
— to collect all useful information for its application in the Member States.

The group may be consulted by the Commission on any changes to the existing system that may be contemplated.

3.   Member States shall take measures to provide the necessary information on the recognition of diplomas within the framework of this Directive. They may be assisted in this task by the information centre on the academic recognition of diplomas and periods of study established by the Member States within the framework of the Resolution of the Council and the Ministers of Education meeting within the Council of 9 February 1976([4]) and, where appropriate, the relevant professional associations or organisations. The Commission shall take the necessary initiatives to ensure the development and coordination of the communication of the necessary information.

Article 10

1.   If, pursuant to the third sentence of the second sub-paragraph of Article 4(1)(b), a Member State proposes not to grant applicants the right to choose between an adaptation period and an aptitude test in respect of a profession within the meaning of this Directive, it shall immediately communicate to the Commission the corresponding draft provision. It

---

[4] OJ No. C38, 19.2.1976, p. 1.

shall at the same time notify the Commission of the grounds which make the enactment of such a provision necessary.

The Commission shall immediately notify the other Member States of any draft it has received; it may also consult the coordinating group referred to in Article 9(2) of the draft.

2.   Without prejudice to the possibility for the Commission and the other Member States of making comments on the draft, the Member State may adopt the provision only if the Commission has not taken a decision to the contrary within three months.

3.   At the request of a Member State or the Commission, Member States shall communicate to them, without delay, the definitive text of a provision arising from the application of this Article.

Article 11

Following the expiry of the period provided for in Article 12, Member States shall communicate to the Commission, every two years, a report on the application of the system introduced.

In addition to general remarks, this report shall contain a statistical summary of the decisions taken and a description of the main problems arising from application of the Directive.

Article 12

Member States shall take the measures necessary to comply with this Directive within two years of its notification. They shall forthwith inform the Commission thereof.

Member States shall communicate to the Commission the texts of the main provisions of national law which they adopt in the field governed by this Directive.

Article 13

Five years at the latest following the date specified in Article 12, the Commission shall report to the European Parliament and the Council on the state of application of the general system for the recognition of higher-education diplomas awarded on completion of professional education and training of at least three years' duration.

After conducting all necessary consultations, the Commission shall, on this occasion, present its conclusions as to any changes that need to be made to the system as it stands. At the same time the Commission shall, where appropriate, submit proposals for improvements in the present system in the interest of further facilitating the freedom of movement, right of establishment and freedom to provide services of the persons covered by this Directive.

Article 14

The Directive is addressed to the Member States.

Done at Brussels, 21 December 1988.

ANNEX

List of professional associations or organizations which satisfy the conditions of the second sub-paragraph of Article 1 (d)

IRELAND (1)

1.   The Institute of Chartered Accountants in Ireland (2)
2.   The Institute of Certified Public Accountants in Ireland (2)
3.   The Association of Certified Accountants (2)
4.   Institution of Engineers of Ireland
5.   Irish Planning Institute

(1) Irish nationals are also members of the following United Kingdom chartered bodies:

> Institute of Chartered Accountants in England and Wales
> Institute of Chartered Accountants of Scotland
> Institute of Actuaries
> Faculty of Actuaries
> The Chartered Institute of Management Accountants
> Institute of Chartered Secretaries and Administrators
> Royal Town Planning Institute
> Royal Institution of Chartered Surveyors
> Chartered Institute of Building.

(2) For the purposes of the activity of auditing only.

UNITED KINGDOM

1. Institute of Chartered Accountants in England and Wales
2. Institute of Chartered Accountants of Scotland
3. Institute of Chartered Accountants in Ireland
4. Chartered Association of Certified Accountants
5. Chartered Institute of Loss Adjusters
6. Chartered Institute of Management Accountants
7. Institute of Chartered Secretaries and Administrators
8. Chartered Insurance Institute
9. Institute of Actuaries
10. Faculty of Actuaries
11. Chartered Institute of Bankers
12. Institute of Bankers in Scotland
13. Royal Institution of Chartered Surveyors
14. Royal Town Planning Institute
15. Chartered Society of Physiotherapy
16. Royal Society of Chemistry
17. British Psychological Society
18. Library Association
19. Institute of Chartered Foresters
20. Chartered Institute of Building
21. Engineering Council
22. Institute of Energy
23. Institution of Structural Engineers
24. Institution of Civil Engineers
25. Institution of Mining Engineers
26. Institution of Mining and Metallurgy
27. Institution of Electrical Engineers
28. Institution of Gas Engineers
29. Institution of Mechanical Engineers
30. Institution of Chemical Engineers
31. Institution of Production Engineers
32. Institution of Marine Engineers
33. Royal Institution of Naval Architects
34. Royal Aeronautical Society
35. Institute of Metals
36. Chartered Institution of Building Services Engineers
37. Institute of Measurement and Control
38. British Computer Society

Council Recommendation 21 December 1988 concerning nationals of Member States who hold a diploma conferred in a third State (89/49/EEC)

[OJ 1989, L19/24]

The Council of the European Communities,

Approving Council Directive 89/48/EEC of 21 December 1988 on a general system for the recognition of higher-education diplomas awarded on completion of professional education and training of at least three years' duration;

Noting that this Directive refers only to diplomas, certificates and other evidence of formal qualifications awarded in Member States to nationals of Member States;

Anxious, however, to take account of the special position of nationals of Member States who hold diplomas, certificates or other evidence of formal qualifications awarded in third States and who are thus in a position comparable to one of those described in Article 3 of the Directive,

Hereby recommends:

that the Governments of the Member States should allow the persons referred to above to take up and pursue regulated professions within the Community by recognising these diplomas, certificates and other evidence of formal qualifications in their territories.

Done at Brussels, 21 December 1988.

Council Directive 92/51/EEC of 18 June 1992 on a second general system for the recognition of professional education and training to supplement Directive 89/48/EEC

[OJ 1992, L209/25]*

The Council of the European Communities,

Having regard to the Treaty establishing the European Economic Community, particular Articles 49, 57(1) and 66 thereof,

Having regard to the proposal from the Commission,[1]

In cooperation with the European Parliament,[2]

Having regard to the opinion of the Economic and Social Committee,[3]

1.   Whereas, pursuant to Article 8a of the Treaty, the internal market shall comprise an area without internal frontiers and whereas, pursuant to Article 3(c) of the Treaty, the abolition, as between Member States, of obstacles to freedom of movement for persons and services constitutes one of the objectives of the Community; whereas, for nationals of the Member States, this means in particular the possibility of pursuing a profession, whether in a self-employed or employed capacity, in a Member State other than that in which they acquired their professional qualifications;

2.   Whereas, for those professions for the pursuit of which the Community has not laid down the necessary minimum level of qualification, Member States reserve the option of

---

* **Editor's Note**: As corrected and amended up to and including Regulation 1882/2003 (OJ 2003 L284/1).

[1] OJ No. C263, 16.10.1989, p. 1 and OJ No. C217, 1.9.1990, p. 4.

[2] OJ No. C149, 18.6.1990, p. 149, and OJ No. C150, 15.6.1992.

[3] OJ No. C75, 26.3.1990, p. 11.

fixing such a level with a view to guaranteeing the quality of services provided in their territory; whereas, however, they may not, without disregarding their obligations laid down in
Articles 5, 48, 52 and 59 of the Treaty, require a national of a Member State to obtain those
qualifications which in general they determine only by reference to those issued under their
own national education and training systems, where the person concerned has already
acquired all or part of those qualifications in another Member State; whereas, as a result, any
host Member State in which a profession is regulated is required to take account of qualifications acquired in another Member State and to determine whether those qualifications
correspond to the qualifications which the Member State concerned requires;

3.   Whereas Council Directives 89/48/EEC of 21 December 1988 on a general system for
the recognition of higher education diplomas awarded on completion of professional
education and training of at least three years' duration[4] facilitates compliance with such
obligations; whereas, however, it is limited to higher education;

4.   Whereas, in order to facilitate the pursuit of all those professional activities which in
a host Member State are dependent on the completion of a certain level of education and
training, a second general system should be introduced to complement the first;

5.   Whereas the complementary general system must be based on the same principles
and contain mutatis mutandis the same rules as the initial general system;

6.   Whereas this Directive is not applicable to those regulated professions which are
covered by specific Directives principally concerned with introducing mutual recognition of
training courses completed before entry into professional life;

7.   Whereas neither is it applicable, furthermore, to those activities covered by specific
Directives principally intended to introduce recognition of technical skills based on experience acquired in another Member State; whereas certain of those Directives apply solely to the
pursuit of activities in a self-employed capacity; whereas, in order to ensure that the pursuit of
such activities as an employed person does not fall within the scope of this Directive, whereby
the pursuit of the same activity would be subject to different legal recognition arrangements
depending on whether it was pursued in a self-employed capacity or as an employed person,
those Directives should be made applicable to persons pursuing the activities in question as
employed persons;

8.   Whereas the complementary general system is entirely without prejudice to the
application of Article 48(4) and Article 55 of the Treaty;

9.   Whereas this complementary system must cover the levels of education and training
not covered by the initial general system, namely that corresponding to other post-secondary
education and training courses and other equivalent education and training, and that corresponding to long or short secondary courses, possibly complemented by professional training
or experience;

10.   Whereas, where in most Member States pursuit of a given regulated profession
is subject to either very short training or the possession of certain personal attributes or
merely general knowledge, the normal mechanism for recognition under this Directive may
be excessively cumbersome; whereas in such cases there should be provision for simplified
mechanisms;

11.   Whereas account should also be taken of the professional training system in the
United Kingdom whereby standards for levels of performance for all professional activities are
established via the 'National Framework of Vocational Qualifications';

12.   Whereas in some Member States there are only relatively few regulated professions;
whereas, however, training for professions which are not regulated may be specifically geared
to the pursuit of the profession, with the structure and level of training being monitored or
approved by the competent authorities of the Member State concerned; whereas this provides
guarantees equivalent to those provided in connection with a regulated profession;

[4] OJ No. L19, 24.1.1989, p. 16.(5), OJ No. L199, 31.7.1985, p. 56.

13.   Whereas the competent authorities of the host Member State should be allowed to determine, in accordance with the relevant provisions of Community law, the detailed rules necessary for implementation of the adoption period and the aptitude test;

14.   Whereas, since it covers two levels of education and training and since the initial general system covers a third level, the complementary general system must lay down whether and under what conditions a person possessing a certain level of education and training may pursue, in another Member State, a profession the qualifications for which are regulated at a different level;

15.   Whereas, for the pursuit of certain professions, certain Member States require the possesion of a diploma within the meaning of Directive 89/48/EEC, while for the same profession other Member States require the completion of professional education or training with a different structure; whereas certain kinds of education and training, while not of a post-secondary nature of minimum duration within the meaning of this Directive, nevertheless result in a comparable professional level and prepare the person for similar responsibilities and activities; whereas such education and training should therefore be classed in the same category as that attested by a diploma; whereas such education and training is very varied and this classification can be achieved only by listing the courses in question; whereas such classification would, where appropriate, establish the recognition of equivalence between such education and training and that covered by Directive 89/48/EEC; whereas some regulated education and training should also be classed at diploma level in a second list;

16.   Whereas, in view of the constantly changing organisation of professional training, there should be a procedure for amending those lists;

17.   Whereas, since it covers occupations the pursuit of which is dependent on the possession of professional or vocational education and training qualifications of secondary level and generally requires manual skills, the complementary general system must also provide for the recognition of such qualifications even where they have been acquired solely through professional experience in a Member State which does not regulate such professions;

18.   Whereas the aim of this general system, like the first general system, is to eliminate obstacles to the taking up and pursuit of regulated professions; whereas work carried out pursuant to Council Decision 85/368/EEC of 16 July 1985 on the comparability of vocational training qualifications between the Member States of the European Community (5), while pursuing a different objective from the elimination of legal obstacles to freedom of movement, namely that of improving the transparency of the labour market, must be used, where appropriate, in the application of this Directive, particularly where it could provide information on the subject, content and duration of professional training;

19.   Whereas professional bodies and professional educational and training establishments should where appropriate, be consulted or be involved in an appropriate way in the decision-making process;

20.   Whereas, like the initial system, such a system, by strengthening the right of a Community national to use his occupational skills in any Member State, supplements and reinforces his right to acquire such skills wherever he wishes;

21.   Whereas the two systems should be evaluated, after a certain period of application, in order to determine how efficiently they operate and, in particular, how they can both be improved,

HAS ADOPTED THIS DIRECTIVE:

CHAPTER I   DEFINITIONS

Article 1

For the purposes of this Directive, the following definitions shall apply:

    (a) diploma: any evidence of education and training or any set of such evidence:

        — which has been awarded by a competent authority in a Member State,

designated in accordance with the laws, regulations or administrative provisions of that State,
— which shows that the holder has successfully completed:
  (i) either a post-secondary course other than that referred to in the second indent of Article 1(a) of Directive 89/48/EEC, of at least one year's duration or of equivalent duration on a part-time basis, one of the conditions of entry of which is, as a general rule, the successful completion of the secondary course required to obtain entry to university or higher education, as well as the professional training which may be required in addition to that post-secondary course;
  (ii) or one of the education and training courses in Annex C, and
— which shows that the holder has the professional qualifications required for the taking up or pursuit of a regulated profession in that Member State, provided that the education and training attested by this evidence was received mainly in the Community, or outside the Community at teaching establishments which provide education and training in accordance with the laws, regulations or administrative provisions of a Member State, or that the holder thereof has three years' professional experience certified by the Member State which recognised third-country evidence of education and training.

The following shall be treated in the same way as a diploma within the meaning of the first sub-paragraph: any evidence of education and training or any set of such evidence awarded by a competent authority in a Member State if it is awarded on the successful completion of education and training received in the Community and recognised by a competent authority in that Member State as being of an equivalent level and if it confers the same rights in respect of the taking up and pursuit of a regulated profession in that Member State;

(b) certificate: any evidence of education and training or any set of such evidence:
— which has been awarded by a competent authority in a Member State, designated in accordance with the laws, regulations or administrative provisions of that State,—which shows that the holder, after having followed a secondary course, has completed: either a course of education or training other than courses referred to in point (a), provided at an educational or training establishment or on the job, or in combination at an educational or training establishment and on the job, and complemented, where appropriate, by the probationary or professional practice required in addition to this course, or the probationary or professional practice required in addition to this secondary course, or
— which shows that the holder, after having followed a secondary course of a technical or vocational nature has completed, where necessary, either a course of education or training as referred to in the previous indent, or the probationary or professional practice required in addition to this secondary course of a technical or vocational nature and
— which shows that the holder has the professional qualifications required for the taking up or pursuit of a regulated profession in that Member State, provided that the education and training attested by this evidence was received mainly in the Community, or outside the Community at teaching establishments which provide education and training in accordance with the laws, regulations or administrative provisions of a Member State, or that the holder thereof has two years' professional experience certified by the Member State which recognised third-country evidence of education and training.

The following shall be treated in the same way as a certificate, within the meaning of the first sub-paragraph: any evidence of education and training or any set of such evidence awarded by a competent authority in a Member State if it is awarded on the successful completion of education and training received in the Community and recognised by a competent authority in a Member State as being of an equivalent level and if it confers the same rights in respect of the taking up and pursuit of a regulated profession in that Member State;

> — comprises a course or courses complemented, where appropriate, by professional training or probationary or professional practice, the structure and level of which are determined by the laws, regulations or administrative provisions of that Member State or which are monitored or approved by the authority designated for that purpose;

(c) attestation of competence; any evidence of qualification:

> — attesting to education and training not forming part of a set constituting a diploma within the meaning of Directive 89/48/EEC or a diploma or certificate within the meaning of this Directive, or
> — awarded following an assessment of the personal qualities, aptitudes or knowledge which it is considered essential that the applicant have for the pursuit of a profession by an authority designated in accordance with the laws, regulations or administrative provisions of a Member State, without proof of prior education and training being required;

(d) host Member State: any Member State in which a national of a Member State applies to pursue a profession subject to regulation in that Member State, other than the State in which he obtained his evidence of education and training or attestation of competence or first pursued the profession in question;

(e) regulated profession: the regulated professional activity or range of activities which constitute this profession in a Member State;

(f) regulated professional activity: a professional activity the taking up or pursuit of which, or one of its modes of pursuit in a Member State, is subject, directly or indirectly, by virtue of laws, regulations or administrative provisions, to the possession of evidence of education and training or an attestation of competence. The following in particular shall constitute a mode of pursuit or a regulated professional activity:

> — pursuit of an activity under a professional title, in so far as the use of such a title is reserved to the holders of evidence of education and training or an attestation of competence governed by laws, regulations or administrative provisions,
> — pursuit of a professional activity relating to health, in so far as remuneration and/or reimbursement for such an activity is subject by virtue of national social security arrangements to the possession of evidence of education and training or an attestation of competence.

Where the first sub-paragraph does not apply, a professional activity shall be deemed to be a regulated professional activity if it is pursued by the members of an association or organisation the purpose of which is, in particular, to promote and maintain a high standard in the professional field concerned and which, to achieve that purpose, is recognised in a special form by a Member State and:

> — awards evidence of education and training to its members,
> — ensures that its members respect the rules of professional conduct which it prescribes, and confers on them the right to use a professional title or designatory letters, or to benefit from a status corresponding to that education and training.

Whenever a Member State grants the recognition referred to in the second sub-paragraph to an association or organisation which satisfies the conditions of that sub-paragraph, it shall inform the Commission thereof;

(g) regulated education and training: any education and training which:

> — is specifically geared to the pursuit of a given profession, and

(h) professional experience: the actual and lawful pursuit of the profession concerned in a Member State;

(i) adaptation period: the pursuit of a regulated profession in the host Member State under the responsibility of a qualified member of that profession, such period of supervised practice possibly being accompanied by further education and training. This period of supervised practice shall be the subject of an assessment. The detailed rules governing the adaptation period and its assessment shall be laid down by the competent authorities in the host Member State.

The status enjoyed in the host Member State by the person undergoing the period of supervised practice, in particular in the matter of right of residence as well as of obligations, social rights and benefits, allowances and remuneration, shall be established by the competent authorities in that Member State in accordance with applicable Community law;

(j) aptitude test: a test limited to the professional knowledge of the applicant, made by the competent authorities of the host Member State with the aim of assessing the ability of the applicant to pursue a regulated profession in that Member State.

In order to permit this test to be carried out, the competent authorities shall draw up a list of subjects which, on the basis of a comparison of the education and training required in the Member State and that received by the applicant, are not covered by the evidence of education and training possessed by the applicant. These subjects may cover both theoretical knowledge and practical skills required for the pursuit of the profession.

This aptitude test must take account of the fact that the applicant is a qualified professional in the Member State of origin or the Member State from which he comes. It shall cover subjects to be selected from those on the list referred to in the second sub-paragraph, knowledge of which is essential to the pursuit of the profession in the host Member State. The test may also include knowledge of the professional rules applicable to the activities in question in the host Member State. The detailed application of the aptitude test shall be determined by the competent authorities of that State.

The status in the host Member State of the applicant who wishes to prepare himself for the aptitude test in that State shall be determined by the competent authorities in that State, in accordance with applicable Community law.

CHAPTER II   SCOPE

Article 2

This Directive shall apply to any national of a Member State wishing to pursue a regulated profession in a host Member State in a self-employed capacity or as an employed person.

This Directive shall apply to neither professions which are the subject of a specific Directive establishing arrangements for the mutual recognition of diplomas by Member States, nor activities covered by a Directive listed in Annex A.

The Directives listed in Annex B shall be made applicable to the pursuit as an employed person of the activities covered by those Directives.

CHAPTER III   SYSTEM FOR RECOGNITION WHERE A HOST MEMBER STATE REQUIRES POSSESSION OF A DIPLOMA WITHIN THE MEANING OF THIS DIRECTIVE OR DIRECTIVE 89/48/EEC

Article 3

Without prejudice to Directive 89/48/EEC, where, in a host Member State, the taking up or pursuit of a regulated profession is subject to possession of a diploma, as defined in this Directive or in Directive 89/48/EEC, the competent authority may not, on the grounds of inadequate qualifications, refuse to authorise a national of a Member State to take up or pursue the profession on the same conditions as those which apply to its own nationals:

(a) if the applicant holds the diploma, as defined in this Directive or in Directive 89/48/EEC, required in another Member State for the taking up or pursuit of the profession in question in its territory, such diploma having been awarded in a Member State; or

(b) if the applicant has pursued the profession in question full-time for two years, or for an equivalent period on a part-time basis, the previous 10 years in another Member State which does not regulate that profession within the meaning of either Article 1(e) and the first sub-paragraph of Article 1(f) of this Directive or Article 1(c) and the first sub-paragraph of Article 1(d) of Directive 89/48/EEC, and possesses evidence of education and training which:

— has been awarded by a competent authority in a Member State, designated in accordance with the laws, regulations or administrative provisions of that State, and

— either shows that the holder has successfully completed a post-secondary course, other than that referred to in the second indent of Article 1(a) of Directive 89/48/EEC, of at least one year's duration, or of equivalent duration on a part-time basis, one of the conditions of entry of which is, as a general rule, the successful completion of the secondary course required to obtain entry into university or higher education, as well as any professional training which is an integral part of that post-secondary course,

— or attests to regulated education and training referred to in Annex D, and

— has prepared the holder for the pursuit of his profession.

However, the two years' professional experience referred to above may not be required where the evidence of education and training held by the applicant and referred to in this point is awarded on completion of regulated education and training.

The following shall be treated in the same way as the evidence of education and training referred to in the first sub-paragraph of this point: any evidence of education and training or any set of such evidence awarded by a competent authority in a Member State if it is awarded on the completion of education and training received in the Community and is recognised by that Member State as being of an equivalent level, provided that the other Member States and the Commission have been notified of this recognition.

By way of derogation from the first sub-paragraph of this Article, the host Member State is not required to apply this Article where the taking up or pursuit of a regulated profession is subject in its country to possession of a diploma as defined in Directive 89/48/EEC, one of the conditions for the issue of which shall be the completion of a post-secondary course of more than four years duration.

Article 4

1. Notwithstanding Article 3, the host Member State may also require the applicant:

(a) to provide evidence of professional experience, where the duration of the education and training adduced in support of his application, as laid down in points (a) and (b) of the first sub-paragraph of Article 3, is at least one year less than that required in the host Member State. In this event, the period of professional experience required may not exceed:

— twice the shortfall in duration of education and training where the shortfall relates to a post-secondary course and/or to a period of probationary practice carried out under the control of a supervising professional person and ending with an examination,

— the shortfall where the shortfall relates to professional practice acquired with the assistance of a qualified member of the profession concerned.

In the case of diplomas within the meaning of the second sub-paragraph of Article 1(a), the duration of education and training recognised as being of an equivalent level shall be determined as for the education and training defined in the first sub-paragraph of Article 1(a).

When these provisions are applied, account must be taken of the professional experience referred to in point (b) of the first sub-paragraph of Article 3.

In any event, the professional experience required may not exceed four years.

Professional experience may not, however, be required of an applicant holding a diploma attesting to a post-secondary course as referred to in the second indent of Article 1(a) or a diploma as defined in Article 1(a) of Directive 89/48/EEC who wishes to pursue his profession in a host Member State which requires the possession of a diploma attesting to one of the courses of education and training as referred to in Annex C;

    (b) to complete an adaptation period not exceeding three years or take an aptitude test where:

— the theoretical and/or practical matters covered by the education and training which he has received as laid down in points (a) or (b) of the first sub-paragraph of Article 3 differ substantially from those covered by the diploma, as defined in this Directive or in Directive 89/48/EEC, required in the host Member State, or

— in the case referred to in point (a) of the first sub-paragraph of Article 3, the profession regulated in the host Member State comprises one or more regulated professional activities which do not form part of the profession regulated in the Member State from which the applicant originates or comes and that difference corresponds to specific education and training required in the host Member State and covers theoretical and/or practical matters which differ substantially from those covered by the diploma, as defined in this Directive or in Directive 89/48/EEC, adduced by the applicant, or

— in the case referred to in point (b) of the first sub-paragraph of Article 3, the profession regulated in the host Member State comprises one or more regulated professional activities which do not form part of the profession pursued by the applicant in the Member State from which he originates or comes, and that difference corresponds to specific education and training required in the host Member State and covers theoretical and/or practical matters which differ substantially from those covered by the evidence of education and training adduced by the applicant.

If the host Member State intends to require the applicant to complete an adaption period or take an aptitude test, it must examine first whether the knowledge acquired by the applicant in the course of his professional experience is such that it fully or partly covers the substantial difference referred to in the first sub-paragraph.

Should the host Member State make use of this possibility, it must give the applicant the right to choose between an adaptation period and an aptitude test. Where the host Member State, which requires a diploma as defined in Directive 89/48/EEC or in this Directive, intends to introduce derogations from an applicant's right to choose, the procedure laid down in Article 14 shall apply.

By way of derogation from the second sub-paragraph of this point, the host Member State may reserve the right to choose between the adaptation period and the aptitude test if

— a profession is involved the pursuit of which requires a precise knowledge of national law and in respect of which the provision of advice and/or assistance concerning national law is an essential and constant feature of the professional activity, or

— where the host Member State makes access to the profession or its pursuit subject to the possession of a diploma as defined in Directive 89/48/EEC, one of the conditions for the award of which is the completion of a post-secondary course of more than three years' duration or an equivalent period on a part-time basis and the applicant holds either a diploma as defined in this Directive or evidence of education and training within the meaning of point (b) of the first sub-paragraph of Article 3 and not covered by Article 3(b) of Directive 89/48/EEC.

2. However, the host Member State may not apply the provisions of paragraph 1(a) and (b) cumulatively.

CHAPTER IV SYSTEM FOR RECOGNITION WHERE A HOST MEMBER STATE REQUIRES POSSESSION OF A DIPLOMA AND THE APPLICANT IS THE HOLDER OF A CERTIFICATE OR HAS RECEIVED CORRESPONDING EDUCATION AND TRAINING

Article 5
Where, in a host Member State the taking up or pursuit of a regulated profession is subject to possession of a diploma, the competent authority may not, on the grounds of inadequate qualifications, refuse to authorise a national of a Member State to take up or pursue that profession on the same conditions as those which apply to its own nationals:

(a) if the applicant holds the certificate required in another Member State for the taking up or pursuit of the same profession in its territory, such certificate having been awarded in a Member State, or

(b) if the applicant has pursued the same profession full-time for two years during the previous 10 years in another Member State which does not regulate that profession, within the meaning of Article 1(e) and the first sub-paragraph of Article 1(f), and possess evidence of education and training:

— which has been awarded by a competent authority in a Member State, designated in accordance with the laws, regulations or administrative provisions of that State, and

— which shows that the holder, after having followed a secondary course, has completed: either a course of professional education or training other than courses referred to in point (a), provided at an educational or training establishment or on the job, or in combination at an educational or training establishment and on the job and complemented, where appropriate, by the probationary or professional practice which is an integral part of that training course, or the probationary or professional practice which is an integral part of that secondary course, or

— which shows that the holder, after having followed a secondary course of a technical or vocational nature has completed, where necessary, either a course of professional education or training as referred to in the previous indent, or the period of probationary or professional practice which is an integral part of that secondary course of a technical or vocational nature and

— which has prepared the holder for the pursuit of this profession.

However, the two years' professional experience referred to above may not be required where the evidence of education and training held by the applicant and referred to in this point is awarded on completion of regulated education and training.

If the host Member State intends to require the applicant to complete an adaptation period or take an aptitude test, it must first examine whether knowledge acquired by the applicant in the course of his professional experience is such that it fully or partly covers the substantial difference between the diploma and the certificate.

Nevertheless, the host Member State may require the applicant to undergo an adaptation period not exceeding three years or take an aptitude test. The host Member State must give the applicant the right to choose between an adaptation period and an aptitude test.

Where the host Member State intends to introduce derogations from an applicant's right to choose, the procedure laid down in Article 14 shall apply.

CHAPTER V   SYSTEM FOR RECOGNITION WHERE A HOST MEMBER STATE
REQUIRES POSSESSION OF A CERTIFICATE

Article 6

Where, in the host Member State, the taking up or pursuit of a regulated profession is subject to possession of a certificate, the competent authority may not, on the grounds of inadequate qualifications, refuse to authorise a national of a Member State to take up or pursue that profession on the same conditions as those which apply to its own nationals:

(a) if the applicant holds the diploma, as defined in this Directive or in Directive 89/48/EEC, or the certificate required in another Member State for the taking up or pursuit of the profession in question in its territory, such diploma having been awarded in a Member State; or

(b) if the applicant has pursued the profession in question full-time for two years or for an equivalent period on a part-time basis during the previous 10 years in another Member State which does not regulate that profession, within the meaning of Article 1(e) and the first sub-paragraph of Article 1(f), and possesses evidence of education and training:

— which has been awarded by a competent authority in a Member State, designated in accordance with the laws, regulations or administrative provisions of that State, and

— which shows that the holder has successfully completed a post-secondary course other than that referred to in the second indent of Article 1(a) of Directive 89/48/EEC, of at least one year's duration or of equivalent duration on a part-time basis, one of the conditions of entry of which is, as a general rule, the completion of the secondary course required to obtain entry to university or higher education, as well as any professional training which is an integral part of that post-secondary course, or

— which shows that the holder, after having followed a secondary course, has completed: either a course of education or training for a profession other than courses referred to in point (a), provided at an educational establishment or on the job, or in combination at an educational establishment and on the job and complemented, where appropriate, by the probationary or professional practice which is an integral part of that training course, or the probationary or professional practice which is an integral part of that secondary course, or

— which shows that the holder, after having followed a secondary course of a technical or vocational nature has completed, where necessary, either a course of education or training for a profession as referred to in the previous indent, or the period of probationary or professional practice which is an integral part of that secondary course of a technical or vocational nature and

— which has prepared the holder for the pursuit of this profession.

However, the two years' professional experience referred to above may not be required where the evidence of education and training held by the applicant and referred to in this point is awarded on completion or regulated education and training.

(c) if the applicant who does not hold any diploma, certificate or other evidence of education and training within the meaning of Article 3(b) or of point (b) of this Article has pursued the profession in question full-time for three consecutive years, or for an equivalent period on a part-time basis, during the previous 10 years in another Member State which does not regulate that profession within the meaning of Article 1(e) and the first sub-paragraph of Article 1(f).

The following shall be treated in the same way as the evidence of education and training referred to under (b) in the first sub-pargraph: any evidence of education and training or any set of such evidence awarded by a competent authority in a Member State if it is awarded on the completion of education and training received in the Community and is recognised by the Member State as being of an equivalent level, provided that the other Member States and the Commission have been notified of this recognition.

Article 7

Without prejudice to Article 6, a host Member State may also require the applicant to:

(a) complete an adaptation period not exceeding two years or to take an aptitude test when the education and training which he received in accordance with points (a) or (b) of the first sub-paragraph of Article 6 relates to theoretical or practical matters differing substantially from those covered by the certificate required in the host Member State, or where there are differences in the fields of activity characterised in the host Member State by specific education and training relating to theoretical or practical matters differing substantially from those covered by the applicant's evidence of formal qualifications.

If the host Member State intends to require the applicant to complete an adaptation period or take an aptitude test, it must first examine whether knowledge acquired by the applicant in the course of his professional experience is such that it fully or partly covers the substantial difference referred to in the first sub-paragraph.

Should the host Member State make use of this possibility, it must give the applicant the right to choose between an adaptation period and an aptitude test. Where the host Member State which requires a certificate intends to introduce derogations as regards an applicant's right to choose, the procedure laid down in Article 14 shall apply;

(b) undergo an adaptation period not exceeding two years or take an aptitude test where, in the instance referred to in point (c) of the first sub-paragraph of Article 6, he does not hold a diploma, certificate or other evidence of education and training. The host Member State may reserve the right to choose between an adaptation period and an aptitude test.

CHAPTER VI   SPECIAL SYSTEMS FOR RECOGNITION OF OTHER QUALIFICATIONS

Article 8

Where, in the host Member State, the taking up or pursuit of a regulated profession is subject to possession of an attestation of competence, the competent authority may not, on the grounds of inadequate qualifications, refuse to authorise a national of a Member State to take up or pursue that profession on the same conditions as those which apply to its own nationals:

(a) if the applicant holds the attestation of competence required in another Member State for the taking up or pursuit of the same profession in its territory, such attestation having been awarded in a Member State; or

(b) if the applicant provides proof of qualifications obtained in other Member States, and giving guarantees, in particular in the matter of health, safety, environmental protection and consumer protection, equivalent to those required by the laws, regulations or administrative provisions of the host Member State.

If the applicant does not provide proof of such an attestation or of such qualifications the laws, regulations or administrative provisions of the host Member State shall apply.

Article 9

Where, in the host Member State, the taking up or pursuit of a regulated profession is subject only to possession of evidence of education attesting to general education at primary or secondary school level, the competent authority may not, on the grounds of inadequate qualifications, refuse to authorise a national of a Member State to take up or pursue that profession on the same conditions as those which apply to its own nationals if the applicant possesses formal qualifications of the corresponding level, awarded in another Member State.

This evidence of formal qualifications must have been awarded by a competent authority in that Member State, designated in accordance with its own laws, regulations or administrative provisions.

CHAPTER VII   OTHER MEASURES TO FACILITATE THE EFFECTIVE EXERCISE OF THE RIGHT OF ESTABLISHMENT, FREEDOM TO PROVIDE SERVICES AND FREEDOM OF MOVEMENT OF EMPLOYED PERSONS

Article 10

1.   Where the competent authority of the host Member State requires of persons wishing to take up a regulated profession proof that they are of good character or repute or that they have not been declared bankrupt, or suspends or prohibits the pursuit of that profession in the event of serious professional misconduct or a criminal offence, that State shall accept as sufficient evidence, in respect of nationals of Member States wishing to pursue that profession in its territory, the production of documents issued by competent authorities in the Member State of origin or the Member State from which the foreign national comes showing that those requirements are met.

Where the competent authorities of the Member State of origin or of the Member State from which the foreign national comes do not issue the documents referred to in the first subparagraph, such documents shall be replaced by a declaration on oath—or, in Member States where there is no provision for declaration on oath, by a solemn declaration—made by the person concerned before a competent judicial or administrative authority or, where appropriate, a notary or qualified professional body of the Member State of origin or the Member State from which the person comes; such authority or notary shall issue written confirmation attesting the authenticity of the declaration on oath or solemn declaration.

2.   Where the competent authority of the host Member State requires of nationals of that Member State wishing to take up or pursue a regulated profession a statement of physical or mental health, that authority shall accept as sufficient evidence in this respect the production of the document required in the Member State of origin or the Member State from which the foreign national comes.

Where the Member State of origin or the Member State from which the foreign national comes does not impose any requirements of this nature on those wishing to take up or pursue the profession in question, the host Member State shall accept from such nationals a statement issued by a competent authority in that State corresponding to the statement issued in the host Member State.

3.   The competent authority of the host Member State may require that the documents and statements referred to in paragraphs 1 and 2 are presented no more than three months after their date of issue.

4.   Where the competent authority of the host Member State requires nationals of that Member State wishing to take up or pursue a regulated profession to take an oath or make solemn declaration and where the form of such oath or declaration cannot be used by nationals of other Member States, that authority shall ensure that an appropriate and equivalent form of oath or declaration is offered to the person concerned.

5.   Where proof of financial standing is required in order to take up or pursue a regulated profession in the host Member State, that Member State shall regard certificates issued by banks in the Member State of origin or in the Member State from where the foreign national comes as equivalent to those issued in its own territory.

6.   Where the competent authority of the host Member State requires of its own nationals wishing to take up or pursue a regulated profession proof that they are insured against the financial risks arising from their professional liability, that Member State shall accept certificates issued by insurance undertakings of other Member States as equivalent to those issued in its own territory. Such certificates shall state that the insurer has complied with the laws and

regulations in force in the host Member State regarding the terms and extent of cover. They may not be presented more than three months after their date of issue.

Article 11

1. The competent authorities of host Member States shall recognise the right of nationals of Member States who fulfil the conditions for the taking up and pursuit of a regulated profession in their territory to use the professional title of the host Member State corresponding to that profession.

2. The competent authority of the host Member State shall recognise the right of nationals of Member States who fulfil the conditions for the taking up and pursuit of a regulated profession in the territory to use their lawful academic title and, where appropriate, the abbreviation thereof deriving from their Member State of origin or the Member State from which they come, in the language of that State. The host Member State may require this title to be followed by the name and location of the establishment or examining board which awarded it.

3. Where a profession is regulated in the host Member State by an association or organisation referred to in Article 1(f), nationals of Member States shall be entitled to use the professional title or designatory letters conferred by that organisation or association only on proof of membership.

Where the association or organisation makes membership subject to certain qualification requirements, it may apply these to nationals of other Member States who are in possession of a diploma within the meaning of Article 1(a), certificate within the meaning of Article 1(b) or evidence of education and training or qualification within the meaning of point (b) of the first sub-paragraph of Article 3, point (b) of the first sub-paragraph of Article 5 or Article 9 in accordance only with this Directive, in particular Articles 3, 4 and 5.

Article 12

1. The host Member State shall accept as means of proof that the conditions laid down in Articles 3 to 9 are satisfied the documents issued by the competent authorities in the Member States, which the person concerned shall submit in support of his application to pursue the profession concerned.

2. The procedure for examining an application to pursue a regulated profession shall be completed as soon as possible and the outcome communicated in a reasoned decision of the competent authority in the host Member State not later than four months after presentation of all the documents relating to the person concerned. A remedy shall be available against this decision or the absence thereof, before a court or tribunal in accordance with the provisions of national law.

CHAPTER VIII   PROCEDURE FOR COORDINATION

Article 13

1. Member States shall designate, within the period provided for in Article 17, the competent authorities empowered to receive the applications and take the decisions referred to in this Directive. They shall communicate this information to the other Member States and to the Commission.

2. Each Member State shall designate a person responsible for coordinating the activities of the authorities referred to in paragraph 1 and shall inform the other Member States and the Commission to that effect. His role shall be to promote uniform application of this Directive to all the professions concerned. This coordinator shall be a member of the coordinating group set up under the aegis of the Commission by Article 9(2) of Directive 89/48/EEC.

The coordinating group set up under the aforementioned provision of Directive 89/48/EEC shall also be required to:

— facilitate the implementation of this Directive, in particular by adopting and publishing opinions on the questions referred to it by the Commission,
— collect all useful information for its application in the Member States, particularly information relating to the establishment of an indicative list of regulated professions and to the disparities between the qualifications awarded in the Member States which a view to assisting the competent authorities of the Member States in their task of assessing whether substantial differences exist.

The group may be consulted by the Commission on any changes to the existing system which may be contemplated.

3.   The Member States shall take measures to provide the necessary information on the recognition of diplomas and certificates and on other conditions governing the taking up of the regulated professions within the framework of this Directive. To carry out this task they may call upon the existing information networks and, where appropriate, the relevant professional associations or organisations. The Commission shall take the necessary initiatives to ensure the development and coordination of the communication of the necessary information.

CHAPTER IX   PROCEDURE FOR DEROGATING FROM THE RIGHT TO CHOOSE BETWEEN ADAPTATION PERIOD AND APTITUDE TEST

Article 14

1.   If, pursuant to the second sentence of the second sub-paragraph of Article 4(1)(b), the third sub-paragraph of Article 5, or the second sentence of the second sub-paragraph of Article 7(a), a Member State proposes not to grant applicants the right to choose between an adaptation period and an aptitude test, it shall immediately communicate to the Commission the corresponding draft provision. It shall at the same time notify the Commission of the grounds which make the enactment of such a provision necessary.

The Commission shall immediately notify the other Member States of any draft which it has received; it may also consult the coordinating group referred to in Article 13(2) on the draft.

2.   Without prejudice to the possibility for the Commission and the other Member States to make comments on the draft, the Member State may adopt the provision only if the Commission has not taken a decision to the contrary within three months.

3.   At the request of a Member State or the Commission, Member States shall communicate to them, without delay, the definitive text of any provision arising from the application of this Article.

CHAPTER X   PROCEDURE FOR AMENDING ANNEXES C AND D

Article 15[1]

1.   The lists of education and training courses set out in Annexes C and D may be amended on the basis of a reasoned request from any Member State concerned to the Commission. All appropriate information and in particular the text of the relevant provisions of national law shall accompany the request. The Member State making the request shall also inform the other Member States.

2.   The Commission shall examine the education and training course in question and those required in the other Member States. It shall verify in particular whether the qualification resulting from the course in question confers on the holder:
— a level of professional education or training of a comparably high level to that of the post-secondary course referred to in point (i) of the second indent of the first subparagraph of Article 1(a), and
— a similar level of responsibility and activity.

[1] Replaced by Regulation 1882/2003 (OJ 2003 L284/1).

3.   The Commission shall be assisted by a committee. The Committee shall adopt its rules of procedure.

4.   Where reference is made to this Article, Articles 4 and 7 of Decision 1999/468/EC(20) shall apply, having regard to the provisions of Article 8 thereof. The period laid down in Article 4(3) of Decision 1999/468/EC shall be set at two months.

5.   The Commission shall inform the Member State concerned of the decision and shall, where appropriate, publish the amended list in the Official Journal of the European Union.

6.   The amendments made to the lists of education and training courses in Annexes C and D on the basis of the procedure laid down above shall be immediately applicable on the date set by the Commission.

CHAPTER XI   OTHER PROVISIONS

Article 16
Following the expiry of the period provided for in Article 17, Member States shall communicate to the Commission, every two years, a report on the application of the system introduced.

In addition to general remarks, this report shall contain a statistical summary of the decisions taken and a description of the main problems arising from the application of this Directive.

Article 17
1.   Member States shall adopt the laws, regulations and administrative provisions necessary for them to comply with the Directive before 18 June 1994. They shall forthwith inform the Commission thereof.

When Member States adopt these measures, the latter shall include a reference to this Directive or be accompanied by such reference at this time of their official publication. The methods of making such a reference shall be laid down by the Member States.

2.   Member States shall communicate to the Commission the texts of the main provisions of national law which they adopt in the field governed by this Directive.

Article 18
Five years at the latest following the date specified in Article 17, the Commission shall report to the European Paliament, the Council and the Economic and Social Committee on the progress of the application of this Directive.

After conducting all necessary consultations, the Commission shall present its conclusions as to any changes which need to be made to this Directive. At the same time the Commission shall, where appropriate, submit proposals for improving the existing rules in the interest of facilitating freedom of movement, right of establishment and freedom to provide services.

Article 19
This Directive is addressed to the Member States.

Done at Luxembourg, 18 June 1992.
For the Council
The President VITOR MARTINS

(Annexes omitted.)

Council Directive of 28 June 1990 on the right of residence (90/364/EEC)

[OJ 1990, L180/26]

[Note: To be repealed on 30 April 2006 when Directive 2004/38 enters into force.]

The Council of the European Communities,

Having regard to the Treaty establishing the European Economic Community, and in particular Article 235 thereof,

(Recitals omitted.)

Whereas Article 3(c) of the Treaty provides that the activities of the Community shall include, as provided in the Treaty, the abolition, as between Member States, of obstacles to freedom of movement for persons;

Whereas Article 8a of the Treaty provides that the internal market must be established by 31 December 1992; whereas the internal market comprises an area without internal frontiers in which the free movement of goods, persons, services and capital is ensured in accordance with the provisions of the Treaty;

Whereas national provisions on the right of nationals of the Member States to reside in a Member State other than their own must be harmonized to ensure such freedom of movement;

Whereas beneficiaries of the right of residence must not become an unreasonable burden on the public finances of the host Member State;

Whereas this right can only be genuinely exercised if it is also granted to members of the family;

Whereas the beneficiaries of this Directive should be covered by administrative arrangements similar to those laid down in particular in Directive 68/360/EEC and Directive 64/221/EEC;

Whereas the Treaty does not provide, for the action concerned, powers other than those of Article 235,

Has adopted this Directive:

Article 1

1. Member States shall grant the right of residence to nationals of Member States who do not enjoy this right under other provisions of Community law and to members of their families as defined in paragraph 2, provided that they themselves and the members of their families are covered by sickness insurance in respect of all risks in the host Member State and have sufficient resources to avoid becoming a burden on the social assistance system of the host Member State during their period of residence.

The resources referred to in the first sub-paragraph shall be deemed sufficient where they are higher than the level of resources below which the host Member State may grant social assistance to its nationals, taking into account the personal circumstances of the applicant and, where appropriate, the personal circumstances of persons admitted pursuant to paragraph 2.

Where the second sub-paragraph cannot be applied in a Member State, the resources of the applicant shall be deemed sufficient if they are higher than the level of the minimum social security pension paid by the host Member State.

2. The following shall, irrespective of their nationality, have the right to install themselves in another Member State with the holder of the right of residence:

    (a) his or her spouse and their descendants who are dependants;

    (b) dependent relatives in the ascending line of the holder of the right of residence and his or her spouse.

Article 2

1. Exercise of the right of residence shall be evidenced by means of the issue of a document known as a 'Residence permit for a national of a Member State of the EEC', the validity of which may be limited to five years on a renewable basis. However, the Member States may, when they deem it to be necessary, require revalidation of the permit at the end of the first two years of residence. Where a member of the family does not hold the nationality of a Member State, he or she shall be issued with a residence document of the same validity as that issued to the national on whom he or she depends.

For the purpose of issuing the residence permit or document, the Member State may require only that the applicant present a valid identity card or passport and provide proof that he or she meets the conditions laid down in Article 1.

2. Articles 2, 3, 6(1)(a) and (2) and Article 9 of Directive 68/360/EEC shall apply mutatis mutandis to the beneficiaries of this Directive.

The spouse and the dependent children of a national of a Member State entitled to the right of residence within the territory of a Member State shall be entitled to take up any employed or self-employed activity anywhere within the territory of that Member State, even if they are not nationals of a Member State.

Member States shall not derogate from the provisions of this Directive save on grounds of public policy, public security or public health. In that event, Directive 64/221/EEC shall apply.

3. This Directive shall not affect existing law on the acquisition of second homes.

Article 3

The right of residence shall remain for as long as beneficiaries of that right fulfil the conditions laid down in Article 1.

Article 4

The Commission shall, not more than three years after the date of implementation of this Directive, and at three-yearly intervals thereafter, draw up a report on the application of this Directive and submit it to the European Parliament and the Council.

Article 5

Member States shall bring into force the laws, regulations and administrative provisions necessary to comply with this Directive not later than 30 June 1992.

They shall forthwith inform the Commission thereof.

Article 6

This Directive is addressed to the Member States.

Done at Luxembourg, 28 June 1990.

(Signature omitted.)

Council Directive of 28 June 1990 on the right of residence for employees and self-employed persons who have ceased their occupational activity (90/365/EEC)

[OJ 1990, L180/28]

[Note: To be repealed on 30 April 2006 when Directive 2004/38 enters into force.]

The Council of the European Communities,

Having regard to the Treaty establishing the European Economic Community, and in particular Article 235 thereof,

(Recitals omitted.)

Whereas Article 3(c) of the Treaty provides that the activities of the Community shall include, as provided in the Treaty, the abolition, as between Member States, of obstacles to freedom of movement for persons;

Whereas Article 8a of the Treaty provides that the internal market must be established by 31 December 1992; whereas the internal market comprises an area without internal frontiers in which the free movement of goods, persons, services and capital is ensured, in accordance with the provisions of the Treaty;

Whereas Articles 48 and 52 of the Treaty provide for freedom of movement for workers and self-employed persons, which entails the right of residence in the Member States in which they pursue their occupational activity; whereas it is desirable that this right of residence also be granted to persons who have ceased their occupational activity even if they have not exercised their right to freeedom of movement during their working life;

Whereas beneficiaries of the right of residence must not become an unreasonable burden on the public finances of the host Member State;

Whereas under Article 10 of Regulation (EEC) No. 1408/71, as amended by Regulation (EEC) No. 1390/81, recipients of invalidity or old age cash benefits or pensions for accidents at work or occupational diseases are entitled to continue to receive these benefits and pensions even if they reside in the territory of a Member State other than that in which the institution responsible for payment is situated;

Whereas this right can only be genuinely exercised if it is also granted to members of the family;

Whereas the beneficiaries of this Directive should be covered by administrative arrangements similar to those laid down in particular by Directive 68/630/EEC and Directive 64/221/EEC;

Whereas the Treaty does not provide, for the action concerned, powers other than those of Article 235,

Has adopted this Directive:

Article 1

1. Member States shall grant the right of residence to nationals of Member States who have pursued an activity as an employee or self-employed person and to members of their families as defined in paragraph 2, provided that they are recipients of an invalidity or early retirement pension, or old age benefits, or of a pension in respect of an industrial accident or disease of an amount sufficient to avoid becoming a burden on the social security system of the host Member State during their period of residence and provided they are covered by sickness insurance in respect of all risks in the host Member State.

The resources of the applicant shall be deemed sufficient where they are higher than the level of resources below which the host Member State may grant social assistance to its nationals, taking into account the personal circumstances of persons admitted pursuant to paragraph 2.

Where the second sub-paragraph cannot be applied in a Member State, the resources of the applicant shall be deemed sufficient if they are higher than the level of the minimum social security pension paid by the host Member State.

2. The following shall, irrespective of their nationality, have the right to install themselves in another Member State with the holder of the right of residence:
   (a) his or her spouse and their descendants who are dependants;
   (b) dependent relatives in the ascending line of the holder of the right of residence and his or her spouse.

Article 2

1. Exercise of the right of residence shall be evidenced by means of the issue of a document known as a 'Residence permit for a national of a Member State of the EEC', whose validity may be limited to five years on a renewable basis. However, the Member States may, when they deem it to be necessary, require revalidation of the permit at the end of the first two years of residence. Where a member of the family does not hold the nationality of a Member State, he or she shall be issued with a residence document of the same validity as that issued to the national on whom he or she depends.

For the purposes of issuing the residence permit or document, the Member State may require only that the applicant present a valid identity card or passport and provide proof that he or she meets the conditions laid down in Article 1.

2. Articles 2, 3, 6(1)(a) and (2) and Article 9 of Directive 68/360/EEC shall apply *mutatis mutandis* to the beneficiaries of this Directive.

The spouse and the dependent children of a national of a Member State entitled to the right of residence within the territory of a Member State shall be entitled to take up any employed or self-employed activity anywhere within the territory of that Member State, even if they are not nationals of a Member State.

Member States shall not derogate from the provisions of this Directive save on grounds of public policy, public security or public health. In that event, Directive 64/221/EEC shall apply.

3. This Directive shall not affect existing law on the acquisition of second homes.

Article 3

The right of residence shall remain for as long as beneficiaries of that right fulfil the conditions laid down in Article 1.

Article 4

The Commission shall, not more than three years after the date of implementation of this Directive, and at three-yearly intervals thereafter, draw up a report on the application of this Directive and submit it to the European Parliament and the Council.

Article 5

Member States shall bring into force the laws, regulations and administrative provisions necessary to comply with this Directive not later than 30 June 1992.

They shall forthwith inform the Commission thereof.

Article 6

This Directive is addressed to the Member States.

Done at Luxembourg, 28 June 1990.

(Signature omitted.)

Council Directive of 29 October 1993 on the right of residence for students (93/96/EEC)

[OJ 1993, L317/59]

[Note: To be repealed on 30 April 2006 when Directive 2004/38 enters into force.]

The Council of the European Communities,

Having regard to the Treaty establishing the European Economic Community, and in particular the second paragraph of Article 7 thereof,

Having regard to the proposal from the Commission,[1] In cooperation with the European Parliament,[2] Having regard to the opinion of the Economic and Social Committee,[3]

Whereas Article 3(c) of the Treaty provides that the activities of the Community shall include, as provided in the Treaty, the abolition, as between Member States, of obstacles to freedom of movement for persons;

Whereas Article 8a of the Treaty provides that the internal market must be established by 31 December 1992; whereas the internal market comprises an area without internal frontiers in which the free movement of goods, persons, services and capital is ensured in accordance with the provisions of the Treaty;

Whereas, as the Court of Justice has held, Articles 128 and 7 of the Treaty prohibit any discrimination between nationals of the Member States as regards access to vocational training in the Community;

Whereas access by a national of one Member State to vocational training in another Member State implies, for that national, a right of residence in that other Member State;

Whereas, accordingly, in order to guarantee access to vocational training, the conditions likely to facilitate the effective exercise of that right of residence should be laid down;

Whereas the right of residence for students forms part of a set of related measures designed to promote vocational training;

Whereas beneficiaries of the right of residence must not become an unreasonable burden on the public finances of the host Member State;

Whereas, in the present state of Community law, as established by the case law of the Court of Justice, assistance granted to students, does not fall within the scope of the Treaty within the meaning of Article 7 thereof;

Whereas the right of residence can only be genuinely exercised if it is also granted to the spouse and their dependent children;

Whereas the beneficiaries of this Directive should be covered by administrative arrangements similar to those laid down in particular in Council Directive 68/360/EEC of 15 October 1968 on the abolition of restrictions on movement and residence within the Community for workers of Member States and their families[4] and Council Directive 64/221/EEC of the 25 February 1964 on the coordination of special measures concerning the movement and residence of foreign nationals which are justified on grounds of public policy, public security or public health;[5]

Whereas this Directive does not apply to students who enjoy the right of residence by virtue of the fact that they are or have been effectively engaged in economic activities or are members of the family of a migrant worker;

Whereas, by its judgment of 7 July 1992 in Case C-295/90, the Court of Justice annulled Council Directive 90/366/EEC of 28 June 1990 on the right of residence for students,[6] while maintaining the effects of the annulled Directive until the entry into force of a directive adopted on the appropriate legal basis;

Whereas the effects of Directive 90/366/EEC should be maintained during the period up to 31 December 1993, the date by which Member States are to have adopted the laws, regulations and administrative provisions necessary to comply with this Directive,

Has adopted this Directive:

Article 1
In order to lay down conditions to facilitate the exercise of the right of residence and with a

---

[1] OJ No. C166, 17.6.1993, p. 16.
[2] OJ No. C255, 20.9.1993, p. 70 and OJ No. C315, 22.11.1993.
[3] OJ No. C304, 10.11.1993, p. 1.
[4] OJ No. L257, 19.10.1968, p. 13. Directive as last amended by the Act of Accession of 1985.
[5] OJ No. 56, 4.4.1964, p. 850/64.
[6] OJ No. L180, 13.7.1990, p. 30.

view to guaranteeing access to vocational training in a non-discriminatory manner for a national of a Member State who has been accepted to attend a vocational training course in another Member State, the Member States shall recognise the right of residence for any student who is a national of a Member State and who does not enjoy that right under other provisions of Community law, and for the student's spouse and their dependent children, where the student assures the relevant national authority, by means of a declaration or by such alternative means as the student may choose that are at least equivalent, that he has sufficient resources to avoid becoming a burden on the social assistance system of the host Member State during their period of residence, provided that the student is enrolled in a recognised educational establishment for the principal purpose of following a vocational training course there and that he is covered by sickness insurance in respect of all risks in the host Member State.

Article 2

1. The right of residence shall be restricted to the duration of the course of studies in question.

The right of residence shall be evidenced by means of the issue of a document known as a 'residence permit for a national of a Member State of the Community', the validity of which may be limited to the duration of the course of studies or to one year where the course lasts longer; in the latter event it shall be renewable annually. Where a member of the family does not hold the nationality of a Member State, he or she shall be issued with a residence document of the same validity as that issued to the national on whom he or she depends.

For the purpose of issuing the residence permit or document, the Member State may require only that the applicant present a valid identity card or passport and provide proof that he or she meets the conditions laid down in Article 1.

2. Articles 2, 3 and 9 of Directive 68/360/EEC shall apply *mutatis mutandis* to the beneficiaries of this Directive.

The spouse and the dependent children of a national of a Member State entitled to the right of residence within the territory of a Member State shall be entitled to take up any employed or self-employed activity anywhere within the territory of that Member State, even if they are not nationals of a Member State.

Member States shall not derogate from the provisions of this directive save on grounds of public policy, public security or public health: in that event, Articles 2 to 9 of Directive 64/221/EEC shall apply.

Article 3

This Directive shall not establish any entitlement to the payment of maintenance grants by the host Member State on the part of students benefiting from the right of residence.

Article 4

The right of residence shall remain for as long as beneficiaries of that right fulfil the conditions laid down in Article 1.

Article 5

The Commission shall, not more than three years after the date of implementation of this Directive, and at three-yearly intervals thereafter, draw up a report on the application of this Directive and submit it to the European Parliament and the Council.

The Commission shall pay particular attention to any difficulties to which the implementation of Article 1 might give rise in the Member States; it shall, if appropriate, submit proposals to the Council with the aim of remedying such difficulties.

Article 6

Member States shall bring into force the laws, regulations and administrative provisions necessary to comply with this Directive not later than 31 December 1993.

They shall forthwith inform the Commission thereof.

For the period preceding that date, the effects of Directive 90/366/EEC shall be maintained.

When Member States adopt those measures, they shall contain a reference to this Directive or shall be accompanied by such a reference on the occasion of their official publication.

The methods of making such references shall be laid down by the Member States.

Article 7

This Directive is addressed to the Member States.

Done at Brussels, 29 October 1993.

(Signature omitted.)

Directive 98/5/EC of the European Parliament and of the Council of 16 February 1998 to facilitate practice of the profession of lawyer on a permanent basis in a Member State other than that in which the qualification was obtained*

The European Parliament and the Council of the European Union,

Having regard to the Treaty establishing the European Community, and in particular Article 49, Article 57(1) and the first and third sentences of Article 57(2) thereof,

Having regard to the proposal from the Commission,[1]

Having regard to the Opinion of the Economic and Social Committee,[2]

Acting in accordance with the procedure laid down in Article 189b of the Treaty,[3]

(1) Whereas, pursuant to Article 7a of the Treaty, the internal market is to comprise an area without internal frontiers; whereas, pursuant to Article 3(c) of the Treaty, the abolition, as between Member States, of obstacles to freedom of movement for persons and services constitutes one of the objectives of the Community; whereas, for nationals of the Member States, this means among other things the possibility of practising a profession, whether in a self-employed or a salaried capacity, in a Member State other than that in which they obtained their professional qualifications;

(2) Whereas, pursuant to Council Directive 89/48/EEC of 21 December 1988 on a general system for the recognition of higher-education diplomas awarded on completion of professional education and training of at least three years' duration,[4] a lawyer who is fully qualified in one Member State may already ask to have his diploma recognised with a view to establishing himself in another Member State in order to practise the profession of lawyer there under the professional title used in that State; whereas the objective of Directive 89/48/EEC is to ensure that a lawyer is integrated into the profession in the host Member State, and the Directive seeks neither to modify the rules regulating the profession in that State nor to remove such a lawyer from the ambit of those rules;

(3) Whereas while some lawyers may become quickly integrated into the profession in the host Member State, *inter alia* by passing an aptitude test as provided for in Directive

---

* OJ No. L77/36 1998 and as amended up to and including OJ 2003 L236/257.

[1] OJ No. C128, 24.5.1995, p. 6 and OJ No. C355, 25.11.1996, p. 19.

[2] OJ No. C256, 2.10.1995, p. 14.

[3] Opinion of the European Parliament of 19 June 1996 (OJ No. C198, 8.7.1996, p. 85), Council Common Position of 24 July 1997 (OJ No. C297, 29.9.1997, p. 6), Decision of the European Parliament of 19 November 1997 (Council Decision of 15 December 1997).

[4] OJ No. L19, 24.1.1989, p. 16.

89/48/EEC, other fully qualified lawyers should be able to achieve such integration after a certain period of professional practice in the host Member State under their home-country professional titles or else continue to practise under their home-country professional titles;

(4) Whereas at the end of that period the lawyer should be able to integrate into the profession in the host Member States after verification that he possesses professional experience in that Member State;

(5) Whereas action along these lines is justified at Community level not only because, compared with the general system for the recognition of diplomas, it provides lawyers with an easier means whereby they can integrate into the profession in a host Member State, but also because, by enabling lawyers to practise under their home-country professional titles on a permanent basis in a host Member State, it meets the needs of consumers of legal services who, owing to the increasing trade flows resulting, in particular, from the internal market, seek advice when carrying out cross-border transactions in which international law, Community law and domestic laws often overlap;

(6) Whereas action is also justified at Community level because only a few Member States already permit in their territory the pursuit of activities of lawyers, otherwise than by way of provision of services, by lawyers from other Member States practising under their home-country professional titles, whereas, however, in the Member States where this possibility exists, the practical details concerning, for example, the area of activity and the obligation to register with the competent authorities differ considerably; whereas such a diversity of situations leads to inequalities and distortions in competition between lawyers from the Member States and constitutes an obstacle to freedom of movement; whereas only a directive laying down the conditions governing practice of the profession, otherwise than by way of provision of services, by lawyers practising under their home-country professional titles is capable of resolving these difficulties and of affording the same opportunities to lawyers and consumers of legal services in all Member States;

(7) Whereas, in keeping with its objective, this Directive does not lay down any rules concerning purely domestic situations, and where it does affect national rules regulating the legal profession it does so no more than is necessary to achieve its purpose effectively; whereas it is without prejudice in particular to national legislation governing access to and practice of the profession of lawyer under the professional title used in the host Member States;

(8) Whereas lawyers covered by the Directive should be required to register with the competent authority in the host Member State in order that that authority may ensure that they comply with the rules of professional conduct in force in that state; whereas the effect of such registration as regards the jurisdictions in which, and the levels and types of court before which lawyers may practise is determined by the law applicable to lawyers in the host Member States;

(9) Whereas lawyers who are not integrated into the profession in the host Member State should practise in that State under their home-country professional titles so as to ensure that consumers are properly informed and to distinguish between such lawyers and lawyers from the host Member State practising under the professional title used there;

(10) Whereas lawyers covered by this Directive should be permitted to give legal advice in particular on the law of their home Member States, on Community law, on international law and on the law of the host Member State; whereas this is already allowed as regards the provision of services under Council Directive 77/249/EEC of 22 March 1977 to facilitate the effective exercise by lawyers of freedom to provide services;[5] whereas, however, provision should be made, as in Directive 77/249/EEC, for the option of excluding from the activities of lawyers practising under their home-country professional titles in the United Kingdom and Ireland the preparation of certain formal documents in the conveyancing and probate

---

[5] OJ No. L78, 26.3.1977, p. 17. Directive as last amended by the 1994 Act of Accession.

spheres; whereas this Directive in no way affects the provisions under which, in every Member State, certain activities are reserved for professions other than the legal profession; whereas the provision in Directive 77/249/EEC concerning the possibility of the host Member State to require a lawyer practising under his home-country professional title to work in conjunction with a local lawyer when representing or defending a client in legal proceedings should also be incorporated in this Directive; whereas the requirement must be interpreted in the light of the case law of the Court of Justice of the European Communities, in particular its judgment of 25 February 1988 in Case 427/85, Commission v Germany;[6]

(11) Whereas to ensure the smooth operation of the justice system Member States should be allowed, by means of specific rules, to reserve access to their highest courts to specialist lawyers, without hindering the integration of Member States' lawyers fulfilling the necessary requirements;

(12) Whereas a lawyer registered under his home-country professional title in the host Member State must remain registered with the competent authority in his home Member State if he is to retain his status of lawyer and be covered by this Directive; whereas for that reason close collaboration between the competent authorities is indispensable, in particular in connection with any disciplinary proceedings;

(13) Whereas lawyers covered by this Directive, whether salaried or self-employed in their home Member States, may practise as salaried lawyers in the host Member State, where that Member State offers that possibility to its own lawyers;

(14) Whereas the purpose pursued by this Directive in enabling lawyers to practise in another Member State under their home-country professional titles is also to make it easier for them to obtain the professional title of that host Member State; whereas under Articles 48 and 52 of the Treaty as interpreted by the Court of Justice the host Member State must take into consideration any professional experience gained in its territory; whereas after effectively and regularly pursuing in the host Member State an activity in the law of that State including Community law for a period of three years, a lawyer may reasonably be assumed to have gained the aptitude necessary to become fully integrated into the legal profession there; whereas at the end of that period the lawyer whocan, subject to verification, furnish evidence of his professional competence in the host Member State should be able to obtain the professional title of that MemberState; whereas if the period of effective and regular professional activity of at least three years includes a shorter period of practice in the law of the host Member State, the authority shall also take into consideration any other knowledge of that State's law, which it may verify during an interview; whereas if evidence of fulfilment of these conditions is not provided, the decision taken by the competent authority of the host State not to grant the State's professional title under the facilitation arrangements linked to those conditions must be substantiated and subject to appeal under national law;

(15) Whereas, for economic and professional reasons, the growing tendency for lawyers in the Community to practise jointly, including in the form of associations, has become a reality; whereas the fact that lawyers belong to a grouping in their home Member State should not be used as a pretext to prevent or deter them from establishing themselves in the host Member States; whereas Member States should be allowed, however, to take appropriate measures with the legitimate aim of safeguarding the profession's independence; whereas certain guarantees should be provided in those Member States which permit joint practice, Have adopted this directive:

Article 1   Object, scope and definitions

1.   The purpose of this Directive is to facilitate practice of the profession of lawyer on a permanent basis in a self-employed or salaried capacity in a Member State other than that in which the professional qualification was obtained.

---

[6] [1988] ECR 1123.

2.   For the purposes of this Directive:
  (a) 'lawyer' means any person who is a national of a Member State and who is author-
       ised to pursue his professional activities under one of the following professional
       titles:

Belgium:	Avocat/Advocaat
Czech Republic:	Advokát
Denmark:	Advokat
Germany:	Rechtsanwalt
Estonia:	Vandeadvokaat
Greece:	Dikigoros
France:	Avocat
Ireland:	Barrister
	Solicitor
Italy:	Avvocato
Cyprus:	Δικηγρο
Latvia:	Zvērinats/Advokāts
Lithuania:	Advokatas
Luxembourg:	Avocat-avoue
Hungary:	Ügyvéd
Malta:	Avukat/Prokuratur Legali
Netherlands:	Advocaat
Austria:	Rechtsanwalt
Poland:	Adwokat/Radca prawny
Portugal:	Advogado
Slovenia:	Odvetnik/Odvetnica
Slovakia:	Advokát/Komerčný právnik
Finland:	Asianajaja — Advokat
Spain:	Abogado
Sweden:	Advokat
United Kingdom:	Advocate
	Barrister
	Solicitor.

  (b) 'home Member State' means the Member State in which a lawyer acquired the
       right to use one of the professional titles referred to in (a) before practising the
       profession of lawyer in another Member State;
  (c) 'host Member State' means the Member State in which a lawyer practises pursuant
       to this Directive;
  (d) 'home-country professional title' means the professional title used in the Member
       State in which a lawyer acquired the right to use that title before practising the
       profession of lawyer in the host Member State;
  (e) 'grouping' means any entity, with or without legal personality, formed under the
       law of a Member State, within which lawyers pursue their professional activities
       jointly under a joint name;
  (f) 'relevant professional title' or 'relevant profession' means the professional title
       or profession governed by the competent authority with whom a lawyer has
       registered under Article 3, and 'competent authority' means that authority.
  3.   This Directive shall apply both to lawyers practising in a self-employed capacity and
to lawyers practising in a salarial capacity in the home Member State and, subject to Article 8,
in the host Member State.

4.   Practice of the profession of lawyer within the meaning of this Directive shall not include the provision of services, which is covered by Directive 77/249/EEC.

Article 2   Right to practise under the home-country professional title

Any lawyer shall be entitled to pursue on a permanent basis, in any other Member State under his home-country professional title, the activities specified in Article 5.

Integration into the profession of lawyer in the host Member State shall be subject to Article 10.

Article 3   Registration with the competent authority

1.   A lawyer who wishes to practise in a Member State other than that in which he obtained his professional qualification shall register with the competent authority in that State.

2.   The competent authority in the host Member State shall register the lawyer upon presentation of a certificate attesting to his registration with the competent authority in the home Member State. It may require that, when presented by the competent authority of the home Member State, the certificate be not more than three months old. It shall inform the competent authority in the home Member State of the registration.

3.   For the purpose of applying paragraph 1:
  — in the United Kingdom and Ireland, lawyers practising under a professional title other than those used in the United Kingdom or Ireland shall register either with the authority responsible for the profession of barrister or advocate or with the authority responsible for the profession of solicitor,
  — in the United Kingdom, the authority responsible for a barrister from Ireland shall be that responsible for the profession of barrister or advocate, and the authority responsible for a solicitor from Ireland shall be that responsible for the profession of solicitor,
  — in Ireland, the authority responsible for a barrister or an advocate from the United Kingdom shall be that responsible for the profession of barrister, and the authority responsible for a solicitor from the United Kingdom shall be that responsible for the profession of solicitor.

4.   Where the relevant competent authority in a host Member State publishes the names of lawyers registered with it, it shall also publish the names of lawyers registered pursuant to this Directive.

Article 4   Practice under the home-country professional title

1.   A lawyer practising in a host Member State under his home-country professional title shall do so under that title, which must be expressed in the official language or one of the official languages of his home Member State, in an intelligible manner and in such a way as to avoid confusion with the professional title of the host Member State.

2.   For the purpose of applying paragraph 1, a host Member State may require a lawyer practising under his home-country professional title to indicate the professional body of which he is a member in his home Member State or the judicial authority before which he is entitled to practise pursuant to the laws of his home Member State. A host Member State may also require a lawyer practising under his home-country professional title to include a reference to his registration with the competent authority in that State.

Article 5   Area of activity

1.   Subject to paragraphs 2 and 3, a lawyer practising under his home-country professional title carries on the same professional activities as a lawyer practising under the relevant processional title used in the host Member State and may, *inter alia*, give advice on the law of his home Member State, on Community law, on international law and on the law of the host Member State. He shall in any event comply with the rules of procedure applicable in the national courts.

2.   Member States which authorise in their territory a prescribed category of lawyers to prepare deeds for obtaining title to administer estates of deceased persons and for creating or transferring interests in land which, in other Member States, are reserved for professions other than that of lawyer may exclude from such activities lawyers practising under a home-country professional title conferred in one of the latter Member States.

3.   For the pursuit of activities relating to the representation or defence of a client in legal proceedings and insofar as the law of the host Member State reserves such activities to lawyers practising under the professional title of that State, the latter may require lawyers practising under their home-country professional titles to work in conjunction with a lawyer who practises before the judicial authority in question and who would, where necessary, be answerable to that authority or with an 'avoué' practising before it.

Nevertheless, in order to ensure the smooth operation of the justice system, Member States may lay down specific rules for access to supreme courts, such as the use of specialist lawyers.

Article 6   Rules of professional conduct applicable

1.   Irrespective of the rules of professional conduct to which he is subject in his home Member State, a lawyer practising under his home-country professional title shall be subject to the same rules of professional conduct as lawyers practising under the relevant professional title of the host Member State in respect of all the activities he pursues in its territory.

2.   Lawyers practising under their home-country professional titles shall be granted appropriate representation in the professional associations of the host Member State. Such representation shall involve at least the right to vote in elections to those associations' governing bodies.

3.   The host Member State may require a lawyer practising under his homecountry professional title either to take out professional indemnity insurance or to become a member of a professional guarantee fund in accordance with the rules which that State lays down for professional activities pursued in its territory. Nevertheless, a lawyer practising under his home-country professional title shall be exempted from that requirement if he can prove that he is covered by insurance taken out or a guarantee provided in accordance with the rules of his home Member State, insofar as such insurance or guarantee is equivalent in terms of the conditions and extent of cover. Where the equivalence is only partial, the competent authority in the host Member State may require that additional insurance or an additional guarantee be contacted to cover the elements which are not already covered by the insurance or guarantee contracted in accordance with the rules of the home Member States.

Article 7   Disciplinary proceedings

1.   In the event of failure by a lawyer practising under his home-country professional title to fulfil the obligations in force in the host Member State, the rules of procedure, penalties and remedies provided for in the host Member State shall apply.

2.   Before initiating disciplinary proceedings against a lawyer practising under his home-country professional title, the competent authority in the host Member State shall inform the competent authority in the home Member State as soon as possible, furnishing it with all the relevant details.

The first sub-paragraph shall apply *mutatis mutandis* where disciplinary proceedings are initiated by the competent authority of the home Member State, which shall inform the competent authority of the host Member State(s) accordingly.

3.   Without prejudice to the decision-making power of the competent authority in the host Member State, that authority shall cooperate throughout the disciplinary proceedings with the competent authority in the home Member State. In particular, the host Member State shall take the measures necessary to ensure that the competent authority in the home Member State can make submissions to the bodies responsible for hearing any appeal.

4.   The competent authority in the home Member State shall decide what action to take, under its own procedural and substantive rules, in the light of a decision of the competent

authority in the host Member State concerning a lawyer practising under his home-country professional title.

5.   Although it is not a prerequisite for the decision of the competent authority in the host Member State, the temporary or permanent withdrawal by the competent authority in the home Member State of the authorisation to practise the profession shall automatically lead to the lawyer concerned being temporarily or permanently prohibited from practising under his home-country professional title in the host Member State.

Article 8   Salaried practice
A lawyer registered in a host Member State under his home-country professional title may practise as a salaried lawyer in the employ of another lawyer, an association or firm of lawyers, or a public or private enterprise to the extent that the host Member State so permits for lawyers registered under the professional title used in that State.

Article 9   Statement of reasons and remedies
Decisions not to effect the registration referred to in Article 3 or to cancel such registration and decisions imposing disciplinary measures shall state the reasons on which they are based.

A remedy shall be available against such decisions before a court or tribunal in accordance with the provisions of domestic law.

Article 10   Like treatment as a lawyer of the host Member State
1.   A lawyer practising under his home-country professional title who has effectively and regularly pursued for a period of at least three years an activity in the host Member State in the law of that State including Community law shall, with a view to gaining admission to the profession of lawyer in the host Member State, be exempted from the conditions set out in Article 4(1)(b) of Directive 89/48/EEC, 'Effective and regular pursuit' means actual exercise of the activity without any interruption other than that resulting from the events of everyday life.

It shall be for the lawyer concerned to furnish the competent authority in the host Member State with proof of such effective regular pursuit for a period of at least three years of an activity in the law of the host Member State. To that end:

(a)   the lawyer shall provide the competent authority in the host Member State with any relevant information and documentation, notably on the number of matters he has dealt with and their nature;

(b)   the competent authority of the host Member State may verify the effective and regular nature of the activity pursued and may, if need be, request the lawyer to provide, orally or in writing, clarification of or further details on the information and documentation mentioned in point (a).

Reasons shall be given for a decision by the competent authority in the host Member State not to grant an exemption where proof is not provided that the requirements laid down in the first sub-paragraph have been fulfilled, and the decision shall be subject to appeal under domestic law.

2.   A lawyer practising under his home-country professional title in a host Member State may, at any time, apply to have his diploma recognised in accordance with Directive 89/48/EEC with a view to gaining admission to the profession of lawyer in the host Member State and practising it under the professional title corresponding to the profession in that Member State.

3.   A lawyer practising under his home-country professional title who has effectively and regularly pursued a professional activity in the host Member State for a period of at least three years but for a lesser period in the law of that Member State may obtain from the competent authority of that State admission to the profession of lawyer in the host Member State and the right to practise it under the professional title corresponding to the profession in that Member State, without having to meet the conditions referred to in Article 4(1)(b) of Directive 89/48/EEC, under the conditions and in accordance with the procedures set out below:

(a) The competent authority of the host Member State shall take into account the effective and regular professional activity pursued during the abovementioned period and any knowledge and professional experience of the law of the host Member State, and any attendance at lectures or seminars on the law of the host Member State, including the rules regulating professional practice and conduct.

(b) The lawyer shall provide the competent authority of the host Member State with any relevant information and documentation, in particular on the matters he has dealt with. Assessment of the lawyer's effective and regular activity in the host Member State and assessment of his capacity to continue the activity he has pursued there shall be carried out by means of an interview with the competent authority of the host Member State in order to verify the regular and effective nature of the activity pursued.

Reasons shall be given for a decision by the competent authority in the host Member State not to grant authorisation where proof is not provided that the requirements laid down in the first sub-paragraph have been fulfilled, and the decision shall be subject to appeal under domestic law.

4.   The competent authority of the host Member State may, by reasoned decision subject to appeal under domestic law, refuse to allow the lawyer the benefit of the provisions of this Article if it considers that this would be against public policy, in particular because of disciplinary proceedings, complaints or incidents of any kind.

5.   The representatives of the competent authority entrusted with consideration of the application shall preserve the confidentiality of any information received.

6.   A lawyer who gains admission to the profession of lawyer in the host Member State in accordance with paragraphs 1, 2 and 3 shall be entitled to use his home-country professional title, expressed in the official language or one of the official languges of his home Member State, alongside the professional title corresponding to the profession of lawyer in the host Member State.

Article 11   Joint practice

Where joint practice is authorised in respect of lawyers carrying on their activities under the relevant professional title in the host Member State, the following provisions shall apply in respect of lawyers wishing to carry on activities under that title or registering with the competent authority:

(1) One or more lawyers who belong to the same grouping in their home Member State and who practise under their home-country professional title in a host Member State may pursue their professional activities in a branch or agency of their grouping in the host Member State. However, where the fundamental rules governing that grouping in the home Member State are incompatible with the fundamental rules laid down by law, regulation or administrative action in the host Member State, the latter rules shall prevail insofar as compliance therewith is justified by the public interest in protecting clients and third parties.

(2) Each Member State shall afford two or more lawyers from the same grouping or the same home Member State who practise in its territory under their home-country professional titles access to a form of joint practice. If the host Member State gives its lawyers a choice between several forms of joint practice, those same forms shall also be made available to the abovementioned lawyers. The manner in which such lawyers practise jointly in the host Member State shall be governed by the laws, regulations and administrative provisions of that State.

(3) The host Member State shall take the measures necessary to permit joint practice also between:

(a) several lawyers from different Member States practising under their home-country professional titles;

(b) one or more lawyers covered by point (a) and one or more lawyers from the host Member State.

The manner in which such lawyers practise jointly in the host Member State shall be governed by the laws, regulations and administrative provisions of that State.

(4) A lawyer who wishes to practise under his home-country professional title shall inform the competent authority in the host Member State of the fact that he is a member of a grouping in his home Member State and furnish any relevant information on that grouping.

(5) Notwithstanding points 1 to 4, a host Member State, insofar as it prohibits lawyers practising under its own relevant professional title from practising the profession of lawyer within a grouping in which some persons are not members of the profession, may refuse to allow a lawyer registered under his home-country professional title to practice in its territory in his capacity as a member of his grouping. The grouping is deemed to include persons who are not members of the profession if

— the capital of the grouping is held entirely or partly, or

— the name under which it practises is used, or

— the decision-making power in that grouping is exercised, *de facto* or *de jure*,

by persons who do not have the status of lawyer within the meaning of Article 1(2).

Where the fundamental rules governing a grouping of lawyers in the home Member State are incompatible with the rules in force in the host Member State or with the provisions of the first sub-paragraph, the host Member State may oppose the opening of a branch or agency within its territory without the restrictions laid down in point (1).

Article 12   Name of the grouping

Whatever the manner in which lawyers practise under their home-country professional titles in the host Member State, they may employ the name of any grouping to which they belong in their home Member State.

The host Member State may require that, in addition to the name referred to in the first sub-paragraph, mention be made of the legal form of the grouping in the home Member State and/or of the names of any members of the grouping practising in the host Member State.

Article 13   Cooperation between the competent authorities in the home and host Member States and confidentiality

In order to facilitate the application of this Directive and to prevent its provisions from being misapplied for the sole purpose of circumventing the rules applicable in the host Member State, the competent authority in the host Member State and the competent authority in the home Member State shall collaborate closely and afford each other mutual assistance.

They shall preserve the confidentiality of the information they exchange.

Article 14   Designation of the competent authorities

Member States shall designate the competent authorities empowered to receive the applications and to take the decisions referred to in this Directive by 14 March 2000. They shall communicate this information to the other Member States and to the Commission.

Article 15   Report by the Commission

Ten years at the latest from the entry into force of this Directive, the Commission shall report to the European Parliament and to the Council on progress in the implementation of the Directive.

After having held all the necessary consultations, it shall on that occasion present its conclusions and any amendments which could be made to the existing system.

Article 16   Implementation

1. Member States shall bring into force the laws, regulations and administrative provisions necessary to comply with this Directive by 14 March 2000. They shall forthwith inform the Commission thereof.

When Member States adopt these measures, they shall contain a reference to this Directive or shall be accompanied by such reference on the occasion of their official publication. The methods of making such reference shall be adopted by Member States.

2. Member States shall communicate to the Commission the texts of the main provisions of domestic law which they adopt in the field covered by this Directive.

Article 17

This Directive shall enter into force on the date of its publication in the *Official Journal of the European Communities*.

Article 18   Addressees

This Directive is addressed to the Member States.

Done at Brussels, 16 February 1998.
For the European Parliament
The President
J. M. GIL-ROBLES

For the Council
The President
J. CUNNINGHAM

Directive 2004/38/EC of the European Parliament and of the Council of 29 April 2004 on the right of citizens of the Union and their family members to move and reside freely within the territory of the Member States

[OJ 2004, L158/77]

(Entry into force 30/4/2006 at which time Regulation (EEC) No. 1612/68 is amended and Directives 64/221/EEC, 68/360/EEC, 72/194/EEC, 73/148/EEC, 75/34/EEC, 75/35/EEC, 90/364/EEC, 90/365/EEC and 93/96/EEC are repealed)

THE EUROPEAN PARLIAMENT AND THE COUNCIL OF THE EUROPEAN UNION,

Having regard to the Treaty establishing the European Community, and in particular Articles 12, 18, 40, 44 and 52 thereof,

Having regard to the proposal from the Commission,[1]

Having regard to the Opinion of the European Economic and Social Committee,[2]

Having regard to the Opinion of the Committee of the Regions,[3]

Acting in accordance with the procedure laid down in Article 251 of the Treaty,[4]

Whereas:

(1) Citizenship of the Union confers on every citizen of the Union a primary and individual right to move and reside freely within the territory of the Member States, subject to the limitations and conditions laid down in the Treaty and to the measures adopted to give it effect.

[1] OJ C 270 E, 25.9.2001, p. 150.
[2] OJ C 149, 21.6.2002, p. 46.
[3] OJ C 192, 12.8.2002, p. 17.
[4] Opinion of the European Parliament of 11 February 2003 (OJ C 43 E, 19.2.2004, p. 42), Council Common Position of 5 December 2003 (OJ C 54 E, 2.3.2004, p. 12) and Position of the European Parliament of 10 March 2004 (not yet published in the Official Journal).

(2) The free movement of persons constitutes one of the fundamental freedoms of the internal market, which comprises an area without internal frontiers, in which freedom is ensured in accordance with the provisions of the Treaty.

(3) Union citizenship should be the fundamental status of nationals of the Member States when they exercise their right of free movement and residence. It is therefore necessary to codify and review the existing Community instruments dealing separately with workers, self-employed persons, as well as students and other inactive persons in order to simplify and strengthen the right of free movement and residence of all Union citizens.

(4) With a view to remedying this sector-by-sector, piecemeal approach to the right of free movement and residence and facilitating the exercise of this right, there needs to be a single legislative act to amend Council Regulation (EEC) No 1612/68 of 15 October 1968 on freedom of movement for workers within the Community,[5] and to repeal the following acts: Council Directive 68/360/EEC of 15 October 1968 on the abolition of restrictions on movement and residence within the Community for workers of Member States and their families,[6] Council Directive 73/148/EEC of 21 May 1973 on the abolition of restrictions on movement and residence within the Community for nationals of Member States with regard to establishment and the provision of services,[7] Council Directive 90/364/EEC of 28 June 1990 on the right of residence,[8] Council Directive 90/365/EEC of 28 June 1990 on the right of residence for employees and self-employed persons who have ceased their occupational activity[9] and Council Directive 93/96/EEC of 29 October 1993 on the right of residence for students.[10]

(5) The right of all Union citizens to move and reside freely within the territory of the Member States should, if it is to be exercised under objective conditions of freedom and dignity, be also granted to their family members, irrespective of nationality. For the purposes of this Directive, the definition of 'family member' should also include the registered partner if the legislation of the host Member State treats registered partnership as equivalent to marriage.

(6) In order to maintain the unity of the family in a broader sense and without prejudice to the prohibition of discrimination on grounds of nationality, the situation of those persons who are not included in the definition of family members under this Directive, and who therefore do not enjoy an automatic right of entry and residence in the host Member State, should be examined by the host Member State on the basis of its own national legislation, in order to decide whether entry and residence could be granted to such persons, taking into consideration their relationship with the Union citizen or any other circumstances, such as their financial or physical dependence on the Union citizen.

(7) The formalities connected with the free movement of Union citizens within the territory of Member States should be clearly defined, without prejudice to the provisions applicable to national border controls.

(8) With a view to facilitating the free movement of family members who are not nationals of a Member State, those who have already obtained a residence card should be exempted from the requirement to obtain an entry visa within the meaning of Council Regulation (EC) No 539/2001 of 15 March 2001 listing the third countries whose nationals must be in possession of visas when crossing the external borders and those whose nationals are exempt from that requirement[11] or, where appropriate, of the applicable national legislation.

[5] OJ L 257, 19.10.1968, p. 2. Regulation as last amended by Regulation (EEC) No 2434/92 (OJ L 245, 26.8.1992, p. 1).

[6] OJ L 257, 19.10.1968, p. 13. Directive as last amended by the 2003 Act of Accession.

[7] OJ L 172, 28.6.1973, p. 14.

[8] OJ L 180, 13.7.1990, p. 26.

[9] OJ L 180, 13.7.1990, p. 28.

[10] OJ L 317, 18.12.1993, p. 59.

[11] 1 OJ L 81, 21.3.2001, p. 1. Regulation as last amended by Regulation (EC) No 453/2003 OJ L 69, 13.3.2003, p. 10).

(9) Union citizens should have the right of residence in the host Member State for a period not exceeding three months without being subject to any conditions or any formalities other than the requirement to hold a valid identity card or passport, without prejudice to a more favourable treatment applicable to job-seekers as recognised by the case-law of the Court of Justice.

(10) Persons exercising their right of residence should not, however, become an unreasonable burden on the social assistance system of the host Member State during an initial period of residence. Therefore, the right of residence for Union citizens and their family members for periods in excess of three months should be subject to conditions.

(11) The fundamental and personal right of residence in another Member State is conferred directly on Union citizens by the Treaty and is not dependent upon their having fulfilled administrative procedures.

(12) For periods of residence of longer than three months, Member States should have the possibility to require Union citizens to register with the competent authorities in the place of residence, attested by a registration certificate issued to that effect.

(13) The residence card requirement should be restricted to family members of Union citizens who are not nationals of a Member State for periods of residence of longer than three months.

(14) The supporting documents required by the competent authorities for the issuing of a registration certificate or of a residence card should be comprehensively specified in order to avoid divergent administrative practices or interpretations constituting an undue obstacle to the exercise of the right of residence by Union citizens and their family members.

(15) Family members should be legally safeguarded in the event of the death of the Union citizen, divorce, annulment of marriage or termination of a registered partnership. With due regard for family life and human dignity, and in certain conditions to guard against abuse, measures should therefore be taken to ensure that in such circumstances family members already residing within the territory of the host Member State retain their right of residence exclusively on a personal basis.

(16) As long as the beneficiaries of the right of residence do not become an unreasonable burden on the social assistance system of the host Member State they should not be expelled. Therefore, an expulsion measure should not be the automatic consequence of recourse to the social assistance system. The host Member State should examine whether it is a case of temporary difficulties and take into account the duration of residence, the personal circumstances and the amount of aid granted in order to consider whether the beneficiary has become an unreasonable burden on its social assistance system and to proceed to his expulsion. In no case should an expulsion measure be adopted against workers, self-employed persons or job-seekers as defined by the Court of Justice save on grounds of public policy or public security.

(17) Enjoyment of permanent residence by Union citizens who have chosen to settle long term in the host Member State would strengthen the feeling of Union citizenship and is a key element in promoting social cohesion, which is one of the fundamental objectives of the Union. A right of permanent residence should therefore be laid down for all Union citizens and their family members who have resided in the host Member State in compliance with the conditions laid down in this Directive during a continuous period of five years without becoming subject to an expulsion measure.

(18) In order to be a genuine vehicle for integration into the society of the host Member State in which the Union citizen resides, the right of permanent residence, once obtained, should not be subject to any conditions.

(19) Certain advantages specific to Union citizens who are workers or self-employed persons and to their family members, which may allow these persons to acquire a right of permanent residence before they have resided five years in the host Member State, should be maintained, as these constitute acquired rights, conferred by Commission Regulation (EEC)

No 1251/70 of 29 June 1970 on the right of workers to remain in the territory of a Member State after having been employed in that State[12] and Council Directive 75/34/EEC of 17 December 1974 concerning the right of nationals of a Member State to remain in the territory of another Member State after having pursued therein an activity in a self-employed capacity.[13]

(20) In accordance with the prohibition of discrimination on grounds of nationality, all Union citizens and their family members residing in a Member State on the basis of this Directive should enjoy, in that Member State, equal treatment with nationals in areas covered by the Treaty, subject to such specific provisions as are expressly provided for in the Treaty and secondary law.

(21) However, it should be left to the host Member State to decide whether it will grant social assistance during the first three months of residence, or for a longer period in the case of job-seekers, to Union citizens other than those who are workers or self-employed persons or who retain that status or their family members, or maintenance assistance for studies, including vocational training, prior to acquisition of the right of permanent residence, to these same persons.

(22) The Treaty allows restrictions to be placed on the right of free movement and residence on grounds of public policy, public security or public health. In order to ensure a tighter definition of the circumstances and procedural safeguards subject to which Union citizens and their family members may be denied leave to enter or may be expelled, this Directive should replace Council Directive 64/221/EEC of 25 February 1964 on the coordination of special measures concerning the movement and residence of foreign nationals, which are justified on grounds of public policy, public security or public health.[14]

(23) Expulsion of Union citizens and their family members on grounds of public policy or public security is a measure that can seriously harm persons who, having availed themselves of the rights and freedoms conferred on them by the Treaty, have become genuinely integrated into the host Member State. The scope for such measures should therefore be limited in accordance with the principle of proportionality to take account of the degree of integration of the persons concerned, the length of their residence in the host Member State, their age, state of health, family and economic situation and the links with their country of origin.

(24) Accordingly, the greater the degree of integration of Union citizens and their family members in the host Member State, the greater the degree of protection against expulsion should be. Only in exceptional circumstances, where there are imperative grounds of public security, should an expulsion measure be taken against Union citizens who have resided for many years in the territory of the host Member State, in particular when they were born and have resided there throughout their life. In addition, such exceptional circumstances should also apply to an expulsion measure taken against minors, in order to protect their links with their family, in accordance with the United Nations Convention on the Rights of the Child, of 20 November 1989.

(25) Procedural safeguards should also be specified in detail in order to ensure a high level of protection of the rights of Union citizens and their family members in the event of their being denied leave to enter or reside in another Member State, as well as to uphold the principle that any action taken by the authorities must be properly justified.

(26) In all events, judicial redress procedures should be available to Union citizens and their family members who have been refused leave to enter or reside in another Member State.

(27) In line with the case-law of the Court of Justice prohibiting Member States from issuing orders excluding for life persons covered by this Directive from their territory, the right of Union citizens and their family members who have been excluded from the territory of a

---

[12] OJ L 142, 30.6.1970, p. 24.
[13] OJ L 14, 20.1.1975, p. 10.
[14] OJ 56, 4.4.1964, p. 850. Directive as last amendede by Directive 75/35/EEC (OJ 14, 20.1.1975, p. 14).

Member State to submit a fresh application after a reasonable period, and in any event after a three year period from enforcement of the final exclusion order, should be confirmed.

(28) To guard against abuse of rights or fraud, notably marriages of convenience or any other form of relationships contracted for the sole purpose of enjoying the right of free movement and residence, Member States should have the possibility to adopt the necessary measures.

(29) This Directive should not affect more favourable national provisions.

(30) With a view to examining how further to facilitate the exercise of the right of free movement and residence, a report should be prepared by the Commission in order to evaluate the opportunity to present any necessary proposals to this effect, notably on the extension of the period of residence with no conditions.

(31) This Directive respects the fundamental rights and freedoms and observes the principles recognised in particular by the Charter of Fundamental Rights of the European Union. In accordance with the prohibition of discrimination contained in the Charter, Member States should implement this Directive without discrimination between the beneficiaries of this Directive on grounds such as sex, race, colour, ethnic or social origin, genetic characteristics, language, religion or beliefs, political or other opinion, membership of an ethnic minority, property, birth, disability, age or sexual orientation,
HAVE ADOPTED THIS DIRECTIVE:

CHAPTER I   GENERAL PROVISIONS

Article 1   Subject
This Directive lays down:
- (a) the conditions governing the exercise of the right of free movement and residence within the territory of the Member States by Union citizens and their family members;
- (b) the right of permanent residence in the territory of the Member States for Union citizens and their family members;
- (c) the limits placed on the rights set out in (a) and (b) on grounds of public policy, public security or public health.

Article 2   Definitions
For the purposes of this Directive:
(1) "Union citizen" means any person having the nationality of a Member State;
(2) "Family member" means:
- (a) the spouse;
- (b) the partner with whom the Union citizen has contracted a registered partnership, on the basis of the legislation of a Member State, if the legislation of the host Member State treats registered partnerships as equivalent to marriage and in accordance with the conditions laid down in the relevant legislation of the host Member State;
- (c) the direct descendants who are under the age of 21 or are dependants and those of the spouse or partner as defined in point (b);
- (d) the dependent direct relatives in the ascending line and those of the spouse or partner as defined in point (b);
(3) "Host Member State" means the Member State to which a Union citizen moves in order to exercise his/her right of free movement and residence.

Article 3   Beneficiaries
1.   This Directive shall apply to all Union citizens who move to or reside in a Member State other than that of which they are a national, and to their family members as defined in point 2 of Article 2 who accompany or join them.

2.   Without prejudice to any right to free movement and residence the persons concerned may have in their own right, the host Member State shall, in accordance with its national legislation, facilitate entry and residence for the following persons:

(a) any other family members, irrespective of their nationality, not falling under the definition in point 2 of Article 2 who, in the country from which they have come, are dependants or members of the household of the Union citizen having the primary right of residence, or where serious health grounds strictly require the personal care of the family member by the Union citizen;

(b) the partner with whom the Union citizen has a durable relationship, duly attested. The host Member State shall undertake an extensive examination of the personal circumstances and shall justify any denial of entry or residence to these people.

CHAPTER II   RIGHT OF EXIT AND ENTRY

Article 4   Right of exit

1.   Without prejudice to the provisions on travel documents applicable to national border controls, all Union citizens with a valid identity card or passport and their family members who are not nationals of a Member State and who hold a valid passport shall have the right to leave the territory of a Member State to travel to another Member State.

2.   No exit visa or equivalent formality may be imposed on the persons to whom paragraph 1 applies.

3.   Member States shall, acting in accordance with their laws, issue to their own nationals, and renew, an identity card or passport stating their nationality.

4.   The passport shall be valid at least for all Member States and for countries through which the holder must pass when travelling between Member States. Where the law of a Member State does not provide for identity cards to be issued, the period of validity of any passport on being issued or renewed shall be not less than five years.

Article 5   Right of entry

1.   Without prejudice to the provisions on travel documents applicable to national border controls, Member States shall grant Union citizens leave to enter their territory with a valid identity card or passport and shall grant family members who are not nationals of a Member State leave to enter their territory with a valid passport. No entry visa or equivalent formality may be imposed on Union citizens.

2.   Family members who are not nationals of a Member State shall only be required to have an entry visa in accordance with Regulation (EC) No 539/2001 or, where appropriate, with national law. For the purposes of this Directive, possession of the valid residence card referred to in Article 10 shall exempt such family members from the visa requirement. Member States shall grant such persons every facility to obtain the necessary visas. Such visas shall be issued free of charge as soon as possible and on the basis of an accelerated procedure.

3.   The host Member State shall not place an entry or exit stamp in the passport of family members who are not nationals of a Member State provided that they present the residence card provided for in Article 10.

4.   Where a Union citizen, or a family member who is not a national of a Member State, does not have the necessary travel documents or, if required, the necessary visas, the Member State concerned shall, before turning them back, give such persons every reasonable opportunity to obtain the necessary documents or have them brought to them within a reasonable period of time or to corroborate or prove by other means that they are covered by the right of free movement and residence.

5.   The Member State may require the person concerned to report his/her presence within its territory within a reasonable and non-discriminatory period of time. Failure to

comply with this requirement may make the person concerned liable to proportionate and non-discriminatory sanctions.

CHAPTER III   RIGHT OF RESIDENCE

Article 6   Right of residence for up to three months
   1.   Union citizens shall have the right of residence on the territory of another Member State for a period of up to three months without any conditions or any formalities other than the requirement to hold a valid identity card or passport.
   2.   The provisions of paragraph 1 shall also apply to family members in possession of a valid passport who are not nationals of a Member State, accompanying or joining the Union citizen.

Article 7   Right of residence for more than three months
   1.   All Union citizens shall have the right of residence on the territory of another Member State for a period of longer than three months if they:
     (a)   are workers or self-employed persons in the host Member State; or
     (b)   have sufficient resources for themselves and their family members not to become a burden on the social assistance system of the host Member State during their period of residence and have comprehensive sickness insurance cover in the host Member State; or
     (c)—are enrolled at a private or public establishment, accredited or financed by the host Member State on the basis of its legislation or administrative practice, for the principal purpose of following a course of study, including vocational training; and
      — have comprehensive sickness insurance cover in the host Member State and assure the relevant national authority, by means of a declaration or by such equivalent means as they may choose, that they have sufficient resources for themselves and their family members not to become a burden on the social assistance system of the host Member State during their period of residence; or
     (d)   are family members accompanying or joining a Union citizen who satisfies the conditions referred to in points (a), (b) or (c).
   2.   The right of residence provided for in paragraph 1 shall extend to family members who are not nationals of a Member State, accompanying or joining the Union citizen in the host Member State, provided that such Union citizen satisfies the conditions referred to in paragraph 1(a), (b) or (c).
   3.   For the purposes of paragraph 1(a), a Union citizen who is no longer a worker or self-employed person shall retain the status of worker or self-employed person in the following circumstances:
     (a)   he/she is temporarily unable to work as the result of an illness or accident;
     (b)   he/she is in duly recorded involuntary unemployment after having been employed for more than one year and has registered as a job-seeker with the relevant employment office;
     (c)   he/she is in duly recorded involuntary unemployment after completing a fixed-term employment contract of less than a year or after having become involuntarily unemployed during the first twelve months and has registered as a job-seeker with the relevant employment office. In this case, the status of worker shall be retained for no less than six months;
     (d)   he/she embarks on vocational training. Unless he/she is involuntarily unemployed, the retention of the status of worker shall require the training to be related to the previous employment.
   4.   By way of derogation from paragraphs 1(d) and 2 above, only the spouse, the registered partner provided for in Article 2(2)(b) and dependent children shall have the right of

residence as family members of a Union citizen meeting the conditions under 1(c) above. Article 3(2) shall apply to his/her dependent direct relatives in the ascending lines and those of his/her spouse or registered partner.

Article 8   Administrative formalities for Union citizens

1.   Without prejudice to Article 5(5), for periods of residence longer than three months, the host Member State may require Union citizens to register with the relevant authorities.

2.   The deadline for registration may not be less than three months from the date of arrival. A registration certificate shall be issued immediately, stating the name and address of the person registering and the date of the registration. Failure to comply with the registration requirement may render the person concerned liable to proportionate and non-discriminatory sanctions.

3.   For the registration certificate to be issued, Member States may only require that

— Union citizens to whom point (a) of Article 7(1) applies present a valid identity card or passport, a confirmation of engagement from the employer or a certificate of employment, or proof that they are self-employed persons;

— Union citizens to whom point (b) of Article 7(1) applies present a valid identity card or passport and provide proof that they satisfy the conditions laid down therein;

— Union citizens to whom point (c) of Article 7(1) applies present a valid identity card or passport, provide proof of enrolment at an accredited establishment and of comprehensive sickness insurance cover and the declaration or equivalent means referred to in point (c) of Article 7(1). Member States may not require this declaration to refer to any specific amount of resources.

4.   Member States may not lay down a fixed amount which they regard as "sufficient resources", but they must take into account the personal situation of the person concerned. In all cases this amount shall not be higher than the threshold below which nationals of the host Member State become eligible for social assistance, or, where this criterion is not applicable, higher than the minimum social security pension paid by the host Member State.

5.   For the registration certificate to be issued to family members of Union citizens, who are themselves Union citizens, Member States may require the following documents to be presented:

(a)   a valid identity card or passport;

(b)   a document attesting to the existence of a family relationship or of a registered partnership;

(c)   where appropriate, the registration certificate of the Union citizen whom they are accompanying or joining;

(d)   in cases falling under points (c) and (d) of Article 2(2), documentary evidence that the conditions laid down therein are met;

(e)   in cases falling under Article 3(2)(a), a document issued by the relevant authority in the country of origin or country from which they are arriving certifying that they are dependants or members of the household of the Union citizen, or proof of the existence of serious health grounds which strictly require the personal care of the family member by the Union citizen;

(f)   in cases falling under Article 3(2)(b), proof of the existence of a durable relationship with the Union citizen.

Article 9   Administrative formalities for family members who are not nationals of a Member State

1.   Member States shall issue a residence card to family members of a Union citizen who are not nationals of a Member State, where the planned period of residence is for more than three months.

2.   The deadline for submitting the residence card application may not be less than three months from the date of arrival.

3.   Failure to comply with the requirement to apply for a residence card may make the person concerned liable to proportionate and non-discriminatory sanctions.

Article 10   Issue of residence cards

1.   The right of residence of family members of a Union citizen who are not nationals of a Member State shall be evidenced by the issuing of a document called "Residence card of a family member of a Union citizen" no later than six months from the date on which they submit the application. A certificate of application for the residence card shall be issued immediately.

2.   For the residence card to be issued, Member States shall require presentation of the following documents:

(a) a valid passport;

(b) a document attesting to the existence of a family relationship or of a registered partnership;

(c) the registration certificate or, in the absence of a registration system, any other proof of residence in the host Member State of the Union citizen whom they are accompanying or joining;

(d) in cases falling under points (c) and (d) of Article 2(2), documentary evidence that the conditions laid down therein are met;

(e) in cases falling under Article 3(2)(a), a document issued by the relevant authority in the country of origin or country from which they are arriving certifying that they are dependants or members of the household of the Union citizen, or proof of the existence of serious health grounds which strictly require the personal care of the family member by the Union citizen;

(f) in cases falling under Article 3(2)(b), proof of the existence of a durable relationship with the Union citizen.

Article 11   Validity of the residence card

1.   The residence card provided for by Article 10(1) shall be valid for five years from the date of issue or for the envisaged period of residence of the Union citizen, if this period is less than five years.

2.   The validity of the residence card shall not be affected by temporary absences not exceeding six months a year, or by absences of a longer duration for compulsory military service or by one absence of a maximum of twelve consecutive months for important reasons such as pregnancy and childbirth, serious illness, study or vocational training, or a posting in another Member State or a third country.

Article 12   Retention of the right of residence by family members in the event of death or departure of the Union citizen

1.   Without prejudice to the second subparagraph, the Union citizen's death or departure from the host Member State shall not affect the right of residence of his/her family members who are nationals of a Member State.

Before acquiring the right of permanent residence, the persons concerned must meet the conditions laid down in points (a), (b), (c) or (d) of Article 7(1).

2.   Without prejudice to the second subparagraph, the Union citizen's death shall not entail loss of the right of residence of his/her family members who are not nationals of a Member State and who have been residing in the host Member State as family members for at least one year before the Union citizen's death.

Before acquiring the right of permanent residence, the right of residence of the persons concerned shall remain subject to the requirement that they are able to show that they are workers or self-employed persons or that they have sufficient resources for themselves and their family members not to become a burden on the social assistance system of the host Member State during their period of residence and have comprehensive sickness insurance cover in the host Member State, or that they are members of the family, already constituted in the host Member State, of a person satisfying these requirements. "Sufficient resources" shall be as defined in Article 8(4).

Such family members shall retain their right of residence exclusively on a personal basis.

3.   The Union citizen's departure from the host Member State or his/her death shall not entail loss of the right of residence of his/her children or of the parent who has actual custody of the children, irrespective of nationality, if the children reside in the host Member State and are enrolled at an educational establishment, for the purpose of studying there, until the completion of their studies.

Article 13   Retention of the right of residence by family members in the event of divorce, annulment of marriage or termination of registered partnership

1.   Without prejudice to the second subparagraph, divorce, annulment of the Union citizen's marriage or termination of his/her registered partnership, as referred to in point 2(b) of Article 2 shall not affect the right of residence of his/her family members who are nationals of a Member State.

Before acquiring the right of permanent residence, the persons concerned must meet the conditions laid down in points (a), (b), (c) or (d) of Article 7(1).

2.   Without prejudice to the second subparagraph, divorce, annulment of marriage or termination of the registered partnership referred to in point 2(b) of Article 2 shall not entail loss of the right of residence of a Union citizen's family members who are not nationals of a Member State where:

(a)   prior to initiation of the divorce or annulment proceedings or termination of the registered partnership referred to in point 2(b) of Article 2, the marriage or registered partnership has lasted at least three years, including one year in the host Member State; or

(b)   by agreement between the spouses or the partners referred to in point 2(b) of Article 2 or by court order, the spouse or partner who is not a national of a Member State has custody of the Union citizen's children; or

(c)   this is warranted by particularly difficult circumstances, such as having been a victim of domestic violence while the marriage or registered partnership was subsisting; or

(d)   by agreement between the spouses or partners referred to in point 2(b) of Article 2 or by court order, the spouse or partner who is not a national of a Member State has the right of access to a minor child, provided that the court has ruled that such access must be in the host Member State, and for as long as is required.

Before acquiring the right of permanent residence, the right of residence of the persons concerned shall remain subject to the requirement that they are able to show that they are workers or self-employed persons or that they have sufficient resources for themselves and their family members not to become a burden on the social assistance system of the host Member State during their period of residence and have comprehensive sickness insurance cover in the host Member State, or that they are members of the family, already constituted in the host Member State, of a person satisfying these requirements. 'Sufficient resources' shall be as defined in Article 8(4).

Such family members shall retain their right of residence exclusively on personal basis.

Article 14   Retention of the right of residence

1.   Union citizens and their family members shall have the right of residence provided for in Article 6, as long as they do not become an unreasonable burden on the social assistance system of the host Member State.

2.   Union citizens and their family members shall have the right of residence provided for in Articles 7, 12 and 13 as long as they meet the conditions set out therein. In specific cases where there is a reasonable doubt as to whether a Union citizen or his/her family members

satisfies the conditions set out in Articles 7, 12 and 13, Member States may verify if these conditions are fulfilled. This verification shall not be carried out systematically.

3.   An expulsion measure shall not be the automatic consequence of a Union citizen's or his or her family member's recourse to the social assistance system of the host Member State.

4. By way of derogation from paragraphs 1 and 2 and without prejudice to the provisions of Chapter VI, an expulsion measure may in no case be adopted against Union citizens or their family members if:

(a) the Union citizens are workers or self-employed persons, or

(b) the Union citizens entered the territory of the host Member State in order to seek employment. In this case, the Union citizens and their family members may not be expelled for as long as the Union citizens can provide evidence that they are continuing to seek employment and that they have a genuine chance of being engaged.

Article 15   Procedural safeguards

1.   The procedures provided for by Articles 30 and 31 shall apply by analogy to all decisions restricting free movement of Union citizens and their family members on grounds other than public policy, public security or public health.

2.   Expiry of the identity card or passport on the basis of which the person concerned entered the host Member State and was issued with a registration certificate or residence card shall not constitute a ground for expulsion from the host Member State.

3.   The host Member State may not impose a ban on entry in the context of an expulsion decision to which paragraph 1 applies.

CHAPTER IV   RIGHT OF PERMANENT RESIDENCE

SECTION I   ELIGIBILITY

Article 16   General rule for Union citizens and their family members

1.   Union citizens who have resided legally for a continuous period of five years in the host Member State shall have the right of permanent residence there. This right shall not be subject to the conditions provided for in Chapter III.

2.   Paragraph 1 shall apply also to family members who are not nationals of a Member State and have legally resided with the Union citizen in the host Member State for a continuous period of five years.

3.   Continuity of residence shall not be affected by temporary absences not exceeding a total of six months a year, or by absences of a longer duration for compulsory military service, or by one absence of a maximum of twelve consecutive months for important reasons such as pregnancy and childbirth, serious illness, study or vocational training, or a posting in another Member State or a third country.

4.   Once acquired, the right of permanent residence shall be lost only through absence from the host Member State for a period exceeding two consecutive years.

Article 17   Exemptions for persons no longer working in the host Member State and their family members

1.   By way of derogation from Article 16, the right of permanent residence in the host Member State shall be enjoyed before completion of a continuous period of five years of residence by:

(a) workers or self-employed persons who, at the time they stop working, have reached the age laid down by the law of that Member State for entitlement to an old age pension or workers who cease paid employment to take early retirement, provided that they have been working in that Member State for at least the preceding twelve months and have resided there continuously for more than three years.

If the law of the host Member State does not grant the right to an old age pension to certain categories of self-employed persons, the age condition shall be deemed to have been met once the person concerned has reached the age of 60;

(b) workers or self-employed persons who have resided continuously in the host Member State for more than two years and stop working there as a result of permanent incapacity to work.

If such incapacity is the result of an accident at work or an occupational disease entitling the person concerned to a benefit payable in full or in part by an institution in the host Member State, no condition shall be imposed as to length of residence;

(c) workers or self-employed persons who, after three years of continuous employment and residence in the host Member State, work in an employed or self-employed capacity in another Member State, while retaining their place of residence in the host Member State, to which they return, as a rule, each day or at least once a week.

For the purposes of entitlement to the rights referred to in points (a) and (b), periods of employment spent in the Member State in which the person concerned is working shall be regarded as having been spent in the host Member State.

Periods of involuntary unemployment duly recorded by the relevant employment office, periods not worked for reasons not of the person's own making and absences from work or cessation of work due to illness or accident shall be regarded as periods of employment.

2.   The conditions as to length of residence and employment laid down in point (a) of paragraph 1 and the condition as to length of residence laid down in point (b) of paragraph 1 shall not apply if the worker's or the self-employed person's spouse or partner as referred to in point 2(b) of Article 2 is a national of the host Member State or has lost the nationality of that Member State by marriage to that worker or self-employed person.

3.   Irrespective of nationality, the family members of a worker or a self-employed person who are residing with him in the territory of the host Member State shall have the right of permanent residence in that Member State, if the worker or self-employed person has acquired himself the right of permanent residence in that Member State on the basis of paragraph 1.

4.   If, however, the worker or self-employed person dies while still working but before acquiring permanent residence status in the host Member State on the basis of paragraph 1, his family members who are residing with him in the host Member State shall acquire the right of permanent residence there, on condition that:

(a) the worker or self-employed person had, at the time of death, resided continuously on the territory of that Member State for two years; or

(b) the death resulted from an accident at work or an occupational disease; or

(c) the surviving spouse lost the nationality of that Member State following marriage to the worker or self-employed person.

Article 18   Acquisition of the right of permanent residence by certain family members who are not nationals of a Member State

Without prejudice to Article 17, the family members of a Union citizen to whom Articles 12(2) and 13(2) apply, who satisfy the conditions laid down therein, shall acquire the right of permanent residence after residing legally for a period of five consecutive years in the host Member State.

SECTION II   ADMINISTRATIVE FORMALITIES

Article 19   Document certifying permanent residence for Union citizens

1.   Upon application Member States shall issue Union citizens entitled to permanent residence, after having verified duration of residence, with a document certifying permanent residence.

2.   The document certifying permanent residence shall be issued as soon as possible.

Article 20   Permanent residence card for family members who are not nationals of a Member State

1.   Member States shall issue family members who are not nationals of a Member State entitled to permanent residence with a permanent residence card within six months of the submission of the application. The permanent residence card shall be renewable automatically every ten years.

2.   The application for a permanent residence card shall be submitted before the residence card expires. Failure to comply with the requirement to apply for a permanent residence card may render the person concerned liable to proportionate and non-discriminatory sanctions.

3.   Interruption in residence not exceeding two consecutive years shall not affect the validity of the permanent residence card.

Article 21   Continuity of residence

For the purposes of this Directive, continuity of residence may be attested by any means of proof in use in the host Member State. Continuity of residence is broken by any expulsion decision duly enforced against the person concerned.

CHAPTER V   PROVISIONS COMMON TO THE RIGHT OF RESIDENCE AND THE RIGHT OF PERMANENT RESIDENCE

Article 22   Territorial scope

The right of residence and the right of permanent residence shall cover the whole territory of the host Member State. Member States may impose territorial restrictions on the right of residence and the right of permanent residence only where the same restrictions apply to their own nationals.

Article 23   Related rights

Irrespective of nationality, the family members of a Union citizen who have the right of residence or the right of permanent residence in a Member State shall be entitled to take up employment or self-employment there.

Article 24   Equal treatment

1.   Subject to such specific provisions as are expressly provided for in the Treaty and secondary law, all Union citizens residing on the basis of this Directive in the territory of the host Member State shall enjoy equal treatment with the nationals of that Member State within the scope of the Treaty. The benefit of this right shall be extended to family members who are not nationals of a Member State and who have the right of residence or permanent residence.

2.   By way of derogation from paragraph 1, the host Member State shall not be obliged to confer entitlement to social assistance during the first three months of residence or, where appropriate, the longer period provided for in Article 14(4)(b), nor shall it be obliged, prior to acquisition of the right of permanent residence, to grant maintenance aid for studies, including vocational training, consisting in student grants or student loans to persons other than workers, self-employed persons, persons who retain such status and members of their families.

Article 25   General provisions concerning residence documents

1.   Possession of a registration certificate as referred to in Article 8, of a document certifying permanent residence, of a certificate attesting submission of an application for a family member residence card, of a residence card or of a permanent residence card, may under no circumstances be made a precondition for the exercise of a right or the completion of an administrative formality, as entitlement to rights may be attested by any other means of proof.

2.   All documents mentioned in paragraph 1 shall be issued free of charge or for a charge not exceeding that imposed on nationals for the issuing of similar documents.

Article 26   Checks

Member States may carry out checks on compliance with any requirement deriving from their national legislation for non-nationals always to carry their registration certificate or residence card, provided that the same requirement applies to their own nationals as regards their identity card. In the event of failure to comply with this requirement, Member States may impose the same sanctions as those imposed on their own nationals for failure to carry their identity card.

CHAPTER VI   RESTRICTIONS ON THE RIGHT OF ENTRY AND THE RIGHT OF RESIDENCE ON GROUNDS OF PUBLIC POLICY, PUBLIC SECURITY OR PUBLIC HEALTH

Article 27   General principles

1.   Subject to the provisions of this Chapter, Member States may restrict the freedom of movement and residence of Union citizens and their family members, irrespective of nationality, on grounds of public policy, public security or public health. These grounds shall not be invoked to serve economic ends.

2.   Measures taken on grounds of public policy or public security shall comply with the principle of proportionality and shall be based exclusively on the personal conduct of the individual concerned.

Previous criminal convictions shall not in themselves constitute grounds for taking such measures.

The personal conduct of the individual concerned must represent a genuine, present and sufficiently serious threat affecting one of the fundamental interests of society. Justifications that are isolated from the particulars of the case or that rely on considerations of general prevention shall not be accepted.

3.   In order to ascertain whether the person concerned represents a danger for public policy or public security, when issuing the registration certificate or, in the absence of a registration system, not later than three months from the date of arrival of the person concerned on its territory or from the date of reporting his/her presence within the territory, as provided for in Article 5(5), or when issuing the residence card, the host Member State may, should it consider this essential, request the Member State of origin and, if need be, other Member States to provide information concerning any previous police record the person concerned may have. Such enquiries shall not be made as a matter of routine. The Member State consulted shall give its reply within two months.

4.   The Member State which issued the passport or identity card shall allow the holder of the document who has been expelled on grounds of public policy, public security, or public health from another Member State to re-enter its territory without any formality even if the document is no longer valid or the nationality of the holder is in dispute.

Article 28   Protection against expulsion

1.   Before taking an expulsion decision on grounds of public policy or public security, the host Member State shall take account of considerations such as how long the individual concerned has resided on its territory, his/her age, state of health, family and economic situation, social and cultural integration into the host Member State and the extent of his/her links with the country of origin.

2.   The host Member State may not take an expulsion decision against Union citizens or their family members, irrespective of nationality, who have the right of permanent residence on its territory, except on serious grounds of public policy or public security.

3.   An expulsion decision may not be taken against Union citizens, except if the decision is based on imperative grounds of public security, as defined by Member States, if they:

   (a)   have resided in the host Member State for the previous ten years; or

(b) are a minor, except if the expulsion is necessary for the best interests of the child, as provided for in the United Nations Convention on the Rights of the Child of 20 November 1989.

Article 29 Public health

1. The only diseases justifying measures restricting freedom of movement shall be the diseases with epidemic potential as defined by the relevant instruments of the World Health Organisation and other infectious diseases or contagious parasitic diseases if they are the subject of protection provisions applying to nationals of the host Member State.

2. Diseases occurring after a three-month period from the date of arrival shall not constitute grounds for expulsion from the territory.

3. Where there are serious indications that it is necessary, Member States may, within three months of the date of arrival, require persons entitled to the right of residence to undergo, free of charge, a medical examination to certify that they are not suffering from any of the conditions referred to in paragraph 1. Such medical examinations may not be required as a matter of routine.

Article 30 Notification of decisions

1. The persons concerned shall be notified in writing of any decision taken under Article 27(1), in such a way that they are able to comprehend its content and the implications for them.

2. The persons concerned shall be informed, precisely and in full, of the public policy, public security or public health grounds on which the decision taken in their case is based, unless this is contrary to the interests of State security.

3. The notification shall specify the court or administrative authority with which the person concerned may lodge an appeal, the time limit for the appeal and, where applicable, the time allowed for the person to leave the territory of the Member State. Save in duly substantiated cases of urgency, the time allowed to leave the territory shall be not less than one month from the date of notification.

Article 31 Procedural safeguards

1. The persons concerned shall have access to judicial and, where appropriate, administrative redress procedures in the host Member State to appeal against or seek review of any decision taken against them on the grounds of public policy, public security or public health.

2. Where the application for appeal against or judicial review of the expulsion decision is accompanied by an application for an interim order to suspend enforcement of that decision, actual removal from the territory may not take place until such time as the decision on the interim order has been taken, except:
— where the expulsion decision is based on a previous judicial decision; or
— where the persons concerned have had previous access to judicial review; or
— where the expulsion decision is based on imperative grounds of public security under Article 28(3).

3. The redress procedures shall allow for an examination of the legality of the decision, as well as of the facts and circumstances on which the proposed measure is based. They shall ensure that the decision is not disproportionate, particularly in view of the requirements laid down in Article 28.

4. Member States may exclude the individual concerned from their territory pending the redress procedure, but they may not prevent the individual from submitting his/her defence in person, except when his/her appearance may cause serious troubles to public policy or public security or when the appeal or judicial review concerns a denial of entry to the territory.

Article 32 Duration of exclusion orders

1. Persons excluded on grounds of public policy or public security may submit an

application for lifting of the exclusion order after a reasonable period, depending on the circumstances, and in any event after three years from enforcement of the final exclusion order which has been validly adopted in accordance with Community law, by putting forward arguments to establish that there has been a material change in the circumstances which justified the decision ordering their exclusion.

The Member State concerned shall reach a decision on this application within six months of its submission.

2.   The persons referred to in paragraph 1 shall have no right of entry to the territory of the Member State concerned while their application is being considered.

Article 33   Expulsion as a penalty or legal consequence

1.   Expulsion orders may not be issued by the host Member State as a penalty or legal consequence of a custodial penalty, unless they conform to the requirements of Articles 27, 28 and 29.

2.   If an expulsion order, as provided for in paragraph 1, is enforced more than two years after it was issued, the Member State shall check that the individual concerned is currently and genuinely a threat to public policy or public security and shall assess whether there has been any material change in the circumstances since the expulsion order was issued.

CHAPTER VII   FINAL PROVISIONS

Article 34   Publicity

Member States shall disseminate information concerning the rights and obligations of Union citizens and their family members on the subjects covered by this Directive, particularly by means of awareness-raising campaigns conducted through national and local media and other means of communication.

Article 35   Abuse of rights

Member States may adopt the necessary measures to refuse, terminate or withdraw any right conferred by this Directive in the case of abuse of rights or fraud, such as marriages of convenience. Any such measure shall be proportionate and subject to the procedural safeguards provided for in Articles 30 and 31.

Article 36   Sanctions

Member States shall lay down provisions on the sanctions applicable to breaches of national rules adopted for the implementation of this Directive and shall take the measures required for their application. The sanctions laid down shall be effective and proportionate. Member States shall notify the Commission of these provisions not later than . . .* and as promptly as possible in the case of any subsequent changes.

Article 37   More favourable national provisions

The provisions of this Directive shall not affect any laws, regulations or administrative provisions laid down by a Member State which would be more favourable to the persons covered by this Directive.

Article 38   Repeals

1.   Articles 10 and 11 of Regulation (EEC) No. 1612/68 shall be repealed with effect from 30 April 2006.

2.   Directives 64/221/EEC, 68/360/EEC, 72/194/EEC, 73/148/EEC, 75/34/EEC, 75/35/EEC, 90/364/EEC, 90/365/EEC and 93/96/EEC shall be repealed with effect from 30 April 2006.

3.   References made to the repealed provisions and Directives shall be construed as being made to this Directive.

---

* Two years from the date of entry into force of this Directive.

Article 39   Report

No later than . . .* the Commission shall submit a report on the application of this Directive to the European Parliament and the Council, together with any necessary proposals, notably on the opportunity to extend the period of time during which Union citizens and their family members may reside in the territory of the host Member State without any conditions. The Member States shall provide the Commission with the information needed to produce the report.

Article 40   Transposition

1.   Member States shall bring into force the laws, regulations and administrative provisions necessary to comply with this Directive by 30 April 2006.

When Member States adopt those measures, they shall contain a reference to this Directive or shall be accompanied by such a reference on the occasion of their official publication. The methods of making such reference shall be laid down by the Member States.

2.   Member States shall communicate to the Commission the text of the provisions of national law which they adopt in the field covered by this Directive together with a table showing how the provisions of this Directive correspond to the national provisions adopted.

Article 41   Entry into force

This Directive shall enter into force on the day of its publication in the Official Journal of the European Union.**

Article 42   Addressees

This Directive is addressed to the Member States.

Done at Strasbourg, 29 April 2004.

For the European Parliament

The President

M. McDOWELL

For the Council

The President

P. COX

* Four years from the date of entry into force of this Directive although the corrected OJ now states 30 April 2006.

** **Editor's Note:** Which was 30 April 2004.

SOCIAL SECURITY

Council Regulation (EEC) No 1408/71 of 14 June 1971 as amended[1]

On the application of social security schemes to employed persons, to self-employed persons and to members of their families moving within the Community[2]

(Preamble omitted.)

TITLE I   GENERAL PROVISIONS

Article 1   Definitions

For the purpose of this Regulation:

(a) 'employed person' and 'self-employed person' mean respectively:

(i) any person who is insured, compulsorily or on an optional continued basis, for one or more of the contingencies covered by the branches of a social security scheme for employed or self-employed persons or by a special scheme for civil servants;

(ii) any person who is compulsorily insured for one or more of the contingencies covered by the branches of social security dealt with in this Regulation, under a social security scheme for all residents or for the whole working population, if such person:

— can be identified as an employed or self-employed person by virtue of the manner in which such scheme is administered or financed, or,

— failing such criteria, is insured for some other contingency specified in Annex I under a scheme for employed or self-employed persons, or under a scheme referred to in (iii), either compulsorily or on an optional continued basis, or, where no such scheme exists in the Member State concerned, complies with the definition given in Annex I;

(iii) any person who is compulsorily insured for several of the contingencies covered by the branches dealt with in this Regulation, under a standard social security scheme for the whole rural population in accordance with the criteria laid down in Annex I;

(iv) any person who is voluntarily insured for one or more of the contingencies covered by the branches dealt with in this Regulation, under a social security scheme of a Member State for employed or self-employed persons or for all residents or for certain categories of residents:

[1] **Editor's Note:** This is now the latest version to appear in which the Regulation has been reissued in a consolidated form as an annex to Regulation 118/97 [OJ No. L28/1 1997]. This includes all amendments up to and including Regulation 1399/99 and replaces the consolidation which previously appeared in OJ No. C325/1 1992. Further amendments to the Annexes have been made by Regulation 1386/2001 (OJ 2001, L187/1) and the 2003 Accession Treaties (OJ 2003, L236/197) but which do not affect the extracts here. Latest Regulation 631/2004 does make changes to these extracts.

[2] Council Regulation (EEC) No. 574/72 [OJ 1972, No. L74/1] lays down the procedure for implementing Regulation (EEC) 1408/71.

    — if such person carries out an activity as an employed or self-employed person, or

    — if such person has previously been compulsorily insured for the same contingency under a scheme for employed or self-employed persons of the same Member State;

(b) 'frontier worker' means any employed or self-employed person who pursues his occupation in the territory of a Member State and resides in the territory of another Member State to which he returns as a rule daily or at least once a week; however, a frontier worker who is posted elsewhere in the territory of the same or another Member State by the undertaking to which he is normally attached, or who engages in the provision of services elsewhere in the territory of the same or another Member State, shall retain the status of frontier worker for a period not exceeding four months, even if he is prevented, during that period, from returning daily or at least once a week to the place where he resides;

(c) 'seasonal worker' means any employed person who goes to the territory of a Member State other than the one in which he is resident to do work there of a seasonal nature for an undertaking or an employer of that State for a period which may on no account exceed eight months, and who stays in the territory of the said State for the duration of his work; work of a seasonal nature shall be taken to mean work which, being dependent on the succession of the seasons, automatically recurs each year;

(ca) 'student' means any person other than an employed or self-employed person or a member of his family or survivor within the meaning of this Regulation who studies or receives vocational training leading to a qualification officially recognised by the authorities of a Member State, and is insured under a general social security scheme or a special social security scheme applicable to students;

(d) 'refugee' shall have the meaning assigned to it in Article 1 of the Convention on the Status of Refugees, signed at Geneva on 28 July 1951;

(e) 'stateless person' shall have the meaning assigned to it in Article 1 of the Convention on the Status of Stateless Persons, signed in New York on 28 September 1954;

(f) (i) 'member of the family' means any person defined or recognised as a member of the family or designated as a member of the household by the legislation under which benefits are provided or, in the cases referred to in Articles 22(1)(a) and 31, by the legislation of the Member State in whose territory such person resides; where, however, the said legislations regard as a member of the family or a member of the household only a person living under the same roof as the employed or self-employed person or student, this condition shall be considered satisfied if the person in question is mainly dependent on that person. Where the legislation of a Member State does not enable members of the family to be distinguished from the other persons to whom it applies, the term 'member of the family' shall have the meaning given to it in Annex I;

    (ii) where, however, the benefits concerned are benefits for disabled persons granted under the legislation of a Member State to all nationals of that State who fulfil the prescribed conditions, the term 'member of the family' means at least the spouse of an employed or self-employed person or student and the children of such person who are either minors or dependent upon such person;

(g) 'survivor' means any person defined or recognised as such by the legislation under which the benefits are granted; where, however, the said legislation regards as a survivor only a person who was living under the same roof as the deceased, this condition shall be considered satisfied if such person was mainly dependent on the deceased;

(h) 'residence' means habitual residence;

(i) 'stay' means temporary residence;

(j) 'legislation' means in respect of each Member State statutes, regulations and other provisions and all other implementing measures, present or future, relating to the branches and schemes of social security covered by Article 4(1) and (2) or those special non-contributory benefits covered by Article 4(2a).

The term excludes provisions of existing or future industrial agreements, whether or not they have been the subject of a decision by the authorities rendering them compulsory or extending their scope. However, in so far as such provisions:

(i) serve to put into effect compulsory insurance imposed by the laws and regulations referred to in the preceding sub-paragraph; or

(ii) set up a scheme administered by the same institution as that which administers the schemes set up by the laws and regulations referred to in the preceding sub-paragraph.

The limitation on the term may at any time be lifted by a declaration of the Member State concerned specifying the schemes of such a kind to which this Regulation applies. Such a declaration shall be notified and published in accordance with the provisions of Article 97.

The provisions of the preceding sub-paragraph shall not have the effect of exempting from the application of this Regulation the schemes to which Regulation No 3 applied.

The term 'legislation' also excludes provisions governing special schemes for self-employed persons the creation of which is left to the initiatives of those concerned or which apply only to a part of the territory of the Member State concerned, irrespective of whether or not the authorities decided to make them compulsory or extend their scope. The special schemes in question are specified in Annex II;

(ja) 'special scheme for civil servants' means any social security scheme which is different from the general social security scheme applicable to employed persons in the Member States concerned and to which all, or certain categories of, civil servants or persons treated as such are directly subject;

(k) 'social security convention' means any bilateral or multilateral instrument which binds or will bind two or more Member States exclusively, and any other multilateral instrument which binds or will bind at least two Member States and one or more other States in the field of social security, for all or part of the branches and schemes set out in Article 4(1) and (2), together with agreements, of whatever kind, concluded pursuant to the said instruments;

(l) 'competent authority' means, in respect of each Member State, the Minister, Ministers or other equivalent authority responsible for social security schemes throughout or in any part of the territory of the State in question;

(m) 'Administrative Commission' means the Commissionreferred to in Article 80;

(n) 'institution' means, in respect of each Member State, the body or authority responsible for administering all or part of the legislation;

(o) 'competent institution' means:

(i) the institution with which the person concerned is insured at the time of the application for benefit; or

(ii) the institution from which the person concerned is entitled or would be entitled to benefits if he or a member or members of his family were resident in the territory of the Member State in which the institution is situated; or

(iii) the institution designated by the competent authority of the Member State concerned; or

(iv) in the case of a scheme relating to an employer's liability in respect of the benefits set out in Article 4(1), either the employer or the insurer involved or, in default thereof, a body or authority designated by the competent authority of the Member State concerned;

(p) 'institution of the place of residence' and 'institution of the place of stay' mean respectively the institution which is competent to provide benefits in the place where the person concerned resides and the institution which is competent to provide benefits in the place where the person concerned resides and the institution which is competent to provide benefits in the place where the person concerned is staying, under the legislation administered by that institution or, where no such institution exists, the institution designated by the competent authority of the Member State in question;

(q) 'competent State' means the Member State in whose territory the competent institution is situated;

(r) 'periods of insurance' means periods of contribution or period of employment or self-employment as defined or recognised as periods of insurance by the legislation under which they were completed or considered as completed, and all periods treated as such, where they are regarded by the said legislation as equivalent to periods of insurance. Periods completed under a special scheme for civil servants are also considered as periods of insurance;

(s) 'periods of employment' and 'periods of self-employment' mean periods so defined or recognised by the legislation under which they were completed, and all periods treated as such, where they are regarded by the said legislation as equivalent to periods of employment or of self-employment. Periods completed under a special scheme for civil servants are also considered as periods of employment;

(sa) 'periods of residence' means periods as defined or recognised as such by the legislation under which they were completed or considered as completed;

(t) 'benefits' and 'pensions' mean all benefits and pensions, including all elements thereof payable out of public funds, revalorisation increases and supplementary allowances, subject to the provisions of Title III, as also lump-sum benefits which may be paid in lieu of pensions, and payments made by way of reimbursement of contributions;

(u) (i) the term 'family benefits' means all benefits in kind or in cash intended to meet family expenses under the legislation provided for in Article 4(1)(h), excluding the special childbirth or adoption allowances referred to in Annex II;

(ii) 'family allowances' means periodical cash benefits granted exclusively by reference to the number and, where appropriate, the age of members of the family;

(v) 'death grants' means any once-for-all payment in the event of death, exclusive of the lump-sum benefits referred to in sub-paragraph (t).

Article 2   Persons covered

1. This Regulation shall apply to employed or self-employed persons and to students who are or have been subject to the legislation of one or more Member States and who are nationals of one of the Member States or who are stateless persons or refugees residing within the territory of one of the Member States, as well as to the members of their families and their survivors.

2. This Regulation shall apply to the survivors of employed or self-employed persons and of students who have been subject to the legislation of one or more Member States, irrespective of the nationality of such employed or self-employed persons, where their survivors are nationals of one of the Member States, or stateless persons or refugees residing within the territory of one of the Member States.

Article 3   Equality of treatment

1.   Subject to the special provisions of this Regulation, persons resident in the territory of one of the Member States to whom this Regulation applies shall be subject to the same obligations and enjoy the same benefits under the legislation of any Member State as the nationals of that State.

2.   The provisions of paragraph 1 shall apply to the right to elect members of the organs of social security institutions or to participate in their nomination, but shall not affect the legislative provisions of any Member State relating to eligibility or methods of nomination of persons concerned to those organs.

3.   Save as provided in Annex III, the provisions of social security conventions which remain in force pursuant to Article 7(2)(c) and the provisions of conventions concluded pursuant to Article 8(1), shall apply to all persons to whom this Regulation applies.

Article 4   Matters covered

1.   This Regulation shall apply to all legislation concerning the following branches of social security:
  (a) sickness and maternity benefits;
  (b) invalidity benefits, including those intended for the maintenance or improvement of earning capacity;
  (c) old-age benefits;
  (d) survivor's benefits;
  (e) benefits in respect of accidents at work and occupational diseases;
  (f) death grants;
  (g) unemployment benefits;
  (h) family benefits.

2.   This Regulation shall apply to all general and special social security schemes, whether contributory or non-contributory, and to schemes concerning the liability of an employer or shipowner in respect of the benefits referred to in paragraph 1.

2a.   This Regulation shall also apply to special non-contributory benefits which are provided under a legislation or schemes other than those referred to in paragraph 1 or excluded by virtue of paragraph 4, where such benefits are intended:
  (a) either to provide supplementary, substitute or ancillary cover against the risks covered by the branches of social security referred to in paragraph 1(a) to (h), or
  (b) solely as specific protection for the disabled.

2b.   This Regulation shall not apply to the provisions in the legislation of a Member State concerning special non-contributory benefits, referred to in Annex II, Section III, the validity of which is confined to part of its territory.

3.   The provisions of Title III of this Regulation shall not, however, affect the legislative provisions of any Member State concerning a shipowner's liability.

4.   This Regulation shall not apply to social and medical assistance, to benefit schemes for victims of war or its consequences.

Article 9   Admission to voluntary or optional continued insurance

1.   The provisions of the legislation of any Member State which make admission to voluntary or optional continued insurance conditional upon residence in the territory of that State shall not apply to persons resident in the territory of another Member State, provided that at some time in their past working life they were subject to the legislation of the first State as employed or as self-employed persons.

2.   Where, under the legislation of a Member State, admission to voluntary or optional continued insurance is conditional upon completion of periods of insurance, the periods of insurance or residence completed under the legislation of another Member State shall be taken into account, to the extent required, as if they were completed under the legislation of the first State.

Article 9a   Prolongation of the reference period
Where, under the legislation of a Member State, recognition of entitlement to a benefit is conditional upon completion of a minimum period of insurance during a specific period preceding the contingency insured against (reference period) and where the aforementioned legislation provides that the periods during which the benefits have been granted under the legislation of that Member State or periods devoted to the upbringing of children in the territory of that Member State shall give rise to prolongation of the reference period, periods during which invalidity pensions or old-age pensions or sickness benefits, unemployment benefits or benefits for accidents at work (except for pensions) have been awarded under the legislation of another Member State and periods devoted to the upbringing of children in the territory of another Member State shall likewise give rise to prolongation of the aforesaid reference period.

Article 10   Waiving of residence clauses—Effect of compulsory insurance on reimbursement of contributions
  1.   Save as otherwise provided in this Regulation invalidity, old-age or survivors' cash benefits, pensions for accidents at work or occupational diseases and death grants acquired under the legislation of one or more Member States shall not be subject to any reduction, modification, suspension, withdrawal or confiscation by reason of the fact that the recipient resides in the territory of a Member State other than that in which the institution responsible for payment is situated.
  The preceding sub-paragraph shall also apply to lump-sum benefits granted in cases of remarriage of a surviving spouse who was entitled to a survivor's pension.
  2.   Where under the legislation of a Member State reimbursement of contributions is conditional upon the person concerned having ceased to be subject to compulsory insurance, this condition shall not be considered satisfied as long as the person concerned is subject to compulsory insurance under the legislation of another Member State.

Article 10a   Special non-contributory benefits
  1.   Notwithstanding the provisions of Article 10 and Title III, persons to whom this Regulation applies shall be granted the special contributory cash benefits referred to in Article 4(2a) exclusively in the territory of the Member State in which they reside, in accordance with the legislation of that State, provided that such benefits are listed in Annex IIa. Such benefits shall be granted by and at the expense of the institution of the place of residence.
  2.   The institution of a Member State under whose legislation entitlement to benefits covered by paragraph 1 is subject to the completion of periods of employment, self-employment or residence shall regard, to the extent necessary, periods of employment, self-employment or residence completed in the territory of any other Member State as periods completed in the territory of the first Member State.
  3.   Where entitlement to a benefit covered by paragraph 1 but granted in the form of a supplement is subject, under the legislation of a Member State, to receipt of a benefit covered by Article 4(1)(a) to (h), and no such benefit is due under that legislation, any corresponding benefit granted under the legislation of any other Member State shall be treated as a benefit granted under the legislation of the first Member State for the purposes of entitlement to the supplement.
  4.   Where the granting of a disability or invalidity benefit covered by paragraph 1 is subject, under the legislation of a Member State to the condition that the disability or invalidity should be diagnosed for the first time in the territory of that Member State, this condition shall be deemed to be fulfilled where such diagnosis is made for the first time in the territory of another Member State.

Article 11   Revalorisation of benefits
Rules for revalorisation provided by the legislation of a Member State shall apply to benefits due under that legislation taking into account the provisions of this Regulation.

Article 12   Prevention of overlapping of benefits

1.   This Regulation can neither confer nor maintain the right to several benefits of the same kind for one and the same period of compulsory insurance. However, this provision shall not apply to benefits in respect of invalidity, old age, death (pensions) or occupational disease which are awarded by the institutions of two or more Member States, in accordance with the provisions of Article 41, 43(2) and (3), 46, 50 and 51 or Article 60(1)(b).

2.   Save as otherwise provided in this Regulation, the provisions of the legislations of a Member State governing the reduction, suspension or withdrawal of benefits in cases of overlapping with other social security benefits or any other form of income may be invoked even where such benefits were acquired under the legislation of another Member State or where such income was acquired in the territory of another Member State.

3.   The provisions of the legislation of a Member State for reduction, suspension or withdrawal of benefit in the case of a person in receipt of invalidity benefits or anticipatory old-age benefits pursuing a professional or trade activity may be invoked against such person even though he is pursuing his activity in the territory of another Member State.

4.   An invalidity pension payable under Netherlands legislation shall, in a case where the Netherlands institution is bound under the provisions of Article 57(5) or 60(2)(b) to contribute also to the cost of benefits for occupational disease granted under the legislation of another Member State be reduced by the amount payable to the institution of the other Member State which is responsible for granting the benefits for occupational disease.

TITLE II   DETERMINATION OF THE LEGISLATION APPLICABLE

Article 13   General rules

1.   Subject to Articles 14c and 14f, persons to whom this Regulation applies shall be subject to the legislation of a single Member State only. That legislation shall be determined in accordance with the provisions of this Title.

2.   Subject to Articles 14 to 17:

(a)   a person employed in the territory of one Member State shall be subject to the legislation of that State even if he resides in the territory of another Member State or if the registered office or place of business of the undertaking or individual employing him is situated in the territory of another Member State;

(b)   a person who is self-employed in the territory of one Member State shall be subject to the legislation of that State even if he resides in the territory of another Member State;

(c)   a person employed on board a vessel flying the flag of a Member State shall be subject to the legislation of that State;

(d)   civil servants and persons treated as such shall be subject to the legislation of the Member State to which the administration employing them is subject;

(e)   a person called up or recalled for service in the armed forces, or for civilian service, of a Member State shall be subject to the legislation of that State. If entitlement under that legislation is subject to the completion of periods of insurance before entry into or after release from such military or civilian service, periods of insurance completed under the legislation of any other Member State shall be taken into account, to the extent necessary, as if they were periods of insurance completed under the legislation of the first State. The employed or self-employed person called up or recalled for service in the armed forces or for civilian service shall retain the status of employed or self-employed person;

(f)   a person to whom the legislation of a Member State ceases to be applicable, without the legislation of another Member State becoming applicable to him in accordance with one of the rules laid down in the aforegoing sub-paragraphs or in accordance with one of the exceptions or special provisions laid down in Articles

14 to 17 shall be subject to the legislation of the Member State in whose territory he resides in accordance with the provisions of that legislation alone.

Article 14 Special rules applicable to persons, other than mariners, engaged in paid employment

Article 13(2)(a) shall apply subject to the following exceptions and circumstances;

1. (a) A person employed in the territory of a Member State by an undertaking to which he is normally attached who is posted by that undertaking to the territory of another Member State to perform work there for that undertaking shall continue to be subject to the legislation of the first Member State, provided that the anticipated duration of that work does not exceed 12 months and that he is not sent to replace another person who has completed his term of posting.

   (b) If the duration of the work to be done extends beyond the duration originally anticipated, owing to unforseeable circumstances, and exceeds 12 months, the legislation of the first Member State shall continue to apply until the completion of such work, provided that the competent authority of the Member State in whose territory the person concerned is posted or the body designated by that authority gives its consent; such consent must be requested before the end of the initial 12-month period. Such consent cannot, however, be given for a period exceeding 12 months.

2. A person normally employed in the territory of two or more Member States shall be subject to the legislation determined as follows:

   (a) A person who is a member of the travelling or flying personnel of an undertaking which, for hire or reward or on its own account, operates international transport services for passengers or goods by rail, road, air or inland waterway and has its registered office or place of business in the territory of a Member State, shall be subject to the legislation of the latter State, with the following restrictions:

      (i) where the said undertaking has a branch or permanent representation in the territory of a Member State other than that in which it has its registered office or place of business, a person employed by such branch or permanent representation shall be subject to the legislation of the Member State in whose territory such branch or permanent representation is situated;

      (ii) where a person is employed principally in the territory of the Member State in which he resides, he shall be subject to the legislation of that State, even if the undertaking which employs him has no registered office or place of business or branch or permanent representation in that territory;

   (b) A person other than that referred to in (a) shall be subject:

      (i) to the legislation of the Member State in whose territory he resides, if he pursues his activity partly in that territory or if he is attached to several undertakings or several employers who have their registered offices or places of business in the territory of different Member States;

      (ii) to the legislation of the Member State in whose territory is situated the registered office or place of business of the undertaking or individual employing him, if he does not reside in the territory of any of the Member States where he is pursuing his activity.

3. A person who is employed in the territory of one Member State by an undertaking which has its registered office or place of business in the territory of another Member State and which straddles the common frontier of these States shall be subject to the legislation of the Member State in whose territory the undertaking has its registered office or place of business.

Article 14a Special rules applicable to persons, other than mariners, who are self-employed

Article 13(2)(b) shall apply subject to the following exceptions and circumstances:

1. (a) A person normally self-employed in the territory of a Member State and who performs work in the territory of another Member State shall continue to be subject to the legislation of the first Member State, provided that the anticipated duration of the work does not exceed 12 months.

(b) If the duration of the work to be done extends beyond the duration originally anticipated, owing to unforeseeable circumstances, and exceeds 12 months, the legislation of the first Member State shall continue to apply until the completion of such work, provided that the competent authority of the Member State in whose territory the person concerned has entered to perform the work in question or the body appointed by that authority gives its consent; such consent must be requested before the end of the initial 12-month period. Such consent cannot, however, be given for a period exceeding 12 months.

2. A person normally employed in the territory of two or more Member States shall be subject to the legislation of the Member State in whose territory he resides if he pursues any part of his activity in the territory of that Member State. If he does not pursue any activity in the territory of the Member State in which he resides, he shall be subject to the legislation of the Member State in whose territory he pursues his main activity. The criteria used to determine the principal activity are laid down in the Regulation referred to in Article 98.

3. A person who is self-employed in an undertaking which has its registered office or place of business in the territory of one Member State and which straddles the common frontier of two Member States shall be subject to the legislation of the Member State in whose territory the undertaking has its registered office or place of business.

4. If the legislation to which a person should be subject in accordance with paragraphs 2 or 3 does not enable that person, even on a voluntary basis, to join a pension scheme, the person concerned shall be subject to the legislation of the other Member State which would apply apart from these particular provisions, or should the legislations of two or more Member States apply in this way, he shall be subject to the legislation decided on by common agreement amongst the Member States concerned or their competent authorities.

Article 15   Rules concerning voluntary insurance or optional continued insurance

1. Articles 13 to 14d shall not apply to voluntary insurance or to optional insurance unless, in respect of one of the branches referred to in Article 4, there exists in any Member State only a voluntary scheme of insurance.

2. Where application of the legislations of two or more Member States entails overlapping of insurance:

— under a compulsory insurance scheme and one or more voluntary or optional continued insurance schemes, the person concerned shall be subject exclusively to the compulsory insurance scheme,

— under two or more voluntary or optional continued insurance schemes, the person concerned may join only the voluntary or optional continued insurance scheme for which he has opted.

3. However, in respect of invalidity, old age and death (pensions), the person concerned may join the voluntary or optional continued insurance scheme of a Member State, even if he is compulsorily subject to the legislation of another Member State, to the extent that such overlapping is explicitly or implicitly admitted in the first Member State.

TITLE III   SPECIAL PROVISIONS RELATING TO THE VARIOUS CATEGORIES OF BENEFITS

CHAPTER 1   SICKNESS AND MATERNITY

SECTION 1   COMMON PROVISIONS

Article 18   Aggregation of periods of insurance, employment or residence

1.   The competent institution of a Member State whose legislation makes the acquisition, retention or recovery of the right to benefits conditional upon the completion of periods of insurance, employment or residence shall, to the extent necessary, take account of periods of insurance, employment or residence completed under the legislation of any other Member State as if they were periods completed under the legislation which it administers.

2.   The provisions of paragraph 1 shall apply to seasonal workers, even in respect of periods prior to any break in insurance exceeding the period allowed by the legislation of the competent State, provided, however, that the person concerned has not ceased to be insured for a period exceeding four months.

SECTION 2   EMPLOYED OR SELF-EMPLOYED PERSONS AND MEMBERS OF THEIR FAMILIES

Article 19   Residence in a Member State other than the competent State— General rules

1.   An employed or self-employed person residing in the territory of a Member State other than the competent State, who satisfies the conditions of the legislation of the competent State for entitlement to benefits, taking account where appropriate of the provisions of Article 18, shall receive in the State in which he is resident:

(a)   benefits in kind provided on behalf of the competent institution by the institution of the place of residence in accordance with the provisions of the legislation administered by that institution as though he were insured with it;

(b)   cash benefits provided by the competent institution in accordance with the legislation which it administers. However, by agreement between the competent institution and the institution of the place of residence, such benefits may be provided by the latter institution on behalf of the former, in accordance with the legislation of the competent State.

2.   The provisions of paragraph 1 shall apply by analogy to members of the family who reside in the territory of a Member State other than the competent State in so far as they are not entitled to such benefits under the legislation of the State in whose territory they reside.

Where the members of the family reside in the territory of a Member State under whose legislation the right to receive benefits in kind is not subject to condition of insurance or employment, benefits in kind which they receive shall be considered as being on behalf of the institution with which the employed or self-employed person is insured, unless the spouse or the person looking after the children pursues a professional or trade activity in the territory of the said Member State.

Article 20   Frontier workers and members of their families—Special rules

A frontier worker may also obtain benefits in the territory of the competent State. Such benefits shall be provided by the competent institution in accordance with the provisions of the legislation of that State, as though the person concerned were resident in that State. Members of his family may receive benefits under the same conditions; however, receipt of such benefits shall, except in urgent cases, be conditional upon an agreement between the States concerned or between the competent authorities of those States or, in its absence, on prior authorisation by the competent institution.

Article 21   Stay in or transfer of residence to the competent State

1.   The employed or self-employed person referred to in Article 19(1) who is staying in the territory of the competent State shall receive benefits in accordance with the provisions of the legislation of that State as though he were resident there, even if he has already received benefits for the same case of sickness or maternity before his stay.

2.   Paragraph 1 shall apply by analogy to the members of the family referred to in Article 19(2).

However, where the latter reside in the territory of a Member State other than the one in whose territory the employed or self-employed person resides, benefits in kind shall be provided by the institution of the place of stay on behalf of the institution of the place of residence of the persons concerned.

3.   Paragraphs 1 and 2 shall not apply to frontier workers and the members of their families.

4.   An employed or self-employed person and members of his family referred to in Article 19 who transfer their residence to the territory of the competent State shall receive benefits in accordance with the provisions of the legislation of that State even if they have already received benefits for the same case of sickness or maternity before transferring their residence.

Article 22   Stay outside the competent State—Return to or transfer of residence to another Member State during sickness or maternity—Need to go to another Member State in order to receive appropriate treatment

1.   An employed or self-employed person who satisfies the conditions of the legislation of the competent State for entitlement to benefits, taking account where appropriate of the provisions of Article 18, and:

(a)   whose condition requires benefits in kind which become necessary on medical grounds during a stay in the territory of another Member State, taking into account the nature of the benefits and the expected length of the stay; or

(b)   who, having become entitled to benefits chargeable to the competent institution, is authorised by that institution to return to the territory of the Member State where he resides, or to transfer his residence to the territory of another Member State; or

(c)   who is authorised by the competent institution to go to the territory of another Member State to receive there the treatment appropriate to his condition,

shall be entitled:

(i)   to benefits in kind provided on behalf of the competent institution by the institution of the place of stay or residence in accordance with the provisions of the legislation which it administers, as though he were insured with it; the length of the period during which benefits are provided shall be governed, however, by the legislation of the competent State;

(ii)   to cash benefits provided by the competent institution in accordance with the provisions of the legislation which it administers. However, by agreement between the competent institution and the institution of the place of stay or residence, such benefits may be provided by the latter institution on behalf of the former, in accordance with the provisions of the legislation of the competent State.

1a.   The Administrative Commission shall establish a list of benefits in kind which, in order to be provided during a stay in another Member State, require, for practical reasons, a prior agreement between the person concerned and the institution providing the care.

2.   The authorisation required under paragraph 1(b) may be refused only if it is established that movement of the person concerned would be prejudicial to his state of health or the receipt of medical treatment.

The authorisation required under paragraph 1(c) may not be refused where the treatment in question is among the benefits provided for by the legislation of the Member State on whose territory the person concerned resides and where he cannot be given such treatment within the time normally necessary for obtaining the treatment in question in the Member State of residence taking account of his current state of health and the probable course of the disease.

3.   Paragraphs 1, 1a and 2 shall apply by analogy to members of the family of an employed or self-employed person.

However, for the purpose of applying paragraph 1(a) and (c)(i) to the members of the family referred to in Article 19(2) who reside in the territory of a Member State other than the one in whose territory the employed or self-employed person resides:

(a)   benefits in kind shall be provided on behalf of the institution of the Member State in whose territory the members of the family are residing by the institution of the place of stay in accordance with the provisions of the legislation which it administers as if the employed or self-employed person were insured there. The period during which benefits are provided shall, however, be that laid down under the legislation of the Member State in whose territory the members of the family are residing;

(b)   the authorisation required under paragraph 1(c) shall be issued by the institution of the Member State in whose territory the members of the family are residing.

4.   The fact that the provisions of paragraph 1 apply to an employed or self-employed person shall not affect the right to benefit of members of his family.

Article 22a   Special rules for certain categories of persons

Notwithstanding Article 2, Article 22(1)(a) and (c) and (1a) shall also apply to persons who are nationals of one of the Member States and are insured under the legislation of a Member State and to the members of their families residing with them.

Article 23   Calculation of cash benefits

1.   The competent institution of a Member State whose legislation provides that the calculation of cash benefits shall be based on average earnings or on average contributions, shall determine such average earnings or contributions exclusively by reference to earnings or contributions completed under the said legislation.

2.   The competent institution of a Member State whose legislation provides that the calculation of cash benefits shall be based on standard earnings, shall take account exclusively of the standard earnings or, where appropriate, of the average of standard earnings for the periods completed under the said legislation.

3.   The competent institution of a Member State under whose legislation the amount of cash benefits varies with the number of members of the family, shall also take into account the members of the family of the person concerned who are resident in the territory of another Member State as if they were resident in the territory of the competent State.

Article 24   Substantial benefits in kind

1.   Where the right of an employed or self-employed person or a member of his family to a prosthesis, a major appliance or other substantial benefits in kind has been recognised by the institution of a Member State before he becomes insured with the institution of another Member State, the said employed or self-employed person shall receive such benefits at the expense of the first institution, even if they are granted after he becomes insured with the second institution.

2.   The Administrative Commission shall draw up the list of benefits to which the provisions of paragraph 1 apply.

SECTION 3   UNEMPLOYED PERSONS AND MEMBERS OF THEIR FAMILIES

Article 25

1.   An unemployed person who was formerly employed or self-employed and to whom the provisions of Article 69(1) or Article 71(1)(b)(ii), second sentence apply and who satisfies the conditions laid down in the legislation of the competent State for entitlement to benefits in kind and cash benefits, taking account where necessary of the provisions of Article 18, shall receive for the period of time referred to in Article 69(1)(c):

(a)   benefits in kind which become necessary on medical grounds for this person during his stay in the territory of the Member State where he is seeking employment, taking account of the nature of the benefits and the expected length of the stay. These benefits in kind shall be provided on behalf of the competent institution by the institution of the Member State in which the person is seeking employment, in accordance with the provisions of the legislation which the latter institution administers, as if he were insured with it;

(b)   cash benefits provided by the competent institution in accordance with the provisions of the legislation which it administers. However, by agreement between the competent institution and the institution of the Member State in which the unemployed person seeks employment, benefits may be provided by the latter institution on behalf of the former institution in accordance with the provisions of the legislation of the competent State. Unemployment benefits under Article 69(1) shall not be granted for the period during which cash benefits are received.

1a.   Article 22(1a) shall apply by analogy.

2.   A totally unemployed person who was formerly employed and to whom the provisions of Article 71(1)(a)(ii) or the first sentence of Article 71(1)(b)(ii) apply, shall receive benefits in kind and in cash in accordance with the provisions of the legislation of the Member State in whose territory he resides, as though he had been subject to that legislation during his last employment, taking account where appropriate of the provisions of Article 18; the cost of such benefits shall be met by the institution of the country of residence.

3.   Where an unemployed person satisfies the conditions of the legislation of the Member State which is responsible for the cost of unemployment benefits for entitlement to sickness and maternity benefits, taking account where appropriate of the provisions of Article 18, the members of his family shall receive these benefits, irrespective of the Member State in whose territory they reside or are staying. Such benefits shall be provided:

(i)   with regard to benefits in kind, by the institution of the place of residence or stay in accordance with the provisions of the legislation which it administers, on behalf of the competent institution of the Member State which is responsible for the cost of unemployment benefits;

(ii)   with regard to cash benefits, by the competent institution of the Member State which is responsible for the cost of unemployment benefits, in accordance with the legislation which it administers.

4.   Without prejudice to any provisions of the legislation of a Member State which permit an extension of the period during which sickness benefits may be granted, the period provided for in paragraph 1 may, in cases of *force majeure*, be extended by the competent institution within the limit fixed by the legislation administered by that institution.

Article 25a   Contributions payable by wholly unemployed persons

The institution which is responsible for granting benefits in kind and cash benefits to the unemployed persons referred to in Article 25(2) and which belongs to a Member State whose legislation provides for deduction of contributions payable by unemployed persons to cover sickness and maternity benefits shall be authorised to make such deductions in accordance with the provisions of its legislation.

CHAPTER 3   OLD AGE AND DEATH (PENSIONS)

Article 44   General provisions for the award of benefits when an employed or self-employed person has been subject to the legislation of two or more Member States
   1.   The rights to benefits of an employed or self-employed person who has been subject to the legislation of two or more Member States, or of his survivors, shall be determined in accordance with the provisions of this Chapter.
   2.   Save as otherwise provided in Article 49, the processing of a claim for an award submitted by the person concerned shall have regard to all the legislations to which the employed or self-employed person has been subject. Exception shall be made to this rule if the person concerned expressly asks for postponement of the award of old-age benefits to which he would be entitled under the legislation of one or more Member States.
   3.   This Chapter shall not apply to increases in or supplements to pensions in respect of children or to orphans' pensions to be granted in accordance with the provisions of Chapter 8.

Article 45   Consideration of periods of insurance or of residence completed under the legislations to which an employed or self-employed person was subject, for the acquisition, retention or recovery of the right to benefits
   1.   Where the legislation of a Member State makes the acquisition, retention or recovery of the right to benefits, under a scheme which is not a special scheme within the meaning of paragraphs 2 or 3, subject to the completion of periods of insurance or of residence, the competent institution of that Member State shall take account, where necessary, of the periods of insurance or of residence under the legislation of any other Member State, be it under a general scheme or under a special scheme and either as an employed person or a self-employed person. For that purpose, it shall take account of these periods as if they had been completed under its own legislation.
   2.   Where the legislation of a Member State makes the granting of certain benefits conditional upon the periods of insurance having been completed only in an occupation which is subject to a special scheme for employed persons or, where appropriate, in a specific employment, periods completed under the legislation of other Member States shall be taken into account for the granting of these benefits only if completed under a corresponding scheme or, failing that, in the same occupation or, where appropriate, in the same employment. If, account having been taken of the periods thus completed, the person concerned does not satisfy the conditions for receipt of these benefits, these periods shall be taken into account for the granting of the benefits under the general scheme or, failing that, under the scheme applicable to manual or clerical workers, as the case may be, subject to the condition that the person has been affiliated to one or other of these schemes.
   3.   Where the legislation of a Member State makes the granting of certain benefits conditional upon the periods of insurance having been completed only in an occupation subject to a special scheme for self-employed persons, periods completed under the legislations of other Member States shall be taken into account for the granting of these benefits only if completed under a corresponding scheme or, failing that, in the same occupation. The special schemes for self-employed persons referred to in this paragraph are listed in Annex I, part B, for each Member State concerned. If, account having been taken of the periods referred to in this paragraph, the person concerned does not satisfy the conditions for receipt of these benefits, these periods shall be taken into account for the granting of the benefit under the general scheme or, failing this, under the scheme applicable to manual or clerical workers, as the case may be, subject to the condition that the person concerned has been affiliated to one or other of these schemes.
   4.   The periods of insurance completed under a special scheme of a Member State shall be taken into account under the general scheme or, failing that, under the scheme applicable to manual or clerical workers, as the case may be, of another Member State for the acquisition,

retention or recovery of the right to benefits, subject to the condition that the person concerned has been affiliated to one or other of these schemes, even if these periods have already been taken into account in the latter State under a scheme referred to in paragraph 2 or in the first sentence of paragraph 3.

5. Where the legislation of a Member State makes the acquisition, retention or recovery of the right to benefits conditional upon the person concerned being insured at the time of the materialisation of the risk, this condition shall be regarded as having been satisfied in the case of insurance under the legislation of another Member State, in accordance with the procedures provided for in Annex VI for each Member State concerned.

6. A period of full unemployment of a worker to whom Article 7(1)(a)(ii) or (b)(ii), first sentence, applies shall be taken into account by the competent institution of the Member State in whose territory the worker concerned resides in accordance with the legislation administered by that institution, as if that legislation applied to him during his last employment.

Where that institution applies legislation providing for deduction of contributions payable by unemployed persons to cover old age pensions and death, it shall be authorised to make such deductions in accordance with the provisions of its legislation.

If the period of full unemployment in the country of residence of the person concerned can be taken into account only if contribution periods have been completed in that country, this condition shall be deemed to be fulfilled if the contribution periods have been completed in another Member State.

Article 46 Award of benefits

1. Where the conditions required by the legislation of a Member State for entitlement to benefits have been satisfied without having to apply Article 45 or Article 40(3), the following rules shall apply:

   (a) the competent institution shall calculate the amount of the benefit that would be due:

      (i) on the one hand, only under the provisions of the legislation which it administers;

      (ii) on the other hand, pursuant to paragraph 2;

   (b) the competent institution may, however, waive the calculation to be carried out in accordance with (a)(ii) if the result of this calculation, apart from differences arising from the use of round figures, is equal to or lower than the result of the calculation carried out in accordance with (a)(i), insofar as that institution does not apply any legislation containing rules against overlapping as referred to in Articles 46b and 46c or if the aforementioned institution applies a legislation containing rules against overlapping in the case referred to in Article 46c, provided that the said legislation lays down that benefits of a different kind shall be taken into consideration only on the basis of the relation of the periods of insurance or of residence completed under that legislation alone to the periods of insurance or of residence required by that legislation in order to qualify for full benefit entitlement.

Annex IV, part C, lists for each Member State concerned the cases where the two calculations would lead to a result of this kind.

2. Where the conditions required by the legislation of a Member State for entitlement to benefits are satisfied only after application of Article 45 and/or Article 40(3), the following rules shall apply:

   (a) the competent institution shall calculate the theoretical amount of the benefit to which the person concerned could lay claim provided all periods of insurance and/ or of residence, which have been completed under the legislation of the Member States to which the employed person or self-employed person was subject, have been completed in the State in question under the legislation which it administers on the date of the award of the benefit. If, under this legislation, the amount of the benefit is independent of the duration of the periods completed, the amount shall be regarded as being the theoretical amount referred to in this paragraph;

(b) the competent institution shall subsequently determine the actual amount of the benefit on the basis of the theoretical amount referred to in the preceding paragraph in accordance with the ratio of the duration of the periods of insurance or of residence completed before the materialisation of the risk under the legislation which it administers to the total duration of the periods of insurance and of residence completed before the materialisation of the risk under the legislations of all the Member States concerned.

3.   The person concerned shall be entitled to the highest amount calculated in accordance with paragraphs 1 and 2 from the competent institution of each Member State without prejudice to any application of the provisions concerning reduction, suspension or withdrawal provided for by the legislation under which this benefit is due.

Where that is the case, the comparison to be carried out shall relate to the amounts determined after the application of the said provisions.

4.   When, in the case of invalidity, old-age or survivor's pensions, the total of the benefits due from the competent institutions of two or more Member States under the provisions of a multilateral social security convention referred to in Article 6(b) does not exceed the total which would be due from such Member States under paragraphs 1 to 3, the person concerned shall benefit from the provisions of this Chapter.

Article 46a   General provisions relating to reduction, suspension or withdrawal applicable to benefits in respect of invalidity, old age or survivors under the legislations of the Member States

1.   For the purposes of this Chapter, overlapping of benefits of the same kind shall have the following meaning: all overlapping of benefits in respect of invalidity, old age and survivors calculated or provided on the basis of periods of insurance and/or residence completed by one and the same person.

2.   For the purposes of this Chapter, overlapping of benefits of different kinds means all overlapping of benefits that cannot be regarded as being of the same kind within the meaning of paragraph 1.

3.   The following rules shall be applicable for the application of provisions on reduction, suspension or withdrawal laid down by the legislation of a Member State in the case of overlapping of a benefit in respect of invalidity, old age or survivors with a benefit of the same kind or a benefit of a different kind or with other income:

(a) account shall be taken of the benefits acquired under the legislation of another Member State or of other income acquired in another Member State only where the legislation of the first Member State provides for the taking into account of benefits or income acquired abroad;

(b) account shall be taken of the amount of benefits to be granted by another Member State before deduction of taxes, social security contributions and other individual levies or deductions;

(c) no account shall be taken of the amount of benefits acquired under the legislation of another Member State which are awarded on the basis of voluntary insurance or continued optional insurance;

(d) where provisions on reduction, suspension or withdrawal are applicable under the legislation of only one Member State on account of the fact that the person concerned receives benefits of a similar or different kind payable under the legislation of other Member States or other income acquired within the territory of other Member States, the benefit payable under the legislation of the first Member State may be reduced only within the limit of the amount of the benefits payable under the legislation or the income acquired within the territory of other Member States.

Article 46b   Special provisions applicable in the case of overlapping of benefits of the same kind under the legislation of two or more Member States

1.   The provisions on reduction, suspension or withdrawal laid down by the legislation of a Member State shall not be applicable to a benefit calculated in accordance with Article 46(2).

2.   The provisions on reduction, suspension or withdrawal laid down by the legislation of a Member State shall apply to a benefit calculated in accordance with Article 46(1)(a)(i) only if the benefit concerned is:

(a)   either a benefit, which is referred to in Annex IV, part D, the amount of which does not depend on the length of the periods of insurance or of residence completed; or

(b)   a benefit, the amount of which is determined on the basis of a credited period deemed to have been completed between the date on which the risk materialised and a later date. In the latter case, the said provisions shall apply in the case of overlapping of such a benefit:

(i)   either with a benefit of the same kind, except where an agreement has been concluded between two or more Member States providing that one and the same credited period may not be taken into account two or more times;

(ii)   or with a benefit of the type referred to in (a).

The benefits and agreements referred to in (b) are mentioned in Annex IV, part D.

Article 46c   Special provisions applicable in the case of overlapping of one or more benefits referred to in Article 46a(1) with one or more benefits of a different kind or with other income, where two or more Member States are concerned

1.   If the receipt of benefits of a different kind or other income entails the reduction, suspension or withdrawal of two or more benefits referred to in Article 46(1)(a)(i), the amounts which would not be paid in strict application of the provisions concerning reduction, suspension or withdrawal provided for by the legislation of the Member States concerned shall be divided by the number of benefits subject to reduction, suspension or withdrawal.

2.   Where the benefit in question is calculated in accordance with Article 46(2), the benefit or benefits of a different kind from other Member States or other income and all other elements provided for by the legislation of the Member State for the application of the provisions in respect of reduction, suspension or withdrawal shall be taken into account in proportion to the periods of insurance and/or residence referred to in Article 46(2)(b), and shall be used for the calculation of the said benefit.

3.   If the receipt of benefits of a different kind or of other income entails reduction, suspension or withdrawal of one or more benefits referred to in Article 46(1)(a)(i), and of one or more benefits referred to in Article 46(2), the following rules shall apply:

(a)   where in a case of a benefit or benefits referred to in Article 46(1)(a)(i), the amounts which would not be paid in strict application of the provisions concerning reduction, suspension or withdrawal provided for by the legislation of the Member States concerned shall be divided by the number of benefits subject to reduction, suspension or withdrawal;

(b)   where in a case of a benefit or benefits calculated in accordance with Article 46(2), the reduction, suspension or withdrawal shall be carried out in accordance with paragraph 2.

4.   Where, in the case referred to in paragraph 1 and 3(a), the legislation of a Member State provides that, for the application of provisions concerning reduction, suspension or withdrawal, account shall be taken of benefits of a different kind and/or other income and all other elements in proportion to the periods of insurance referred to in Article 46(2)(b), the division provided for in the said paragraphs shall not apply in respect of that Member State.

5.   All the abovementioned provisions shall apply *mutatis mutandis* where the legislation of one or more Member States provides that the right to a benefit cannot be acquired in the case where the person concerned is in receipt of a benefit of a different kind, payable under the legislation of another Member State, or of other income.

Article 50   Award of a supplement where the total of benefits payable under the legislations of the various Member States does not amount to the minimum laid down by the legislation of the State in whose territory the receipient resides

A recipient of benefits to whom the Chapter applies may not, in the State in whose territory he resides and under whose legislation a benefit is payable to him, be awarded a benefit which is less than the minimum benefit fixed by that legislation for a period of insurance or residence equal to all the periods of insurance taken into account for the payment in accordance with the preceding Articles. The competent institution of that State shall, if necessary, pay him throughout the period of his residence in its territory a supplement equal to the difference between the total of the benefits payable under this Chapter and the amount of the minimum benefit.

Article 51   Revalorisation and recalculation of benefits

1.   If, by reason of an increase in the cost of living or changes in the level of wages or salaries or other reasons for adjustment, the benefits of the States concerned are altered by a fixed percentage or amount, such percentage or amount must be applied directly to the benefits determined under Article 46, without the need for a recalculation in accordance with that Article.

2.   On the other hand, if the method of determining benefits or the rules for calculating benefits should be altered, a recalculation shall be carried out in accordance with Article 46.

CHAPTER 4   ACCIDENTS AT WORK AND OCCUPATIONAL
DISEASES SECTION 1   RIGHT TO BENEFITS

Article 52   Residence in a Member State other than the competent State— General rules

An employed or self-employed person who sustains an accident at work or contracts an occupational disease, and who is residing in the territory of a Member State other than the competent State, shall receive in the State in which he is residing:

(a)   benefits in kind, provided on behalf of the competent institution by the institutions of his place of residence in accordance with the provisions of the legislation which it administers as if he were insured with it;

(b)   cash benefits provided by the competent institution in accordance with the provisions of the legislation which it administers. However, by agreement between the competent institution and the institution of the place of residence, these benefits may be provided by the latter institution on behalf of the former in accordance with the legislation of the competent State.

CHAPTER 6   UNEMPLOYMENT BENEFITS

SECTION 1   COMMON PROVISIONS

Article 67   Aggregation of periods of insurance or employment

1.   The competent institution of a Member State whose legislation makes the acquisition, retention or recovery of the right to benefits subject to the completion of periods of insurance shall take into account, to the extent necessary, periods of insurance or employment completed as an employed person under the legislation of any other Member State, as though they

were periods of insurance completed under the legislation which it administers, provided, however, that the periods of employment would have been counted as periods of insurance had they been completed under that legislation.

2.   The competent institution of a Member State whose legislation makes the acquisition, retention or recovery of the right to benefits subject to the completion of periods of employment shall take into account, to the extent necessary, periods of insurance or employment completed as an employed person under the legislation of any other Member State, as though they were periods of employment completed under the legislation which it administers.

3.   Except in the cases referred to in Article 71(1)(a)(ii) and (b)(ii), application of the provisions of paragraphs 1 and 2 shall be subject to the condition that the person concerned should have completed lastly:

— in the case of paragraph 1, periods of insurance,

— in the case of paragraph 2, periods of employment,

in accordance with the provisions of the legislation under which the benefits are claimed.

4.   Where the length of the period during which benefits may be granted depends on the length of periods of insurance or employment, the provisions of paragraph 1 or 2 shall apply, as appropriate.

Article 68   Calculation of benefits

1.   The competent institution of a Member State whose legislation provides that the calculation of benefits should be based on the amount of the previous wage or salary shall take into account exclusively the wage or salary received by the person concerned in respect of his last employment in the territory of the State. However, if the person concerned had been in his last employment in that territory for less than four weeks, the benefits shall be calculated on the basis of the normal wage or salary corresponding, in the place where the unemployed person is residing or staying, to an equivalent or similar employment to his last employment in the territory of another Member State.

2.   The competent institution of a Member State whose legislation provides that the amount of benefits varies with the number of members of the family, shall take into account also members of the family of the person concerned who are residing in the territory of another Member State, as though they were residing in the territory of the competent State. This provision shall not apply if, in the country of residence of the members of the family, another person is entitled to unemployment benefits for the calculation of which the members of the family are taken into consideration.

SECTION 2   UNEMPLOYED PERSONS GOING TO A MEMBER STATE
OTHER THAN THE COMPETENT STATE

Article 69   Conditions and limits for the retention of the right to benefits

1.   An employed or self-employed person who is wholly unemployed and who satisfies the conditions of the legislation of a Member State for entitlement to benefits and who goes to one or more other Member States in order to seek employment there shall retain his entitlement to such benefits under the following conditions and within the following limits:

(a) Before his departure, he must have been registered as a person seeking work and have remained available to the employment services of the competent State for at least four weeks after becoming unemployed. However, the competent services or institutions may authorise his departure before such time has expired;

(b) He must register as a person seeking work with the employment services of each of the Member States to which he goes and be subject to the control procedure organised therein. This condition shall be considered satisfied for the period before registration if the person concerned registered within seven days of the date when he ceased to be available to the employment services of the State he left. In exceptional cases, this period may be extended by the competent services or institutions;

(c) Entitlement to benefits shall continue for a maximum period of three months from the date when the person concerned ceased to be available to the employment services of the State which he left, provided that the total duration of the benefits does not exceed the duration of the period of benefits he was entitled to under the legislation of that State. In the case of a seasonal worker such duration shall, moreover, be limited to the period remaining until the end of the season for which he was engaged.

2. If the person concerned returns to the competent State before the expiry of the period during which he is entitled to benefits under the provisions of paragraph 1(c), he shall continue to be entitled to benefits under the legislation of that State; he shall lose all entitlement to benefits under the legislation of the competent State if he does not return there before the expiry of that period. In exceptional cases, this time limit may be extended by the competent services or institutions.

3. The provisions of paragraph 1 may be invoked only once between two periods of employment.

4. Where the competent State is Belgium, an unemployed person who returns there after the expiry of the three month period laid down in paragraph 1(c), shall not requalify for benefits in that country until he has been employed there for at least three months.

Article 70   Provision of benefits and reimbursements

1. In the cases referred to in Article 69(1), benefits shall be provided by the institution of each of the States to which an unemployed person goes to seek employment.

The competent institution of the Member State to whose legislation an employed or self-employed person was subject at the time of his last employment shall be obliged to reimburse the amount of such benefits.

2. The reimbursements referred to in paragraph 1 shall be determined and made in accordance with the procedure laid down by the implementing Regulation referred to in Article 98, on proof of actual expenditure, or by lump sum payments.

3. Two or more Member States, or the competent authorities of those States, may provide for other methods of reimbursement or payment, or may waive all reimbursement between the institutions coming under their jurisdiction.

SECTION 3   UNEMPLOYED PERSONS WHO, DURING THEIR LAST EMPLOYMENT, WERE RESIDING IN A MEMBER STATE OTHER THAN THE COMPETENT STATE

Article 71

1. An unemployed person who was formerly employed and who, during his last employment, was residing in the territory of a Member State other than the competent State shall receive benefits in accordance with the following provisions:

(a) (i)   A frontier worker who is partially or intermittently unemployed in the undertaking which employs him, shall receive benefits in accordance with the provisions of the legislation of the competent State as if he were residing in the territory of that State; these benefits shall be provided by the competent institution;

(ii)   A frontier worker who is wholly unemployed shall receive benefits in accordance with the provisions of the legislation of the Member State in whose territory he resides as though he had been subject to that legislation while last employed; these benefits shall be provided by the institution of the place of residence at its own expense;

(b) (i) An employed person, other than a frontier worker, who is partially, intermittently or wholly unemployed and who remains available to his employer or to the employment services in the territory of the competent State shall receive benefits in accordance with the provisions of the legislation of that State as though he were residing in its territory; these benefits shall be provided by the competent institution;

   (ii) An employed person, other than a frontier worker, who is wholly unemployed and who makes himself available for work to the employment services in the territory of the Member State in which he resides, or who returns to that territory, shall receive benefits in accordance with the legislation of that State as if he had last been employed there; the institution of the place of residence shall provide such benefits at its own expense. However, if such an employed person has become entitled to benefits at the expense of the competent institution of the Member State to whose legislation he was last subject, he shall receive benefits under the provisions of Article 69. Receipt of benefits under the legislation of the State in which he resides shall be suspended for any period during which the unemployed person may, under the provisions of Article 69, make a claim for benefits under the legislation to which he was last subject.

2.   An unemployed person may not claim benefits under the legislation of the Member State in whose territory he resides while he is entitled to benefits under the provisions of paragraph 1(a)(i) or (b)(i).

CHAPTER 7   FAMILY BENEFITS

Article 72   Aggregation of periods of insurance, employment or self-employment

Where the legislation of a Member State makes acquisition of the right to benefits conditional upon completion of periods of insurance, employment or self-employment, the competent institution of that State shall take into account for this purpose, to the extent necessary, periods of insurance, employment or self-employment completed in any other Member State, as if they were periods completed under the legislation which it administers.

Article 72a   Employed persons who have become fully unemployed

An employed person who has become fully unemployed and to whom Article 71(1)(a)(ii) or (b)(ii), first sentence, apply shall, for the members of his family residing in the territory of the same Member State as he, receive family benefits in accordance with the legislation of that State, as if he had been subject to that legislation during his last employment, taking account, where appropriate, of the provisions of Article 72. These benefits shall be provided by, and at the expense of, the institution of the place of residence.

Where that institution applies legislation providing for deduction of contributions payable by unemployed persons to cover family benefits, it shall be authorised to make such deductions in accordance with the provisions of its legislation.

Article 73   Employed or self-employed persons the members of whose families reside in a Member State other than the competent State

An employed or self-employed person subject to the legislation of a Member State shall be entitled, in respect of the members of his family who are residing in another Member State, to the family benefits provided for by the legislation of the former State, as if they were residing in that State, subject to the provisions of Annex VI.

Article 74   Unemployed persons the members of whose families reside in a Member State other than the competent State

An unemployed person who was formerly employed or self-employed and who draws unemployment benefits under the legislation of a Member State shall be entitled, in respect of the members of his family residing in another Member State, to the family benefits provided for by the legislation of the former State, as if they were residing in that State, subject to the provisions of Annex VI.

Article 93   Rights of institutions responsible for benefits against liable third parties

1.   If a person receives benefits under the legislation of one Member State in respect of an injury resulting from an occurrence in the territory of another State, any rights of the institution responsible for benefits against a third party bound to compensate for the injury shall be governed by the following rules:

(a) Where the institution responsible for benefits is, by virtue of the legislation which it administers, subrogated to the rights which the recipient has against the third party, such subrogation shall be recognised by each Member State;

(b) Where the said institution has direct rights against the third party, such rights shall be recognised by each Member State.

2.   If a person receives benefits under the legislation of one Member State in respect of an injury resulting from an occurrence in the territory of another Member State, the provisions of the said legislation which determine in which cases the civil liability of employers or of the persons employed by them is to be excluded shall apply with regard to the said person or to the competent institution.

The provisions of paragraph 1 shall also apply to any rights of the institution responsible for benefit against an employer or the persons employed by him in cases where their liability is not excluded.

3.   Where, in accordance with the provisions of Article 36(3) and/or Article 63(3), two or more Member States or the competent authorities of those States have concluded an agreement to waive reimbursement between institutions under their jurisdiction, any rights arising against a liable third party shall be governed by the following rules:

(a) Where the institution of the Member State of stay or residence awards benefits to a person in respect of an injury which was sustained within its territory, that institution, in accordance with the legislation which it administers, shall exercise the right to subrogation or direct action against the third party liable to provide compensation for the injury;

(b) For the purpose of implementing (a);

(i) the person receiving benefits shall be deemed to be insured with the institution of the place of stay or residence, and

(ii) that institution shall be deemed to be the debtor institution;

(c) The provisions of paragraphs 1 and 2 shall remain applicable in respect of any benefits not covered by the waiver agreement referred to in this paragraph.

(All remaining provisions omitted.)

SOCIAL POLICY: EQUAL PAY AND TREATMENT

Council Directive of 10 February 1975 on the approximation of the laws of the Member States relating to the application of the principle of equal pay for men and women (75/117/EEC)

[OJ 1975, L45/19]

(Preamble omitted.)

Article 1

The principle of equal pay for men and women outlined in Article 119 of the Treaty, hereinafter called 'principle of equal pay', means, for the same work or for work to which equal value is attributed, the elimination of all discrimination on grounds of sex with regard to all aspects and conditions of remuneration.

In particular, where a job classification system is used for determining pay, it must be based on the same criteria for both men and women and so drawn up as to exclude any discrimination on grounds of sex.

Article 2

Member States shall introduce into their national legal systems such measures as are necessary to enable all employees who consider themselves wronged by failure to apply the principle of equal pay to pursue their claims by judicial process after possible recourse to other competent authorities.

Article 3

Member States shall abolish all discrimination between men and women arising from laws, regulations or administrative provisions which is contrary to the principle of equal pay.

Article 4

Member States shall take the necessary measures to ensure that provisions appearing in collective agreements, wage scales, wage agreements or individual contracts of employment which are contrary to the principle of equal pay shall be, or may be declared, null and void or may be amended.

Article 5

Member States shall take the necessary measures to protect employees against dismissal by the employer as a reaction to a complaint within the undertaking or to any legal proceedings aimed at enforcing compliance with the principle of equal pay.

Article 6

Member States shall, in accordance with their national circumstances and legal systems, take the measures necessary to ensure that the principle of equal pay is applied. They shall see that effective means are available to take care that this principle is observed.

Article 7

Member States shall take care that the provisions adopted pursuant to this Directive, together with the relevant provisions already in force, are brought to the attention of employees by all appropriate means, for example at their place of employment.

(All remaining provisions omitted.)

Council Directive of 9 February 1976 on the implementation of the principle of equal treatment for men and women as regards access to employment, vocational training and promotion, and working conditions (76/207/EEC) [OJ 1976 L39/40] as amended by Directive 2002/73

[OJ 2002, L269/15]*

THE COUNCIL OF THE EUROPEAN COMMUNITIES,

Having regard to the Treaty establishing the European Economic Community, and in particular Article 235 thereof,

Having regard to the proposal from the Commission,

Having regard to the opinion of the European Parliament[1],

Having regard to the opinion of the Economic and Social Committee[2],

Whereas the Council, in its resolution of 21 January 1974 concerning a social action programme[3], included among the priorities action for the purpose of achieving equality between men and women as regards access to employment and vocational training and promotion and as regards working conditions, including pay;

Whereas, with regard to pay, the Council adopted on 10 February 1975 Directive 75/117/EEC on the approximation of the laws of the Member States relating to the application of the principle of equal pay for men and women[4];

Whereas Community action to achieve the principle of equal treatment for men and women in respect of access to employment and vocational training and promotion and in respect of other working conditions also appears to be necessary; whereas, equal treatment for male and female workers constitutes one of the objectives of the Community, in so far as the harmonization of living and working conditions while maintaining their improvement are inter alia to be furthered; whereas the Treaty does not confer the necessary specific powers for this purpose;

Whereas the definition and progressive implementation of the principle of equal treatment in matters of social security should be ensured by means of subsequent instruments,

HAS ADOPTED THIS DIRECTIVE:

Article 1

1. The purpose of this Directive is to put into effect in the Member States the principle of equal treatment for men and women as regards access to employment, including promotion, and to vocational training and as regards working conditions and, on the conditions referred to in paragraph 2, social security. This principle is hereinafter referred to as 'the principle of equal treatment.'

1a. Member States shall actively take into account the objective of equality between men and women when formulating and implementing laws, regulations, administrative provisions, policies and activities in the areas referred to in paragraph 1.

* **Editor's Note**: The amendments made by Directive 2002/73 (OJ 2002 L269/15) take effect as from 5 October 2005.

[1] OJ No C 111, 20.5.1975, p. 14.
[2] OJ No C 286, 15.12.1975, p. 8.
[3] OJ No C 13, 12.2.1974, p. 1.
[4] OJ No L 45, 19.2.1975, p. 19.

2.   With a view to ensuring the progressive implementation of the principle of equal treatment in matters of social security, the Council, acting on a proposal from the Commission, will adopt provisions defining its substance, its scope and the arrangements for its application.

Article 2

1.   For the purposes of the following provisions, the principle of equal treatment shall mean that there shall be no discrimination whatsoever on grounds of sex either directly or indirectly by reference in particular to marital or family status.

2.   For the purposes of this Directive, the following definitions shall apply:
— direct discrimination: where one person is treated less favourably on grounds of sex than another is, has been or would be treated in a comparable situation,
— indirect discrimination: where an apparently neutral provision, criterion or practice would put persons of one sex at a particular disadvantage compared with persons of the other sex, unless that provision, criterion or practice is objectively justified by a legitimate aim, and the means of achieving that aim are appropriate and necessary,
— harassment: where an unwanted conduct related to the sex of a person occurs with the purpose or effect of violating the dignity of a person, and of creating an intimidating, hostile, degrading, humiliating or offensive environment,
— sexual harassment: where any form of unwanted verbal, non-verbal or physical conduct of a sexual nature occurs, with the purpose or effect of violating the dignity of a person, in particular when creating an intimidating, hostile, degrading, humiliating or offensive environment.

3.   Harassment and sexual harassment within the meaning of this Directive shall be deemed to be discrimination on the grounds of sex and therefore prohibited.

A person's rejection of, or submission to, such conduct may not be used as a basis for a decision affecting that person.

4.   An instruction to discriminate against persons on grounds of sex shall be deemed to be discrimination within the meaning of this Directive.

5.   Member States shall encourage, in accordance with national law, collective agreements or practice, employers and those responsible for access to vocational training to take measures to prevent all forms of discrimination on grounds of sex, in particular harassment and sexual harassment at the workplace.

6.   Member States may provide, as regards access to employment including the training leading thereto, that a difference of treatment which is based on a characteristic related to sex shall not constitute discrimination where, by reason of the nature of the particular occupational activities concerned or of the context in which they are carried out, such a characteristic constitutes a genuine and determining occupational requirement, provided that the objective is legitimate and the requirement is proportionate.

7.   This Directive shall be without prejudice to provisions concerning the protection of women, particularly as regards pregnancy and maternity.

A woman on maternity leave shall be entitled, after the end of her period of maternity leave, to return to her job or to an equivalent post on terms and conditions which are no less favourable to her and to benefit from any improvement in working conditions to which she would be entitled during her absence. Less favourable treatment of a woman related to pregnancy or maternity leave within the meaning of Directive 92/85/EEC shall constitute discrimination within the meaning of this Directive.

This Directive shall also be without prejudice to the provisions of Council Directive 96/34/EC of 3 June 1996 on the framework agreement on parental leave concluded by UNICE, CEEP and the ETUC[1] and of Council Directive 92/85/EEC of 19 October 1992 on the introduction

[1] OJ L 145, 19.6.1996, p. 4.

of measures to encourage improvements in the safety and health at work of pregnant workers and workers who have recently given birth or are breastfeeding (tenth individual Directive within the meaning of Article 16(1) of Directive 89/391/EEC)[2]. It is also without prejudice to the right of Member States to recognise distinct rights to paternity and/or adoption leave. Those Member States which recognise such rights shall take the necessary measures to protect working men and women against dismissal due to exercising those rights and ensure that, at the end of such leave, they shall be entitled to return to their jobs or to equivalent posts on terms and conditions which are no less favourable to them, and to benefit from any improvement in working conditions to which they would have been entitled during their absence.

8.   Member States may maintain or adopt measures within the meaning of Article 141(4) of the Treaty with a view to ensuring full equality in practice between men and women.

Article 3

1.   Application of the principle of equal treatment means that there shall be no direct or indirect discrimination on the grounds of sex in the public or private sectors, including public bodies, in relation to:

(a) conditions for access to employment, to self-employment or to occupation, including selection criteria and recruitment conditions, whatever the branch of activity and at all levels of the professional hierarchy, including promotion;

(b) access to all types and to all levels of vocational guidance, vocational training, advanced vocational training and retraining, including practical work experience;

(c) employment and working conditions, including dismissals, as well as pay as provided for in Directive 75/117/EEC;

(d) membership of, and involvement in, an organisation of workers or employers, or any organisation whose members carry on a particular profession, including the benefits provided for by such organisations.

2.   To that end, Member States shall take the necessary measures to ensure that:

(a) any laws, regulations and administrative provisions contrary to the principle of equal treatment are abolished;

(b) any provisions contrary to the principle of equal treatment which are included in contracts or collective agreements, internal rules of undertakings or rules governing the independent occupations and professions and workers' and employers' organisations shall be, or may be declared, null and void or are amended.

Articles 4 and 5 (deleted by Directive 2002/73)

Article 6

1.   Member States shall ensure that judicial and/or administrative procedures, including where they deem it appropriate conciliation procedures, for the enforcement of obligations under this Directive are available to all persons who consider themselves wronged by failure to apply the principle of equal treatment to them, even after the relationship in which the discrimination is alleged to have occurred has ended.

2.   Member States shall introduce into their national legal systems such measures as are necessary to ensure real and effective compensation or reparation as the Member States so determine for the loss and damage sustained by a person injured as a result of discrimination contrary to Article 3, in a way which is dissuasive and proportionate to the damage suffered; such compensation or reparation may not be restricted by the fixing of a prior upper limit, except in cases where the employer can prove that the only damage suffered by an applicant as a result of discrimination within the meaning of this Directive is the refusal to take his/her job application into consideration.

3.   Member States shall ensure that associations, organisations or other legal entities

[2] OJ L 348, 28.11.1992, p. 1.

which have, in accordance with the criteria laid down by their national law, a legitimate interest in ensuring that the provisions of this Directive are complied with, may engage, either on behalf or in support of the complainants, with his or her approval, in any judicial and/or administrative procedure provided for the enforcement of obligations under this Directive.

4.   Paragraphs 1 and 3 are without prejudice to national rules relating to time limits for bringing actions as regards the principle of equal treatment.

Article 7
Member States shall introduce into their national legal systems such measures as are necessary to protect employees, including those who are employees' representatives provided for by national laws and/or practices, against dismissal or other adverse treatment by the employer as a reaction to a complaint within the undertaking or to any legal proceedings aimed at enforcing compliance with the principle of equal treatment.

Article 8
Member States shall take care that the provisions adopted pursuant to this Directive, together with the relevant provisions already in force, are brought to the attention of employees by all appropriate means, for example at their place of employment.

Article 8a
1.   Member States shall designate and make the necessary arrangements for a body or bodies for the promotion, analysis, monitoring and support of equal treatment of all persons without discrimination on the grounds of sex. These bodies may form part of agencies charged at national level with the defence of human rights or the safeguard of individuals' rights.

2.   Member States shall ensure that the competences of these bodies include:
   (a)   without prejudice to the right of victims and of associations, organisations or other legal entities referred to in Article 6(3), providing independent assistance to victims of discrimination in pursuing their complaints about discrimination;
   (b)   conducting independent surveys concerning discrimination;
   (c)   publishing independent reports and making recommendations on any issue relating to such discrimination.

Article 8b
1.   Member States shall, in accordance with national traditions and practice, take adequate measures to promote social dialogue between the social partners with a view to fostering equal treatment, including through the monitoring of workplace practices, collective agreements, codes of conduct, research or exchange of experiences and good practices.

2.   Where consistent with national traditions and practice, Member States shall encourage the social partners, without prejudice to their autonomy, to promote equality between women and men and to conclude, at the appropriate level, agreements laying down anti-discrimination rules in the fields referred to in Article 1 which fall within the scope of collective bargaining. These agreements shall respect the minimum requirements laid down by this Directive and the relevant national implementing measures.

3.   Member States shall, in accordance with national law, collective agreements or practice, encourage employers to promote equal treatment for men and women in the workplace in a planned and systematic way.

4.   To this end, employers should be encouraged to provide at appropriate regular intervals employees and/or their representatives with appropriate information on equal treatment for men and women in the undertaking. Such information may include statistics on proportions of men and women at different levels of the organisation and possible measures to improve the situation in cooperation with employees' representatives.

Article 8c
Member States shall encourage dialogue with appropriate non-governmental organisations which have, in accordance with their national law and practice, a legitimate interest in contributing to the fight against discrimination on grounds of sex with a view to promoting the principle of equal treatment.

Article 8d
Member States shall lay down the rules on sanctions applicable to infringements of the national provisions adopted pursuant to this Directive, and shall take all measures necessary to ensure that they are applied.

The sanctions, which may comprise the payment of compensation to the victim, must be effective, proportionate and dissuasive. The Member States shall notify those provisions to the Commission by 5 October 2005 at the latest and shall notify it without delay of any subsequent amendment affecting them.

Article 8e
1.   Member States may introduce or maintain provisions which are more favourable to the protection of the principle of equal treatment than those laid down in this Directive.

2.   The implementation of this Directive shall under no circumstances constitute grounds for a reduction in the level of protection against discrimination already afforded by Member States in the fields covered by this Directive.

Article 9
1.   Member States shall put into force the laws, regulations and administrative provisions necessary in order to comply with this Directive within 30 months of its notification and shall immediately inform the Commission thereof.

However, as regards the first part of Article 3(2)(c) and the first part of Article 5(2)(c), Member States shall carry out a first examination and if necessary a first revision of the laws, regulations and administrative provisions referred to therein within four years of notification of this Directive.

2.   Member States shall periodically assess the occupational activities referred to in Article 2 (2) in order to decide, in the light of social developments, whether there is justification for maintaining the exclusions concerned. They shall notify the Commission of the results of this assessment.

3.   Member States shall also communicate to the Commission the texts of laws, regulations and administrative provisions which they adopt in the field covered by this Directive.

Article 10
Within two years following expiry of the 30-month period laid down in the first subparagraph of Article 9(1), Member States shall forward all necessary information to the Commission to enable it to draw up a report on the application of this Directive for submission to the Council.

Article 11
This Directive is addressed to the Member States.

Council Directive of 19 December 1978 on the progressive implementation of the principle of equal treatment for men and women in matters of social security (79/7/EEC)

[OJ 1979, L6/24]

(Preamble omitted.)

Article 1

The purpose of this Directive is the progressive implementation, in the field of social security and other elements of social protection provided for in Article 3, of the principle of equal treatment for men and women in matters of social security, hereinafter referred to as 'the principle of equal treatment'.

Article 2

This Directive shall apply to the working population—including self-employed persons, workers and self-employed persons whose activity is interrupted by illness, accident or involuntary unemployment and persons seeking employment—and to retired or invalided workers and self-employed persons.

Article 3

1. This Directive shall apply to:
   (a) statutory schemes which provide protection against the following risks:
       — sickness,
       — invalidity,
       — old age,
       — accidents at work and occupational diseases,
       — unemployment;
   (b) social assistance, in so far as it is intended to supplement or replace the schemes referred to in (a).

2. This Directive shall not apply to the provisions concerning survivors' benefits nor to those concerning family benefits, except in the case of family benefits granted by way of increases of benefits due in respect of the risks referred to in paragraph 1(a).

3. With a view to ensuring implementation of the principle of equal treatment in occupational schemes, the Council, acting on a proposal from the Commission, will adopt provisions defining its substance, its scope and the arrangements for its application.

Article 4

1. The principle of equal treatment means that there shall be no discrimination what-soever on ground of sex either directly, or indirectly by reference in particular to marital or family status, in particular as concerns:
   — the scope of the schemes and the conditions of access thereto,
   — the obligation to contribute and the calculation of contributions,
   — the calculation of benefits including increases due in respect of a spouse and for dependants and the conditions governing the duration and retention of entitlement to benefits.

2. The principle of equal treatment shall be without prejudice to the provisions relating to the protection of women on the grounds of maternity.

Article 5
Member States shall take the measures necessary to ensure that any laws, regulations and administrative provisions contrary to the principle of equal treatment are abolished.

Article 6
Member States shall introduce into their national legal systems such measures as are necessary to enable all persons who consider themselves wronged by failure to apply the principle of equal treatment to pursue their claims by judicial process, possibly after recourse to other competent authorities.

Article 7
　　1.　This Directive shall be without prejudice to the right of Member States to exclude from its scope:
　　　(a) the determination of pensionable age for the purposes of granting old-age and retirement pensions and the possible consequences thereof for other benefits;
　　　(b) advantages in respect of old-age pension schemes granted to persons who have brought up children; the acquisition of benefit entitlements following periods of interruption of employment due to the bringing up of children;
　　　(c) the granting of old-age or invalidity benefit entitlements by virtue of the derived entitlements of a wife;
　　　(d) the granting of increases of long-term invalidity, old-age, accidents at work and occupational disease benefits for a dependent wife;
　　　(e) the consequences of the exercise, before the adoption of this Directive, of a right of option not to acquire rights or incur obligations under a statutory scheme.
　　2.　Member States shall periodically examine matters excluded under paragraph 1 in order to ascertain, in the light of social developments in the matter concerned, whether there is justification for maintaining the exclusions concerned.

Article 8
　　1.　Member States shall bring into force the laws, regulations and administrative provisions necessary to comply with this Directive within six years of its notification. They shall immediately inform the Commission thereof.
　　2.　Member States shall communicate to the Commission the text of laws, regulations and administrative provisions which they adopt in the field covered by this Directive, including measures adopted pursuant to Article 7(2).
　　They shall inform the Commission of their reasons for maintaining any existing provisions on the matters referred to in Article 7(1) and of the possibilities for reviewing them at a later date.

Article 9
Within seven years of notification of this Directive, Member States shall forward all information necessary to the Commission to enable it to draw up a report on the application of this Directive for submission to the Council and to propose such further measures as may be required for the implementation of the principle of equal treatment.

Article 10
This Directive is addressed to the Member States.

Done at Brussels, 19 December 1978.

Council Directive of 24 July 1986 on the implementation of the principle of equal treatment for men and women in occupational social security schemes (86/378/EEC)

[OJ 1986, L225/40][1]

The Council of the European Communities,

Having regard to the Treaty establishing the European Economic Community, and in particular Articles 100 and 235 thereof,

Having regard to the proposal from the Commission,

Having regard to the opinion of the European Parliament,

Having regard to the opinion of the Economic and Social Committee,

Whereas the Treaty provides that each Member State shall ensure the application of the principle that men and women should receive equal pay for equal work; whereas 'pay' should be taken to mean the ordinary basic or minimum wage or salary and any other consideration, whether in cash or in kind, which the worker receives, directly or indirectly, from his employer in respect of his employment;

Whereas, although the principle of equal pay does indeed apply directly in cases where discrimination can be determined solely on the basis of the criteria of equal treatment and equal pay, there are also situations in which implementation of this principle implies the adoption of additional measures which more clearly define its scope;

Whereas Article 1(2) of Council Directive 76/207/EEC of 9 February 1976 on the implementation of the principle of equal treatment for men and women as regards access to employment, vocational training and promotion, and working conditions provides that, with a view to ensuring the progressive implementation of the principle of equal treatment in matters of social security, the Council, acting on a proposal from the Commission, will adopt provisions defining its substance, its scope and the arrrangements for its application; whereas the Council adopted to this end Directive 79/7/EEC of 19 December 1978 on the progressive implementation of the principle of equal treatment for men and women in matters of social security;

Whereas Article 3(3) of Directive 79/7/EEC provides that, with a view to ensuring implementation of the principle of equal treatment in occupational schemes, the Council, acting on a proposal from the Commission, will adopt provisions defining its substance, its scope and the arrangements for its application;

Whereas the principle of equal treatment should be implemented in occupational social security schemes which provide protection against the risks specified in Article 3(1) of Directive 79/7/EEC as well as those which provide employees with any other consideration in cash or in kind within the meaning of the Treaty;

Whereas implementation of the principle of equal treatment does not prejudice the provisions relating to the protection of women by reason of maternity,

Has adopted this directive:

Article 1

The object of this Directive is to implement, in occupational social security schemes, the principle of equal treatment for men and women, hereinafter referred to as 'the principle of equal treatment'.

---

[1] **Editor's Note:** As amended by Corrigendum 1986 L283/27, Directive 96/97 (OJ No. L46/20) and Corrigendum OJ 1997 L241/8. The non-amending parts of Directive 96/97 are reproduced following Directive 86/613 below. Also note that a Commission consolidated version of this Directive now exists (1986 L0378) http://europa.eu.int/eur-lex/en/consleg/main/1986/en_1986L0378_index.html.

Article 2

1. 'Occupational social security schemes' means schemes not governed by Directive 79/7/EEC whose purpose is to provide workers, whether employees or self-employed, in an undertaking or group of undertakings, area of economic activity or occupational sector or group of such sectors with benefits intended to supplement the benefits provided by statutory social security schemes or to replace them, whether membership of such schemes is compulsory or optional.

2. This Directive does not apply to:
   (a) individual contracts for self-employed workers;
   (b) schemes for self-employed workers having only one member;
   (c) in the case of salaried workers, insurance contracts to which the employer is not a party;
   (d) optional provisions of occupational schemes offered to participants individually to guarantee them:
      — either additional benefits, or
      — a choice of date on which the normal benefits for self-employed workers will start, or a choice between several benefits;
   (e) occupational schemes in so far as benefits are financed by contributions paid by workers on a voluntary basis.

3. This Directive does not preclude an employer granting to persons who have already reached the retirement age for the purposes of granting a pension by virtue of an occupational scheme, but who have not yet reached the retirement age for the purposes of granting a statutory retirement pension, a pension supplement, the aim of which is to make equal or more nearly equal the overall amount of benefit paid to these persons in relation to the amount paid to persons of the other sex in the same situation who have already reached the statutory retirement age, until the persons benefiting from the supplement reach the statutory retirement age.

Article 3

This Directive shall apply to members of the working population including self-employed persons, persons whose activity is interrupted by illness, maternity, accident or involuntary unemployment and persons seeking employment, to retired and disabled workers and to those claiming under them, in accordance with national law and/or practice.

Article 4

This Directive shall apply to:
   (a) occupational schemes which provide protection against the following risks:
      — sickness,
      — invalidity,
      — old age, including early retirement,
      — industrial accidents and occupational diseases,
      — unemployment;
   (b) occupational schemes which provide for other social benefits, in cash or in kind, and in particular survivors' benefits and family allowances, if such benefits are accorded to employed persons and thus constitute a consideration paid by the employer to the worker by reason of the latter's employment.

Article 5

1. Under the conditions laid down in the following provisions, the principle of equal treatment implies that there shall be no discrimination on the basis of sex, either directly or indirectly, by reference in particular to marital or family status, especially as regards:
      — the scope of the schemes and the conditions of access to them;
      — the obligation to contribute and the calculation of contributions;

— the calculation of benefits, including supplementary benefits due in respect of a spouse or dependants, and the conditions governing the duration and retention of entitlement to benefits.

2.   The principle of equal treatment shall not prejudice the provisions relating to the protection of women by reason of maternity.

Article 6

1.   Provisions contrary to the principle of equal treatment shall include those based on sex, either directly or indirectly, in particular by reference to marital or family for:

- (a) determining the persons who may participate in an occupational scheme;
- (b) fixing the compulsory or optional nature of participation in an occupational scheme;
- (c) laying down different rules as regards the age of entry into the scheme or the minimum period of employment or membership of the scheme required to obtain the benefits thereof;
- (d) laying down different rules, except as provided for in points (h) and (i), for the reimbursement of contributions where a worker leaves a scheme without having fulfilled the conditions guaranteeing him a deferred right to long-term benefits;
- (e) setting different conditions for the granting of benefits of restricting such benefits to workers of one or other of the sexes;
- (f) fixing different retirement ages;
- (g) suspending the retention or acquisition of rights during periods of maternity leave or leave for family reasons which are granted by law or agreement and are paid by the employer;
- (h) setting different levels of benefit, except insofar as may be necessary to take account of actuarial calculation factors which differ according to sex in the case of defined contribution schemes.

   In the case of funded defined-benefit schemes, certain elements (examples of which are annexed) may be unequal where the inequality of the amounts results from the effects of the use of actuarial factors differing according to sex at the time when the scheme's funding is implemented;
- (i) setting different levels of worker contribution;
    - — in the case of defined-contribution schemes if the aim is to equalize the amount of the final benefits or to make them more nearly equal for both sexes,
    - — in the case of funded defined-benefit schemes where the employer's contributions are intended to ensure the adequacy of the funds necessary to cover the cost of the benefits defined,
- (j) laying down different standards or standards applicable only to workers of a specified sex, except as provided for in sub-paragraphs (h) and (i), as regards the guarantee or retention of entitlement to deferred benefits when a worker leaves a scheme.

2.   Where the granting of benefits within the scope of this Directive is left to the discretion of the scheme's management bodies, the latter must comply with the principle of equal treatment.

Article 7

Member States shall take all necessary steps to ensure that:

- (a) provisions contrary to the principle of equal treatment in legally compulsory collective agreements, staff rules of undertakings or any other arrangements relating to occupational schemes are null and void, or may be declared null and void or amended;

(b) schemes containing such provisions may not be approved or extended by administrative measures.

Article 8

1. Member States shall take all necessary steps to ensure that the provisions of occupational schemes contrary to the principle of equal treatment are revised by 1 January 1993 at the latest.

2. This Directive shall not preclude rights and obligations relating to a period of membership of an occupational scheme prior to revision of that scheme from remaining subject to the provisions of the scheme in force during that period.

Article 9

As regards schemes for self-employed workers, Member States may defer compulsory application of the principle of equal treatment with regard to:

(a) determination of pensionable age for the granting of old-age or retirement pensions, and the possible implications for other benefits:
— either until the date on which such equality is achieved in statutory schemes,
— or, at the latest, until such equality is required by a directive;
(b) survivors' pensions until Community law establishes the principle of equal treatment in statutory social security schemes in that regard;
(c) the application of the first sub-paragraph of point (i) of Article 6(1) to take account of the different actuarial calculation factors, at the latest until 1 January 1999.

Article 9a

Where men and women may claim a flexible pensionable age under the same conditions, this shall not be deemed to be incompatible with this Directive.

Article 10

Member States shall introduce into their national legal systems such measures as are necessary to enable all persons who consider themselves injured by failure to apply the principle of equal treatment to pursue their claims before the courts, possibly after bringing the matters before other competent authorities.

Article 11

Member States shall take all the necessary steps to protect worker against dismissal where this constitutes a response on the part of the employer to a complaint made at undertaking level or to the institution of legal proceedings aimed at enforcing compliance with the principle of equal treatment.

Article 12

1. Member States shall bring into force such laws, regulations and administrative provisions as are necessary in order to comply with this Directive at the latest three years after notification thereof. They shall immediately inform the Commission thereof.

2. Member States shall communicate to the Commission at the latest five years after notification of this Directive all information necessary to enable the Commission to draw up a report on the application of this Directive for submission to the Council.

Article 13

This Directive is addressed to the Member States.

Done at Brussels, 24 July 1986.

Council Directive 86/613 of 11 December 1986 on the application of the principle of equal treatment between men and women engaged in an activity, including agriculture, in a self-employed capacity, and on the protection of self-employed women during pregnancy and motherhood (86/613/EEC)

[OJ 1986, L359/56]

The Council of the European Communities,

Having regard to the Treaty establishing the European Economic Community, and in particular Articles 100 and 235 thereof,

Having regard to the proposal from the Commission,

Having regard to the opinion of the European Parliament,

Having regard to the opinion of the Economic and Social Committee,

Whereas, in its resolution of 12 July 1982 on the promotion of equal opportunities for women, the Council approved the general objectives of the Commission communication concerning a new Community action programme on the promotion of equal opportunities for women (1982 to 1985) and expressed the will to implement appropriate measures to achieve them;

Whereas action 5 of the programme referred to above concerns the application of the principle of equal treatment to self-employed women and to women in agriculture;

Whereas the implementation of the principle of equal pay for men and women workers, as laid down in Article 119 of the Treaty, forms an integral part of the establishment and functioning of the common market;

Whereas on 10 February 1975 the Council adopted Directive 75/117/EEC on the approximation of the laws of the Member States relating to the application of the principle of equal pay for men and women;

Whereas, as regards other aspects of equality of treatment between men and women, on 9 February 1976 the Council adopted Directive 76/207/EEC on the implementation of the principle of equal treatment for men and women as regards access to employment, vocational training and promotion, and working conditions and on 19 December 1978 Directive 79/7/EEC on the progressive implementation of the principle of equal treatment for men and women in matters of social security;

Whereas, as regards persons engaged in a self-employed capacity, in an activity in which their spouses are also engaged, the implementation of the principle of equal treatment should be pursued through the adoption of detailed provisions designed to cover the specific situation of these persons;

Whereas differences persist between the Member States in this field, whereas, therefore it is necessary to approximate national provisions with regard to the application of the principle of equal treatment;

Whereas in certain respects the Treaty does not confer the powers necessary for the specific actions required;

Whereas the implementation of the principle of equal treatment is without prejudice to measures concerning the protection of women during pregnancy and motherhood,

Has adopted this directive:

SECTION I AIMS AND SCOPE

Article 1

The purpose of this Directive is to ensure, in accordance with the following provisions, application in the Member States of the principle of equal treatment as between men and women engaged in an activity in a self-employed capacity, or contributing to the pursuit of such an activity, as regards those aspects not covered by Directives 76/207/EEC and 79/7/EEC.

Article 2

This Directive covers:
   (a) self-employed workers, i.e., all persons pursuing a gainful activity for their own account, under the conditions laid down by national law, including farmers and members of the liberal professions;
   (b) their spouses, not being employees or partners, where they habitually, under the conditions laid down by national law, participate in the activities of the self-employed worker and perform the same tasks or ancillary tasks.

Article 3

For the purposes of this Directive the principle of equal treatment implies the absence of all discrimination on grounds of sex, either directly or indirectly, by reference in particular to marital or family status.

SECTION II EQUAL TREATMENT BETWEEN SELF-EMPLOYED MALE AND FEMALE
WORKERS—POSITION OF THE SPOUSES WITHOUT PROFESSIONAL STATUS OF
SELF-EMPLOYED WORKERS—PROTECTION OF SELF-EMPLOYED WORKERS OR
WIVES OF SELF-EMPLOYED WORKERS DURING PREGNANCY AND MOTHERHOOD

Article 4

As regards self-employed persons, Member States shall take the measures necessary to ensure the elimination of all provisions which are contrary to the principle of equal treatment as defined in Directive 76/207/EEC, especially in respect of the establishment, equipment or extension of a business or the launching or extension of any other form of self-employed activity including financial facilities.

Article 5

Without prejudice to the specific conditions for access to certain activities which apply equally to both sexes, Member States shall take the measures necessary to ensure that the conditions for the formation of a company between spouses are not more restrictive than the conditions for the formation of a company between unmarried persons.

Article 6

Where a contributory social security system for self-employed workers exists in a Member State, that Member State shall take the necessary measures to enable the spouses referred to in Article 2(b) who are not protected under the self-employed worker's social security scheme to join a contributory social security scheme voluntarily.

Article 7

Member States shall undertake to examine under what conditions recognition of the work of the spouses referred to in Article 2(b) may be encouraged and, in the light of such examination, consider any appropriate steps for encouraging such recognition.

Article 8

Member States shall undertake to examine whether, and under what conditions, female self-employed workers and the wives of self-employed workers may, during interruptions in their occupational activity owing to pregnancy or motherhood,

— have access to services supplying temporary replacements or existing national social services, or
— be entitled to cash benefits under a social security scheme or under any other public social protection system.

SECTION III   GENERAL AND FINAL PROVISIONS

Article 9
Member States shall introduce into their national legal systems such measures as are necessary to enable all persons who consider themselves wronged by failure to apply the principle of equal treatment in self-employed activities to pursue their claims by judicial process, possibly after recourse to other competent authorities.

Article 10
Member States shall ensure that the measures adopted pursuant to this Directive, together with the relevant provisions already in force, are brought to the attention of bodies representing self-employed workers and vocational training centres.

Article 11
The Council shall review this Directive, on a proposal from the Commission, before 1 July 1993.

Article 12
1.   Member States shall bring into force the laws, regulations and administrative provisions necessary to comply with this Directive not later than 30 June 1989. However, if a Member State which, in order to comply with Article 5 of this Directive, has to amend its legislation on matrimonial rights and obligations, the date on which such Member State must comply with Article 5 shall be 30 June 1991.

2.   Member States shall immediately inform the Commission of the measures taken to comply with this Directive.

Article 13
Member States shall forward to the Commission, not later than 30 June 1991, all the information necessary to enable it to draw up a report on the application of this directive for submission to the Council.

Article 14
This Directive is addressed to the Member States.

Done at Brussels, 11 December 1986.

Council Directive 96/34/EC of 3 June 1996 on the framework agreement on parental leave concluded by UNICE, CEEP and the ETUC
[OJ 1996, L145/9]*

THE COUNCIL OF THE EUROPEAN UNION,
Having regard to the Agreement on social policy, annexed to the Protocol (No. 14) on social policy, annexed to the Treaty establishing the European Community, and in particular Article 4(2) thereof,

* **Editor's Note:** As amended and extended to the UK by Directive 97/75 (OJ 1998, L10/24).

Having regard to the proposal from the Commission,

(1) Whereas on the basis of the Protocol on social policy, the Member States, with the exception of the United Kingdom of Great Britain and Northern Ireland, (hereinafter referred to as 'the Member States'), wishing to pursue the course mapped out by the 1989 Social Charter have concluded an Agreement on social policy amongst themselves;

(2) Whereas management and labour may, in accordance with Article 4(2) of the Agreement on social policy, request jointly that agreements at Community level be implemented by a Council decision on a proposal from the Commission;

(3) Whereas paragraph 16 of the Community Charter of the Fundamental Social Rights of Workers on equal treatment for men and women provides, inter alia, that 'measures should also be developed enabling men and women to reconcile their occupational and family obligations;

(4) Whereas the Council, despite the existence of a broad consensus, has not been able to act on the proposal for a Directive on parental leave for family reasons (1), as amended (2) on 15 November 1984;

(5) Whereas the Commission, in accordance with Article 3(2) of the Agreement on social policy, consulted management and labour on the possible direction of Community action with regard to reconciling working and family life;

(6) Whereas the Commission, considering after such consultation that Community action was desirable, once again consulted management and labour on the substance of the envisaged proposal in accordance with Article 3(3) of the said Agreement;

(7) Whereas the general cross-industry organisations (UNICE, CEEP and the ETUC) informed the Commission in their joint letter of 5 July 1995 of their desire to initiate the procedure provided for by Article 4 of the said Agreement;

(8) Whereas the said cross-industry organisations concluded, on 14 December 1995, a framework agreement on parental leave; whereas they have forwarded to the Commission their joint request to implement this framework agreement by a Council Decision on a proposal from the Commission in accordance with Article 4(2) of the said Agreement;

(9) Whereas the Council, in its Resolution of 6 December 1994 on certain aspects for a European Union social policy; a contribution to economic and social convergence in the Union (3), asked the two sides of industry to make use of the possibilities for concluding agreements, since they are as a rule closer to social reality and to social problems; whereas in Madrid, the members of the European Council from those States which have signed the Agreement on social policy welcomed the conclusion of this framework agreement;

(10) Whereas the signatory parties wanted to conclude a framework agreement setting out minimum requirements on parental leave and time off from work on grounds of force majeure and referring back to the Member States and/or management and labour for the definition of the conditions under which parental leave would be implemented, in order to take account of the situation, including the situation with regard to family policy, existing in each Member State, particularly as regards the conditions for granting parental leave and exercise of the right to parental leave;

(11) Whereas the proper instrument for implementing this framework agreement is a Directive within the meaning of Article 189 of the Treaty; whereas it is therefore binding on the Member States as to the result to be achieved, but leaves them the choice of form and methods;

(12) Whereas, in keeping with the principle of subsidiarity and the principle of proportionality as set out in Article 3b of the Treaty, the objectives of this Directive cannot be sufficiently achieved by the Member States and can therefore be better achieved by the Community; whereas this Directive is confined to the minimum required to achieve these objectives and does not go beyond what is necessary to achieve that purpose;

(13) Whereas the Commission has drafted its proposal for a Directive, taking into account the representative status of the signatory parties, their mandate and the legality of the

clauses of the framework agreement and compliance with the relevant provisions concerning small and medium-sized undertakings;

(14) Whereas the Commission, in accordance with its Communication of 14 December 1993 concerning the implementation of the Protocol on social policy, informed the European Parliament by sending it the text of the framework agreement, accompanied by its proposal for a Directive and the explanatory memorandum;

(15) Whereas the Commission also informed the Economic and Social Committee by sending it the text of the framework agreement, accompanied by its proposal for a Directive and the explanatory memorandum;

(16) Whereas clause 4 point 2 of the framework agreement states that the implementation of the provisions of this agreement does not constitute valid grounds for reducing the general level of protection afforded to workers in the field of this agreement. This does not prejudice the right of Member States and/or management and labour to develop different legislative, regulatory or contractual provisions, in the light of changing circumstances (including the introduction of non-transferability), as long as the minimum requirements provided for in the present agreement are complied with;

(17) Whereas the Community Charter of the Fundamental Social Rights of Workers recognises the importance of the fight against all forms of discrimination, especially based on sex, colour, race, opinions and creeds;

(18) Whereas Article F(2) of the Treaty on European Union provides that 'the Union shall respect fundamental rights, as guaranteed by the European Convention for the Protection of Human Rights and Fundamental Freedoms signed in Rome on 4 November 1950 and as they result from the constitutional traditions common to the Member States, as general principles of Community law;

(19) Whereas the Member States can entrust management and labour, at their joint request, with the implementation of this Directive, as long as they take all the necessary steps to ensure that they can at all times guarantee the results imposed by this Directive;

(20) Whereas the implementation of the framework agreement contributes to achieving the objectives under Article 1 of the Agreement on social policy,

HAS ADOPTED THIS DIRECTIVE:

Article 1   Implementation of the framework agreement

The purpose of this Directive is to put into effect the annexed framework agreement on parental leave concluded on 14 December 1995 between the general cross-industry organisations (UNICE, CEEP and the ETUC).

Article 2   Final provisions

1.   The Member States shall bring into force the laws, regulations and administrative provisions necessary to comply with this Directive by 3 June 1998 at the latest or shall ensure by that date at the latest that management and labour have introduced the necessary measures by agreement, the Member States being required to take any necessary measure enabling them at any time to be in a position to guarantee the results imposed by this Directive. They shall forthwith inform the Commission thereof.

1a.   As regards the United Kingdom of Great Britain and Northern Ireland, the date of 3 June 1998 in paragraph 1 shall be replaced by 15 December 1999.

2.   The Member States may have a maximum additional period of one year, if this is necessary to take account of special difficulties or implementation by a collective agreement.

They must forthwith inform the Commission of such circumstances.

3.   When Member States adopt the measures referred to in paragraph 1, they shall contain a reference to this Directive or be accompanied by such reference on the occasion of their official publication. The methods of making such reference shall be laid down by Member States.

Article 3

This Directive is addressed to the Member States.

Done at Luxembourg, 3 June 1996.
For the Council The President T. TREU

ANNEX   FRAMEWORK AGREEMENT ON PARENTAL LEAVE

PREAMBLE

The enclosed framework agreement represents an undertaking by UNICE, CEEP and the ETUC to set out minimum requirements on parental leave and time off from work on grounds of force majeure, as an important means of reconciling work and family life and promoting equal opportunities and treatment between men and women.

ETUC, UNICE and CEEP request the Commission to submit this framework agreement to the Council for a Council Decision making these minimum requirements binding in the Member States of the European Community, with the exception of the United Kingdom of Great Britain and Northern Ireland.

I   GENERAL CONSIDERATIONS

1.   Having regard to the Agreement on social policy annexed to the Protocol on social policy, annexed to the Treaty establishing the European Community, and in particular Articles 3(4) and 4(2) thereof;

2.   Whereas Article 4(2) of the Agreement on social policy provides that agreements concluded at Community level shall be implemented, at the joint request of the signatory parties, by a Council Decision on a proposal from the Commission;

3.   Whereas the Commission has announced its intention to propose a Community measure on the reconciliation of work and family life;

4.   Whereas the Community Charter of Fundamental Social Rights stipulates at point 16 dealing with equal treatment that measures should be developed to enable men and women to reconcile their occupational and family obligations;

5.   Whereas the Council Resolution of 6 December 1994 recognises that an effective policy of equal opportunities presupposes an integrated overall strategy allowing for better organisation of working hours and greater flexibility, and for an easier return to working life, and notes the important role of the two sides of industry in this area and in offering both men and women an opportunity to reconcile their work responsibilities with family obligations;

6.   Whereas measures to reconcile work and family life should encourage the introduction of new flexible ways of organising work and time which are better suited to the changing needs of society and which should take the needs of both undertakings and workers into account;

7.   Whereas family policy should be looked at in the context of demographic changes, the effects of the ageing population, closing the generation gap and promoting women's participation in the labour force;

8.   Whereas men should be encouraged to assume an equal share of family responsibilities, for example they should be encouraged to take parental leave by means such as awareness programmes;

9.   Whereas the present agreement is a framework agreement setting out minimum requirements and provisions for parental leave, distinct from maternity leave, and for time off from work on grounds of force majeure, and refers back to Member States and social partners for the establishment of the conditions of access and detailed rules of application in order to take account of the situation in each Member State;

10. Whereas Member States should provide for the maintenance of entitlements to benefits in kind under sickness insurance during the minimum period of parental leave;

11. Whereas Member States should also, where appropriate under national conditions and taking into account the budgetary situation, consider the maintenance of entitlements to relevant social security benefits as they stand during the minimum period of parental leave;

12. Whereas this agreement takes into consideration the need to improve social policy requirements, to enhance the competitiveness of the Community economy and to avoid imposing administrative, financial and legal constraints in a way which would impede the creation and development of small and medium-sized undertakings;

13. Whereas management and labour are best placed to find solutions that correspond to the needs of both employers and workers and must therefore have conferred on them a special role in the implementation and application of the present agreement,

THE SIGNATORY PARTIES HAVE AGREED THE FOLLOWING:

II CONTENT

Clause 1: Purpose and scope

1. This agreement lays down minimum requirements designed to facilitate the reconciliation of parental and professional responsibilities for working parents.

2. This agreement applies to all workers, men and women, who have an employment contract or employment relationship as defined by the law, collective agreements or practices in force in each Member State.

Clause 2: Parental leave

1. This agreement grants, subject to clause 2.2, men and women workers an individual right to parental leave on the grounds of the birth or adoption of a child to enable them to take care of that child, for at least three months, until a given age up to 8 years to be defined by Member States and/or management and labour.

2. To promote equal opportunities and equal treatment between men and women, the parties to this agreement consider that the right to parental leave provided for under clause 2.1 should, in principle, be granted on a non-transferable basis.

3. The conditions of access and detailed rules for applying parental leave shall be defined by law and/or collective agreement in the Member States, as long as the minimum requirements of this agreement are respected. Member States and/or management and labour may, in particular:

(a) decide whether parental leave is granted on a full-time or part-time basis, in a piecemeal way or in the form of a time-credit system;

(b) make entitlement to parental leave subject to a period of work qualification and/or a length of service qualification which shall not exceed one year;

(c) adjust conditions of access and detailed rules for applying parental leave to the special circumstances of adoption;

(d) establish notice periods to be given by the worker to the employer when exercising the right to parental leave, specifying the beginning and the end of the period of leave;

(e) define the circumstances in which an employer, following consultation in accordance with national law, collective agreements and practices, is allowed to postpone the granting of parental leave for justifiable reasons related to the operation of the undertaking (e.g. where work is of a seasonal nature, where a replacement cannot be found within the notice period, where a significant proportion of the workforce applies for parental leave at the same time, where a specific function is of strategic importance). Any problem arising from the application of this provision should be dealt with in accordance with national law, collective agreements and practices;

(f) in addition to (e), authorise special arrangements to meet the operational and organisational requirements of small undertakings.

4. In order to ensure that workers can exercise their right to parental leave, Member States and/or management and labour shall take the necessary measures to protect workers against dismissal on the grounds of an application for, or the taking of, parental leave in accordance with national law, collective agreements or practices.

5. At the end of parental leave, workers shall have the right to return to the same job or, if that is not possible, to an equivalent or similar job consistent with their employment contract or employment relationship.

6. Rights acquired or in the process of being acquired by the worker on the date on which parental leave starts shall be maintained as they stand until the end of parental leave. At the end of parental leave, these rights, including any changes arising from national law, collective agreements or practice, shall apply.

7. Member States and/or management and labour shall define the status of the employment contract or employment relationship for the period of parental leave.

8. All matters relating to social security in relation to this agreement are for consideration and determination by Member States according to national law, taking into account the importance of the continuity of the entitlements to social security cover under the different schemes, in particular health care.

Clause 3: Time off from work on grounds of *force majeure*

1. Member States and/or management and labour shall take the necessary measures to entitle workers to time off from work, in accordance with national legislation, collective agreements and/or practice, on grounds of *force majeure* for urgent family reasons in cases of sickness or accident making the immediate presence of the worker indispensable.

2. Member States and/or management and labour may specify the conditions of access and detailed rules for applying clause 3.1 and limit this entitlement to a certain amount of time per year and/or per case.

Clause 4: Final provisions

1. Member States may apply or introduce more favourable provisions that those set out in this agreement.

2. Implementation of the provisions of this agreement shall not constitute valid grounds for reducing the general level of protection afforded to workers in the field covered by this agreement. This shall not prejudice the right of Member States and/or management and labour to develop different legislative, regulatory or contractual provisions, in the light of changing circumstances (including the introduction of non-transferability), as long as the minimum requirements provided for in the present agreement are complied with.

3. The present agreement shall not prejudice the right of management and labour to conclude, at the appropriate level including European level, agreements adapting and/or complementing the provisions of this agreement in order to take into account particular circumstances.

4. Member States shall adopt the laws, regulations and administrative provisions necessary to comply with the Council decision within a period of two years from its adoption or shall ensure that management and labour (1) introduce the necessary measures by way of agreement by the end of this period. Member States may, if necessary to take account of particular difficulties or implementation by collective agreement, have up to a maximum of one additional year to comply with this decision.

5. The prevention and settlement of disputes and grievances arising from the application of this agreement shall be dealt with in accordance with national law, collective agreements and practices.

6.   Without prejudice to the respective role of the Commission, national courts and the Court of Justice, any matter relating to the interpretation of this agreement at European level should, in the first instance, be referred by the Commission to the signatory parties who will give an opinion.

7.   The signatory parties shall review the application of this agreement five years after the date of the Council decision if requested by one of the parties to this agreement.

Done at Brussels, 14 December 1995.

Fritz VERZETNITSCH, President of the ETUC
Emilio GABAGLIO, Secretary-General ETUC
Bld Emile Jacqmain 155
B-1210 Brussels

Antonio Castellano AUYANET, President of the CEEP
Roger GOURVES, Secretary-General CEEP
Rue de la Charite 15
B-1040 Brussels

Francois PERIGOT, President of the UNICE
Zygmunt TYSZKIEWICZ, Secretary-General UNICE
Rue Joseph II 40
B-1040 Brussels.

Council Directive 96/97/EC of 20 December 1996 amending Directive 86/378/EEC on the implementation of the principle of equal treatment for men and women in occupational social security schemes

[OJ 1997, L46/20; corrected by OJ 1999, L151/39]

The Council of the European Union,
  Having regard to the Treaty establishing the European Community, and in particular Article 100 thereof,
  Having regard to the proposal from the Commission,[1]
  Having regard to the opinion of the European Parliament,[2]
  Having regard to the opinion of the Economic and Social Committee,[3]
  Whereas Article 119 of the Treaty provides that each Member State shall ensure the application of the principle that men and women should receive equal pay for equal work; whereas 'pay' should be taken to mean the ordinary basic or minimum wage or salary and any other consideration, whether in cash or in kind, which the worker receives, directly or indirectly, from his employer in respect of his employment;
  Whereas, in its judgment of 17 May 1990, in Case 262/88: *Barber* v *Guardian Royal Exchange Assurance Group*,[4] the Court of Justice of the European Communities acknowledges that all

---

[1] OJ No. C218, 23.8.1995, p. 5.
[2] Opinion delivered on 12 November 1996 [OJ No. C362, 2.12.1996].
[3] OJ No. C18, 22.1.1996, p. 132.
[4] [1990] ECR I-1889.

forms of occupational pension constitute an element of pay within the meaning of Article 119 of the Treaty;

Whereas, in the abovementioned judgment, as clarified by the judgment of 14 December 1993 (Case C-110/91: *Moroni* v *Collo GmbH*),[5] the Court interprets Article 119 of the Treaty in such a way that discrimination between men and women in occupational social security schemes is prohibited in general and not only in respect of establishing the age of entitlement to a pension or when an occupational pension is offered by way of compensation for compulsory retirement on economic grounds;

Whereas, in accordance with Protocol 2 concerning Article 119 of the Treaty annexed to the Treaty establishing the European Community, benefits under occupational social security schemes shall not be considered as remuneration if and in so far as they are attributable to periods of employment prior to 17 May 1990, except in the case of workers or those claiming under them who have, before that date, initiated legal proceedings or raised an equivalent claim under the applicable national law;

Whereas, in its judgments of 28 September 1994[6] (Case C-57/93: *Vroege* v *NCIV Instituut voor Volkshuisvesting BV* and Case C-128/93: *Fisscher* v *Voorhuis Hengelo BV*), the Court ruled that the abovementioned Protocol did not affect the right to join an occupational pension scheme, which continues to be governed by the judgment of 13 May 1986 in Case 170/84: *Bilka-Kaufhaus GmbH* v *Hartz*,[7] and that the limitation of the effects in time of the judgment of 17 May 1990 in Case C-262/88: *Barber* v *Guardian Royal Exchange Assurance Group* does not apply to the right to join an occupational pension scheme; whereas the Court also ruled that the national rules relating to time limits for bringing actions under national law may be relied on against workers who assert their right to join an occupational pension scheme, provided that they are not less favourable for that type of action than for similar actions of a domestic nature and that they do not render the exercise of rights conferred by Community law impossible in practice; whereas the Court has also pointed out that the fact that a worker can claim retroactively to join an occupational pension scheme does not allow the worker to avoid paying the contributions relating to the period of membership concerned;

Whereas the exclusion of workers on the grounds of the nature of their work contracts from access to a company or sectoral social security scheme may constitute indirect discrimination against women;

Whereas, in its judgment of 9 November 1993 (Case C-132/92: *Birds Eye Walls Ltd* v *Friedel M. Roberts*),[8] the Court has also specified that it is not contrary to Article 119 of the Treaty, when calculating the amount of a bridging pension which is paid by an employer to male and female employees who have taken early retirement on grounds of ill health and which is intended to compensate, in particular, for loss of income resulting from the fact that they have not yet reached the age required for payment of the State pension which they will subsequently receive and to reduce the amount of the bridging pension accordingly, even though, in the case of men and women aged between 60 and 65, the result is that a female ex-employee receives a smaller bridging pension than that paid to her male counterpart, the difference being equal to the amount of the State pension to which she is entitled as from the age of 60 in respect of the periods of service completed with that employer;

Whereas, in its judgment of 6 October 1993 (Case C-109/91: *Ten Oever* v *Stichting Bedrijfpensioenfonds voor het Glazenwassersen Schoonmaakbedrijf*)[9] and in its judgments of 14 December

---

[5] [1993] ECR I-6591.
[6] [1994] ECR I-4541 and (1994) ECR I-483, respectively.
[7] [1996] ECR I-1607.
[8] [1993] ECR I-5579.
[9] [1993] ECR I-4879.

1993 (Case C-110/91: *Moroni* v *Collo GmbH*), 22 December 1993 (Case C-152/91: *Neath* v *Hugh Steeper Ltd*)[10] and 28 September 1994 (Case C-200/91: *Coloroll Pension Trustees Limited* v *Russell and Others*),[11] the Court confirms that, by virtue of the judgment of 17 May 1990 (Case C-262/88: *Barber* v *Guardian Royal Exchange Assurance Group*), the direct effect of Article 119 of the Treaty may be relied on, for the purpose of claiming equal treatment in the matter of occupational pensions, only in relation to benefits payable in respect of periods of service subsequent to 17 May 1990, except in the case of workers or those claiming under them who have, before that date, initiated legal proceedings or raised an equivalent claim under the applicable national law;

Whereas, in its abovementioned judgments (Case C-109/91: *Ten Oever* v *Stichting Bedrijfpensioenfonds voor het Glazenwassersen Schoonmaakbedrijf* and Case C-200/91: *Coloroll Pension Trustees Limited* v *Russell and Others*), the Court confirms that the limitation of the effects in time of the Barber judgment applies to survivors' pensions and, consequently, equal treatment in this matter may be claimed only in relation to periods of service subsequent to 17 May 1990, except in the case of those who have, before that date, initiated legal proceedings or raised an equivalent claim under the applicable national law;

Whereas, moreover, in its judgments in Case C-152/91 and Case C-200/91, the Court specifies that the contributions of male and female workers to a defined-benefit pension scheme must be the same, since they are covered by Article 119 of the Treaty, whereas inequality of employers' contributions paid under funded defined-benefit schemes, which is due to the use of actuarial factors differing according to sex, is not to be assessed in the light of that same provision;

Whereas, in its judgments of 28 September 1994[12] (Case C-408/92: *Smith* v *Advel Systems* and Case C-28/93: *Van den Akker* v *Stichting Shell Pensioenfonds*), the Court points out that Article 119 of the Treaty precludes an employer who adopts measures necessary to comply with the *Barber* judgment of 17 May 1990 (C-262/88) from raising the retirement age for women to that which exists for men in relation to periods of service completed between 17 May 1990 and the date on which those measures come into force; on the other hand, as regards periods of service completed after the latter date, Article 119 does not prevent an employer from taking that step; as regards periods of service prior to 17 May 1990, Community law imposed no obligation which would justify retroactive reduction of the advantages which women enjoyed;

Whereas, in its abovementioned judgment in Case C-200/91: *Coloroll Pension Trustees Limited* v *Russell and Others*), the Court ruled that additional benefits stemming from contributions paid by employees on a purely voluntary basis are not covered by Article 119 of the Treaty;

Whereas, among the measures included in its third medium-term action programme on equal opportunities for women and men (1991 to 1995),[13] the Commission emphasises once more the adoption of suitable measures to take account of the consequences of the judgment of 17 May 1990 in Case 262/88 (*Barber* v *Guardian Royal Exchange Assurance Group*);

Whereas that judgment automatically invalidates certain provisions of Council Directive 86/378/EEC of 24 July 1986 on the implementation of the principle of equal treatment for men and women in occupational social security schemes[14] in respect of paid workers;

Whereas Article 119 of the Treaty is directly applicable and can be invoked before the

---

[10] [1993] ECR I-6953.
[11] [1994] ECR I-4389.
[12] [1994] ECR I-4435 and [1994] ECR I-4527, respectively.
[13] OJ No. C142, 31.5.1991, p. 1.
[14] OJ No. L225, 12.8.1986, p. 40.

national courts against any employer, whether a private person or a legal person, and whereas it is for these courts to safeguard the rights which that provision confers on individuals;

Whereas, on grounds of legal certainty, it is necesary to amend Directive 86/378/EEC in order to adapt the provisions which are affected by the Barber case-law,

Has adopted this directive:

Article 1[1]

Article 2

1. Any measure implementing this Directive, as regards paid workers, must cover all benefits derived from periods of employment subsequent to 17 May 1990 and shall apply retroactively to that date, without prejudice to workers or those claiming under them who have, before that date, initiated legal proceedings or raised an equivalent claim under national law. In that event, the implementation measures must apply retroactively to 8 April 1976 and must cover all the benefits derived from periods of employment after that date. For Member States which acceded to the Community after 8 April 1976 and before 17 May 1990, that date shall be replaced by the date on which Article 119 of the Treaty became applicable on their territory.

2. The second sentence of paragraph 1 shall not prevent national rules relating to time limits for bringing actions under national law from being relied on against workers or those claiming under them who initiated legal proceedings or raise an equivalent claim under national law before 17 May 1990, provided that they are not less favourable for that type of action than for similar actions of a domestic nature and that they do not render the exercise of Commnity law impossible in practice.

3. For Member States whose accession took place after 17 May 1990 and who were on 1 January 1994 Contracting Parties to the Agreement on the European Economic Area, the date of 17 May 1990 in the first sentence of paragraph 1 of this Article is replaced by 1 January 1994.

Article 3

1. Member States shall bring into force the laws, regulations and administrative provisions necessary to comply with this Directive by 1 July 1997. They shall forthwith inform the Commission thereof.

When Member States adopt these provisions, they shall contain a reference to this Directive or be accompanied by such reference on the occasion of their official publication. The methods of making such a reference shall be laid down by the Member States.

2. Member States shall communicate to the Commission, at the latest two years after the entry into force of this Directive, all information necessary to enable the Commission to draw up a report on the application of this Directive.

Article 4

This Directive shall enter into force on the 20th day following that of its publication in the *Official Journal of the European Communities*.

Article 5

This Directive is addressed to the Member States.

Done at Brussels, 20 December 1996.
For the Council
The President
S. BARRETT

---

[1] **Editor's Note:** Article 1 amended Directive 86/378 and is not reproduced here.

Council Directive 97/80/EC of 15 December 1997 on the burden of proof in cases of discrimination based on sex

[OJ 1998, L14/6]*

THE COUNCIL OF THE EUROPEAN UNION,

Having regard to the Agreement on social policy annexed to the Protocol (No. 14) on social policy annexed to the Treaty establishing the European Community, and in particular Article 2(2) thereof,

Having regard to the proposal from the Commission,[1]

Having regard to the opinion of the Economic and Social Committee,[2]

Acting, in accordance with the procedure laid down in Article 189c of the Treaty, in cooperation with the European Parliament,[3]

(1) Whereas, on the basis of the Protocol on social policy annexed to the Treaty, the Member States, with the exception of the United Kingdom of Great Britain and Northern Ireland (hereinafter called 'the Member States'), wishing to implement the 1989 Social Charter, have concluded an Agreement on social policy;

(2) Whereas the Community Charter of the Fundamental Social Rights of Workers recognises the importance of combating every form of discrimination, including discrimination on grounds of sex, colour, race, opinions and beliefs;

(3) Whereas paragraph 16 of the Community Charter of the Fundamental Social Rights of Workers on equal treatment for men and women, provides, inter alia, that 'action should be intensified to ensure the implementation of the principle of equality for men and women as regards, in particular, access to employment, remuneration, working conditions, social protection, education, vocational training and career development;

(4) Whereas, in accordance with Article 3(2) of the Agreement on social policy, the Commission has consulted management and labour at Community level on the possible direction of Community action on the burden of proof in cases of discrimination based on sex;

(5) Whereas the Commission, considering Community action advisable after such consultation, once again consulted management and labour on the content of the proposal contemplated in accordance with Article 3(3) of the same Agreement; whereas the latter have sent their opinions to the Commission;

(6) Whereas, after the second round of consultation, neither management nor labour have informed the Commission of their wish to initiate the process—possibly leading to an agreement—provided for in Article 4 of the same Agreement;

(7) Whereas, in accordance with Article 1 of the Agreement, the Community and the Member States have set themselves the objective, inter alia, of improving living and working conditions; whereas effective implementation of the principle of equal treatment for men and women would contribute to the achievement of that aim;

(8) Whereas the principle of equal treatment was stated in Article 119 of the Treaty, in Council Directive 75/117/EEC of 10 February 1975 on the approximation of the laws of the

---

* **Editor's Note:** As amended and extended to the UK by Directive 98/52 (OJ 1998, L14/205).

[1] OJ C 332, 7.11.1996, p. 11 and OJ C 185, 18.6.1997, p. 21.

[2] OJ C 133, 28.4.1997, p. 34.

[3] Opinion of the European Parliament of 10 April 1997 (OJ C 132, 28.4.1997, p. 215), Common Position of the Council of 24 July 1997 (OJ C 307, 8.10.1997, p. 6) and Decision of the European Parliament of 6 November 1997 (OJ C 358, 24.11.1997).

Member States relating to the application of the principle of equal pay for men and women[4] and in Council Directive 76/207/EEC of 9 February 1976 on the implementation of the principle of equal treatment for men and women as regards access to employment, vocational training and promotion and working conditions;[5]

(9) Whereas Council Directive 92/85/EEC of 19 October 1992 on the introduction of measures to encourage improvements in the safety and health at work of pregnant workers and workers who have recently given birth or are breastfeeding[6] also contributes to the effective implementation of the principle of equal treatment for men and women; whereas that Directive should not work to the detriment of the aforementioned Directives on equal treatment; whereas, therefore, female workers covered by that Directive should likewise benefit from the adaptation of the rules on the burden of proof;

(10) Whereas Council Directive 96/34/EC of 3 June 1996 on the framework agreement on parental leave concluded by UNICE, CEEP and the ETUC,[7] is also based on the principle of equal treatment for men and women;

(11) Whereas the references to 'judicial process' and 'court' cover mechanisms by means of which disputes may be submitted for examination and decision to independent bodies which may hand down decisions that are binding on the parties to those disputes;

(12) Whereas the expression 'out-of-court procedures' means in particular procedures such as conciliation and mediation;

(13) Whereas the appreciation of the facts from which it may be presumed that there has been direct or indirect discrimination is a matter for national judicial or other competent bodies, in accordance with national law or practice;

(14) Whereas it is for the Member States to introduce, at any appropriate stage of the proceedings, rules of evidence which are more favourable to plaintiffs;

(15) Whereas it is necessary to take account of the specific features of certain Member States' legal systems, inter alia where an inference of discrimination is drawn if the respondent fails to produce evidence that satisfies the court or other competent authority that there has been no breach of the principle of equal treatment;

(16) Whereas Member States need not apply the rules on the burden of proof to proceedings in which it is for the court or other competent body to investigate the facts of the case; whereas the procedures thus referred to are those in which the plaintiff is not required to prove the facts, which it is for the court or competent body to investigate;

(17) Whereas plaintiffs could be deprived of any effective means of enforcing the principle of equal treatment before the national courts if the effect of introducing evidence of an apparent discrimination were not to impose upon the respondent the burden of proving that his practice is not in fact discriminatory;

(18) Whereas the Court of Justice of the European Communities has therefore held that the rules on the burden of proof must be adapted when there is a prima facie case of discrimination and that, for the principle of equal treatment to be applied effectively, the burden of proof must shift back to the respondent when evidence of such discrimination is brought;

(19) Whereas it is all the more difficult to prove discrimination when it is indirect; whereas it is therefore important to define indirect discrimination;

(20) Whereas the aim of adequately adapting the rules on the burden of proof has not been achieved satisfactorily in all Member States and, in accordance with the principle of subsidiarity stated in Article 3b of the Treaty and with that of proportionality, that aim must

[4] OJ L 45, 19.2.1975, p. 19.
[5] OJ L 39, 14.2.1976, p. 40.
[6] OJ L 348, 28.11.1992, p. 1.
[7] OJ L 145, 19.6.1996, p. 4.

be attained at Community level; whereas this Directive confines itself to the minimum action required and does not go beyond what is necessary for that purpose,

HAS ADOPTED THIS DIRECTIVE:

Article 1   Aim

The aim of this Directive shall be to ensure that the measures taken by the Member States to implement the principle of equal treatment are made more effective, in order to enable all persons who consider themselves wronged because the principle of equal treatment has not been applied to them to have their rights asserted by judicial process after possible recourse to other competent bodies.

Article 2   Definitions

1.   For the purposes of this Directive, the principle of equal treatment shall mean that there shall be no discrimination whatsoever based on sex, either directly or indirectly.

2.   For purposes of the principle of equal treatment referred to in paragraph 1, indirect discrimination shall exist where an apparently neutral provision, criterion or practice disadvantages a substantially higher proportion of the members of one sex unless that provision, criterion or practice is appropriate and necessary and can be justified by objective factors unrelated to sex.

Article 3   Scope

1.   This Directive shall apply to:
   (a) the situations covered by Article 119 of the Treaty and by Directives 75/117/EEC, 76/207/EEC and, insofar as discrimination based on sex is concerned, 92/85/EEC and 96/34/EC;
   (b) any civil or administrative procedure concerning the public or private sector which provides for means of redress under national law pursuant to the measures referred to in (a) with the exception of out-of-court procedures of a voluntary nature or provided for in national law.

2.   This Directive shall not apply to criminal procedures, unless otherwise provided by the Member States.

Article 4   Burden of proof

1.   Member States shall take such measures as are necessary, in accordance with their national judicial systems, to ensure that, when persons who consider themselves wronged because the principle of equal treatment has not been applied to them establish, before a court or other competent authority, facts from which it may be presumed that there has been direct or indirect discrimination, it shall be for the respondent to prove that there has been no breach of the principle of equal treatment.

2.   This Directive shall not prevent Member States from introducing rules of evidence which are more favourable to plaintiffs.

3.   Member States need not apply paragraph 1 to proceedings in which it is for the court or competent body to investigate the facts of the case.

Article 5   Information

Member States shall ensure that measures taken pursuant to this Directive, together with the provisions already in force, are brought to the attention of all the persons concerned by all appropriate means.

Article 6   Non-regression

Implementation of this Directive shall under no circumstances be sufficient grounds for a reduction in the general level of protection of workers in the areas to which it applies, without prejudice to the Member States' right to respond to changes in the situation by introducing laws, regulations and administrative provisions which differ from those in force on the notification of this Directive, provided that the minimum requirements of this Directive are complied with.

Article 7   Implementation
The Member States shall bring into force the laws, regulations and administrative provisions necessary for them to comply with this Directive by 1 January 2001. They shall immediately inform the Commission thereof.

As regards the United Kingdom of Great Britain and Northern Ireland, the date of 1 January 2001 in paragraph 1 shall be replaced by 22 July 2001.

When the Member States adopt those measures they shall contain a reference to this Directive or shall be accompanied by such a reference on the occasion of their official publication. The methods of making such references shall be laid down by the Member States.

The Member States shall communicate to the Commission, within two years of the entry into force of this Directive, all the information necessary for the Commission to draw up a report to the European Parliament and the Council on the application of this Directive.

Article 8
This Directive is addressed to the Member States.

Done at Brussels, 15 December 1997.
For the Council
The President
J.-C. JUNCKER

Council Directive 2000/43 of 29 June 2000 implementing the principle of equal treatment between persons irrespective of racial or ethnic origin
[OJ 2000, L180/22]

THE COUNCIL OF THE EUROPEAN UNION,
Having regard to the Treaty establishing the European Community and in particular Article 13 thereof,
Having regard to the proposal from the Commission,[1]
Having regard to the opinion of the European Parliament,[2]
Having regard to the opinion of the Economic and Social Committee,[3]
Having regard to the opinion of the Committee of the Regions,[4]
Whereas:

(1) The Treaty on European Union marks a new stage in the process of creating an ever closer union among the peoples of Europe.

(2) In accordance with Article 6 of the Treaty on European Union, the European Union is founded on the principles of liberty, democracy, respect for human rights and fundamental freedoms, and the rule of law, principles which are common to the Member States, and should

---

[1] Not yet published in the Official Journal.
[2] Opinion delivered on 18.5.2000 (not yet published in the Official Journal).
[3] Opinion delivered on 12.4.2000 (not yet published in the Official Journal).
[4] Opinion delivered on 31.5.2000 (not yet published in the Official Journal).

respect fundamental rights as guaranteed by the European Convention for the protection of Human Rights and Fundamental Freedoms and as they result from the constitutional traditions common to the Member States, as general principles of Community Law.

(3) The right to equality before the law and protection against discrimination for all persons constitutes a universal right recognised by the Universal Declaration of Human Rights, the United Nations Convention on the Elimination of all forms of Discrimination Against Women, the International Convention on the Elimination of all forms of Racial Discrimination and the United Nations Covenants on Civil and Political Rights and on Economic, Social and Cultural Rights and by the European Convention for the Protection of Human Rights and Fundamental Freedoms, to which all Member States are signatories.

(4) It is important to respect such fundamental rights and freedoms, including the right to freedom of association. It is also important, in the context of the access to and provision of goods and services, to respect the protection of private and family life and transactions carried out in this context.

(5) The European Parliament has adopted a number of Resolutions on the fight against racism in the European Union.

(6) The European Union rejects theories which attempt to determine the existence of separate human races. The use of the term 'racial origin' in this Directive does not imply an acceptance of such theories.

(7) The European Council in Tampere, on 15 and 16 October 1999, invited the Commission to come forward as soon as possible with proposals implementing Article 13 of the EC Treaty as regards the fight against racism and xenophobia.

(8) The Employment Guidelines 2000 agreed by the European Council in Helsinki, on 10 and 11 December 1999, stress the need to foster conditions for a socially inclusive labour market by formulating a coherent set of policies aimed at combating discrimination against groups such as ethnic minorities.

(9) Discrimination based on racial or ethnic origin may undermine the achievement of the objectives of the EC Treaty, in particular the attainment of a high level of employment and of social protection, the raising of the standard of living and quality of life, economic and social cohesion and solidarity. It may also undermine the objective of developing the European Union as an area of freedom, security and justice.

(10) The Commission presented a communication on racism, xenophobia and anti-Semitism in December 1995.

(11) The Council adopted on 15 July 1996 Joint Action (96/443/JHA) concerning action to combat racism and xenophobia[5] under which the Member States undertake to ensure effective judicial cooperation in respect of offences based on racist or xenophobic behaviour.

(12) To ensure the development of democratic and tolerant societies which allow the participation of all persons irrespective of racial or ethnic origin, specific action in the field of discrimination based on racial or ethnic origin should go beyond access to employed and self-employed activities and cover areas such as education, social protection including social security and health-care, social advantages and access to and supply of goods and services.

(13) To this end, any direct or indirect discrimination based on racial or ethnic origin as regards the areas covered by this Directive should be prohibited throughout the Community. This prohibition of discrimination should also apply to nationals of third countries, but does not cover differences of treatment based on nationality and is without prejudice to provisions governing the entry and residence of third-country nationals and their access to employment and to occupation.

---

[5] OJ L 185, 24.7.1996, p. 5.

(14) In implementing the principle of equal treatment irrespective of racial or ethnic origin, the Community should, in accordance with Article 3(2) of the EC Treaty, aim to eliminate inequalities, and to promote equality between men and women, especially since women are often the victims of multiple discrimination.

(15) The appreciation of the facts from which it may be inferred that there has been direct or indirect discrimination is a matter for national judicial or other competent bodies, in accordance with rules of national law or practice. Such rules may provide in particular for indirect discrimination to be established by any means including on the basis of statistical evidence.

(16) It is important to protect all natural persons against discrimination on grounds of racial or ethnic origin. Member States should also provide, where appropriate and in accordance with their national traditions and practice, protection for legal persons where they suffer discrimination on grounds of the racial or ethnic origin of their members.

(17) The prohibition of discrimination should be without prejudice to the maintenance or adoption of measures intended to prevent or compensate for disadvantages suffered by a group of persons of a particular racial or ethnic origin, and such measures may permit organisations of persons of a particular racial or ethnic origin where their main object is the promotion of the special needs of those persons.

(18) In very limited circumstances, a difference of treatment may be justified where a characteristic related to racial or ethnic origin constitutes a genuine and determining occupational requirement, when the objective is legitimate and the requirement is proportionate. Such circumstances should be included in the information provided by the Member States to the Commission.

(19) Persons who have been subject to discrimination based on racial and ethnic origin should have adequate means of legal protection. To provide a more effective level of protection, associations or legal entities should also be empowered to engage, as the Member States so determine, either on behalf or in support of any victim, in proceedings, without prejudice to national rules of procedure concerning representation and defence before the courts.

(20) The effective implementation of the principle of equality requires adequate judicial protection against victimisation.

(21) The rules on the burden of proof must be adapted when there is a prima facie case of discrimination and, for the principle of equal treatment to be applied effectively, the burden of proof must shift back to the respondent when evidence of such discrimination is brought.

(22) Member States need not apply the rules on the burden of proof to proceedings in which it is for the court or other competent body to investigate the facts of the case. The procedures thus referred to are those in which the plaintiff is not required to prove the facts, which it is for the court or competent body to investigate.

(23) Member States should promote dialogue between the social partners and with non-governmental organisations to address different forms of discrimination and to combat them.

(24) Protection against discrimination based on racial or ethnic origin would itself be strengthened by the existence of a body or bodies in each Member State, with competence to analyse the problems involved, to study possible solutions and to provide concrete assistance for the victims.

(25) This Directive lays down minimum requirements, thus giving the Member States the option of introducing or maintaining more favourable provisions. The implementation of this Directive should not serve to justify any regression in relation to the situation which already prevails in each Member State.

(26) Member States should provide for effective, proportionate and dissuasive sanctions in case of breaches of the obligations under this Directive.

(27) The Member States may entrust management and labour, at their joint request, with the implementation of this Directive as regards provisions falling within the scope of

collective agreements, provided that the Member States take all the necessary steps to ensure that they can at all times guarantee the results imposed by this Directive.

(28) In accordance with the principles of subsidiarity and proportionality as set out in Article 5 of the EC Treaty, the objective of this Directive, namely ensuring a common high level of protection against discrimination in all the Member States, cannot be sufficiently achieved by the Member States and can therefore, by reason of the scale and impact of the proposed action, be better achieved by the Community. This Directive does not go beyond what is necessary in order to achieve those objectives,

HAS ADOPTED THIS DIRECTIVE:

CHAPTER I   GENERAL PROVISIONS

Article 1   Purpose
The purpose of this Directive is to lay down a framework for combating discrimination on the grounds of racial or ethnic origin, with a view to putting into effect in the Member States the principle of equal treatment.

Article 2   Concept of discrimination
1.   For the purposes of this Directive, the principle of equal treatment shall mean that there shall be no direct or indirect discrimination based on racial or ethnic origin.
2.   For the purposes of paragraph 1:
   (a)   direct discrimination shall be taken to occur where one person is treated less favourably than another is, has been or would be treated in a comparable situation on grounds of racial or ethnic origin;
   (b)   indirect discrimination shall be taken to occur where an apparently neutral provision, criterion or practice would put persons of a racial or ethnic origin at a particular disadvantage compared with other persons, unless that provision, criterion or practice is objectively justified by a legitimate aim and the means of achieving that aim are appropriate and necessary.
3.   Harassment shall be deemed to be discrimination within the meaning of paragraph 1, when an unwanted conduct related to racial or ethnic origin takes place with the purpose or effect of violating the dignity of a person and of creating an intimidating, hostile, degrading, humiliating or offensive environment. In this context, the concept of harassment may be defined in accordance with the national laws and practice of the Member States.
4.   An instruction to discriminate against persons on grounds of racial or ethnic origin shall be deemed to be discrimination within the meaning of paragraph 1.

Article 3   Scope
1.   Within the limits of the powers conferred upon the Community, this Directive shall apply to all persons, as regards both the public and private sectors, including public bodies, in relation to:
   (a)   conditions for access to employment, to self-employment and to occupation, including selection criteria and recruitment conditions, whatever the branch of activity and at all levels of the professional hierarchy, including promotion;
   (b)   access to all types and to all levels of vocational guidance, vocational training, advanced vocational training and retraining, including practical work experience;
   (c)   employment and working conditions, including dismissals and pay;
   (d)   membership of and involvement in an organisation of workers or employers, or any organisation whose members carry on a particular profession, including the benefits provided for by such organisations;
   (e)   social protection, including social security and healthcare;

(f) social advantages;

(g) education;

(h) access to and supply of goods and services which are available to the public, including housing.

2.   This Directive does not cover difference of treatment based on nationality and is without prejudice to provisions and conditions relating to the entry into and residence of third-country nationals and stateless persons on the territory of Member States, and to any treatment which arises from the legal status of the third-country nationals and stateless persons concerned.

Article 4   Genuine and determining occupational requirements

Notwithstanding Article 2(1) and (2), Member States may provide that a difference of treatment which is based on a characteristic related to racial or ethnic origin shall not constitute discrimination where, by reason of the nature of the particular occupational activities concerned or of the context in which they are carried out, such a characteristic constitutes a genuine and determining occupational requirement, provided that the objective is legitimate and the requirement is proportionate.

Article 5   Positive action

With a view to ensuring full equality in practice, the principle of equal treatment shall not prevent any Member State from maintaining or adopting specific measures to prevent or compensate for disadvantages linked to racial or ethnic origin.

Article 6   Minimum requirements

1.   Member States may introduce or maintain provisions which are more favourable to the protection of the principle of equal treatment than those laid down in this Directive.

2.   The implementation of this Directive shall under no circumstances constitute grounds for a reduction in the level of protection against discrimination already afforded by Member States in the fields covered by this Directive.

CHAPTER II   REMEDIES AND ENFORCEMENT

Article 7   Defence of rights

1.   Member States shall ensure that judicial and/or administrative procedures, including where they deem it appropriate conciliation procedures, for the enforcement of obligations under this Directive are available to all persons who consider themselves wronged by failure to apply the principle of equal treatment to them, even after the relationship in which the discrimination is alleged to have occurred has ended.

2.   Member States shall ensure that associations, organisations or other legal entities, which have, in accordance with the criteria laid down by their national law, a legitimate interest in ensuring that the provisions of this Directive are complied with, may engage, either on behalf or in support of the complainant, with his or her approval, in any judicial and/or administrative procedure provided for the enforcement of obligations under this Directive.

3.   Paragraphs 1 and 2 are without prejudice to national rules relating to time limits for bringing actions as regards the principle of equality of treatment.

Article 8   Burden of proof

1.   Member States shall take such measures as are necessary, in accordance with their national judicial systems, to ensure that, when persons who consider themselves wronged because the principle of equal treatment has not been applied to them establish, before a court or other competent authority, facts from which it may be presumed that there has been direct or indirect discrimination, it shall be for the respondent to prove that there has been no breach of the principle of equal treatment.

2.   Paragraph 1 shall not prevent Member States from introducing rules of evidence which are more favourable to plaintiffs.

3.   Paragraph 1 shall not apply to criminal procedures.

4.   Paragraphs 1, 2 and 3 shall also apply to any proceedings brought in accordance with Article 7(2).

5.   Member States need not apply paragraph 1 to proceedings in which it is for the court or competent body to investigate the facts of the case.

Article 9   Victimisation

Member States shall introduce into their national legal systems such measures as are necessary to protect individuals from any adverse treatment or adverse consequence as a reaction to a complaint or to proceedings aimed at enforcing compliance with the principle of equal treatment.

Article 10   Dissemination of information

Member States shall take care that the provisions adopted pursuant to this Directive, together with the relevant provisions already in force, are brought to the attention of the persons concerned by all appropriate means throughout their territory.

Article 11   Social dialogue

1.   Member States shall, in accordance with national traditions and practice, take adequate measures to promote the social dialogue between the two sides of industry with a view to fostering equal treatment, including through the monitoring of workplace practices, collective agreements, codes of conduct, research or exchange of experiences and good practices.

2.   Where consistent with national traditions and practice, Member States shall encourage the two sides of the industry without prejudice to their autonomy to conclude, at the appropriate level, agreements laying down anti-discrimination rules in the fields referred to in Article 3 which fall within the scope of collective bargaining. These agreements shall respect the minimum requirements laid down by this Directive and the relevant national implementing measures.

Article 12   Dialogue with non-governmental organisations

Member States shall encourage dialogue with appropriate non-governmental organisations which have, in accordance with their national law and practice, a legitimate interest in contributing to the fight against discrimination on grounds of racial and ethnic origin with a view to promoting the principle of equal treatment.

CHAPTER III   BODIES FOR THE PROMOTION OF EQUAL TREATMENT

Article 13

1.   Member States shall designate a body or bodies for the promotion of equal treatment of all persons without discrimination on the grounds of racial or ethnic origin. These bodies may form part of agencies charged at national level with the defence of human rights or the safeguard of individuals' rights.

2.   Member States shall ensure that the competences of these bodies include:

— without prejudice to the right of victims and of associations, organisations or other legal entities referred to in Article 7(2), providing independent assistance to victims of discrimination in pursuing their complaints about discrimination,

— conducting independent surveys concerning discrimination,

— publishing independent reports and making recommendations on any issue relating to such discrimination.

CHAPTER IV   FINAL PROVISIONS

Article 14   Compliance

Member States shall take the necessary measures to ensure that:

(a) any laws, regulations and administrative provisions contrary to the principle of equal treatment are abolished;

(b) any provisions contrary to the principle of equal treatment which are included in individual or collective contracts or agreements, internal rules of undertakings, rules governing profit-making or non-profit-making associations, and rules governing the independent professions and workers' and employers' organisations, are or may be declared, null and void or are amended.

Article 15   Sanctions

Member States shall lay down the rules on sanctions applicable to infringements of the national provisions adopted pursuant to this Directive and shall take all measures necessary to ensure that they are applied. The sanctions, which may comprise the payment of compensation to the victim, must be effective, proportionate and dissuasive. The Member States shall notify those provisions to the Commission by 19 July 2003 at the latest and shall notify it without delay of any subsequent amendment affecting them.

Article 16   Implementation

Member States shall adopt the laws, regulations and administrative provisions necessary to comply with this Directive by 19 July 2003 or may entrust management and labour, at their joint request, with the implementation of this Directive as regards provisions falling within the scope of collective agreements. In such cases, Member States shall ensure that by 19 July 2003, management and labour introduce the necessary measures by agreement, Member States being required to take any necessary measures to enable them at any time to be in a position to guarantee the results imposed by this Directive. They shall forthwith inform the Commission thereof.

When Member States adopt these measures, they shall contain a reference to this Directive or be accompanied by such a reference on the occasion of their official publication. The methods of making such a reference shall be laid down by the Member States.

Article 17   Report

1.   Member States shall communicate to the Commission by 19 July 2005, and every five years thereafter, all the information necessary for the Commission to draw up a report to the European Parliament and the Council on the application of this Directive.

2.   The Commission's report shall take into account, as appropriate, the views of the European Monitoring Centre on Racism and Xenophobia, as well as the viewpoints of the social partners and relevant non-governmental organisations. In accordance with the principle of gender mainstreaming, this report shall, inter alia, provide an assessment of the impact of the measures taken on women and men. In the light of the information received, this report shall include, if necessary, proposals to revise and update this Directive.

Article 18   Entry into force

This Directive shall enter into force on the day of its publication in the Official Journal of the European Communities.

Article 19   Addressees

This Directive is addressed to the Member States.

Done at Luxembourg, 29 June 2000.

For the Council
The President
M. ARCANJO

Council Directive 2000/78 of 27 November 2000 establishing a general framework for equal treatment in employment and occupation

[OJ 2000, L303/16]

THE COUNCIL OF THE EUROPEAN UNION,

Having regard to the Treaty establishing the European Community, and in particular Article 13 thereof,

Having regard to the proposal from the Commission,[1]

Having regard to the Opinion of the European Parliament,[2]

Having regard to the Opinion of the Economic and Social Committee,[3]

Having regard to the Opinion of the Committee of the Regions,[4]

Whereas:

(1) In accordance with Article 6 of the Treaty on European Union, the European Union is founded on the principles of liberty, democracy, respect for human rights and fundamental freedoms, and the rule of law, principles which are common to all Member States and it respects fundamental rights, as guaranteed by the European Convention for the Protection of Human Rights and Fundamental Freedoms and as they result from the constitutional traditions common to the Member States, as general principles of Community law.

(2) The principle of equal treatment between women and men is well established by an important body of Community law, in particular in Council Directive 76/207/EEC of 9 February 1976 on the implementation of the principle of equal treatment for men and women as regards access to employment, vocational training and promotion, and working conditions.[5]

(3) In implementing the principle of equal treatment, the Community should, in accordance with Article 3(2) of the EC Treaty, aim to eliminate inequalities, and to promote equality between men and women, especially since women are often the victims of multiple discrimination.

(4) The right of all persons to equality before the law and protection against discrimination constitutes a universal right recognised by the Universal Declaration of Human Rights, the United Nations Convention on the Elimination of All Forms of Discrimination against Women, United Nations Covenants on Civil and Political Rights and on Economic, Social and Cultural Rights and by the European Convention for the Protection of Human Rights and Fundamental Freedoms, to which all Member States are signatories. Convention No 111 of the International Labour Organisation (ILO) prohibits discrimination in the field of employment and occupation.

(5) It is important to respect such fundamental rights and freedoms. This Directive does not prejudice freedom of association, including the right to establish unions with others and to join unions to defend one's interests.

(6) The Community Charter of the Fundamental Social Rights of Workers recognises the importance of combating every form of discrimination, including the need to take appropriate action for the social and economic integration of elderly and disabled people.

---

[1] OJ C 177 E, 27.6.2000, p. 42.
[2] Opinion delivered on 12 October 2000 (not yet published in the Official Journal).
[3] OJ C 204, 18.7.2000, p. 82.
[4] OJ C 226, 8.8.2000, p. 1.
[5] OJ L 39, 14.2.1976, p. 40.

(7) The EC Treaty includes among its objectives the promotion of coordination between employment policies of the Member States. To this end, a new employment chapter was incorporated in the EC Treaty as a means of developing a coordinated European strategy for employment to promote a skilled, trained and adaptable workforce.

(8) The Employment Guidelines for 2000 agreed by the European Council at Helsinki on 10 and 11 December 1999 stress the need to foster a labour market favourable to social integration by formulating a coherent set of policies aimed at combating discrimination against groups such as persons with disability. They also emphasise the need to pay particular attention to supporting older workers, in order to increase their participation in the labour force.

(9) Employment and occupation are key elements in guaranteeing equal opportunities for all and contribute strongly to the full participation of citizens in economic, cultural and social life and to realising their potential.

(10) On 29 June 2000 the Council adopted Directive 2000/43/EC[6] implementing the principle of equal treatment between persons irrespective of racial or ethnic origin. That Directive already provides protection against such discrimination in the field of employment and occupation.

(11) Discrimination based on religion or belief, disability, age or sexual orientation may undermine the achievement of the objectives of the EC Treaty, in particular the attainment of a high level of employment and social protection, raising the standard of living and the quality of life, economic and social cohesion and solidarity, and the free movement of persons.

(12) To this end, any direct or indirect discrimination based on religion or belief, disability, age or sexual orientation as regards the areas covered by this Directive should be prohibited throughout the Community. This prohibition of discrimination should also apply to nationals of third countries but does not cover differences of treatment based on nationality and is without prejudice to provisions governing the entry and residence of third-country nationals and their access to employment and occupation.

(13) This Directive does not apply to social security and social protection schemes whose benefits are not treated as income within the meaning given to that term for the purpose of applying Article 141 of the EC Treaty, nor to any kind of payment by the State aimed at providing access to employment or maintaining employment.

(14) This Directive shall be without prejudice to national provisions laying down retirement ages.

(15) The appreciation of the facts from which it may be inferred that there has been direct or indirect discrimination is a matter for national judicial or other competent bodies, in accordance with rules of national law or practice. Such rules may provide, in particular, for indirect discrimination to be established by any means including on the basis of statistical evidence.

(16) The provision of measures to accommodate the needs of disabled people at the workplace plays an important role in combating discrimination on grounds of disability.

(17) This Directive does not require the recruitment, promotion, maintenance in employment or training of an individual who is not competent, capable and available to perform the essential functions of the post concerned or to undergo the relevant training, without prejudice to the obligation to provide reasonable accommodation for people with disabilities.

(18) This Directive does not require, in particular, the armed forces and the police, prison or emergency services to recruit or maintain in employment persons who do not have

---

[6] OJ L 180, 19.7.2000, p. 22.

the required capacity to carry out the range of functions that they may be called upon to perform with regard to the legitimate objective of preserving the operational capacity of those services.

(19) Moreover, in order that the Member States may continue to safeguard the combat effectiveness of their armed forces, they may choose not to apply the provisions of this Directive concerning disability and age to all or part of their armed forces. The Member States which make that choice must define the scope of that derogation.

(20) Appropriate measures should be provided, i.e. effective and practical measures to adapt the workplace to the disability, for example adapting premises and equipment, patterns of working time, the distribution of tasks or the provision of training or integration resources.

(21) To determine whether the measures in question give rise to a disproportionate burden, account should be taken in particular of the financial and other costs entailed, the scale and financial resources of the organisation or undertaking and the possibility of obtaining public funding or any other assistance.

(22) This Directive is without prejudice to national laws on marital status and the benefits dependent thereon.

(23) In very limited circumstances, a difference of treatment may be justified where a characteristic related to religion or belief, disability, age or sexual orientation constitutes a genuine and determining occupational requirement, when the objective is legitimate and the requirement is proportionate. Such circumstances should be included in the information provided by the Member States to the Commission.

(24) The European Union in its Declaration No 11 on the status of churches and non-confessional organisations, annexed to the Final Act of the Amsterdam Treaty, has explicitly recognised that it respects and does not prejudice the status under national law of churches and religious associations or communities in the Member States and that it equally respects the status of philosophical and non-confessional organisations. With this in view, Member States may maintain or lay down specific provisions on genuine, legitimate and justified occupational requirements which might be required for carrying out an occupational activity.

(25) The prohibition of age discrimination is an essential part of meeting the aims set out in the Employment Guidelines and encouraging diversity in the workforce. However, differences in treatment in connection with age may be justified under certain circumstances and therefore require specific provisions which may vary in accordance with the situation in Member States. It is therefore essential to distinguish between differences in treatment which are justified, in particular by legitimate employment policy, labour market and vocational training objectives, and discrimination which must be prohibited.

(26) The prohibition of discrimination should be without prejudice to the maintenance or adoption of measures intended to prevent or compensate for disadvantages suffered by a group of persons of a particular religion or belief, disability, age or sexual orientation, and such measures may permit organisations of persons of a particular religion or belief, disability, age or sexual orientation where their main object is the promotion of the special needs of those persons.

(27) In its Recommendation 86/379/EEC of 24 July 1986 on the employment of disabled people in the Community,[7] the Council established a guideline framework setting out examples of positive action to promote the employment and training of disabled people, and in its Resolution of 17 June 1999 on equal employment opportunities for people with disabilities,[8] affirmed the importance of giving specific attention inter alia to recruitment, retention, training and lifelong learning with regard to disabled persons.

---

[7] OJ L 225, 12.8.1986, p. 43.
[8] OJ C 186, 2.7.1999, p. 3.

(28) This Directive lays down minimum requirements, thus giving the Member States the option of introducing or maintaining more favourable provisions. The implementation of this Directive should not serve to justify any regression in relation to the situation which already prevails in each Member State.

(29) Persons who have been subject to discrimination based on religion or belief, disability, age or sexual orientation should have adequate means of legal protection. To provide a more effective level of protection, associations or legal entities should also be empowered to engage in proceedings, as the Member States so determine, either on behalf or in support of any victim, without prejudice to national rules of procedure concerning representation and defence before the courts.

(30) The effective implementation of the principle of equality requires adequate judicial protection against victimisation.

(31) The rules on the burden of proof must be adapted when there is a prima facie case of discrimination and, for the principle of equal treatment to be applied effectively, the burden of proof must shift back to the respondent when evidence of such discrimination is brought. However, it is not for the respondent to prove that the plaintiff adheres to a particular religion or belief, has a particular disability, is of a particular age or has a particular sexual orientation.

(32) Member States need not apply the rules on the burden of proof to proceedings in which it is for the court or other competent body to investigate the facts of the case. The procedures thus referred to are those in which the plaintiff is not required to prove the facts, which it is for the court or competent body to investigate.

(33) Member States should promote dialogue between the social partners and, within the framework of national practice, with non-governmental organisations to address different forms of discrimination at the workplace and to combat them.

(34) The need to promote peace and reconciliation between the major communities in Northern Ireland necessitates the incorporation of particular provisions into this Directive.

(35) Member States should provide for effective, proportionate and dissuasive sanctions in case of breaches of the obligations under this Directive.

(36) Member States may entrust the social partners, at their joint request, with the implementation of this Directive, as regards the provisions concerning collective agreements, provided they take any necessary steps to ensure that they are at all times able to guarantee the results required by this Directive.

(37) In accordance with the principle of subsidiarity set out in Article 5 of the EC Treaty, the objective of this Directive, namely the creation within the Community of a level playing-field as regards equality in employment and occupation, cannot be sufficiently achieved by the Member States and can therefore, by reason of the scale and impact of the action, be better achieved at Community level. In accordance with the principle of proportionality, as set out in that Article, this Directive does not go beyond what is necessary in order to achieve that objective,

HAS ADOPTED THIS DIRECTIVE:

CHAPTER I   GENERAL PROVISIONS

Article 1   Purpose
The purpose of this Directive is to lay down a general framework for combating discrimination on the grounds of religion or belief, disability, age or sexual orientation as regards employment and occupation, with a view to putting into effect in the Member States the principle of equal treatment.

Article 2   Concept of discrimination

    1.   For the purposes of this Directive, the 'principle of equal treatment' shall mean that there shall be no direct or indirect discrimination whatsoever on any of the grounds referred to in Article 1.

    2.   For the purposes of paragraph 1:

      (a)   direct discrimination shall be taken to occur where one person is treated less favourably than another is, has been or would be treated in a comparable situation, on any of the grounds referred to in Article 1;

      (b)   indirect discrimination shall be taken to occur where an apparently neutral provision, criterion or practice would put persons having a particular religion or belief, a particular disability, a particular age, or a particular sexual orientation at a particular disadvantage compared with other persons unless:

         (i)   that provision, criterion or practice is objectively justified by a legitimate aim and the means of achieving that aim are appropriate and necessary, or

         (ii)   as regards persons with a particular disability, the employer or any person or organisation to whom this Directive applies, is obliged, under national legislation, to take appropriate measures in line with the principles contained in Article 5 in order to eliminate disadvantages entailed by such provision, criterion or practice.

    3.   Harassment shall be deemed to be a form of discrimination within the meaning of paragraph 1, when unwanted conduct related to any of the grounds referred to in Article 1 takes place with the purpose or effect of violating the dignity of a person and of creating an intimidating, hostile, degrading, humiliating or offensive environment. In this context, the concept of harassment may be defined in accordance with the national laws and practice of the Member States.

    4.   An instruction to discriminate against persons on any of the grounds referred to in Article 1 shall be deemed to be discrimination within the meaning of paragraph 1.

    5.   This Directive shall be without prejudice to measures laid down by national law which, in a democratic society, are necessary for public security, for the maintenance of public order and the prevention of criminal offences, for the protection of health and for the protection of the rights and freedoms of others.

Article 3   Scope

    1.   Within the limits of the areas of competence conferred on the Community, this Directive shall apply to all persons, as regards both the public and private sectors, including public bodies, in relation to:

      (a)   conditions for access to employment, to self-employment or to occupation, including selection criteria and recruitment conditions, whatever the branch of activity and at all levels of the professional hierarchy, including promotion;

      (b)   access to all types and to all levels of vocational guidance, vocational training, advanced vocational training and retraining, including practical work experience;

      (c)   employment and working conditions, including dismissals and pay;

      (d)   membership of, and involvement in, an organisation of workers or employers, or any organisation whose members carry on a particular profession, including the benefits provided for by such organisations.

    2.   This Directive does not cover differences of treatment based on nationality and is without prejudice to provisions and conditions relating to the entry into and residence of third-country nationals and stateless persons in the territory of Member States, and to any treatment which arises from the legal status of the third-country nationals and stateless persons concerned.

    3.   This Directive does not apply to payments of any kind made by state schemes or similar, including state social security or social protection schemes.

4. Member States may provide that this Directive, in so far as it relates to discrimination on the grounds of disability and age, shall not apply to the armed forces.

Article 4   Occupational requirements

1. Notwithstanding Article 2(1) and (2), Member States may provide that a difference of treatment which is based on a characteristic related to any of the grounds referred to in Article 1 shall not constitute discrimination where, by reason of the nature of the particular occupational activities concerned or of the context in which they are carried out, such a characteristic constitutes a genuine and determining occupational requirement, provided that the objective is legitimate and the requirement is proportionate.

2. Member States may maintain national legislation in force at the date of adoption of this Directive or provide for future legislation incorporating national practices existing at the date of adoption of this Directive pursuant to which, in the case of occupational activities within churches and other public or private organisations the ethos of which is based on religion or belief, a difference of treatment based on a person's religion or belief shall not constitute discrimination where, by reason of the nature of these activities or of the context in which they are carried out, a person's religion or belief constitute a genuine, legitimate and justified occupational requirement, having regard to the organisation's ethos. This difference of treatment shall be implemented taking account of Member States' constitutional provisions and principles, as well as the general principles of Community law, and should not justify discrimination on another ground.

Provided that its provisions are otherwise complied with, this Directive shall thus not prejudice the right of churches and other public or private organisations, the ethos of which is based on religion or belief, acting in conformity with national constitutions and laws, to require individuals working for them to act in good faith and with loyalty to the organisation's ethos.

Article 5   Reasonable accommodation for disabled persons

In order to guarantee compliance with the principle of equal treatment in relation to persons with disabilities, reasonable accommodation shall be provided. This means that employers shall take appropriate measures, where needed in a particular case, to enable a person with a disability to have access to, participate in, or advance in employment, or to undergo training, unless such measures would impose a disproportionate burden on the employer. This burden shall not be disproportionate when it is sufficiently remedied by measures existing within the framework of the disability policy of the Member State concerned.

Article 6   Justification of differences of treatment on grounds of age

1. Notwithstanding Article 2(2), Member States may provide that differences of treatment on grounds of age shall not constitute discrimination, if, within the context of national law, they are objectively and reasonably justified by a legitimate aim, including legitimate employment policy, labour market and vocational training objectives, and if the means of achieving that aim are appropriate and necessary.

Such differences of treatment may include, among others:

(a) the setting of special conditions on access to employment and vocational training, employment and occupation, including dismissal and remuneration conditions, for young people, older workers and persons with caring responsibilities in order to promote their vocational integration or ensure their protection;

(b) the fixing of minimum conditions of age, professional experience or seniority in service for access to employment or to certain advantages linked to employment;

(c) the fixing of a maximum age for recruitment which is based on the training requirements of the post in question or the need for a reasonable period of employment before retirement.

2. Notwithstanding Article 2(2), Member States may provide that the fixing for occupational social security schemes of ages for admission or entitlement to retirement or invalidity benefits, including the fixing under those schemes of different ages for employees or groups or categories of employees, and the use, in the context of such schemes, of age criteria in actuarial calculations, does not constitute discrimination on the grounds of age, provided this does not result in discrimination on the grounds of sex.

Article 7   Positive action

1. With a view to ensuring full equality in practice, the principle of equal treatment shall not prevent any Member State from maintaining or adopting specific measures to prevent or compensate for disadvantages linked to any of the grounds referred to in Article 1.

2. With regard to disabled persons, the principle of equal treatment shall be without prejudice to the right of MemberStates to maintain or adopt provisions on the protection of health and safety at work or to measures aimed at creating or maintaining provisions or facilities for safeguarding or promoting their integration into the working environment.

Article 8   Minimum requirements

1. Member States may introduce or maintain provisions which are more favourable to the protection of the principle of equal treatment than those laid down in this Directive.

2. The implementation of this Directive shall under no circumstances constitute grounds for a reduction in the level of protection against discrimination already afforded by Member States in the fields covered by this Directive.

CHAPTER II   REMEDIES AND ENFORCEMENT

Article 9   Defence of rights

1. Member States shall ensure that judicial and/or administrative procedures, including where they deem it appropriate conciliation procedures, for the enforcement of obligations under this Directive are available to all persons who consider themselves wronged by failure to apply the principle of equal treatment to them, even after the relationship in which the discrimination is alleged to have occurred has ended.

2. Member States shall ensure that associations, organisations or other legal entities which have, in accordance with the criteria laid down by their national law, a legitimate interest in ensuring that the provisions of this Directive are complied with, may engage, either on behalf or in support of the complainant, with his or her approval, in any judicial and/or administrative procedure provided for the enforcement of obligations under this Directive.

3. Paragraphs 1 and 2 are without prejudice to national rules relating to time limits for bringing actions as regards the principle of equality of treatment.

Article 10   Burden of proof

1. Member States shall take such measures as are necessary, in accordance with their national judicial systems, to ensure that, when persons who consider themselves wronged because the principle of equal treatment has not been applied to them establish, before a court or other competent authority, facts from which it may be presumed that there has been direct or indirect discrimination, it shall be for the respondent to prove that there has been no breach of the principle of equal treatment.

2. Paragraph 1 shall not prevent Member States from introducing rules of evidence which are more favourable to plaintiffs.

3. Paragraph 1 shall not apply to criminal procedures.

4. Paragraphs 1, 2 and 3 shall also apply to any legal proceedings commenced in accordance with Article 9(2).

5. Member States need not apply paragraph 1 to proceedings in which it is for the court or competent body to investigate the facts of the case.

Article 11   Victimisation

Member States shall introduce into their national legal systems such measures as are necessary to protect employees against dismissal or other adverse treatment by the employer as a reaction to a complaint within the undertaking or to any legal proceedings aimed at enforcing compliance with the principle of equal treatment.

Article 12   Dissemination of information

Member States shall take care that the provisions adopted pursuant to this Directive, together with the relevant provisions already in force in this field, are brought to the attention of the persons concerned by all appropriate means, for example, at the workplace, throughout their territory.

Article 13   Social dialogue

1.   Member States shall, in accordance with their national traditions and practice, take adequate measures to promote dialogue between the social partners with a view to fostering equal treatment, including through the monitoring of workplace practices, collective agreements, codes of conduct and through research or exchange of experiences and good practices.

2.   Where consistent with their national traditions and practice, Member States shall encourage the social partners, without prejudice to their autonomy, to conclude at the appropriate level agreements laying down anti-discrimination rules in the fields referred to in Article 3 which fall within the scope of collective bargaining. These agreements shall respect the minimum requirements laid down by this Directive and by the relevant national implementing measures.

Article 14   Dialogue with non-governmental organisations

Member States shall encourage dialogue with appropriate non-governmental organisations which have, in accordance with their national law and practice, a legitimate interest in contributing to the fight against discrimination on any of the grounds referred to in Article 1 with a view to promoting the principle of equal treatment.

CHAPTER III   PARTICULAR PROVISIONS

Article 15   Northern Ireland

1.   In order to tackle the under-representation of one of the major religious communities in the police service of Northern Ireland, differences in treatment regarding recruitment into that service, including its support staff, shall not constitute discrimination insofar as those differences in treatment are expressly authorised by national legislation.

2.   In order to maintain a balance of opportunity in employment for teachers in Northern Ireland while furthering the reconciliation of historical divisions between the major religious communities there, the provisions on religion or belief in this Directive shall not apply to the recruitment of teachers in schools in Northern Ireland in so far as this is expressly authorised by national legislation.

CHAPTER IV   FINAL PROVISIONS

Article 16   Compliance

Member States shall take the necessary measures to ensure that:

(a) any laws, regulations and administrative provisions contrary to the principle of equal treatment are abolished;

(b) any provisions contrary to the principle of equal treatment which are included in contracts or collective agreements, internal rules of undertakings or rules governing the independent occupations and professions and workers' and employers' organisations are, or may be, declared null and void or are amended.

Article 17   Sanctions

Member States shall lay down the rules on sanctions applicable to infringements of the national provisions adopted pursuant to this Directive and shall take all measures necessary to ensure that they are applied. The sanctions, which may comprise the payment of compensation to the victim, must be effective, proportionate and dissuasive. Member States shall notify those provisions to the Commission by 2 December 2003 at the latest and shall notify it without delay of any subsequent amendment affecting them.

Article 18   Implementation

Member States shall adopt the laws, regulations and administrative provisions necessary to comply with this Directive by 2 December 2003 at the latest or may entrust the social partners, at their joint request, with the implementation of this Directive as regards provisions concerning collective agreements. In such cases, Member States shall ensure that, no later than 2 December 2003, the social partners introduce the necessary measures by agreement, the Member States concerned being required to take any necessary measures to enable them at any time to be in a position to guarantee the results imposed by this Directive. They shall forthwith inform the Commission thereof.

In order to take account of particular conditions, Member States may, if necessary, have an additional period of 3 years from 2 December 2003, that is to say a total of 6 years, to implement the provisions of this Directive on age and disability discrimination. In that event they shall inform the Commission forthwith. Any Member State which chooses to use this additional period shall report annually to the Commission on the steps it is taking to tackle age and disability discrimination and on the progress it is making towards implementation. The Commission shall report annually to the Council.

When Member States adopt these measures, they shall contain a reference to this Directive or be accompanied by such reference on the occasion of their official publication. The methods of making such reference shall be laid down by Member States.

Article 19   Report

1.   Member States shall communicate to the Commission, by 2 December 2005 at the latest and every five years thereafter, all the information necessary for the Commission to draw up a report to the European Parliament and the Council on the application of this Directive.

2.   The Commission's report shall take into account, as appropriate, the viewpoints of the social partners and relevant non-governmental organisations. In accordance with the principle of gender mainstreaming, this report shall, inter alia, provide an assessment of the impact of the measures taken on women and men. In the light of the information received, this report shall include, if necessary, proposals to revise and update this Directive.

Article 20   Entry into force

This Directive shall enter into force on the day of its publication in the Official Journal of the European Communities.

Article 21   Addressees

This Directive is addressed to the Member States.

Done at Brussels, 27 November 2000.

For the Council
The President
E. GUIGOU

SOCIAL POLICY: WORKER PROTECTION

Council Directive 2001/23 of 12 March 2001 on the approximation of the laws of the Member States relating to the safeguarding of employees' rights in the event of transfers of undertakings, businesses or parts of undertakings or businesses

[OJ 2001, L82/16]*

THE COUNCIL OF THE EUROPEAN UNION,

Having regard to the Treaty establishing the European Community, and in particular Article 94 thereof,

Having regard to the proposal from the Commission,

Having regard to the opinion of the European Parliament,[1]

Having regard to the opinion of the Economic and Social Committee,[2]

Whereas:

(1) Council Directive 77/187/EEC of 14 February 1977 on the approximation of the laws of the Member States relating to the safeguarding of employees' rights in the event of transfers of undertakings, businesses or parts of undertakings or businesses[3] has been substantially amended.[4] In the interests of clarity and rationality, it should therefore be codified.

(2) Economic trends are bringing in their wake, at both national and Community level, changes in the structure of undertakings, through transfers of undertakings, businesses or parts of undertakings or businesses to other employers as a result of legal transfers or mergers.

(3) It is necessary to provide for the protection of employees in the event of a change of employer, in particular, to ensure that their rights are safeguarded.

(4) Differences still remain in the Member States as regards the extent of the protection of employees in this respect and these differences should be reduced.

(5) The Community Charter of the Fundamental Social Rights of Workers adopted on 9 December 1989 ('Social Charter') states, in points 7, 17 and 18 in particular that: 'The completion of the internal market must lead to an improvement in the living and working conditions of workers in the European Community. The improvement must cover, where necessary, the development of certain aspects of employment regulations such as procedures for collective redundancies and those regarding bankruptcies. Information, consultation and participation for workers must be developed along appropriate lines, taking account of the practice in force in the various Member States. Such information, consultation and participation must be implemented in due time, particularly in connection with restructuring operations in undertakings or in cases of mergers having an impact on the employment of workers'.

(6) In 1977 the Council adopted Directive 77/187/EEC to promote the harmonisation of the relevant national laws ensuring the safeguarding of the rights of employees and

---

* **Editor's Note:** This Directive repeals and replaces Council Directive 77/187/EEC (OJ L 61, 5.3.1977, p. 26) and Council Directive 98/50/EC (OJ L 201, 17.7.1998, p. 88).

[1] Opinion delivered on 25 October 2000 (not yet published in the Official Journal).

[2] OJ C 367, 20.12.2000, p. 21.

[3] OJ L 61, 5.3.1977, p. 26.

[4] See Annex I, Part A.

requiring transferors and transferees to inform and consult employees' representatives in good time.

(7) That Directive was subsequently amended in the light of the impact of the internal market, the legislative tendencies of the Member States with regard to the rescue of undertakings in economic difficulties, the case-law of the Court of Justice of the European Communities, Council Directive 75/129/EEC of 17 February 1975 on the approximation of the laws of the Member States relating to collective redundancies[5] and the legislation already in force in most Member States.

(8) Considerations of legal security and transparency required that the legal concept of transfer be clarified in the light of the case-law of the Court of Justice. Such clarification has not altered the scope of Directive 77/187/EEC as interpreted by the Court of Justice.

(9) The Social Charter recognises the importance of the fight against all forms of discrimination, especially based on sex, colour, race, opinion and creed.

(10) This Directive should be without prejudice to the time limits set out in Annex I Part B within which the Member States are to comply with Directive 77/187/EEC, and the act amending it,

HAS ADOPTED THIS DIRECTIVE:

CHAPTER I   SCOPE AND DEFINITIONS

Article 1

1. (a) This Directive shall apply to any transfer of an undertaking, business, or part of an undertaking or business to another employer as a result of a legal transfer or merger.
   (b) Subject to sub-paragraph (a) and the following provisions of this Article, there is a transfer within the meaning of this Directive where there is a transfer of an economic entity which retains its identity, meaning an organised grouping of resources which has the objective of pursuing an economic activity, whether or not that activity is central or ancillary.
   (c) This Directive shall apply to public and private undertakings engaged in economic activities whether or not they are operating for gain. An administrative reorganisation of public administrative authorities, or the transfer of administrative functions between public administrative authorities, is not a transfer within the meaning of this Directive.

2.   This Directive shall apply where and in so far as the undertaking, business or part of the undertaking or business to be transferred is situated within the territorial scope of the Treaty.

3.   This Directive shall not apply to seagoing vessels.

Article 2

1.   For the purposes of this Directive:
   (a) 'transferor' shall mean any natural or legal person who, by reason of a transfer within the meaning of Article 1(1), ceases to be the employer in respect of the undertaking, business or part of the undertaking or business;
   (b) 'transferee' shall mean any natural or legal person who, by reason of a transfer within the meaning of Article 1(1), becomes the employer in respect of the undertaking, business or part of the undertaking or business;
   (c) 'representatives of employees' and related expressions shall mean the repre-

---

[5] OJ L 48, 22.2.1975, p. 29. Directive replaced by Directive 98/59/EC (OJ L 225, 12.8.1998, p. 6).

sentatives of the employees provided for by the laws or practices of the Member States;

(d) 'employee' shall mean any person who, in the Member State concerned, is protected as an employee under national employment law.

2.   This Directive shall be without prejudice to national law as regards the definition of contract of employment or employment relationship. However, Member States shall not exclude from the scope of this Directive contracts of employment or employment relationships solely because:

(a) of the number of working hours performed or to be performed,

(b) they are employment relationships governed by a fixed-duration contract of employment within the meaning of Article 1(1) of Council Directive 91/383/EEC of 25 June 1991 supplementing the measures to encourage improvements in the safety and health at work of workers with a fixed-duration employment relationship or a temporary employment relationship,[6] or

(c) they are temporary employment relationships within the meaning of Article 1(2) of Directive 91/383/EEC, and the undertaking, business or part of the undertaking or business transferred is, or is part of, the temporary employment business which is the employer.

CHAPTER II   SAFEGUARDING OF EMPLOYEES' RIGHTS

Article 3

1.   The transferor's rights and obligations arising from a contract of employment or from an employment relationship existing on the date of a transfer shall, by reason of such transfer, be transferred to the transferee.

Member States may provide that, after the date of transfer, the transferor and the transferee shall be jointly and severally liable in respect of obligations which arose before the date of transfer from a contract of employment or an employment relationship existing on the date of the transfer.

2.   Member States may adopt appropriate measures to ensure that the transferor notifies the transferee of all the rights and obligations which will be transferred to the transferee under this Article, so far as those rights and obligations are or ought to have been known to the transferor at the time of the transfer. A failure by the transferor to notify the transferee of any such right or obligation shall not affect the transfer of that right or obligation and the rights of any employees against the transferee and/or transferor in respect of that right or obligation.

3.   Following the transfer, the transferee shall continue to observe the terms and conditions agreed in any collective agreement on the same terms applicable to the transferor under that agreement, until the date of termination or expiry of the collective agreement or the entry into force or application of another collective agreement. Member States may limit the period for observing such terms and conditions with the proviso that it shall not be less than one year.

4. (a) Unless Member States provide otherwise, paragraphs 1 and 3 shall not apply in relation to employees' rights to old-age, invalidity or survivors' benefits under supplementary company or intercompany pension schemes outside the statutory social security schemes in Member States.

(b) Even where they do not provide in accordance with sub-paragraph (a) that paragraphs 1 and 3 apply in relation to such rights, Member States shall adopt the measures necessary to protect the interests of employees and of persons no longer employed in the transferor's business at the time of the transfer in respect of rights

---

[6] OJ L 206, 29.7.1991, p. 19.

conferring on them immediate or prospective entitlement to old age benefits, including survivors' benefits, under supplementary schemes referred to in sub-paragraph (a).

Article 4

1. The transfer of the undertaking, business or part of the undertaking or business shall not in itself constitute grounds for dismissal by the transferor or the transferee. This provision shall not stand in the way of dismissals that may take place for economic, technical or organisational reasons entailing changes in the workforce. Member States may provide that the first sub-paragraph shall not apply to certain specific categories of employees who are not covered by the laws or practice of the Member States in respect of protection against dismissal.

2. If the contract of employment or the employment relationship is terminated because the transfer involves a substantial change in working conditions to the detriment of the employee, the employer shall be regarded as having been responsible for termination of the contract of employment or of the employment relationship.

Article 5

1. Unless Member States provide otherwise, Articles 3 and 4 shall not apply to any transfer of an undertaking, business or part of an undertaking or business where the transferor is the subject of bankruptcy proceedings or any analogous insolvency proceedings which have been instituted with a view to the liquidation of the assets of the transferor and are under the supervision of a competent public authority (which may be an insolvency practitioner authorised by a competent public authority).

2. Where Articles 3 and 4 apply to a transfer during insolvency proceedings which have been opened in relation to a transferor (whether or not those proceedings have been instituted with a view to the liquidation of the assets of the transferor) and provided that such proceedings are under the supervision of a competent public authority (which may be an insolvency practitioner determined by national law) a Member State may provide that:

(a) notwithstanding Article 3(1), the transferor's debts arising from any contracts of employment or employment relationships and payable before the transfer or before the opening of the insolvency proceedings shall not be transferred to the transferee, provided that such proceedings give rise, under the law of that Member State, to protection at least equivalent to that provided for in situations covered by Council Directive 80/987/EEC of 20 October 1980 on the approximation of the laws of the Member States relating to the protection of employees in the event of the insolvency of their employer,[7] and, or alternatively, that,

(b) the transferee, transferor or person or persons exercising the transferor's functions, on the one hand, and the representatives of the employees on the other hand may agree alterations, in so far as current law or practice permits, to the employees' terms and conditions of employment designed to safeguard employment opportunities by ensuring the survival of the undertaking, business or part of the undertaking or business.

3. A Member State may apply paragraph 20(b) to any transfers where the transferor is in a situation of serious economic crisis, as defined by national law, provided that the situation is declared by a competent public authority and open to judicial supervision, on condition that such provisions already existed in national law on 17 July 1998.

The Commission shall present a report on the effects of this provision before 17 July 2003 and shall submit any appropriate proposals to the Council.

---

[7] OJ L 283, 20.10.1980, p. 23. Directive as last amended by the 1994 Act of Accession.

4.   Member States shall take appropriate measures with a view to preventing misuse of insolvency proceedings in such a way as to deprive employees of the rights provided for in this Directive.

Article 6

1.   If the undertaking, business or part of an undertaking or business preserves its autonomy, the status and function of the representatives or of the representation of the employees affected by the transfer shall be preserved on the same terms and subject to the same conditions as existed before the date of the transfer by virtue of law, regulation, administrative provision or agreement, provided that the conditions necessary for the constitution of the employee's representation are fulfilled.

The first sub-paragraph shall not apply if, under the laws, regulations, administrative provisions or practice in the Member States, or by agreement with the representatives of the employees, the conditions necessary for the reappointment of the representatives of the employees or for the reconstitution of the representation of the employees are fulfilled.

Where the transferor is the subject of bankruptcy proceedings or any analogous insolvency proceedings which have been instituted with a view to the liquidation of the assets of the transferor and are under the supervision of a competent public authority (which may be an insolvency practitioner authorised by a competent public authority), Member States may take the necessary measures to ensure that the transferred employees are properly represented until the new election or designation of representatives of the employees.

If the undertaking, business or part of an undertaking or business does not preserve its autonomy, the Member States shall take the necessary measures to ensure that the employees transferred who were represented before the transfer continue to be properly represented during the period necessary for the reconstitution or reappointment of the representation of employees in accordance with national law or practice.

2.   If the term of office of the representatives of the employees affected by the transfer expires as a result of the transfer, the representatives shall continue to enjoy the protection provided by the laws, regulations, administrative provisions or practice of the Member States.

CHAPTER III   INFORMATION AND CONSULTATION

Article 7

1.   The transferor and transferee shall be required to inform the representatives of their respective employees affected by the transfer of the following:
— the date or proposed date of the transfer,
— the reasons for the transfer,
— the legal, economic and social implications of the transfer for the employees,
— any measures envisaged in relation to the employees.

The transferor must give such information to the representatives of his employees in good time, before the transfer is carried out.

The transferee must give such information to the representatives of his employees in good time, and in any event before his employees are directly affected by the transfer as regards their conditions of work and employment.

2.   Where the transferor or the transferee envisages measures in relation to his employees, he shall consult the representatives of his employees in good time on such measures with a view to reaching an agreement.

3.   Member States whose laws, regulations or administrative provisions provide that representatives of the employees may have recourse to an arbitration board to obtain a decision on the measures to be taken in relation to employees may limit the obligations laid down in paragraphs 1 and 2 to cases where the transfer carried out gives rise to a change in the

business likely to entail serious disadvantages for a considerable number of the employees. The information and consultations shall cover at least the measures envisaged in relation to the employees.

The information must be provided and consultations take place in good time before the change in the business as referred to in the first sub-paragraph is effected.

4.   The obligations laid down in this Article shall apply irrespective of whether the decision resulting in the transfer is taken by the employer or an undertaking controlling the employer.

In considering alleged breaches of the information and consultation requirements laid down by this Directive, the argument that such a breach occurred because the information was not provided by an undertaking controlling the employer shall not be accepted as an excuse.

5.   Member States may limit the obligations laid down in paragraphs 1, 2 and 3 to undertakings or businesses which, in terms of the number of employees, meet the conditions for the election or nomination of a collegiate body representing the employees.

6.   Member States shall provide that, where there are no representatives of the employees in an undertaking or business through no fault of their own, the employees concerned must be informed in advance of:

— the date or proposed date of the transfer,
— the reason for the transfer,
— the legal, economic and social implications of the transfer for the employees,
— any measures envisaged in relation to the employees.

CHAPTER IV   FINAL PROVISIONS

Article 8
This Directive shall not affect the right of Member States to apply or introduce laws, regulations or administrative provisions which are more favourable to employees or to promote or permit collective agreements or agreements between social partners more favourable to employees.

Article 9
Member States shall introduce into their national legal systems such measures as are necessary to enable all employees and representatives of employees who consider themselves wronged by failure to comply with the obligations arising from this Directive to pursue their claims by judicial process after possible recourse to other competent authorities.

Article 10
The Commission shall submit to the Council an analysis of the effect of the provisions of this Directive before 17 July 2006. It shall propose any amendment which may seem necessary.

Article 11
Member States shall communicate to the Commission the texts of the laws, regulations and administrative provisions which they adopt in the field covered by this Directive.

Article 12
Directive 77/187/EEC, as amended by the Directive referred to in Annex I, Part A, is repealed, without prejudice to the obligations of the Member States concerning the time limits for implementation set out in Annex I, Part B.

References to the repealed Directive shall be construed as references to this Directive and shall be read in accordance with the correlation table in Annex II.

Article 13

This Directive shall enter into force on the 20th day following its publication in the Official Journal of the European Communities.

Article 14

This Directive is addressed to the Member States.

Done at Brussels, 12 March 2001.

For the Council
The President
B. RINGHOLM

ANNEX I   PART A

Repealed Directive and its amending Directive (referred to in Article 12) Council Directive 77/187/EEC (OJ L61, 5.3.1977, p. 26)
    Council Directive 98/50/EC (OJ L201, 17.7.1998, p. 88)

PART B

Deadlines for transposition into national law (referred to in Article 12)

Directive	Deadline for transposition
77/187/EEC	16 February 1979
98/50/EC	17 July 2001

ANNEX II   CORRELATION TABLE

Directive 77/187/EEC	Article 1
This Directive	Article 1
Directive 77/187/EEC Article 2	
This Directive	Article 2
Directive 77/187/EEC Article 3	
This Directive	Article 2
Directive 77/187/EEC Article 4	
This Directive	Article 4
Directive 77/187/EEC Article 4a	
This Directive	Article 5
Directive 77/187/EEC Article 5	
This Directive	Article 6
Directive 77/187/EEC Article 6	
This Directive	Article 7
Directive 77/187/EEC Article 7	
This Directive	Article 8
Directive 77/187/EEC Article 7a	
This Directive	Article 9

Directive 77/187/EEC Article 7b
This Directive   Article 10

Directive 77/187/EEC Article 8
This Directive   Article 11

Directive 77/187/EEC —
This Directive   Article 12

Directive 77/187/EEC —
This Directive   Article 13

Directive 77/187/EEC —
This Directive   Article 14

Directive 77/187/EEC —
This Directive   ANNEX I

Directive 77/187/EEC —
This Directive   ANNEX II

Council Directive 80/987/EEC of 20 October 1980 on the protection of employees in the event of the insolvency of their employer

[OJ 1980, No. L283/23]*

The Council of the European Communities,

Having regard to the Treaty establishing the European Economic Community, and in particular Article 100 thereof,

Having regard to the proposal from the Commission[1],

Having regard to the opinion of the European Parliament[2],

Having regard to the opinion of the Economic and Social Committee[3],

Whereas it is necessary to provide for the protection of employees in the event of the insolvency of their employer, in particular in order to guarantee payment of their outstanding claims, while taking account of the need for balanced economic and social development in the Community;

Whereas differences still remain between the member states as regards the extent of the protection of employees in this respect; whereas efforts should be directed towards reducing these differences, which can have a direct effect on the functioning of the common market;

Whereas the approximation of laws in this field should, therefore, be promoted while the improvement within the meaning of Article 117 of the Treaty is maintained;

Whereas as a result of the geographical situation and the present job structures in that area, the labour market in Greenland is fundamentally different from that of the other areas of the Community;

Whereas to the extent that the Hellenic Republic is to become a member of the European Economic Community on 1 January 1981 in accordance with the act concerning the conditions of accession of the Hellenic Republic and the adjustments to the Treaties, it is appropri-

---

* **Editor's Note:** As amended by Directive 87/164 [OJ 1987 No. L66/11] and substantially revised by Directive 2002/74 [OJ 2002 L270/10].

    [1] OJ No C 135, 9.6.1978, p. 2.
    [2] OJ No C 39, 12.2.1979, p. 26.
    [3] OJ No C 105, 26.4.1979, p. 15.

ate to stipulate in the annex to the Directive under the heading 'Greece', those categories of employees whose claims may be excluded in accordance with Article 1(2) of the Directive,

HAS ADOPTED THIS DIRECTIVE:

SECTION I   SCOPE AND DEFINITIONS

Article 1

1.   This Directive shall apply to employees' claims arising from contracts of employment or employment relationships and existing against employers who are in a state of insolvency within the meaning of Article 2(1).

2.   Member States may, by way of exception, exclude claims by certain categories of employee from the scope of this Directive, by virtue of the existence of other forms of guarantee if it is established that these offer the persons concerned a degree of protection equivalent to that resulting from this Directive.

3.   Where such provision already applies in their national legislation, Member States may continue to exclude from the scope of this Directive:

(a)   domestic servants employed by a natural person;

(b)   share-fishermen.

Article 2

1.   For the purposes of this Directive, an employer shall be deemed to be in a state of insolvency where a request has been made for the opening of collective proceedings based on insolvency of the employer, as provided for under the laws, regulations and administrative provisions of a Member State, and involving the partial or total divestment of the employer's assets and the appointment of a liquidator or a person performing a similar task, and the authority which is competent pursuant to the said provisions has:

(a)   either decided to open the proceedings, or

(b)   established that the employer's undertaking or business has been definitively closed down and that the available assets are insufficient to warrant the opening of the proceedings.

2.   This Directive is without prejudice to national law as regards the definition of the terms 'employee', 'employer', 'pay', 'right conferring immediate entitlement' and 'right conferring prospective entitlement'.

However, the Member States may not exclude from the scope of this Directive:

(a)   part-time employees within the meaning of Directive 97/81/EC;

(b)   workers with a fixed-term contract within the meaning of Directive 1999/70/EC;

(c)   workers with a temporary employment relationship within the meaning of Article 1(2) of Directive 91/383/EEC.

3.   Member States may not set a minimum duration for the contract of employment or the employment relationship in order for workers to qualify for claims under this Directive.

4.   This Directive does not prevent Member States from extending workers' protection to other situations of insolvency, for example where payments have been de facto stopped on a permanent basis, established by proceedings different from those mentioned in paragraph 1 as provided for under national law. Such procedures shall not however create a guarantee obligation for the institutions of the other Member States in the cases referred to in Section IIIa.

SECTION II   PROVISIONS CONCERNING GUARANTEE INSTITUTIONS

Article 3

Member States shall take the measures necessary to ensure that guarantee institutions guarantee, subject to Article 4, payment of employees' outstanding claims resulting from contracts of employment or employment relationships, including, where provided for by national law, severance pay on termination of employment relationships. The claims taken over by the guarantee institution shall be the outstanding pay claims relating to a period prior to and/or, as applicable, after a given date determined by the Member States.

Article 4

1.   Member States shall have the option to limit the liability of the guarantee institutions referred to in Article 3.

2.   When Member States exercise the option referred to in paragraph 1, they shall specify the length of the period for which outstanding claims are to be met by the guarantee institution. However, this may not be shorter than a period covering the remuneration of the last three months of the employment relationship prior to and/or after the date referred to in Article 3. Member States may include this minimum period of three months in a reference period with a duration of not less than six months.

Member States having a reference period of not less than 18 months may limit the period for which outstanding claims are met by the guarantee institution to eight weeks. In this case, those periods which are most favourable to the employee are used for the calculation of the minimum period.

3.   Furthermore, Member States may set ceilings on the payments made by the guarantee institution. These ceilings must not fall below a level which is socially compatible with the social objective of this Directive.

When Member States exercise this option, they shall inform the Commission of the methods used to set the ceiling.

Article 5

Member States shall lay down detailed rules for the organization, financing and operation of the guarantee institutions, complying with the following principles in particular:

   (a)   the assets of the institutions shall be independent of the employers' operating capital and be inaccessible to proceedings for insolvency;

   (b)   employers shall contribute to financing, unless it is fully covered by the public authorities;

   (c)   the institutions' liabilities shall not depend on whether or not obligations to contribute to financing have been fulfilled.

SECTION III   PROVISIONS CONCERNING SOCIAL SECURITY

Article 6

Member States may stipulate that Articles 3, 4 and 5 shall not apply to contributions due under national statutory social security schemes or under supplementary company or inter-company pension schemes outside the national statutory social security schemes.

Article 7

Member States shall take the measures necessary to ensure that non-payment of compulsory contributions due from the employer, before the onset of his insolvency, to their insurance institutions under national statutory social security schemes does not adversely affect employees' benefit entitlement in respect of these insurance institutions inasmuch as the employees' contributions were deducted at source from the remuneration paid.

Article 8

Member States shall ensure that the necessary measures are taken to protect the interests of employees and of persons having already left the employer's undertaking or business at the date of the onset of the employer's insolvency in respect of rights conferring on them immediate or prospective entitlement to old-age benefits, including survivors' benefits, under supplementary company or inter-company pension schemes outside the national statutory social security schemes.

SECTION IIIa   PROVISIONS CONCERNING TRANSNATIONAL SITUATIONS

Article 8a

1. When an undertaking with activities in the territories of at least two Member States is in a state of insolvency within the meaning of Article 2(1), the institution responsible for meeting employees' outstanding claims shall be that in the Member State in whose territory they work or habitually work.

2. The extent of employees' rights shall be determined by the law governing the competent guarantee institution.

3. Member States shall take the measures necessary to ensure that, in the cases referred to in paragraph 1, decisions taken in the context of insolvency proceedings referred to in Article 2(1), which have been requested in another Member State, are taken into account when determining the employer's state of insolvency within the meaning of this Directive.

Article 8b

1. For the purposes of implementing Article 8a, Member States shall make provision for the sharing of relevant information between their competent administrative authorities and/ or the guarantee institutions mentioned in Article 3, making it possible in particular to inform the guarantee institution responsible for meeting the employees' outstanding claims.

2. Member States shall notify the Commission and the other Member States of the contact details of their competent administrative authorities and/or guarantee institutions. The Commission shall make these communications publicly accessible.

SECTION IV   GENERAL AND FINAL PROVISIONS

Article 9

This Directive shall not affect the option of Member States to apply or introduce laws, Regulations or administrative provisions which are more favourable to employees. Implementation of this Directive shall not under any circumstances be sufficient grounds for a regression in relation to the current situation in the Member States and in relation to the general level of protection of workers in the area covered by it.

Article 10

This Directive shall not affect the option of Member States:

    (a) to take the measures necessary to avoid abuses;

    (b) to refuse or reduce the liability referred to in Article 3 or the guarantee obligation referred to in Article 7 if it appears that fulfilment of the obligation is unjustifiable because of the existence of special links between the employee and the employer and of common interests resulting in collusion between them;

    (c) to refuse or reduce the liability referred to in Article 3 or the guarantee obligation referred to in Article 7 in cases where the employee, on his or her own or together with his or her close relatives, was the owner of an essential part of the employer's undertaking or business and had a considerable influence on its activities.

Article 10a

Member States shall notify the Commission and the other Member States of the types of national insolvency proceedings falling within the scope of this Directive, and of any amendments relating thereto. The Commission shall publish these communications in the Official Journal of the European Communities.

Article 11
    1.   Member States shall bring into force the laws, Regulations and administrative provisions necessary to comply with this Directive within 36 months of its notification. They shall forthwith inform the Commission thereof.
    2.   Member States shall communicate to the Commission the texts of the laws, Regulations and administrative provisions which they adopt in the field governed by this Directive.

Article 12
Within 18 months of the expiry of the period of 36 months laid down in Article 11(1), Member States shall forward all relevant information to the Commission in order to enable it to draw up a report on the application of this Directive for submission to the Council.

Article 13
This Directive is addressed to the Member States.
done at Luxembourg, 20 October 1980.

For the Council, the President, J. Santer

Council Directive of 12 June 1989 on the introduction of measures to encourage imporvements in the safety and health of workers at work (89/391/EEC)*

[OJ 1989, L183/1]

The Council of the European Communities,
    Having regard to the Treaty establishing the European Economic Community, and in particular Article 118a thereof,

(Recitals and Preamble omitted.)

Has adopted this Directive:

SECTION I   GENERAL PROVISIONS

Article 1   Object
    1.   The object of this Directive is to introduce measures to encourage improvements in the safety and health of workers at work.
    2.   To that end it contains general principles concerning the prevention of occupational risks, the protection of safety and health, the elimination of risk and accident factors, the informing, consultation, balanced participation in accordance with national laws and/or practices and training of workers and their representatives, as well as general guidelines for the implementation of the said principles.
    3.   This Directive shall be without prejudice to existing or future national and Community provisions which are more favourable to protection of the safety and health of workers at work.

Article 2   Scope
    1.   This Directive shall apply to all sectors of activity, both public and private (industrial, agricultural, commercial, administrative, service, educational, cultural, leisure, etc.).

* **Editor's Note**: Amended by Regulation 2003/1882, OJ 2003 L284/1.

2.   This Directive shall not be applicable where characteristics peculiar to certain specific public service activities, such as the armed forces or the police, or to certain specific activities in the civil protection services inevitably conflict with it.

In that event, the safety and health of workers must be ensured as far as possible in the light of the objectives of this Directive.

Article 3   Definitions

For the purposes of this Directive, the following terms shall have the following meanings:
- (a) worker: any person employed by an employer, including trainees and apprentices but excluding domestic servants;
- (b) employer: any natural or legal person who has an employment relationship with the worker and has responsibility for the undertaking and/or establishment;
- (c) workers' representative with specific responsibility for the safety and health of workers: any person elected, chosen or designated in accordance with national laws and/or practices to represent workers where problems arise relating to the safety and health protection of workers at work;
- (d) prevention: all the steps or measures taken or planned at all stages of work in the undertaking to prevent or reduce occupational risks.

Article 4

1.   Member States shall take the necessary steps to ensure that employers, workers and workers' representatives are subject to the legal provisions necessary for the implementation of this Directive.

2.   In particular, Member States shall ensure adequate controls and supervision.

SECTION II   EMPLOYERS' OBLIGATIONS

Article 5   General provision

1.   The employer shall have a duty to ensure the safety and health of workers in every aspect related to the work.

2.   Where, pursuant to Article 7(3), an employer enlists competent external services or persons, this shall not discharge him from his responsibilities in this area.

3.   The workers' obligations in the field of safety and health at work shall not affect the principle of the responsibility of the employer.

4.   This Directive shall not restrict the option of Member States to provide for the exclusion or the limitation of employers' responsibility where occurrences are due to unusual and unforeseeable circumstances, beyond the employers' control, or to exceptional events, the consequences of which could not have been avoided despite the exercise of all due care.

Member States need not exercise the option referred to in the first sub-paragraph.

Article 6   General obligations on employers

1.   Within the context of his responsibilities, the employer shall take the measures necessary for the safety and health protection of workers, including prevention of occupational risks and provision of information and training, as well as provision of the necessary organisation and means.

The employer shall be alert to the need to adjust these measures to take account of changing circumstances and aim to improve existing situations.

2.   The employer shall implement the measures referred to in the first sub-paragraph of paragraph 1 on the basis of the following general principles of prevention:
- (a) avoiding risks;
- (b) evaluating the risks which cannot be avoided;
- (c) combating the risks at source;
- (d) adapting the work to the individual, especially as regards the design of work places, the choice of work equipment and the choice of working and production

methods, with a view, in particular, to alleviating monotonous work and work at a predetermined work-rate and to reducing their effect on health;

(e) adapting to technical progress;

(f) replacing the dangerous by the non-dangerous or the less dangerous;

(g) developing a coherent overall prevention policy which covers technology, organisation of work, working conditions, social relationships and the influence of factors related to the working environment;

(h) giving collective protective measures priority over individual protective measures;

(i) giving appropriate instructions to the workers.

3. Without prejudice to the other provisions of this Directive, the employer shall, taking into account the nature of the activities of the enterprise and/or establishment:

(a) evaluate the risks to the safety and health of workers, *inter alia* in the choice of work equipment, the chemical substances or preparations used, and the fitting-out of work places.

Subsequent to this evaluation and as necessary, the preventive measures and the working and production methods implemented by the employer must:

— assure an improvement in the level of protection afforded to workers with regard to safety and health,

— be integrated into all the activities of the undertaking and/or establishment and at all hierarchical levels;

(b) where he entrusts tasks to a worker, take into consideration the worker's capabilities as regards health and safety;

(c) ensure that the planning and introduction of new technologies are the subject of consultation with the workers and/or their representatives, as regards the consequences of the choice of equipment, the working conditions and the working environment for the safety and health of workers;

(d) take appropriate steps to ensure that only workers who have received adequate instructions may have access to areas where there is serious and specific danger.

4. Without prejudice to the other provisions of this Directive, where several undertakings share a work place, the employers shall cooperate in implementing the safety, health and occupational hygiene provisions and, taking into account the nature of the activities, shall coordinate their actions in matters of the protection and prevention of occupational risks, and shall inform one another and their respective workers and/or workers' representatives of those risks.

5. Measures related to safety, hygiene and health at work may in no circumstances involve the workers in financial cost.

Article 7 Protective and preventive services

1. Without prejudice to the obligations referred to in Articles 5 and 6, the employer shall designate one or more workers to carry out activities related to the protection and prevention of occupational risks for the undertaking and/or establishment.

2. Designated workers may not be placed at any disadvantage because of their activities related to the protection and prevention of occupational risks.
Designated workers shall be allowed adequate time to enable them to fulfil their obligations arising from this Directive.

3. If such protective and preventive measures cannot be organised for lack of competent personnel in the undertaking and/or establishment, the employer shall enlist competent external services or persons.

4. Where the employer enlists such services or persons, he shall inform them of the factors known to affect, or suspected of affecting, the safety and health of the workers and they must have access to the information referred to in Article 10(2).

5. In all cases:

— the workers designated must have the necessary capabilities and the necessary means,
— the external services or persons consulted must have the necessary aptitudes and the necessary personal and professional means, and
— the workers designated and the external services or persons consulted must be sufficient in number

to deal with the organisation of protective and preventive measures, taking into account the size of the undertaking and/or establishment and/or the hazards to which the workers are exposed and their distribution throughout the entire undertaking and/or establishment.

6.   The protection from, and prevention of, the health and safety risks which form the subject of this Article shall be the responsibility of one or more workers, of one service or of separate services whether from inside or outside the undertaking and/or establishment.

The worker(s) and/or agency(ies) must work together whenever necessary.

7.   Member States may define, in the light of the nature of the activities and size of the undertakings, the categories of undertakings in which the employer, provided he is competent, may himself take responsibility for the measures referred to in paragraph 1.

8.   Member States shall define the necessary capabilities and aptitudes referred to in paragraph 5.

They may determine the sufficient number referred to in paragraph 5.

Article 8   **First aid, fire-fighting and evacuation of workers, serious and imminent danger**

1.   The employer shall:
— take the necessary measures for first aid, fire-fighting and evacuation of workers, adapted to the nature of the activities and the size of the undertaking and/or establishment and taking into account other persons present,
— arrange any necessary contacts with external services, particularly as regards first aid, emergency medical care, rescue work and fire-fighting.

2.   Pursuant to paragraph 1, the employer shall, *inter alia*, for first aid, fire-fighting and the evacuation of workers, designate the workers required to implement such measures.

The number of such workers, their training and the equipment available to them shall be adequate, taking account of the size and/or specific hazards of the undertaking and/or establishment.

3.   The employer shall:
(a) as soon as possible, inform all workers who are, or may be, exposed to serious and imminent danger of the risk involved and of the steps taken or to be taken as regards protection;
(b) take action and give instructions to enable workers in the event of serious, imminent and unavoidable danger to stop work and/or immediately to leave the work place and proceed to a place of safety;
(c) save in exceptional cases for reasons duly substantiated, refrain from asking workers to resume work in a working situation where there is still a serious and imminent danger.

4.   Workers who, in the event of serious, imminent and unavoidable danger, leave their workstation and/or a dangerous area may not be placed at any disadvantage because of their action and must be protected against any harmful and unjustified consequences, in accordance with national laws and/or practices.

5.   The employer shall ensure that all workers are able, in the event of serious and imminent danger to their own safety and/or that of other persons, and where the immediate superior responsible cannot be contacted, to take the appropriate steps in the light of their knowledge and the technical means at their disposal, to avoid the consequences of such danger.

Their actions shall not place them at any disadvantage, unless they acted carelessly or there was negligence on their part.

Article 9   Various obligations on employers

1. The employer shall:
    (a) be in possession of an assessment of the risks to safety and health at work, including those facing groups of workers exposed to particular risks;
    (b) decide on the protective measures to be taken and, if necessary, the protective equipment to be used;
    (c) keep a list of occupational accidents resulting in a worker being unfit for work for more than three working days;
    (d) draw up, for the responsible authorities and in accordance with national laws and/or practices, reports on occupational accidents suffered by his workers.

2. Member States shall define, in the light of the nature of the activities and size of the undertakings, the obligations to be met by the different categories of undertakings in respect of the drawing-up of the documents provided for in paragraph 1(a) and (b) and when preparing the documents provided for in paragraph 1(c) and (d).

Article 10   Worker information

1. The employer shall take appropriate measures so that workers and/or their representatives in the undertaking and/or establishment receive, in accordance with national laws and/or practices which may take account, *inter alia*, of the size of the undertaking and/or establishment, all the necessary information concerning:
    (a) the safety and health risks and protective and preventive measures and activities in respect of both the undertaking and/or establishment in general and each type of workstation and/or job;
    (b) the measures taken pursuant to Article 8(2).

2. The employer shall take appropriate measures so that employers of workers from any outside undertakings and/or establishments engaged in work in his undertaking and/or establishment receive, in accordance with national laws and/or practices, adequate information concerning the points referred to in paragraph 1(a) and (b) which is to be provided to the workers in question.

3. The employer shall take appropriate measures so that workers with specific functions in protecting the safety and health of workers, and workers' representatives with specific responsibility for the safety and health of workers shall have access, to carry out their functions and in accordance with national laws and/or practices, to:
    (a) the risk assessment and protective measures referred to in Article 9(1)(a) and (b);
    (b) the list and reports referred to in Article 9(1)(c) and (d);
    (c) the information yielded by protective and preventive measures, inspection agencies and bodies responsible for safety and health.

Article 11   Consultation and participation of workers

1. Employers shall consult workers and/or their representatives and allow them to take part in discussions on all questions relating to safety and health at work.

This presupposes:
    — the consultation of workers,
    — the right of workers and/or their representatives to make proposals,
    — balanced participation in accordance with national laws and/or practices.

2. Workers or workers' representatives with specific responsibility for the safety and health of workers shall take part in a balanced way, in accordance with national laws and/or practices, or shall be consulted in advance and in good time by the employer with regard to:
    (a) any measure which may substantially affect safety and health;
    (b) the designation of workers referred to in Articles 7(1) and 8(2) and the activities referred to in Article 7(1);

(c) the information referred to in Articles 9(1) and 10;

(d) the enlistment, where appropriate, of the competent services or persons outside the undertaking and/or establishment, as referred to in Article 7(3);

(e) the planning and organisation of the training referred to in Article 12.

3. Workers' representatives with specific responsibility for the safety and health of workers shall have the right to ask the employer to take appropriate measures and to submit proposals to him to that end to mitigate hazards for workers and/or to remove sources of danger.

4. The workers referred to in paragraph 2 and the workers' representatives referred to in paragraphs 2 and 3 may not be placed at a disadvantage because of their respective activities referred to in paragraphs 2 and 3.

5. Employers must allow workers' representatives with specific responsibility for the safety and health of workers adequate time off work, without loss of pay, and provide them with the necessary means to enable such representatives to exercise their rights and functions deriving from this Directive.

6. Workers and/or their representatives are entitled to appeal, in accordance with national law and/or practice, to the authority responsible for safety and health protection at work if they consider that the measures taken and the means employed by the employer are inadequate for the purposes of ensuring safety and health at work.

Workers' representatives must be given the opportunity to submit their observations during inspection visits by the competent authority.

Article 12   Training of workers

1. The employer shall ensure that each worker receives adequate safety and health training, in particular in the form of information and instructions specific to his workstation or job:

— on recruitment,

— in the event of a transfer or a change of job,

— in the event of the introduction of new work equipment or a change in equipment,—in the event of the introduction of any new technology.

The training shall be:

— adapted to take account of new or changed risks, and

— repeated periodically if necessary.

2. The employer shall ensure that workers from outside undertakings and/or establishments engaged in work in his undertaking and/or establishment have in fact received appropriate instructions regarding health and safety risks during their activities in his undertaking and/or establishment.

3. Workers' representatives with a specific role in protecting the safety and health of workers shall be entitled to appropriate training.

4. The training referred to in paragraphs 1 and 3 may not be at the workers' expense or at that of the workers' representatives.

The training referred to in paragraph 1 must take place during working hours.

The training referred to in paragraph 3 must take place during working hours or in accordance with national practice either within or outside the undertaking and/or the establishment.

SECTION III   WORKERS' OBLIGATIONS

Article 13

1. It shall be the responsibility of each worker to take care as far as possible of his own safety and health and that of other persons affected by his acts or commissions at work in accordance with his training and the instructions given by his employer.

2. To this end, workers must in particular, in accordance with their training and the instructions given by their employer:

(a) make correct use of machinery, apparatus, tools, dangerous substances, transport equipment and other means of production;

(b) make correct use of the personal protective equipment supplied to them and, after use, return it to its proper place;

(c) refrain from disconnecting, changing or removing arbitrarily safety devices fitted, e.g., to machinery, apparatus, tools, plant and buildings, and use such safety devices correctly;

(d) immediately inform the employer and/or the workers with specific responsibility for the safety and health of workers of any work situation they have reasonable grounds for considering represents a serious and immediate danger to safety and health and of any shortcomings in the protection arrangements;

(e) cooperate, in accordance with national practice, with the employer and/or workers with specific responsibility for the safety and health of workers, for as long as may be necessary to enable any tasks or requirements imposed by the competent authority to protect the safety and health of workers at work to be carried out;

(f) cooperate, in accordance with national practice, with the employer and/or workers with specific responsibility for the safety and health of workers, for as long as may be necessary to enable the employer to ensure that the working environment and working conditions are safe and pose no risk to safety and health within their field of activity.

SECTION IV   MISCELLANEOUS PROVISIONS

Article 14   Health surveillance

1.   To ensure that workers receive health surveillance appropriate to the health and safety risks they incur at work, measures shall be introduced in accordance with national law and/or practices.

2.   The measures referred to in paragraph 1 shall be such that each worker, if he so wishes, may receive health surveillance at regular intervals.

3.   Health surveillance may be provided as part of a national health system.

Article 15   Risk groups

Particularly sensitive risk groups must be protected against the dangers which specifically affect them.

Article 16   Individual Directives—Amendments—General scope of this Directive

1.   The Council, acting on a proposal from the Commission based on Article 118a of the Treaty, shall adopt individual Directives, *inter alia*, in the areas listed in the Annex.

2.   This Directive and, without prejudice to the procedure referred to in Article 17 concerning technical adjustments, the individual Directives may be amended in accordance with the procedure provided for in Article 118a of the Treaty.

3.   The provisions of this Directive shall apply in full to all the areas covered by the individual Directives, without prejudice to more stringent and/or specific provisions contained in these individual Directives.

Article 17   Committee

1.   For the purely technical adjustments to the individual Directives provided for in Article 16(1) to take account of:

— the adoption of Directives in the field of technical harmonisation and standardisation, and/or

— technical progress, changes in international regulations or specifications, and new findings,

the Commission shall be assisted by a committee.

2.   Articles 5 and 7 of Decision 1999/468/EC(42) shall apply, having regard to the provisions of Article 8 thereof.

The period laid down in Article 5(6) of Decision 1999/468/EC shall be set at three months.

3.   The Committee shall adopt its rules of procedure.

Article 18   Final provisions

1.   Member States shall bring into force the laws, regulations and administrative provisions necessary to comply with this Directive by 31 December 1992.

They shall forthwith inform the Commission thereof.

2.   Member States shall communicate to the Commission the texts of the provisions of national law which they have already adopted or adopt in the field covered by this Directive.

3.   Member States shall report to the Commission every five years on the practical implementation of the provisions of this Directive, indicating the points of view of employers and workers.

The Commission shall inform the European Parliament, the Council, the Economic and Social Committee and the Advisory Committee on Safety, Hygiene and Health Protection at Work.

4.   The Commission shall submit periodically to the European Parliament, the Council and the Economic and Social Committee a report on the implementation of this Directive, taking into account paragraphs 1 to 3.

Article 19

This Directive is addressed to the Member States.

Done at Luxembourg, 12 June 1989.

(Signature omitted.)

ANNEX

List of areas referred to in Article 16(1)
> — Work places[1]
> — Work equipment
> — Personal protective equipment
> — Work with visual display units
> — Handling of heavy loads involving risk of back injury
> — Temporary or mobile work sites[2]
> — Fisheries and agriculture

---

[1] Council Directive of 19 October 1992 (92/85/EEC) [No. L348/1] in the area of pregnant workers and workers who have recently given birth or are breastfeeding.

[2] Council Directive of 24 June 1992 (92/57/EEC) [No. L245/6] implementing minimum health and safety requirements in this area.

Council Directive 92/85 of 19 October 1992 on the introduction of measures to encourage improvements in the safety and health at work of pregnant workers and workers who have recently given birth or are breastfeeding (tenth individual Directive within the meaning of Article 16(1) of Directive 89/391/EEC)

[OJ 1992, L348/1]

The Council of the European Communities,

Having regard to the Treaty establishing the European Economic Community, and in particular Article 118a thereof,

Having regard to the proposal from the Commission, drawn up after consultation with the Advisory Committee on Safety, Hygiene and Health Protection at work,[1]

In cooperation with the European Parliament,[2]

Having regard to the opinion of the Economic and Social Committee,[3]

Whereas Article 118a of the Treaty provides that the Council shall adopt, by means of directives, minimum requirements for encouraging improvements, especially in the working environment, to protect the safety and health of workers;

Whereas this Directive does not justify any reduction in levels of protection already achieved in individual Member States, the Member States being committed, under the Treaty, to encouraging improvements in conditions in this area and to harmonising conditions while maintaining the improvements made;

Whereas, under the terms of Article 118a of the Treaty, the said directives are to avoid imposing administrative, financial and legal constraints in a way which would hold back the creation and development of small and medium-sized undertakings;

Whereas, pursuant to Decision 74/325/EEC,[4] as last amended by the 1985 Act of Accession, the Advisory Committee on Safety, Hygiene and Health protection at Work is consulted by the Commission on the drafting of proposals in this field;

Whereas the Community Charter of the fundamental social rights of workers, adopted at the Strasbourg European Council on 9 December 1989 by the Heads of State or Government of 11 Member States, lays down, in paragraph 19 in particular, that:

'Every worker must enjoy satisfactory health and safety conditions in his working environment. Appropriate measures must be taken in order to achieve further harmonisation of conditions in this area while maintaining the improvements made';

Whereas the Commission, in its action programme for the implementation of the Community Charter of the fundamental social rights of workers, has included among its aims the adoption by the Council of a Directive on the protection of pregnant women at work;

Whereas Article 15 of Council Directive 89/391/EEC of 12 June 1989 on the introduction of measures to encourage improvements in the safety and health of workers at work[5] provides that particularly sensitive risk groups must be protected against the dangers which specifically affect them;

[1] OJ No. C281, 9 November 1990, p. 3 and OJ No. C25 1 February 1991, p. 9.
[2] OJ No. C19, 28 January 1992, p. 177 and OJ No. C150, 15 June 1992, p. 99.
[3] OJ No. C41, 18 February 1991, p. 29.
[4] OJ No. L185, 9 July 1974, p. 15.
[5] OJ No. L183, 29 June 1989, p. 1.

Whereas pregnant workers, workers who have recently given birth or who are breastfeeding must be considered a specific risk group in many respects, measures must be taken with regard to their safety and health;

Whereas the protection of the safety and health of pregnant workers, workers who have recently given birth or workers who are breastfeeding should not treat women on the labour market unfavourably nor work to the detriment of directives concerning equal treatment for men and women;

Whereas some types of activities may pose a specific risk, for pregnant workers, workers who have recently given birth or workers who are breastfeeding, of exposure to dangerous agents, processes or working conditions; whereas such risks must therefore be assessed and the result of such assessment communicated to female workers and/or their representatives;

Whereas, further, should the result of this assessment reveal the existence of a risk to the safety or health of the female worker, provision must be made for such worker to be protected;

Whereas pregnant workers and workers who are breastfeeding must not engage in activities which have been assessed as revealing a risk of exposure, jeopardizing safety and health, to certain particularly dangerous agents or working conditions;

Whereas provision should be made for pregnant workers, workers who have recently given birth or workers who are breastfeeding not to be required to work at night where such provision is necessary from the point of view of their safety and health;

Whereas the vulnerability of pregnant workers, workers who have recently given birth or who are breastfeeding makes it necessary for them to be granted the right to maternity leave of at least 14 continuous weeks, allocated before and/or after confinement, and renders necessary the compulsory nature of maternity leave of at least two weeks, allocated before and/or after confinement;

Whereas the risk of dismissal for reasons associated with their condition may have harmful effects on the physical and mental state of pregnant workers, workers who have recently given birth or who are breastfeeding; whereas provision should be made for such dismissal to be prohibited;

Whereas measures for the organisation of work concerning the protection of the health of pregnant workers, workers who have recently given birth or workers who are breastfeeding would serve no purpose unless accompanied by the maintenance of rights linked to the employment contract, including maintenance of payment and/or entitlement to an adequate allowance;

Whereas, moreover, provision concerning maternity leave would also serve no purpose unless accompanied by the maintenance of rights linked to the employment contract and/or entitlement to an adequate allowance;

Whereas the concept of an adequate allowance in the case of maternity leave must be regarded as a technical point of reference with a view to fixing the minimum level of protection and should in no circumstances be interpreted as suggesting an analogy between pregnancy and illness,

Has adopted this Directive:

SECTION I PURPOSE AND DEFINITIONS

Article 1 Purpose

1. The purpose of this Directive, which is the tenth individual Directive within the meaning of Article 16(1) of Directive 89/391/EEC, is to implement measures to encourage improvements in the safety and health at work of pregnant workers and workers who have recently given birth or who are breastfeeding.

2. The provisions of Directive 89/391/EEC, except for Article 2(2) thereof, shall apply in full to the whole area covered by paragraph 1, without prejudice to any more stringent and/or specific provisions contained in this Directive.

3. This Directive may not have the effect of reducing the level of protection afforded to pregnant workers, workers who have recently given birth or who are breastfeeding as compared with the situation which exists in each Member State on the date on which this Directive is adopted.

Article 2   Definitions

For the purposes of this Directive:

- (a) *pregnant worker* shall mean a pregnant worker who informs her employer of her condition, in accordance with national legislation and/or national practice;
- (b) *worker who has recently given birth* shall mean a worker who has recently given birth within the meaning of national legislation and/or national practice and who informs her employer of her condition, in accordance with that legislation and/or practice;
- (c) *worker who is breastfeeding* shall mean a worker who is breastfeeding within the meaning of national legislation and/or national practice and who informs her employer of her condition, in accordance with that legislation and/or practice.

SECTION II   GENERAL PROVISIONS

Article 3   Guidelines

1. In consultation with the Member States and assisted by the Advisory Committee on Safety, Hygiene and Health Protection at Work, the Commission shall draw up guidelines on the assessment of the chemical, physical and biological agents and industrial processes considered hazardous for the safety or health of workers within the meaning of Article 2.

The guidelines referred to in the first sub-paragraph shall also cover movements and postures, mental and physical fatigue and other types of physical and mental stress connected with the work done by workers within the meaning of Article 2.

2. The purpose of the guidelines referred to in paragraph 1 is to serve as a basis for the assessment referred to in Article 4(1).

To this end, MemberStates shall bring these guidelines to the attention of all employers and all female workers and/or their representatives in the respective Member State.

Article 4   Assessment and information

1. For all activities liable to involve a specific risk of exposure to the agents, processes or working conditions of which a non-exhaustive list is given in Annex I, the employer shall assess the nature, degree and duration of exposure, in the undertaking and/or establishment concerned, of workers within the meaning of Article 2, either directly or by way of the protective and preventive services referred to in Article 7 of Directive 89/391/EEC, in order to:

- — assess any risks to the safety or health and any possible effect on the pregnancy or breastfeeding of workers within the meaning of Article 2,
- — decide what measures should be taken.

2. Without prejudice to Article 10 of Directive 89/391/EEC, workers within the meaning of Article 2 and workers likely to be in one of the situations referred to in Article 2 in the undertaking and/or establishment concerned and/or their representatives shall be informed of the results of the assessment referred to in paragraph 1 and of all measures to be taken concerning health and safety at work.

Article 5   Action further to the results of the assessment

1. Without prejudice to Article 6 of Directive 89/391/EEC, if the results of the assessment referred to in Article 4(1) reveal risk to the safety or health or an effect on the pregnancy

or breastfeeding of a worker within the meaning of Article 2, the employer shall take the necessary measures to ensure that, by temporarily adjusting the working conditions and/or the working hours of the worker concerned, the exposure of that worker to such risks is avoided.

2.   If the adjustment of her working conditions and/or working hours is not technically and/or objectively feasible, or cannot reasonably be required on duly substantiated grounds, the employer shall take the necessary measures to move the worker concerned to another job.

3.   If moving her to another job is not technically and/or objectively feasible or cannot reasonably be required on duly substantiated grounds, the worker concerned shall be granted leave in accordance with national legislation and/or national practice for the whole of the period necessary to protect her safety or health.

4.   The provisions of this Article shall apply *mutatis mutandis* to the case where a worker pursuing an activity which is forbidden pursuant to Article 6 becomes pregnant or starts breastfeeding and informs her employer thereof.

Article 6   Cases in which exposure is prohibited

In addition to the general provisions concerning the protection of workers, in particular those relating to the limit values for occupational exposure:

1.   pregnant workers within the meaning of Article 2(a) may under no circumstances be obliged to perform duties for which the assessment has revealed a risk of exposure, which would jeopardise safety or health, to the agents and working conditions listed in Annex II, Section A;

2.   workers who are breastfeeding, within the meaning of Article 2(c), may under no circumstances be obliged to perform duties for which the assessment has revealed a risk of exposure, which would jeopardise safety or health, to the agents and working conditions listed in Annex II, Section B.

Article 7   Night work

1.   Member States shall take the necessary measures to ensure that workers referred to in Article 2 are not obliged to perform night work during their pregnancy and for a period following childbirth which shall be determined by the national authority competent for safety and health, subject to submission, in accordance with the procedures laid down by the Member States, of a medical certificate stating that this is necessary for the safety or health of the worker concerned.

2.   The measures referred to in paragraph 1 must entail the possibility, in accordance with national legislation and/or national practice, of:

(a)   transfer to daytime work; or

(b)   leave from work or extension of maternity leave where such a transfer is not technically and/or objectively feasible or cannot reasonably be required on duly substantiated grounds.

Article 8   Maternity leave

1.   Member States shall take the necessary measures to ensure that workers within the meaning of Article 2 are entitled to a continuous period of maternity leave of at least 14 weeks allocated before and/or after confinement in accordance with national legislation and/or practice.

2.   The maternity leave stipulated in paragraph 1 must include compulsory maternity leave of at least two weeks allocated before and/or after confinement in accordance with national legislation and/or practice.

Article 9   Time off for ante-natal examinations

Member States shall take the necessary measures to ensure that pregnant workers within the meaning of Article 2(a) are entitled to, in accordance with national legislation and/or practice, time off, without loss of pay, in order to attend ante-natal examinations, if such examinations have to take place during working hours.

Article 10 Prohibition of dismissal

In order to guarantee workers, within the meaning of Article 2, the exercise of their health and safety protection rights as recognised under this Article, it will be provided that:

1. Member States shall take the necessary measures to prohibit the dismissal of workers, within the meaning of Article 2, during the period from the beginning of their pregnancy to the end of the maternity leave referred to in Article 8(1), save in exceptional cases not connected with their condition which are permitted under national legislation and/or practice and, where applicable, provided that the competent authority has given its consent;

2. if a worker, within the meaning of Article 2, is dismissed during the period referred to in point 1, the employer must cite duly substantiated grounds for her dismissal in writing;

3. Member States shall take the necessary measures to protect workers, within the meaning of Article 2, from consequences of dismissal which is unlawful by virtue of point 1.

Article 11 Employment rights

In order to guarantee workers within the meaning of Article 2 the exercise of their health and safety protection rights as recognised in this Article, it shall be provided that:

1. in the cases referred to in Articles 5, 6 and 7, the employment rights relating to the employment contract, including the maintenance of a payment to, and/or entitlement to an adequate allowance for, workers within the meaning of Article 2, must be ensured in accordance with national legislation and/or national practice;

2. in the case referred to in Article 8, the following must be ensured:
   - (a) the rights connected with the employment contract of workers within the meaning of Article 2, other than those referred to in point (b) below;
   - (b) maintenance of a payment to, and/or entitlement to an adequate allowance for, workers within the meaning of Article 2;

3. the allowance referred to in point 2(b) shall be deemed adequate if it guarantees income at least equivalent to that which the worker concerned would receive in the event of a break in her activities on grounds connected with her state of health, subject to any ceiling laid down under national legislation;

4. Member States may make entitlement to pay or the allowance referred to in points 1 and 2(b) conditional upon the worker concerned fulfilling the conditions of eligibility for such benefits laid down under national legislation.

These conditions may under no circumstances provide for periods of previous employment in excess of 12 months immediately prior to the presumed date of confinement.

Article 12 Defence of rights

Member States shall introduce into their national legal systems such measures as are necessary to enable all workers who should themselves wronged by failure to comply with the obligations arising from the Directive to pursue their claims by judicial process (and/or, in accordance with national laws and/or practice) by recourse to other competent authorities.

Article 13 Amendments to the Annexes

1. Strictly technical adjustments to Annex I as a result of technical progress, changes in international regulations or specifications and new findings in the area covered by this Directive shall be adopted in accordance with the procedure laid down in Article 17 of Directive 89/391/EEC.

2. Annex II may be amended only in accordance with the procedure laid down in Article 118a of the Treaty.

Article 14   Final provisions
1.   Member States shall bring into force the laws, regulations and administrative provisions necessary to comply with this Directive not later than two years after the adoption thereof or ensure, at the latest two years after adoption of this Directive, that the two sides of industry introduce the requisite provisions by means of collective agreements, with Member States being required to make all the necessary provisions to enable them at all times to guarantee the results laid down by this Directive. They shall forthwith inform the Commission thereof.
2.   When Member States adopt the measures referred to in paragraph 1, they shall contain a reference of this Directive or shall be accompanied by such reference on the occasion of their official publication. The methods of making such a reference shall be laid down by the Member States.
3.   Member States shall communicate to the Commission the texts of the essential provisions of national law which they have already adopted or adopt in the field governed by this Directive.
4.   Member States shall report to the Commission every five years on the practical implementation of the provisions of this Directive, indicating the points of view of the two sides of industry.
However, Member States shall report for the first time to the Commission on the practical implementation of the provisions of this Directive, indicating the points of view of the two sides of industry, four years after its adoption.
The Commission shall inform the European Parliament, the Council, the Economic and Social Committee and the Advisory Committee on Safety, Hygiene and Health Protection at Work.
5.   The Commission shall periodically submit to the European Parliament, the Council and the Economic and Social Committee a report on the implementation of this Directive, taking into account paragraphs 1, 2 and 3.
6.   The Council will re-examine the Directive, on the basis of an assessment carried out on the basis of the reports referred to in the second sub-paragraph of paragraph 4 and, should the need arise, of a proposal, to be submitted by the Commission at the latest five years after adoption of the Directive.

Article 15
This Directive is addressed to the Member States.
Done at Luxembourg, 19 October 1992.
For the Council, The President, D. Curry

ANNEX I   NON-EXHAUSTIVE LIST OF AGENTS, PROCESSES AND
WORKING CONDITIONS

REFERRED TO IN ARTICLE 4(1)

A.   Agents
1.   *Physical agents* where these are regarded as agents causing foetal lesions and/or likely to disrupt placental attachment, and in particular:
   (a) shocks, vibration or movement;
   (b) handling of loads entailing risks, particularly of a dorsolumbar nature;
   (c) noise;
   (d) ionizing radiation;
   (e) non-ionizing radiation;
   (f) extremes of cold or heat;
   (g) movements and postures, travelling—either inside or outside the establishment—mental and physical fatigue and other physical burdens connected with the activity of the worker within the meaning of Article 2 of the Directive.

2.   *Biological agents*

Biological agents of risk groups 2, 3 and 3 within the meaning of Article 2(d) numbers 2, 3 and 4 of Directive 90/679/EEC, in so far as it is known that these agents or the therapeutic measures necessitated by such agents endanger the health of pregnant women and the unborn child and in so far as they do not yet appear in Annex II.

3.   *Chemical agents*

The following chemical agents in so far as it is known that they endanger the health of pregnant womenand the unborn child and in so far as they do not yet appear in Annex II:

   (a) substances labelled R 40, R 45, R 46, and R 47 under Directive 67/548/EEC in so far as they do not yet appear in Annex II;

   (b) chemical agents in Annex I to Directive 90/394/EEC;

   (c) mercury and mercury derivatives;

   (d) antimitotic drugs;

   (e) carbon monoxide;

   (f) chemical agents of known and dangerous percutaneous absorption.

B.   Processes

Industrial processes listed in Annex I to Directive 90/394/EEC.

C.   Working conditions

Underground mining work.

ANNEX II   NON-EXHAUSTIVE LIST OF AGENTS AND WORKING CONDITIONS

REFERRED TO IN ARTICLE 6

A.   Pregnant workers within the meaning of Article 2(a)

1. Agents

(a)   *Physical agents*

Work in hyperbaric atmosphere, e.g., pressurised enclosures and underwater diving.

(b)   *Biological agents*

The following biological agents:

    — toxoplasma,

    — rubella virus,

unless the pregnant workers are proved to be adequately protected against such agents by immunisation.

(c)   *Chemical agents*

Lead and lead derivatives in so far as these agents are capable of being absorbed by the human organism.

2. Working conditions

Underground mining work.

B.   Workers who are breastfeeding within the meaning of Article 2(c)

1. Agents

(a)   *Chemical agents*

Lead and lead derivatives in so far as these agents are capable of being absorbed by the human organism.

2. Working conditions

Underground mining work.

Council Directive 94/33 EC of 22 June 1994 on the protection of young people at work
[OJ 1994, L216/12]

The Council of the European Union,

Having regard to the Treaty establishing the European Community, and in particular Article 118a thereof,

Having regard to the proposal from the Commission,[1]

Having regard to the opinion of the Economic and Social Committee,[2]

Acting in accordance with the procedure referred to in Article 189c of the Treaty[3]

Whereas Article 118a of the Treaty provides that the Council shall adopt, by means of directives, minimum requirements to encourage improvements, especially in the working environment, as regards the health and safety of workers;

Whereas, under that Article, such directives must avoid imposing administrative, financial and legal constraints in a way which would hold back the creation and development of small and medium-sized undertakings;

Whereas points 20 and 22 of the Community Charter of the Fundamental Social Rights of Workers, adopted by the European Council in Strasbourg on 9 December 1989, state that:

20.   Without prejudice to such rules as may be more favourable to young people, in particular those ensuring their preparation for work through vocational training, and subject to derogations limited to certain light work, the minimum employment age must not be lower than the minimum school-leaving age and, in any case, not lower than 15 years;

22.   Appropriate measures must be taken to adjust labour regulations applicable to young workers so that their specific development and vocational training and access to employment needs are met. The duration of work must, in particular, be limited—without it being possible to circumvent this limitation through recourse to overtime—and night work prohibited in the case of workers of under eighteen years of age, save in the case of certain jobs laid down in national legislation or regulations.

Whereas account should be taken of the principles of the International Labour Organisation regarding the protection of young people at work, including those relating to the minimum age for access to employment or work;

Whereas, in this Resolution on child labour,[4] the European Parliament summarised the various aspects of work by young people and stressed its effects on their health, safety and physical and intellectual development, and pointed to the need to adopt a Directive harmonising national legislation in the field;

Whereas Article 15 of Council Directive 89/391/EEC of 12 June 1989 on the introduction of measures to encourage improvements in the safety and health of workers at work[5] provides that particularly sensitive risk groups must be protected against the dangers which specifically affect them;

Whereas children and adolescents must be considered specific risk groups, and measures must be taken with regard to their safety and health;

---

[1] OJ No. C84, 4.4.1992, p. 7.

[2] OJ No. C313, 30.11.1992, p. 70.

[3] Opinion of the European Parliament of 17 December 1992 (OJ No. C21, 25.1.1993, p. 167). Council Common Position of 23 November 1993 (not yet published in the Official Journal) and Decision of the European Parliament of 9 March 1994 (OJ No. C91, 28.3.1994, p. 89).

[4] OJ No. C190, 20.7.1987, p. 44.

[5] OJ No. L183, 29.6.1989, p. 1.

Whereas the vulnerability of children calls for Member States to prohibit their employment and ensure that the minimum working or employment age is not lower than the minimum age at which compulsory schooling as imposed by national law ends or 15 years in any event; whereas derogations from the prohibition on child labour may be admitted only in special cases and under the conditions stipulated in this Directive;

Whereas, under no circumstances, may such derogations be detrimental to regular school attendance or prevent children benefiting fully from their education;

Whereas, in view of the nature of the transition from childhood to adult life, work by adolescents should be strictly regulated and protected;

Whereas every employer should guarantee young people working conditions appropriate to their age;

Whereas employers should implement the measures necessary to protect the safety and health of young people onthe basis of an assessment of work-related hazards to the young;

Whereas Member States should protect young people against any specific risks arising from their lack of experience, absence of awareness of existing or potential risks, or from their immaturity;

Whereas Member States should therefore prohibit the employment of young people for the work specified by this Directive;

Whereas the adoption of specific minimal requirements in respect of the organisation of working time is likely to improve working conditions for young people;

Whereas the maximum working time of young people should be strictly limited and night work by young people should be prohibited, with the exception of certain jobs specified by national legislation or rules;

Whereas Member States should take the appropriate measures to ensure that the working time of adolescents receiving school education does not adversely affect their ability to benefit from that education;

Whereas time spent on training by young persons working under a theoretical and/or practical combined work/training scheme or an in-plant work-experience should be counted as working time;

Whereas, in order to ensure the safety and health of young people, the latter should be granted minimum daily, weekly and annual periods of rest and adequate breaks;

Whereas, with respect to the weekly rest period, due account should be taken of the diversity of cultural, ethnic, religious and other factors prevailing in the Member States;

Whereas in particular, it is ultimately for each Member State to decide whether Sunday should be included in the weekly rest period, and if so to what extent;

Whereas appropriate work experience may contribute to the aim of preparing young people for adult working and social life, provided it is ensured that any harm to their safety, health and development is avoided;

Whereas, although derogations from the bans and limitations imposed by this Directive would appear indispensable for certain activities or particular situations, applications thereof must not prejudice the principles underlying the established protection system;

Whereas this Directive constitutes a tangible step towards developing the social dimension of the internal market;

Whereas the application in practice of the system of protection laid down by this Directive will require that Member States implement a system of effective and proportionate measures;

Whereas the implementation of some provisions of this Directive poses particular problems for one Member State with regard to its system of protection for young people at work; whereas that Member State should therefore be allowed to refrain from implementing the relevant provisions for a suitable period,

HAS ADOPTED THIS DIRECTIVE:

SECTION I

Article 1   Purpose

1.   Member States shall take the necessary measures to prohibit work by children. They shall ensure, under the conditions laid down by this Directive, that the minimum working or employment age is not lower than the minimum age at which compulsory full-time schooling as imposed by national law ends or 15 years in any event.

2.   Member States ensure that work by adolescents is strictly regulated and protected under the conditions laid down in this Directive.

3.   Member States shall ensure in general that employers guarantee that young people have working conditions which suit their age.

They shall ensure that young people are protected against economic exploitation and against any work likely to harm their safety, health or physical, mental, moral or social development or to jeopardise their education.

Article 2   Scope

1.   This Directive shall apply to any person under 18 years of age having an employment contract or an employment relationship defined by the law in force in a Member State and/or governed by the law in force in a Member State.

2.   Member States may make legislative or regulatory provision for this Directive not to apply, within the limits and under the conditions which they set by legislative or regulatory provision, to occasional work or short-term work involving:

    (a) domestic service in a private household, or

    (b) work regarded as not being harmful, damaging or dangerous to young people in a family undertaking.

Article 3   Definitions

For the purposes of this Directive:

    (a) 'young person' shall mean any person under 18 years of age referred to in Article 2(1);

    (b) 'child' shall mean any young person of less than 15 years of age or who is still subject to compulsory full-time schooling under national law;

    (c) 'adolescent' shall mean any young person of at least 15 years of age but less than 18 years of age who is no longer subject to compulsory full-time schooling under national law;

    (d) 'light work' shall mean all work which, on account of the inherent nature of the tasks which it involves and the particular conditions under which they are performed:

        (i) is not likely to be harmful to the safety, health or development of children, and

        (ii) is not such as to be harmful to their attendance at school, their participation in vocational guidance or training programmes approved by the competent authority or their capacity to benefit from the instruction received;

    (e) 'working time' shall mean any period during which the young person is at work, at the employer's disposal and carrying out his activity or duties in accordance with national legislation and/or practice;

    (f) 'rest period' shall mean any period which is not working time.

Article 4   Prohibition of work by children

1.   Member States shall adopt the measures necessary to prohibit work by children.

2.   Taking into account the objectives set out in Article 1, Member States may make legislative or regulatory provision for the prohibition of work by children not to apply to:

  (a) children pursuing the activities set out in Article 5;

  (b) children of at least 14 years of age working under a combined work/training scheme or an in-plant work-experience scheme, provided that such work is done in accordance with the conditions laid down by the competent authority;

  (c) children of at least 14 years of age performing light work other than that covered by Article 5; light work other than that covered by Article 5 may, however, be performed by children of 13 years of age for a limited number of hours per week in the case of categories of work determined by national legislation.

3.   Member States that make use of the opinion referred to in paragraph 2(c) shall determine, subject to the provisions of this Directive, the working conditions relating to the light work in question.

Article 5   Cultural or similar activities

1.   The employment of children for the purposes of performance in cultural, artistic, sports or advertising activities shall be subject to prior authorisation to be given by the competent authority in individual cases.

2.   Member States shall by legislative or regulatory provision lay down the working conditions for children in the cases referred to in paragraph 1 and the details of the prior authorisation procedure, on condition that the activities:

  (i)   are not likely to be harmful to the safety, health or development of children, and

  (ii) are not such as to be harmful to their attendance at school, their participation in vocational guidance or training programmes approved by the competent authority or their capacity to benefit from the instruction received.

3.   By way of derogation from the procedure laid down in paragraph 1, in the case of children of at least 13 years of age, Member States may authorise, by legislative or regulatory provision, in accordance with conditions which they shall determine, the employment of children for the purposes of performance in cultural, artistic, sports or advertising activities.

4.   The Member States which have a specific authorisation system for modelling agencies with regard to the activities of children may retain that system.

SECTION II

Article 6   General obligations on employers

1.   Without prejudice to Article 4(1), the employer shall adopt the measures necessary to protect the safety and health of young people, taking particular account of the specific risks referred to in Article 7(1).

2.   The employer shall implement the measures provided for in paragraph 1 on the basis of an assessment of the hazards to young people in connection with their work. The assessment must be made before young people begin work and when there is any major change in working conditions and must pay particular attention to the following points:

  (a) the fitting-out and layout of the workplace and the workstation;

  (b) the nature, degree and duration of exposure to physical, biological and chemical agents;

  (c) the form, range and use of work equipment, in particular agents, machines, apparatus and devices, and the way in which they are handled;

  (d) the arrangement of work processes and operations and the way in which these are combined (organisation of work);

  (e) the level of training and instruction given to young people.

Where this assessment shows that there is a risk to the safety, the physical or mental health or development of young people, an appropriate free assessment and monitoring of their health shall be provided at regular intervals without prejudice to Directive 89/391/EEC. The free health assessment and monitoring may form part of a national health system.

3.   The employer shall inform young people of possible risks and of all measures adopted concerning their safety and health.

Furthermore, he shall inform the legal representatives of children of possible risks and of all measures adopted concerning children's safety and health.

4.   The employer shall involve the protective and preventive services referred to in Article 7 of Directive 89/391/EEC in the planning, implementation and monitoring of the safety and health conditions applicable to young people.

Article 7   Vulnerability of young people—Prohibition of work

1.   Member States shall ensure that young people are protected from any specific risks to their safety, health and development which are a consequence of their lack of experience, of absence of awareness of existing or potential risks or of the fact that young people have not yet fully matured.

2.   Without prejudice to Article 4(1), Member States shall to this end prohibit the employment of young people for:

(a)   work which is objectively beyond their phyiscal or psychological capacity;

(b)   work involving harmful exposure to agents which are toxic, carcinogenic, cause heritable genetic damage, or harm to the unborn child or which in any other way chronically affect human health;

(c)   work involving harmful exposure to radiation;

(d)   work involving the risk of accidents which it may be assumed cannot be recognised or avoided by young persons owing to their insufficient attention to safety or lack of experience or training; or

(e)   work in which there is a risk to health from extreme cold or heat, or from noise or vibration. Work which is likely to entail specific risks for young people within the meaning of paragraph 1 includes:
   — work involving harmful exposure to the physical, biological and chemical agents referred to in point I of the Annex, and
   — processes and work referred to in point II of the Annex.

3.   Member States may, by legislative or regulatory provision, authorise derogations from paragraph 2 in the case of adolescents where such derogations are indispensable for their vocational training, provided that protection of their safety and health is ensured by the fact that the work is performed under the supervision of a competent person within the meaning of Article 7 of Directive 89/391/EEC and provided that the protection afforded by that Directive is guaranteed.

SECTION III

Article 8   Working time

1.   Member States which make use of the option in Article 4(2)(b) or (c) shall adopt the measures necessary to limit the working time of children to:

(a)   eight hours a day and 40 hours a week for work performed under a combined work/training scheme or an in-plant work-experience scheme;

(b)   two hours on a school day and 12 hours a week for work performed in term-time outside the hours fixed for school attendance, provided that this is not prohibited by national legislation and/or practice; in no circumstances may the daily working time exceed seven hours; this limit may be raised to eight hours in the case of children who have reached the age of 15;

    (c) seven hours a day and 35 hours a week for work performed during a period of at least a week when school is not operating; these limits may be raised to eight hours a day and 40 hours a week in the case of children who have reached the age of 15;

    (d) seven hours a day and 35 hours a week for light work performed by children no longer subject to compulsory full-time schooling under national law.

2.   Member States shall adopt the measures necessary to limit the working time of adolescents to eight hours a day and 40 hours a week.

3.   The time spent on training by a young person working under a theoretical and/or practical combined work/training scheme or an in-plant work-experience scheme shall be counted as working time.

4.   Where a young person is employed by more than one employer, working days and working time shall be cumulative.

5.   Member States may, by legislative or regulatory provision, authorise derogations from paragraph 1(a) and paragraph 2 either by way of exception or where there are objective grounds for so doing. Member States shall, by legislative or regulatory provision, determine the conditions, limits and procedure for implementing such derogations.

Article 9   Night work

1. (a) Member States which make use of the option in Article 4(2)(b) or (c) shall adopt the measures necessary to prohibit work by children between 8 p.m. and 6 a.m.

    (b) Member States shall adopt the measures necessary to prohibit work by adolescents either between 10 p.m. and 6 a.m. or between 11 p.m. and 7 a.m.

2. (a) Member States may, by legislative or regulatory provision, authorise work by adolescents in specific areas of activity during the period in which night work is prohibited as referred to in paragraph 1(b). In that event, Member States shall take appropriate measures to ensure that the adolescent is supervised by an adult where such supervision is necessary for the adolescent's protection.

    (b) If point (a) is applied, work shall continue to be prohibited between midnight and 4 a.m.

However, Member States may, by legislative or regulatory provision, authorise work by adolescents during the period in which night work is prohibited in the following cases, where there are objective grounds for so doing and provided that adolescents are allowed suitable compensatory rest time and that the objectives set out in Article 1 are not called into question:

    — work performed in the shipping or fisheries sectors;
    — work performed in the context of the armed forces or the police;
    — work performed in hospitals or similar establishments;
    — cultural, artistic, sports or advertising activities.

3.   Prior to any assignment to night work and at regular intervals thereafter, adolescents shall be entitled to a free assessment of their health and capacities, unless the work they do during the period during which work is prohibited is of an exceptional nature.

Article 10   Rest period

1. (a) Member States which make use of the option in Article 4(2)(b) or (c) shall adopt the measures necessary to ensure that, for each 24-hour period, children are entitled to a minimum rest period of 14 consecutive hours.

    (b) Member States shall adopt the measures necessary to ensure that, for each 24-hour period, adolescents are entitled to a minimum rest period of 12 consecutive hours.

2.   Member States shall adopt the measures necessary to ensure that, for each seven-day period:

    — children in respect of whom they have made use of the option in Article 4(2)(b) or (c), and
    — adolescents

are entitled to a minimum rest period of two days, which shall be consecutive if possible. Where justified by technical or organisation reasons, the minimum rest period may be reduced, but may in no circumstances be less than 36 consecutive hours. The minimum rest period referred to in the first and second sub-paragraphs shall in principle include Sunday.

3.   Member States may, by legislative or regulatory provision, provide for the minimum rest periods referred to in paragraphs 1 and 2 to be interrupted in the case of activities involving periods of work that are split up over the day or are of short duration.

4.   Member States may make legislative or regulatory provision for derogations from paragraph 1(b) and paragraph 2 in respect of adolescents in the following cases, where there are objective grounds for so doing and provided that they are granted appropriate compensatory rest time and that the objectives set out in Article 1 are not called into question:

    (a)   work performed in the shipping or fisheries sectors;
    (b)   work performed in the context of the armed forces or the police;
    (c)   work performed in hospitals or similar establishments;
    (d)   work performed in agriculture;
    (e)   work performed in the tourism industry or in the hotel, restaurant and café sector;
    (f)   activities involving periods of work split up over the day.

Article 11   Annual rest
Member States which make use of the option referred to in Article 4(2)(b) or (c) shall see to it that a period free of any work is included, as far as possible, in the school holidays of children subject to compulsory full-time schooling under national law.

Article 12   Breaks
Member States shall adopt the measures necessary to ensure that, where daily working time is more than four and a half hours, young people are entitled to a break of at least 30 minutes, which shall be consecutive if possible.

Article 13   Work by adolescents in the event of *force majeure*
Member States may, by legislative or regulatory provision, authorise derogations from Article 8(2), Article 9(1)(b), Article 10(1)(b) and, in the case of adolescents, Article 12, for work in the circumstances referred to in Article 5(4) of Directive 89/391/EEC, provided that such work is of a temporary nature and must be performed immediately, that adult workers are not available and that the adolescents are allowed equivalent compensatory rest time within the following three weeks.

SECTION IV

Article 14   Measures
Each Member State shall lay down any necessary measures to be applied in the event of failure to comply with the provisions adopted in order to implement this Directive; such measures must be effective and proportionate.

Article 15   Adaptation of the Annex
Adaptations of a strictly technical nature to the Annex in the light of technical progress, changes in international rules or specifications and advances in knowledge in the field covered by this Directive shall be adopted in accordance with the procedure provided for in Article 17 of Directive 89/391/EEC.

Article 16   Non-reducing clause

Without prejudice to the right of Member States to develop, in the light of changing circumstances, different provisions on the protection of young people, as long as the minimum requirements provided for by this Directive are complied with, the implementation of this Directive shall not constitute valid grounds for reducing the general level of protection afforded to young people.

Article 17   Final provisions

1. (a) Member States shall bring into force the laws, regulations and administrative provisions necessary to comply with this Directive not later than 22 June 1996 or ensure, by that date at the latest, that the two sides of industry introduce the requisite provisions by means of collective agreements, with Member States being required to make all the necessary provisions to enable them at all times to guarantee the results laid down by this Directive.

   (b) The United Kingdom may refrain from implementing the first sub-paragraph of Article 8(1)(b) with regard to the provision relating to the maximum weekly working time, and also Article 8(2) and Article 9(1)(b) and (2) for a period of four years from the date specified in sub-paragraph (a).

   The Commission shall submit a report on the effects of this provision.

   The Council, acting in accordance with the conditions laid down by the Treaty, shall decide whether this period should be extended.

   (c) Member States shall forthwith inform the Commission thereof.

2. When Member States adopt the measures referred to in paragraph 1, such measures shall contain a reference to this Directive or shall be accompanied by such reference on the occasion of their official publication. The methods of making such reference shall be laid down by Member States.

3. Member States shall communicate to the Commission the texts of the main provisions of national law which they have already adopted or adopt in the field governed by this Directive.

4. Member States shall report to the Commission every five years on the practical implementation of the provisions of this Directive, indicating the viewpoints of the two sides of industry.

   The Commission shall inform the European Parliament, the Council and the Economic and Social Committee thereof.

5. The Commission shall periodically submit to the European Parliament, the Council and the Economic and Social Committee a report on the application of this Directive taking into account paragraphs 1, 2, 3 and 4.

Article 18

This Directive is addressed to the Member States.

Done at Luxembourg, 22 June 1994.
For the Council, The President
E. YIANNOPOULOS

ANNEX

Non-exhaustive list of agents, processes and work (Article 7(2), second sub-paragraph)

I   Agents

1. Physical agents:
   (a) Ionizing radiation;
   (b) Work in a high-pressure atmosphere, e.g., in pressurised containers, diving.

2. Biological agents
   (a) Biological agents belonging to groups 3 and 4 within the meaning of Article 2(d) of Council Directive 90/679/EEC of 26 November 1990 on the protection of workers from risks related to exposure to biological agents at work (Seventh individual Directive within the meaning of Article 16(1) of Directive 89/391/EEC).[1]
3. Chemical agents
   (a) Substances and preparations classified according to Council Directive 67/548/EEC of 27 June 1967 on the approximation of laws, regulations and administrative provisions relating to the classification, packaging and labelling of dangerous substances[2] with amendments and Council Directive 88/379/EEC of 7 June 1988 on the approximation of the laws, regulations and administrative provisions of the Member States relating to the classification, packaging and labelling of dangerous preparations[3] as toxic (T), very toxic (Tx), corrosive (C) or explosive (E);
   (b) Substances and preparations classified according to Directives 67/548/EEC and 88/379/EEC as harmful (Xn) and with one or more of the following risk phrases:—
   danger of very serious irreversible effects (R39),
   — possible risk of irreversible effects (R40),
   — may cause sensitisation by inhalation (R42),
   — may cause sensitisation by skin contact (R43),
   — may cause cancer (R45),
   — may cause heritable genetic damage (R46),
   — danger of serious damage to health by prolonged exposure (R48),
   — may impair fertility (R60),
   — may cause harm to the unborn child (R61);
   (c) Substances and preparations classified according to Directives 67/548/EEC and 88/379/EEC as irritant (Xi) and with one or more of the following risk phrases:—
   highly flammable (R12),
   — may cause sensitisation by inhalation (R42),
   — may cause sensitisation by skin contact (R43),
   (d) Substances and preparations referred to Article 2(c) of Council Directive 90/394/EEC of 28 June 1990 on the protection of workers from the risks related to exposure to carcinogens at work (Sixth individual Directive within the meaning of Article 16(1) of Directive 89/391/EEC;[4]
   (e) Lead and compounds thereof, inasmuch as the agents in question are absorbable by the human organism;
   (f) Asbestos.

II Processes and work

1. Processes at work referred to in Annex I to Directive 90/394/EEC.
2. Manufacture and handling of devices, fireworks or other objects containing explosives.
3. Work with fierce or poisonous animals.
4. Animal slaughtering on an industrial scale.
5. Work involving the handling of equipment for the production, storage or application of compressed, liquified or dissolved gases.

---

[1] OJ No. L374, 31.12.1990, p. 1.
[2] OJ No. L196, 16.8.1967, p. 1. Directive as last amended by Directive 93/679/EEC (OJ No. L268, 29.10.1993, p. 71).
[3] OJ No. L187, 16.7.1988, p. 14. Directive as last amended by Directive 93/18/EEC (OJ No. L104, 29.4.1993, p. 46).
[4] OJ No. L196, 26.7.1990, p. 1.

6. Work with vats, tanks, reservoirs or carboys containing chemical agents referred to in 1.3.

7. Work involving a risk of structural collapse.

8. Work involving high-voltage electrical hazards.

9. Work the pace of which is determined by machinery and involving payment by results.

Council Directive 94/45/EC of 22 September 1994 on the establishment of a European Works Council or a procedure in Community-scale undertakings and Community-scale groups of undertakings for the purposes of informing and consulting employees

[OJ 1994, L254/64]*

THE COUNCIL OF THE EUROPEAN UNION,

Having regard to the Agreement on social policy annexed to Protocol 14 on social policy annexed to the Treaty establishing the European Community, and in particular Article 2(2) thereof,

Having regard to the proposal from the Commission,[1]

Having regard to the opinion of the Economic and Social Committee,[2]

Acting in accordance with the procedure referred to in Article 189c of the Treaty,[3]

Whereas, on the basis of the Protocol on Social Policy annexed to the Treaty establishing the European Community, the Kingdom of Belgium, the Kingdom of Denmark, the Federal Republic of Germany, the Hellenic Republic, the Kingdom of Spain, the French Republic, Ireland, the Italian Republic, the Grand Duchy of Luxembourg, the Kingdom of the Netherlands and the Portuguese Republic (hereinafter referred to as 'the Member States'), desirous of implementing the Social Charter of 1989, have adopted an Agreement on Social Policy;

Whereas Article 2(2) of the said Agreement authorises the Council to adopt minimum requirements by means of directives;

Whereas, pursuant to Article 1 of the Agreement, one particular objective of the Community and the Member States is to promote dialogue between management and labour;

Whereas point 17 of the Community Charter of Fundamental Social Rights of Workers provides, inter alia, that information, consultation and participation for workers must be developed along appropriate lines, taking account of the practices in force in different Member States; whereas the Charter states that 'this shall apply especially in companies or groups of companies having establishments or companies in two or more Member States';

Whereas the Council, despite the existence of a broad consensus among the majority of Member States, was unable to act on the proposal for a Council Directive on the establishment of a European Works Council in Community-scale undertakings or groups of

---

* **Editor's Note:** As amended and extended to the UK by Directive 97/74 (OJ 1997, L10/22).

[1] OJ No. C135, 18.5.1994, p. 8 and OJ No. C199, 21.7.1994, p. 10.

[2] Opinion delivered on 1 June 1994 (not yet published in the Official Journal).

[3] Opinion of the European Parliament of 4 May 1994 (OJ No. C205, 25.7.1994) and Council common position of 18 July 1994 (OJ No. C244, 31.8.1994, p. 37).

undertakings for the purposes of informing and consulting employees,[4] as amended on 3 December 1991;[5]

Whereas the Commission, pursuant to Article 3(2) of the Agreement on Social Policy, has consulted management and labour at Community level on the possible direction of Community action on the information and consultation of workers in Community-scale undertakings and Community-scale groups of undertakings;

Whereas the Commission, considering after this consultation that Community action was advisable, has again consulted management and labour on the content of the planned proposal, pursuant to Article 3(3) of the said Agreement, and management and labour have presented their opinions to the Commission;

Whereas, following this second phase of consultation, management and labour have not informed the Commission of their wish to initiate the process which might lead to the conclusion of an agreement, as provided for in Article 4 of the Agreement;

Whereas the functioning of the internal market involves a process of concentrations of undertakings, cross-border mergers, take-overs, joint ventures and, consequently, a transnationalisation of undertakings and groups of undertakings;

Whereas, if economic activities are to develop in a harmonious fashion, undertakings and groups of undertakings operating in two or more Member States must inform and consult the representatives of those of their employees that are affected by their decisions;

Whereas procedures for informing and consulting employees as embodied in legislation or practice in the Member States are often not geared to the transnational structure of the entity which takes the decisions affecting those employees;

Whereas this may lead to the unequal treatment of employees affected by decisions within one and the same undertaking or group of undertakings;

Whereas appropriate provisions must be adopted to ensure that the employees of Community-scale undertakings are properly informed and consulted when decisions which affect them are taken in a Member State other than that in which they are employed;

Whereas, in order to guarantee that the employees of undertakings or groups of undertakings operating in two or more Member States are properly informed and consulted, it is necessary to set up European Works Councils or to create other suitable procedures for the transnational information and consultation of employees;

Whereas it is accordingly necessary to have a definition of the concept of controlling undertaking relating solely to this Directive and not prejudging definitions of the concepts of group or control which might be adopted in texts to be drafted in the future;

Whereas the mechanisms for informing and consulting employees in such undertakings or groups must encompass all of the establishments or, as the case may be, the group's undertakings located within the Member States, regardless of whether the undertaking or the group's controlling undertaking has its central management inside or outside the territory of the Member States;

Whereas, in accordance with the principle of autonomy of the parties, it is for the representatives of employees and the management of the undertaking or the group's controlling undertaking to determine by agreement the nature, composition, the function, mode of operation, procedures and financial resources of European Works Councils or other information and consultation procedures so as to suit their own particular circumstances;

Whereas, in accordance with the principle of subsidiarity, it is for the Member States to determine who the employees' representatives are and in particular to provide, if they consider appropriate, for a balanced representation of different categories of employees;

Whereas, however, provision should be made for certain subsidiary requirements to apply

---

[4] OJ No. C39, 15.2.1991, p. 10.
[5] OJ No. C336, 31.12.1991, p. 11.

should the parties so decide or in the event of the central management refusing to initiate negotiations or in the absence of agreement subsequent to such negotiations;

Whereas, moreover, employees' representatives may decide not to seek the setting-up of a European Works Council or the parties concerned may decide on other procedures for the transnational information and consultation of employees;

Whereas, without prejudice to the possibility of the parties deciding otherwise, the European Works Council set up in the absence of agreement between the parties must, in order to fulfil the objective of this Directive, be kept informed and consulted on the activities of the undertaking or group of undertakings so that it may assess the possible impact on employees' interests in at least two different Member States;

Whereas, to that end, the undertaking or controlling undertaking must be required to communicate to the employees' appointed representatives general information concerning the interests of employees and information relating more specifically to those aspects of the activities of the undertaking or group of undertakings which affect employees' interests; whereas the European Works Council must be able to deliver an opinion at the end of that meeting;

Whereas certain decisions having a significant effect on the interests of employees must be the subject of information and consultation of the employees' appointed representatives as soon as possible;

Whereas provision should be made for the employees' representatives acting within the framework of the Directive to enjoy, when exercising their functions, the same protection and guarantees similar to those provided to employees' representatives by the legislation and/or practice of the country of employment;

Whereas they must not be subject to any discrimination as a result of the lawful exercise of their activities and must enjoy adequate protection as regards dismissal and other sanctions;

Whereas the information and consultation provisions laid down in this Directive must be implemented in the case of an undertaking or a group's controlling undertaking which has its central management outside the territory of the Member States by its representative agent, to be designated if necessary, in one of the Member States or, in the absence of such an agent, by the establishment or controlled undertaking employing the greatest number of employees in the Member States;

Whereas special treatment should be accorded to Community-scale undertakings and groups of undertakings in which there exists, at the time when this Directive is brought into effect, an agreement, covering the entire workforce, providing for the transnational information and consultation of employees;

Whereas the Member States must take appropriate measures in the event of failure to comply with the obligations laid down in this Directive,

HAS ADOPTED THIS DIRECTIVE:

SECTION I   GENERAL

Article 1   Objective

1. The purpose of this Directive is to improve the right to information and to consultation of employees in Community-scale undertakings and Community-scale groups of undertakings.

2. To that end, a European Works Council or a procedure for informing and consulting employees shall be established in every Community-scale undertaking and every Community-scale group of undertakings, where requested in the manner laid down in Article 5(1), with the purpose of informing and consulting employees under the terms, in the manner and with the effects laid down in this Directive.

3.   Notwithstanding paragraph 2, where a Community-scale group of undertakings within the meaning of Article 2(1)(c) comprises one or more undertakings or groups of undertakings which are Community-scale undertakings or Community-scale groups of undertakings within the meaning of Article 2(1)(a) or (c), a European Works Council shall be established at the level of the group unless the agreements referred to in Article 6 provide otherwise.

4.   Unless a wider scope is provided for in the agreements referred to in Article 6, the powers and competence of European Works Councils and the scope of information and consultation procedures established to achieve the purpose specified in paragraph 1 shall, in the case of a Community-scale undertaking, cover all the establishments located within the Member States and, in the case of a Community-scale group of undertakings, all group undertakings located within the Member States.

5.   Member States may provide that this Directive shall not apply to merchant navy crews.

Article 2   Definitions

1.   For the purposes of this Directive:
   (a) 'Community-scale undertaking' means any undertaking with at least 1,000 employees within the Member States and at least 150 employees in each of at least two Member States;
   (b) 'group of undertakings' means a controlling undertaking and its controlled undertakings;
   (c) 'Community-scale group of undertakings' means a group of undertakings with the following characteristics:
      — at least 1,000 employees within the Member States,
      — at least two group undertakings in different Member States, and
      — at least one group undertaking with at least 150 employees in one Member State, and
      — at least one other group undertaking with at least 150 employees in another Member State;
   (d) 'employees' representatives' means the employees' representatives provided for by national law and/or practice;
   (e) 'central management' means the central management of the Community-scale undertaking or, in the case of a Community-scale group of undertakings, of the controlling undertaking;
   (f) 'consultation' means the exchange of views and establishment of dialogue between employees' representatives and central management or any more appropriate level of management;
   (g) 'European Works Council' means the council established in accordance with Article 1(2) or the provisions of the Annex, with the purpose of informing and consulting employees;
   (h) 'special negotiating body' means the body established in accordance with Article 5(2) to negotiate with the central management regarding the establishment of a European Works Council or a procedure for informing and consulting employees in accordance with Article 1(2).

2.   For the purposes of this Directive, the prescribed thresholds for the size of the work-force shall be based on the average number of employees, including part-time employees, employed during the previous two years calculated according to national legislation and/or practice.

Article 3   Definition of 'controlling undertaking'

1.   For the purposes of this Directive, 'controlling undertaking' means an undertaking which can exercise a dominant influence over another undertaking ('the controlled under-

taking') by virtue, for example, of ownership, financial participation or the rules which govern it.

2.   The ability to exercise a dominant influence shall be presumed, without prejudice to proof to the contrary, when, in relation to another undertaking directly or indirectly:*

(a) holds a majority of that undertaking's subscribed capital; or

(b) controls a majority of the votes attached to that undertaking's issued share capital; or

(c) can appoint more than half of the members of that undertaking's administrative, management or supervisory body.

3.   For the purposes of paragraph 2, a controlling undertaking's rights as regards voting and appointment shall include the rights of any other controlled undertaking and those of any person or body acting in his or its own name but on behalf of the controlling undertaking or of any other controlled undertaking.

4.   Notwithstanding paragraphs 1 and 2, an undertaking shall not be deemed to be a 'controlling undertaking' with respect to another undertaking in which it has holdings where the former undertaking is a company referred to in Article 3(5)(a) or (c) of Council Regulation (EEC) No. 4064/89 of 21 December 1989 on the control of concentrations between undertakings.[6]

5.   A dominant influence shall not be presumed to be exercised solely by virtue of the fact that an office holder is exercising his functions, according to the law of a Member State relating to liquidation, winding up, insolvency, cessation of payments, compositions or analogous proceedings.

6.   The law applicable in order to determine whether an undertaking is a 'controlling undertaking' shall be the law of the Member State which governs that undertaking. Where the law governing that undertaking is not that of a Member State, the law applicable shall be the law of the Member State within whose territory the representative of the undertaking or, in the absence of such a representative, the central management of the group undertaking which employs the greatest number of employees is situated.

7.   Where, in the case of a conflict of laws in the application of paragraph 2, two or more undertakings from a group satisfy one or more of the criteria laid down in that paragraph, the undertaking which satisfies the criterion laid down in point (c) thereof shall be regarded as the controlling undertaking, without prejudice to proof that another undertaking is able to exercise a dominant influence.

SECTION II   ESTABLISHMENT OF A EUROPEAN WORKS COUNCIL OR AN
EMPLOYEE INFORMATION AND CONSULTATION PROCEDURE

Article 4   Responsibility for the establishment of a European Works Council or an employee information and consultation procedure

1.   The central management shall be responsible for creating the conditions and means necessary for the setting up of a European Works Council or an information and consultation procedure, as provided for in Article 1(2), in a Community-scale undertaking and a Community-scale group of undertakings.

2.   Where the central management is not situated in a Member State, the central management's representative agent in a Member State, to be designated if necessary, shall

---

* **Editor's Note:** Although not present in either the printed OJ version or any online versions of this Directive, it is presumed the words 'an undertaking' or 'a controlling undertaking' should appear here to make better sense.

[6] OJ No. L395, 30.12.1989, p. 1.

take on the responsibility referred to in paragraph 1. In the absence of such a representative, the management of the establishment or group undertaking employing the greatest number of employees in any one Member State shall take on the responsibility referred to in paragraph 1.

3. For the purposes of this Directive, the representative or representatives or, in the absence of any such representatives, the management referred to in the second sub-paragraph of paragraph 2, shall be regarded as the central management.

Article 5 Special negotiating body

1. In order to achieve the objective in Article 1(1), the central management shall initiate negotiations for the establishment of a European Works Council or an information and consultation procedure on its own initiative or at the written request of at least 100 employees or their representatives in at least two undertakings or establishments in at least two different Member States.

2. For this purpose, a special negotiating body shall be established in accordance with the following guidelines:

(a) The Member States shall determine the method to be used for the election or appointment of the members of the special negotiating body who are to be elected or appointed in their territories.

Member States shall provide that employees in undertakings and/or establishments in which there are no employees' representatives through no fault of their own, have the right to elect or appoint members of the special negotiating body.

The second sub-paragraph shall be without prejudice to national legislation and/or practice laying downthresholds for the establishment of employee representation bodies.

(b) The special negotiating body shall have a minimum of three and a maximum of 18 members.

(c) In these elections or appointments, it must be ensured:
   — firstly, that each Member State in which the Community-scale undertaking has one or more establishments or in which the Community-scale group of undertakings has the controlling undertaking or one or more controlled undertakings is represented by one member,
   — secondly, that there are supplementary members in proportion to the number of employees working in the establishments, the controlling under-taking or the controlled undertakings as laid down by the legislation of the Member State within the territory of which the central management is situated.

(d) The central management and local management shall be informed of the composition of the special negotiating body.

3. The special negotiating body shall have the task of determining, with the central management, by written agreement, the scope, composition, functions, and term of office of the European Works Council(s) or the arrangements for implementing a procedure for the information and consultation of employees.

4. With a view to the conclusion of an agreement in accordance with Article 6, the central management shall convene a meeting with the special negotiating body. It shall inform the local managements accordingly.

For the purpose of the negotiations, the special negotiating body may be assisted by experts of its choice.

5. The special negotiating body may decide, by at least two-thirds of the votes, not to open negotiations in accordance with paragraph 4, or to terminate the negotiations already opened.

Such a decision shall stop the procedure to conclude the agreement referred to in Article 6. Where such a decision has been taken, the provisions in the Annex shall not apply.

A new request to convene the special negotiating body may be made at the earliest two years after the abovementioned decision unless the parties concerned lay down a shorter period.

6.   Any expenses relating to the negotiations referred to in paragraphs 3 and 4 shall be borne by the central management so as to enable the special negotiating body to carry out its task in an appropriate manner.

In compliance with this principle, Member States may lay down budgetary rules regarding the operation of the special negotiating body. They may in particular limit the funding to cover one expert only.

Article 6   Content of the agreement

1.   The central management and the special negotiating body must negotiate in a spirit of cooperation with a view to reaching an agreement on the detailed arrangements for implementing the information and consultation of employees provided for in Article 1(1).

2.   Without prejudice to the autonomy of the parties, the agreement referred to in paragraph 1 between the central management and the special negotiating body shall determine:

(a)   the undertakings of the Community-scale group of undertakings or the establishments of the Community-scale undertaking which are covered by the agreement;

(b)   the composition of the European Works Council, the number of members, the allocation of seats and the term of office;

(c)   the functions and the procedure for information and consultation of the European Works Council;

(d)   the venue, frequency and duration of meetings of the European Works Council;

(e)   the financial and material resources to be allocated to the European Works Council;

(f)   the duration of the agreement and the procedure for its renegotiation.

3.   The central management and the special negotiating body may decide, in writing, to establish one or more information and consultation procedures instead of a European Works Council.

The agreement must stipulate by what method the employees' representatives shall have the right to meet to discuss the information conveyed to them.

This information shall relate in particular to transnational questions which significantly affect workers' interests.

4.   The agreements referred to in paragraphs 2 and 3 shall not, unless provision is made otherwise therein, be subject to the subsidiary requirements of the Annex.

5.   For the purposes of concluding the agreements referred to in paragraphs 2 and 3, the special negotiating body shall act by a majority of its members.

Article 7   Subsidiary requirements

1.   In order to achieve the objective in Article 1(1), the subsidiary requirements laid down by the legislation of the Member State in which the central management is situated shall apply:

— where the central management and the special negotiating body so decide, or— where the central management refuses to commence negotiations within six months of the request referred to in Article 5(1), or

— where, after three years from the date of this request, they are unable to conclude an agreement as laid down in Article 6 and the special negotiating body has not taken the decision provided for in Article 5(5).

2.   The subsidiary requirements referred to in paragraph 1 as adopted in the legislation of the Member States must satisfy the provisions set out in the Annex.

SECTION III   MISCELLANEOUS PROVISIONS

Article 8   Confidential information

1. Member States shall provide that members of special negotiating bodies or of European Works Councils and any experts who assist them are not authorised to reveal any information which has expressly been provided to them in confidence.

The same shall apply to employees' representatives in the framework of an information and consultation procedure.

This obligation shall continue to apply, wherever the persons referred to in the first and second sub-paragraphs are, even after the expiry of their terms of office.

2. Each Member State shall provide, in specific cases and under the conditions and limits laid down by national legislation, that the central management situated in its territory is not obliged to transmit information when its nature is such that, according to objective criteria, it would seriously harm the functioning of the undertakings concerned or would be prejudicial to them.

A Member State may make such dispensation subject to prior administrative or judicial authorisation.

3. Each Member State may lay down particular provisions for the central management of undertakings in its territory which pursue directly and essentially the aim of ideological guidance with respect to information and the expression of opinions, on condition that, at the date of adoption of this Directive such particular provisions already exist in the national legislation.

Article 9   Operation of European Works Council and information and consultation procedure for workers

The central management and the European Works Council shall work in a spirit of cooperation with due regard to their reciprocal rights and obligations.

The same shall apply to cooperation between the central management and employees' representatives in the framework of an information and consultation procedure for workers.

Article 10   Protection of employees' representatives

Members of special negotiating bodies, members of European Works Councils and employees' representatives exercising their functions under the procedure referred to in Article 6(3) shall, in the exercise of their functions, enjoy the same protection and guarantees provided for employees' representatives by the national legislation and/or practice in force in their country of employment.

This shall apply in particular to attendance at meetings of special negotiating bodies or European Works Councils or any other meetings within the framework of the agreement referred to in Article 6(3), and the payment of wages for members who are on the staff of the Community-scale undertaking or the Community-scale group of undertakings for the period of absence necessary for the performance of their duties.

Article 11   Compliance with this Directive

1. Each Member State shall ensure that the management of establishments of a Community-scale undertaking and the management of undertakings which form part of a Community-scale group of undertakings which are situated within its territory and their employees' representatives or, as the case may be, employees abide by the obligations laid down by this Directive, regardless of whether or not the central management is situated within its territory.

2. Member States shall ensure that the information on the number of employees referred to in Article 2(1)(a) and (c) is made available by undertakings at the request of the parties concerned by the application of this Directive.

3. Member States shall provide for appropriate measures in the event of failure to

comply with this Directive; in particular, they shall ensure that adequate administrative or judicial procedures are available to enable the obligations deriving from this Directive to be enforced.

4.   Where Member States apply Article 8, they shall make provision for administrative or judicial appeal procedures which the employees' representatives may initiate when the central management requires confidentiality or does not give information in accordance with that Article.

Such procedures may include procedures designed to protect the confidentiality of the information in question.

Article 12   Link between this Directive and other provisions

1.   This Directive shall apply without prejudice to measures taken pursuant to Council Directive 75/129/EEC of 17 February 1975 on the approximation of the laws of the Member States relating to collective redundancies,[7] and to Council Directive 77/187/EEC of 14 February 1977 on the approximation of the laws of the Member States relating to the safeguarding of employees' rights in the event of transfers of undertakings, businesses or parts of businesses.[8]

2.   This Directive shall be without prejudice to employees' existing rights to information and consultation under national law.

Article 13   Agreements in force

1.   Without prejudice to paragraph 2, the obligations arising from this Directive shall not apply to Community-scale undertakings or Community-scale groups of undertakings in which, on the date laid down in Article 14(1) for the implementation of this Directive or the date of its transposition in the Member State in question, where this is earlier than the abovementioned date, there is already an agreement, covering the entire workforce, providing for the transnational information and consultation of employees.

2.   When the agreements referred to in paragraph 1 expire, the parties to those agreements may decide jointly to renew them.

Where this is not the case, the provisions of this Directive shall apply.

Article 14   Final provisions

1.   Member States shall bring into force the laws, regulations and administrative provisions necessary to comply with this Directive no later than 22 September 1996 or shall ensure by that date at the latest that management and labour introduce the required provisions by way of agreement, the Member States being obliged to take all necessary steps enabling them at all times to guarantee the results imposed by this Directive. They shall forthwith inform the Commission thereof.

2.   When Member States adopt these measures, they shall contain a reference to this Directive or shall be accompanied by such reference on the occasion of their official publication. The methods of making such reference shall be laid down by Member States.

Article 15   Review by the Commission

Not later than 22 September 1999, the Commission shall, in consultation with the Member States and with management and labour at European level, review its operation and, in particular examine whether the workforce size thresholds are appropriate with a view to proposing suitable amendments to the Council, where necessary.

---

[7] OJ No. L48, 22.2.1975, p. 29. Regulation as last amended by Directive 92/56/EEC (OJ No. L245, 26.8.1992, p. 3).

[8] OJ No. L61, 5.3.1977, p. 26.

Article 16

This Directive is addressed to the Member States.

Done at Brussels, 22 September 1994. For the Council

The President

N. BLUEM

ANNEX

SUBSIDIARY REQUIREMENTS referred to in Article 7 of the Directive

1. In order to achieve the objective in Article 1(1) of the Directive and in the cases provided for in Article 7(1) of the Directive, the establishment, composition and competence of a European Works Council shall be governed by the following rules:

(a) The competence of the European Works Council shall be limited to information and consultation on the matters which concern the Community-scale under-taking or Community-scale group of undertakings as a whole or at least two of its establishments or group undertakings situated in different Member States. In the case of undertakings or groups of undertakings referred to in Article 4(2), the competence of the European Works Council shall be limited to those matters concerning all their establishments or group undertakings situated within the Member States or concerning at least two of their establishments or group undertakings situated in different Member States.

(b) The European Works Council shall be composed of employees of the Community-scale undertaking or Community-scale group of undertakings elected or appointed from their number by the employees' representatives or, in the absence thereof, by the entire body of employees.

The election or appointment of members of the European Works Council shall be carried out in accordance with national legislation and/or practice.

(c) The European Works Council shall have a minimum of three members and a maximum of 30. Where its size so warrants, it shall elect a select committee from among its members, comprising at most three members. It shall adopt its own rules of procedure.

(d) In the election or appointment of members of the European Works Council, it must be ensured:
   — firstly, that each Member State in which the Community-scale undertaking has one or more establishments or in which the Community-scale group of undertakings has the controlling undertaking or one or more controlled undertakings is represented by one member,
   — secondly, that there are supplementary members in proportion to the number of employees working in the establishments, the controlling undertaking or the controlled undertakings as laid down by the legislation of the Member State within the territory of which the central management is situated.

(e) The central management and any other more appropriate level of management shall be informed of the composition of the European Works Council.

(f) Four years after the European Works Council is established it shall examine whether to open negotiations for the conclusion of the agreement referred to in Article 6 of the Directive or to continue to apply the subsidiary requirements adopted in accordance with this Annex.

Articles 6 and 7 of the Directive shall apply, mutatis mutandis, if a decision has been taken to negotiate an agreement according to Article 6 of the Directive, in which case 'special negotiating body' shall be replaced by 'European Works Council'.

2.   The European Works Council shall have the right to meet with the central management once a year, to be informed and consulted, on the basis of a report drawn up by the central management, on the progress of the business of the Community-scale undertaking or Community-scale group of undertakings and its prospects. The local managements shall be informed accordingly.

The meeting shall relate in particular to the structure, economic and financial situation, the probable development of the business and of production and sales, the situation and probable trend of employment, investments, and substantial changes concerning organisation, introduction of new working methods or production processes, transfers of production, mergers, cut-backs or closures of undertakings, establishments or important parts thereof, and collective redundancies.

3.   Where there are exceptional circumstances affecting the employees' interests to a considerable extent, particularly in the event of relocations, the closure of establishments or undertakings or collective redundancies, the select committee or, where no such committee exists, the European Works Council shall have the right to be informed. It shall have the right to meet, at its request, the central management, or any other more appropriate level of management within the Community-scale undertaking or group of undertakings having its own powers of decision, so as to be informed and consulted on measures significantly affecting employees' interests. Those members of the European Works Council who have been elected or appointed by the establishments and/or undertakings which are directly concerned by the measures in question shall also have the right to participate in the meeting organised with the select committee.

This information and consultation meeting shall take place as soon as possible on the basis of a report drawn up by the central management or any other appropriate level of management of the Community-scale undertaking or group of undertakings, on which an opinion may be delivered at the end of the meeting or within a reasonable time.

This meeting shall not affect the prerogatives of the central management.

4.   The Member States may lay down rules on the chairing of information and consultation meetings.

Before any meeting with the central management, the European Works Council or the select committee, where necessary enlarged in accordance with the second paragraph of point 3, shall be entitled to meet without the management concerned being present.

5.   Without prejudice to Article 8 of the Directive, the members of the European Works Council shall inform the representatives of the employees of the establishments or of the undertakings of a Community-scale group of undertakings or, in the absence of representatives, the workforce as a whole, of the content and outcome of the information and consultation procedure carried out in accordance with this Annex.

6.   The European Works Council or the select committee may be assisted by experts of its choice, in so far as this is necessary for it to carry out its tasks.

7.   The operating expenses of the European Works Council shall be borne by the central management.

The central management concerned shall provide the members of the European Works Council with such financial and material resources as enable them to perform their duties in an appropriate manner.

In particular, the cost of organising meetings and arranging for interpretation facilities and the accommodation and travelling expenses of members of the European Works Council and its select committee shall be met by the central management unless otherwise agreed.

In compliance with these principles, the Member States may lay down budgetary rules regarding the operation of the European Works Council. They may in particular limit funding to cover one expert only.

Council Directive 97/81/EC of 15 December 1997 concerning the framework agreement on part-time work concluded by UNICE, CEEP and the ETUC*

[OJ 1998, L14/9]

THE COUNCIL OF THE EUROPEAN UNION,

Having regard to the Agreement on social policy annexed to the Protocol (No. 14) on social policy, annexed to the Treaty establishing the European Community, and in particular Article 4(2) thereof,

Having regard to the proposal from the Commission,

(1) Whereas on the basis of the Protocol on social policy annexed to the Treaty establishing the European Community, the Member States, with the exception of the United Kingdom of Great Britain and Northern Ireland (hereinafter referred to as 'the Member States'), wishing to continue along the path laid down in the 1989 Social Charter, have concluded an agreement on social policy;

(2) Whereas management and labour (the social partners) may, in accordance with Article 4(2) of the Agreement on social policy, request jointly that agreements at Community level be implemented by a Council decision on a proposal from the Commission;

(3) Whereas point 7 of the Community Charter of the Fundamental Social Rights of Workers provides, inter alia, that 'the completion of the internal market must lead to an improvement in the living and working conditions of workers in the European Community. This process must result from an approximation of these conditions while the improvement is being maintained, as regards in particular . . . forms of employment other than open-ended contracts, such as fixed-term contracts, part-time working, temporary work and seasonal work';

(4) Whereas the Council has not reached a decision on the proposal for a Directive on certain employment relationships with regard to distortions of competition,[1] as amended,[2] nor on the proposal for a Directive on certain employment relationships with regard to working conditions;[3]

(5) Whereas the conclusions of the Essen European Council stressed the need to take measures to promote employment and equal opportunities for women and men, and called for measures with a view to increasing the employment-intensiveness of growth, in particular by a more flexible organisation of work in a way which fulfils both the wishes of employees and the requirements of competition;

(6) Whereas the Commission, in accordance with Article 3(2) of the Agreement on social policy, has consulted management and labour on the possible direction of Community action with regard to flexible working time and job security;

(7) Whereas the Commission, considering after such consultation that Community action was desirable, once again consulted management and labour at Community level on the substance of the envisaged proposal in accordance with Article 3(3) of the said Agreement;

(8) Whereas the general cross-industry organisations, the Union of Industrial and Employer's Confederations of Europe (UNICE), the European Centre of Enterprises with Public Participation (CEEP) and the European Trade Union Confederation (ETUC) informed the Commission in their joint letter of 19 June 1996 of their desire to initiate the procedure provided for in Article 4 of the Agreement on social policy; whereas they asked the Com-

---

* **Editor's Note:** As extended to the UK by Council Directive 98/23/EC.

[1] OJ C 224, 8.9.1990, p. 6.

[2] OJ C 305, 5.12.1990, p. 8.

[3] OJ C 224, 8.9.1990, p. 4.

mission, in a joint letter dated 12 March 1997, for a further three months; whereas the Commission complied with this request;

(9) Whereas the said cross-industry organisations concluded, on 6 June 1997, a Framework Agreement on part-time work; whereas they forwarded to the Commission their joint request to implement this Framework Agreement by a Council decision on a proposal from the Commission, in accordance with Article 4(2) of the said Agreement;

(10) Whereas the Council, in its Resolution of 6 December 1994 on prospects for a European Union social policy: contribution to economic and social convergence in the Union,[4] asked management and labour to make use of the opportunities for concluding agreements, since they are as a rule closer to social reality and to social problems;

(11) Whereas the signatory parties wished to conclude a framework agreement on part-time work setting out the general principles and minimum requirements for part-time working; whereas they have demonstrated their desire to establish a general framework for eliminating discrimination against part-time workers and to contribute to developing the potential for part-time work on a basis which is acceptable for employers and workers alike;

(12) Whereas the social partners wished to give particular attention to part-time work, while at the same time indicating that it was their intention to consider the need for similar agreements for other flexible forms of work;

(13) Whereas, in the conclusions of the Amsterdam European Council, the Heads of State and Government of the European Union strongly welcomed the agreement concluded by the social partners on part-time work;

(14) Whereas the proper instrument for implementing the Framework Agreement is a Directive within the meaning of Article 189 of the Treaty; whereas it therefore binds the Member States as to the result to be achieved, whilst leaving national authorities the choice of form and methods;

(15) Whereas, in accordance with the principles of subsidiarity and proportionality as set out in Article 3(b) of the Treaty, the objectives of this Directive cannot be sufficiently achieved by the Member States and can therefore be better achieved by the Community; whereas this Directive does not go beyond what is necessary for the attainment of those objectives;

(16) Whereas, with regard to terms used in the Framework Agreement which are not specifically defined therein, this Directive leaves Member States free to define those terms in accordance with national law and practice, as is the case for other social policy Directives using similar terms, providing that the said definitions respect the content of the Framework Agreement;

(17) Whereas the Commission has drafted its proposal for a Directive, in accordance with its Communication of 14 December 1993 concerning the application of the Protocol (No. 14) on social policy and its Communication of 18 September 1996 concerning the development of the social dialogue at Community level, taking into account the representative status of the signatory parties and the legality of each clause of the Framework Agreement;

(18) Whereas the Commission has drafted its proposal for a Directive in compliance with Article 2(2) of the Agreement on social policy which provides that Directives in the social policy domain 'shall avoid imposing administrative, financial and legal constraints in a way which would hold back the creation and development of small and medium-sized undertakings';

(19) Whereas the Commission, in accordance with its Communication of 14 December 1993 concerning the application of the Protocol (No. 14) on social policy, informed the European Parliament by sending it the text of its proposal for a Directive containing the Framework Agreement;

(20) Whereas the Commission also informed the Economic and Social Committee;

---

[4] OJ C 368, 23.12.1994, p. 6.

(21) Whereas Clause 6.1 of the Framework Agreement provides that Member States and/or the social partners may maintain or introduce more favourable provisions;

(22) Whereas Clause 6.2 of the Framework Agreement provides that implementation of this Directive may not serve to justify any regression in relation to the situation which already exists in each Member State;

(23) Whereas the Community Charter of the Fundamental Social Rights of Workers recognises the importance of the fight against all forms of discrimination, especially based on sex, colour, race, opinion and creed;

(24) Whereas Article F(2) of the Treaty on European Union states that the Union shall respect fundamental rights, as guaranteed by the European Convention for the Protection of Human Rights and Fundamental Freedoms and as they result from the constitutional traditions common to the Member States, as general principles of Community law;

(25) Whereas the Member States may entrust the social partners, at their joint request, with the implementation of this Directive, provided that the Member States take all the necessary steps to ensure that they can at all times guarantee the results imposed by this Directive;

(26) Whereas the implementation of the Framework Agreement contributes to achieving the objectives under Article 1 of the Agreement on social policy,

HAS ADOPTED THIS DIRECTIVE:

Article 1
The purpose of this Directive is to implement the Framework Agreement on part-time work concluded on 6 June 1997 between the general cross-industry organisations (UNICE, CEEP and the ETUC) annexed hereto.

Article 2
1. Member States shall bring into force the laws, regulations and administrative provisions necessary to comply with this Directive not later than 20 January 2000, or shall ensure that, by that date at the latest, the social partners have introduced the necessary measures by agreement, the Member States being required to take any necessary measures to enable them at any time to be in a position to guarantee the results imposed by this Directive. They shall forthwith inform the Commission thereof.

Member States may have a maximum of one more year, if necessary, to take account of special difficulties or implementation by a collective agreement.

They shall inform the Commission forthwith in such circumstances. When Member States adopt the measures referred to in the first sub-paragraph, they shall contain a reference to this Directive or shall be accompanied by such reference on the occasion of their official publication. The methods of making such a reference shall be laid down by the Member States.

1a. As regards the United Kingdom of Great Britain and Northern Ireland, the date of 20 January 2000 in paragraph 1 shall be replaced by the date of 7 April 2000.

2. Member States shall communicate to the Commission the text of the main provisions of domestic law which they have adopted or which they adopt in the field governed by this Directive.

Article 3
This Directive shall enter into force on the day of its publication in the Official Journal of the European Communities.

Article 4
This Directive is addressed to the Member States.

Done at Brussels, 15 December 1997. For the Council
The President
J.-C. JUNCKER

ANNEX   UNION OF INDUSTRIAL AND EMPLOYERS' CONFEDERATIONS OF
EUROPE, EUROPEAN TRADE UNION CONFEDERATION, EUROPEAN CENTRE
OF ENTERPRISES WITH PUBLIC PARTICIPATION FRAMEWORK AGREEMENT
ON PART-TIME WORK

Preamble

This Framework Agreement is a contribution to the overall European strategy on employment. Part-time work has had an important impact on employment in recent years. For this reason, the parties to this agreement have given priority attention to this form of work. It is the intention of the parties to consider the need for similar agreements relating to other forms of flexible work.

Recognising the diversity of situations in Member States and acknowledging that part-time work is a feature of employment in certain sectors and activities, this Agreement sets out the general principles and minimum requirements relating to part-time work. It illustrates the willingness of the social partners to establish a general framework for the elimination of discrimination against part-time workers and to assist the development of opportunities for part-time working on a basis acceptable to employers and workers.

This Agreement relates to employment conditions of part-time workers recognising that matters concerning statutory social security are for decision by the Member States. In the context of the principle of non-discrimination, the parties to this Agreement have noted the Employment Declaration of the Dublin European Council of December 1996, wherein the Council inter alia emphasised the need to make social security systems more employment-friendly by 'developing social protection systems capable of adapting to new patterns of work and of providing appropriate protection to people engaged in such work'. The parties to this Agreement consider that effect should be given to this Declaration.

ETUC, UNICE and CEEP request the Commission to submit this Framework Agreement to the Council for a decision making these requirements binding in the Member States which are party to the Agreement on social policy annexed to the Protocol (No. 14) on social policy annexed to the Treaty establishing the European Community.

The parties to this Agreement ask the Commission, in its proposal to implement this Agreement, to request that Member States adopt the laws, regulations and administrative provisions necessary to comply with the Council decision within a period of two years from its adoption or ensure[5] that the social partners establish the necessary measures by way of agreement by the end of this period. Member States may, if necessary to take account of particular difficulties or implementation by collective agreement, have up to a maximum of one additional year to comply with this provision.

Without prejudice to the role of national courts and the Court of Justice, the parties to this agreement request that any matter relating to the interpretation of this agreement at European level should, in the first instance, be referred by the Commission to them for an opinion.

General considerations

1.   Having regard to the Agreement on social policy annexed to the Protocol (No. 14) on social policy annexed to the Treaty establishing the European Community, and in particular Articles 3(4) and 4(2) thereof;

2.   Whereas Article 4(2) of the Agreement on social policy provides that agreements concluded at Community level may be implemented, at the joint request of the signatory parties, by a Council decision on a proposal from the Commission.

3.   Whereas, in its second consultation document on flexibility of working time and security for workers, the Commission announced its intention to propose a legally binding Community measure;

---

[5] Within the meaning of Article 2(4) of the Agreement on social policy of the Treaty establishing the European Community.

4.   Whereas the conclusions of the European Council meeting in Essen emphasised the need for measures to promote both employment and equal opportunities for women and men, and called for measures aimed at 'increasing the employment intensiveness of growth, in particular by more flexible organisation of work in a way which fulfils both the wishes of employees and the requirements of competition';

5.   Whereas the parties to this agreement attach importance to measures which would facilitate access to part-time work for men and women in order to prepare for retirement, reconcile professional and family life, and take up education and training opportunities to improve their skills and career opportunities for the mutual benefit of employers and workers and in a manner which would assist the development of enterprises;

6.   Whereas this Agreement refers back to Member States and social partners for the arrangements for the application of these general principles, minimum requirements and provisions, in order to take account of the situation in each Member State;

7.   Whereas this Agreement takes into consideration the need to improve social policy requirements, to enhance the competitiveness of the Community economy and to avoid imposing administrative, financial and legal constraints in a way which would hold back the creation and development of small and medium-sized undertakings;

8.   Whereas the social partners are best placed to find solutions that correspond to the needs of both employers and workers and must therefore be given a special role in the implementation and application of this Agreement.

THE SIGNATORY PARTIES HAVE AGREED THE FOLLOWING:

Clause 1:   Purpose
The purpose of this Framework Agreement is:
  (a) to provide for the removal of discrimination against part-time workers and to improve the quality of part-time work;
  (b) to facilitate the development of part-time work on a voluntary basis and to contribute to the flexible organisation of working time in a manner which takes into account the needs of employers and workers.

Clause 2:   Scope
1.   This Agreement applies to part-time workers who have an employment contract or employment relationship as defined by the law, collective agreement or practice in force in each Member State.

2.   Member States, after consultation with the social partners in accordance with national law, collective agreements or practice, and/or the social partners at the appropriate level in conformity with national industrial relations practice may, for objective reasons, exclude wholly or partly from the terms of this Agreement part-time workers who work on a casual basis. Such exclusions should be reviewed periodically to establish if the objective reasons for making them remain valid.

Clause 3:   Definitions
For the purpose of this agreement:
1.   The term 'part-time worker' refers to an employee whose normal hours of work, calculated on a weekly basis or on average over a period of employment of up to one year, are less than the normal hours of work of a comparable full-time worker.

2.   The term 'comparable full-time worker' means a full-time worker in the same establishment having the same type of employment contract or relationship, who is engaged in the same or a similar work/occupation, due regard being given to other considerations which may include seniority and qualification/skills.

Where there is no comparable full-time worker in the same establishment, the comparison shall be made by reference to the applicable collective agreement or, where there is no applicable collective agreement, in accordance with national law, collective agreements or practice.

Clause 4:   Principle of non-discrimination

1.   In respect of employment conditions, part-time workers shall not be treated in a less favourable manner than comparable full-time workers solely because they work part time unless different treatment is justified on objective grounds.

2.   Where appropriate, the principle of pro rata temporis shall apply.

3.   The arrangements for the application of this clause shall be defined by the Member States and/or social partners, having regard to European legislation, national law, collective agreements and practice.

4.   Where justified by objective reasons, Member States after consultation of the social partners in accordance with national law, collective agreements or practice and/or social partners may, where appropriate, make access to particular conditions of employment subject to a period of service, time worked or earnings qualification.

Qualifications relating to access by part-time workers to particular conditions of employment should be reviewed periodically having regard to the principle of non-discrimination as expressed in Clause 4.1.

Clause 5:   Opportunities for part-time work

1.   In the context of Clause 1 of this Agreement and of the principle of non-discrimination between part-time and full-time workers:

 (a) Member States, following consultations with the social partners in accordance with national law or practice, should identify and review obstacles of a legal or administrative nature which may limit the opportunities for part-time work and, where appropriate, eliminate them;

 (b) the social partners, acting within their sphere of competence and through the procedures set out in collective agreements, should identify and review obstacles which may limit opportunities for part-time work and, where appropriate, eliminate them.

2.   A worker's refusal to transfer from full-time to part-time work or vice-versa should not in itself constitute a valid reason for termination of employment, without prejudice to termination in accordance with national law, collective agreements and practice, for other reasons such as may arise from the operational requirements of the establishment concerned.

3.   As far as possible, employers should give consideration to:

 (a) requests by workers to transfer from full-time to part-time work that becomes available in the establishment;

 (b) requests by workers to transfer from part-time to full-time work or to increase their working time should the opportunity arise;

 (c) the provision of timely information on the availability of part-time and full-time positions in the establishment in order to facilitate transfers from full-time to part-time or vice versa;

 (d) measures to facilitate access to part-time work at all levels of the enterprise, including skilled and managerial positions, and where appropriate, to facilitate access by part-time workers to vocational training to enhance career opportunities and occupational mobility;

 (e) the provision of appropriate information to existing bodies representing workers about part-time working in the enterprise.

Clause 6:   Provisions on implementation

1.   Member States and/or social partners may maintain or introduce more favourable provisions than set out in this agreement.

2.   Implementation of the provisions of this Agreement shall not constitute valid grounds for reducing the general level of protection afforded to workers in the field of this agreement. This does not prejudice the right of Member States and/or social partners to develop different legislative, regulatory or contractual provisions, in the light of changing

circumstances, and does not prejudice the application of Clause 5.1 as long as the principle of non-discrimination as expressed in Clause 4.1 is complied with.

3.   This Agreement does not prejudice the right of the social partners to conclude, at the appropriate level, including European level, agreements adapting and/or complementing the provisions of this Agreement in a manner which will take account of the specific needs of the social partners concerned.

4.   This Agreement shall be without prejudice to any more specific Community provisions, and in particular Community provisions concerning equal treatment or opportunities for men and women.

5.   The prevention and settlement of disputes and grievances arising from the application of this Agreement shall be dealt with in accordance with national law, collective agreements and practice.

6.   The signatory parties shall review this Agreement, five years after the date of the Council decision, if requested by one of the parties to this Agreement.

Council Directive 98/59/EC of 20 July 1998 on the approximation of the laws of the Member States relating to collective redundancies

[OJ 1998, L225/16]*

THE COUNCIL OF THE EUROPEAN UNION,

Having regard to the Treaty establishing the European Community, and in particular Article 100 thereof,

Having regard to the proposal from the Commission,

Having regard to the opinion of the European Parliament,[1]

Having regard to the opinion of the Economic and Social Committee,[2]

(1) Whereas for reasons of clarity and rationality Council Directive 75/129/EEC of 17 February 1975 on the approximation of the laws of the Member States relating to collective redundancies[3] should be consolidated;

(2) Whereas it is important that greater protection should be afforded to workers in the event of collective redundancies while taking into account the need for balanced economic and social development within the Community;

(3) Whereas, despite increasing convergence, differences still remain between the provisions in force in the Member States concerning the practical arrangements and procedures for such redundancies and the measures designed to alleviate the consequences of redundancy for workers;

(4) Whereas these differences can have a direct effect on the functioning of the internal market;

(5) Whereas the Council resolution of 21 January 1974 concerning a social action programme[4] made provision for a directive on the approximation of Member States' legislation on collective redundancies;

(6) Whereas the Community Charter of the fundamental social rights of workers, adopted at the European Council meeting held in Strasbourg on 9 December 1989 by the

---

* **Editor's Note:** This repeals Directive 75/129 as amended by Directive 92/56.

[1] OJ C 210, 6.7.1998.

[2] OJ C 158, 26.5.1997, p. 11.

[3] OJ L 48, 22.2.1975, p. 29. Directive as amended by Directive 92/56/EEC (OJ L 245, 26.8.1992, p. 3).

[4] OJ C 13, 12.2.1974, p. 1.

Heads of State or Government of 11 Member States, states, inter alia, in point 7, first paragraph, first sentence, and second paragraph; in point 17, first paragraph; and in point 18, third indent: '7. The completion of the internal market must lead to an improvement in the living and working conditions of workers in the European Community.

The improvement must cover, where necessary, the development of certain aspects of employment regulations such as procedures for collective redundancies and those regarding bankruptcies.

17.   Information, consultation andparticipation for workers must be developed along appropriate lines, taking account of the practices in force in the various Member States.

18.   Such information, consultation and participation must be implemented in due time, particularly in the following cases:

— in cases of collective redundancy procedures';

(7) Whereas this approximation must therefore be promoted while the improvement is being maintained within the meaning of Article 117 of the Treaty;

(8) Whereas, in order to calculate the number of redundancies provided for in the definition of collective redundancies within the meaning of this Directive, other forms of termination of employment contracts on the initiative of the employer should be equated to redundancies, provided that there are at least five redundancies;

(9) Whereas it should be stipulated that this Directive applies in principle also to collective redundancies resulting where the establishment's activities are terminated as a result of a judicial decision;

(10) Whereas the Member States should be given the option of stipulating that workers' representatives may call on experts on grounds of the technical complexity of the matters which are likely to be the subject of the informing and consulting;

(11) Whereas it is necessary to ensure that employers' obligations as regards information, consultation and notification apply independently of whether the decision on collective redundancies emanates from the employer or from an undertaking which controls that employer;

(12) Whereas Member States should ensure that workers' representatives and/or workers have at their disposal administrative and/or judicial procedures in order to ensure that the obligations laid down in this Directive are fulfilled;

(13) Whereas this Directive must not affect the obligations of the Member States concerning the deadlines for transposition of the Directives set out in Annex I, Part B.

HAS ADOPTED THIS DIRECTIVE:

SECTION I   DEFINITIONS AND SCOPE

Article 1

1.   For the purposes of this Directive:

(a) 'collective redundancies means dismissals effected by an employer for one or more reasons not related to the individual workers concerned where, according to the choice of the Member States, the number of redundancies is:

(i) either, over a period of 30 days:

— at least 10 in establishments normally employing more than 20 and less than 100 workers,

— at least 10% of the number of workers in establishments normally employing at least 100 but less than 300 workers,

— at least 30 in establishments normally employing 300 workers or more,

(ii) or, over a period of 90 days, at least 20, whatever the number of workers normally employed in the establishments in question;

(b) 'workers' representatives means the workers' representatives provided for by the laws or practices of the Member States.

For the purpose of calculating the number of redundancies provided for in the first sub-paragraph of point (a), terminations of an employment contract which occur on the employer's initiative for one or more reasons not related to the individual workers concerned shall be assimilated to redundancies, provided that there are at least five redundancies.

2.   This Directive shall not apply to:

(a) collective redundancies effected under contracts of employment concluded for limited periods of time or for specific tasks except where such redundancies take place prior to the date of expiry or the completion of such contracts;

(b) workers employed by public administrative bodies or by establishments governed by public law (or, in Member States where this concept is unknown, by equivalent bodies);

(c) the crews of seagoing vessels.

SECTION II   INFORMATION AND CONSULTATION

Article 2

1.   Where an employer is contemplating collective redundancies, he shall begin consultations with the workers' representatives in good time with a view to reaching an agreement.

2.   These consultations shall, at least, cover ways and means of avoiding collective redundancies or reducing the number of workers affected, and of mitigating the consequences by recourse to accompanying social measures aimed, inter alia, at aid for redeploying or retraining workers made redundant.

Member States may provide that the workers' representatives may call on the services of experts in accordance with national legislation and/or practice.

3.   To enable workers' representatives to make constructive proposals, the employers shall in good time during the course of the consultations:

(a) supply them with all relevant information and

(b) in any event notify them in writing of:

(i)   the reasons for the projected redundancies;

(ii) the number of categories of workers to be made redundant;

(iii) the number and categories of workers normally employed;

(iv) the period over which the projected redundancies are to be effected;

(v)   the criteria proposed for the selection of the workers to be made redundant in so far as national legislation and/or practice confers the power therefore upon the employer;

(vi) the method for calculating any redundancy payments other than those arising out of national legislation and/or practice.

The employer shall forward to the competent public authority a copy of, at least, the elements of the written communication which are provided for in the first sub-paragraph, point (b), subpoints (i) to (v).

4.   The obligations laid down in paragraphs 1, 2 and 3 shall apply irrespective of whether the decision regarding collective redundancies is being taken by the employer or by an undertaking controlling the employer.

In considering alleged breaches of the information, consultation and notification requirements laid down by this Directive, account shall not be taken of any defence on the part of the employer on the ground that the necessary information has not been provided to the employer by the undertaking which took the decision leading to collective redundancies.

SECTION III   PROCEDURE FOR COLLECTIVE REDUNDANCIES

Article 3

1.   Employers shall notify the competent public authority in writing of any projected collective redundancies.

However, Member States may provide that in the case of planned collective redundancies arising from termination of the establishment's activities as a result of a judicial decision, the employer shall be obliged to notify the competent public authority in writing only if the latter so requests.

This notification shall contain all relevant information concerning the projected collective redundancies and the consultations with workers' representatives provided for in Article 2, and particularly the reasons for the redundancies, the number of workers to be made redundant, the number of workers normally employed and the period over which the redundancies are to be effected.

2.   Employers shall forward to the workers' representatives a copy of the notification provided for in paragraph 1.

The workers' representatives may send any comments they may have to the competent public authority.

Article 4

1.   Projected collective redundancies notified to the competent public authority shall take effect not earlier than 30 days after the notification referred to in Article 3(1) without prejudice to any provisions governing individual rights with regard to notice of dismissal.

Member States may grant the competent public authority the power to reduce the period provided for in the preceding sub-paragraph.

2.   The period provided for in paragraph 1 shall be used by the competent public authority to seek solutions to the problems raised by the projected collective redundancies.

3.   Where the initial period provided for in paragraph 1 is shorter than 60 days, Member States may grant the competent public authority the power to extend the initial period to 60 days following notification where the problems raised by the projected collective redundancies are not likely to be solved within the initial period.

Member States may grant the competent public authority wider powers of extension. The employer must be informed of the extension and the grounds for it before expiry of the initial period provided for in paragraph 1.

4.   Member States need not apply this Article to collective redundancies arising from termination of the establishment's activities where this is the result of a judicial decision.

SECTION IV   FINAL PROVISIONS

Article 5

This Directive shall not affect the right of Member States to apply or to introduce laws, regulations or administrative provisions which are more favourable to workers or to promote or to allow the application of collective agreements more favourable to workers.

Article 6

Member States shall ensure that judicial and/or administrative procedures for the enforcement of obligations under this Directive are available to the workers' representatives and/or workers.

Article 7

Member States shall forward to the Commission the text of any fundamental provisions of national law already adopted or being adopted in the area governed by this Directive.

Article 8
1.   The Directives listed in Annex I, Part A, are hereby repealed without prejudice to the obligations of the Member States concerning the deadlines for transposition of the said Directive set out in Annex I, Part B.

2.   References to the repealed Directives shall be construed as references to this Directive and shall be read in accordance with the correlation table in Annex II.

Article 9
This Directive shall enter into force on the 20th day following its publication in the Official Journal of the European Communities.

Article 10
This Directive is addressed to the Member States.

Done at Brussels, 20 July 1998. For the Council
The President
W. MOLTERER

ANNEX I   PART A

Repealed Directives (referred to by Article 8) Council Directive 75/129/EEC and its following amendment: Council Directive 92/56/EEC.

PART B   DEADLINES FOR TRANSPOSITION INTO NATIONAL LAW

(referred to by Article 8)

Directive	Deadline for transposition
75/129/EEC (OJ L48, 22.2.1975, p. 29)	19 February 1977
92/56/EEC (OJ L245, 26.8.1992, p. 3)	24 June 1994

ANNEX II   CORRELATION TABLE

Directive 75/129/EEC	This Directive
Article 1(1), first sub-paragraph, point (a), first indent, point 1	Article 1(1), first sub-paragraph, point (a), first indent
Article 1(1), first sub-paragraph, point (a), first indent, point 2	Article 1(1), first sub-paragraph, point (a)(i), second indent
Article 1(1), first sub-paragraph, point (a), first indent, point 3	Article 1(1), first sub-paragraph, point (a)(i), third indent
Article 1(1), first sub-paragraph, point (b)	Article 1(1), first sub-paragraph, point (b)
Article 1(1), second sub-paragraph	Article 1(1), second sub-paragraph
Article 1(2)	Article 1(2)
Article 2	Article 2
Article 3	Article 3
Article 4	Article 4

Article 5	Article 5
Article 5a	Article 6
Article 6(1)	—
Article 6(2)	Article 7
Article 7	—
—	Article 8
—	Article 9
—	Article 10
—	Annex I
—	Annex II

Council Directive 1999/70/EC of 28 June 1999 concerning the framework agreement on fixed-term work concluded by ETUC, UNICE and CEEP

[OJ 1999, L175/43]*

THE COUNCIL OF THE EUROPEAN UNION,

Having regard to the Treaty establishing the European Community, and in particular Article 139(2) thereof,

Having regard to the proposal from the Commission,

Whereas:

(1) Following the entry into force of the Treaty of Amsterdam the provisions of the Agreement on social policy annexed to the Protocol on social policy, annexed to the Treaty establishing the European Community have been incorporated into Articles 136 to 139 of the Treaty establishing the European Community;

(2) Management and labour (the social partners) may, in accordance with Article 139(2) of the Treaty, request jointly that agreements at Community level be implemented by a Council decision on a proposal from the Commission;

(3) Point 7 of the Community Charter of the Fundamental Social Rights of Workers provides, *inter alia*, that 'the completion of the internal market must lead to an improvement in the living and working conditions of workers in the European Community. This process must result from an approximation of these conditions while the improvement is being maintained, as regards in particular forms of employment other than open-ended contracts, such as fixed-term contracts, part-time working, temporary work and seasonal work';

(4) The Council has been unable to reach a decision on the proposal for a Directive on certain employment relationships with regard to distortions of competition([1]), nor on the proposal for a Directive on certain employment relationships with regard to working conditions([2]);

(5) The conclusions of the Essen European Council stressed the need to take measures with a view to 'increasing the employment-intensiveness of growth, in particular by a more flexible organisation of work in a way which fulfils both the wishes of employees and the requirements of competition';

(6) The Council Resolution of 9 February 1999 on the 1999 Employment Guidelines

---

* **Editor's Note**. As corrected by OJ 1999 L244/64.

[1] OJ C 224, 8.9.1990, p. 6. and OJ C 305, 5.12.1990, p. 8.

[2] OJ C 224, 8.9.1990, p. 4.

invites the social partners at all appropriate levels to negotiate agreements to modernise the organisation of work, including flexible working arrangements, with the aim of making undertakings productive and competitive and achieving the required balance between flexibility and security;

(7) The Commission, in accordance with Article 3(2) of the Agreement on social policy, has consulted management and labour on the possible direction of Community action with regard to flexible working time and job security;

(8) The Commission, considering after such consultation that Community action was desirable, once again consulted management and labour on the substance of the envisaged proposal in accordance with Article 3(3) of the said Agreement;

(9) The general cross-industry organisations, namely the Union of Industrial and Employers' Confederations of Europe (UNICE), the European Centre of Enterprises with Public Participation (CEEP) and the European Trade Union Confederation (ETUC), informed the Commission in a joint letter dated 23 March 1998 of their desire to initiate the procedure provided for in Article 4 of the said Agreement; they asked the Commission, in a joint letter, for a further period of three months; the Commission complied with this request extending the negotiation period to 30 March 1999;

(10) The said cross-industry organisations on 18 March 1999 concluded a framework agreement on fixed-term work; they forwarded to the Commission their joint request to implement the framework agreement by a Council Decision on a proposal from the Commission, in accordance with Article 4(2) of the Agreement on social policy;

(11) The Council, in its Resolution of 6 December 1994 on 'certain aspects for a European Union social policy: a contribution to economic and social convergence in the Union'([3]), asked management and labour to make use of the opportunities for concluding agreements, since they are as a rule closer to social reality and to social problems;

(12) The signatory parties, in the preamble to the framework agreement on part-time work concluded on 6 June 1997, announced their intention to consider the need for similar agreements relating to other forms of flexible work;

(13) Management and labour wished to give particular attention to fixed-term work, while at the same time indicating that it was their intention to consider the need for a similar agreement relating to temporary agency work;

(14) The signatory parties wished to conclude a framework agreement on fixed-term work setting out the general principles and minimum requirements for fixed-term employment contracts and employment relationships; they have demonstrated their desire to improve the quality of fixed-term work by ensuring the application of the principle of non-discrimination, and to establish a framework to prevent abuse arising from the use of successive fixed-term employment contracts or relationships;

(15) The proper instrument for implementing the framework agreement is a directive within the meaning of Article 249 of the Treaty; it therefore binds the Member States as to the result to be achieved, whilst leaving them the choice of form and methods;

(16) In accordance with the principles of subsidiarity and proportionality as set out in Article 5 of the Treaty, the objectives of this Directive cannot be sufficiently achieved by the Member States and can therefore be better achieved by the Community; this Directive limits itself to the minimum required for the attainment of those objectives and does not go beyond what is necessary for that purpose;

(17) As regards terms used in the framework agreement but not specifically defined therein, this Directive allows Member States to define such terms in conformity with national law or practice as is the case for other Directives on social matters using similar terms, provided that the definitions in question respect the content of the framework agreement;

(18) The Commission has drafted its proposal for a Directive, in accordance with its

[3] OJ C 368, 23.12.1994, p. 6.

Communication of 14 December 1993 concerning the application of the agreement on social policy and its Communication of 20 May 1998 on adapting and promoting the social dialogue at Community level, taking into account the representative status of the contracting parties, their mandate and the legality of each clause of the framework agreement; the contracting parties together have a sufficiently representative status;

(19) The Commission informed the European Parliament and the Economic and Social Committee by sending them the text of the agreement, accompanied by its proposal for a Directive and the explanatory memorandum, in accordance with its communication concerning the implementation of the Protocol on social policy;

(20) On 6 May 1999 the European Parliament adopted a Resolution on the framework agreement between the social partners;

(21) The implementation of the framework agreement contributes to achieving the objectives in Article 136 of the Treaty,

HAS ADOPTED THIS DIRECTIVE:

Article 1

The purpose of the Directive is to put into effect the framework agreement on fixed-term contracts concluded on 18 March 1999 between the general cross-industry organisations (ETUC, UNICE and CEEP) annexed hereto.

Article 2

Member States shall bring into force the laws, regulations and administrative provisions necessary to comply with this Directive by 10 July 2001, or shall ensure that, by that date at the latest, management and labour have introduced the necessary measures by agreement, the Member States being required to take any necessary measures to enable them at any time to be in a position to guarantee the results imposed by this Directive. They shall forthwith inform the Commission thereof. Member States may have a maximum of one more year, if necessary, and following consultation with management and labour, to take account of special difficulties or implementation by a collective agreement. They shall inform the Commission forthwith in such circumstances.

When Member States adopt the provisions referred to in the first paragraph, these shall contain a reference to this Directive or shall be accompanied by such reference at the time of their official publication. The procedure for such reference shall be adopted by the Member States.

Article 3

This Directive shall enter into force on the day of its publication in the *Official Journal of the European Communities*.

Article 4

This Directive is addressed to the Member States.

Done at Luxembourg, 28 June 1999.

For the Council
The President
M. NAUMANN

ANNEX

ETUC-UNICE-CEEP FRAMEWORK AGREEMENT ON FIXED-TERM WORK

Preamble

This framework agreement illustrates the role that the social partners can play in the European employment strategy agreed at the 1997 Luxembourg extraordinary summit and, following the framework agreement on part-time work, represents a further contribution towards achieving a better balance between 'flexibility in working time and security for workers'.

The parties to this agreement recognise that contracts of an indefinite duration are, and will continue to be, the general form of employment relationship between employers and workers. They also recognise that fixed-term employment contracts respond, in certain circumstances, to the needs of both employers and workers.

This agreement sets out the general principles and minimum requirements relating to fixed-term work, recognising that their detailed application needs to take account of the realities of specific national, sectoral and seasonal situations. It illustrates the willingness of the Social Partners to establish a general framework for ensuring equal treatment for fixed-term workers by protecting them against discrimination and for using fixed-term employment contracts on a basis acceptable to employers and workers.

This agreement applies to fixed-term workers with the exception of those placed by a temporary work agency at the disposition of a user enterprise. It is the intention of the parties to consider the need for a similar agreement relating to temporary agency work.

This agreement relates to the employment conditions of fixed-term workers, recognising that matters relating to statutory social security are for decision by the Member States. In this respect the Social Partners note the Employment Declaration of the Dublin European Council in 1996 which emphasised *inter alia*, the need to develop more employment-friendly social security systems by 'developing social protection systems capable of adapting to new patterns of work and providing appropriate protection to those engaged in such work'. The parties to this agreement reiterate the view expressed in the 1997 part-time agreement that Member States should give effect to this Declaration without delay.

In addition, it is also recognised that innovations in occupational social protection systems are necessary in order to adapt them to current conditions, and in particular to provide for the transferability of rights.

The ETUC, UNICE and CEEP request the Commission to submit this framework agreement to the Council for a decision making these requirements binding in the Member States which are party to the Agreement on social policy annexed to the Protocol (No 14) on social policy annexed to the Treaty establishing the European Community.

The parties to this agreement ask the Commission, in its proposal to implement the agreement, to request Member States to adopt the laws, regulations and administrative provisions necessary to comply with the Council Decision within two years from its adoption or ensure([1]) that the social partners establish the necessary measures by way of agreement by the end of this period. Member States may, if necessary and following consultation with the social partners, and in order to take account of particular difficulties or implementation by collective agreement, have up to a maximum of one additional year to comply with this provision.

The parties to this agreement request that the social partners are consulted prior to any legislative, regulatory or administrative initiative taken by a Member State to conform to the present agreement.

Without prejudice to the role of national courts and the Court of Justice, the parties to this agreement request that any matter relating to the interpretation of this agreement at European level should in the first instance be referred by the Commission to them for an opinion.

General considerations

1. Having regard to the Agreement on social policy annexed to the Protocol (No 14) on social policy annexed to the Treaty establishing the European Community, and in particular Article 3.4 and 4.2 thereof;

---

[1] Within the meaning of Article 2.4 of the Agreement on social policy annexed to the Protocol (No. 14) on social policy annexed to the Treaty establishing the European Community.

2.   Whereas Article 4.2 of the Agreement on social policy provides that agreements concluded at Community level may be implemented, at the joint request of the signatory parties, by a Council decision on a proposal from the Commission;

3.   Whereas, in its second consultation document on flexibility in working time and security for workers, the Commission announced its intention to propose a legally-binding Community measure;

4.   Whereas in its opinion on the proposal for a Directive on part-time work, the European Parliament invited the Commission to submit immediately proposals for directives on other forms of flexible work, such as fixed-term work and temporary agency work;

5.   Whereas in the conclusions of the extraordinary summit on employment adopted in Luxembourg, the European Council invited the social partners to negotiate agreements to 'modernise the organisation of work, including flexible working arrangements, with the aim of making undertakings productive and competitive and achieving the required balance between flexibility and security';

6.   Whereas employment contracts of an indefinite duration are the general form of employment relationships and contribute to the quality of life of the workers concerned and improve performance;

7.   Whereas the use of fixed-term employment contracts based on objective reasons is a way to prevent abuse;

8.   Whereas fixed-term employment contracts are a feature of employment in certain sectors, occupations and activities which can suit both employers and workers;

9.   Whereas more than half of fixed-term workers in the European Union are women and this agreement can therefore contribute to improving equality of opportunities between women and men;

10.   Whereas this agreement refers back to Member States and social partners for the arrangements for the application of its general principles, minimum requirements and provisions, in order to take account of the situation in each Member State and the circumstances of particular sectors and occupations, including the activities of a seasonal nature;

11.   Whereas this agreement takes into consideration the need to improve social policy requirements, to enhance the competitiveness of the Community economy and to avoid imposing administrative, financial and legal constraints in a way which would hold back the creation and development of small and medium-sized undertakings;

12.   Whereas the social partners are best placed to find solutions that correspond to the needs of both employers and workers and shall therefore be given a special role in the implementation and application of this agreement.

THE SIGNATORY PARTIES HAVE AGREED THE FOLLOWING

Purpose (clause 1)
The purpose of this framework agreement is to:
  (a) improve the quality of fixed-term work by ensuring the application of the principle of non-discrimination;
  (b) establish a framework to prevent abuse arising from the use of successive fixed-term employment contracts or relationships.

Scope (clause 2)
1.   This agreement applies to fixed-term workers who have an employment contract or employment relationship as defined in law, collective agreements or practice in each Member State.

2.   Member States after consultation with the social partners and/or the social partners may provide that this agreement does not apply to:
  (a) initial vocational training relationships and apprenticeship schemes;

(b) employment contracts and relationships which have been concluded within the framework of a specific public or publicly-supported training, integration and vocational retraining programme.

Definitions (clause 3)

1.   For the purpose of this agreement the term 'fixed-term worker' means a person having an employment contract or relationship entered into directly between an employer and a worker where the end of the employment contract or relationship is determined by objective conditions such as reaching a specific date, completing a specific task, or the occurrence of a specific event.

2.   For the purpose of this agreement, the term 'comparable permanent worker' means a worker with an employment contract or relationship of indefinite duration, in the same establishment, engaged in the same or similar work/occupation, due regard being given to qualifications/skills. Where there is no comparable permanent worker in the same establishment, the comparison shall be made by reference to the applicable collective agreement, or where there is no applicable collective agreement, in accordance with national law, collective agreements or practice.

Principle of non-discrimination (clause 4)

1.   In respect of employment conditions, fixed-term workers shall not be treated in a less favourable manner than comparable permanent workers solely because they have a fixed-term contract or relation unless different treatment is justified on objective grounds.

2.   Where appropriate, the principle of pro rata temporis shall apply.

3.   The arrangements for the application of this clause shall be defined by the Member States after consultation with the social partners and/or the social partners, having regard to Community law and national law, collective agreements and practice.

4.   Period-of service qualifications relating to particular conditions of employment shall be the same for fixed-term workers as for permanent workers except where different length-of service qualifications are justified on objective grounds.

Measures to prevent abuse (clause 5)

1.   To prevent abuse arising from the use of successive fixed-term employment contracts or relationships, Member States, after consultation with social partners in accordance with national law, collective agreements or practice, and/or the social partners, shall, where there are no equivalent legal measures to prevent abuse, introduce in a manner which takes account of the needs of specific sectors and/or categories of workers, one or more of the following measures:

(a) objective reasons justifying the renewal of such contracts or relationships;

(b) the maximum total duration of successive fixed-term employment contracts or relationships;

(c) the number of renewals of such contracts or relationships.

2.   Member States after consultation with the social partners and/or the social partners shall, where appropriate, determine under what conditions fixed-term employment contracts or relationships:

(a) shall be regarded as 'successive'

(b) shall be deemed to be contracts or relationships of indefinite duration.

Information and employment opportunities (clause 6)

1.   Employers shall inform fixed-term workers about vacancies which become available in the undertaking or establishment to ensure that they have the same opportunity to secure permanent positions as other workers. Such information may be provided by way of a general announcement at a suitable place in the undertaking or establishment.

2.   As far as possible, employers should facilitate access by fixed-term workers to

appropriate training opportunities to enhance their skills, career development and occupational mobility.

Information and consultation (clause 7)

1.   Fixed-term workers shall be taken into consideration in calculating the threshold above which workers' representative bodies provided for in national and Community law may be constituted in the undertaking as required by national provisions.

2.   The arrangements for the application of clause 7.1 shall be defined by Member States after consultation with the social partners and/or the social partners in accordance with national law, collective agreements or practice and having regard to clause 4.1.

3.   As far as possible, employers should give consideration to the provision of appropriate information to existing workers' representative bodies about fixed-term work in the undertaking.

Provisions on implementation (clause 8)

1.   Member States and/or the social partners can maintain or introduce more favourable provisions for workers than set out in this agreement.

2.   This agreement shall be without prejudice to any more specific Community provisions, and in particular Community provisions concerning equal treatment or opportunities for men and women.

3.   Implementation of this agreement shall not constitute valid grounds for reducing the general level of protection afforded to workers in the field of the agreement.

4.   The present agreement does not prejudice the right of the social partners to conclude at the appropriate level, including European level, agreements adapting and/or complementing the provisions of this agreement in a manner which will take note of the specific needs of the social partners concerned.

5.   The prevention and settlement of disputes and grievances arising from the application of this agreement shall be dealt with in accordance with national law, collective agreements and practice.

6.   The signatory parties shall review the application of this agreement five years after the date of the Council decision if requested by one of the parties to this agreement.

Fritz VERZETNITSCH
President of the ETUC
Georges JACOBS
President of UNICE
Antonio CASTELLANO AUYANET
President of CEEP
Emilio GABAGLIO.
General-Secretary of the ETUC
Dirk F. HUDIG
Secretary-General of UNICE
Jytte FREDENSBORG
Secretary-General of CEEP
18 March 1999

Directive 2002/14/EC of the European Parliament and of the Council of 11 March 2002 establishing a general framework for informing and consulting employees in the European Community

[OJ 2000, L80/29]

THE EUROPEAN PARLIAMENT AND THE COUNCIL OF THE EUROPEAN UNION,

Having regard to the Treaty establishing the European Community, and in particular Article 137(2) thereof,

Having regard to the proposal from the Commission([1]),

Having regard to the opinion of the Economic and Social Committee([2]),

Having regard to the opinion of the Committee of the Regions([3]),

Acting in accordance with the procedure referred to in Article 251([4]), and in the light of the joint text approved by the Conciliation Committee on 23 January 2002,

Whereas:

(1) Pursuant to Article 136 of the Treaty, a particular objective of the Community and the Member States is to promote social dialogue between management and labour.

(2) Point 17 of the Community Charter of Fundamental Social Rights of Workers provides, *inter alia*, that information, consultation and participation for workers must be developed along appropriate lines, taking account of the practices in force in different Member States.

(3) The Commission consulted management and labour at Community level on the possible direction of Community action on the information and consultation of employees in undertakings within the Community.

(4) Following this consultation, the Commission considered that Community action was advisable and again consulted management and labour on the contents of the planned proposal; management and labour have presented their opinions to the Commission.

(5) Having completed this second stage of consultation, management and labour have not informed the Commission of their wish to initiate the process potentially leading to the conclusion of an agreement.

(6) The existence of legal frameworks at national and Community level, intended to ensure that employees are involved in the affairs of the undertaking employing them and in decisions which affect them, has not always prevented serious decisions affecting employees from being taken and made public without adequate procedures having been implemented beforehand to inform and consult them.

(7) There is a need to strengthen dialogue and promote mutual trust within undertakings in order to improve risk anticipation, make work organisation more flexible and facilitate employee access to training within the undertaking while maintaining security, make employees aware of adaptation needs, increase employees' availability to undertake measures and activities to increase their employability, promote employee involvement in the operation and future of the undertaking and increase its competitiveness.

---

[1] OJ C 2, 5.1.1999, p. 3.

[2] OJ C 258, 10.9.1999, p. 24.

[3] OJ C 144, 16.5.2001, p. 58.

[4] Opinion of the European Parliament of 14 April 1999 (OJ C 219, 30.7.1999, p. 223), confirmed on 16 September 1999 (OJ C 54, 25.2.2000, p. 55), Council Common Position of 27 July 2001 (OJ C 307, 31.10.2001, p. 16) and Decision of the European Parliament of 23 October 2001 (not yet published in the Official Journal). Decision of the European Parliament of 5 February 2002 and Decision of the Council of 18 February 2002.

(8) There is a need, in particular, to promote and enhance information and consultation on the situation and likely development of employment within the undertaking and, where the employer's evaluation suggests that employment within the undertaking may be under threat, the possible anticipatory measures envisaged, in particular in terms of employee training and skill development, with a view to offsetting the negative developments or their consequences and increasing the employability and adaptability of the employees likely to be affected.

(9) Timely information and consultation is a prerequisite for the success of the restructuring and adaptation of undertakings to the new conditions created by globalisation of the economy, particularly through the development of new forms of organisation of work.

(10) The Community has drawn up and implemented an employment strategy based on the concepts of 'anticipation', 'prevention' and 'employability', which are to be incorporated as key elements into all public policies likely to benefit employment, including the policies of individual undertakings, by strengthening the social dialogue with a view to promoting change compatible with preserving the priority objective of employment.

(11) Further development of the internal market must be properly balanced, maintaining the essential values on which our societies are based and ensuring that all citizens benefit from economic development.

(12) Entry into the third stage of economic and monetary union has extended and accelerated the competitive pressures at European level. This means that more supportive measures are needed at national level.

(13) The existing legal frameworks for employee information and consultation at Community and national level tend to adopt an excessively a posteriori approach to the process of change, neglect the economic aspects of decisions taken and do not contribute either to genuine anticipation of employment developments within the undertaking or to risk prevention.

(14) All of these political, economic, social and legal developments call for changes to the existing legal framework providing for the legal and practical instruments enabling the right to be informed and consulted to be exercised.

(15) This Directive is without prejudice to national systems regarding the exercise of this right in practice where those entitled to exercise it are required to indicate their wishes collectively.

(16) This Directive is without prejudice to those systems which provide for the direct involvement of employees, as long as they are always free to exercise the right to be informed and consulted through their representatives.

(17) Since the objectives of the proposed action, as outlined above, cannot be adequately achieved by the Member States, in that the object is to establish a framework for employee information and consultation appropriate for the new European context described above, and can therefore, in view of the scale and impact of the proposed action, be better achieved at Community level, the Community may adopt measures in accordance with the principle of subsidiarity as set out in Article 5 of the Treaty. In accordance with the principle of proportionality, as set out in that Article, this Directive does not go beyond what is necessary in order to achieve these objectives.

(18) The purpose of this general framework is to establish minimum requirements applicable throughout the Community while not preventing Member States from laying down provisions more favourable to employees.

(19) The purpose of this general framework is also to avoid any administrative, financial or legal constraints which would hinder the creation and development of small and medium-sized undertakings. To this end, the scope of this Directive should be restricted, according to the choice made by Member States, to undertakings with at least 50 employees or establishments employing at least 20 employees.

(20) This takes into account and is without prejudice to other national measures and

practices aimed at fostering social dialogue within companies not covered by this Directive and within public administrations.

(21) However, on a transitional basis, Member States in which there is no established statutory system of information and consultation of employees or employee representation should have the possibility of further restricting the scope of the Directive as regards the numbers of employees.

(22) A Community framework for informing and consulting employees should keep to a minimum the burden on undertakings or establishments while ensuring the effective exercise of the rights granted.

(23) The objective of this Directive is to be achieved through the establishment of a general framework comprising the principles, definitions and arrangements for information and consultation, which it will be for the Member States to comply with and adapt to their own national situation, ensuring, where appropriate, that management and labour have a leading role by allowing them to define freely, by agreement, the arrangements for informing and consulting employees which they consider to be best suited to their needs and wishes.

(24) Care should be taken to avoid affecting some specific rules in the field of employee information and consultation existing in some national laws, addressed to undertakings or establishments which pursue political, professional, organisational, religious, charitable, educational, scientific or artistic aims, as well as aims involving information and the expression of opinions.

(25) Undertakings and establishments should be protected against disclosure of certain particularly sensitive information.

(26) The employer should be allowed not to inform and consult where this would seriously damage the undertaking or the establishment or where he has to comply immediately with an order issued to him by a regulatory or supervisory body.

(27) Information and consultation imply both rights and obligations for management and labour at undertaking or establishment level.

(28) Administrative or judicial procedures, as well as sanctions that are effective, dissuasive and proportionate in relation to the seriousness of the offence, should be applicable in cases of infringement of the obligations based on this Directive.

(29) This Directive should not affect the provisions, where these are more specific, of Council Directive 98/59/EC of 20 July 1998 on the approximation of the laws of the Member States relating to collective redundancies([5]) and of Council Directive 2001/23/EC of 12 March 2001 on the approximation of the laws of the Member States relating to the safeguarding of employees' rights in the event of transfers of undertakings, businesses or parts of undertakings or businesses([6]).

(30) Other rights of information and consultation, including those arising from Council Directive 94/45/EEC of 22 September 1994 on the establishment of a European Works Council or a procedure in Community-scale undertakings and Community-scale groups of undertakings for the purposes of informing and consulting employees([7]), should not be affected by this Directive.

(31) Implementation of this Directive should not be sufficient grounds for a reduction in the general level of protection of workers in the areas to which it applies,

HAVE ADOPTED THIS DIRECTIVE:

Article 1   Object and principles

1.   The purpose of this Directive is to establish a general framework setting out minimum

---

[5] OJ L 225, 12.8.1998, p. 16.
[6] OJ L 82, 22.3.2001, p. 16.
[7] OJ L 254, 30.9.1994, p. 64. Directive as amended by Directive 97/74/EC (OJ L 10, 16.1.1998, p. 22).

requirements for the right to information and consultation of employees in undertakings or establishments within the Community.

2.   The practical arrangements for information and consultation shall be defined and implemented in accordance with national law and industrial relations practices in individual Member States in such a way as to ensure their effectiveness.

3.   When defining or implementing practical arrangements for information and consultation, the employer and the employees' representatives shall work in a spirit of cooperation and with due regard for their reciprocal rights and obligations, taking into account the interests both of the undertaking or establishment and of the employees.

Article 2   Definitions

For the purposes of this Directive:

(a) 'undertaking' means a public or private undertaking carrying out an economic activity, whether or not operating for gain, which is located within the territory of the Member States;

(b) 'establishment' means a unit of business defined in accordance with national law and practice, and located within the territory of a Member State, where an economic activity is carried out on an ongoing basis with human and material resources;

(c) 'employer' means the natural or legal person party to employment contracts or employment relationships with employees, in accordance with national law and practice;

(d) 'employee' means any person who, in the Member State concerned, is protected as an employee under national employment law and in accordance with national practice;

(e) 'employees' representatives' means the employees' representatives provided for by national laws and/or practices;

(f) 'information' means transmission by the employer to the employees' representatives of data in order to enable them to acquaint themselves with the subject matter and to examine it;

(g) 'consultation' means the exchange of views and establishment of dialogue between the employees' representatives and the employer.

Article 3   Scope

1.   This Directive shall apply, according to the choice made by Member States, to:

(a) undertakings employing at least 50 employees in any one Member State, or

(b) establishments employing at least 20 employees in any one Member State.

Member States shall determine the method for calculating the thresholds of employees employed.

2.   In conformity with the principles and objectives of this Directive, Member States may lay down particular provisions applicable to undertakings or establishments which pursue directly and essentially political, professional organisational, religious, charitable, educational, scientific or artistic aims, as well as aims involving information and the expression of opinions, on condition that, at the date of entry into force of this Directive, provisions of that nature already exist in national legislation.

3.   Member States may derogate from this Directive through particular provisions applicable to the crews of vessels plying the high seas.

Article 4   Practical arrangements for information and consultation

1.   In accordance with the principles set out in Article 1 and without prejudice to any provisions and/or practices in force more favourable to employees, the Member States shall determine the practical arrangements for exercising the right to information and consultation at the appropriate level in accordance with this Article.

2. Information and consultation shall cover:
   (a) information on the recent and probable development of the undertaking's or the establishment's activities and economic situation;
   (b) information and consultation on the situation, structure and probable development of employment within the undertaking or establishment and on any anticipatory measures envisaged, in particular where there is a threat to employment;
   (c) information and consultation on decisions likely to lead to substantial changes in work organisation or in contractual relations, including those covered by the Community provisions referred to in Article 9(1).

3. Information shall be given at such time, in such fashion and with such content as are appropriate to enable, in particular, employees' representatives to conduct an adequate study and, where necessary, prepare for consultation.

4. Consultation shall take place:
   (a) while ensuring that the timing, method and content thereof are appropriate;
   (b) at the relevant level of management and representation, depending on the subject under discussion;
   (c) on the basis of information supplied by the employer in accordance with Article 2(f) and of the opinion which the employees' representatives are entitled to formulate;
   (d) in such a way as to enable employees' representatives to meet the employer and obtain a response, and the reasons for that response, to any opinion they might formulate;
   (e) with a view to reaching an agreement on decisions within the scope of the employer's powers referred to in paragraph 2(c).

Article 5 Information and consultation deriving from an agreement

Member States may entrust management and labour at the appropriate level, including at undertaking or establishment level, with defining freely and at any time through negotiated agreement the practical arrangements for informing and consulting employees. These agreements, and agreements existing on the date laid down in Article 11, as well as any subsequent renewals of such agreements, may establish, while respecting the principles set out in Article 1 and subject to conditions and limitations laid down by the Member States, provisions which are different from those referred to in Article 4.

Article 6 Confidential information

1. Member States shall provide that, within the conditions and limits laid down by national legislation, the employees' representatives, and any experts who assist them, are not authorised to reveal to employees or to third parties, any information which, in the legitimate interest of the undertaking or establishment, has expressly been provided to them in confidence. This obligation shall continue to apply, wherever the said representatives or experts are, even after expiry of their terms of office. However, a Member State may authorise the employees' representatives and anyone assisting them to pass on confidential information to employees and to third parties bound by an obligation of confidentiality.

2. Member States shall provide, in specific cases and within the conditions and limits laid down by national legislation, that the employer is not obliged to communicate information or undertake consultation when the nature of that information or consultation is such that, according to objective criteria, it would seriously harm the functioning of the undertaking or establishment or would be prejudicial to it.

3. Without prejudice to existing national procedures, Member States shall provide for administrative or judicial review procedures for the case where the employer requires confidentiality or does not provide the information in accordance with paragraphs 1 and 2. They may also provide for procedures intended to safeguard the confidentiality of the information in question.

Article 7   Protection of employees' representatives

Member States shall ensure that employees' representatives, when carrying out their functions, enjoy adequate protection and guarantees to enable them to perform properly the duties which have been assigned to them.

Article 8   Protection of rights

1.   Member States shall provide for appropriate measures in the event of non-compliance with this Directive by the employer or the employees' representatives. In particular, they shall ensure that adequate administrative or judicial procedures are available to enable the obligations deriving from this Directive to be enforced.

2.   Member States shall provide for adequate sanctions to be applicable in the event of infringement of this Directive by the employer or the employees' representatives. These sanctions must be effective, proportionate and dissuasive.

Article 9   Link between this Directive and other Community and national provisions

1.   This Directive shall be without prejudice to the specific information and consultation procedures set out in Article 2 of Directive 98/59/EC and Article 7 of Directive 2001/23/EC.

2.   This Directive shall be without prejudice to provisions adopted in accordance with Directives 94/45/EC and 97/74/EC.

3.   This Directive shall be without prejudice to other rights to information, consultation and participation under national law.

4.   Implementation of this Directive shall not be sufficient grounds for any regression in relation to the situation which already prevails in each Member State and in relation to the general level of protection of workers in the areas to which it applies.

Article 10   Transitional provisions

Notwithstanding Article 3, a Member State in which there is, at the date of entry into force of this Directive, no general, permanent and statutory system of information and consultation of employees, nor a general, permanent and statutory system of employee representation at the workplace allowing employees to be represented for that purpose, may limit the application of the national provisions implementing this Directive to:

(a) undertakings employing at least 150 employees or establishments employing at least 100 employees until 23 March 2007, and

(b) undertakings employing at least 100 employees or establishments employing at least 50 employees during the year following the date in point (a).

Article 11   Transposition

1.   Member States shall adopt the laws, regulations and administrative provisions necessary to comply with this Directive not later than 23 March 2005 or shall ensure that management and labour introduce by that date the required provisions by way of agreement, the Member States being obliged to take all necessary steps enabling them to guarantee the results imposed by this Directive at all times. They shall forthwith inform the Commission thereof.

2.   Where Member States adopt these measures, they shall contain a reference to this Directive or shall be accompanied by such reference on the occasion of their official publication. The methods of making such reference shall be laid down by the Member States.

Article 12   Review by the Commission

Not later than 23 March 2007, the Commission shall, in consultation with the Member States and the social partners at Community level, review the application of this Directive with a view to proposing any necessary amendments.

Article 13   Entry into force

This Directive shall enter into force on the day of its publication in the Official Journal of the European Communities.

Article 14   Addressees
This Directive is addressed to the Member States.

Done at Brussels, 11 March 2002.

For the European Parliament
The President
P. COX

For the Council
The President
J. PIQUÉ i CAMPS

Joint Declaration of the European Parliament, the Council and the Commission on Employee Representation

'With regard to employee representation, the European Parliament, the Council and the Commission recall the judgements of the European Court of Justice of 8 June 1994 in Cases C-382/92 (Safeguarding of employees rights in the event of transfers of undertakings) and C-383/92 (Collective redundancies).'

Directive 2003/88/EC of the European Parliament and of the Council of 4 November 2003 concerning certain aspects of the organisation of working time
[OJ 2003, L299/9] *

THE EUROPEAN PARLIAMENT AND THE COUNCIL OF THE EUROPEAN UNION,
   Having regard to the Treaty establishing the European Community, and in particular Article 137(2) thereof,
   Having regard to the proposal from the Commission,
   Having regard to the opinion of the European Economic and Social Committee,[1]
   Having consulted the Committee of the Regions,
   Acting in accordance with the procedure referred to in Article 251 of the Treaty,[2]
   Whereas:
   (1) Council Directive 93/104/EC of 23 November 1993, concerning certain aspects of the organisation of working time,[3] which lays down minimum safety and health requirements for the organisation of working time, in respect of periods of daily rest, breaks, weekly rest, maximum weekly working time, annual leave and aspects of night work, shift work and patterns of work, has been significantly amended. In order to clarify matters, a codification of the provisions in question should be drawn up.
   (2) Article 137 of the Treaty provides that the Community is to support and complement the activities of the Member States with a view to improving the working environment to protect workers' health and safety. Directives adopted on the basis of that Article are to avoid imposing administrative, financial and legal constraints in a way which would hold back the creation and development of small and medium-sized undertakings.
   (3) The provisions of Council Directive 89/391/EEC of 12 June 1989 on the introduction

---

   * **Editor's Note:** This Directive repeals and replaces Directives 93/104 and 2000/34.
   [1] OJ C 61, 14.3.2003, p. 123.
   [2] Opinion of the European Parliament of 17 December 2002 (not yet published in the Official Journal) and Council Decision of 22 September 2003.
   [3] OJ L 307, 13.12.1993, p. 18. Directive as amended by Directive 2000/34/EC of the European Parliament and of the Council (OJ L 195, 1.8.2000, p. 41).

of measures to encourage improvements in the safety and health of workers at work[4] remain fully applicable to the areas covered by this Directive without prejudice to more stringent and/ or specific provisions contained herein.

(4) The improvement of workers' safety, hygiene and health at work is an objective which should not be subordinated to purely economic considerations.

(5) All workers should have adequate rest periods. The concept of 'rest' must be expressed in units of time, i.e. in days, hours and/or fractions thereof. Community workers must be granted minimum daily, weekly and annual periods of rest and adequate breaks. It is also necessary in this context to place a maximum limit on weekly working hours.

(6) Account should be taken of the principles of the International Labour Organisation with regard to the organisation of working time, including those relating to night work.

(7) Research has shown that the human body is more sensitive at night to environmental disturbances and also to certain burdensome forms of work organisation and that long periods of night work can be detrimental to the health of workers and can endanger safety at the workplace.

(8) There is a need to limit the duration of periods of night work, including overtime, and to provide for employers who regularly use night workers to bring this information to the attention of the competent authorities if they so request.

(9) It is important that night workers should be entitled to a free health assessment prior to their assignment and thereafter at regular intervals and that whenever possible they should be transferred to day work for which they are suited if they suffer from health problems.

(10) The situation of night and shift workers requires that the level of safety and health protection should be adapted to the nature of their work and that the organisation and functioning of protection and prevention services and resources should be efficient.

(11) Specific working conditions may have detrimental effects on the safety and health of workers. The organisation of work according to a certain pattern must take account of the general principle of adapting work to the worker.

(12) A European Agreement in respect of the working time of seafarers has been put into effect by means of Council Directive 1999/63/EC of 21 June 1999 concerning the Agreement on the organisation of working time of seafarers concluded by the European Community Shipowners' Association (ECSA) and the Federation of Transport Workers' Unions in the European Union (FST)[5] based on Article 139(2) of the Treaty. Accordingly, the provisions of this Directive should not apply to seafarers.

(13) In the case of those 'share-fishermen' who are employees, it is for the Member States to determine, pursuant to this Directive, the conditions for entitlement to, and granting of, annual leave, including the arrangements for payments.

(14) Specific standards laid down in other Community instruments relating, for example, to rest periods, working time, annual leave and night work for certain categories of workers should take precedence over the provisions of this Directive.

(15) In view of the question likely to be raised by the organisation of working time within an undertaking, it appears desirable to provide for flexibility in the application of certain provisions of this Directive, whilst ensuring compliance with the principles of protecting the safety and health of workers.

(16) It is necessary to provide that certain provisions may be subject to derogations implemented, according to the case, by the Member States or the two sides of industry. As a general rule, in the event of a derogation, the workers concerned must be given equivalent compensatory rest periods.

(17) This Directive should not affect the obligations of the Member States concerning the deadlines for transposition of the Directives set out in Annex I, part B,

---

[4] OJ L 183, 29.6.1989, p. 1.
[5] OJ L 167, 2.7.1999, p. 33.

HAVE ADOPTED THIS DIRECTIVE:

CHAPTER 1   SCOPE AND DEFINITIONS

Article 1   Purpose and scope

1.   This Directive lays down minimum safety and health requirements for the organisation of working time.

2.   This Directive applies to:
   (a)   minimum periods of daily rest, weekly rest and annual leave, to breaks and maximum weekly working time; and
   (b)   certain aspects of night work, shift work and patterns of work.

3.   This Directive shall apply to all sectors of activity, both public and private, within the meaning of Article 2 of Directive 89/391/EEC, without prejudice to Articles 14, 17, 18 and 19 of this Directive.

This Directive shall not apply to seafarers, as defined in Directive 1999/63/EC without prejudice to Article 2(8) of this Directive.

4.   The provisions of Directive 89/391/EEC are fully applicable to the matters referred to in paragraph 2, without prejudice to more stringent and/or specific provisions contained in this Directive.

Article 2   Definitions

For the purposes of this Directive, the following definitions shall apply:

1.   'working time' means any period during which the worker is working, at the employer's disposal and carrying out his activity or duties, in accordance with national laws and/or practice;

2.   'rest period' means any period which is not working time;

3.   'night time' means any period of not less than seven hours, as defined by national law, and which must include, in any case, the period between midnight and 5.00;

4.   'night worker' means:
   (a)   on the one hand, any worker, who, during night time, works at least three hours of his daily working time as a normal course; and
   (b)   on the other hand, any worker who is likely during night time to work a certain proportion of his annual working time, as defined at the choice of the Member State concerned:
      (i)   by national legislation, following consultation with the two sides of industry; or
      (ii)   by collective agreements or agreements concluded between the two sides of industry at national or regional level;

5.   'shift work' means any method of organising work in shifts whereby workers succeed each other at the same work stations according to a certain pattern, including a rotating pattern, and which may be continuous or discontinuous, entailing the need for workers to work at different times over a given period of days or weeks;

6.   'shift worker' means any worker whose work schedule is part of shift work;

7.   'mobile worker' means any worker employed as a member of travelling or flying personnel by an undertaking which operates transport services for passengers or goods by road, air or inland waterway;

8.   'offshore work' means work performed mainly on or from offshore installations (including drilling rigs), directly or indirectly in connection with the exploration, extraction or exploitation of mineral resources, including hydrocarbons, and diving in connection with such activities, whether performed from an offshore installation or a vessel;

9.   'adequate rest' means that workers have regular rest periods, the duration of which is expressed in units of time and which are sufficiently long and continuous to ensure that, as a

result of fatigue or other irregular working patterns, they do not cause injury to themselves, to fellow workers or to others and that they do not damage their health, either in the short term or in the longer term.

CHAPTER 2   MINIMUM REST PERIODS – OTHER ASPECTS OF THE ORGANISATION OF WORKING TIME

Article 3   Daily rest
Member States shall take the measures necessary to ensure that every worker is entitled to a minimum daily rest period of 11 consecutive hours per 24-hour period.

Article 4   Breaks
Member States shall take the measures necessary to ensure that, where the working day is longer than six hours, every worker is entitled to a rest break, the details of which, including duration and the terms on which it is granted, shall be laid down in collective agreements or agreements between the two sides of industry or, failing that, by national legislation.

Article 5   Weekly rest period
Member States shall take the measures necessary to ensure that, per each seven-day period, every worker is entitled to a minimum uninterrupted rest period of 24 hours plus the 11 hours' daily rest referred to in Article 3.

If objective, technical or work organisation conditions so justify, a minimum rest period of 24 hours may be applied.

Article 6   Maximum weekly working time
Member States shall take the measures necessary to ensure that, in keeping with the need to protect the safety and health of workers:
- (a) the period of weekly working time is limited by means of laws, regulations or administrative provisions or by collective agreements or agreements between the two sides of industry;
- (b) the average working time for each seven-day period, including overtime, does not exceed 48 hours.

Article 7   Annual leave
1.   Member States shall take the measures necessary to ensure that every worker is entitled to paid annual leave of at least four weeks in accordance with the conditions for entitlement to, and granting of, such leave laid down by national legislation and/or practice.

2.   The minimum period of paid annual leave may not be replaced by an allowance in lieu, except where the employment relationship is terminated.

CHAPTER 3   NIGHT WORK – SHIFT WORK – PATTERNS OF WORK

Article 8   Length of night work
Member States shall take the measures necessary to ensure that:
- (a) normal hours of work for night workers do not exceed an average of eight hours in any 24-hour period;
- (b) night workers whose work involves special hazards or heavy physical or mental strain do not work more than eight hours in any period of 24 hours during which they perform night work.

For the purposes of point (b), work involving special hazards or heavy physical or mental strain shall be defined by national legislation and/or practice or by collective agreements or agreements concluded between the two sides of industry, taking account of the specific effects and hazards of night work.

Article 9   Health assessment and transfer of night workers to day work
   1. Member States shall take the measures necessary to ensure that:
     (a) night workers are entitled to a free health assessment before their assignment and thereafter at regular intervals;
     (b) night workers suffering from health problems recognised as being connected with the fact that they perform night work are transferred whenever possible to day work to which they are suited.
   2. The free health assessment referred to in paragraph 1(a) must comply with medical confidentiality.
   3. The free health assessment referred to in paragraph 1(a) may be conducted within the national health system.

Article 10   Guarantees for night-time working
   Member States may make the work of certain categories of night workers subject to certain guarantees, under conditions laid down by national legislation and/or practice, in the case of workers who incur risks to their safety or health linked to night-time working.

Article 11   Notification of regular use of night workers
Member States shall take the measures necessary to ensure that an employer who regularly uses night workers brings this information to the attention of the competent authorities if they so request.

Article 12   Safety and health protection
Member States shall take the measures necessary to ensure that:
     (a) night workers and shift workers have safety and health protection appropriate to the nature of their work;
     (b) appropriate protection and prevention services or facilities with regard to the safety and health of night workers and shift workers are equivalent to those applicable to other workers and are available at all times.

Article 13   Pattern of work
Member States shall take the measures necessary to ensure that an employer who intends to organise work according to a certain pattern takes account of the general principle of adapting work to the worker, with a view, in particular, to alleviating monotonous work and work at a predetermined work-rate, depending on the type of activity, and of safety and health requirements, especially as regards breaks during working time.

CHAPTER 4   MISCELLANEOUS PROVISIONS

Article 14   More specific Community provisions
This Directive shall not apply where other Community instruments contain more specific requirements relating to the organisation of working time for certain occupations or occupational activities.

Article 15   More favourable provisions
This Directive shall not affect Member States' right to apply or introduce laws, regulations or administrative provisions more favourable to the protection of the safety and health of workers or to facilitate or permit the application of collective agreements or agreements concluded between the two sides of industry which are more favourable to the protection of the safety and health of workers.

Article 16   Reference periods
Member States may lay down:
     (a) for the application of Article 5 (weekly rest period), a reference period not exceeding 14 days;

(b) for the application of Article 6 (maximum weekly working time), a reference period not exceeding four months.

The periods of paid annual leave, granted in accordance with Article 7, and the periods of sick leave shall not be included or shall be neutral in the calculation of the average;

(c) for the application of Article 8 (length of night work), a reference period defined after consultation of the two sides of industry or by collective agreements or agreements concluded between the two sides of industry at national or regional level.

If the minimum weekly rest period of 24 hours required by Article 5 falls within that reference period, it shall not be included in the calculation of the average.

CHAPTER 5   DEROGATIONS AND EXCEPTIONS

Article 17   Derogations

1.   With due regard for the general principles of the protection of the safety and health of workers, Member States may derogate from Articles 3 to 6, 8 and 16 when, on account of the specific characteristics of the activity concerned, the duration of the working time is not measured and/or predetermined or can be determined by the workers themselves, and particularly in the case of:

(a) managing executives or other persons with autonomous decision-taking powers;

(b) family workers; or

(c) workers officiating at religious ceremonies in churches and religious communities.

2.   Derogations provided for in paragraphs 3, 4 and 5 may be adopted by means of laws, regulations or administrative provisions or by means of collective agreements or agreements between the two sides of industry provided that the workers concerned are afforded equivalent periods of compensatory rest or that, in exceptional cases in which it is not possible, for objective reasons, to grant such equivalent periods of compensatory rest, the workers concerned are afforded appropriate protection.

3.   In accordance with paragraph 2 of this Article derogations may be made from Articles 3, 4, 5, 8 and 16:

(a) in the case of activities where the worker's place of work and his place of residence are distant from one another, including offshore work, or where the worker's different places of work are distant from one another;

(b) in the case of security and surveillance activities requiring a permanent presence in order to protect property and persons, particularly security guards and caretakers or security firms;

(c) in the case of activities involving the need for continuity of service or production, particularly:

(i)   services relating to the reception, treatment and/or care provided by hospitals or similar establishments, including the activities of doctors in training, residential institutions and prisons;

(ii)   dock or airport workers;

(iii)   press, radio, television, cinematographic production, postal and telecommunications services, ambulance, fire and civil protection services;

(iv)   gas, water and electricity production, transmission and distribution, household refuse collection and incineration plants;

(v)   industries in which work cannot be interrupted on technical grounds;

(vi)   research and development activities;

(vii) agriculture;

(viii) workers concerned with the carriage of passengers on regular urban transport services;

(d) where there is a foreseeable surge of activity, particularly in:

(i) agriculture;

(ii) tourism;

(iii) postal services;

(e) in the case of persons working in railway transport:

(i) whose activities are intermittent;

(ii) who spend their working time on board trains; or

(iii) whose activities are linked to transport timetables and to ensuring the continuity and regularity of traffic;

(f) in the circumstances described in Article 5(4) of Directive 89/391/EEC;

(g) in cases of accident or imminent risk of accident.

4. In accordance with paragraph 2 of this Article derogations may be made from Articles 3 and 5:

(a) in the case of shift work activities, each time the worker changes shift and cannot take daily and/or weekly rest periods between the end of one shift and the start of the next one;

(b) in the case of activities involving periods of work split up over the day, particularly those of cleaning staff.

5. In accordance with paragraph 2 of this Article, derogations may be made from Article 6 and Article 16(b), in the case of doctors in training, in accordance with the provisions set out in the second to the seventh subparagraphs of this paragraph.

With respect to Article 6 derogations referred to in the first subparagraph shall be permitted for a transitional period of five years from 1 August 2004.

Member States may have up to two more years, if necessary, to take account of difficulties in meeting the working time provisions with respect to their responsibilities for the organisation and delivery of health services and medical care. At least six months before the end of the transitional period, the Member State concerned shall inform the Commission giving its reasons, so that the Commission can give an opinion, after appropriate consultations, within the three months following receipt of such information. If the Member State does not follow the opinion of the Commission, it will justify its decision. The notification and justification of the Member State and the opinion of the Commission shall be published in the Official Journal of the European Union and forwarded to the European Parliament.

Member States may have an additional period of up to one year, if necessary, to take account of special difficulties in meeting the responsibilities referred to in the third subparagraph. They shall follow the procedure set out in that subparagraph.

Member States shall ensure that in no case will the number of weekly working hours exceed an average of 58 during the first three years of the transitional period, an average of 56 for the following two years and an average of 52 for any remaining period.

The employer shall consult the representatives of the employees in good time with a view to reaching an agreement, wherever possible, on the arrangements applying to the transitional period. Within the limits set out in the fifth subparagraph, such an agreement may cover:

(a) the average number of weekly hours of work during the transitional period; and

(b) the measures to be adopted to reduce weekly working hours to an average of 48 by the end of the transitional period.

With respect to Article 16(b) derogations referred to in the first subparagraph shall be permitted provided that the reference period does not exceed 12 months, during the first part of the transitional period specified in the fifth subparagraph, and six months thereafter.

Article 18 Derogations by collective agreements

Derogations may be made from Articles 3, 4, 5, 8 and 16 by means of collective agreements or agreements concluded between the two sides of industry at national or regional level or, in conformity with the rules laid down by them, by means of collective agreements or agreements concluded between the two sides of industry at a lower level.

Member States in which there is no statutory system ensuring the conclusion of collective agreements or agreements concluded between the two sides of industry at national or regional level, on the matters covered by this Directive, or those Member States in which there is a specific legislative framework for this purpose and within the limits thereof, may, in accordance with national legislation and/or practice, allow derogations from Articles 3, 4, 5, 8 and 16 by way of collective agreements or agreements concluded between the two sides of industry at the appropriate collective level.

The derogations provided for in the first and second subparagraphs shall be allowed on condition that equivalent compensating rest periods are granted to the workers concerned or, in exceptional cases where it is not possible for objective reasons to grant such periods, the workers concerned are afforded appropriate protection.

Member States may lay down rules:

(a) for the application of this Article by the two sides of industry; and

(b) for the extension of the provisions of collective agreements or agreements concluded in conformity with this Article to other workers in accordance with national legislation and/or practice.

Article 19   Limitations to derogations from reference periods

The option to derogate from Article 16(b), provided for in Article 17(3) and in Article 18, may not result in the establishment of a reference period exceeding six months.

However, Member States shall have the option, subject to compliance with the general principles relating to the protection of the safety and health of workers, of allowing, for objective or technical reasons or reasons concerning the organisation of work, collective agreements or agreements concluded between the two sides of industry to set reference periods in no event exceeding 12 months.

Before 23 November 2003, the Council shall, on the basis of a Commission proposal accompanied by an appraisal report, re-examine the provisions of this Article and decide what action to take.

Article 20   Mobile workers and offshore work

1.   Articles 3, 4, 5 and 8 shall not apply to mobile workers.

Member States shall, however, take the necessary measures to ensure that such mobile workers are entitled to adequate rest, except in the circumstances laid down in Article 17(3)(f) and (g).

2.   Subject to compliance with the general principles relating to the protection of the safety and health of workers, and provided that there is consultation of representatives of the employer and employees concerned and efforts to encourage all relevant forms of social dialogue, including negotiation if the parties so wish, Member States may, for objective or technical reasons or reasons concerning the organisation of work, extend the reference period referred to in Article 16(b) to 12 months in respect of workers who mainly perform offshore work.

3.   Not later than 1 August 2005 the Commission shall, after consulting the Member States and management and labour at European level, review the operation of the provisions with regard to offshore workers from a health and safety perspective with a view to presenting, if need be, the appropriate modifications.

Article 21   Workers on board seagoing fishing vessels

1.   Articles 3 to 6 and 8 shall not apply to any worker on board a seagoing fishing vessel flying the flag of a Member State.

Member States shall, however, take the necessary measures to ensure that any worker on board a seagoing fishing vessel flying the flag of a Member State is entitled to adequate rest and to limit the number of hours of work to 48 hours a week on average calculated over a reference period not exceeding 12 months.

2.   Within the limits set out in paragraph 1, second subparagraph, and paragraphs 3 and 4 Member States shall take the necessary measures to ensure that, in keeping with the need to protect the safety and health of such workers:

(a)   the working hours are limited to a maximum number of hours which shall not be exceeded in a given period of time; or

(b)   a minimum number of hours of rest are provided within a given period of time.

The maximum number of hours of work or minimum number of hours of rest shall be specified by law, regulations, administrative provisions or by collective agreements or agreements between the two sides of the industry.

3.   The limits on hours of work or rest shall be either:

(a)   maximum hours of work which shall not exceed:

(i)   14 hours in any 24-hour period; and

(ii)   72 hours in any seven-day period;

or

(b)   minimum hours of rest which shall not be less than:

(i)   10 hours in any 24-hour period; and

(ii)   77 hours in any seven-day period.

4.   Hours of rest may be divided into no more than two periods, one of which shall be at least six hours in length, and the interval between consecutive periods of rest shall not exceed 14 hours.

5.   In accordance with the general principles of the protection of the health and safety of workers, and for objective or technical reasons or reasons concerning the organisation of work, Member States may allow exceptions, including the establishment of reference periods, to the limits laid down in paragraph 1, second subparagraph, and paragraphs 3 and 4. Such exceptions shall, as far as possible, comply with the standards laid down but may take account of more frequent or longer leave periods or the granting of compensatory leave for the workers. These exceptions may be laid down by means of:

(a)   laws, regulations or administrative provisions provided there is consultation, where possible, of the representatives of the employers and workers concerned and efforts are made to encourage all relevant forms of social dialogue; or

(b)   collective agreements or agreements between the two sides of industry.

6.   The master of a seagoing fishing vessel shall have the right to require workers on board to perform any hours of work necessary for the immediate safety of the vessel, persons on board or cargo, or for the purpose of giving assistance to other vessels or persons in distress at sea.

7.   Members States may provide that workers on board seagoing fishing vessels for which national legislation or practice determines that these vessels are not allowed to operate in a specific period of the calendar year exceeding one month, shall take annual leave in accordance with Article 7 within that period.

Article 22   Miscellaneous provisions

1.   A Member State shall have the option not to apply Article 6, while respecting the general principles of the protection of the safety and health of workers, and provided it takes the necessary measures to ensure that:

(a)   no employer requires a worker to work more than 48 hours over a seven-day period, calculated as an average for the reference period referred to in Article 16(b), unless he has first obtained the worker's agreement to perform such work;

(b)   no worker is subjected to any detriment by his employer because he is not willing to give his agreement to perform such work;

(c)   the employer keeps up-to-date records of all workers who carry out such work;

(d) the records are placed at the disposal of the competent authorities, which may, for reasons connected with the safety and/or health of workers, prohibit or restrict the possibility of exceeding the maximum weekly working hours;

(e) the employer provides the competent authorities at their request with information on cases in which agreement has been given by workers to perform work exceeding 48 hours over a period of seven days, calculated as an average for the reference period referred to in Article 16(b).

Before 23 November 2003, the Council shall, on the basis of a Commission proposal accompanied by an appraisal report, re-examine the provisions of this paragraph and decide on what action to take.

2.   Member States shall have the option, as regards the application of Article 7, of making use of a transitional period of not more than three years from 23 November 1996, provided that during that transitional period:

(a) every worker receives three weeks' paid annual leave in accordance with the conditions for the entitlement to, and granting of, such leave laid down by national legislation and/or practice; and

(b) the three-week period of paid annual leave may not be replaced by an allowance in lieu, except where the employment relationship is terminated.

3.   If Member States avail themselves of the options provided for in this Article, they shall forthwith inform the Commission thereof.

CHAPTER 6   FINAL PROVISIONS

Article 23   **Level of Protection**

Without prejudice to the right of Member States to develop, in the light of changing circumstances, different legislative, regulatory or contractual provisions in the field of working time, as long as the minimum requirements provided for in this Directive are complied with, implementation of this Directive shall not constitute valid grounds for reducing the general level of protection afforded to workers.

Article 24   **Reports**

1.   Member States shall communicate to the Commission the texts of the provisions of national law already adopted or being adopted in the field governed by this Directive.

2.   Member States shall report to the Commission every five years on the practical implementation of the provisions of this Directive, indicating the viewpoints of the two sides of industry.

The Commission shall inform the European Parliament, the Council, the European Economic and Social Committee and the Advisory Committee on Safety, Hygiene and Health Protection at Work thereof.

3.   Every five years from 23 November 1996 the Commission shall submit to the European Parliament, the Council and the European Economic and Social Committee a report on the application of this Directive taking into account Articles 22 and 23 and paragraphs 1 and 2 of this Article.

Article 25   **Review of the operation of the provisions with regard to workers on board seagoing fishing vessels**

Not later than 1 August 2009 the Commission shall, after consulting the Member States and management and labour at European level, review the operation of the provisions with regard to workers on board seagoing fishing vessels, and, in particular examine whether these provisions remain appropriate, in particular, as far as health and safety are concerned with a view to proposing suitable amendments, if necessary.

Article 26   Review of the operation of the provisions with regard to workers concerned with the carriage of passengers

Not later than 1 August 2005 the Commission shall, after consulting the Member States and management and labour at European level, review the operation of the provisions with regard to workers concerned with the carriage of passengers on regular urban transport services, with a view to presenting, if need be, the appropriate modifications to ensure a coherent and suitable approach in the sector.

Article 27   Repeal

1.   Directive 93/104/EC, as amended by the Directive referred to in Annex I, part A, shall be repealed, without prejudice to the obligations of the Member States in respect of the deadlines for transposition laid down in Annex I, part B.

2.   The references made to the said repealed Directive shall be construed as references to this Directive and shall be read in accordance with the correlation table set out in Annex II.

Article 28   Entry into force

This Directive shall enter into force on 2 August 2004.

Article 29   Addressees

This Directive is addressed to the Member States.

Done at Brussels, 4 November 2003.

For the European Parliament
The President
P. Cox

For the Council
The President
G. Tremonti

ANNEX I
PART A   REPEALED DIRECTIVE AND ITS AMENDMENT (Article 27)

Council Directive 93/104/EC   (OJ L 307, 13.12.1993, p. 18)
Directive 2000/34/EC of the European Parliament and of the Council (OJ L 195, 1.8.2000, p. 41)

PART B   DEADLINES FOR TRANSPOSITION INTO NATIONAL LAW (Article 27)

Directive	Deadline for transposition
93/104/EC	23 November 1996
2000/34/EC	1 August 2003[1]

ANNEX II

CORRELATION TABLE

Directive 93/104/EC	This Directive
Articles 1 to 5	Articles 1 to 5

[1] August 2004 in the case of doctors in training. See Article 2 of Directive 2000/34/EC.

[1] Directive 2000/34/EC, Article 3.
[2] Directive 2000/34/EC, Article 4.

COMPETITION

Regulation No. 17—First Regulation implementing Articles 81 and 82 of the Treaty

[OJ Sp. Ed. 1962, No. 204/62, p. 87]*

Article 8   Duration and revocation of decisions under Article 85(3)

3.   The Commission may revoke or amend its decision or prohibit specified acts by the parties:

   (a) where there has been a change in any of the facts which were basic to the making of the decision;
   (b) where the parties commit a breach of any obligation attached to the decision;
   (c) where the decision is based on incorrect information or was induced by deceit;
   (d) where the parties abuse the exemption from the provisions of Article 85(1) of the Treaty granted to them by the decision.

In cases to which sub-paragraphs (b), (c) or (d) apply, the decision may be revoked with retroactive effect.

Commission Notice on agreements of minor importance which do not appreciably restrict competition under Article 81(1) of the Treaty Establishing the European Community (*de minimis*)([1])

[OJ 2001, C368/13]

I

1.   Article 81(1) prohibits agreements between undertakings which may affect trade between Member States and which have as their object or effect the prevention, restriction or distortion of competition within the common market. The Court of Justice of the European Communities has clarified that this provision is not applicable where the impact of the agreement on intra-Community trade or on competition is not appreciable.

2.   In this notice the Commission quantifies, with the help of market share thresholds, what is not an appreciable restriction of competition under Article 81 of the EC Treaty. This negative definition of appreciability does not imply that agreements between undertakings which exceed the thresholds set out in this notice appreciably restrict competition. Such

---

*   **Editor's Note:** Following the entry into force of Regulation 1/2003, included below, Article 8(3) is the only Article which remains, temporarily, in force.

[1]   **Editor's Note:** This notice replaces the notice on agreements of minor importance published in OJ C 372, 9.12.1997. Permission to reproduce this document is gratefully acknowledged but please note that 'Only European Community legislation printed in the paper edition of the Official Journal of the European Union is deemed authentic'.

agreements may still have only a negligible effect on competition and may therefore not be prohibited by Article 81(1)([2]).

3.   Agreements may in addition not fall under Article 81(1) because they are not capable of appreciably affecting trade between Member States. This notice does not deal with this issue. It does not quantify what does not constitute an appreciable effect on trade. It is however acknowledged that agreements between small and medium-sized undertakings, as defined in the Annex to Commission Recommendation 96/280/EC([3]), are rarely capable of appreciably affecting trade between Member States. Small and medium-sized undertakings are currently defined in that recommendation as undertakings which have fewer than 250 employees and have either an annual turnover not exceeding EUR 40 million or an annual balance-sheet total not exceeding EUR 27 million.

4.   In cases covered by this notice the Commission will not institute proceedings either upon application or on its own initiative. Where undertakings assume in good faith that an agreement is covered by this notice, the Commission will not impose fines. Although not binding on them, this notice also intends to give guidance to the courts and authorities of the Member States in their application of Article 81.

5.   This notice also applies to decisions by associations of undertakings and to concerted practices.

6.   This notice is without prejudice to any interpretation of Article 81 which may be given by the Court of Justice or the Court of First Instance of the European Communities.

II

7.   The Commission holds the view that agreements between undertakings which affect trade between Member States do not appreciably restrict competition within the meaning of Article 81(1):

   (a) if the aggregate market share held by the parties to the agreement does not exceed 10% on any of the relevant markets affected by the agreement, where the agreement is made between undertakings which are actual or potential competitors on any of these markets (agreements between competitors)([4]); or

   (b) if the market share held by each of the parties to the agreement does not exceed 15 % on any of the relevant markets affected by the agreement, where the agreement is made between undertakings which are not actual or potential competitors on any of these markets (agreements between non-competitors).

[2] See, for instance, the judgment of the Court of Justice in Joined Cases C-215/96 and C-216/96 *Bagnasco (Carlos)* v *Banca Popolare di Novara and Casa di Risparmio di Genova e Imperia* (1999) ECR I-135, points 34–35. This notice is also without prejudice to the principles for assessment under Article 81(1) as expressed in the Commission notice 'Guidelines on the applicability of Article 81 of the EC Treaty to horizontal cooperation agreements', OJ C 3, 6.1.2001, in particular points 17–31 inclusive, and in the Commission notice 'Guidelines on vertical restraints', OJ C 291, 13.10.2000, in particular points 5–20 inclusive.

[3] OJ L 107, 30.4.1996, p. 4. This recommendation will be revised. It is envisaged to increase the annual turnover threshold from EUR 40 million to EUR 50 million and the annual balance-sheet total threshold from EUR 27 million to EUR 43 million.

[4] On what are actual or potential competitors, see the Commission notice 'Guidelines on the applicability of Article 81 of the EC Treaty to horizontal cooperation agreements', OJ C 3, 6.1.2001, paragraph 9. A firm is treated as an actual competitor if it is either active on the same relevant market or if, in the absence of the agreement, it is able to switch production to the relevant products and market them in the short term without incurring significant additional costs or risks in response to a small and permanent increase in relative prices (immediate supply-side substitutability). A firm is treated as a potential competitor if there is evidence that, absent the agreement, this firm could and would be likely to undertake the necessary additional investments or other necessary switching costs so that it could enter the relevant market in response to a small and permanent increase in relative prices.

In cases where it is difficult to classify the agreement as either an agreement between competitors or an agreement between non-competitors the 10% threshold is applicable.

8.   Where in a relevant market competition is restricted by the cumulative effect of agreements for the sale of goods or services entered into by different suppliers or distributors (cumulative foreclosure effect of parallel networks of agreements having similar effects on the market), the market share thresholds under point 7 are reduced to 5%, both for agreements between competitors and for agreements between non-competitors. Individual suppliers or distributors with a market share not exceeding 5% are in general not considered to contribute significantly to a cumulative foreclosure effect([5]). A cumulative foreclosure effect is unlikely to exist if less than 30% of the relevant market is covered by parallel (networks of) agreements having similar effects.

9.   The Commission also holds the view that agreements are not restrictive of competition if the market shares do not exceed the thresholds of respectively 10%, 15% and 5% set out in point 7 and 8 during two successive calendar years by more than 2 percentage points.

10.   In order to calculate the market share, it is necessary to determine the relevant market. This consists of the relevant product market and the relevant geographic market. When defining the relevant market, reference should be had to the notice on the definition of the relevant market for the purposes of Community competition law([6]). The market shares are to be calculated on the basis of sales value data or, where appropriate, purchase value data. If value data are not available, estimates based on other reliable market information, including volume data, may be used.

11.   Points 7, 8 and 9 do not apply to agreements containing any of the following hardcore restrictions:

(1) as regards agreements between competitors as defined in point 7, restrictions which, directly or indirectly, in isolation or in combination with other factors under the control of the parties, have as their object([7])

    (a)   the fixing of prices when selling the products to third parties;

    (b)   the limitation of output or sales;

    (c)   the allocation of markets or customers;

(2) as regards agreements between non-competitors as defined in point 7, restrictions which, directly or indirectly, in isolation or in combination with other factors under the control of the parties, have as their object:

    (a)   the restriction of the buyer's ability to determine its sale price, without prejudice to the possibility of the supplier imposing a maximum sale price or recommending a sale price, provided that they do not amount to a fixed or minimum sale price as a result of pressure from, or incentives offered by, any of the parties;

    (b)   the restriction of the territory into which, or of the customers to whom, the buyer may sell the contract goods or services, except the following restrictions which are not hardcore:

      — the restriction of active sales into the exclusive territory or to an exclusive customer group reserved to the supplier or allocated by the supplier to another

---

[5]   See also the Commission notice 'Guidelines on vertical restraints', OJ C 291, 13.10.2000, in particular paragraphs 73, 142, 143 and 189. While in the guidelines on vertical restraints in relation to certain restrictions reference is made not only to the total but also to the tied market share of a particular supplier or buyer, in this notice all market share thresholds refer to total market shares.

[6]   OJ C 372, 9.12.1997, p. 5.

[7]   Without prejudice to situations of joint production with or without joint distribution as defined in Article 5, paragraph 2, of Commission Regulation (EC) No. 2658/2000 and Article 5, paragraph 2, of Commission Regulation (EC) No. 2659/2000, OJ L 304, 5.12.2000, pp. 3 and 7 respectively.

buyer, where such a restriction does not limit sales by the customers of the buyer,

— the restriction of sales to end users by a buyer operating at the wholesale level of trade,

— the restriction of sales to unauthorised distributors by the members of a selective distribution system, and

— the restriction of the buyer's ability to sell components, supplied for the purposes of incorporation, to customers who would use them to manufacture the same type of goods as those produced by the supplier;

(c) the restriction of active or passive sales to end users by members of a selective distribution system operating at the retail level of trade, without prejudice to the possibility of prohibiting a member of the system from operating out of an unauthorised place of establishment;

(d) the restriction of cross-supplies between distributors within a selective distribution system, including between distributors operating at different levels of trade;

(e) the restriction agreed between a supplier of components and a buyer who incorporates those components, which limits the supplier's ability to sell the components as spare parts to end users or to repairers or other service providers not entrusted by the buyer with the repair or servicing of its goods;

(3) as regards agreements between competitors as defined in point 7, where the competitors operate, for the purposes of the agreement, at a different level of the production or distribution chain, any of the hardcore restrictions listed in paragraph (1) and (2) above.

12. (1) For the purposes of this notice, the terms 'undertaking', 'party to the agreement', 'distributor', 'supplier' and 'buyer' shall include their respective connected undertakings.

(2) 'Connected undertakings' are:

(a) undertakings in which a party to the agreement, directly or indirectly:

— has the power to exercise more than half the voting rights, or

— has the power to appoint more than half the members of the supervisory board, board of management or bodies legally representing the undertaking, or

— has the right to manage the undertaking's affairs;

(b) undertakings which directly or indirectly have, over a party to the agreement, the rights or powers listed in (a);

(c) undertakings in which an undertaking referred to in (b) has, directly or indirectly, the rights or powers listed in (a);

(d) undertakings in which a party to the agreement together with one or more of the undertakings referred to in (a), (b) or (c), or in which two or more of the latter undertakings, jointly have the rights or powers listed in (a);

(e) undertakings in which the rights or the powers listed in (a) are jointly held by:

— parties to the agreement or their respective connected undertakings referred to in (a) to (d), or

— one or more of the parties to the agreement or one or more of their connected undertakings referred to in (a) to (d) and one or more third parties.

(3) For the purposes of paragraph 2(e), the market share held by these jointly held undertakings shall be apportioned equally to each undertaking having the rights or the powers listed in paragraph 2(a).

Council Regulation (EC) No 659/1999 of 22 March 1999 laying down detailed rules for the application of Article 93 of the EC Treaty
[OJ 1999, L83/1]

THE COUNCIL OF THE EUROPEAN UNION,

Having regard to the Treaty establishing the European Community, and in particular Article 94 thereof,

Having regard to the proposal from the Commission,[1]

Having regard to the opinion of the European Parliament,[2]

Having regard to the opinion of the Economic and Social Committee,[3]

(1) Whereas, without prejudice to special procedural rules laid down in regulations for certain sectors, this Regulation should apply to aid in all sectors; whereas, for the purpose of applying Articles 77 and 92 of the Treaty, the Commission has specific competence under Article 93 thereof to decide on the compatibility of State aid with the common market when reviewing existing aid, when taking decisions on new or altered aid and when taking action regarding non-compliance with its decisions or with the requirement as to notification;

(2) Whereas the Commission, in accordance with the case-law of the Court of Justice of the European Communities, has developed and established a consistent practice for the application of Article 93 of the Treaty and has laid down certain procedural rules and principles in a number of communications; whereas it is appropriate, with a view to ensuring effective and efficient procedures pursuant to Article 93 of the Treaty, to codify and reinforce this practice by means of a regulation;

(3) Whereas a procedural regulation on the application of Article 93 of the Treaty will increase transparency and legal certainty;

(4) Whereas, in order to ensure legal certainty, it is appropriate to define the circumstances under which aid is to be considered as existing aid; whereas the completion and enhancement of the internal market is a gradual process, reflected in the permanent development of State aid policy; whereas, following these developments, certain measures, which at the moment they were put into effect did not constitute State aid, may since have become aid;

(5) Whereas, in accordance with Article 93(3) of the Treaty, any plans to grant new aid are to be notified to the Commission and should not be put into effect before the Commission has authorised it;

(6) Whereas, in accordance with Article 5 of the Treaty, Member States are under an obligation to cooperate with the Commission and to provide it with all information required to allow the Commission to carry out its duties under this Regulation;

(7) Whereas the period within which the Commission is to conclude the preliminary examination of notified aid should be set at two months from the receipt of a complete notification or from the receipt of a duly reasoned statement of the Member State concerned that it considers the notification to be complete because the additional information requested by the Commission is not available or has already been provided; whereas, for reasons of legal certainty, that examination should be brought to an end by a decision;

(8) Whereas in all cases where, as a result of the preliminary examination, the Commission cannot find that the aid is compatible with the common market, the formal investigation procedure should be opened in order to enable the Commission to gather all the information it needs to assess the compatibility of the aid and to allow the interested parties to submit their

---

[1] OJ C 116, 16.4.1998, p. 13.
[2] Opinion delivered on 14 January 1999 (not yet published in the Official Journal).
[3] (3) OJ C 284, 14.9.1998, p. 10.

comments; whereas the rights of the interested parties can best be safeguarded within the framework of the formal investigation procedure provided for under Article 93(2) of the Treaty;

(9) Whereas, after having considered the comments submitted by the interested parties, the Commission should conclude its examination by means of a final decision as soon as the doubts have been removed; whereas it is appropriate, should this examination not be concluded after a period of 18 months from the opening of the procedure, that the Member State concerned has the opportunity to request a decision, which the Commission should take within two months;

(10) Whereas, in order to ensure that the State aid rules are applied correctly and effectively, the Commission should have the opportunity of revoking a decision which was based on incorrect information;

(11) Whereas, in order to ensure compliance with Article 93 of the Treaty, and in particular with the notification obligation and the standstill clause in Article 93(3), the Commission should examine all cases of unlawful aid; whereas, in the interests of transparency and legal certainty, the procedures to be followed in such cases should be laid down; whereas when a Member State has not respected the notification obligation or the standstill clause, the Commission should not be bound by time limits;

(12) Whereas in cases of unlawful aid, the Commission should have the right to obtain all necessary information enabling it to take a decision and to restore immediately, where appropriate, undistorted competition; whereas it is therefore appropriate to enable the Commission to adopt interim measures addressed to the Member State concerned; whereas the interim measures may take the form of information injunctions, suspension injunctions and recovery injunctions; whereas the Commission should be enabled in the event of non-compliance with an information injunction, to decide on the basis of the information available and, in the event of non-compliance with suspension and recovery injunctions, to refer the matter to the Court of Justice direct, in accordance with the second subparagraph of Article 93(2) of the Treaty;

(13) Whereas in cases of unlawful aid which is not compatible with the common market, effective competition should be restored; whereas for this purpose it is necessary that the aid, including interest, be recovered without delay; whereas it is appropriate that recovery be effected in accordance with the procedures of national law; whereas the application of those procedures should not, by preventing the immediate and effective execution of the Commission decision, impede the restoration of effective competition; whereas to achieve this result, Member States should take all necessary measures ensuring the effectiveness of the Commission decision;

(14) Whereas for reasons of legal certainty it is appropriate to establish a period of limitation of 10 years with regard to unlawful aid, after the expiry of which no recovery can be ordered;

(15) Whereas misuse of aid may have effects on the functioning of the internal market which are similar to those of unlawful aid and should thus be treated according to similar procedures; whereas unlike unlawful aid, aid which has possibly been misused is aid which has been previously approved by the Commission; whereas therefore the Commission should not be allowed to use a recovery injunction with regard to misuse of aid;

(16) Whereas it is appropriate to define all the possibilities in which third parties have to defend their interests in State aid procedures;

(17) Whereas in accordance with Article 93(1) of the Treaty, the Commission is under an obligation, in cooperation with Member States, to keep under constant review all systems of existing aid; whereas in the interests of transparency and legal certainty, it is appropriate to specify the scope of cooperation under that Article;

(18) Whereas, in order to ensure compatibility of existing aid schemes with the common market and in accordance with Article 93(1) of the Treaty, the Commission should propose

appropriate measures where an existing aid scheme is not, or is no longer, compatible with the common market and should initiate the procedure provided for in Article 93(2) of the Treaty if the Member State concerned declines to implement the proposed measures;

(19) Whereas, in order to allow the Commission to monitor effectively compliance with Commission decisions and to facilitate cooperation between the Commission and Member States for the purpose of the constant review of all existing aid schemes in the Member States in accordance with Article 93(1) of the Treaty, it is necessary to introduce a general reporting obligation with regard to all existing aid schemes;

(20) Whereas, where the Commission has serious doubts as to whether its decisions are being complied with, it should have at its disposal additional instruments allowing it to obtain the information necessary to verify that its decisions are being effectively complied with; whereas for this purpose on-site monitoring visits are an appropriate and useful instrument, in particular for cases where aid might have been misused; whereas therefore the Commission must be empowered to undertake on-site monitoring visits and must obtain the cooperation of the competent authorities of the Member States where an undertaking opposes such a visit;

(21) Whereas, in the interests of transparency and legal certainty, it is appropriate to give public information on Commission decisions while, at the same time, maintaining the principle that decisions in State aid cases are addressed to the Member State concerned; whereas it is therefore appropriate to publish all decisions which might affect the interests of interested parties either in full or in a summary form or to make copies of such decisions available to interested parties, where they have not been published or where they have not been published in full; whereas the Commission, when giving public information on its decisions, should respect the rules on professional secrecy, in accordance with Article 214 of the Treaty;

(22) Whereas the Commission, in close liaison with the Member States, should be able to adopt implementing provisions laying down detailed rules concerning the procedures under this Regulation; whereas, in order to provide for cooperation between the Commission and the competent authorities of the Member States, it is appropriate to create an Advisory Committee on State aid to be consulted before the Commission adopts provisions pursuant to this Regulation,

HAS ADOPTED THIS REGULATION:

CHAPTER I   GENERAL

Article 1   Definitions

For the purpose of this Regulation:

    (a) 'aid' shall mean any measure fulfilling all the criteria laid down in Article 92(1) of the Treaty;

    (b) 'existing aid' shall mean:

        (i) without prejudice to Articles 144 and 172 of the Act of Accession of Austria, Finland and Sweden, all aid which existed prior to the entry into force of the Treaty in the respective Member States, that is to say, aid schemes and individual aid which were put into effect before, and are still applicable after, the entry into force of the Treaty;

        (ii) authorised aid, that is to say, aid schemes and individual aid which have been authorised by the Commission or by the Council;

        (iii) aid which is deemed to have been authorised pursuant to Article 4(6) of this Regulation or prior to this Regulation but in accordance with this procedure;

        (iv) aid which is deemed to be existing aid pursuant to Article 15;

        (v) aid which is deemed to be an existing aid because it can be established that at the time it was put into effect it did not constitute an aid, and subsequently became an aid due to the evolution of the common market and without having been altered by the Member State. Where certain measures become aid following the liberalisation of an activity by Community law, such measures shall not be considered as existing aid after the date fixed for liberalisation;

(c) 'new aid' shall mean all aid, that is to say, aid schemes and individual aid, which is not existing aid, including alterations to existing aid;

(d) 'aid scheme' shall mean any act on the basis of which, without further implementing measures being required, individual aid awards may be made to undertakings defined within the act in a general and abstract manner and any act on the basis of which aid which is not linked to a specific project may be awarded to one or several undertakings for an indefinite period of time and/or for an indefinite amount;

(e) 'individual aid' shall mean aid that is not awarded on the basis of an aid scheme and notifiable awards of aid on the basis of an aid scheme;

(f) 'unlawful aid' shall mean new aid put into effect in contravention of Article 93(3) of the Treaty;

(g) 'misuse of aid' shall mean aid used by the beneficiary in contravention of a decision taken pursuant to Article 4(3) or Article 7(3) or (4) of this Regulation;

(h) 'interested party' shall mean any Member State and any person, undertaking or association of undertakings whose interests might be affected by the granting of aid, in particular the beneficiary of the aid, competing undertakings and trade associations.

CHAPTER II   PROCEDURE REGARDING NOTIFIED AID

Article 2   Notification of new aid

1.   Save as otherwise provided in regulations made pursuant to Article 94 of the Treaty or to other relevant provisions thereof, any plans to grant new aid shall be notified to the Commission in sufficient time by the Member State concerned. The Commission shall inform the Member State concerned without delay of the receipt of a notification.

2.   In a notification, the Member State concerned shall provide all necessary information in order to enable the Commission to take a decision pursuant to Articles 4 and 7 (hereinafter referred to as 'complete notification').

Article 3   Standstill clause

Aid notifiable pursuant to Article 2(1) shall not be put into effect before the Commission has taken, or is deemed to have taken, a decision authorising such aid.

Article 4   Preliminary examination of the notification and decisions of the Commission

1.   The Commission shall examine the notification as soon as it is received. Without prejudice to Article 8, the Commission shall take a decision pursuant to paragraphs 2, 3 or 4.

2.   Where the Commission, after a preliminary examination, finds that the notified measure does not constitute aid, it shall record that finding by way of a decision.

3.   Where the Commission, after a preliminary examination, finds that no doubts are raised as to the compatibility with the common market of a notified measure, in so far as it falls within the scope of Article 92(1) of the Treaty, it shall decide that the measure is compatible with the common market (hereinafter referred to as a 'decision not to raise objections'). The decision shall specify which exception under the Treaty has been applied.

4.   Where the Commission, after a preliminary examination, finds that doubts are raised as to the compatibility with the common market of a notified measure, it shall decide to initiate proceedings pursuant to Article 93(2) of the Treaty (hereinafter referred to as a 'decision to initiate the formal investigation procedure').

5.   The decisions referred to in paragraphs 2, 3 and 4 shall be taken within two months. That period shall begin on the day following the receipt of a complete notification. The notification will be considered as complete if, within two months from its receipt, or from the receipt of any additional information requested, the Commission does not request any further information. The period can be extended with the consent of both the Commission and the Member State concerned. Where appropriate, the Commission may fix shorter time limits.

6.   Where the Commission has not taken a decision in accordance with paragraphs 2, 3 or 4 within the period laid down in paragraph 5, the aid shall be deemed to have been authorised by the Commission. The Member State concerned may thereupon implement the measures in question after giving the Commission prior notice thereof, unless the Commission takes a decision pursuant to this Article within a period of 15 working days following receipt of the notice.

Article 5   Request for information

1.   Where the Commission considers that information provided by the Member State concerned with regard to a measure notified pursuant to Article 2 is incomplete, it shall request all necessary additional information. Where a Member State responds to such a request, the Commission shall inform the Member State of the receipt of the response.

2.   Where the Member State concerned does not provide the information requested within the period prescribed by the Commission or provides incomplete information, the Commission shall send a reminder, allowing an appropriate additional period within which the information shall be provided.

3.   The notification shall be deemed to be withdrawn if the requested information is not provided within the prescribed period, unless before the expiry of that period, either the period has been extended with the consent of both the Commission and the Member State concerned, or the Member State concerned, in a duly reasoned statement, informs the Commission that it considers the notification to be complete because the additional information requested is not available or has already been provided. In that case, the period referred to in Article 4(5) shall begin on the day following receipt of the statement. If the notification is deemed to be withdrawn, the Commission shall inform the Member State thereof.

Article 6   Formal investigation procedure

1.   The decision to initiate the formal investigation procedure shall summarise the relevant issues of fact and law, shall include a preliminary assessment of the Commission as to the aid character of the proposed measure and shall set out the doubts as to its compatibility with the common market. The decision shall call upon the Member State concerned and upon other interested parties to submit comments within a prescribed period which shall normally not exceed one month. In duly justified cases, the Commission may extend the prescribed period.

2.   The comments received shall be submitted to the Member State concerned. If an interested party so requests, on grounds of potential damage, its identity shall be withheld from the Member State concerned. The Member State concerned may reply to the comments submitted within a prescribed period which shall normally not exceed one month. In duly justified cases, the Commission may extend the prescribed period.

Article 7   Decisions of the Commission to close the formal investigation procedure

1.   Without prejudice to Article 8, the formal investigation procedure shall be closed by means of a decision as provided for in paragraphs 2 to 5 of this Article.

2.   Where the Commission finds that, where appropriate following modification by the Member State concerned, the notified measure does not constitute aid, it shall record that finding by way of a decision.

3.   Where the Commission finds that, where appropriate following modification by the Member State concerned, the doubts as to the compatibility of the notified measure with the

common market have been removed, it shall decide that the aid is compatible with the common market (hereinafter referred to as a 'positive decision'). That decision shall specify which exception under the Treaty has been applied.

4.   The Commission may attach to a positive decision conditions subject to which an aid may be considered compatible with the common market and may lay down obligations to enable compliance with the decision to be monitored (hereinafter referred to as a 'conditional decision').

5.   Where the Commission finds that the notified aid is not compatible with the common market, it shall decide that the aid shall not be put into effect (hereinafter referred to as a 'negative decision').

6.   Decisions taken pursuant to paragraphs 2, 3, 4 and 5 shall be taken as soon as the doubts referred to in Article 4(4) have been removed. The Commission shall as far as possible endeavour to adopt a decision within a period of 18 months from the opening of the procedure. This time limit may be extended by common agreement between the Commission and the Member State concerned.

7.   Once the time limit referred to in paragraph 6 has expired, and should the Member State concerned so request, the Commission shall, within two months, take a decision on the basis of the information available to it. If appropriate, where the information provided is not sufficient to establish compatibility, the Commission shall take a negative decision.

Article 8   Withdrawal of notification

1.   The Member State concerned may withdraw the notification within the meaning of Article 2 in due time before the Commission has taken a decision pursuant to Article 4 or 7.

2.   In cases where the Commission initiated the formal investigation procedure, the Commission shall close that procedure.

Article 9   Revocation of a decision

The Commission may revoke a decision taken pursuant to Article 4(2) or (3), or Article 7(2), (3), (4), after having given the Member State concerned the opportunity to submit its comments, where the decision was based on incorrect information provided during the procedure which was a determining factor for the decision. Before revoking a decision and taking a new decision, the Commission shall open the formal investigation procedure pursuant to Article 4(4). Articles 6, 7 and 10, Article 11(1), Articles 13, 14 and 15 shall apply mutatis mutandis.

CHAPTER III   PROCEDURE REGARDING UNLAWFUL AID

Article 10   Examination, request for information and information injunction

1.   Where the Commission has in its possession information from whatever source regarding alleged unlawful aid, it shall examine that information without delay.

2.   If necessary, it shall request information from the Member State concerned. Article 2(2) and Article 5(1) and (2) shall apply mutatis mutandis.

3.   Where, despite a reminder pursuant to Article 5(2), the Member State concerned does not provide the information requested within the period prescribed by the Commission, or where it provides incomplete information, the Commission shall by decision require the information to be provided (hereinafter referred to as an 'information injunction'). The decision shall specify what information is required and prescribe an appropriate period within which it is to be supplied.

Article 11   Injunction to suspend or provisionally recover aid

1.   The Commission may, after giving the Member State concerned the opportunity to submit its comments, adopt a decision requiring the Member State to suspend any unlawful aid until the Commission has taken a decision on the compatibility of the aid with the common market (hereinafter referred to as a 'suspension injunction').

2.   The Commission may, after giving the Member State concerned the opportunity to submit its comments, adopt a decision requiring the Member State provisionally to recover any unlawful aid until the Commission has taken a decision on the compatibility of the aid with the common market (hereinafter referred to as a 'recovery injunction'), if the following criteria are fulfilled:

— according to an established practice there are no doubts about the aid character of the measure concerned

and

— there is an urgency to act

and

— there is a serious risk of substantial and irreparable damage to a competitor.

Recovery shall be effected in accordance with the procedure set out in Article 14(2) and (3). After the aid has been effectively recovered, the Commission shall take a decision within the time limits applicable to notified aid.

The Commission may authorise the Member State to couple the refunding of the aid with the payment of rescue aid to the firm concerned.

The provisions of this paragraph shall be applicable only to unlawful aid implemented after the entry into force of this Regulation.

Article 12   Non-compliance with an injunction decision

If the Member State fails to comply with a suspension injunction or a recovery injunction, the Commission shall be entitled, while carrying out the examination on the substance of the matter on the basis of the information available, to refer the matter to the Court of Justice of the European Communities direct and apply for a declaration that the failure to comply constitutes an infringement of the Treaty.

Article 13   Decisions of the Commission

1.   The examination of possible unlawful aid shall result in a decision pursuant to Article 4(2), (3) or (4). In the case of decisions to initiate the formal investigation procedure, proceedings shall be closed by means of a decision pursuant to Article 7. If a Member State fails to comply with an information injunction, that decision shall be taken on the basis of the information available.

2.   In cases of possible unlawful aid and without prejudice to Article 11(2), the Commission shall not be bound by the time-limit set out in Articles 4(5), 7(6) and 7(7).

3.   Article 9 shall apply mutatis mutandis.

Article 14   Recovery of aid

1.   Where negative decisions are taken in cases of unlawful aid, the Commission shall decide that the Member State concerned shall take all necessary measures to recover the aid from the beneficiary (hereinafter referred to as a 'recovery decision'). The Commission shall not require recovery of the aid if this would be contrary to a general principle of Community law.

2.   The aid to be recovered pursuant to a recovery decision shall include interest at an appropriate rate fixed by the Commission. Interest shall be payable from the date on which the unlawful aid was at the disposal of the beneficiary until the date of its recovery.

3.   Without prejudice to any order of the Court of Justice of the European Communities pursuant to Article 185 of the Treaty, recovery shall be effected without delay and in accordance with the procedures under the national law of the Member State concerned, provided that they allow the immediate and effective execution of the Commission's decision. To this effect and in the event of a procedure before national courts, the Member States concerned shall take all necessary steps which are available in their respective legal systems, including provisional measures, without prejudice to Community law.

Article 15   Limitation period

1.   The powers of the Commission to recover aid shall be subject to a limitation period of ten years.

2.   The limitation period shall begin on the day on which the unlawful aid is awarded to the beneficiary either as individual aid or as aid under an aid scheme. Any action taken by the Commission or by a Member State, acting at the request of the Commission, with regard to the unlawful aid shall interrupt the limitation period. Each interruption shall start time running afresh. The limitation period shall be suspended for as long as the decision of the Commission is the subject of proceedings pending before the Court of Justice of the European Communities.

3.   Any aid with regard to which the limitation period has expired, shall be deemed to be existing aid.

CHAPTER IV   PROCEDURE REGARDING MISUSE OF AID

Article 16   Misuse of aid

Without prejudice to Article 23, the Commission may in cases of misuse of aid open the formal investigation procedure pursuant to Article 4(4). Articles 6, 7, 9 and 10, Article 11(1), Articles 12, 13, 14 and 15 shall apply mutatis mutandis.

CHAPTER V   PROCEDURE REGARDING EXISTING AID SCHEMES

Article 17   Cooperation pursuant to Article 93(1) of the Treaty

1.   The Commission shall obtain from the Member State concerned all necessary information for the review, in cooperation with the Member State, of existing aid schemes pursuant to Article 93(1) of the Treaty.

2.   Where the Commission considers that an existing aid scheme is not, or is no longer, compatible with the common market, it shall inform the Member State concerned of its preliminary view and give the Member State concerned the opportunity to submit its comments within a period of one month. In duly justified cases, the Commission may extend this period.

Article 18   Proposal for appropriate measures

Where the Commission, in the light of the information submitted by the Member State pursuant to Article 17, concludes that the existing aid scheme is not, or is no longer, compatible with the common market, it shall issue a recommendation proposing appropriate measures to the Member State concerned. The recommendation may propose, in particular:

    (a)   substantive amendment of the aid scheme,
       or
    (b)   introduction of procedural requirements,
       or
    (c)   abolition of the aid scheme.

Article 19   Legal consequences of a proposal for appropriate measures

1.   Where the Member State concerned accepts the proposed measures and informs the Commission thereof, the Commission shall record that finding and inform the Member State thereof. The Member State shall be bound by its acceptance to implement the appropriate measures.

2.   Where the Member State concerned does not accept the proposed measures and the Commission, having taken into account the arguments of the Member State concerned, still considers that those measures are necessary, it shall initiate proceedings pursuant to Article 4(4). Articles 6, 7 and 9 shall apply mutatis mutandis.

CHAPTER VI   INTERESTED PARTIES

Article 20   Rights of interested parties

1.   Any interested party may submit comments pursuant to Article 6 following a Commission decision to initiate the formal investigation procedure. Any interested party which has submitted such comments and any beneficiary of individual aid shall be sent a copy of the decision taken by the Commission pursuant to Article 7.

2.   Any interested party may inform the Commission of any alleged unlawful aid and any alleged misuse of aid. Where the Commission considers that on the basis of the information in its possession there are insufficient grounds for taking a view on the case, it shall inform the interested party thereof. Where the Commission takes a decision on a case concerning the subject matter of the information supplied, it shall send a copy of that decision to the interested party.

3.   At its request, any interested party shall obtain a copy of any decision pursuant to Articles 4 and 7, Article 10(3) and Article 11.

CHAPTER VII   MONITORING

Article 21   Annual reports

1.   Member States shall submit to the Commission annual reports on all existing aid schemes with regard to which no specific reporting obligations have been imposed in a conditional decision pursuant to Article 7(4).

2.   Where, despite a reminder, the Member State concerned fails to submit an annual report, the Commission may proceed in accordance with Article 18 with regard to the aid scheme concerned.

Article 22   On-site monitoring

1.   Where the Commission has serious doubts as to whether decisions not to raise objections, positive decisions or conditional decisions with regard to individual aid are being complied with, the Member State concerned, after having been given the opportunity to submit its comments, shall allow the Commission to undertake on-site monitoring visits.

2.   The officials authorised by the Commission shall be empowered, in order to verify compliance with the decision concerned:
   (a) to enter any premises and land of the undertaking concerned;
   (b) to ask for oral explanations on the spot;
   (c) to examine books and other business records and take, or demand, copies.
   The Commission may be assisted if necessary by independent experts.

3.   The Commission shall inform the Member State concerned, in good time and in writing, of the on-site monitoring visit and of the identities of the authorised officials and experts. If the Member State has duly justified objections to the Commission's choice of experts, the experts shall be appointed in common agreement with the Member State. The officials of the Commission and the experts authorised to carry out the on-site monitoring shall produce an authorisation in writing specifying the subject-matter and purpose of the visit.

4.   Officials authorised by the Member State in whose territory the monitoring visit is to be made may be present at the monitoring visit.

5.   The Commission shall provide the Member State with a copy of any report produced as a result of the monitoring visit.

6.   Where an undertaking opposes a monitoring visit ordered by a Commission decision pursuant to this Article, the Member State concerned shall afford the necessary assistance to the officials and experts authorised by the Commission to enable them to carry out the monitoring visit. To this end the Member States shall, after consulting the Commission, take the necessary measures within eighteen months after the entry into force of this Regulation.

Article 23   Non-compliance with decisions and judgments

1.   Where the Member State concerned does not comply with conditional or negative decisions, in particular in cases referred to in Article 14, the Commission may refer the matter to the Court of Justice of the European Communities direct in accordance with Article 93(2) of the Treaty.

2.   If the Commission considers that the Member State concerned has not complied with a judgment of the Court of Justice of the European Communities, the Commission may pursue the matter in accordance with Article 171 of the Treaty.

CHAPTER VIII   COMMON PROVISIONS

Article 24   Professional secrecy

The Commission and the Member States, their officials and other servants, including independent experts appointed by the Commission, shall not disclose information which they have acquired through the application of this Regulation and which is covered by the obligation of professional secrecy.

Article 25   Addressee of decisions

Decisions taken pursuant to Chapters II, III, IV, V and VII shall be addressed to the Member State concerned. The Commission shall notify them to the Member State concerned without delay and give the latter the opportunity to indicate the Commission which information it considers to be covered by the obligation of professional secrecy.

Article 26   Publication of decisions

1.   The Commission shall publish in the Official Journal of the European Communities a summary notice of the decisions which it takes pursuant to Article 4(2) and (3) and Article 18 in conjunction with Article 19(1). The summary notice shall state that a copy of the decision may be obtained in the authentic language version or versions.

2.   The Commission shall publish in the Official Journal of the European Communities the decisions which it takes pursuant to Article 4(4) in their authentic language version. In the Official Journal published in languages other than the authentic language version, the authentic language version will be accompanied by a meaningful summary in the language of that Official Journal.

3.   The Commission shall publish in the Official Journal of the European Communities the decisions which it takes pursuant to Article 7.

4.   In cases where Article 4(6) or Article 8(2) applies, a short notice shall be published in the Official Journal of the European Communities.

5.   The Council, acting unanimously, may decide to publish decisions pursuant to the third subparagraph of Article 93(2) of the Treaty in the Official Journal of the European Communities.

Article 27   Implementing provisions

The Commission, acting in accordance with the procedure laid down in Article 29, shall have the power to adopt implementing provisions concerning the form, content and other details of notifications, the form, content and other details of annual reports, details of time-limits and the calculation of time-limits, and the interest rate referred to in Article 14(2).

Article 28   Advisory Committee on State aid

An Advisory Committee on State aid (hereinafter referred to as the 'Committee') shall be set up. It shall be composed of representatives of the Member States and chaired by the representative of the Commission.

Article 29   Consultation of the Committee

1.   The Commission shall consult the Committee before adopting any implementing provision pursuant to Article 27.

2.   Consultation of the Committee shall take place at a meeting called by the Commission. The drafts and documents to be examined shall be annexed to the notification. The meeting shall take place no earlier than two months after notification has been sent. This period may be reduced in the case of urgency.

3.   The Commission representative shall submit to the Committee a draft of the measures to be taken. The Committee shall deliver an opinion on the draft, within a time-limit which the chairman may lay down according to the urgency of the matter, if necessary by taking a vote.

4.   The opinion shall be recorded in the minutes; in addition, each Member State shall have the right to ask to have its position recorded in the minutes. The Committee may recommend the publication of this opinion in the Official Journal of the European Communities.

5.   The Commission shall take the utmost account of the opinion delivered by the Committee. It shall inform the Committee on the manner in which its opinion has been taken into account.

Article 30   Entry into force
This Regulation shall enter into force on the twentieth day following that of its publication in the Official Journal of the European Communities.

This Regulation shall be binding in its entirety and directly applicable in all Member States.
Done at Brussels, 22 March 1999.
For the Council
The President
G. VERHEUGEN

Commission Regulation (EC) No. 2790/1999 of 22 December 1999 on the application of Article 81(3) of the Treaty to categories of vertical agreements and concerted practices*
[OJ 1999, L336/21]

THE COMMISSION OF THE EUROPEAN COMMUNITIES,
   Having regard to the Treaty establishing the European Community,
   Having regard to Council Regulation No 19/65/EEC of 2 March 1965 on the application of Article 85(3) of the Treaty to certain categories of agreements and concerted practices,[1] as last amended by Regulation (EC) No 1215/1999,[2] and in particular Article 1 thereof,
   Having published a draft of this Regulation,[3]
   Having consulted the Advisory Committee on Restrictive Practices and Dominant Positions,
   Whereas:
   (1) Regulation No 19/65/EEC empowers the Commission to apply Article 81(3) of the Treaty (formerly Article 85(3)) by regulation to certain categories of vertical agreements and corresponding concerted practices falling within Article 81(1).
   (2) Experience acquired to date makes it possible to define a category of vertical agreements which can be regarded as normally satisfying the conditions laid down in Article 81(3).

---

* **Editor's Note:** As amended by the 2003 Accession Treaty (OJ 2003, L236/344).
[1] OJ 36, 6.3.1965, p. 533/65.
[2] OJ L 148, 15.6.1999, p. 1.
[3] OJ C 270, 24.9.1999, p. 7.

(3) This category includes vertical agreements for the purchase or sale of goods or services where these agreements are concluded between non-competing undertakings, between certain competitors or by certain associations of retailers of goods; it also includes vertical agreements containing ancillary provisions on the assignment or use of intellectual property rights; for the purposes of this Regulation, the term 'vertical agreements' includes the corresponding concerted practices.

(4) For the application of Article 81(3) by regulation, it is not necessary to define those vertical agreements which are capable of falling within Article 81(1); in the individual assessment of agreements under Article 81(1), account has to be taken of several factors, and in particular the market structure on the supply and purchase side.

(5) The benefit of the block exemption should be limited to vertical agreements for which it can be assumed with sufficient certainty that they satisfy the conditions of Article 81(3).

(6) Vertical agreements of the category defined in this Regulation can improve economic efficiency within a chain of production or distribution by facilitating better coordination between the participating undertakings; in particular, they can lead to a reduction in the transaction and distribution costs of the parties and to an optimisation of their sales and investment levels.

(7) The likelihood that such efficiency-enhancing effects will outweigh any anti-competitive effects due to restrictions contained in vertical agreements depends on the degree of market power of the undertakings concerned and, therefore, on the extent to which those undertakings face competition from other suppliers of goods or services regarded by the buyer as interchangeable or substitutable for one another, by reason of the products' characteristics, their prices and their intended use.

(8) It can be presumed that, where the share of the relevant market accounted for by the supplier does not exceed 30%, vertical agreements which do not contain certain types of severely anti-competitive restraints generally lead to an improvement in production or distribution and allow consumers a fair share of the resulting benefits; in the case of vertical agreements containing exclusive supply obligations, it is the market share of the buyer which is relevant in determining the overall effects of such vertical agreements on the market.

(9) Above the market share threshold of 30%, there can be no presumption that vertical agreements falling within the scope of Article 81(1) will usually give rise to objective advantages of such a character and size as to compensate for the disadvantages which they create for competition.

(10) This Regulation should not exempt vertical agreements containing restrictions which are not indispensable to the attainment of the positive effects mentioned above; in particular, vertical agreements containing certain types of severely anti-competitive restraints such as minimum and fixed resale-prices, as well as certain types of territorial protection, should be excluded from the benefit of the block exemption established by this Regulation irrespective of the market share of the undertakings concerned.

(11) In order to ensure access to or to prevent collusion on the relevant market, certain conditions are to be attached to the block exemption; to this end, the exemption of non-compete obligations should be limited to obligations which do not exceed a definite duration; for the same reasons, any direct or indirect obligation causing the members of a selective distribution system not to sell the brands of particular competing suppliers should be excluded from the benefit of this Regulation.

(12) The market-share limitation, the non-exemption of certain vertical agreements and the conditions provided for in this Regulation normally ensure that the agreements to which the block exemption applies do not enable the participating undertakings to eliminate competition in respect of a substantial part of the products in question.

(13) In particular cases in which the agreements falling under this Regulation nevertheless have effects incompatible with Article 81(3), the Commission may withdraw the benefit of the block exemption; this may occur in particular where the buyer has significant market

power in the relevant market in which it resells the goods or provides the services or where parallel networks of vertical agreements have similar effects which significantly restrict access to a relevant market or competition therein; such cumulative effects may for example arise in the case of selective distribution or non-compete obligations.

(14) Regulation No 19/65/EEC empowers the competent authorities of Member States to withdraw the benefit of the block exemption in respect of vertical agreements having effects incompatible with the conditions laid down in Article 81(3), where such effects are felt in their respective territory, or in a part thereof, and where such territory has the characteristics of a distinct geographic market;

Member States should ensure that the exercise of this power of withdrawal does not prejudice the uniform application throughout the common market of the Community competition rules or the full effect of the measures adopted in implementation of those rules.

(15) In order to strengthen supervision of parallel networks of vertical agreements which have similar restrictive effects and which cover more than 50% of a given market, the Commission may declare this Regulation inapplicable to vertical agreements containing specific restraints relating to the market concerned, thereby restoring the full application of Article 81 to such agreements.

(16) This Regulation is without prejudice to the application of Article 82.

(17) In accordance with the principle of the primacy of Community law, no measure taken pursuant to national laws on competition should prejudice the uniform application throughout the common market of the Community competition rules or the full effect of any measures adopted in implementation of those rules, including this Regulation,

HAS ADOPTED THIS REGULATION:

Article 1

For the purposes of this Regulation:

(a) 'competing undertakings' means actual or potential suppliers in the same product market; the product market includes goods or services which are regarded by the buyer as interchangeable with or substitutable for the contract goods or services, by reason of the products' characteristics, their prices and their intended use;

(b) 'non-compete obligation' means any direct or indirect obligation causing the buyer not to manufacture, purchase, sell or resell goods or services which compete with the contract goods or services, or any direct or indirect obligation on the buyer to purchase from the supplier or from another undertaking designated by the supplier more than 80% of the buyer's total purchases of the contract goods or services and their substitutes on the relevant market, calculated on the basis of the value of its purchases in the preceding calendar year;

(c) 'exclusive supply obligation' means any direct or indirect obligation causing the supplier to sell the goods or services specified in the agreement only to one buyer inside the Community for the purposes of a specific use or for resale;

(d) 'Selective distribution system' means a distribution system where the supplier undertakes to sell the contract goods or services, either directly or indirectly, only to distributors selected on the basis of specified criteria and where these distributors undertake not to sell such goods or services to unauthorised distributors;

(e) 'intellectual property rights' includes industrial property rights, copyright and neighbouring rights;

(f) 'know-how' means a package of non-patented practical information, resulting from experience and testing by the supplier, which is secret, substantial and identified: in this context, 'secret' means that the know-how, as a body or in the precise configuration and assembly of its components, is not generally known or easily accessible;

'substantial' means that the know-how includes information which is indispensable to the buyer for the use, sale or resale of the contract goods or services;

'identified' means that the know-how must be described in a sufficiently comprehensive manner so as to make it possible to verify that it fulfils the criteria of secrecy and substantiality;

(g) 'buyer' includes an undertaking which, under an agreement falling within Article 81(1) of the Treaty, sells goods or services on behalf of another undertaking.

Article 2

1. Pursuant to Article 81(3) of the Treaty and subject to the provisions of this Regulation, it is hereby declared that Article 81(1) shall not apply to agreements or concerted practices entered into between two or more undertakings each of which operates, for the purposes of the agreement, at a different level of the production or distribution chain, and relating to the conditions under which the parties may purchase, sell or resell certain goods or services ('vertical agreements').

This exemption shall apply to the extent that such agreements contain restrictions of competition falling within the scope of Article 81(1) ('vertical restraints').

2. The exemption provided for in paragraph 1 shall apply to vertical agreements entered into between an association of undertakings and its members, or between such an association and its suppliers, only if all its members are retailers of goods and if no individual member of the association, together with its connected undertakings, has a total annual turnover exceeding EUR 50 million; vertical agreements entered into by such associations shall be covered by this Regulation without prejudice to the application of Article 81 to horizontal agreements concluded between the members of the association or decisions adopted by the association.

3. The exemption provided for in paragraph 1 shall apply to vertical agreements containing provisions which relate to the assignment to the buyer or use by the buyer of intellectual property rights, provided that those provisions do not constitute the primary object of such agreements and are directly related to the use, sale or resale of goods or services by the buyer or its customers. The exemption applies on condition that, in relation to the contract goods or services, those provisions do not contain restrictions of competition having the same object or effect as vertical restraints which are not exempted under this Regulation.

4. The exemption provided for in paragraph 1 shall not apply to vertical agreements entered into between competing undertakings; however, it shall apply where competing undertakings enter into a non-reciprocal vertical agreement and:

(a) the buyer has a total annual turnover not exceeding EUR 100 million, or

(b) the supplier is a manufacturer and a distributor of goods, while the buyer is a distributor not manufacturing goods competing with the contract goods, or

(c) the supplier is a provider of services at several levels of trade, while the buyer does not provide competing services at the level of trade where it purchases the contract services.

5. This Regulation shall not apply to vertical agreements the subject matter of which falls within the scope of any other block exemption regulation.

Article 3

1. Subject to paragraph 2 of this Article, the exemption provided for in Article 2 shall apply on condition that the market share held by the supplier does not exceed 30% of the relevant market on which it sells the contract goods or services.

2. In the case of vertical agreements containing exclusive supply obligations, the exemption provided for in Article 2 shall apply on condition that the market share held by the buyer does not exceed 30% of the relevant market on which it purchases the contract goods or services.

Article 4

The exemption provided for in Article 2 shall not apply to vertical agreements which, directly or indirectly, in isolation or in combination with other factors under the control of the parties, have as their object:

(a) the restriction of the buyer's ability to determine its sale price, without prejudice to the possibility of the supplier's imposing a maximum sale price or recommending a sale price, provided that they do not amount to a fixed or minimum sale price as a result of pressure from, or incentives offered by, any of the parties;

(b) the restriction of the territory into which, or of the customers to whom, the buyer may sell the contract goods or services, except:
   — the restriction of active sales into the exclusive territory or to an exclusive customer group reserved to the supplier or allocated by the supplier to another buyer, where such a restriction does not limit sales by the customers of the buyer,
   — the restriction of sales to end users by a buyer operating at the wholesale level of trade,
   — the restriction of sales to unauthorised distributors by the members of a selective distribution system, and
   — the restriction of the buyer's ability to sell components, supplied for the purposes of incorporation, to customers who would use them to manufacture the same type of goods as those produced by the supplier;

(c) the restriction of active or passive sales to end users by members of a selective distribution system operating at the retail level of trade, without prejudice to the possibility of prohibiting a member of the system from operating out of an unauthorised place of establishment;

(d) the restriction of cross-supplies between distributors within a selective distribution system, including between distributors operating at different level of trade;

(e) the restriction agreed between a supplier of components and a buyer who incorporates those components, which limits the supplier to selling the components as spare parts to end-users or to repairers or other service providers not entrusted by the buyer with the repair or servicing of its goods.

Article 5

The exemption provided for in Article 2 shall not apply to any of the following obligations contained in vertical agreements:

(a) any direct or indirect non-compete obligation, the duration of which is indefinite or exceeds five years. A non-compete obligation which is tacitly renewable beyond a period of five years is to be deemed to have been concluded for an indefinite duration. However, the time limitation of five years shall not apply where the contract goods or services are sold by the buyer from premises and land owned by the supplier or leased by the supplier from third parties not connected with the buyer, provided that the duration of the noncompete obligation does not exceed the period of occupancy of the premises and land by the buyer;

(b) any direct or indirect obligation causing the buyer, after termination of the agreement, not to manufacture, purchase, sell or resell goods or services, unless such obligation:
   — relates to goods or services which compete with the contract goods or services, and
   — is limited to the premises and land from which the buyer has operated during the contract period, and
   — is indispensable to protect know-how transferred by the supplier to the buyer, and provided that the duration of such non-compete obligation is limited to a

period of one year after termination of the agreement; this obligation is without prejudice to the possibility of imposing a restriction which is unlimited in time on the use and disclosure of know-how which has not entered the public domain;

(c) any direct or indirect obligation causing the members of a selective distribution system not to sell the brands of particular competing suppliers.

Article 6

The Commission may withdraw the benefit of this Regulation, pursuant to Article 7(1) of Regulation No 19/65/EEC, where it finds in any particular case that vertical agreements to which this Regulation applies nevertheless have effects which are incompatible with the conditions laid down in Article 81(3) of the Treaty, and in particular where access to the relevant market or competition therein is significantly restricted by the cumulative effect of parallel networks of similar vertical restraints implemented by competing suppliers or buyers.

Article 7

Where in any particular case vertical agreements to which the exemption provided for in Article 2 applies have effects incompatible with the conditions laid down in Article 81(3) of the Treaty in the territory of a Member State, or in a part thereof, which has all the characteristics of a distinct geographic market, the competent authority of that Member State may withdraw the benefit of application of this Regulation in respect of that territory, under the same conditions as provided in Article 6.

Article 8

1.   Pursuant to Article 1a of Regulation No 19/65/EEC, the Commission may by regulation declare that, where parallel networks of similar vertical restraints cover more than 50% of a relevant market, this Regulation shall not apply to vertical agreements containing specific restraints relating to that market.

2.   A regulation pursuant to paragraph 1 shall not become applicable earlier than six months following its adoption.

Article 9

1.   The market share of 30% provided for in Article 3(1) shall be calculated on the basis of the market sales value of the contract goods or services and other goods or services sold by the supplier, which are regarded as interchangeable or substitutable by the buyer, by reason of the products' characteristics, their prices and their intended use; if market sales value data are not available, estimates based on other reliable market information, including market sales volumes, may be used to establish the market share of the undertaking concerned. For the purposes of Article 3(2), it is either the market purchase value or estimates thereof which shall be used to calculate the market share.

2.   For the purposes of applying the market share, the threshold provided for in Article 3 the following rules shall apply:

(a) the market share shall be calculated on the basis of data relating to the preceding calendar year;

(b) the market share shall include any goods or services supplied to integrated distributors for the purposes of sale;

(c) if the market share is initially not more than 30% but subsequently rises above that level without exceeding 35%, the exemption provided for in Article 2 shall continue to apply for a period of two consecutive calendar years following the year in which the 30% market share threshold was first exceeded;

(d) if the market share is initially not more than 30% but subsequently rises above 35%, the exemption provided for in Article 2 shall continue to apply for one calendar year following the year in which the level of 35% was first exceeded;

(e) the benefit of points (c) and (d) may not be combined so as to exceed a period of two calendar years.

Article 10

1. For the purpose of calculating total annual turnover within the meaning of Article 2(2) and (4), the turnover achieved during the previous financial year by the relevant party to the vertical agreement and the turnover achieved by its connected undertakings in respect of all goods and services, excluding all taxes and other duties, shall be added together. For this purpose, no account shall be taken of dealings between the party to the vertical agreement and its connected undertakings or between its connected undertakings.

2. The exemption provided for in Article 2 shall remain applicable where, for any period of two consecutive financial years, the total annual turnover threshold is exceeded by no more than 10%.

Article 11

1. For the purposes of this Regulation, the terms 'undertaking', 'supplier' and 'buyer' shall include their respective connected undertakings.

2. 'Connected undertakings' are:
   (a) undertakings in which a party to the agreement, directly or indirectly:
      — has the power to exercise more than half the voting rights, or
      — has the power to appoint more than half the members of the supervisory board, board of management or bodies legally representing the undertaking, or
      — has the right to manage the undertaking's affairs;
   (b) undertakings which directly or indirectly have, over a party to the agreement, the rights or powers listed in (a);
   (c) undertakings in which an undertaking referred to in (b) has, directly or indirectly, the rights or powers listed in (a);
   (d) undertakings in which a party to the agreement together with one or more of the undertakings referred to in (a), (b) or (c), or in which two or more of the latter undertakings, jointly have the rights or powers listed in (a);
   (e) undertakings in which the rights or the powers listed in (a) are jointly held by:
      — parties to the agreement or their respective connected undertakings referred to in (a) to (d), or
      — one or more of the parties to the agreement or one or more of their connected undertakings referred to in (a) to (d) and one or more third parties.

3. For the purposes of Article 3, the market share held by the undertakings referred to in paragraph 2(e) of this Article shall be apportioned equally to each undertaking having the rights or the powers listed in paragraph 2(a).

Article 12

1. The exemptions provided for in Commission Regulations (EEC) No 1983/83,[4] (EEC) No 1984/83[5] and (EEC) No 4087/88[6] shall continue to apply until 31 May 2000.

2. The prohibition laid down in Article 81(1) of the EC Treaty shall not apply during the period from 1 June 2000 to 31 December 2001 in respect of agreements already in force on 31 May 2000 which do not satisfy the conditions for exemption provided for in this Regulation but which satisfy the conditions for exemption provided for in Regulations (EEC) No 1983/83, (EEC) No 1984/83 or (EEC) No 4087/88.

Article 12a

The prohibition in Article 81(1) of the Treaty shall not apply to agreements which were in existence at the date of accession of the Czech Republic, Estonia, Cyprus, Latvia, Lithuania,

---

[4] OJ L 173, 30.6.1983, p. 1.
[5] OJ L 173, 30.6.1983, p. 5.
[6] OJ L 359, 28.12.1988, p. 46.

Hungary, Malta, Poland, Slovenia and Slovakia and which, by reason of accession, fall within the scope of Article 81(1) if, within six months from the date of accession, they are so amended that they comply with the conditions laid down in this Regulation.

Article 13

This Regulation shall enter into force on 1 January 2000.

It shall apply from 1 June 2000, except for Article 12(1) which shall apply from 1 January 2000.

This Regulation shall expire on 31 May 2010.

This Regulation shall be binding in its entirety and directly applicable in all Member States.

Done at Brussels, 22 December 1999.

For the Commission

Mario MONTI

Member of the Commission

Commission Regulation (EC) No. 2658/2000 of 29 November 2000 on the application of Article 81(3) of the Treaty to categories of specialisation agreements

[OJ 2000, L304/3]*

THE COMMISSION OF THE EUROPEAN COMMUNITIES,

Having regard to the Treaty establishing the European Community,

Having regard to Council Regulation (EEC) No 2821/71 of 20 December 1971 on the application of Article 85(3) of the Treaty to categories of agreements, decisions and concerted practices,[1] as last amended by the Act of Accession of Austria, Finland and Sweden, and in particular Article 1(1)(c) thereof,

Having published a draft of this Regulation,[2]

Having consulted the Advisory Committee on Restrictive Practices and Dominant Positions,

Whereas:

(1) Regulation (EEC) No 2821/71 empowers the Commission to apply Article 81(3) (formerly Article 85(3)) of the Treaty by regulation to certain categories of agreements, decisions and concerted practices falling within the scope of Article 81(1) which have as their object specialisation, including agreements necessary for achieving it.

(2) Pursuant to Regulation (EEC) No 2821/71, in particular, the Commission has adopted Regulation (EEC) No 417/85 of 19 December 1984 on the application of Article 85(3) of the Treaty to categories of specialisation agreements,[3] as last amended by Regulation (EC) No 2236/97.[4] Regulation (EEC) No 417/85 expires on 31 December 2000.

(3) A new regulation should meet the two requirements of ensuring effective protection of competition and providing adequate legal security for undertakings. The pursuit of these objectives should take account of the need to simplify administrative supervision and the legislative framework to as great an extent as possible. Below a certain level of market power it can, for the application of Article 81(3), in general be presumed that the positive effects of specialisation agreements will outweigh any negative effects on competition.

(4) Regulation (EEC) No 2821/71 requires the exempting regulation of the Commission to define the categories of agreements, decisions and concerted practices to which it applies,

---

* **Editor's Note**: As amended by the 2003 Accession Treaty (OJ 2003, L236/344).

[1] OJ L 285, 29.12.1971, p. 46.

[2] OJ C 118, 27.4.2000, p. 3.

[3] OJ L 53, 22.2.1985, p. 1.

[4] OJ L 306, 11.11.1997, p. 12.

to specify the restrictions or clauses which may, or may not, appear in the agreements, decisions and concerted practices, and to specify the clauses which must be contained in the agreements, decisions and concerted practices or the other conditions which must be satisfied.

(5) It is appropriate to move away from the approach of listing exempted clauses and to place greater emphasis on defining the categories of agreements which are exempted up to a certain level of market power and on specifying the restrictions or clauses which are not to be contained in such agreements. This is consistent with an economics-based approach which assesses the impact of agreements on the relevant market.

(6) For the application of Article 81(3) by regulation, it is not necessary to define those agreements which are capable of falling within Article 81(1). In the individual assessment of agreements under Article 81(1), account has to be taken of several factors, and in particular the market structure on the relevant market.

(7) The benefit of the block exemption should be limited to those agreements for which it can be assumed with sufficient certainty that they satisfy the conditions of Article 81(3).

(8) Agreements on specialisation in production generally contribute to improving the production or distribution of goods, because the undertakings concerned can concentrate on the manufacture of certain products and thus operate more efficiently and supply the products more cheaply. Agreements on specialisation in the provision of services can also be said to generally give rise to similar improvements. It is likely that, given effective competition, consumers will receive a fair share of the resulting benefit.

(9) Such advantages can arise equally from agreements whereby one participant gives up the manufacture of certain products or provision of certain services in favour of another participant ('unilateral specialisation'), from agreements whereby each participant gives up the manufacture of certain products or provision of certain services in favour of another participant ('reciprocal specialisation') and from agreements whereby the participants undertake to jointly manufacture certain products or provide certain services ('joint production').

(10) As unilateral specialisation agreements between non-competitors may benefit from the block exemption provided by Commission Regulation (EC) No 2790/1999 of 22 December 1999 on the application of Article 81(3) of the Treaty to categories of vertical agreements and concerted practices,[5] the application of the present Regulation to unilateral specialisation agreements should be limited to agreements between competitors.

(11) All other agreements entered into between undertakings relating to the conditions under which they specialise in the production of goods and/or services should fall within the scope of this Regulation. The block exemption should also apply to provisions contained in specialisation agreements which do not constitute the primary object of such agreements, but are directly related to and necessary for their implementation, and to certain related purchasing and marketing arrangements.

(12) To ensure that the benefits of specialisation will materialise without one party leaving the market downstream of production, unilateral and reciprocal specialisation agreements should only be covered by this Regulation where they provide for supply and purchase obligations. These obligations may, but do not have to, be of an exclusive nature.

(13) It can be presumed that, where the participating undertakings' share of the relevant market does not exceed 20%, specialisation agreements as defined in this Regulation will, as a general rule, give rise to economic benefits in the form of economies of scale or scope or better production technologies, while allowing consumers a fair share of the resulting benefits.

(14) This Regulation should not exempt agreements containing restrictions which are not indispensable to attain the positive effects mentioned above. In principle certain severe anti-competitive restraints relating to the fixing of prices charged to third parties, limitation of output or sales, and allocation of markets or customers should be excluded from the benefit

---

[5] OJ L 336, 29.12.1999, p. 21.

of the block exemption established by this Regulation irrespective of the market share of the undertakings concerned.

(15) The market share limitation, the non-exemption of certain agreements and the conditions provided for in this Regulation normally ensure that the agreements to which the block exemption applies do not enable the participating undertakings to eliminate competition in respect of a substantial part of the products or services in question.

(16) In particular cases in which the agreements falling under this Regulation neverthe-less have effects incompatible with Article 81(3) of the Treaty, the Commission may withdraw the benefit of the block exemption.

(17) In order to facilitate the conclusion of specialisation agreements, which can have a bearing on the structure of the participating undertakings, the period of validity of this Regulation should be fixed at 10 years.

(18) This Regulation is without prejudice to the application of Article 82 of the Treaty.

(19) In accordance with the principle of the primacy of Community law, no measure taken pursuant to national laws on competition should prejudice the uniform application throughout the common market of the Community competition rules or the full effect of any measures adopted in implementation of those rules, including this Regulation,

HAS ADOPTED THIS REGULATION:

Article 1 Exemption

1. Pursuant to Article 81(3) of the Treaty and subject to the provisions of this Regulation, it is hereby declared that Article 81(1) shall not apply to the following agreements entered into between two or more undertakings (hereinafter referred to as 'the parties') which relate to the conditions under which those undertakings specialise in the production of products (hereinafter referred to as 'specialisation agreements'):

   (a) unilateral specialisation agreements, by virtue of which one party agrees to cease production of certain products or to refrain from producing those products and to purchase them from a competing undertaking, while the competing undertaking agrees to produce and supply those products; or

   (b) reciprocal specialisation agreements, by virtue of which two or more parties on a reciprocal basis agree to cease or refrain from producing certain but different products and to purchase these products from the other parties, who agree to supply them; or

   (c) joint production agreements, by virtue of which two or more parties agree to produce certain products jointly.

This exemption shall apply to the extent that such specialisation agreements contain restrictions of competition falling within the scope of Article 81(1) of the Treaty.

2. The exemption provided for in paragraph 1 shall also apply to provisions contained in specialisation agreements, which do not constitute the primary object of such agreements, but are directly related to and necessary for their implementation, such as those concerning the assignment or use of intellectual property rights.

The first sub-paragraph does, however, not apply to provisions which have the same object as the restrictions of competition enumerated in Article 5(1).

Article 2 Definitions

For the purposes of this Regulation:

1. 'Agreement' means an agreement, a decision of an association of undertakings or a concerted practice.

2. 'Participating undertakings' means undertakings party to the agreement and their respective connected undertakings.

3. 'Connected undertakings' means:

   (a) undertakings in which a party to the agreement, directly or indirectly:

        (i)   has the power to exercise more than half the voting rights, or

        (ii) has the power to appoint more than half the members of the supervisory board, board of management or bodies legally representing the undertaking, or

        (iii) has the right to manage the undertaking's affairs;

    (b) undertakings which directly or indirectly have, over a party to the agreement, the rights or powers listed in (a);

    (c) undertakings in which an undertaking referred to in (b) has, directly or indirectly, the rights or powers listed in (a);

    (d) undertakings in which a party to the agreement together with one or more of the undertakings referred to in (a), (b) or (c), or in which two or more of the latter undertakings, jointly have the rights or powers listed in (a);

    (e) undertakings in which the rights or the powers listed in (a) are jointly held by:

        (i)   parties to the agreement or their respective connected undertakings referred to in (a) to (d), or

        (ii) one or more of the parties to the agreement or one or more of their connected undertakings referred to in (a) to (d) and one or more third parties.

4.   'Product' means a good and/or a service, including both intermediary goods and/or services and final goods and/or services, with the exception of distribution and rental services.

5.   'Production' means the manufacture of goods or the provision of services and includes production by way of subcontracting.

6.   'Relevant market' means the relevant product and geographic market(s) to which the products, which are the subject matter of a specialisation agreement, belong.

7.   'Competing undertaking' means an undertaking that is active on the relevant market (an actual competitor) or an undertaking that would, on realistic grounds, undertake the necessary additional investments or other necessary switching costs so that it could enter the relevant market in response to a small and permanent increase in relative prices (a potential competitor).

8.   'Exclusive supply obligation' means an obligation not to supply a competing undertaking other than a party to the agreement with the product to which the specialisation agreement relates.

9.   'Exclusive purchase obligation' means an obligation to purchase the product to which the specialisation agreement relates only from the party which agrees to supply it.

Article 3   Purchasing and marketing arrangements

The exemption provided for in Article 1 shall also apply where:

    (a) the parties accept an exclusive purchase and/or exclusive supply obligation in the context of a unilateral or reciprocal specialisation agreement or a joint production agreement, or

    (b) the parties do not sell the products which are the object of the specialisation agreement independently but provide for joint distribution or agree to appoint a third party distributor on an exclusive or non-exclusive basis in the context of a joint production agreement provided that the third party is not a competing undertaking.

Article 4   Market share threshold

The exemption provided for in Article 1 shall apply on condition that the combined market share of the participating undertakings does not exceed 20% of the relevant market.

Article 5   Agreements not covered by the exemption

1.   The exemption provided for in Article 1 shall not apply to agreements which, directly or indirectly, in isolation or in combination with other factors under the control of the parties, have as their object:

    (a) the fixing of prices when selling the products to third parties;

    (b) the limitation of output or sales; or

    (c) the allocation of markets or customers.

  2. Paragraph 1 shall not apply to:

    (a) provisions on the agreed amount of products in the context of unilateral or recipro-cal specialisation agreements or the setting of the capacity and production volume of a production joint venture in the context of a joint production agreement;

    (b) the setting of sales targets and the fixing of prices that a production joint venture charges to its immediate customers in the context of point (b) of Article 3.

Article 6   Application of the market share threshold

  1. For the purposes of applying the market share threshold provided for in Article 4 the following rules shall apply:

    (a) the market share shall be calculated on the basis of the market sales value; if market sales value data are not available, estimates based on other reliable market information, including market sales volumes, may be used to establish the market share of the undertaking concerned;

    (b) the market share shall be calculated on the basis of data relating to the preceding calendar year;

    (c) the market share held by the undertakings referred to in point 3(e) of Article 2 shall be apportioned equally to each undertaking having the rights or the powers listed in point 3(a) of Article 2.

  2. If the market share referred to in Article 4 is initially not more than 20% but sub-sequently rises above this level without exceeding 25%, the exemption provided for in Article 1 shall continue to apply for a period of two consecutive calendar years following the year in which the 20% threshold was first exceeded.

  3. If the market share referred to in Article 4 is initially not more than 20% but sub-sequently rises above 25%, the exemption provided for in Article 1 shall continue to apply for one calendar year following the year in which the level of 25% was first exceeded.

  4. The benefit of paragraphs 2 and 3 may not be combined so as to exceed a period of two calendar years.

Article 7   Withdrawal

The Commission may withdraw the benefit of this Regulation, pursuant to Article 7 of Regulation (EEC) No 2821/71, where, either on its own initiative or at the request of a Member State or of a natural or legal person claiming a legitimate interest, it finds in a particular case that an agreement to which the exemption provided for in Article 1 applies nevertheless has effects which are incompatible with the conditions laid down in Article 81(3) of the Treaty, and in particular where:

    (a) the agreement is not yielding significant results in terms of rationalisation or consumers are not receiving a fair share of the resulting benefit, or

    (b) the products which are the subject of the specialisation are not subject in the common market or a substantial part thereof to effective competition from identi-cal products or products considered by users to be equivalent in view of their characteristics, price and intended use.

Article 8   Transitional period

The prohibition laid down in Article 81(1) of the Treaty shall not apply during the period from 1 January 2001 to 30 June 2002 in respect of agreements already in force on 31 December 2000 which do not satisfy the conditions for exemption provided for in this Regulation but which satisfy the conditions for exemption provided for in Regulation (EEC) No 417/85.

Article 8a

The prohibition in Article 81(1) of the Treaty shall not apply to agreements which were in existence at the date of accession of the Czech Republic, Estonia, Cyprus, Latvia, Lithuania,

Hungary, Malta, Poland, Slovenia and Slovakia and which, by reason of accession, fall within the scope of Article 81(1) if, within six months from the date of accession, they are so amended that they comply with the conditions laid down in this Regulation.

Article 9   Period of validity
This Regulation shall enter into force on 1 January 2001.

It shall expire on 31 December 2010.

This Regulation shall be binding in its entirety and directly applicable in all Member States.

Done at Brussels, 29 November 2000.

For the Commission
Mario MONTI
Member of the Commission

Commission Regulation (EC) No. 2659/2000 of 29 November 2000 on the application of Article 81(3) of the Treaty to categories of research and development agreements*

[OJ 2000, L304/7]

THE COMMISSION OF THE EUROPEAN COMMUNITIES,

Having regard to the Treaty establishing the European Community,

Having regard to Council Regulation (EEC) No 2821/71 of 20 December 1971 on application of Article 85(3) of the Treaty to categories of agreements, decisions and concerted practices,[1] as last amended by the Act of Accession of Austria, Finland and Sweden, and in particular Article 1(1)(b) thereof,

Having published a draft of this Regulation,[2]

Having consulted the Advisory Committee on Restrictive Practices and Dominant Positions,

Whereas:

(1) Regulation (EEC) No 2821/71 empowers the Commission to apply Article 81(3) (formerly Article 85(3)) of the Treaty by regulation to certain categories of agreements, decisions and concerted practices falling within the scope of Article 81(1) which have as their object the research and development of products or processes up to the stage of industrial application, and exploitation of the results, including provisions regarding intellectual property rights.

(2) Article 163(2) of the Treaty calls upon the Community to encourage undertakings, including small and medium-sized undertakings, in their research and technological development activities of high quality, and to support their efforts to cooperate with one another. Pursuant to Council Decision 1999/65/EC of 22 December 1998 concerning the rules for the participation of undertakings, research centres and universities and for the dissemination of research results for the implementation of the fifth framework programme of the European Community (1998–2002)[3] and Commission Regulation (EC) No 996/1999[4] on the implementation of Decision 1999/65/EC, indirect research and technological

---

* **Editor's Note**: As amended by the 2003 Accession Treaty (OJ 2003, L236/344).
[1] OJ L 285, 29.12.1971, p. 46.
[2] OJ C 118, 27.4.2000, p. 3.
[3] OJ L 26, 1.2.1999, p. 46.
[4] OJ L 122, 12.5.1999, p. 9.

development (RTD) actions suppported under the fifth framework programme of the Community are required to be carried out cooperatively.

(3) Agreements on the joint execution of research work or the joint development of the results of the research, up to but not including the stage of industrial application, generally do not fall within the scope of Article 81(1) of the Treaty. In certain circumstances, however, such as where the parties agree not to carry out other research and development in the same field, thereby forgoing the opportunity of gaining competitive advantages over the other parties, such agreements may fall within Article 81(1) and should therefore be included within the scope of this Regulation.

(4) Pursuant to Regulation (EEC) No 2821/71, the Commission has, in particular, adopted Regulation (EEC) No 418/85 of 19 December 1984 on the application of Article 85(3) of the Treaty to categories of research and development agreements,[5] as last amended by Regulation (EC) No 2236/97.[6] Regulation (EEC) No 418/85 expires on 31 December 2000.

(5) A new regulation should meet the two requirements of ensuring effective protection of competition and providing adequate legal security for undertakings. The pursuit of these objectives should take account of the need to simplify administrative supervision and the legislative framework to as great an extent possible. Below a certain level of market power it can, for the application of Article 81(3), in general be presumed that the positive effects of research and development agreements will outweigh any negative effects on competition.

(6) Regulation (EEC) No 2821/71 requires the exempting regulation of the Commission to define the categories of agreements, decisions and concerted practices to which it applies, to specify the restrictions or clauses which may, or may not, appear in the agreements, decisions and concerted practices, and to specify the clauses which must be contained in the agreements, decisions and concerted practices or the other conditions which must be satisfied.

(7) It is appropriate to move away from the approach of listing exempted clauses and to place greater emphasis on defining the categories of agreements which are exempted up to a certain level of market power and on specifying the restrictions or clauses which are not to be contained in such agreements. This is consistent with an economics based approach which assesses the impact of agreements on the relevant market.

(8) For the application of Article 81(3) by regulation, it is not necessary to define those agreements which are capable of falling within Article 81(1). In the individual assessment of agreements under Article 81(1), account has to be taken of several factors, and in particular the market structure on the relevant market.

(9) The benefit of the block exemption should be limited to those agreements for which it can be assumed with sufficient certainty that they satisfy the conditions of Article 81(3).

(10) Cooperation in research and development and in the exploitation of the results generally promotes technical and economic progress by increasing the dissemination of know-how between the parties and avoiding duplication of research and development work, by stimulating new advances through the exchange of complementary know-how, and by rationalising the manufacture of the products or application of the processes arising out of the research and development.

(11) The joint exploitation of results can be considered as the natural consequence of joint research and development. It can take different forms such as manufacture, the exploitation of intellectual property rights that substantially contribute to technical or economic progress, or the marketing of new products.

(12) Consumers can generally be expected to benefit from the increased volume and effectiveness of research and development through the introduction of new or improved products or services or the reduction of prices brought about by new or improved processes.

(13) In order to attain the benefits and objectives of joint research and development

[5] OJ L 53, 22.2.1985, p. 5.
[6] OJ L 306, 11.11.1997, p. 12.

the benefit of this Regulation should also apply to provisions contained in research and development agreements which do not constitute the primary object of such agreements, but are directly related to and necessary for their implementation.

(14) In order to justify the exemption, the joint exploitation should relate to products or processes for which the use of the results of the research and development is decisive, and each of the parties is given the opportunity of exploiting any results that interest it. However, where academic bodies, research institutes or undertakings which supply research and development as a commercial service without normally being active in the exploitation of results participate in research and development, they may agree to use the results of research and development solely for the purpose of further research. Similarly, non-competitors may agree to limit their right to exploitation to one or more technical fields of application to facilitate cooperation between parties with complementary skills.

(15) The exemption granted under this Regulation should be limited to research and development agreements which do not afford the undertakings the possibility of eliminating competition in respect of a substantial part of the products or services in question. It is necessary to exclude from the block exemption agreements between competitors whose combined share of the market for products or services capable of being improved or replaced by the results of the research and development exceeds a certain level at the time the agreement is entered into.

(16) In order to guarantee the maintenance of effective competition during joint exploitation of the results, provision should be made for the block exemption to cease to apply if the parties' combined share of the market for the products arising out of the joint research and development becomes too great. The exemption should continue to apply, irrespective of the parties' market shares, for a certain period after the commencement of joint exploitation, so as to await stabilisation of their market shares, particularly after the introduction of an entirely new product, and to guarantee a minimum period of return on the investments involved.

(17) This Regulation should not exempt agreements containing restrictions which are not indispensable to attain the positive effects mentioned above. In principle certain severe anti-competitive restraints such as limitations on the freedom of parties to carry out research and development in a field unconnected to the agreement, the fixing of prices charged to third parties, limitations on output or sales, allocation of markets or customers, and limitations on effecting passive sales for the contract products in territories reserved for other parties should be excluded from the benefit of the block exemption established by this Regulation irrespective of the market share of the undertakings concerned.

(18) The market share limitation, the non-exemption of certain agreements, and the conditions provided for in this Regulation normally ensure that the agreements to which the block exemption applies do not enable the participating undertakings to eliminate competition in respect of a substantial part of the products or services in question.

(19) In particular cases in which the agreements falling under this Regulation nevertheless have effects incompatible with Article 81(3) of the Treaty, the Commission may withdraw the benefit of the block exemption.

(20) Agreements between undertakings which are not competing manufacturers of products capable of being improved or replaced by the results of the research and development will only eliminate effective competition in research and development in exceptional circumstances. It is therefore appropriate to enable such agreements to benefit from the block exemption irrespective of market share and to address such exceptional cases by way of withdrawal of its benefit.

(21) As research and development agreements are often of a long-term nature, especially where the cooperation extends to the exploitation of the results, the period of validity of this Regulation should be fixed at 10 years.

(22) This Regulation is without prejudice to the application of Article 82 of the Treaty.

(23) In accordance with the principle of the primacy of Community law, no measure

taken pursuant to national laws on competition should prejudice the uniform application throughout the common market of the Community competition rules or the full effect of any measures adopted in implementation of those rules, including this Regulation,

HAS ADOPTED THIS REGULATION:

Article 1   Exemption

1.   Pursuant to Article 81(3) of the Treaty and subject to the provisions of this Regulation, it is hereby declared that Article 81(1) shall not apply to agreements entered into between two or more undertakings (hereinafter referred to as 'the parties') which relate to the conditions under which those undertakings pursue:

  (a) joint research and development of products or processes and joint exploitation of the results of that research and development;
  (b) joint exploitation of the results of research and development of products or processes jointly carried out pursuant to a prior agreement between the same parties; or
  (c) joint research and development of products or processes excluding joint exploitation of the results.

This exemption shall apply to the extent that such agreements (hereinafter referred to as 'research and development agreements') contain restrictions of competition falling within the scope of Article 81(1).

2.   The exemption provided for in paragraph 1 shall also apply to provisions contained in research and development agreements which do not constitute the primary object of such agreements, but are directly related to and necessary for their implementation, such as an obligation not to carry out, independently or together with third parties, research and development in the field to which the agreement relates or in a closely connected field during the execution of the agreement.

The first sub-paragraph does, however, not apply to provisions which have the same object as the restrictions of competition enumerated in Article 5(1).

Article 2   Definitions

For the purposes of this Regulation:

1.   'agreement' means an agreement, a decision of an association of undertakings or a concerted practice;

2.   'participating undertakings' means undertakings party to the research and development agreement and their respective connected undertakings;

3.   'connected undertakings' means:

  (a) undertakings in which a party to the research and development agreement, directly or indirectly:
    (i)   has the power to exercise more than half the voting rights,
    (ii) has the power to appoint more than half the members of the supervisory board, board of management or bodies legally representing the undertaking, or
    (iii) has the right to manage the undertaking's affairs;
  (b) undertakings which directly or indirectly have, over a party to the research and development agreement, the rights or powers listed in (a);
  (c) undertakings in which an undertaking referred to in (b) has, directly or indirectly, the rights or powers listed in (a);
  (d) undertakings in which a party to the research and development agreement together with one or more of the undertakings referred to in (a), (b) or (c), or in which two or more of the latter undertakings, jointly have the rights or powers listed in (a);

(e) undertakings in which the rights or the powers listed in (a) are jointly held by:

    (i) parties to the research and development agreement or their respective connected undertakings referred to in (a) to (d), or

    (ii) one or more of the parties to the research and development agreement or one or more of their connected undertakings referred to in (a) to (d) and one or more third parties;

4. 'research and development' means the acquisition of know-how relating to products or processes and the carrying out of theoretical analysis, systematic study or experimentation, including experimental production, technical testing of products or processes, the establishment of the necessary facilities and the obtaining of intellectual property rights for the results;

5. 'product' means a good and/or a service, including both intermediary goods and/or services and final goods and/or services;

6. 'contract process' means a technology or process arising out of the joint research and development;

7. 'contract product' means a product arising out of the joint research and development or manufactured or provided applying the contract processes;

8. 'exploitation of the results' means the production or distribution of the contract products or the application of the contract processes or the assignment or licensing of intellectual property rights or the communication of know-how required for such manufacture or application;

9. 'intellectual property rights' includes industrial property-rights, copyright and neighbouring rights;

10. 'know-how' means a package of non-patented practical information, resulting from experience and testing, which is secret, substantial and identified: in this context, 'secret' means that the know-how is not generally known or easily accessible; 'substantial' means that the know-how includes information which is indispensable for the manufacture of the contract products or the application of the contract processes; 'identified' means that the know-how is described in a sufficiently comprehensive manner so as to make it possible to verify that it fulfils the criteria of secrecy and substantiality;

11. research and development, or exploitation of the results, are carried out 'jointly' where the work involved is:

    (a) carried out by a joint team, organisation or undertaking,

    (b) jointly entrusted to a third party, or

    (c) allocated between the parties by way of specialisation in research, development, production or distribution;

12. 'competing undertaking' means an undertaking that is supplying a product capable of being improved or replaced by the contract product (an actual competitor) or an undertaking that would, on realistic grounds, undertake the necessary additional investments or other necessary switching costs so that it could supply such a product in response to a small and permanent increase in relative prices (a potential competitor);

13. 'relevant market for the contract products' means the relevant product and geographic market(s) to which the contract products belong.

Article 3 Conditions for exemption

1. The exemption provided for in Article 1 shall apply subject to the conditions set out in paragraphs 2 to 5.

2. All the parties must have access to the results of the joint research and development for the purposes of further research or exploitation. However, research institutes, academic bodies, or undertakings which supply research and development as a commercial service without normally being active in the exploitation of results may agree to confine their use of the results for the purposes of further research.

3.   Without prejudice to paragraph 2, where the research and development agreement provides only for joint research and development, each party must be free independently to exploit the results of the joint research and development and any pre-existing know-how necessary for the purposes of such exploitation. Such right to exploitation may be limited to one or more technical fields of application, where the parties are not competing undertakings at the time the research and development agreement is entered into.

4.   Any joint exploitation must relate to results which are protected by intellectual property rights or constitute know-how, which substantially contribute to technical or economic progress and the results must be decisive for the manufacture of the contract products or the application of the contract processes.

5.   Undertakings charged with manufacture by way of specialisation in production must be required to fulfil orders for supplies from all the parties, except where the research and development agreement also provides for joint distribution.

Article 4   Market share threshold and duration of exemption

1.   Where the participating undertakings are not competing undertakings, the exemption provided for in Article 1 shall apply for the duration of the research and development. Where the results are jointly exploited, the exemption shall continue to apply for seven years from the time the contract products are first put on the market within the common market.

2.   Where two or more of the participating undertakings are competing undertakings, the exemption provided for in Article 1 shall apply for the period referred to in paragraph 1 only if, at the time the research and development agreement is entered into, the combined market share of the participating undertakings does not exceed 25% of the relevant market for the products capable of being improved or replaced by the contract products.

3.   After the end of the period referred to in paragraph 1, the exemption shall continue to apply as long as the combined market share of the participating undertakings does not exceed 25% of the relevant market for the contract products.

Article 5   Agreements not covered by the exemption

1.   The exemption provided for in Article 1 shall not apply to research and development agreements which, directly or indirectly, in isolation or in combination with other factors under the control of the parties, have as their object:

(a) the restriction of the freedom of the participating undertakings to carry out research and development independently or in cooperation with third parties in a field unconnected with that to which the research and development relates or, after its completion, in the field to which it relates or in a connected field;

(b) the prohibition to challenge after completion of the research and development the validity of intellectual property rights which the parties hold in the common market and which are relevant to the research and development or, after the expiry of the research and development agreement, the validity of intellectual property rights which the parties hold in the common market and which protect the results of the research and development, without prejudice to the possibility to provide for termination of the research and development agreement in the event of one of the parties challenging the validity of such intellectual property rights;

(c) the limitation of output or sales;

(d) the fixing of prices when selling the contract product to third parties;

(e) the restriction of the customers that the participating undertakings may serve, after the end of seven years from the time the contract products are first put on the market within the common market;

(f) the prohibition to make passive sales of the contract products in territories reserved for other parties;

    (g) the prohibition to put the contract products on the market or to pursue an active sales policy for them in territories within the common market that are reserved for other parties after the end of seven years from the time the contract products are first put on the market within the common market;

    (h) the requirement not to grant licences to third parties to manufacture the contract products or to apply the contract processes where the exploitation by at least one of the parties of the results of the joint research and development is not provided for or does not take place;

    (i) the requirement to refuse to meet demand from users or resellers in their respective territories who would market the contract products in other territories within the common market; or

    (j) the requirement to make it difficult for users or resellers to obtain the contract products from other resellers within the common market, and in particular to exercise intellectual property rights or take measures so as to prevent users or resellers from obtaining, or from putting on the market within the common market, products which have been lawfully put on the market within the Community by another party or with its consent.

2.   Paragraph 1 shall not apply to:

    (a) the setting of production targets where the exploitation of the results includes the joint production of the contract products;

    (b) the setting of sales targets and the fixing of prices charged to immediate customers where the exploitation of the results includes the joint distribution of the contract products.

Article 6   Application of the market share threshold

1.   For the purposes of applying the market share threshold provided for in Article 4 the following rules shall apply:

    (a) the market share shall be calculated on the basis of the market sales value; if market sales value data are not available, estimates based on other reliable market information, including market sales volumes, may be used to establish the market share of the undertaking concerned;

    (b) the market share shall be calculated on the basis of data relating to the preceding calendar year;

    (c) the market share held by the undertakings referred to in point 3(e) of Article 2 shall be apportioned equally to each undertaking having the rights or the powers listed in point 3(a) of Article 2.

2.   If the market share referred to in Article 4(3) is initially not more than 25% but subsequently rises above this level without exceeding 30%, the exemption provided for in Article 1 shall continue to apply for a period of two consecutive calendar years following the year in which the 25% threshold was first exceeded.

3.   If the market share referred to in Article 4(3) is initially not more than 25% but subsequently rises above 30%, the exemption provided for in Article 1 shall continue to apply for one calendar year following the year in which the level of 30% was first exceeded.

4.   The benefit of paragraphs 2 and 3 may not be combined so as to exceed a period of two calendar years.

Article 7   Withdrawal

The Commission may withdraw the benefit of this Regulation, pursuant to Article 7 of Regulation (EEC) No 2821/71, where, either on its own initiative or at the request of a Member State or of a natural or legal person claiming a legitimate interest, it finds in a particular case that a research and development agreement to which the exemption provided for in Article 1 applies nevertheless has effects which are incompatible with the conditions laid down in Article 81(3) of the Treaty, and in particular where:

(a) the existence of the research and development agreement substantially restricts the scope for third parties to carry out research and development in the relevant field because of the limited research capacity available elsewhere;

(b) because of the particular structure of supply, the existence of the research and development agreement substantially restricts the access of third parties to the market for the contract products;

(c) without any objectively valid reason, the parties do not exploit the results of the joint research and development;

(d) the contract products are not subject in the whole or a substantial part of the common market to effective competition from identical products or products considered by users as equivalent in view of their characteristics, price and intended use;

(e) the existence of the research and development agreement would eliminate effective competition in research and development on a particular market.

Article 8   Transitional period

The prohibition laid down in Article 81(1) of the Treaty shall not apply during the period from 1 January 2001 to 30 June 2002 in respect of agreements already in force on 31 December 2000 which do not satisfy the conditions for exemption provided for in this Regulation but which satisfy the conditions for exemption provided for in Regulation (EEC) No 418/85.

Article 8a

The prohibition in Article 81(1) of the Treaty shall not apply to agreements which were in existence at the date of accession of the Czech Republic, Estonia, Cyprus, Latvia, Lithuania, Hungary, Malta, Poland, Slovenia and Slovakia and which, by reason of accession, fall within the scope of Article 81(1) if, within six months from the date of accession, they are so amended that they comply with the conditions laid down in this Regulation.

Article 9   Period of validity

This Regulation shall enter into force on 1 January 2001.

It shall expire on 31 December 2010.

This Regulation shall be binding in its entirety and directly applicable in all Member States.

Done at Brussels, 29 November 2000.

For the Commission
Mario MONTI
Member of the Commission

Commission Notice on the definition of relevant market for the purposes of Community competition law

[OJ 1997, C372/5]*

I.   INTRODUCTION

1.   The purpose of this notice is to provide guidance as to how the Commission applies the concept of relevant product and geographic market in its ongoing enforcement of Community competition law, in particular the application of Council Regulation No 17 and (EEC) No 4064/89, their equivalents in other sectoral applications such as transport, coal and

steel, and agriculture, and the relevant provisions of the EEA Agreement ([1]). Throughout this notice, references to Articles 85 and 86 of the Treaty and to merger control are to be understood as referring to the equivalent provisions in the EEA Agreement and the ECSC Treaty.

2.   Market definition is a tool to identify and define the boundaries of competition between firms. It serves to establish the framework within which competition policy is applied by the Commission. The main purpose of market definition is to identify in a systematic way the competitive constraints that the undertakings involved ([2]) face. The objective of defining a market in both its product and geographic dimension is to identify those actual competitors of the undertakings involved that are capable of constraining those undertakings' behaviour and of preventing them from behaving independently of effective competitive pressure. It is from this perspective that the market definition makes it possible *inter alia* to calculate market shares that would convey meaningful information regarding market power for the purposes of assessing dominance or for the purposes of applying Article 85.

3.   It follows from point 2 that the concept of 'relevant market' is different from other definitions of market often used in other contexts. For instance, companies often use the term 'market' to refer to the area where it sells its products or to refer broadly to the industry or sector where it belongs.

4.   The definition of the relevant market in both its product and its geographic dimensions often has a decisive influence on the assessment of a competition case. By rendering public the procedures which the Commission follows when considering market definition and by indicating the criteria and evidence on which it relies to reach a decision, the Commission expects to increase the transparency of its policy and decision-making in the area of competition policy.

5.   Increased transparency will also result in companies and their advisers being able to better anticipate the possibility that the Commission may raise competition concerns in an individual case. Companies could, therefore, take such a possibility into account in their own internal decision-making when contemplating, for instance, acquisitions, the creation of joint ventures, or the establishment of certain agreements. It is also intended that companies should be in a better position to understand what sort of information the Commission considers relevant for the purposes of market definition.

6.   The Commission's interpretation of 'relevant market' is without prejudice to the interpretation which may be given by the Court of Justice or the Court of First Instance of the European Communities.

II.   DEFINITION OF RELEVANT MARKET

Definition of relevant product market and relevant geographic market
7.   The Regulations based on Article 85 and 86 of the Treaty, in particular in section 6 of Form A/B with respect to Regulation No 17, as well as in section 6 of Form CO with respect to Regulation (EEC) No 4064/89 on the control of concentrations having a Community dimension have laid down the following definitions, 'Relevant product markets' are defined as follows:

'A relevant product market comprises all those products and/or services which are

---

[1] The focus of assessment in State aid cases is the aid recipient and the industry/sector concerned rather than identification of competitive constraints faced by the aid recipient. When consideration of market power and therefore of the relevant market are raised in any particular case, elements of the approach outlined here might serve as a basis for the assessment of State aid cases.
[2] For the purposes of this notice, the undertakings involved will be, in the case of a concentration, the parties to the concentration; in investigations within the meaning of Article 86 of the Treaty, the undertaking being investigated or the complainants; for investigations within the meaning of Article 85, the parties to the Agreement.

regarded as interchangeable or substitutable by the consumer, by reason of the products' characteristics, their prices and their intended use'.

8. 'Relevant geographic markets' are defined as follows:

'The relevant geographic market comprises the area in which the undertakings concerned are involved in the supply and demand of products or services, in which the conditions of competition are sufficiently homogeneous and which can be distinguished from neighbouring areas because the conditions of competition are appreciably different in those area'.

9. The relevant market within which to assess a given competition issue is therefore established by the combination of the product and geographic markets. The Commission interprets the definitions in paragraphs 7 and 8 (which reflect the case-law of the Court of Justice and the Court of First Instance as well as its own decision-making practice) according to the orientations defined in this notice.

Concept of relevant market and objectives of Community competition policy

10. The concept of relevant market is closely related to the objectives pursued under Community competition policy. For example, under the Community's merger control, the objective in controlling structural changes in the supply of a product/service is to prevent the creation or reinforcement of a dominant position as a result of which effective competition would be significantly impeded in a substantial part of the common market. Under the Community's competition rules, a dominant position is such that a firm or group of firms would be in a position to behave to an appreciable extent independently of its competitors, customers and ultimately of its consumers ([3]). Such a position would usually arise when a firm or group of firms accounted for a large share of the supply in any given market, provided that other factors analysed in the assessment (such as entry barriers, customers' capacity to react, etc.) point in the same direction.

11. The same approach is followed by the Commission in its application of Article 86 of the Treaty to firms that enjoy a single or collective dominant position. Within the meaning of Regulation No 17, the Commission has the power to investigate and bring to an end abuses of such a dominant position, which must also be defined by reference to the relevant market. Markets may also need to be defined in the application of Article 85 of the Treaty, in particular, in determining whether an appreciable restriction of competition exists or in establishing if the condition pursuant to Article 85(3)(b) for an exemption from the application of Article 85(1) is met.

12. The criteria for defining the relevant market are applied generally for the analysis of certain types of behaviour in the market and for the analysis of structural changes in the supply of products. This methodology, though, might lead to different results depending on the nature of the competition issue being examined. For instance, the scope of the geographic market might be different when analysing a concentration, where the analysis is essentially prospective, from an analysis of past behaviour. The different time horizon considered in each case might lead to the result that different geographic markets are defined for the same products depending on whether the Commission is examining a change in the structure of supply, such as a concentration or a cooperative joint venture, or examining issues relating to certain past behaviour.

Basic principles for market definition

Competitive constraints

13. Firms are subject to three main sources or competitive constraints: demand substitutability, supply substitutability and potential competition. From an economic point of view, for the definition of the relevant market, demand substitution constitutes the most

---

[3] Definition given by the Court of Justice in its judgment of 13 February 1979 in Case 85/76, *Hoffmann-La Roche* [1979] ECR 461, and confirmed in subsequent judgments.

immediate and effective disciplinary force on the suppliers of a given product, in particular in relation to their pricing decisions. A firm or a group of firms cannot have a significant impact on the prevailing conditions of sale, such as prices, if its customers are in a position to switch easily to available substitute products or to suppliers located elsewhere. Basically, the exercise of market definition consists in identifying the effective alternative sources of supply for the customers of the undertakings involved, in terms both of products/services and of geographic location of suppliers.

14. The competitive constraints arising from supply side substitutability other then those described in paragraphs 20 to 23 and from potential competition are in general less immediate and in any case require an analysis of additional factors. As a result such constraints are taken into account at the assessment stage of competition analysis.

Demand substitution

15. The assessment of demand substitution entails a determination of the range of products which are viewed as substitutes by the consumer. One way of making this determination can be viewed as a speculative experiment, postulating a hypothetical small, lasting change in relative prices and evaluating the likely reactions of customers to that increase. The exercise of market definition focuses on prices for operational and practical purposes, and more precisely on demand substitution arising from small, permanent changes in relative prices. This concept can provide clear indications as to the evidence that is relevant in defining markets.

16. Conceptually, this approach means that, starting from the type of products that the undertakings involved sell and the area in which they sell them, additional products and areas will be included in, or excluded from, the market definition depending on whether competition from these other products and areas affect or restrain sufficiently the pricing of the parties' products in the short term.

17. The question to be answered is whether the parties' customers would switch to readily available substitutes or to suppliers located elsewhere in response to a hypothetical small (in the range 5% to 10%) but permanent relative price increase in the products and areas being considered. If substitution were enough to make the price increase unprofitable because of the resulting loss of sales, additional substitutes and areas are included in the relevant market. This would be done until the set of products and geographical areas is such that small, permanent increases in relative prices would be profitable. The equivalent analysis is applicable in cases concerning the concentration of buying power, where the starting point would then be the supplier and the price test serves to identify the alternative distribution channels or outlets for the supplier's products. In the application of these principles, careful account should be taken of certain particular situations as described within paragraphs 56 and 58.

18. A practical example of this test can be provided by its application to a merger of, for instance, soft-drink bottlers. An issue to examine in such a case would be to decide whether different flavours of soft drinks belong to the same market. In practice, the question to address would be whether consumers of flavour A would switch to other flavours when confronted with a permanent price increase of 5% to 10% for flavour A. If a sufficient number of consumers would switch to, say, flavour B, to such an extent that the price increase for flavour A would not be profitable owing to the resulting loss of sales, then the market would comprise at least flavours A and B. The process would have to be extended in addition to other available flavours until a set of products is identified for which a price rise would not induce a sufficient substitution in demand.

19. Generally, and in particular for the analysis of merger cases, the price to take into account will be the prevailing market price. This may not be the case where the prevailing price has been determined in the absence of sufficient competition. In particular for the investigation of abuses of dominant positions, the fact that the prevailing price might already have been substantially increased will be taken into account.

Supply substitution

20.   Supply-side substitutability may also be taken into account when defining markets in those situations in which its effects are equivalent to those of demand substitution in terms of effectiveness and immediacy. This means that suppliers are able to switch production to the relevant products and market them in the short term ([4]) without incurring significant additional costs or risks in response to small and permanent changes in relative prices. When these conditions are met, the additional production that is put on the market will have a disciplinary effect on the competitive behaviour of the companies involved. Such an impact in terms of effectiveness and immediacy is equivalent to the demand substitution effect.

21.   These situations typically arise when companies market a wide range of qualities or grades of one product; even if, for a given final customer or group of consumers, the different qualities are not substitutable, the different qualities will be grouped into one product market, provided that most of the suppliers are able to offer and sell the various qualities immediately and without the significant increases in costs described above. In such cases, the relevant product market will encompass all products that are substitutable in demand and supply, and the current sales of those products will be aggregated so as to give the total value or volume of the market. The same reasoning may lead to group different geographic areas.

22.   A practical example of the approach to supply-side substitutability when defining product markets is to be found in the case of paper. Paper is usually supplied in a range of different qualities, from standard writing paper to high quality papers to be used, for instance, to publish art books. From a demand point of view, different qualities of paper cannot be used for any given use, i.e. an art book or a high quality publication cannot be based on lower quality papers. However, paper plants are prepared to manufacture the different qualities, and production can be adjusted with negligible costs and in a short time-frame. In the absence of particular difficulties in distribution, paper manufacturers are able therefore, to compete for orders of the various qualities, in particular if orders are placed with sufficient lead time to allow for modification of production plans. Under such circumstances, the Commission would not define a separate market for each quality of paper and its respective use. The various qualities of paper are included in the relevant market, and their sales added up to estimate total market value and volume.

23.   When supply-side substitutability would entail the need to adjust significantly existing tangible and intangible assets, additional investments, strategic decisions or time delays, it will not be considered at the stage of market definition. Examples where supply-side substitution did not induce the Commission to enlarge the market are offered in the area of consumer products, in particular for branded beverages. Although bottling plants may in principle bottle different beverages, there are costs and lead times involved (in terms of advertising, product testing and distribution) before the products can actually be sold. In these cases, the effects of supply-side substitutability and other forms of potential competition would then be examined at a later stage.

Potential competition

24.   The third source of competitive constraint, potential competition, is not taken into account when defining markets, since the conditions under which potential competition will actually represent an effective competitive constraint depend on the analysis of specific factors and circumstances related to the conditions of entry. If required, this analysis is only carried out at a subsequent stage, in general once the position of the companies involved in the relevant market has already been ascertained, and when such position gives rise to concerns from a competition point of view.

---

[4] That is such a period that does not entail a significant adjustment of existing tangible and intangible assets (see paragraph 23).

III. EVIDENCE RELIED ON TO DEFINE RELEVANT MARKETS

The process of defining the relevant market in practice

Product dimension

25.   There is a range of evidence permitting an assessment of the extent to which substitution would take place. In individual cases, certain types of evidence will be determinant, depending very much on the characteristics and specificity of the industry and products or services that are being examined. The same type of evidence may be of no importance in other cases. In most cases, a decision will have to be based on the consideration of a number of criteria and different items of evidence. The Commission follows an open approach to empirical evidence, aimed at making an effective use of all available information which may be relevant in individual cases. The Commission does not follow a rigid hierarchy of different sources of information or types of evidence.

26.   The process of defining relevant markets may be summarized as follows: on the basis of the preliminary information available or information submitted by the undertakings involved, the Commission will usually be in a position to broadly establish the possible relevant markets within which, for instance, a concentration or a restriction of competition has to be assessed. In general, and for all practical purposes when handling individual cases, the question will usually be to decide on a few alternative possible relevant markets. For instance, with respect to the product market, the issue will often be to establish whether product A and product B belong or do not belong to the same product market. it is often the case that the inclusion of product B would be enough to remove any competition concerns.

27.   In such situations it is not necessary to consider whether the market includes additional products, or to reach a definitive conclusion on the precise product market. If under the conceivable alternative market definitions the operation in question does not raise competition concerns, the question of market definition will be left open, reducing thereby the burden on companies to supply information.

Geographic dimension

28.   The Commission's approach to geographic market definition might be summarized as follows: it will take a preliminary view of the scope of the geographic market on the basis of broad indications as to the distribution of market shares between the parties and their competitors, as well as a preliminary analysis of pricing and price differences at national and Community or EEA level. This initial view is used basically as a working hypothesis to focus the Commission's enquiries for the purposes of arriving at a precise geographic market definition.

29.   The reasons behind any particular configuration of prices and market shares need to be explored. Companies might enjoy high market shares in their domestic markets just because of the weight of the past, and conversely, a homogeneous presence of companies throughout the EEA might be consistent with national or regional geographic markets. The initial working hypothesis will therefore be checked against an analysis of demand characteristics (importance of national or local preferences, current patterns of purchases of customers, product differentiation/brands, other) in order to establish whether companies in different areas do indeed constitute a real alternative source of supply for consumers. The theoretical experiment is again based on substitution arising from changes in relative prices, and the question to answer is again whether the customers of the parties would switch their orders to companies located elsewhere in the short term and at a negligible cost.

30.   If necessary, a further check on supply factors will be carried out to ensure that those companies located in differing areas do not face impediments in developing their sales on competitive terms throughout the whole geographic market. This analysis will include an examination of requirements for a local presence in order to sell in that area the conditions of access to distribution channels, costs associated with setting up a distribution network, and the presence or absence of regulatory barriers arising from public procurement, price

regulations, quotas and tariffs limiting trade or production, technical standards, monopolies, freedom of establishment, requirements for administrative authorizations, packaging regulations, etc. In short, the Commission will identify possible obstacles and barriers isolating companies located in a given area from the competitive pressure of companies located outside that area, so as to determine the precise degree of market interpenetration at national, European or global level.

31.   The actual pattern and evolution of trade flows offers useful supplementary indications as to the economic importance of each demand or supply factor mentioned above, and the extent to which they may or may not constitute actual barriers creating different geographic markets. The analysis of trade flows will generally address the question of transport costs and the extent to which these may hinder trade between different areas, having regard to plant location, costs of production and relative price levels.

Market integration in the Community

32.   Finally, the Commission also takes into account the continuing process of market integration, in particular in the Community, when defining geographic markets, especially in the area of concentrations and structural joint ventures. The measures adopted and implemented in the internal market programme to remove barriers to trade and further integrate the Community markets cannot be ignored when assessing the effects on competition of a concentration or a structural joint venture. A situation where national markets have been artificially isolated from each other because of the existence of legislative barriers that have now been removed will generally lead to a cautious assessment of past evidence regarding prices, market shares or trade patterns. A process of market integration that would, in the short term, lead to wider geographic markets may therefore be taken into consideration when defining the geographic market for the purposes of assessing concentrations and joint ventures.

The process of gathering evidence

33.   When a precise market definition is deemed necessary, the Commission will often contact the main customers and the main companies in the industry to enquire into their views about the boundaries of product and geographic markets and to obtain the necessary factual evidence to reach a conclusion. The Commission might also contact the relevant professional associations, and companies active in upstream markets, so as to be able to define, in so far as necessary, separate product and geographic markets, for different levels of production or distribution of the products/services in question. It might also request additional information to the undertakings involved.

34.   Where appropriate, the Commission will address written requests for information to the market players mentioned above. These requests will usually include questions relating to the perceptions of companies about reactions to hypothetical price increases and their views of the boundaries of the relevant market. They will also ask for provision of the factual information the Commission deems necessary to reach a conclusion on the extent of the relevant market. The Commission might also discuss with marketing directors or other officers of those companies to gain a better understanding on how negotiations between suppliers and customers take place and better understand issues relating to the definition of the relevant market. Where appropriate, they might also carry out visits or inspections to the premises of the parties, their customers and/or their competitors, in order to better understand how products are manufactured and sold.

35.   The type of evidence relevant to reach a conclusion as to the product market can be categorized as follows:

Evidence to define markets—product dimension

36.   An analysis of the product characteristics and its intended use allows the Commission, as a first step, to limit the field of investigation of possible substitutes. However, product characteristics and intended use are insufficient to show whether two products are demand

substitutes. Functional interchangeability or similarity in characteristics may not, in them-selves, provide sufficient criteria, because the responsiveness of customers to relative price changes may be determined by other considerations as well. For example, there may be different competitive constraints in the original equipment market for car components and in spare parts, thereby leading to a separate delineation of two relevant markets. Conversely, differences in product characteristics are not in themselves sufficient to exclude demand substitutability, since this will depend to a large extent on how customers value different characteristics.

37.   The type of evidence the Commission considers relevant to assess whether two products are demand substitutes can be categorized as follows:

38.   Evidence of substitution in the recent past. In certain cases, it is possible to analyse evidence relating to recent past events or shocks in the market that offer actual examples of substitution between two products. When available, this sort of information will normally be fundamental for market definition. If there have been changes in relative prices in the past (all else being equal), the reactions in terms of quantities demanded will be determinant in establishing substitutability. Launches of new products in the past can also offer useful information, when it is possible to precisely analyse which products have lost sales to the new product.

39.   There are a number of quantitative tests that have specifically been designed for the purpose of delineating markets. These tests consist of various econometric and statistical approaches estimates of elasticities and cross-price elasticities ([5]) for the demand of a product, tests based on similarity of price movements over time, the analysis of causality between price series and similarity of price levels and/or their convergence. The Commission takes into account the available quantitative evidence capable of withstanding rigorous scrutiny for the purposes of establishing patterns of substitution in the past.

40.   Views of customers and competitors. The Commission often contacts the main customers and competitors of the companies involved in its enquiries, to gather their views on the boundaries of the product market as well as most of the factual information it requires to reach a conclusion on the scope of the market. Reasoned answers of customers and competitors as to what would happen if relative prices for the candidate products were to increase in the candidate geographic area by a small amount (for instance of 5% to 10%) are taken into account when they are sufficiently backed by factual evidence.

41.   Consumer preferences. In the case of consumer goods, it may be difficult for the Commission to gather the direct views of end consumers about substitute products. Marketing studies that companies have commissioned in the past and that are used by companies in their own decision-making as to pricing of their products and/or marketing actions may provide useful information for the Commission's delineation of the relevant market. Consumer surveys on usage patterns and attitudes, data from consumer's purchasing patterns, the views expressed by retailers and more generally, market research studies submitted by the parties and their competitors are taken into account to establish whether an economically significant proportion of consumers consider two products as substitutable, also taking into account the importance of brands for the products in question. The methodology followed in consumer surveys carried out *ad hoc* by the undertakings involved or their competitors for the purposes of a merger procedure or a procedure pursuant to Regulation No 17 will usually be scrutinized with utmost care. Unlike pre-existing studies, they have not been prepared in the normal course of business for the adoption of business decisions.

42.   Barriers and costs associated with switching demand to potential substitutes. There are a number of barriers and costs that might prevent the Commission from considering two

---

[5] Own-price elasticity of demand for product X is a measure of the responsiveness of demand for X to percentage change in its own price. Cross-price elasticity between products X and Y is the responsiveness of demand for product X to percentage change in the price of product Y.

prima facie demand substitutes as belonging to one single product market. It is not possible to provide an exhaustive list of all the possible barriers to substitution and of switching costs. These barriers or obstacles might have a wide range of origins, and in its decisions, the Commission has been confronted with regulatory barriers or other forms of State intervention, constraints arising in downstream markets, need to incur specific capital investment or loss in current output in order to switch to alternative inputs, the location of customers, specific investment in production process, learning and human capital investment, retooling costs or other investments, uncertainty about quality and reputation of unknown suppliers, and others.

43.   Different categories of customers and price discrimination. The extent of the product market might be narrowed in the presence of distinct groups of customers. A distinct group of customers for the relevant product may constitute a narrower, distinct market when such a group could be subject to price discrimination. This will usually be the case when two conditions are met: (a) it is possible to identify clearly which group an individual customer belongs to at the moment of selling the relevant products to him, and (b) trade among customers or arbitrage by third parties should not be feasible.

Evidence for defining markets—geographic dimension

44.   The type of evidence the Commission considers relevant to reach a conclusion as to the geographic market can be categorized as follows:

45.   Past evidence of diversion of orders to other areas. In certain cases, evidence on changes in prices between different areas and consequent reactions by customers might be available. Generally, the same quantitative tests used for product market definition might as well be used in geographic market definition, bearing in mind that international comparisons of prices might be more complex due to a number of factors such as exchange rate movements, taxation and product differentiation.

46.   Basic demand characteristics. The nature of demand for the relevant product may in itself determine the scope of the geographical market. Factors such as national preferences or preferences for national brands, language, culture and life style, and the need for a local presence have a strong potential to limit the geographic scope of competition.

47.   Views of customers and competitors. Where appropriate, the Commission will contact the main customers and competitors of the parties in its enquiries, to gather their views on the boundaries of the geographic market as well as most of the factual information it requires to reach a conclusion on the scope of the market when they are sufficiently backed by factual evidence.

48.   Current geographic pattern of purchases. An examination of the customers' current geographic pattern of purchases provides useful evidence as to the possible scope of the geographic market. When customers purchase from companies located anywhere in the Community or the EEA on similar terms, or they procure their supplies through effective tendering procedures in which companies from anywhere in the Community or the EEA submit bids, usually the geographic market will be considered to be Community-wide.

49.   Trade flows/pattern of shipments. When the number of customers is so large that it is not possible to obtain through them a clear picture of geographic purchasing patterns, information on trade flows might be used alternatively, provided that the trade statistics are available with a sufficient degree of detail for the relevant products. Trade flows, and above all, the rationale behind trade flows provide useful insights and information for the purpose of establishing the scope of the geographic market but are not in themselves conclusive.

50.   Barriers and switching costs associated to divert orders to companies located in other areas. The absence of trans-border purchases or trade flows, for instance, does not necessarily mean that the market is at most national in scope. Still, barriers isolating the national market have to identified before it is concluded that the relevant geographic market in such a case is

national. Perhaps the clearest obstacle for a customer to divert its orders to other areas is the impact of transport costs and transport restrictions arising from legislation or from the nature of the relevant products. The impact of transport costs will usually limit the scope of the geographic market for bulky, low-value products, bearing in mind that a transport disadvantage might also be compensated by a comparative advantage in other costs (labour costs or raw materials). Access to distribution in a given area, regulatory barriers still existing in certain sectors, quotas and custom tariffs might also constitute barriers isolating a geographic area from the competitive pressure of companies located outside that area. Significant switching costs in procuring supplies from companies located in other countries constitute additional sources of such barriers.

51.   On the basis of the evidence gathered, the Commission will then define a geographic market that could range from a local dimension to a global one, and there are examples of both local and global markets in past decisions of the Commission.

52.   The paragraphs above describe the different factors which might be relevant to define markets. This does not imply that in each individual case it will be necessary to obtain evidence and assess each of these factors. Often in practice the evidence provided by a subset of these factors will be sufficient to reach a conclusion, as shown in the past decisional practice of the Commission.

IV.   CALCULATION OF MARKET SHARE

53.   The definition of the relevant market in both its product and geographic dimensions allows the identification the suppliers and the customers/consumers active on that market. On that basis, a total market size and market shares for each supplier can be calculated on the basis of their sales of the relevant products in the relevant area. In practice, the total market size and market shares are often available from market sources, i.e. companies' estimates, studies commissioned from industry consultants and/or trade associations. When this is not the case, or when available estimates are not reliable, the Commission will usually ask each supplier in the relevant market to provide its own sales in order to calculate total market size and market shares.

54.   If sales are usually the reference to calculate market shares, there are nevertheless other indications that, depending on the specific products or industry in question, can offer useful information such as, in particular, capacity, the number of players in bidding markets, units of fleet as in aerospace, or the reserves held in the case of sectors such as mining.

55.   As a rule of thumb, both volume sales and value sales provide useful information. In cases of differentiated products, sales in value and their associated market share will usually be considered to better reflect the relative position and strength of each supplier.

V.   ADDITIONAL CONSIDERATIONS

56.   There are certain areas where the application of the principles above has to be undertaken with care. This is the case when considering primary and secondary markets, in particular, when the behaviour of undertakings at a point in time has to be analysed pursuant to Article 86. The method of defining markets in these cases is the same, i.e. assessing the responses of customers based on their purchasing decisions to relative price changes, but taking into account as well, constraints on substitution imposed by conditions in the connected markets. A narrow definition of market for secondary products, for instance, spare parts, may result when compatibility with the primary product is important. Problems of finding compatible secondary products together with the existence of high prices and a long lifetime of the primary products may render relative price increases of secondary products profitable. A different market definition may result if significant substitution between

secondary products is possible or if the characteristics of the primary products make quick and direct consumer responses to relative price increases of the secondary products feasible.

57.   In certain cases, the existence of chains of substitution might lead to the definition of a relevant market where products or areas at the extreme of the market are not directly substitutable. An example might be provided by the geographic dimension of a product with significant transport costs. In such cases, deliveries from a given plant are limited to a certain area around each plant by the impact of transport costs. In principle, such an area could constitute the relevant geographic market. However, if the distribution of plants is such that there are considerable overlaps between the areas around different plants, it is possible that the pricing of those products will be constrained by a chain substitution effect, and lead to the definition of a broader geographic market. The same reasoning may apply if product B is a demand substitute for products A and C. Even if products A and C are not direct demand substitutes, they might be found to be in the same relevant product market since their respective pricing might be constrained by substitution to B.

58.   From a practical perspective, the concept of chains of substitution has to be corroborated by actual evidence, for instance related to price interdependence at the extremes of the chains of substitution, in order to lead to an extension of the relevant market in an individual case. Price levels at the extremes of the chains would have to be of the same magnitude as well.

Council Regulation (EC) No. 1/2003 of 16 December 2002 on the implementation of the rules on competition laid down in Articles 81 and 82 of the Treaty

[OJ 2003, L1/1]*

THE COUNCIL OF THE EUROPEAN UNION,

Having regard to the Treaty establishing the European Community, and in particular Article 83 thereof,

Having regard to the proposal from the Commission,[1]

Having regard to the opinion of the European Parliament,[2]

Having regard to the opinion of the European Economic and Social Committee,[3]

Whereas:

(1) In order to establish a system which ensures that competition in the common market is not distorted, Articles 81 and 82 of the Treaty must be applied effectively and uniformly in the Community. Council Regulation No 17 of 6 February 1962, First Regulation implementing Articles 81 and 82[4] of the Treaty,[5] has allowed a Community competition policy to develop that has helped to disseminate a competition culture within the Community. In the light of experience, however, that Regulation should now be replaced by legislation designed to meet the challenges of an integrated market and a future enlargement of the Community.

---

* **Editor's Note:** This Regulation replaced Regulation 17 with effect from 1 May 2004. As amended by Regulation 411/2004 (OJ 2004, L68/1).

[1] OJ C 365 E, 19.12.2000, p. 284.

[2] OJ C 72 E, 21.3.2002, p. 305.

[3] OJ C 155, 29.5.2001, p. 73.

[4] The title of Regulation No 17 has been adjusted to take account of the renumbering of the Articles of the EC Treaty, in accordance with Article 12 of the Treaty of Amsterdam; the original reference was to Articles 85 and 86 of the Treaty.

[5] OJ 13, 21.2.1962, p. 204/62. Regulation as last amended by Regulation (EC) No 1216/1999 (OJ L 148, 15.6.1999, p. 5).

(2) In particular, there is a need to rethink the arrangements for applying the exception from the prohibition on agreements, which restrict competition, laid down in Article 81(3) of the Treaty. Under Article 83(2)(b) of the Treaty, account must be taken in this regard of the need to ensure effective supervision, on the one hand, and to simplify administration to the greatest possible extent, on the other.

(3) The centralised scheme set up by Regulation No 17 no longer secures a balance between those two objectives. It hampers application of the Community competition rules by the courts and competition authorities of the Member States, and the system of notification it involves prevents the Commission from concentrating its resources on curbing the most serious infringements. It also imposes considerable costs on undertakings.

(4) The present system should therefore be replaced by a directly applicable exception system in which the competition authorities and courts of the Member States have the power to apply not only Article 81(1) and Article 82 of the Treaty, which have direct applicability by virtue of the case-law of the Court of Justice of the European Communities, but also Article 81(3) of the Treaty.

(5) In order to ensure an effective enforcement of the Community competition rules and at the same time the respect of fundamental rights of defence, this Regulation should regulate the burden of proof under Articles 81 and 82 of the Treaty. It should be for the party or the authority alleging an infringement of Article 81(1) and Article 82 of the Treaty to prove the existence thereof to the required legal standard. It should be for the undertaking or association of undertakings invoking the benefit of a defence against a finding of an infringement to demonstrate to the required legal standard that the conditions for applying such defence are satisfied. This Regulation affects neither national rules on the standard of proof nor obligations of competition authorities and courts of the Member States to ascertain the relevant facts of a case, provided that such rules and obligations are compatible with general principles of Community law.

(6) In order to ensure that the Community competition rules are applied effectively, the competition authorities of the Member States should be associated more closely with their application. To this end, they should be empowered to apply Community law.

(7) National courts have an essential part to play in applying the Community competition rules. When deciding disputes between private individuals, they protect the subjective rights under Community law, for example, by awarding damages to the victims of infringements. The role of the national courts here complements that of the competition authorities of the Member States. They should therefore be allowed to apply Articles 81 and 82 of the Treaty in full.

(8) In order to ensure the effective enforcement of the Community competition rules and the proper functioning of the cooperation mechanisms contained in this Regulation, it is necessary to oblige the competition authorities and courts of the Member States to also apply Articles 81 and 82 of the Treaty where they apply national competition law to agreements and practices which may affect trade between Member States. In order to create a level playing field for agreements, decisions by associations of undertakings and concerted practices within the internal market, it is also necessary to determine pursuant to Article 83(2)(e) of the Treaty the relationship between national laws and Community competition law. To that effect it is necessary to provide that the application of national competition laws to agreements, decisions or concerted practices within the meaning of Article 81(1) of the Treaty may not lead to the prohibition of such agreements, decisions and concerted practices if they are not also prohibited under Community competition law. The notions of agreements, decisions and concerted practices are autonomous concepts of Community competition law covering the coordination of behaviour of undertakings on the market as interpreted by the Community Courts. Member States should not under this Regulation be precluded from adopting and applying on their territory stricter national competition laws which prohibit or impose sanctions on unilateral conduct engaged in by undertakings. These stricter national laws may

include provisions which prohibit or impose sanctions on abusive behaviour toward economically dependent undertakings. Furthermore, this Regulation does not apply to national laws which impose criminal sanctions on natural persons except to the extent that such sanctions are the means whereby competition rules applying to undertakings are enforced.

(9) Articles 81 and 82 of the Treaty have as their objective the protection of competition on the market. This Regulation, which is adopted for the implementation of these Treaty provisions, does not preclude Member States from implementing on their territory national legislation, which protects other legitimate interests provided that such legislation is compatible with general principles and other provisions of Community law. Insofar as such national legislation pursues predominantly an objective different from that of protecting competition on the market, the competition authorities and courts of the Member States may apply such legislation on their territory. Accordingly, Member States may under this Regulation implement on their territory national legislation that prohibits or imposes sanctions on acts of unfair trading practice, be they unilateral or contractual. Such legislation pursues a specific objective, irrespective of the actual or presumed effects of such acts on competition on the market. This is particularly the case of legislation which prohibits undertakings from imposing on their trading partners, obtaining or attempting to obtain from them terms and conditions that are unjustified, disproportionate or without consideration.

(10) Regulations such as 19/65/EEC,[6] (EEC) No 2821/71,[7] (EEC) No 3976/87,[8] (EEC) No 1534/91,[9] or (EEC) No 479/92[10] empower the Commission to apply Article 81(3) of the Treaty by Regulation to certain categories of agreements, decisions by associations of undertakings and concerted practices. In the areas defined by such Regulations, the Commission has adopted and may continue to adopt so called "block" exemption Regulations by which it declares Article 81(1) of the Treaty inapplicable to categories of agreements, decisions and concerted practices. Where agreements, decisions and concerted practices to which such Regulations apply nonetheless have effects that are incompatible with Article 81(3) of the Treaty, the Commission and the competition authorities of the Member States should have the power to withdraw in a particular case the benefit of the block exemption Regulation.

---

[6] Council Regulation No 19/65/EEC of 2 March 1965 on the application of Article 81(3) (the titles of the Regulations have been adjusted to take account of the renumbering of the Articles of the EC Treaty, in accordance with Article 12 of the Treaty of Amsterdam; the original reference was to Article 85(3) of the Treaty) of the Treaty to certain categories of agreements and concerted practices (OJ 36, 6.3.1965, p. 533). Regulation as last amended by Regulation (EC) No 1215/1999 (OJ L 148, 15.6.1999, p. 1).

[7] Council Regulation (EEC) No 2821/71 of 20 December 1971 on the application of Article 81(3) (the titles of the Regulations have been adjusted to take account of the renumbering of the Articles of the EC Treaty, in accordance with Article 12 of the Treaty of Amsterdam; the original reference was to Article 85(3) of the Treaty) of the Treaty to categories of agreements, decisions and concerted practices (OJ L 285, 29.12.1971, p. 46). Regulation as last amended by the Act of Accession of 1994.

[8] Council Regulation (EEC) No 3976/87 of 14 December 1987 on the application of Article 81(3) (the titles of the Regulations have been adjusted to take account of the renumbering of the Articles of the EC Treaty, in accordance with Article 12 of the Treaty of Amsterdam; the original reference was to Article 85(3) of the Treaty) of the Treaty to certain categories of agreements and concerted practices in the air transport sector (OJ L 374, 31.12.1987, p. 9). Regulation as last amended by the Act of Accession of 1994.

[9] Council Regulation (EEC) No 1534/91 of 31 May 1991 on the application of Article 81(3) (the titles of the Regulations have been adjusted to take account of the renumbering of the Articles of the EC Treaty, in accordance with Article 12 of the Treaty of Amsterdam; the original reference was to Article 85(3) of the Treaty) of the Treaty to certain categories of agreements, decisions and concerted practices in the insurance sector (OJ L 143, 7.6.1991, p. 1).

[10] Council Regulation (EEC) No 479/92 of 25 February 1992 on the application of Article 81(3) (the titles of the Regulations have been adjusted to take account of the renumbering of the Articles of the EC Treaty, in accordance with Article 12 of the Treaty of Amsterdam; the original reference was to Article 85(3) of the Treaty) of the Treaty to certain categories of agreements, decisions and concerted practices between liner shipping companies (Consortia) (OJ L 55, 29.2.1992, p. 3). Regulation amended by the Act of Accession of 1994.

(11) For it to ensure that the provisions of the Treaty are applied, the Commission should be able to address decisions to undertakings or associations of undertakings for the purpose of bringing to an end infringements of Articles 81 and 82 of the Treaty. Provided there is a legitimate interest in doing so, the Commission should also be able to adopt decisions which find that an infringement has been committed in the past even if it does not impose a fine. This Regulation should also make explicit provision for the Commission's power to adopt decisions ordering interim measures, which has been acknowledged by the Court of Justice.

(12) This Regulation should make explicit provision for the Commission's power to impose any remedy, whether behavioural or structural, which is necessary to bring the infringement effectively to an end, having regard to the principle of proportionality. Structural remedies should only be imposed either where there is no equally effective behavioural remedy or where any equally effective behavioural remedy would be more burdensome for the undertaking concerned than the structural remedy. Changes to the structure of an undertaking as it existed before the infringement was committed would only be proportionate where there is a substantial risk of a lasting or repeated infringement that derives from the very structure of the undertaking.

(13) Where, in the course of proceedings which might lead to an agreement or practice being prohibited, undertakings offer the Commission commitments such as to meet its concerns, the Commission should be able to adopt decisions which make those commitments binding on the undertakings concerned. Commitment decisions should find that there are no longer grounds for action by the Commission without concluding whether or not there has been or still is an infringement. Commitment decisions are without prejudice to the powers of competition authorities and courts of the Member States to make such a finding and decide upon the case. Commitment decisions are not appropriate in cases where the Commission intends to impose a fine.

(14) In exceptional cases where the public interest of the Community so requires, it may also be expedient for the Commission to adopt a decision of a declaratory nature finding that the prohibition in Article 81 or Article 82 of the Treaty does not apply, with a view to clarifying the law and ensuring its consistent application throughout the Community, in particular with regard to new types of agreements or practices that have not been settled in the existing case-law and administrative practice.

(15) The Commission and the competition authorities of the Member States should form together a network of public authorities applying the Community competition rules in close cooperation. For that purpose it is necessary to set up arrangements for information and consultation. Further modalities for the cooperation within the network will be laid down and revised by the Commission, in close cooperation with the Member States.

(16) Notwithstanding any national provision to the contrary, the exchange of information and the use of such information in evidence should be allowed between the members of the network even where the information is confidential. This information may be used for the application of Articles 81 and 82 of the Treaty as well as for the parallel application of national competition law, provided that the latter application relates to the same case and does not lead to a different outcome. When the information exchanged is used by the receiving authority to impose sanctions on undertakings, there should be no other limit to the use of the information than the obligation to use it for the purpose for which it was collected given the fact that the sanctions imposed on undertakings are of the same type in all systems. The rights of defence enjoyed by undertakings in the various systems can be considered as sufficiently equivalent. However, as regards natural persons, they may be subject to substantially different types of sanctions across the various systems. Where that is the case, it is necessary to ensure that information can only be used if it has been collected in a way which respects the same level of protection of the rights of defence of natural persons as provided for under the national rules of the receiving authority.

(17) If the competition rules are to be applied consistently and, at the same time, the

network is to be managed in the best possible way, it is essential to retain the rule that the competition authorities of the Member States are automatically relieved of their competence if the Commission initiates its own proceedings. Where a competition authority of a Member State is already acting on a case and the Commission intends to initiate proceedings, it should endeavour to do so as soon as possible. Before initiating proceedings, the Commission should consult the national authority concerned.

(18) To ensure that cases are dealt with by the most appropriate authorities within the network, a general provision should be laid down allowing a competition authority to suspend or close a case on the ground that another authority is dealing with it or has already dealt with it, the objective being that each case should be handled by a single authority. This provision should not prevent the Commission from rejecting a complaint for lack of Community interest, as the case-law of the Court of Justice has acknowledged it may do, even if no other competition authority has indicated its intention of dealing with the case.

(19) The Advisory Committee on Restrictive Practices and Dominant Positions set up by Regulation No 17 has functioned in a very satisfactory manner. It will fit well into the new system of decentralised application. It is necessary, therefore, to build upon the rules laid down by Regulation No 17, while improving the effectiveness of the organisational arrangements. To this end, it would be expedient to allow opinions to be delivered by written procedure. The Advisory Committee should also be able to act as a forum for discussing cases that are being handled by the competition authorities of the Member States, so as to help safeguard the consistent application of the Community competition rules.

(20) The Advisory Committee should be composed of representatives of the competition authorities of the Member States. For meetings in which general issues are being discussed, Member States should be able to appoint an additional representative. This is without prejudice to members of the Committee being assisted by other experts from the Member States.

(21) Consistency in the application of the competition rules also requires that arrangements be established for cooperation between the courts of the Member States and the Commission. This is relevant for all courts of the Member States that apply Articles 81 and 82 of the Treaty, whether applying these rules in lawsuits between private parties, acting as public enforcers or as review courts. In particular, national courts should be able to ask the Commission for information or for its opinion on points concerning the application of Community competition law. The Commission and the competition authorities of the Member States should also be able to submit written or oral observations to courts called upon to apply Article 81 or Article 82 of the Treaty. These observations should be submitted within the framework of national procedural rules and practices including those safeguarding the rights of the parties. Steps should therefore be taken to ensure that the Commission and the competition authorities of the Member States are kept sufficiently well informed of proceedings before national courts.

(22) In order to ensure compliance with the principles of legal certainty and the uniform application of the Community competition rules in a system of parallel powers, conflicting decisions must be avoided. It is therefore necessary to clarify, in accordance with the case-law of the Court of Justice, the effects of Commission decisions and proceedings on courts and competition authorities of the Member States. Commitment decisions adopted by the Commission do not affect the power of the courts and the competition authorities of the Member States to apply Articles 81 and 82 of the Treaty.

(23) The Commission should be empowered throughout the Community to require such information to be supplied as is necessary to detect any agreement, decision or concerted practice prohibited by Article 81 of the Treaty or any abuse of a dominant position prohibited by Article 82 of the Treaty. When complying with a decision of the Commission, undertakings cannot be forced to admit that they have committed an infringement, but they are in any event obliged to answer factual questions and to provide documents, even if this information

may be used to establish against them or against another undertaking the existence of an infringement.

(24) The Commission should also be empowered to undertake such inspections as are necessary to detect any agreement, decision or concerted practice prohibited by Article 81 of the Treaty or any abuse of a dominant position prohibited by Article 82 of the Treaty. The competition authorities of the Member States should cooperate actively in the exercise of these powers.

(25) The detection of infringements of the competition rules is growing ever more difficult, and, in order to protect competition effectively, the Commission's powers of investigation need to be supplemented. The Commission should in particular be empowered to interview any persons who may be in possession of useful information and to record the statements made. In the course of an inspection, officials authorised by the Commission should be empowered to affix seals for the period of time necessary for the inspection. Seals should normally not be affixed for more than 72 hours. Officials authorised by the Commission should also be empowered to ask for any information relevant to the subject matter and purpose of the inspection.

(26) Experience has shown that there are cases where business records are kept in the homes of directors or other people working for an undertaking. In order to safeguard the effectiveness of inspections, therefore, officials and other persons authorised by the Commission should be empowered to enter any premises where business records may be kept, including private homes. However, the exercise of this latter power should be subject to the authorisation of the judicial authority.

(27) Without prejudice to the case-law of the Court of Justice, it is useful to set out the scope of the control that the national judicial authority may carry out when it authorises, as foreseen by national law including as a precautionary measure, assistance from law enforcement authorities in order to overcome possible opposition on the part of the undertaking or the execution of the decision to carry out inspections in non-business premises. It results from the case-law that the national judicial authority may in particular ask the Commission for further information which it needs to carry out its control and in the absence of which it could refuse the authorisation. The case-law also confirms the competence of the national courts to control the application of national rules governing the implementation of coercive measures.

(28) In order to help the competition authorities of the Member States to apply Articles 81 and 82 of the Treaty effectively, it is expedient to enable them to assist one another by carrying out inspections and other fact-finding measures.

(29) Compliance with Articles 81 and 82 of the Treaty and the fulfilment of the obligations imposed on undertakings and associations of undertakings under this Regulation should be enforceable by means of fines and periodic penalty payments. To that end, appropriate levels of fine should also be laid down for infringements of the procedural rules.

(30) In order to ensure effective recovery of fines imposed on associations of undertakings for infringements that they have committed, it is necessary to lay down the conditions on which the Commission may require payment of the fine from the members of the association where the association is not solvent. In doing so, the Commission should have regard to the relative size of the undertakings belonging to the association and in particular to the situation of small and medium-sized enterprises. Payment of the fine by one or several members of an association is without prejudice to rules of national law that provide for recovery of the amount paid from other members of the association.

(31) The rules on periods of limitation for the imposition of fines and periodic penalty payments were laid down in Council Regulation (EEC) No 2988/74,[11] which also concerns

---

[11] Council Regulation (EEC) No 2988/74 of 26 November 1974 concerning limitation periods in proceedings and the enforcement of sanctions under the rules of the European Economic Community relating to transport and competition (OJ L 319, 29.11.1974, p. 1).

penalties in the field of transport. In a system of parallel powers, the acts, which may interrupt a limitation period, should include procedural steps taken independently by the competition authority of a Member State. To clarify the legal framework, Regulation (EEC) No 2988/74 should therefore be amended to prevent it applying to matters covered by this Regulation, and this Regulation should include provisions on periods of limitation.

(32) The undertakings concerned should be accorded the right to be heard by the Commission, third parties whose interests may be affected by a decision should be given the opportunity of submitting their observations beforehand, and the decisions taken should be widely publicised. While ensuring the rights of defence of the undertakings concerned, in particular, the right of access to the file, it is essential that business secrets be protected. The confidentiality of information exchanged in the network should likewise be safeguarded.

(33) Since all decisions taken by the Commission under this Regulation are subject to review by the Court of Justice in accordance with the Treaty, the Court of Justice should, in accordance with Article 229 thereof be given unlimited jurisdiction in respect of decisions by which the Commission imposes fines or periodic penalty payments.

(34) The principles laid down in Articles 81 and 82 of the Treaty, as they have been applied by Regulation No 17, have given a central role to the Community bodies. This central role should be retained, whilst associating the Member States more closely with the application of the Community competition rules. In accordance with the principles of subsidiarity and proportionality as set out in Article 5 of the Treaty, this Regulation does not go beyond what is necessary in order to achieve its objective, which is to allow the Community competition rules to be applied effectively.

(35) In order to attain a proper enforcement of Community competition law, Member States should designate and empower authorities to apply Articles 81 and 82 of the Treaty as public enforcers. They should be able to designate administrative as well as judicial authorities to carry out the various functions conferred upon competition authorities in this Regulation. This Regulation recognises the wide variation which exists in the public enforcement systems of Member States. The effects of Article 11(6) of this Regulation should apply to all competition authorities. As an exception to this general rule, where a prosecuting authority brings a case before a separate judicial authority, Article 11(6) should apply to the prosecuting authority subject to the conditions in Article 35(4) of this Regulation. Where these conditions are not fulfilled, the general rule should apply. In any case, Article 11(6) should not apply to courts insofar as they are acting as review courts.

(36) As the case-law has made it clear that the competition rules apply to transport, that sector should be made subject to the procedural provisions of this Regulation. Council Regulation No 141 of 26 November 1962 exempting transport from the application of Regulation No 17[12] should therefore be repealed and Regulations (EEC) No 1017/68,[13] (EEC) No 4056/86[14] and (EEC) No 3975/87[15] should be amended in order to delete the specific procedural provisions they contain.

---

[12] OJ 124, 28.11.1962, p. 2751/62; Regulation as last amended by Regulation No. 1002/67/EEC (OJ 306, 16.12.1967, p. 1).

[13] Council Regulation (EEC) No. 1017/68 of 19 July 1968 applying rules of competition to transport by rail, road and inland waterway (OJ L 175, 23.7.1968, p. 1). Regulation as last amended by the Act of Accession of 1994.

[14] Council Regulation (EEC) No. 4056/86 of 22 December 1986 laying down detailed rules for the application of Articles 81 and 82 (the title of the Regulation has been adjusted to take account of the renumbering of the Articles of the EC Treaty, in accordance with Article 12 of the Treaty of Amsterdam; the original reference was to Articles 85 and 86 of the Treaty) of the Treaty to maritime transport (OJ L 378, 31.12.1986, p. 4). Regulation as last amended by the Act of Accession of 1994.

[15] Council Regulation (EEC) No 3975/87 of 14 December 1987 laying down the procedure for the application of the rules on competition to undertakings in the air transport sector (OJ L 374, 31.12.1987, p. 1). Regulation as last amended by Regulation (EEC) No 2410/92 (OJ L 240, 24.8.1992, p. 18).

(37) This Regulation respects the fundamental rights and observes the principles recognised in particular by the Charter of Fundamental Rights of the European Union. Accordingly, this Regulation should be interpreted and applied with respect to those rights and principles.

(38) Legal certainty for undertakings operating under the Community competition rules contributes to the promotion of innovation and investment. Where cases give rise to genuine uncertainty because they present novel or unresolved questions for the application of these rules, individual undertakings may wish to seek informal guidance from the Commission. This Regulation is without prejudice to the ability of the Commission to issue such informal guidance,

HAS ADOPTED THIS REGULATION:

CHAPTER I   PRINCIPLES

Article 1   Application of Articles 81 and 82 of the Treaty

1.   Agreements, decisions and concerted practices caught by Article 81(1) of the Treaty which do not satisfy the conditions of Article 81(3) of the Treaty shall be prohibited, no prior decision to that effect being required.

2.   Agreements, decisions and concerted practices caught by Article 81(1) of the Treaty which satisfy the conditions of Article 81(3) of the Treaty shall not be prohibited, no prior decision to that effect being required.

3.   The abuse of a dominant position referred to in Article 82 of the Treaty shall be prohibited, no prior decision to that effect being required.

Article 2   Burden of proof

In any national or Community proceedings for the application of Articles 81 and 82 of the Treaty, the burden of proving an infringement of Article 81(1) or of Article 82 of the Treaty shall rest on the party or the authority alleging the infringement. The undertaking or association of undertakings claiming the benefit of Article 81(3) of the Treaty shall bear the burden of proving that the conditions of that paragraph are fulfilled.

Article 3   Relationship between Articles 81 and 82 of the Treaty and national competition laws

1.   Where the competition authorities of the Member States or national courts apply national competition law to agreements, decisions by associations of undertakings or concerted practices within the meaning of Article 81(1) of the Treaty which may affect trade between Member States within the meaning of that provision, they shall also apply Article 81 of the Treaty to such agreements, decisions or concerted practices. Where the competition authorities of the Member States or national courts apply national competition law to any abuse prohibited by Article 82 of the Treaty, they shall also apply Article 82 of the Treaty.

2.   The application of national competition law may not lead to the prohibition of agreements, decisions by associations of undertakings or concerted practices which may affect trade between Member States but which do not restrict competition within the meaning of Article 81(1) of the Treaty, or which fulfil the conditions of Article 81(3) of the Treaty or which are covered by a Regulation for the application of Article 81(3) of the Treaty. Member States shall not under this Regulation be precluded from adopting and applying on their territory stricter national laws which prohibit or sanction unilateral conduct engaged in by undertakings.

3.   Without prejudice to general principles and other provisions of Community law, paragraphs 1 and 2 do not apply when the competition authorities and the courts of the Member States apply national merger control laws nor do they preclude the application of provisions of national law that predominantly pursue an objective different from that pursued by Articles 81 and 82 of the Treaty.

CHAPTER II POWERS

Article 4   Powers of the Commission

For the purpose of applying Articles 81 and 82 of the Treaty, the Commission shall have the powers provided for by this Regulation.

Article 5   Powers of the competition authorities of the Member States

The competition authorities of the Member States shall have the power to apply Articles 81 and 82 of the Treaty in individual cases. For this purpose, acting on their own initiative or on a complaint, they may take the following decisions:
— requiring that an infringement be brought to an end,
— ordering interim measures,
— accepting commitments,
— imposing fines, periodic penalty payments or any other penalty provided for in their national law.

Where on the basis of the information in their possession the conditions for prohibition are not met they may likewise decide that there are no grounds for action on their part.

Article 6   Powers of the national courts

National courts shall have the power to apply Articles 81 and 82 of the Treaty.

CHAPTER III   COMMISSION DECISIONS

Article 7   Finding and termination of infringement

1.   Where the Commission, acting on a complaint or on its own initiative, finds that there is an infringement of Article 81 or of Article 82 of the Treaty, it may by decision require the undertakings and associations of undertakings concerned to bring such infringement to an end. For this purpose, it may impose on them any behavioural or structural remedies which are proportionate to the infringement committed and necessary to bring the infringement effectively to an end. Structural remedies can only be imposed either where there is no equally effective behavioural remedy or where any equally effective behavioural remedy would be more burdensome for the undertaking concerned than the structural remedy. If the Commission has a legitimate interest in doing so, it may also find that an infringement has been committed in the past.

2.   Those entitled to lodge a complaint for the purposes of paragraph 1 are natural or legal persons who can show a legitimate interest and Member States.

Article 8   Interim measures

1. In cases of urgency due to the risk of serious and irreparable damage to competition, the Commission, acting on its own initiative may by decision, on the basis of a prima facie finding of infringement, order interim measures.

2.   A decision under paragraph 1 shall apply for a specified period of time and may be renewed in so far this is necessary and appropriate.

Article 9   Commitments

1.   Where the Commission intends to adopt a decision requiring that an infringement be brought to an end and the undertakings concerned offer commitments to meet the concerns expressed to them by the Commission in its preliminary assessment, the Commission may by decision make those commitments binding on the undertakings. Such a decision may be adopted for a specified period and shall conclude that there are no longer grounds for action by the Commission.

2.   The Commission may, upon request or on its own initiative, reopen the proceedings:
(a) where there has been a material change in any of the facts on which the decision was based;

(b) where the undertakings concerned act contrary to their commitments; or

(c) where the decision was based on incomplete, incorrect or misleading information provided by the parties.

Article 10 Finding of inapplicability

Where the Community public interest relating to the application of Articles 81 and 82 of the Treaty so requires, the Commission, acting on its own initiative, may by decision find that Article 81 of the Treaty is not applicable to an agreement, a decision by an association of undertakings or a concerted practice, either because the conditions of Article 81(1) of the Treaty are not fulfilled, or because the conditions of Article 81(3) of the Treaty are satisfied.

The Commission may likewise make such a finding with reference to Article 82 of the Treaty.

CHAPTER IV COOPERATION

Article 11

Cooperation between the Commission and the competition authorities of the Member States

1. The Commission and the competition authorities of the Member States shall apply the Community competition rules in close cooperation.

2. The Commission shall transmit to the competition authorities of the Member States copies of the most important documents it has collected with a view to applying Articles 7, 8, 9, 10 and Article 29(1). At the request of the competition authority of a Member State, the Commission shall provide it with a copy of other existing documents necessary for the assessment of the case.

3. The competition authorities of the Member States shall, when acting under Article 81 or Article 82 of the Treaty, inform the Commission in writing before or without delay after commencing the first formal investigative measure. This information may also be made available to the competition authorities of the other Member States.

4. No later than 30 days before the adoption of a decision requiring that an infringement be brought to an end, accepting commitments or withdrawing the benefit of a block exemption Regulation, the competition authorities of the Member States shall inform the Commission. To that effect, they shall provide the Commission with a summary of the case, the envisaged decision or, in the absence thereof, any other document indicating the proposed course of action. This information may also be made available to the competition authorities of the other Member States. At the request of the Commission, the acting competition authority shall make available to the Commission other documents it holds which are necessary for the assessment of the case. The information supplied to the Commission may be made available to the competition authorities of the other Member States. National competition authorities may also exchange between themselves information necessary for the assessment of a case that they are dealing with under Article 81 or Article 82 of the Treaty.

5. The competition authorities of the Member States may consult the Commission on any case involving the application of Community law.

6. The initiation by the Commission of proceedings for the adoption of a decision under Chapter III shall relieve the competition authorities of the Member States of their competence to apply Articles 81 and 82 of the Treaty. If a competition authority of a Member State is already acting on a case, the Commission shall only initiate proceedings after consulting with that national competition authority.

Article 12 Exchange of information

1. For the purpose of applying Articles 81 and 82 of the Treaty the Commission and the competition authorities of the Member States shall have the power to provide one another with and use in evidence any matter of fact or of law, including confidential information.

2. Information exchanged shall only be used in evidence for the purpose of applying Article 81 or Article 82 of the Treaty and in respect of the subject-matter for which it was collected by the transmitting authority. However, where national competition law is applied in the same case and in parallel to Community competition law and does not lead to a different outcome, information exchanged under this Article may also be used for the application of national competition law.

3. Information exchanged pursuant to paragraph 1 can only be used in evidence to impose sanctions on natural persons where:

— the law of the transmitting authority foresees sanctions of a similar kind in relation to an infringement of Article 81 or Article 82 of the Treaty or, in the absence thereof,

— the information has been collected in a way which respects the same level of protection of the rights of defence of natural persons as provided for under the national rules of the receiving authority. However, in this case, the information exchanged cannot be used by the receiving authority to impose custodial sanctions.

Article 13   Suspension or termination of proceedings

1. Where competition authorities of two or more Member States have received a complaint or are acting on their own initiative under Article 81 or Article 82 of the Treaty against the same agreement, decision of an association or practice, the fact that one authority is dealing with the case shall be sufficient grounds for the others to suspend the proceedings before them or to reject the complaint. The Commission may likewise reject a complaint on the ground that a competition authority of a Member State is dealing with the case.

2. Where a competition authority of a Member State or the Commission has received a complaint against an agreement, decision of an association or practice which has already been dealt with by another competition authority, it may reject it.

Article 14   Advisory Committee

1. The Commission shall consult an Advisory Committee on Restrictive Practices and Dominant Positions prior to the taking of any decision under Articles 7, 8, 9, 10, 23, Article 24(2) and Article 29(1).

2. For the discussion of individual cases, the Advisory Committee shall be composed of representatives of the competition authorities of the Member States. For meetings in which issues other than individual cases are being discussed, an additional Member State representative competent in competition matters may be appointed. Representatives may, if unable to attend, be replaced by other representatives.

3. The consultation may take place at a meeting convened and chaired by the Commission, held not earlier than 14 days after dispatch of the notice convening it, together with a summary of the case, an indication of the most important documents and a preliminary draft decision. In respect of decisions pursuant to Article 8, the meeting may be held seven days after the dispatch of the operative part of a draft decision. Where the Commission dispatches a notice convening the meeting which gives a shorter period of notice than those specified above, the meeting may take place on the proposed date in the absence of an objection by any Member State. The Advisory Committee shall deliver a written opinion on the Commission's preliminary draft decision. It may deliver an opinion even if some members are absent and are not represented. At the request of one or several members, the positions stated in the opinion shall be reasoned.

4. Consultation may also take place by written procedure. However, if any Member State so requests, the Commission shall convene a meeting. In case of written procedure, the Commission shall determine a time-limit of not less than 14 days within which the Member States are to put forward their observations for circulation to all other Member States. In case of decisions to be taken pursuant to Article 8, the time-limit of 14 days is replaced by seven

days. Where the Commission determines a time-limit for the written procedure which is shorter than those specified above, the proposed time-limit shall be applicable in the absence of an objection by any Member State.

5.   The Commission shall take the utmost account of the opinion delivered by the Advisory Committee. It shall inform the Committee of the manner in which its opinion has been taken into account.

6.   Where the Advisory Committee delivers a written opinion, this opinion shall be appended to the draft decision. If the Advisory Committee recommends publication of the opinion, the Commission shall carry out such publication taking into account the legitimate interest of undertakings in the protection of their business secrets.

7.   At the request of a competition authority of a Member State, the Commission shall include on the agenda of the Advisory Committee cases that are being dealt with by a competition authority of a Member State under Article 81 or Article 82 of the Treaty. The Commission may also do so on its own initiative. In either case, the Commission shall inform the competition authority concerned.

A request may in particular be made by a competition authority of a Member State in respect of a case where the Commission intends to initiate proceedings with the effect of Article 11(6).

The Advisory Committee shall not issue opinions on cases dealt with by competition authorities of the Member States. The Advisory Committee may also discuss general issues of Community competition law.

Article 15   Cooperation with national courts

1.   In proceedings for the application of Article 81 or Article 82 of the Treaty, courts of the Member States may ask the Commission to transmit to them information in its possession or its opinion on questions concerning the application of the Community competition rules.

2.   Member States shall forward to the Commission a copy of any written judgment of national courts deciding on the application of Article 81 or Article 82 of the Treaty. Such copy shall be forwarded without delay after the full written judgment is notified to the parties.

3.   Competition authorities of the Member States, acting on their own initiative, may submit written observations to the national courts of their Member State on issues relating to the application of Article 81 or Article 82 of the Treaty. With the permission of the court in question, they may also submit oral observations to the national courts of their Member State. Where the coherent application of Article 81 or Article 82 of the Treaty so requires, the Commission, acting on its own initiative, may submit written observations to courts of the Member States. With the permission of the court in question, it may also make oral observations.

For the purpose of the preparation of their observations only, the competition authorities of the Member States and the Commission may request the relevant court of the Member State to transmit or ensure the transmission to them of any documents necessary for the assessment of the case.

4.   This Article is without prejudice to wider powers to make observations before courts conferred on competition authorities of the Member States under the law of their Member State.

Article 16   Uniform application of Community competition law

1.   When national courts rule on agreements, decisions or practices under Article 81 or Article 82 of the Treaty which are already the subject of a Commission decision, they cannot take decisions running counter to the decision adopted by the Commission. They must also avoid giving decisions which would conflict with a decision contemplated by the Commission in proceedings it has initiated. To that effect, the national court may assess whether

it is necessary to stay its proceedings. This obligation is without prejudice to the rights and obligations under Article 234 of the Treaty.

2. When competition authorities of the Member States rule on agreements, decisions or practices under Article 81 or Article 82 of the Treaty which are already the subject of a Commission decision, they cannot take decisions which would run counter to the decision adopted by the Commission.

CHAPTER V POWERS OF INVESTIGATION

Article 17 Investigations into sectors of the economy and into types of agreements

1. Where the trend of trade between Member States, the rigidity of prices or other circumstances suggest that competition may be restricted or distorted within the common market, the Commission may conduct its inquiry into a particular sector of the economy or into a particular type of agreements across various sectors. In the course of that inquiry, the Commission may request the undertakings or associations of undertakings concerned to supply the information necessary for giving effect to Articles 81 and 82 of the Treaty and may carry out any inspections necessary for that purpose.

The Commission may in particular request the undertakings or associations of undertakings concerned to communicate to it all agreements, decisions and concerted practices.

The Commission may publish a report on the results of its inquiry into particular sectors of the economy or particular types of agreements across various sectors and invite comments from interested parties.

2. Articles 14, 18, 19, 20, 22, 23 and 24 shall apply mutatis mutandis.

Article 18 Requests for information

1. In order to carry out the duties assigned to it by this Regulation, the Commission may, by simple request or by decision, require undertakings and associations of undertakings to provide all necessary information.

2. When sending a simple request for information to an undertaking or association of undertakings, the Commission shall state the legal basis and the purpose of the request, specify what information is required and fix the time-limit within which the information is to be provided, and the penalties provided for in Article 23 for supplying incorrect or misleading information.

3. Where the Commission requires undertakings and associations of undertakings to supply information by decision, it shall state the legal basis and the purpose of the request, specify what information is required and fix the time-limit within which it is to be provided. It shall also indicate the penalties provided for in Article 23 and indicate or impose the penalties provided for in Article 24. It shall further indicate the right to have the decision reviewed by the Court of Justice.

4. The owners of the undertakings or their representatives and, in the case of legal persons, companies or firms, or associations having no legal personality, the persons author-ised to represent them by law or by their constitution shall supply the information requested on behalf of the undertaking or the association of undertakings concerned. Lawyers duly authorised to act may supply the information on behalf of their clients. The latter shall remain fully responsible if the information supplied is incomplete, incorrect or misleading.

5. The Commission shall without delay forward a copy of the simple request or of the decision to the competition authority of the Member State in whose territory the seat of the undertaking or association of undertakings is situated and the competition authority of the Member State whose territory is affected.

6. At the request of the Commission the governments and competition authorities of the Member States shall provide the Commission with all necessary information to carry out the duties assigned to it by this Regulation.

Article 19   Power to take statements   ᷏

1.   In order to carry out the duties assigned to it by this Regulation, the Commission may interview any natural or legal person who consents to be interviewed for the purpose of collecting information relating to the subject-matter of an investigation.

2.   Where an interview pursuant to paragraph 1 is conducted in the premises of an undertaking, the Commission shall inform the competition authority of the Member State in whose territory the interview takes place. If so requested by the competition authority of that Member State, its officials may assist the officials and other accompanying persons authorised by the Commission to conduct the interview.

Article 20   The Commission's powers of inspection

1.   In order to carry out the duties assigned to it by this Regulation, the Commission may conduct all necessary inspections of undertakings and associations of undertakings.

2.   The officials and other accompanying persons authorised by the Commission to conduct an inspection are empowered:

    (a) to enter any premises, land and means of transport of undertakings and associations of undertakings;

    (b) to examine the books and other records related to the business, irrespective of the medium on which they are stored;

    (c) to take or obtain in any form copies of or extracts from such books or records;

    (d) to seal any business premises and books or records for the period and to the extent necessary for the inspection;

    (e) to ask any representative or member of staff of the undertaking or association of undertakings for explanations on facts or documents relating to the subject-matter and purpose of the inspection and to record the answers.

3.   The officials and other accompanying persons authorised by the Commission to conduct an inspection shall exercise their powers upon production of a written authorisation specifying the subject matter and purpose of the inspection and the penalties provided for in Article 23 in case the production of the required books or other records related to the business is incomplete or where the answers to questions asked under paragraph 2 of the present Article are incorrect or misleading. In good time before the inspection, the Commission shall give notice of the inspection to the competition authority of the Member State in whose territory it is to be conducted.

4.   Undertakings and associations of undertakings are required to submit to inspections ordered by decision of the Commission. The decision shall specify the subject matter and purpose of the inspection, appoint the date on which it is to begin and indicate the penalties provided for in Articles 23 and 24 and the right to have the decision reviewed by the Court of Justice. The Commission shall take such decisions after consulting the competition authority of the Member State in whose territory the inspection is to be conducted.

5.   Officials of as well as those authorised or appointed by the competition authority of the Member State in whose territory the inspection is to be conducted shall, at the request of that authority or of the Commission, actively assist the officials and other accompanying persons authorised by the Commission. To this end, they shall enjoy the powers specified in paragraph 2.

6.   Where the officials and other accompanying persons authorised by the Commission find that an undertaking opposes an inspection ordered pursuant to this Article, the Member State concerned shall afford them the necessary assistance, requesting where appropriate the assistance of the police or of an equivalent enforcement authority, so as to enable them to conduct their inspection.

7.   If the assistance provided for in paragraph 6 requires authorisation from a judicial authority according to national rules, such authorisation shall be applied for. Such authorisation may also be applied for as a precautionary measure.

8.   Where authorisation as referred to in paragraph 7 is applied for, the national judicial authority shall control that the Commission decision is authentic and that the coercive measures envisaged are neither arbitrary nor excessive having regard to the subject matter of the inspection. In its control of the proportionality of the coercive measures, the national judicial authority may ask the Commission, directly or through the Member State competition authority, for detailed explanations in particular on the grounds the Commission has for suspecting infringement of Articles 81 and 82 of the Treaty, as well as on the seriousness of the suspected infringement and on the nature of the involvement of the undertaking concerned. However, the national judicial authority may not call into question the necessity for the inspection nor demand that it be provided with the information in the Commission's file. The lawfulness of the Commission decision shall be subject to review only by the Court of Justice.

Article 21   Inspection of other premises

1.   If a reasonable suspicion exists that books or other records related to the business and to the subject-matter of the inspection, which may be relevant to prove a serious violation of Article 81 or Article 82 of the Treaty, are being kept in any other premises, land and means of transport, including the homes of directors, managers and other members of staff of the undertakings and associations of undertakings concerned, the Commission can by decision order an inspection to be conducted in such other premises, land and means of transport.

2.   The decision shall specify the subject matter and purpose of the inspection, appoint the date on which it is to begin and indicate the right to have the decision reviewed by the Court of Justice. It shall in particular state the reasons that have led the Commission to conclude that a suspicion in the sense of paragraph 1 exists. The Commission shall take such decisions after consulting the competition authority of the Member State in whose territory the inspection is to be conducted.

3.   A decision adopted pursuant to paragraph 1 cannot be executed without prior authorisation from the national judicial authority of the Member State concerned. The national judicial authority shall control that the Commission decision is authentic and that the coercive measures envisaged are neither arbitrary nor excessive having regard in particular to the seriousness of the suspected infringement, to the importance of the evidence sought, to the involvement of the undertaking concerned and to the reasonable likelihood that business books and records relating to the subject matter of the inspection are kept in the premises for which the authorisation is requested. The national judicial authority may ask the Commission, directly or through the Member State competition authority, for detailed explanations on those elements which are necessary to allow its control of the proportionality of the coercive measures envisaged.

However, the national judicial authority may not call into question the necessity for the inspection nor demand that it be provided with information in the Commission's file. The lawfulness of the Commission decision shall be subject to review only by the Court of Justice.

4.   The officials and other accompanying persons authorised by the Commission to conduct an inspection ordered in accordance with paragraph 1 of this Article shall have the powers set out in Article 20(2)(a), (b) and (c). Article 20(5) and (6) shall apply mutatis mutandis.

Article 22   Investigations by competition authorities of Member States

1.   The competition authority of a Member State may in its own territory carry out any inspection or other fact-finding measure under its national law on behalf and for the account of the competition authority of another Member State in order to establish whether there has been an infringement of Article 81 or Article 82 of the Treaty. Any exchange and use of the information collected shall be carried out in accordance with Article 12.

2.   At the request of the Commission, the competition authorities of the Member States shall undertake the inspections which the Commission considers to be necessary under Article 20(1) or which it has ordered by decision pursuant to Article 20(4). The officials of

the competition authorities of the Member States who are responsible for conducting these inspections as well as those authorised or appointed by them shall exercise their powers in accordance with their national law.

If so requested by the Commission or by the competition authority of the Member State in whose territory the inspection is to be conducted, officials and other accompanying persons authorised by the Commission may assist the officials of the authority concerned.

CHAPTER VI   PENALTIES

Article 23   Fines

1.   The Commission may by decision impose on undertakings and associations of undertakings fines not exceeding 1% of the total turnover in the preceding business year where, intentionally or negligently:

(a) they supply incorrect or misleading information in response to a request made pursuant to Article 17 or Article 18(2);

(b) in response to a request made by decision adopted pursuant to Article 17 or Article 18(3), they supply incorrect, incomplete or misleading information or do not supply information within the required time-limit;

(c) they produce the required books or other records related to the business in incomplete form during inspections under Article 20 or refuse to submit to inspections ordered by a decision adopted pursuant to Article 20(4);

(d) in response to a question asked in accordance with Article 20(2)(e),

— they give an incorrect or misleading answer,

— they fail to rectify within a time-limit set by the Commission an incorrect, incomplete or misleading answer given by a member of staff, or

— they fail or refuse to provide a complete answer on facts relating to the subject-matter and purpose of an inspection ordered by a decision adopted pursuant to Article 20(4);

(e) seals affixed in accordance with Article 20(2)(d) by officials or other accompanying persons authorised by the Commission have been broken.

2.   The Commission may by decision impose fines on undertakings and associations of undertakings where, either intentionally or negligently:

(a) they infringe Article 81 or Article 82 of the Treaty; or

(b) they contravene a decision ordering interim measures under Article 8; or

(c) they fail to comply with a commitment made binding by a decision pursuant to Article 9.

For each undertaking and association of undertakings participating in the infringement, the fine shall not exceed 10% of its total turnover in the preceding business year.

Where the infringement of an association relates to the activities of its members, the fine shall not exceed 10% of the sum of the total turnover of each member active on the market affected by the infringement of the association.

3.   In fixing the amount of the fine, regard shall be had both to the gravity and to the duration of the infringement.

4.   When a fine is imposed on an association of undertakings taking account of the turnover of its members and the association is not solvent, the association is obliged to call for contributions from its members to cover the amount of the fine.

Where such contributions have not been made to the association within a time-limit fixed by the Commission, the Commission may require payment of the fine directly by any of the undertakings whose representatives were members of the decision-making bodies concerned of the association.

After the Commission has required payment under the second subparagraph, where necessary to ensure full payment of the fine, the Commission may require payment of the balance by any of the members of the association which were active on the market on which the infringement occurred.

However, the Commission shall not require payment under the second or the third subparagraph from undertakings which show that they have not implemented the infringing decision of the association and either were not aware of its existence or have actively distanced themselves from it before the Commission started investigating the case.

The financial liability of each undertaking in respect of the payment of the fine shall not exceed 10% of its total turnover in the preceding business year.

5. Decisions taken pursuant to paragraphs 1 and 2 shall not be of a criminal law nature.

Article 24   Periodic penalty payments

1. The Commission may, by decision, impose on undertakings or associations of undertakings periodic penalty payments not exceeding 5% of the average daily turnover in the preceding business year per day and calculated from the date appointed by the decision, in order to compel them:

(a) to put an end to an infringement of Article 81 or Article 82 of the Treaty, in accordance with a decision taken pursuant to Article 7;

(b) to comply with a decision ordering interim measures taken pursuant to Article 8;

(c) to comply with a commitment made binding by a decision pursuant to Article 9;

(d) to supply complete and correct information which it has requested by decision taken pursuant to Article 17 or Article 18(3);

(e) to submit to an inspection which it has ordered by decision taken pursuant to Article 20(4).

2. Where the undertakings or associations of undertakings have satisfied the obligation which the periodic penalty payment was intended to enforce, the Commission may fix the definitive amount of the periodic penalty payment at a figure lower than that which would arise under the original decision. Article 23(4) shall apply correspondingly.

CHAPTER VII   LIMITATION PERIODS

Article 25   Limitation periods for the imposition of penalties

1. The powers conferred on the Commission by Articles 23 and 24 shall be subject to the following limitation periods:

(a) three years in the case of infringements of provisions concerning requests for information or the conduct of inspections;

(b) five years in the case of all other infringements.

2. Time shall begin to run on the day on which the infringement is committed. However, in the case of continuing or repeated infringements, time shall begin to run on the day on which the infringement ceases.

3. Any action taken by the Commission or by the competition authority of a Member State for the purpose of the investigation or proceedings in respect of an infringement shall interrupt the limitation period for the imposition of fines or periodic penalty payments. The limitation period shall be interrupted with effect from the date on which the action is notified to at least one undertaking or association of undertakings which has participated in the infringement. Actions which interrupt the running of the period shall include in particular the following:

(a) written requests for information by the Commission or by the competition authority of a Member State;

(b) written authorisations to conduct inspections issued to its officials by the Commission or by the competition authority of a Member State;

(c) the initiation of proceedings by the Commission or by the competition authority of a Member State;

(d) notification of the statement of objections of the Commission or of the competition authority of a Member State.

4.   The interruption of the limitation period shall apply for all the undertakings or associations of undertakings which have participated in the infringement.

5.   Each interruption shall start time running afresh. However, the limitation period shall expire at the latest on the day on which a period equal to twice the limitation period has elapsed without the Commission having imposed a fine or a periodic penalty payment. That period shall be extended by the time during which limitation is suspended pursuant to paragraph 6.

6.   The limitation period for the imposition of fines or periodic penalty payments shall be suspended for as long as the decision of the Commission is the subject of proceedings pending before the Court of Justice.

Article 26   Limitation period for the enforcement of penalties

1.   The power of the Commission to enforce decisions taken pursuant to Articles 23 and 24 shall be subject to a limitation period of five years.

2.   Time shall begin to run on the day on which the decision becomes final.

3.   The limitation period for the enforcement of penalties shall be interrupted:

(a) by notification of a decision varying the original amount of the fine or periodic penalty payment or refusing an application for variation;

(b) by any action of the Commission or of a Member State, acting at the request of the Commission, designed to enforce payment of the fine or periodic penalty payment.

4.   Each interruption shall start time running afresh.

5.   The limitation period for the enforcement of penalties shall be suspended for so long as:

(a) time to pay is allowed;

(b) enforcement of payment is suspended pursuant to a decision of the Court of Justice.

CHAPTER VIII   HEARINGS AND PROFESSIONAL SECRECY

Article 27   Hearing of the parties, complainants and others

1.   Before taking decisions as provided for in Articles 7, 8, 23 and Article 24(2), the Commission shall give the undertakings or associations of undertakings which are the subject of the proceedings conducted by the Commission the opportunity of being heard on the matters to which the Commission has taken objection. The Commission shall base its decisions only on objections on which the parties concerned have been able to comment. Complainants shall be associated closely with the proceedings.

2.   The rights of defence of the parties concerned shall be fully respected in the proceedings. They shall be entitled to have access to the Commission's file, subject to the legitimate interest of undertakings in the protection of their business secrets. The right of access to the file shall not extend to confidential information and internal documents of the Commission or the competition authorities of the Member States. In particular, the right of access shall not extend to correspondence between the Commission and the competition authorities of the Member States, or between the latter, including documents drawn up pursuant to Articles 11 and 14. Nothing in this paragraph shall prevent the Commission from disclosing and using information necessary to prove an infringement.

3.   If the Commission considers it necessary, it may also hear other natural or legal persons. Applications to be heard on the part of such persons shall, where they show a sufficient interest, be granted. The competition authorities of the Member States may also ask the Commission to hear other natural or legal persons.

4.   Where the Commission intends to adopt a decision pursuant to Article 9 or Article 10, it shall publish a concise summary of the case and the main content of the commitments or of

the proposed course of action. Interested third parties may submit their observations within a time limit which is fixed by the Commission in its publication and which may not be less than one month. Publication shall have regard to the legitimate interest of undertakings in the protection of their business secrets.

Article 28   Professional secrecy

1.   Without prejudice to Articles 12 and 15, information collected pursuant to Articles 17 to 22 shall be used only for the purpose for which it was acquired.

2.   Without prejudice to the exchange and to the use of information foreseen in Articles 11, 12, 14, 15 and 27, the Commission and the competition authorities of the Member States, their officials, servants and other persons working under the supervision of these authorities as well as officials and civil servants of other authorities of the Member States shall not disclose information acquired or exchanged by them pursuant to this Regulation and of the kind covered by the obligation of professional secrecy. This obligation also applies to all representatives and experts of Member States attending meetings of the Advisory Committee pursuant to Article 14.

CHAPTER IX   EXEMPTION REGULATIONS

Article 29   Withdrawal in individual cases

1.   Where the Commission, empowered by a Council Regulation, such as Regulations 19/65/EEC, (EEC) No 2821/71, (EEC) No 3976/87, (EEC) No 1534/91 or (EEC) No 479/92, to apply Article 81(3) of the Treaty by regulation, has declared Article 81(1) of the Treaty inapplicable to certain categories of agreements, decisions by associations of undertakings or concerted practices, it may, acting on its own initiative or on a complaint, withdraw the benefit of such an exemption Regulation when it finds that in any particular case an agreement, decision or concerted practice to which the exemption Regulation applies has certain effects which are incompatible with Article 81(3) of the Treaty.

2.   Where, in any particular case, agreements, decisions by associations of undertakings or concerted practices to which a Commission Regulation referred to in paragraph 1 applies have effects which are incompatible with Article 81(3) of the Treaty in the territory of a Member State, or in a part thereof, which has all the characteristics of a distinct geographic market, the competition authority of that Member State may withdraw the benefit of the Regulation in question in respect of that territory.

CHAPTER X   GENERAL PROVISIONS

Article 30   Publication of decisions

1.   The Commission shall publish the decisions, which it takes pursuant to Articles 7 to 10, 23 and 24.

2.   The publication shall state the names of the parties and the main content of the decision, including any penalties imposed. It shall have regard to the legitimate interest of undertakings in the protection of their business secrets.

Article 31   Review by the Court of Justice

The Court of Justice shall have unlimited jurisdiction to review decisions whereby the Commission has fixed a fine or periodic penalty payment. It may cancel, reduce or increase the fine or periodic penalty payment imposed.

Article 32   Exclusions

This Regulation shall not apply to:

        (a) international tramp vessel services as defined in Article 1(3)(a) of Regulation (EEC) No 4056/86;

(b) a maritime transport service that takes place exclusively between ports in one and the same Member State as foreseen in Article 1(2) of Regulation (EEC) No 4056/86.

Article 33   Implementing provisions

1.   The Commission shall be authorised to take such measures as may be appropriate in order to apply this Regulation. The measures may concern, *inter alia*:

(a) the form, content and other details of complaints lodged pursuant to Article 7 and the procedure for rejecting complaints;

(b) the practical arrangements for the exchange of information and consultations provided for in Article 11;

(c) the practical arrangements for the hearings provided for in Article 27.

2.   Before the adoption of any measures pursuant to paragraph 1, the Commission shall publish a draft thereof and invite all interested parties to submit their comments within the time-limit it lays down, which may not be less than one month. Before publishing a draft measure and before adopting it, the Commission shall consult the Advisory Committee on Restrictive Practices and Dominant Positions.

CHAPTER XI   TRANSITIONAL, AMENDING AND FINAL PROVISIONS

Article 34   Transitional provisions

1.   Applications made to the Commission under Article 2 of Regulation No 17, notifications made under Articles 4 and 5 of that Regulation and the corresponding applications and notifications made under Regulations (EEC) No 1017/68, (EEC) No 4056/86 and (EEC) No 3975/87 shall lapse as from the date of application of this Regulation.

2.   Procedural steps taken under Regulation No 17 and Regulations (EEC) No 1017/68, (EEC) No 4056/86 and (EEC) No 3975/87 shall continue to have effect for the purposes of applying this Regulation.

Article 35   Designation of competition authorities of Member States

1.   The Member States shall designate the competition authority or authorities responsible for the application of Articles 81 and 82 of the Treaty in such a way that the provisions of this regulation are effectively complied with. The measures necessary to empower those authorities to apply those Articles shall be taken before 1 May 2004. The authorities designated may include courts.

2.   When enforcement of Community competition law is entrusted to national administrative and judicial authorities, the Member States may allocate different powers and functions to those different national authorities, whether administrative or judicial.

3.   The effects of Article 11(6) apply to the authorities designated by the Member States including courts that exercise functions regarding the preparation and the adoption of the types of decisions foreseen in Article 5. The effects of Article 11(6) do not extend to courts insofar as they act as review courts in respect of the types of decisions foreseen in Article 5.

4.   Notwithstanding paragraph 3, in the Member States where, for the adoption of certain types of decisions foreseen in Article 5, an authority brings an action before a judicial authority that is separate and different from the prosecuting authority and provided that the terms of this paragraph are complied with, the effects of Article 11(6) shall be limited to the authority prosecuting the case which shall withdraw its claim before the judicial authority when the Commission opens proceedings and this withdrawal shall bring the national proceedings effectively to an end.

Article 36   Amendment of Regulation (EEC) No 1017/68

Regulation (EEC) No 1017/68 is amended as follows:

1.   Article 2 is repealed;

2.   in Article 3(1), the words 'The prohibition laid down in Article 2' are replaced by the words 'The prohibition in Article 81(1) of the Treaty';
3.   Article 4 is amended as follows:
  (a) In paragraph 1, the words 'The agreements, decisions and concerted practices referred to in Article 2' are replaced by the words 'Agreements, decisions and concerted practices pursuant to Article 81(1) of the Treaty';
  (b) Paragraph 2 is replaced by the following:

'2.   If the implementation of any agreement, decision or concerted practice covered by paragraph 1 has, in a given case, effects which are incompatible with the requirements of Article 81(3) of the Treaty, undertakings or associations of undertakings may be required to make such effects cease.'

4.   Articles 5 to 29 are repealed with the exception of Article 13(3) which continues to apply to decisions adopted pursuant to Article 5 of Regulation (EEC) No 1017/68 prior to the date of application of this Regulation until the date of expiration of those decisions;
5.   In Article 30, paragraphs 2, 3 and 4 are deleted.

Article 37   Amendment of Regulation (EEC) No 2988/74
In Regulation (EEC) No 2988/74, the following Article is inserted:

'Article 7a   Exclusion
This Regulation shall not apply to measures taken under Council Regulation (EC) No 1/2003 of 16 December 2002 on the implementation of the rules on competition laid down in Articles 81 and 82 of the Treaty[16].'

Article 38   Amendment of Regulation (EEC) No 4056/86
Regulation (EEC) No 4056/86 is amended as follows:
1.   Article 7 is amended as follows:
  (a) Paragraph 1 is replaced by the following:

'1.   Breach of an obligation
Where the persons concerned are in breach of an obligation which, pursuant to Article 5, attaches to the exemption provided for in Article 3, the Commission may, in order to put an end to such breach and under the conditions laid down in Council Regulation (EC) No 1/2003 of 16 December 2002 on the implementation of the rules on competition laid down in Articles 81 and 82 of the Treaty[17] adopt a decision that either prohibits them from carrying out or requires them to perform certain specific acts, or withdraws the benefit of the block exemption which they enjoyed.'

  (b) Paragraph 2 is amended as follows:
    (i) In point (a), the words 'under the conditions laid down in Section II' are replaced by the words 'under the conditions laid down in Regulation (EC) No 1/2003';
    (ii) The second sentence of the second subparagraph of point (c)(i) is replaced by the following:

'At the same time it shall decide, in accordance with Article 9 of Regulation (EC) No 1/2003, whether to accept commitments offered by the undertakings concerned with a view, *inter alia*, to obtaining access to the market for non-conference lines.'

2.   Article 8 is amended as follows:
  (a) Paragraph 1 is deleted.

[16] OJ L 1, 4.1.2003, p. 1.
[17] OJ L 1, 4.1.2003, p. 1.

(b) In paragraph 2 the words 'pursuant to Article 10' are replaced by the words 'pursuant to Regulation (EC) No 1/2003'.

(c) Paragraph 3 is deleted;

3. Article 9 is amended as follows:

(a) In paragraph 1, the words 'Advisory Committee referred to in Article 15' are replaced by the words 'Advisory Committee referred to in Article 14 of Regulation (EC) No 1/2003';

(b) In paragraph 2, the words 'Advisory Committee as referred to in Article 15' are replaced by the words 'Advisory Committee referred to in Article 14 of Regulation (EC) No 1/2003';

4. Articles 10 to 25 are repealed with the exception of Article 13(3) which continues to apply to decisions adopted pursuant to Article 81(3) of the Treaty prior to the date of application of this Regulation until the date of expiration of those decisions;

5. in Article 26, the words 'the form, content and other details of complaints pursuant to Article 10, applications pursuant to Article 12 and the hearings provided for in Article 23(1) and (2)' are deleted.

Article 39   Amendment of Regulation (EEC) No 3975/87
Articles 3 to 19 of Regulation (EEC) No 3975/87 are repealed with the exception of Article 6(3) which continues to apply to decisions adopted pursuant to Article 81(3) of the Treaty prior to the date of application of this Regulation until the date of expiration of those decisions.

Article 40   Amendment of Regulations No 19/65/EEC, (EEC) No 2821/71 and (EEC) No 1534/91
Article 7 of Regulation No 19/65/EEC, Article 7 of Regulation (EEC) No 2821/71 and Article 7 of Regulation (EEC) No 1534/91 are repealed.

Article 41   Amendment of Regulation (EEC) No 3976/87
Regulation (EEC) No 3976/87 is amended as follows:

1. Article 6 is replaced by the following:

'Article 6
The Commission shall consult the Advisory Committee referred to in Article 14 of Council Regulation (EC) No 1/2003 of 16 December 2002 on the implementation of the rules on competition laid down in Articles 81 and 82 of the Treaty[18] before publishing a draft Regulation and before adopting a Regulation.'

2. Article 7 is repealed.

Article 42   Amendment of Regulation (EEC) No 479/92
Regulation (EEC) No 479/92 is amended as follows:

1. Article 5 is replaced by the following:

'Article 5
Before publishing the draft Regulation and before adopting the Regulation, the Commission shall consult the Advisory Committee referred to in Article 14 of Council Regulation (EC) No 1/2003 of 16 December 2002 on the implementation of the rules on competition laid down in Articles 81 and 82 of the Treaty[19].'

2. Article 6 is repealed.

Article 43   Repeal of Regulations No 17 and No 141
1. Regulation No 17 is repealed with the exception of Article 8(3) which continues to apply to decisions adopted pursuant to Article 81(3) of the Treaty prior to the date of application of this Regulation until the date of expiration of those decisions.

[18] OJ L 1, 4.1.2003, p. 1.
[19] OJ L 1, 4.1.2003, p. 1.

2. Regulation No 141 is repealed.

3. References to the repealed Regulations shall be construed as references to this Regulation.

Article 44 Report on the application of the present Regulation

Five years from the date of application of this Regulation, the Commission shall report to the European Parliament and the Council on the functioning of this Regulation, in particular on the application of Article 11(6) and Article 17.

On the basis of this report, the Commission shall assess whether it is appropriate to propose to the Council a revision of this Regulation.

Article 45 Entry into force

This Regulation shall enter into force on the 20th day following that of its publication in the Official Journal of the European Communities.

It shall apply from 1 May 2004.

This Regulation shall be binding in its entirety and directly applicable in all Member States.

Done at Brussels, 16 December 2002.

For the Council
The President
M. Fischer Boel

Council Regulation (EC) No. 139/2004 of 20 January 2004 on the control of concentrations between undertakings (the EC Merger Regulation)

[OJ 2004, L24/22]*

THE COUNCIL OF THE EUROPEAN UNION,

Having regard to the Treaty establishing the European Community, and in particular Articles 83 and 308 thereof,

Having regard to the proposal from the Commission,[1]

Having regard to the opinion of the European Parliament,[2]

Having regard to the opinion of the European Economic and Social Committee,[3]

Whereas:

(1) Council Regulation (EEC) No 4064/89 of 21 December 1989 on the control of concentrations between undertakings[4] has been substantially amended. Since further amendments are to be made, it should be recast in the interest of clarity.

(2) For the achievement of the aims of the Treaty, Article 3(1)(g) gives the Community the objective of instituting a system ensuring that competition in the internal market is not distorted. Article 4(1) of the Treaty provides that the activities of the Member States and the Community are to be conducted in accordance with the principle of an open market economy

---

* **Editor's Note:** This Regulation replaces and repeals Regulations 4064/89 and 1310/97.

[1] OJ C 20, 28.1.2003, p. 4.

[2] Opinion delivered on 9.10.2003 (not yet published in the Official Journal).

[3] Opinion delivered on 24.10.2003 (not yet published in the Official Journal).

[4] OJ L 395, 30.12.1989, p. 1. Corrected version in OJ L 257, 21.9.1990, p. 13. Regulation as last amended by Regulation (EC) No 1310/97 (OJ L 180, 9.7.1997, p. 1). Corrigendum in OJ L 40, 13.2.1998, p. 17.

with free competition. These principles are essential for the further development of the internal market.

(3) The completion of the internal market and of economic and monetary union, the enlargement of the European Union and the lowering of international barriers to trade and investment will continue to result in major corporate reorganisations, particularly in the form of concentrations.

(4) Such reorganisations are to be welcomed to the extent that they are in line with the requirements of dynamic competition and capable of increasing the competitiveness of European industry, improving the conditions of growth and raising the standard of living in the Community.

(5) However, it should be ensured that the process of reorganisation does not result in lasting damage to competition; Community law must therefore include provisions governing those concentrations which may significantly impede effective competition in the common market or in a substantial part of it.

(6) A specific legal instrument is therefore necessary to permit effective control of all concentrations in terms of their effect on the structure of competition in the Community and to be the only instrument applicable to such concentrations. Regulation (EEC) No 4064/89 has allowed a Community policy to develop in this field. In the light of experience, however, that Regulation should now be recast into legislation designed to meet the challenges of a more integrated market and the future enlargement of the European Union. In accordance with the principles of subsidiarity and of proportionality as set out in Article 5 of the Treaty, this Regulation does not go beyond what is necessary in order to achieve the objective of ensuring that competition in the common market is not distorted, in accordance with the principle of an open market economy with free competition.

(7) Articles 81 and 82, while applicable, according to the case-law of the Court of Justice, to certain concentrations, are not sufficient to control all operations which may prove to be incompatible with the system of undistorted competition envisaged in the Treaty. This Regulation should therefore be based not only on Article 83 but, principally, on Article 308 of the Treaty, under which the Community may give itself the additional powers of action necessary for the attainment of its objectives, and also powers of action with regard to concentrations on the markets for agricultural products listed in Annex I to the Treaty.

(8) The provisions to be adopted in this Regulation should apply to significant structural changes, the impact of which on the market goes beyond the national borders of any one Member State. Such concentrations should, as a general rule, be reviewed exclusively at Community level, in application of a 'one-stop shop' system and in compliance with the principle of subsidiarity. Concentrations not covered by this Regulation come, in principle, within the jurisdiction of the Member States.

(9) The scope of application of this Regulation should be defined according to the geographical area of activity of the undertakings concerned and be limited by quantitative thresholds in order to cover those concentrations which have a Community dimension. The Commission should report to the Council on the implementation of the applicable thresholds and criteria so that the Council, acting in accordance with Article 202 of the Treaty, is in a position to review them regularly, as well as the rules regarding pre-notification referral, in the light of the experience gained; this requires statistical data to be provided by the Member States to the Commission to enable it to prepare such reports and possible proposals for amendments. The Commission's reports and proposals should be based on relevant information regularly provided by the Member States.

(10) A concentration with a Community dimension should be deemed to exist where the aggregate turnover of the undertakings concerned exceeds given thresholds; that is the case irrespective of whether or not the undertakings effecting the concentration have their seat or their principal fields of activity in the Community, provided they have substantial operations there.

(11) The rules governing the referral of concentrations from the Commission to Member States and from Member States to the Commission should operate as an effective corrective mechanism in the light of the principle of subsidiarity; these rules protect the competition interests of the Member States in an adequate manner and take due account of legal certainty and the 'one-stop shop' principle.

(12) Concentrations may qualify for examination under a number of national merger control systems if they fall below the turnover thresholds referred to in this Regulation. Multiple notification of the same transaction increases legal uncertainty, effort and cost for undertakings and may lead to conflicting assessments. The system whereby concentrations may be referred to the Commission by the Member States concerned should therefore be further developed.

(13) The Commission should act in close and constant liaison with the competent authorities of the Member States from which it obtains comments and information.

(14) The Commission and the competent authorities of the Member States should together form a network of public authorities, applying their respective competences in close cooperation, using efficient arrangements for information-sharing and consultation, with a view to ensuring that a case is dealt with by the most appropriate authority, in the light of the principle of subsidiarity and with a view to ensuring that multiple notifications of a given concentration are avoided to the greatest extent possible. Referrals of concentrations from the Commission to Member States and from Member States to the Commission should be made in an efficient manner avoiding, to the greatest extent possible, situations where a concentration is subject to a referral both before and after its notification.

(15) The Commission should be able to refer to a Member State notified concentrations with a Community dimension which threaten significantly to affect competition in a market within that Member State presenting all the characteristics of a distinct market. Where the concentration affects competition on such a market, which does not constitute a substantial part of the common market, the Commission should be obliged, upon request, to refer the whole or part of the case to the Member State concerned. A Member State should be able to refer to the Commission a concentration which does not have a Community dimension but which affects trade between Member States and threatens to significantly affect competition within its territory. Other Member States which are also competent to review the concentration should be able to join the request. In such a situation, in order to ensure the efficiency and predictability of the system, national time limits should be suspended until a decision has been reached as to the referral of the case. The Commission should have the power to examine and deal with a concentration on behalf of a requesting Member State or requesting Member States.

(16) The undertakings concerned should be granted the possibility of requesting referrals to or from the Commission before a concentration is notified so as to further improve the efficiency of the system for the control of concentrations within the Community. In such situations, the Commission and national competition authorities should decide within short, clearly defined time limits whether a referral to or from the Commission ought to be made, thereby ensuring the efficiency of the system. Upon request by the undertakings concerned, the Commission should be able to refer to a Member State a concentration with a Community dimension which may significantly affect competition in a market within that Member State presenting all the characteristics of a distinct market; the undertakings concerned should not, however, be required to demonstrate that the effects of the concentration would be detrimental to competition. A concentration should not be referred from the Commission to a Member State which has expressed its disagreement to such a referral. Before notification to national authorities, the undertakings concerned should also be able to request that a concentration without a Community dimension which is capable of being reviewed under the national competition laws of at least three Member States be referred to the Commission. Such requests for pre-notification referrals to the Commission would be particularly pertinent in

situations where the concentration would affect competition beyond the territory of one Member State. Where a concentration capable of being reviewed under the competition laws of three or more Member States is referred to the Commission prior to any national notification, and no Member State competent to review the case expresses its disagreement, the Commission should acquire exclusive competence to review the concentration and such a concentration should be deemed to have a Community dimension. Such pre-notification referrals from Member States to the Commission should not, however, be made where at least one Member State competent to review the case has expressed its disagreement with such a referral.

(17) The Commission should be given exclusive competence to apply this Regulation, subject to review by the Court of Justice.

(18) The Member States should not be permitted to apply their national legislation on competition to concentrations with a Community dimension, unless this Regulation makes provision therefore. The relevant powers of national authorities should be limited to cases where, failing intervention by the Commission, effective competition is likely to be significantly impeded within the territory of a Member State and where the competition interests of that Member State cannot be sufficiently protected otherwise by this Regulation. The Member States concerned must act promptly in such cases; this Regulation cannot, because of the diversity of national law, fix a single time limit for the adoption of final decisions under national law.

(19) Furthermore, the exclusive application of this Regulation to concentrations with a Community dimension is without prejudice to Article 296 of the Treaty, and does not prevent the Member States from taking appropriate measures to protect legitimate interests other than those pursued by this Regulation, provided that such measures are compatible with the general principles and other provisions of Community law.

(20) It is expedient to define the concept of concentration in such a manner as to cover operations bringing about a lasting change in the control of the undertakings concerned and therefore in the structure of the market. It is therefore appropriate to include, within the scope of this Regulation, all joint ventures performing on a lasting basis all the functions of an autonomous economic entity. It is moreover appropriate to treat as a single concentration transactions that are closely connected in that they are linked by condition or take the form of a series of transactions in securities taking place within a reasonably short period of time.

(21) This Regulation should also apply where the undertakings concerned accept restrictions directly related to, and necessary for, the implementation of the concentration. Commission decisions declaring concentrations compatible with the common market in application of this Regulation should automatically cover such restrictions, without the Commission having to assess such restrictions in individual cases. At the request of the undertakings concerned, however, the Commission should, in cases presenting novel or unresolved questions giving rise to genuine uncertainty, expressly assess whether or not any restriction is directly related to, and necessary for, the implementation of the concentration. A case presents a novel or unresolved question giving rise to genuine uncertainty if the question is not covered by the relevant Commission notice in force or a published Commission decision.

(22) The arrangements to be introduced for the control of concentrations should, without prejudice to Article 86(2) of the Treaty, respect the principle of non-discrimination between the public and the private sectors. In the public sector, calculation of the turnover of an undertaking concerned in a concentration needs, therefore, to take account of undertakings making up an economic unit with an independent power of decision, irrespective of the way in which their capital is held or of the rules of administrative supervision applicable to them.

(23) It is necessary to establish whether or not concentrations with a Community dimension are compatible with the common market in terms of the need to maintain and develop effective competition in the common market. In so doing, the Commission must place its

appraisal within the general framework of the achievement of the fundamental objectives referred to in Article 2 of the Treaty establishing the European Community and Article 2 of the Treaty on European Union.

(24) In order to ensure a system of undistorted competition in the common market, in furtherance of a policy conducted in accordance with the principle of an open market economy with free competition, this Regulation must permit effective control of all concentrations from the point of view of their effect on competition in the Community. Accordingly, Regulation (EEC) No 4064/89 established the principle that a concentration with a Community dimension which creates or strengthens a dominant position as a result of which effective competition in the common market or in a substantial part of it would be significantly impeded should be declared incompatible with the common market.

(25) In view of the consequences that concentrations in oligopolistic market structures may have, it is all the more necessary to maintain effective competition in such markets. Many oligopolistic markets exhibit a healthy degree of competition. However, under certain circumstances, concentrations involving the elimination of important competitive constraints that the merging parties had exerted upon each other, as well as a reduction of competitive pressure on the remaining competitors, may, even in the absence of a likelihood of coordination between the members of the oligopoly, result in a significant impediment to effective competition. The Community courts have, however, not to date expressly interpreted Regulation (EEC) No 4064/89 as requiring concentrations giving rise to such non-coordinated effects to be declared incompatible with the common market. Therefore, in the interests of legal certainty, it should be made clear that this Regulation permits effective control of all such concentrations by providing that any concentration which would significantly impede effective competition, in the common market or in a substantial part of it, should be declared incompatible with the common market. The notion of 'significant impediment to effective competition' in Article 2(2) and (3) should be interpreted as extending, beyond the concept of dominance, only to the anti-competitive effects of a concentration resulting from the non-coordinated behaviour of undertakings which would not have a dominant position on the market concerned.

(26) A significant impediment to effective competition generally results from the creation or strengthening of a dominant position. With a view to preserving the guidance that may be drawn from past judgments of the European courts and Commission decisions pursuant to Regulation (EEC) No 4064/89, while at the same time maintaining consistency with the standards of competitive harm which have been applied by the Commission and the Community courts regarding the compatibility of a concentration with the common market, this Regulation should accordingly establish the principle that a concentration with a Community dimension which would significantly impede effective competition, in the common market or in a substantial part thereof, in particular as a result of the creation or strengthening of a dominant position, is to be declared incompatible with the common market.

(27) In addition, the criteria of Article 81(1) and (3) of the Treaty should be applied to joint ventures performing, on a lasting basis, all the functions of autonomous economic entities, to the extent that their creation has as its consequence an appreciable restriction of competition between undertakings that remain independent.

(28) In order to clarify and explain the Commission's appraisal of concentrations under this Regulation, it is appropriate for the Commission to publish guidance which should provide a sound economic framework for the assessment of concentrations with a view to determining whether or not they may be declared compatible with the common market.

(29) In order to determine the impact of a concentration on competition in the common market, it is appropriate to take account of any substantiated and likely efficiencies put forward by the undertakings concerned. It is possible that the efficiencies brought about by the concentration counteract the effects on competition, and in particular the potential harm to consumers, that it might otherwise have and that, as a consequence, the concentration would

not significantly impede effective competition, in the common market or in a substantial part of it, in particular as a result of the creation or strengthening of a dominant position. The Commission should publish guidance on the conditions under which it may take efficiencies into account in the assessment of a concentration.

(30) Where the undertakings concerned modify a notified concentration, in particular by offering commitments with a view to rendering the concentration compatible with the common market, the Commission should be able to declare the concentration, as modified, compatible with the common market. Such commitments should be proportionate to the competition problem and entirely eliminate it. It is also appropriate to accept commitments before the initiation of proceedings where the competition problem is readily identifiable and can easily be remedied. It should be expressly provided that the Commission may attach to its decision conditions and obligations in order to ensure that the undertakings concerned comply with their commitments in a timely and effective manner so as to render the concentration compatible with the common market. Transparency and effective consultation of Member States as well as of interested third parties should be ensured throughout the procedure.

(31) The Commission should have at its disposal appropriate instruments to ensure the enforcement of commitments and to deal with situations where they are not fulfilled. In cases of failure to fulfil a condition attached to the decision declaring a concentration compatible with the common market, the situation rendering the concentration compatible with the common market does not materialise and the concentration, as implemented, is therefore not authorised by the Commission. As a consequence, if the concentration is implemented, it should be treated in the same way as a non-notified concentration implemented without authorisation. Furthermore, where the Commission has already found that, in the absence of the condition, the concentration would be incompatible with the common market, it should have the power to directly order the dissolution of the concentration, so as to restore the situation prevailing prior to the implementation of the concentration. Where an obligation attached to a decision declaring the concentration compatible with the common market is not fulfilled, the Commission should be able to revoke its decision. Moreover, the Commission should be able to impose appropriate financial sanctions where conditions or obligations are not fulfilled.

(32) Concentrations which, by reason of the limited market share of the undertakings concerned, are not liable to impede effective competition may be presumed to be compatible with the common market. Without prejudice to Articles 81 and 82 of the Treaty, an indication to this effect exists, in particular, where the market share of the undertakings concerned does not exceed 25 % either in the common market or in a substantial part of it.

(33) The Commission should have the task of taking all the decisions necessary to establish whether or not concentrations with a Community dimension are compatible with the common market, as well as decisions designed to restore the situation prevailing prior to the implementation of a concentration which has been declared incompatible with the common market.

(34) To ensure effective control, undertakings should be obliged to give prior notification of concentrations with a Community dimension following the conclusion of the agreement, the announcement of the public bid or the acquisition of a controlling interest. Notification should also be possible where the undertakings concerned satisfy the Commission of their intention to enter into an agreement for a proposed concentration and demonstrate to the Commission that their plan for that proposed concentration is sufficiently concrete, for example on the basis of an agreement in principle, a memorandum of understanding, or a letter of intent signed by all undertakings concerned, or, in the case of a public bid, where they have publicly announced an intention to make such a bid, provided that the intended agreement or bid would result in a concentration with a Community dimension. The implementation of concentrations should be suspended until a final decision of the Commission has been

taken. However, it should be possible to derogate from this suspension at the request of the undertakings concerned, where appropriate. In deciding whether or not to grant a derogation, the Commission should take account of all pertinent factors, such as the nature and gravity of damage to the undertakings concerned or to third parties, and the threat to competition posed by the concentration. In the interest of legal certainty, the validity of transactions must nevertheless be protected as much as necessary.

(35) A period within which the Commission must initiate proceedings in respect of a notified concentration and a period within which it must take a final decision on the compatibility or incompatibility with the common market of that concentration should be laid down. These periods should be extended whenever the undertakings concerned offer commitments with a view to rendering the concentration compatible with the common market, in order to allow for sufficient time for the analysis and market testing of such commitment offers and for the consultation of Member States as well as interested third parties. A limited extension of the period within which the Commission must take a final decision should also be possible in order to allow sufficient time for the investigation of the case and the verification of the facts and arguments submitted to the Commission.

(36) The Community respects the fundamental rights and observes the principles recognised in particular by the Charter of Fundamental Rights of the European Union.[5] Accordingly, this Regulation should be interpreted and applied with respect to those rights and principles.

(37) The undertakings concerned must be afforded the right to be heard by the Commission when proceedings have been initiated; the members of the management and supervisory bodies and the recognised representatives of the employees of the undertakings concerned, and interested third parties, must also be given the opportunity to be heard.

(38) In order properly to appraise concentrations, the Commission should have the right to request all necessary information and to conduct all necessary inspections throughout the Community. To that end, and with a view to protecting competition effectively, the Commission's powers of investigation need to be expanded. The Commission should, in particular, have the right to interview any persons who may be in possession of useful information and to record the statements made.

(39) In the course of an inspection, officials authorised by the Commission should have the right to ask for any information relevant to the subject matter and purpose of the inspection; they should also have the right to affix seals during inspections, particularly in circumstances where there are reasonable grounds to suspect that a concentration has been implemented without being notified; that incorrect, incomplete or misleading information has been supplied to the Commission; or that the undertakings or persons concerned have failed to comply with a condition or obligation imposed by decision of the Commission. In any event, seals should only be used in exceptional circumstances, for the period of time strictly necessary for the inspection, normally not for more than 48 hours.

(40) Without prejudice to the case-law of the Court of Justice, it is also useful to set out the scope of the control that the national judicial authority may exercise when it authorises, as provided by national law and as a precautionary measure, assistance from law enforcement authorities in order to overcome possible opposition on the part of the undertaking against an inspection, including the affixing of seals, ordered by Commission decision. It results from the case-law that the national judicial authority may in particular ask of the Commission further information which it needs to carry out its control and in the absence of which it could refuse the authorisation. The case-law also confirms the competence of the national courts to control the application of national rules governing the implementation of coercive measures. The competent authorities of the Member States should cooperate actively in the exercise of the Commission's investigative powers.

---

[5] (5) OJ C 364, 18.12.2000, p. 1.

(41) When complying with decisions of the Commission, the undertakings and persons concerned cannot be forced to admit that they have committed infringements, but they are in any event obliged to answer factual questions and to provide documents, even if this information may be used to establish against themselves or against others the existence of such infringements.

(42) For the sake of transparency, all decisions of the Commission which are not of a merely procedural nature should be widely publicised. While ensuring preservation of the rights of defence of the undertakings concerned, in particular the right of access to the file, it is essential that business secrets be protected. The confidentiality of information exchanged in the network and with the competent authorities of third countries should likewise be safeguarded.

(43) Compliance with this Regulation should be enforceable, as appropriate, by means of fines and periodic penalty payments. The Court of Justice should be given unlimited jurisdiction in that regard pursuant to Article 229 of the Treaty.

(44) The conditions in which concentrations, involving undertakings having their seat or their principal fields of activity in the Community, are carried out in third countries should be observed, and provision should be made for the possibility of the Council giving the Commission an appropriate mandate for negotiation with a view to obtaining non-discriminatory treatment for such undertakings.

(45) This Regulation in no way detracts from the collective rights of employees, as recognised in the undertakings concerned, notably with regard to any obligation to inform or consult their recognised representatives under Community and national law.

(46) The Commission should be able to lay down detailed rules concerning the implementation of this Regulation in accordance with the procedures for the exercise of implementing powers conferred on the Commission. For the adoption of such implementing provisions, the Commission should be assisted by an Advisory Committee composed of the representatives of the Member States as specified in Article 23,

HAS ADOPTED THIS REGULATION:

Article 1   Scope

1. Without prejudice to Article 4(5) and Article 22, this Regulation shall apply to all concentrations with a Community dimension as defined in this Article.

2. A concentration has a Community dimension where:

(a) the combined aggregate worldwide turnover of all the undertakings concerned is more than EUR 5000 million; and

(b) the aggregate Community-wide turnover of each of at least two of the undertakings concerned is more than EUR 250 million,

unless each of the undertakings concerned achieves more than two-thirds of its aggregate Community-wide turnover within one and the same Member State.

3. A concentration that does not meet the thresholds laid down in paragraph 2 has a Community dimension where:

(a) the combined aggregate worldwide turnover of all the undertakings concerned is more than EUR 2500 million;

(b) in each of at least three Member States, the combined aggregate turnover of all the undertakings concerned is more than EUR 100 million;

(c) in each of at least three Member States included for the purpose of point (b), the aggregate turnover of each of at least two of the undertakings concerned is more than EUR 25 million; and

(d) the aggregate Community-wide turnover of each of at least two of the undertakings concerned is more than EUR 100 million,

unless each of the undertakings concerned achieves more than two-thirds of its aggregate Community-wide turnover within one and the same Member State.

4.   On the basis of statistical data that may be regularly provided by the Member States, the Commission shall report to the Council on the operation of the thresholds and criteria set out in paragraphs 2 and 3 by 1 July 2009 and may present proposals pursuant to paragraph 5.

5.   Following the report referred to in paragraph 4 and on a proposal from the Commission, the Council, acting by a qualified majority, may revise the thresholds and criteria mentioned in paragraph 3.

Article 2   Appraisal of concentrations

1.   Concentrations within the scope of this Regulation shall be appraised in accordance with the objectives of this Regulation and the following provisions with a view to establishing whether or not they are compatible with the common market.

In making this appraisal, the Commission shall take into account:

(a) the need to maintain and develop effective competition within the common market in view of, among other things, the structure of all the markets concerned and the actual or potential competition from undertakings located either within or outwith the Community;

(b) the market position of the undertakings concerned and their economic and financial power, the alternatives available to suppliers and users, their access to supplies or markets, any legal or other barriers to entry, supply and demand trends for the relevant goods and services, the interests of the intermediate and ultimate consumers, and the development of technical and economic progress provided that it is to consumers' advantage and does not form an obstacle to competition.

2.   A concentration which would not significantly impede effective competition in the common market or in a substantial part of it, in particular as a result of the creation or strengthening of a dominant position, shall be declared compatible with the common market.

3.   A concentration which would significantly impede effective competition, in the common market or in a substantial part of it, in particular as a result of the creation or strengthening of a dominant position, shall be declared incompatible with the common market.

4.   To the extent that the creation of a joint venture constituting a concentration pursuant to Article 3 has as its object or effect the coordination of the competitive behaviour of undertakings that remain independent, such coordination shall be appraised in accordance with the criteria of Article 81(1) and (3) of the Treaty, with a view to establishing whether or not the operation is compatible with the common market.

5.   In making this appraisal, the Commission shall take into account in particular:

— whether two or more parent companies retain, to a significant extent, activities in the same market as the joint venture or in a market which is downstream or upstream from that of the joint venture or in a neighbouring market closely related to this market,

— whether the coordination which is the direct consequence of the creation of the joint venture affords the undertakings concerned the possibility of eliminating competition in respect of a substantial part of the products or services in question.

Article 3   Definition of concentration

1.   A concentration shall be deemed to arise where a change of control on a lasting basis results from:

(a) the merger of two or more previously independent undertakings or parts of undertakings, or

(b) the acquisition, by one or more persons already controlling at least one undertaking, or by one or more undertakings, whether by purchase of securities or assets, by contract or by any other means, of direct or indirect control of the whole or parts of one or more other undertakings.

2. Control shall be constituted by rights, contracts or any other means which, either separately or in combination and having regard to the considerations of fact or law involved, confer the possibility of exercising decisive influence on an undertaking, in particular by:
  (a) ownership or the right to use all or part of the assets of an undertaking;
  (b) rights or contracts which confer decisive influence on the composition, voting or decisions of the organs of an undertaking.
3. Control is acquired by persons or undertakings which:
  (a) are holders of the rights or entitled to rights under the contracts concerned; or
  (b) while not being holders of such rights or entitled to rights under such contracts, have the power to exercise the rights deriving therefrom.
4. The creation of a joint venture performing on a lasting basis all the functions of an autonomous economic entity shall constitute a concentration within the meaning of paragraph 1(b).
5. A concentration shall not be deemed to arise where:
  (a) credit institutions or other financial institutions or insurance companies, the normal activities of which include transactions and dealing in securities for their own account or for the account of others, hold on a temporary basis securities which they have acquired in an undertaking with a view to reselling them, provided that they do not exercise voting rights in respect of those securities with a view to determining the competitive behaviour of that undertaking or provided that they exercise such voting rights only with a view to preparing the disposal of all or part of that undertaking or of its assets or the disposal of those securities and that any such disposal takes place within one year of the date of acquisition; that period may be extended by the Commission on request where such institutions or companies can show that the disposal was not reasonably possible within the period set;
  (b) control is acquired by an office-holder according to the law of a Member State relating to liquidation, winding up, insolvency, cessation of payments, compositions or analogous proceedings;
  (c) the operations referred to in paragraph 1(b) are carried out by the financial holding companies referred to in Article 5(3) of Fourth Council Directive 78/660/EEC of 25 July 1978 based on Article 54(3)(g) of the Treaty on the annual accounts of certain types of companies[6] provided however that the voting rights in respect of the holding are exercised, in particular in relation to the appointment of members of the management and supervisory bodies of the undertakings in which they have holdings, only to maintain the full value of those investments and not to determine directly or indirectly the competitive conduct of those undertakings.

Article 4   Prior notification of concentrations and pre-notification referral at the request of the notifying parties

1. Concentrations with a Community dimension defined in this Regulation shall be notified to the Commission prior to their implementation and following the conclusion of the agreement, the announcement of the public bid, or the acquisition of a controlling interest.

Notification may also be made where the undertakings concerned demonstrate to the Commission a good faith intention to conclude an agreement or, in the case of a public bid, where they have publicly announced an intention to make such a bid, provided that the intended agreement or bid would result in a concentration with a Community dimension.

---

[6] (6) OJ L 222, 14. 8. 1978, p. 11. Directive as last amended by Directive 2003/51/EC of the European Parliament and of the Council (OJ L 178, 17.7.2003, p. 16).

For the purposes of this Regulation, the term 'notified concentration' shall also cover intended concentrations notified pursuant to the second subparagraph. For the purposes of paragraphs 4 and 5 of this Article, the term 'concentration' includes intended concentrations within the meaning of the second subparagraph.

2.   A concentration which consists of a merger within the meaning of Article 3(1)(a) or in the acquisition of joint control within the meaning of Article 3(1)(b) shall be notified jointly by the parties to the merger or by those acquiring joint control as the case may be. In all other cases, the notification shall be effected by the person or undertaking acquiring control of the whole or parts of one or more undertakings.

3.   Where the Commission finds that a notified concentration falls within the scope of this Regulation, it shall publish the fact of the notification, at the same time indicating the names of the undertakings concerned, their country of origin, the nature of the concentration and the economic sectors involved. The Commission shall take account of the legitimate interest of undertakings in the protection of their business secrets.

4.   Prior to the notification of a concentration within the meaning of paragraph 1, the persons or undertakings referred to in paragraph 2 may inform the Commission, by means of a reasoned submission, that the concentration may significantly affect competition in a market within a Member State which presents all the characteristics of a distinct market and should therefore be examined, in whole or in part, by that Member State.

The Commission shall transmit this submission to all Member States without delay. The Member State referred to in the reasoned submission shall, within 15 working days of receiving the submission, express its agreement or disagreement as regards the request to refer the case. Where that Member State takes no such decision within this period, it shall be deemed to have agreed.

Unless that Member State disagrees, the Commission, where it considers that such a distinct market exists, and that competition in that market may be significantly affected by the concentration, may decide to refer the whole or part of the case to the competent authorities of that Member State with a view to the application of that State's national competition law.

The decision whether or not to refer the case in accordance with the third subparagraph shall be taken within 25 working days starting from the receipt of the reasoned submission by the Commission. The Commission shall inform the other Member States and the persons or undertakings concerned of its decision. If the Commission does not take a decision within this period, it shall be deemed to have adopted a decision to refer the case in accordance with the submission made by the persons or undertakings concerned.

If the Commission decides, or is deemed to have decided, pursuant to the third and fourth subparagraphs, to refer the whole of the case, no notification shall be made pursuant to paragraph 1 and national competition law shall apply. Article 9(6) to (9) shall apply mutatis mutandis.

5.   With regard to a concentration as defined in Article 3 which does not have a Community dimension within the meaning of Article 1 and which is capable of being reviewed under the national competition laws of at least three Member States, the persons or undertakings referred to in paragraph 2 may, before any notification to the competent authorities, inform the Commission by means of a reasoned submission that the concentration should be examined by the Commission.

The Commission shall transmit this submission to all Member States without delay.

Any Member State competent to examine the concentration under its national competition law may, within 15 working days of receiving the reasoned submission, express its disagreement as regards the request to refer the case.

Where at least one such Member State has expressed its disagreement in accordance with the third subparagraph within the period of 15 working days, the case shall not be referred. The Commission shall, without delay, inform all Member States and the persons or undertakings concerned of any such expression of disagreement.

Where no Member State has expressed its disagreement in accordance with the third sub-paragraph within the period of 15 working days, the concentration shall be deemed to have a Community dimension and shall be notified to the Commission in accordance with paragraphs 1 and 2. In such situations, no Member State shall apply its national competition law to the concentration.

6.   The Commission shall report to the Council on the operation of paragraphs 4 and 5 by 1 July 2009. Following this report and on a proposal from the Commission, the Council, acting by a qualified majority, may revise paragraphs 4 and 5.

Article 5   Calculation of turnover

1.   Aggregate turnover within the meaning of this Regulation shall comprise the amounts derived by the undertakings concerned in the preceding financial year from the sale of products and the provision of services falling within the undertakings' ordinary activities after deduction of sales rebates and of value added tax and other taxes directly related to turnover. The aggregate turnover of an undertaking concerned shall not include the sale of products or the provision of services between any of the undertakings referred to in paragraph 4.

Turnover, in the Community or in a Member State, shall comprise products sold and services provided to undertakings or consumers, in the Community or in that Member State as the case may be.

2.   By way of derogation from paragraph 1, where the concentration consists of the acquisition of parts, whether or not constituted as legal entities, of one or more undertakings, only the turnover relating to the parts which are the subject of the concentration shall be taken into account with regard to the seller or sellers.

However, two or more transactions within the meaning of the first subparagraph which take place within a two-year period between the same persons or undertakings shall be treated as one and the same concentration arising on the date of the last transaction.

3.   In place of turnover the following shall be used:

(a)   for credit institutions and other financial institutions, the sum of the following income items as defined in Council Directive 86/635/EEC,[7] after deduction of value added tax and other taxes directly related to those items, where appropriate:
    (i)   interest income and similar income;
    (ii)   income from securities:
        —   income from shares and other variable yield securities,
        —   income from participating interests,
        —   income from shares in affiliated undertakings;
    (iii) commissions receivable;
(iv)   net profit on financial operations;
(v)   other operating income.
    The turnover of a credit or financial institution in the Community or in a Member State shall comprise the income items, as defined above, which are received by the branch or division of that institution established in the Community or in the Member State in question, as the case may be;
(b)   for insurance undertakings, the value of gross premiums written which shall comprise all amounts received and receivable in respect of insurance contracts issued by or on behalf of the insurance undertakings, including also outgoing reinsurance premiums, and after deduction of taxes and parafiscal contributions or levies charged by reference to the amounts of individual premiums or the total volume of premiums; as regards Article 1(2)(b) and (3)(b), (c) and (d) and the final part of Article 1(2) and (3), gross premiums received from Community residents and from residents of one Member State respectively shall be taken into account.

---

[7]   (7) OJ L 372, 31.12.1986, p. 1. Directive as last amended by Directive 2003/51/EC of the European Parliament and of the Council.

4. Without prejudice to paragraph 2, the aggregate turnover of an undertaking concerned within the meaning of this Regulation shall be calculated by adding together the respective turnovers of the following:

(a) the undertaking concerned;

(b) those undertakings in which the undertaking concerned, directly or indirectly:

(i) owns more than half the capital or business assets, or

(ii) has the power to exercise more than half the voting rights, or

(iii) has the power to appoint more than half the members of the supervisory board, the administrative board or bodies legally representing the undertakings, or

(iv) has the right to manage the undertakings' affairs;

(c) those undertakings which have in the undertaking concerned the rights or powers listed in (b);

(d) those undertakings in which an undertaking as referred to in (c) has the rights or powers listed in (b);

(e) those undertakings in which two or more undertakings as referred to in (a) to (d) jointly have the rights or powers listed in (b).

5. Where undertakings concerned by the concentration jointly have the rights or powers listed in paragraph 4(b), in calculating the aggregate turnover of the undertakings concerned for the purposes of this Regulation:

(a) no account shall be taken of the turnover resulting from the sale of products or the provision of services between the joint undertaking and each of the undertakings concerned or any other undertaking connected with any one of them, as set out in paragraph 4(b) to (e);

(b) account shall be taken of the turnover resulting from the sale of products and the provision of services between the joint undertaking and any third undertakings. This turnover shall be apportioned equally amongst the undertakings concerned.

Article 6   Examination of the notification and initiation of proceedings

1. The Commission shall examine the notification as soon as it is received.

(a) Where it concludes that the concentration notified does not fall within the scope of this Regulation, it shall record that finding by means of a decision.

(b) Where it finds that the concentration notified, although falling within the scope of this Regulation, does not raise serious doubts as to its compatibility with the common market, it shall decide not to oppose it and shall declare that it is compatible with the common market.

A decision declaring a concentration compatible shall be deemed to cover restrictions directly related and necessary to the implementation of the concentration.

(c) Without prejudice to paragraph 2, where the Commission finds that the concentration notified falls within the scope of this Regulation and raises serious doubts as to its compatibility with the common market, it shall decide to initiate proceedings. Without prejudice to Article 9, such proceedings shall be closed by means of a decision as provided for in Article 8(1) to (4), unless the undertakings concerned have demonstrated to the satisfaction of the Commission that they have abandoned the concentration.

2. Where the Commission finds that, following modification by the undertakings concerned, a notified concentration no longer raises serious doubts within the meaning of paragraph 1(c), it shall declare the concentration compatible with the common market pursuant to paragraph 1(b).

The Commission may attach to its decision under paragraph 1(b) conditions and obligations intended to ensure that the undertakings concerned comply with the commitments they have entered into vis-à-vis the Commission with a view to rendering the concentration compatible with the common market.

3. The Commission may revoke the decision it took pursuant to paragraph 1(a) or (b) where:

(a) the decision is based on incorrect information for which one of the undertakings is responsible or where it has been obtained by deceit,

or

(b) the undertakings concerned commit a breach of an obligation attached to the decision.

4. In the cases referred to in paragraph 3, the Commission may take a decision under paragraph 1, without being bound by the time limits referred to in Article 10(1).

5. The Commission shall notify its decision to the undertakings concerned and the competent authorities of the Member States without delay.

Article 7   Suspension of concentrations

1. A concentration with a Community dimension as defined in Article 1, or which is to be examined by the Commission pursuant to Article 4(5), shall not be implemented either before its notification or until it has been declared compatible with the common market pursuant to a decision under Articles 6(1)(b), 8(1) or 8(2), or on the basis of a presumption according to Article 10(6).

2. Paragraph 1 shall not prevent the implementation of a public bid or of a series of transactions in securities including those convertible into other securities admitted to trading on a market such as a stock exchange, by which control within the meaning of Article 3 is acquired from various sellers, provided that:

(a) the concentration is notified to the Commission pursuant to Article 4 without delay; and

(b) the acquirer does not exercise the voting rights attached to the securities in question or does so only to maintain the full value of its investments based on a derogation granted by the Commission under paragraph 3.

3. The Commission may, on request, grant a derogation from the obligations imposed in paragraphs 1 or 2. The request to grant a derogation must be reasoned. In deciding on the request, the Commission shall take into account inter alia the effects of the suspension on one or more undertakings concerned by the concentration or on a third party and the threat to competition posed by the concentration. Such a derogation may be made subject to conditions and obligations in order to ensure conditions of effective competition. A derogation may be applied for and granted at any time, be it before notification or after the transaction.

4. The validity of any transaction carried out in contravention of paragraph 1 shall be dependent on a decision pursuant to Article 6(1)(b) or Article 8(1), (2) or (3) or on a presumption pursuant to Article 10(6).

This Article shall, however, have no effect on the validity of transactions in securities including those convertible into other securities admitted to trading on a market such as a stock exchange, unless the buyer and seller knew or ought to have known that the transaction was carried out in contravention of paragraph 1.

Article 8   Powers of decision of the Commission

1. Where the Commission finds that a notified concentration fulfils the criterion laid down in Article 2(2) and, in the cases referred to in Article 2(4), the criteria laid down in Article 81(3) of the Treaty, it shall issue a decision declaring the concentration compatible with the common market.

A decision declaring a concentration compatible shall be deemed to cover restrictions directly related and necessary to the implementation of the concentration.

2. Where the Commission finds that, following modification by the undertakings concerned, a notified concentration fulfils the criterion laid down in Article 2(2) and, in the

cases referred to in Article 2(4), the criteria laid down in Article 81(3) of the Treaty, it shall issue a decision declaring the concentration compatible with the common market.

The Commission may attach to its decision conditions and obligations intended to ensure that the undertakings concerned comply with the commitments they have entered into vis-à-vis the Commission with a view to rendering the concentration compatible with the common market. A decision declaring a concentration compatible shall be deemed to cover restrictions directly related and necessary to the implementation of the concentration.

3.   Where the Commission finds that a concentration fulfils the criterion defined in Article 2(3) or, in the cases referred to in Article 2(4), does not fulfil the criteria laid down in Article 81(3) of the Treaty, it shall issue a decision declaring that the concentration is incompatible with the common market.

4.   Where the Commission finds that a concentration:

(a) has already been implemented and that concentration has been declared incompatible with the common market, or

(b) has been implemented in contravention of a condition attached to a decision taken under paragraph 2, which has found that, in the absence of the condition, the concentration would fulfil the criterion laid down in Article 2(3) or, in the cases referred to in Article 2(4), would not fulfil the criteria laid down in Article 81(3) of the Treaty, the Commission may:

— require the undertakings concerned to dissolve the concentration, in particular through the dissolution of the merger or the disposal of all the shares or assets acquired, so as to restore the situation prevailing prior to the implementation of the concentration; in circumstances where restoration of the situation prevailing before the implementation of the concentration is not possible through dissolution of the concentration, the Commission may take any other measure appropriate to achieve such restoration as far as possible,

— order any other appropriate measure to ensure that the undertakings concerned dissolve the concentration or take other restorative measures as required in its decision.

In cases falling within point (a) of the first subparagraph, the measures referred to in that subparagraph may be imposed either in a decision pursuant to paragraph 3 or by separate decision.

5.   The Commission may take interim measures appropriate to restore or maintain conditions of effective competition where a concentration:

(a) has been implemented in contravention of Article 7, and a decision as to the compatibility of the concentration with the common market has not yet been taken;

(b) has been implemented in contravention of a condition attached to a decision under Article 6(1)(b) or paragraph 2 of this Article;

(c) has already been implemented and is declared incompatible with the common market.

6.   The Commission may revoke the decision it has taken pursuant to paragraphs 1 or 2 where:

(a) the declaration of compatibility is based on incorrect information for which one of the undertakings is responsible or where it has been obtained by deceit; or

(b) the undertakings concerned commit a breach of an obligation attached to the decision.

7.   The Commission may take a decision pursuant to paragraphs 1 to 3 without being bound by the time limits referred to in Article 10(3), in cases where:

(a) it finds that a concentration has been implemented

(i) in contravention of a condition attached to a decision under Article 6(1)(b), or

(ii) in contravention of a condition attached to a decision taken under paragraph 2 and in accordance with Article 10(2), which has found that, in the absence of the condition, the concentration would raise serious doubts as to its compatibility with the common market; or

(b) a decision has been revoked pursuant to paragraph 6.

8.   The Commission shall notify its decision to the undertakings concerned and the competent authorities of the Member States without delay.

Article 9   Referral to the competent authorities of the Member States

1.   The Commission may, by means of a decision notified without delay to the undertakings concerned and the competent authorities of the other Member States, refer a notified concentration to the competent authorities of the Member State concerned in the following circumstances.

2.   Within 15 working days of the date of receipt of the copy of the notification, a Member State, on its own initiative or upon the invitation of the Commission, may inform the Commission, which shall inform the undertakings concerned, that:

(a) a concentration threatens to affect significantly competition in a market within that Member State, which presents all the characteristics of a distinct market, or

(b) a concentration affects competition in a market within that Member State, which presents all the characteristics of a distinct market and which does not constitute a substantial part of the common market.

3.   If the Commission considers that, having regard to the market for the products or services in question and the geographical reference market within the meaning of paragraph 7, there is such a distinct market and that such a threat exists, either:

(a) it shall itself deal with the case in accordance with this Regulation; or

(b) it shall refer the whole or part of the case to the competent authorities of the Member State concerned with a view to the application of that State's national competition law.

If, however, the Commission considers that such a distinct market or threat does not exist, it shall adopt a decision to that effect which it shall address to the Member State concerned, and shall itself deal with the case in accordance with this Regulation.

In cases where a Member State informs the Commission pursuant to paragraph 2(b) that a concentration affects competition in a distinct market within its territory that does not form a substantial part of the common market, the Commission shall refer the whole or part of the case relating to the distinct market concerned, if it considers that such a distinct market is affected.

4.   A decision to refer or not to refer pursuant to paragraph 3 shall be taken:

(a) as a general rule within the period provided for in Article 10(1), second subparagraph, where the Commission, pursuant to Article 6(1)(b), has not initiated proceedings; or

(b) within 65 working days at most of the notification of the concentration concerned where the Commission has initiated proceedings under Article 6(1)(c), without taking the preparatory steps in order to adopt the necessary measures under Article 8(2), (3) or (4) to maintain or restore effective competition on the market concerned.

5.   If within the 65 working days referred to in paragraph 4(b) the Commission, despite a reminder from the Member State concerned, has not taken a decision on referral in accordance with paragraph 3 nor has taken the preparatory steps referred to in paragraph 4(b), it shall be deemed to have taken a decision to refer the case to the Member State concerned in accordance with paragraph 3(b).

6.   The competent authority of the Member State concerned shall decide upon the case without undue delay.

Within 45 working days after the Commission's referral, the competent authority of the Member State concerned shall inform the undertakings concerned of the result of the preliminary competition assessment and what further action, if any, it proposes to take. The Member State concerned may exceptionally suspend this time limit where necessary information has not been provided to it by the undertakings concerned as provided for by its national competition law.

Where a notification is requested under national law, the period of 45 working days shall begin on the working day following that of the receipt of a complete notification by the competent authority of that Member State.

7.   The geographical reference market shall consist of the area in which the undertakings concerned are involved in the supply and demand of products or services, in which the conditions of competition are sufficiently homogeneous and which can be distinguished from neighbouring areas because, in particular, conditions of competition are appreciably different in those areas. This assessment should take account in particular of the nature and characteristics of the products or services concerned, of the existence of entry barriers or of consumer preferences, of appreciable differences of the undertakings' market shares between the area concerned and neighbouring areas or of substantial price differences.

8.   In applying the provisions of this Article, the Member State concerned may take only the measures strictly necessary to safeguard or restore effective competition on the market concerned.

9.   In accordance with the relevant provisions of the Treaty, any Member State may appeal to the Court of Justice, and in particular request the application of Article 243 of the Treaty, for the purpose of applying its national competition law.

Article 10   Time limits for initiating proceedings and for decisions

1.   Without prejudice to Article 6(4), the decisions referred to in Article 6(1) shall be taken within 25 working days at most. That period shall begin on the working day following that of the receipt of a notification or, if the information to be supplied with the notification is incomplete, on the working day following that of the receipt of the complete information. That period shall be increased to 35 working days where the Commission receives a request from a Member State in accordance with Article 9(2)or where, the undertakings concerned offer commitments pursuant to Article 6(2) with a view to rendering the concentration compatible with the common market.

2.   Decisions pursuant to Article 8(1) or (2) concerning notified concentrations shall be taken as soon as it appears that the serious doubts referred to in Article 6(1)(c) have been removed, particularly as a result of modifications made by the undertakings concerned, and at the latest by the time limit laid down in paragraph 3.

3.   Without prejudice to Article 8(7), decisions pursuant to Article 8(1) to (3) concerning notified concentrations shall be taken within not more than 90 working days of the date on which the proceedings are initiated. That period shall be increased to 105 working days where the undertakings concerned offer commitments pursuant to Article 8(2), second subparagraph, with a view to rendering the concentration compatible with the common market, unless these commitments have been offered less than 55 working days after the initiation of proceedings. The periods set by the first subparagraph shall likewise be extended if the notifying parties make a request to that effect not later than 15 working days after the initiation of proceedings pursuant to Article 6(1)(c). The notifying parties may make only one such request. Likewise, at any time following the initiation of proceedings, the periods set by the first subparagraph may be extended by the Commission with the agreement of the notifying parties. The total duration of any extension or extensions effected pursuant to this subparagraph shall not exceed 20 working days.

4.   The periods set by paragraphs 1 and 3 shall exceptionally be suspended where, owing to circumstances for which one of the undertakings involved in the concentration is

responsible, the Commission has had to request information by decision pursuant to Article 11 or to order an inspection by decision pursuant to Article 13.

The first subparagraph shall also apply to the period referred to in Article 9(4)(b).

5. Where the Court of Justice gives a judgment which annuls the whole or part of a Commission decision which is subject to a time limit set by this Article, the concentration shall be re-examined by the Commission with a view to adopting a decision pursuant to Article 6(1).

The concentration shall be re-examined in the light of current market conditions.

The notifying parties shall submit a new notification or supplement the original notification, without delay, where the original notification becomes incomplete by reason of intervening changes in market conditions or in the information provided. Where there are no such changes, the parties shall certify this fact without delay.

The periods laid down in paragraph 1 shall start on the working day following that of the receipt of complete information in a new notification, a supplemented notification, or a certification within the meaning of the third subparagraph.

The second and third subparagraphs shall also apply in the cases referred to in Article 6(4) and Article 8(7).

6. Where the Commission has not taken a decision in accordance with Article 6(1)(b), (c), 8(1), (2) or (3) within the time limits set in paragraphs 1 and 3 respectively, the concentration shall be deemed to have been declared compatible with the common market, without prejudice to Article 9.

Article 11   Requests for information

1. In order to carry out the duties assigned to it by this Regulation, the Commission may, by simple request or by decision, require the persons referred to in Article 3(1)(b), as well as undertakings and associations of undertakings, to provide all necessary information.

2. When sending a simple request for information to a person, an undertaking or an association of undertakings, the Commission shall state the legal basis and the purpose of the request, specify what information is required and fix the time limit within which the information is to be provided, as well as the penalties provided for in Article 14 for supplying incorrect or misleading information.

3. Where the Commission requires a person, an undertaking or an association of undertakings to supply information by decision, it shall state the legal basis and the purpose of the request, specify what information is required and fix the time limit within which it is to be provided. It shall also indicate the penalties provided for in Article 14 and indicate or impose the penalties provided for in Article 15. It shall further indicate the right to have the decision reviewed by the Court of Justice.

4. The owners of the undertakings or their representatives and, in the case of legal persons, companies or firms, or associations having no legal personality, the persons authorised to represent them by law or by their constitution, shall supply the information requested on behalf of the undertaking concerned. Persons duly authorised to act may supply the information on behalf of their clients. The latter shall remain fully responsible if the information supplied is incomplete, incorrect or misleading.

5. The Commission shall without delay forward a copy of any decision taken pursuant to paragraph 3 to the competent authorities of the Member State in whose territory the residence of the person or the seat of the undertaking or association of undertakings is situated, and to the competent authority of the Member State whose territory is affected. At the specific request of the competent authority of a Member State, the Commission shall also forward to that authority copies of simple requests for information relating to a notified concentration.

6. At the request of the Commission, the governments and competent authorities of the Member States shall provide the Commission with all necessary information to carry out the duties assigned to it by this Regulation.

7.   In order to carry out the duties assigned to it by this Regulation, the Commission may interview any natural or legal person who consents to be interviewed for the purpose of collecting information relating to the subject matter of an investigation. At the beginning of the interview, which may be conducted by telephone or other electronic means, the Commission shall state the legal basis and the purpose of the interview.

Where an interview is not conducted on the premises of the Commission or by telephone or other electronic means, the Commission shall inform in advance the competent authority of the Member State in whose territory the interview takes place. If the competent authority of that Member State so requests, officials of that authority may assist the officials and other persons authorised by the Commission to conduct the interview.

Article 12   Inspections by the authorities of the Member States

1.   At the request of the Commission, the competent authorities of the Member States shall undertake the inspections which the Commission considers to be necessary under Article 13(1), or which it has ordered by decision pursuant to Article 13(4). The officials of the competent authorities of the Member States who are responsible for conducting these inspections as well as those authorised or appointed by them shall exercise their powers in accordance with their national law.

2.   If so requested by the Commission or by the competent authority of the Member State within whose territory the inspection is to be conducted, officials and other accompanying persons authorised by the Commission may assist the officials of the authority concerned.

Article 13   The Commission's powers of inspection

1.   In order to carry out the duties assigned to it by this Regulation, the Commission may conduct all necessary inspections of undertakings and associations of undertakings.

2.   The officials and other accompanying persons authorised by the Commission to conduct an inspection shall have the power:

  (a) to enter any premises, land and means of transport of undertakings and associations of undertakings;
  (b) to examine the books and other records related to the business, irrespective of the medium on which they are stored;
  (c) to take or obtain in any form copies of or extracts from such books or records;
  (d) to seal any business premises and books or records for the period and to the extent necessary for the inspection;
  (e) to ask any representative or member of staff of the undertaking or association of undertakings for explanations on facts or documents relating to the subject matter and purpose of the inspection and to record the answers.

3.   Officials and other accompanying persons authorised by the Commission to conduct an inspection shall exercise their powers upon production of a written authorisation specifying the subject matter and purpose of the inspection and the penalties provided for in Article 14, in the production of the required books or other records related to the business which is incomplete or where answers to questions asked under paragraph 2 of this Article are incorrect or misleading. In good time before the inspection, the Commission shall give notice of the inspection to the competent authority of the Member State in whose territory the inspection is to be conducted.

4.   Undertakings and associations of undertakings are required to submit to inspections ordered by decision of the Commission. The decision shall specify the subject matter and purpose of the inspection, appoint the date on which it is to begin and indicate the penalties provided for in Articles 14 and 15 and the right to have the decision reviewed by the Court of Justice. The Commission shall take such decisions after consulting the competent authority of the Member State in whose territory the inspection is to be conducted.

5.   Officials of, and those authorised or appointed by, the competent authority of

the Member State in whose territory the inspection is to be conducted shall, at the request of that authority or of the Commission, actively assist the officials and other accompanying persons authorised by the Commission. To this end, they shall enjoy the powers specified in paragraph 2.

6.   Where the officials and other accompanying persons authorised by the Commission find that an undertaking opposes an inspection, including the sealing of business premises, books or records, ordered pursuant to this Article, the Member State concerned shall afford them the necessary assistance, requesting where appropriate the assistance of the police or of an equivalent enforcement authority, so as to enable them to conduct their inspection.

7.   If the assistance provided for in paragraph 6 requires authorisation from a judicial authority according to national rules, such authorisation shall be applied for. Such authorisation may also be applied for as a precautionary measure.

8.   Where authorisation as referred to in paragraph 7 is applied for, the national judicial authority shall ensure that the Commission decision is authentic and that the coercive measures envisaged are neither arbitrary nor excessive having regard to the subject matter of the inspection. In its control of proportionality of the coercive measures, the national judicial authority may ask the Commission, directly or through the competent authority of that Member State, for detailed explanations relating to the subject matter of the inspection. However, the national judicial authority may not call into question the necessity for the inspection nor demand that it be provided with the information in the Commission's file. The lawfulness of the Commission's decision shall be subject to review only by the Court of Justice.

Article 14   Fines

1.   The Commission may by decision impose on the persons referred to in Article 3(1)b, undertakings or associations of undertakings, fines not exceeding 1% of the aggregate turnover of the undertaking or association of undertakings concerned within the meaning of Article 5 where, intentionally or negligently:

   (a) they supply incorrect or misleading information in a submission, certification, notification or supplement thereto, pursuant to Article 4, Article 10(5) or Article 22(3);

   (b) they supply incorrect or misleading information in response to a request made pursuant to Article 11(2);

   (c) in response to a request made by decision adopted pursuant to Article 11(3), they supply incorrect, incomplete or misleading information or do not supply information within the required time limit;

   (d) they produce the required books or other records related to the business in incomplete form during inspections under Article 13, or refuse to submit to an inspection ordered by decision taken pursuant to Article 13(4);

   (e) in response to a question asked in accordance with Article 13(2)(e),
   — they give an incorrect or misleading answer,
   — they fail to rectify within a time limit set by the Commission an incorrect, incomplete or misleading answer given by a member of staff, or
   — they fail or refuse to provide a complete answer on facts relating to the subject matter and purpose of an inspection ordered by a decision adopted pursuant to Article 13(4);

   (f) seals affixed by officials or other accompanying persons authorised by the Commission in accordance with Article 13(2)(d) have been broken.

2.   The Commission may by decision impose fines not exceeding 10% of the aggregate turnover of the undertaking concerned within the meaning of Article 5 on the persons referred to in Article 3(1)b or the undertakings concerned where, either intentionally or negligently, they:

(a) fail to notify a concentration in accordance with Articles 4 or 22(3) prior to its implementation, unless they are expressly authorised to do so by Article 7(2) or by a decision taken pursuant to Article 7(3);

(b) implement a concentration in breach of Article 7;

(c) implement a concentration declared incompatible with the common market by decision pursuant to Article 8(3) or do not comply with any measure ordered by decision pursuant to Article 8(4) or (5);

(d) fail to comply with a condition or an obligation imposed by decision pursuant to Articles 6(1)(b), Article 7(3) or Article 8(2), second subparagraph.

3.   In fixing the amount of the fine, regard shall be had to the nature, gravity and duration of the infringement.

4.   Decisions taken pursuant to paragraphs 1, 2 and 3 shall not be of a criminal law nature.

Article 15   Periodic penalty payments

1.   The Commission may by decision impose on the persons referred to in Article 3(1)b, undertakings or associations of undertakings, periodic penalty payments not exceeding 5% of the average daily aggregate turnover of the undertaking or association of undertakings concerned within the meaning of Article 5 for each working day of delay, calculated from the date set in the decision, in order to compel them:

(a) to supply complete and correct information which it has requested by decision taken pursuant to Article 11(3);

(b) to submit to an inspection which it has ordered by decision taken pursuant to Article 13(4);

(c) to comply with an obligation imposed by decision pursuant to Article 6(1)(b), Article 7(3) or Article 8(2), second subparagraph; or;

(d) to comply with any measures ordered by decision pursuant to Article 8(4) or (5).

2.   Where the persons referred to in Article 3(1)(b), undertakings or associations of undertakings have satisfied the obligation which the periodic penalty payment was intended to enforce, the Commission may fix the definitive amount of the periodic penalty payments at a figure lower than that which would arise under the original decision.

Article 16   Review by the Court of Justice

The Court of Justice shall have unlimited jurisdiction within the meaning of Article 229 of the Treaty to review decisions whereby the Commission has fixed a fine or periodic penalty payments; it may cancel, reduce or increase the fine or periodic penalty payment imposed.

Article 17   Professional secrecy

1.   Information acquired as a result of the application of this Regulation shall be used only for the purposes of the relevant request, investigation or hearing.

2.   Without prejudice to Article 4(3), Articles 18 and 20, the Commission and the competent authorities of the Member States, their officials and other servants and other persons working under the supervision of these authorities as well as officials and civil servants of other authorities of the Member States shall not disclose information they have acquired through the application of this Regulation of the kind covered by the obligation of professional secrecy.

3.   Paragraphs 1 and 2 shall not prevent publication of general information or of surveys which do not contain information relating to particular undertakings or associations of undertakings.

Article 18   Hearing of the parties and of third persons

1.   Before taking any decision provided for in Article 6(3), Article 7(3), Article 8(2) to (6), and Articles 14 and 15, the Commission shall give the persons, undertakings and associations of undertakings concerned the opportunity, at every stage of the procedure up to the

consultation of the Advisory Committee, of making known their views on the objections against them.

2.   By way of derogation from paragraph 1, a decision pursuant to Articles 7(3) and 8(5) may be taken provisionally, without the persons, undertakings or associations of undertakings concerned being given the opportunity to make known their views beforehand, provided that the Commission gives them that opportunity as soon as possible after having taken its decision.

3.   The Commission shall base its decision only on objections on which the parties have been able to submit their observations. The rights of the defence shall be fully respected in the proceedings. Access to the file shall be open at least to the parties directly involved, subject to the legitimate interest of undertakings in the protection of their business secrets.

4.   In so far as the Commission or the competent authorities of the Member States deem it necessary, they may also hear other natural or legal persons. Natural or legal persons showing a sufficient interest and especially members of the administrative or management bodies of the undertakings concerned or the recognised representatives of their employees shall be entitled, upon application, to be heard.

Article 19   Liaison with the authorities of the Member States

1.   The Commission shall transmit to the competent authorities of the Member States copies of notifications within three working days and, as soon as possible, copies of the most important documents lodged with or issued by the Commission pursuant to this Regulation. Such documents shall include commitments offered by the undertakings concerned vis-à-vis the Commission with a view to rendering the concentration compatible with the common market pursuant to Article 6(2) or Article 8(2), second subparagraph.

2.   The Commission shall carry out the procedures set out in this Regulation in close and constant liaison with the competent authorities of the Member States, which may express their views upon those procedures. For the purposes of Article 9 it shall obtain information from the competent authority of the Member State as referred to in paragraph 2 of that Article and give it the opportunity to make known its views at every stage of the procedure up to the adoption of a decision pursuant to paragraph 3 of that Article; to that end it shall give it access to the file.

3.   An Advisory Committee on concentrations shall be consulted before any decision is taken pursuant to Article 8(1) to (6), Articles 14 or 15 with the exception of provisional decisions taken in accordance with Article 18(2).

4.   The Advisory Committee shall consist of representatives of the competent authorities of the Member States. Each Member State shall appoint one or two representatives; if unable to attend, they may be replaced by other representatives. At least one of the representatives of a Member State shall be competent in matters of restrictive practices and dominant positions.

5.   Consultation shall take place at a joint meeting convened at the invitation of and chaired by the Commission. A summary of the case, together with an indication of the most important documents and a preliminary draft of the decision to be taken for each case considered, shall be sent with the invitation. The meeting shall take place not less than 10 working days after the invitation has been sent. The Commission may in exceptional cases shorten that period as appropriate in order to avoid serious harm to one or more of the undertakings concerned by a concentration.

6.   The Advisory Committee shall deliver an opinion on the Commission's draft decision, if necessary by taking a vote. The Advisory Committee may deliver an opinion even if some members are absent and unrepresented. The opinion shall be delivered in writing and appended to the draft decision. The Commission shall take the utmost account of the opinion delivered by the Committee. It shall inform the Committee of the manner in which its opinion has been taken into account.

7.   The Commission shall communicate the opinion of the Advisory Committee, together with the decision, to the addressees of the decision. It shall make the opinion public

together with the decision, having regard to the legitimate interest of undertakings in the protection of their business secrets.

Article 20　Publication of decisions

1.　The Commission shall publish the decisions which it takes pursuant to Article 8(1) to (6), Articles 14 and 15 with the exception of provisional decisions taken in accordance with Article 18(2) together with the opinion of the Advisory Committee in the Official Journal of the European Union.

2.　The publication shall state the names of the parties and the main content of the decision; it shall have regard to the legitimate interest of undertakings in the protection of their business secrets.

Article 21　Application of the Regulation and jurisdiction

1.　This Regulation alone shall apply to concentrations as defined in Article 3, and Council Regulations (EC) No 1/2003,[8] (EEC) No 1017/68,[9] (EEC) No 4056/86[10] and (EEC) No 3975/87[11] shall not apply, except in relation to joint ventures that do not have a Community dimension and which have as their object or effect the coordination of the competitive behaviour of undertakings that remain independent.

2.　Subject to review by the Court of Justice, the Commission shall have sole jurisdiction to take the decisions provided for in this Regulation.

3.　No Member State shall apply its national legislation on competition to any concentration that has a Community dimension.

The first subparagraph shall be without prejudice to any Member State's power to carry out any enquiries necessary for the application of Articles 4(4), 9(2) or after referral, pursuant to Article 9(3), first subparagraph, indent (b), or Article 9(5), to take the measures strictly necessary for the application of Article 9(8).

4.　Notwithstanding paragraphs 2 and 3, Member States may take appropriate measures to protect legitimate interests other than those taken into consideration by this Regulation and compatible with the general principles and other provisions of Community law. Public security, plurality of the media and prudential rules shall be regarded as legitimate interests within the meaning of the first subparagraph.

Any other public interest must be communicated to the Commission by the Member State concerned and shall be recognised by the Commission after an assessment of its compatibility with the general principles and other provisions of Community law before the measures referred to above may be taken. The Commission shall inform the Member State concerned of its decision within 25 working days of that communication.

Article 22　Referral to the Commission

1.　One or more Member States may request the Commission to examine any concentration as defined in Article 3 that does not have a Community dimension within the meaning of Article 1 but affects trade between Member States and threatens to significantly affect competition within the territory of the Member State or States making the request.

Such a request shall be made at most within 15 working days of the date on which the concentration was notified, or if no notification is required, otherwise made known to the Member State concerned.

2.　The Commission shall inform the competent authorities of the Member States and the undertakings concerned of any request received pursuant to paragraph 1 without delay. Any other Member State shall have the right to join the initial request within a period of 15 working days of being informed by the Commission of the initial request.

---

[8]　OJ L 1, 4.1.2003, p. 1.

[9]　OJ L 175, 23. 7. 1968, p. 1. Regulation as last amended by Regulation (EC) No. 1/2003 (OJ L 1, 4.1.2003, p. 1).

[10]　OJ L 378, 31. 12. 1986, p. 4. Regulation as last amended by Regulation (EC) No. 1/2003.

[11]　OJ L 374. 31. 12. 1987, p. 1. Regulation as last amended by Regulation (EC) No. 1/2003.

All national time limits relating to the concentration shall be suspended until, in accordance with the procedure set out in this Article, it has been decided where the concentration shall be examined. As soon as a Member State has informed the Commission and the undertakings concerned that it does not wish to join the request, the suspension of its national time limits shall end.

3. The Commission may, at the latest 10 working days after the expiry of the period set in paragraph 2, decide to examine, the concentration where it considers that it affects trade between Member States and threatens to significantly affect competition within the territory of the Member State or States making the request. If the Commission does not take a decision within this period, it shall be deemed to have adopted a decision to examine the concentration in accordance with the request.

The Commission shall inform all Member States and the undertakings concerned of its decision. It may request the submission of a notification pursuant to Article 4.

The Member State or States having made the request shall no longer apply their national legislation on competition to the concentration.

4. Article 2, Article 4(2) to (3), Articles 5, 6, and 8 to 21 shall apply where the Commission examines a concentration pursuant to paragraph 3. Article 7 shall apply to the extent that the concentration has not been implemented on the date on which the Commission informs the undertakings concerned that a request has been made.

Where a notification pursuant to Article 4 is not required, the period set in Article 10(1) within which proceedings may be initiated shall begin on the working day following that on which the Commission informs the undertakings concerned that it has decided to examine the concentration pursuant to paragraph 3.

5. The Commission may inform one or several Member States that it considers a concentration fulfils the criteria in paragraph 1. In such cases, the Commission may invite that Member State or those Member States to make a request pursuant to paragraph 1.

Article 23   Implementing provisions

1. The Commission shall have the power to lay down in accordance with the procedure referred to in paragraph 2:

(a) implementing provisions concerning the form, content and other details of notifications and submissions pursuant to Article 4;

(b) implementing provisions concerning time limits pursuant to Article 4(4), (5) Articles 7, 9, 10 and 22;

(c) the procedure and time limits for the submission and implementation of commitments pursuant to Article 6(2) and Article 8(2);

(d) implementing provisions concerning hearings pursuant to Article 18.

2. The Commission shall be assisted by an Advisory Committee, composed of representatives of the Member States.

(a) Before publishing draft implementing provisions and before adopting such provisions, the Commission shall consult the Advisory Committee.

(b) Consultation shall take place at a meeting convened at the invitation of and chaired by the Commission. A draft of the implementing provisions to be taken shall be sent with the invitation. The meeting shall take place not less than 10 working days after the invitation has been sent.

(c) The Advisory Committee shall deliver an opinion on the draft implementing provisions, if necessary by taking a vote. The Commission shall take the utmost account of the opinion delivered by the Committee.

Article 24   Relations with third countries

1. The Member States shall inform the Commission of any general difficulties encountered by their undertakings with concentrations as defined in Article 3 in a third country.

2. Initially not more than one year after the entry into force of this Regulation and, thereafter periodically, the Commission shall draw up a report examining the treatment accorded to undertakings having their seat or their principal fields of activity in the Community, in the terms referred to in paragraphs 3 and 4, as regards concentrations in third countries. The Commission shall submit those reports to the Council, together with any recommendations.

3. Whenever it appears to the Commission, either on the basis of the reports referred to in paragraph 2 or on the basis of other information, that a third country does not grant undertakings having their seat or their principal fields of activity in the Community, treatment comparable to that granted by the Community to undertakings from that country, the Commission may submit proposals to the Council for an appropriate mandate for negotiation with a view to obtaining comparable treatment for undertakings having their seat or their principal fields of activity in the Community.

4. Measures taken under this Article shall comply with the obligations of the Community or of the Member States, without prejudice to Article 307 of the Treaty, under international agreements, whether bilateral or multilateral.

Article 25   Repeal

1. Without prejudice to Article 26(2), Regulations (EEC) No 4064/89 and (EC) No 1310/97 shall be repealed with effect from 1 May 2004.

2. References to the repealed Regulations shall be construed as references to this Regulation and shall be read in accordance with the correlation table in the Annex.

Article 26   Entry into force and transitional provisions

1. This Regulation shall enter into force on the 20th day following that of its publication in the Official Journal of the European Union.

It shall apply from 1 May 2004.

2. Regulation (EEC) No 4064/89 shall continue to apply to any concentration which was the subject of an agreement or announcement or where control was acquired within the meaning of Article 4(1) of that Regulation before the date of application of this Regulation, subject, in particular, to the provisions governing applicability set out in Article 25(2) and (3) of Regulation (EEC) No 4064/89 and Article 2 of Regulation (EEC) No 1310/97.

3. As regards concentrations to which this Regulation applies by virtue of accession, the date of accession shall be substituted for the date of application of this Regulation.

This Regulation shall be binding in its entirety and directly applicable in all Member States. Done at Brussels, 20 January 2004.

For the Council
The President
C. McCREEVY

ANNEX   CORRELATION TABLE

Regulation (EEC) No 4064/89	This Regulation
Article 1(1), (2) and (3)	Article 1(1), (2) and (3)
Article 1(4)	Article 1(4)
Article 1(5)	Article 1(5)
Article 2(1)	Article 2(1)
—	Article 2(2)
Article 2(2)	Article 2(3)
Article 2(3)	Article 2(4)
Article 2(4)	Article 2(5)
Article 3(1)	Article 3(1)

Article 3(2)   Article 3(4)
Article 3(3)   Article 3(2)
Article 3(4)   Article 3(3)
—   Article 3(4)
Article 3(5)   Article 3(5)
Article 4(1) first sentence   Article 4(1) first subparagraph
Article 4(1) second sentence   —

—   Article 4(1) second and third subparagraphs
Article 4(2) and (3)   Article 4(2) and (3)
—   Article 4(4) to (6)
Article 5(1) to (3)   Article 5(1) to (3)
Article 5(4), introductory words   Article 5(4), introductory words
Article 5(4) point (a)   Article 5(4) point (a)
Article 5(4) point (b), introductory words   Article 5(4) point (b), introductory words
Article 5(4) point (b), first indent   Article 5(4) point (b)(i)
Article 5(4) point (b), second indent   Article 5(4) point (b)(ii)
Article 5(4) point (b), third indent   Article 5(4) point (b)(iii)
Article 5(4) point (b), fourth indent   Article 5(4) point (b)(iv)
Article 5(4) points (c), (d) and (e)   Article 5(4) points (c), (d) and (e)
Article 5(5)   Article 5(5)
Article 6(1), introductory words   Article 6(1), introductory words
Article 6(1) points (a) and (b)   Article 6(1) points (a) and (b)
Article 6(1) point (c)   Article 6(1) point (c), first sentence
Article 6(2) to (5)   Article 6(2) to (5)
Article 7(1)   Article 7(1)
Article 7(3)   Article 7(2)
Article 7(4)   Article 7(3)
Article 7(5)   Article 7(4)
Article 8(1)   Article 6(1) point (c), second sentence
Article 8(2)   Article 8(1) and (2)
Article 8(3)   Article 8(3)
Article 8(4)   Article 8(4)
—   Article 8(5)
Article 8(5)   Article 8(6)
Article 8(6)   Article 8(7)
—   Article 8(8)
Article 9(1) to (9)   Article 9(1) to (9)
Article 9(10)   —
Article 10(1) and (2)   Article 10(1) and (2)
Article 10(3)   Article 10(3) first subparagraph, first sentence
—   Article 10(3) first subparagraph, second sentence
—   Article 10(3) second subparagraph
Article 10(4)   Article 10(4) first subparagraph
—   Article 10(4), second subparagraph
Article 10(5)   Article 10(5), first and fourth subparagraphs
—   Article 10(5), second, third and fifth subparagraphs
Article 10(6)   Article 10(6)
Article 11(1)   Article 11(1)
Article 11(2)   —
Article 11(3)   Article 11(2)
Article 11(4)   Article 11(4) first sentence
—   Article 11(4) second and third sentences
Article 11(5) first sentence   —
Article 11(5) second sentence   Article 11(3)
Article 11(6)   Article 11(5)
—   Article 11(6) and (7)
Article 12   Article 12
Article 13(1) first subparagraph   Article 13(1)
Article 13(1) second subparagraph, intro words   Article 13(2) introductory words

Commission Regulation (EC) No 773/2004 of 7 April 2004 relating to the conduct of proceedings by the Commission pursuant to Articles 81 and 82 of the EC Treaty

[OJ 2004 L123/18]

THE COMMISSION OF THE EUROPEAN COMMUNITIES,

Having regard to the Treaty establishing the European Community,

Having regard to the Agreement on the European Economic Area,

Having regard to Council Regulation (EC) No 1/2003 of 16 December 2002 on the implementation of the rules on competition laid down in Articles 81 and 82 of the Treaty,[1] and in particular Article 33 thereof,

After consulting the Advisory Committee on Restrictive Practices and Dominant Positions,

Whereas:

(1) Regulation (EC) No 1/2003 empowers the Commission to regulate certain aspects of proceedings for the application of Articles 81 and 82 of the Treaty. It is necessary to lay down rules concerning the initiation of proceedings by the Commission as well as the handling of complaints and the hearing of the parties concerned.

(2) According to Regulation (EC) No 1/2003, national courts are under an obligation to avoid taking decisions which could run counter to decisions envisaged by the Commission in the same case. According to Article 11(6) of that Regulation, national competition authorities are relieved from their competence once the Commission has initiated proceedings for the adoption of a decision under Chapter III of Regulation (EC) No 1/2003. In this context, it is important that courts and competition authorities of the Member States are aware of the initiation of proceedings by the Commission. The Commission should therefore be able to make public its decisions to initiate proceedings.

(3) Before taking oral statements from natural or legal persons who consent to be interviewed, the Commission should inform those persons of the legal basis of the interview and its voluntary nature. The persons interviewed should also be informed of the purpose of the interview and of any record which may be made. In order to enhance the accuracy of the statements, the persons interviewed should also be given an opportunity to correct the statements recorded. Where information gathered from oral statements is exchanged pursuant to Article 12 of Regulation (EC) No 1/2003, that information should only be used in evidence to impose sanctions on natural persons where the conditions set out in that Article are fulfilled.

(4) Pursuant to Article 23(1)(d) of Regulation (EC) No 1/2003 fines may be imposed on undertakings and associations of undertakings where they fail to rectify within the time limit fixed by the Commission an incorrect, incomplete or misleading answer given by a member of their staff to questions in the course of inspections. It is therefore necessary to provide the undertaking concerned with a record of any explanations given and to establish a procedure enabling it to add any rectification, amendment or supplement to the explanations given by the member of staff who is not or was not authorised to provide explanations on behalf of the undertaking. The explanations given by a member of staff should remain in the Commission file as recorded during the inspection.

(5) Complaints are an essential source of information for detecting infringements of competition rules. It is important to define clear and efficient procedures for handling complaints lodged with the Commission.

---

[1] OJ L 1, 4.1.2003, p. 1. Regulation as amended by Regulation (EC) No 411/2004 (OJ L 68, 6.3.2004, p. 1).

(6) In order to be admissible for the purposes of Article 7 of Regulation (EC) No 1/2003, a complaint must contain certain specified information.

(7) In order to assist complainants in submitting the necessary facts to the Commission, a form should be drawn up. The submission of the information listed in that form should be a condition for a complaint to be treated as a complaint as referred to in Article 7 of Regulation (EC) No 1/2003.

(8) Natural or legal persons having chosen to lodge a complaint should be given the possibility to be associated closely with the proceedings initiated by the Commission with a view to finding an infringement. However, they should not have access to business secrets or other confidential information belonging to other parties involved in the proceedings.

(9) Complainants should be granted the opportunity of expressing their views if the Commission considers that there are insufficient grounds for acting on the complaint. Where the Commission rejects a complaint on the grounds that a competition authority of a Member State is dealing with it or has already done so, it should inform the complainant of the identity of that authority.

(10) In order to respect the rights of defence of undertakings, the Commission should give the parties concerned the right to be heard before it takes a decision.

(11) Provision should also be made for the hearing of persons who have not submitted a complaint as referred to in Article 7 of Regulation (EC) No 1/2003 and who are not parties to whom a statement of objections has been addressed but who can nevertheless show a sufficient interest. Consumer associations that apply to be heard should generally be regarded as having a sufficient interest, where the proceedings concern products or services used by the end-consumer or products or services that constitute a direct input into such products or services. Where it considers this to be useful for the proceedings, the Commission should also be able to invite other persons to express their views in writing and to attend the oral hearing of the parties to whom a statement of objections has been addressed. Where appropriate, it should also be able to invite such persons to express their views at that oral hearing.

(12) To improve the effectiveness of oral hearings, the Hearing Officer should have the power to allow the parties concerned, complainants, other persons invited to the hearing, the Commission services and the authorities of the Member States to ask questions during the hearing.

(13) When granting access to the file, the Commission should ensure the protection of business secrets and other confidential information. The category of 'other confidential information' includes information other than business secrets, which may be considered as confidential, insofar as its disclosure would significantly harm an undertaking or person. The Commission should be able to request undertakings or associations of undertakings that submit or have submitted documents or statements to identify confidential information.

(14) Where business secrets or other confidential information are necessary to prove an infringement, the Commission should assess for each individual document whether the need to disclose is greater than the harm which might result from disclosure.

(15) In the interest of legal certainty, a minimum time-limit for the various submissions provided for in this Regulation should be laid down.

(16) This Regulation replaces Commission Regulation (EC) No 2842/98 of 22 December 1998 on the hearing of parties in certain proceedings under Articles 85 and 86 of the EC Treaty,[2] which should therefore be repealed.

(17) This Regulation aligns the procedural rules in the transport sector with the general rules of procedure in all sectors. Commission Regulation (EC) No 2843/98 of 22 December 1998 on the form, content and other details of applications and notifications provided for in

[2] OJ L 354, 30.12.1998, p. 18.

Council Regulations (EEC) No 1017/68, (EEC) No 4056/86 and (EEC) No 3975/87 applying the rules on competition to the transport sector[3] should therefore be repealed.

(18) Regulation (EC) No 1/2003 abolishes the notification and authorisation system. Commission Regulation (EC) No 3385/94 of 21 December 1994 on the form, content and other details of applications and notifications provided for in Council Regulation No 17[4] should therefore be repealed,

HAS ADOPTED THIS REGULATION:

CHAPTER I   SCOPE

Article 1   Subject-matter and scope
This regulation applies to proceedings conducted by the Commission for the application of Articles 81 and 82 of the Treaty.

CHAPTER II   INITIATION OF PROCEEDINGS

Article 2   Initiation of proceedings
1.   The Commission may decide to initiate proceedings with a view to adopting a decision pursuant to Chapter III of Regulation (EC) No 1/2003 at any point in time, but no later than the date on which it issues a preliminary assessment as referred to in Article 9(1) of that Regulation or a statement of objections or the date on which a notice pursuant to Article 27(4) of that Regulation is published, whichever is the earlier.

2.   The Commission may make public the initiation of proceedings, in any appropriate way. Before doing so, it shall inform the parties concerned.

3.   The Commission may exercise its powers of investigation pursuant to Chapter V of Regulation (EC) No 1/2003 before initiating proceedings.

4.   The Commission may reject a complaint pursuant to Article 7 of Regulation (EC) No 1/2003 without initiating proceedings.

CHAPTER III   INVESTIGATIONS BY THE COMMISSION

Article 3   Power to take statements
1.   Where the Commission interviews a person with his consent in accordance with Article 19 of Regulation (EC) No 1/2003, it shall, at the beginning of the interview, state the legal basis and the purpose of the interview, and recall its voluntary nature. It shall also inform the person interviewed of its intention to make a record of the interview.

2.   The interview may be conducted by any means including by telephone or electronic means.

3.   The Commission may record the statements made by the persons interviewed in any form. A copy of any recording shall be made available to the person interviewed for approval. Where necessary, the Commission shall set a time-limit within which the person interviewed may communicate to it any correction to be made to the statement.

Article 4   Oral questions during inspections
1.   When, pursuant to Article 20(2)(e) of Regulation (EC) No 1/2003, officials or other accompanying persons authorised by the Commission ask representatives or members of staff of an undertaking or of an association of undertakings for explanations, the explanations given may be recorded in any form.

---

[3] OJ L 354, 30.12.1998, p. 22.
[4] OJ L 377, 31.12.1994, p. 28.

2.   A copy of any recording made pursuant to paragraph 1 shall be made available to the undertaking or association of undertakings concerned after the inspection.

3.   In cases where a member of staff of an undertaking or of an association of undertakings who is not or was not authorised by the undertaking or by the association of undertakings to provide explanations on behalf of the undertaking or association of undertakings has been asked for explanations, the Commission shall set a time-limit within which the undertaking or the association of undertakings may communicate to the Commission any rectification, amendment or supplement to the explanations given by such member of staff. The rectification, amendment or supplement shall be added to the explanations as recorded pursuant to paragraph 1.

CHAPTER IV   HANDLING OF COMPLAINTS

Article 5   Admissibility of complaints

1.   Natural and legal persons shall show a legitimate interest in order to be entitled to lodge a complaint for the purposes of Article 7 of Regulation (EC) No 1/2003.

Such complaints shall contain the information required by Form C, as set out in the Annex. The Commission may dispense with this obligation as regards part of the information, including documents, required by Form C.

2.   Three paper copies as well as, if possible, an electronic copy of the complaint shall be submitted to the Commission. The complainant shall also submit a non-confidential version of the complaint, if confidentiality is claimed for any part of the complaint.

3.   Complaints shall be submitted in one of the official languages of the Community.

Article 6   Participation of complainants in proceedings

1.   Where the Commission issues a statement of objections relating to a matter in respect of which it has received a complaint, it shall provide the complainant with a copy of the non-confidential version of the statement of objections and set a time-limit within which the complainant may make known its views in writing.

2.   The Commission may, where appropriate, afford complainants the opportunity of expressing their views at the oral hearing of the parties to which a statement of objections has been issued, if complainants so request in their written comments.

Article 7   Rejection of complaints

1.   Where the Commission considers that on the basis of the information in its possession there are insufficient grounds for acting on a complaint, it shall inform the complainant of its reasons and set a time-limit within which the complainant may make known its views in writing. The Commission shall not be obliged to take into account any further written submission received after the expiry of that time-limit.

2.   If the complainant makes known its views within the time-limit set by the Commission and the written submissions made by the complainant do not lead to a different assessment of the complaint, the Commission shall reject the complaint by decision.

3.   If the complainant fails to make known its views within the time-limit set by the Commission, the complaint shall be deemed to have been withdrawn.

Article 8   Access to information

1.   Where the Commission has informed the complainant of its intention to reject a complaint pursuant to Article 7(1) the complainant may request access to the documents on which the Commission bases its provisional assessment. For this purpose, the complainant may however not have access to business secrets and other confidential information belonging to other parties involved in the proceedings.

2.   The documents to which the complainant has had access in the context of proceedings conducted by the Commission under Articles 81 and 82 of the Treaty may only be used by

the complainant for the purposes of judicial or administrative proceedings for the application of those Treaty provisions.

Article 9   Rejections of complaints pursuant to Article 13 of Regulation (EC) No 1/2003

Where the Commission rejects a complaint pursuant to Article 13 of Regulation (EC) No 1/2003, it shall inform the complainant without delay of the national competition authority which is dealing or has already dealt with the case.

CHAPTER V   EXERCISE OF THE RIGHT TO BE HEARD

Article 10   Statement of objections and reply

1.   The Commission shall inform the parties concerned in writing of the objections raised against them. The statement of objections shall be notified to each of them.

2.   The Commission shall, when notifying the statement of objections to the parties concerned, set a time-limit within which these parties may inform it in writing of their views. The Commission shall not be obliged to take into account written submissions received after the expiry of that time-limit.

3.   The parties may, in their written submissions, set out all facts known to them which are relevant to their defence against the objections raised by the Commission. They shall attach any relevant documents as proof of the facts set out. They shall provide a paper original as well as an electronic copy or, where they do not provide an electronic copy, 28 paper copies of their submission and of the documents attached to it. They may propose that the Commission hear persons who may corroborate the facts set out in their submission.

Article 11   Right to be heard

1.   The Commission shall give the parties to whom it has addressed a statement of objections the opportunity to be heard before consulting the Advisory Committee referred to in Article 14(1) of Regulation (EC) No 1/2003.

2.   The Commission shall, in its decisions, deal only with objections in respect of which the parties referred to in paragraph 1 have been able to comment.

Article 12   Right to an oral hearing

The Commission shall give the parties to whom it has addressed a statement of objections the opportunity to develop their arguments at an oral hearing, if they so request in their written submissions.

Article 13   Hearing of other persons

1.   If natural or legal persons other than those referred to in Articles 5 and 11 apply to be heard and show a sufficient interest, the Commission shall inform them in writing of the nature and subject matter of the procedure and shall set a time-limit within which they may make known their views in writing.

2.   The Commission may, where appropriate, invite persons referred to in paragraph 1 to develop their arguments at the oral hearing of the parties to whom a statement of objections has been addressed, if the persons referred to in paragraph 1 so request in their written comments.

3.   The Commission may invite any other person to express its views in writing and to attend the oral hearing of the parties to whom a statement of objections has been addressed. The Commission may also invite such persons to express their views at that oral hearing.

Article 14   Conduct of oral hearings

1.   Hearings shall be conducted by a Hearing Officer in full independence.

2.   The Commission shall invite the persons to be heard to attend the oral hearing on such date as it shall determine.

3.   The Commission shall invite the competition authorities of the Member States to take part in the oral hearing. It may likewise invite officials and civil servants of other authorities of the Member States.

4.   Persons invited to attend shall either appear in person or be represented by legal representatives or by representatives authorised by their constitution as appropriate. Undertakings and associations of undertakings may also be represented by a duly authorised agent appointed from among their permanent staff.

5.   Persons heard by the Commission may be assisted by their lawyers or other qualified persons admitted by the Hearing Officer.

6.   Oral hearings shall not be public. Each person may be heard separately or in the presence of other persons invited to attend, having regard to the legitimate interest of the undertakings in the protection of their business secrets and other confidential information.

7.   The Hearing Officer may allow the parties to whom a statement of objections has been addressed, the complainants, other persons invited to the hearing, the Commission services and the authorities of the Member States to ask questions during the hearing.

8.   The statements made by each person heard shall be recorded. Upon request, the recording of the hearing shall be made available to the persons who attended the hearing. Regard shall be had to the legitimate interest of the parties in the protection of their business secrets and other confidential information.

CHAPTER VI   ACCESS TO THE FILE AND TREATMENT OF CONFIDENTIAL INFORMATION

Article 15   Access to the file and use of documents

1.   If so requested, the Commission shall grant access to the file to the parties to whom it has addressed a statement of objections. Access shall be granted after the notification of the statement of objections.

2.   The right of access to the file shall not extend to business secrets, other confidential information and internal documents of the Commission or of the competition authorities of the Member States. The right of access to the file shall also not extend to correspondence between the Commission and the competition authorities of the Member States or between the latter where such correspondence is contained in the file of the Commission.

3.   Nothing in this Regulation prevents the Commission from disclosing and using information necessary to prove an infringement of Articles 81 or 82 of the Treaty.

4.   Documents obtained through access to the file pursuant to this Article shall only be used for the purposes of judicial or administrative proceedings for the application of Articles 81 and 82 of the Treaty.

Article 16   Identification and protection of confidential information

1.   Information, including documents, shall not be communicated or made accessible by the Commission in so far as it contains business secrets or other confidential information of any person.

2.   Any person which makes known its views pursuant to Article 6(1), Article 7(1), Article 10(2) and Article 13(1) and (3) or subsequently submits further information to the Commission in the course of the same procedure, shall clearly identify any material which it considers to be confidential, giving reasons, and provide a separate non-confidential version by the date set by the Commission for making its views known.

3.   Without prejudice to paragraph 2 of this Article, the Commission may require undertakings and associations of undertakings which produce documents or statements pursuant to Regulation (EC) No 1/2003 to identify the documents or parts of documents which they consider to contain business secrets or other confidential information belonging to them and to identify the undertakings with regard to which such documents are to be considered

confidential. The Commission may likewise require undertakings or associations of undertakings to identify any part of a statement of objections, a case summary drawn up pursuant to Article 27(4) of Regulation (EC) No 1/2003 or a decision adopted by the Commission which in their view contains business secrets.

The Commission may set a time-limit within which the undertakings and associations of undertakings are to:

(a) substantiate their claim for confidentiality with regard to each individual document or part of document, statement or part of statement;

(b) provide the Commission with a non-confidential version of the documents or statements, in which the confidential passages are deleted;

(c) provide a concise description of each piece of deleted information.

4.   If undertakings or associations of undertakings fail to comply with paragraphs 2 and 3, the Commission may assume that the documents or statements concerned do not contain confidential information.

CHAPTER VII   GENERAL AND FINAL PROVISIONS

Article 17   Time-limits

1.   In setting the time-limits provided for in Article 3(3), Article 4(3), Article 6(1), Article 7(1), Article 10(2) and Article 16(3), the Commission shall have regard both to the time required for preparation of the submission and to the urgency of the case.

2.   The time-limits referred to in Article 6(1), Article 7(1) and Article 10(2) shall be at least four weeks. However, for proceedings initiated with a view to adopting interim measures pursuant to Article 8 of Regulation (EC) No 1/2003, the time-limit may be shortened to one week.

3.   The time-limits referred to in Article 3(3), Article 4(3) and Article 16(3) shall be at least two weeks.

4.   Where appropriate and upon reasoned request made before the expiry of the original time-limit, time-limits may be extended.

Article 18   Repeals

Regulations (EC) No 2842/98, (EC) No 2843/98 and (EC) No 3385/94 are repealed.

References to the repealed regulations shall be construed as references to this regulation.

Article 19   Transitional provisions

Procedural steps taken under Regulations (EC) No 2842/98 and (EC) No 2843/98 shall continue to have effect for the purpose of applying this Regulation.

Article 20   Entry into force

This Regulation shall enter into force on 1 May 2004.

This Regulation shall be binding in its entirety and directly applicable in all Member States.

Done at Brussels, 7 April 2004.

For the Commission Mario Monti Member of the Commission

ANNEX FORM C   COMPLAINT PURSUANT TO ARTICLE 7 OF REGULATION (EC) No 1/2003

I.   Information regarding the complainant and the undertaking(s) or association of undertakings giving rise to the complaint

1.   Give full details on the identity of the legal or natural person submitting the complaint. Where the complainant is an undertaking, identify the corporate group to which it belongs and provide a concise overview of the nature and scope of its business activities.

Provide a contact person (with telephone number, postal and e-mail-address) from which supplementary explanations can be obtained.

2. Identify the undertaking(s) or association of undertakings whose conduct the complaint relates to, including, where applicable, all available information on the corporate group to which the undertaking(s) complained of belong and the nature and scope of the business activities pursued by them. Indicate the position of the complainant vis-à-vis the undertaking(s) or association of undertakings complained of (e.g. customer, competitor).

II. Details of the alleged infringement and evidence

3. Set out in detail the facts from which, in your opinion, it appears that there exists an infringement of Article 81 or 82 of the Treaty and/or Article 53 or 54 of the EEA agreement. Indicate in particular the nature of the products (goods or services) affected by the alleged infringements and explain, where necessary, the commercial relationships concerning these products. Provide all available details on the agreements or practices of the undertakings or associations of undertakings to which this complaint relates. Indicate, to the extent possible, the relative market positions of the undertakings concerned by the complaint.

4. Submit all documentation in your possession relating to or directly connected with the facts set out in the complaint (for example, texts of agreements, minutes of negotiations or meetings, terms of transactions, business documents, circulars, correspondence, notes of telephone conversations . . .). State the names and address of the persons able to testify to the facts set out in the complaint, and in particular of persons affected by the alleged infringement. Submit statistics or other data in your possession which relate to the facts set out, in particular where they show developments in the marketplace (for example information relating to prices and price trends, barriers to entry to the market for new suppliers etc.).

5. Set out your view about the geographical scope of the alleged infringement and explain, where that is not obvious, to what extent trade between Member States or between the Community and one or more EFTA States that are contracting parties of the EEA Agreement may be affected by the conduct complained of.

III. Finding sought from the Commission and legitimate interest

6. Explain what finding or action you are seeking as a result of proceedings brought by the Commission.

7. Set out the grounds on which you claim a legitimate interest as complainant pursuant to Article 7 of Regulation (EC) No 1/2003. State in particular how the conduct complained of affects you and explain how, in your view, intervention by the Commission would be liable to remedy the alleged grievance.

IV. Proceedings before national competition authorities or national courts

8. Provide full information about whether you have approached, concerning the same or closely related subject-matters, any other competition authority and/or whether a lawsuit has been brought before a national court. If so, provide full details about the administrative or judicial authority contacted and your submissions to such authority.

Declaration that the information given in this form and in the Annexes thereto is given entirely in good faith.

Date and signature.

Commission Regulation (EC) No 772/2004 of 7 April 2004 on the application of Article 81(3) of the Treaty to categories of technology transfer agreements

[OJ 2004, L123/11]

THE COMMISSION OF THE EUROPEAN COMMUNITIES,

Having regard to the Treaty establishing the European Community,

Having regard to Council Regulation No 19/65/EEC of 2 March 1965 on application of Article 85(3) of the Treaty to certain categories of agreements and concerted practices,[1] and in particular Article 1 thereof,

Having published a draft of this Regulation,[2]

After consulting the Advisory Committee on Restrictive Practices and Dominant Positions,

Whereas:

(1) Regulation No 19/65/EEC empowers the Commission to apply Article 81(3) of the Treaty by Regulation to certain categories of technology transfer agreements and corresponding concerted practices to which only two undertakings are party which fall within Article 81(1).

(2) Pursuant to Regulation No 19/65/EEC, the Commission has, in particular, adopted Regulation (EC) No 240/96 of 31 January 1996 on the application of Article 85(3) of the Treaty to certain categories of technology transfer agreements.[3]

(3) On 20 December 2001 the Commission published an evaluation report on the transfer of technology block exemption Regulation (EC) No 240/96.[4] This generated a public debate on the application of Regulation (EC) No 240/96 and on the application in general of Article 81(1) and (3) of the Treaty to technology transfer agreements. The response to the evaluation report from Member States and third parties has been generally in favour of reform of Community competition policy on technology transfer agreements. It is therefore appropriate to repeal Regulation (EC) No 240/96.

(4) This Regulation should meet the two requirements of ensuring effective competition and providing adequate legal security for undertakings. The pursuit of these objectives should take account of the need to simplify the regulatory framework and its application. It is appropriate to move away from the approach of listing exempted clauses and to place greater emphasis on defining the categories of agreements which are exempted up to a certain level of market power and on specifying the restrictions or clauses which are not to be contained in such agreements. This is consistent with an economics-based approach which assesses the impact of agreements on the relevant market. It is also consistent with such an approach to make a distinction between agreements between competitors and agreements between non-competitors.

(5) Technology transfer agreements concern the licensing of technology. Such agreements will usually improve economic efficiency and be pro-competitive as they can reduce duplication of research and development, strengthen the incentive for the initial research and development, spur incremental innovation, facilitate diffusion and generate product market competition.

(6) The likelihood that such efficiency-enhancing and pro-competitive effects will outweigh any anti-competitive effects due to restrictions contained in technology transfer

[1] OJ 36, 6.3.1965, p. 533/65. Regulation as last amended by Regulation (EC) No 1/2003 (OJ L 1, 4.1.2003, p. 1).
[2] OJ C 235, 1.10.2003, p. 10.
[3] OJ L 31, 9.2.1996, p. 2. Regulation as amended by the 2003 Act of Accession.
[4] COM(2001) 786 final.

agreements depends on the degree of market power of the undertakings concerned and, therefore, on the extent to which those undertakings face competition from undertakings owning substitute technologies or undertakings producing substitute products.

(7) This Regulation should only deal with agreements where the licensor permits the licensee to exploit the licensed technology, possibly after further research and development by the licensee, for the production of goods or services. It should not deal with licensing agreements for the purpose of subcontracting research and development. It should also not deal with licensing agreements to set up technology pools, that is to say, agreements for the pooling of technologies with the purpose of licensing the created package of intellectual property rights to third parties.

(8) For the application of Article 81(3) by regulation, it is not necessary to define those technology transfer agreements that are capable of falling within Article 81(1). In the individual assessment of agreements pursuant to Article 81(1), account has to be taken of several factors, and in particular the structure and the dynamics of the relevant technology and product markets.

(9) The benefit of the block exemption established by this Regulation should be limited to those agreements which can be assumed with sufficient certainty to satisfy the conditions of Article 81(3). In order to attain the benefits and objectives of technology transfer, the benefit of this Regulation should also apply to provisions contained in technology transfer agreements that do not constitute the primary object of such agreements, but are directly related to the application of the licensed technology.

(10) For technology transfer agreements between competitors it can be presumed that, where the combined share of the relevant markets accounted for by the parties does not exceed 20% and the agreements do not contain certain severely anti-competitive restraints, they generally lead to an improvement in production or distribution and allow consumers a fair share of the resulting benefits.

(11) For technology transfer agreements between non-competitors it can be presumed that, where the individual share of the relevant markets accounted for by each of the parties does not exceed 30% and the agreements do not contain certain severely anti-competitive restraints, they generally lead to an improvement in production or distribution and allow consumers a fair share of the resulting benefits.

(12) There can be no presumption that above these market-share thresholds technology transfer agreements do fall within the scope of Article 81(1). For instance, an exclusive licensing agreement between non-competing undertakings does often not fall within the scope of Article 81(1). There can also be no presumption that, above these market-share thresholds, technology transfer agreements falling within the scope of Article 81(1) will not satisfy the conditions for exemption. However, it can also not be presumed that they will usually give rise to objective advantages of such a character and size as to compensate for the disadvantages which they create for competition.

(13) This Regulation should not exempt technology transfer agreements containing restrictions which are not indispensable to the improvement of production or distribution. In particular, technology transfer agreements containing certain severely anti-competitive restraints such as the fixing of prices charged to third parties should be excluded from the benefit of the block exemption established by this Regulation irrespective of the market shares of the undertakings concerned. In the case of such hardcore restrictions the whole agreement should be excluded from the benefit of the block exemption.

(14) In order to protect incentives to innovate and the appropriate application of intellectual property rights, certain restrictions should be excluded from the block exemption. In particular exclusive grant back obligations for severable improvements should be excluded. Where such a restriction is included in a licence agreement only the restriction in question should be excluded from the benefit of the block exemption.

(15) The market-share thresholds, the non-exemption of technology transfer agreements

containing severely anti-competitive restraints and the excluded restrictions provided for in this Regulation will normally ensure that the agreements to which the block exemption applies do not enable the participating undertakings to eliminate competition in respect of a substantial part of the products in question.

(16) In particular cases in which the agreements falling under this Regulation nevertheless have effects incompatible with Article 81(3), the Commission should be able to withdraw the benefit of the block exemption. This may occur in particular where the incentives to innovate are reduced or where access to markets is hindered.

(17) Council Regulation (EC) No 1/2003 of 16 December 2002 on the implementation of the rules on competition laid down in Articles 81 and 82 of the Treaty[5] empowers the competent authorities of Member States to withdraw the benefit of the block exemption in respect of technology transfer agreements having effects incompatible with Article 81(3), where such effects are felt in their respective territory, or in a part thereof, and where such territory has the characteristics of a distinct geographic market. Member States must ensure that the exercise of this power of withdrawal does not prejudice the uniform application throughout the common market of the Community competition rules or the full effect of the measures adopted in implementation of those rules.

(18) In order to strengthen supervision of parallel networks of technology transfer agreements which have similar restrictive effects and which cover more than 50% of a given market, the Commission should be able to declare this Regulation inapplicable to technology transfer agreements containing specific restraints relating to the market concerned, thereby restoring the full application of Article 81 to such agreements.

(19) This Regulation should cover only technology transfer agreements between a licensor and a licensee. It should cover such agreements even if conditions are stipulated for more than one level of trade, by, for instance, requiring the licensee to set up a particular distribution system and specifying the obligations the licensee must or may impose on resellers of the products produced under the licence. However, such conditions and obligations should comply with the competition rules applicable to supply and distribution agreements. Supply and distribution agreements concluded between a licensee and its buyers should not be exempted by this Regulation.

(20) This Regulation is without prejudice to the application of Article 82 of the Treaty,

HAS ADOPTED THIS REGULATION:

Article 1   Definitions

1. For the purposes of this Regulation, the following definitions shall apply:
    (a) 'agreement' means an agreement, a decision of an association of undertakings or a concerted practice;
    (b) 'technology transfer agreement' means a patent licensing agreement, a know-how licensing agreement, a software copyright licensing agreement or a mixed patent, know-how or software copyright licensing agreement, including any such agreement containing provisions which relate to the sale and purchase of products or which relate to the licensing of other intellectual property rights or the assignment of intellectual property rights, provided that those provisions do not constitute the primary object of the agreement and are directly related to the production of the contract products; assignments of patents, know-how, software copyright or a combination thereof where part of the risk associated with the exploitation of the technology remains with the assignor, in particular where the sum payable in consideration of the assignment is dependent on the turnover obtained by the assignee in respect of products produced with the assigned technology, the

quantity of such products produced or the number of operations carried out employing the technology, shall also be deemed to be technology transfer agreements;

(c) 'reciprocal agreement' means a technology transfer agreement where two undertakings grant each other, in the same or separate contracts, a patent licence, a know-how licence, a software copyright licence or a mixed patent, know-how or software copyright licence and where these licences concern competing technologies or can be used for the production of competing products;

(d) 'non-reciprocal agreement' means a technology transfer agreement where one undertaking grants another undertaking a patent licence, a know-how licence, a software copyright licence or a mixed patent, know-how or software copyright licence, or where two undertakings grant each other such a licence but where these licences do not concern competing technologies and cannot be used for the production of competing products;

(e) 'product' means a good or a service, including both intermediary goods and services and final goods and services;

(f) 'contract products' means products produced with the licensed technology;

(g) 'intellectual property rights' includes industrial property rights, know-how, copyright and neighbouring rights;

(h) 'patents' means patents, patent applications, utility models, applications for registration of utility models, designs, topographies of semiconductor products, supplementary protection certificates for medicinal products or other products for which such supplementary protection certificates may be obtained and plant breeder's certificates;

(i) 'know-how' means a package of non-patented practical information, resulting from experience and testing, which is:

(i) secret, that is to say, not generally known or easily accessible,

(ii) substantial, that is to say, significant and useful for the production of the contract products, and

(iii) identified, that is to say, described in a sufficiently comprehensive manner so as to make it possible to verify that it fulfils the criteria of secrecy and substantiality;

(j) 'competing undertakings' means undertakings which compete on the relevant technology market and/or the relevant product market, that is to say:

(i) competing undertakings on the relevant technology market, being undertakings which license out competing technologies without infringing each others' intellectual property rights (actual competitors on the technology market); the relevant technology market includes technologies which are regarded by the licensees as interchangeable with or substitutable for the licensed technology, by reason of the technologies' characteristics, their royalties and their intended use,

(ii) competing undertakings on the relevant product market, being undertakings which, in the absence of the technology transfer agreement, are both active on the relevant product and geographic market(s) on which the contract products are sold without infringing each others' intellectual property rights (actual competitors on the product market) or would, on realistic grounds, undertake the necessary additional investments or other necessary switching costs so that they could timely enter, without infringing each others' intellectual property rights, the(se) relevant product and geographic market(s) in response to a small and permanent increase in relative prices (potential competitors on the product market); the relevant product market comprises products which are regarded by the buyers as interchangeable with or substitutable for the contract products, by reason of the products' characteristics, their prices and their intended use;

(k) 'selective distribution system' means a distribution system where the licensor undertakes to license the production of the contract products only to licensees selected on the basis of specified criteria and where these licensees undertake not to sell the contract products to unauthorised distributors;

(l) 'exclusive territory' means a territory in which only one undertaking is allowed to produce the contract products with the licensed technology, without prejudice to the possibility of allowing within that territory another licensee to produce the contract products only for a particular customer where this second licence was granted in order to create an alternative source of supply for that customer;

(m) 'exclusive customer group' means a group of customers to which only one undertaking is allowed actively to sell the contract products produced with the licensed technology;

(n) 'severable improvement' means an improvement that can be exploited without infringing the licensed technology.

2.   The terms 'undertaking', 'licensor' and 'licensee' shall include their respective connected undertakings.

'Connected undertakings' means:

(a) undertakings in which a party to the agreement, directly or indirectly:
   (i)   has the power to exercise more than half the voting rights, or
   (ii) has the power to appoint more than half the members of the supervisory board, board of management or bodies legally representing the undertaking, or
   (iii) has the right to manage the undertaking's affairs;

(b) undertakings which directly or indirectly have, over a party to the agreement, the rights or powers listed in (a);

(c) undertakings in which an undertaking referred to in (b) has, directly or indirectly, the rights or powers listed in (a);

(d) undertakings in which a party to the agreement together with one or more of the undertakings referred to in (a), (b) or (c), or in which two or more of the latter undertakings, jointly have the rights or powers listed in (a);

(e) undertakings in which the rights or the powers listed in (a) are jointly held by:
   (i)   parties to the agreement or their respective connected undertakings referred to in (a) to (d), or
   (ii) one or more of the parties to the agreement or one or more of their connected undertakings referred to in (a) to (d) and one or more third parties.

Article 2   Exemption

Pursuant to Article 81(3) of the Treaty and subject to the provisions of this Regulation, it is hereby declared that Article 81(1) of the Treaty shall not apply to technology transfer agreements entered into between two undertakings permitting the production of contract products.

This exemption shall apply to the extent that such agreements contain restrictions of competition falling within the scope of Article 81(1). The exemption shall apply for as long as the intellectual property right in the licensed technology has not expired, lapsed or been declared invalid or, in the case of know-how, for as long as the know-how remains secret, except in the event where the know-how becomes publicly known as a result of action by the licensee, in which case the exemption shall apply for the duration of the agreement.

Article 3   Market-share thresholds

1.   Where the undertakings party to the agreement are competing undertakings, the exemption provided for in Article 2 shall apply on condition that the combined market share of the parties does not exceed 20% on the affected relevant technology and product market.

2.   Where the undertakings party to the agreement are not competing undertakings,

the exemption provided for in Article 2 shall apply on condition that the market share of each of the parties does not exceed 30% on the affected relevant technology and product market.

3.   For the purposes of paragraphs 1 and 2, the market share of a party on the relevant technology market(s) is defined in terms of the presence of the licensed technology on the relevant product market(s). A licensor's market share on the relevant technology market shall be the combined market share on the relevant product market of the contract products produced by the licensor and its licensees.

Article 4   Hardcore restrictions

1.   Where the undertakings party to the agreement are competing undertakings, the exemption provided for in Article 2 shall not apply to agreements which, directly or indirectly, in isolation or in combination with other factors under the control of the parties, have as their object:

(a)   the restriction of a party's ability to determine its prices when selling products to third parties;

(b)   the limitation of output, except limitations on the output of contract products imposed on the licensee in a non-reciprocal agreement or imposed on only one of the licensees in a reciprocal agreement;

(c)   the allocation of markets or customers except:

(i)   the obligation on the licensee(s) to produce with the licensed technology only within one or more technical fields of use or one or more product markets,

(ii)   the obligation on the licensor and/or the licensee, in a non-reciprocal agreement, not to produce with the licensed technology within one or more technical fields of use or one or more product markets or one or more exclusive territories reserved for the other party,

(iii)   the obligation on the licensor not to license the technology to another licensee in a particular territory,

(iv)   the restriction, in a non-reciprocal agreement, of active and/or passive sales by the licensee and/or the licensor into the exclusive territory or to the exclusive customer group reserved for the other party,

(v)   the restriction, in a non-reciprocal agreement, of active sales by the licensee into the exclusive territory or to the exclusive customer group allocated by the licensor to another licensee provided the latter was not a competing undertaking of the licensor at the time of the conclusion of its own licence,

(vi)   the obligation on the licensee to produce the contract products only for its own use provided that the licensee is not restricted in selling the contract products actively and passively as spare parts for its own products,

(vii)the obligation on the licensee, in a non-reciprocal agreement, to produce the contract products only for a particular customer, where the licence was granted in order to create an alternative source of supply for that customer;

(d)   the restriction of the licensee's ability to exploit its own technology or the restriction of the ability of any of the parties to the agreement to carry out research and development, unless such latter restriction is indispensable to prevent the disclosure of the licensed know-how to third parties.

2.   Where the undertakings party to the agreement are not competing undertakings, the exemption provided for in Article 2 shall not apply to agreements which, directly or indirectly, in isolation or in combination with other factors under the control of the parties, have as their object:

(a)   the restriction of a party's ability to determine its prices when selling products to third parties, without prejudice to the possibility of imposing a maximum sale price or recommending a sale price, provided that it does not amount to a fixed or minimum sale price as a result of pressure from, or incentives offered by, any of the parties;

(b) the restriction of the territory into which, or of the customers to whom, the licensee may passively sell the contract products, except:

   (i) the restriction of passive sales into an exclusive territory or to an exclusive customer group reserved for the licensor,

   (ii) the restriction of passive sales into an exclusive territory or to an exclusive customer group allocated by the licensor to another licensee during the first two years that this other licensee is selling the contract products in that territory or to that customer group,

   (iii) the obligation to produce the contract products only for its own use provided that the licensee is not restricted in selling the contract products actively and passively as spare parts for its own products,

   (iv) the obligation to produce the contract products only for a particular customer, where the licence was granted in order to create an alternative source of supply for that customer,

   (v) the restriction of sales to end-users by a licensee operating at the wholesale level of trade,

   (vi) the restriction of sales to unauthorised distributors by the members of a selective distribution system;

(c) the restriction of active or passive sales to end-users by a licensee which is a member of a selective distribution system and which operates at the retail level, without prejudice to the possibility of prohibiting a member of the system from operating out of an unauthorised place of establishment.

3. Where the undertakings party to the agreement are not competing undertakings at the time of the conclusion of the agreement but become competing undertakings afterwards, paragraph 2 and not paragraph 1 shall apply for the full life of the agreement unless the agreement is subsequently amended in any material respect.

Article 5   Excluded restrictions

1. The exemption provided for in Article 2 shall not apply to any of the following obligations contained in technology transfer agreements:

(a) any direct or indirect obligation on the licensee to grant an exclusive licence to the licensor or to a third party designated by the licensor in respect of its own severable improvements to or its own new applications of the licensed technology;

(b) any direct or indirect obligation on the licensee to assign, in whole or in part, to the licensor or to a third party designated by the licensor, rights to its own severable improvements to or its own new applications of the licensed technology;

(c) any direct or indirect obligation on the licensee not to challenge the validity of intellectual property rights which the licensor holds in the common market, without prejudice to the possibility of providing for termination of the technology transfer agreement in the event that the licensee challenges the validity of one or more of the licensed intellectual property rights.

2. Where the undertakings party to the agreement are not competing undertakings, the exemption provided for in Article 2 shall not apply to any direct or indirect obligation limiting the licensee's ability to exploit its own technology or limiting the ability of any of the parties to the agreement to carry out research and development, unless such latter restriction is indispensable to prevent the disclosure of the licensed know-how to third parties.

Article 6   Withdrawal in individual cases

1. The Commission may withdraw the benefit of this Regulation, pursuant to Article 29(1) of Regulation (EC) No 1/2003, where it finds in any particular case that a technology

transfer agreement to which the exemption provided for in Article 2 applies nevertheless has effects which are incompatible with Article 81(3) of the Treaty, and in particular where:

(a) access of third parties' technologies to the market is restricted, for instance by the cumulative effect of parallel networks of similar restrictive agreements prohibiting licensees from using third parties' technologies;

(b) access of potential licensees to the market is restricted, for instance by the cumulative effect of parallel networks of similar restrictive agreements prohibiting licensors from licensing to other licensees;

(c) without any objectively valid reason, the parties do not exploit the licensed technology.

2. Where, in any particular case, a technology transfer agreement to which the exemption provided for in Article 2 applies has effects which are incompatible with Article 81(3) of the Treaty in the territory of a Member State, or in a part thereof, which has all the characteristics of a distinct geographic market, the competition authority of that Member State may withdraw the benefit of this Regulation, pursuant to Article 29(2) of Regulation (EC) No 1/2003, in respect of that territory, under the same circumstances as those set out in paragraph 1 of this Article.

Article 7   Non-application of this Regulation

1. Pursuant to Article 1a of Regulation No 19/65/EEC, the Commission may by regulation declare that, where parallel networks of similar technology transfer agreements cover more than 50% of a relevant market, this Regulation is not to apply to technology transfer agreements containing specific restraints relating to that market.

2. A regulation pursuant to paragraph 1 shall not become applicable earlier than six months following its adoption.

Article 8   Application of the market-share thresholds

1. For the purposes of applying the market-share thresholds provided for in Article 3 the rules set out in this paragraph shall apply. The market share shall be calculated on the basis of market sales value data. If market sales value data are not available, estimates based on other reliable market information, including market sales volumes, may be used to establish the market share of the undertaking concerned. The market share shall be calculated on the basis of data relating to the preceding calendar year. The market share held by the undertakings referred to in point (e) of the second subparagraph of Article 1(2) shall be apportioned equally to each undertaking having the rights or the powers listed in point (a) of the second subparagraph of Article 1(2).

2. If the market share referred to in Article 3(1) or (2) is initially not more than 20% respectively 30% but subsequently rises above those levels, the exemption provided for in Article 2 shall continue to apply for a period of two consecutive calendar years following the year in which the 20% threshold or 30% threshold was first exceeded.

Article 9   Repeal

Regulation (EC) No 240/96 is repealed.

References to the repealed Regulation shall be construed as references to this Regulation.

Article 10   Transitional period

The prohibition laid down in Article 81(1) of the Treaty shall not apply during the period from 1 May 2004 to 31 March 2006 in respect of agreements already in force on 30 April 2004 which do not satisfy the conditions for exemption provided for in this Regulation but which, on 30 April 2004, satisfied the conditions for exemption provided for in Regulation (EC) No 240/96.

Article 11   Period of validity

This Regulation shall enter into force on 1 May 2004.

It shall expire on 30 April 2014.

This Regulation shall be binding in its entirety and directly applicable in all Member States.

Done at Brussels, 7 April 2004.

For the Commission Mario Monti Member of the Commission

CONSUMER PROTECTION

Council Directive of 25 July 1985 on the approximation of the laws, regulations and administrative provisions of the Member States concerning liability for defective products (85/374/ EEC)

[OJ 1985, L210/29]*

THE COUNCIL OF THE EUROPEAN COMMUNITIES,

Having regard to the Treaty establishing the European Economic Community, and in particular Article 100 thereof,

Having regard to the proposal from the Commission,[1]

Having regard to the opinion of the European Parliament,[2]

Having regard to the opinion of the Economic and Social Committee,[3]

Whereas approximation of the laws of the Member States concerning the liability of the producer for damage caused by the defectiveness of his products is necessary because the existing divergences may distort competition and affect the movement of goods within the common market and entail a differing degree of protection of the consumer against damage caused by a defective product to his health or property;

Whereas liability without fault on the part of the producer is the sole means of adequately solving the problem, peculiar to our age of increasing technicality, of a fair apportionment of the risks inherent in modern technological production;

Whereas liability without fault should apply only to movables which have been industrially produced; whereas, as a result, it is appropriate to exclude liability for agricultural products and game, except where they have undergone a processing of an industrial nature which could cause a defect in these products;

Whereas the liability provided for in this Directive should also apply to movables which are used in the construction of immovables or are installed in immovables;

Whereas protection of the consumer requires that all producers involved in the production process should be made liable, in so far as their finished product, component part or any raw material supplied by them was defective; whereas, for the same reason, liability should extend to importers of products into the Community and to persons who present themselves as producers by affixing their name, trade mark or other distinguishing feature or who supply a product the producer of which cannot be identified;

Whereas, in situations where several persons are liable for the same damage, the protection of the consumer requires that the injured person should be able to claim full compensation for the damage from any one of them;

---

* **Editor's Note:** Amended by Directive 99/34, OJ 1999, L141/20.

[1] OJ No. C241, 14. 10. 1976, p. 9 and OJ No. C271, 26. 10. 1979, p. 3.

[2] OJ No. C127, 21. 5. 1979, p. 61.

[3] OJ No. C114, 7. 5. 1979, p. 15.

Whereas, to protect the physical well-being and property of the consumer, the defectiveness of the product should be determined by reference not to its fitness for use but to the lack of the safety which the public at large is entitled to expect; whereas the safety is assessed by excluding any misuse of the product not reasonable under the circumstances;

Whereas a fair apportionment of risk between the injured person and the producer implies that the producer should be able to free himself from liability if he furnishes proof as to the existence of certain exonerating circumstances;

Whereas the protection of the consumer requires that the liability of the producer remains unaffected by acts or omissions of other persons having contributed to cause the damage; whereas, however, the contributory negligence of the injured person may be taken into account to reduce or disallow such liability;

Whereas the protection of the consumer requires compensation for death and personal injury as well as compensation for damage to property; whereas the latter should nevertheless be limited to goods for private use or consumption and be subject to a deduction of a lower threshold of a fixed amount in order to avoid litigation in an excessive number of cases; whereas this Directive should not prejudice compensation for pain and suffering and other non-material damages payable, where appropriate, under the law applicable to the case;

Whereas a uniform period of limitation for the bringing of action for compensation is in the interests both of the injured person and of the producer;

Whereas products age in the course of time, higher safety standards are developed and the state of science and technology progresses; whereas, therefore, it would not be reasonable to make the producer liable for an unlimited period for the defectiveness of his product; whereas, therefore, liability should expire after a reasonable length of time, without prejudice to claims pending at law;

Whereas, to achieve effective protection of consumers, no contractual derogation should be permitted as regards the liability of the producer in relation to the injured person;

Whereas under the legal systems of the Member States an injured party may have a claim for damages based on grounds of contractual liability or on grounds of non-contractual liability other than that provided for in this Directive; in so far as these provisions also serve to attain the objective of effective protection of consumers, they should remain unaffected by this Directive; whereas, in so far as effective protection of consumers in the sector of pharmaceutical products is already also attained in a Member State under a special liability system, claims based on this system should similarly remain possible;

Whereas, to the extent that liability for nuclear injury or damage is already covered in all Member States by adequate special rules, it has been possible to exclude damage of this type from the scope of this Directive;

Whereas, since the exclusion of primary agricultural products and game from the scope of this Directive may be felt, in certain Member States, in view of what is expected for the protection of consumers, to restrict unduly such protection, it should be possible for a Member State to extend liability to such products;

Whereas, for similar reasons, the possibility offered to a producer to free himself from liability if he proves that the state of scientific and technical knowledge at the time when he put the product into circulation was not such as to enable the existence of a defect to be discovered may be felt in certain Member States to restrict unduly the protection of the consumer; whereas it should therefore be possible for a Member State to maintain in its legislation or to provide by new legislation that this exonerating circumstance is not admitted; whereas, in the case of new legislation, making use of this derogation should, however, be subject to a Community stand-still procedure, in order to raise, if possible, the level of protection in a uniform manner throughout the Community;

Whereas, taking into account the legal traditions in most of the Member States, it is inappropriate to set any financial ceiling on the producer's liability without fault; whereas, in so far as there are, however, differing traditions, it seems possible to admit that a Member

State may derogate from the principle of unlimited liability by providing a limit for the total liability of the producer for damage resulting from a death or personal injury and caused by identical items with the same defect, provided that this limit is established at a level sufficiently high to guarantee adequate protection of the consumer and the correct functioning of the common market;

Whereas the harmonization resulting from this cannot be total at the present stage, but opens the way towards greater harmonization; whereas it is therefore necessary that the Council receive at regular intervals, reports from the Commission on the application of this Directive, accompanied, as the case may be, by appropriate proposals;

Whereas it is particularly important in this respect that a re-examination be carried out of those parts of the Directive relating to the derogations open to the Member States, at the expiry of a period of sufficient length to gather practical experience on the effects of these derogations on the protection of consumers and on the functioning of the common market,

HAS ADOPTED THIS DIRECTIVE:

Article 1
The producer shall be liable for damage caused by a defect in his product.

Article 2
For the purpose of this Directive, 'product' means all movables even if incorporated into another movable or into an immovable. 'Product' includes electricity.

Article 3
1. 'Producer' means the manufacturer of a finished product, the producer of any raw material or the manufacturer of a component part and any person who, by putting his name, trade mark or other distinguishing feature on the product presents himself as its producer.

2. Without prejudice to the liability of the producer, any person who imports into the Community a product for sale, hire, leasing or any form of distribution in the course of his business shall be deemed to be a producer within the meaning of this Directive and shall be responsible as a producer.

3. Where the producer of the product cannot be identified, each supplier of the product shall be treated as its producer unless he informs the injured person, within a reasonable time, of the identity of the producer or of the person who supplied him with the product. The same shall apply, in the case of an imported product, if this product does not indicate the identity of the importer referred to in paragraph 2, even if the name of the producer is indicated.

Article 4
The injured person shall be required to prove the damage, the defect and the causal relationship between defect and damage.

Article 5
Where, as a result of the provisions of this Directive, two or more persons are liable for the same damage, they shall be liable jointly and severally, without prejudice to the provisions of national law concerning the rights of contribution or recourse.

Article 6
1. A product is defective when it does not provide the safety which a person is entitled to expect, taking all circumstances into account, including:
   (a) the presentation of the product;
   (b) the use to which it could reasonably be expected that the product would be put;
   (c) the time when the product was put into circulation.
2. A product shall not be considered defective for the sole reason that a better product is subsequently put into circulation.

Article 7

The producer shall not be liable as a result of this Directive if he proves:

  (a) that he did not put the product into circulation; or
  (b) that, having regard to the circumstances, it is probable that the defect which caused the damage did not exist at the time when the product was put into circulation by him or that this defect came into being afterwards; or
  (c) that the product was neither manufactured by him for sale or any form of distribution for economic purpose nor manufactured or distributed by him in the course of his business; or
  (d) that the defect is due to compliance of the product with mandatory regulations issued by the public authorities; or
  (e) that the state of scientific and technical knowledge at the time when he put the product into circulation was not such as to enable the existence of the defect to be discovered; or
  (f) in the case of a manufacturer of a component, that the defect is attributable to the design of the product in which the component has been fitted or to the instructions given by the manufacturer of the product.

Article 8

1.   Without prejudice to the provisions of national law concerning the right of contribution or recourse, the liability of the producer shall not be reduced when the damage is caused both by a defect in product and by the act or omission of a third party.

2.   The liability of the producer may be reduced or disallowed when, having regard to all the circumstances, the damage is caused both by a defect in the product and by the fault of the injured person or any person for whom the injured person is responsible.

Article 9

For the purpose of Article 1, 'damage' means:

  (a) damage caused by death or by personal injuries;
  (b) damage to, or destruction of, any item of property other than the defective product itself, with a lower threshold of 500 ECU, provided that the item of property:
      (i) is of a type ordinarily intended for private use or consumption, and
      (ii) was used by the injured person mainly for his own private use or consumption.

This Article shall be without prejudice to national provisions relating to non-material damage.

Article 10

1.   Member States shall provide in their legislation that a limitation period of three years shall apply to proceedings for the recovery of damages as provided for in this Directive. The limitation period shall begin to run from the day on which the plaintiff became aware, or should reasonably have become aware, of the damage, the defect and the identity of the producer.

2.   The laws of Member States regulating suspension or interruption of the limitation period shall not be affected by this Directive.

Article 11

Member States shall provide in their legislation that the rights conferred upon the injured person pursuant to this Directive shall be extinguished upon the expiry of a period of 10 years from the date on which the producer put into circulation the actual product which caused the damage, unless the injured person has in the meantime instituted proceedings against the producer.

Article 12

The liability of the producer arising from this Directive may not, in relation to the injured person, be limited or excluded by a provision limiting his liability or exempting him from liability.

Article 13

This Directive shall not affect any rights which an injured person may have according to the rules of the law of contractual or non-contractual liability or a special liability system existing at the moment when this Directive is notified.

Article 14

This Directive shall not apply to injury or damage arising from nuclear accidents and covered by international conventions ratified by the Member States.

Article 15

1. Each Member State may:
    (b) by way of derogation from Article 7(e), maintain or, subject to the procedure set out in paragraph 2 of this Article, provide in this legislation that the producer shall be liable even if he proves that the state of scientific and technical knowledge at the time when he put the product into circulation was not such as to enable the existence of a defect to be discovered.

2. A Member State wishing to introduce the measure specified in paragraph 1(b) shall communicate the text of the proposed measure to the Commission. The Commission shall inform the other Member States thereof. The Member State concerned shall hold the proposed measure in abeyance for nine months after the Commission is informed and provided that in the meantime the Commission has not submitted to the Council a proposal amending this Directive on the relevant matter. However, if within three months of receiving the said information, the Commission does not advise the Member State concerned that it intends submitting such a proposal to the Council, the Member State may take the proposed measure immediately. If the Commission does submit to the Council such a proposal amending this Directive within the aforementioned nine months, the Member State concerned shall hold the proposed measure in abeyance for a further period of 18 months from the date on which the proposal is submitted.

3. Ten years after the date of notification of this Directive, the Commission shall submit to the Council a report on the effect that rulings by the courts as to the application of Article 7 (e) and of paragraph 1(b) of this Article have on consumer protection and the functioning of the common market. In the light of this report the Council, acting on a proposal from the Commission and pursuant to the terms of Article 100 of the Treaty, shall decide whether to repeal Article 7(e).

Article 16

1. Any Member State may provide that a producer's total liability for damage resulting from a death or personal injury and caused by identical items with the same defect shall be limited to an amount which may not be less than 70 million ECU.

2. Ten years after the date of notification of this Directive, the Commission shall submit to the Council a report on the effect on consumer protection and the functioning of the common market of the implementation of the financial limit on liability by those Member States which have used the option provided for in paragraph 1. In the light of this report the Council, acting on a proposal from the Commission and pursuant to the terms of Article 100 of the Treaty, shall decide whether to repeal paragraph 1.

Article 17

This Directive shall not apply to products put into circulation before the date on which the provisions referred to in Article 19 enter into force.

Article 18

1.   For the purposes of this Directive, the ECU shall be that defined by Regulation (EEC) No 3180/78,[4] as amended by Regulation (EEC) No 2626/84.[5] The equivalent in national currency shall initially be calculated at the rate obtaining on the date of adoption of this Directive.

2.   Every five years the Council, acting on a proposal from the Commission, shall examine and, if need be, revise the amounts in this Directive, in the light of economic and monetary trends in the Community.

Article 19

1.   Member States shall bring into force, not later than three years from the date of notification of this Directive, the laws, regulations and administrative provisions necessary to comply with this Directive. They shall forthwith inform the Commission thereof.[6]

2.   The procedure set out in Article 15(2) shall apply from the date of notification of this Directive.

Article 20

Member States shall communicate to the Commission the texts of the main provisions of national law which they subsequently adopt in the field governed by this Directive.

Article 21

Every five years the Commission shall present a report to the Council on the application of this Directive and, if necessary, shall submit appropriate proposals to it.

Article 22

This Directive is addressed to the Member States.

Done at Brussels, 25 July 1985.

For the Council

The President

J. POOS

Council Directive of 20 December 1985 to protect the consumer in respect of contracts negotiated away from business premises (85/577/EEC)

[OJ 1985, L372/31]

THE COUNCIL OF THE EUROPEAN COMMUNITIES,

Having regard to the Treaty establishing the European Economic Community, and in particular Article 100 thereof,

Having regard to the proposal from the Commission,[1]

Having regard to the opinion of the European Parliament,[2]

Having regard to the opinion of the Economic and Social Committee,[3]

---

[4] OJ No. L379, 30.12.1978, p. 1.
[5] OJ No. L247, 16.9.1984, p. 1.
[6] This Directive was notified to the Member States on 30 July 1985.

[1] OJ No. C22, 29.1.1977, p. 6; OJ No. C127, 1.6.1978, p. 6.
[2] OJ No. C241, 10.10.1977, p. 26
[3] OJ No. C180, 18.7.1977, p. 39.

Whereas it is a common form of commercial practice in the Member States for the conclusion of a contract or a unilateral engagement between a trader and consumer to be made away from the business premises of the trader, and whereas such contracts and engagements are the subject of legislation which differs from one Member State to another;

Whereas any disparity between such legislation may directly affect the functioning of the common market; whereas it is therefore necessary to approximate laws in this field;

Whereas the preliminary programme of the European Economic Community for a consumer protection and information policy[4] provides *inter alia*, under paragraphs 24 and 25, that appropriate measures be taken to protect consumers against unfair commercial practices in respect of doorstep selling; whereas the second programme of the European Economic Community for a consumer protection and information policy[5] confirmed that the action and priorities defined in the preliminary programme would be pursued;

Whereas the special feature of contracts concluded away from the business premises of the trader is that as a rule it is the trader who initiates the contract negotiations, for which the consumer is unprepared or which he does not except; whereas the consumer is often unable to compare the quality and price of the offer with other offers;

Whereas this surprise element generally exists not only in contracts made at the doorstep but also in other forms of contract concluded by the trader away from his business premises;

Whereas the consumer should be given a right of cancellation over a period of at least seven days in order to enable him to assess the obligations arising under the contract;

Whereas appropriate measures should be taken to ensure that the consumer is informed in writing of this period for reflection;

Whereas the freedom of Member States to maintain or introduce a total or partial prohibition on the conclusion of contracts away from business premises, inasmuch as they consider this to be in the interest of consumers, must not be affected;

HAS ADOPTED THIS DIRECTIVE:

Article 1

1.   This Directive shall apply to contracts under which a trader supplies goods or services to a consumer and which are concluded:
- during an excursion organised by the trader away from his business premises, or
- during a visit by a trader
  - (i)   to the consumer's home or to that of another consumer;
  - (ii) to the consumer's place of work; where the visit does not take place at the express request of the consumer.

2.   This Directive shall also apply to contracts for the supply of goods or services other than those concerning which the consumer requested the visit of the trader, provided that when he requested the visit the consumer did not know, or could not reasonably have known, that the supply of those other goods or services formed part of the trader's commercial or professional activities.

3.   This Directive shall also apply to contracts in respect of which an offer was made by the consumer under conditions similar to those described in paragraph 1 or paragraph 2 although the consumer was not bound by that offer before its acceptance by the trader.

4.   This Directive shall also apply to offers made contractually by the consumer under conditions similar to those described in paragraph 1 or paragraph 2 where the consumer is bound by his offer.

Article 2

For the purposes of this Directive:

[4] OJ No. C92, 25.4.1975, p. 2.
[5] OJ No. C133, 3.6.1981, p. 1.

'consumer' means a natural person who, in transactions covered by this Directive, is acting for purposes which can be regarded as outside his trade or profession;

'trader' means a natural or legal person who, for the transaction in question, acts in his commercial or professional capacity, and anyone acting in the name or on behalf of a trader.

Article 3

1.   The Member States may decide that this Directive shall apply only to contracts for which the payment to be made by the consumer exceeds a specified amount. This amount may not exceed 60 ECU. The Council, acting on a proposal from the Commission, shall examine and, if necessary, revise this amount for the first time no later than four years after notification of the Directive and thereafter every two years, taking into account economic and monetary developments in the Community.

2.   This Directive shall not apply to:

(a) contracts for the construction, sale and rental of immovable property or contracts concerning other rights relating to immovable property. Contracts for the supply of goods and for their incorporation in immovable property or contracts for repairing immovable property shall fall within the scope of this Directive;

(b) contracts for the supply of foodstuffs or beverages or other goods intended for current consumption in the household and supplied by regular roundsmen;

(c) contracts for the supply of goods or services, provided that all three of the following conditions are met:

(i)   the contract is concluded on the basis of a trader's catalogue which the consumer has a proper opportunity of reading in the absence of the trader's representative,

(ii) there is intended to be continuity of contact between the trader's representative and the consumer in relation to that or any subsequent transaction,

(iii) both the catalogue and the contract clearly inform the consumer of his right to return goods to the supplier within a period of not less than seven days of receipt or otherwise to cancel the contract within that period without obligation of any kind other than to take reasonable care of the goods;

(d) insurance contracts;

(e) contracts for securities.

3.   By way of derogation from Article 1(2), Member States may refrain from applying this Directive to contracts for the supply of goods or services having a direct connection with the goods or services concerning which the consumer requested the visit of the trader.

Article 4

In the case of transactions within the scope of Article 1, traders shall be required to give consumers written notice of their right of cancellation within the period laid down in Article 5, together with the name and address of a person against whom that right may be exercised. Such notice shall be dated and shall state particulars enabling the contract to be identified. It shall be given to the consumer:

(a) in the case of Article 1(1), at the time of conclusion of the contract;

(b) in the case of Article 1(2), not later than the time of conclusion of the contract;

(c) in the case of Article 1(3) and 1(4), when the offer is made by the consumer.

Member States shall ensure that their national legislation lays down appropriate consumer protection measures in cases where the information referred to in this Article is not supplied.

Article 5

1.   The consumer shall have the right to renounce the effects of his undertaking by sending notice within a period of not less than seven days from receipt by the consumer

of the notice referred to in Article 4, in accordance with the procedure laid down by national law. It shall be sufficient if the notice is dispatched before the end of such period.

2.   The giving of the notice shall have the effect of releasing the consumer from any obligations under the cancelled contract.

Article 6
The consumer may not waive the rights conferred on him by this Directive.

Article 7
If the consumer exercises his right of renunciation, the legal effects of such renunciation shall be governed by national laws, particularly regarding the reimbursement of payments for goods or services provided and the return of goods received.

Article 8
This Directive shall not prevent Member States from adopting or maintaining more favourable provisions to protect consumers in the field which it covers.

Article 9
1.   Member States shall take the measures necessary to comply with this Directive within 24 months of its notification.[6] They shall forthwith inform the Commission thereof.

2.   Member States shall ensure that the texts of the main provisions of national law which they adopt in the field covered by this Directive are communicated to the Commission.

Article 10
This Directive is addressed to the Member States.

Done at Brussels, 20 December 1985.
For the Council
The President
R. KRIEPS

Council Directive of 13 June 1990 on package travel, package holidays and package tours (90/314/EEC)
[OJ 1990, L158/59]

THE COUNCIL OF THE EUROPEAN COMMUNITIES,

Having regard to the Treaty establishing the European Economic Community, and in particular Article 100a thereof,

Having regard to the proposal from the Commission,[1]

In cooperation with the European Parliament,[2]

Having regard to the opinion of the Economic and Social Committee,[3]

Whereas one of the main objectives of the Community is to complete the internal market, of which the tourist sector is an essential part;

Whereas the national laws of Member States concerning package travel, package holidays and package tours, hereinafter referred to as 'packages', show many disparities and national practices in this field are markedly different, which gives rise to obstacles to the freedom to provide services in respect of packages and distortions of competition amongst operators established in different Member States;

---

[6] This Directive was notified to the Member States on 23 December 1985.

[1] OJ No. C96, 12.4.1988, p. 5.
[2] OJ No. C69, 20.3.1989, p. 102 and OJ No. C149, 18.6.1990.
[3] OJ No. C102, 24.4.1989, p. 27.

Whereas the establishment of common rules on packages will contribute to the elimination of these obstacles and thereby to the achievement of a common market in services, thus enabling operators established in one Member State to offer their services in other Member States and Community consumers to benefit from comparable conditions when buying a package in any Member State;

Whereas paragraph 36(b) of the Annex to the Council resolution of 19 May 1981 on a second programme of the European Economic Community for a consumer protection and information policy[4] invites the Commission to study, *inter alia*, tourism and, if appropriate, to put forward suitable proposals, with due regard for their significance for consumer protection and the effects of differences in Member States' legislation on the proper functioning of the common market;

Whereas in the resolution on a Community policy on tourism on 10 April 1984[5] the Council welcomed the Commission's initiative in drawing attention to the importance of tourism and took note of the Commission's initial guidelines for a Community policy on tourism;

Whereas the Commission communication to the Council entitled 'A New Impetus for Consumer Protection Policy', which was approved by resolution of the Council on 6 May 1986,[6] lists in paragraph 37, among the measures proposed by the Commission, the harmonization of legislation on packages;

Whereas tourism plays an increasingly important role in the economies of the Member States; whereas the package system is a fundamental part of tourism; whereas the package travel industry in Member States would be stimulated to greater growth and productivity if at least a minimum of common rules were adopted in order to give it a Community dimension; whereas this would not only produce benefits for Community citizens buying packages organised on the basis of those rules, but would attract tourists from outside the Community seeking the advantages of guaranteed standards in packages;

Whereas disparities in the rules protecting consumers in different Member States are a disincentive to consumers in one Member State from buying packages in another Member State;

Whereas this disincentive is particularly effective in deterring consumers from buying packages outside their own Member State, and more effective than it would be in relation to the acquisition of other services, having regard to the special nature of the services supplied in a package which generally involve the expenditure of substantial amounts of money in advance and the supply of the services in a State other than that in which the consumer is resident;

Whereas the consumer should have the benefit of the protection introduced by this Directive irrespective of whether he is a direct contracting party, a transferee or a member of a group on whose behalf another person has concluded a contract in respect of a package;

Whereas the organiser of the package and/or the retailer of it should be under obligation to ensure that in descriptive matter relating to packages which they respectively organise and sell, the information which is given is not misleading and brochures made available to consumers contain information which is comprehensible and accurate;

Whereas the consumer needs to have a record of the terms of contract applicable to the package; whereas this can conveniently be achieved by requiring that all the terms of the contract be stated in writing of such other documentary form as shall be comprehensible and accessible to him, and that he be given a copy thereof;

Whereas the consumer should be at liberty in certain circumstances to transfer to a willing third person a booking made by him for a package;

Whereas the price established under the contract should not in principle be subject to revision except where the possibility of upward or downward revision is expressly provided

---

[4] OJ No. C165, 23.6.1981, p. 24.
[5] OJ No. C115, 30.4.1984, p. 1.
[6] OJ No. C118, 7.3.1986, p. 28.

for in the contract; whereas that possibility should nonetheless be subject to certain conditions;

Whereas the consumer should in certain circumstances be free to withdraw before departure from a package travel contract;

Whereas there should be a clear definition of the rights available to the consumer in circumstances where the organiser of the package cancels it before the agreed date of departure;

Whereas if, after the consumer has departed, there occurs a significant failure of performance of the services for which he has contracted or the organiser perceives that he will be unable to procure a significant part of the services to be provided; the organiser should have certain obligations towards the consumer;

Whereas the organiser and/or retailer party to the contract should be liable to the consumer for the proper performance of the obligations arising from the contract; whereas, moreover, the organiser and/or retailer should be liable for the damage resulting for the consumer from failure to perform or improper performance of the contract unless the defects in the performance of the contract are attributable neither to any fault of theirs nor to that of another supplier of services;

Whereas in cases where the organiser and/or retailer is liable for failure to perform or improper performance of the services involved in the package, such liability should be limited in accordance with the international conventions governing such services, in particular the Warsaw Convention of 1929 in International Carriage by Air, the Berne Convention of 1961 on Carriage by Rail, the Athens Convention of 1974 on Carriage by Sea and the Paris Convention of 1962 on the Liability of Hotel-keepers; whereas, moreover, with regard to damage other than personal injury, it should be possible for liability also to be limited under the package contract provided, however, that such limits are not unreasonable;

Whereas certain arrangements should be made for the information of consumers and the handling of complaints;

Whereas both the consumer and the package travel industry would benefit if organisers and/or retailers were placed under an obligation to provide sufficient evidence of security in the event of insolvency;

Whereas Member States should be at liberty to adopt, or retain, more stringent provisions relating to package travel for the purpose of protecting the consumer,

HAS ADOPTED THIS DIRECTIVE:

Article 1

The purpose of this Directive is to approximate the laws, regulations and administrative provisions of the Member States relating to packages sold or offered for sale in the territory of the Community.

Article 2

For the purposes of this Directive:

1.   'package' means the pre-arranged combination of not fewer than two of the following when sold or offered for sale at an inclusive price and when the service covers a period of more than twenty-four hours or includes overnight accommodation:

   (a) transport;
   (b) accommodation;
   (c) other tourist services not ancillary to transport or accommodation and accounting for a significant proportion of the package. The separate billing of various components of the same package shall not absolve the organiser or retailer from the obligations under this Directive;

2.   'organiser' means the person who, other than occasionally, organises packages and sells or offers them for sale, whether directly or through a retailer;

3.   'retailer' means the person who sells or offers for sale the package put together by the organiser;

4.   'consumer' means the person who takes or agrees to take the package ('the principal contractor'), or any person on whose behalf the principal contractor agrees to purchase the package ('the other beneficiaries') or any person to whom the principal contractor or any of the other beneficiaries transfers the package ('the transferee');

5.   'contract' means the agreement linking the consumer to the organiser and/or the retailer.

Article 3

1.   Any descriptive matter concerning a package and supplied by the organiser or the retailer to the consumer, the price of the package and any other conditions applying to the contract must not contain any misleading information.

2.   When a brochure is made available to the consumer, it shall indicate in a legible, comprehensible and accurate manner both the price and adequate information concerning:

   (a) the destination and the means, characteristics and categories of transport used;

   (b) the type of accommodation, its location, category or degree of comfort and its main features, its approval and tourist classification under the rules of the host Member State concerned;

   (c) the meal plan;

   (d) the itinerary;

   (e) general information on passport and visa requirements for nationals of the Member State or States concerned and health formalities required for the journey and the stay;

   (f) either the monetary amount or the percentage of the price which is to be paid on account, and the timetable for payment of the balance;

   (g) whether a minimum number of persons is required for the package to take place and, if so, the deadline for informing the consumer in the event of cancellation. The particulars contained in the brochure are binding on the organiser or retailer, unless:

     — changes in such particulars have been clearly communicated to the consumer before conclusion of the contract, in which case the brochure shall expressly state so,

     — changes are made later following an agreement between the parties to the contract.

Article 4

1. (a) The organiser and/or the retailer shall provide the consumer, in writing or any other appropriate form, before the contract is concluded, with general information on passport and visa requirements applicable to nationals of the Member State or States concerned and in particular on the periods for obtaining them, as well as with information on the health formalities required for the journey and the stay;

   (b) The organiser and/or retailer shall also provide the consumer, in writing or any other appropriate form, with the following information in good time before the start of the journey:

     (i) the times and places of intermediate stops and transport connections as well as details of the place to be occupied by the traveller, e.g. cabin or berth on ship, sleeper compartment on train;

     (ii) the name, address and telephone number of the organiser's and/or retailer's local representative or, failing that, of local agencies on whose assistance a consumer in difficulty could call. Where no such representatives or agencies exist, the consumer must in any case be provided with an emergency telephone number or any other information that will enable him to contract the organiser and/or the retailer;

(iii) in the case of journeys or stays abroad by minors, information enabling direct contact to be established with the child or the person responsible at the child's place of stay;

(iv) information on the optional conclusion of an insurance policy to cover the cost of cancellation by the consumer or the cost of assistance, including repatriation, in the event of accident or illness.

2.   Member States shall ensure that in relation to the contract the following principles apply:

(a) depending on the particular package, the contract shall contain at least the elements listed in the Annex;

(b) all the terms of the contract are set out in writing or such other form as is comprehensible and accessible to the consumer and must be communicated to him before the conclusion of the contract; the consumer is given a copy of these terms;

(c) the provision under (b) shall not preclude the belated conclusion of last-minute reservations or contracts.

3.   Where the consumer is prevented from proceeding with the package, he may transfer his booking, having first given the organiser or the retailer reasonable notice of his intention before departure, to a person who satisfies all the conditions applicable to the package. The transferor of the package and the transferee shall be jointly and severally liable to the organiser or retailer party to the contract for payment of the balance due and for any additional costs arising from such transfer.

4. (a)   The prices laid down in the contract shall not be subject to revision unless the contract expressly provides for the possibility of upward or downward revision and states precisely how the revised price is to be calculated, and solely to allow for variations in:

— transportation costs, including the cost of fuel,
— dues, taxes or fees chargeable for certain services, such as landing taxes or embarkation or disembarkation fees at ports and airports,
— the exchange rates applied to the particular package.

(b)   During the twenty days prior to the departure date stipulated, the price stated in the contract shall not be increased.

5.   If the organiser finds that before the departure he is constrained to alter significantly any of the essential terms, such as the price, he shall notify the consumer as quickly as possible in order to enable him to take appropriate decisions and in particular:

— either to withdraw from the contract without penalty,
— or to accept a rider to the contract specifying the alterations made and their impact on the price.

The consumer shall inform the organiser or the retailer of his decision as soon as possible.

6.   If the consumer withdraws from the contract pursuant to paragraph 5, or if, for whatever cause, other than the fault of the consumer, the organiser cancels the package before the agreed date of departure, the consumer shall be entitled:

(a) either to take a substitute package of equivalent or higher quality where the organiser and/or retailer is able to offer him such a substitute. If the replacement package offered is of lower quality, the organiser shall refund the difference in price to the consumer;

(b) or to be repaid as soon as possible all sums paid by him under the contract. In such a case, he shall be entitled, if appropriate, to be compensated by either the organiser or the retailer, whichever the relevant Member State's law requires, for non-performance of the contract, except where:

    (i) cancellation is on the grounds that the number of persons enrolled for the package is less than the minimum number required and the consumer is informed of the cancellation, in writing, within the period indicated in the package description; or

    (ii) cancellation, excluding overbooking, is for reasons of *force majeure*, i.e. unusual and unforeseeable circumstances beyond the control of the party by whom it is pleaded, the consequences of which could not have been avoided even if all due care had been exercised.

    7. Where, after departure, a significant proportion of the services contracted for is not provided or the organiser perceives that he will be unable to procure a significant proportion of the services to be provided, the organiser shall make suitable alternative arrangements, at no extra cost to the consumer, for the continuation of the package, and where appropriate compensate the consumer for the difference between the services offered and those supplied. If it is impossible to make such arrangements or these are not accepted by the consumer for good reasons, the organiser shall, where appropriate, provide the consumer, at no extra cost, with equivalent transport back to the place of departure, or to another return-point to which the consumer has agreed and shall, where appropriate, compensate the consumer.

Article 5

    1. Member States shall take the necessary steps to ensure that the organiser and/or retailer party to the contract is liable to the consumer for the proper performance of the obligations arising from the contract, irrespective of whether such obligations are to be performed by that organiser and/or retailer or by other suppliers of services without prejudice to the right of the organiser and/or retailer to pursue those other suppliers of services.

    2. With regard to the damage resulting for the consumer from the failure to perform or the improper performance of the contract, Member States shall take the necessary steps to ensure that the organiser and/or retailer is/are liable unless such failure to perform or improper performance is attributable neither to any fault of theirs nor to that of another supplier of services, because:

— the failures which occur in the performance of the contract are attributable to the consumer,

— such failures are attributable to a third party unconnected with the provision of the services contracted for, and are unforeseeable or unavoidable,

— such failures are due to a case of *force majeure* such as that defined in Article 4 (6), second sub-paragraph (ii), or to an event which the organiser and/or retailer or the supplier of services, even with all due care, could not foresee or forestall.

In the cases referred to in the second and third indents, the organiser and/or retailer party to the contract shall be required to give prompt assistance to a consumer in difficulty. In the matter of damages arising from the non-performance or improper performance of the services involved in the package, the Member States may allow compensation to be limited in accordance with the international conventions governing such services. In the matter of damage other than personal injury resulting from the non-performance or improper performance of the services involved in the package, the Member States may allow compensation to be limited under the contract. Such limitation shall not be unreasonable.

    3. Without prejudice to the fourth sub-paragraph of paragraph 2, there may be no exclusion by means of a contractual clause from the provisions of paragraphs 1 and 2.

    4. The consumer must communicate any failure in the performance of a contract which he perceives on the spot to the supplier of the services concerned and to the organiser and/or retailer in writing or any other appropriate form at the earliest opportunity. This obligation must be stated clearly and explicitly in the contract.

Article 6

In cases of complaint, the organiser and/or retailer or his local representative, if there is one, must make prompt efforts to find appropriate solutions.

Article 7

The organiser and/or retailer party to the contract shall provide sufficient evidence of security for the refund of money paid over and for the repatriation of the consumer in the event of insolvency.

Article 8

Member States may adopt or return more stringent provisions in the field covered by this Directive to protect the consumer.

Article 9

1.   Member States shall bring into force the measures necessary to comply with this Directive before 31 December 1992. They shall forthwith inform the Commission thereof.

2.   Member States shall communicate to the Commission the texts of the main provisions of national law which they adopt in the field governed by this Directive. The Commission shall inform the other Member States thereof.

Article 10

This Directive is addressed to the Member States.

Done at Luxembourg, 13 June 1990.

For the Council

The President

D. J. O'MALLEY

ANNEX

Elements to be included in the contract if relevant to the particular package;

(a)   the travel destination(s) and, where periods of stay are involved, the relevant periods, with dates;

(b)   the means, characteristics and categories of transport to be used, the dates, times and points of departure and return;

(c)   where the package includes accommodation, its location, its tourist category or degree of comfort, its main features, its compliance with the rules of the host Member State concerned and the meal plan;

(d)   whether a minimum number of persons is required for the package to take place and, if so, the deadline for informing the consumer in the event of cancellation;

(e)   the itinerary;

(f)   visits, excursions or other services which are included in the total price agreed for the package;

(g)   the name and address of the organiser, the retailer and, where appropriate, the insurer;

(h)   the price of the package, an indication of the possibility of price revisions under Article 4(4) and an indication of any dues, taxes or fees chargeable for certain services (landing, embarkation or disembarkation fees at ports and airports, tourist taxes) where such costs are not included in the package;

(i)   the payment schedule and method of payment;

(j)   special requirements which the consumer has communicated to the organiser or retailer when making the booking, and which both have accepted;

(k)   periods within which the consumer must make any complaint concerning failure to perform or improper performance of the contract.

Council Directive 93/13/EEC of 5 April 1993 on unfair terms in consumer contracts

[OJ 1993, L95/29]

THE COUNCIL OF THE EUROPEAN COMMUNITIES,

Having regard to the Treaty establishing the European Economic Community, and in particular Article 100 A thereof,

Having regard to the proposal from the Commission,[1]

In cooperation with the European Parliament,[2]

Having regard to the opinion of the Economic and Social Committee,[3]

Whereas it is necessary to adopt measures with the aim of progressively establishing the internal market before 31 December 1992; whereas the internal market comprises an area without internal frontiers in which goods, persons, services and capital move freely;

Whereas the laws of Member States relating to the terms of contract between the seller of goods or supplier of services, on the one hand, and the consumer of them, on the other hand, show many disparities, with the result that the national markets for the sale of goods and services to consumers differ from each other and that distortions of competition may arise amongst the sellers and suppliers, notably when they sell and supply in other Member States;

Whereas, in particular, the laws of Member States relating to unfair terms in consumer contracts show marked divergences;

Whereas it is the responsibility of the Member States to ensure that contracts concluded with consumers do not contain unfair terms;

Whereas, generally speaking, consumers do not know the rules of law which, in Member States other than their own, govern contracts for the sale of goods or services; whereas this lack of awareness may deter them from direct transactions for the purchase of goods or services in another Member State;

Whereas, in order to facilitate the establishment of the internal market and to safeguard the citizen in his role as consumer when acquiring goods and services under contracts which are governed by the laws of Member States other than his own, it is essential to remove unfair terms from those contracts;

Whereas sellers of goods and suppliers of services will thereby be helped in their task of selling goods and supplying services, both at home and throughout the internal market; whereas competition will thus be stimulated, so contributing to increased choice for Community citizens as consumers;

Whereas the two Community programmes for a consumer protection and information policy[4] underlined the importance of safeguarding consumers in the matter of unfair terms of contract; whereas this protection ought to be provided by laws and regulations which are either harmonised at Community level or adopted directly at that level;

Whereas in accordance with the principle laid down under the heading 'Protection of the economic interests of the consumers', as stated in those programmes: 'acquirers of goods and services should be protected against the abuse of power by the seller or supplier, in particular against one-sided standard contracts and the unfair exclusion of essential rights in contracts';

Whereas more effective protection of the consumer can be achieved by adopting uniform rules of law in the matter of unfair terms; whereas those rules should apply to all contracts

---

[1] OJ No. C73, 24.3.1992, p. 7.

[2] OJ No. C326, 16.12.1991, p. 108 and OJ No. C21, 25.1.1993.

[3] OJ No. C159, 17.6.1991, p. 34.

[4] OJ No. C92, 25.4.1975, p. 1 and OJ No. C133, 3.6.1981, p. 1.

concluded between sellers or suppliers and consumers; whereas as a result *inter alia* contracts relating to employment, contracts relating to succession rights, contracts relating to rights under family law and contracts relating to the incorporation and organization of companies or partnership agreements must be excluded from this Directive;

Whereas the consumer must receive equal protection under contracts concluded by word of mouth and written contracts regardless, in the latter case, of whether the terms of the contract are contained in one or more documents;

Whereas, however, as they now stand, national laws allow only partial harmonization to be envisaged; whereas, in particular, only contractual terms which have not been individually negotiated are covered by this Directive; whereas Member States should have the option, with due regard for the Treaty, to afford consumers a higher level of protection through national provisions that are more stringent than those of this Directive;

Whereas the statutory or regulatory provisions of the Member States which directly or indirectly determine the terms of consumer contracts are presumed not to contain unfair terms; whereas, therefore, it does not appear to be necessary to subject the terms which reflect mandatory statutory or regulatory provisions and the principles or provisions of international conventions to which the Member States or the Community are party; whereas in that respect the wording 'mandatory statutory or regulatory provisions' in Article 1(2) also covers rules which, according to the law, shall apply between the contracting parties provided that no other arrangements have been established;

Whereas Member States must however ensure that unfair terms are not included, particularly because this Directive also applies to trades, business or professions of a public nature;

Whereas it is necessary to fix in a general way the criteria for assessing the unfair character of contract terms;

Whereas the assessment, according to the general criteria chosen, of the unfair character of terms, in particular in sale or supply activities of a public nature providing collective services which take account of solidarity among users, must be supplemented by a means of making an overall evaluation of the different interests involved; whereas this constitutes the requirement of good faith; whereas, in making an assessment of good faith, particular regard shall be had to the strength of the bargaining positions of the parties, whether the consumer had an inducement to agree to the term and whether the goods or services were sold or supplied to the special order of the consumer; whereas the requirement of good faith may be satisfied by the seller or supplier where he deals fairly and equitably with the other party whose legitimate interests he has to take into account;

Whereas, for the purposes of this Directive, the annexed list of terms can be of indicative value only and, because of the cause of the minimal character of the Directive, the scope of these terms may be the subject of amplification or more restrictive editing by the Member States in their national laws;

Whereas the nature of goods or services should have an influence on assessing the unfairness of contractual terms;

Whereas, for the purposes of this Directive, assessment of unfair character shall not be made of terms which describe the main subject matter of the contract nor the quality/price ratio of the goods or services supplied; whereas the main subject matter of the contract and the price/quality ratio may nevertheless be taken into account in assessing the fairness of other terms; whereas it follows, *inter alia*, that in insurance contracts, the terms which clearly define or circumscribe the insured risk and the insurer's liability shall not be subject to such assessment since these restrictions are taken into account in calculating the premium paid by the consumer;

Whereas contracts should be drafted in plain, intelligible language, the consumer should actually be given an opportunity to examine all the terms and, if in doubt, the interpretation most favourable to the consumer should prevail;

Whereas Member States should ensure that unfair terms are not used in contracts concluded with consumers by a seller or supplier and that if, nevertheless, such terms are so used, they will not bind the consumer, and the contract will continue to bind the parties upon those terms if it is capable of continuing in existence without the unfair provisions;

Whereas there is a risk that, in certain cases, the consumer may be deprived of protection under this Directive by designating the law of a non-Member country as the law applicable to the contract; whereas provisions should therefore be included in this Directive designed to avert this risk;

Whereas persons or organisations, if regarded under the law of a Member State as having a legitimate interest in the matter, must have facilities for initiating proceedings concerning terms of contract drawn up for general use in contracts concluded with consumers, and in particular unfair terms, either before a court or before an administrative authority competent to decide upon complaints or to initiate appropriate legal proceedings; whereas this possibility does not, however, entail prior verification of the general conditions obtaining in individual economic sectors;

Whereas the courts or administrative authorities of the Member States must have at their disposal adequate and effective means of preventing the continued application of unfair terms in consumer contracts,

HAS ADOPTED THIS DIRECTIVE:

Article 1

1.   The purpose of this Directive is to approximate the laws, regulations and administrative provisions of the Member States relating to unfair terms in contracts concluded between a seller or supplier and a consumer.

2.   The contractual terms which reflect mandatory statutory or regulatory provisions and the provisions or principles of international conventions to which the Member States or the Community are party, particularly in the transport area, shall not be subject to the provisions of this Directive.

Article 2

For the purposes of this Directive:
- (a) 'unfair terms' means the contractual terms defined in Article 3;
- (b) 'consumer' means any natural person who, in contracts covered by this Directive, is acting for purposes which are outside his trade, business or profession;
- (c) 'seller or supplier' means any natural or legal person who, in contracts covered by this Directive, is acting for purposes relating to his trade, business or profession, whether publicly owned or privately owned.

Article 3

1.   A contractual term which has not been individually negotiated shall be regarded as unfair if, contrary to the requirement of good faith, it causes a significant imbalance in the parties' rights and obligations arising under the contract, to the detriment of the consumer.

2.   A term shall always be regarded as not individually negotiated where it has been drafted in advance and the consumer has therefore not been able to influence the substance of the term, particularly in the context of a pre-formulated standard contract. The fact that certain aspects of a term or one specific term have been individually negotiated shall not exclude the application of this Article to the rest of a contract if an overall assessment of the contract indicates that it is nevertheless a pre-formulated standard contract. Where any seller or supplier claims that a standard term has been individually negotiated, the burden of proof in this respect shall be incumbent on him.

3.   The Annex shall contain an indicative and non-exhaustive list of the terms which may be regarded as unfair.

Article 4

1. Without prejudice to Article 7, the unfairness of a contractual term shall be assessed, taking into account the nature of the goods or services for which the contract was concluded and by referring, at the time of conclusion of the contract, to all the circumstances attending the conclusion of the contract and to all the other terms of the contract or of another contract on which it is dependent.

2. Assessment of the unfair nature of the terms shall relate neither to the definition of the main subject matter of the contract nor to the adequacy of the price and remuneration, on the one hand, as against the services or goods supplies in exchange, on the other, in so far as these terms are in plain intelligible language.

Article 5

In the case of contracts where all or certain terms offered to the consumer are in writing, these terms must always be drafted in plain, intelligible language. Where there is doubt about the meaning of a term, the interpretation most favourable to the consumer shall prevail. This rule on interpretation shall not apply in the context of the procedures laid down in Article 7(2).

Article 6

1. Member States shall lay down that unfair terms used in a contract concluded with a consumer by a seller or supplier shall, as provided for under their national law, not be binding on the consumer and that the contract shall continue to bind the parties upon those terms if it is capable of continuing in existence without the unfair terms.

2. Member States shall take the necessary measures to ensure that the consumer does not lose the protection granted by this Directive by virtue of the choice of the law of a non-Member country as the law applicable to the contract if the latter has a close connection with the territory of the Member States.

Article 7

1. Member States shall ensure that, in the interests of consumers and of competitors, adequate and effective means exist to prevent the continued use of unfair terms in contracts concluded with consumers by sellers or suppliers.

2. The means referred to in paragraph 1 shall include provisions whereby persons or organisations, having a legitimate interest under national law in protecting consumers, may take action according to the national law concerned before the courts or before competent administrative bodies for a decision as to whether contractual terms drawn up for general use are unfair, so that they can apply appropriate and effective means to prevent the continued use of such terms.

3. With due regard for national laws, the legal remedies referred to in paragraph 2 may be directed separately or jointly against a number of sellers or suppliers from the same economic sector or their associations which use or recommend the use of the same general contractual terms or similar terms.

Article 8

Member States may adopt or retain the most stringent provisions compatible with the Treaty in the area covered by this Directive, to ensure a maximum degree of protection for the consumer.

Article 9

The Commission shall present a report to the European Parliament and to the Council concerning the application of this Directive five years at the latest after the date in Article 10(1).

Article 10

1. Member States shall bring into force the laws, regulations and administrative

provisions necessary to comply with this Directive no later than 31 December 1994. They shall forthwith inform the Commission thereof. These provisions shall be applicable to all contracts concluded after 31 December 1994.

2.   When Member States adopt these measures, they shall contain a reference to this Directive or shall be accompanied by such reference on the occasion of their official publication. The methods of making such a reference shall be laid down by the Member States.

3.   Member States shall communicate the main provisions of national law which they adopt in the field covered by this Directive to the Commission.

Article 11
This Directive is addressed to the Member States.

Done at Luxembourg, 5 April 1993.
For the Council
The President
N. HELVEG PETERSEN

ANNEX   TERMS REFERRED TO IN ARTICLE 3(3)

1.   Terms which have the object or effect of:
   (a) excluding or limiting the legal liability of a seller or supplier in the event of the death of a consumer or personal injury to the latter resulting from an act or omission of that seller or supplier;
   (b) inappropriately excluding or limiting the legal rights of the consumer vis-à-vis the seller or supplier or another party in the event of total or partial non-performance or inadequate performance by the seller or supplier of any of the contractual obligations, including the option of offsetting a debt owed to the seller or supplier against any claim which the consumer may have against him;
   (c) making an agreement binding on the consumer whereas provision of services by the seller or supplier is subject to a condition whose realisation depends on his own will alone;
   (d) permitting the seller or supplier to retain sums paid by the consumer where the latter decides not to conclude or perform the contract, without providing for the consumer to receive compensation of an equivalent amount from the seller or supplier where the latter is the party cancelling the contract;
   (e) requiring any consumer who fails to fulfil his obligation to pay a disproportionately high sum in compensation;
   (f) authorising the seller or supplier to dissolve the contract on a discretionary basis where the same facility is not granted to the consumer, or permitting the seller or supplier to retain the sums paid for services not yet supplied by him where it is the seller or supplier himself who dissolves the contract;
   (g) enabling the seller or supplier to terminate a contract of indeterminate duration without reasonable notice except where there are serious grounds for doing so;
   (h) automatically extending a contract of fixed duration where the consumer does not indicate otherwise, when the deadline fixed for the consumer to express this desire not to extend the contract is unreasonably early;
   (i) irrevocably binding the consumer to terms with which he had no real opportunity of becoming acquainted before the conclusion of the contract;
   (j) enabling the seller or supplier to alter the terms of the contract unilaterally without a valid reason which is specified in the contract;
   (k) enabling the seller or supplier to alter unilaterally without a valid reason any characteristics of the product or service to be provided;

(l) providing for the price of goods to be determined at the time of delivery or allowing a seller of goods or supplier of services to increase their price without in both cases giving the consumer the corresponding right to cancel the contract if the final price is too high in relation to the price agreed when the contract was concluded;

(m) giving the seller or supplier the right to determine whether the goods or services supplied are in conformity with the contract, or giving him the exclusive right to interpret any term of the contract;

(n) limiting the seller's or supplier's obligation to respect commitments undertaken by his agents or making his commitments subject to compliance with a particular formality;

(o) obliging the consumer to fulfil all his obligations where the seller or supplier does not perform his;

(p) giving the seller or supplier the possibility of transferring his rights and obligations under the contract, where this may serve to reduce the guarantees for the consumer, without the latter's agreement;

(q) excluding or hindering the consumer's right to take legal action or exercise any other legal remedy, particularly by requiring the consumer to take disputes exclusively to arbitration not covered by legal provisions, unduly restricting the evidence available to him or imposing on him a burden of proof which, according to the applicable law, should lie with another party to the contract.

2. Scope of subparagraphs (g), (j) and (l)

(a) Subparagraph (g) is without hindrance to terms by which a supplier of financial services reserves the right to terminate unilaterally a contract of indeterminate duration without notice where there is a valid reason, provided that the supplier is required to inform the other contracting party or parties thereof immediately.

(b) Subparagraph (j) is without hindrance to terms under which a supplier of financial services reserves the right to alter the rate of interest payable by the consumer or due to the latter, or the amount of other charges for financial services without notice where there is a valid reason, provided that the supplier is required to inform the other contracting party or parties thereof at the earliest opportunity and that the latter are free to dissolve the contract immediately. Subparagraph (j) is also without hindrance to terms under which a seller or supplier reserves the right to alter unilaterally the conditions of a contract of indeterminate duration, provided that he is required to inform the consumer with reasonable notice and that the consumer is free to dissolve the contract.

(c) Subparagraphs (g), (j) and (l) do not apply to:
  — transactions in transferable securities, financial instruments and other products or services where the price is linked to fluctuations in a stock exchange quotation or index or a financial market rate that the seller or supplier does not control;
  — contracts for the purchase or sale of foreign currency, traveller's cheques or international money orders denominated in foreign currency;

(d) Subparagraph (l) is without hindrance to price-indexation clauses, where lawful, provided that the method by which prices vary is explicitly described.

Directive 2001/95/EEC of the European Parliament and of the Council of 3 December 2001 on general product safety

[OJ 2002, No. L11/4]*

THE EUROPEAN PARLIAMENT AND THE COUNCIL OF THE EUROPEAN UNION,

Having regard to the Treaty establishing the European Economic Community, and in particular Articles 95 thereof,

Having regard to the proposal from the Commission,[1]

Having regard to the opinion of the Economic and Social Committee,[2]

Acting in accordance with the procedure referred to in Article 251 of the Treaty,[3] in the light of the joint text approved by the Conciliation Committee on 2 August 2001,

Whereas:

(1) Under Article 16 of Council Directive 92/59/EEC of 29 June 1992 on general product safety,[4] the Council was to decide, four years after the date set for the implementation of the said Directive, on the basis of a report of the Commission on the experience acquired, together with appropriate proposals, whether to adjust Directive 92/59/EEC. It is necessary to amend Directive 92/59/EEC in several respects, in order to complete, reinforce or clarify some of its provisions in the light of experience as well as new and relevant developments on consumer product safety, together with the changes made to the Treaty, especially in Articles 152 concerning public health and 153 concerning consumer protection, and in the light of the precautionary principle. Directive 92/59/EEC should therefore be recast in the interest of clarity. This recasting leaves the safety of services outside the scope of this Directive, since the Commission intends to identify the needs, possibilities and priorities for Community action on the safety of services and liability of service providers, with a view to presenting appropriate proposals.

(2) It is important to adopt measures with the aim of improving the functioning of the internal market, comprising an area without internal frontiers in which the free movement of goods, persons, services and capital is assured.

(3) In the absence of Community provisions, horizontal legislation of the Member States on product safety, imposing in particular a general obligation on economic operators to market only safe products, might differ in the level of protection afforded to consumers. Such disparities, and the absence of horizontal legislation in some Member States, would be liable to create barriers to trade and distortion of competition within the internal market.

(4) In order to ensure a high level of consumer protection, the Community must contribute to protecting the health and safety of consumers. Horizontal Community legislation introducing a general product safety requirement, and containing provisions on the general obligations of producers and distributors, on the enforcement of Community product safety requirements and on rapid exchange of information and action at Community level in certain cases, should contribute to that aim.

(5) It is very difficult to adopt Community legislation for every product which exists or which may be developed; there is a need for a broad-based, legislative framework of a horizontal

---

* **Editor's Note:** This Directive replaces Directive 92/59 with effect from 15 January 2004.

[1] OJ C 337 E, 28.11.2000, p. 109 and OJ C 154 E, 29.5.2000, p. 265.

[2] OJ C 367, 20.12.2000, p. 34.

[3] Opinion of the European Parliament of 15.11.2000 (OJ C 223, 8.8.2001, p. 154), Council Common Position of 12.2.2001 (OJ C 93, 23.3.2001, p. 24) and Decision of the European Parliament of 16.5.2001 (not yet published in the Official Journal). Decision of the European Parliament of 4.10.2001 and Council Decision of 27.9.2001.

[4] OJ L 228, 11.8.1992, p. 24.

nature to deal with such products, and also to cover lacunae, in particular pending revision of the existing specific legislation, and to complement provisions in existing or forthcoming specific legislation, in particular with a view to ensuring a high level of protection of safety and health of consumers, as required by Article 95 of the Treaty.

(6) It is therefore necessary to establish at Community level a general safety requirement for any product placed on the market, or otherwise supplied or made available to consumers, intended for consumers, or likely to be used by consumers under reasonably foreseeable conditions even if not intended for them. In all these cases the products under consideration can pose risks for the health and safety of consumers which must be prevented. Certain second-hand goods should nevertheless be excluded by their very nature.

(7) This Directive should apply to products irrespective of the selling techniques, including distance and electronic selling.

(8) The safety of products should be assessed taking into account all the relevant aspects, in particular the categories of consumers which can be particularly vulnerable to the risks posed by the products under consideration, in particular children and the elderly.

(9) This Directive does not cover services, but in order to secure the attainment of the protection objectives in question, its provisions should also apply to products that are supplied or made available to consumers in the context of service provision for use by them. The safety of the equipment used by service providers themselves to supply a service to consumers does not come within the scope of this Directive since it has to be dealt with in conjunction with the safety of the service provided. In particular, equipment on which consumers ride or travel which is operated by a service provider is excluded from the scope of this Directive.

(10) Products which are designed exclusively for professional use but have subsequently migrated to the consumer market should be subject to the requirements of this Directive because they can pose risks to consumer health and safety when used under reasonably foreseeable conditions.

(11) In the absence of more specific provisions, within the framework of Community legislation covering safety of the products concerned, all the provisions of this Directive should apply in order to ensure consumer health and safety.

(12) If specific Community legislation sets out safety requirements covering only certain risks or categories of risks, with regard to the products concerned the obligations of economic operators in respect of these risks are those determined by the provisions of the specific legislation, while the general safety requirement of this Directive should apply to the other risks.

(13) The provisions of this Directive relating to the other obligations of producers and distributors, the obligations and powers of the Member States, the exchanges of information and rapid intervention situations and dissemination of information and confidentiality apply in the case of products covered by specific rules of Community law, if those rules do not already contain such obligations.

(14) In order to facilitate the effective and consistent application of the general safety requirement of this Directive, it is important to establish European voluntary standards covering certain products and risks in such a way that a product which conforms to a national standard transposing a European standard is to be presumed to be in compliance with the said requirement.

(15) With regard to the aims of this Directive, European standards should be established by European standardisation bodies, under mandates set by the Commission assisted by appropriate Committees. In order to ensure that products in compliance with the standards fulfil the general safety requirement, the Commission assisted by a committee composed of representatives of the Member States, should fix the requirements that the standards must meet. These requirements should be included in the mandates to the standardisation bodies.

(16) In the absence of specific regulations and when the European standards established under mandates set by the Commission are not available or recourse is not made to such standards, the safety of products should be assessed taking into account in particular national

standards transposing any other relevant European or international standards, Commission recommendations or national standards, international standards, codes of good practice, the state of the art and the safety which consumers may reasonably expect. In this context, the Commission's recommendations may facilitate the consistent and effective application of this Directive pending the introduction of European standards or as regards the risks and/or products for which such standards are deemed not to be possible or appropriate.

(17) Appropriate independent certification recognised by the competent authorities may facilitate proof of compliance with the applicable product safety criteria.

(18) It is appropriate to supplement the duty to observe the general safety requirement by other obligations on economic operators because action by such operators is necessary to prevent risks to consumers under certain circumstances.

(19) The additional obligations on producers should include the duty to adopt measures commensurate with the characteristics of the products, enabling them to be informed of the risks that these products may present, to supply consumers with information enabling them to assess and prevent risks, to warn consumers of the risks posed by dangerous products already supplied to them, to withdraw those products from the market and, as a last resort, to recall them when necessary, which may involve, depending on the provisions applicable in the Member States, an appropriate form of compensation, for example, exchange or reimbursement.

(20) Distributors should help in ensuring compliance with the applicable safety requirements. The obligations placed on distributors apply in proportion to their respective responsibilities. In particular, it may prove impossible, in the context of charitable activities, to provide the competent authorities with information and documentation on possible risks and origin of the product in the case of isolated used objects provided by private individuals.

(21) Both producers and distributors should cooperate with the competent authorities in action aimed at preventing risks and inform them when they conclude that certain products supplied are dangerous. The conditions regarding the provision of such information should be set in this Directive to facilitate its effective application, while avoiding an excessive burden for economic operators and the authorities.

(22) In order to ensure the effective enforcement of the obligations incumbent on producers and distributors, the Member States should establish or designate authorities which are responsible for monitoring product safety and have powers to take appropriate measures, including the power to impose effective, proportionate and dissuasive penalties, and ensure appropriate coordination between the various designated authorities.

(23) It is necessary in particular for the appropriate measures to include the power for Member States to order or organise, immediately and efficiently, the withdrawal of dangerous products already placed on the market and as a last resort to order, coordinate or organise the recall from consumers of dangerous products already supplied to them. Those powers should be applied when producers and distributors fail to prevent risks to consumers in accordance with their obligations. Where necessary, the appropriate powers and procedures should be available to the authorities to decide and apply any necessary measures rapidly.

(24) The safety of consumers depends to a great extent on the active enforcement of Community product safety requirements. The Member States should, therefore, establish systematic approaches to ensure the effectiveness of market surveillance and other enforcement activities and should ensure their openness to the public and interested parties.

(25) Collaboration between the enforcement authorities of the Member States is necessary in ensuring the attainment of the protection objectives of this Directive. It is, therefore, appropriate to promote the operation of a European network of the enforcement authorities of the Member States to facilitate, in a coordinated manner with other Community procedures, in particular the Community Rapid Information System (RAPEX), improved collaboration at operational level on market surveillance and other enforcement activities, in particular risk assessment, testing of products, exchange of expertise and scientific knowledge, execution of joint surveillance projects and tracing, withdrawing or recalling dangerous products.

(26) It is necessary, for the purpose of ensuring a consistent, high level of consumer health and safety protection and preserving the unity of the internal market, that the Commission be informed of any measure restricting the placing on the market of a product or requiring its withdrawal or recall from the market. Such measures should be taken in compliance with the provisions of the Treaty, and in particular Articles 28, 29 and 30 thereof.

(27) Effective supervision of product safety requires the setting-up at national and Community levels of a system of rapid exchange of information in situations of serious risk requiring rapid intervention in respect of the safety of a product. It is also appropriate in this Directive to set out detailed procedures for the operation of the system and to give the Commission, assisted by an advisory committee, power to adapt them.

(28) This Directive provides for the establishment of non-binding guidelines aimed at indicating simple and clear criteria and practical rules which may change, in particular for the purpose of allowing efficient notification of measures restricting the placing on the market of products in the cases referred to in this Directive, whilst taking into account the range of situations dealt with by Member States and economic operators. The guidelines should in particular include criteria for the application of the definition of serious risks in order to facilitate consistent implementation of the relevant provisions in case of such risks.

(29) It is primarily for Member States, in compliance with the Treaty and in particular with Articles 28, 29 and 30 thereof, to take appropriate measures with regard to dangerous products located within their territory.

(30) However, if the Member States differ as regards the approach to dealing with the risk posed by certain products, such differences could entail unacceptable disparities in consumer protection and constitute a barrier to intra-Community trade.

(31) It may be necessary to deal with serious product-safety problems requiring rapid intervention which affect or could affect, in the immediate future, all or a significant part of the Community and which, in view of the nature of the safety problem posed by the product, cannot be dealt with effectively in a manner commensurate with the degree of urgency, under the procedures laid down in the specific rules of Community law applicable to the products or category of products in question.

(32) It is therefore necessary to provide for an adequate mechanism allowing, as a last resort, for the adoption of measures applicable throughout the Community, in the form of a decision addressed to the Member States, to cope with situations created by products presenting a serious risk. Such a decision should entail a ban on the export of the product in question, unless in the case in point exceptional circumstances allow a partial ban or even no ban to be decided upon, particularly when a system of prior consent is established. In addition, the banning of exports should be examined with a view to preventing risks to the health and safety of consumers. Since such a decision is not directly applicable to economic operators, Member States should take all necessary measures for its implementation. Measures adopted under such a procedure are interim measures, save when they apply to individually identified products or batches of products. In order to ensure the appropriate assessment of the need for, and the best preparation of such measures, they should be taken by the Commission, assisted by a committee, in the light of consultations with the Member States, and, if scientific questions are involved falling within the competence of a Community scientific committee, with the scientific committee competent for the risk concerned.

(33) The measures necessary for the implementation of this Directive should be adopted in accordance with Council Decision 1999/468/EC of 28 June 1999 laying down the procedures for the exercise of implementing powers conferred on the Commission.[5]

(34) In order to facilitate effective and consistent application of this Directive, the various aspects of its application may need to be discussed within a committee.

---

[5] OJ L 184, 17.7.1999, p. 23.

(35) Public access to the information available to the authorities on product safety should be ensured. However, professional secrecy, as referred to in Article 287 of the Treaty, must be protected in a way which is compatible with the need to ensure the effectiveness of market surveillance activities and of protection measures.

(36) This Directive should not affect victims' rights within the meaning of Council Directive 85/374/EEC of 25 July 1985 on the approximation of the laws, regulations and administrative provisions of the Member States concerning liability for defective products.[6]

(37) It is necessary for Member States to provide for appropriate means of redress before the competent courts in respect of measures taken by the competent authorities which restrict the placing on the market of a product or require its withdrawal or recall.

(38) In addition, the adoption of measures concerning imported products, like those concerning the banning of exports, with a view to preventing risks to the safety and health of consumers must comply with the Community's international obligations.

(39) The Commission should periodically examine the manner in which this Directive is applied and the results obtained, in particular in relation to the functioning of market surveillance systems, the rapid exchange of information and measures adopted at Community level, together with other issues relevant for consumer product safety in the Community, and submit regular reports to the European Parliament and the Council on the subject.

(40) This Directive should not affect the obligations of Member States concerning the deadline for transposition and application of Directive 92/59/EEC,

HAVE ADOPTED THIS DIRECTIVE:

CHAPTER I

OBJECTIVE—SCOPE—DEFINITIONS

Article 1

1. The purpose of this Directive is to ensure that products placed on the market are safe.

2. This Directive shall apply to all the products defined in Article 2(a). Each of its provisions shall apply in so far as there are no specific provisions with the same objective in rules of Community law governing the safety of the products concerned.

Where products are subject to specific safety requirements imposed by Community legislation, this Directive shall apply only to the aspects and risks or categories of risks not covered by those requirements. This means that:

   (a) Articles 2(b) and (c), 3 and 4 shall not apply to those products insofar as concerns the risks or categories of risks covered by the specific legislation;
   (b) Articles 5 to 18 shall apply except where there are specific provisions governing the aspects covered by the said Articles with the same objective.

Article 2

For the purposes of this Directive:

   (a) 'product' shall mean any product—including in the context of providing a service—which is intended for consumers or likely, under reasonably foreseeable conditions, to be used by consumers even if not intended for them, and is supplied or made available, whether for consideration or not, in the course of a commercial activity, and whether new, used or reconditioned.

   This definition shall not apply to second-hand products supplied as antiques or as products to be repaired or reconditioned prior to being used, provided that

---

[6] OJ L 210, 7.8.1985, p. 29. Directive as amended by Directive 1999/34/EC of the European Parliament and of the Council (OJ L 141, 4.6.1999, p. 20).

the supplier clearly informs the person to whom he supplies the product to that effect;

(b) "safe product" shall mean any product which, under normal or reasonably foreseeable conditions of use including duration and, where applicable, putting into service, installation and maintenance requirements, does not present any risk or only the minimum risks compatible with the product's use, considered to be acceptable and consistent with a high level of protection for the safety and health of persons, taking into account the following points in particular:

(i) the characteristics of the product, including its composition, packaging, instructions for assembly and, where applicable, for installation and maintenance;

(ii) the effect on other products, where it is reasonably foreseeable that it will be used with other products;

(iii) the presentation of the product, the labelling, any warnings and instructions for its use and disposal and any other indication or information regarding the product;

(iv) the categories of consumers at risk when using the product, in particular children and the elderly.

The feasibility of obtaining higher levels of safety or the availability of other products presenting a lesser degree of risk shall not constitute grounds for considering a product to be "dangerous";

(c) "dangerous product" shall mean any product which does not meet the definition of "safe product" in (b);

(d) "serious risk" shall mean any serious risk, including those the effects of which are not immediate, requiring rapid intervention by the public authorities;

(e) "producer" shall mean:

(i) the manufacturer of the product, when he is established in the Community, and any other person presenting himself as the manufacturer by affixing to the product his name, trade mark or other distinctive mark, or the person who reconditions the product;

(ii) the manufacturer's representative, when the manufacturer is not established in the Community or, if there is no representative established in the Community, the importer of the product;

(iii) other professionals in the supply chain, insofar as their activities may affect the safety properties of a product;

(f) "distributor" shall mean any professional in the supply chain whose activity does not affect the safety properties of a product;

(g) "recall" shall mean any measure aimed at achieving the return of a dangerous product that has already been supplied or made available to consumers by the producer or distributor;

(h) "withdrawal" shall mean any measure aimed at preventing the distribution, display and offer of a product dangerous to the consumer.

CHAPTER II

GENERAL SAFETY REQUIREMENT, CONFORMITY ASSESSMENT CRITERIA AND EUROPEAN STANDARDS

Article 3

1. Producers shall be obliged to place only safe products on the market.

2. A product shall be deemed safe, as far as the aspects covered by the relevant national legislation are concerned, when, in the absence of specific Community provisions governing

the safety of the product in question, it conforms to the specific rules of national law of the Member State in whose territory the product is marketed, such rules being drawn up in conformity with the Treaty, and in particular Articles 28 and 30 thereof, and laying down the health and safety requirements which the product must satisfy in order to be marketed.

A product shall be presumed safe as far as the risks and risk categories covered by relevant national standards are concerned when it conforms to voluntary national standards transposing European standards, the references of which have been published by the Commission in the Official Journal of the European Communities in accordance with Article 4. The Member States shall publish the references of such national standards.

3   In circumstances other than those referred to in paragraph 2, the conformity of a product to the general safety requirement shall be assessed by taking into account the following elements in particular, where they exist:

(a) voluntary national standards transposing relevant European standards other than those referred to in paragraph 2;

(b) the standards drawn up in the Member State in which the product is marketed;

(c) Commission recommendations setting guidelines on product safety assessment;

(d) product safety codes of good practice in force in the sector concerned;

(e) the state of the art and technology;

(f) reasonable consumer expectations concerning safety.

4.   Conformity of a product with the criteria designed to ensure the general safety requirement, in particular the provisions mentioned in paragraphs 2 or 3, shall not bar the competent authorities of the Member States from taking appropriate measures to impose restrictions on its being placed on the market or to require its withdrawal from the market or recall where there is evidence that, despite such conformity, it is dangerous.

Article 4

1.   For the purposes of this Directive, the European standards referred to in the second subparagraph of Article 3(2) shall be drawn up as follows:

(a) the requirements intended to ensure that products which conform to these standards satisfy the general safety requirement shall be determined in accordance with the procedure laid down in Article 15(2);

(b) on the basis of those requirements, the Commission shall, in accordance with Directive 98/34/EC of the European Parliament and of the Council of 22 June 1998 laying down a procedure for the provision of information in the field of technical standards and regulations and of rules on information society services[7] call on the European standardisation bodies to draw up standards which satisfy these requirements;

(c) on the basis of those mandates, the European standardisation bodies shall adopt the standards in accordance with the principles contained in the general guidelines for cooperation between the Commission and those bodies;

(d) the Commission shall report every three years to the European Parliament and the Council, within the framework of the report referred to in Article 19(2), on its programmes for setting the requirements and the mandates for standardisation provided for in subparagraphs (a) and (b) above. This report will, in particular, include an analysis of the decisions taken regarding requirements and mandates for standardisation referred to in subparagraphs (a) and (b) and regarding the standards referred to in subparagraph (c). It will also include information on the products for which the Commission intends to set the requirements and the mandates in question, the product risks to be considered and the results of any preparatory work launched in this area.

[7] OJ L 204, 21.7.1998, p. 37. Directive amended by Directive 98/48/EC (OJ L 217, 5.8.1998, p. 18).

2.   The Commission shall publish in the Official Journal of the European Communities the references of the European standards adopted in this way and drawn up in accordance with the requirements referred to in paragraph 1.

If a standard adopted by the European standardisation bodies before the entry into force of this Directive ensures compliance with the general safety requirement, the Commission shall decide to publish its references in the Official Journal of the European Communities.

If a standard does not ensure compliance with the general safety requirement, the Commission shall withdraw reference to the standard from publication in whole or in part.

In the cases referred to in the second and third subparagraphs, the Commission shall, on its own initiative or at the request of a Member State, decide in accordance with the procedure laid down in Article 15(2) whether the standard in question meets the general safety requirement. The Commission shall decide to publish or withdraw after consulting the Committee established by Article 5 of Directive 98/34/EC. The Commission shall notify the Member States of its decision.

CHAPTER III

OTHER OBLIGATIONS OF PRODUCERS AND OBLIGATIONS OF DISTRIBUTORS

Article 5

1.   Within the limits of their respective activities, producers shall provide consumers with the relevant information to enable them to assess the risks inherent in a product throughout the normal or reasonably foreseeable period of its use, where such risks are not immediately obvious without adequate warnings, and to take precautions against those risks.

The presence of warnings does not exempt any person from compliance with the other requirements laid down in this Directive.

Within the limits of their respective activities, producers shall adopt measures commensurate with the characteristics of the products which they supply, enabling them to:

(a) be informed of risks which these products might pose;

(b) choose to take appropriate action including, if necessary to avoid these risks, withdrawal from the market, adequately and effectively warning consumers or recall from consumers.

   The measures referred to in the third subparagraph shall include, for example:

(a) an indication, by means of the product or its packaging, of the identity and details of the producer and the product reference or, where applicable, the batch of products to which it belongs, except where not to give such indication is justified and

(b) in all cases where appropriate, the carrying out of sample testing of marketed products, investigating and, if necessary, keeping a register of complaints and keeping distributors informed of such monitoring.

   Action such as that referred to in (b) of the third subparagraph shall be undertaken on a voluntary basis or at the request of the competent authorities in accordance with Article 8(1)(f). Recall shall take place as a last resort, where other measures would not suffice to prevent the risks involved, in instances where the producers consider it necessary or where they are obliged to do so further to a measure taken by the competent authority. It may be effected within the framework of codes of good practice on the matter in the Member State concerned, where such codes exist.

2.   Distributors shall be required to act with due care to help to ensure compliance with the applicable safety requirements, in particular by not supplying products which they know or should have presumed, on the basis of the information in their possession and as

professionals, do not comply with those requirements. Moreover, within the limits of their respective activities, they shall participate in monitoring the safety of products placed on the market, especially by passing on information on product risks, keeping and providing the documentation necessary for tracing the origin of products, and cooperating in the action taken by producers and competent authorities to avoid the risks. Within the limits of their respective activities they shall take measures enabling them to cooperate efficiently.

3.   Where producers and distributors know or ought to know, on the basis of the information in their possession and as professionals, that a product that they have placed on the market poses risks to the consumer that are incompatible with the general safety requirement, they shall immediately inform the competent authorities of the Member States thereof under the conditions laid down in Annex I, giving details, in particular, of action taken to prevent risk to the consumer.

The Commission shall, in accordance with the procedure referred to in Article 15(3), adapt the specific requirements relating to the obligation to provide information laid down in Annex I.

4.   Producers and distributors shall, within the limits of their respective activities, cooperate with the competent authorities, at the request of the latter, on action taken to avoid the risks posed by products which they supply or have supplied. The procedures for such cooperation, including procedures for dialogue with the producers and distributors concerned on issues related to product safety, shall be established by the competent authorities.

CHAPTER IV

SPECIFIC OBLIGATIONS AND POWERS OF THE MEMBER STATES

Article 6

1.   Member States shall ensure that producers and distributors comply with their obligations under this Directive in such a way that products placed on the market are safe.

2.   Member States shall establish or nominate authorities competent to monitor the compliance of products with the general safety requirements and arrange for such authorities to have and use the necessary powers to take the appropriate measures incumbent upon them under this Directive.

3.   Member States shall define the tasks, powers, organisation and cooperation arrangements of the competent authorities. They shall keep the Commission informed, and the Commission shall pass on such information to the other Member States.

Article 7

Member States shall lay down the rules on penalties applicable to infringements of the national provisions adopted pursuant to this Directive and shall take all measures necessary to ensure that they are implemented. The penalties provided for shall be effective, proportionate and dissuasive. Member States shall notify those provisions to the Commission by 15 January 2004 and shall also notify it, without delay, of any amendment affecting them.

Article 8

1.   For the purposes of this Directive, and in particular of Article 6 thereof, the competent authorities of the Member States shall be entitled to take, *inter alia*, the measures in (a) and in (b) to (f) below, where appropriate:

(a) for any product:

(i)   to organise, even after its being placed on the market as being safe, appropriate checks on its safety properties, on an adequate scale, up to the final stage of use or consumption;

(ii) to require all necessary information from the parties concerned;

(iii) to take samples of products and subject them to safety checks;

(b) for any product that could pose risks in certain conditions:
   (i) to require that it be marked with suitable, clearly worded and easily com-
       prehensible warnings, in the official languages of the Member State in which
       the product is marketed, on the risks it may present;
   (ii) to make its marketing subject to prior conditions so as to make it safe;
(c) for any product that could pose risks for certain persons:
       to order that they be given warning of the risk in good time and in an
   appropriate form, including the publication of special warnings;
(d) for any product that could be dangerous:
       for the period needed for the various safety evaluations, checks and controls,
   temporarily to ban its supply, the offer to supply it or its display;
(e) for any dangerous product:
       to ban its marketing and introduce the accompanying measures required to
   ensure the ban is complied with;
(f) for any dangerous product already on the market:
   (i) to order or organise its actual and immediate withdrawal, and alert consumers
       to the risks it presents;
   (ii) to order or coordinate or, if appropriate, to organise together with producers
        and distributors its recall from consumers and its destruction in suitable
        conditions.

2.   When the competent authorities of the Member States take measures such as those
provided for in paragraph 1, in particular those referred to in (d) to (f), they shall act in
accordance with the Treaty, and in particular Articles 28 and 30 thereof, in such a way as to
implement the measures in a manner proportional to the seriousness of the risk, and taking
due account of the precautionary principle.

In this context, they shall encourage and promote voluntary action by producers and
distributors, in accordance with the obligations incumbent on them under this Directive,
and in particular Chapter III thereof, including where applicable by the development of codes
of good practice.

If necessary, they shall organise or order the measures provided for in paragraph 1(f) if the
action undertaken by the producers and distributors in fulfilment of their obligations is
unsatisfactory or insufficient. Recall shall take place as a last resort. It may be effected within
the framework of codes of good practice on the matter in the Member State concerned, where
such codes exist.

3.   In particular, the competent authorities shall have the power to take the necessary
action to apply with due dispatch appropriate measures such as those mentioned in paragraph
1, (b) to (f), in the case of products posing a serious risk. These circumstances shall be determined by the Member States, assessing each individual case on its merits, taking into account
the guidelines referred to in point 8 of Annex II.

4.   The measures to be taken by the competent authorities under this Article shall be
addressed, as appropriate, to:
   (a) the producer;
   (b) within the limits of their respective activities, distributors and in particular the
       party responsible for the first stage of distribution on the national market;
   (c) any other person, where necessary, with a view to cooperation in action taken to
       avoid risks arising from a product.

Article 9

1.   In order to ensure effective market surveillance, aimed at guaranteeing a high level of
consumer health and safety protection, which entails cooperation between their competent
authorities, Member States shall ensure that approaches employing appropriate means and
procedures are put in place, which may include in particular:

(a) establishment, periodical updating and implementation of sectoral surveillance programmes by categories of products or risks and the monitoring of surveillance activities, findings and results;

(b) follow-up and updating of scientific and technical knowledge concerning the safety of products;

(c) periodical review and assessment of the functioning of the control activities and their effectiveness and, if necessary, revision of the surveillance approach and organisation put in place.

2.   Member States shall ensure that consumers and other interested parties are given an opportunity to submit complaints to the competent authorities on product safety and on surveillance and control activities and that these complaints are followed up as appropriate. Member States shall actively inform consumers and other interested parties of the procedures established to that end.

Article 10

1.   The Commission shall promote and take part in the operation in a European network of the authorities of the Member States competent for product safety, in particular in the form of administrative cooperation.

2.   This network operation shall develop in a coordinated manner with the other existing Community procedures, particularly RAPEX. Its objective shall be, in particular, to facilitate:

(a) the exchange of information on risk assessment, dangerous products, test methods and results, recent scientific developments as well as other aspects relevant for control activities;

(b) the establishment and execution of joint surveillance and testing projects;

(c) the exchange of expertise and best practices and cooperation in training activities;

(d) improved cooperation at Community level with regard to the tracing, withdrawal and recall of dangerous products.

CHAPTER V

EXCHANGES OF INFORMATION AND RAPID INTERVENTION SITUATIONS

Article 11

1.   Where a Member State takes measures which restrict the placing on the market of products—or require their withdrawal or recall—such as those provided for in Article 8(1)(b) to (f), the Member State shall, to the extent that such notification is not required under Article 12 or any specific Community legislation, inform the Commission of the measures, specifying its reasons for adopting them. It shall also inform the Commission of any modification or lifting of such measures.

If the notifying Member State considers that the effects of the risk do not or cannot go beyond its territory, it shall notify the measures concerned insofar as they involve information likely to be of interest to Member States from the product safety standpoint, and in particular if they are in response to a new risk which has not yet been reported in other notifications.

In accordance with the procedure laid down in Article 15(3) of this Directive, the Commission shall, while ensuring the effectiveness and proper functioning of the system, adopt the guidelines referred to in point 8 of Annex II. These shall propose the content and standard form for the notifications provided for in this Article, and, in particular, shall provide precise criteria for determining the conditions for which notification is relevant for the purposes of the second subparagraph.

2.   The Commission shall forward the notification to the other Member States, unless it

concludes, after examination on the basis of the information contained in the notification, that the measure does not comply with Community law. In such a case, it shall immediately inform the Member State which initiated the action.

Article 12

1. Where a Member State adopts or decides to adopt, recommend or agree with producers and distributors, whether on a compulsory or voluntary basis, measures or actions to prevent, restrict or impose specific conditions on the possible marketing or use, within its own territory, of products by reason of a serious risk, it shall immediately notify the Commission thereof through RAPEX. It shall also inform the Commission without delay of modification or withdrawal of any such measure or action.

If the notifying Member State considers that the effects of the risk do not or cannot go beyond its territory, it shall follow the procedure laid down in Article 11, taking into account the relevant criteria proposed in the guidelines referred to in point 8 of Annex II.

Without prejudice to the first subparagraph, before deciding to adopt such measures or to take such action, Member States may pass on to the Commission any information in their possession regarding the existence of a serious risk.

In the case of a serious risk, they shall notify the Commission of the voluntary measures laid down in Article 5 of this Directive taken by producers and distributors.

2. On receiving such notifications, the Commission shall check whether they comply with this Article and with the requirements applicable to the functioning of RAPEX, and shall forward them to the other Member States, which, in turn, shall immediately inform the Commission of any measures adopted.

3. Detailed procedures for RAPEX are set out in Annex II. They shall be adapted by the Commission in accordance with the procedure referred to in Article 15(3).

4. Access to RAPEX shall be open to applicant countries, third countries or international organisations, within the framework of agreements between the Community and those countries or international organisations, according to arrangements defined in these agreements. Any such agreements shall be based on reciprocity and include provisions on confidentiality corresponding to those applicable in the Community.

Article 13

1. If the Commission becomes aware of a serious risk from certain products to the health and safety of consumers in various Member States, it may, after consulting the Member States, and, if scientific questions arise which fall within the competence of a Community Scientific Committee, the Scientific Committee competent to deal with the risk concerned, adopt a decision in the light of the result of those consultations, in accordance with the procedure laid down in Article 15(2), requiring Member States to take measures from among those listed in Article 8(1)(b) to (f) if, at one and the same time:

(a) it emerges from prior consultations with the Member States that they differ significantly on the approach adopted or to be adopted to deal with the risk; and

(b) the risk cannot be dealt with, in view of the nature of the safety issue posed by the product, in a manner compatible with the degree of urgency of the case, under other procedures laid down by the specific Community legislation applicable to the products concerned; and

(c) the risk can be eliminated effectively only by adopting appropriate measures applicable at Community level, in order to ensure a consistent and high level of protection of the health and safety of consumers and the proper functioning of the internal market.

2. The decisions referred to in paragraph 1 shall be valid for a period not exceeding one year and may be confirmed, under the same procedure, for additional periods none of which shall exceed one year.

However, decisions concerning specific, individually identified products or batches of products shall be valid without a time limit.

3.   Export from the Community of dangerous products which have been the subject of a decision referred to in paragraph 1 shall be prohibited unless the decision provides otherwise.

4.   Member States shall take all necessary measures to implement the decisions referred to in paragraph 1 within less than 20 days, unless a different period is specified in those decisions.

5.   The competent authorities responsible for carrying out the measures referred to in paragraph 1 shall, within one month, give the parties concerned an opportunity to submit their views and shall inform the Commission accordingly.

CHAPTER VI

COMMITTEE PROCEDURES

Article 14

1.   The measures necessary for the implementation of this Directive relating to the matters referred to below shall be adopted in accordance with the regulatory procedure provided for in Article 15(2):

(a)   the measures referred to in Article 4 concerning standards adopted by the European standardisation bodies;

(b)   the decisions referred to in Article 13 requiring Member States to take measures as listed in Article 8(1)(b) to (f).

2.   The measures necessary for the implementation of this Directive in respect of all other matters shall be adopted in accordance with the advisory procedure provided for in Article 15(3).

Article 15

1.   The Commission shall be assisted by a Committee.

2.   Where reference is made to this paragraph, Articles 5 and 7 of Decision 1999/468/EC shall apply, having regard to the provisions of Article 8 thereof.

The period laid down in Article 5(6) of Decision 1999/468/EC shall be set at 15 days.

3.   Where reference is made to this paragraph, Articles 3 and 7 of Decision 1999/468/EC shall apply, having regard to the provisions of Article 8 thereof.

4.   The Committee shall adopt its rules of procedure.

CHAPTER VII

FINAL PROVISIONS

Article 16

1.   Information available to the authorities of the Member States or the Commission relating to risks to consumer health and safety posed by products shall in general be available to the public, in accordance with the requirements of transparency and without prejudice to the restrictions required for monitoring and investigation activities. In particular the public shall have access to information on product identification, the nature of the risk and the measures taken.

However, Member States and the Commission shall take the steps necessary to ensure that their officials and agents are required not to disclose information obtained for the purposes of this Directive which, by its nature, is covered by professional secrecy in duly justified cases, except for information relating to the safety properties of products which must be made public if circumstances so require, in order to protect the health and safety of consumers.

2. Protection of professional secrecy shall not prevent the dissemination to the competent authorities of information relevant for ensuring the effectiveness of market monitoring and surveillance activities. The authorities receiving information covered by professional secrecy shall ensure its protection.

Article 17

This Directive shall be without prejudice to the application of Directive 85/374/EEC.

Article 18

1. Any measure adopted under this Directive and involving restrictions on the placing of a product on the market or requiring its withdrawal or recall must state the appropriate reasons on which it is based. It shall be notified as soon as possible to the party concerned and shall indicate the remedies available under the provisions in force in the Member State in question and the time limits applying to such remedies.

The parties concerned shall, whenever feasible, be given an opportunity to submit their views before the adoption of the measure. If this has not been done in advance because of the urgency of the measures to be taken, they shall be given such opportunity in due course after the measure has been implemented.

Measures requiring the withdrawal of a product or its recall shall take into consideration the need to encourage distributors, users and consumers to contribute to the implementation of such measures.

2. Member States shall ensure that any measure taken by the competent authorities involving restrictions on the placing of a product on the market or requiring its withdrawal or recall can be challenged before the competent courts.

3. Any decision taken by virtue of this Directive and involving restrictions on the placing of a product on the market or requiring its withdrawal or its recall shall be without prejudice to assessment of the liability of the party concerned, in the light of the national criminal law applying in the case in question.

Article 19

1. The Commission may bring before the Committee referred to in Article 15 any matter concerning the application of this Directive and particularly those relating to market monitoring and surveillance activities.

2. Every three years, following 15 January 2004, the Commission shall submit a report on the implementation of this Directive to the European Parliament and the Council.

The report shall in particular include information on the safety of consumer products, in particular on improved traceability of products, the functioning of market surveillance, standardisation work, the functioning of RAPEX and Community measures taken on the basis of Article 13. To this end the Commission shall conduct assessments of the relevant issues, in particular the approaches, systems and practices put in place in the Member States, in the light of the requirements of this Directive and the other Community legislation relating to product safety. The Member States shall provide the Commission with all the necessary assistance and information for carrying out the assessments and preparing the reports.

Article 20

The Commission shall identify the needs, possibilities and priorities for Community action on the safety of services and submit to the European Parliament and the Council, before 1 January 2003, a report, accompanied by proposals on the subject as appropriate.

Article 21

1.   Member States shall bring into force the laws, regulations and administrative provisions necessary in order to comply with this Directive with effect from 15 January 2004. They shall forthwith inform the Commission thereof.

When Member States adopt those measures, they shall contain a reference to this Directive or be accompanied by such reference on the occasion of their official publication. The methods of making such reference shall be laid down by Member States.

2.   Member States shall communicate to the Commission the provisions of national law which they adopt in the field covered by this Directive.

Article 22

Directive 92/59/EEC is hereby repealed from 15 January 2004, without prejudice to the obligations of Member States concerning the deadlines for transposition and application of the said Directive as indicated in Annex III.

References to Directive 92/59/EEC shall be construed as references to this Directive and shall be read in accordance with the correlation table in Annex IV.

Article 23

This Directive shall enter into force on the day of its publication in the Official Journal of the European Communities.

Article 24

This Directive is addressed to the Member States.

Done at Brussels, 3 December 2001.

For the European Parliament The President N. Fontaine

For the Council The President F. Vandenbroucke

ANNEX I

REQUIREMENTS CONCERNING INFORMATION ON PRODUCTS THAT DO NOT COMPLY WITH THE GENERAL SAFETY REQUIREMENT TO BE PROVIDED TO THE COMPETENT AUTHORITIES BY PRODUCERS AND DISTRIBUTORS

1.   The information specified in Article 5(3), or where applicable by specific requirements of Community rules on the product concerned, shall be passed to the competent authorities appointed for the purpose in the Member States where the products in question are or have been marketed or otherwise supplied to consumers.

2.   The Commission, assisted by the Committee referred to in Article 15, shall define the content and draw up the standard form of the notifications provided for in this Annex, while ensuring the effectiveness and proper functioning of the system. In particular, it shall put forward, possibly in the form of a guide, simple and clear criteria for determining the special conditions, particularly those concerning isolated circumstances or products, for which notification is not relevant in relation to this Annex.

3.   In the event of serious risks, this information shall include at least the following:
   (a)   information enabling a precise identification of the product or batch of products in question;
   (b)   a full description of the risk that the products in question present;

    (c) all available information relevant for tracing the product;

    (d) a description of the action undertaken to prevent risks to consumers.

ANNEX II

PROCEDURES FOR THE APPLICATION OF RAPEX AND GUIDELINES FOR NOTIFICATIONS

    1. RAPEX covers products as defined in Article 2(a) that pose a serious risk to the health and safety of consumers.

    Pharmaceuticals, which come under Directives 75/319/EEC[1] and 81/851/EEC,[2] are excluded from the scope of RAPEX.

    2. RAPEX is essentially aimed at a rapid exchange of information in the event of a serious risk. The guidelines referred to in point 8 define specific criteria for identifying serious risks.

    3. Member States notifying under Article 12 shall provide all available details. In particular, the notification shall contain the information stipulated in the guidelines referred to in point 8 and at least:

    (a) information enabling the product to be identified;

    (b) a description of the risk involved, including a summary of the results of any tests/analyses and of their conclusions which are relevant to assessing the level of risk;

    (c) the nature and the duration of the measures or action taken or decided on, if applicable;

    (d) information on supply chains and distribution of the product, in particular on destination countries.

Such information must be transmitted using the special standard notification form and by the means stipulated in the guidelines referred to in point 8.

When the measure notified pursuant to Article 11 or Article 12 seeks to limit the marketing or use of a chemical substance or preparation, the Member States shall provide as soon as possible either a summary or the references of the relevant data relating to the substance or preparation considered and to known and available substitutes, where such information is available. They will also communicate the anticipated effects of the measure on consumer health and safety together with the assessment of the risk carried out in accordance with the general principles for the risk evaluation of chemical substances as referred to in Article 10(4) of Regulation (EEC) No 793/93[3] in the case of an existing substance or in Article 3(2) of Directive 67/548/EEC[4] in the case of a new substance. The guidelines referred to in point 8 shall define the details and procedures for the information requested in that respect.

    4. When a Member State has informed the Commission, in accordance with Article 12(1), third subparagraph, of a serious risk before deciding to adopt measures, it must inform the Commission within 45 days whether it confirms or modifies this information.

    5. The Commission shall, in the shortest time possible, verify the conformity with the provisions of the Directive of the information received under RAPEX and, may, when it

---

[1] OJ L 147, 9.6.1975, p. 13. Directive as last amended by Commission Directive 2000/38/EC (OJ L 139, 10.6.2000, p. 28).

[2] OJ L 317, 6.11.1981, p. 1. Directive as last amended by Commission Directive 2000/37/EC (OJ L 139, 10.6.2000, p. 25).

[3] OJ L 84, 5.4.1993, p. 1.

[4] OJ 196, 16.8.1967, p. 1/67. Directive as last amended by Commission Directive 2000/33/EC (OJ L 136, 8.6.2000, p. 90).

considers it to be necessary and in order to assess product safety, carry out an investigation on its own initiative. In the case of such an investigation, Member States shall supply the Commission with the requested information to the best of their ability.

6.   Upon receipt of a notification referred to in Article 12, the Member States are requested to inform the Commission, at the latest within the set period of time stipulated in the guidelines referred to in point 8, of the following:

(a)   whether the product has been marketed in their territory;

(b)   what measures concerning the product in question they may be adopting in the light of their own circumstances, stating the reasons, including any differing assessment of risk or any other special circumstance justifying their decision, in particular lack of action or of follow-up;

(c)   any relevant supplementary information they have obtained on the risk involved, including the results of any tests or analyses carried out.

 The guidelines referred to in point 8 shall provide precise criteria for notifying measures limited to national territory and shall specify how to deal with notifications concerning risks which are considered by the Member State not to go beyond its territory.

7.   Member States shall immediately inform the Commission of any modification or lifting of the measure(s) or action(s) in question.

8.   The Commission shall prepare and regularly update, in accordance with the procedure laid down in Article 15(3), guidelines concerning the management of RAPEX by the Commission and the Member States.

9.   The Commission may inform the national contact points regarding products posing serious risks, imported into or exported from the Community and the European Economic Area.

10.   Responsibility for the information provided lies with the notifying Member State.

11.   The Commission shall ensure the proper functioning of the system, in particular classifying and indexing notifications according to the degree of urgency. Detailed procedures shall be laid down by the guidelines referred to in point 8.

ANNEX III

PERIOD FOR THE TRANSPOSITION AND APPLICATION OF THE REPEALED DIRECTIVE

(REFERRED TO IN THE FIRST SUBPARAGRAPH OF ARTICLE 22)

Directive	*Period for transposition*	*Period for bringing into application*
Directive 92/59/EEC	29 June 1994	29 June 1994

ANNEX IV

CORRELATION TABLE

(REFERRED TO IN THE SECOND SUBPARAGRAPH OF ARTICLE 22)

This Directive	Directive 92/59/EEC
Article 1	Article 1
Article 2	Article 2
Article 3	Article 4
Article 4	–
Article 5	Article 3
Article 6	Article 5
Article 7	Article 5(2)
Article 8	Article 6
Article 9	—
Article 10	—
Article 11	Article 7
Article 12	Article 8
Article 13	Article 9
Articles 14 and 15	Article 10
Article 16	Article 12
Article 17	Article 13
Article 18	Article 14
Article 19	Article 15
Article 20	—
Article 21	Article 17
Article 22	Article 18
Article 23	Article 19
Annex I	—
Annex II	Annex
Annex III	—
Annex IV	—

INTELLECTUAL PROPERTY AND INFORMATION TECHNOLOGY

Council Directive 89/552 of 3 October 1989 on the coordination of certain provisions laid down by law, regulation or administrative action in Member States concerning the pursuit of television broadcasting activities

[OJ 1989, L298/23]*

THE COUNCIL OF THE EUROPEAN COMMUNITIES,

Having regard to the Treaty establishing the European Economic Community, and in particular Articles 57 (2) and 66 thereof,

* **Editor's Note:** As amended by Directive 97/36 [OJ No. L220/60].

Having regard to the proposal from the Commission,[1]

In cooperation with the European Parliament,[2]

Having regard to the opinion of the Economic and Social Committee,[3]

Whereas the objectives of the Community as laid down in the Treaty include establishing an even closer union among the peoples of Europe, fostering closer relations between the States belonging to the Community, ensuring the economic and social progress of its countries by common action to eliminate the barriers which divide Europe, encouraging the constant improvement of the living conditions of its peoples as well as ensuring the preservation and strengthening of peace and liberty;

Whereas the Treaty provides for the establishment of a common market, including the abolition, as between Member States, of obstacles to freedom of movement for services and the institution of a system ensuring that competition in the common market is not distorted;

Whereas broadcasts transmitted across frontiers by means of various technologies are one of the ways of pursuing the objectives of the Community; whereas measures should be adopted to permit and ensure the transition from national markets to a common programme production and distribution market and to establish conditions of fair competition without prejudice to the public interest role to be discharged by the television broadcasting services;

Whereas the Council of Europe has adopted the European Convention on Transfrontier Television;

Whereas the Treaty provides for the issuing of directives for the coordination of provisions to facilitate the taking up of activities as self-employed persons;

Whereas television broadcasting constitutes, in normal circumstances, a service within the meaning of the Treaty;

Whereas the Treaty provides for free movement of all services normally provided against payment, without exclusion on grounds of their cultural or other content and without restriction of nationals of Member States established in a Community country other than that of the person for whom the services are intended;

Whereas this right as applied to the broadcasting and distribution of television services is also a specific manifestation in Community law of a more general principle, namely the freedom of expression as enshrined in Article 10(1) of the Convention for the Protection of Human Rights and Fundamental Freedoms ratified by all Member States; whereas for this reason the issuing of directives on the broadcasting and distribution of television programmes must ensure their free movement in the light of the said Article and subject only to the limits set by paragraph 2 of that Article and by Article 56(1) of the Treaty;

Whereas the laws, regulations and administrative measures in Member States concerning the pursuit of activities as television broadcasters and cable operators contain disparities, some of which may impede the free movement of broadcasts within the Community and may distort competition within the common market;

Whereas all such restrictions on freedom to provide broadcasting services within the Community must be abolished under the Treaty;

Whereas such abolition must go hand in hand with coordination of the applicable laws; whereas this coordination must be aimed at facilitating the pursuit of the professional activities concerned and, more generally, the free movement of information and ideas within the Community;

Whereas it is consequently necessary and sufficient that all broadcasts comply with the law of Member State from which they emanate;

---

[1] OJ C 179, 17.7.1986, p. 4.

[2] OJ C 49, 22.2.1988, p. 53, and OJ C 158, 26.6.1989.

[3] OJ C 232, 31.8.1987, p. 29.

Whereas this Directive lays down the minimum rules needed to guarantee freedom of transmission in broadcasting; whereas, therefore, it does not affect the responsibility of the Member States and their authorities with regard to the organization—including the systems of licensing, administrative authorization or taxation—financing and the content of programmes; whereas the independence of cultural developments in the Member States and the preservation of cultural diversity in the Community therefore remain unaffected;

Whereas it is necessary, in the common market, that all broadcasts emanating from and intended for reception within the Community and in particular those intended for reception in another Member State, should respect the law of the originating Member State applicable to broadcasts intended for reception by the public in that Member State and the provisions of this Directive;

Whereas the requirement that the originating Member State should verify that broadcasts comply with national law as coordinated by this Directive is sufficient under Community law to ensure free movement of broadcasts without secondary control on the same grounds in the receiving Member States; whereas, however, the receiving Member State may, exceptionally and under specific conditions provisionally suspend the retransmission of televised broadcasts;

Whereas it is essential for the Member States to ensure the prevention of any acts which may prove detrimental to freedom of movement and trade in television programmes or which may promote the creation of dominant positions which would lead to restrictions on pluralism and freedom of televised information and of the information sector as a whole;

Whereas this Directive, being confined specifically to television broadcasting rules, is without prejudice to existing or future Community acts of harmonization, in particular to satisfy mandatory requirements concerning the protection of consumers and the fairness of commercial transactions and competition;

Whereas co-ordination is nevertheless needed to make it easier for persons and industries producing programmes having a cultural objective to take up and pursue their activities;

Whereas minimum requirements in respect of all public or private Community television programmes for European audio-visual productions have been a means of promoting production, independent production and distribution in the abovementioned industries and are complementary to other instruments which are already or will be proposed to favour the same objective;

Whereas it is therefore necessary to promote markets of sufficient size for television productions in the Member States to recover necessary investments not only by establishing common rules opening up national markets but also by envisaging for European productions where practicable and by appropriate means a majority proportion in television programmes of all Member States; whereas, in order to allow the monitoring of the application of these rules and the pursuit of the objectives, Member States will provide the Commission with a report on the application of the proportions reserved for European works and independent productions in this Directive; whereas for the calculation of such proportions account should be taken of the specific situation of the Hellenic Republic and the Portuguese Republic; whereas the Commission must inform the other Member States of these reports accompanied, where appropriate by an opinion taking account of, in particular, progress achieved in relation to previous years, the share of first broadcasts in the programming, the particular circumstances of new television broadcasters and the specific situation of countries with a low audio-visual production capacity or restricted language area;

Whereas for these purposes 'European works' should be defined without prejudice to the possibility of Member States laying down a more detailed definition as regards television broadcasters under their jurisdiction in accordance with Article 3(1) in compliance with Community law and account being taken of the objectives of this Directive; Whereas it is important to seek appropriate instruments and procedures in accordance with Community law in order to promote the implementation of these objectives with a view to adopting suitable measures to encourage the activity and development of European audio-visual production and distribution, particularly in countries with a low production capacity or restricted language area;

Whereas national support schemes for the development of European production may be applied in so far as they comply with Community law;

Whereas a commitment, where practicable, to a certain proportion of broadcasts for independent productions, created by producers who are independent of broadcasters, will stimulate new sources of television production, especially the creation of small and medium-sized enterprises; whereas it will offer new opportunities and outlets to the marketing of creative talents of employment of cultural professions and employees in the cultural field; whereas the definition of the concept of independent producer by the Member States should take account of that objective by giving due consideration to small and medium-sized producers and making it possible to authorize financial participation by the co-production subsidiaries of television organizations;

Whereas measures are necessary for Member States to ensure that a certain period elapses between the first cinema showing of a work and the first television showing;

Whereas in order to allow for an active policy in favour of a specific language, Member States remain free to lay down more detailed or stricter rules in particular on the basis of language criteria, as long as these rules are in conformity with Community law, and in particular are not applicable to the retransmission of broadcasts originating in other Member States;

Whereas in order to ensure that the interests of consumers as television viewers are fully and properly protected, it is essential for television advertising to be subject to a certain number of minimum rules and standards and that the Member States must maintain the right to set more detailed or stricter rules and in certain circumstances to lay down different conditions for television broadcasters under their jurisdiction;

Whereas Member States, with due regard to Community law and in relation to broadcasts intended solely for the national territory which may not be received, directly or indirectly, in one or more Member States, must be able to lay down different conditions for the insertion of advertising and different limits for the volume of advertising in order to facilitate these particular broadcasts;

Whereas it is necessary to prohibit all television advertising promoting cigarettes and other tobacco products including indirect forms of advertising which, whilst not directly mentioning the tobacco product, seek to circumvent the ban on advertising by using brand names, symbols or other distinctive features of tobacco products or of undertakings whose known or main activities include the production or sale of such products;

Whereas it is equally necessary to prohibit all television advertising for medicinal products and medical treatment available only on prescription in the Member State within whose jurisdiction the broadcaster falls and to introduce strict criteria relating to the television advertising of alcoholic products;

Whereas in view of the growing importance of sponsorship in the financing of programmes, appropriate rules should be laid down;

Whereas it is, furthermore, necessary to introduce rules to protect the physical, mental and moral development of minors in programmes and in television advertising;

Whereas although television broadcasters are normally bound to ensure that programmes present facts and events fairly, it is nevertheless important that they should be subject to specific obligations with respect to the right of reply or equivalent remedies so that any person whose legitimate interests have been damaged by an assertion made in the course of a broadcast television programme may effectively exercise such right or remedy.

HAS ADOPTED THIS DIRECTIVE:

CHAPTER I　DEFINITIONS

Article 1　For the purpose of this Directive:

(a)　'television broadcasting' means the initial transmission by wire or over the air, including that by satellite, in unencoded or encoded form, of television programmes intended for reception by the public. It includes the communication of programmes between undertakings with a view to their being relayed to the public. It does not include communication services providing items of information or other messages on individual demand such as telecopying, electronic data banks and other similar services;

(b)　"broadcaster" means the natural or legal person who has editorial responsibility for the composition of schedules of television programmes within the meaning of (a) and who transmits them or has them transmitted by third parties;

(c)　"television advertising" means any form of announcement broadcast whether in return for payment or for similar consideration or broadcast for self-promotional purposes by a public or private undertaking in connection with a trade, business, craft or profession in order to promote the supply of goods or services, including immovable property, rights and obligations, in return for payment;

(d)　'surreptitious advertising' means the representation in words or pictures of goods, services, the name, the trade mark or the activities of a producer of goods or a provider of services in programmes when such representation is intended by the broadcaster to serve advertising and might mislead the public as to its nature. Such representation is considered to be intentional in particular if it is done in return for payment or for similar consideration;

(e)　'sponsorship' means any contribution made by a public or private undertaking not engaged in television broadcasting activities or in the production of audiovisual works, to the financing of television programmes with a view to promoting its name, its trade mark, its image, its activities or its products.

(f)　"teleshopping" means direct offers broadcast to the public with a view to the supply of goods or services, including immovable property, rights and obligations, in return for payment.

CHAPTER II　GENERAL PROVISIONS

Article 2

1.　Each Member State shall ensure that all television broadcasts transmitted by broadcasters under its jurisdiction comply with the rules of the system of law applicable to broadcasts intended for the public in that Member State.

2.　For the purposes of this Directive the broadcasters under the jurisdiction of a Member State are:

— those established in that Member State in accordance with paragraph 3;

— those to whom paragraph 4 applies.

3.　For the purposes of this Directive, a broadcaster shall be deemed to be established in a Member State in the following cases:

(a)　the broadcaster has its head office in that Member State and the editorial decisions about programme schedules are taken in that Member State;

(b)　if a broadcaster has its head office in one Member State but editorial decisions on programme schedules are taken in another Member State, it shall be deemed to be established in the Member State where a significant part of the workforce involved in the pursuit of the television broadcasting activity operates; if a significant part of the workforce involved in the pursuit of the television broadcasting activity operates in each of those Member States, the broadcaster shall be deemed to be established in the Member State where it has its head office; if a significant part of the workforce involved in the pursuit of the television broadcasting activity operates in neither of those Member States, the broadcaster shall be deemed to be established in the Member State where it first began broadcasting in accordance with the system of law of that Member State, provided that it maintains a stable and effective link with the economy of that Member State;

(c) if a broadcaster has its head office in a Member State but decisions on programme schedules are taken in a third country, or vice-versa, it shall be deemed to be established in the Member State concerned, provided that a significant part of the workforce involved in the pursuit of the television broadcasting activity operates in that Member State.

4.   Broadcasters to whom the provisions of paragraph 3 are not applicable shall be deemed to be under the jurisdiction of a Member State in the following cases:

(a) they use a frequency granted by that Member State;

(b) although they do not use a frequency granted by a Member State they do use a satellite capacity appertaining to that Member State;

(c) although they use neither a frequency granted by a Member State nor a satellite capacity appertaining to a Member State they do use a satellite up-link situated in that Member State.

5.   If the question as to which Member State has jurisdiction cannot be determined in accordance with paragraphs 3 and 4, the competent Member State shall be that in which the broadcaster is established within the meaning of Articles 52 and following of the Treaty establishing the European Community.

6.   This Directive shall not apply to broadcasts intended exclusively for reception in third countries, and which are not received directly or indirectly by the public in one or more Member States.

Article 2a

1.   Member States shall ensure freedom of reception and shall not restrict retransmissions on their territory of television broadcasts from other Member States for reasons which fall within the fields coordinated by this Directive.

2.   Member States may, provisionally, derogate from paragraph 1 if the following conditions are fulfilled:

(a) a television broadcast coming from another Member State manifestly, seriously and gravely infringes Article 22 (1) or (2) and/or Article 22a;

(b) during the previous 12 months, the broadcaster has infringed the provision(s) referred to in (a) on at least two prior occasions;

(c) the Member State concerned has notified the broadcaster and the Commission in writing of the alleged infringements and of the measures it intends to take should any such infringement occur again;

(d) consultations with the transmitting Member State and the Commission have not produced an amicable settlement within 15 days of the notification provided for in (c), and the alleged infringement persists.

The Commission shall, within two months following notification of the measures taken by the Member State, take a decision on whether the measures are compatible with Community law. If it decides that they are not, the Member State will be required to put an end to the measures in question as a matter of urgency.

3.   Paragraph 2 shall be without prejudice to the application of any procedure, remedy or sanction to the infringements in question in the Member State which has jurisdiction over the broadcaster concerned.

Article 3

1.   Member States shall remain free to require television broadcasters under their jurisdiction to comply with more detailed or stricter rules in the areas covered by this Directive.

2.   Member States shall, by appropriate means, ensure, within the framework of their
legislation, that television broadcasters under their jurisdiction effectively comply with the
provisions of this Directive.

3.   The measures shall include the appropriate procedures for third parties directly
affected, including nationals of other Member States, to apply to the competent judicial or
other authorities to seek effective compliance according to national provisions.

Article 3a

1.   Each Member State may take measures in accordance with Community law to ensure
that broadcasters under its jurisdiction do not broadcast on an exclusive basis events which
are regarded by that Member State as being of major importance for society in such a way as
to deprive a substantial proportion of the public in that Member State of the possibility of
following such events via live coverage or deferred coverage on free television. If it does so, the
Member State concerned shall draw up a list of designated events, national or non-national,
which it considers to be of major importance for society. It shall do so in a clear and transparent manner in due and effective time. In so doing the Member State concerned shall also
determine whether these events should be available via whole or partial live coverage, or
where necessary or appropriate for objective reasons in the public interest, whole or partial
deferred coverage.

2.   Member States shall immediately notify to the Commission any measures taken or
to be taken pursuant to paragraph 1. Within a period of three months from the notification,
the Commission shall verify that such measures are compatible with Community law
and communicate them to the other Member States. It shall seek the opinion of the Committee established pursuant to Article 23a. It shall forthwith publish the measures taken in the
Official Journal of the European Communities and at least once a year the consolidated list of
the measures taken by Member States.

3.   Member States shall ensure, by appropriate means, within the framework of their
legislation that broadcasters under their jurisdiction do not exercise the exclusive rights
purchased by those broadcasters following the date of publication of this Directive in such a
way that a substantial proportion of the public in another Member State is deprived of the
possibility of following events which are designated by that other Member State in accordance
with the preceding paragraphs via whole or partial live coverage or, where necessary or
appropriate for objective reasons in the public interest, whole or partial deferred coverage on
free television as determined by that other Member State in accordance with paragraph 1.

CHAPTER III   PROMOTION OF DISTRIBUTION AND PRODUCTION
OF TELEVISION PROGRAMMES

Article 4

1.   Member States shall ensure where practicable and by appropriate means, that
broadcasters reserve for European works, within the meaning of Article 6, a majority proportion of their transmission time, excluding the time appointed to news, sports events,
games, advertising, teletext services and teleshopping. This proportion, having regard to the
broadcaster's informational, educational, cultural and entertainment responsibilities to its
viewing public, should be achieved progressively, on the basis of suitable criteria.

2.   Where the proportion laid down in paragraph 1 cannot be attained, it must not
be lower than the average for 1988 in the Member State concerned. However, in respect of
the Hellenic Republic and the Portuguese Republic, the year 1988 shall be replaced by the
year 1990. 3. From 3 October 1991, the Member States shall provide the Commission every

two years with a report on the application of this Article and Article 5. That report shall in particular include a statistical statement on the achievement of the proportion referred to in this Article and Article 5 for each of the television programmes falling within the jurisdiction of the Member State concerned, the reasons, in each case, for the failure to attain that proportion and the measures adopted or envisaged in order to achieve it.

The Commission shall inform the other Member States and the European Parliament of the reports, which shall be accompanied, where appropriate, by an opinion. The Commission shall ensure the application of this Article and Article 5 in accordance with the provisions of the Treaty. The Commission may take account in its opinion, in particular, of progress achieved in relation to previous years, the share of first broadcast works in the programming, the particular circumstances of new television broadcasters and the specific situation of countries with a low audiovisual production capacity or restricted language area.

4.   The Council shall review the implementation of this Article on the basis of a report from the Commission accompanied by any proposals for revision that it may deem appropriate no later than the end of the fifth year from the adoption of the Directive. To that end, the Commission report shall, on the basis of the information provided by Member States under paragraph 3, take account in particular of developments in the Community market and of the international context.

Article 5

Member States shall ensure, where practicable and by appropriate means, that broadcasters reserve at least 10% of their transmission time, excluding the time appointed to news, sports events, games, advertising, teletext services and teleshopping, or alternately, at the discretion of the Member State, at least 10% of their programming budget, for European works created by producers who are independent of broadcasters. This proportion, having regard to broadcasters' informational, educational, cultural and entertainment responsibilities to its viewing public, should be achieved progressively, on the basis of suitable criteria; it must be achieved by earmarking an adequate proportion for recent works, that is to say works transmitted within five years of their production.

Article 6

1.   Within the meaning of this chapter, 'European works' means the following:
   (a)   works originating from Member States;
   (b)   works originating from European third States party to the European Convention on Transfrontier Television of the Council of Europe and fulfilling the conditions of paragraph 2;
   (c)   works originating from other European third countries and fulfilling the conditions of paragraph 3.

Application of the provisions of (b) and (c) shall be conditional on works originating from Member States not being the subject of discriminatory measures in the third countries concerned.

2.   The works referred to in paragraph 1 (a) and (b) are works mainly made with authors and workers residing in one or more States referred to in paragraph 1 (a) and (b) provided that they comply with one of the following three conditions:
   (a)   they are made by one or more producers established in one or more of those States; or
   (b)   production of the works is supervised and actually controlled by one or more producers established in one or more of those States; or
   (c)   the contribution of co-producers of those States to the total co-production costs is preponderant and the co-production is not controlled by one or more producers established outside those States.

3.   The works referred to in paragraph 1 (c) are works made exclusively or in co-production with producers established in one or more Member States by producers established in one or more European third countries with which the Community has concluded agreements relating to the audiovisual sector, if those works are mainly made with authors and workers residing in one or more European States.

4.   Works that are not European works within the meaning of paragraph 1 but that are produced within the framework of bilateral co-production treaties concluded between Member States and third countries shall be deemed to be European works provided that the Community co-producers supply a majority share of the total cost of the production and that the production is not controlled by one or more producers established outside the territory of the Member States.

5.   Works which are not European works within the meaning of paragraphs 1 and 4, but made mainly with authors and workers residing in one or more Member States, shall be considered to be European works to an extent corresponding to the proportion of the contribution of Community co-producers to the total production costs.

Article 7
Member States shall ensure that broadcasters under their jurisdiction do not broadcast cinematographic works outside periods agreed with the rights holders.

Article 8*

Article 9
This Chapter shall not apply to television broadcasts that are intended for local audiences and do not form part of a national network.

CHAPTER IV   TELEVISION ADVERTISING, SPONSORSHIP AND TELESHOPPING

Article 10
1.   Television advertising and teleshopping shall be readily recognizable as such and kept quite separate from other parts of the programme service by optical and/or acoustic means.

2.   Isolated advertising and teleshopping spots shall remain the exception.

3.   Advertising and teleshopping shall not use subliminal techniques.

4.   Surreptitious advertising and teleshopping shall be prohibited.

Article 11
1.   Advertising and teleshopping spots shall be inserted between programmes. Provided the conditions set out in paragraphs 2 to 5 are fulfilled, advertising and teleshopping spots may also be inserted during programmes in such a way that the integrity and value of the programme, taking into account natural breaks in and the duration and nature of the programme, and the rights of the rights holders are not prejudiced.

2.   In programmes consisting of autonomous parts, or in sports programmes and similarly structured events and performances containing intervals, advertising and teleshopping spots shall only be inserted between the parts or in the intervals.

3.   The transmission of audiovisual works such as feature films and films made for television (excluding series, serials, light entertainment programmes and documentaries), provided their scheduled duration is more than 45 minutes, may be interrupted once for each period of 45 minutes. A further interruption shall be allowed if their scheduled duration is at least 20 minutes longer than two or more complete periods of 45 minutes.

---

* **Editor's Note:** Deleted by Directive 97/36 [OJ No. L220/60].

4. Where programmes, other than those covered by paragraph 2, are interrupted by advertising or teleshopping spots, a period of at least 20 minutes should elapse between each successive advertising break within the programme.

5. Advertising and teleshopping shall not be inserted in any broadcast of a religious service. News and current affairs programmes, documentaries, religious programmes and children's programmes, when their scheduled duration is less than 30 minutes, shall not be interrupted by advertising or by teleshopping. If their scheduled duration is 30 minutes or longer, the provisions of the previous paragraphs shall apply.

Article 12
Television advertising and teleshopping shall not:
> (a) prejudice respect for human dignity:
> (b) include any discrimination on grounds of race, sex or nationality;
> (c) be offensive to religious or political beliefs;
> (d) encourage behaviour prejudicial to health or to safety;
> (e) encourage behaviour prejudicial to the protection of the environment.

Article 13
All forms of television advertising and teleshopping for cigarettes and other tobacco products shall be prohibited.

Article 14
1. Television advertising for medicinal products and medical treatment available only on prescription in the Member State within whose jurisdiction the broadcaster falls shall be prohibited.

2. Teleshopping for medicinal products which are subject to a marketing authorization within the meaning of Council Directive 65/65/EEC of 26 January 1965 on the approximation of provisions laid down by law, regulation or administrative action relating to medicinal products (*), as well as teleshopping for medical treatment, shall be prohibited.

Article 15
Television advertising and teleshopping for alcoholic beverages shall comply with the following criteria:
> (a) it may not be aimed specifically at minors or, in particular, depict minors consuming these beverages;
> (b) it shall not link the consumption of alcohol to enhanced physical performance or to driving;
> (c) it shall not create the impression that the consumption of alcohol contributes towards social or sexual success;
> (d) it shall not claim that alcohol has therapeutic qualities or that it is a stimulant, a sedative or a means of resolving personal conflicts;
> (e) it shall not encourage immoderate consumption of alcohol or present abstinence or moderation in a negative light;
> (f) it shall not place emphasis on high alcoholic content as being a positive quality of the beverages.

Article 16
1. Television advertising shall not cause moral or physical detriment to minors, and shall therefore comply with the following criteria for their protection:

(*) OJ No. 22, 9.2.1965, p. 369. Directive as last amended by Directive 93/39/EEC (OJ No. L214, 24.8.1993, p. 22).

(a) it shall not directly exhort minors to buy a product or a service by exploiting their inexperience or credulity;

(b) it shall not directly encourage minors to persuade their parents or others to purchase the goods or services being advertised;

(c) it shall not exploit the special trust minors place in parents, teachers or other persons;

(d) it shall not unreasonably show minors in dangerous situations.

2.   Teleshopping shall comply with the requirements referred to in paragraph 1 and, in addition, shall not exhort minors to contract for the sale or rental of goods and services.

Article 17

1.   Sponsored television programmes shall meet the following requirements:

(a) the content and scheduling of sponsored programmes may in no circumstances be influenced by the sponsor in such a way as to affect the responsibility and editorial independence of the broadcaster in respect of programmes;

(b) they must be clearly identified as such by the name and/or logo of the sponsor at the beginning and/or the end of the programmes;

(c) they must not encourage the purchase or rental of the products or services of the sponsor or a third party, in particular by making special promotional references to those products or services.

2.   Television programmes may not be sponsored by undertakings whose principal activity is the manufacture or sale of cigarettes and other tobacco products.

3.   Sponsorship of television programmes by undertakings whose activities include the manufacture or sale of medicinal products and medical treatment may promote the name or the image of the undertaking but may not promote specific medicinal products or medical treatments available only on prescription in the Member State within whose jurisdiction the broadcaster falls.

4.   News and current affairs programmes may not be sponsored.

Article 18

1.   The proportion of transmission time devoted to teleshopping spots, advertising spots and other forms of advertising, with the exception of teleshopping windows within the meaning of Article 18a, shall not exceed 20 % of the daily transmission time.

The transmission time for advertising spots shall not exceed 15 % of the daily transmission time.

2.   The proportion of advertising spots and teleshopping spots within a given clock hour shall not exceed 20 %.

3.   For the purposes of this Article, advertising does not include:

— announcements made by the broadcaster in connection with its own programmes and ancillary products directly derived from those programmes;

— public service announcements and charity appeals broadcast free of charge.

Article 18a

1.   Windows devoted to teleshopping broadcast by a channel not exclusively devoted to teleshopping shall be of a minimum uninterrupted duration of 15 minutes.

2.   The maximum number of windows per day shall be eight. Their overall duration shall not exceed three hours per day. They must be clearly identified as teleshopping windows by optical and acoustic means.

Article 19

Chapters I, II, IV, V, VI, VIa and VII shall apply mutatis mutandis to channels exclusively devoted to teleshopping. Advertising on such channels shall be allowed within the daily limits established by Article 18(1). Article 18(2) shall not apply.

Article 19a

Chapters I, II, IV, V, VI, VIa and VII shall apply mutatis mutandis to channels exclusively devoted to self-promotion. Other forms of advertising on such channels shall be allowed within the limits established by Article 18(1) and (2). This provision in particular shall be subject to review in accordance with Article 26.

Article 20

Without prejudice to Article 3, Member States may, with due regard for Community law, lay down conditions other than those laid down in Article 11(2) to (5) and Articles 18 and 18a in respect of broadcasts intended solely for the national territory which cannot be received, directly or indirectly by the public, in one or more other Member States.

Article 21*

CHAPTER V   PROTECTION OF MINORS AND PUBLIC ORDER

Article 22

1.   Member States shall take appropriate measures to ensure that television broadcasts by broadcasters under their jurisdiction do not include any programmes which might seriously impair the physical, mental or moral development of minors, in particular programmes that involve pornography or gratuitous violence.

2.   The measures provided for in paragraph 1 shall also extend to other programmes which are likely to impair the physical, mental or moral development of minors, except where it is ensured, by selecting the time of the broadcast or by any technical measure, that minors in the area of transmission will not normally hear or see such broadcasts.

3.   Furthermore, when such programmes are broadcast in unencoded form Member States shall ensure that they are preceded by an acoustic warning or are identified by the presence of a visual symbol throughout their duration.

Article 22a

Member States shall ensure that broadcasts do not contain any incitement to hatred on grounds of race, sex, religion or nationality.

Article 22b

1.   The Commission shall attach particular importance to application of this Chapter in the report provided for in Article 26.

2.   The Commission shall within one year from the date of publication of this Directive, in liaison with the competent Member State authorities, carry out an investigation of the possible advantages and drawbacks of further measures with a view to facilitating the control exercised by parents or guardians over the programmes that minors may watch. This study shall consider, *inter alia*, the desirability of:

— the requirement for new television sets to be equipped with a technical device enabling parents or guardians to filter out certain programmes;
— the setting up of appropriate rating systems,
— encouraging family viewing policies and other educational and awareness measures,
— taking into account experience gained in this field in Europe and elsewhere as well as the views of interested parties such as broadcasters, producers, educationalists, media specialists and relevant associations.

* **Editor's Note:** Deleted by Directive 97/36 [OJ No. L220/60].

CHAPTER VI   RIGHT OF REPLY

Article 23
1.   Without prejudice to other provisions adopted by the Member States under civil, administrative or criminal law, any natural or legal person, regardless of nationality, whose legitimate interests, in particular reputation and good name, have been damaged by an assertion of incorrect facts in a television programme must have a right of reply or equivalent remedies. Member States shall ensure that the actual exercise of the right of reply or equivalent remedies is not hindered by the imposition of unreasonable terms or conditions. The reply shall be transmitted within a reasonable time subsequent to the request being substantiated and at a time and in a manner appropriate to the broadcast to which the request refers.
2.   A right of reply or equivalent remedies shall exist in relation to all broadcasters under the jurisdiction of a Member State.
3.   Member States shall adopt the measures needed to establish the right of reply or the equivalent remedies and shall determine the procedure to be followed for the exercise thereof. In particular, they shall ensure that a sufficient time span is allowed and that the procedures are such that the right or equivalent remedies can be exercised appropriately by natural or legal persons resident or established in other Member States.
4.   An application for exercise of the right of reply or the equivalent remedies may be rejected if such a reply is not justified according to the conditions laid down in paragraph 1, would involve a punishable act, would render the broadcaster liable to civil law proceedings or would transgress standards of public decency.
5.   Provision shall be made for procedures whereby disputes as to the exercise of the right of reply or the equivalent remedies can be subject to judicial review.

CHAPTER VIa   CONTACT COMMITTEE

Article 23a
1.   A contact committee shall be set up under the aegis of the Commission. It shall be composed of representatives of the competent authorities of the Member States. It shall be chaired by a representative of the Commission and meet either on his initiative or at the request of the delegation of a Member State.
2.   The tasks of this committee shall be:
   (a) to facilitate effective implementation of this Directive through regular consultation on any practical problems arising from its application, and particularly from the application of Article 2, as well as on any other matters on which exchanges of views are deemed useful;
   (b) to deliver own-initiative opinions or opinions requested by the Commission on the application by the Member States of the provisions of this Directive;
   (c) to be the forum for an exchange of views on what matters should be dealt with in the reports which Member States must submit pursuant to Article 4 (3), on the methodology of these, on the terms of reference for the independent study referred to in Article 25a, on the evaluation of tenders for this and on the study itself;
   (d) to discuss the outcome of regular consultations which the Commission holds with representatives of broadcasting organizations, producers, consumers, manufacturers, service providers and trade unions and the creative community;
   (e) to facilitate the exchange of information between the Member States and the Commission on the situation and the development of regulatory activities regarding television broadcasting services, taking account of the Community's audiovisual policy, as well as relevant developments in the technical field;

(f) to examine any development arising in the sector on which an exchange of views appears useful.

CHAPTER VII   FINAL PROVISIONS

Article 24

In fields which this Directive does not coordinate, it shall not affect the rights and obligations of Member States resulting from existing conventions dealing with telecommunications or broadcasting.

Article 25

1. Member States shall bring into force the laws, regulations and administrative provisions necessary to comply with this Directive not later than 3 October 1991. They shall forthwith inform the Commission thereof.

2.   Member States shall communicate to the Commission the text of the main provisions of national law which they adopt in the fields governed by this Directive.

Article 25a

A further review as provided for in Article 4 (4) shall take place before 30 June 2002. It shall take account of an independent study on the impact of the measures in question at both Community and national level.

Article 26

Not later than 31 December 2000, and every two years thereafter, the Commission shall submit to the European Parliament, the Council and the Economic and Social Committee a report on the application of this Directive as amended and, if necessary, make further proposals to adapt it to developments in the field of television broadcasting, in particular in the light of recent technological developments.

Article 27

This Directive is addressed to the Member States.

Done at Luxembourg, 3 October 1989.

For the Council
The President
R. DUMAS

Council Directive 91/250 of 14 May 1991 on the legal protection of computer programs
[OJ 1991, L122/42]*

THE COUNCIL OF THE EUROPEAN COMMUNITIES,

Having regard to the Treaty establishing the European Economic Community and in particular Article 100a thereof,

Having regard to the proposal from the Commission,[1]

---

* **Editor's Note:** As amended by Directive 93/98 [OJ 1993, L290/9].
[1] OJ C 91, 12.4.1989, p. 4; and OJ C 320, 20.12.1990, p. 22.

In cooperation with the European Parliament,[2]

Having regard to the opinion of the Economic and Social Committee,[3]

Whereas computer programs are at present not clearly protected in all Member States by existing legislation and such protection, where it exists, has different attributes;

Whereas the development of computer programs requires the investment of considerable human, technical and financial resources while computer programs can be copied at a fraction of the cost needed to develop them independently;

Whereas computer programs are playing an increasingly important role in a broad range of industries and computer program technology can accordingly be considered as being of fundamental importance for the Community's industrial development;

Whereas certain differences in the legal protection of computer programs offered by the laws of the Member States have direct and negative effects on the functioning of the common market as regards computer programs and such differences could well become greater as Member States introduce new legislation on this subject;

Whereas existing differences having such effects need to be removed and new ones prevented from arising, while differences not adversely affecting the functioning of the common market to a substantial degree need not be removed or prevented from arising;

Whereas the Community's legal framework on the protection of computer programs can accordingly in the first instance be limited to establishing that Member States should accord protection to computer programs under copyright law as literary works and, further, to establishing who and what should be protected, the exclusive rights on which protected persons should be able to rely in order to authorize or prohibit certain acts and for how long the protection should apply;

Whereas, for the purpose of this Directive, the term 'computer program' shall include programs in any form, including those which are incorporated into hardware; whereas this term also includes preparatory design work leading to the development of a computer program provided that the nature of the preparatory work is such that a computer program can result from it at a later stage;

Whereas, in respect of the criteria to be applied in determining whether or not a computer program is an original work, no tests as to the qualitative or aesthetic merits of the program should be applied;

Whereas the Community is fully committed to the promotion of international standardization;

Whereas the function of a computer program is to communicate and work together with other components of a computer system and with users and, for this purpose, a logical and, where appropriate, physical interconnection and interaction is required to permit all elements of software and hardware to work with other software and hardware and with users in all the ways in which they are intended to function;

Whereas the parts of the program which provide for such interconnection and interaction between elements of software and hardware are generally known as 'interfaces';

Whereas this functional interconnection and interaction is generally known as 'interoperability'; whereas such interoperability can be defined as the ability to exchange information and mutually to use the information which has been exchanged;

Whereas, for the avoidance of doubt, it has to be made clear that only the expression of a computer program is protected and that ideas and principles which underlie any element of a program, including those which underlie its interfaces, are not protected by copyright under this Directive;

[2] OJ C 231, 17.9.1990, p. 78; and Decision of 17 April 1991, not yet published in the Official Journal.
[3] OJ C 329, 30.12.1989, p. 4.

Whereas, in accordance with this principle of copyright, to the extent that logic, algorithms and programming languages comprise ideas and principles, those ideas and principles are not protected under this Directive;

Whereas, in accordance with the legislation and jurisprudence of the Member States and the international copyright conventions, the expression of those ideas and principles is to be protected by copyright;

Whereas, for the purposes of this Directive, the term 'rental' means the making available for use, for a limited period of time and for profit-making purposes, of a computer program or a copy thereof; whereas this term does not include public lending, which, accordingly, remains outside the scope of this Directive;

Whereas the exclusive rights of the author to prevent the unauthorized reproduction of his work have to be subject to a limited exception in the case of a computer program to allow the reproduction technically necessary for the use of that program by the lawful acquirer;

Whereas this means that the acts of loading and running necessary for the use of a copy of a program which has been lawfully acquired, and the act of correction of its errors, may not be prohibited by contract; whereas, in the absence of specific contractual provisions, including when a copy of the program has been sold, any other act necessary for the use of the copy of a program may be performed in accordance with its intended purpose by a lawful acquirer of that copy;

Whereas a person having a right to use a computer program should not be prevented from performing acts necessary to observe, study or test the functioning of the program, provided that these acts do not infringe the copyright in the program;

Whereas the unauthorized reproduction, translation, adaptation or transformation of the form of the code in which a copy of a computer program has been made available constitutes an infringement of the exclusive rights of the author;

Whereas, nevertheless, circumstances may exist when such a reproduction of the code and translation of its form within the meaning of Article 4(a) and (b) are indispensable to obtain the necessary information to achieve the interoperability of an independently created program with other programs;

Whereas it has therefore to be considered that in these limited circumstances only, performance of the acts of reproduction and translation by or on behalf of a person having a right to use a copy of the program is legitimate and compatible with fair practice and must therefore be deemed not to require the authorization of the rightholder;

Whereas an objective of this exception is to make it possible to connect all components of a computer system, including those of different manufacturers, so that they can work together;

Whereas such an exception to the author's exclusive rights may not be used in a way which prejudices the legitimate interests of the rightholder or which conflicts with a normal exploitation of the program;

Whereas, in order to remain in accordance with the provisions of the Berne Convention for the Protection of Literary and Artistic Works, the term of protection should be the life of the author and fifty years from the first of January of the year following the year of his death or, in the case of an anonymous or pseudonymous work, 50 years from the first of January of the year following the year in which the work is first published;

Whereas protection of computer programs under copyright laws should be without prejudice to the application, in appropriate cases, of other forms of protection; whereas, however, any contractual provisions contrary to Article 6 or to the exceptions provided for in Article 5(2) and (3) should be null and void;

Whereas the provisions of this Directive are without prejudice to the application of the competition rules under Articles 85 and 86 of the Treaty if a dominant supplier refuses to make information available which is necessary for interoperability as defined in this Directive;

Whereas the provisions of this Directive should be without prejudice to specific requirements of Community law already enacted in respect of the publication of interfaces in the telecommunications sector or Council Decisions relating to standardization in the field of information technology and telecommunication;

Whereas this Directive does not affect derogations provided for under national legislation in accordance with the Berne Convention on points not covered by this Directive,

HAS ADOPTED THIS DIRECTIVE:

Article 1   Object of protection

1.   In accordance with the provisions of this Directive, Member States shall protect computer programs, by copyright, as literary works within the meaning of the Berne Convention for the Protection of Literary and Artistic Works. For the purposes of this Directive, the term 'computer programs' shall include their preparatory design material.

2.   Protection in accordance with this Directive shall apply to the expression in any form of a computer program. Ideas and principles which underlie any element of a computer program, including those which underlie its interfaces, are not protected by copyright under this Directive.

3.   A computer program shall be protected if it is original in the sense that it is the author's own intellectual creation. No other criteria shall be applied to determine its eligibility for protection.

Article 2   Authorship of computer programs

1.   The author of a computer program shall be the natural person or group of natural persons who has created the program or, where the legislation of the Member State permits, the legal person designated as the rightholder by that legislation. Where collective works are recognized by the legislation of a Member State, the person considered by the legislation of the Member State to have created the work shall be deemed to be its author.

2.   In respect of a computer program created by a group of natural persons jointly, the exclusive rights shall be owned jointly.

3.   Where a computer program is created by an employee in the execution of his duties or following the instructions given by his employer, the employer exclusively shall be entitled to exercise all economic rights in the program so created, unless otherwise provided by contract.

Article 3   Beneficiaries of protection

Protection shall be granted to all natural or legal persons eligible under national copyright legislation as applied to literary works.

Article 4   Restricted Acts

Subject to the provisions of Articles 5 and 6, the exclusive rights of the rightholder within the meaning of Article 2, shall include the right to do or to authorize:

(a) the permanent or temporary reproduction of a computer program by any means and in any form, in part or in whole. Insofar as loading, displaying, running, transmission or storage of the computer program necessitate such reproduction, such acts shall be subject to authorization by the rightholder;

(b) the translation, adaptation, arrangement and any other alteration of a computer program and the reproduction of the results thereof, without prejudice to the rights of the person who alters the program;

(c) any form of distribution to the public, including the rental, of the original computer program or of copies thereof. The first sale in the Community of a copy of a program by the rightholder or with his consent shall exhaust the distribution right within the Community of that copy, with the exception of the right to control further rental of the program or a copy thereof.

Article 5   Exceptions to the restricted acts

1.   In the absence of specific contractual provisions, the acts referred to in Article 4(a) and (b) shall not require authorization by the rightholder where they are necessary for the use of the computer program by the lawful acquirer in accordance with its intended purpose, including for error correction.

2.   The making of a back-up copy by a person having a right to use the computer program may not be prevented by contract insofar as it is necessary for that use.

3.   The person having a right to use a copy of a computer program shall be entitled, without the authorization of the rightholder, to observe, study or test the functioning of the program in order to determine the ideas and principles which underlie any element of the program if he does so while performing any of the acts of loading, displaying, running, transmitting or storing the program which he is entitled to do.

Article 6   Decompilation

1.   The authorization of the rightholder shall not be required where reproduction of the code and translation of its form within the meaning of Article 4(a) and (b) are indispensable to obtain the information necessary to achieve the interoperability of an independently created computer program with other programs, provided that the following conditions are met:

(a)   these acts are performed by the licensee or by another person having a right to use a copy of a program, or on their behalf by a person authorized to do so;

(b)   the information necessary to achieve interoperability has not previously been readily available to the persons referred to in subparagraph (a); and

(c)   these acts are confined to the parts of the original program which are necessary to achieve interoperability.

2.   The provisions of paragraph 1 shall not permit the information obtained through its application:

(a)   to be used for goals other than to achieve the interoperability of the independently created computer program;

(b)   to be given to others, except when necessary for the interoperability of the independently created computer program; or

(c)   to be used for the development, production or marketing of a computer program substantially similar in its expression, or for any other act which infringes copyright.

3.   In accordance with the provisions of the Berne Convention for the protection of Literary and Artistic Works, the provisions of this Article may not be interpreted in such a way as to allow its application to be used in a manner which unreasonably prejudices the right holder's legitimate interests or conflicts with a normal exploitation of the computer program.

Article 7   Special measures of protection

1.   Without prejudice to the provisions of Articles 4, 5 and 6, Member States shall provide, in accordance with their national legislation, appropriate remedies against a person committing any of the acts listed in subparagraphs (a), (b) and (c) below:

(a)   any act of putting into circulation a copy of a computer program knowing, or having reason to believe, that it is an infringing copy;

(b)   the possession, for commercial purposes, of a copy of a computer program knowing, or having reason to believe, that it is an infringing copy;

(c)   any act of putting into circulation, or the possession for commercial purposes of, any means the sole intended purpose of which is to facilitate the unauthorized removal or circumvention of any technical device which may have been applied to protect a computer program.

2.   Any infringing copy of a computer program shall be liable to seizure in accordance with the legislation of the Member State concerned.

3.   Member States may provide for the seizure of any means referred to in paragraph 1(c).

Article 8   (Repealed)[4]

Article 9   Continued application of other legal provisions
   1.   The provisions of this Directive shall be without prejudice to any other legal provisions such as those concerning patent rights, trade-marks, unfair competition, trade secrets, protection of semi-conductor products or the law of contract. Any contractual provisions contrary to Article 6 or to the exceptions provided for in Article 5(2) and (3) shall be null and void.
   2.   The provisions of this Directive shall apply also to programs created before 1 January 1993 without prejudice to any acts concluded and rights acquired before that date.

Article 10   Final provisions
   1.   Member States shall bring into force the laws, regulations and administrative provisions necessary to comply with this Directive before 1 January 1993. When Member States adopt these measures, the latter shall contain a reference to this Directive or shall be accompanied by such reference on the occasion of their official publication. The methods of making such a reference shall be laid down by the Member States.
   2.   Member States shall communicate to the Commission the provisions of national law which they adopt in the field governed by this Directive.

Article 11
This Directive is addressed to the Member States. Done at Brussels, 14 May 1991.

For the Council
The President
J. F. POOS

Council Directive 92/100/EEC of 19 November 1992 on rental right and lending right and on certain rights related to copyright in the field of intellectual property

[OJ 1992, L 346/61]*

THE COUNCIL OF THE EUROPEAN COMMUNITIES,
   Having regard to the Treaty establishing the European Economic Community, and in particular Articles 57(2), 66 and 100a thereof,
   Having regard to the proposal from the Commission,[1]
   In cooperation with the European Parliament,[2]
   Having regard to the opinion of the Economic and Social Committee,[3]

   Whereas differences exist in the legal protection provided by the laws and practices of the Member States for copyright works and subject matter of related rights protection as regards

---

[4]   **Editor's Note:** Repealed by Article 11 of Directive 93/98 [OJ 1993, L290/9].

*   **Editor's Note:** As amended by Directives 93/98 [OJ 1993, L209/9] and 2001/29 [OJ 2001, L167/10].
[1]   OJ C 53, 28.2.1991, p. 35 and OJ C 128, 20.5.1992, p. 8.
[2]   OJ C 67, 16.3.1992, p. 92 and Decision of 28 October 1992 (not yet published in the Official Journal).
[3]   OJ C 269, 14.10.1991, p. 54.

rental and lending; whereas such differences are sources of barriers to trade and distortions of competition which impede the achievement and proper functioning of the internal market;

Whereas such differences in legal protection could well become greater as Member States adopt new and different legislation or as national case-law interpreting such legislation develops differently;

Whereas such differences should therefore be eliminated in accordance with the objective of introducing an area without internal frontiers as set out in Article 8a of the Treaty so as to institute, pursuant to Article 3(f) of the Treaty, a system ensuring that competition in the common market is not distorted;

Whereas rental and lending of copyright works and the subject matter of related rights protection is playing an increasingly important role in particular for authors, performers and producers of phonograms and films; whereas piracy is becoming an increasing threat;

Whereas the adequate protection of copyright works and subject matter of related rights protection by rental and lending rights as well as the protection of the subject matter of related rights protection by the fixation right, reproduction right, distribution right, right to broadcast and communication to the public can accordingly be considered as being of fundamental importance for the Community's economic and cultural development;

Whereas copyright and related rights protection must adapt to new economic developments such as new forms of exploitation;

Whereas the creative and artistic work of authors and performers necessitates an adequate income as a basis for further creative and artistic work, and the investments required particularly for the production of phonograms and films are especially high and risky;

Whereas the possibility for securing that income and recouping that investment can only effectively be guaranteed through adequate legal protection of the rightholders concerned;

Whereas these creative, artistic and entrepreneurial activities are, to a large extent, activities of self-employed persons; whereas the pursuit of such activities must be made easier by providing a harmonized legal protection within the Community;

Whereas, to the extent that these activities principally constitute services, their provision must equally be facilitated by the establishment in the Community of a harmonized legal framework;

Whereas the legislation of the Member States should be approximated in such a way so as not to conflict with the international conventions on which many Member States' copyright and related rights laws are based;

Whereas the Community's legal framework on the rental right and lending right and on certain rights related to copyright can be limited to establishing that Member States provide rights with respect to rental and lending for certain groups of rightholders and further to establishing the rights of fixation, reproduction, distribution, broadcasting and communication to the public for certain groups of rightholders in the field of related rights protection;

Whereas it is necessary to define the concepts of rental and lending for the purposes of this Directive;

Whereas it is desirable, with a view to clarity, to exclude from rental and lending within the meaning of this Directive certain forms of making available, as for instance making available phonograms or films (cinematographic or audiovisual works or moving images, whether or not accompanied by sound) for the purpose of public performance or broadcasting, making available for the purpose of exhibition, or making available for on-the-spot reference use;

Whereas lending within the meaning of this Directive does not include making available between establishments which are accessible to the public;

Whereas, where lending by an establishment accessible to the public gives rise to a payment the amount of which does not go beyond what is necessary to cover the operating costs of the establishment, there is no direct or indirect economic or commercial advantage within the meaning of this Directive;

Whereas it is necessary to introduce arrangements ensuring that an unwaivable equitable remuneration is obtained by authors and performers who must retain the possibility to entrust the administration of this right to collecting societies representing them;

Whereas the equitable remuneration may be paid on the basis of one or several payments an any time on or after the conclusion of the contract;

Whereas the equitable remuneration must take account of the importance of the contribution of the authors and performers concerned to the phonogram or film;

Whereas it is also necessary to protect the rights at least of authors as regards public lending by providing for specific arrangements; whereas, however, any measures based on Article 5 of this Directive have to comply with Community law, in particular with Article 7 of the Treaty;

Whereas the provisions of Chapter II do not prevent Member States from extending the presumption set out in Article 2(5) to the exclusive rights included in that chapter; whereas furthermore the provisions of Chapter II do not prevent Member States from providing for a rebuttable presumption of the authorization of exploitation in respect of the exclusive rights of performers provided for in those articles, in so far as such presumption is compatible with the International Convention for the Protection of Performers, Producers of Phonograms and Broadcasting Organizations (hereinafter referred to as the Rome Convention);

Whereas Member States may provide for more far-reaching protection for owners of rights related to copyright than that required by Article 8 of this Directive;

Whereas the harmonized rental and lending rights and the harmonized protection in the field of rights related to copyright should not be exercised in a way which constitutes a disguised restriction on trade between Member States or in a way which is contrary to the rule of media exploitation chronology, as recognized in the Judgment handed down in Société Cinéthèque v. FNCF,[4]

HAS ADOPTED THIS DIRECTIVE:

CHAPTER I   RENTAL AND LENDING RIGHT

Article 1   Object of harmonization

1.   In accordance with the provisions of this Chapter, Member States shall provide, subject to Article 5, a right to authorize or prohibit the rental and lending of originals and copies of copyright works, and other subject matter as set out in Article 2(1).

2.   For the purposes of this Directive, 'rental' means making available for use, for a limited period of time and for direct or indirect economic or commercial advantage.

3.   For the purposes of this Directive, 'lending' means making available for use, for a limited period of time and not for direct or indirect economic or commercial advantage, when it is made through establishments which are accessible to the public.

4.   The rights referred to in paragraph 1 shall not be exhausted by any sale or other act of distribution of originals and copies of copyright works and other subject matter as set out in Article 2(1).

Article 2   Rightholders and subject matter of rental and lending right

1.   The exclusive right to authorize or prohibit rental and lending shall belong:
— to the author in respect of the original and copies of his work,
— to the performer in respect of fixations of his performance,
— to the phonogram producer in respect of his phonograms, and
— to the producer of the first fixation of a film in respect of the original and copies of his film. For the purposes of this Directive, the term 'film' shall designate a cinematographic or audiovisual work or moving images, whether or not accompanied by sound.

---

[4] Cases 60/84 and 61/84, ECR 1985, p. 2605.

2.   For the purposes of this Directive the principal director of a cinematographic or audiovisual work shall be considered as its author or one of its authors. Member States may provide for others to be considered as its co-authors.

3.   This Directive does not cover rental and lending rights in relation to buildings and to works of applied art.

4.   The rights referred to in paragraph 1 may be transferred, assigned or subject to the granting of contractual licences.

5.   Without prejudice to paragraph 7, when a contract concerning film production is concluded, individual or collectively, by performers with a film producer, the performer covered by this contract shall be presumed, subject to contractual clauses to the contrary, to have transferred his rental right, subject to Article 4.

6.   Member States may provide for a similar presumption as set out in paragraph 5 with respect to authors.

7.   Member States may provide that the signing of a contract concluded between a performer and a film producer concerning the production of a film has the effect of authorizing rental, provided that such contract provides for an equitable remuneration within the meaning of Article 4. Member States may also provide that this paragraph shall apply mutatis mutandis to the rights included in Chapter II.

Article 3   Rental of computer programs
This Directive shall be without prejudice to Article 4(c) of Council Directive 91/250/EEC of 14 May 1991 on the legal protection of computer programs.[5]

Article 4   Unwaivable right to equitable remuneration
1.   Where an author or performer has transferred or assigned his rental right concerning a phonogram or an original or copy of a film to a phonogram or film producer, that author or performer shall retain the right to obtain an equitable remuneration for the rental.

2.   The right to obtain an equitable remuneration for rental cannot be waived by authors or performers.

3.   The administration of this right to obtain an equitable remuneration may be entrusted to collecting societies representing authors or performers.

4.   Member States may regulate whether and to what extent administration by collecting societies of the right to obtain an equitable remuneration may be imposed, as well as the question from whom this remuneration may be claimed or collected.

Article 5   Derogation from the exclusive public lending right
1.   Member States may derogate from the exclusive right provided for in Article 1 in respect of public lending, provided that at least authors obtain a remuneration for such lending. Member States shall be free to determine this remuneration taking account of their cultural promotion objectives.

2.   When Member States do not apply the exclusive lending right provided for in Article 1 as regards phonograms, films and computer programs, they shall introduce, at least for authors, a remuneration.

3.   Member States may exempt certain categories of establishments from the payment of the remuneration referred to in paragraphs 1 and 2.

4.   The Commission, in cooperation with the Member States, shall draw up before 1 July 1997 a report on public lending in the Community. It shall forward this report to the European Parliament and to the Council.

---

[5] OJ No. 122, 17.5.1999, p. 42.

CHAPTER II   RIGHTS RELATED TO COPYRIGHT

Article 6   Fixation right

1.   Member States shall provide for performers the exclusive right to authorize or prohibit the fixation of their performances.

2.   Member States shall provide for broadcasting organizations the exclusive right to authorize or prohibit the fixation of their broadcasts, whether these broadcasts are transmitted by wire or over the air, including by cable or satellite.

3.   A cable distributor shall not have the right provided for in paragraph 2 where it merely retransmits by cable the broadcasts of broadcasting organizations.

Article 7*

Article 8   Broadcasting and communication to the public

1.   Member States shall provide for performers the exclusive right to authorize or prohibit the broadcasting by wireless means and the communication to the public of their performances, except where the performance is itself already a broadcast performance or is made from a fixation.

2.   Member States shall provide a right in order to ensure that a single equitable remuneration is paid by the user, if a phonogram published for commercial purposes, or a reproduction of such phonogram, is used for broadcasting by wireless means or for any communication to the public, and to ensure that this remuneration is shared between the relevant performers and phonogram producers. Member States may, in the absence of agreement between the performers and phonogram producers, lay down the conditions as to the sharing of this remuneration between them.

3.   Member States shall provide for broadcasting organizations the exclusive right to authorize or prohibit the rebroadcasting of their broadcasts by wireless means, as well as the communication to the public of their broadcasts if such communication is made in places accessible to the public against payment of an entrance fee.

Article 9   Distribution right

1.   Member States shall provide
— for performers, in respect of fixations of their performances,
— for phonogram producers, in respect of their phonograms,
— for producers of the first fixations of films, in respect of the original and copies of their films,
— for broadcasting organizations, in respect of fixations of their broadcast as set out in Article 6(2), the exclusive right to make available these objects, including copies thereof, to the public by sale or otherwise, hereafter referred to as the 'distribution right'.

2.   The distribution right shall not be exhausted within the Community in respect of an object as referred to in paragraph 1, except where the first sale in the Community of that object is made by the rightholder or with his consent.

3.   The distribution right shall be without prejudice to the specific provisions of Chapter I, in particular Article 1(4).

4.   The distribution right may be transferred, assigned or subject to the granting of contractual licences.

Article 10   Limitations to rights

1.   Member States may provide for limitations to the rights referred to in Chapter II in respect of:
(a) private use;
(b) use of short excerpts in connection with the reporting of current events;

* **Editor's Note:** Repealed by Directive 2001/29 [OJ 2001, L167/10].

(c) ephemeral fixation by a broadcasting organization by means of its own facilities and for its own broadcasts;

(d) use solely for the purposes of teaching or scientific research.

2.   Irrespective of paragraph 1, any Member State may provide for the same kinds of limitations with regard to the protection of performers, producers of phonograms, broadcasting organizations and of producers of the first fixations of films, as it provides for in connection with the protection of copyright in literary and artistic works. However, compulsory licences may be provided for only to the extent to which they are compatible with the Rome Convention.

3.   The limitations shall only be applied in certain special cases which do not conflict with a normal exploitation of the subject-matter and do not unreasonably prejudice the legitimate interests of the rightholder.*

CHAPTER III   DURATION

Article 11**   (Repealed)

Article 12   (Repealed)

CHAPTER IV   COMMON PROVISIONS

Article 13   Application in time

1.   This Directive shall apply in respect of all copyright works, performances, phonograms, broadcasts and first fixations of films referred to in this Directive which are, on 1 July 1994, still protected by the legislation of the Member States in the field of copyright and related rights or meet the criteria for protection under the provisions of this Directive on that date.

2.   This Directive shall apply without prejudice to any acts of exploitation performed before 1 July 1994.

3.   Member States may provide that the rightholders are deemed to have given their authorization to the rental or lending of an object referred to in Article 2 (1) which is proven to have been made available to third parties for this purpose or to have been acquired before 1 July 1994. However, in particular where such an object is a digital recording, Member States may provide that rightholders shall have a right to obtain an adequate remuneration for the rental or lending of that object.

4.   Member States need not apply the provisions of Article 2(2) to cinematographic or audiovisual works created before 1 July 1994.

5.   Member States may determine the date as from which the Article 2(2) shall apply, provided that that date is no later than 1 July 1997.

6.   This Directive shall, without prejudice to paragraph 3 and subject to paragraphs 8 and 9, not affect any contracts concluded before the date of its adoption.

7.   Member States may provide, subject to the provisions of paragraphs 8 and 9, that when rightholders who acquire new rights under the national provisions adopted in implementation of this Directive have, before 1 July 1994, given their consent for exploitation, they shall be presumed to have transferred the new exclusive rights.

8.   Member States may determine the date as from which the unwaivable right to an equitable remuneration referred to in Article 4 exists, provided that that date is no later than 1 July 1997.

9.   For contracts concluded before 1 July 1994, the unwaivable right to an equitable

---

* **Editor's Note:** Article 10(3) amended by Directive 2001/29 [OJ 2001, L167/10].

** **Editor's Note:** Articles 11 and 12 repealed by Directive 93/98 [OJ 1993, L209/9].

remuneration provided for in Article 4 shall apply only where authors or performers or those representing them have submitted a request to that effect before 1 January 1997. In the absence of agreement between rightholders concerning the level of remuneration, Member States may fix the level of equitable remuneration.

Article 14   Relation between copyright and related rights
Protection of copyright-related rights under this Directive shall leave intact and shall in no way affect the protection of copyright.

Article 15   Final provisions
1.   Member States shall bring into force the laws, regulations and administrative provisions necessary to comply with this Directive not later than 1 July 1994. They shall forthwith inform the Commission thereof.

When Member States adopt these measures, they shall contain a reference to this Directive or shall be accompanied by such reference at the time of their official publication.

The methods of making such a reference shall be laid down by the Member States.

2.   Member States shall communicate to the Commission the main provisions of domestic law which they adopt in the field covered by this Directive.

Article 16
This Directive is addressed to the Member States.

Done at Brussels, 19 November 1992.

For the Council
The President
E. LEIGH

Council Directive 93/83/EEC of 27 September 1993 on the coordination of certain rules concerning copyright and rights related to copyright applicable to satellite broadcasting and cable retransmission
[OJ 1993, L248/15]

THE COUNCIL OF THE EUROPEAN COMMUNITIES,
Having regard to the Treaty establishing the European Economic Community, and in particular Articles 57(2) and 66 thereof,
Having regard to the proposal from the Commission,[1]
In cooperation with the European Parliament,[2]
Having regard to the opinion of the Economic and Social Committee,[3]

(1) Whereas the objectives of the Community as laid down in the Treaty include establishing an ever closer union among the peoples of Europe, fostering closer relations between the States belonging to the Community and ensuring the economic and social progress of the Community countries by common action to eliminate the barriers which divide Europe;

(2) Whereas, to that end, the Treaty provides for the establishment of a common market and an area without internal frontiers; whereas measures to achieve this include the abolition of obstacles to the free movement of services and the institution of a system ensuring that competition in the common market is not distorted;

[1] OJ C 255, 1.10.1991, p. 3 and OJ C 25, 28.1.1993, p. 43.
[2] OJ C 305, 23.11.1992, p. 129 and OJ C 255, 20.9.1993.
[3] OJ C 98, 21.4.1992, p. 44.

Whereas, to that end, the Council may adopt directives for the coordination of the provisions laid down by law, regulation or administrative action in Member States concerning the taking up and pursuit of activities as self-employed persons;

(3) Whereas broadcasts transmitted across frontiers within the Community, in particular by satellite and cable, are one of the most important ways of pursuing these Community objectives, which are at the same time political, economic, social, cultural and legal;

(4) Whereas the Council has already adopted Directive 89/552/EEC of 3 October 1989 on the coordination of certain provisions laid down by law, regulation or administrative action in Member States concerning the pursuit of television broadcasting activities,[4] which makes provision for the promotion of the distribution and production of European television programmes and for advertising and sponsorship, the protection of minors and the right of reply;

(5) Whereas, however, the achievement of these objectives in respect of cross-border satellite broadcasting and the cable retransmission of programmes from other Member States is currently still obstructed by a series of differences between national rules of copyright and some degree of legal uncertainty; whereas this means that holders of rights are exposed to the threat of seeing their works exploited without payment of remuneration or that the individual holders of exclusive rights in various Member States block the exploitation of their rights; whereas the legal uncertainty in particular constitutes a direct obstacle in the free circulation of programmes within the Community;

(6) Whereas a distinction is currently drawn for copyright purposes between communication to the public by direct satellite and communication to the public by communications satellite; whereas, since individual reception is possible and affordable nowadays with both types of satellite, there is no longer any justification for this differing legal treatment;

(7) Whereas the free broadcasting of programmes is further impeded by the current legal uncertainty over whether broadcasting by a satellite whose signals can be received directly affects the rights in the country of transmission only or in all countries of reception together; whereas, since communications satellites and direct satellites are treated alike for copyright purposes, this legal uncertainty now affects almost all programmes broadcast in the Community by satellite;

(8) Whereas, furthermore, legal certainty, which is a prerequisite for the free movement of broadcasts within the Community, is missing where programmes transmitted across frontiers are fed into and retransmitted through cable networks;

(9) Whereas the development of the acquisition of rights on a contractual basis by authorization is already making a vigorous contribution to the creation of the desired European audiovisual area;

Whereas the continuation of such contractual agreements should be ensured and their smooth application in practice should be promoted wherever possible;

(10) Whereas at present cable operators in particular cannot be sure that they have actually acquired all the programme rights covered by such an agreement;

(11) Whereas, lastly, parties in different Member States are not all similarly bound by obligations which prevent them from refusing without valid reason to negotiate on the acquisition of the rights necessary for cable distribution or allowing such negotiations to fail;

(12) Whereas the legal framework for the creation of a single audiovisual area laid down in Directive 89/552/EEC must, therefore, be supplemented with reference to copyright;

(13) Whereas, therefore, an end should be put to the differences of treatment of the transmission of programmes by communications satellite which exist in the Member States, so that the vital distinction throughout the Community becomes whether works and other protected subject matter are communicated to the public; whereas this will also ensure equal treatment of the suppliers of cross-border broadcasts, regardless of whether they use a direct broadcasting satellite or a communications satellite;

---

[4] OJ L 298, 17.10.1989, p. 23.

(14) Whereas the legal uncertainty regarding the rights to be acquired which impedes cross-border satellite broadcasting should be overcome by defining the notion of communication to the public by satellite at a Community level; whereas this definition should at the same time specify where the act of communication takes place; whereas such a definition is necessary to avoid the cumulative application of several national laws to one single act of broadcasting; whereas communication to the public by satellite occurs only when, and in the Member State where, the programme-carrying signals are introduced under the control and responsibility of the broadcasting organization into an uninterrupted chain of communication leading to the satellite and down towards the earth; whereas normal technical procedures relating to the programme-carrying signals should not be considered as interruptions to the chain of broadcasting;

(15) Whereas the acquisition on a contractual basis of exclusive broadcasting rights should comply with any legislation on copyright and rights related to copyright in the Member State in which communication to the public by satellite occurs;

(16) Whereas the principle of contractual freedom on which this Directive is based will make it possible to continue limiting the exploitation of these rights, especially as far as certain technical means of transmission or certain language versions are concerned;

(17) Whereas, in arriving at the amount of the payment to be made for the rights acquired, the parties should take account of all aspects of the broadcast, such as the actual audience, the potential audience and the language version;

(18) Whereas the application of the country-of-origin principle contained in this Directive could pose a problem with regard to existing contracts; whereas this Directive should provide for a period of five years for existing contracts to be adapted, where necessary, in the light of the Directive; whereas the said country-of-origin principle should not, therefore, apply to existing contracts which expire before 1 January 2000; whereas if by that date parties still have an interest in the contract, the same parties should be entitled to renegotiate the conditions of the contract;

(19) Whereas existing international co-production agreements must be interpreted in the light of the economic purpose and scope envisaged by the parties upon signature; whereas in the past international co-production agreements have often not expressly and specifically addressed communication to the public by satellite within the meaning of this Directive a particular form of exploitation; whereas the underlying philosophy of many existing international co-production agreements is that the rights in the co-production are exercised separately and independently by each co-producer, by dividing the exploitation rights between them along territorial lines; whereas, as a general rule, in the situation where a communication to the public by satellite authorized by one co-producer would prejudice the value of the exploitation rights of another co-producer, the interpretation of such an existing agreement would normally suggest that the latter co-producer would have to give his consent to the authorization, by the former co-producer, of the communication to the public by satellite; whereas the language exclusivity of the latter co-producer will be prejudiced where the language version or versions of the communication to the public, including where the version is dubbed or subtitled, coincide(s) with the language or the languages widely understood in the territory allotted by the agreement to the latter co-producer; whereas the notion of exclusivity should be understood in a wider sense where the communication to the public by satellite concerns a work which consists merely of images and contains no dialogue or subtitles; whereas a clear rule is necessary in cases where the international co-production agreement does not expressly regulate the division of rights in the specific case of communication to the public by satellite within the meaning of this Directive;

(20) Whereas communications to the public by satellite from non-member countries will under certain conditions be deemed to occur within a Member State of the Community;

(21) Whereas it is necessary to ensure that protection for authors, performers, producers of phonograms and broadcasting organizations is accorded in all Member States and that this

protection is not subject to a statutory licence system; whereas only in this way is it possible to ensure that any difference in the level of protection within the common market will not create distortions of competition;

(22) Whereas the advent of new technologies is likely to have an impact on both the quality and the quantity of the exploitation of works and other subject matter;

(23) Whereas in the light of these developments the level of protection granted pursuant to this Directive to all rightholders in the areas covered by this Directive should remain under consideration;

(24) Whereas the harmonization of legislation envisaged in this Directive entails the harmonization of the provisions ensuring a high level of protection of authors, performers, phonogram producers and broadcasting organizations; whereas this harmonization should not allow a broadcasting organization to take advantage of differences in levels of protection by relocating activities, to the detriment of audiovisual productions;

(25) Whereas the protection provided for rights related to copyright should be aligned on that contained in Council Directive 92/100/EEC of 19 November 1992 on rental right and lending right and on certain rights related to copyright in the field of intellectual property[5] for the purposes of communication to the public by satellite;

Whereas, in particular, this will ensure that peformers and phonogram producers are guaranteed an appropriate remuneration for the communication to the public by satellite of their performances or phonograms;

(26) Whereas the provisions of Article 4 do not prevent Member States from extending the presumption set out in Article 2(5) of Directive 92/100/EEC to the exclusive rights referred to in Article 4;

Whereas, furthermore, the provisions of Article 4 do not prevent Member States from providing for a rebuttable presumption of the authorization of exploitation in respect of the exclusive rights of performers referred to in that Article, insofar as such presumption is compatible with the International Convention for the Protection of Performers, Producers of Phonograms and Broadcasting Organizations;

(27) Whereas the cable retransmission of programmes from other Member States is an act subject to copyright and, as the case may be, rights related to copyright;

Whereas the cable operator must, therefore, obtain the authorization from every holder of rights in each part of the programme retransmitted;

Whereas, pursuant to this Directive, the authorizations should be granted contractually unless a temporary exception is provided for in the case of existing legal licence schemes;

(28) Whereas, in order to ensure that the smooth operation of contractual arrangements is not called into question by the intervention of outsiders holding rights in individual parts of the programme, provision should be made, through the obligation to have recourse to a collecting society, for the exclusive collective exercise of the authorization right to the extent that this is required by the special features of cable retransmission;

Whereas the authorization right as such remains intact and only the exercise of this right is regulated to some extent, so that the right to authorize a cable retransmission can still be assigned;

Whereas this Directive does not affect the exercise of moral rights;

(29) Whereas the exemption provided for in Article 10 should not limit the choice of holders of rights to transfer their rights to a collecting society and thereby have a direct share in the remuneration paid by the cable distributor for cable retransmission;

(30) Whereas contractual arrangements regarding the authorization of cable retransmission should be promoted by additional measures;

Whereas a party seeking the conclusion of a general contract should, for its part, be obliged to submit collective proposals for an agreement;

---

[5] OJ L 346, 27.11.1992, p. 61.

Whereas, furthermore, any party shall be entitled, at any moment, to call upon the assistance of impartial mediators whose task is to assist negotiations and who may submit proposals;

Whereas any such proposals and any opposition thereto should be served on the parties concerned in accordance with the applicable rules concerning the service of legal documents, in particular as set out in existing international conventions;

Whereas, finally, it is necessary to ensure that the negotiations are not blocked without valid justification or that individual holders are not prevented without valid justification from taking part in the negotiations;

Whereas none of these measures for the promotion of the acquisition of rights calls into question the contractual nature of the acquisition of cable retransmission rights;

(31) Whereas for a transitional period Member States should be allowed to retain existing bodies with jurisdiction in their territory over cases where the right to retransmit a programme by cable to the public has been unreasonably refused or offered on unreasonable terms by a broadcasting organization;

Whereas it is understood that the right of parties concerned to be heard by the body should be guaranteed and that the existence of the body should not prevent the parties concerned from having normal access to the courts;

(32) Whereas, however, Community rules are not needed to deal with all of those matters, the effects of which perhaps with some commercially insignificant exceptions, are felt only inside the borders of a single Member State;

(33) Whereas minimum rules should be laid down in order to establish and guarantee free and uninterrupted cross-border broadcasting by satellite and simultaneous, unaltered cable retransmission of programmes broadcast from other Member States, on an essentially contractual basis;

(34) Whereas this Directive should not prejudice further harmonization in the field of copyright and rights related to copyright and the collective administration of such rights;

Whereas the possibility for Member States to regulate the activities of collecting societies should not prejudice the freedom of contractual negotiation of the rights provided for in this Directive, on the understanding that such negotiation takes place within the framework of general or specific national rules with regard to competition law or the prevention of abuse of monopolies;

(35) Whereas it should, therefore, be for the Member States to supplement the general provisions needed to achieve the objectives of this Directive by taking legislative and administrative measures in their domestic law, provided that these do not run counter to the objectives of this Directive and are compatible with Community law;

(36) Whereas this Directive does not affect the applicability of the competition rules in Articles 85 and 86 of the Treaty,

HAS ADOPTED THIS DIRECTIVE:

CHAPTER I   DEFINITIONS

Article 1   Definitions

1. For the purpose of this Directive, 'satellite' means any satellilte operating on frequency bands which, under telecommunications law, are reserved for the broadcast of signals for reception by the public or which are reserved for closed, point-to-point communication. In the latter case, however, the circumstances in which individual reception of the signals takes place must be comparable to those which apply in the first case.

2. (a)   For the purpose of this Directive, 'communication to the public by satellite' means the act of introducing, under the control and responsibility of the broadcasting organization, the programme-carrying signals intended for reception by the

public into an uninterrupted chain of communication leading to the satellite and down towards the earth.

(b) The act of communication to the public by satellite occurs solely in the Member State where, under the control and responsibility of the broadcasting organization, the programme-carrying signals are introduced into an uninterrupted chain of communication leading to the satellite and down towards the earth.

(c) If the programme-carrying signals are encrypted, then there is communication to the public by satellite on condition that the means for decrypting the broadcast are provided to the public by the broadcasting organization or with its consent.

(d) Where an act of communication to the public by satellite occurs in a non-Community State which does not provide the level of protection provided for under Chapter II,

(i) if the programme-carrying signals are transmitted to the satellite from an uplink situation situated in a Member State, that act of communication to the public by satellite shall be deemed to have occurred in that Member State and the rights provided for under Chapter II shall be exercisable against the person operating the uplink station; or

(ii) if there is no use of an uplink station situated in a Member State but a broadcasting organization established in a Member State has commissioned the act of communication to the public by satellite, that act shall be deemed to have occurred in the Member State in which the broadcasting organization has its principal establishment in the Community and the rights provided for under Chapter II shall be exercisable against the broadcasting organization.

3.   For the purposes of this Directive, 'cable retransmission' means the simultaneous, unaltered and unabridged retransmission by a cable or microwave system for reception by the public of an initial transmission from another Member State, by wire or over the air, including that by satellite, of television or radio programmes intended for reception by the public.

4.   For the purposes of this Directive 'collecting society' means any organization which manages or administers copyright or rights related to copyright as its sole purpose or as one of its main purposes.

5.   For the purposes of this Directive, the principal director of a cinematographic or audiovisual work shall be considered as its author or one of its authors. Member States may provide for others to be considered as its co-authors.

CHAPTER II   BROADCASTING OF PROGRAMMES BY SATELLITE

Article 2   Broadcasting right

Member States shall provide an exclusive right for the author to authorize the communication to the public by satellite of copyright works, subject to the provisions set out in this chapter.

Article 3   Acquisition of broadcasting rights

1.   Member States shall ensure that the authorization referred to in Article 2 may be acquired only be agreement.

2.   A Member State may provide that a collective agreement between a collecting society and a broadcasting organization concerning a given category of works may be extended to rightholders of the same category who are not represented by the collecting society, provided that:

— the communication to the public by satellite simulcasts a terrestrial broadcast by the same broadcaster, and

— the unrepresented rightholder shall, at any time, have the possibility of excluding the extension of the collective agreement to his works and of exercising his rights either individually or collectively.

3.   Paragraph 2 shall not apply to cinematographic works, including works created by a process analogous to cinematography.

4.   Where the law of a Member State provides for the extension of a collective agreement in accordance with the provisions of paragraph 2, that Member States shall inform the Commission which broadcasting organizations are entitled to avail themselves of that law. The Commission shall publish this information in the Official Journal of the European Communities (C series).

Article 4   Rights of performers, phonogram producers and broadcasting organizations

1.   For the purposes of communication to the public by satellite, the rights of performers, phonogram producers and broadcasting organizations shall be protected in accordance with the provisions of Articles 6, 7, 8 and 10 of Directive 92/100/EEC.

2.   For the purposes of paragraph 1, 'broadcasting by wireless means' in Directive 92/100/EEC shall be understood as including communication to the public by satellite.

3.   With regard to the exercise of the rights referred to in paragraph 1, Articles 2(7) and 12 of Directive 92/100/EEC shall apply.

Article 5   Relation between copyright and related rights

Protection of copyright-related rights under this Directive shall leave intact and shall in no way affect the protection of copyright.

Article 6   Minimum protection

1.   Member States may provide for more far-reaching protection for holders of rights related to copyright than that required by Article 8 of Directive 92/100/EEC.

2.   In applying paragraph 1 Member States shall observe the definitions contained in Article 1 (1) and (2).

Article 7   Transitional provisions

1.   With regard to the application in time of the rights referred to in Article 4(1) of this Directive, Article 13(1), (2), (6) and (7) of Directive 92/100/EEC shall apply. Article 13(4) and (5) of Directive 92/100/EEC shall apply mutatis mutandis.

2.   Agreements concerning the exploitation of works and other protected subject matter which are in force on the date mentioned in Article 14(1) shall be subject to the provisions of Articles 1(2), 2 and 3 as from 1 January 2000 if they expire after that date.

3.   When an international co-production agreement concluded before the date mentioned in Article 14(1) between a co-producer from a Member State and one or more co-producers from other Member States or third countries expressly provides for a system of division of exploitation rights between the co-producers by geographical areas for all means of communication to the public, without distinguishing the arrangement applicable to communication to the public by satellite from the provisions applicable to the other means of communication, and where communication to the public by satellite of the co-production would prejudice the exclusivity, in particular the language exclusivity, of one of the co-producers or his assignees in a given territory, the authorization by one of the co-producers or his assignees for a communication to the public by satellite shall require the prior consent of the holder of that exclusivity, whether co-producer or assignee.

CHAPTER III   CABLE RETRANSMISSION

Article 8   Cable retransmission right

1.   Member States shall ensure that when programmes from other Member States are retransmitted by cable in their territory the applicable copyright and related rights are observed and that such retransmission takes place on the basis of individual or collective contractual agreements between copyright owners, holders of related rights and cable operators.

2.   Notwithstanding paragraph 1, Member States may retain until 31 December 1997 such statutory licence systems which are in operation or expressly provided for by national law on 31 July 1991.

Article 9   Exercise of the cable retransmission right

1.   Member States shall ensure that the right of copyright owners and holders or related rights to grant or refuse authorization to a cable operator for a cable retransmission may be exercised only through a collecting society.

2.   Where a rightholder has not transferred the management of his rights to a collecting society, the collecting society which manages rights of the same category shall be deemed to be mandated to manage his rights. Where more than one collecting society manages rights of that category, the rightholder shall be free to choose which of those collecting societies is deemed to be mandated to manage his rights. A rightholder referred to in this paragraph shall have the same rights and obligations resulting from the agreement between the cable operator and the collecting society which is deemed to be mandated to manage his rights as the rightholders who have mandated that collecting society and he shall be able to claim those rights within a period, to be fixed by the Member State concerned, which shall not be shorter than three years from the date of the cable retransmission which includes his work or other protected subject matter.

3.   A Member State may provide that, when a rightholder authorizes the initial transmission within its territory of a work or other protected subject matter, he shall be deemed to have agreed not to exercise his cable retransmission rights on an individual basis but to exercise them in accordance with the provisions of this Directive.

Article 10   Exercise of the cable retransmission right by broadcasting organizations

Member States shall ensure that Article 9 does not apply to the rights exercised by a broadcasting organization in respect of its own transmission, irrespective of whether the rights concerned are its own or have been transferred to it by other copyright owners and/or holders of related rights.

Article 11   Mediators

1.   Where no agreement is concluded regarding authorization of the cable retransmission of a broadcast. Member States shall ensure that either party may call upon the assistance of one or more mediators.

2.   The task of the mediators shall be to provide assistance with negotiation. They may also submit proposals to the parties.

3.   It shall be assumed that all the parties accept a proposal as referred to in paragraph 2 if none of them expresses its opposition within a period of three months. Notice of the proposal and of any opposition thereto shall be served on the parties concerned in accordance with the applicable rules concerning the service of legal documents.

4.   The mediators shall be so selected that their independence and impartiality are beyond reasonable doubt.

Article 12   Prevention of the abuse of negotiating positions

1.   Member States shall ensure by means of civil or administrative law, as appropriate, that the parties enter and conduct negotiations regarding authorization for cable retransmission in good faith and do not prevent or hinder negotiation without valid justification.

2.   A Member State which, on the date mentioned in Article 14(1), has a body with jurisdiction in its territory over cases where the right to retransmit a programme by cable to the public in that Member State has been unreasonably refused or offered on unreasonable terms by a broadcasting organization may retain that body.

3.   Paragraph 2 shall apply for a transitional period of eight years from the date mentioned in Article 14(1).

CHAPTER IV   GENERAL PROVISIONS

Article 13   Collective administration of rights

This Directive shall be without prejudice to the regulation of the activities of collecting societies by the Member States.

Article 14   Final provisions

1.   Member States shall bring into force the laws, regulations and administrative provisions necessary to comply with this Directive before 1 January 1995. They shall immediately inform the Commission thereof.

When Member States adopt these measures, the latter shall contain a reference to this Directive or shall be accompanied by such reference at the time of their official publication. The methods of making such a reference shall be laid down by the Member States.

2.   Member States shall communicate to the Commission the provisions of national law which they adopt in the field covered by this Directive.

3.   Not later than 1 January 2000, the Commission shall submit to the European Parliament, the Council and the Economic and Social Committee a report on the application of this Directive and, if necessary, make further proposals to adapt it to developments in the audio and audiovisual sector.

Article 15

This Directive is addressed to the Member States.

Done at Brussels, 27 September 1993.

For the Council
The President
R. URBAIN

Council Directive 93/98/EEC of 29 October 1993 harmonizing the term of protection of copyright and certain related rights

[OJ 1993, L290/9]*

THE COUNCIL OF THE EUROPEAN COMMUNITIES,

Having regard to the Treaty establishing the European Economic Community, and in particular Articles 57(2), 66 and 100a thereof,

Having regard to the proposal from the Commission,[1]

In cooperation with the European Parliament,[2]

Having regard to the opinion of the Economic and Social Committee,[3]

---

* **Editor's Note:** As amended by Directive 2001/29 [OJ 2001, L167/10].

[1] OJ C 92, 11.4.1992, p. 6 and OJ C 27, 30.1.1993, p. 7.

[2] OJ C 337, 21.12.1992, p. 205 and Decision of 27 October 1993 (not yet published in the Official Journal).

[3] OJ C 287, 4.11.1992, p. 53.

(1) Whereas the Berne Convention for the protection of literary and artistic works and the International Convention for the protection of performers, producers of phonograms and broadcasting organizations (Rome Convention) lay down only minimum terms of protection of the rights they refer to, leaving the Contracting States free to grant longer terms; whereas certain Member States have exercised this entitlement; whereas in addition certain Member States have not become party to the Rome Convention;

(2) Whereas there are consequently differences between the national laws governing the terms of protection of copyright and related rights, which are liable to impede the free movement of goods and freedom to provide services, and to distort competition in the common market; whereas therefore with a view to the smooth operation of the internal market, the laws of the Member States should be harmonized so as to make terms of protection identical throughout the Community;

(3) Whereas harmonization must cover not only the terms of protection as such, but also certain implementing arrangements such as the date from which each term of protection is calculated;

(4) Whereas the provisions of this Directive do not affect the application by the Member States of the provisions of Article 14a (2) (b), (c) and (d) and (3) of the Berne Convention;

(5) Whereas the minimum term of protection laid down by the Berne Convention, namely the life of the author and 50 years after his death, was intended to provide protection for the author and the first two generations of his descendants; whereas the average lifespan in the Community has grown longer, to the point where this term is no longer sufficient to cover two generations;

(6) Whereas certain Member States have granted a term longer than 50 years after the death of the author in order to offset the effects of the world wars on the exploitation of authors' works;

(7) Whereas for the protection of related rights certain Member States have introduced a term of 50 years after lawful publication or lawful communication to the public;

(8) Whereas under the Community position adopted for the Uruguay Round negotiations under the General Agreement on Tariffs and Trade (GATT) the term of protection for producers of phonograms should be 50 years after first publication;

(9) Whereas due regard for established rights is one of the general principles of law protected by the Community legal order; whereas, therefore, a harmonization of the terms of protection of copyright and related rights cannot have the effect of reducing the protection currently enjoyed by rightholders in the Community; whereas in order to keep the effects of transitional measures to a minimum and to allow the internal market to operate in practice, the harmonization of the term of protection should take place on a long term basis;

(10) Whereas in its communication of 17 January 1991 'Follow-up to the Green Paper—Working programme of the Commission in the field of copyright and neighbouring rights' the Commission stresses the need to harmonize copyright and neighbouring rights at a high level of protection since these rights are fundamental to intellectual creation and stresses that their protection ensures the maintenance and development of creativity in the interest of authors, cultural industries, consumers and society as a whole;

(11) Whereas in order to establish a high level of protection which at the same time meets the requirements of the internal market and the need to establish a legal environment conducive to the harmonious development of literary and artistic creation in the Community, the term of protection for copyright should be harmonized at 70 years after the death of the author or 70 years after the work is lawfully made available to the public, and for related rights at 50 years after the event which sets the term running;

(12) Whereas collections are protected according to Article 2(5) of the Berne Convention when, by reason of the selection and arrangement of their content, they constitute intellectual creations; whereas those works are protected as such, without prejudice to the

copyright in each of the works forming part of such collections, whereas in consequence specific terms of protection may apply to works included in collections;

(13) Whereas in all cases where one or more physical persons are identified as authors the term of protection should be calculated after their death; whereas the question of authorship in the whole or a part of a work is a question of fact which the national courts may have to decide;

(14) Whereas terms of protection should be calculated from the first day of January of the year following the relevant event, as they are in the Berne and Rome Conventions;

(15) Whereas Article 1 of Council Directive 91/250/EEC of 14 May 1991 on the legal protection of computer programs[4] provides that Member States are to protect computer programs, by copyright, as literary works within the meaning of the Berne Convention; whereas this Directive harmonizes the term of protection of literary works in the Community; whereas Article 8 of Directive 91/250/EEC, which merely makes provisional arrangements governing the term of protection of computer programs, should accordingly be repealed;

(16) Whereas Articles 11 and 12 of Council Directive 92/100/EEC of 19 November 1992 on rental right and lending right and on certain rights related to copyright in the field of intellectual property[5] make provision for minimum terms of protection only, subject to any further harmonization; whereas this Directive provides such further harmonization; whereas these Articles should accordingly be repealed;

(17) Whereas the protection of photographs in the Member States is the subject of varying regimes; whereas in order to achieve a sufficient harmonization of the term of protection of photographic works, in particular of those which, due to their artistic or professional character, are of importance within the internal market, it is necessary to define the level of originality required in this Directive; whereas a photographic work within the meaning of the Berne Convention is to be considered original if it is the author's own intellectual creation reflecting his personality, no other criteria such as merit or purpose being taken into account; whereas the protection of other photographs should be left to national law;

(18) Whereas, in order to avoid differences in the term of protection as regards related rights it is necessary to provide the same starting point for the calculation of the term throughout the Community; whereas the performance, fixation, transmission, lawful publication, and lawful communication to the public, that is to say the means of making a subject of a related right perceptible in all appropriate ways to persons in general, should be taken into account for the calculation of the term of protection regardless of the country where this performance, fixation, transmission, lawful publication, or lawful communication to the public takes place;

(19) Whereas the rights of broadcasting organizations in their broadcasts, whether these broadcasts are transmitted by wire or over the air, including by cable or satellite, should not be perpetual; whereas it is therefore necessary to have the term of protection running from the first transmission of a particular broadcast only; whereas this provision is understood to avoid a new term running in cases where a broadcast is identical to a previous one;

(20) Whereas the Member States should remain free to maintain or introduce other rights related to copyright in particular in relation to the protection of critical and scientific publications; whereas, in order to ensure transparency at Community level, it is however necessary for Member States which introduce new related rights to notify the Commission;

(21) Whereas it is useful to make clear that the harmonization brought about by this Directive does not apply to moral rights;

(22) Whereas, for works whose country of origin within the meaning of the Berne Convention is a third country and whose author is not a Community national, comparison of

---

[4] OJ L 122, 17.5.1991, p. 42.
[5] OJ L 346, 27.11.1992, p. 61.

terms of protection should be applied, provided that the term accorded in the Community does not exceed the term laid down in this Directive;

(23) Whereas where a rightholder who is not a Community national qualifies for protection under an international agreement the term of protection of related rights should be the same as that laid down in this Directive, except that it should not exceed that fixed in the country of which the rightholder is a national;

(24) Whereas comparison of terms should not result in Member States being brought into conflict with their international obligations;

(25) Whereas, for the smooth functioning of the internal market this Directive should be applied as from 1 July 1995;

(26) Whereas Member States should remain free to adopt provisions on the interpretation, adaptation and further execution of contracts on the exploitation of protected works and other subject matter which were concluded before the extension of the term of protection resulting from this Directive;

(27) Whereas respect of acquired rights and legitimate expectations is part of the Community legal order; whereas Member States may provide in particular that in certain circumstances the copyright and related rights which are revived pursuant to this Directive may not give rise to payments by persons who undertook in good faith the exploitation of the works at the time when such works lay within the public domain,

HAS ADOPTED THIS DIRECTIVE:

Article 1   Duration of authors' rights

1.   The rights of an author of a literary or artistic work within the meaning of Article 2 of the Berne Convention shall run for the life of the author and for 70 years after his death, irrespective of the date when the work is lawfully made available to the public.

2.   In the case of a work of joint authorship the term referred to in paragraph 1 shall be calculated from the death of the last surviving author.

3.   In the case of anonymous or pseudonymous works, the term of protection shall run for 70 years after the work is lawfully made available to the public. However, when the pseudonym adopted by the author leaves no doubt as to his identity, or if the author discloses his identity during the period referred to in the first sentence, the term of protection applicable shall be that laid down in paragraph 1.

4.   Where a Member State provides for particular provisions on copyright in respect of collective works or for a legal person to be designated as the rightholder, the term of protection shall be calculated according to the provisions of paragraph 3, except if the natural persons who have created the work as such are identified as such in the versions of the work which are made available to the public. This paragraph is without prejudice to the rights of identified authors whose identifiable contributions are included in such works, to which contributions paragraph 1 or 2 shall apply.

5.   Where a work is published in volumes, parts, instalments, issues or episodes and the term of protection runs from the time when the work was lawfully made available to the public, the term of protection shall run for each such item separately.

6.   In the case of works for which the term of protection is not calculated from the death of the author or authors and which have not been lawfully made available to the public within 70 years from their creation, the protection shall terminate.

Article 2   Cinematographic or audiovisual works

1.   The principal director of a cinematographic or audiovisual work shall be considered as its author or one of its authors. Member States shall be free to designate other co-authors.

2.   The term of protection of cinematographic or audiovisual works shall expire 70 years after the death of the last of the following persons to survive, whether or not these persons are

designated as co-authors: the principal director, the author of the screenplay, the author of the dialogue and the composer of music specifically created for use in the cinematographic or audiovisual work.

Article 3   Duration of related rights

1.   The rights of performers shall expire 50 years after the date of the performance. However, if a fixation of the performance is lawfully published or lawfully communicated to the public within this period, the rights shall expire 50 years from the date of the first such publication or the first such communication to the public, whichever is the earlier.

2.   The rights of producers of phonograms shall expire 50 years after the fixation is made. However, if the phonogram has been lawfully published within this period, the said rights shall expire 50 years from the date of the first lawful publication. If no lawful publication has taken place within the period mentioned in the first sentence, and if the phonogram has been lawfully communicated to the public within this period, the said rights shall expire 50 years from the date of the first lawful communication to the public. However, where through the expiry of the term of protection granted pursuant to this paragraph in its version before amendment by Directive 2001/29/EC of the European Parliament and of the Council of 22 May 2001 on the harmonisation of certain aspects of copyright and related rights in the information society(11) the rights of producers of phonograms are no longer protected on 22 December 2002, this paragraph shall not have the effect of protecting those rights anew.*

3.   The rights of producers of the first fixation of a film shall expire 50 years after the fixation is made.

However, if the film is lawfully published or lawfully communicated to the public during this period, the rights shall expire 50 years from the date of the first such publication or the first such communication to the public, whichever is the earlier. The term 'film' shall designate a cinematographic or audiovisual work or moving images, whether or not accompanied by sound.

4.   The rights of broadcasting organizations shall expire 50 years after the first transmission of a broadcast, whether this broadcast is transmitted by wire or over the air, including by cable or satellite.

Article 4   Protection of previously unpublished works

Any person who, after the expiry of copyright protection, for the first time lawfully publishes or lawfully communicates to the public a previously unpublished work, shall benefit from a protection equivalent to the economic rights of the author. The term of protection of such rights shall be 25 years from the time when the work was first lawfully published or lawfully communicated to the public.

Article 5   Critical and scientific publications

Member States may protect critical and scientific publications of works which have come into the public domain. The maximum term of protection of such rights shall be 30 years from the time when the publication was first lawfully published.

Article 6   Protection of photographs

Photographs which are original in the sense that they are the author's own intellectual creation shall be protected in accordance with Article 1. No other criteria shall be applied to determine their eligibility for protection. Member States may provide for the protection of other photographs.

Article 7   Protection vis-à-vis third countries

1.   Where the country off origin of a work, within the meaning of the Berne Convention, is a third country, and the author of the work is not a Community national, the term of

---

* **Editor's Note:** As amended by Directive 2001/29 [OJ 2001, L167/10].

protection granted by the Member States shall expire on the date of expiry of the protection granted in the country of origin of the work, but may not exceed the term laid down in Article 1.

2.   The terms of protection laid down in Article 3 shall also apply in the case of rightholders who are not Community nationals, provided Member States grant them protection.

However, without prejudice to the international obligations of the Member States, the term of protection granted by Member States shall expire no later than the date of expiry of the protection granted in the country of which the rightholder is a national and may not exceed the term laid down in Article 3.

3.   Member States which, at the date of adoption of this Directive, in particular pursuant to their international obligations, granted a longer term of protection than that which would result from the provisions, referred to in paragraphs 1 and 2 may maintain this protection until the conclusion of international agreements on the term of protection by copyright or related rights.

Article 8   Calculation of terms
The terms laid down in this Directive are calculated from the first day of January of the year following the event which gives rise to them.

Article 9   Moral rights
This Directive shall be without prejudice to the provisions of the Member States regulating moral rights.

Article 10   Application in time
1.   Where a term of protection, which is longer than the corresponding term provided for by this Directive, is already running in a Member State on the date referred to in Article 13(1), this Directive shall not have the effect of shortening that term of protection in that Member State.

2.   The terms of protection provided for in this Directive shall apply to all works and subject matter which are protected in at least one Member State, on the date referred to in Article 13(1), pursuant to national provisions on copyright or related rights or which meet the criteria for protection under Directive 92/100/EEC.

3.   This Directive shall be without prejudice to any acts of exploitation performed before the date referred to in Article 13(1). Member States shall adopt the necessary provisions to protect in particular acquired rights of third parties.

4.   Member States need not apply the provisions of Article 2(1) to cinematographic or audiovisual works created before 1 July 1994.

5.   Member States may determine the date as from which Article 2(1) shall apply, provided that date is no later than 1 July 1997.

Article 11   Technical adaptation
1.   Article 8 of Directive 91/250/EEC is hereby repealed.

2.   Articles 11 and 12 of Directive 92/100/EEC are hereby repealed.

Article 12   Notification procedure
Member States shall immediately notify the Commission of any governmental plan to grant new related rights, including the basic reasons for their introduction and the term of protection envisaged.

Article 13   General provisions
1.   Member States shall bring into force the laws, regulations and administrative provisions necessary to comply with Articles 1 to 11 of this Directive before 1 July 1995.

When Member States adopt these provisions, they shall contain a reference to this

Directive or shall be accompanied by such reference at the time of their official publication. The methods of making such a reference shall be laid down by the Member States.

Member States shall communicate to the Commission the texts of the provisions of national law which they adopt in the field governed by this Directive.

2.   Member States shall apply Article 12 from the date of notification of this Directive.

Article 14
This Directive is addressed to the Member States.

Done at Brussels, 29 October 1993.

For the Council
The President
R. URBAIN

Directive 96/9/EC of the European Parliament and of the Council of 11 March 1996 on the legal protection of databases
[OJ 1996, No. L77/20]

The European Parliament and the Council of the European Union,

Having regard to the Treaty establishing the European Community, and in particular Article 57(2), 66 and 100a thereof,

Having regard to the proposal from the Commission,[1]

Having regard to the opinion of the Economic and Social Committee,[2]

Acting in accordance with the procedure laid down in Article 189b of the Treaty,[3]

(1) Whereas databases are at present not sufficiently protected in all Member States by existing legislation; whereas such protection, where it exists, has different attributes;

(2) Whereas such differences in the legal protection of databases offered by the legislation of the Member States have direct negative effects on the functioning of the internal market as regards databases and in particular on the freedom of natural and legal persons to provide on-line database goods and services on the basis of harmonised legal arrangements throughout the Community; whereas such differences could well become more pronounced as Member States introduce new legislation in this field, which is now taking on an increasingly international dimension;

(3) Whereas existing differences distorting the functioning of the internal market need to be removed and new ones prevented from arising, while differences not adversely affecting the functioning of the internal market or the development of an information market within the Community need not be removed or prevented from arising;

(4) Whereas copyright protection for databases exists in varying forms in the Member States according to legislation or case-law, and whereas, if differences in legislation in the scope and conditions of protection remain between the Member States, such unharmonised intellectual property rights can have the effect of preventing the free movement of goods or services within the Community;

---

[1] OJ 1992 C156/4 and OJ 1993 C308/1.
[2] OJ C 19, 25.1.1993, p. 3.
[3] OJ 1993 C194/144, and OJ 1995 C288/14.

(5) Whereas copyright remains an appropriate form of exclusive right for authors who have created databases;

(6) Whereas, nevertheless, in the absence of a harmonised system of unfair-competition legislation or of case-law, other measures are required in addition to prevent the unauthorised extraction and/or re-utilisation of the contents of a database;

(7) Whereas the making of databases requires the investment of considerable human, technical and financial resources while such databases can be copied or accessed at a fraction of the cost needed to design them independently;

(8) Whereas the unauthorised extraction and/or re-utilisation of the contents of a database constitute acts which can have serious economic and technical consequences;

(9) Whereas databases are a vital tool in the development of an information market within the Community; whereas this tool will also be of use in many other fields;

(10) Whereas the exponential growth, in the Community and worldwide, in the amount of information generated and processed annually in all sectors of commerce and industry calls for investment in all the Member States in advanced information processing systems;

(11) Whereas there is at present a very great imbalance in the level of investment in the database sector both as between the Member States and between the Community and the world's largest database-producing third countries;

(12) Whereas such an investment in modern information storage and processing systems will not take place within the Community unless a stable and uniform legal protection regime is introduced for the protection of the rights of makers of databases;

(13) Whereas this Directive protects collections, sometimes called 'compilations, of works, data or other materials which are arranged, stored and accessed by means which include electronic, electromagnetic or electro-optical processes or analogous processes;

(14) Whereas protection under this Directive should be extended to cover non-electronic databases;

(15) Whereas the criteria used to determine whether a database should be protected by copyright should be defined to the fact that the selection or the arrangement of the contents of the database is the author's own intellectual creation; whereas such protection should cover the structure of the database;

(16) Whereas no criterion other than originality in the sense of the author's intellectual creation should be applied to determine the eligibility of the database for copyright protection, and in particular no aesthetic or qualitative criteria should be applied;

(17) Whereas the term 'database should be understood to include literary, artistic, musical or other collections of works or collections of other material such as texts, sound, images, numbers, facts, and data; whereas it should cover collections of independent works, data or other materials which are systematically or methodically arranged and can be individually accessed; whereas this means that a recording or an audio-visual, cinemato-graphic, literary or musical work as such does not fall within the scope of this Directive;

(18) Whereas this Directive is without prejudice to the freedom of authors to decide whether, or in what manner, they will allow their works to be included in a database, in particular whether or not the authorisation given is exclusive; whereas the protection of databases by the *sui generis* right is without prejudice to existing rights over their contents, and whereas in particular where an author or the holder of a related right permits some of his works or subject matter to be included in a database pursuant to a non-exclusive agreement, a third party may make use of those works or subject matter subject to the required consent of the author or of the holder of the related right without the *sui generis* right of the maker of the database being invoked to prevent him doing so, on condition that those works or subject matter are neither extracted from the database nor re-utilised on the basis thereof;

(19) Whereas, as a rule, the compilation of several recordings of musical performances on a CD does not come within the scope of this Directive, both because, as a compilation, it

does not meet the conditions for copyright protection and because it does not represent a substantial enough investment to be eligible under the *sui generis* right;

(20) Whereas protection under this Directive may also apply to the materials necessary for the operation or consultation of certain databases such as thesaurus and indexation systems;

(21) Whereas the protection provided for in this Directive relates to databases in which works, data or other materials have been arranged systematically or methodically; whereas it is not necessary for those materials to have been physically stored in an organised manner;

(22) Whereas electronic databases within the meaning of this Directive may also include devices such as CD-ROM and CD-i;

(23) Whereas the term 'database' should not be taken to extend to computer programs used in the making or operation of a database, which are protected by Council Directive 91/250/ EEC of 14 May 1991 on the legal protection of computer programs;[4]

(24) Whereas the rental and lending of databases in the field of copyright and related rights are governed exclusively by Council Directive 92/100/EEC of 19 November 1992 on rental right and lending right and on certain rights related to copyright in the field of intellectual property;[5]

(25) Whereas the term of copyright is already governed by Council Directive 93/98/EEC of 29 October 1993 harmonizing the term of protection of copyright and certain related rights;[6]

(26) Whereas works protected by copyright and subject matter protected by related rights, which are incorporated into a database, remain nevertheless protected by the respective exclusive rights and may not be incorporated into, or extracted from, the database without the permission of the rightholder or his successors in title;

(27) Whereas copyright in such works and related rights in subject matter thus incorporated into a database are in no way affected by the existence of a separate right in the selection or arrangement of these works and subject matter in a database;

(28) Whereas the moral rights of the natural person who created the database belong to the author and should be exercised according to the legislation of the Member States and the provisions of the Berne Convention for the Protection of Literary and Artistic Works; whereas such moral rights remain outside the scope of this Directive;

(29) Whereas the arrangements applicable to databases created by employees are left to the discretion of the Member States; whereas, therefore nothing in this Directive prevents Member States from stipulating in their legislation that where a database is created by an employee in the execution of his duties or following the instructions given by his employer, the employer exclusively shall be entitled to exercise all economic rights in the database so created, unless otherwise provided by contract;

(30) Whereas the author's exclusive rights should include the right to determine the way in which his work is exploited and by whom, and in particular to control the distribution of his work to unauthorised persons;

(31) Whereas the copyright protection of databases includes making databases available by means other than the distribution of copies;

(32) Whereas Member States are required to ensure that their national provisions are at least materially equivalent in the case of such acts subject to restrictions as are provided for by this Directive;

(33) Whereas the question of exhaustion of the right of distribution does not arise in the case of on-line databases, which come within the field of provision of services; whereas this also applies with regard to a material copy of such a database made by the user of such a

---

[4] OJ 1991 L122/42.
[5] OJ L 346, 27.11.1992, p. 61.
[6] (3) OJ L 290, 24.11.1993, p. 9.

service with the consent of the rightholder; whereas, unlike CD-ROM or CD-i, where the intellectual property is incorporated in a material medium, namely an item of goods, every on-line service is in fact an act which will have to be subject to authorisation where the copyright so provides;

(34) Whereas, nevertheless, once the rightholder has chosen to make available a copy of the database to a user, whether by an on-line service or by other means of distribution, that lawful user must be able to access and use the database for the purposes and in the way set out in the agreement with the rightholder, even if such access and use necessitate performance of otherwise restricted acts;

(35) Whereas a list should be drawn up of exceptions to restricted acts, taking into account the fact that copyright as covered by this Directive applies only to the selection or arrangements of the contents of a database; whereas Member States should be given the option of providing for such exceptions in certain cases; whereas, however, this option should be exercised in accordance with the Berne Convention and to the extent that the exceptions relate to the structure of the database; whereas a distinction should be drawn between exceptions for private use and exceptions for reproduction for private purposes, which concerns provisions under national legislation of some Member States on levies on blank media or recording equipment;

(36) Whereas the term 'scientific research' within the meaning of this Directive covers both the natural sciences and the human sciences;

(37) Whereas Article 10(1) of the Berne Convention is not affected by this Directive;

(38) Whereas the increasing use of digital recording technology exposes the database maker to the risk that the contents of his database may be copied and rearranged electronically, without his authorisation, to produce a database of identical content which, however, does not infringe any copyright in the arrangement of his database;

(39) Whereas, in addition to aiming to protect the copyright in the original selection or arrangement of the contents of a database, this Directive seeks to safeguard the position of makers of databases against misappropriation of the results of the financial and professional investment made in obtaining and collection the contents by protecting the whole or substantial parts of a database against certain acts by a user or competitor;

(40) Whereas the object of this *sui generis* right is to ensure protection of any investment in obtaining, verifying or presenting the contents of a database for the limited duration of the right; whereas such investment may consist in the deployment of financial resources and/or the expending of time, effort and energy;

(41) Whereas the objective of the *sui generis* right is to give the maker of a database the option of preventing the unauthorised extraction and/or re-utilisation of all or a substantial part of the contents of that database; whereas the maker of a database is the person who takes the initiative and the risk of investing; whereas this excludes subcontractors in particular from the definition of maker;

(42) Whereas the special right to prevent unauthorised extraction and/or re-utilisation relates to acts by the user which go beyond his legitimate rights and thereby harm the investment; whereas the right to prohibit extraction and/or re-utilisation of all or a substantial part of the contents relates not only to the manufacture of a parasitical competing product but also to any user who, through his acts, causes significant detriment, evaluated qualitatively or quantitatively, to the investment;

(43) Whereas, in the case of on-line transmission, the right to prohibit re-utilisation is not exhausted either as regards the database or as regards a material copy of the database or of part thereof made by the addressee of the transmission with the consent of the rightholder;

(44) Whereas, when on-screen display of the contents of a database necessitates the permanent or temporary transfer of all or a substantial part of such contents to another medium, that act should be subject to authorisation by the rightholder;

(45) Whereas the right to prevent unauthorised extraction and/or re-utilisation does not in any way constitute an extension of copyright protection to mere facts or data;

(46) Whereas the existence of a right to prevent the unauthorised extraction and/or re-utilisation of the whole or a substantial part of works, data or materials from a database should not give rise to the creation of a new right in the works, data or materials themselves;

(47) Whereas, in the interests of competition between suppliers of information products and services, protection by the *sui generis* right must not be afforded in such a way as to facilitate abuses of a dominant position, in particular as regards the creation and distribution of new products and services which have an intellectual, documentary, technical, economic or commercial added value; whereas, therefore, the provisions of this Directive are without prejudice to the application of Community or national competition rules;

(48) Whereas the objective of this Directive, which is to afford an appropriate and uniform level of protection of databases as a means to secure the remuneration of the maker of the database, is different from the aim of Directive 95/46/EC of the European Parliament and of the Council of 24 October 1995 on the protection of individuals with regard to the processing of personal data and on the free movement of such data,[7] which is to guarantee free circulation of personal data on the basis of harmonised rules designed to protect fundamental rights, notably the right to privacy which is recognised in Article 8 of the European Convention for the Protection of Human Rights and Fundamental Freedoms; whereas the provisions of this Directive are without prejudice to data protection legislation;

(49) Whereas, notwithstanding the right to prevent extraction and/or re-utilisation of all or a substantial part of a database, it should be laid down that the maker of a database or rightholder may not prevent a lawful user of the database from extracting and re-utilising insubstantial parts; whereas, however, that user may not unreasonably prejudice either the legitimate interests of the holder of the *sui generis* right or the holder of copyright or a related right in respect of the works or subject matter contained in the database;

(50) Whereas the Member States should be given the option of providing for exceptions to the right to prevent the unauthorised extraction and/or re-utilisation of a substantial part of the contents of a database in the case of extraction for private purposes, for the purposes of illustration for teaching or scientific research, or where extraction and/or re-utilisation are/is carried out in the interests of public security or for the purposes of an administrative or judicial procedure; whereas such operations must not prejudice the exclusive rights of the maker to exploit the database and their purpose must not be commercial;

(51) Whereas the Member States, where they avail themselves of the option to permit a lawful user of a database to extract a substantial part of the contents for the purposes of illustration for teaching or scientific research, may limit that permission to certain categories of teaching or scientific research institution;

(52) Whereas those Member States which have specific rules providing for a right comparable to the *sui generis* right provided for in this Directive should be permitted to retain, as far as the new right is concerned, the exceptions traditionally specified by such rules;

(53) Whereas the burden of proof regarding the date of completion of the making of a database lies with the maker of the database;

(54) Whereas the burden of proof that the criteria exist for concluding that a substantial modification of the contents of a database is to be regarded as a substantial new investment lies with the maker of the database resulting from such investment;

(55) Whereas a substantial new investment involving a new term of protection may include a substantial verification of the contents of the database;

(56) Whereas the right to prevent unauthorised extraction and/or re-utilisation in respect of a database should apply to databases whose makers are nationals or habitual residents of

[7] OJ L 281, 23.11.1995, p. 31.

third countries or to those produced by legal persons not established in a Member State, within the meaning of the Treaty, only if such third countries offer comparable protection to databases produced by nationals of a Member State or persons who have their habitual residence in the territory of the Community;

(57) Whereas, in addition to remedies provided under the legislation of the Member States for infringements of copyright or other rights, Member States should provide for appropriate remedies against unauthorised extraction and/or re-utilisation of the contents of a database;

(58) Whereas, in addition to the protection given under this Directive to the structure of the database by copyright, and to its contents against unauthorised extraction and/or re-utilisation under the *sui generis* right, other legal provisions in the Member States relevant to the supply of database goods and services continue to apply;

(59) Whereas this Directive is without prejudice to the application to databases composed of audio-visual works of any rules recognised by a Member State's legislation concerning the broadcasting of audio-visual programmes;

(60) Whereas some Member States currently protect under copyright arrangements databases which do not meet the criteria for eligibility for copyright protection laid down in this Directive; whereas, even if the databases concerned are eligible for protection under the right laid down in this Directive to prevent unauthorised extraction and/or re-utilisation of their contents, the term of protection under that right is considerably shorter than that which they enjoy under the national arrangements currently in force; whereas harmonization of the criteria for determining whether a database is to be protected by copyright may not have the effect of reducing the term of protection currently enjoyed by the rightholders concerned; whereas a derogation should be laid down to that effect; whereas the effects of such derogation must be confined to the territories of the Member States concerned,

HAVE ADOPTED THIS DIRECTIVE:

CHAPTER I   SCOPE

Article 1   Scope

1.   This Directive concerns the legal protection of databases in any form.

2.   For the purposes of this Directive, 'database' shall mean a collection of independent works, data or other materials arranged in a systematic or methodical way and individually accessible by electronic or other means.

3.   Protection under this Directive shall not apply to computer programs used in the making or operation of databases accessible by electronic means.

Article 2   Limitations on the scope

This Directive shall apply without prejudice to Community provisions relating to:

    (a)   the legal protection of computer programs;

    (b)   rental right, lending right and certain rights related to copyright in the field of intellectual property;

    (c)   the term of protection of copyright and certain related rights.

CHAPTER II   COPYRIGHT

Article 3   Object of protection

1.   In accordance with this Directive, databases which, by reason of the selection or arrangement of their contents, constitute the author's own intellectual creation shall be protected as such by copyright. No other criteria shall be applied to determine their eligibility for that protection.

2.   The copyright protection of databases provided for by this Directive shall not extend to their contents and shall be without prejudice to any rights subsisting in those contents themselves.

Article 4   Database authorship
1.   The author of a database shall be the natural person or group of natural persons who created the base or, where the legislation of the Member States so permits, the legal person designated as the rightholder by that legislation.

2.   Where collective works are recognised by the legislation of a Member State, the economic rights shall be owned by the person holding the copyright.

3.   In respect of a database created by a group of natural persons jointly, the exclusive rights shall be owned jointly.

Article 5   Restricted acts
In respect of the expression of the database which is protectable by copyright, the author of a database shall have the exclusive right to carry out or to authorise:

   (a)   temporary or permanent reproduction by any means and in any form, in whole or in part;
   (b)   translation, adaptation, arrangement and any other alteration;
   (c)   any form of distribution to the public of the database or of copies thereof. The first sale in the Community of a copy of the database by the rightholder or with his consent shall exhaust the right to control resale of that copy within the Community;
   (d)   any communication, display or performance to the public;
   (e)   any reproduction, distribution, communication, display or performance to the public of the results of the acts referred to in (b).

Article 6   Exceptions to restricted acts
1.   The performance by the lawful user of a database or of a copy thereof of any of the acts listed in Article 5 which is necessary for the purposes of access to the contents of the databases and normal use of the contents by the lawful user shall not require the authorisation of the author of the database. Where the lawful user is authorised to use only part of the database, this provision shall apply only to that part.

2.   Member States shall have the option of providing for limitations on the rights set out in Article 5 in the following cases:

   (a)   in the case of reproduction for private purposes of a non-electronic database;
   (b)   where there is use for the sole purpose of illustration for teaching or scientific research, as long as the source is indicated and to the extent justified by the non-commercial purpose to be achieved;
   (c)   where there is use for the purposes of public security of for the purposes of an administrative or judicial procedure;
   (d)   where other exceptions to copyright which are traditionally authorised under national law are involved, without prejudice to points (a), (b) and (c).

3.   In accordance with the Berne Convention for the protection of Literary and Artistic Works, this Article may not be interpreted in such a way as to allow its application to be used in a manner which unreasonably prejudices the rightholder's legitimate interests or conflicts with normal exploitation of the database.

CHAPTER III   *SUI GENERIS* RIGHT

Article 7   Object of protection
1.   Member States shall provide for a right for the maker of a database which shows that there has been qualitatively and/or quantitatively a substantial investment in either the

obtaining, verification or presentation of the contents to prevent extraction and/or re-utilisation of the whole or of a substantial part, evaluated qualitatively and/or quantitatively, of the contents of that database.

2.   For the purposes of this Chapter:

(a) 'extraction' shall mean the permanent or temporary transfer of all or a substantial part of the contents of a database to another medium by any means or in any form;

(b) 're-utilisation' shall mean any form of making available to the public all or a substantial part of the contents of a database by the distribution of copies, by renting, by on-line or other forms of transmission. The first sale of a copy of a database within the Community by the rightholder or with his consent shall exhaust the right to control resale of that copy within the Community;

Public lending is not an act of extraction or re-utilisation.

3.   The right referred to in paragraph 1 may be transferred, assigned or granted under contractual licence.

4.   The right provided for in paragraph 1 shall apply irrespective of the eligibility of that database for protection by copyright or by other rights. Moreover, it shall apply irrespective of eligibility of the contents of that database for protection by copyright or by other rights. Protection of databases under the right provided for in paragraph 1 shall be without prejudice to rights existing in respect of their contents.

5.   The repeated and systematic extraction and/or re-utilisation of insubstantial parts of the contents of the database implying acts which conflict with a normal exploitation of that database or which unreasonably prejudice the legitimate interests of the maker of the database shall not be permitted.

Article 8   Rights and obligations of lawful users

1.   The maker of a database which is made available to the public in whatever manner may not prevent a lawful user of the database from extracting and/or re-utilising insubstantial parts of its contents, evaluated qualitatively and/or quantitatively, for any purposes whatsoever. Where the lawful user is authorised to extract and/or re-utilise only part of the database, this paragraph shall apply only to that part.

2.   A lawful user of a database which is made available to the public in whatever manner may not perform acts which conflict with normal exploitation of the database or unreasonably prejudice the legitimate interests of the maker of the database.

3.   A lawful user of a database which is made available to the public in any manner may not cause prejudice to the holder of a copyright or related right in respect of the works or subject matter contained in the database.

Article 9   Exceptions to the *sui generis* right

Member States may stipulate that lawful users of a database which is made available to the public in whatever manner may, without the authorisation of its maker, extract or re-utilise a substantial part of its contents:

(a) in the case of extraction for private purposes of the contents of a non-electronic database;

(b) in the case of extraction for the purposes of illustration for teaching or scientific research, as long as the source is indicated and to the extent justified by the non-commercial purpose to be achieved;

(c) in the case of extraction and/or re-utilisation for the purposes of public security or an administrative or judicial procedure.

Article 10   Term of protection

1.   The right provided for in Article 7 shall run from the date of completion of the making of the database. It shall expire fifteen years from the first of January of the year following the date of completion.

2.   In the case of a database which is made available to the public in whatever manner before expiry of the period provided for in paragraph 1, the term of protection by that right shall expire fifteen years from the first of January of the year following the date when the database was first made available to the public.

3.   Any substantial change, evaluated qualitatively or quantitatively, to the contents of a database, including any substantial change resulting from the accumulation of successive additions, deletions or alterations, which would result in the database being considered to be a substantial new investment, evaluated qualitatively or quantitatively, shall qualify the database resulting from that investment for its own term of protection.

Article 11   Beneficiaries of protection under the *sui generis* right

1.   The right provided for in Article 7 shall apply to database whose makers or right-holders are nationals of a Member State or who have their habitual residence in the territory of the Community.

2.   Paragraph 1 shall also apply to companies and firms formed in accordance with the law of a Member State and having their registered office, central administration or principal place of business within the Community; however, where such a company or firm has only its registered office in the territory of the Community, its operations must be genuinely linked on an ongoing basis with the economy of a Member State.

3.   Agreements extending the right provided for in Article 7 to databases made in third countries and falling outside the provisions of paragraphs 1 and 2 shall be concluded by the Council acting on a proposal from the Commission. The term of any protection extended to databases by virtue of that procedure shall not exceed that available pursuant to Article 10.

CHAPTER IV   COMMON PROVISIONS

Article 12   Remedies

Member States shall provide appropriate remedies in respect of infringements of the rights provided for in this Directive.

Article 13   Continued application of other legal provisions

This Directive shall be without prejudice to provisions concerning in particular copyright, rights related to copyright or any other rights or obligations subsisting in the data, works or other materials incorporated into a database, patent rights, trade marks, design rights, the protection of national treasures, laws on restrictive practices and unfair competition, trade secrets, security, confidentiality, data protection and privacy, access to public documents, and the law of contract.

Article 14   Application over time

1.   Protection pursuant to this Directive as regards copyright shall also be available in respect of databases created prior to the date referred to Article 16(1) which on that date fulfil the requirements laid down in this Directive as regards copyright protection of databases.

2.   Notwithstanding paragraph 1, where a database protected under copyright arrangements in a Member State on the date of publication of this Directive does not fulfil the eligibility criteria for copyright protection laid down in Article 3(1), this Directive shall not result in any curtailing in that Member State of the remaining term of protection afforded under those arrangements.

3.   Protection pursuant to the provisions of this Directive as regards the right provided for in Article 7 shall also be available in respect of databases the making of which was completed not more than fifteen years prior to the date referred to in Article 16(1) and which on that date fulfil the requirements laid down in Article 7.

4.   The protection provided for in paragraphs 1 and 3 shall be without prejudice to any acts concluded and rights acquired before the date referred to in those paragraphs.

5.   In the case of a database the making of which was completed not more than fifteen years prior to the date referred to in Article 16(1), the term of protection by the right provided for in Article 7 shall expire fifteen years from the first of January following that date.

Article 15   Binding nature of certain provisions

Any contractual provision contrary to Articles 6(1) and 8 shall be null and void.

Article 16   Final provisions

1.   Member States shall bring into force the laws, regulations and administrative provisions necessary to comply with this Directive before 1 January 1998.

When Member States adopt these provisions, they shall contain a reference to this Directive or shall be accompanied by such reference on the occasion of their official publication. The methods of making such reference shall be laid down by Member States.

2.   Member States shall communicate to the Commission the text of the provisions of domestic law which they adopt in the field governed by this Directive. 3. Not later than at the end of the third year after the date referred to in paragraph 1, and every three years thereafter, the Commission shall submit to the European Parliament, the Council and the Economic and Social Committee a report on the application of this Directive, in which, *inter alia*, on the basis of specific information supplied by the Member States, it shall examine in particular the application of the *sui generis* right, including Articles 8 and 9, and shall verify especially whether the application of this right has led to abuse of a dominant position or other interference with free competition which would justify appropriate measures being taken, including the establishment of non-voluntary licensing arrangements. Where necessary, it shall submit proposals for adjustment of this Directive in line with developments in the area of databases.

Article 17

This Directive is addressed to the Member States.

Done at Strasbourg, 11 March 1996.

For the European Parliament
The President
K. HAENSCH
For the Council

The President
L. DINI

Directive 2001/29/EC of the European Parliament and of the Council of 22 May 2001 on the harmonisation of certain aspects of copyright and related rights in the information society

[OJ 2001 L167/10]*

THE EUROPEAN PARLIAMENT AND THE COUNCIL OF THE EUROPEAN UNION,

Having regard to the Treaty establishing the European Community, and in particular Articles 47(2), 55 and 95 thereof,

* **Editor's Note:** As corrected by Corrigendum OJ 2002 L6/70.

Having regard to the proposal from the Commission,[1]
Having regard to the opinion of the Economic and Social Committee,[2]
Acting in accordance with the procedure laid down in Article 251 of the Treaty,[3]
Whereas:

(1) The Treaty provides for the establishment of an internal market and the institution of a system ensuring that competition in the internal market is not distorted. Harmonisation of the laws of the Member States on copyright and related rights contributes to the achievement of these objectives.

(2) The European Council, meeting at Corfu on 24 and 25 June 1994, stressed the need to create a general and flexible legal framework at Community level in order to foster the development of the information society in Europe. This requires, *inter alia*, the existence of an internal market for new products and services. Important Community legislation to ensure such a regulatory framework is already in place or its adoption is well under way. Copyright and related rights play an important role in this context as they protect and stimulate the development and marketing of new products and services and the creation and exploitation of their creative content.

(3) The proposed harmonisation will help to implement the four freedoms of the internal market and relates to compliance with the fundamental principles of law and especially of property, including intellectual property, and freedom of expression and the public interest.

(4) A harmonised legal framework on copyright and related rights, through increased legal certainty and while providing for a high level of protection of intellectual property, will foster substantial investment in creativity and innovation, including network infrastructure, and lead in turn to growth and increased competitiveness of European industry, both in the area of content provision and information technology and more generally across a wide range of industrial and cultural sectors. This will safeguard employment and encourage new job creation.

(5) Technological development has multiplied and diversified the vectors for creation, production and exploitation. While no new concepts for the protection of intellectual property are needed, the current law on copyright and related rights should be adapted and supplemented to respond adequately to economic realities such as new forms of exploitation.

(6) Without harmonisation at Community level, legislative activities at national level which have already been initiated in a number of Member States in order to respond to the technological challenges might result in significant differences in protection and thereby in restrictions on the free movement of services and products incorporating, or based on, intellectual property, leading to a refragmentation of the internal market and legislative inconsistency. The impact of such legislative differences and uncertainties will become more significant with the further development of the information society, which has already greatly increased transborder exploitation of intellectual property. This development will and should further increase. Significant legal differences and uncertainties in protection may hinder economies of scale for new products and services containing copyright and related rights.

(7) The Community legal framework for the protection of copyright and related rights must, therefore, also be adapted and supplemented as far as is necessary for the smooth functioning of the internal market. To that end, those national provisions on copyright and related rights which vary considerably from one Member State to another or which cause legal uncertainties hindering the smooth functioning of the internal market and the proper

---

[1] OJ C 108, 7.4.1998, p. 6 and OJ C 180, 25.6.1999, p. 6.
[2] OJ C 407, 28.12.1998, p. 30.
[3] Opinion of the European Parliament of 10 February 1999 (OJ C 150, 28.5.1999, p. 171), Council Common Position of 28 September 2000 (OJ C 344, 1.12.2000, p. 1) and Decision of the European Parliament of 14 February 2001 (not yet published in the Official Journal). Council Decision of 9 April 2001.

development of the information society in Europe should be adjusted, and inconsistent national responses to the technological developments should be avoided, whilst differences not adversely affecting the functioning of the internal market need not be removed or prevented.

(8) The various social, societal and cultural implications of the information society require that account be taken of the specific features of the content of products and services.

(9) Any harmonisation of copyright and related rights must take as a basis a high level of protection, since such rights are crucial to intellectual creation. Their protection helps to ensure the maintenance and development of creativity in the interests of authors, performers, producers, consumers, culture, industry and the public at large. Intellectual property has therefore been recognised as an integral part of property.

(10) If authors or performers are to continue their creative and artistic work, they have to receive an appropriate reward for the use of their work, as must producers in order to be able to finance this work. The investment required to produce products such as phonograms, films or multimedia products, and services such as 'on-demand' services, is considerable. Adequate legal protection of intellectual property rights is necessary in order to guarantee the availability of such a reward and provide the opportunity for satisfactory returns on this investment.

(11) A rigorous, effective system for the protection of copyright and related rights is one of the main ways of ensuring that European cultural creativity and production receive the necessary resources and of safeguarding the independence and dignity of artistic creators and performers.

(12) Adequate protection of copyright works and subject-matter of related rights is also of great importance from a cultural standpoint. Article 151 of the Treaty requires the Community to take cultural aspects into account in its action.

(13) A common search for, and consistent application at European level of, technical measures to protect works and other subject-matter and to provide the necessary information on rights are essential insofar as the ultimate aim of these measures is to give effect to the principles and guarantees laid down in law.

(14) This Directive should seek to promote learning and culture by protecting works and other subject-matter while permitting exceptions or limitations in the public interest for the purpose of education and teaching.

(15) The Diplomatic Conference held under the auspices of the World Intellectual Property Organisation (WIPO) in December 1996 led to the adoption of two new Treaties, the "WIPO Copyright Treaty" and the "WIPO Performances and Phonograms Treaty", dealing respectively with the protection of authors and the protection of performers and phonogram producers. Those Treaties update the international protection for copyright and related rights significantly, not least with regard to the so-called "digital agenda", and improve the means to fight piracy world-wide. The Community and a majority of Member States have already signed the Treaties and the process of making arrangements for the ratification of the Treaties by the Community and the Member States is under way. This Directive also serves to implement a number of the new international obligations.

(16) Liability for activities in the network environment concerns not only copyright and related rights but also other areas, such as defamation, misleading advertising, or infringement of trademarks, and is addressed horizontally in Directive 2000/31/EC of the European Parliament and of the Council of 8 June 2000 on certain legal aspects of information society services, in particular electronic commerce, in the internal market ("Directive on electronic commerce"),[4] which clarifies and harmonises various legal issues relating to information society services including electronic commerce. This Directive should be implemented within a timescale similar to that for the implementation of the Directive on electronic commerce, since that Directive provides a harmonised framework of principles and provisions relevant

---

[4] OJ L 178, 17.7.2000, p. 1.

inter alia to important parts of this Directive. This Directive is without prejudice to provisions relating to liability in that Directive.

(17) It is necessary, especially in the light of the requirements arising out of the digital environment, to ensure that collecting societies achieve a higher level of rationalisation and transparency with regard to compliance with competition rules.

(18) This Directive is without prejudice to the arrangements in the Member States concerning the management of rights such as extended collective licences.

(19) The moral rights of rightholders should be exercised according to the legislation of the Member States and the provisions of the Berne Convention for the Protection of Literary and Artistic Works, of the WIPO Copyright Treaty and of the WIPO Performances and Phonograms Treaty. Such moral rights remain outside the scope of this Directive.

(20) This Directive is based on principles and rules already laid down in the Directives currently in force in this area, in particular Directives 91/250/EEC,[5] 92/100/EEC,[6] 93/83/EEC,[7] 93/98/EEC[8] and 96/9/EC,[9] and it develops those principles and rules and places them in the context of the information society. The provisions of this Directive should be without prejudice to the provisions of those Directives, unless otherwise provided in this Directive.

(21) This Directive should define the scope of the acts covered by the reproduction right with regard to the different beneficiaries. This should be done in conformity with the acquis communautaire. A broad definition of these acts is needed to ensure legal certainty within the internal market.

(22) The objective of proper support for the dissemination of culture must not be achieved by sacrificing strict protection of rights or by tolerating illegal forms of distribution of counterfeited or pirated works.

(23) This Directive should harmonise further the author's right of communication to the public. This right should be understood in a broad sense covering all communication to the public not present at the place where the communication originates. This right should cover any such transmission or retransmission of a work to the public by wire or wireless means, including broadcasting. This right should not cover any other acts.

(24) The right to make available to the public subject-matter referred to in Article 3(2) should be understood as covering all acts of making available such subject-matter to members of the public not present at the place where the act of making available originates, and as not covering any other acts.

(25) The legal uncertainty regarding the nature and the level of protection of acts of on-demand transmission of copyright works and subject-matter protected by related rights over networks should be overcome by providing for harmonised protection at Community level. It should be made clear that all rightholders recognised by this Directive should have an exclusive right to make available to the public copyright works or any other subject-matter by way of interactive on-demand transmissions. Such interactive on-demand transmissions are characterised by the fact that members of the public may access them from a place and at a time individually chosen by them.

---

[5] Council Directive 91/250/EEC of 14 May 1991 on the legal protection of computer programs (OJ L 122, 17.5.1991, p. 42). Directive as amended by Directive 93/98/EEC.

[6] Council Directive 92/100/EEC of 19 November 1992 on rental right and lending right and on certain rights related to copyright in the field of intellectual property (OJ L 346, 27.11.1992, p. 61). Directive as amended by Directive 93/98/EEC.

[7] Council Directive 93/83/EEC of 27 September 1993 on the coordination of certain rules concerning copyright and rights related to copyright applicable to satellite broadcasting and cable retransmission (OJ L 248, 6.10.1993, p. 15).

[8] Council Directive 93/98/EEC of 29 October 1993 harmonising the term of protection of copyright and certain related rights (OJ L 290, 24.11.1993, p. 9).

[9] Directive 96/9/EC of the European Parliament and of the Council of 11 March 1996 on the legal protection of databases (OJ L 77, 27.3.1996, p. 20).

(26) With regard to the making available in on-demand services by broadcasters of their radio or television productions incorporating music from commercial phonograms as an integral part thereof, collective licensing arrangements are to be encouraged in order to facilitate the clearance of the rights concerned.

(27) The mere provision of physical facilities for enabling or making a communication does not in itself amount to communication within the meaning of this Directive.

(28) Copyright protection under this Directive includes the exclusive right to control distribution of the work incorporated in a tangible article. The first sale in the Community of the original of a work or copies thereof by the rightholder or with his consent exhausts the right to control resale of that object in the Community. This right should not be exhausted in respect of the original or of copies thereof sold by the rightholder or with his consent outside the Community. Rental and lending rights for authors have been established in Directive 92/100/EEC. The distribution right provided for in this Directive is without prejudice to the provisions relating to the rental and lending rights contained in Chapter I of that Directive.

(29) The question of exhaustion does not arise in the case of services and on-line services in particular. This also applies with regard to a material copy of a work or other subject-matter made by a user of such a service with the consent of the rightholder. Therefore, the same applies to rental and lending of the original and copies of works or other subject-matter which are services by nature. Unlike CD-ROM or CD-I, where the intellectual property is incorporated in a material medium, namely an item of goods, every on-line service is in fact an act which should be subject to authorisation where the copyright or related right so provides.

(30) The rights referred to in this Directive may be transferred, assigned or subject to the granting of contractual licences, without prejudice to the relevant national legislation on copyright and related rights.

(31) A fair balance of rights and interests between the different categories of rightholders, as well as between the different categories of rightholders and users of protected subject-matter must be safeguarded. The existing exceptions and limitations to the rights as set out by the Member States have to be reassessed in the light of the new electronic environment. Existing differences in the exceptions and limitations to certain restricted acts have direct negative effects on the functioning of the internal market of copyright and related rights. Such differences could well become more pronounced in view of the further development of transborder exploitation of works and cross-border activities. In order to ensure the proper functioning of the internal market, such exceptions and limitations should be defined more harmoniously. The degree of their harmonisation should be based on their impact on the smooth functioning of the internal market.

(32) This Directive provides for an exhaustive enumeration of exceptions and limitations to the reproduction right and the right of communication to the public. Some exceptions or limitations only apply to the reproduction right, where appropriate. This list takes due account of the different legal traditions in Member States, while, at the same time, aiming to ensure a functioning internal market. Member States should arrive at a coherent application of these exceptions and limitations, which will be assessed when reviewing implementing legislation in the future.

(33) The exclusive right of reproduction should be subject to an exception to allow certain acts of temporary reproduction, which are transient or incidental reproductions, forming an integral and essential part of a technological process and carried out for the sole purpose of enabling either efficient transmission in a network between third parties by an intermediary, or a lawful use of a work or other subject-matter to be made. The acts of reproduction concerned should have no separate economic value on their own. To the extent that they meet these conditions, this exception should include acts which enable browsing as well as acts of caching to take place, including those which enable transmission systems to function efficiently, provided that the intermediary does not modify the information and does not interfere with the lawful use of technology, widely recognised and used by industry, to obtain

data on the use of the information. A use should be considered lawful where it is authorised by the rightholder or not restricted by law.

(34) Member States should be given the option of providing for certain exceptions or limitations for cases such as educational and scientific purposes, for the benefit of public institutions such as libraries and archives, for purposes of news reporting, for quotations, for use by people with disabilities, for public security uses and for uses in administrative and judicial proceedings.

(35) In certain cases of exceptions or limitations, rightholders should receive fair compensation to compensate them adequately for the use made of their protected works or other subject-matter. When determining the form, detailed arrangements and possible level of such fair compensation, account should be taken of the particular circumstances of each case. When evaluating these circumstances, a valuable criterion would be the possible harm to the rightholders resulting from the act in question. In cases where rightholders have already received payment in some other form, for instance as part of a licence fee, no specific or separate payment may be due. The level of fair compensation should take full account of the degree of use of technological protection measures referred to in this Directive. In certain situations where the prejudice to the rightholder would be minimal, no obligation for payment may arise.

(36) The Member States may provide for fair compensation for rightholders also when applying the optional provisions on exceptions or limitations which do not require such compensation.

(37) Existing national schemes on reprography, where they exist, do not create major barriers to the internal market. Member States should be allowed to provide for an exception or limitation in respect of reprography.

(38) Member States should be allowed to provide for an exception or limitation to the reproduction right for certain types of reproduction of audio, visual and audio-visual material for private use, accompanied by fair compensation. This may include the introduction or continuation of remuneration schemes to compensate for the prejudice to rightholders. Although differences between those remuneration schemes affect the functioning of the internal market, those differences, with respect to analogue private reproduction, should not have a significant impact on the development of the information society. Digital private copying is likely to be more widespread and have a greater economic impact. Due account should therefore be taken of the differences between digital and analogue private copying and a distinction should be made in certain respects between them.

(39) When applying the exception or limitation on private copying, Member States should take due account of technological and economic developments, in particular with respect to digital private copying and remuneration schemes, when effective technological protection measures are available. Such exceptions or limitations should not inhibit the use of technological measures or their enforcement against circumvention.

(40) Member States may provide for an exception or limitation for the benefit of certain non-profit making establishments, such as publicly accessible libraries and equivalent institutions, as well as archives. However, this should be limited to certain special cases covered by the reproduction right. Such an exception or limitation should not cover uses made in the context of on-line delivery of protected works or other subject-matter. This Directive should be without prejudice to the Member States' option to derogate from the exclusive public lending right in accordance with Article 5 of Directive 92/100/EEC. Therefore, specific contracts or licences should be promoted which, without creating imbalances, favour such establishments and the disseminative purposes they serve.

(41) When applying the exception or limitation in respect of ephemeral recordings made by broadcasting organisations it is understood that a broadcaster's own facilities include those of a person acting on behalf of and under the responsibility of the broadcasting organisation.

(42) When applying the exception or limitation for non-commercial educational and scientific research purposes, including distance learning, the non-commercial nature of the activity in question should be determined by that activity as such. The organisational structure and the means of funding of the establishment concerned are not the decisive factors in this respect.

(43) It is in any case important for the Member States to adopt all necessary measures to facilitate access to works by persons suffering from a disability which constitutes an obstacle to the use of the works themselves, and to pay particular attention to accessible formats.

(44) When applying the exceptions and limitations provided for in this Directive, they should be exercised in accordance with international obligations. Such exceptions and limitations may not be applied in a way which prejudices the legitimate interests of the rightholder or which conflicts with the normal exploitation of his work or other subject-matter. The provision of such exceptions or limitations by Member States should, in particular, duly reflect the increased economic impact that such exceptions or limitations may have in the context of the new electronic environment. Therefore, the scope of certain exceptions or limitations may have to be even more limited when it comes to certain new uses of copyright works and other subject-matter.

(45) The exceptions and limitations referred to in Article 5(2), (3) and (4) should not, however, prevent the definition of contractual relations designed to ensure fair compensation for the rightholders insofar as permitted by national law.

(46) Recourse to mediation could help users and rightholders to settle disputes. The Commission, in cooperation with the Member States within the Contact Committee, should undertake a study to consider new legal ways of settling disputes concerning copyright and related rights.

(47) Technological development will allow rightholders to make use of technological measures designed to prevent or restrict acts not authorised by the rightholders of any copyright, rights related to copyright or the sui generis right in databases. The danger, however, exists that illegal activities might be carried out in order to enable or facilitate the circumvention of the technical protection provided by these measures. In order to avoid fragmented legal approaches that could potentially hinder the functioning of the internal market, there is a need to provide for harmonised legal protection against circumvention of effective technological measures and against provision of devices and products or services to this effect.

(48) Such legal protection should be provided in respect of technological measures that effectively restrict acts not authorised by the rightholders of any copyright, rights related to copyright or the *sui generis* right in databases without, however, preventing the normal operation of electronic equipment and its technological development. Such legal protection implies no obligation to design devices, products, components or services to correspond to technological measures, so long as such device, product, component or service does not otherwise fall under the prohibition of Article 6. Such legal protection should respect proportionality and should not prohibit those devices or activities which have a commercially significant purpose or use other than to circumvent the technical protection. In particular, this protection should not hinder research into cryptography.

(49) The legal protection of technological measures is without prejudice to the application of any national provisions which may prohibit the private possession of devices, products or components for the circumvention of technological measures.

(50) Such a harmonised legal protection does not affect the specific provisions on protection provided for by Directive 91/250/EEC. In particular, it should not apply to the protection of technological measures used in connection with computer programs, which is exclusively addressed in that Directive. It should neither inhibit nor prevent the development or use of any means of circumventing a technological measure that is necessary to enable acts to be

undertaken in accordance with the terms of Article 5(3) or Article 6 of Directive 91/250/EEC. Articles 5 and 6 of that Directive exclusively determine exceptions to the exclusive rights applicable to computer programs.

(51) The legal protection of technological measures applies without prejudice to public policy, as reflected in Article 5, or public security. Member States should promote voluntary measures taken by rightholders, including the conclusion and implementation of agreements between rightholders and other parties concerned, to accommodate achieving the objectives of certain exceptions or limitations provided for in national law in accordance with this Directive. In the absence of such voluntary measures or agreements within a reasonable period of time, Member States should take appropriate measures to ensure that rightholders provide beneficiaries of such exceptions or limitations with appropriate means of benefiting from them, by modifying an implemented technological measure or by other means. However, in order to prevent abuse of such measures taken by rightholders, including within the framework of agreements, or taken by a Member State, any technological measures applied in implementation of such measures should enjoy legal protection.

(52) When implementing an exception or limitation for private copying in accordance with Article 5(2)(b), Member States should likewise promote the use of voluntary measures to accommodate achieving the objectives of such exception or limitation. If, within a reasonable period of time, no such voluntary measures to make reproduction for private use possible have been taken, Member States may take measures to enable beneficiaries of the exception or limitation concerned to benefit from it. Voluntary measures taken by rightholders, including agreements between rightholders and other parties concerned, as well as measures taken by Member States, do not prevent rightholders from using technological measures which are consistent with the exceptions or limitations on private copying in national law in accordance with Article 5(2)(b), taking account of the condition of fair compensation under that provision and the possible differentiation between various conditions of use in accordance with Article 5(5), such as controlling the number of reproductions. In order to prevent abuse of such measures, any technological measures applied in their implementation should enjoy legal protection.

(53) The protection of technological measures should ensure a secure environment for the provision of interactive on-demand services, in such a way that members of the public may access works or other subject-matter from a place and at a time individually chosen by them. Where such services are governed by contractual arrangements, the first and second subparagraphs of Article 6(4) should not apply. Non-interactive forms of online use should remain subject to those provisions.

(54) Important progress has been made in the international standardisation of technical systems of identification of works and protected subject-matter in digital format. In an increasingly networked environment, differences between technological measures could lead to an incompatibility of systems within the Community. Compatibility and interoperability of the different systems should be encouraged. It would be highly desirable to encourage the development of global systems.

(55) Technological development will facilitate the distribution of works, notably on networks, and this will entail the need for rightholders to identify better the work or other subject-matter, the author or any other rightholder, and to provide information about the terms and conditions of use of the work or other subject-matter in order to render easier the management of rights attached to them. Rightholders should be encouraged to use markings indicating, in addition to the information referred to above, *inter alia* their authorisation when putting works or other subject-matter on networks.

(56) There is, however, the danger that illegal activities might be carried out in order to remove or alter the electronic copyright-management information attached to it, or otherwise to distribute, import for distribution, broadcast, communicate to the public or make available to the public works or other protected subject-matter from which such information has

been removed without authority. In order to avoid fragmented legal approaches that could potentially hinder the functioning of the internal market, there is a need to provide for harmonised legal protection against any of these activities.

(57) Any such rights-management information systems referred to above may, depending on their design, at the same time process personal data about the consumption patterns of protected subject-matter by individuals and allow for tracing of on-line behaviour. These technical means, in their technical functions, should incorporate privacy safeguards in accordance with Directive 95/46/EC of the European Parliament and of the Council of 24 October 1995 on the protection of individuals with regard to the processing of personal data and the free movement of such data.[10]

(58) Member States should provide for effective sanctions and remedies for infringements of rights and obligations as set out in this Directive. They should take all the measures necessary to ensure that those sanctions and remedies are applied. The sanctions thus provided for should be effective, proportionate and dissuasive and should include the possibility of seeking damages and/or injunctive relief and, where appropriate, of applying for seizure of infringing material.

(59) In the digital environment, in particular, the services of intermediaries may increasingly be used by third parties for infringing activities. In many cases such intermediaries are best placed to bring such infringing activities to an end. Therefore, without prejudice to any other sanctions and remedies available, rightholders should have the possibility of applying for an injunction against an intermediary who carries a third party's infringement of a protected work or other subject-matter in a network. This possibility should be available even where the acts carried out by the intermediary are exempted under Article 5. The conditions and modalities relating to such injunctions should be left to the national law of the Member States.

(60) The protection provided under this Directive should be without prejudice to national or Community legal provisions in other areas, such as industrial property, data protection, conditional access, access to public documents, and the rule of media exploitation chronology, which may affect the protection of copyright or related rights.

(61) In order to comply with the WIPO Performances and Phonograms Treaty, Directives 92/100/EEC and 93/98/EEC should be amended,

HAVE ADOPTED THIS DIRECTIVE:

CHAPTER I   OBJECTIVE AND SCOPE

Article 1   Scope

1.   This Directive concerns the legal protection of copyright and related rights in the framework of the internal market, with particular emphasis on the information society.

2.   Except in the cases referred to in Article 11, this Directive shall leave intact and shall in no way affect existing Community provisions relating to:
- (a) the legal protection of computer programs;
- (b) rental right, lending right and certain rights related to copyright in the field of intellectual property;
- (c) copyright and related rights applicable to broadcasting of programmes by satellite and cable retransmission;
- (d) the term of protection of copyright and certain related rights;
- (e) the legal protection of databases.

---

[10] OJ L 281, 23.11.1995, p. 31.

CHAPTER II   RIGHTS AND EXCEPTIONS

Article 2   Reproduction right

Member States shall provide for the exclusive right to authorise or prohibit direct or indirect, temporary or permanent reproduction by any means and in any form, in whole or in part:

    (a) for authors, of their works;

    (b) for performers, of fixations of their performances;

    (c) for phonogram producers, of their phonograms;

    (d) for the producers of the first fixations of films, in respect of the original and copies of their films;

    (e) for broadcasting organisations, of fixations of their broadcasts, whether those broadcasts are transmitted by wire or over the air, including by cable or satellite.

Article 3   Right of communication to the public of works and right of making available to the public other subject-matter

1.   Member States shall provide authors with the exclusive right to authorise or prohibit any communication to the public of their works, by wire or wireless means, including the making available to the public of their works in such a way that members of the public may access them from a place and at a time individually chosen by them.

2.   Member States shall provide for the exclusive right to authorise or prohibit the making available to the public, by wire or wireless means, in such a way that members of the public may access them from a place and at a time individually chosen by them:

    (a) for performers, of fixations of their performances;

    (b) for phonogram producers, of their phonograms;

    (c) for the producers of the first fixations of films, of the original and copies of their films;

    (d) for broadcasting organisations, of fixations of their broadcasts, whether these broadcasts are transmitted by wire or over the air, including by cable or satellite.

3.   The rights referred to in paragraphs 1 and 2 shall not be exhausted by any act of communication to the public or making available to the public as set out in this Article.

Article 4   Distribution right

1.   Member States shall provide for authors, in respect of the original of their works or of copies thereof, the exclusive right to authorise or prohibit any form of distribution to the public by sale or otherwise.

2.   The distribution right shall not be exhausted within the Community in respect of the original or copies of the work, except where the first sale or other transfer of ownership in the Community of that object is made by the rightholder or with his consent.

Article 5   Exceptions and limitations

1.   Temporary acts of reproduction referred to in Article 2, which are transient or incidental, which are an integral and essential part of a technological process and the sole purpose of which is to enable

    (a) a transmission in a network between third parties by an intermediary, or

    (b) a lawful use

       of a work or other subject-matter to be made, and which have no independent economic significance, shall be exempted from the reproduction right provided for in Article 2.

2.   Member States may provide for exceptions or limitations to the reproduction right provided for in Article 2 in the following cases:

    (a) in respect of reproductions on paper or any similar medium, effected by the use of any kind of photographic technique or by some other process having similar effects, with the exception of sheet music, provided that the rightholders receive fair compensation;

(b) in respect of reproductions on any medium made by a natural person for private use and for ends that are neither directly nor indirectly commercial, on condition that the rightholders receive fair compensation which takes account of the application or non-application of technological measures referred to in Article 6 to the work or subject-matter concerned;

(c) in respect of specific acts of reproduction made by publicly accessible libraries, educational establishments or museums, or by archives, which are not for direct or indirect economic or commercial advantage;

(d) in respect of ephemeral recordings of works made by broadcasting organisations by means of their own facilities and for their own broadcasts; the preservation of these recordings in official archives may, on the grounds of their exceptional documentary character, be permitted;

(e) in respect of reproductions of broadcasts made by social institutions pursuing non-commercial purposes, such as hospitals or prisons, on condition that the rightholders receive fair compensation.

3.   Member States may provide for exceptions or limitations to the rights provided for in Articles 2 and 3 in the following cases:

(a) use for the sole purpose of illustration for teaching or scientific research, as long as the source, including the author's name, is indicated, unless this turns out to be impossible and to the extent justified by the non-commercial purpose to be achieved;

(b) uses, for the benefit of people with a disability, which are directly related to the disability and of a non-commercial nature, to the extent required by the specific disability;

(c) reproduction by the press, communication to the public or making available of published articles on current economic, political or religious topics or of broadcast works or other subject-matter of the same character, in cases where such use is not expressly reserved, and as long as the source, including the author's name, is indicated, or use of works or other subject-matter in connection with the reporting of current events, to the extent justified by the informatory purpose and as long as the source, including the author's name, is indicated, unless this turns out to be impossible;

(d) quotations for purposes such as criticism or review, provided that they relate to a work or other subject-matter which has already been lawfully made available to the public, that, unless this turns out to be impossible, the source, including the author's name, is indicated, and that their use is in accordance with fair practice, and to the extent required by the specific purpose;

(e) use for the purposes of public security or to ensure the proper performance or reporting of administrative, parliamentary or judicial proceedings;

(f) use of political speeches as well as extracts of public lectures or similar works or subject-matter to the extent justified by the informatory purpose and provided that the source, including the author's name, is indicated, except where this turns out to be impossible;

(g) use during religious celebrations or official celebrations organised by a public authority;

(h) use of works, such as works of architecture or sculpture, made to be located permanently in public places;

(i) incidental inclusion of a work or other subject-matter in other material;

(j) use for the purpose of advertising the public exhibition or sale of artistic works, to the extent necessary to promote the event, excluding any other commercial use;

(k) use for the purpose of caricature, parody or pastiche;

(l)   use in connection with the demonstration or repair of equipment;

(m) use of an artistic work in the form of a building or a drawing or plan of a building for the purposes of reconstructing the building;

(n) use by communication or making available, for the purpose of research or private study, to individual members of the public by dedicated terminals on the premises of establishments referred to in paragraph 2(c) of works and other subject-matter not subject to purchase or licensing terms which are contained in their collections;

(o) use in certain other cases of minor importance where exceptions or limitations already exist under national law, provided that they only concern analogue uses and do not affect the free circulation of goods and services within the Community, without prejudice to the other exceptions and limitations contained in this Article.

4.   Where the Member States may provide for an exception or limitation to the right of reproduction pursuant to paragraphs 2 and 3, they may provide similarly for an exception or limitation to the right of distribution as referred to in Article 4 to the extent justified by the purpose of the authorised act of reproduction.

5.   The exceptions and limitations provided for in paragraphs 1, 2, 3 and 4 shall only be applied in certain special cases which do not conflict with a normal exploitation of the work or other subject-matter and do not unreasonably prejudice the legitimate interests of the rightholder.

CHAPTER III PROTECTION OF TECHNOLOGICAL MEASURES AND
RIGHTS-MANAGEMENT INFORMATION

Article 6   Obligations as to technological measures

1.   Member States shall provide adequate legal protection against the circumvention of any effective technological measures, which the person concerned carries out in the knowledge, or with reasonable grounds to know, that he or she is pursuing that objective.

2.   Member States shall provide adequate legal protection against the manufacture, import, distribution, sale, rental, advertisement for sale or rental, or possession for commercial purposes of devices, products or components or the provision of services which:

(a) are promoted, advertised or marketed for the purpose of circumvention of, or

(b) have only a limited commercially significant purpose or use other than to circumvent, or

(c) are primarily designed, produced, adapted or performed for the purpose of enabling or facilitating the circumvention of, any effective technological measures.

3.   For the purposes of this Directive, the expression "technological measures" means any technology, device or component that, in the normal course of its operation, is designed to prevent or restrict acts, in respect of works or other subject-matter, which are not authorised by the rightholder of any copyright or any right related to copyright as provided for by law or the *sui generis* right provided for in Chapter III of Directive 96/9/EC. Technological measures shall be deemed "effective" where the use of a protected work or other subject-matter is controlled by the rightholders through application of an access control or protection process, such as encryption, scrambling or other transformation of the work or other subject-matter or a copy control mechanism, which achieves the protection objective.

4.   Notwithstanding the legal protection provided for in paragraph 1, in the absence of voluntary measures taken by rightholders, including agreements between rightholders and other parties concerned, Member States shall take appropriate measures to ensure that rightholders make available to the beneficiary of an exception or limitation provided for in

national law in accordance with Article 5(2)(a), (2)(c), (2)(d), (2)(e), (3)(a), (3)(b) or (3)(e) the means of benefiting from that exception or limitation, to the extent necessary to benefit from that exception or limitation and where that beneficiary has legal access to the protected work or subject-matter concerned.

A Member State may also take such measures in respect of a beneficiary of an exception or limitation provided for in accordance with Article 5(2)(b), unless reproduction for private use has already been made possible by rightholders to the extent necessary to benefit from the exception or limitation concerned and in accordance with the provisions of Article 5(2)(b) and (5), without preventing rightholders from adopting adequate measures regarding the number of reproductions in accordance with these provisions.

The technological measures applied voluntarily by rightholders, including those applied in implementation of voluntary agreements, and technological measures applied in implementation of the measures taken by Member States, shall enjoy the legal protection provided for in paragraph 1.

The provisions of the first and second subparagraphs shall not apply to works or other subject-matter made available to the public on agreed contractual terms in such a way that members of the public may access them from a place and at a time individually chosen by them.

When this Article is applied in the context of Directives 92/100/EEC and 96/9/EC, this paragraph shall apply mutatis mutandis.

Article 7   Obligations concerning rights-management information

1.   Member States shall provide for adequate legal protection against any person knowingly performing without authority any of the following acts:
  (a) the removal or alteration of any electronic rights-management information;
  (b) the distribution, importation for distribution, broadcasting, communication or making available to the public of works or other subject-matter protected under this Directive or under Chapter III of Directive 96/9/EC from which electronic rights-management information has been removed or altered without authority,

  if such person knows, or has reasonable grounds to know, that by so doing he is inducing, enabling, facilitating or concealing an infringement of any copyright or any rights related to copyright as provided by law, or of the *sui generis* right provided for in Chapter III of Directive 96/9/EC.

2.   For the purposes of this Directive, the expression "rights-management information" means any information provided by rightholders which identifies the work or other subject-matter referred to in this Directive or covered by the *sui generis* right provided for in Chapter III of Directive 96/9/EC, the author or any other rightholder, or information about the terms and conditions of use of the work or other subject-matter, and any numbers or codes that represent such information.

The first subparagraph shall apply when any of these items of information is associated with a copy of, or appears in connection with the communication to the public of, a work or other subject matter referred to in this Directive or covered by the *sui generis* right provided for in Chapter III of Directive 96/9/EC.

CHAPTER IV   COMMON PROVISIONS

Article 8   Sanctions and remedies

1.   Member States shall provide appropriate sanctions and remedies in respect of infringements of the rights and obligations set out in this Directive and shall take all the measures necessary to ensure that those sanctions and remedies are applied. The sanctions thus provided for shall be effective, proportionate and dissuasive.

2.   Each Member State shall take the measures necessary to ensure that rightholders whose interests are affected by an infringing activity carried out on its territory can bring an action for damages and/or apply for an injunction and, where appropriate, for the seizure of infringing material as well as of devices, products or components referred to in Article 6(2).

3.   Member States shall ensure that rightholders are in a position to apply for an injunction against intermediaries whose services are used by a third party to infringe a copyright or related right.

Article 9   Continued application of other legal provisions
This Directive shall be without prejudice to provisions concerning in particular patent rights, trade marks, design rights, utility models, topographies of semi-conductor products, type faces, conditional access, access to cable of broadcasting services, protection of national treasures, legal deposit requirements, laws on restrictive practices and unfair competition, trade secrets, security, confidentiality, data protection and privacy, access to public documents, the law of contract.

Article 10   Application over time
1.   The provisions of this Directive shall apply in respect of all works and other subject-matter referred to in this Directive which are, on 22 December 2002, protected by the Member States' legislation in the field of copyright and related rights, or which meet the criteria for protection under the provisions of this Directive or the provisions referred to in Article 1(2).

2.   This Directive shall apply without prejudice to any acts concluded and rights acquired before 22 December 2002.

Article 11   Technical adaptations
1.   Directive 92/100/EEC is hereby amended as follows:
   (a)   Article 7 shall be deleted;
   (b)   Article 10(3) shall be replaced by the following: "3. The limitations shall only be applied in certain special cases which do not conflict with a normal exploitation of the subject-matter and do not unreasonably prejudice the legitimate interests of the rightholder."

2.   Article 3(2) of Directive 93/98/EEC shall be replaced by the following:

"2.   The rights of producers of phonograms shall expire 50 years after the fixation is made. However, if the phonogram has been lawfully published within this period, the said rights shall expire 50 years from the date of the first lawful publication. If no lawful publication has taken place within the period mentioned in the first sentence, and if the phonogram has been lawfully communicated to the public within this period, the said rights shall expire 50 years from the date of the first lawful communication to the public.

However, where through the expiry of the term of protection granted pursuant to this paragraph in its version before amendment by Directive 2001/29/EC of the European Parliament and of the Council of 22 May 2001 on the harmonisation of certain aspects of copyright and related rights in the information society[11] the rights of producers of phonograms are no longer protected on 22 December 2002, this paragraph shall not have the effect of protecting those rights anew."

Article 12   Final provisions
1.   Not later than 22 December 2004 and every three years thereafter, the Commission shall submit to the European Parliament, the Council and the Economic and Social Committee a report on the application of this Directive, in which, *inter alia*, on the basis of specific

[11]   OJ L 167, 22.6.2001, p. 10.

information supplied by the Member States, it shall examine in particular the application of Articles 5, 6 and 8 in the light of the development of the digital market. In the case of Article 6, it shall examine in particular whether that Article confers a sufficient level of protection and whether acts which are permitted by law are being adversely affected by the use of effective technological measures. Where necessary, in particular to ensure the functioning of the internal market pursuant to Article 14 of the Treaty, it shall submit proposals for amendments to this Directive.

　　2.　Protection of rights related to copyright under this Directive shall leave intact and shall in no way affect the protection of copyright.

　　3.　A contact committee is hereby established. It shall be composed of representatives of the competent authorities of the Member States. It shall be chaired by a representative of the Commission and shall meet either on the initiative of the chairman or at the request of the delegation of a Member State.

　　4.　The tasks of the committee shall be as follows:
　　(a)　to examine the impact of this Directive on the functioning of the internal market, and to highlight any difficulties;
　　(b)　to organise consultations on all questions deriving from the application of this Directive;
　　(c)　to facilitate the exchange of information on relevant developments in legislation and case-law, as well as relevant economic, social, cultural and technological developments;
　　(d)　to act as a forum for the assessment of the digital market in works and other items, including private copying and the use of technological measures.

Article 13　Implementation

　　1.　Member States shall bring into force the laws, regulations and administrative provisions necessary to comply with this Directive before 22 December 2002. They shall forthwith inform the Commission thereof.

　　When Member States adopt these measures, they shall contain a reference to this Directive or shall be accompanied by such reference on the occasion of their official publication. The methods of making such reference shall be laid down by Member States.

　　2.　Member States shall communicate to the Commission the text of the provisions of domestic law which they adopt in the field governed by this Directive.

Article 14　Entry into force

This Directive shall enter into force on the day of its publication in the Official Journal of the European Communities.

Article 15　Addressees

This Directive is addressed to the Member States.

Done at Brussels, 22 May 2001.

For the European Parliament
The President
N. Fontaine

For the Council
The President
M. Winberg

PART III

UK Legislation

European Communities Act 1972*

1.—(1)   This Act may be cited as the European Communities Act 1972.

(2) In this Act and, except in so far as the context otherwise requires, in any other Act (including any Act of the Parliament of Northern Ireland)—

'the Communities' means the European Economic Community, the European Coal and Steel Community and the European Atomic Energy Community;

'the Treaties' or 'the Community Treaties' means, subject to subsection (3) below, the pre-accession treaties, that is to say, those described in Part I of Schedule I to this Act, taken with

(a) the treaty relating to the accession of the United Kingdom to the European Economic Community and to the European Atomic Energy Community, signed at Brussels on the 22nd January 1972; and

(b) the decision, of the same date, of the Council of the European Communities relating to the accession of the United Kingdom to the European Coal and Steel Community; and

(c) the treaty relating to the accession of the Hellenic Republic to the European Economic Community and to the European Atomic Energy Community, signed at Athens on 28th May 1979; and

(d) the decision, of 24th May 1979, of the Council relating to the accession of the Hellenic Republic to the European Coal and Steel Community; and

(e) the decisions of the Council of 7th May 1985, 24th June 1988 and 31st October 1994, on the Communities' system of own resources; and

(g) the treaty relating to the accession of the Kingdom of Spain and the Portuguese Republic to the European Economic Community and to the European Atomic Energy Community, signed at Lisbon and Madrid on 12th June 1985; and

(h) the decision, of 11th June 1985, of the Council relating to the accession of the Kingdom of Spain and the Portuguese Republic to the European Coal and Steel Community; and

(j) the following provisions of the Single European Act signed at Luxembourg and The Hague on 17th and 28th February 1986, namely Title II (amendment of the treaties establishing the Communities) and, so far as they relate to any of the Communities or any Community institution, the preamble and Titles II (common provisions) and IV (general and final provisions); and

(k) Titles II, III and IV of the Treaty on European Union signed at Maastricht on 7th February 1992, together with the other provisions of the Treaty so far as they relate to those Titles, and the Protocols adopted at Maastricht on the date and annexed to the Treaty establishing the European Community with the exception of the Protocol on Social Policy on page 117 of Cm 1934; and

---

* **Editor's Note:** As amended up to the European Union (Accessions) Act 2003 (2003 c. 35), s. 1.

(l) the decision, of 1st February 1993, of the Council amending the Act concerning the election of the representatives of the European Parliament by direct universal suffrage annexed to Council Decision 76/787/ECSC, EEC, Euratom of 20th September 1976; and

(m) the Agreement on the European Economic Area signed at Oporto on 2nd May 1992 together with the Protocol adjusting the Agreement signed at Brussels on 17th March 1993; and

(n) the treaty concerning the accession of the Kingdom of Norway, the Republic of Austria, the Republic of Finland and the Kingdom of Sweden to the European Union, signed at Corfu on 24th June 1994; and

(o) the following provisions of the Treaty signed at Amsterdam on 2nd October 1997 amending the Treaty on European Union, the Treaties establishing the European Communities and certain related Acts—
(i) Articles 2 to 9,
(ii) Article 12, and
(iii) the other provisions of the Treaty so far as they relate to those Articles, and the Protocols adopted on that occasion other than the Protocol on Article J.7 of the Treaty on European Union, and

(p) the following provisions of the Treaty signed at Nice on 26th February 2001 amending the Treaty on European Union, the Treaties establishing the European Communities and certain related Acts—
(i) Articles 2 to 10, and
(ii) the other provisions of the Treaty so far as they relate to those Articles, and the Protocols adopted on that occasion;

(q) the treaty concerning the accession of the Czech Republic, the Republic of Estonia, the Republic of Cyprus, the Republic of Latvia, the Republic of Lithuania, the Republic of Hungary, the Republic of Malta, the Republic of Poland, the Republic of Slovenia and the Slovak Republic to the European Union, signed at Athens on 16th April 2003;
and any other treaty entered into by any of the Communities, with or without any of the Member States, or entered into, as a treaty ancillary to any of the Treaties, by the United Kingdom;
and any expression defined in Schedule I to this Act has the meaning there given to it.

(3) If Her Majesty by Order in Council declares that a treaty specified in the Order is to be regarded as one of the Community Treaties as herein defined, the Order shall be conclusive that it is to be so regarded; but a treaty entered into by the United Kingdom after the 22nd January 1972, other than a pre-accession treaty to which the United Kingdom acceeds on terms settled on or before that date, shall not be so regarded unless it is so specified, nor be so specified unless a draft of the Order in Council has been approved by resolution of each House of Parliament.

(4) For purposes of subsections (2) and (3) above, 'treaty' includes any international agreement, and any protocol or annex to a treaty or international agreement.

2.—(1) All such rights, powers, liabilities, obligations and restrictions from time to time created or arising by or under the Treaties, and all such remedies and procedures from time to time provided for by or under the Treaties, as in accordance with the Treaties are without further enactment to be given legal effect or used in the United Kingdom shall be recognised and available in law, and be enforced, allowed and followed accordingly; and the expression 'enforceable Community right' and similar expressions shall be read as referring to one to which this subsection applies.

(2) Subject to Schedule 2 to this Act, at any time after its passing Her Majesty may by Order in Council, and any designated Minister or department may by regulations, make provision—
(a) for the purpose of implementing any Community obligation of the United Kingdom, or enabling any such obligation to be implemented, or of enabling any

rights enjoyed or to be enjoyed by the United Kingdom under or by virtue of the Treaties to be exercised; or

(b) for the purpose of dealing with matters arising out of or related to any such obligation or rights or the coming into force, or the operation from time to time, of subsection (1) above;

and in the exercise of any statutory power or duty, including any power to give directions or to legislate by means of orders, rules, regulations or other subordinate instrument, the person entrusted with the power or duty may have regard to the objects of the Communities and to any such obligation or rights as aforesaid.

In this subsection 'designated Minister or department' means such Minister of the Crown or government department as may from time to time be designated by Order in Council in relation to any matter or for any purpose, but subject to such restrictions or conditions (if any) as may be specified by the Order in Council.

(3) There shall be charged on and issued out of the Consolidated Fund or, if so determined by the Treasury, the National Loans Fund the amounts required to meet any Community obligation to make payments to any of the Communities or member States, or any Community obligation in respect of contributions to the capital or reserves of the European Investment Bank or in respect of loans to the Bank, or to redeem any notes or obligations issued or created in respect of any such Community obligation; and, except as otherwise provided by or under any enactment,—

(a) any other expenses incurred under or by virtue of the Treaties or this Act by any Minister of the Crown or government department may be paid out of moneys provided by Parliament and;

(b) any sums received under or by virtue of the Treaties or this Act by any Minister of the Crown or government department save for such sums as may be required for disbursements permitted by any other enactment, shall be paid into the Consolidated Fund or, if so determined by the Treasury, the National Loans Fund.

(4) The provision that may be made under subsection (2) above includes, subject to Schedule 2 to this Act, any such provision (of any such extent) as might be made by Act of Parliament, and any enactment passed or to be passed, other than one contained in this part of this Act, shall be construed and have effect subject to the foregoing provisions of this section; but, except as may be provided by any Act passed after this Act, Schedule 2 shall have effect in connection with the powers conferred by this and the following sections of this Act to make Orders in Council and regulations.

(5) ...[1] and the references in that subsection to a Minister of the Crown or Government department and to a statutory power or duty shall include a Minister or department of the Government of Northern Ireland and a power or duty arising under or by virtue of an Act of the Parliament of Northern Ireland.

(6) A law passed by the legislature of any of the Channel Islands or of the Isle of Man, or a colonial Law (within the meaning of the Colonial Laws Validity Act 1865) passed or made for Gibraltar, if expressed to be passed or made in the implementation of the Treaties and of the obligations of the United Kingdom thereunder, shall not be void or inoperative by reason of any inconsistency with or repugnancy to an Act of Parliament, passed or to be passed, that extends to the Island or Gibraltar or any provision having the force and effect of an Act there (but not including this section), nor by reason of its having some operation outside the Island or Gibraltar; and any such Act or provision that extends to the Island or Gibraltar shall be construed and have effect subject to the provisions of any such law.

3.—(1) For the purposes of all legal proceedings any question as to the meaning or effect of any of the Treaties, or as to the validity, meaning or effect of any Community instrument, shall be treated as a question of law (and, if not referred to the European Court, be

---

[1] Words repealed by the Northern Ireland Constitution Act 1973 (c. 36 SIF 29:3), Sch. 6 Pt. I.

for determination as such in accordance with the principles laid down by and any relevant [²decision of the European Court or any court attached thereto]).

Notes:

S. 2(2)(a)(b) excluded (N.I.) by Northern Ireland Constitution Act 1973 (c. 36, SIF 29:3), s. 2(2), Sch. 2 para. 3.

Reference in s. 2(5) to 'that subsection' means s. 2(2) of this Act. Reference to a Minister of the Government of Northern Ireland to be construed, as respects the discharge of functions, as a reference to the head of a Northern Ireland department: Northern Ireland Constitution Act 1973 (c. 36, SIF 29:3), Sch. 5 para. 7(2).

(2) Judicial notice shall be taken of the Treaties, of the Official Journal of the Communities and of any decision of, or expression of opinion by, the European Court [³or any court attached thereto] on any such question as aforesaid; and the Official Journal shall be admissible as evidence of any instrument or other act thereby communicated of any of the Communities or of any Community institution.

(3) Evidence of any instrument issued by a Community institution, including any judgment or order of the European Court [⁴or any court attached thereto], or of any document in the custody of a Community institution, or any entry in or extract from such a document, may be given in any legal proceedings by production of a copy certified as a true copy by an official of that institution; and any document purporting to be such a copy shall be received in evidence without proof of the official position or handwriting of the person signing the certificate.

(4) Evidence of any Community instrument may also be given in any legal proceedings—

(a) by production of a copy purporting to be printed by the Queen's Printer;

(b) where the instrument is in the custody of a government department (including a department of the Government of Northern Ireland), by production of a copy certified on behalf of the department to be a true copy by an officer of the department generally or specially authorised so to do;

and any document purporting to be such a copy as is mentioned in paragraph (b) above of an instrument in the custody of a department shall be received in evidence without proof of the official position or handwriting of the person signing the certificate, or of his authority to do so, or of the document being in the custody of the Department.

(5) In any legal proceedings in Scotland evidence of any matter given in a manner authorised by this section shall be sufficient evidence of it.

SCHEDULE 1

PART II   OTHER DEFINITIONS

'Economic Community', 'Coal and Steel Community' and 'Euratom' mean respectively the European Economic Community, the European Coal and Steel Community and the European Atomic Energy Community.

'Community customs duty' means, in relation to any goods, such duty of customs as may from time to time be fixed for those goods by directly applicable Community provision as the duty chargeable on importation into Member States.

'Community institution' means any institution of any of the Communities or common to the Communities; and any reference to an institution of a particular Community shall include one common to the Communities when it acts for that Community, and similarly with references to a committee, officer or servant of a particular Community.

---

² Words substituted by the European Communities (Amendment) Act 1986 (c. 58, SIF 29:5), s. 2(a).
³ Words inserted by the European Communities (Amendment) Act 1986 (c. 58, SIF 29:5), s. 2(b).
⁴ Words inserted by the European Communities (Amendment) Act 1986 (c. 58, SIF 29:5), s. 2(b).

'Community instrument' means any instrument issued by a Community institution.

'Community obligation' means any obligation created or arising by or under the Treaties, whether an enforceable Community obligation or not.

'Enforceable Community right' and similar expressions shall be construed in accordance with section 2(1) of this Act.

'Entry date' means the date on which the United Kingdom becomes a member of the Communities.

Note: *Entry date: the United Kingdom became a member of the Communities on 1.1.1973.*

'European Court' means the Court of Justice of the European Communities.

'Member', in the expression 'Member State', refers to membership of the Communities.

SCHEDULE 2   PROVISIONS AS TO SUBORDINATE LEGISLATION

1.—(1)   The powers conferred by section 2(2) of this Act to make provision for the purposes mentioned in section 2(2)(a) and (b) shall not include power—
  (a) to make any provision imposing or increasing taxation; or
  (b) to make any provision taking effect from a date earlier than that of the making of the instrument containing the provision; or
  (c) to confer any power to legislate by means of orders, rules, regulations or other subordinate instrument, other than rules of procedure for any court or tribunal; or
  (d) to create any new criminal offence punishable with imprisonment for more than two years or punishable on summary conviction with imprisonment for more than three months or with a fine of more than [5level 5 on the standard scale] (if not calculated on a daily basis) or with a fine of more than [6£100 a day].

(2) Subparagraph (1)(c) above shall not be taken to preclude the modification of a power to legislate conferred otherwise than under section 2(2), or the extension of any such power to purposes of the like nature as those for which it was conferred; and a power to give directions as to matters of administration is not to be regarded as a power to legislate within the meaning of sub-paragraph (1)(c).

2.—(1)   Subject to paragraph 3 below, where a provision contained in any section of this Act confers power to make regulations (otherwise than by modification or extension of an existing power), the power shall be exercisable by statutory instrument.

(2) Any statutory instrument containing an Order in Council or regulations made in the exercise of a power so conferred, if made without a draft having been approved by resolution of each House of Parliament, shall be subject to annulment in pursuance of a resolution of either House.

3.   Nothing in paragraph 2 above shall apply to any Order in Council made by the Governor of Northern Ireland or to any regulation made by a Minister or department of the Government of Northern Ireland; but where a provision contained in any section of this Act confers power to make such an Order in Council or regulations, then any Order in Council or regulations made in the exercise of that power, if made without a draft having been approved by resolution of each House of the Parliament of Northern Ireland, shall be subject to negative resolution within the meaning of section 41(6) of the Interpretation Act (Northern Ireland) 1954 as if the Order or regulations were a statutory instrument within the meaning of that Act.

---

[5] Words substituted (E.W.S.) (N.I.) by virtue of (E.W.) Criminal Justice Act 1982 (c. 48, SIF 39:1), ss. 38, 46, (S.) Criminal Procedure (Scotland) Act 1975 (c. 21, SIF 39:1), ss. 289F, 289G and (N.I.) by SI 1984/703 (N.I.3), arts 5, 6.
[6] Words substituted by Criminal Law Act 1977 (c. 45, SIF 39:1). s. 32(3).

INDEX